LORETTE WILMOT LIBRARY
Nazareth College of Rochester

Stephen Seleman

A LATIN-ENGLISH DICTIONARY
of
ST. THOMAS AQUINAS

A LATIN-ENGLISH

DICTIONARY

of

ST. THOMAS AQUINAS

A LATIN-ENGLISH
DICTIONARY

of

ST. THOMAS AQUINAS

based on

The *Summa Theologica*
and selected passages of his other works

by

Roy J. Deferrari, Ph.D., LL.D., L.H.D., D.Ed.

GARDINER PROFESSOR OF GREEK AND LATIN

AT THE CATHOLIC UNIVERSITY OF AMERICA, WASHINGTON, D.C.

ST. PAUL EDITIONS

IMPRIMATUR:

His Eminence,

† RICHARD CARDINAL CUSHING

January 25, 1960

AUTHOR'S FOREWORD

In the Foreword of "A Lexicon of St. Thomas Aquinas" we say in part: "We assume, then, that the only satisfactory way to study the philosophy and the theology of St. Thomas is through the medium of his own language and not exclusively or even predominantly through the language of translators and interpreters. With this thought in mind, the authors plan in the near future a handy small edition of this lexicon for students who wish to read the works of St. Thomas in their original language."

The present work is this so-called handy, small edition of the Lexicon, but, to be entirely accurate in our terminology, we call it a Latin-English Dictionary of St. Thomas Aquinas, since it will not contain any passages from the works of St. Thomas to illustrate the various uses of words. It will, however, contain every word and all its meanings as presented in the Lexicon. If the user of the Dictionary should wish to see examples of St. Thomas's use of words or phrases, he can easily consult the Lexicon for this purpose. This work is intended as a handy instrument for the rapid translation of the works of the Angelic Doctor, and in particular of his Summa Theologica.

ROY J. DEFERRARI

A

a, ab, *prep.* with *abl.*, (1) *from,* indicating agency, *by,* (2) *from, from out of,* (3) *in relation to,* (4) *on account of, for the sake of.* On **principium a quo,** see *principium.*—On **terminus a quo,** see *terminus.*—On **prius, a quo non convertitur consequentia essendi or subsistendi,** see *prior.*

Aaron, *indecl.* or onis, *m., Aaron, brother of Moses;* of the tribe of Levi and first high-priest of the Hebrews.

abacus, i, *m., a square tablet, abacus,* found only once in the S.T.

abbas, atis, *m.,* originally a Syrian word meaning *father,* and at first used in Latin of any monk respected for his old age or for the sanctity of his life. It is most frequently used to mean *the head of an ecclesiastical community of men, abbot,* and so in the S.T.

abbatissa, ae, *f., the head of an ecclesiastical community of women, abbess.*

abbreviatio, onis, *f., an abbreviation, an abridgement.*

Abdias, ae, *m., Abdias,* the governor of the house of Achab.

abdicatio, onis, *f., renunciation, disowning.*

abdico, are, avi, atum, 1, *v. a.,* to *renounce, disown.*

abditus, a, um, *P. a., hidden, remote.*

abduco, ere, xi, ctum, 3, *v. a.,* (1) *to lead away,* (2) *to take away forcibly, ravish.*—The following expressions with *abducere* in this (1) sense are common: (a), **abducere a Deo,** *to lead away from God.*—(b), **abducere a finali bono,** *to lead away from the final good.*—(c), **abducere a ratione,** *to lead away from reason.*

Abel, *indecl.* or elis and **Abelus,** i, *m., Abel, son of Adam.*

abeo, ire, ivi or ii, itum, *v. n., to depart, turn aside from, depart.* —**abire in infinitum,** *to depart into infinity.*

aberro, are, avi, atum, 1, *v. n. to wander away from, to wander, to stray.*

abhorreo, ere, ui, 2, *v. n.* and *a., to shudder at, abhor.*

abicio, ere, ieci, iectum, 3, *v. a., to cast away, throw aside.*—**abiectus,** a, um, *P. a., abject, worthless.*—**abiecte,** *adv., abjectly.*

abigo, ere, egi, actum, 3, *v. a., to drive away, get rid of.*

Abiron, *indecl., m., Abiron, the son of Eliab.*

abiectio, onis, *f., a throwing away, rejection, renunciation.*—**abiectio temporalium (rerum),** *renuntiation of temporal goods.*

abiuratio, onis, *f., a forswearing, abjuration.*

abiuro, are, avi, atum, 1, *v. a., to deny anything on oath, forswear, abjure.*

ablacto, are, avi, atum, 1, *v. a., to wean.*

ablatio, onis, *f., a taking away, removal, ablation.*

ablativus, a, um, *adj.,* (1) *possessing the power of taking away, removing, ablative,* (2) **ablativus** with or without **casus,** *the ablative case.*

abluo, ere, ui, utum, 3, *v. a.,* (1) *to wash away, wash,* (2) of religious rites, *to wash away sin, purify.*

ablutio, onis, *f.,* (1) *a washing away* or *cleansing,* (2) *offscourings,* (3) *a spiritual washing away* or *cleansing.*—Common expressions are: (a), **ablutio exterior corporalis,** *exterior corporal ablution.*—(b), **ablutio interior spiritualis,** *interior spiritual ablution.*—(c), **ablutio peccatorum,** *ablution* or *washing away of sins.*

ablutivus, a, um, *adj., capable of washing away, lavational.*

aboleo, ere, evi (ui), itum, 2, *v. a.,* (1) *to destroy, abolish,* (2) in the *pass., to die, decay.*

abolitio, onis, *f., abolishing, abolition.*

abominabilis, e, *adj., deserving to be abhorred, abominable.*

abominatio, onis, *f., an abominating, an abomination.*

abominor, ari, atus, 1, *v. dep., to abominate, abhor.*

abortivus, a, um, *adj., born prematurely, abortive.*

Abraham or **Abram,** *indecl.* or *ae., m., Abraham.*

abrenuntiatio, onis, *f., renunciation.*

abrenuntio, are, avi, atum, 1, *v. n., to disclaim, renounce,* used with the *dat.*

abrogo, are, avi, atum, 1, *v. a., to repeal, abrogate.*

abruptum, i, *n., steep ascent,* used in quotation from Gregory.

Absalon, *indecl., m., Absalon, the son of David.*

abscedo, ere, cessi, cessum, 3, *v. n., to depart, disappear.*

abscindo, ere, cidi, cissum, 3, *v. a., to tear asunder, separate, cut away.*

abscissio, onis, *f., a breaking off, cutting off, abscission.*

abscondo, ere, condi, and condidi, conditum and consum, 3, *v. a., to conceal carefully, hide.*—**absconditus,** a, um, *P. a., hidden, secret,* often used substantively. —**absconse,** *adv., secretly.*

absconsio, onis, *f., hiding, absconsement.*

absentia, ae, *f., absence.*

absento, are, avi, atum, 1, *v. a., to be absent.*

absisto, ere, stiti, no sup., 3, *v. n., to withdraw from, cease,* used in S.T. only in quot.

absolute, *adv.,* see *absolvo.*

absolutio, onis, *f., an absolving, acquittal, absolution.*—**sacramentum absolutionis,** *sacrament of absolution.*—**absolutio sacramentalis,** *sacramental absolution.*

absolutus, a, um, *P. a.,* see *absolvo.*

absolvo, ere, vi, utum, 3, *v. a.,* (1) lit., *to free from,* (2) *to absolve, acquit.*—**absolutus,** a, um, *P. a.,* (1) *cut off, freed,* synonym of *abstractus* and *separatus,* (2) *having no relation to anything else, relationless, independent, simple, absolute,* the opposite of *condicionalis, condicionatus, relativus,* and *relatus.*—On **bonum absolutum,** see *bonus* under 3; on **esse absolutum,** see *esse;* on **forma absoluta,** see *forma* under 2; on **malum absolutum,** see *malus* under 3; on **natura absoluta,** see *natura;* on **numerus absolutus,** see *numerus;* on **potentia absoluta,** see *potentia* under 2; on **quidditas absoluta,** see *quidditas;* on **ratio absoluta,** see *ratio* under 2; on **vita absoluta,** see *vita* under 3.—On **aequalitas absoluta,** see *aequalitas* under 1; on **apprehensio absoluta,** see *apprehensio* under 2; on **attributum absolutum,** see *attributum;* on **bonitas absoluta,** see *bonitas* under 1; on **certitudo absoluta,** see *certitudo* under 2 and 3; on **cognitio absoluta,** see *cognitio* under 2; on **comparatio absoluta,** see *comparatio* under 2; on **consideratio absoluta,** see *consideratio;* on **contradictio absoluta,** see *contradictio;* on **definitio absoluta,** see *definitio* under 2; on **distributio absoluta,** see *distributio* under 1; on **ens absolutum,** see *ens;* on **falsum absolutum,** see *falsus;* on **generatio absoluta,** see *generatio* under 1; on **identitas absoluta,** see *identitas;* on **impotentia absoluta,** see *impotentia;* on **intentio**

absoluta, see *intentio* under 2; on **iudicium absolutum,** see *iudicium* under 3; on **motus absolutus appetitus,** see *motus* under 2; on **multitudo absoluta,** see *multitudo* under 1; on **necessitas absoluta,** see *necessitas* under 1-3; on **negatio absoluta,** see *negatio* under 2; on **nomen absolutum,** see *nomen* under 1; on **oppositio absoluta,** see *oppositio* under 2; on **perfectio absoluta,** see *perfectio* under 2 and 3; on **positio absoluta,** see *positio* under 2; on **possibile absolutum,** see *possibilis* under 1; on **potentia absoluta,** see *potentia* under 3 and 4; on **privatio absoluta,** see *privatio* under 2; on **proprietas absoluta,** see *proprietas* under 1; on **quantitas absoluta,** see *quantitas* under 1; on **ratio absoluta,** see *ratio* under 4 and 7; on **relatio absoluta,** see *relatio;* on **res absoluta,** see *res;* on **sanctitas absoluta,** see *sanctitas;* on **scientia absoluta,** see *scientia* under 2; on **substantia absoluta,** see *substantia* under 8; on **totalitas absoluta,** see *totalitas;* on **veritas absoluta,** see *veritas* under 1; on **verum absolutum,** see *verus* under 1; on **violentia absoluta,** see *violentia* under 1; on **virtus absoluta,** see *virtus* under 1; on **voluntas absoluta,** see *voluntas* under 3.—**quod est per essentiam suam relativum, posterius est absoluto,** see *relativus.*—**relatio non potest esse**

absque aliquo absoluto, see *relatio.*—absolutum, i, *n., the independent, the absolute.*—absolute, *adv. separately, without regard to any particular circumstance, independently, absolutely, simply,* synonym of *simpliciter,* the opposite of *ex seu sub condicione, exsistente aliqua condicione, in comparatione seu per comparationem, in ordine ad aliquid, cum relatione, relative, quantum ad aliquid, secundum quid, suppositione facta, sub suppositione.*

absonus, a, um, adj. deviating from *the right tone, unsuitable, incongruous.*

absorbeo, ere, bui, rarely psi, ptum, 2, *v. a., to swallow down, engross, absorb.*

absque, *prep.,* with *abl., without.* —absque hoc quod, with *subj., without that, except that not.* —Common phrases are: (a), absque auxilio, *without aid.*— (b), absque culpa, *without fault.* —(c), absque dubio, *without doubt.*—(d), absque gratia, *without grace.*—(e), absque necessitate, *without necessity.*—(f), absque peccato, *without sin.*

absterreo, ere, ui, itum, 2, *v. a., to drive away by terrifying, frighten away.*

abstinentia, ae, *f.,* (1) *abstinence, a refraining from anything, abstaining from food* as sobrietas is abstaining from drink, (2) *abstinence* or *renunciation* in the sense of a virtue, the opposite of *gula,* (3) *ieiunium (fasting) as a part of abstinence.* For the difference between *abstintentia* and *castitas* see *castitas;* for the difference between *abstintentia* and *continentia* see *continentia.* —On votum abstinentiae see *votum* under 1.

abstineo, ere, ui, tentum, 2, *v. a.* and *n., to keep away, to abstain from a thing,* used with the (1) *abl.* and *ab,* (2) the gerund and gerundive with *ab,* (3) *ne* and *subj.,* (4) *quin* and the *subj.,* (5) *absol.*

abstracte, *adv.,* see *abstraho.*

abstractio, onis, *f., abstraction, separation, deduction,* a synonym of *resolutio,* used (1) primarily in a psychological sense for the operations of the cognitive faculties and (2) secondarily in a logical or epistemological sense, i.e., the drawing of the general from the particular, generalization, a synonym of *resolutio* and the opposite of *concretio,* (3) the mystical sense, a synonym of *alienatio.*—On cognoscere in abstractione et per abstractionem, see *cognoscere* under 2; on dicere per abstractionem, see *dicere* under 3; on fieri abstractionem, see *fieri;* on modus abstractionis, see *modus* under 2; on via abstractionis, see *via* under 3.—Kinds of *abstractio* in this (2) sense are: (a), abstractio a materia seu a materialibus condicionibus, *ab-*

straction from matter or *material conditions.*—(b), **abstractio a materia individuali, abstractio a materia sensibili,** and **abstractio a materia intelligibili,** *abstraction* (of form) *from individual matter, that from sensible matter, that from intelligible matter.* Cf. *materia* under 3.—(c), **abstractio a materia intellegibili,** see *abstractio a materia individuali.*—(d) **abstractio a materia sensibili,** see *abstractio a materia individuali.*—(e), **abstractio a materialibus condicionibus,** see *abstractio a materia.*—(f), **abstractio formae a materia seu speciei a materia** and **abstractio universalis a particulari,** *abstraction of form from matter* (formal abstraction) and *that of the general from the particular* (total abstraction).—(g), **abstractio intellectus seu per intellectum,** *abstraction of the intellect,* which is the opposite of *abstractio sensus seu per sensum,* i.e., sensible abstraction.—(h), **abstractio maior** and **abstractio minor,** *the greater or more extensively continued abstraction and the smaller or less extensively continued abstraction.*—(i), **abstractio minor,** see *abstractio maior.*—(j), **abstractio per intellectum,** see *abstractio intellectus.*—(k), **abstractio speciei a materia,** see *abstractio formae a materia.*—(l), **abstractio universalis a particulari,** see *abstractio formae a materia.*—

abstractio non est nisi unitorum, *only that can be abstracted which is united or bound with something else.*

abstractive, *adv., after the manner or in the sense of abstraction, abstractively,* a synonym of *abstracte.* On **dicere abstractive,** see *dicere* under 3; on **sumere abstractive,** see *sumere* under 3.

abstractus, a, um, *P. a.,* see *abstraho.*

abstraho, ere, xi, ctum, 3, *v. a.,* (1) *to abstract, separate, to take one thing without another,* in the ontological sense, (2) *to abstract, separate, deduct,* in the psychological sense, (3) *to abstract, separate, deduct,* in the epistemological sense, (4) *to abstract, separate, deduct,* in the mystical sense, a synonym of *alienare,* (5) and generally, *to grasp, understand.*—On **intellectus abstrahens,** see *intellectus* under 3.—Kinds of *abstrahere* in this sense are: (a), **abstrahere a materia** and **abstrahere a motu,** *to abstract something from matter and from motion.*—(b), **abstrahere a materia communi** and **abstrahere a materia individuali seu signata,** *to abstract* (form) *from common and from individual or marked matter.* Cf. *materia* under 3.—(c), **abstrahere a materia individuali,** see *abstrahere a materia communi.*—(d), **abstrahere a materia intellegibili** and **abstrahere a materia sensibili,** *to ab-*

stract (form) *from intelligible and from sensible material.* Cf. *materia* under 3.—(e), **abstrahere a materia sensibili,** see *abstrahere a materia intelligibili.* —(f), **abstrahere a materia signata,** see *abstrahere a materia communi.*—(g), **abstrahere a motu,** see *abstrahere a materia.* —(h), **abstrahere formam a materia seu abstrahere speciem a materia,** and **abstrahere totum a parte seu universale a particuli,** *to abstract form from matter, formal abstraction, and the whole from the part or the general from the particular, total abstraction.*—(i), **abstrahere per intellectum,** *to abstract by means of the intellect.*—(j), **abstrahere per modum compositionis et divisionis** and **abstrahere per modum simplicitatis,** *to abstract something after the manner of composition and division or of affirmation and negation,* i.e., by the second act of the mind, judgment, and *after the manner of simplicity* or *in the simple manner,* i.e., by the first act of the mind, simple apprehension. —(k), **abstrahere per modum simplicitatis,** see *abstrahere per modum compositionis et divisionis.*—(l), **abstrahere speciem a materia,** see *abstrahere formam a materia.*—(m), **abstrahere totum a parte,** see *abstrahere formam a materia.*—(n), **abstrahere universale a particuli,** see *abstrahere formam a materia.*—

abstrahentium non est mendacium, the translation of the Aristotelian phrase: *oude ginetai pseudos chorizonton, those who simply abstract something from a thing without at the same time designating it as separated from the thing commit no untruth.*— **abstractus,** a, um, *P. a., absracted, deducted, separated,* in the ontological psychological, epistemological and mystical senses of the word, a synonym of *absolutus* and *separatus.* On **bonum abstractum,** see *bonus* under 3; on **consideratio abstracta,** see *consideratio;* on **dicere ut in abstracto,** see *dicere* under 3; on **forma abstracta,** see *forma* under 2; on **homo abstractus,** see *homo;* on **intellectus abstractus,** see *intellectus* under 3; on **linea abstracta,** see *linea* under 1; on **nomen abstractum,** see *nomen* under 1; on **numerus abstractus,** see *numerus;* on **quidditas abstracta,** see *quidditas;* on **similitudo abstracta,** see *similitudo* under 2; on **species a re abstracta,** see *species* under 5; on **unum abstractum,** see *unus.*—With *abstractum* in the epistemological sense, the opposite of *concretum,* is understood *a materia,* i.e., that which is abstracted from the matter or the individual determination of a thing by means of the intellect, the essence of a thing.—On **definere in abstracto,** see *definere* under 2; on **dicere in abstracto,**

see *dicere* under 3; on **praedicare in abstracto**, see *praedicare* under 2; on **significare in abstracto seu ut in abstracto**, see *significare.*—quanto aliquid est simplicius et abstractius, tanto secundum se est nobilius et altius, *the simpler and more general anything is, the nobler and more sublime it is in itself.* —**abstractum**, i, *n., the abstract,* the opposite of *concretum.*—**abstracte**, *adv., in the manner or the sense of a generalization, abstractly,* a synonym of *abstractive* and *in abstracto,* the opposite of *concrete, concretive, in concretione,* and *in concreto.* On **accipere abstracte**, see *accipere* under 3; on **cognoscere abstracte**, see *cognoscere* under 2; on **significare abstracte**, see *significare;* on **sumere abstracte**, see *sumere* under 3.

absum, abesse, afui, afuturus, *v. n., to be away from, be absent,* the opposite of *adsum.*—**absit**, *far be it, God forbid.* Used (1) *absolutely* (2) introducing *ut* or *quod clause* with the *subj.,* but always in quotation.—**absens**, entis, *P. a., absent,* opposite of *praesens.*

absumo, ere, mpsi, mptum, 3, *v. a., to consume, annihilate.*

absurdus, a, um, *adj., irrational, absurd.*—Common phrases are: (a), **quod est absurdum,**—(b), **quod videtur absurdum.**—**absurde**, *adv., irrationally, absurdly.*

absynthium, i, *n., wormwood.*

abundantia, ae, *f., abundance, fulness, richness,* usually with the *gen.* Common phrases are (a), **abundantia suae bonitatis.**—(b) **abundantia charitatis.**—(c), **abundantia divini amoris.**—(d), **abundantia divitiarum.**—(e), **abundantia gratiae.**—(f), **abundantia meritorum.**

abunde, *adv., in great profusion* or *abundance, abundantly.*

abundo, are, avi, atum, 1, *v. n.,* (1) *to abound, have to overflowing, to flow* or *overflow,* (2) *to have an abundance of, to abound in,* used with the *abl.* with or without the *prep.* in.— **abundans**, antis, *P. a., overflowing, abounding, abundant.*— **abundanter**, *adv., abundantly, copiously.*

abusio, onis, *f., abuse, misuse.*

abusive, *adv.,* see *abusivus.*

abusivus, a, um, *adj., misapplied, abusive,* does not occur in the S.T. On **comparatio abusiva**, see *comparatio* under 2; on **locutio abusiva**, see *locutio* under 4; on **praedicatio abusiva**, see *praedicatio* under 2.—**abusive**, *adv., in a misapplied or abusive manner, abusively.* On **agere abusive**, see *agere* under 1.

abusus, us, *m., misuse, abuse.*

abutor, i, usus, 3, *v. dep., to make use of for any purpose, misuse, abuse.*

abyssus, i, *f., a bottomless pit, an abyss.*

academicus, i, *m., an academic philosopher. Contra Academicos,* the name of a work of St. Augustine.

Accaron, indecl., *m.*, *Accaron.*

accedo, ere, cessi, cessum, 3, *v. n.*, (1) *to come near, to approach,* used (a) *absolutely,* (b) with *ad* in literal and figurative senses, (c) impersonally, (2) esp., *to approach the sacraments,* with *ad, to enter upon,* (3) *to approach for sexual intercourse,* used with *ad,* (4) *be added,* only in quotation, (5) *to happen, befall,* with *dat.* (6) *to approach in likeness,* with *ad.—*

acceleratio, onis, *f.*, *a hastening, an acceleration.*

accelero, are, avi, atum, (also adc.), 1, *v. a.*, *to hasten, accelerate.*

accendo, ere, ndi, nsum, 3, *v. a.*, (1) *to set on fire, kindle, light,* (2) *to incite, rouse up.*

accensio, onis, *f.*, *excitement, stirring up, inflaming, kindling.*

acceptabilis, e, *adj.*, *acceptable, worthy of acceptance.*

acceptatio, onis, *f.*, (1) *acceptance, acceptation, reception,* a synonym of *acceptio,* (2) *ingratiation, winning favor.*

acceptio, onis, *f.*, (1) *acceptance, the act of receiving, reception,* the opposite of *datio,* (2) *comprehension, apprehension, understanding,* (3) *consideration, partiality, bias,* (4) *imputation, insinuation, acceptance.* — One kind of *acceptio* in this (1) sense is: **acceptio supernaturalis,** *supernatural reception.* One kind of *acceptio* in this (2) sense is:

acceptio simplex, *the simple comprehension* or *presentation* of a thing, so called because it is not bound with any predicate of the thing.

acceptivus, a, um, *adj.*, *inclined to accept, acceptive.*

accepto, are, avi, atum, 1, *v. freq. a,* *to take, receive, accept.*

acceptor, oris, *m.*, *acceptor, respecter, a viewer with partiality.*

accessio, onis, *f.*, *access, attack.*

accessorius, a, um, *adj.*, *aiding* or *contributing in a secondary way, accessory,* a synonym of *secundarius,* a, um, and the opposite of *principalis.*

accessus, us, *m.*, *approach* in (1) literal and (2) figurative senses, opposite of *recessus.*—Common phrases are: **accessus ad Deum,** *approach to God.*—**accessus ad terminum,** *approach to a term* or *end.*

accidens, entis, *P. a.*, fr. *accido,* used as a substantive n., (1) *a happening, occurrence, incident, event,* (2) *something that is added, that comes to hand* in the broader sense of the word, i.e., that which for its existence depends on another than its own subject, one of the nine predicaments, the opposite of *substantia, non-substantial.—* (3) *something that is added, that comes to hand* in the narrower sense of the word, i.e., that which belongs to a thing but is placed outside its essence, one of the predicables, the opposite of *proprium, non-essential.*—On **bonum in accidente,** see *bonus* under 2; on **definitio accidentis,** see *definitio* under 2; on **distingui accidente,** see *distinguere;* on **diversitas accidentis,** see *diversitas;* on **diversus secundum accidens,** see *diversus;* on **esse accidentis,** see *esse;* on **multum secundum accidens,** see *multus* under 1; on **praedicare de accidente,** see *praedicare* under 2; on **problema de accidente,** see *problema;* on **scire secundum accidens,** see *scire* under 2.— Kinds of *accidens* in this (2) sense are: (a), **accidens commune** and **accidens proprium,** the *common,* i.e., predicamental, *and the peculiar* or *predicable accident.*—(b), **accidens completum,** *the complete* or *completely formed accident.*—(c), **accidens compositum seu copulatum** and **accidens simplex seu simpliciter,** *the accident which in its definition is joined or bound with a fixed subject* and *the simple accident which is not bound with a fixed subject.*—(d), **accidens copulatum,** see *accidens compositum.*—(e), **accidens exterius,** *the exterior* or *obvious accident.*— (f), **accidens extraneum seu quod omnino per accidens se habet** and **accidens per se,** *the adventitious predicamental accident* or *that which happened incidentally* and *the predicable accident that befits a thing as such and according to its nature and*

essence.—(g), **accidens gratuitum totius naturae** and **accidens individuale seu individuans, seu individui,** *the predicable accident imparted to the nature of an entire species and the individual* or *individualizing accident,* i.e., *the accident that befits an individual as such.*—(h), **accidens individuale seu individuans** see *accidens gratuitum totius naturae.*—(i), **accidens individui,** see *accidens gratuitum totius naturae.*—(j), **accidens innaturale** and **accidens naturale,** *the unnatural* and *the natural accident.*—(k), **accidens inseparabile** and **accidens separabile,** *the inseparable* and *the separable accident.*—(l), **accidens manens** and **accidens non manens seu pertransiens,** *the permanent* and *the nonpermanent* or *transient accident.*—(m), **accidens naturale,** see *accidens innaturale.*— (n), **accidens non manens,** see *accidens manens.*—(o), **accidens per se,** see *accidens extraneum.* —(p), **accidens pertransiens,** see *accidens manens.*—(q), **accidens proprium,** see *accidens commune.*—(r), **accidens quod omnino per accidens se habet,** see *accidens extraneum.*—(s), **accidens sensibile seu sensu perceptibile,** *the sensibly perceptible accident.*—(t), **accidens a sensu perceptibile,** see *accidens sensibile.* —(u), **accidens separabile,** see *accidens inseparabile.*—(v), **accidens simplex seu simpliciter,** see *accidens compositum.*—accidens magis proprie dicitur entis, quam ens, *it is more properly said of accident that it is of a being than that it is a being, because it never exists for itself but always in another as in its subject.* **accidens non excedit suum subiectum seu non extendit se ultra suum subiectum,** *accident proceeds and extends itself according to the kind and manner of its operation, never beyond the nature of its subject.* **accidentis non est accidens,** *an accident cannot serve another accident as subject,* at least not *per se,* i.e., not through itself. **agere non est accidentium, sed substantiarum,** see *agere* under 1.—**nullum accidens invenitur sine substantia, sed aliqua substantia invenitur sine accidente,** *there is no accident without a substance serving it as subject, but there is a substance without accidents,* i.e., *God.*—For examples, see under sense 2 above. On **fallacia accidentis,** see *fallacia* under 2; on **per accidens seu secundum accidens,** see *per* under 1; on **sophisma accidentis,** see *sophisma.*

accidentalis, e, *adj., accidental, unessential, not belonging to the substance,* the opposite of *essentialis* and *substantialis.* See *accidens* under 3.—On **bonitas accidentalis,** see *bonitas* under 1; on **bonum accidentale seu secundum esse accidentale,** see *bonus* under 2; on **causa accidentalis,** see *causa* under 2; on **compositio accidentalis,** see *compositio* under 1; on **differentia accidentalis,** see *differentia;* on **dispositio accidentalis,** see *dispositio* under 4; on **diversitas accidentalis,** see *diversitas;* on **esse accidentale,** see *esse;* on **forma accidentalis,** see *forma* under 2; on **gloria accidentalis,** see *gloria* under 2; on **habitudo accidentalis,** see *habitudo;* on **immutatio accidentalis,** see *immutatio* under 2; on **modus accidentalis,** see *modus* under 1 and 2; on **pars accidentalis,** see *pars* under 1; on **perfectio accidentalis,** see *perfectio* under 2 and 4; on **potentia accidentalis,** see *potentia* under 4; on **praedicatio accidentalis,** see *praedicatio* under 2; on **praedictum accidentale,** see *praedictum* under 1; on **praemium accidentale,** see *praemium;* on **proprietas accidentalis,** see *proprietas* under 1; on **qualitas accidentalis,** see *qualitas;* on **quantitas accidentalis,** see *quantitas* under 2; on **suppositio accidentalis,** see *suppositio* under 4; on **unio accidentalis,** see *unio;* on **unire modo accidentali,** see *unire;* on **veritas accidentalis,** see *veritas* under 1. —**accidentaliter,** *adv., in an unessential* or *accidental way, by the way, accidentally, incidentally,* the opposite of *essentialiter* and *substantialiter.*—On **dicere accidentaliter,** see *dicere* under

3: on **praedicare accidentaliter,** see *praedicare* under 2; on **unire accidentaliter,** see *unire.*

accidentaliter, *adv.,* see *accidentalis.*

accido, ere, cidi, no sup. 3, *v. n.,* *to come to pass, happen, occur, befall.* (I). May be used (1) *absolutely,* (2) with *in* and *abl.,* (3) with the *dat.,* construed (4) with *quod.* and *indic.* or *subj.,* (5) rarely with *ut* and *subj.,* (6) *quin* and *subj.,* (7) with *inf.* (II). Also rarely, *to fall upon, reach, attain, be added,* used with *ad.*

accingo, ere, nxi, nctum, 3, *v. a.,* used in *pass.* as *middle, to gird oneself, make oneself ready for anything, prepare.*

accipio, ere, cepi, ceptum, 3, *v. a.,* (1) *to accept, receive, take,* (2) *to take from, take away,* (3) *to take, grasp, comprehend, understand,* a synonym of *sumere* and *tenere,* (4) *to take consideration of, be partial towards,* (5) *to accept, impute, imply, assume.* —On **occasio accepta,** see *occasio.*—On **species a re accepta,** see *species* under 5.—Kinds of *accipere* in this (3) sense are: (a), **accipere absolute,** *to comprehend something absolutely, simply.*—(b), **accipere abstracte** and **accipere concretive,** *to grasp something in the abstract* and *in the concrete sense.*—(c), **accipere aequivoce, accipere analogice,** and **accipere univoce,** *to understand something equivo*cally, analogically, *and* homogeneously.*—(d)* **accipere analogice,** see *accipere aequivoce.*— (e), **accipere collective,** *to comprehend something in a collective sense.*—(f), **accipere complexe,** *to understand something comprehensively.*—(g), **accipere concretive,** see *accipere abstracte.*—(h), **accipere habitualiter,** *to understand something in the manner of a habitus,* i.e., *not actually or advertently.*—(i), **accipere metaphorice** and **accipere proprie,** *to understand something metaphorically* and *properly.*—(j), **accipere negative seu remotive, accipere privative,** and **accipere positive,** *to understand something in the sense of a removal or negation, in that of a deficiency, and in that of an affirmation.*—(k), **accipere positive,** see *accipere negative.*—(l), **accipere privative,** see *accipere negative.*—(m), **accipere proprie,** see *accipere metaphorice.*—(n), **accipere remotive,** see *accipere negative.*—(o), **accipere simpliciter,** see *accipere absolute.*— (p), **accipere singulariter,** *to understand something in the sense of the singular.*—(q), **accipere sub disiunctione,** *to understand something in the sense of a distinction or separation.*— (r), **accipere univoce,** see *accipere aequivoce.*—**acceptus,** a, um, *P. a.,* (1) *received, accepted, understood,* (2) *acceptable, agreeable.*

accipiter, tris, *m., hawk.*

acclinis, e. *adj., inclined to, leaning on,* used with the *dat.*

accommodatio, onis, *f., accommodation, adjustment.*

accommodatus, a, um, *P. a.,* see *accommodo.*

accommode, *adv.,* see *accommodus.*

accommodo, are, avi, atum, 1, *v. a., to fit* or *adapt one thing to another, accommodate,* used with *ad, dat.,* and *absol.*—**accommodatus,** a, um, *P. a., fitted* or *adapted to, conformable* or *appropriate to,* a synonym of *accommodus.* On **distributio accommodata,** see *distributio* under 1.

accommodus, a, um, *adj., fit, suitable,* used with the *dat.,* and with *ad,* a synonym of *accommodatus.*—**accommode,** *adv., fitly, suitably.*

accresco, ere, evi, etum, 3, *v. n.,* (1) *to grow, become larger by growth, increase,* (2) *to be added to by way of increase or growth,* used with the *dat.*

accumbo, (adc.), ere, cubui, cubitum 3, *v. n., to lay oneself down in a reclining position, lie.*

accumulo, (adc.), are, avi, atum, 1, *v. a., to add to a heap, accumulate.*

accurate, *adv., carefully, nicely, exactly,* a synonym of *studiose.*

accusabilis, e, *adj. blameworthy, reprehensible.*

accusatio, onis, *f.,* (1) *complaint, accusation, indictment,* (2) *bill of indictment, action, suit.*

accusator, oris, *m.,* (1) *one who calls another to account, an accuser,* (2) *plaintiff,* opposite of *reus.*

accuso, are avi, atum, 1, *v. a.,* (1) *to call one to account, reproach, blame,* (2) also metaph. of things, *to find fault with, denounce,* (3) *to call one to account publicly, arraign, indict, charge,* used with *acc.* of person, and *de* with the *abl.* of the charge.

acedia sive acidia, ae, *f., sloth, abhorrence, aversion, disgust for spiritual blessings* because the attainment of these require physical exertion, the opposite of *gaudium spirituale.*—*Acedia* is a kind of *tristitia.* Cf. *tristitia* under 1. It is one of the seven capital sins. Cf. *vitium.* Its daughters are the following six: *malitia, rancor, pusillanimitas, desperatio, torpor circa praecepta, evagatio mentis ad illicita.*

acedior, ari, 1, *v. dep., to be morose, be peevish.*

acer, cris, cre, *adj., sharp, severe, vehement.*—**acriter,** *adv., sharply, severely, vehemently.*

acerbitas, atis, *f., sharpness, severity, violence.*

acerbus, a, um, *adj., harsh, grievous, painful.*

acervus, i, *m., a multitude of objects,* sometimes of the same kind, *rising in a heap, a heap.*

acesco, ere, acui, 3, *v. inch., to become* or *turn sour.*

acetum, i, *n.*, *sour wine, wine, vinegar.*

Achab, *m.*, *indecl. Achab, king of Samaria, husband of Jezabel.*

Acham or **Achar** or **Achan,** *m.*, *indecl., Achan, the son of Charmi, the son of Zabdi, the son of Zare of the tribe of Juda.*

Achaz, *m.*, *indecl., Achaz,* the son of Joathan, the son of Ozias, King of Juda.

Achilles, is, *m.*, *Achilles,* the celebrated Greek hero in the Trojan war distinguished for strength and beauty; son of Peleus, king of Thessaly, and of Thetis.

Achior, *m.*, *Achior,* captain of all the children of Ammon.

Achis, *m.*, *indecl., Achis,* king of Geth.

Achos, Greek *achos, eos, to,* in Greek, *distress, pain of body* or *mind;* in Latin, *a kind of anxietas, anxious care.* According to Nemesius, Latin interpreter of Gregory of Nyssa, it is *aegritudo vocis usum adimens.*

acidus, a, um, *adj., sour, tart, acid.*

acies, ei, *f.,* (1) *line of battle, battle array, battle,* (2) *acuteness of mind, concentration, force, power.*

acinus, i, *m., a berry,* especially *the grape.*

acolythus, i, *m., an acolyte,* the highest of the minor orders, the cleric who serves the ministers at Mass.

acquiesco, ere, evi, etum, 3, *v. n., to be satisfied with, to acquiesce in* or *give assent to.*

acquiro, ere, sivi, situm, 3, *v. a., to get, obtain, acquire,* used *absol.,* and with *acc.*

acquisitio, onis, *f., acquisition, accession.*

acquisitivus, a, um, *adj., having a tendency to acquire, acquisitive, productive.*

acrimonia, ae, *f., sharpness, acrimony, irritation.*

acriter, *adv.,* see *acer.*

actio, onis, *f.,* (1) *a doing, performing, action* in the general sense of the word, a synonym of *actus* and *operatio,* the opposite of *passio,* (2) *immanent action,* i.e., *actio manens,* a synonym of *operatio,* the opposite of *factio.* This action is in the category of *quality,* also called metaphysical, (3) *transient action,* i.e. *actio transiens,* a synonym of *factio.* This is the Aristotelian category, called predicamental.—On the difference between *actio* and *passio,* see *passio* under 2. On **bonitas actionis,** see *bonitas* under 1; on **bonum actionis seu in actione,** see *bonus* under 2; on **defectus actionis,** see *defectus* under 2; on **malum actionis seu in actione,** see *malus* under 2; on **potentia actionis,** see *potentia* under 1; on **principium actionis,** see *principium;* on **principium primum et propinquum seu proximum actionis,** see *principium;* on **verbum exceptae actionis,** see *verbum* under 2; on **veritas actionis,** see *veritas* under 1; on voluntarium secundum actionem, see *voluntarius* under 3. *Actio transiens* is one of the nine categories of *accidens*. Cf. *accidens* under 2; i.e., it is one of the ten categories of Aristotle; see *genus* under 2 and *praedicamentum* under 2.—Kinds of *actio* in this (1) sense are: (a) actio artificialis and actio naturae seu naturalis, *the artistic* and *the natural action* or *the action of art* and *that of nature.*—(b), actio bona, actio indifferens, and also actio mala, *the normally good, the morally indifferent,* and *the morally bad action.*— (c), actio casualis, *accidental action.* Cf. *casualis.*—(d), actio civilis, *public* or *political action.* —(e), actio connaturalis, *action that conforms to the nature of a thing* or *that is according to its nature.*—(f), actio consistens in agente, see *actio exiens.*— (g), actio contemplativa seu contemplatoria and actio exterior, *contemplative* or *ascetic action* which is an action of the spirit and therefore *an interior action,* and *the exterior action* which is fulfilled in the sphere of the visible.—(h), actio corporalis and actio spiritualis, *the corporal* or *physical action* and *the spiritual* or *immaterial action.* Cf. *spiritualis.*—(i), actio debita, *due* or *obligatory action.* —(j), actio defectiva seu deficiens, *the defective* or *deficient*

action.—(k), actio determinata, *the definite* or *determined action.*—(l), actio disponens and actio perficiens, *the preparing* and *accomplishing action.*—(m), actio essentialis and actio personalis, *the essential* and *the personal action.*—(n), actio excepta, *the exceptional or impersonal action.*—(o), actio exiens seu progrediens seu tendens seu transiens in alterum seu in materiam exteriorem and actio manens seu consistens seu quiescens in agente, *the transient action* or *that which goes forth and fulfills itself in something alien and the immanent action* or *that which remains within the agent.*—(p), actio exterior, see *actio contemplativa.*—(q), actio hierarchia, *hierarchical action* or *action performed by members of a hierarchy as such.*—(r), actio hominis and actio humana, *the action of man* or *human action.* —(s), actio humana, see *actio hominis.*—(t), actio indifferens, see *actio bona.*—(u), actio indiscreta, *the undifferentiated* or *undistinguished action.*—(v), actio in distans, *action upon the distant* or *action in the distance.* —(w), actio instantanea and actio successiva, *action that takes place in a moment* and *action that takes place in successive moments.*—(x), actio intellectualis, *intellectual action,* by which is to be understood both the action of the intellect itself and that which comes under the influence of the intellect of another.—(y), **actio intellegibilis**, *intellectual action* or *action of the intellect*.—(z), **actio liberalis**, *free action* or *action befitting the free*.—(a²), **actio ludicra**, *the action of jest* or *play*.—(b²), **actio manens**, see *actio exiens*.—(c²), **actio meritoria**, *meritorious action*.—(d²), **actio mixta**, **actio violenta**, and **actio voluntaria seu voluntatis**, *the mixed action* (from force and free will), *the forced action*, and *the voluntary action*.—(e²) **actio moralis** and **actio physica**, *the moral or ethical action* and *the physical action* or *the action accomplished by a thing as a being of nature*.—(f²), **actio naturae**, see *actio artificialis*.—(g²), **actio naturalis**, see *actio artificialis*.—(h²), **actio personalis**, see *actio essentialis*.—(i²), **actio perficiens**, see *actio disponens*.—(j²), **actio physica**, see *actio moralis*.—(k²), **actio progrediens**, see *actio exiens*.—(l²), **actio propria**, *the action proper to a thing* or *the appropriate action of a thing, characteristic action*.—(m²), **actio sacramentalis**, *sacramental action*.—(n²), **actio spiritualis**, see *actio corporalis*.—(o²), **actio successiva**, see *actio instantanea*.—(p²), **actio tendens in alterum**, see *actio exiens*.—(q²), **actio transiens**, see *actio exiens*.—(r²), **actio voluntaria**, see *actio mixta*.—(s²), **actio voluntatis**, see *actio mixta*.— *the*

action of the active principle, when it is received as an act upon the passive, is a reality of the latter and a form or *a beginning of a form of the same*.—**actio consequitur modum actus in agente**, *action regulates itself according to the measure of the reality in the agent*.—**actio cuiuslibet rei sequitur naturam ipsius**, *the action of anything is is directed according to its own nature and essence*.—**actiones in particularibus seu singularibus sunt**, *actions are always accomplished in particular* or *individual things, not in the general*, in that they are always directed to and terminate in an individual.—**actiones sunt individuorum seu singularium seu suppositorum**, *actions have their subjects in individuals* or *individual things* or *individual substances, not in their parts* or *forms* or *faculties*.—**actio proprie non attribuitur instrumento, sed principali agenti**, *an action in its proper meaning is to be ascribed not to the instrument but to the chief cause*.—**cuius est potentia, eius est actio**, see *potentia* under 2.—**eiusdem est potentia et actio**, see *potentia* under 2.—**posita actione sequitur effectus**, *when action is established* or *accomplished, the effect follows*.

active, *adv.*, see *activus*.

activus, a, um, *adj., concerning a deed* or *an effect* or *an action,*

doing, effecting, active, a synonym of *practicus,* the opposite
of *contemplativus, speculativus,*
and *theoricus* on the one hand,
on the other to *passivus* and
receptivus as well as *factivus*
and *operativus;* in grammar,
active voice. On **beatitudo activa,** see *beatitudo* under 1; on
causa activa, see *causa* under 1;
on **defectus activi principii,** see
defectus under 2; on **determinatio activa,** see *determinatio* under 1; on **dispositio activa,** see
dispositio under 4; on **felicitas
activa,** see *felicitas;* on **forma
activa,** see *forma* under 2; on
generatio activa, see *generatio*
under 1; on **habitus activus,** see
habitus under 4; on **impotentia
activa,** see *impotentia;* on **intellectus activus,** see *intellectus*
under 3; on **notio activa,** see
notio under 2; on **omnipotentia
activa,** see *omnipotentia* under
1; on **operatio activa,** see *operatio* under 2; on **organum activum,** see *organum;* on **origo
activa,** see *origo;* on **potentia
activa,** see *potentia* under 1 and
2; on **potestas activa,** see *potestas* under 1; on **principium activum et primum activum,** see
principium; on **privatio activa,**
see *privatio* under 1; on **qualitas
activa,** see *qualitas;* on **relatio
activa,** see *relatio;* on **religio activa,** see *religio* under 2; on
**scandalum activum, activum per
accidens et activum per se,** see
scandalum under 2; on **scientia**

activa, see *scientia* under 1; on
sphaera activa, see *sphaera* under 3; on **verbum activum,** see
verbum under 2; on **virtus activa,** see *virtus* under 1 and 5;
on **vita activa,** see *vita* under 3.
—**activum, i,** *n., the active principle, cause.*—**activum naturale,**
the natural cause.—**active,** *adv.,
in the manner and sense of action, actively,* the opposite of
passive and *receptive.* On **corrumpere active,** see *corrumpere*
under 2; on **creatio active accepta seu significata,** see *creatio*
under 2; on **generatio active
sumpta,** see *generatio* under 1;
on **origo active significata,** see
origo; on **possibile active,** see
possibile under 1; on **recipere
active,** see *recipere;* on **significare active,** see *significare.*

actor, oris, *m.,* 1) *doer, performer,
maker,* the opposite of *factor*
although sometimes its synonym,
(2) in judicial language, *one
who brings an action, plaintiff,*
the opposite of *reus,* (3) *administrator.*

actualis, e, *adj.,* (1) *active, actual,*
understood in the sense of an
activity, consisting in an activity, appearing in the form of an
activity, concerning an activity,
the opposite of *habitualis* and
virtualis, (2) *active, actual,* i.e.,
taking place in reality, being in
the state of reality, the opposite
of *possibilis* and *potentialis.*—
On **amor actualis,** see *amor* under 1; on **applicatio actualis,**

see *applicatio* under 3; on **apprehensio actualis**, see *apprehensio* under 2; on **caritas actualis**, see *caritas;* on **cogitatio actualis**, see *cogitatio* under 2; on **cognitio actualis**, see *cognitio* under 2; on **concupiscentia actualis**, see *concupiscentia* under 2; on **continuitas actualis**, see *continuitas* under 2; on **culpa actualis**, see *culpa;* on **cupiditas actualis**, see *cupiditas;* on **delectatio actualis**, see *delectatio;* on **dispositio actualis**, see *dispositio;* on **divisio actualis**, see *divisio;* on **intentio actualis**, see *intentio* under 2; on **libido actualis**, see *libido* under 2; on **macula actualis**, see *macula;* on **malitia actualis**, see *malitia* under 3; on **meritum actuale**, see *meritum* under 1; on **notitia actualis**, see *notitia* under 2; on **ordinatio actualis**, see *ordinatio* under 3; on **paupertas actualis**, see *paupertas* under 2; on **peccatum actuale**, see *peccatum* under 2; on **respectus actualis**, see *respectus;* on **scientia actualis**, see *scientia* under 1; on **visio actualis**, see *visio* under 1; on **voluntas actualis**, see *voluntas* under 3.—On **bonum actuale**, see *bonus* under 3; on **causa actualis**, see *causa* under 2; on **cognitio actualis**, see *cognitio* under 2; on **compositio actualis**, see *compositio* under 1; on **confessio actualis**, see *confessio* under 2; on **consideratio actualis**, see *consideratio;* on **diversitas actualis**, see *diversitas;* on **inspi-**

ratio actualis, see *inspiratio;* on **intellegentia actualis**, see *intellegentia* under 2; on **motio actualis**, see *motio;* on **operatio actualis**, see *operatio* under 2; on **relatio actualis**, see *relatio;* on **representatio actualis**, see *representatio;* on **sanctificatio actualis**, see *sanctificatio* under 1.

actualiter, *adv.*, (1) *after the manner* or *in the sense of an action, actively,* the opposite of *habitualiter* and *virtualiter,* (2) *in a real way, in reality, actually,* the opposite of *potentialiter.*— On **considerare actualiter**, see *considerare;* on **intellegere actualiter**, see *intellegere* under 1.

actualitas, atis, *f.*, (1) *realization, efficacy,* (2) *actual realization, actuality,* a synonym of *esse,* the opposite of *potentialitas.*

actualiter, *adv.*, see *actualis.*

actuo, are, avi, atum, 1, *v. a., to activate, realize, put in a state of reality.*

actuosus, a, um, *adj., pertaining to the active, full of activity, busy.*

actus, us, *m.*, (1) *action, activity, act,* a synonym of *actio* and *operatio,* the opposite of *habitus* and *potentia,* (2) *reality, real being,* the opposite of *potentia* and *potestas,* (3) *deed, activity, Acts of the Apostles.*—On **bonitas actus moralis et ex essentia actus**, see *bonitas* under 1; on **bonum in actibus humanis**, see *bonus* under 2; on **circumstantia actus**, see *circumstantia* under

2

1; on **continuatio actus,** see *continuatio* under 2; on .**delectatio secundum actum,** see *delectatio;* on **imperfectio actus,** see *imperfectio;* on **libertas quantum ad actum,** see *libertas* under 2; on **perfectio actus,** see *perfectio* under 2; on **qualitas actus,** see *qualitas;* on **quantitas actus,** see *quantitas* under 2; on **significare per modum actus,** see *significare;* on **substantia actus,** see *substantia* under 8; on **voluntas praecedens actum,** see *voluntas* under c.—Kinds of **actus** in this (1) sense are: (a), **actus absolute bonus,** *the simply morally good act,* which is opposed to the relatively morally good act.—(b), **actus bestialis,** *the bestial or brutal act,* so-called because it makes man like a beast.—(c), **actus bonus, actus indifferens,** and **actus malus,** *the morally good, the morally indifferent, and the morally evil act.*—(d), **actus carnalis,** *the carnal act or the act accomplished by the flesh.*—(e), **actus casualis,** *the incidental act or the act occasioned by chance.*—(f), **actus clavis seu clavium,** *the act of the* (ecclesiastical) *power of the keys.*—(g), **actus coactus** and **actus voluntarius,** *the forced* and *the voluntary act.*—(h), **actus coniugalis seu matrimonialis seu martimonii,** the *matrimonial or connubial act.*—(i), **actus continuus,** *the continuous or unbroken act.*—(j), **actus cul-**

pae, *the act of guilt* or *involving guilt.*—(k), **actus deficiens seu imperfectus** and **actus perfectus,** *the defective or imperfect act* and *the perfect act.*—(l), **actus deformis,** *the formless act.*—(m), **actus demeritorius** and **actus meritorius,** *the unmeritorious and the meritorious act.*—(n), **actus deordinatus seu inordinatus** and **actus ordinatus seu regulatus,** *the act not regulated* (by reason) or *the disordered act* and *the act regulated* (by reason) or *the ordered act.*—(o), **actus elicitus** and **actus imperatus,** *the act called forth by a faculty* or *accomplished by it* and *the act commanded or ordered by it.* Both of these usually belong to different faculties but at times they may stem from one and the same, namely the will.—(p), **actus essentialis** and **actus personalis,** *the essential* and *the personal act,* i.e., the act which comes from the nature or essence of a thing and that which is accomplished by a person as such.—(q), **actus exterior** and **actus interior seu intrinsecus,** *the exterior act,* i.e. the act which appears in the exterior or corresponds in the exterior to a faculty, and *the inner act,* i.e., the act which is accomplished within a thing or a faculty. Cf. *voluntas* under 2.—(r), **actus figuralis,** *the figurative or symbolic act.*—(s), **actus formae,** *the act of the (substan-*

tial) *form of a thing.* Cf. **effectus formae** under *effectus* and **principium primum actionis** under *actio* 1.—(t), **actus formaliter bonus** and **actus materialiter bonus,** *the act morally good, formally* and *materially.*—(u), **actus generativus** and **actus praeparativus,** *the generative* or *productive act* and *the preparatory act.* —(v), **actus hierarchicus,** *the hierarchical act* or *the act accomplished by the member of a hierarchy as such.*—(w), **actus hominis** and **actus humanus,** *the act of a human being* and *the human act.*—(x), **actus humanus,** see *actus hominis.*—(y), **actus illicitus,** *the morally prohibited act.*—(z), **actus imperatus,** see *actus elicitus.*—(a²), **actus imperfectus,** see *actus deficiens.*—(b²), **actus indifferens,** see *actus bonus.*—(c²), **actus indifferens ad vitam seu minimus** and **actus necessarius ad vitam seu principalis,** *the act indifferent* or *least necessary for life* and *the act necessary and of first importance for life.*—(d²), **actus indirectus** and **actus rectus,** *the indirect* and *the direct act.*—(e²), **actus individuus seu particularis seu singularis,** *the individual* or *particular* or *single act.*—(f²), **actus inordinatus,** see *actus deordinatus.*—(g²), **actus interior seu intrinsecus,** see *actus exterior.*— (h²), **actus laudabilis,** *the praiseworthy act.*—(i²), **actus legitimus,** *the lawful act* or *the act*

administered by the law.—(j²), **actus materialiter bonus,** see *actus formaliter bonus.*—(k²), **actus matrimonialis,** see *actus coniugalis.*—(l²), **actus matrimonii,** see *actus coniugalis.*—(m²), **actus mercenarius,** *the mercenary act.* —(n²), **actus meritorius,** see *actus demeritorius.*—(o²), **actus minimus,** see *actus indifferens ad vitam.*—(p²), **actus miraculosus,** *the miraculous act.*—(q²), **actus moralis, actus naturae,** *the moral* and *the physical act,* or *the activity that belongs to the sphere of morals and that which proceeds from a human nature.*— (r²), **actus naturae,** see *actus moralis.*—(s²), **actus necessarius ad vitam,** see *actus indifferens ad vitam.*—(t²), **actus notionalis,** *the notional act,* i.e., *that activity in God which establishes a notio.*—(u²), **actus ordinatus,** see *actus deordinatus.*—(v²), **actus particularis,** see *actus individuus.*—(w²), **actus per accidens bonus** and **actus per se bonus,** *the morally good act by reason of an accident* and *the morally good act by reason of itself* or *as such.*—(x²), **actus perfectus,** see *actus deficiens.*—(y²), **actus permanens** and **actus transiens,** *the permanent* or *lasting act* and *the transient* or *passing act.*— (z²), **acts per se bonus,** see *actus per accidens bonus.*—(a³), **actus personalis,** see *actus essentialis.* —(b³), **actus praeparativus,** see *actus generativus.*—(c³), **actus** principalis ad vitam, see *actus indifferens ad vitam.*—(d³), actus privatus and actus publicus, *the private* and *the public act.*—(e³), actus publicus, see *actus privatus.*—(f³), actus purus, *the pure act* or that with which nothing is mixed.—(g³), actus rectus, see *actus indirectus.*—(h³), actus regulatus, see *actus deordinatus.*—(i³), actus sacramentalis, *the sacramental act.*—(j³), actus scientiae, see *scientia* under 1.—(k³), actus simplex, *the simple* or *absolute act.*—(l³), actus singularis, see *actus individuus.*—(m³), actus spiritualis, *the immaterial* or *spiritual act.*—(n³), actus syllogisticus, *the syllogistic act, the act of drawing conclusions.*—(o³), actus transiens, see *actus permanens.*—(p³), actus virtuosus seu virtutis and actus vitiosus seu vitii, *the virtuous* and *the immoral* or *sinful act* and *the act of virtue* and *that of vice* or *of sin.*—(q³), actus virtutis, see *actus virtuosus.*—(r³), actus vitii, see *actus virtuosus.*—(s³), actus voluntarius, see *actus coactus.*—(t³), actus voluntatis, see *voluntas* under 4.—actus circa singularia or in particularibus est actus, *acts are accomplished only in individual things* and *under special circumstances.* Cf. *actio* under 1. actus cuiuslibet potentiae accipitur secundum ordinem potentiae ad suum obiectum, *the act of every potentiality is conceived and understood according to the relation of potentiality to its object.* actus distinguuntur ad invicem penes terminos et penes principia, *acts are distinguished among each other according to their objects* and *according to their faculties* or *principles.* Cf. *ratio potentiae diversificatur etc.* actus referuntur ad supposita, *acts are referred to individual substances as to their subjects.* Cf. actus sunt suppositorum. actus speciem recipiunt ex obiectis, *acts are specified through their objects,* or *formally different objects establish different kinds of actions.* In this connection note the following: sicut actus exterior accipit speciem ab obiecto circa quod est (see obiectum), ita actus interior voluntatis accipit speciem a fine sicut a proprio obiecto. actus sunt praevii potentiis sc. ratione seu secundum rationem definitivam, the translation of the Aristotelian passage: *proteron gar eisi ton dunameon hai energeiai kai hai praxeis kata ton logon.* (De Anim. II. 4. 415. a. 18 ff), *actions according to conception or definition are previous to the corresponding faculties, because their concept is contained in the definition of the faculty and therefore precedes it.* actus sunt suppositorum seu individuorum seu particularium seu singularium subsistentium, *actions have their subjects in individual sub-*

stances. Cf. above: *actus refe-runtur ad supposita.* actus terminatur ad aliquid simile agenti, *action aims at something as its result* or *product which is similar to the act.* cuius est actus eius est potentia, the inverted translation of the Aristotelian passage: *hou gar he dunamis, toutou kai he energeia, to whatever as its subject the act belongs, this is also subject of the faculty belonging to it.* cuius est habitus, eius est actus, see *habitus* under 4. cuius est potentia, eius est actus et e contrario, see *potentia* under 2; diversitas actus quandoque indicat diversitatem potentiarum, quandoque non, *diversity of action points sometimes to a diversity of faculty and sometimes not.* Cf. *potentia* under 1. eiusdem est potentia, cuius est actus procedens a potentia, see *potentia* under 2. habitus propter actus sunt, see *habitus* under 4. in particularibus est actus, see above: *actus circa singularia sunt.* non possunt esse unius potentiae simul plures actus, see *potentia* under 2. quales sunt habitus tales actus reddunt, see *habitus* under 4.—On causa in actu, see *causa* under 2; on cognoscere actu seu in actu, see *cognoscere* under 2; on contrarietas secundum actum, see *contrarietas* under 1; on convenientia potentiae ad actum, see *convenientia* under 2; on diversus actus, see *diversus;* on divi-

sio in actu, see *divisio;* on effectus in actu, see *effectus;* on ens actus, ens in actu et ens in actu simpliciter, see *ens;* on esse actu seu in actu, see *esse;* on exsistere actu, see *exsistere;* on infinitum actu seu in actu, see *infinitus;* on intellectus in ..ctu, see *intellectus* under 3; on intellegibile actu seu in actu, see *intellegibilis* under 2; on ponere in actu, see *ponere* under 2; on posterius secundum actum, see *posterior* under 2; on prius secundum actum, see *prior* under 1; on puritas actus, see *puritas* under 2; on scientia in actu, see *scientia* under 1; on scire in actu, see *scire* under 1; on sensus in actu, see *sensus* under 3; on sentire actu, see *sentire* under 1; on unum actu, see *unus;* on velle actu, see *velle* under 1; on verum actu, see *verum* under 1; on vita secundum actum, see *vita* under 2; on volitum actu, see *volitus;* on voluntas secundum actum, see *voluntas* under 3. Kinds of *actus* in this sense are: (a), actus completus seu perfectus and actus incompletus seu imperfectus, *the complete* or *finished* and *the incomplete* or *unfinished reality.* Cf. actus imperfectus et perfectus under 1.—(b), actus debitus, *the due or proper reality.*—(c), actus exsistendi, *the reality of being* or *existence.*—(d), actus imperfecti and actus perfecti, *the reality of the imperfect* or *that not yet fully passed into the state of reality, and the reality of the perfect or that of the fully passed into the state of reality,* i.e., motion in the proper and that in the improper sense of the word. Cf. *motus* under 1 and 2.—(e), **actus imperfectus,** see *actus completus.*—(f), **actus incompletus,** see *actus completus.*—(g), **actus participatus seu receptus,** *communicated or shared or received reality which is opposed to essential reality.*—(h), **actus perfecti,** see *actus imperfecti.*—(i), **actus perfectissimi,** *the most complete or the most perfect reality,* which is actually identical with *actus purus seu totus.*—**actus perfectus,** see *actus imperfectus.*—(j), **actus permanens seu quietus,** *the constant* (see *actus permanens* under 1) or *the quiet reality,* the opposite of *motus.*—(k), **actus potentiae permixtus** and **actus purus seu totus,** *the reality mingled with possibility or possible being,* and *the pure or total reality* which is nothing else than reality (actus tantum). Cf. *actus purus* under 1.—(l), **actus primus** and **actus secundus,** *the first* and *the second reality,* i.e., the reality which is the first of all realities, namely God.—(m), **actus proprius,** *the reality proper to a thing, the proper reality.*—(n), **actus purus,** see *potentiae permixtus.*—(o), **actus quietus,** see *actus permanens.*—(p), **actus receptus,** see *actus participatus.*

—(q), **actus secundus,** see *actus primus.*—(r), **actus superadditus,** *the reality added* (to the nature of a thing).—(s), **actus totus,** see *actus potentiae mixtus.*—(t), **actus ultimus,** *the last reality* by which it is to be understood as the opposite of *actus primus,* as *actus secundus,* i.e., the reality to be understood as the last and highest perfection of the being of a thing.—**actus est prior potentia ratione,** *reality or actuality is according to its conception and definition prior to the possibility or practicability.*—**actus est prior potentia substantia seu secundum substantiam, id est perfectione,** or, **actus est prior quam potentia, secundum substantiam et formam,** or, **actus secundum naturam est prior potentia,** *the reality or actuality is according to the nature or the essence or the form,* i.e., *according to its perfection or completion, prior to the possibility or practicability.*—**actus est prior potentia tempore,** or, **actus generatione et tempore est posterior potentia,** *reality or actuality is according to time and generation prior to possibility or practicality, and likewise the reverse holds good, whereby one speaks simply of reality and potentiality, or with reference to something.*—**actus est prior quam potentia secundum substantiam et formam,** see above: *actus est prior potentia substantia* etc. **actus et potentia** dividunt quodlibet genus entium, *every supreme genus of being is divided into the actual and potential of the genus concerned.* actus generatione et tempore est posterior potentia, see above: *actus est prior potentia tempore.* —actus secundum naturam est prior potentia, see above: *actus est prior potentia substantia,* etc. —agens agendo aliquid actu facit, see *agens.*—agere sequitur ad esse in actu, see *agere* under 1.—ens dividitur per potentiam et actum, see *ens.*—in bonis actus est melior potentia, . . . , in malis est actus peior potentia, *in the case of good things reality is better than potentiality, but in the case of evil things reality is worse than potentiality.*—nihil agit nisi secundum quod est actu, or, omne agens agit, inquantum actu est, or, unumquodque agit, secundum quod est actu, *every cause is effective only in so far as it exists in the state of reality.*—nihil secundum idem est potentia et actu, see *potentia* under 4.—non reducitur, quod est in potentia, in actum, nisi per id, quod est in actus, see *potentia* under 4.—omne, quod est in potentia, reducitur ad actum per id, quod est actu ens, see *potentia* under 4.—omne agens agit, inquantum est actu, see above: *nihil agit, nisi* etc.— potentia et actus sunt de primis differentiis entis, see *potentia* under 4.—proprius actus in pro-

pria materia fit, *every proper reality comes in a proper matter as in the subject bringing it into existence.*—proprius actus respondet propriae potentiae, *every reality corresponds to a proper potentiality.*—unumquodque agit, secundum quod est actu, see above: *nihil agit, nisi* etc.—unumquodque genus dividitur per potentiam ei actum, see *potentia* under 4.—quod est in potentia, naturaliter movetur ab alio, quod est actu, see *potentia* under 4.

acuitas, atis, *f., sharpness,* literally or figuratively.

aculeus, i, *m., a sting.*

acumen, inis, *n., a point, sharpness.*

acus, um, *f., a needle* or *pin.*

acutus, a, um, *v.* acuo, *P. a., sharpened, made pointed, sharp, pointed, keen,* used literally and figuratively.—acute, *adv., sharply, keenly.*

ad, *prep.* with *acc.,* (1) *at, near, to, till, for,* (2) *in relation to, with regard to, like, according to.*— Common phrases with *ad* in this sense are: (a), ad hoc, *for this purpose, to this end.*—(b), ad hoc quod, with *subj., for this, that, in order that.*—(c), ad invicem, *to each other, to one another.*—(d), terminus ad quem, see *terminus.*—(e), usque ad, *all the way to, continuous to.*— Common phrases with *ad* in this sense are: ad aliquid, *in relation to something,* a synonym of relativum, Aristotelian *on pros ti,* denotes relation to something or the existence of the relationship, one of the ten categories of Aristotle (see *genus* under 2, and *praedicamentum* under 2), On **distingui secundum ad aliquid**, see *distinguere;* on **magnus ad aliquid**, see *magnus;* on **oppositum ut ad aliquid**, see *opponere;* on **significare ut ad aliqiud**, see *significare.*—Kinds of *ad aliquid* are: (a), **ad aliquid ratione alterius seu secundum aliud** and **ad aliquid secundum se**, *the possessing a relationship to something in accordance with another or on the basis of another and the possessing a relationship to something in accordance with itself or as a result of its own essence.* —(b), **ad aliquid . secundum aliud**, see *ad aliquid ratione alterius.*—(c), **ad aliquid secundum rationem tantum** and **ad aliquid secundum rem**, *the possessing a relationship to something simply according to thought* or *simply in thought and the possessing a relationship to something according to fact and in reality.*— (d), **ad aliquid secundum rem**, see *ad aliquid rationem tantum.* —(e), **ad aliquid secundum se**, see *ad aliquid ratione alterius.*— **se habere ad**, *to hold oneself to, be related to, regard.*— **quantum** or **inquantum ad**, *in so far as concerns.*

adaequate, *adv.*, see *adaequo.*

adaequatio, onis, *f.*, *a making equal, equalizing, equalization, equation.*

adaequo, are, avi, atum, 1, *v. a.* and *n.*, *to make equal to, equalize, equate, equal.*—**adaequatus**, a, um, *P. a.*, *equalized, exactly suited* or *fitted, corresponding perfectly, adequate.* On **effectus adaequatus**, see *effectus;* on **forma adaequata**, see *forma;* on **ratio adaequata**, see *ratio.*

Adam, *indecl. m.*, or *gen. Adae,* also **Adamus**, i, *Adam*, the first man.

Adamantus, or **Adimantus**, i, *m.*, **Adamantus**, originally *Adantus* (*Adantos*), one of the twelve disciples of Manes or Manichaeus. Plotius (Contra Man. 1. 14) wrote the name as Adamantus. In the Greek form of Anathema he seems to be called Adam.

adamas, antis, *m.*, *adamant, magnet.*

adaperio, ire, ui, ertum, 4, *v. a.*, *to open, throw open.*

adapertio, onis, *f.*, *the act of opening, opening.*

adaptatio, onis, *f.*, *adapting, adaptation.*

adapto, are, avi, atum, 1, *v. a.*, *to fit, adapt, adjust,* used with the *dat.*

adaugeo, ere, xi, ctum, 2, *v. a.*, *to make greater by adding to, increase, augment.*

addico, ere, xi, ctum, 3, *v. a.*, *to give one's consent to a thing, adjudge, sentence,* with *dat.*, rarely with *ad* and *acc.*—**addic-**

tus, a, um, *P. a., dedicated, sentenced, destined.*

addisco, ere, didici, *no sup.*, 3, *v. a., to learn, be informed.*

additamentum, i, *n., addition, increase.*

additio, onis, *f., an adding to, addition,* the opposite of *subtractio* and *divisio.*

addo, ere, didi, ditum, 3, *v. a., to add to by way of increase, join* or *annex to, augment,* with *dat.* or *ad* and *acc.* or *super* and *acc.* or *supra* and *acc.*—**additus,** a, um, *P. a., added.*

adduco, ere, xi, ctum, 3, *v. a., to bring, prompt, induce, persuade, incite to,* used with *ad* or *in* and the *acc.,* with *ad* and gerund, also *absol.,* with *dat.* and with the *inf.* in quotation.—**adductus,** a, um, *P. a., adduced, cited, quoted.*

adeo, ire, ii, and rarely ivi, itum, 4, *v. n.* and *a., to go to, approach,* with *acc.*

adeo, *adv., to such an extent, so,* (1) with *adj.* alone, (2) with *quod* and *indic.* or *subj.,* (3) with *ut* and *subj.,* (4) with *quin* and *subj.*—**adeo quod,** *so much so that, so that,* with *indicative.*

adeps, ipis, *comm., the soft fat* or *grease of animals, suet, lard.*

adeptio, onis, *f., an obtaining, attainment.*

adhaerentia, ae, *f., power to cling, coherence.*

adhaereo, ere, haesi, haesum, 2, *v. n., to cling to, adhere to,* used with the *dat.* or *absol.*

adhaesio, onis, *f., an adhering, adhesion.*

adhibeo, ere, ui, itum, 2, *v. n., to bring* or *add to, apply, employ,* (1) used with *ad* and *acc.,* (2) *circa* and *acc.,* (3) *contra* and *acc.,* (4) *in* and the *abl.,* (5) *dat.* alone, (6) *absol.*

adhibitio, onis, *f., an employing, application.*

adhortor, ari, atus, 1, *v. dep., to encourage, exhort,* with *ad* and the *acc.,* used only in quot.

adhuc, *adv.,* (1) *thus far, until now, as yet,* (2) in temporal sense, *still, yet,* (3) *besides, furthermore,* (4) the equivalent of *eti* in comparisions for emphasis, *still, yet.*—**tamen adhuc,** *yet, still.*

adicio, see *adjicio.*

Adimantus, i, *m.,* see *Adamantus.*

adimo, ere, emi, emptum, 3, *v. a., to take away, destroy.*

adimpleo, ere, evi, etum, 2, *v. a., to fulfil, perform.*

adimpletio, onis, *f., a completing, fulfilling, completion, fulfilment.*

adinvenio, ire, veni, ventum, 4, *v. a., to find out, discover, devise.*

adinventio, onis, *f., a finding out, discovering, discovery, innovation.*

adinventivus, a, um, *adj., inventive.*

adipiscibilis, e, *adj., attainable by effort, obtainable.*

adipiscor, i, eptus, 3, *v. dep., to attain to by effort, obtain, acquire.*

aditus, us, *m., a going to, approach, access, admittance, entrance,* often used with *ad* and *acc., in* and *acc.,* and the *gen.*

adiectio, onis, *f., an adding to, addition.*

adiective, *adv.,* see *adiectivus.*

adiectivus, a um, *adj., that is added, adjective,* the opposite of *substantivus.* On **numen adiectivum,** see *nomen* under 1.— Kinds of *adiectivum* are: (a), **adiectivum essentiale** and **adiectivum personale,** *the essential and the personal adjective,* or *the adjective that expresses something essential and that which expresses something personal.*— (d), **adiectivum negativum,** *negative adjective, an adjective that expresses something negatively.*—(c), **adiectivum notionale,** *a notional adjective, an adjective that expresses a notion regarding God.*—(d), **adiectivum personale,** see *adiectivum essentiale.*—**adiective,** *adv., after the manner* or *in the sense of an adjective, adjectively,* the opposite of *substantive.* On **dicere adiective,** see *dicere;* on **significare adiective,** see *significare;* on **sumere adiective,** see *sumere;* on **tenere adiective,** see *tenere.*

adjicio, ere, ieci, iectum, 3, *v. a., to add* or *apply to a thing by way of increase, add a new thought* to what has already been said, *add* used with *ad* and *acc.,* (2) with *dat.,* (3) with

super and *acc.,* (4) simply with direct object.

adiudico, are, avi, atum, 1, *v. a., to adjudge, adjudicate, assign,* used with *acc.* and *dat,* or *in.*

adiunctio, onis, *f., a joining* or *binding to, addition.*

adiungo, ere, nxi, nctum, 3, *v. a., to add, join,* (1) with *dat.,* (2) rarely with *in* and *abl.,* (3) with direct object alone.—**adiunctus,** a, um, *P. a., joined, added, connected with.*—**adiunctum,** i, *n., something added, an adjunct.*

adiuratio, onis, *f., a swearing to, swearing, adjuration.*

adiuro, are, avi, atum, 1, *v. a., to swear to, confirm by an oath, adjure.* See on *adiuratio.*

adiutor, oris, *m., one who helps, a helper, an assistant.*

adiutorium, i, *n., help, aid, assistance, support.*

adiuvabilis, e, *adj., capable of being helped.*

adiuvo, are, iuvi, iutum 1, *v. a., to give aid, help, assist, support.* —**adiuvans,** antis, *P. a., helping, assisting,* sometimes used substantively.

adminiculor, ari, atus, 1, *v. dep., to support, prop,* used with *dat.*

adminiculum, i, *n., a prop, stay, support.*

administratio, onis, *f., ministration, direction, management, care, administration.*

administrative, *adv., administratively, in the manner* or *sense of an administrator* or *executor.*

administrator, oris, *m., he that is near to help* or *assist, manager, administrator.*

administratorius, a, um, *adj., performing the duties of an assistant, ministering, helping.*

administro, are, avi, atum, 1, *v. a., to manage, guide, administer, direct.*

admirablilis, e, *adj., worthy of admiration, admirable, wonderful.*

admiratio, onis, *f., an admiring, admiration, wonder, surprise, amazement.*

admirativus, a, um, *adj., admiring.*

admiror, ari, atus, 1, *v. dep., to wonder* or *be astonished at, regard with admiration, admire.*

admisceo, ere, scui, xtum, 2, *v. a., to add to by mingling, mix with, add to, admix.* Used (1) with *dat.* usually, (2) with *in* and *abl.,* (3) also *absol.*—**admixtus,** a, um, *P. a., that is mingled with something, mixed.*

admitto, ere, misi, missum, 3, *v. a., to suffer to come to a place, admit, allow, permit.* Used (1) usually with *ad* and *acc.* (2) with *in* and *acc.,* (2) *absol.*

admixtio, onis, *f., a mingling, an admixture, mixture.*

admoneo, ere, ui, itum, 2, *v. a., to remind, suggest, advise, warn, admonish,* (1) in general construed *absolutely,* also (2) with *acc.* of person, (3) with *acc.* of person and *de* and *abl.* of thing, (4) with *acc.* of person and *ut* (ne) and *subj.,* or *ad* and *gerund.*

admonitio, onis, *f.,* (1) *a reminding, calling to mind, suggestion,* (2) *a friendly, mild admonition,* (3) *correction, chastisement,* (4) *instruction.*

adoleo, ere, ui, ultum, 2, *v. a., to offer in worship, sacrifice, burn.*

adolescens, entis, *m., a young man.*

adolescentia, ae, *f., the time of youth, from the fifteenth to the thirtieth year, between the year of puer* and *iuvenis, adolescence.*

adolescentula, ae, *f., a very young maiden.*

adolescentulus, i, *m., a very young man.*

Adonai, *m., indecl., Adonai.*

adoptatio, onis, *f., an adopting, receiving,* as a child.

adoptio, onis, *f., a taking* or *receiving of one in the place of a child, an adopting, adoption.* On **filiatio adoptionis,** see *filiatio;* on **filius adoptionis seu per gratiam adoptionis,** see *filius* under 1; on **gratia adoptionis,** see *gratia* under 2.—Kinds of **adoptio** are *adoptio perfecta* or *arrogatio* and *adoptio simplex, the perfect* and *the simple* or *imperfect adoption of a child.*

adoptivus, a, um, *adj., pertaining, to adoption, made* or *acquired by adoption, adoptive, adopted.*

adopto, are, avi, atum, 1, *v. a., to take one in place of a child* or *grandchild, adopt.*

adoratio, onis, *f.,* (1) *worship, adoration, veneration of a superior being,* (2) *manifestation of adoration, exterior sign of* *the veneration of a superior being.*—Kinds of *adoratio* in this (1) sense are: (a), **adoratio corporalis seu exterior** and **adoratio spiritualis seu interior,** *the bodily* or *exterior adoration* and *the spiritual* or *interior adoration.* —(b), **adoratio duliae,** and **adoratio latriae,** *the adoration of service* and *the adoration of service to God,* i.e., the adoration of an exalted creature and the adoration of the Creator.— (c), **adoratio exterior,** see *adoratio corporalis.*—(d), **adoratio interior,** see *adoratio corporalis.* —(e), **adoratio latriae,** see *adoratio duliae.*—(f), **adoratio spiritualis,** see *adoratio corporalis.*

adorator, oris, *m., one who adores, a worshipper.*

adorior, iri, ortus, 4, *v. dep., to approach, undertake.*

adorno, are, avi, atum, 1, *v. a., to decorate, adorn, embellish.*

adoro, are, avi, atum, 1, *v. a., to reverence, honor, adore, worship,* used with *acc.* and *absol.* —**adorans,** antis, *m., adorer, worshipper.*

Adrianus, i, *m.,* also **Hadrianus,** i, *m., Adrian* or *Hadrian* (772-795), in 787 presided through a legate over the Seventh General Council held at Nicaea, when the Catholic doctrine regarding the use and veneration of images was upheld.

adscisco, ere, ivi, itum, 3, *v. a., to receive, admit.*

adscribo, ere, psi, ptum, 3, *v. a.,* (1) *to impute, ascribe, attribute,* construed with the *dat.,* (2) *enroll, admit,* with *ad* and *acc.*

adsto, are, stiti, no sup., 1, *v. n.,* also *asto, to stand at* or *near a person* or *thing, stand by.*

adstringo, ere, inxi, ictum, 3, *v. a., to bind, put under obligation, oblige, necessitate.*—**adstrictus,** a, um, *P. a., bound to, obligated, bound.*

adstruo, ere, struxi, structum, 3, *v. a., to affirm, establish.*

adsum, adesse, adfui, *v. n., to be present, be at hand.* Used (1) with *dat.,* (2) in the *abl.,* (3) *absol.*

adulatio, onis, *f., low, cringing flattery, adulation,* the opposite of *detractio* and *litigium,* a synonym of *placiditas,* SS. Q. 115 deals with *adulatio.*

adulator, oris, *m., a low cringing flatterer,* a synonym of *blanditor.*

adulor, ari, atus, 1, *v. dep., to flatter in a cringing manner, fawn upon,* used with *dat.* or *absol.*

adulter, eri, *m., an adulterer.*

adultera, ae, *f., adulteress.*

adulterinus, a, um, *adj., adulterous.*

adulterium, ii, *n.,* (1) *adultery* in the narrow sense of the word, the same as *adulterium carnale* under 2, a species or kind of *luxuria* and *iniustitia* and sometimes also of *avaritia,* (2) *adultery* in the broad sense of the word.—Kinds of *adulte-*

rium in this (2) sense are: **adulterium carnale** and **adulterium spirituale,** *the carnal* and *the spiritual adulterium* or *the violation of the matrimonium carnale* and *the violation of the matrimonium spirituale.* Cf. *matrimonium.*

adultero, are, avi, atum, 1, *v. n.* and *a., to commit adultery, pollute, defile.*

adultus, a, um, *P. a., grown up, adult.*

adunatio, onis, *f., a making into one, uniting, union.*

aduno, are, avi, atum, 1, *v. a., to make one, unite.*

aduro, ere, usi, ustum, 3, *v. a., to kindle, burn, scorch, dry up.*

adustio, onis, *f., a kindling, burning.*

adustivus, a, um, *adj., of burning, burning.*

advena, ae, *m.,* and *f., a foreigner, stranger.*

advenio, ire, veni, ventum, 4, *v. a., to come to, reach, arrive at,* (1) used *absol.,* (2) with *dat.,* (3) with *ad* and *acc.,* (4) with *in* and *acc.,* and (5) with *supra* and *acc.*

adventitius, a, um, *adj., that is present by coming, foreign, adventitious.*

adventus, us, *m., a coming, approach, arrival.*

adverbialiter, *adv., in the manner of an adverb, adverbially.*

adverbium, ii, *n., an adverb.*

adversarius, i, *m., an antagonist, opponent, adversary.*

adversative, *adv., in the manner or the sense of opposition, adversatively.* On **ponere adversative,** see *ponere* under 2.

adversitas, atis, *f., misfortune, suffering, adversity.*

adversor, ari, atus, 1, *v. dep., to stand opposite to one, oppose, resist.*—**adversans,** ntis, *m., adversary.*

adversum, i, *n., misfortune, disaster, adversity.*

adversus, *prep.* with *acc., facing, against.*

adverto, ere, ti, sum, 3, *v. a., to direct the mind to, heed, observe, notice*—**adversus,** a, um, *P. a., unfavorable, adverse.*—**adversum,** i, *n., something adverse, adversity, calamity.*—**ex adverso,** *adv. phrase, on the other hand.*

advesperascit, ere, avit, 3, *v. impers.* and *inch., it approaches evening, twilight is coming on.*

advocatio, onis, *f., legal assistance, counsel at law, legal counsel.*

advocatus, i, *m.,* also **advocata,** ae, *f., legal assistant, counsellor, advocate.*

advoco, are, avi, atum, 1, *v. a., to call someone* to a place or to someone for counsel or aid; in judicial language, *avail oneself* of some one in a cause as *aid, assistant, witness, counsellor; call in.* Used with *ad* and *acc.,* also *absol.*

advolo, are, avi, atum, 1, *v. n., to fly to* or *towards,* used with *in* and *acc.*

advolvo, ere, vi, volutum, 3, *v. a.*, *to roll to* or *toward,* with *dat.*

aedificatio, onis, *f.*, (1) abstr., *the act of building, a building* or *constructing,* used (a), *absol.,* (b) with the *gen.*, (2) concr., *a building, structure, edifice,* (3) fig., *building up, instructing, edification,* used (a) *absol.,* (b) with *gen.*

aedificativus, a, um, *adj., building, constructing,* a synonym of *aedificatorius.* On **ars aedificativa,** see *ars* under 2.

aedificator, oris, *m., a builder.*

aedificatorius, a, um, *adj., building, constructing,* a synonym of *aedificativus.* On **ars aedificatoria,** see *ars* under 2.

aedificium, i, *n., a building of any kind, an edifice, structure,* used (1) concretely, (2) figuratively. —**spirituale aedificium,** *spiritual edifice.*

aedifico, are, avi, atum, 1, *v. a.*, (1) lit., *to erect a building, build,* used (a) *absol.,* (b) with *object,* (2) in gen., *to build* or *erect anything,* (3) fig., *to build up, establish, instruct, edify,* used (a) *absol.,* (b) with *object.*

aeger, gra, grum, *adj., ill, sick, unwell,* the opposite of *sanus,* used lit. and fig.

aegritudinalis, e, *adj., sickly, caused by disease, unhealthy.*

aegritudo, inis, *f., illness, sickness,* either of body or mind or soul, the opposite of *sanitas,* a synonym of *infirmitas* and *morbus.*

aegrotatio, onis, *f., illness, sickness, disease, infirmity,* properly only of body, while *aegritudo* and *morbus* also designate that of mind and soul.

aegrotativus, a, um, *adj., inclined to sickness.*

aegroto, are, avi, atum, 1, *v. n.*, *to be ill, sick,* in the S.T. used only of the body.

aegrotus, a, um, *adj., ill, sick, diseased,* a synonym of *aeger,* used in the S.T. only of the body.

Aegyptia, ae, *f., an Egyptian woman.*

Aegyptiacus, a, um, *adj., Egyptian.*

Aegyptius, ii, *m., an Egyptian.*

Aegyptus, i, *f., Egypt.*

aemulatio, onis, *f., an assiduous striving to equal* or *excel another in anything, emulation.*

aemulator, oris, *m., a zealous imitator, emulator.*

aemulor, ari, atus, 1, *v. dep., to rival, endeavor to equal* or *to excel, emulate.*

aemulus, a, um, *adj., emulating, rivalling, emulous,* as a substantive, *rival.*

Aeneis, idis or idos, *f., the Aeneid of Vergil.*

aeneus, a, um, *adj., of copper* or *bronze.*

aenigma, atis, *n., that which is dark, obscure* or *inexplicable, a riddle, enigma, obscurity,* a synonym of *obscuritas.*

aenigmaticus, a um, *adj., like an enigma, obscure, enigmatic,* a synonym of *obscurus.* On **cognitio aenigmatica,** see *cognitio*

under 2; on **visio aenigmatica,**
see *visio* under 1.

aequabilis, e, *adj., equal, consistent, uniform, equable.*

aequalis, e, *adj.,* (1) *equally
great, equal in the sense of
bodily size,* the opposite of
inaequalis, (2) *equally great,
equal* in a figurative sense.
See *aequalitas.*—Kinds of *aequale* in this (1) sense are: (a),
aequale secundum proportionem and **aequale secundum
quantitatem** or **quantitatem absolutam,** *equally great according
to relation* and *equally great
according to greatness* or *absolute greatness.*—(b), **aequale
secundum quantitatem** or **quantitatem absolutam,** seé (a).—(c),
aequale simpliciter, *simply* or
entirely equally great. On **amicitia inter aequales,** see *amicitia*
under 1; on **complexio aequalis,**
see *complexio* under 2; on
iurisdictio aequalis, see *iurisdictio;* on **iustitia aequalis,** see
iustitia under 1; on **iustum
aequale** and **iustus aequalis,** see
iustus; on **terminus aequalis,** see
terminus under 4.—**ex aequali,**
equally.—**aequaliter,** *adv., equally, uniformly, in equal measure,
in like manner.* On **praedicare
aequaliter et aequaliter ad invicem** see *praedicare* under 2;
on **procedere aequaliter,** see
procedere under 4.

aequalitas, atis, *f.,* (1) *equal
greatness, equality in bodily
size,* the opposite of *inaequalitas,*
(2) *equal greatness, equality* in
a figurative sense, the opposite
of *inaequalitas* and *disparitas,*
(3) *equality, uniformity* of a
thing.—On **proportio aequalitatis,**
see *proportio* under 1.—Kinds of
aequalitas in this (1) sense are:
(a), **aequalitas absoluta seu
omnimoda seu simpliciter** and
aequalitas aliqualis seu secundum quid, *the simple* or *complete equality,* and *the equality
in a certain measure* or *in a relative way.*—(b), **aequalitas aequiperantiae,** *the equality of
comparison in all and in every
respect,* the opposite of *aequalitas seu proportio partium ad invicem.*—(c), **aequalitas aliqualis,**
see *aequalitas absoluta.*—(d), **aequalitas arithmetica seu secundum arithmeticam medietatem
seu quantitatis** and **aequalitas
geometrica seu proportionis,** *the
arithmetical* and *the geometrical
equality* or *the equality of the
absolute* and *that of proportion.*
—(e), **aequalitas geometrica,** see
aequalitas arithmetica.—(f), **aequalitas omnimoda,** see *aequalitas absoluta.*—(g), **aequalitas
proportionis,** see *aequalitas arithmetica.*—(h), **aequalitas quantitatis,** see *aequalitas arithmetica.*—(i), **aequalitas secundum
arithmeticam medietatem,** see
aequalitas arithmetica.—(j), **aequalitas secundum quantitatem
absolutam** and **aequalitas secundum quantitatem comparatam,** *the equality of absolute*

quantity and *that of compared quantity* or *relative size*. Cf. **aequalitas arithmetica**.—(k), **aequalitas secundum quantitatem comparatam**, see *aequalitas secundum quantitatem absolutam*.—(1), **aequalitas secundum quid**, see *aequalitas absoluta*.—(m), **aequalitas simpliciter**, see *aequalitas absoluta*.—On **comparatio aequalitatis**, see *comparatio* under 2; on **iustitia aequalitas**, see *iustitia*; on **relatio aequalitatis**, see *relatio*.—Kinds of **aequalitas** in this (2) sense are: (a), **aequalitas mutua**, *the common* or *mutual equality of two things*.—(b), **aequalitas secundum quantitatem virtualem**, *equality according to the greatness of a power*.

aequaliter, *adv.*, see *aequalis*.

aequanimitas, atis, *f.*, *calmness, patience, equanimity*.

aequanimiter, *adv.*, *calmly, with equanimity*.

aeque, *adv.*, see *aequus*.

aequidistantia, ae, *f.*, *an equal distance*.

aequinoctialis, e, *adj.*, *pertaining to the equinox, equinoctial*, with *circulus* = *the equator*.

aequinoctium, i, *n.*, *the time of equal days* and *nights, equinox*.

aequiparantia, ae, *f.*, *complete equalization, coordination, equality*, a synonym of *adaequatio*. On **aequalitas aequiparatiae**, see *aequalitas* under 1; on **relatio aequiparantiae**, see *relatio;* on **similitudo aequiparantiae seu secundum aequiperantiam**, see *similtudo* under 1.

aequipero, (also **aequipar**), are, avi, atum, 1, *v. a.* and *n.*, *to put a thing on an equality with another thing, equalize*, with *dat.*

aequipolleo, ere, *v. n.*, *to be of equal value* or *significance*. On *enuntiatio aequipollens*, see *enuntiatio* under 2; on **propositio aequipollens**, see *propositio* under 2.

aequitas, atis, *f.*, *the virtue of doing what is right* and *just, justice, equity*, a synonym of *epikeia* and *iustitia*, the opposite of *iniquitas and iniustitia*.—Kinds of *aequitas* are: **aequitas moralis** and **aequitas naturalis**, *the moral* or *ethical justice*, and *the natural justice*, i.e., *the justice which man gradually acquires* and *that which is his by nature*.

aequivalentia, ae, *f.*, *equivalence, the state of being equal in value*.

aequivaleo, ere, 2, *v. a.*, *to have equal power, be equivalent*.

aequivocatio, onis, *f.*, (1) *same name* or *title*, same name of two or more things which in their concept and essence are different; the opposite of *univocatio*, in which not only the name but the thing signified by the name is the same. This diversity may be (2) *ambiguity*, a complete difference or (3) *analogy*, a relative or proportional difference. It does not imply the pejorative and malicious sense of our English *equivocation*.—On **falla-**

cia aequivocationis, see *fallacia* under 2; on **significare per modum aequivocationis,** see *significare.*—Kinds of *aequivocatio* in this (2) sense are: **aequivocatio pura seu multum distans** and **aequivocatio propinqua seu proxima,** *the pure* or *the purely accidental* and therefore *remotely* (ab unitate generis) *existing* or *distant homonymity* (likeness of name) in sense 2, and the *closely* or *very closely existing homonymity because of the greater* or *smaller similarity of the things designated by the same name.*

aequivoce, *adv.,* see *aequivocus.*

aequivoco, are, avi, atum, 1, *v. a.* and *n., to use in an equivocal sense, equivocate, but not with intent to deceive.*

aequivocus, a, um, *adj.,* (1) *homonymous,* of like name in the broad sense of the word; all things are so called which share the same name but not the same idea and essence, whether they are alike or not; opposite of *univocus,* and therefore inclusive of analogous, see below, (2) *homonymous, of like name* in the narrow sense of the word, applied to those things which bear the same name but are not only different in idea and essence, but are not similar to each other, a synonym of *aequivocus a casu,* opposite of *analogicus* or *analogus.*—On **agens aequivocum,** see *agens;*

on **causa aequivoca,** see *causa* under (b); on **effectus aequivocus,** see *effectus;* on **generatio aequivoca,** see *generatio* under 1. One kind of *aequivocus* in the broad sense of the word is **aequivocus a casu seu per casum et fortunam seu omnino seu pure,** *accidently* or *wholly* or *purely* and *simply homonymous,* the opposite of *analogicum seu analogum,* which is called **aequivocus a consilio.**—*Omne aequivocum reducitur ad univocum,* every *aequivocum* is to be traced back to an *univocum,* i.e., essentially different things are designated by the same name because there are essentially similar things to which the name in question is first applied. On **dictio aequivoca,** see *dictio* under 2; on **nomen aequivocum** or **pure aequivocum,** see *nomen* under 1; on **praedicatio aequivoca,** see *praedicatio* under 2.—**aequivoce,** *adv.,* (1) *in the manner* or *sense of homonymy,* (2) *in the manner* or *sense of pure* or *complete homonymy,* synonym of *omnino* or *pure aequivoce.*—On **causa aequivoce agens,** see *causa* under 2; on **commune aequivoce,** see *communis* under 1; on **dicere omnino seu proprie seu pure aequivoce,** see *dicere* under 3; on **praedicare omnino seu pure aequivoce,** see *praedicare* under 2.—On **accipere aequivoce,** see *accipere* under 3;

on **dicere aequivoce,** see *dicere* under 3; on **praedicare aequivoce,** see *praedicare* under 2; on **sumere aequivoce,** see *sumere* under 3.

aequo, are avi, atum, 1, *v. a.* and *n., to make one thing equal to another, make oneself equal to another, consider equal, equal, rival,* used with *acc.* alone or with *acc.* and *dat.*

aequor, oris, *n., an even, level surface, the sea, waters.*

aequus, a, um, *adj.,* (1) *equal, equally great,* (2) *right, just, fair,* a synonym of *epiikes.—* ex aequo, *equally, in the manner of equality* or *of equal size. In the sense of equal* or *equally large measure.* On **significare ex aequo,** see *significare.* —On **ars aequi,** see *ars* under 2; on **iudicium aequi,** see *iudicium* under 2.—**aeque,** *adv., in like manner, equally.*

aer, aeris *m., the air, atmosphere, the lower atmosphere* as distinguished from *aether,* the upper pure air.

aereus, a, um, *adj., pertaining to the air, aerial, airy, high,* usually *aerius.*

aeromantia, ae, *f., divination from the state of the air, aeromancy.*

aerugo, inis, *f., the rust of copper, verdigris.*

aerumna, ae, *f., toil, hardship, distress.*

aerumnosus, a, um, *adj., full of trouble, wretched, miserable.*

aes, aeris, *n.,* (1) *any crude metal dug out of earth, copper, bronze,* (2) *money.*

aestas, atis, *f., the summer season,* as one half of the year from March twenty-second to September twenty-second; the other half was *hiems;* also in a restricted sense, the *summer,* the three months from the entrance of the sun into Cancer to the autumn equinox.

aestimatio, onis, *f., estimation, valuation, analysis, opinion,* a synonym of *existimatio.* On **agens per aestimationem,** see *agens.*—Kinds of *aestimatio* are: (a), **aestimatio confusa,** *obscure* or *confused estimation,* as opposed to **aestimatio distincta,** *clear* and *definite estimation.—* (b), **aestimatio corrupta seu falsa,** and **aestimatio recta seu vera seu iusta,** *the corrupted* or *false* and *the right* or *true* or *just estimation.—*(c), **aestimatio falsa,** see *aestimatio corrupta.—*(d), **aestimatio grossa,** *the rough* or *approximate estimation.—*(e), **aestimatio iusta,** see *aestimatio corrupta.—*(f), **aestimatio naturalis,** *the natural estimation* or *the estimation suggested by nature.—*(g), **aestimatio particularis,** *particular estimation, estimation with reference to the particular* or *individual.—*(h), **aestimatio recta,** see *aestimatio corrupta.—*(i), **aestimatio vera,** see *aestimatio corrupta.*

aestimativus, a, um, *adj.*, *estimating*, *valuating*, *analysing*, *sentient faculty of valuation* or *sentient power of judgment*, that faculty of the animal by which it recognizes the individual relations of usefulness and harmfulness which confront it but are not comprehensible to the external senses; always used in the S.T. in the feminine gender agreeing with *potentia*, *virtus*, *vis*, either expressed or understood.—On **potentia aestimativa**, see *potentia* under 2; on **virtus aestimativa**, see *virtus* under 1; on **vis aestimativa**, see *vis* under 1. This faculty is also called **aestimativa naturalis**, *natural sentient power of evaluation*. On the difference between *vis aestimativa* of the animal and the corresponding *vis cogitativa* of man, see *cogitativus*.

aestimator, oris, n., *one who estimates the value of things, an estimator, a judge.*

aestimo, are, avi, atum, 1, *v. a.*, (1) *to determine* or *estimate the extrinsic* (money) *value of a thing, value, appraise,* used with *abl.* or *gen.* of value, (2) *to estimate the intrinsic* (moral) *worth of a thing, value, hold,* used with the *gen.;* with *pro.* and *abl.* of value; with *ex* and *abl., abl.* alone; *secundum* with *acc.* of the standard by which a thing is estimated.

aestivalis, e, *adj., pertaining to summer, summer-like.*

aestuo, are, avi, atum, 1, *v. n., to be in agitation or violent commotion, rage, burn with desire* or *passion.*—**aestuantius,** *more ardently.*

aestuosus, a, um, *adj., very hot.*

aestus, um, *m.,* (1) *fire, glow, heat,* (2) *fire* or *heat of any passion.*

aestas, atis, *f.,* (1) *the period of life, time of life, life, age,* (2) *a space of time, an age, generation, time,* (3) *the time* or *period of life for the man himself, the age for the men living in it.* Kinds of *aetas* in this (1) sense are: (a), **aetas corporalis,** *corporeal age, age of the body.*—(b), **infantilis aetas,** *infantile age, age of infancy.*—(c), **aetas iuvenalis,** *youthful* or *juvenile age.*—(d), **aetas legitima,** *legal age.*—(e), **aetas perfecta,** *perfect age.*—(f), **aetas puerilis,** *boyish age, age of boyhood.*—(g), **aetas spiritualis,** *spiritual age.*

aeternaliter, *adv., forever, incessantly, eternally, for all eternity, from eternity,* the opposite of *temporaliter.*

aeternitas, atis, *f., eternity,* the measure of the duration of a wholly immutable being. On the relationship between **aeternitas** and **aevum,** see *aevum.* On **nunc aeternitatis,** see *nunc;* on **ratio aeternitatis,** see *ratio* under 14; on **speculum aeternitatis,** see *speculum* under 1; on **veritas aeternitatis,** see *veritas* under 4. —Kinds of *aeternitas* are: (a), **aeternitas divina,** *divine eternity,*

eternity of God.—(b), **aeternitas mundi,** *eternity of the world.*—(c), **aeternitas participata,** *the eternity participated in* and *shared by the creature,* the opposite of *eternity of God.*

aeternus, a, um, *adj.,* (1) *eternal* in the true sense of the word, without succession of past, present, and future; see *aeternitas,* (2) *eternal* in the false sense of the word, i.e., *endless, unceasing,* the opposite of *temporalis* and a synonym of *diuturnus,* (3) *existing from primeval times,* (4) *immemorial, preceding primeval times.*—ab **aeterno,** *from eternity,* without beginning in time. On **dicere ab aeterno,** see *dicere* under 3; on **electio aeterna,** see *electio* under 2; on **filiatio aeterna,** see *filiatio;* on **fruitio aeterna,** see *fruitio;* on **electio aeterna,** see *electio;* on **generatio aeterna,** see *generatio* under 1; on **intellectus aeternus,** see *intellectus* under 3; on **lex aeterna,** see *lex* under 1; on **missio aeterna,** see *missio;* on **nativitas aeterna,** see *nativitas;* on **poena aeterna,** see *poena;* on **praedicare ab aeterno,** see *praedicare* under 2; on **processio aeterna,** see *processio;* on **ratio aeterna,** see *ratio* under 8; on **speculum aeternum,** see *speculum* under 1; on **suppositum aeternum,** see *suppositum* under 1; on **verbum aeternum,** see, *verbum* under 1; on **veritas aeterna,** see *veritas* under 1; on **voluntas aeterna,** see *voluntas*

under 3.—Kinds of *aeternum* in this (1) sense are: (a), **aeternum participative,** *eternity by participation.*—(b), **aeternum secundum quid,** *eternal in some respect.*—(c), **aeternum simpliciter,** *simply* or *absolutely eternal.* See (a) and (b).—**in aeternum,** *into eternity, forever, for an age,* a synonym of *in saeculum.* On **auctoritas aeterna,** see *auctoritas* under 4; on **beatitudo aeterna,** see *beatitudo* under 1; on **bonum aeternum,** see *bonus* under 3; on **mors aeterna,** see *mors;* on **peccatum aeternum,** see *peccatum* under 2; on **sacerdotium aeternum,** see *sacerdotium;* on **tempus aeternum,** see *tempus;* on **vita aeterna,** see *vita.*

aether, eris, *n., the upper pure bright air, aether.*

aethereus, (also **aetherius**), a, um, *adj., pertaining to the ether, ethereal, fiery,* a synonym of *empyreus.*

Aethiopia, ae, *f., Ethiopia,* a country in Africa on both sides of the equator.

Aethiops, opis, *m., Aethiopian.*

aetiologia, ae, *f., the teaching of causes* and *reasons, etiology.*

aeviternus, a, um, *adj., particiating in an aevum* or *age, aeviternal.*

aevum, i, *n.,* (1) *eternity in the* unreal sense of the word, a synonym of *aeternitas participata;* the measure of the duration of an incorruptible, and substantially immutable, but created being, i.e., an angel. Strictly speaking, there is only one *ae-vum,* the duration of the highest angel or spiritual substance, (2) *space of time,* a synonym of *saeculum.*—On **nunc aevi,** see *nunc.*

affabilitas, atis, *f., affability, friendliness, kindness, courtesy,* a synonym of *amicitia.*

affatus, us, *m., a speaking to, address.*

affectio, onis, *f., the relation to* or *disposition toward a thing produced in a person by some influence, agitation, inclination, affection, striving after, desire,* a synonym of *affectus* and *passio.* On **passio secundum affectionem,** see *passio* under 2; on **voluntas affectionis,** see *voluntas* under 3.—Kinds of *affectio* are: (a), **affectio animae,** *affection of soul.*—(b), **affectio animi,** *affection of the soul, spiritual faculty of desire.*—(c), **affectio bestialis,** *animal* or *bestial affection.*—(d), **affectio charitatis,** *affection of love.*—(e), **affectio carnalis,** *carnal affection* and *inclination.*—(f), **affectio cordis,** *affection* or *feeling of the heart.* —(g), **affectio devota,** *pious* or *devout affection.*—(h), **affectio exterior,** *exterior affection.*—(i), **affectio indebita,** *undue affection.*—(j), **affectio inordinata,** *inordinated* or *unregulated affection.*—(k), **affectio intellectiva,** *transcendental affection.*—(l), **affectio interior,** *interior affection.* —(m), **affectio ordinata,** *regu-lated affection.*—(n), **affectio quieta,** *calm* or *subdued affection.*—(o), **affectio sensitiva** or **sensualis,** *sensitive* or *sensual affection.* Cf. **affectio intellectiva.** —(p), **affectio terrena,** *earthly inclination* or *affection.*

affectivus, a, um, *adj., passionate, desiring intensely* or *passionately,* see *affectio* and *affectus,* a synonym of *affectualis.* On **cognitio affectiva,** see *cognitio* under 2; on **conclusio affectiva,** see *conclusio* under 2; on **pars affectiva,** see *pars* under 1; on **passio affectiva,** see *passio* under 2; on **potentia affectiva,** see *potentia* under 2; on **unio affectiva,** see *unio;* on **virtus affectiva,** see *virtus* under 1; on **vis affectiva,** see *vis* under 1.

affecto, are, avi, atum, 1, *v. freq., to exert one's self, to obtain, strive after, desire, covet.*—**affectatus,** a, um, *P. a., desired, coveted.* On **ignorantia affectata,** see *ignorantia.*

affectualis, e, *adj., affectionate, passionate,* a synonym of *affectivus.* On **unio affectualis,** see *unio.*

affectus, us, *m.,* (1) *state, condition, situation,* a synonym of *passio,* (2) *affectionate state* or *mood, inclination, desire, longing,* a synonym of *affectio* and *passio,* (3) *faculty of desire.*— On **approximatio secundum affectum,** see *approximatio;* on **magnitudo affectus,** see *magnitudo* under 3; on **perfectio se-**

cundum affectum, see *perfectio*
under 2; on **unio affectus sive
secundum affectum,** see *unio;*
on **unitas affectus,** see *unitas.*—
Kinds of *affectus* in this (2)
sense are: (a), **affectus dilectionis,** *the affection of love* or *the
affection consisting of love* (in
voluntate).—(b), **affectus misericordiae,** *the affection of sympathy* or *the affection consisting
of sympathy.*—(c), **affectus passionis seu secundum passionem**
and **affectus secundum rationem,**
*the affection of physical suffer-
ing* or that which takes place
merely by some physical change,
i.e., *the purely sensuous affection,* and *the affection which is
according to reason* and *is guided by it.*—(d), **affectus praesentis
saeculi,** *affection for* or *an attachment to this world* and *its
goods.* Cf. *luxuria.*—(e), **affectus
secundum passionem,** see *affectus passionis.*—(f), **affectus secundum rationem,** see *affectus
passionis.*—(g), **affectus simplex,**
the simple affection or *the roused
activity of the will,* called simple
because in contrast with the
proper affection it is *absque
passione vel animi concitatione*
and comes into being without
any physical change. Cf. *simplex actus voluntatis* under *voluntas* 2.—(h), **affectus terreno-
rum,** *an affection* or *attachment
for the earthly.*—(i), **affectus
uxorius,** *affection for wife.* On
emanatio affectus, see *emanatio;*

on **motus affectus,** see *motus*
under 2; on **passio affectus,** see
passio under 2.

affero, affere, attuli, allatum, *v. n.,*
(1) *to bring, bear, cause,* used
with *acc.* alone, with *dat.,* with
de and *abl.,* with *in* and *acc.,*
(2) *affirm, assert, adduce.*

afficio, ere, affeci, affectum, 3,
*v. a., to exert an influence on
body or mind so that it is*
brought into such or such a
state, *affect a person, affect,* (1)
used with *acc.* and *abl.* or in
pass. with *abl.,* (2) with *ad* and
acc., (3) with *secundum* and
acc., (4) with *circa* and *acc.,*
(5) with *in* and *acc.*

affigo, ere, ixi, ixum, 3, *v. a., to fix*
or *fasten to, attach to,* used with
dat. or *in* and *abl.*

affinis, e, *adj., that is neighboring*
or *a neighbor to, adjacent to,
near by family relationship,* the
opposite of *consanguineus,* used
(1) with *dat.,* (2) with *gen.,*
(3) *substantively.*

affinitas, atis, *f.,* (1) *relationship,*
(2) *affinity by marriage,* the
opposite of *consanguinitas.* On
gradus affinitatis, see *gradus.*

affirmatio, onis, *f.,* (1) *affirmation,
affirmative expression, positive
assertion,* a synonym of *positio*
and the opposite of *negatio, privatio,* and *remotio,* (2) *positive
settlement* of a thing, the opposite of *negatio.*—On **via affirmationis,** see *via* under 1; on **virtus
affirmationis,** see *virtus* under 6.
—Kinds of *affirmatio* in this (1)

sense are: (a), **affirmatio de prae-dicato finito, affirmatio de prae-dicato infinito,** and **affirmatio de praedicato privativo seu affir-matio privativa,** *the affirmation with a limited, that with an un-limited,* and *that with privative predicate.* Cf. *praedicatum.*— (b), **affirmatio de praedicato in-finito,** see *affirmatio de praedi-cato finito.*—(c), **affirmatio de praedicato privativo,** see *affirm-atio de praedicato finito.*—(d), **affirmatio incompacta,** *the af-firmation not entirely true.*—(e), **affirmatio privativa,** see *affirma-tio de praedicato infinito.*—(f), **affirmatio secundum quid** and **affirmatio simplex seu simplici-ter,** *the relative affirmation* or *the affirmation in a certain re-spect,* e.g., homo est iniustus, and *the simple* or *absolute af-firmation,* e.g., homo est iniustus. —(g), **affirmatio simplex seu sim-pliciter,** see *affirmatio secun-dum quid.*—(h), **affirmatio una,** *a single affirmation.*—**ad plura sese extendit negatio quam af-firmatio,** *the denial of a decision has a greater sphere than the assertion of its opposite.*—**affir-matio et negatio non sunt simul vera,** *affirmation* and *denial, which are opposed to each other, are not true at the same time.*— **affirmatio naturaliter est prior negatione,** or, **affirmatio secun-dum propriam rationem prior est negatione,** *affirmation is by na-ture* and *essence prior to nega-*

tion.—**in deo affirmationes sunt incompactae,** *affirmations made with reference to God are not entirely true.*—**si affirmatio est causa affirmationis, et negatio est causa negationis,** and the reverse, **si negato est causa ne-gationis, affirmatio est causa af-firmationis** (Cf. Aristotle's Anal. post. I. 13, 78. b. 17-21), *if the affirmation of something is the proper basis for the affirmation of something else, then also is the denial of the one the proper basis for the denial of the other,* and *vice versa.*—On **oppositio af-firmationis et negationis,** see *op-positio* under 2.—Kinds of *affir-matio* in this (2) sense are: **affir-matio imaginata, affirmatio in-tellecta,** and **affirmatio realis,** *the sensibly presented, the intel-lectually presented,* and *the truly positive settlement of a thing.*

affirmative, *adv.,* see *affirmativus.*

affirmativus, a, um, *adj., affirming, affirmative, asserting positively,* the opposite of *negativus* and *privativus.* On **demonstratio af-firmativa,** see *demonstratio* un-der 3; on **differentia affirmativa,** see *differentia;* on **enuntiatio af-firmativa,** see *enuntiatio* under 2; on **intellectus affirmativus,** see *intellectus* under 8; on **locus affirmativus,** see *locus* under 4; on **mandatum affirmativum,** see *mandatum;* on **praeceptum af-firmativum,** see *praeceptum;* on **praedicatum affirmativum,** see *praedicatum* under 1; on **propo-**

sitio affirmativa, see *propositio* under 2; on syllogismus affirmativus, see *syllogismus.*—affirmativa sc. enuntiatio or propositio, *the affirmative* or *positive expression* or *proposition.*—Kinds of affirmativa propositio or enuntiatio are: (a), affirmativa de praedicato finito, affirmativa de praedicato infinito seu infinita, and affirmativa de praedicato privativo seu privativa, *the affirmation with a limited, that with an unlimited* and *that with a private predicate.* Cf. *praedicatum* under 1.—(b), affirmativa de praedicato infinito, see *affirmativa de praedicato finito.*—(c), affirmativa de praedicato privativo, see *affirmativa de praedicato finito.*—(d), affirmativa infinita, see *affirmativa de praedicato finito.*—(e), affirmativa privativa, see *affirmativa de praedicato finito.*—(f), affirmativa simplex seu simpliciter, *the simple affirmation* or *the absolute affirmation* which is opposed to *affirmatio secundum quid,* i.e., the relative affirmation or the affirmation in a certain respect. Cf. affirmatio secundum quid under *affirmatio* under 1.—affirmative, *adv., in the manner* or *sense of an affirmation, affirmatively,* the opposite of *negative* and *privative.* On cognoscere affirmative, see *cognoscere;* on dicere affirmative, see *dicere;* on intellegere affirmative, see *intellegere;*

on significare affirmative, see *significare.*

affirmo, are, avi, atum, 1, *v. a., to present in words, assert, affirm, declare,* the opposite of *nego.*

afflatus, us, *m., afflation of the Holy Spirit, inspiration.*

afflictio, onis, *f., pain, suffering, torment.*

afflictivus, a, um, *adj., wounding, afflicting.* On amor afflictivus, see *amor* under 1; on passio afflictiva, see *passio;* on poena afflictiva, see *poena.*

affligo, ere, ixi, ictum, 3, *v. a., to strike* or *beat* a thing, *ruin, prostrate, afflict.*

affluenter, *adv., richly, affluently.*

affluentia, ae, *f., affluence abundance, profusion.*

affor, ari, atus, 1, *v. dep., to speak to, address, accost.*

Africa, ae, *f., Africa.*

Africanus, i, *m.,* Sextus Julius *Africanus,* a learned Christian writer of the third century who passed the greater part of his life at Emmaus in Palestine and afterwards lived at Alexandria. His principal work was a *Chronicon* in five books, from the creation of the world, which he placed in 5499 B.C., to A.D. 221. This work is lost but part of it is extracted by Eusebius in his *Chronicon,* and many fragments of it are preserved by other writers.

Agabus i, *m., Agabus.*

Agag, *indecl., n.,* Agag, *king of Amalec.*

Agamemnon, onis, *m.*, *Agamemnon, King of Mycenae,* son of Atreus and Aerope.

Agapitus (also *Agapetus*), i, *m.*, *Agapitus* or *Agapetus.*

Agar, *indecl. f.*, *Agar,* an Egyptian handmaid of Sara, the wife of Abraham.

Agatha, ae, *f.*, *Agatha,* a virgin martyred at Catalana in Sicily under Decius, Feb. 5, 251, according to her *Acta;* but under Diocletian according to the Martyrol. and Aldehelm (de Virgin. 22).

Agathensis, e, *adj., of Agde. Concilium Agathense, Council of Agde.*

Agatho, onis, *m.*, *Pope Agatho.*

agens, entis, see *ago.*

ager, agri, *m.*, (1) *improved* or *productive land, a field,* (2) metaph. for *Ecclesia, the field of the Lord* with its harvest of saved souls.

Ageruchia, ae, *f.*, *Ageruchia,* a high born lady of Gaul, to whom St. Jerome addressed a letter (CXXIII in Migne collection) on monogamy.

Aggaeus, i, *m.*, *Aggaeus,* one of those who returned from the first year of the reign of King Cyrus. Cf. the Prophecy of Aggeus in the Old Testament.

aggenero, are, 1, *v. a.*, fig., *to cause, engender, produce.*

aggravatio, onis, *f.*, (1) *heaviness, load,* (2) fig., *depression, aggravation.*

aggravo, are, avi, atum, 1. *v. a.*, (1) *to add to the weight of, make heavier, weigh down,* (2) fig., *make worse* or *more dangerous, aggravate,* (3) *oppress, burden, annoy.*

aggredior, i, gressus, 3, *v. dep.*, (1) *to go to, approach,* (2) *go against, attack, approach,* (3) *go to, set about, undertake, begin.*

aggregatio, onis, *f.*, *aggregation, sum.*

aggrego, are, avi, atum, 1, *v. a.*, (1) *to attach to, add to, reckon among, bring together,* a synonym of *adiungere,* (2) in *pass.*, *to attach one's self to, join.*

aggressio, onis, *f.*, *attack, assault.*

agibilis, e, *adj., feasible, practicable,* in the order of immanent activity, the opposite of *factibilis.* On **bonum agibile,** see *bonus* under 3.—**agibile,** is, *n., that can be done, the doable,* i.e., *the immanent action,* as opposed to *factibile, that can be made.* On **ratio agibilium,** see *ratio* under 6.—Kinds of *agibile* are: (a), **agibile circa bona vel mala unius hominis** and **agibile circa bona vel mala totius multitudinis civilis,** *action with reference to the good* and *the evil things of an individual person* and *that with reference to such on the part of the entire multitude* or *of the state.*—(b), **agibile circa bona vel mala totius multitudinis civilis,** see *agibile circa bona vel mala* *unius hominis.*—(c), **agibile particulare,** *the particular* or *single action.*—**prudentia est recta ratio agibilium,** see *prudentia* under 1.

agilis, e, *adj., that moves easily, agile.*

agilitas, atis, *f., mobility, nimbleness, quickness, agility.*—*agilitas* is one of the four *dotes* or characteristics of the glorified body at the resurrection.

hagios, a, on, adj., pure, unsoiled, unearthly.

agitatio, onis, *f., contemplation, consideration,* the opposite of *administratio.*

agito, are, avi, atum, 1, *v. freq. a.,* (1) *to stir, rouse,* (2) *to ponder consider.*

agmen, inis, *n., a collected multitude in motion, an army on the march, multitude.*

Agnes, etis, *f., Agnes,* a virgin 12 or 13 years old, beheaded at Rome under Diocletian, celebrated by Ambrose, Jerome, Augustine, and others.

agnitio, onis, *f., recognition, acknowledgment, knowledge.*

agnosco, ere, novi, agnitum, 3, *v. a.,* (1) *to declare, announce, acknowledge,* (2) *understand, recognize, know, perceive.*—**veritas agnita,** *known truth.*

agnus, i, *m., lamb.*—**Agnus Dei,** *lamb of God.*—**agnus paschalis,** *paschal lamb.*

ago, ere, egi, actum, 3, *v. a.,* (1) *to be active, do, treat, have effect, operate,* a synonym of *facere,* the opposite of *pati,* (2)

do, act in the sense of an immanent activity, the opposite of *facere,* (3) *effect, bring about, accomplish,* in the sense of a transient action, a synonym of *facere,* (4) *drive on, put into action, spur on,* in the sense of (2), (5) *treat, negotiate, settle,* (6) *bring to, lead.*—Common phrases are: (a), **agere gratias,** *to give thanks.*—(b), **agere vitam,** *to lead* or *live a life.*—(c) **agere poenitentiam,** *to do* or *perform penance.* On **intelligentia agens,** see *intellegentia* under 1; on **medium agere,** see *medium* under 2; on **potentia ad agere,** see *potentia* under 1; on **principium agendi, principium agens et principium agens propter finem,** see *principium;* on **sensus agens,** see *sensus* under 3.—Kinds of *ager* in this (1) sense are: (a), **agere abusive** and **agere proprie,** *to be active in the misused* or *improper sense of the word* and *in the proper sense of the word.*—(b), **agere a casu** and **agere a fortuna,** *to be active incidentally.* Cf. *casus* under 3.—(c), **agere a fortuna,** see *agere a casu.*—(d), **agere a necessitate seu ex necessitate seu in necessitate seu per necessitatem naturae seu per naturam** and **agere per intellectum seu per intellectum et voluntatem seu per voluntatem seu per arbitrium voluntatis seu per electionem voluntatis,** *to be active through force of nature* or *in consequence of an urge of nature,* and *to be active with reason* or *through reason* and *free will* or *in consequence of a free decision* or *choice of the will.*—(e), **agere consequenter** and **a primo,** *to be active in consequence of something,* and *to be active in the first place.*—(f), **agere effective seu efficienter, agere formaliter,** and **agere per modum causae finalis,** *to be active efficiently, in a formal way,* and *after the manner of the final cause.* Efficient action does not mean "highly useful"; it means productive or operative of an effect. Formal action has very little action in it; it means what makes any particular thing *that* thing and not something else, as whiteness formally makes snow white. Final causality is the influence some desirable goal has on an agent, moving him to seek after it.—(g), **agere efficienter,** see *agere effective.*—(h), **agere ex necessitate,** see *agere a necessitate.*—(i), **agere formaliter,** see *agere effective.*—(j), **agere in necessitate,** see *agere a necessitate.*—(k), **agere per accidens** and **agere per se,** *to be active by accident* or *indirectly* and *to be active of itself* or *according to its own nature* or *as such.*—(l), **agere per intellectum seu per intellectum et voluntatem,** see *agere a necessitate.*—(m), **agere per modum causae finalis,** see

agere effective.*—(n), **agere per modum efficientiae, agere per modum meriti, agere per modum satisfactionis, agere per modum redemptionis, and **agere per modum sacrificii,** *to be active after the manner of effecting, after the manner of deserving* or *merit, after the manner of satisfying, after the manner of redemption,* and *after the manner of sacrifice.*—(o), **agere per modum meriti,** see *agere per modum efficientiae.*—(p), **agere per modum redemptionis,** see *agere per modum efficientiae.*—(q), **agere per modum sacrificii,** see *agere per modum efficientiae.*—(r), **agere per modum satisfactionis,** see *agere per modum efficientiae.*—(s), **agere per naturam,** see *agere a necessitate.*—(t), **agere per necessitatem,** see *agere a necessitate.*—(u), **agere per necessitatem naturae,** see *agere a necessitate.*—(v), **agere per se,** see *agere per accidens.*—(w), **agere per voluntatem,** see *agere a necessitate.*—(x), **agere petitorio** and **agere possessorio,** *to be active in a petitory* and *in a possessory manner.* Cf. 4 Sent. 41 exp.—(y), **agere possessorio,** see *agere petitorio.*—(z), **agere primo,** see *agere consequenter.*—(a²), **agere proprie,** see *agere abusive.*—(b²), **agere secundum partem** and **agere secundum se totum,** *to be active according to one of its parts* and *according to its whole,* or *to be partially* and *wholly active.*—(c²), agere secundum quid and agere simpliciter, *to be active in a certain respect* and *to be active simply or absolutely.*—(d²), agere secundum se totum, see *agere secundum partem.*—(e²), agere simpliciter, see *agere secundum quid.*—(f²), agere ut praeeligens and agere ut ratiocinans, *to be active in a selective manner* and *in a deliberate manner,* or *to be active selectively* and *to be so deliberately.*—Agens agendo aliquid actu facit, see *agens.*—agens omne propter finem agit, see *agens.*—agere non est accidentium, sed substantiarum or, agere non est, nisi rei per se subsistentia, *being active* or *effecting is not an affair of accidents but of substances* or *of things existing by themselves* and *not in another.* Cf. actiones seu actus sunt suppositorum under *actio* under 1, and *actus* under 1.—agere sequitur ad esse in actu or, esse est prius natura, quam agere *activity follows upon reality* or *the being of a thing is by nature earlier than its activity.*—agit unumquodque ratione formae, *everything is active on the basis* and *by reason of its form.* Cf. omne agens agit per suam formam under *agens.*—eius est agere, cuius est esse, *that which has being has also activity,* i.e., *substance.* Cf. above: agere non est accidentium etc.—esse est

prius natura quam agere, see above *agere sequitur ad esse* etc.—nihil agit nisi secundum suam speciem, or, nihil agit ultra suam speciem, or, nulla res potest agere ultra suam speciem, *nothing is active beyond the limits of its species* and *outside its activities* unless it is active as an instrumental cause, per quem modum aliquid potest agere ultra suam speciem, non quasi virtute propria, sed virtute principalis agentis.—nihil agit nisi secundum quod est actu, see *actus* under 2.—nihil agit ultra suam speciem, see above: *nihil agit, nisi secundum* etc.—nihil agit ultra suam virtutem, *nothing is active beyond its strength;* cf. *nulla virtus activa agit ultra suum genus,* under *virtus* under 1.—non quaecumque apta nata sunt agere et pati ad invicem, sed solum illa, quae sunt contraria vel habent contrarietatem, *only those things are suited to influence each other, which according to their substance are not opposed to each other* and *carry in themselves opposing accidents.*—nulla res potest agere ultra suam speciem, see above: *nihil agit, nisi secundum* etc.—nullum agens corporale efficienter agit nisi per contactum, see *agens.*—omne agens agit, inquantum actu est, see *actus* under 2.—omne agens agit sibi simile, see *agens.*—omne agens assimilat sibi patiens, see *agens.*—omne, quod agit, potens esse agere, *all that is active possesses also the potentiality corresponding to it.*—unumquodque agit secundum quod est actu, see *actus* under 2.—On malitia acta, see *malitia.*—On potentia agens et acta, see *potentia* under 2.—(animalia) magis aguntur quam agunt, or, irrationalis magis aguntur ad operandum, quam seipsa agant, *animals or irrational beings are rather driven to their activities than they drive themselves.* sicut aliquid agitur naturaliter, sic aptum natum est agi, or, sicut agitur unumquodque cursu naturae, ita natur est, or, unumquodque, sicut agitur naturaliter, sic actum natum est agi, the translation of the Aristotelian passage: *hos prattetai houto pephuke* (Phys. II. 8,199. a. 9ff.), *as a thing activates itself naturally or according to the direction of nature, so it is also disposed to activity by nature.*—agens, entis, P. a., *doing, active, effecting,* the opposite of *patiens* and *passivus;* commonly used as a *substantive, agent, cause.* On bonum agentis, see *bonus* under 2; on causa agens, see *causa* under 1; on defectus agentis, see *defectus* under 2; on finis agentis, see *finis* under 2; on imperfectio agentis, see *imperfectio;* on intellectus agens, see *intellectus* under 3; on movere per modum agentis, see *movere;* on ordo

agentis, see *ordo* under 1; on praeparatio agens, see *praeparatio* under 1.—Kinds of *agens* in the sense of cause or effective cause are: (a), agens aequivocum and agens univocum, the cause which in relation to this effect is only remotely or relatively and therefore analogously or ambiguously a cause at all, or is capable of producing more than one kind of effect, and that which has species and essence in common with the effect. Thus the sun is the equivocal cause of heat, inasmuch as it moves the univocal cause—heated body—to produce its proper effect, heat; or the sun is the equivocal cause of the generation of this man, inasmuch as the sun disposes the matter and moves the univocal cause, the father, to impress the form or species of man in this matter.—(b), agens analogicum, *the agent similarly* or *relatively like* the univocal cause of an effect inasmuch as it influences and contributes to the production of the effect, but is specifically or even generically different from the effect, more often called in St. Thomas the *agens aequivocum.*—(c), agens artificiale, agens naturale, and agens per gratiam seu per caritatem, *the artistically active cause, the naturally active cause,* and *the cause active from love* or *grace.* —(d), agens consubstantiale, *the cause which is of like substance* (with its effect).—(e), **agens contractum seu finitum** and **agens indeterminatum,** *the cause which is restricted or limited in its action* and *that which is unrestricted.*—(f), **agens corporale seu corporeum** and **agens incorporeum,** *the physical* and *the immaterial cause.*—(g), **agens creatum** and **agens divinum,** *the created or produced cause* and *the divine cause.*—(h), **agens deficiens,** *the cause which is lacking or defective in its power.*— (i), **agens divinum,** see *agens creatum.*—(j), **agens exterius seu extrinsecum** and **agens interius,** *the exterior cause or the cause produced from without,* and *the interior cause.*—(k), **agens finitum** see *agens contractum.*—(l), **agens immediatum seu proximum seu propinquum,** and **agens remotum,** *the immediate or proximate cause and the remote cause calculated from that upon which it is to bring into effect.*—(m), **agens imperfectum** and **agens perfectum,** *the imperfect and the perfect cause.* —(n), **agens incorporeum,** see *agens corporale.*—(o), **agens indeterminatum,** see *agens contractum.*—(p), **agens inferius** and **agens superius,** *the lower or subordinate* and *the higher or or superior cause.*—(q), **agens instrumentale** and **agens principale seu principaliter,** *the instrumental* and *the chief cause.*

—(r), **agens insufficiens** and **agens sufficiens,** *the cause insufficient to produce an effect for itself,* and *the sufficient cause.*—(s), **agens intellectuale seu per intellectum seu per intellectum et voluntatem seu voluntarium,** and **agens naturale seu per naturam seu physicum,** *the rational cause or the cause that acts with reason* and *free will,* and *the natural cause or the cause guided by the blind force of nature.*—(t), **agens interius,** see *agens exterius.*—(u), **agens materiale,** *the material or physical cause.*—(v), **agens naturale,** see *agens artificiale, agens intellectuale,* and *agens supernaturale.*—(w), **agens organicum,** the organic cause.—(x), **agens particulare** and **agens universale,** *the particular* and *the general cause,* i.e., the cause which is able to bring forth a smaller sphere of effects and that which can bring forth all possible effects.—(y), **agens per aestimationem,** *the active cause or the basis of valuation* and *judgment.* —(z), **agens per caritatem,** see *agens artificiale.*—(a²), **agens perfectum,** see *agens imperfectum.* —(b²), **agens per gratiam,** see *agens artificiale.*—(c²), **agens per se,** *the cause active through itself,* presupposing the first motion from God.—(d²), **agens per voluntatem,** see *agens intellectuale.*—(e²), **agens physicum,** see *agens intellectuale.*—(f²), **agens** primum seu supremum and agens secundum seu secundarium, *the first* or *the highest cause* and *the second cause* or *the cause of second rank.*—(g^2), agens principale seu principaliter, see *agens instrumentale.*—(h^2), agens propinquum, see *agens immediatum.*—(i^2), agens proprium, *the proper* or *particular cause of a thing.*—(j^2), agens proximum, see *agens immediatum.*—(k^2), agens remotum, see *agens immediatum.*—(l^2), agens secundarium seu secundum, see *agens primum.*—(m^2) agens secundum necessitatem and agens secundum voluntatem, *the cause acting by natural necessity* and *that acting by free will.*—(n^2) agens secundum voluntatem, see *agens secundum necessitatem.*—(o^2), agens sufficiens, see *agens insufficiens.*—(p^2), agens superius, see *agens inferius.*—(q^2), agens supernaturale and agens naturale, *the supernatural* and *the natural cause.*—(r^2), agens supremum, see *agens primum.*—(s^2), agens universale, see *agens particulare.*—(t^2), agens univocum, see *agens aequivocum.*—(u^2), agens voluntarium, see *agens intellectuale.*—agens agendo aliquid actu fecit, *the acting cause through its activity effects something.* agens est honorabilius seu nobilius seu praestantius patiente, the translation of the Aristotelian passage: *aei gar timoteron to poioun tou*

paschontos, every active cause is more honorable or *more noble* or *more excellent than that which suffers something through its activity,* because it is in the same relation to the sufferer as the giver to the receiver, already possessing that which the sufferer is first to receive through its action. agens et patiens oportet esse simul, *the active cause and that upon which it is to act must exist at the same time* and *in the same place.* agens omne propter finem agit, *every active cause is busy for the sake of one end.* agens proximum oportet esse coniunctum, *the proximate cause must be bound with that upon which it is to bring about an effect.* nullum agens corporale efficienter agit, nisi per contactum, *a physical cause is operative as an active cause only when it is in contact with that upon which it is to bring about an effect.* omne agens agit, inquantum actu est, see *actus* under 2. omne agens agit per suam formam, *every active cause operates in consequence of* and *according to the form dwelling in it,* quae vel est essentia eius vel pars essentiae. omne agens agit sibi simile, or, omne agens assimilat sibi patiens, *every cause brings forth in that upon which it operates something similar to itself,* and this has its basis in that the effect already virtually virtualiter) exists in its cause. **Omne agens, excepto primo agente, in suo opere indiget subiecto, quod sit susceptibile suae actionis,** *with the exception of the first cause every cause needs an object for its action, which receives the effect.* **quodcumque agens est praesens tantum uni suorum effectum,** *the action of a cause which produces several effects always exists simultaneously only with one of them.*

agon, onis, *m.,* *contest* or *combat in the public games, Christian contest* or *combat, the contest* or *combat of this world.*

agonia, ae, *f.,* *anxiety.*

agonizo, are, avi, atum, *to engage in a conflict, strive.*

agresta, ae, *f.,* *juice of unripe grapes.*

agrestis, e, *adj.,* a synonym of *rusticus, rural, rustic, wild, boorish, rude.—***agrestis,** is, *m., farmer, peasant.*

agricola, ae, *f., a farmer, ploughman, countryman, peasant, boor.*

agricultura, ae, *f., agriculture.*

Agrippa, ae, *m., Agrippa,* the name of a king of Judea. He was the grandson of Herod the Great and son of Aristobulus and Berenice. He was sent to Rome by his grandfather but was forced to leave because of debts. But he returned to Rome and became a favorite of Tiberius and Caligula. In 37, Caligula ascended the throne and,

when he was assassinated, Agrippa supported Claudius who made him king of Judea. He governed satisfactorily to the Jews and persecuted James and Peter. He died suddenly at an exhibition of games at Caesarea, possibly by assassination.

Ahias, ae, *m.,* the prophet *Ahias* the Silonite.

aio, *verb, defect., say, affirm, assert.*

aithein, *to burn.*

ala, ae, *f., wing.*

alacritas, atis, *f., briskness, alacrity, promptness.*

alapa, ae, *f., a stroke or blow upon the cheek with the open hand, a box on the ear.*

alatus, a, um, *adj., furnished with wings, winged.*

alba, ae, *f., an alb, a white linen vestment.*

albedo, inis, *f., white color, whiteness.*

albo, are, *v. a., to make white,* in *pass. to become white.*

albugo, inis, *f., a white spot, a disease of the eye, film, albugo.*

Albumazar, also **Albumasar,** *indecl. m., Albumazar,* or *Abu-Maaschor,* 805-885, an Arabian astronomer. He was born in Balkh, lived in Bagdad, and died in Wasid of Central Asia. Three of his works were translated into Latin: De Magnis Coniunctionibus, Introductorium in Astronomiam, Flores Astrologici.

albus, a, um, *adj., white,* the opposite of *niger.*—**album,** i, *n., whiteness, white color, white* a synonym of *albedo.*

alchimia, also **alchymia,** ae, *f., alchemy, the art of making* or *changing base metals into pure metals, especially gold and silver, chemistry.*

alchimicus, a, um, *adj.,* also *alchymicus, alchemistic, chemical.*—**alchimicus,** i, *m., alchemist, chemist,* a synonym of *alchimista.*

alchimista, also **alchymista,** ae, *m., alchemist, chemist,* a synonym of *alchimicus.*

Alcibiades, is, *m., Alcibiades, an Athenian general in the time of the Peloponnesian War, a pupil of Socrates; a work of Plato,* so used in PP. Q. 76. Art. 1 c.

Alcuinus, i, *m., Alcuin, eminent educator, scholar, and theologian,* born about 735, died May 19, 804. Cf. SS. Q. 164. Art. 2 ad 1.

alea, ae, *f., a game with dice.*

aleator, oris, *m., a player with dice, a gamester.*

Alexander, dri, *m., Alexander,* the name of several popes quoted by St. Thomas. Note also the work, De Rhetorica ad Alexandrum, ascribed to Aristotle, PT. Q. 55. Art. 5 c.

Alexandria, ae, *f., the name of several towns in antiquity, Alexandria* in Egypt.

Alexandrinus, a, um, *adj., pertaining to Alexandria.*

Alexius, i, *m., Alexius, saint* and *confessor.* According to legend, he was the son of a noble Roman who ran away on the night of his marriage to Edessa where he lived the life of an ascetic in poverty for seventeen years. He returned to Rome and unknown to his family lived near his former home as a beggar. The Greek version is very similar. The West celebrates his feast on July 17; the East on March 17. Veneration for him was brought to Rome by Sergius at the end of the tenth century.

Algazel, is, *m., Algazel,* Al-Ghazali, Mohammed Abu Hamid, born at Tus 1058, an Arabian philosopher and theologian. In 1091 he was made professor in the College of Baghdad. Over a four year period he wrote against the Ismaelites (assassins), then resigned the chair, lead an ascetic life with a leaning toward scepticism, then towards mysticism, and finally began attacking philosophers, especially the beliefs in eternity, the reality of the divine attributes, and the immortality of the soul. At the Sultan's wish he accepted a professorship in the College of Nizam ul-Mulk at Nishapur. He died at Tas, December, 1111. Sixty-nine works are accredited to him, of which the main ones are a treatise on eschatology, "Revival of Sciences," and several treatises on ethics.

alibi, *adv., elsewhere, somewhere else, in* or *at another's place.*

alicubi, *adv., somewhere, anywhere, at any place.*

alienatio, onis, *f., separation, desertion, alienation.*—**alienatio (a sensibus),** *alienation from the senses, a sensibus* may or may not be expressed, *loss of consciousness.*

alienigena, ae, *m., a stranger, foreigner, alien.*

alieno, are, avi, atum, 1, *v. a., to cast off, alienate, estrange.*

alienus, a, um, *adj., of another, foreign, alien.*—**de alieno (bono),** *from the property of another.*

alietas, atis, *f., dissimilarity, unlikeness,* i.e., dissimilarity according to the *suppositum.*

alimentum, i, *n., nourishment, nutriment, food, provisions.*

alioquin, *adv., in other respects, for the rest, otherwise.*

Alipius, also **Alypius,** i, *m., Alipius,* an acquaintance of St. Augustine mentioned in the Confessions 6. 7.

aliqualis, e, *adj., constituted in some way, some sort of, of some kind, some, such and such.* On **aequalitas aliqualis,** *relative equality,* see *aequalitas* under 1. —**aliqualiter,** *adv., in some way, in some measure.* On **iustum aliqualiter,** see *iustus;* on **unum aliqualiter,** see *unus.*

aliqualiter, *adv.,* see *aliqualis.*

aliquamdiu, *adv., awhile, for a while, for sometime.*

aliquando, *adv., at some time* or *other, once, at any time, ever.*

aliquanto, *adv., somewhat, in some degree, a little, considerably,* used in the S.T. only when giving references to other works.

aliquantulus, a, um, *adj., little, small.*—**aliquantulum,** *adv., somewhat, a little.*

aliquatenus, *adv., to a certain degree* or *extent, in some measure,*

aliqui, aliqua, aliquod, *indef. adj., some, any.*

aliquis, aliquid, *indef. subst. pron., somebody* or *other, someone, anyone, something, anything.* On **ad aliquid,** see *ad* under 2; on **bonum aliquid,** see *bonus* under 3; on **corruptio aliqua,** see *corruptio* under 2; on **demonstratio ad aliquid,** see *demonstratio* under 3; on **dictio aliqua,** see *dictio* under 2; on **distingui secundum aliquid,** see *distinguere;* on **esse aliquid, alicuius et in aliquo,** see *esse;* on **fieri ex aliquo,** see *fieri;* on **generatio alicuius et aliqua,** see *generatio* under 1; on **hoc aliquid,** see *hic;* on **impossibile aliquid,** see *impossibilis;* on **malum aliquid,** see *malus* under 1; on **perfectum secundum aliquid sui et secundum aliquid exterius adiacens** or **per aliquid exterius adveniens,** see *perfectus* under 1; on **posse ad aliquid, in aliquo, super aliquid et supra aliquid,** see *posse;* on **possibile aliquid,** see *possibilis* under 1; on **significare ut in aliquo,** see *significare;* on **suppositio ad aliquid,**

see *suppositio* under 3.—**aliquid demonstratum sive monstratum,** *something apparent* or *definite,* i.e., *something special,* a synonym of *hoc aliquid* or *hoc signatum.* See *hic.*

aliquoties, *adv., several times, at different times.*

aliquotus, a, um, *adj., certain, some.*

aliter, *adv.,* see *alius.*

aliunde, *adv., from another* or *some other place, person* or *thing,* (1) used *absolutely,* (2) with *quam.*

alius, a, ud, *adj.,* and *subst., being unlike, different, another.* On the difference between *alius* and *alter,* see *alter* under 2. On **ad aliquid secundum aliud,** see *ad* under 2; on **causa per aliud,** see *causa* under 2; on **cognoscere in aliud,** see *cognoscere* under 2; on **continuum per se secundum aliud,** see *continuum* under 2; on **ens per aliud,** see *ens;* on **esse ab alio, in alio,** and **esse per aliud,** see *esse;* on **fieri aliud et ex alio,** see *fieri;* on **necessarius per aliud,** see *necessarius* under 1; on **necessitas ex alio,** see *necessitas* under 1; on **perfectum secundum aliud,** see *perfectus* under 1; on **praedicare ad aliud,** see *praedicare* under 2; on **propter aliud,** see *propter.*— Kinds of *alius* are: (a), **alius numero,** the Aristotelian *heteros arithmo, different according to number* and *individuum.*—(b), **alius secundum accidens, alius**

secundum rationem, and **alius secundum subiectum,** *different according to something secondary, different according to an idea* or *essence,* and *different according to subject* or *possessor.* See **aliter secundum accidens,** under *alter.*—(c), **alius secundum quid** and **alius simpliciter,** *different in some respect, different simply* or *absolutely.*—(d), **alius secundum rationem,** see *alius secundum accidens.*—(e), **alius secundum subiectum,** see *alius secundum accidens.*—(f), **alius simpliciter,** see *alius secundum quid.*—**aliter,** *adv., otherwise, in another manner,* used (1) *absol.,* (2) with *quam, otherwise than,* (3) with *non quam, not otherwise than,* (4) with the *abl., differently from,* (5) with *non nisi, by no other means, on no other condition, not otherwise except.*—**aliter . . . aliter,** *one in one way . . . another in another.*

allego, are, avi, atum, 1, *v. a., to bring forward, relate, allege.*— **allegata,** orum, *n., things alleged, evidence.*

allegoria, ae, *f., an allegory, a figurative representation of a thought* or *of an abstract truth.* —**secundum allegoriam,** *allegorically,* a synonym of *allegorice.*

allegorice, *adv.,* see *allegoricus.*

allegoricus, a, um, *adj., symbolical, allegorical.* On **causa allegorica,** see *causa* under 3; on **sensus allegoricus,** see *sensus* under 8; on significatio allegorica, see *significatio* under 1.—**allegorice,** *adv.,* *allegorically.*

allevio, are, avi, atum, 1, *v .a.,* *to make light, lighten, relieve, alleviate,* a synonym of *allevo,* are.

allevo, are, avi, atum, 1, *v. a., to lift up, lighten, alleviate, mitigate,* a synonym of *allevio,* are.

allicio, ere, lexi, lectum, 3, *v. a., to draw to oneself, attract.*

alligatio, onis, *f., a binding* or *tying to.*

alligo, are, avi, atum, 1, *v. a., to bind to, bind.*

allocutio, onis, *f., a speaking to, an accosting, an address,* a synonym of *alloquium.*

alloquium, ii, *n., a speaking to, an address,* a synonym of *allocutio.*

alloquor, i, cutus, 3, *v. dep. a., to speak to, address, exhort.*

Almariani, orum, *m.,* also **Almarici, Amauriani,** *Amalricians,* an heretical sect founded towards the end of the twelfth century, by Amaury de Bene or de Chartres (Latin, *Almaricus, Amalricus, Amauricus*), a cleric and professor in the University of Paris, who died between 1204 and 1207. The Amalricians, like their founder, professed a kind of pantheism, holding as the fundamental principle of their system that God and the universe are one; that God is everything and everything is God.

almificus, a, um, *adj., glorious, celebrated for sanctity.*

alo, ere, alui, altum, and alitum, 3, *v. a., to nourish, cherish, promote, increase.*

aloe, es, *f., the aloe.*

Alphaeus, i, *m., Alphaeus.* Father of James the Apostle or James the Lesser, the same person as Cleophas, husband of Mary, sister or sister-in-law of the Blessed Virgin Mary.

Alpharabius, i, *m., Alpharabius.* Cf. PTS. Q. 92, Art. 1 c. Muhammad ibn-Muhammad ibn-Tarkhan abu-Nasr al-Farabi (Alpharabius) was born in Transoxiana, educated under a Christian physician and a Christian translator in Baghdad, and flourished as a Sufi at Aleppo in the brilliant court of Sayf-al-Dawlah at al Hamdani. He died at Damascus in 950 at the age of eigthy. His system of philosophy, as revealed by his several treatises on Plato and Aristotle, was a syncretism of Platonism, Aristotelianism, and Sufism, and won for him the enviable title of "the second teacher" after the great Aristotle.

altar, (altare), aris, *n., altar.*

alte, *adv., high.*

alter, tera, terum, *adj.,* (1) *the other of two, another,* (2) *being otherwise, accidentally different, qualitatively different.*—**alter** ... **alter,** (a) *the one* ... *the other,* (b) *one* ... *another.*—**unus** ... **alter,** (a) *the one* ... *the other,* a synonym of *alter* ... *alter,* (b) *one* ... *another.*—On **apprehen-**

sio alterius, see *apprehensio* under 2; on **auctoritas alterius,** see
auctoritas under 4; on **bonum
alterius,** see *bonus* under a and
c; on **propter alterum,** see *propter.*—On **ad aliquid ratione alterius,** see *ad* under 2; on **fieri
alterum et ex altero,** see *fieri;*
on **verbum alterum,** see *verbum*
under 1.—Kinds of *alter* in this
(2) sense are: (a), **alter genere,**
Aristotelian *heteros genei, different according to its genus* or
kind.—(b), **alter secundum accidens, alter secundum rationem,**
and **alter secundum subiectum,**
*different according to accident,
different according to idea* or *essence, different according to
subject* or *suppositum.*—(c), **alter
secundum rationem,** see *alter
secundum accidens.*—(d), **alter
secundum subiectum,** see *alter
secundum accidens.*

alterabilis, e, *adj., subject to
change, alterable, changeable,* a
synonym of *mutabilis.*

alteratio, onis, *f.,* (1) *making different, change, alteration of the
sensible quality, physical agitation* or *excitement,* a synonym
of *passio,* (2) *making different,
change, alteration of quality in
the general sense of the word.*—
On the difference between **alteratio** and **generatio,** see *generatio* under 1. On **fieri alteratione,**
see *fieri;* on **motus alterationis,**
see *motus* under 1.—Kinds of
alteratio in this (2) sense are:
(a), **alteratio animae** or **animalis**

and **alteratio corporalis,** *alteration of the soul* and *that of the
body* or *animal and purely corporal alteration,* of which the
former has its subject in the
soul, the latter in the body.—(b),
alteratio animalis, see *alteratio
animae.*—(c), **alteratio corporalis,** see *alteratio animae.*—(d),
alteratio naturalis and **alteratio
violenta,** *natural alteration* or
that conformable to nature and
forced alteration.—(e), **alteratio
passiva** and **alteratio perfectiva,**
passive and *perfecting alteration*
or the alteration that consists in
an actual passivity and that
which consists in the perfecting
of the altered thing. See also
passio corruptiva under *passio*
under 2.—(f), **alteratio perfectiva,** see *alteratio passiva.*—(g),
alteratio violenta, see *alteratio
naturalis.*—**alterationis terminus
est generatio,** *the goal of the
alteration of the quality of a
thing is the production of another thing.*

alterativus, a, um, *adj., changing.*
Cf. *alteratio* and *qualitas.* Cf. *alteratio* and *qualitas.* On **qualitas
alterativa,** see *qualitas.*

alteritas, atis, *f., unlikeness, difference,* especially in accidents,
accidental difference. Cf. *alter.*

alternatio, onis, *f., an interchange,
alternation.*

alterno, are, avi, atum, 1, *v. a.* and
*n., to do one thing and then an-
other, do a thing by turns, inter-*

change with something, alternate.

alternus, a, um, *adj., one after the other, by turns, interchangeable, alternate.*

altero, are, avi, atum, 1, *v. a.* and *n., to alter, make different, change quality* in the particular and general sense of the word. See *alteratio.* On **corpus primum alterans,** see *corpus;* on **qualitas alterans,** see *qualitas.—***alterans primum,** *the first changing principle,* namely the heavens and all the heavenly bodies.—Kinds of **alterare** are: **alterare extra naturam** and **alterare secundum naturam,** *to change without the aid of nature and to change according to nature* or *according to the course of nature.*

alteruter, alterutra, alterutrum, *adj., one of two, the one* or *the other, either.*

altitudo, dinis, *f., height* or *highness* in both the literal and figurative senses.—Kinds of *altitudo* are: **altitudo terrena** and **altitudo virtutis,** *earthly highness* and *highness of virtue,* i.e., the highness which bestows upon man the possession of earthly goods and that which bestows virtue upon him.

Altissiodorensis, also **Autissiodorensis** and **Antissiodorensis,** is, *m., Altissiodorensis,* William of Auxerre, Archdeacon of Beauvais, a thirteenth-century theologian and professor at the University of Paris. He was one of the three theologians appointed in 1231 by Gregory IX to prepare an amended edition of the physical and metaphysical works of Aristotle which had been placed under a ban by the Council of 1210 because of the errors which were contained in the inaccurate translations and in the Arabian commentaries accompanying them. He is the author of a work entitled "Summa Aurea", which is not, as it is sometimes described, a mere compendium of the "Book of Sentences" by Peter the Lombard.

altus, a, um, *adj.,* (1) lit., *high, deep,* (2) trop., *high, lofty, noble, august.—***altum,** i, *n., a height, high heaven,* especially in the phrase **in altum,** *on high.*

alvus, i, *f., the belly, a paunch, womb.*

amabilis, e, *adj., that deserves to be loved, worthy of love, lovely, amiable.*

Amalec et **Amalech,** *indecl. noun, m.,* the grandson of Esau through Eliphaz and Thamna, the concubine, one of the first kings of Edom.

Amalecitae, arum, *m., Amalecites,* a tribe which, from the days of Exodus until the time of King Saul, roamed over the region from the southern boundary of Juda to the Egyptian frontier and the peninsula of Sinai. They are not counted among the kindred of the Israelites, and probably were among the inhabitants of the region, whom the Hebrew and Armenian immigrants found already in the land. Israel first met with the Amalecites in the region near Sinai, when Amalec naturally tried to prevent the entrance of a new tribe into the region.

Aman, *indecl. noun, m.*, the persecutor of Achiacharus, the son of Hammedatha, appears in the Book of Esther as the enemy of the Jews and the chief minister of Assuerus.

amarissime, *adv., most bitterly.*

amaritudo, inis, *f., bitterness, severity, sadness.*

amarus, a, um, *adj.,* (1) of taste, *bitter, pungent,* opposite of *dulcis,* (2) trop., *calamitous, unpleasant, sad,* (3) of persons, *sullen, morose.*

Amasias, ae, *m., Amasias,* eighth king of Juda, son of Joas and Joadan or Joaden, came to the throne in the second year of the reign of Joas, king of Israel, and ruled for twenty-nine years.

amatio, onis, *f., love in the sense of affection,* at times also in the sense of a *simple emotion.—* Kinds of *amatio* are: (a), **amatio corporalis,** *physical* or *sensual love.* Cf. C. G. 3. 118.—(b), **amatio mutua** and **amatio simplex,** *mutual love* and *simple* or *one-sided love.*—(c), **amatio simplex,** see *amatio mutua.*

amativus, a, um, *adj., loving,* as *subst., lover.*

amator, oris, *m.,* (1) *lover, friend,* in honorable sense, (2) *lover,* in dishonorable sense.

amatorius, a, um, *adj., amatory, amorous.*

ambidexter, tra, trum, *adj., ambidextrous.*

ambigo, ere, 3, *v. n.,* (1) *to be undecided, doubt,* (2) *argue, dispute,* used by St. Thomas only in quotation.

ambiguus, a, um, *adj., uncertain, doubtful.—***ambiguum,** i, *n., doubt, uncertainty.*

ambio, ire, ivi and ii, itum, 4, *v. n.* and *a.,* (1) *to surround, encircle,* (2) *comprise,* (3) *strive after, seek.*

ambitio, onis, *f., a desire for honor, ambition.*

ambitiosus, a, um, *adj., honor-loving, ambitious.* See *ambitio.*

ambitus, us, *m.,* (1) *circumference, compass,* (2) *ambition,* (3) *greed.*

ambo, bae, bo, *num., both,* used usually of objects naturally in pairs, as the parts of the body.

Ambrosius, i, *m., St. Ambrose,* bishop of Milan, (A.D. 374-397). He was born probably in 340 and he died on Good Friday night, 397. The chief sources of his life are his own works and a biography written by his secretary, Paulinus. St. Thomas quotes from the works of St. Ambrose freely throughout the S.T., especially from the following works: De Officiis, Super Lucam, De Paradiso, the various essays on virginity, De Spiritu Sanctu, De Incarnatione Domini, De Sacramentis, De Mysteriis, De Fide.

ambulatio, onis, *f., a walking about, a walk.*

ambulo, are, avi, atum, 1, *v. n., to go about, walk.*

amen, Gr. *amen, adv., truly, surely, verily, so be it.*

amens, mentis, *adj., out of one's senses, beside one's self, senseless, mad, insane, frantic, distracted.*

amentia, ae, *f., the being out of one's senses, beside one's self, madness, insanity.*

amica, ae, *f., a female friend, a concubine, a mistress.*

amicabilis, e, *adj., friendly, belonging to friendship, rising from friendship, proving friendship.* On **debitum amicabile,** see *debitus* under 1; on **opus amicabile,** see *opus* under 4.

amicio, ire, icui or ixi, ictum, 4, *v. a., to throw around, wrap about, cover.*

amicitia, ae, *f.,* (1) *friendship in the sense of a habitus,* (2) *friendship in the sense of an act, proof of friendship, manifestation of friendship,* (3) *friendliness, affability,* a synonym of *affabilitas.* —On **amor amicitiae,** see *amor* under 1; on **bonum amicitiae,** see *bonus* under 3; on **debitum amicitiae,** see *debitus* under 1; on **dilectio amicitiae,** see *dilectio* under 1; on **voluntas amicitiae,** see *voluntas* under 3.—Kinds of *amicitia* in this (1) sense are: (a),

amicitia charitatis, *friendship or love for God, friendship of man with God.*—(b), **amicitia cognata seu cognatorum seu consanguineorum,** *friendship of blood relationship.*—(c), **amicitia commilitantium,** *friendship of fellow-soldiers.*—(d), **amicitia concivium seu politica,** *friendship of fellow-citizens or political friendship.*—(e), **amicitia coniugalis** and **amicitia fraterna,** *friendship of husband* and *wife* and *of brother* and *sister.*—(f), **amicitia connutritiva seu hetaerica,** *friendship of persons nurtured together* or *as companions in youth.*—(g), **amicitia consanguineorum,** see *amicitia cognata.*—(h), **amicitia delectabilis, amicitia honesti seu honesta,** and **amicitia utilis,** *agreeable, honorable* and *useful friendship, friendship in which a friend is loved because of the pleasure which the relationship affords, friendship for the sake of a friend, friendship on account of which advantages are obtained.*—(i), **amicitia fraterna,** see *amicitia coniugalis.*—(j), **amicitia hetaerica,** see *amicitia connutritiva.*—(k), **amicitia hominis ad Deum,** *man's friendship in relation to God.* —(l), **amicitia hominum ad invicem,** *friendship of men in relation to each other.*—(m), **amicitia honesta** or **honesti,** see *amicitia delectabilis.*—(n), **amicitia imperfecta** and **amicitia perfecta,**

imperfect and *perfect friend-ship,* so called because in the first case a friend is loved in an imperfect manner, i.e., for the sake of something else, and in the latter in a perfect man-ner, i.e., for the sake of friend-ship itself.—(o), **amicitia inter aequales** and **amicitia inter inaequales,** *friendship between equals* and *between unequals.*—(p), **amicitia inter inaequales,** see *amicitia inter aequales.*—(q), **amicitia liberalis** and **amicitia servilis,** *friendship betweeen the free* or *free born* and *between those not free* or *slaves.*—(r), **amicitia materna** and **amicitia paterna,** *maternal* and *paternal friendship, friendship of mother* and *father for their children.*—(s), **amicitia naturalis,** *natural friendship, friendship according to nature.*—(t), **amicitia paterna,** see *amicitia materna.*—(u), **amicitia per accidens** and **amicitia per se,** *friendship for some sec-ondary reason* and *friendship for its own sake.*—(v), **amicitia peregrinantium** or **peregrinorum,** *friendship of travelling compan-ions.*—(w), **amicitia perfecta,** see *amicitia imperfecta.*—(x), **amici-tia per se,** see *amicitia per acci-dens.*—(y), **amicitia politica,** see *amicitia convicium.*—(z), **amici-tia principalis,** *the principal* or *most excellent friendship.*—(a²), **amicitia regalis,** *royal friendship* or *the friendship of a king for one of his subjects.*—(b²), **amici-**

tia secundum superabundantiam, seu amicitia superabundantiae, *friendship in superabundance.*—(c²), **amicitia superabundantiae,** see *amicitia secundum · abun-dantiam.*—(d²), **amicitia servilis,** see *amicitia liberalis.*—(e²), **ami-citia utilis,** see *amicitia delec-tabilis.*

amictus, us, *m., mantle, cloak.*

amicus, a, um, *adj., friendly, kind, amicable.*

amicus, i, *m., a friend,* the oppo-site of *inimicus.*

Aminadab, *indecl. noun, m., Ami-nadab,* son of Ram, of the tribe of Juda. His daughter Elizabeth became the wife of the high priest Aaron, and his son Na-hasson was the chief of his tribe at the time of the depar-ture from Egypt. He lived under the difficult servitude of the Pharaohs and must have died before the *exodus.* He is count-ed among the ancestors of Our Lord Jesus Christ.

amissibilis, e, *adj., that may be lost.*

amissibiliter, *adv.,* see *amissibilis.*

amissio, onis, *f., a losing, a loss.*

amita, ae, *f., a sister of a grand-father, a great aunt.*

amitto, ere, misi, missum, 3, *v. a., dismiss, lose.*

Ammon, *indecl., m., Ammon,* son of Lot and of his second daugh-ter, father of the Ammonites. The descendants of Ammon were called sons of Ammon.

Ammonitae et **Ammonites,** arum, *m., Ammonites,* a nation in Eastern Palestine. As to their origin from Lot, compare Genesis 19, 38. It is possible that Ammon is derived from the name of a tribal divinity. According to the pedigree presented in Genesis 19, 37 and 38, the Ammonites were closely related to the Israelites and still more so to their neighbors in the south, the Moabites.

amo, are, avi, atum, 1, *v. a., to like, love,* the opposite of *odi.* See *amor.*—**amans,** antis, *P. a.,* with *gen.,* or *absol., fond, loving, kind, pleasing,* and *subst.* a *friend, lover.*—**amatus,** a, um, *P. a., loved, beloved;* and *subst., loved one.*

amoenitas, atis, *f., pleasantness, loveliness, delightfulness.*

amor, oris, *m.,* (1) *love,* the opposite of *odium,* (2) *love* embodied in a person, i.e., the Holy Ghost. On the relation of *amor, charitas,* and *dilectio,* see *dilectio.* On **communicatio per modum amoris,** see *communicatio* under 1; on **lex amoris,** see *lex* under 1; on **magnitudo amoris,** see *magnitudo* under 3; on **procedere per modum amoris,** see *procedere* under 4; on **processio amoris,** see *processio;* on **servitus amoris,** see *servitus* under 1; on **servus amoris,** see *servus;* on **unio amoris,** see *unio.*—Kinds of *amor* in this (1) sense are: (a), **amor actualis,** *love in the sense of action.*—(b), **amor amicitiae sive benevolentiae** and **amor concupiscentiae,** *love of friendship* or *of benevolence, love of desire.*—(c), **amor angelicus** and **amor divinus,** *angelic* and *divine love* or *love of angels* and *love of God.*—(d), **amor animalis sive carnalis sive carnis sive sensitivus** and **amor rationalis sive spiritualis sive intellectualis,** *animal* or *carnal* or *sensual love* and *rational* or *spiritual* or *intellectual love.*—(e), **amor benevolentiae,** see *amor amicitiae.*—(f), **amor boni,** *love of good.*—(g), **amor charitatis** and **amor communiter dictus,** *love, in the sense of charity* and *so-called love in general.*—(h), **amor carnalis,** see *amor animalis.*—(i), **amor carnis,** see *amor animalis.*—(j), **amor communiter dictus,** see *amor caritatis.*—(k), **amor concupiscentiae,** see *amor amicitiae.*—(l), **amor congregativus sive unitivus,** *the joining* or *uniting love,* i.e., *the love for God,* the opposite of *amor disgregativus,* i.e., *the dissipating* or *self-love.*—(m), **amor corruptivus seu deteriorativus seu laesivus,** and **amor meliorativus seu perfectivus,** *the love that debases* or *injures the lover* and *the love that makes him better and more perfect.*—(n), **amor Dei** and **amor peccati,** *love for God* and *love for sin.*—(o), **amor deteriorativus,** see *amor corruptivus.*—(p), **amor divinus,** see *amor angelicus.*—

(q), **amor divitiarum,** *love of riches.*—(r), **amor gratuitus** and **amor mercenarius,** *the love bestowed gratuitously* and *the hired* or *mercenary love.*—(s), **amor honoris,** *love of honor.*—(t), **amor imperfectus** and **amor perfectus,** *the imperfect* and *the perfect love.*—(u), **amor inordinatus** and **amor ordinatus,** *unregulated* or *sinful love* and *regulated* or *virtuous love.*—(v), **amor intellectualis,** see *amor animalis.*—(w), **amor iustitiae,** *love of justice.*—(x), **amor laesivus,** see *amor corruptivus.*—(y), **amor libidinosus,** *sensual* or *lustful love.*—(z), **amor meliorativus,** see *amor corruptivus.*—(a^2), **amor mercenarius,** see *amor gratuitus.*—(b^2), **amor mundanus** and **amor supermundanus,** *worldly* or *mundane love* and *spiritual* or *supermundane love.*—(c^2), **amor naturalis,** *natural love.*—(d^2), **amor peccati,** see *amor Dei.*—(e^2), **amor pecuniae,** *love of money,* see *amor divitiarum.*—(f^2), **amor perfectivus,** see *amor corruptivus.*—(g^2), **amor perfectus,** see *amor imperfectus.*—(h^2), **amor personalis,** *personal love,* i.e., love constituted in a person.—(i^2), **amor rationalis,** see *amor animalis.*—(j^2), **amor sensitivus,** see *amor animalis.*—(k^2), **amor socialis,** *convivial* or *social love.*—(l^2), **amor spiritualis,** see *amor animalis.*—(m^2), **amor sui,** *love of self.* Cf. *luxuria.*—(n^2), **amor supermundanus,** see *amor*

mundanus.—**Amor Dei est congregativus,** *love of God is unifying.*—**Amor est vis unitiva et concretiva,** *love is a force which unites* and *joins solidly.*

Amos, *indecl., m., Amos,* the earliest of the prophets whose writings have come down to us, and the initiator of one of the greatest movements in spiritual history. He was a herdsman or small sheep farmer in Tekoa, a small town in the uplands some six miles south of Bethlehem. Amos was prophesying in those years in which Uzziah and Jeroboam II were reigning contemporaneously, B.C. 775-750.

amotio, onis, *f., a removing, removal.*

amoveo, ere, movi, motum, 2, *v. a., to remove from, put* or *take away, withdraw.*

amphora, ae, *f., a vessel,* usually made of clay, with two handles or ears, for liquids, especially wine, *a flagon, pitcher, flask, bottle.*

amplector, i, exus, 3, *v. dep., to surround, encompass, embrace, take in.*

amplexus, us, *m., embrace, encircling, surrounding.*

ampliatio, onis, *f., an extending, enlarging.*

amplificatio, onis, *f., enlarging, increasing, amplification.*

amplifico, are, avi, atum, 1, *v. a., to widen, to extend, enlarge, increase,* (2) *amplify, enlarge upon.*

amplio, are, avi, atum, 1, *v. a., to*

extend, enlarge, increase, amplify.

amplitudo, inis, *f., wide extent, amplitude, size, bulk.*

amplus, a, um, *adj.,* (1), *great, abundant, ample,* rarely used in the positive in the S.T., (2) frequently used in the comparative degree, especially (a) as substantive in the sense of *more, a greater quantity* or *number,* and (b) as adverb in the sense of *more often, to a greater extent,* also (3) rarely in the superlative degree.

amputo, are, avi, atum, 1, *v. a., to lop off, curtail, shorten, diminish.*

amylum, or **amulum,** i, *n., starch.*

an, *conj., whether, or.* On **cognoscere an est,** see *cognoscere* under 2; on **quaestio an est,** see *quaestio.*

Anacletus, i, *m., Anaclete,* Saint and second or third bishop of Rome, a martyr under Domitian. Others say that he succeeded Clement I as fifth Bishop of Rome and was martyred under Trajan. His day is July 13.

anadochus, i, *m., Greek anadochos, a taking upon oneself, giving security for,* in the S.T., *a godparent, sponsor.*

anagoge, es, *f.,* see *anagogia.*

anagogia, ae, *f.,* or *anagoge, Greek anagoge,* (1) *a leading up, leading back,* (2) *a leading up, referring to, directing to heavenly things, mystical interpretation, anagoge.*

anagogicus, a, um, *adj., leading up, directing to the heavenly, mystical, anagogic, anagogical.* See *anagogia.* On **causa anagogica,** see *causa* under 3; on **sensus anagogicus,** see *sensus* under 8; on **significatio anagogica,** see *significatio* under 1.

analogia, ae, *f., comparative likeness, analogy.* On **communis secundum analogiam,** see *communis* under 1; on **communitas analogiae,** see *communitas* under 1; on **dicere secundum analogiam,** see *dicere* under 3; on **idem secundum analogiam,** see *idem;* on **similitudo analogiae,** see *similitudo* under 1; on **unum secundum analogiam,** see *unus.* —Kinds of *analogia* are described in various ways: (a), **analogia communissima,** *the most general analogy.*—(b), **analogia secundum convenientiam in aliquo uno** and **analogia secundum quod unum imitatur aliud,** *analogy according to the agreement of two or more things in one thing,* and *analogy of two things according to which one imitates the other.*—(c), **analogia secundum covenientiam proportionalitatis** and **analogia secundum covenientiam proportionis,** *analogy of relative likeness and that according to agreement of proportion,* in other words, *analogy, in the sense of the like condition or relation of two things to each other,* and *analogy in the sense of the like condition of two* *things with references to something else.*—(d), **analogia secundum convenientiam proportionis,** see *analogia secundum convenientiam proportionalitatis.*—(e), **analogia secundum esse, analogia secundum intentionem tantum,** and **analogia secundum esse et intentionem,** *analogy according to being, that merely according to the idea, and that according to being and idea.*—(f), **analogia secundum esse et intentionem,** see *analogia secundum esse.*—(g), **analogia secundum intentionem tantum,** see *analogia secundum esse.*—(h), **analogia secundum quod unum imitatur aliud,** see *analogia secundum convenientiam in aliquo uno.*

analogice, *adv.,* see *analogicus.*

analogicus, a, um, *adj., pertaining to analogy,* see *analogia, relatively alike, relative,* a synonym of *analogus.* On **agens analogicum** see *agens;* on **communitas analogica,** see *communitas* under 1; on **praedicatio analogica,** see *praedicatio* under 2.—**analogice,** *adv., after the manner* and *in the sense of analogy, analogically.* On **accipere analogice,** see *accipere* under 3; on **commune analogice,** see *communis* under 1; on **dicere analogice,** see *dicere* under 3; on **praedicare analogice,** see *praedicare* under 2; on **sumere analogice,** see *sumere* under 3.

analogus, a, um, *adj., analogous, proportionate,* see *analogia, relatively alike, relative,* a synonym of *analogicus.* On **commune analogum,** see *communis* under 1; on **genus analogum,** see *genus* under 2; on **numen analogum,** see *nomen* under 1.

analytice, *adv.,* see *analyticus.*

analyticus, a, um, *adj., analytic,* not used in the S.T., (1) *taking to pieces, analyzing, dissolving, concerning dissoluton,* a synonym of *resolutorius,* the opposite of *compositivus,* (2) *analytica, resolutoria,* the Analytica of Aristotle.—(1), on **ratio analytica,** see *ratio* under 13; on **scientia analytica,** see *scientia* under 1. *Analytica* sc. *pars logicae,* synonym of *Iudicativa;* Analytics, that part of Logic which has for its object the conclusion which comes of necessity and with certainty.—**analytice,** *adv., after the manner and in the sense of analysis* or *dissolution, analytically,* Aristotle's *analyticos,* synonym of *modo seu processu resolutorio,* the opposite of *composite, modo seu processu compositivo,* and *logice.*

Ananias, ae, *m., Ananias,* one of the members of the early Church at Jerusalem who conspired with his wife, Sapphira, to make a false statement respecting their gift of property to the community of the brethren and was with her struck dead.

anas, anatis, *f., duck.*

anathema, atis, *n.*, Greek *anathema* or *anathema,* (1) *anathema, an accursed thing,* (2) *the person cursed.*

anathematizo, are, 1, *v. a.,* Greek *anathematizo, to anathematize, put under the ban.*

Anaxagoras, ae, *m., Anaxagoras,* born at Clazomenae c. 500 B.C., died at Lampsacus in Ionia c. 430 B.C. It appears that he wrote a work entitled, like most of the ancient philosophical treatises *peri physeos.* Plato speaks of it in the Apology. Simplicius could still procure a copy of it in the sixth century of our era. It is to Simplicius that we owe such fragments as have come down to us. He taught that being is the result of the interaction of ultimate elements under control of the divine mind.

anchora, ae, *f., an anchor.*

ancilla, ae, *f., a maid-servant, handmaid, female slave.*

Ancyra, ae, *f., Ancyra,* modern *Angora,* a titular see of Galatia in Asia Minor, suffragan of Laodicea. It was said to have been founded by Midas, was the chief place of the Gallic conquerors of Asia Minor, (c. 277 B.C.). It is also famous for the official record of the Acts of Augustus, known as the "Monumentum Ancyranum."

andragathia, ae, *f.,* Greek *andragathia, manly* or *mature consideration* and *care.*

Andreas, ae, *m., Andrew.* (1) St. Andrew, the Apostle, son of Jonas or John (Matt. 16. 17; John 1. 42) was born in Bethsaida of Galilee (John 1. 44). He was brother of Simon Peter (Matt. 10. 2; John 1. 40). Both were fishermen (Matt. 4. 18; Mark 1. 16). From the fourth Gospel we learn that Andrew was a disciple of the Baptist whose testimony first led him and John the Evangelist to follow Jesus (John 1. 35-40).—(2) dicitur enim in legenda B. Andreae, PP. Q. 36. Art. 2. The Andrew referred to here may be either St. Andrew, a martyr of the Faith in Lampascus during the persecution of Decius or St. Andrew of Crete who was born at Damascus about the middle of the seventh century and died July 4. 740. It is probably the latter. St. Andrew of Crete attained the front rank of ecclesiastical orators of the Byzantine epoch. We know of twenty-two published and twenty-one of his unpublished sermons.

Andronicus, i, *m., Andronicus* of Rhodes, an eclectic of the Peripatetic School. He edited the works of Aristotle about 70 B.C. The story of the fate of Aristotle's works as narrated by Strabo (13. 1. 54) and repeated with the addition of a few details by Plutarch (Sulla, 26) is regarded as reliable. It tells how the library of Aristotle fell into the hands of Theophrastus by whom it was bequeathed to Neleus of Scepsis. After the death of Neleus the manuscripts were hidden in a cellar where they remained for almost two centuries. When Athens was captured by the Romans in 84 B.C., the library was brought to Rome by Sulla. A Roman grammarian named Tyrannion secured several copies, thus enabling Andronicus of Rhodes to collect the treatises and publish them. It must not, however, be inferred that the manuscripts hidden in the cellar for two hundred years were the only existing copy of Aristotle's works.

angelicus, a, um, *adj., belonging to angels, angelic.*

angelus, i, *m., an angel.* Important sections of the S.T. devoted exclusively to the *angeli* are the following: PP. Q. 50, De substantia angelorum absolute; Q. 51, De angelis in comparatione ad corpus; Q. 52, De angelis in comparatione ad locum; Q. 53, De motu locali angelorum; Q. 54, De virtute cognoscitiva angeli; Q. 55, De medio cognitionis angelicae; Q. 56, De cognitione angelica ex parte rerum immaterialium; Q. 57, De cognitione angelorum quantum ad res materiales; Q. 58, De modo cognitionis angelicae; Q. 59, De voluntate angelorum; Q. 60, De amore, seu dilectione angeli; Q. 61, De productione angelorum in esse naturae; Q. 62, De productione angeli in esse gratiae, et gloriae; Q. 63, De malitia angelorum quoad culpam; Q. 106, Quomodo una creatura aliam moveat, et primo de angelorum illuminatione; Q. 107, De locutionibus angelorum; Q. 108, De ordinatione angelorum secundum hierarchias et ordines; Q. 109, De ordinatione malorum angelorum; Q. 110, De praesidentia angelorum super creaturam corporalem; Q. 111, De actione angelorum in homines; Q. 112, De missione angelorum; Q. 113, De custodia bonorum angelorum et impugnatione malorum.

angli, orum, *m., Angles,* a low German tribe who occupied the district of Angeln in Schleswig-Holstein and extended to the West as far as the North Sea. With the Jutes and the Saxons, the Angles passed over in great numbers to Britain during the fifth century and settled in East Anglia, Northumbria, and Mercia. From them England derives its name.

anguilla, ae, *f., dim., an eel.*

angularis, e, *adj., having corners or angles, angular.*

angulus, i, *m., an angle, a corner.*

angustia, ae, *f., difficulty, distress.*

augustio, are, avi, atum, 1, *v. a., to make narrow, straiten.*

angustus, a, um, *adj., narrow, strait, close, contracted.*

anhelo, are, avi, atum, 1, *v. n.* and
a., *to draw the breath with great
difficulty, pant, puff, gasp.*

anhomoemerus, a, um, *adj.*, *consisting of unlike parts*, the opposite of *homoeomerus, homogeneus*, and *uniformis*, not found in
the S.T. On **corpus anhomoeomerum**, see *corpus.*

anima, ae, *f.*, (1) *soul* in the particular and narrower sense of
the word, not confined to the human soul, but the first act of any
organic physical body, having
life, (2) *soul* in the unreal and
broader sense of the word, i.e.,
the inner principle of the local
motion of a thing. *hothen proton
he kata topon kinesis, psyche*,
Aristotle's, De anim. 2. 4, 415.
b. 21 f. On **alteratio animae**, see
alteratio under 2; on **bonum animae**, see *bonus* under 3; on **defectus animae**, see *defectus* under 1; on **dispositio animae**, see
dispositio under 4; on **dos animae**, see *dos* under 2; on **ens in
anima**, see *ens;* on **esse in anima**, see *esse;* on **gloria animae**,
see *gloria* under 2; on **habitus
animae**, see *habitus* under 4; on
infirmitas animae, see *infirmitas*
under 1; on **intellectus animae**,
see *intellectus* under 3; on **intentio animae**, see *intentio* under 4; on **macula animae**, see
macula; on **malum animae**, see
malus under 3; on **oculus in anima**, see *oculus;* on **opus animae**,
see *opus* under 4; on **pars animae**, see *pars* under 1; on **passio**

**animae, in anima, animae nutri-
tivae et animae tantum**, see *passio* under 2; on **potentia animae
et solius animae**, see *potentia* under 2; on **proprietas solius animae**, see *proprietas* under 1; on
regimen animae, see *regimen;*
on **res extra animam**, see *res;* on
resurrectio animae, see *resurrectio;* on **servitus quantum ad animam**, see *servitus* under 1; on
verbum impressum animae see
verbum under 1; on **virtus animae**, see *virtus* under 1; on **vita
animae**, see *vita* under 1.—Kinds
of *anima* in this (1) sense are:
(a), **pars animae appetitiva**, *the
appetitive part of the soul.*—(b),
anima beata and **anima beati**,
blessed soul and *soul of the
blessed.*—(c), **anima beati**, see
anima beata.—(d), **anima bestiae
seu bestialis seu bruti seu brutalis, anima hominis seu humana**,
and **anima plantae**, *the animal
soul, the soul of man,* and *the
soul of the plant.*—(e), **anima
bestialis**, see *anima bestiae.*—(f),
anima brutalis, see *anima bestiae.*—(g), **anima bruti**, see *anima bestiae.*—(h), **anima generativa seu nutritiva** and **anima motiva**, *the producing* or *sustaining soul* and *the soul causing
local motion,* or *the soul with
power of production* and *sustenance* and *that with the power of local movement,* in other
words, *the vegetative soul* and
the sensitive soul.—(i), **anima
Christi**, *soul of Christ.*—(j), **ani-**

ma **Dei,** *soul of God.*—(k), **anima glorificata** and **anima non glorificata,** *the glorified* and *the unglorified soul of man.*—(l), **anima hominis,** see *animae bestiae.* —(m), **anima humana,** see *anima bestiae.*—(n), **anima imperfecta** and **anima perfecta,** *imperfect soul,* i.e., with relation to man, the vegetative and sensitive soul, and *perfect soul,* i.e., rational or human soul.—(o), **anima intellectiva seu intellectualis seu rationalis, anima sensibilis seu sensitiva seu sensificans seu irrationalis** and **anima vegetabilis seu vegetativa seu vivificans,** *the intellective* or *rational soul, the sensitive* or *irrational soul* and *the vegetative,* or *life-giving soul,* which are to be understood on the one hand in the sense that each of them signifes, if in a context concerning man, the human soul in a particular part of its powers, on the other hand in the sense that the first signifies the human soul in all its powers, the second the animal soul, and the third the soul of the plants.—(p), **anima intellectualis,** see *anima intellectiva.*— (q), **anima irrationalis,** see *anima intellectiva.*—(r), **anima motiva,** see *anima generativa.*—(s), **anima non glorificata,** see *anima glorificata.*—(t), **anima nutritiva,** see *anima generativa.*—(u), **anima perfecta,** see *anima imperfecta.*—(v), **anima plantae,** see *anima bestiae.*—(w), **anima ra-**

tionalis, see *anima intellectiva.*— (x), **anima sancta** and **anima sancti,** *holy soul* and *soul of a holy one, a saint.*—(y), **anima sancti,** see *anima sancta.*—(z), **anima sensibilis,** see *anima intellectiva.*—(a²), **anima sensificans,** see *anima intellectiva.*—(b²), **anima sensitiva,** see *anima intellectiva.*—(c²), **anima vegetabilis,** see *anima intellectiva.*—(d²), **anima vegetativa,** see *anima intellectiva.*—(e²), **anima vivificans,** see *anima intellectiva.*—**Anima est quodammodo omnia,** *the soul is in a certain sense everything,* a translation of the Aristotelian passage *he psyche ta onta pos esti panta,* De Anim. 3. 8. 431. b. 21.—(2), *anima* taken in this sense is distinquished thus: (a), **anima caelestis seu caeli,** *the soul of heaven.*—(b), **anima caeli,** see *anima caelestis.*—(c), **anima mundi seu orbis,** *the soul of the world.*—(d), **anima orbis,** see *anima mundi.*—(e), **anima primi caeli,** *the soul of the first* or *upper heaven.*

animadversio, onis, *f., reproach, censure.*

animadverto, ere, ti, sum, 3, *v. a., to give heed to, notice, observe, consider.*

animal, alis, *n.,* (1) *animal* in the broader sense of the word, i.e., *a being endowed with senses, a sensitive nature,* (2) *animal* in the narrower sense of the word, i.e., *an irrational being of sense,* a synonym of *brutum.*—On **ani-**

mali esse, see *esse.*—Kinds of *animal* in the broader sense of the word are: (a), animal brutum seu irrationale and animal rationale, *the irrational* and *rational animal.*—(b), animal civile seu politicum seu sociale seu sociabile seu gregale and animal solitarium, *the political* or *social* or *sociable or gregarious and the solitary or single animal.*—(c), animal coniugale, *the conjugal animal, the animal living with another.*—(d), animal corpore aereum and animal inferius, *animal with an aerial body* and *an animal living on earth.*—(e), animal domesticum, *domestic animal.*—(f), animal gregale, see *animal civile.*—(g), animal inferius, see *animal corpore aereum.*—(h), animal irrationale, see *animal brutum.*—(i), animal naturale and animal separatum, *the natural animal* or *the animal found in nature* and *the separated animal* or *the animal separated from its environment.*—(j), animal politicum, see *animal civile.*—(k), animal rationale, see *animal brutum.*—(l), animal risibile, *an animal that can laugh.*—(m), animal separatum, see *animal naturale.*—(n), animal sociale seu sociabile, see *animal civile.*—(o), animal solitarium, see *animal civile.* Homo est naturaliter animal domesticum, see *homo.* Homo naturaliter seu secundum suam naturam est animal civile seu politicum seu so-

ciale seu sociabile, see *homo.*—On circulus animalium, see *circulus* under 1; on vita animalis, see *vita* under 1.—Kinds of *animal* in the narrower sense are: (a), animal annulosi corporis seu annulosum, *the animal with a body like a ring* or *ring-shaped.*—(b), animal aquaticum, animal terrenum seu terrestre, and animal caeleste, *the animal of the water, of the land* and *of the heavens,* i.e., *winged.*—(c), animal caeleste, see *animal aquaticum.*—(d), animal domesticum seu mansuetum and animal ferox seu saevum, *the domestic* or *tamed animal* and *the wild animal.*—(e), animal durae testae, animal mollis testae, and animal molle, *the animal with a hard shell, the animal with a soft shell,* and *the mollusk.*—(f), animal ferox, see *animal domesticum.*—(g), animal gressibile seu progressivum, and animal immobile, *the animal that can walk* or *move from place to place* and *the attached animal, the one grown to the ground.*—(h), animal ignobile and animal nobile, *the ignobile* and *the noble animal.*—(i), animal immobile, see *animal gressibile.*—(j), animal immolatitium, *the sacrificial animal.*—(k), animal immundum and animal mundum, *the unclean* and *the clean animal* in the sense of the Mosaic law.—(l), animal imperfectum and animal perfectum, *the imperfect* and *the perfect animal* of which the former is called imperfect because it is either grown to the ground like a plant or it does not express the animal nature in all its capacities, or because it does not represent in a most perfect manner the nature of its kind; the latter is called perfect either because it can move locally or expresses animal nature perfectly or possesses all essential and unessential characteristics of its kind.—(m), animal mansuetum, see *animal domesticum.*—(n), animal molle, see *animal durae testae.*—(o), animal mollis testae, see *animal durae testae.*—(p), animal nobile, see *animal ignobile.*—(q), animal perfectum, see *animal imperfectum.*—(r), animal pictum and animal verum, *the painted* and *the true animal.*—(s), animal progressivum, see *animal gressibile.*—(t), animal saevum, see *animal domesticum.*—(u), animal silvestre, *the animal of the forest.*—(v), animal terrenum, see *animal aquaticum.*—(w), animal terrestre, see *animal aquaticum.*—(x), animal totalum, *the animal existing entirely, the animal existing on its whole body, the animal not divided into its members or parts.*—(y), animal venenosum, *poisonous animal.*—(z), animal verum, see *animal pictum.*—(a²), animal volatile, see *animal aquaticum.*—animalia magis aguntur, quam agunt, see *agere* under 4.

—Animal sumitur a natura sensitiva per modum concretionis, see *concretio* under 3.

animalis, e, *adj.,* (1), *soulful,* synonym of *animatus,* opposite of *inanimatus,* (2) *sensuous, endowed with senses,* synonym of *animatus* and *sensitivus,* the opposite of *inanimatus* on the one hand and *spiritualis* on the other, (3) *brutal, bestial, brutalized.*—On habitus animalis, see *habitus* under 4; on immutatio animalis, see *immutatio* under 2.—(2), on amor animalis, see *amor* under 1; on appetitus animalis, see *appetitus* under 1; on apprehensio animalis, see *apprehensio* under 2; on causa animalis, see *causa* under 2; on concupiscentia animalis, see *concupiscentia* under 1; on delectatio animalis, see *delectatio;* on generatio animalis, see *generatio* under 1; on homo animalis, see *homo;* on intentio animalis, see *intentio* under 2; on motus animalis, see *motus* under 2; on nativitas animalis, see *nativitas;* on operatio animalis see *operatio* under 2; on organum animale, see *organum;* on passio animalis, see *passio* under 2; on proprietas animalis, see *proprietas* under 1; on sapientia animalis, see *sapientia* under 1; on spiritus animalis, see *spiritus;* on virtus animalis, see *virtus* under 1; on vis animalis, see *vis* under 1; on vita animalis, see *vita* under 1.—On corpus animale, see *corpus;* on sapientia animalis, see *sapientia* under 1.—animaliter, *adv., in a soulful* or *sensitive manner, feelingly,* synonym of *sensitive,* the opposite of *spiritualiter.*

animalitas, atis, *f., animalism, sensuality, the nature and essence of a being endowed with senses.*

animaliter, *adv.,* see *animalis.*

animans antis, *m., f.,* and *n., any living, animate being, an animal,* a synonym of *animal.*

animatio, onis, *f., a quickening, an animating, animation.*

animatus, a, um, *P. a.,* see *animo.*

animo, are, avi, atum, 1, *v. a.* and *n., to quicken, animate endow with a soul.*—animatus, a, um, *P. a.,* (1) *animated, living,* a synonym of *animalis* and *vivus,* the opposite of *inanimatus,* (2), *sensitive, discerning by sense, being sensible of, perceiving,* also the opposite of *inanimatus.* —On corpus animatum, see *corpus;* on esse animatum, see *esse;* on instrumentum animatum, see *instrumentum;* on iustitia animata, see *iustitia* under 4; on iustum animatum, see *iustus;* on res animata, see *res;* on substantia animata, see *substantia* under 2.—primum animatum, i, *n., the first animated, the primary animate,* i.e., that matter which the soul actualizes first.

animositas, atis, *f.,* (1) *boldness, courage, spirit,* (2) *wrath, enmity.*

animosus, a, um, *adj., full of courage, bold, spirited, undaunted.*

animus, i, *m.,* (1), *intellect, reason,* i.e., the rational part of the human soul; cf. pars animae under *pars,* (2) *feeling,* i.e., the sensitive faculty of desire, (3) *courage,* (4) *intention.*—On conceptio animi, see *conceptio* under 3; on libertas animi, see *libertas* under 1; on verbum animi sinu cogitatum, see *verbum* under 1; on virtus purgati animi, see *virtus* under 5; on vitium animi, see *vitium* under 2.—On motus animi, see *motus* under 2; on passio animi, see *passio* under 2; on remissio animi, see *remissio* under 1. Moderatio animi and austeritas animi, *mildness* or *gentleness of heart* and *severity* or *hardness of heart.*

Anna, ae, *f., Anna.* The Anna mentioned in the S.T. was the daughter of Phanuel and belonged to the ancient tribe of Asher. She lived for more than a hundred years, was a wife for seven years and a widow for eighty-four. She gave herself to a lively devotion frequenting the temple and worshipping with supplications day and night. At the presentation of the Infant Messias (Luke 2. 22-24), she entered the sacred court, and hearing Simeon's prophecy and benediction took up the refrain of praise.

annales, ium, *m., annals.*

annecto, ere, nexui, nexum, 3, *v. a.* to *tie* or *bind to, connect, annex.—***annexum,*** i, *n., something annexed* or *connected.*

annexio, onis, *f., a tying* or *binding to, a connecting.*

annexus, us, *m., a tying* or *binding to, a connection.*

annihilatio, onis, *f., annihilation.*

annihilo, are, 1, *v. a., to bring to nothing, annihilate.*

anniversarius, a, um, *adj., returning* or *renewed annually, annual, yearly.*

annuatim, *adv., annually.*

annullo, are, avi, 1, *v. a., to annihilate, annul.*

annulus, i, *m.,* (anulus), *ring.*

annumeratio, onis, *f., a numbering, counting.*

annumero, are, avi, atum, 1, *v. a., to add to, include with, reckon with.*

annuntiatio, onis, *f., an announcing, announcement, annunciation.*

annuntio, are, avi, 1, *v. a., to announce, make known, relate, proclaim.*

annuo, ere, ui, utum, 3, *v. n., to nod, assent to, approve.*

annus, i, *m., a year.*

annuus, a, um, *adj., annual.*

Anomaei or **Anomoei,** orum, *m., Anomoeans,* so called from their doctrine that the Son is not consubstantial (*anomoios*) with the Father.

Anselmus, i, *m., Anselm,* Saint, Archbishop of Canterbury, doctor of the Church. He was born at Aosta, a Burgundian town on the confines of Lombardy, 1033-34; died April 21, 1109. Collections of his works were published soon after the invention of printing.

ante, *prep.* and *adv., before,* the opposite of *post.*

antea, *temp. adv., before, formerly, earlier, aforetime.*

anteactus, a, um, *adj., that has been done before, former.*

antecedens, entis, *P. a.,* see *antecedo.*

antecedenter, *adv.,* see *antecedo.*

antecedo, ere, cessi, cessum, 3, *v. n., to precede, excel,* used with *abl.* of respect, with or without *in.*—***antecedens,*** entis, *P. a.,* (1) *preceding,* the opposite of *consequens,* (2) *antecedent* clause in a conditional sentence, also the opposite of *consequens.*—On **bonum antecedens,** see *bonus* under 2; on **ignorantia antecedens,** see *ignorantia* under 1; on **voluntas antecedens,** see *voluntas* under 3.—**omnis condicionalis, cuius antecedens est necessarium absolute, consequens est necessarium absolute,** see *necessarius* under 2.—**antecedenter,** *adv., in a preceding way, antecedently,* the opposite of *consequenter.* On **ad beatitudinem pertinere antecedenter,** see *beatitudo* under 1; on **velle antecedenter,** see *velle* under 1.

antecello, ere, 3, *v. n., to distinguish one's self above any one,* *excel, be superior to,* used with *dat., abl.,* and with *in.*

antecessio, onis, *f., that which goes before, precedence, antecedent cause* as opposed to final cause.

antecessor, oris, *m., forerunner, predecessor.*

antedicta, orum, *n., things mentioned before.*

antefero, ferre, tuli, latum, 3, *v. a., to bear* or *carry before, prefer.*

antepono, ere, posui, positum, 3, *v. a., place before, prefer.*

Antepraedicamenta, orum, *n., the first three chapters of Aristotle's Categories.*

antequam, *adv., before,* used with (1) *indicative* and (2) *subjunctive.*

anterior, ius, *adj., comp., previous, former, anterior, opposite of posterior.*

anthropomorphitae, arum, *m., anthropomorphists, anthropomorphites, devotees of anthropomorphism,* the name applied to that tendency which endows the gods, or God, with the nature of men or man.

Antichristus, i, *m., the Antichrist.* PT. Q. 8. Art. 8 deals with the subject, *utrum Antichristus possit etiam dici caput omnium malorum.*

anticipatio, onis, *f., anticipation,* a voluntary reaction to a stimulus before the latter occurs.

anticipo, are, avi, atum, 1, *v. a., to take before, anticipate.*

Antiochenus, a, um, *adj., of* or

belonging to Antiochia, Antiochene.

Antiochia, (**Antiochea**), ae, *f., Antioch.*

Antiochus, i, *m., Antiochus IV.* In 175 B.C. he seized the Syrian throne and began a series of conquests which were to rival his father's. In the course of his battles he had become suspicious of Judaea and determined to force that country into complete subjection to his will. His motives were probably more political than religious but as a part of his program he undertook to compel the Jews to worship heathen gods as well as, if not in place of, Jehovah. His plans were put into active operation towards the end of 170. B.C. The events of the period of persecutions are related in 2 Machabees. Antiochus IV died on an expedition against the Parthians in B.C. 164.

antique, *adv.,* see *antiquus.*

antiquitas, atis, *f., the quality of being antiquus, age, antiquity.* —**Antiquitates Iudaeae,** *the Jewish antiquities* of Flavius Josephus, historian born A.D. 37 at Jerusalem, died about 101. The work in twenty books contains the whole history of the Jews from the creation to the outbreak of the revolt in A.D. 66.

antiquitus, *adv., from ancient times.*

antiquus, a, um, *adj., old, ancient, former.—antique, adv., in former times, of old,* a synonym of *antiquitus.*

Antonius, ii, *m., Antonius,* saint, the patriarch of Monasticism, born in 251 in the village of Koma near Thebais of a wealthy Coptic family. For information concerning his life, we rely almost exclusively on his biography by Athanasius.

antonomastice, *adv., in the manner* or *sense of antonomasia,* a figure of speech which is used when a name appropriate to several different things is applied to that of one of them to which it is preeminently suitable.

anus, us, *f., old woman* (married or unmarried).

anxietas, atis, *f., solicitude, mental distress* or *agitation* either in dread or anticipation of some sorrow or trial, or as a general apprehension of misfortune.

anxio, are, 1, *v. a., to make uneasy* or *anxious.*

aperio, ire, erui, ertum, 4, *v. a., to uncover, make* or *lay bare, open,* the opposite of *claudere. —apertus,* a, um, *P. a., opened, open, free.—aperte, adv., openly, clearly, plainly.*

aperte, *adv.,* see *aperio.*

apertio, onis, *f., an opening, unfolding,* the opposite of *clausio.*

apertura, ae, *f., an opening, aperture.*

aphilotimia, ae, *f., (aphilotimia), without love of honor.*

Aphricanus, i, *m., Africanus.* See *Africanus.*

apirocalia, (*apurocalia*), ae, *f., a passionate inclination to overdo the expenditure of anything,* a synonym of *banausia,* and *consumptio,* the opposite of *magnificentia* and *parvificentia.*

apis or-es, is, *f., a bee.*

apocalypsis, is, *f., (apokalypsis), a disclosing, revelation. The Revelation, The Apocalypse.*

apocryphus, a, um, *adj., the apocryphal books incorporated with the Bible.*

Apollinaris, is, *m., Apollinaris* the Younger, author of a theory according to which Christ had a human body and a human sensitive soul but no human rational mind, the Divine Logus taking the place of this. He was bishop of Laodicea and flourished in the latter half of the fourth century. At first he was highly esteemed by men like St. Athanasius, St. Basil, and St. Jerome for his classical culture, his biblical learning, his defense of Christianity, and his loyaty to the Nicene faith.

Apollinaristae, arum, *m., the Apollianists, followers of Apollinaris* and his Christological theory. See Apollinaris.

Apollinarius, ii, *m., Apollinaris.*

Apollo, inis, *m., Apollo,* son of Jupiter and Latona, twin-brother of Diana, and god of the sun;

on account of his omniscience, god of divination; also known as god of archery, god of the pestilence, god of the healing art, god of poetry and music.

apostasia, ae, *f., falling away* or *separation from God.*—Kinds of *apostasia* are: (a), **apostasia absolute dicta** or **simpliciter dicta,** *apostasy absolutely* or *simply so called.*—(b), **apostasia a fide** or **perfidiae, apostasia ordinis** and **apostasia religionis,** *apostasy from faith* or *of perfidy, apostasy through the renunciation of holy orders* and *of the religious state.* See **apostasia absolute dicta**—(c), **apostasia ordinis,** see *apostasia a fide.*—(d), **apostasia perfidiae,** see *apostasia a fide.*—(e), **apostasia simpliciter dicta,** see *apostasia absolute dicta.*

apostata, ae, *m., an apostate.*

apostato, are, 1, *v. n., to forsake one's religion, apostatize.* See *apostasia.*

apostolatus, us, *m., the office of an apostle, apostolate, apostleship.*

Apostolici, orum, *m., followers of the Apostles, the Apostolici,* the name of a Christian sect.

apostolicus, a, um, *adj., relating to an apostle, apostolic.*

apostolus, i, *m.,* (1) *an apostle,* (2) *the Apostle,* i.e., St. Paul.

apparatus, us, *m., a preparing, providing, preparation, splendor.*

apparentia, ae, *f., appearance, semblance.* On **causa apparentiae,** see *causa* under 4; on simi-

litudo apparentiae, see *similitudo* under 1.

appareo, ere, ui, itum, 2, *v. n., to appear, become visible, make one's appearance.*—**apparet,** impers., *it is evident, clear, manifest.*

apparentia, ium, *n. pl., things that appear, appearances.*—**non apparentia,** *things that appear not, the unseen.*—**argumentum non apparentium,** *the evidence of things that appear not.*

apparatio, onis, *f., apparition, appearance.*

appellatio, onis, *f.,* (1) *a name, title, appellation,* (2) in judic. lang., *an appeal.*

appellativus, a, um, *adj., appellative, called; nomen appellativum,* the opposite of *nomen proprium.* On **nomen appellativum,** see *nomen.*

appello, are, avi, atum, 1, *v. n.,* (1) *to call, term, entitle, declare, name,* (2) in judic. language, *appeal to one.*

appendix, icis, *f., appendix of a literary work.*

appendo, ere, endi, ensum, 3, *v. a., to hang something upon something, attach to, append.*

appetibilis, e, *adj., desirable, appetibile.* Kinds of *appetibile* are: (a), **appetibile absolute** and **appetibile in ordine ad aliud,** *absolutely* or *simply* and *in a certain respect desirable.*—(b), **appetibile in ordine ad aliud,** see *appetibile absolute.*—(c), **appetibile primum** and **ap-**

petibile secundum, *the desirable in the first and foremost place, and that in the second place.*—(d), appetibile secundum, see *appetibile primum.*—(e), appetibile secundum sensum, *the desirable through a sense.*

appetibilitas, atis, *f.*, *desirability, desirableness.* On ratio appetibilitatis, see *ratio* under 14.

appetitivus, a, um, *adj.*, *striving, desiring.* On intellectus appetitivi et appetitivus, see *electio* and *intellectus;* on motus appetitivus, see *motus;* on pars appetitiva, see *pars;* on potentia appetitiva, see *potentia;* on virtus appetitiva, see *virtus;* on vis appetitiva, see *vis.* Appetitivum, sc. *genus potentiarum animae* or *principium,* the translation of Aristotelian *orektikon* (De Anim. 2. 3. 414 a. 31; 3. 7. 431. a. 13), denotes either (1) the entirety of the desire of an animal being, including the will in man, i.e., simply, according to all phases of its activity, or, on the other hand, (2) in contrast to *fugitivum,* those faculties only in so far as they tend to good.

appetitus, us, *m.*, (1), *a striving, desire,* a synonym of *concupiscentia,* (2) *the appetitive faculty.*—On velle appetitu naturali, see *velle* under 1.—Kinds of *appetitus* in this (1) sense are: (a), appetitus animalis seu sensitivus, appetitus intelligibilis seu

intellectivus seu intellectualis seu rationalis seu voluntarius and appetitus naturalis, *animal* or *sensual* or *irrational desire, the supersensible* or *rational* (the *orexis dianoetike* of Aristotle) or *voluntary desire,* and *the natural desire* which sometimes occurs without knowledge of the desire and sometimes signifes that faculty of desire which arises from nature. Cf. appetitus animalis under 2.—(b), appetitus consiliativus seu deliberatus seu praeconsiliati and appetitus impetuosus, the *orexis bouleutike* of Aristotle, *the deliberating* or *deliberated desire* or *desire for something previously considered,* and *impetuous* or *violent desire.*—(c), appetitus deliberatus, see *appetitus consiliativus.*—(d), appetitus impetuosus, see *appetitus consiliativus.*—(e), appetitus inquisitivus, *the investigating desire* or *the desire based on an investigation.*—(f), appetitus intellectivi seu intellectivus seu intellectualis seu intellegibilis seu appetitus animalis. Cf. appetitus intellectivus under 2.—(g), appetitus libidinosus seu libidinis, *sensual desire.*—(h), appetitus naturalis, see *appetitus animalis.* Cf. *appetitus naturalis* under 2.—(i), appetitus perversus and appetitus rectus, *the wrong* and *the right desire.*—(j), appetitus preconsiliati, see *appetitus consiliativus.*—(k), appetitus rationalis, see *appetitus animalis.* Cf. **appetitus rationalis** under 2.—(l), **appetitus, rectus,** see *appetitus perversus.*—(m), **appetitus sensitivus,** see *appetitus animalis.* Cf. **appetitus sensitivus** under 2.—(n), **appetitus simplex,** *the simple desire.* Cf. **actus simplex,** under *actus* under 2 and *velle* under 2.—(o), **appetitus voluntarius,** see **appetitus animalis.**—**appetitus sequitur apprehensionem,** *desire follows knowledge* and *directs itself towards it.* **impossibile est naturae appetitum vanum esse,** see *vanus* under 3.—On **delectatio appetitus intellectivi et sensitivi seu sensibilis,** see *delectatio;* on **libido appetitus sensitivi,** see *libido* under 2; on **motus appetitus absolutus et in ordine ad alterum,** see *motus* under 2; on **passio appetitus sensitivi,** see *passio* under 2.—Kinds of *appetitus* in this (2) sense are: (a), **appetitus animalis seu bestialis seu brutalis seu sensitivus seu sensibilis seu sensualis seu irrationalis, appetitus intellectivus seu intellectualis seu rationalis** and **appetitus naturalis,** *the animal* or *sensitive* or *irrational faculty of desire, the supersensible* or *rational faculty of desire,* and *the natural faculty of desire.* Cf. **appetitus animalis** under 1.—(b), **appetitus bestialis,** see *appetitus animalis.*—(c), **appetitus brutalis,** see *appetitus animalis.*—(d), **appetitus carnalis seu carnis,** *the carnal* or *the cor-*

poral faculty of desire.—(e), **appetitus carnis,** see *appetitus carnalis.*—(f), **appetitus humanus,** *the human faculty of desire* or *the will.*—(g), **appetitus inferior** and **appetitus superior,** *the lower* and *the higher,* or *the sensitive and supersensitive faculty of desire* in man.—(h), **appetitus intellectivus seu intellectualis,** see *appetitus animalis.*—(i), **appetitus irrationalis,** see *appetitus animalis.*—(j), **appetitus materiae,** *the faculty of desire in material.*—(k), **appetitus naturalis,** see *appetitus animalis.* Cf. *appetitus animalis* under 1.—(l), **appetitus passivus,** *the passive faculty of desire* or *that capable of receiving impressions.*—(m), **appetitus rationalis,** see *appetitus animalis.* Cf. *appetitus ratonalis* under 1.—(n), **appetitus rationis** and **appetitus sensus,** *the faculty of desire of the rational part of man's soul* and *that of the sensible part of man's soul.* Cf. **pars animae** under *pars* under 1.—(o), **appetitus sensibilis seu sensitivus seu sensualis,** see *appetitus animalis.* Cf. **appetitus sensitivus** under 1.—(p), **appetitus sensualitatis,** *the faculty of the desire of the sensual* or *the sensual faculty of desire.*—(q), **appetitus superior,** see *appetitus inferior.*

appeto, ere, ivi, itum, 3, *v. a., to strive after something, strive after, desire.*—Kinds of *appetere* are: (a), **appetere explicite** and appetere implicite, *to desire in an open* or *explicit manner* and *to desire in a restrained* or *implicit manner.*—(b), appetere implicite, see *appetere explicite.*—(c), appetere inordinate, *to desire inordinately* or *without measure.*—(d), appetere naturaliter, *to desire* or *seek naturally.*—(e), appetere propter aliud and appetere propter se or sibi, *to seek for something as ordered to something else* and *to seek for something for its self.*—(f), appetere propter se, see *appetere propter aliud.*—Bonum est, quod omnia appetunt, see *bonus* under 3.

applicabilis, e, *adj., to be applied, applicable.*

applicatio, onis, *f.*, (1) *adjustment, conformity, close accommodation,* (2) *application, devotedness,* (3) *employment, application.*—A special kind of *applicatio* which belongs here is: applicatio actualis, *application in the sense of an activity.*

applico, are, avi and ui, atum and itum, 1, *v. a.*, (1) *to adjust, make conform* or *fit, accommodate closely,* (2) *to apply, devote,* (3) *to employ, make use of* or *apply.*—On magnum applicatum alicui rei, see *magnus.*

appono, ere, posui, positum, 3, *v. a., to apply to, add, unite,* the opposite of *subtraho.*

apporto, are, avi, atum, 1, *v. a., to bring, carry, conduct, convey to.* Used in the S.T. only in quot.

appositio, onis, *f., a setting before, application, adding.*

appositive, *adv.*, see *appositivus.*

appositivus, a, um, *adj., by way of addition, in apposition.*—appositive, *adv., by way of addition, in apposition.*

apprehendo, ere, di, sum, 3, *v. a.*, (1) *to grasp, take hold of,* (2) *to grasp with intellectual power, perceive, understand.*—On forma apprehensa, see *forma* under 2; on intellectus quidditatem rei apprehendens, see *intellectus* under 4; on simplex apprehensum, see *simplex* under 1.— Kinds of *apprehendere* in this (2) sense are: (a), apprehendere absolute, *to understand absolutely.*—(b), apprehendere directe and apprehendere per reflexionem, *to understand directly* and *to understand reflexively.*—(c), apprehendere distincte, *to understand exactly.*—(d), apprehendere per imaginationem, apprehendere per sensum, and apprehendere per intellectum, *to understand by means of the imagination, by means of an external sense, by means of the reason.*—(e), apprehendere per intellectum, see *apprehendere per imaginationem.*—(b), apprehendere naturaliter, *to understand naturally.*—(g), apprehendere simpliciter, *to understand simply.*—(h), apprehendere per modum complexi and apprehendere per modum incomplexi or simplicis, *to understand according to the manner of the complex* and *the not complex or simple.*—(i), apprehendere per modum incomplexi, see *apprehendere per modum complexi.*—(j), apprehendere per modum simplicis, see *apprehendere per modum complexi.*—(k), apprehendere per reflexionem, see *apprehendere directe.*—(l), apprehendere per sensum, see *apprehendere per imaginationem.*

apprehensibilis, e, *adj., that can be understood, intelligible.*

apprehensio, onis, *f.*, (1) *seizure, grasping,* (2) *grasping by means of intellectual power, perception, understanding.*—On ordo apprehensionis, see *ordo* under 1; on via apprehensionis, see *via.*— Kinds of *apprehensio* in this (2) sense are: (a), apprehensio absoluta sive simplex and apprehensio inquisitiva, *the absolute* or *simple understanding and the searching understanding.* i.e., to grasp something intuitively and to grasp as a result of a process of reasoning.—(b), apprehensio actualis, *an understanding consisting of an activity.*—(c), apprehensio alterius sive non-coniuncta and apprehensio propria sive coniuncta, *the knowledge of another* and *the knowledge of oneself either united* or *not united with the desiring being.*—(d), apprehensio animalis sive apprehensivae sensualis sive sensitiva

sive sensus and apprehensio intellectiva sive intellectualis sive intellectus sive rationis, *the animal* or *sensitive* and *supersensible knowledge, the knowledge of reason.*—(e), apprehensio apprehensio appresensivae sensualis, see *apprehensio animalis.*— (f), apprehensio certa or vera, *certain* or *true understanding.*— (g), apprehensio coniuncta, see *apprehensio alterius.*—(h), apprehensio connaturalis, *natural understanding* or *the understanding coinciding with the nature of a faculty.*—(i), apprehensio exterior and apprehensio interior, *exterior* and *interior understanding,* or *the understanding of an exterior* and *of an interior object.*—(j), apprehensio imaginaria seu imaginationis seu phantastica, *understanding of the power of imagination,* or *sensible representation.*—(k), apprehensio imaginaonis, see *apprehensio imaginaria.* —(l), apprehensio inquisitiva, see *apprehensio absoluta.*—(m), apprehensio intellectiva or intellectualis, see *apprehensio animalis.* —(n), apprehensio intellectus, see *apprehensio animalis.*—(o), apprehensio interior, see *apprehensio exterior.*—(p), apprehensio non-coniuncta, see *apprehensio alterius.*—(q), apprehensio particularis and apprehensio universalis, *particular* and *general* or *universal understanding.*—(r), apprehensio phantastica, see *apprehensio imaginaria.*—(s), appre-

hensio propria, see *apprehensio
alterius.*—(t), apprehensio rationis, see *apprehensio animalis.*—
(u), apprehensio sensitiva, see
apprehensio animalis.—(v), apprehensio sensus, see *apprehensio animalis.*—(w), apprehensio
simplex, see *apprehensio absoluta.*—(x), apprehensio superficialis, *superficial understanding.*—
(y), apprehensio universalis, see
apprehensio particularis.—(z), apprehensio vera, see *apprehensio
certa.*

apprehensivus, a, um, *adj., grasping, comprehending, knowing.*
On pars apprehensiva, see *pars*
under 1; on potentia apprehensiva, see *potentia* under 2; on
ratio apprehensiva, see *ratio* under 1; on virtus apprehensiva,
see *virtus* under 1; on vis apprehensiva, see *vis* under 1.—appre-
hensivum, sc. *genus animae, the
genus or the whole of the sensible faculty of a being.*

appretio, are, avi, atum, 1, *v. a., to
value, estimate at a price, appraise, rate,* used only as deponent in the S.T.

approbatio, onis, *f., an approving,
probation.* On notitia approbationis, see *notitia* under 2; on
providentia approbationis, see
providentia; on scientia approbationis, see *scientia* under 2.

approbo, are, avi, atum, 1, *v. a.,
to assent to as good, approve,
prove,* the opposite of *reprobo.*

appropinquatio, onis, *f., an approach, drawing near.*

appropinquo, are, avi, atum, 1, *v.
n., to come near, draw nigh to,
approach,* used with *ad* and *acc.,*
the *dat.* alone, and *absolutely.*

appropriate, *adv., in the manner* or
*the sense of ascribing a special
characteristic, appropriately.*

appropriatio, onis, *f., appropriation, ascribing, the attributing
of a special characteristic.*

approprio, are, 1, *v. n.,* (1) *to appropriate, take one's own possession,* (2) *appropriate, ascribe,
attribute as a special peculiarity.*
See *appropriatio.*—On causa appropriata, see *causa* under 2; on
opus appropriatum, see *opus* under 4; on ratio appropriata, see
ratio under 11; on sapientia appropriata, see *sapientia* under 1.
—Kinds of *appropriare* in this (2)
sense are: appropriare causaliter
sive per causam and appropriare
essentialiter, *to ascribe something to another in the sense of
cause* or *in the sense of essence.*

approximatio, onis, *f., approximation.*—Kinds of *approximatio* are:
(a), approximatio localis and approximatio spiritualis, *local* or
physical and *spiritual approximation.*—(b), approximatio per
similitudinem naturae and approximatio secundum affectum,
*approximation as the result of
a similarity of nature* and *approximation according to affection*
or *desire.*—(c), approximatio secundum affectum, see *approximatio per similitudinem naturae.*

—(d), **approximatio spiritualis,** see *approximatio localis.*

Aprilis, is, *m.,* (sc. mensis), *April.*

aptissime, *adv., most fittingly, most suitably.*

aptitudo, inis, *f., suitability, fitness, inclination, proneness towards.*

apto, are, avi, atum, 1, *v. a., to fit, adapt, accommodate, apply, adjust.*

aptus, a, um, *adj., suited, suitable, proper, fit, adapted, apposite.*

apud, *prep.* with *acc., at, near, about, around, before.*

Apuleius, i, *m., Apuleius, a native of Madaura in Africa,* who was a bombastic writer of the second century. His principal work yet extant is called Metamorphoseon sive de Asino Aureo libri XI.

aqua, ae, *f., water.* Certain kinds of aqua are: (a), **aqua baptismalis,** *baptismal water.*—(b), **aqua benedicta,** *holy water.*—(c), **aqua pura** and **aqua simplex,** *pure water* and *plain water.*—(d), **aqua rosacea,** *rose water.*—(e), **aqua simplex,** see *aqua pura.*

Aquarii, iorum, *m., (Hydroparastatai), Aquarians,* a name given to several sects in the early Church but chiefly to the followers of Tatian, of whom Theodoret says: "Tatian, after the death of his master, Justin the Martyr, set himself up as the author of a heresy. Among the things he rejected were marriage, and the use of animal food, and wine.

Tatian is the father of the Aquarians and of the Encratites. They are called Hydroparastatae, because they offer water instead of wine; and Encratites, because they neither drink wine nor eat animal food." St. Augustine, (De Haeresibus, 64) says: "The Aquarians are so called because in the cup of the Sacrament they offer water, not that which the whole Church offers."

aquaticus, a, um, *adj., living, growing, found in* or *by the water, aquatic.*

aqueus, a, um, *adj., aqueous,* a synonym of *crystallinus.*

aquila, ae, *f., an eagle.*

aquilo, onis, *m., north wind, the north.*

aquilonaris, e, *adj., northerly, northern.*

aquosus, a, um, *adj., abounding in water, humid, watery.*

ara, ae, *f., altar.*

Arabicus, a, um, *adj., Arabic,* used in neuter as subst. for *the Arabic language.*

aranea, ae, *f., a spider.*

aratrum, i, *n., a plough.*

Aratus, i, *m., Aratus,* of Soli, afterwards Pompeiopolis, in Cilicia, or, according to one authority, of Tarsus, flourished B.C. 270, and spent all the latter part of his life at the court of Antigonus Gonatas, king of Macedonia. He wrote two astronomical poems, entitled Phaenomena (*Phainomena*), consisting of 732 verses, and Diosemeia (*Diosemeia*) of 422.

Arausicanus, a, um, *adj.,* with *concilium, the Council of Orange.* Two councils were held at Orange (Arausio), a town in the present department of Vaucluse in Southern France. The first met Nov. 8, 441 in the church called "Ecclesia Iustinianensis" or "Iustianensis." The council is designated either by the name of the church "synodus Iustinianensis" or by that of the episcopal city, "Arausicana Ia" (first of Orange.) For the canons issued by the Council, see the Catholic Encyclopaedia. The second council was held on July 3, 529 to publish a decision in matters of faith.

Arbee, *indecl., f.,* city of *Arbee,* same as Hebron. Sara, the wife of Abraham, died and was buried there in a tomb which Abraham bought from Ephron.

arbiter, tri, *m., an umpire, arbiter, judge.*

arbitrarius, a, um, *adj., depending on the will, of one's own choice, arbitrary.*

arbitrium, ii, *n.,* (1) *sentence of the arbiter* or *judge, arbitration, decision,* (2) *free decision, free judgment, pleasure* or *option,* (3) *capacity* or *inclination to make a decision,* (4) *faculty of decision.*—Kinds of *arbitrium* in this sense are: **arbitrium liberum** and **arbitrium non liberum,** *decision that is free* and *that which is not free.* Cf. **arbitrium liberum** under 3 and 4. On **voluntas ex** libero arbitrio rationis proveniens, see *voluntas* under 3. **Liberum arbitrium dicitur quasi liberum iudicium,** *a free decision is in a certain measure a free opinion but no iudicium,* **quo sententiat homo de conclusionibus in scientiis speculativis,** *but an opinion in the sense of* electio *which likewise dicitur quoddam iudicium.* **Liberum arbitrium est liberum de ratione iudicium,** *a free decision is a free judgment proceeding from reason in so far indeed as the decision is reached on the basis of deliberation, and the deliberation is concluded on the part of reason by a true judgment.* **Liberum arbitrium est liberum de voluntate iudicium,** *a free decision is a free judgment proceeding from the will,* in so far indeed as the decision of the will or the choice made by the will is considered a kind of judgment. On **agere per arbitrium voluntatis,** see *agere* under 1.— Cf. *liberum arbitrium* under 1 and 4. **Liberum arbitrium dicitur esse facultas voluntatis et rationis,** *freedom of choice is said to be the faculty of the will and reason.* On **iudicium liberi arbitrii,** see *iudicium* under 4; on **libertas liberi arbitrii,** see *libertas* under 1; on **motus liberi arbitrii,** see *motus* under 2.—Kinds of *liberi arbitrii* in this (4) sense are: **liberum arbitrium Dei sive divinum, liberum arbitrium an-**

geli sive angelicum and liberum arbitrium hominis sive humanum, *the free will of God, that of the angels, that of man.*—Liberum arbitrium est causa sui motus, *free will is the cause of its own motion or activity.*

arbitror, ari, atus, 1, *v. dep.*, *to be of the opinion, believe, think, suppose.*

arbor, oris, *f.*, *tree.*

arbustum, i, *n.*, *shrub.*

arca, ae, *f.*, *chest, coffer, the ark* of the testament, anything in the shape of a box, *Noah's ark.*

arceo, ere, cui, ctum, 2, *to keep off, prevent from*, (1) used *absol.*, (2) with *a* or *ab* and *abl.*, (3) with *a* or *ab* and *abl.* of *gerund* and *gerundive*, (4) with *ne* and *subj.*

archangelus, i, *m.*, *an archangel.*

archidiaconatus, us, *m.*, *archdeaconry.*

archidiaconus, i, *m.*, *archdeacon.*

archiepiscopus, i, *m.*, *archbishop.*

archisynagogus, i, *m.*, *ruler of the synagague.*

architecton, onis, *m.*, *a master-builder, architect,* a synonym of *architectus* and *architector.*

architectonice, *adv.*, see *architectonicus.*

architectonicus, a, um, *adj.*, *architectural, masterly, commanding, dominant, ordering, superordinate,* a synonym of *dominativus* and *principativus.* On **architectonica**, see *ars* under 2; on **notitia architectonica**, see *notitia* under 2; on **prudentia architecto-**

nica, see *prudentia* under 1; on **ratio architectonica**, see *ratio* under 6; on **scientia architectonica**, see *scientia* under 1; on **virtus architectonica**, see *virtus* under 5.—architectonice, *adv.*, *after the manner* or *in the sense of the architect, of the master, of the commander, of the ruler.*

architector, oris, *m.*, *master-builder, architect,* a synonym of *architecton* and *architectus.*

architectura, ae, *f.*, *the art of building, architecture.*

architectus, i, *m.*, *master-builder, an architect,* a synonym of *architecton* and *architector.*

arctatio, onis, *f.*, *inconvenience, stricture.*

arctitudo, inis, *f.*, *strictness.*

arcto, are, avi, atum, 1, *v. a.*, *to bind, obligate, restrict.*

arctus, a, um, *adj.*, *close, strait, narrow, confined, short, brief, strict, severe.*

arcus, us, *m.*, *bow.*

ardeo, ere, rsi, rsum, 2, *v. n.*, *burn, blaze, glow.*—**ardens**, entis, *P. a.*, *burning, fiery, ardent, hot.*—**ardenter**, *adv.*, *in a burning, fiery, eager, passionate manner, ardently.*

ardor, oris, *m.*, *heat, burning, ardor.*

arduitas, atis, *f.*, *arduousness.*

arduus, a, um, *adj.*, *arduous, difficult.*

area, ae, *f.*, *a vacant space, place.*

arefacio, ere, feci, factum, 3, *v. a.*, *to wither up, break down.*

arena, ae, *f.*, *sand.*

aresco, ere, 3, *v. n. inch., to become dry, dry up, wither, be dry.*

argenteus, a, um, *adj., of* or *from silver, made of silver.*

argentum, i, *n.,* (1) *silver,* (2) *money.*

argumentatio, onis, *f., advancing of proof, procedure of testimony, testimony* or *evidence* in the wider sense of the word, a synonym of *argumentum* and *locus.* One kind of *argumentatio* is *argumentatio localis, evidence* or *proof from passages* or *expressions.*

argumentativus, a, um, *adj., proving, proving the truth of something by a syllogism, possible of being proven by a syllogism, argumentative.* On **modus argumentativus,** see *modus* under b; on **probatio argumentativa,** see *probatio* under 2; on **ratio argumentativa,** see *ratio* under 13.

argumentor, ari, atum, *v. dep., to adduce proof of a thing, prove, adduce something as proof, make a conclusion.*

argumentum, i, *n.,* (1) *proof* in the wider sense of the word, a synonym of *argumentatio* and *locus,* (2) *evidence, sign, mark,* (3) *brief statement of contents, summary,* (4) *means of revelation, the insight of the producing light,* (5) *conviction, certainty.* —Kinds of *argumentum* in this (1) sense are: (a), **argumentum ab auctoritate,** *proof from authority.*—(b), **argumentum a maiori** and **argumentum a mi-** nori, *proof from the greater* and *from the lesser.*—(c), **argumentum a minori,** see *argumentum a maiori.*—(d), **argumentum extraneum,** *exterior proof* or *proof taken from something exterior.*— (e), **argumentum negativum,** *negative proof.*—(f), **argumentum probabile,** *proof of probability,* see *argumentum extraneum.*— (g), **argumentum rhetoricum,** *rhetorical proof.*—(h), **argumentum solubile,** *soluble* or *refutable proof.*—(i), **argumentum sophisticum,** *the sophistic* or *deceitful proof.* Under this heading belongs: **argumentum expressum,** *the explicit* or *distinct sign.*

arguo, ere, ui, utum, 3, *v. a.,* (1) *to make clear, show, prove, argue, declare, assert,* (2) *to accuse, denounce, censure, blame* with *de* and the *abl.*

Ariani, orum, *m., Arians, followers of Arius,* the heresiarch. Arius was born in Africa (the exact locality is disputed) in A.D. 256. In his early days he was a pupil of Lucian of Antioch, a celebrated Christian teacher, and a martyr of the faith. By some, Arius is said to have derived his heresy from Lucian. The heresy is concerned with the exact nature of the relation between the Father and the Son.

Arianus, a, um, *adj., pertaining* or *belonging to the Arian heresy.*

ariditas, atis, *f., dryness, drought.*

aridus, a, um, *adj., dry, withered, arid, parched.*

aries, ietis, *m.*, *a male sheep, a ram.*

Arimathaea, ae, *f.*, *Arimathaea,* a city in Judea, from which came Joseph, a noble counsellor who went to Pilate and begged the body of Jesus.

aristocratia, ae, *f.*, *government by the best, rule by the best, aristocracy.*

aristocraticus, a, um, *adj.*, *aristocratic.* Cf. *aristocratia.*

Aristophanes, is, *m.*, the most distinguished comic poet of Greece, from Lindus, on the island of Rhodes, a contemporary of Socrates.

Aristoteles, is, *m.*, *Aristotle,* a very learned and distinguished pupil of Plato, from Stagira, in Macedonia, teacher of Alexander the Great, and founder of the Peripatetic philosophy, often referred to by St. Thomas as *the* philosopher.

arithmeticus, a, um, *adj.*, *concerning number, belonging to it, arithmetic.* On aequalitas arithmetica, see *aequalitas* under 1; on medium arithmeticum, see *medium* under 1; on proportio arithmetica, see *proportio* under 1; on proportionalitas arithmetica, see *proportionalitas.*—arithmeticus, i, *m.*, *arithmetician.*—arithmetica, ae, *f.*, = *arithmetice* (*sc. techne*), *arithmetic, science of numbers.*

Arius, i, *m.*, an heresiarch, born about A.D. 250, died 336. He is said to have been a Libyan by descent. Arius learned his religious views from Lucian, the presbyter of Antioch and afterwards the martyr. He took sides with Meletius, an Egyptian schismatic, against Peter, Bishop of Alexandria, but a reconciliation followed, and Peter ordained Arius deacon. Because of new disputes, the Bishop excommunicated this restless churchman. However, he gained the friendship of Achillas, Peter's successor; was made presbyter by him in 313, and received the charge of a well-known district in Alexandria, called Baucalis. This entitled Arius to expound the Scriptures officially, and he exercised much influence when, in 318, his quarrel with Bishop Alexander broke out over the fundamental truth of our Lord's divine Sonship and substance.

arma, orum, *n.*, *implements of war, arms, both of offense and defense.*

armatura, ae, *f.*, *armour.*

Armentarius, ii, *m.*, *Armentarius.* St. Augustine (Classis III, Ep. 127), addresses a letter to a certain Armentarius and to his wife Paulina, who have taken the vow of chastity. In this letter he extols their action and urges them to remain faithful to this vow. St. Thomas refers to this letter several times.

armentarius, a, um, *adj.*, *pertaining to a herd of cattle.*

armentum, i, *n., cattle for plough-ing, a herd.*

armiger, gera, gerum, *adj., bearing weapons, armed, warlike.*

armo, are, avi, atum, 1, *v. a., to fur-nish with weapons, arm, equip.*

armus, i, *m., the shoulder where it is fitted to the shoulder blade, the forequarter,* usually *the shoulder of an animal,* while *umerus is that of men.*

aro, are, avi, atum, 1, *v. a., to plough, till.*

aroma, atis, *n., a spice.*

aromaticus, a, um, *adj., composed of spice, aromatic, fragrant.*

arreptitius, a, um, *adj., raving, pos-sessed of an evil spirit.*

arrha, ae, *f., money given to ratify a contract, a pledge, an earnest. Arrha* is a part of the purchase money, while *pignus* is a pledge to be restored when the con-tract for the security of which it is given has been performed.

arrideo, ere, risi, risum, 2, *v. n., to laugh at, smile at.*

arripio, ere, ripui, reptum, 3, *v. a., to seize, snatch, lay hold of, take possession of, seize upon with eagerness* or *haste.*

arroganter, *adv., arrogantly, haugh-tily, proudly, insolently.*

arrogantia, ae, *f., arrogance, con-ceitedness, pride, haughtiness.*

arrogatio, onis, *f., a taking to one's self, adoption.*

arrogo, are, avi, atum, 1, *v. a., to appropriate, claim as one's own, assume.*

ars, artis, *f.,* (1) *art* or *knowledge* in the broader sense, synonym of *scientia,* (2) *art* or *knowledge* in the narrower sense, i.e., skill, dexterity, and adroitness in pro-ducing a work, (3), *art, artificial-ity.*—Kinds of *ars* in this (1) sense are: **ars factiva seu operativa, ars practica** and **ars speculativa seu theorica,** *creative* or *effec-tive art, practical* and *specula-tive* or *theoretical art.* On the difference between *ars, intellec-tus, prudentia,* and *scientia,* see *scientia.* On the difference be-tween *ars* and *natura,* see *na-tura.* **materia artis,** *the matter of art,* i.e., *that to which art directs itself.*—**Operatio artis,** *the action of art.* Cf. **operatio artis** under *operatio.* On **constituere per artem,** see *constituere* under 2; on **continuum per artem,** see *continuum* under 2; on **fieri ab arte,** see *fieri;* on **forma artis,** see *forma* under 2; on **generare per artem,** see *generare;* on **generatio secundum artem,** see *generatio* under 1; on **opus artis,** see *opus* under 4; on **peccatum artis,** see *peccatum* under 1.— Kinds of *ars* in the sense of art properly so called are: (a), **ars aedificativa seu aedificatoria,** *architecture.*—(b), **ars aequi** and **ars boni,** *art of the worthy* and *the right* and *art of the good,* i.e., the art that is prepared to bring forth what is worthy and right, to produce what is mor-ally good,—(c), **ars architectonica**

seu imperans seu principalis seu superior and ars famulans seu subministrativa seu subserviens seu exsequens seu subalternata seu inferior, *the commanding* or *principal* or *superordinate* and *the serving* or *effecting* or *subordinate art.* Cf. also *artifex.*—(d), ars boni, see *ars aequi.*—(e), ars campsoria, seu nummularia seu obolostatica, *the art of the money-changer.*—(f), ars carpentaria, *the art of a carpenter.*—(g), ars civilis seu politica, *statesmanship* or *the art of the statesman.*—(h), ars coniecturalis, *the art of attaining exactness in practical things.* Cf. also *eustochia.*—(i), ars coquorum seu pulmentaria, *the art of cooking.* —(j), ars demonstrationis seu ars demonstrativa, *the art of argumentation.*—(k), ars demonstrativa, see *ars demonstrationis.*— (l), ars equestris, *the art of horseback riding.*—(m), ars divina, *divine art* or *God's art.*—(n), ars exercitiva, *the art of gymnastics.* —(o), ars exsequens, see *ars architectonica.*—(p), ars fabrilis, *the art* or *skill of the blacksmith.* —(q), ars faciendi vestes, *the art* or *skill of the tailor.*—(r), ars factiva and ars usualis, *the art that makes* or *builds something* and *uses* or *applies it,* i.e., the art of preparing the necessary material for a work and the art of applying the material to the work.—(s), ars famulans, see *ars architectonica.*—(t), ars figuli, *the art of*

pottery.—(u), ars figurandi seu figurativa, *the instructive art.*— (v), ars furnaria, *the art of baking.*—(w), ars gubernativa seu gubernatoria and ars navifactiva, *the art of the pilot* and *shipbuilder.*—(x), ars humana, *the art of man.*—(y), ars imperans, see *ars architectonica.*—(z), ars inferior, see *ars architectonica.*—(a²), ars legispositiva, *art of legislation.*— (b²), ars liberalis and ars servilis seu mechanica, *the free* and *the unfree* or *mechanical art.*—(c²), ars logica, *logic.*—(d²), ars magica, *the art of magic.*—(e²), ars mechanica, see *ars liberalis.*—(f²), ars medicinalis or medicinae and and ars pigmentaria, *the art of medicine* or *healing* and *of salve mixing* or *pharmacy.*—(g²), ars militaris, *the art* or *skill of war.* —(h²), ars navifactiva, see *ars gubernativa.*—(i²), ars necromantica, *the black art* or *the art of the evocation* or *conjuration of the dead.*—(j²), ars negotiativa, *skill in trade.*—(k²), ars notoria, *the publishing art,* i.e., the art of learning and making things known that are unknown.—(l²), ars noxiae superstitionis and ars nugatoriae superstitionis, *the art of harmful* and *foolish superstition.*—(m²), ars nugatoriae superstitionis, see *ars noxiae superstitionis.*—(n²), ars numismatica, *the art of numismatics.*—(o²), ars nummularia, see *ars campsoria.* —(p²), ars obolostatica, see *ars campsoria.*—(q²), ars oeconomica, *the art of housekeeping* or *home-management.*—(r^2), **ars pecunaria,** *the art of money,* i.e., the art which has as its object everything that pertains to money.— (s^2), **ars pecuniativa,** *the art of making money.*—(t^2), **ars pecuniativa mercativa, mercenaria et oneraria,** *the art of making money by selling goods, by hiring,* and *by transportation of freight.* —(u^2), **ars pigmentaria,** see *ars medicinalis.*—(v^2), **ars politica,** see *ars civilis.*—(w^2), **ars pulmentaria,** see *ars coquorum.*—(x^2), **ars rhetorica,** *the art of the rhetor* or *the orator.*—(y^2), **ars servilis,** see *ars liberalis.*—(z^2), **ars subalternata,** see *ars principalis.*—(a^3), **ars subministrativa,** see *ars principalis.*—(b^3), **ars subserviens,** see *ars principalis.*—(c^3), **ars superior,** see *ars principalis.*—(d^3), **ars textoria,** *the art of weaving.*—(e^3), **ars translativa,** *the transferring* or *transferred art of making money.* —(f^3), **ars usualis,** see *ars factiva.*—**Ars est ministra naturae,** *art is the servant of nature,* in so far as supplet defectum naturae in illis, in quibus natura deficit. **Ars imitatur naturam,** also **ars imitatur naturam inquantum potest,** a translation of the Aristotelian phrase: *he techne mimeitur ten physin,* art imitates nature, in so far as it can but only *in his, quae possint fieri* et arte et natura; ... si quis enim ex frigida causa infirmatur, natura

eum calefaciendo sanat, unde et medicus, si eum curare debeat, calefaciendo sanat. **Ars non est in artificatio, quod fit per artem,** the translation of the Aristotelian passage: *he men oun techne arche en allo, art is not in the artistic work which is made by art but in something different from it, namely, in the artist.* Cf. *natura.* **Ars se habet semper ad bonum,** *art always aims at something good and perfect.*

Arsenius, ii, *m., Arsenius,* saint and anchorite, was born at Rome in 354 and died at Troe in Egypt in 450. Theodosius the Great asked the Emperor Gratian and Pope Damasus to send him a tutor from the West for his son Arcadius. They selected Arsenius who was well-read in Greek literature and a member of a noble Roman family. He was said to have been a deacon of the Church.

arteria, ae, *f., the wind pipe, artery.*

arthron, ou, *n., joint.*

articulatio, onis, *f., articulation, dissection, difference.*

articulus, i, *m.,* (1) *joint, member, part,* (2) *point of time, moment,* (3), *position, situation.*—**Articulus fidei,** *article of faith.*—**articulus mortis,** *the moment of death.*—**articulus necessitatis,** *the moment of necessity.*

artifex, ficis, *m., artist, craftsman,* one who acts according to the intellectual habit of *ars,* art, which for St. Thomas may be either an art or a craft in our sense.—Kinds of *artifex* are: (a), **artifex inferior** and **artifex superior,** *inferior* or *lower craftsman* and *superior* or *higher craftsman.*—(b), **artifex princeps seu imperans seu dirigens** and **artifex usualis seu exsequens,** *the principal* or *directing* or *leading artist* and *the assistant* or *producing artist* or *craftsman.* Cf. **ars architectonica,** under *ars* under 2.

artificialis, e, *adj., artistic, artificial.* On **actio artificialis,** see *actio* under 1; on **agens artificialis,** see *agens;* on **corpus artificialis,** see *corpus;* on **corruptio artificialis,** see *corruptio* under 2; on **forma artificialis,** see *forma* under 2; on **generatio artificialis,** see *generatio* under 1; on **modus artificialis,** see *modus* under 2; on **operatio artificialis,** see *operatio* under 2; on **opus artificiale,** see *opus* under 4; on **peccatum artificiale,** see *peccatum* under 1; on **res artificialis,** see *res.*—**artificialiter,** *adv., in an artistic, scientific manner,* a synonym of *artificiose.*

artificialiter, *adv.,* see *artificialis.*

artificiatus, a, um, *adj., wrought by art.*

artificiose, *adv.,* see *artificiosus.*

artificiosus, a, um, *adj., accomplished in art, skilful, artistic.*—

artificiose, *adv., in an artistic, scientific manner, artistically,* a synonym of *artificialiter.*

artificium, ii, *n., a profession, trade, employment, handicraft, art, workmanship, work.*

Artotyritae, arum, *m., (artos,* bread; *tyros,* cheese), *the Artotyritae.* One of a Montanist sect which according to its opponents used bread and cheese in the celebration of the Lord's Supper, because the first men offered the fruits of the earth and their flock.

aruspicium, ii, *n., inspection of victims, auspicy.*

arx, arcis, *f., heights, summit, pinnacle,* used in S.T. only in a figurative sense.

Asa, *indecl., m., Asa,* king of Juda, born in 975 B.C., son and successor of Abias, king of Juda. He died in 933 B.C., after reigning for forty-one years and was succeeded by his son, Josephat.

ascendo, ere, scendi, scensum, 3, *v. n., ascend, mount up,* used both lit. and fig., constr. with *in* and *acc., inter* and *acc., ad* and *acc., super* and *acc.,* and *absol.,* the opposite of *descendo.*

ascensio, onis, *f.,* (1) *an ascending, ascent,* the opposite of *descensio,* (2) *the Ascension* of Christ, *ascension into heaven.*

ascensor, oris, *m., one that ascends,* a rider in a vehicle or on a horse.

ascensus, us, *m., an ascending, ascent,* the opposite of *descensus.*

ascisco, ere, ivi, itum, 3, *v. a.*, see *adscisco.*

ascribi, ere, psi, ptum, 3, *v. a.*, see *adscribo.*

asina, ae, *f.*, *a she-ass.*

asinus, i, *m.*, *an ass.*

aspectus, us, *m.*, *sight, glance.* **primo aspectu,** with or without prep. *in, at first sight, at first glance.*

asper, era, erum, *adj.*, (1) *rough, uneven, harsh, severe,* (2) of taste, *rough, harsh, sour, bitter.* —**aspere,** *adv.*, *roughly, harshly.*

aspere, *adv.*, see *asper.*

aspergo, ere, ersi, ersum, 3, *v. a.*, *to sprinkle, spatter over.*

asperitas, atis, *f.*, *severity, difficulty, adversity.*

aspernor, ari, atus, 1, *v. dep. a.*, *to disdain, spurn, reject.*

aspersio, onis, *f.*, *a sprinkling upon, a sprinkling.*

aspersorium, ii, *n.*, *aspersory,* an instrument with which to sprinkle.

aspicio, ere, spexi, spectum, 3, *v. a.*, *to behold, look at, see,* used *absol.* and with *ad* and *acc.*

assecutio, onis, *f.*, *a carrying out, attainment.*

assensio, onis, *f.*, *consent, assent,* a synonym of *assensus.*

assensus, us, *m.*, *consent, assent,* especially on the part of the mind, a synonym of *assensio,* the opposite of *dissensus.* On the difference between *assensus* and *consensus,* see *assentire.*— **assensus inquisitus,** *consent arising from investigation.*

assentatio, onis, *f.*, *a flattering assent, flattery, adulation,* a synonym of *adulatio.*

assentio, ire, si, sum, 4, *to consent, assent,* in the first place an act of the mind but also an act of the will, the opposite of *dissentire.*

assequor, i, secutus, 3, *v. dep.*, *to gain, obtain, procure.*

assero, ere, serui, sertum, 3, *v. a.*, *to maintain, assert, affirm, declare,* the opposite of *nego.*

assertio, onis, *f.*, *an assertion, declaration.*

assertive, *adv.*, *in the manner* or *sense of a concluding assertion, taking leave of something that has been settled, assertively,* of the same meaning as *determinando,* the opposite of *inquisitive, inquirendo,* and *dubitando.*

assertorius, a, um, *adj.*, *declaratory, of the nature of assertion, assertory,* in the S.T. always used with *iuramentum,* the opposite of *promissorius.*

assessio, onis, *f.*, *a sitting by* or *near the judge, an assisting of the judge, the acting as assistant judge, assesion.*

assessor, oris, *m.*, *the assistant of a judge, an assessor.*

assessorie, *adv.*, *in the manner of an assistant, especially of an assistant judge, assessorially,* see *assessor.*

assidue, *adv.*, see *assiduus.*

assiduitas, atis, *f.*, *a frequent occurrence, repetition,, assiduity, unremitting application,* with or without the *gen.* of the thing, a synonym of *frequentia.*

assiduus, a, um, *adj., continual, constant, without intermission, assiduous.*—**assidue,** *adv., continually, constantly, without intermission, assiduously.*

assignatio, onis, *f., assignment, allotment, assignation.*

assigno, are, avi, atum, 1, *v. a., to assign, allot, ascribe, indicate, point out.*

assimilatio, onis, *f., assimilation.* On **via assimilationis,** see *via* under 3.—Kinds of *assimilatio* are: **assimilatio per informationem** and **assimilatio secundum convenientiam,** *assimilation through reception of a likeness* and *assimilation according to agreement in nature* and *essence.*

assimilativus, a, um, *adj., tending to* or *characterized by* or *causing assimilation, assimilative.*

assimilo, are, avi, atum, 1, *v. a.* and *n.,* (1) *to consider as similar, compare,* (2) *assimilate,* to become like, but not identical with.

assisto, ere, astiti, *no sup.,* 3, *v. n., to stand by one, defend, assist, aid,* used with *dat.,* a synonym of *ministro.*

asso, are, 1, *v. a., to roast, broil.*

associatio, onis, *f., union with, association.*

associo, are, avi, atum, 1, *v. a., to unite with* a person or thing, *associate with.*

assuefacio, ere, feci, factum, 3, *v. a., to use* or *accustom* to something, *habituate, inure,* constr. with *ad* and *acc.,* with *dat., absol.*

assuefactio, onis, *f., becoming accustomed* or *inured* to a thing.

Assuerus, i, *m., Assuerus,* who married the queen Esther. He probably is to be identified with Darius, the son of Hystaspis, who began to rule eight years after the death of Cyrus.

assuesco, ere, evi, etum, 3, *v. a., to become habituated* or *inured to.*

assuetudo, inis, *f., a being accustomed* to a thing, *custom, habit.*

assumo, ere, mpsi, mptum, 3, *v. a.,* (1) *to take to one's self, accept, take for one's self, receive,* (2) *take from, draw from,* (3) *take, seize,* (4) *add to, accept* as a basis for a conclusion, the Aristotelian *lambanein.* On **communicabilitas assumentis** see *communicabilitas;* on **corpus assumere,** see *corpus;* on **instrumentum assumere,** see *instrumentum.*

assumptibilis, e, *adj., acceptable, admissible, assumable.* On **communicabilitas assumptibilis,** see *communicabilitas;* on **communitas assumptibilis,** see *communitas* under 1.

assumptio, onis, *f.,* (1) *assumption, admission, adoption,* (2) *taking on, drawing in,* (3) *seizure, grasping, adoption,* (4) *basis for a conclusion,* (5) *the sacrament* *of the altar.*—On the difference between *assumptio* and *unio*, see *unio.*—Kinds of *assumptio* in this (1) sense are: (a), **assumptio in natura** and **assumptio in persona,** *assumption respecting a nature* and *assumption respecting a person.*—(b), **assumptio in persona,** see *assumptio in natura.*—(c), **assumptio legitima,** *the legitimate adoption of a child.*

assurgo, ere, surrexi, surrectum, 3, *v. n., to rise, come to mind.*

assus, a, um, *adj., roasted.*

Assyrii, orum, *m., the Assyrians.*

astrologia, ae, *f., knowledge of the stars, astronomy.*

astrologus, i, *m.,* (1) *an astronomer,* a synonym of *astronomus,* (2) *astrologer.*

astronomia, ae, *f., knowledge of the stars, astronomy.*

astronomicus, a, um, *adj., astronomical.*

astrum, i, *n., a star, constellation.*

astruo, ere, see *adstruo.*

astute, *adv.,* see *astutus.*

astutia, ae, *f.,* (1) figuratively, *the quality of dexterity, adroitness, understanding, prudence,* in a good sense, (2) properly, *cunning, slyness, subtlety, craft,* in the use of means to an end, in a bad sense.

astutus, a, um, *adj., shrewd, sly, cunning.*—**astutus,** i, *m., a knowing, shrewd person.*—**astute,** *adv., cunningly.*

asunetoi, on, *m.,* (Grk., *asunetoi*),

persons who are insensate or marked by a lack of reason.

at, *conj., but, on the contrary, in oppostion to this.* Passim.

atavus, i, *m., the father of a great- great- grandfather, or great- great- grandmother, an ancestor, forefather.*

Athanasius, ii, *m., Athanasius,* a celebrated archbishop of Alexandria in the time of the Emperor Constantine; a zealous persecutor of the Arians, who was persecuted by them in return; he died A.D. 377.

Athenae, arum, *f., Athens,* the capital of Attica.

Athenienses, ium, *m., the inhabitants of Athens, Athenians.*

athleta, ae, *comm., a wrestler, athlete.*

atomus, a, um, *adj., indivisible.*

atomus, i, *f., something indivisible, atom.*—**in atomo,** i.e., **in individuo,** *in an individual.*

atque, *conj., and also, and besides, and even, and.*

atramentum, i, *n., ink.*

atrium, ii, *n.,* (1) *an entrance hall in front of the Jewish tabernacle, atrium,* (2) *the Holy of Holies of the tabernacle,* (3) *a consecrated place to which fugitives from justice might flee as a refuge.*

atrocitas, atis, *f., the quality of atrox, cruelty.*

atrox, ocis, *adj., cruel, fierce, atrocious.*

attaedians, antis, *adj., wearisome, irksome.*

attamen, *adv.*, see *tamen.*

attendo, ere, tendi, tentum, 3, *v. a.*, (1) *to attend to something, mind,* (2) *to take into account, to fix one's eye upon, mean,* (3) *observe, perceive.*

attente, *adv., attentively, carefully.*

attentio, onis; *f., attention.*—Kinds of *attentio* are: (a), **attentio actualis** and **attentio secundum virtutem,** *actual attention* or *attention taking place in reality* and *virtual attention* or *attention continuing because of the power of a previous attention.*—(b), **attentio ad finem orationis, attentio ad petitionem ipsam seu ad sensum verborum** and **attentio ad verba,** *attention on the aim of prayer, on the petition in prayer,* or *on the thought contained in it* and *on the words of the prayer.* —(c), **attentio ad petitionem ipsam,** see *attentio ad finem orationis.*—(d), **attentio ad sensum verborum,** see *attentio ad finem orationis.*—(e), **attentio ad verba,** see *attentio ad finem orationis.*— (f), **attentio secundum virtutem,** see *attentio actualis.*

attento, are, avi, atum, 1, *v. a.*, (1) *to do, try, make trial of, attempt,* (2) *to attempt to lead someone from right, tempt, entice to evil.*

attenuo, are, avi, atum, 1, *v. a., to diminish, lessen, to render weak, thin.*

attero, ere, trivi, tritum, 3, *v. a.*, (1) *to weaken, exhaust, wear out, waste,* (2) *masticate, chew,* (3) *pass away* or *out of exis-*

tence.—**attrita,** orum, *n., objects ground* or *rubbed by friction.*

attestatio, onis, *f., an attesting, attestation, testimony.*

attestor, ari, atus, 1, *v. dep., to bear witness to, attest, prove, confirm, corroborate.*

attinentia, ae, *f., relationship, kinship.* On **genus attinentiae,** see *genus* under 2; on **gradus attinentiae,** see *gradus* under 1; on **processus attinentiae,** see *processus* under 1; on **propinquitas attinentiae,** see *propinquitas* under 2; on **species attinentiae,** see *species* under 8.

attineo, ere, tinui, tentum, 2, *v. a.* and *n., to pertain to, be related to,* constr. with the *dat.* or *ad* and *acc.*

attingo, ere, tigi, tactum, 3, *v. a., to attain to, pertain to, come in contact with, reach,* constr. with *acc.*, with *ad* and *acc.*, and *absol.*

attolo, ere, no perf. or sup., 3, *v. a., to lift* or *raise up, raise, elevate.*

attondeo, ere, tondi, tonsum, 2, *v. a., to shave, shear, clip, crop.*

attractivus, a, um, *adj., attractive, pleasing.*

attraho, ere, traxi, tractum, 3, *v. a., to draw, lead, bring, move, attract.*

attribuo, ere, ui, utum, 3, *v. a., to attribute* or *impute to one, charge with, ascribe to.*

attributio, onis, *f., attribution, assignment of a quality* as something peculiar.

attributum, i, *n., attribute,* i.e., that quality which benefits a thing in a peculiar and original manner, so that, if other things share in it, it befits that thing above all and for the most part. On **communitas attributi**, see *communitas* under 1.— Kinds of *attributum* are: (a), **attributum absolutum**, *the irrelative attribute.*—(b), **attributum divinum**, *the divine attribute.*—(c), **attributum essentiale seu naturale** and **attributum personale**, *the essential* or *natural* and *the personal attribute.*—(d), **attributum naturale**, see *attributum essentiale.*—(e), **attributum participatum**, *the imparted* or *shared attribute.*—(f), **attributum personale**, see *attributum essentiale.*—(g), **attributum potentiae**, *the attribute of power.*

attritio, onis, *f.*, (1) *rubbing, imperfect grinding, breaking*, (2) *incomplete compunction of heart, imperfect sorrow for sins.* On the difference between *attritio* and *contritio*, see *contritio* under 2.

auctor, oris, *comm.*, (1) *author, originator*, (2) *teacher.*

auctoritas, atis, *f.*, (1) *source, authorship*, (2) *the statement of an important person, a passage from a distinguished book*, (3) *authority, weight*, (4) *might, power.*—On **clavis auctoritatis**, see *clavis* under 2; on **potestas auctoritatis**, see *potestas* under 3. **per auctoritatem**, *in the manner of authorship* or *of the principal cause, authoritatively, a* synonym of *auctoritative, per modum auctoritatis* or *principalis agentis*, the opposite of *instrumentaliter* or *per modum instrumenti* or *ministraliter.*—Kinds of *auctoritas* in this (3) sense are: (a), **auctoritas adquisita** and **auctoritas naturalis**, *the acquired power* and *the power of nature* or *natural power.*—(b), **auctoritas aeterna**, *the eternal power.*—See *auctoritas adquisita.*—(c), **auctoritas alterius** and **auctoritas propria**, *the power of another* and *one's own power.*—(d), **auctoritas commissa** and **auctoritas ordinaria**, *power committed to someone* and *ordinary power* or *power befitting one according to the usual order.*—(e), **auctoritas divina** and **auctoritas humana**, *divine power* and *human power.*—(f), **auctoritas dominii** and **auctoritas secundaria**, *the power of authority* or *of a lord* and *secundary* or *subordinate power.*—(g), **auctoritas humana**, see *auctoritas divina.*—(h), **auctoritas immediata**, *immediate power.*—(i), **auctoritas naturalis**, see *auctoritas adquisita.*—(j), **auctoritas ordinaria**, see *auctoritas commissa.* —(k), **auctoritas plena**, *full power.*—(l), **auctoritas primaeva**, *primitive* or *original power.* —(m), **auctoritas propria**, see *auctoritas alterius.*—(n), **auctoritas publica**, *public power* or *power of the state.*—(o), **auctoritas secundaria**, see *auctoritas dominii.*

auctoritative, *adv., after the manner* or *in the sense of the author, authoritatively,* a synonym of *per auctoritatem* or *per modum auctoritatis,* the opposite of *ministerialiter* and *instrumentaliter.*

audacia, ae, *f.,* (1) in a good sense, *daring, intrepidity, courage, valor,* (2) in a bad sense, *audacity, presumption, temerity, insolence, impudence.*

audacter, *adv.,* see *audax.*

audax, acis, *adj., daring,* in a good sense, but oftener in a bad sense, *bold, courageous, spirited; audacious, rash, presumptuous, foolhardy.*—**audacter,** *adv., boldly, courageously, audaciously.*—*sup. audacissime.*

audeo, ere, ausum, 2, *v. a.* and *n., to venture, dare, be bold, be courageous.*

audibilis, e, *adj., possible of being heard, audible.*

audio, ire, ivi, itum, 4, *v. a.,* (1) *to hear, perceive* or *understand by hearing, learn,* (2) *hear, listen to, obey, heed.*—**confessionem audire,** *to hear confession,* i.e., on the part of a duly authorized person.—**audire missam,** *to hear mass,* i.e., take part in the holy sacrifice of the mass.—**audiens,** entis, *m.,* or *f., he who listens, a listener.*

auditio, onis, *f., a hearing, a listening to.*

auditor, oris, *m.,* (1) *a hearer, auditor,* (2) *one that hears a teacher, a pupil, a disciple.*

auditus, us, *m.,* (1) *the hearing, sense of hearing,* (2) *the act of hearing, hearing,* (3) *something heard.*

aufero, auferre, abstuli, ablatum, 3, *v. a., to take* or *bear off, carry off, withdraw, remove.*

augeo, ere, auxi, auctum, 2, *v. a.* and *n., to increase, augment, enlarge, strengthen,* the opposite of *minuo.*

augmentatio, onis, *f., increase, growth, augmentation,* a synonym of *augmentum.*

augmentativus, a, um, *adj., that causes growth, concerned with growth, augmentative.* On **potentia augmentativa,** see *potentia* under 2; on **virtus augmentativa,** see *virtus* under 1; on **vis augmentativa,** see *vis* under 1.

augmento, are, 1, *v.* and *a., to increase, enlarge,* the opposite of *diminuo* and *minuo.*

augmentum, i, *n., an increase, growth, augmentation,* the opposite of *decrementum* and *diminutio.*

augur, uris, *comm., an augur, diviner, soothsayer.*

augurium, ii, *n., the observation* and *interpretation of omens, augury, any kind of divination, prophecy, soothsaying, interpretation.*

auguror, ari, atus, 1, *v. dep., to perform the services* or *fill the office of an augur, take auguries, prophesy.*

Augustinus, i, *m., Aurelius Augustinus,* Saint and Bishop of Hippo Regius in North Africa, born at Thagaste in Numidia Proconsularis on November 13, 354 and died in Hippo Regius on August 28, 430 during the seige of that city by Gaiseric. St. Thomas shows a very wide and thorough knowledge of the works of St. Augustine, quoting from nearly all his works, the finished and polished works such as the Confessions, City of God, and On the Trinity, the unrevised sermons and letters, and nearly all the minor works.

Augustus, a, um, *adj., of* or *relating to Augustus* or *the emporer,* but especially (*Mensis*) *Augustus, the month of August.*

Augustus, i, *m., Augustus.*—(1), *Augustus Caesar,* the first Roman emperor, was born on the 23rd of September, 63 B.C. He was the son of C. Octavius by Atia, a daughter of Julia, the sister of C. Julius Caesar. He died at Nola on the 29th of August, 14 A.D.—(2), *Constantinus Augustus, Flavius Valerius Aurelius Constantinus,* surnamed Magnus or the Great was born on February 27th, probably in 274, at Naissus (Nissa), in Dardania or Upper Moesia. His mother was the Christian Helena. He died on Whitsunday 337, in the 31st year of his reign, dating it from July 25, 306.—(3), *Theodosius Augustus, Theodosius the Great,* Roman Emperor of the East, A.D. 378-395, was the son of the general Theodosius. He was born in Spain about 346 and died at Milan on the 17th of January, 395 A.D.—(4), *Leo Augustus,* surnamed the Great, was born c. 400, in the country of the Bessi in Thrace. He was proclaimed emperor February 7, 457, and was crowned by Anatolius, patriarch of Constantinople, being the first Christian sovereign to receive his crown from the hands of a priest. He died in 461.—(5), *Martianus (Marcianus) Augustus,* Emperor of the East (A.D. 450-457) was the son of a poor but respectable man who had served in the imperial armies. He was born either in Thrace or in Illyrium about 391 A.D., and succeeded Theodosius the Younger who died in 450. The latter's widow, the celebrated Pulcheria, offered her hand and the imperial title to Marcian, on condition that he would not prevent her continuing the state of virginity which she had hitherto enjoyed. He gladly agreed. He died on June 26th, 457.

aula, ae, *f., a palace, royal court.*

Aulus, i, *m., Aulus, the praenomen of Aulus Gellius, a grammarian of the first half of the second century of the Christian era, author of the Noctes Atticae.*

aura, ae, *f., sound, voice, echo.*

aurea, ae, *f., sc. corona,* (1) *golden crown,* (2) *essential happiness of man in heaven.*

Aurelianensis, e, *adj.*, sc. *urbs, the Aurelian city,* the present city of *Orleans.* St. Thomas quotes a council at Orleans. *Concilium Aurelianense.*

Aurelius, i, *m.*, *Aurelius,* archbishop of Carthage from 388 to 423. His episcopate coincided with the last great effort made by the Donatists to uphold a losing cause, and with the first appearance of Pelagianism. St. Thomas refers to letters written by St. Augustine to Aurelius.

aureola, ae, *f.*, sc. *corona,* (1) *a golden wreath* or *halo,* (2) *glory,* (3) *unessential happiness of man in heaven.*

aureus, a, um, *adj.*, *gold, golden.*

aurichalcum, i, *n.*, *yellow copper ore, brass.*

auricula, ae, *f.*, *the external ear, ear-lap.*

auriga, ae, *comm.*, *a charioteer, driver.*

auris, is, *f.*, *the ear,* as the organ of hearing, while *auricula* is the external ear.

aurora, ae, *f.*, *the dawn, daybreak, morning.*

aurum, i, *n.*, (1) *gold, gold-plate, things made of gold,* (2) *money, wealth.*

ausculto, are, avi, atum, 1, *v. freq.*, *to listen, give heed, learn by hearing.*

ausivus, a, um, *adj.*, *that causes boldness, makes men bold.*

auspicium, ii, *n.*, *divination by observing the flight of birds, augury from birds, auspices.*

austeritas, atis, *f.*, *severity, austerity, rigor.*

austerus, a, um, *adj.*, (1) *of taste, harsh, sour, tart,* (2) *severe, rigid, strict, austere.*

australis, e, *adj.*, *southern.*

aut, *conj.*, used singly, *or;* repeated, *either . . . or; aut . . . vel, either . . . or.*

autem, *conj.*, *on the other hand, but yet, however, nevertheless,* never found at the beginning of a clause, but after one or more words.

authenticus, a, um, *adj.*, *that comes from the author, authentic, original, genuine.*

autumnus, i, *m.*, *the season of abundance, autumn.*

auxiliatio, onis, *f.*, *a helping, aiding.*

auxilior, ari, atus, 1, *v. dep.*, *to help, aid, assist, succor,* constr. with *dat.*

auxilium, ii, *n.*, *help, aid, assistance, support, succor.*—Kinds of *auxilium* are: (a), **daemonis auxilium,** *a demon's help.*—(b), **auxilium Dei** or **auxilium divinum,** *God's help* or *divine help.*—(c), **auxilium divinum,** see *auxilium Dei.*—(d), **auxilium exterius** and **auxilium interius,** *exterior help* and *interior help.*—(e), **auxilium gratiae,** *help of grace.*—(f), **humanum auxilium,** *human help.*—(g), **auxilium medicinae,** *help of medicine.*

avaritia, ae, *f.*, (1) *greediness, covetousness, avarice* in the wider sense of the word, a synonym of *cupiditas*, (2) *greediness, covetousness, avarice* in the true and narrower sense of the word, a synonym of *illiberalitas*, the opposite of *largitas, liberalitas*, and *prodigalitas*, (3) *covetousness, desire for another's wife.*— Kinds of *avaritia* in this (1) sense are: **avaritia communiter dicta sive generaliter accepta sive generalis**, and **avarita proprie sumpta sive specialis**, *avarice commonly so called* or *generally accepted*, or *general avarice* and *avarice taken in a particular sense* or *special avarice*.

avarus, a, um, *adj., covetous, greedy, avaricious*, a synonym of *illiberalis*. On **iniustus avarus**, see *iniustus*.

Avempace, *indecl. m., Ibn Badsha* or *Ibn Badja*, called by the scholastics *Aven-Pace* and *Avempace*, an Arabian philosopher, physician, astronomer, mathematician, and poet. He was born at Saragossa toward the end of the 11th century and died at Fez in 1138.

aveo, ere, 2, *v. a., to be* or *fare well*, used only in the *imper. ave, Hail.*

Averroes, *indecl., m.*, Mahommed Ibn Roschd, Arabian philosopher, astronomer, and writer on jurisprudence. He was born at Cordova in 1126. He studied law, theology, medicine, mathematics, and philosophy. He became physician to the Khalsfah Jaqub Jusuf and was charged with writing a commentary on Aristotle, which he carried out not so much with originality but with the greatest detail. The works of Averroes were one of the main sources of medieval Aristotelianism before and even after the original texts had been translated.

aversio, onis, *f., a turning away*, the opposite of *conversio.*—Kinds of *aversio* are: (a), **aversio a Deo**, *turning away from God.*— (b), **aversio a fine ultimo**, *a turning away from the last end.*—(c), **aversio a incommutabili bono**, *a turning away from the unchangeable good.*

averto, ere, ti, sum, 3, *v. a., to turn away, remove, avert*, the opposite of *converto.*

Avicebron, *indecl., m., Avicebron*, the first Jewish philosopher in Spain. He was born in Malaga in 1020 and died in 1070. He was a poet, philosopher, and moralist. His main work, *Fons Vitae*, was very influential and was much quoted by the scholastics. His doctrine of a spiritual substance individualizing also the pure spirits or separate forms was opposed by St. Thomas as early as his first treatise, *De Ente*. It found favor, however, later with the medieval Augustinians in the 13th century.

Avicenna, ae, *m., Avicenna*. He was born in 980 in the country of Bacchara. He began to write

while still very young and completed more than a hundred
works before his death. He
taught in Ssaphan, was physician to several Persian princes,
and died at Hamadan in 1037.
Logic, physic, mathematics, and
metaphysics form the parts of
his comprehensive encyclopedia
in eighteen volumes. His philosophy is Aristotelian with noticeable Neo-Platonic influences. St.
Albert the Great and St. Thomas
Aquinas professed great admiration for Avicenna whom the
Arabs used to call the "third
Aristotle."

aviditas, atis, *f., an eagerness* for
something, *avidity, longing, vehement desire.*

avidus, a, um, *adj., longing eagerly* for something, *desirous, eager, earnest, greedy.* As an adjective in the S.T. only in quotation.

avis, is, *f., a bird.*

avoco, are, avi, atum, 1, *v. a., to
call off,* or *away.*

avolo, are, avi, atum, 1, *v. n., to
fly forth* or *away.*

avus, i, *m., grandfather, grandsire.*

Aymo, (Haimo or **Aimo** or **Aymo,)**
indecl. m., Aymo, Benedictine
monk of Fulda and Bishop of
Halberstadt. He studied with
Rabanus Maurus under Alcuin.
He died in 813. St. Thomas in
the S.T. refers to his commentary on the Apocalypse.

Azarias, ae, *m., Azarias,* also called
Ozias. He was born in 829 B.
C., the son of Amasias, king of
Juda. At the death of his father
and when only sixteen years
old he began his reign. He
reigned well at first but later,
overcome by pride, he interfered with the sacerdotal duties
of the high priest in the temple
of the Lord. He was cast out of
the temple and died a leper in
776 B.C. His son Joathan succeeded him.

azymus, a, um, *adj., (azumas), unleavened,* also fig., *unleavened,*
i.e., *morally uncorrupted, pure.*
—**azyma,** orum, *n., the Jewish
feast of unleavened bread.*

B

Baal, *m., indecl., Baal,* a Syrian
deity.

Babylon, onis, *f., Babylon,* the an-
cient and renowned chief city of
Babylonia, on both sides of the
Euphrates, whose ruins are at
Hille, in Irak Arabi.

Babylonia, ae, *f., Babylonia,* the
Syrian province named after its

capital, Babylon, between the
Euphrates and the Tigris; sometimes used for all Syria, Assyria,
and Mesopotamia; now Irak
Arabi.

Babylonicus, a, um, *adj.,* same as
Babylonius, Babylonian.

bactroperita, ae, *m., furnished with*
or *carrying a staff* and *pouch;*

staff and *pouch-carrier; a nick-name for a Cynic philosopher.*

baculus, i, *m.,* (1) *a stick, staff,* as a support in walking, (2) *a sceptre of a bishop* or *abbot, crozier.*

baiulus, i, *m., he who bears burdens, porter, carrier.*

Bala, ae, *f., Bala,* daughter of Retea, maid of Rachel and third wife of Jacob.

Balaam, *m., indecl. Balaam,* son of Beor.

balbus, a, um, *adj., stammering, stuttering.*

balbutio, ire, 4, *v. n.* and *a.,* to *stammer, stutter.*

ballivus, (balivus), i, *m., a bailiff, chief magistrate.*

balneor, ari, atus, 1, *v. n.* and *a., dep.,* to *bathe.*

balneum, i, *n., a bath, a place for bathing.*

balsamum, i, *n., a fragrant gum of the balsam-tree, balsam.*

Balthasar, (Baltassar), *indecl. m., Balthasar,* son of Nabuchodonosor the Great, whom he succeeded as king of Babylon.

baltheus, (balteus), i, *m., a girdle, belt.*

banausia, ae, *f., mania* or *passion, the making of a greatly disproportionate expense,* a synonym of *apirocalia* and *consumptio,* the opposite of *magnificentia* and *parvificentia.*

banausus, a, um, *adj., passing every measure of expense, prolific,* the opposite of *magnificus* and *parvificus,* does not occur in the S.T.

bannum, i, *n., public pronouncement;* in pl. *banna, banns, publication* of an intended marriage.

baptisma, atis, *n.,* or **baptismus,** i, *m.,* (1) *baptism in general* and in the broader sense of the word, (2) *baptism in the particular* and in the narrower sense of the word.—Kinds of *baptismus* in this (1) sense are: (a), **baptismus Christi sive Spiritus sive Spiritus Sancti sive noster** and **baptismus Ioannis sive poenitentiae,** *the baptism of Christ* or *of the Holy Ghost* or *our Christian baptism* and *the baptism of St. John* or *the baptism of penance.* —(b), **baptismus Ioannis,** see *baptismus Christi.*—(c), **baptismus Iudaeorum,** *baptism of the Jews.* —(d), **baptismus Ioannis,** see *baptismus Christi.*—(e), **baptismus Pharisaeorum,** *baptism of the Pharisees.*—(f), **baptismus poenitentiae,** see *baptismus Christi.*— (g), **baptismus Spiritus** or **Spiritus Sancti,** see *baptismus Christi.*—On **character baptismi,** see *character* under 2; on **poenitentia ante baptismum,** see *poenitentia* under 1.—Kinds of *baptismus* in this (2) sense are: (a), **baptismus aquae seu fluminis,** *baptism of water.*—(b), **baptismus flaminis,** *baptism of desire.*—(c), **baptismus sanguinis,** *baptism of blood.*

baptismalis, e, *adj., pertaining to baptism, baptismal.*

Baptista, ae, *m., the baptizer,* in the S.T. it is always used with *Ioannes, John the Baptist.*

baptisterium, ii, *n.*, *a baptistery, a baptismal font.*

baptizatio, onis, *f.*, *baptizing.*

baptizo, are, avi, atum, 1, *v. a.*, *to baptize.*

barba, ae, *f.*, *the beard,* usually distinguished from mustache and whiskers but sometimes including both.

barbarus, a, um, *adj.*, *barbarous, uncivilized.*—**barbarus,** i, *m.*, *a foreigner, stranger, barbarian.*

Barnabus, ae, *m.*, *Barnabus,* a surname given by the Apostles to Joseph the Levite whose first recorded deed was the selling of his property and the giving of its proceeds to the Christian community. He was St. Paul's colaborer in preaching the gospel.

Bartholomaeus, i, *m.*, *Bartholomew,* Saint, one of the Twelve Apostles. The name means "son of Tolmai." An Apocryphal gospel of Bartholomew existed in the early ages.

Baruch, *indecl. noun, m., Baruch,* the son of Neriah, friend and amanuensis of the prophet Jeremias. An apocryphal work, the Book of Baruch, has come down to us bearing his name. It contains a promise of future glory for Israel and predicts the rebuilding of Jerusalem.

basilica, ae, *a basilica,* a church of the basilican type, or one to which the title has been given as an honor by the Pope.

Basilius, i, *m.*, *Basil the Great.* Saint and Archbishop of Caesa-

rea. He was born in Caesarea of Cappadocia in 329 or 330 and died there on January 1, 379, in the fiftieth year of his age. He has been called the Church's most effective instrument, after St. Anthanasius, in the final victory over Arianism. St. Thomas in the S.T. quotes from the letters; the homilies on the Hexaemeron, on Faith, on Psalm XXVIII. 7, on the Book of Proverbs, on St. Luke's Gospel, the Contra Eunomium, and the De Constitutione Monachorum. By far the greatest number of quotations are from the homilies on the Hexaemeron.

basis, is and eos, *f.*, *a base* or *support for a laver.*

beatificatio, onis, *f.*, *beatification, the state of being blessed.*

beatifico, are, 1, *v. a.*, *to make happy, bless, give a sight of the glories of heaven, beatify.*

beatificus, a, um, *adj.*, *beatific, blissful, imparting great happiness* or *blessedness.*

beatitudo, inis, *f.*, *blissfulness, salvation, beatitude, felicity,* a synonym of *felicitas.* This happiness can be considered under various aspects, (1) as a *state* of being happy, (2) as an *object,* the attainment of which will make one happy, (3) as the *action or operation* by which the objective happiness is attained, and (4) antonomastically, as an *extremely good and virtuous operation* proceeding from the impulse of the Holy Ghost in the Gifts. Cf. PS. Q. 69.— On **meritum beatitudinis,** see *meritum* under 1; on **scientia beatitudinis,** see *scientia* under 2; on **status beatitudinis finalis seu futurae,** see **status** under 3; on **visio beatitudinis,** see *visio* under 1.—Kinds of *beatitude* in this first (1) sense are: (a), **beatitudo activa seu activae vitae** and **beatitudo contemplativa,** *active* and *contemplative happiness* or *the happiness of the active* and *that of the contemplative life.* See also *vita* under 3.—(b), **beatitudo angeli, beatitudo hominis,** and **beatitudo Dei,** *happiness of the angel, that of man,* and *that of God.*—(c), **beatitudo animae,** *blessedness of the soul.*—(d), **beatitudo completa seu perfecta** and **beatitudo imperfecta seu inchoata,** *the complete* or *perfect happiness* and *the imperfect* or *incomplete happiness,* of which the former consists in the immediate contemplation of God, and the latter of indirect knowledge of God. Ultima autem perfectio quae est finis totius universi, est perfecta beatitudo sanctorum (this includes the act, the object, and the state), quae erit in ultima consummatione saeculi.—(e), **beatitudo contemplativa,** see *beatitudo activa.*—(f), **beatitudo Dei,** see *beatitudo angeli.*—(g), **beatitudo divina,** *divine happiness.*—(h), **be-**

atitudo futura** and **beatitudo praesentis vitae,** *the future* or *heavenly happiness* and *the present* or *earthly happiness.*—(i), **beatitudo hominis,** or **beatitudo humana,** see *beatitudo angeli.*—(j), **beatitudo imperfecta,** see *beatitudo completa.*—(k), **beatitudo inchoata,** see *beatitudo completa.*—(l), **beatitudo patriae** and **beatitudo viae seu terrena,** *the happiness of the heavenly fatherland* and *that on the way there,* or *the happiness of heaven* and *that on earth.*—(m), **beatitudo perfecta,** see *beatitudo completa.*—(n), **beatitudo praesentis vitae,** see *beatitudo futura.*—(o), **beatitudo propinqua,** and **beatitudo remota,** *the near* or *immediate happiness* and *the distant happiness.*—(p), **beatitudo sanctorum,** *the happiness of the saints,* see *beatitudo animae.*—(q), **beatitudo spei,** *the happiness of hope,* that happiness which consists first in hope and is in contrast to the happiness attained in reality.—(r), **beatitudo spiritualis,** *spiritual happiness.*—(s), **beatitudo tenuis,** *trivial* or *insignificant happiness.*—(t), **beatitudo terrena,** see *beatitudo patriae.*—(u), **beatitudo viae,** see *beatitudo patriae.*—**Homo naturaliter desiderat beatitudinem,** *man according to his nature longs for happiness but only in general, not in particular, because all do not realize where their true happiness lies.*

St. Thomas treats of these objects in particular in PS. Q. 2.— (a), **beatitudo aeterna, seu perpetua,** *eternal* or *everlasting happiness.*—(b), **beatitudo apparens seu falsa seu opinata** and **beatitudo vera,** *the apparent* or *false* or *supposed happiness* and *the true* and *actual happiness,* the former of which consists in the possession and enjoyment of a created good which is not really objective happiness, the latter in the knowledge and contemplation of God who is the true object, the possession of which makes man truly happy.—(c), **beatitudo bestialis,** *the animal or bestial happiness of man.*—(d), **beatitudo falsa,** see *beatitudo apparens;* also beatitudo divina under 1.—(e), **beatitudo opinata,** see *beatitudo apparens.*—(f), **beatitudo perpetua,** see *beatitudo aeterna.*—(g), **beatitudo supernaturalis,** *the supernatural happiness,* which is opposed to the natural.—(h), **beatitudo vera,** see *beatitudo apparens.*—Various kinds of *beatitude* in this (3) sense are: (a), **beatitudo creata** and **beatitudo increata,** *the created* and *uncreated happiness* or *the happiness of the creature* and *that of its Creator.* —(b), **finalis seu ultima beatitudo,** *the final* or *highest happiness.*—(c), **beatitudo increata,** see *beatitudo creata.*—(d), **beatitudo participata** and **beatitudo**

per essentiam, *imparted* or *shared happiness* and *essential happiness;* in other words that happiness imparted by God to a creature and that happiness of God which is not communicable to him.—(e), **beatitudo per essentiam,** see *beatitudo participata.*—On the connection between **beatitudo** and **donum** and **fructus Spiritus Sancti** and **virtus,** see *fructus.*— The kinds of *beatitude* in the sense of the perfect act are the following eight: **paupertas spiritus,** see *paupertas;* **pietas; luctus,** i.e., *sorrow for past sins,* **esuries et sitis iustitiae,** i.e. *hunger* and *thirst after justice;* **misericordia; munditia cordis,** see *munditia;* **pacificatio,** i.e., *peace making;* **persecutio passiva,** i.e., *being persecuted.*

beatus, a, um, *P. a.,* (1) *blissful, happy,* (2) *blissful, happy in heaven.*—Kinds of *beatus* in this (1) sense are: (a), **beatus participative** and **beatus per essentiam suam,** *happy through participation in another's happiness or happy through one's own essence* or *through one's self.*—(b), **beatus per essentiam suam,** see *beatus participative.*—(c), **beatus secundum quid** and **beatus simpliciter,** *happy relatively* or *in a certain respect* and *simply* or *absolutely happy.*—(d), **beatus simpliciter,** see *beatus secundum quid.*—On **cognitio beata,** see *cognitio* under 2; on **con-**

templatio beata, see *contempla-*
tio; on dilectio beata, see *dilec-*
tio under 1; on fruitio beata, see
fruitio; on intellectus beatus, see
intellectus under 3; on scientia
beata, see *scientia* under 2; on
virgo beata, see *virgo;* on visio
beata see *visio* under 1; on vita
beata, see *vita* under 1.—*Superl ,*
beatissimus, a, um, *most bless-*
ed, most holy, a title of the
higher clergy.

Beda, ae, *m., Bede,* the Venerable
Bede. He was born in 676 probably at Yarrow where he died
on May 26, 735. Bede's attain-
ments were very great. Grammar, rhetoric, poetry, hagiogra-
phy, arithmetic, chronology, and
speculations on natural science
furnished material for his pen.
In addition he wrote his famous
works on history and the interpretation of Scripture. In the
S.T., St. Thomas refers frequently to Bede's commentaries
on the New Testament, especially those on St. Luke and
St. Mark. References are also
made to the *Expositio in Gene-*
sim, Expositio in Exodum, He-
xaemeron, De Tabernaculo,
Hom. Dom. Palmarum, Hom. in
festo Annuntiationis B. Mariae,
and *De Remediis Peccatorum,*
the last referred to as Bede's
Penitential.

Beelzebub, *indecl., m., Beelzebub,*
the chief of the evil spirits.

Behemot, *indecl., m., Behemot,* a
name for the devil.

Belial, *indecl., m., Belial,* a chief
of the evil spirits.

bellicus, a, um, *adj., pertaining to*
war, military.

bello, are, avi, atum, 1, *v. n., to*
wage or *carry on war, fight in*
war.

bellua, (belua), ae, *f., a beast, mon-*
ster.

bellum, i, *n., war, warfare, battle.*

bene, *adv.,* see *bonus.*

benedico, ere, xi, ctum, *v. n.* and
a., to bless, consecrate, hallow,
the opposite of *maledico.*—aqua
benedicta, *blessed water, holy*
water.—oleum benedictum, *bless-*
ed oil, holy oil.—benedictus, i,
m., an approved or *holy person.*

benedictio, onis, *f., a benediction,*
blessing, the opposite of *male-*
dictio.

Benedictus, i, *m., Benedict,* Saint
and abbot of Monte Cassino,
called "patriarch of the monks of
the West." He was born about
A.D. 480 at Nursia (Norcia),
anciently belonging to the Sa-
bines, an episcopal city in the
duchy of Spoleto in Umbria. His
death is variously computed
from 539 to A.D. 543. His character is best attested by his "Regula Monachorum," if, as is
reasonable to suppose, this work
is really his own composition.

benefacio, ere, feci, factum, 3, *v.*
n., used with *dat.* and *absol., to*
do a good action to, benefit, im-
part benefits, the opposite of
malefacio.

benefactivus, a, um, *adj., doing*

good, benefiting, beneficent, a synonym of *beneficus.*

benefactor, oris, *m., he who confers a favor, a benefactor.*

beneficientia, ae, *f., beneficence, doing good* in the wider and the narrower sense of the word. On the relationship of *beneficientia* to *benevolentia,* see *benevolentia.*

beneficiatus, i, *m., one who has been benefited, one who receives a favor, beneficiary.*

beneficium, ii, *n.,* (1) *benefit, kindness,* the opposite of *maleficium,* (2) *benefice,* an ecclesiastical position or office to which a stipend or salary is attached.— Kinds of *beneficium* in this (1) sense are: (a), **beneficium commune** and **beneficium particulare seu privatum,** *the general* and *particular* or *individual benefit.*—(b), **beneficium Dei seu beneficium divinum,** *benefit from God and divine benefit.*—(c), **beneficium divinum,** see *beneficium Dei.*—(d), **beneficium exterius,** *exterior benefit.*—(e), **beneficium generale,** *general benefit.*—(f), **beneficium gratuitum,** *the benefit bestowed out of pure favor.*—(g), **beneficium naturale,** *natural benefit.*—(h), **beneficium particulare,** see *beneficium commune.*—(i), **beneficium privatum,** see *beneficium commune.*—(j), **beneficium publicum,** *public benefit.*—(k), **beneficium speciale,** *special benefit.*— (l), **beneficium spirituale,** *spirit-*

ual benefit.—**beneficium ecclesiasticum,** *ecclesiastical benefice* or *income.*

beneficus, a, um, *adj., generous, liberal, beneficent, obliging, favorable.*

beneplacitum, i, *n., good pleasure, gracious purpose.*

benevolentia, ae, *f., good-will, benevolence.* On **amor benevolentiae,** see *amor* under 1.—**benevolentia non habet distentionem et appetitum, id est, aliquem impetum inclinationis,** *goodwill does not imply impetuosity* or *desire, that is, an eager inclination,* the translation of the Aristotelian passage: *ou gar echei (sc. he philesis) diatasin oud' orexin.* Goodwill has no sensitive desire.

benevolus, a, um, *adj., well-wishing, benevolent, kind, friendly, favorable.*

benigne, *adv.,* see *benignus.*

benignitas, atis, *f., kindness, kindheartedness, friendliness.* On the difference between *benignitas* and *bonitas,* see *bonitas.* The *benignitas* of man is one of the *fructus Spiritus Sancti;* see *fructus* under 2. **Benignitas amicabilis,** *friendly kindheartedness.*

benignor, ari, 1, *v. dep., to rejoice, take delight.*

benignus, a, um, *adj., kind, good, friendly, pleasing, favorable, benignant.*—**benigne,** *adv., in a friendly manner kindly, benevolently, benignly.*

Berengarius, ii, *m., Berengarius* of Tours. He was born at Tours about 999 and died on the island of St. Cosme, near the city, in 1088. According to some of his contemporaries, Berengarius held erroneous opinions about the spiritual power, marriage, the baptism of children, and other points of doctrine. His fundamental doctrine and error, however, concern the Holy Eucharist.

Berenice, es, *f., Berenice,* the daughter of the Jewish king Agrippa I and sister of Agrippa the Younger, accused of incest.

Bernardus, i, *m., Bernard* of Clairvaux, Saint, was born in 1090, at Fontaines, near Dijon, France, and died at Clairvaux on August 21, 1153. He founded 163 monasteries in different parts of Europe. He was the first Cistercian monk to be placed on the calendar of saints and was canonized by Alexander III on January 18, 1174. Pope Pius VIII gave him the title of Doctor of the Church. In the S.T. St. Thomas quotes chiefly from the De Consideratione. He also quotes from the De Natura Amoris, De Gratia et Libero Arbitrio, De Gradibus Humilitatis, De Praecepto et Dispensatione, De Diligendo Deo, and from the sermons De SS. Innocentibus, in Cantica, and De Coena Domini.

Bersabee, (Bethsabee), *f., indecl.,* also **Bersabea,** ea, *f., Bersabee,* the wife of Urias, born 1056

B.C. After the death of Urias, she married David. See 2 Reg. 11 and 12; also 3 Reg. 1 and 2.

bestia, ae, *f., the irrational animal, wild animal, beast,* a synonym of *brutum.* On **anima bestiae,** see *anima;* on **character bestiae,** see *character.*—Kinds of *bestia* are: (a), **bestia domestica,** *the domestic animal.*—(b), **bestia sylvestris,** *the animal of the forest, wild animal.* See *bestia domestica.*

bestialis, e, *adj., animal, beastly* in the strict and in the transferred sense of the word, a synonym of *brutalis.* On **actus bestialis,** see *actus* under 1; on **affectio bestialis,** see *affectio;* on **anima bestialis,** see *anima* under 1; on **appetitus bestialis,** see *appetitus* under 2; on **corpus bestiale,** see *corpus;* on **delectatio bestialis,** see *delectatio;* on **dispositio bestiale,** see *dispositio* under 4; on **homo bestialis,** see *homo;* on **incontinentia bestialis,** see *incontinentia;* on **malitia bestialis,** see *malitia* under 3; on **multitudo bestialis,** see *multitudo* under 4; on **operatio bestalis,** see *operatio* under 2; on **vita bestialis,** see *vita* under 3.

bestialitas, atis, *f.,* (1) *animal cruelty,* (2) *bestial desire, animal passion,* (3) *sexual intercourse with an animal.*

Bethlehem, (Bethleem), *n., indecl., Bethlehem,* a town of the tribe of Juda, the birthplace of David and of Christ, now Beit el Lahm.

biblia, ae, *f., the Bible.*

bibo, ere, bibi, (post-class. fut. bi-biturus), 3, *v. a., to drink.*

bicubitus, a, um, *adj., of two cubits.*

biduum, ii, *n., a period or space of two days, two days.*

biennium, ii, *n., a period or space of two years, two years.*

bigae, arum, *f., a two-horsed car or chariot.*

bigamia, ae, *f., bigamy,* having more than one spouse, whether simultaneously or in succession.

bigamus, i, *m., a man twice married,* see *bigamia.*

bilinguis, e, *adj., double-tongued, hypocritical, deceitful, false, treacherous.*

bimatus, us, *m., the age of two years.*

bimus, a, um, *adj., two years old, of two years.*

binarius, a, um, *adj., that contains or consists of two.*

binomius, a, um, *adj., having two names.*

bipes, pedis, *adj., two-footed.*

bis, *adj., num., twice, at two times, on two occasions.*

blandimentum, i, *n., flattering words, blandishment, flattery.*

blandior, iri, itus, 4, *v. dep., to flatter, soothe, correct, caress.*

blanditia, ae, *f., a caressing, flattering, flattery.*

blanditor, oris, *m., a flatterer.*

blandus, a, um, *adj., flattering, fawning, caressing.*

blasphemia, ae, *f., blasphemy.*—Kinds of *blasphemia* are: (a), **blasphemia cordis** or **interior**

and **blasphemia oris** or **vocalis,** *the blasphemy of thought* or *inner blasphemy* and *expressed* or *exterior blasphemy.*—(b), **blasphemia interior,** see *blasphemia cordis.*—(c), **blasphemia oris,** see *blasphemia cordis.*—(d), **blasphemia perfecta,** *the perfect* or *complete blasphemy.*—(e), **blasphemia vocalis,** see *blasphemia cordis.*

blasphemo, are, avi, atum, 1, *v. a., to revile, reproach, blaspheme.*

blasphemus, a, um, *adj., reviling, defaming, blasphemous,* used in the S.T. usually as *subst.,* i.e., **blasphemus,** i, *m., blasphemer.*

Boetius, (**Boethius**), ii, *m., Boethius,* a distinguished philosopher and theologian under Theodoric. He was born about 470 A.D. and was beheaded A.D. 524 in prison, where he composed his most distinguished work, De Consolatione Philosophiae Libri V. In the S.T., St. Thomas quotes most frequently from this work, but he also quotes much from De Duabus Naturis, the De Trinitate, and the De Hebdomadibus or An Omne Quod Est Sit Bonum. He also refers to the Commentary on Cicero's Topica, the Commentarium Praedicamentorum, the De Institutione Arithmetica, and the In Categorias Aristotelis.

Bonifacius, ii, *m., Boniface.* (1), Boniface I, Saint and Pope. He was elected on December 28, 418 and died at Rome on September 4, 422. Little is known of him previous to his election. He strongly supported St. Augustine in combating Pelagianism. When he received two letters from a Pelagian source calumniating St. Augustine he sent them to him. In recognition of this solicitude, Augustine dedicated to Boniface his rejoinder contained in "Contra Duas Epistolas Pelagianorum, Libri Quatuor." St. Thomas quotes this work frequently.—(2), Boniface IV, Saint and Pope from 608 to 615. During his pontificate Mellitus, the first bishop of London, went to Rome to consult him on matters pertaining to the Church in England. St. Thomas quotes him on the monastic life. Cf. SS. Q. 187. Art. 1 and 2.— (3), Saint Boniface, Bishop of Maintz, called the "Apostle of Germany." He was born in Wessex in the last quarter of the 7th century and was then named Winfried. His success in evangelizing central Europe was amazing. There is a letter of Pope Gregory to this Boniface declaring: "Persons baptized by adulterous and unworthy priests and without interrogation as to their faith are not to be rebaptized; children taken from their parents, of whose baptism there is no proof, are to be baptized."

St. Thomas quotes this letter in PT. Q. 67. Art. 5.

bonitas, atis, *f.*, (1) *goodness* in the abstract and in the concrete senses of the word, a synonym of *completio, perfectio,* and *virtus,* also synonym of *bonum,* the opposite of *malitia* and *malum,* (2) *kindness, kindheartedness, goodness.*—On **gradus in bonitatis,** see *gradus* under 1; on **rectitudo bonitatis,** see *rectitudo* under 3.—Kinds of *bonitas* in this (1) meaning are: (a), **bonitas absoluta seu completa seu omnimoda seu perfecta** and **bonitas deficiens seu imperfecta,** *the absolute* or *perfect* and *the defective* or *imperfect goodness.* —(b), **bonitas absoluta** and **bonitas dependens ab alio,** *unconditioned* or *independent goodness,* and *goodness dependent on something.*—(c), **bonitas absoluta seu simpliciter** and **bonitas secundum quid,** *absolute* or *simple goodness* and *goodness in a certain respect.*—(d), **bonitas accidentalis seu extra essentiam rei** and **bonitas substantialis seu essentialis seu de essentia rei,** *the unessential* or *accidental goodness* and *the essential goodness* or *that belonging to the very nature of something.*—(e), **bonitas actionis** and **bonitas effectus,** *the goodness of an action* and *of an effect.*—(f), **bonitas actus,** *goodness of an act.*—(g), **bonitas exterioris et bonitas interioris actus,** *goodness of the exterior* and *goodness of the interior act.*—(h), bonitas actus interioris, see *bonitas actus exterioris.*—(i), bonitas actus moralis seu bonitas moralis and bonitas rei naturalis, *the goodness of a virtuous action* and *that of the natural thing,* or *the moral goodness* and *the physical* or *metaphysical goodness.*—(j), bonitas adquisita, bonitas naturae seu naturalis and bonitas superaddita, *acquired goodness, natural goodness* or *that existing by nature,* and *that added to nature.*—(k), bonitas aestimata and bonitas vera, *pretended* or *reputed goodness* and *real goodness.*—(l), bonitas circumstantiarum seu ex circumstantiis, bonitas ex fine, bonitas ex genere seu materia, bonitas ex forma habitus and bonitas ex essentia actus, *goodness arising from circumstances, that arising from the purpose of the doer, that arising from its kind* or *matter, i.e., from its object,* and *that arising from the form of its respective habitus,* and *that arising from the essence of a moral act.*—(m), bonitas civilis, *civic goodness* or *the goodness of a citizen.*—(n), bonitas communis seu universalis and bonitas particularis, *the general goodness* and *the specific goodness.*—(o), bonitas completa, see *bonitas absoluta.*—(p), bonitas creata seu creaturae and bonitas increata seu divina seu Dei, *the created* and *the uncreated goodness,* or *the goodness of the creature*

and *that of God.* Cf. bonitas divina.—(q), bonitas creaturae, see *bonitas creata.*—(r), bonitas Dei, see *bonitas creata.*—(s), bonitas de essentia rei, see *bonitas accidentalis.*—(t), bonitas deficiens, see *bonitas absoluta.*—(u), bonitas dependens ab alio, see *bonitas absoluta.*—(v), bonitas divina, see *bonitas creata.*—(w), bonitas essentialis, see *bonitas accidentalis.* —(x), bonitas essentialis seu per essentiam seu pura and bonitas participata seu per participationem, *essential goodness* or *that which constitutes its being* or *pure goodness* and *the shared* or *imparted goodness.*—(y), bonitas ex circumstantiis, see *bonitas circumstantiarum.*—(z), bonitas ex essentia actus, see *bonitas circumstantiarum.*—(a^2), bonitas ex fine, see *bonitas circumstantiarum.*—(b^2), bonitas ex forma habitus, see *bonitas circumstantiarum.*—(c^2), bonitas ex genere, see *bonitas circumstantiarum.*—(d^2), bonitas ex materia, see *bonitas circumstantiarum.*—(e^2), bonitas ex obiecto, *goodness derived from the object.* See bonitas ex fine.—(f^2), bonitas extra essentiam rei, see *bonitas accidentalis.*—(g^2), bonitas hominis, *the goodness of man.*—(h^2), bonitas infinita, *infinite goodness.*—(i^2), bonitas imperfecta, see *bonitas absoluta.*—(j^2), bonitas increata, see *bonitas creata.*—(k^2), bonitas inhaerens, *goodness adhering to a thing as its subject* or *inherent goodness*, the opposite of *sub-sistens*, i.e., that goodness exist-ing for itself.—(l²), **bonitas inten-tionis**, *goodness of intention.*—(m²), **bonitas moralis**, see *bonitas actus moralis.*—(n²), **bonitas na-turae**, see *bonitas adquisita.*—(o²), **bonitas naturalis**, see *bonitas ad-quisita.*—(p²), **bonitas participata**, see *bonitas essentialis.*—(q²), **bo-nitas particularis**, see *bonitas communis.*—(r²), **bonitas per es-sentiam**, see *bonitas essentialis.*—(s²), **bonitas per participationem**, see *bonitas essentialis.*—(t²), **bo-nitas perfecta**, *perfect goodness.* See *bonitas absoluta.*—(u²), **boni-tas prima seu summa**, *the first* or *highest goodness.*—(v²), **bonitas prima** and **bonitas ultima**, *the first* and *the last goodness of a thing.*—(w²), **bonitas prima actus moralis** and **bonitas prima rei naturalis**, *the first goodness* or *that coming first into considera-tion in a moral action* and *that of a thing by nature.*—(x²), **boni-tas prima rei naturalis**, see *boni-tas prima actus moralis.*—(y²), **bo-nitas pura**, see *bonitas essentialis.* —(z²), **bonitas rei naturalis**, see *bonitas actus moralis.*—(a³), **boni-tas summa**, see *bonitas prima.*—(b³), **bonitas substantialis**, see *bo-nitas accidentalis.*—(c³), **bonitas super addita**, see *bonitas adqui-sita.*—(d³), **bonitas ultima**, see *bo-nitas prima.*—(e³), **bonitas univer-salis**, see *bonitas communis.*—(f³), **bonitas vera**, see *bonitas aesti-mata.*—(g³), **bonitas voluntatis**,

goodness of the will. With man *bonitas* is one of the fruits of the Holy Ghost. Cf. *fructus* under 2.—Kinds of *bonitas* in this sense are: (a), **bonitas divina**, *divine goodness.* Cf. *divina.*—(b), **boni-tas per se**, *goodness which is so through itself* and *its own being,* or *goodness itself.*

Bonosiaci, orum, *m.*, *the Bonosiaci* or *Bonosiani*, *the Bonosians*, an heretical sect whose founder was Bonosus, Bishop of Sardica in Illyria at the end of the fourth century. Gregory the Great re-jected their baptism because the name of the Trinity was not invoked.

bonus, a, um, *adj.*, (1) *good* in the general sense of the word, that which all desire, the opposite of *malus*, (2) *good in itself, objec-tively good*, i.e., that which is good in so far as it refers to a su-perior will (the divine); in other words good as it is or has been desired, a synonym of *perfectus*, likewise the opposite of *malus*, (3) *good for something, subjec-tively good*, i.e., that which is good in so far as it tends to per-fect the subject and is therefore desirable; likewise the opposite of *malus.*—Kinds of bonum in its general meaning are: (a), **bonum absolute seu in se seu secundum se** and **bonum alterius**, *the abso-lute good* or *good in itself* or *good according to its own nature.* Cf. *bonum absolute acceptum* under 2, and *the good of anoth-*

er, (cf. *bonum alterius* under 3) i.e., the objective good and the subjective good.—(b), **bonum alterius**, see *bonum absolute*.—(c), **bonum in se**, see *bonum absolute*.—(d) **bonum quod convertitur cum ente** and **bonum quod est in genere qualitatis**, *good which is convertible with being* et **nullum rem supra ens addit** (Pot. 9. 7 ad 5), a synonym of **bonum absolute seu in se seu secundum se**, and *the good which belongs to the category of quality* (cf. *genus* under 2) and is added to being when it is said of it a "res" or close modification, (these last two kinds of *bonum* are identical with the first two mentioned according to the thing).—(e), **bonum quod est in genere qualitatis**, see *bonum convertitur cum ente*.—(f), **bonum secundum se**, see *bonum absolute*. Cf. *bonum ex suppositione alterius* under 3. —**per se bonum**, *good existing for itself*, as Plato assumed it. On **actio bona**, see *actio* under 1; on **actus bonus**, see *actus* under 1; on **ars bona**, see *ars* under 2; on **commutatio bona**, see *commutatio* under 2; on **conscientia bona**, see *conscientia* under 3; on **concupiscentia bona**, see *concupiscentia* under 1; on **delectatio bona**, see *delectatio;* on **electio bona**, see *electio* under 1; on **finis bonus**, see *finis* under 2; on **fortuna bona**, see *fortuna* under 1; on **habitus bonus**, see *habitus* under 4; on **ho-**

mo simpliciter bonus, see *homo;* on **intentio bona**, see *intentio* under 2; on **ira bona**, see *ira* under 1; on **libertas ad bonum**, see *libertas* under 2; on **mos bonus**, see *mos* under 2; on **opus bonum**, see *opus* under 4; on **oratio bona**, see *oratio* under 3; on **passio bona**, see *passio* under 3; on **ratio bona**, see *ratio* under 14; on **sensus bonus**, see *sensus* under 4; on **spiritus bonus**, see *spiritus;* on **stultitia bona**, see *stultitia;* on **superbia bona**, see *superbia* under 2; on **voluntas bona**, see *voluntas* under 3.— Kinds of *bonum* in the sense of good objectively or the objective good or the objective goodness are: (a), **bonum accidentale seu in accidente seu secundum esse accidentale** and **bonum substantiale seu in substantia seu quantum ad substantiam seu essentiale seu secundum esse essentiale**, *the unessential good of a thing* or *the good of a thing which is placed in one of its accidents*, i.e., its accidental perfection, and that which is placed in its own substance.—(b), **bonum actionis** and **bonum agentis**, *the good of an action* and *that of the doer*, in other words, the good which consists in the perfection of the work and the good which consists in the perfection of the doer.—(c), **bonum agentis**, see *bonum actionis*.—(d), **bonum antecedens** and **bonum consequens**, *the antecedent* and *consequent* *good.*—(e), **bonum completum seu consummatum seu perfectum** and **bonum defectivum seu deficiens seu imperfectum,** *the complete* or *final* or *perfect good* and *the defective* or *imperfect good.* See *bonum imperfectum* under 3.—(f), **bonum consequens,** see *bonum antecedens.*—(g), **bonum consummatum,** see *bonum completum.*—(h), **bonum continentiae,** *the good that consists in continence.*—(i), **bonum defectivum seu deficiens,** see *bonum completum.*—(j), **bonum essentiale,** see *bonum accidentale.*—(k), **bonum essentiale seu essentialiter seu per essentiam** and **bonum participative** or **bonum participatione seu secundum participationem aliquam,** *the essentially good, the good through participation with the first.*—(l), **bonum essentialiter,** see *bonum essentiale.*—(m), **bonum ex causa, bonum ex circumstantiis, bonum ex fine,** and **bonum ex genere seu secundum speciem suam,** *the good originating from its cause, from its circumstances, from its genus* or *kind,* i.e., from the object of a moral action.—(n), **bonum ex circumstantiis,** see *bonum ex causa.*—(o), **bonum ex fine,** see *bonum ex causa.*—(p), **bonum ex genere,** see *bonum ex causa.*—(q), **bonum formaliter seu formaliter dictum** and **bonum materialiter dictum,** *the good in the formal* and *that in the material sense of the word.*

(r), **bonum hominis,** *the good* or *the goodness of man.*—(s), **bonum imperfectum,** see *bonum completum.*—(t), **bonum in accidente,** see *bonum accidentale.*—(u), **bonum in actionibus** and **bonum in rebus,** *the good in actions* and *the good in things* or *the goodness in doing* and *the goodness in the being of the thing.*—(v), **bonum in actibus humanis seu in actionibus moralibus seu in moralibus seu morale seu moris,** and **bonum in rebus naturalibus seu in naturalibus seu naturae seu naturale,** *the moral* or *virtuous good* and *the natural* or *physical good.* Cf. *bonum naturale* under 3.—(w), **bonum inhaerens seu in ipsis rebus** and **bonum subsistens seu separatum,** *the good inherent in a thing as its subject* or *the accidental good existing in things* and *that existing for itself* or *the good separated from the things of the world.* Cf. **per se bonum** above.—(x), **bonum in ipsis rebus,** see *bonum inhaerens.*—(y), **bonum in moralibus,** see *bonum in actionibus moralibus.*—(z), **bonum in naturalibus,** see *bonum in actionibus moralibus.*—(a^2), **bonum in rebus,** see *bonum in actionibus.*—(b^2), **bonum in rebus naturalibus,** see *bonum in actionibus.*—(c^2), **bonum in substantia,** see *bonum accidentale.*—(d^2), **bonum materialiter dictum,** see *bonum formaliter dictum.*—(e^2), **bonum melius seu super-**

abundans and **bonum necessarium**, *the better good* or *the good extending beyond the measure of necessity* and *the necessary good;* in other words, the advised and the prescribed morally good work.—(f²), **bonum meritorium**, *the meritorius good.*—(g²), **bonum morale**, see *bonum in actionibus moralibus.*—(h²), **bonum moris**, see *bonum in actionibus moralibus.*—(i²), **bonum naturae**, see *bonum in actionibus moralibus.*—(j²), **bonum necessarium**, see *bonum melius.*—(k²), **bonum ordinis seu quantum ad ordinem in finem**, *the good of order* or *the good consisting in the ordering of an action towards its goal.*—(l²), **bonum participative**, see *bonum essentiale.*—(m²), **bonum per accidens** and **bonum per se**, *the good which comes from something incidental* and *the good through itself* and *its own substance.*—(n²), **bonum per essentiam**, see *bonum essentiale.*—(o²), **bonum perfectum**, see *bonum completum.* Cf. *bonum perfectum* under 3.—(p²), **bonum per participationem**, see *bonum essentiale.*—(q²), **bonum per se**, see *bonum per accidens.*—(r²), **bonum per suam substantiam**, see *bonum accidentale.*—(s²), **bonum primum**, *the first Good,* namely, *God.*—(t²), **bonum quantum ad ordinem in finem**, see *bonum ordinis.*—(u²), **bonum quantum ad substantiam**, see *bonum accidentale.*—(v²), **bonum secundum esse**

accidentale, see *bonum accidentale.*—(w²), **bonum secundum esse essentiale**, see *bonum accidentale.*—(x²), **bonum secundum legis positionem** and **bonum secundum naturalem ordinem**, *the good according to the provision of the law* and *the good according to the natural order,* or *the legal* and *the natural good.*—(y²), **bonum secundum naturalem ordinem**, see *bonum secundum legis positionem.*—(z²), **bonum secundum quandam similitudinem** and **bonum vere**, *the good according to a kind of resemblance* and *the good in the true sense of the word* or *the unreal* and *the real good.* Cf. **bonum vere** under 2.—(a³), **bonum secundum quid** and **bonum simpliciter**, *the good in a certain respect* or *the relatively good,* and *the simple or plainly good,* that which has all the perfection, substantial and accidental, which is due to it. Cf. **bonum secundum quid** under 3.—(b³), **bonum secundum speciem suam**, see **bonum ex causa**.—(c³), **bonum separatum**, see *bonum inhaerens.*—(d³), **bonum simpliciter**, see **bonum secundum quid**.—(e³), **bonum subsistens**, see *bonum inhaerens.*—(f³), **bonum substantiale**, see *bonum accidentale.*—(g³), **bonum summe seu summum**, *the highest good.* Cf. *bonum summum* under 3.—(h³), **bonum superabundans**, see *bonum melius.*—(i³), **bonum virtutis seu virtutis** moralis, *the good* or *the good-ness of virtue,* i.e., the goodness peculiar to virtue or the good-ness of a moral act arising from the side of virtue which is the principal of the act. Cf. **bonum virtutis** under 3.—(jᵃ), **bonum virtutis moralis,** see *bonum virtutis.*—**bonum causatur seu est ex integra causa, malum autem ex singularibus seu singulis defectibus,** or **bonum constat ex una causa perfecta, sed malum omnifariam contingit ex particularibus defectibus,** or, **bonum contingit ex tota integra causa, malum autem ex singularibus defectibus,** or **bonum contingit ex una et integra causa, malum autem ex singularibus defectibus,** or **bonum est ex causa una et integra, malum autem ex particularibus defectibus,** or, **bonum est ex tota et integra causa malum autem ex singularibus defectibus,** or **bonum est ex una et tota causa, malum autem ex singularibus defectibus,** or **bonum autem causatur ex integra causa,** *the good originates from a single cause* and *also from a single cause only when it is whole and undamaged; the bad results when there is any defect in any of the elements producing the good;* in other words, the moral-ly good act is accomplished only when the object as well as the circumstances and end under which it is accomplished are morally good, but the morally bad when the object or any one of the circumstances is affected with a fault, sicut pulchritudo causatur ex hoc, quod omnia corporis membra decenter se habent, quorum si unum tantum fuerit indecenter dispositum, turpitudinem inducit.—**Bonum communiter acceptum est simplicius quam essentia,** *the good of a thing, as it is under-stood generally, is in its conception simpler,* i.e., more extensive, *than the essence of the same,* quia communius (est), cum dicatur non solum de essentia, sed etiam de eo, quod per essentiam subsistit, et iterum de accidentibus.—**bonum contingit uno modo, sed malum omnifariam seu multipliciter,** the translation of the Aristotelian passage *to men hamartein pollachos estin, . . . , to de katorthoun monachos, the morally good comes into existence in a single manner, the morally bad in all possible ways,* or *at least in manifold ways.—* **Bonum convertitur cum ente,** see *bonum* under 1 and *convertere* under 1.—**Bonum dicitur per informationem entis,** *something is called good as a result of its form;* in other words, because it is provided with a form, cum autem unumquodque sit id, quod est, per suam formam, forma autem praesupponit quaedam et quaedam ad ipsam ex necessitate consequuntur, ad hoc quod aliquid sit perfectum et bonum, necesse est, quod formam habeat et ea, quae praeexiguntur ad eam, et ea, quae consequuntur ad ipsam.—**Bonum est diffusivum seu communicativum sui esse,** or, **bonum secundum suam rationem est diffusivum sui esse;** *it is characteristic of the good in consequence of its essence to spread its influence and to be imparted,* cum autem dicitur, quod bonum est diffusivum secundum sui rationem, non est intelligenda effusio, secundum quod importat operationem causae efficientis, sed secundum quod importat habitudinem causae finalis.—**Bonum est vehementius in agendo quam malum,** or, **bonum fortius est ad movendum, quam malum,** *the good has a greater power than the bad in operation,* quia malum non agit, nisi virtute boni.— **Bonum non indiget malo, sed e converso,** *the good does not require the bad* or *evil for its existence,* but the evil does require the good, because evil according to its definition is a *privatio boni* and so must adhere to a good as its subject.— **Quilibet singularis defectus causat malum, bonum autem causatur ex integra causa,** see above: Bonum causatur ex integra, etc.—**Verum et bonum subiecto quidem convertuntur, ...,** sed secundum rationem invicem se excedunt, *the true* and *the*

good are according to the subject exchangeable things, quia omne verum est bonum et omne bonum est verum; *according to the conception* or *idea they exceed each other,* sicut intellectus et voluntas invicem se excedunt, nam intellectus intellegit voluntatem et multa alia et voluntas appetit ea, quae pertinent ad intellectum, et multa alia.—(3), *bonum est, quod omnia appetunt,* the translation of the Aristotelian passage *t'agathon, hore pant'ephietai.* Ratio enim boni in hoc consistit, quod aliquid sit appetibile.—Kinds of bonum in the (3) sense of subjectively good are the following: (a), **bonum absolute acceptum seu simpliciter acceptum seu absolutum** and **bonum arctum seu arduum seu cum arduitate et elevatione seu cum arduitate et difficultate adipiscendi, seu sub ratione arduitatis et difficultate,** *the good free of difficulties* or *imagined as free of such* and *the good connected with difficulties* or *imagined as connected with such;* in other words, the good attained in an easy and that in a difficult way.—(b), **bonum absolutum,** see *bonum absolute acceptum.*—(c), **bonum abstractum seu non participatur** and **bonum participatum seu participabile,** *the good which is abstracted* or *deducted* or *not shared* and *the good which is shared* or *imparted.*—(d), **bonum actuale,** *the* *good present in reality.*—(e), **bonum additum** and **bonum privatum substractum,** *the added* and *the deprived* or *subtracted good.* See also *bonum commune.*—(f), **bonum adeptum seu habitum** and **bonum non habitum,** *the attained* and *the not attained good.* —(g), **bonum ad naturam communem pertinens seu naturae** (sc. hominis) **seu naturae humanae** and **bonum personale,** *the good of common human nature* and *the personal good of man.* —(h), **bonum adquisitum per motum** and **bonum adquisitum sine motu,** *the good acquired by means of motion* and *the good acquired without motion.* —(i), **bonum adquisitum sine motu,** see *bonum adquisitum per motum.*—(j), **bonum aestimatum apparens seu verisimile** and **bonum vere seu verum,** *the supposed* or *apparent* or *probable good* and *the true* or *real good.*—(k), **bonum aeternum** and **bonum temporale,** *the eternal* and *the temporal good.*—(l), **bonum agibile seu operabile,** *the active good* or *the good carried out by action.*—(m), **bonum alicui seu huic seu quoad hunc** and **bonum simpliciter,** *the good for anyone* or *for this* or *that person* and *the simply good* and *the good for all.*—(n), **bonum alienum seu alterius** and **bonum proprium,** *the strange* or *the good of another* and *the particular* or *proper good.*—(o),

bonum alterius, see *bonum alienum.*—(p), **bonum amatum,** *the good that is loved.*—(q), **bonum amicitiae,** *the good consisting in friendship.*—(r), **bonum animae seu spirituale, bonum corporis seu secundum corpus seu corporale** and **bonum exterius seu exteriorum rerum seu in exterioribus rebus consistens,** *the good of the soul, that of the body,* and *that consisting in an exterior thing* or *the spiritual, the corporal* and *the exterior good of man.*—(s), **bonum apparens,** see *bonum aestimatum.*—(t), **bonum arctum** see *bonum absolute acceptum.*—(u), **bonum arduum,** see *bonum absolute acceptum.*—(v), **bonum caeleste** and **bonum terrenum,** *the heavenly* and *the earthly good.*—(w), **bonum caritatis,** *the good consisting of the love of God.*—(x), **bonum carnis,** *the good of the flesh* or *of man according to his flesh.*—(y), **bonum commune seu publicum** and **bonum singulare seu privatum,** *the common* or *public good* and *the good of the individual* or *private good.* Cf. **bonum additum.**—(z), **bonum commune seu secundum communem boni rationem seu universale** and **bonum particulare seu particulatum,** *the common good* or *according to the common plan of good* or *universal good* and *the particular* or *the good produced as a particular good.*—(a²), **bo-**

num commutabile seu corruptibile and **bonum incommutabile,**
the changeable or *passing good*
and *the unchangeable good.*—
(b^2), **bonum completivum seu
perfectivum,** *the completing* or
perfecting good.—(c^2), **bonum
coniugale seu matrimonii,** *the
conjugal good* or *the good of
matrimony.*—(d^2), **bonum coniunctum** and **bonum exterius
seu extrinsecum,** *the good connected with the one who desires
it* or *that attained by him,* and
the good still outside him.—(e^2),
bonum connaturale seu naturale
and **bonum supernaturale,** *the
good commensurate with the
nature of him who desires* or
the natural good and *the supernatural good.*—(f^2), **bonum contractum seu determinatum seu
finitum** and **bonum infinitum,**
the restricted or *determined* or
limited or *finite good* and *the
infinite good.*—(g^2), **bonum corporale,** see *bonum animae.*—
(h^2), **bonum corporis,** see *bonum animae.*—(i^2), **bonum corruptibile,** see *bonum commutabile.*—(j^2), **bonum creditum** and
bonum increatum, *the created
good* and *the uncreated good.*
—(k^2), **bonum creaturae,** *the
good of the creature.*—(l^2), **bonum cui fit** and **bonum facienti,**
*the good with reference to him
who receives it* and *the good
with reference to him who performs it.*—(m^2), **bonum cum
arduitate et difficultate adipi-**

scendi seu cum arduitate et elevatione, see *bonum absolute
acceptum.*—(n^2), **bonum delectabile, bonum honestum,** and
bonum utile, *the amusing* or
pleasing, the suitable or *noble,*
(see *bonum honorabile*), and
the useful good; in other words,
the pleasing, the decent, and
the useful.—(o^2), **bonum delectabile secundum sensum,** *the
sensible, pleasurable* or *pleasing
good.*—(p^2), **bonum determinatum,** see *bonum contractum.*—
(q^2), **bonum divinum,** *the divine
Good or God.*—(r^2), **bonum domesticum,** and **bonum patriae seu
politicum,** *the domestic* and *the
political good,* or *the welfare
of the family* and *of the state*
or *the fatherland.*—(s^2), **bonum
ecclesiae seu ecclesiasticum,** *the
material property of an ecclesiastical group.*—(t^2), **bonum ex
suppositione alterius** and **bonum
secundum se seu simpliciter,** *the
good resulting from the supposition of something else* and
the good according to itself or
absolute good. Cf. **bonum alicui,**
and **bonum secundum quid.**—
(u^2), **bonum exterius,** see **bonum
animae** and **bonum coniunctum.**
—(v^2), **bonum extrinsecum,** see
bonum coniunctum.—(w^2), **bonum facienti,** see *bonum cui fit.*
—(x^2), **bonum finale seu ultimum** and **bonum proximum,** *the
last* or *the final good of man* and
the proximate good; in other
words, *the good which man fi-*

nally strives for and attains, and *the good which he temporarily strives for and attains.*—(y²), **bonum finitum,** see *bonum contractum.*—(z²), **bonum fortunae,** *the good of accident* or *good luck,* through which only one of the exterior goods (see *bonum exterius*) is to be understood, because the attainment and keeping of it depends so much on good luck.—(a³) **bonum futurum** and **bonum praesens seu habitum,** *the future* and *the present good* or *that which is possessed.* —(b³), **bonum gentis,** *the good* or *welfare of the people.* Cf. C. G. 1. 41.—(c³), **bonum gloriae, bonum gratiae,** and **bonum naturae seu secundum naturam,** *the good of heavenly splendor, the good of grace,* and *the good of nature,* (cf. *bonum ad communem naturam pertinens*) in other words, the good which for man consists of heavenly splendor or belongs to it; the good which for man rests here below in the grace of God or is granted him by grace, and the good which belongs to his nature or is in accordance with it.—(d³), **bonum gratiae,** see *bonum gloriae.*—(e³), **bonum habitum,** see *bonum futurum.*—(f³), **bonum hominis seu humanum,** *the good of man* or *human good.* Cf. **bonum hominis.**—(g³), **bonum hominis secundum quid** and **bonum hominis simpliciter,** *the good of man in a certain respect* and *the good of man simply.*—

(h³), **bonum hominis simpliciter,** see *bonum hominis secundum quid.*—(i³), **bonum honestum,** *that good which is fitting,* or *decent,* or *strictly in accordance with the nature which seeks it for itself not as a means to some further good,* as opposed to *bonum utile.* See *bonum delectabile.*—(j³), **bonum honorabile,** and **bonum laudabile,** *the honorable* and *the praiseworthy good.* See *bonum honestum.*—(k³), **bonum huic,** see *bonum alicui.*—(l³), **bonum huius mundi,** *the good of this world.*—(m³), **bonum humanum,** see *bonum hominis.*—(n³), **bonum imaginabile seu imaginarium seu imaginatum,** *the sensibly represented* or *the imagined good.*—(o³), **bonum imperfectum** and **bonum perfectum,** *the imperfect* and *the perfect good.* See **bonum completum** under 2. —(p³), **bonum incommutabile,** see *bonum commutabile.*—(q³), **bonum increatum,** see **bonum creatum.**—(r³), **bonum individui seu unius individui seu proprii individui** and **bonum speciei,** *the good of an individual* or *of a single individual* or *of a particular individual and the good of the entire kind.*—(s³), **bonum infinitum,** see *bonum contractum.*—(t³), **bonum intellectuale seu intellegibile seu secundum intellectum seu secundum rationem** and **bonum sensibile seu secundum sensum,** *the supersensible* or *spiritual good* and *the sensi-*

ble or *physical good.*—(u³), bonum intellectus seu rationis, bonum voluntatis and bonum sensus, *the good of reason,* which consists of the true or of the truth; *the good of the will,* which consists of the good, or *the goodness of the thing;* and the *good of sense* which consists of the suitable on every occasion.—(v³), bonum laudabile, see *bonum honorabile.*—(w³), bonum matrimonii, see *bonum coniugale.*—(x³), bonum multitudinis seu totius seu totius mulititudinis civilis and bonum unius seu unius hominis, *the good of the multitude* or *of the whole* or *of the state,* and *the good of the individual* or *the citizen.*—(y³), bonum naturae, see *bonum ad naturam communem pertinens* and *bonum gloriae.* Cf. *bonum naturae* under 2.—(z³), bonum naturae humanae, see *bonum ad naturam communem pertinens.*—(a⁴), bonum naturae singularis and bonum universi, *the good of a single nature of a being* and *the good of the universe.*—(b⁴), bonum naturale, see *bonum connaturale.* Cf. *bonum naturale* under 2.—(c⁴), bonum non-habitum, see *bonum actuale.*—(d⁴), bonum non-participatum, see *bonum abstractum.*—(e⁴), bonum operabile, see *bonum agibile.*—(f⁴), bonum participabile, see *bonum abstractum.*—(g⁴), bonum participatum, see *bonum abstractum.*—(h⁴), bonum particulare,

see *bonum commune.*—(i⁴), bonum particulatum, see *bonum commune.*—(j⁴), bonum patriae, see *bonum domesticum.*—(k⁴), bonum patrimoniale, *the paternal good.*—(l⁴), bonum perfectivum, see *bonum completivum.*—(m⁴), bonum perfectum, see *bonum imperfectum.* Cf. *bonum perfectum* under 2.—(n⁴), bonum personale, see *bonum ad naturam communem pertinens.*—(o⁴), bonum politicum, see *bonum domesticum.*—(p⁴), bonum praesens, see *bonum futurum.*—(q⁴), bonum principale, and bonum secundarium, *the principal* and *the subordinate good.*—(r⁴), bonum privatum, see *bonum additum* and *bonum commune.*—(s⁴), bonum proprii individui, see *bonum individui.*—(t⁴), bonum proprium, see *bonum alienum.*—(u⁴), bonum proximum, see *bonum finale.*—(v⁴), bonum publicum, see *bonum commune.*—(w⁴), bonum quoad hunc, see *bonum alicui.*—(x⁴), bonum rationis, see *bonum intellectus.*—(y⁴), bonum secundarium, see *bonum principale.*—(z⁴), bonum secundum communem boni rationem, see *bonum commune.*—(a⁵), bonum secundum corpus, see *bonum animae.*—(b⁵), bonum secundum intellectum, see *bonum intellectuale.*—(c⁵), bonum secundum quid and bonum simpliciter, *the respective good* or *the good in a certain respect* and *the simple* or *the absolute good.* Cf. bonum ex suppositione alterius and bonum alicui; also *bonum secundum quid and bonum simpliciter* under 2.—(d⁵), bonum secundum rationem, see *bonum intellectuale.*—(e⁵), bonum secundum se, see *bonum ex suppositione alterius.*—(f⁵), bonum secundum sensum, see *bonum intellectuale.* —(g⁵), bonum sensibile, see *bonum intellectuale.*—(h⁵), bonum sensus, see *bonum intellectus.—* (i⁵), bonum simpliciter, see *bonum alicui, bonum ex suppositione alterius* and *bonum secundum quid.* Cf. *bonum simpliciter* under 2.—(j⁵), bonum simpliciter acceptum, see *bonum absolute acceptum.*—(k⁵), bonum singulare, see *bonum commune.*—(l⁵), bonum speciei, see *bonum individui.*—(m⁵), bonum spirituale, see *bonum animae.*—(n⁵), bonum sub ratione arduitatis et difficultatis, see *bonum absolute acceptum.*—(o⁵), bonum subtractum, see *bonum additum.*—(p⁵), bonum summum, *the highest good.* Cf. *bonum summum* under 2.—(q⁵), bonum summum in aliquo genere vel ordine rerum and bonum summum simpliciter, *the highest good in any kind* or *order of things* and *the highest simple* or *absolute good.*—(r⁵), bonum summum in aliquo ordine rerum, see *bonum summum in aliquo genere rerum.*—(s⁵), bonum summum simpliciter, see *bonum summum in aliquo genere rerum.*—(t⁵), bonum tem-

porale, see *bonum aeternum.—* (u⁵), bonum terrenum, see *bonum caeleste.*—(v⁵), bonum totius multitudinis civilis, see *bonum multitudinis.—*(w⁵), bonum totius, see *bonum multitudinis.—*(x⁵), bonum ultimum, see *bonum finale.*—(y⁵), bonum unius seu unius hominis, see *bonum multitudinis.*—(z⁵), bonum unius individui, see *bonum individui.*—(a⁶) bonum universale, see *bonum commune.*—(b⁶), bonum universale simpliciter, *the simple* or *absolute universal good,* namely God, the opposite of *bonum universale secundum quid,* that is, the respective or in a certain respect general good, under which is to be understood a created good, which places itself in opposition to another created good as a general good. (c⁶), bonum universi, see *bonum naturae singularis.*—(d⁶), bonum vere, see *bonum aestimatum.—* (e⁶), bonum verisimile, see *bonum aestimatum.—*(f⁶), bonum verum, see *bonum aestimatum.—* (g⁶), bonum virtutis, *the good of virtue,* in other words, the good of man which for him is laid in virtue. Cf. *bonum virtutis* under 2.— *Comp.,* melior, melius, *better.—*Cf. SS. Q. 161. Art. 2; SS. Q. 163. Art. 4 (bis); PT. Q. 82. Art. 6 (passim); PT. Q. 86. Art. 5 (bis); PT. Q. 90. Art. 4; et passim.—*Sup.,* optimus, a, um, *best.—Adv., posit.,* bene, *well, honorably, satisfactorily, prosper-*

ously, correctly, the opposite of *male.—Comp.,* **melius,** *better.—Sup.,* **optime,** *best.*

Booz, *indecl. noun, m., Boaz,* a wealthy Bethlehemite, the son of Salmon and grandfather of Jesse. He became the second husband of the widowed Ruth.

bos, bovis, *comm., an ox, a cow.*

botrus, i, *f., the grape.*

boulesis, see *bulesis.*

bouly, Grk. *boule, f., counsel, good counsel.*

bovinus, a, um, *adj., of,* or *pertaining to oxen* or *cows, bovine.*

brachium, (**bracchium**), ii, *n., the arm,* from the shoulder to the hand or to the wrist.

bravium, i, *n., a reward, prize.*

brevio, are, avi, atum, 1, *v. a., to shorten, abbreviate, abridge,* the opposite of *prolongo.*

brevis, e, *adj., short, little, small,* of space, time, extent, the opposite of *diuturnus.*—**breviter,** *adv., briefly, shortly.*—**in brevi,** (tempore), *in a short time.*

brevitas, atis, *f.,* (1) of time, *shortness, brevity,* the opposite of *longitudo,* (2) of words, *conciseness, brevity,* (3) *littleness, smallness,* generally, a synonym of *parvitas.*

bria, ae, *f., a measure,* a synonym of *mensura.*

brutalis, e, *adj., animal, beastly,* a synonym of *bestialis.* On **anima brutalis,** see *anima* under 1; on **appetitus brutalis,** see *appetitus* under 2; on **irascibilis brutalis,** see *irascibilis;* on **vita brutalis,** see *vita* under 3.—**brutaliter,** *adv., in the manner of an animal, brutally.*

brutaliter, *adv.,* see *brutalis.*

brutum, i, *n.,* see *brutus.*

brutus, a, um, *adj., irrational,* in the S.T. used only with *animal.*—**brutum,** i, *n., animal, beast,* a synonym of *animal* and *bestia.* On **delectatio brutorum,** see *delectatio.*

bubo, onis, *f., an owl.*

buccella, ae, *f., a small mouthful, morsel.*

buccina, ae, *f., a crooked horn* or *trumpet.*

buccino, are, avi, atum, 1, *v. n., to blow the buccina.*

bucolicus, a, um, *adj., pertaining to shepherds, pastoral, bucolic.*

Bulgari, orum, *m., the Bulgarians.* The *Responsa Nicolai ad consulta Bulgarorum* is the reply given by Pope Nicholas I to Boris, Prince of Bulgaria, on matters of Church discipline.

bulisis, (**bulesis**), Grk. *boulesis, f., free-will.*

butyrum, i, *n., butter.*

byssus, *f., cotton, cotton material, a fine kind of flax,* a synonym of *linum.*

C

Cabilonensis, e, *adj., of* or *belonging to Cabillonum,* (Chalon-sur-Saone). The *Concilium Cabilo-* *nense,* held in 813, decreed that during Lent fasting should be observed until the celebration

of the office of Vespers, which
in the Lenten season is said
after the ninth hour.

cachinnus, i, *m.*, *a laugh in derision, jeering.*

cacumen, inis, *n.*, *the peak, top, utmost point.*

cadaver, eris, *n.*, *a dead body of
man* or *brute, corpse, carcass.*

cadaverinus, a, um, *adj.*, *(cadaver)*,
of carrion, cadaverous.

cado, ere, cecidi, casum, 3, *v. n.*,
(1) *to fall, fall down,* (2) *fall
upon, find,* (3) *fall into, fall in
with,* (4) *fall under, belong to,*
(5) *fall between,* (6) *fall away,
become separated,* (7) *fall into
sin, sin.*

caducus, a, um, *adj.*, *perishable,
falling,* a synonym of *temporalis,
terrenus.*—**morbus caducus,** *epilepsy.*

Caecilia, ae, *f.*, *Cecilia,* Saint, a
Roman virgin who suffered mar-
tyrdom in 230 under Alexander
Severus.

Caecilius, ii, *m.*, *Caecilius,* Bishop
of Bilta, to whom Cyprian ad-
dresses a letter on the irregularity prevalent in some churches
where water, instead of wine
mixed with water was offered at
the Mass.

caecitas, atis, *f.*, *blindness.* Kinds
of *blindness* are: **caecitas corporalis** and **caecitas mentis,** *physical blindness* and *spiritual blindness.* Cf. *luxuria.*

caeco, are, avi, atum, 1, *v. a.*, *to
blind, make blind.*

caecus, a, um, *adj.*, (1) *unseeing,
blind* physically, (2) *blind* spir-
itually.

caedes, is, *f.*, *slaughter, murder.*

caedo, ere, cecidi, caesum, 3, *v. a.*
to strike, cut, hew.

caelebs, libis, *adj.*, *unmarried, ce-
libate.*

Caelestinus, i, *m.*, *Celestine I,*
Saint, Pope. Nothing is known
of his early history except that
he was a Roman and that his
father's name was Priscus. He
succeeded Saint Boniface I as
Pope, September 10, 422 and
died July 26, 432.

caelestis, e, *adj.*, *heavenly,* opposite of *terrenus.* On **anima caelestis,** see *anima* under 2; on **bonum caeleste,** see *bonus* under
3; on **corpus caeleste,** see *corpus;*
on **desiderium caeleste,** see *desiderium* under 1; on **ecclesia
caelestis,** see *ecclesia* under 1;
on **filius caelestis,** see *filius* under 1; on **gloria caelestis,** see
gloria under 1; on **hierarchia caelestis,** see *hierarchia;* on **homo
caelestis,** see *homo;* on **intellectus caelestis,** see *intellectus* under 1; on **motus caelestis,** see
motus under 1; on **natura caelestis,** see *natura;* on **pater caelestis,** see *pater;* on **regnum caeleste,** see *regnum;* on **spiritus
caelestis,** see *spiritus;* on **substantia caelestis,** see *substantia*
under 2; on **vita caelestis,** see
vita under 3.

caelibatus, us, *m.*, *celibacy, the
single life.*

caelum, i, *n.,* (*caelus,* i, *m.,*), also *coel–, heaven* in the real and the unreal sense of the word.— **caeli,** orum, *m., the heavens, heaven.*—**regnum caelorum,** *kingdom of heaven.* On **anima caeli et primi caeli,** see *anima* under 2. On **clavis caeli,** see *clavis* under 2; on **motus caeli seu in caelum,** see *motus* under 1; on **regnum caeli,** see *regnum;* on **virtus caeli,** see *virtus* under 1.— Kinds of *caelum* are: (a), **caelum aereum,** *airy heaven.*—(b), **caelum aethereum,** *ethereal heaven.* —(c), **caelum aqueum,** *watery heaven.*—(d), **caelum corporeum,** *physical heaven.*—(e), **caelum crystallinum,** *crystal heaven.*—(f), **caelum empyreum seu igneum seu intellectuale,** *fiery* or *supersensible* or *intellectual heaven.*— (g), **caelum igneum,** see *caelum empyreum.*—(h), **caelum intellectuale,** see *caelum empyreum.*— (i), **caelum Olympium,** *Olympic heaven.*—(j), **caelum primum, caelum secundum,** and **caelium tertium,** *the first* (cf. *caelum supremum*), *the second,* and the *third heaven.*—(k), **caelum sanctae Trinitatis,** *the heaven of the Holy Trinity.*—(l), **caelum secundum,** see *caelum primum.*—(m), **caelum sidereum,** *starry sky, firmament,* synonym of *firmamentum.*—(n), **caelum sphaericum,** *the spherical heaven.*—(o), **caelum superius,** *higher heaven.*— (p), **caelum supremum,** *uppermost* or *highest heaven.* Cf. **caelum primum.**—(q), **caelum tertium,** see *caelum primum.*—(r), **caelum Trinitatis,** *the heaven of the Trinity.* See *caelum sanctae Trinitatis.*

caementum, i, *n., cement.*

caemeterium, ii, *n., a cemetery.*

caenaculum, i, *n.,* see *coenaculum.*

Caere, *indecl., f., Caere,* a very ancient city in Etruria, previously called Agylla.

caeremonia, ae, *f., a formal act, rite, observance,* certain external works whereby man makes profession of his subjection to God, a synonym of *cultus.*

caeremonialis, e, *adj., pertaining to religious rites, ceremonial.*— **caeremonialia,** ium, *n., a ceremonial,* a system of rules observed on certain occasions, as at a time of worship.

Caesar, aris, *m., Caesar,* the name of a patrician family of the Julian gens, which traced its origin to Iulus, the son of Aeneas. The name was assumed by Augustus as the adopted son of the dictator C. Julius Caesar, and was by Augustus handed down to his adopted son Tiberius. It continued to be used by Caligula, Claudius, and Nero, as members either by adoption or female descent of Caesar's family. Though the family became extinct with Nero, succeeding emperors used the name to stamp themselves as members of the reigning house. The first three alone are mentioned in the

S.T. (1), *Caius Julius Caesar,* the Dictator, was probably born on July 12, 100 B.C., and was assassinated March, 15, 44 B.C.— (2), Gaius Octavius, after his a-doption by his great-uncle, *Gaius Iulius Caesar Octavianus;* the title of *Augustus* was given him by the senate and the people in 27 as a mark of special rank and claim to veneration; the first Roman emperor, born on the 23rd of September, 63 B.C., and died at Nola on the 29th of August, 14 A.D.—(3), *Tiberius Claudius Nero Caesar,* was born on the 16th of November, B.C. 42, and died on the 16th of March, 37, at the villa of Lucullus, in Misenum. He reigned from 14 to 37 A.D., in which period occurred the Crucifixion.

Caesariensis, e, *adj., of Caesarea, Caesarean.*

caesaries, ei, *f., the hair.*

caeterus, (**cet-**), a, um, *adj., the other, that which exists besides, can be added to what is already named of a like kind with it, the remainder, the rest.*—**caeteri,** orum, *m., others, the rest.*— **caetera,** orum, *n., other things.* —**de caetero,** *as for the rest, for the future.*—**caetera huiusmodi,** *other things of this kind, other similar things.*—**in caeteris,** *in other things, in other respects.* —**inter caetera,** *among other things, among others.*—**caeteris paribus,** *other things being e-qual.*

Cain, *indecl. m., Cain,* first son of Adam and Eve.

Caiphas, ae, *m., Caiphas,* the seventy-first high priest of the Jews. He followed the teaching of the Saducaei and succeeded Simon, the son of Camith, in the priesthood. He was most hostile to Jesus, whose death he occasioned by furnishing false witnesses.

Caius, i, *m., Caius.*—(1) a Roman jurist quoted in the *Corpus Juris Canonici.* Cf. SS. Q. 57. Art. 3. —(2) a monk unknown except for four letters addressed to him by Dionysius, the Pseudo-Aeropagite. These letters are, for the most part, answers to questions concerning Catholic doctrine. They also contain practical directions and exhortations concerning conduct towards infidels, regarding mildness and humility, and on other points.

calamus, i, *m., a branch, the arm* or *branch of a candelabrum.*

calcaneum, i, *n., the heel.*

calceamentum, i, *n., a covering for the foot, a shoe.*

calceo, are, avi, atum, 1, *v. a., to* put on shoes.

calceus, i, *m., a shoe, half-boot.*— **ars calceorum,** *the art of making shoes, shoemaking.*

calco, are, avi, atum, 1, *v. a., to tread upon something, tread under foot.*

calculo, are, 1, *v. a., to calculate, compute, reckon.*

calculus, i, *m., a live coal.*

calefacio, ere, feci, factum, 3, *v. a.*, (1) *to make warm* or *hot, warm, heat,* opposite of *infrigido,* (2) *warm spiritually.*

calefactibilis, e, *adj., capable of being warmed* or *made hot.*

calefactibilitas, atis, *f., an inherent quality of things which renders them receptive of heat, capability of being warmed* or *heated.*

calefactio, onis, *f., a warming, heating,* the opposite of *infrigidatio.*

calefactivus, a, um, *adj., calefacient, causing heat* or *warmth.*

calesco, ere, 3, *v. inch. n., to grow warm* or *hot,* the opposite of *frigesco.*

calidas, atis, *f., warmth, heat,* the opposite of *frigiditas.*

calidus, a, um, *adj., hot, warm,* opposite of *frigidus.*—**calidum,** i, *n., the hot, heat.*

caliga, ae, *f., a shoe of leather, a half-boot, a soldier's boot.*

caliginosus, a, um, *adj., full of mist, covered with mist, dark, obscure, gloomy.*

caligo, inis, *f., a thick atmosphere, a mist, vapor, fog, darkness, obscurity.*

calix, icis, *m.,* (1) *cup, goblet, drinking-vessel, chalice,* (2) *Christ's passion.*

calor, oris, *m.,* (1) *warmth, heat, glow,* opposite of *frigus,* (2) *heat of passion,* (3) *heat of fever.*

Calosyrius, ii, *m., Calosyrius,* Cyril of Alexandria in his eighty-third letter to Calosyrius censures the opinion of certain Egyptian monks who maintained that God had a human body, since man was made to the image of God.

calumnia, ae, *f., a false accusation, malicious charge, false* or *malicious information.*

calumniator, oris, *m., a pettifogger, calumniator.*

calumnior, ari, atus, 1, *v. dep. act., to depreciate, misrepresent, calumniate, blame unjustly.*

calumniose, *adv.,* see *calumniosus.*

calumniosus, a, um, *adj., full of tricks* or *artifices, calumnious.*— **calumniose,** *adv., artfully, by trickery, calumniously.*

calvaria, ae, *f.,* (1) *the skull of a man,* (2) *the place where the condemned are beheaded,* (3) *Calvary,* the place where Jesus Christ was crucified.

cambium, ii, *n., humidity,* in the course of transformation.

camelus, i, *m., a camel.*

caminus, i, *m., furnace.*

campsorius, a, um, *adj., referring to exchange of money.* On **communicatio campsoria,** see *communicatio* under 3; on **commutatio campsoria,** see *commutatio* under 2.

campus, i, *m., an even, flat place, a plain field.*

candela, ae, *f., a light made of wax* or *tallow, wax light, tallow-candle, taper.*

candelabrum, i, *n., a candlestick, branched candlestick, chandelier, candelabrum.*

candens, entis, *P. a., glowing with heat, glowing hot.*

candidus, a, um, *adj., white, clear, bright,* opposite of *niger.*

candor, oris, *m.,* (1) *clearness, radiance, brightness, brilliancy, splendor,* (2) *candor, purity, integrity, sincerity.*

caninus, a, um, *adj., of* or *pertaining to a dog, canine.*

canis, is, *comm.,* (1) *a dog,* (2) *a notorious sinner.*

canistrum, i, *n., a basket woven from reeds, a bread-basket, a canister.*

cano, ere, cecini, cantum, 3, *v. n., to sing, sound, play,* synonym of *canto.*

canon, onis, *m.,* (1) *rule, standard of conduct, regulation, precept,* (2) *summary, record, inventory.* —Kinds of *canon* in this (1) sense are: (a), **canon Apostolorum seu apostolicus,** *precept of the Apostles.* —(b), **canon missae,** *the unchangeable part of Holy Mass.* —(c), **canon sacer,** *holy* or *church precept.*

canonicatus, us, *m., a canonry.*

canonicus, a, um, *adj.,* (1) *according to a precept of the Church, belonging to it, canonical,* (2) *belonging to the summary* or *record of Holy Scripture, canonical.* —On **electio canonica,** see *electio* under 1; on **ius canonicum,** see *ius* under 1.—On **liber canonicus,** see *liber* under 3; on **scriptura canonica,** see *scriptura* under 2.—**Canonica** sc. **epistula,** *a letter placed in the canon of sacred scripture.* —**canonicus,** i, *m., a canon, canonry,*

prebendary. —Kinds of *canonicus* in this (2) sense are: **canonicus regularis** and **canonicus simplex,** *the regular* and *the simple canon.*

canorus, a, um, *adj., melodious, harmonious.*

canticum, i, *n.,* (1) *a song,* (2) *Canticum Canticorum, Song of Songs, the Canticles.*

canto, are, avi, atum, 1, *v. n.* and *a., to sound, sing, play,* synonym of *cano.*

cantor, oris, *m., a singer.*

Cantuariensis, e, *adj., of Canterbury. Thomas Cantuariensis, Thomas of Canterbury,* Thomas Becket, saint and martyr, Archbishop of Canterbury, born at London December 21, 1118 (?), died at Canterbury, December 29, 1170.

cantus, us, *m., song, singing.*

capacitas, atis, *f., mental capacity, admissibility, susceptibility.*

capax, acis, *adj., capacious, susceptible, fit for.*

capella, ae, *f., a chapel.*

capesso, ere, ivi, itum, 3, *v. a., to lay hold of with the mind, comprehend, understand.*

Capharnaum, i, *n., Capharnaum,* a maritime city on the shore of the Sea of Galilee. And leaving the city Nazareth, he came and dwelt in Capharnaum on the sea coast, in the borders of Zabulon and of Nephthalim, Matt. 4. 13.

capillus, i, *m., the hair of the head, hair,* synonym of *pilus.*

capio, ere, cepi, captum, 3, *v. a.*, to take in hand, take hold of, lay hold of, take, seize, understand.

capitalis, e, *adj.*, (1) *concerning the head*, (2) *principal, acting in the manner of the head*, (3) *like the principal part.*—On **peccatum capitale**, see *peccatum* under 2; on **poena capitalis**, see *poena;* on **sententia capitalis**, see *sententia* under 2. On **peccatum capitale**, see *peccatum* under 2; on **vitium capitale**, see *vitium* under 2.

capitatus, a, um, *adj.*, *having a head*.

capitulatim, *adj.*, *by heads, summarily*. Aristotelian *en kephalaio* (De Anim. 3. 10. 433 b. 21), synonym of *summarie* and *summatim*, not in the S.T.

capitulum, i, *n.*, (1) *chief section, principal division*, (2) *a summarizing chapter*, (3) *general meeting of a body, a chapter*.

cappatus, a, um, *adj.*, *covered with a cloak, cloaked*.

capra, ae, *f.*, a *she-goat*.

caprea, ae, *f.*, *a kind of wild she-goat, a roe*.

caprinus, a, um, *adj.*, *of* or *pertaining to goats*.

captio, onis, *f.*, (1) *a catching, seizing*, (2) *apprehension*.

captiose, *adv.*, *captiously, insidiously*.

captivitas, atis, *f.*, *captivity, bondage*.

captivo, are, 1, *v. a.*, *to take captive*.

captivus, a, um, *adj.*, *captive, prisoner*.

capto, are, avi, atum, 1, *v. freq. act*, *to strive after, try* or *seek to obtain*.

captus, us, *m.*, *a taking, seizing*.

Capuanus, a, um, *adj.*, *of Capua*.

caput, itis, *n.*, *head*, in the literal and figurative sense of the word. On **gratia capitis**, see *gratia* under 2; on **poena capitis**, see *poena.*—Kinds of caput are: (a), **caput angelorum**, *the head of angels.*—(b), **caput Christi**, *the head of Christ.*—(c), **caput corporis naturalis seu naturale** and **corpus in spiritualibus**, *the head of a natural body* or *the natural head* and *the head in spiritual things* or *the spiritual head.*— (d), **caput ecclesiae**, *the head of the Church.*—(e), **caput hominum**, *the head of men* or *mankind.*—(f), **caput mulieris**, *the head of a woman.*—(g), **caput in spiritualibus**, see *caput corporis naturalis.*—(h), **caput naturale**, see *caput corporis naturalis.*—(i), **caput omnium malorum**, *the head of all evil*.

carbo, onis, *f.*, *coal, charcoal*.

carcer, eris, *m.*, *a prison, jail*.

cardinalis, e, *adj.*, *of* or *pertaining to a door-hinge, that on which something turns* or *depends, principal, chief*. On **virtus cardinalis**, see *virtus* under 5.

cardo, inis, *m.*, *the hinge of a door*.

carentia, ae, *f.*, *a lack* or *want of something, deprivation, forfei-*

ture, something lost to its owner by way of penalty, a synonym of *privatio,* constr. with the *gen.*

careo, ere, ui, itum, 2, *v. n., to be cut off from, be without, want, lack,* constr. regularly with *abl.*

carisia, ae, *f., (caristia, charistia), high market value.*

caritas, atis, *f.,* see *charitas.*

carmen, inis, *n., a song.*

carnalis, e, *adj.,* (1) *carnal* in the proper sense of the word, the opposite of *spiritualis,* (2) *carnal* in the improper sense of the word, i.e., referring or relating to the flesh, influenced or controlled by the flesh, following sensual appetite, also the opposite of *spiritualis.*—On **actus carnalis,** see *actus,* under 1; on **adulterium carnale,** see *adulterium* under 2; on **amor carnalis,** see *amor* under 1; on **appetitus carnalis,** see *appetitus* under 2; on **concupiscentia carnalis,** see *concupiscentia* under 2; on **corpus carnale,** see *corpus;* on **corruptio carnalis,** see *corruptio* under 3; on **delectatio carnalis,** see *delectatio;* on **desiderium carnale,** see *desiderium* under 1; on **generatio carnalis,** see *generatio* under 1; on **matrimonium carnale,** see *matrimonium;* on **mors carnalis,** see *mors;* on **nativitas carnalis,** see *nativitas;* on **observantia carnalis,** see *observantia* under 4; on **opus carnale,** see *opus* under 4; on **pater carnalis,** see *pater;* on **peccatum car-**

nale, see *peccatum* under 2; on **propinquitas carnalis,** see *propinquitas* under 2; on **sacrificium carnale,** see *sacrificium;* on **servitus carnalis,** see *servitus* under 1; on **vitium carnale,** see *vitium* under 2.—On **affectio carnalis,** see *affectio;* on **collatio carnalis,** see *collatio* under 3; on **conversatio carnalis,** see *conversatio* under 2; on **homo carnalis,** see *homo;* on **intentio carnalis,** see *intentio* under 2; on **opus carnale,** see *opus* under 4.—**carnaliter,** *adv., carnally.*

carnalitas, atis, *f., carnality, any carnal propensity* or *act,* the opposite of *spiritualitas.*

carnaliter, *adv.,* see *carnalis.*

carneus, a, um, *adj., of flesh, carnal,* the opposite of *spiritalis* and *spiritualis.*

carnifex, ficis, *m., an executioner.*

caro, carnis, *f.,* (1) *flesh* in the proper sense of the word, the opposite of *spiritus,* (2) *flesh* in the improper sense of the word, *carnal inclination, carnal disposition* of man, also the opposite of *spiritus.*—On **appetitus carnis,** see *appetitus* under 2; on **bonum carnis,** see *bonus* under 3; on **concupiscentia carnis,** see *concupiscentia* under 2; on **corruptio carnis,** see *corruptio* under 3; on **delectabile carnis,** see *delectabilis;* on **delectatio carnis,** see *delectatio;* on **desiderium carnis,** see *desiderium* under 1; on **carni esse,** see *esse;* on **incorruptio carnis,** see *incorruptio* under 2; on integritas carnis, see *integritas;* on lex carnis, see *lex* under 1; on oculus carnis, see *oculus;* on opus carnis, see *opus* under 4; on passio carnis, see *passio* under 2; on resurrectio carnis, see *resurrectio;* on sensus carnis, *sensus* under 2; on voluptas carnis, see *voluptas.*—The following kinds of *caro* belong here: (a), caro bestialis, *the flesh of beasts.* —(b), caro humana, *human flesh.* —(c), caro immortalis and caro mortalis, *immortal* and *mortal flesh.*—(d), caro impassibilis and caro passibilis, *flesh incapable of suffering* and *flesh capable of suffering.*—(e), caro mortalis, see *caro immortalis.*—(f), caro passibilis, see *caro impassibilis.* —(g), caro phantastica and caro vera, *imaginary flesh* and *true flesh.*—(h), caro vera, see *caro phantastica.*—stimulus carnis, *the sting of the flesh* or *impure carnal desire.* On amor carnis, see *amor* under 1; on concupiscentia carnis, see *concupiscentia* under 2; on opus carnis, see *opus* under 4; on prudentia carnis, see *prudentia* under 1; on tentatio carnis, see *tentatio* under 2.

Carolus, i, *m., Charles,* here *Charlemagne,* King of the Franks, first sovereign of the Christian Empire of the West; born April 2, 742; died at Aachen, January, 28, 814. The place of his birth (whether Aachen or Liege) has never been fully ascertained, while the traditional date has been set a year or more later by recent writers.

carpentarius, ii, *m., a carpenter.*

carpo, ere, psi, ptum, 3, *to censure, dispraise, find fault with.*

cartallus, i, *m., a basket.*

Carthaginiensis, e, *adj. Carthaginian.*

carus, a, um, *adj.,* (1) *dear, precious, esteemed, valued,* (2) *dear, costly, at a high price,* the opposite of *vilis.*—cari, orum, *m., loved ones.*—care, *adv., dearly, at a high price.*

caseus, i, *m., cheese.*

Cassianus, i, *m., Ioannes Cassianus, John Cassian,* a monk and ascetic writer of Southern Gaul and the first to introduce the rules of Eastern monasticism into the West; born probably in Provence about 360; died about 435, probably near Marseilles. His two principal works deal with the cenobitic life and the principal or deadly sins. They are entitled "De institutis coenobiorum et de octo principalium vitiorum remediis libri XII", and "Collationes XXIV". Cassian himself describes the relation between the two works, saying: "These books, i.e., the Institutes, are mainly taken up with what belongs to the outer man and the customs of the coenobia, the others, i.e., the *Collationes* or Conferences, deal rather with the training of the inner man and the perfection of the heart."

St. Thomas refers to both works in the S.T.

Cassiodorus, i, *m., Flavius Magnus Aurelius Cassiodorus Senator,* the last being a surname; a Roman writer, statesman, and monk, born about 490; died about 583. During his public career Cassiodorus tried to reconcile two races, the Goths and the Romans; in his religous retreat he labored with greater success to harmonize the culture of the ancient with that of the Christian world. There are references in the S.T. to his commentaries (*complexiones*) on the Psalms.

Cassius, i, *m., Cassius,* a contributor to the *Digestae* or *Pandecta* of the *Corpus Iuris Civilis,* of Justinian I.

casso, are, avi, atum, 1, *v. a., to frustrate, bring to naught, make void.*

cassus, a, um, *adj., empty, void, useless, fruitless.*

castellum, i, *n., Castellum Emmaus,* a titular see in Palaestrina Prima, suffragan of Caesarea. It is mentioned for the first time in 166-165 B.C. when Judas Machabeus defeated there the army of Gorgias. When the Crusaders entered Emmaus in 1099 on their way to Jerusalem, the village was already known as Castellum Emmaus.

castigatio, onis, *f., a correction, chastising, punishment.*

castigo, are, avi, atum, 1, *v. a., to correct, chastise, punish, blame, reprove, censure.*

castitas, atis, *f.,* (1) *purity* in the general sense of the word, (2) *purity* in the narrow and particular sense of the word, *chastity,* the opposite of *luxuria.*—Kinds of *castitas* in the general sense of the word are: **castitas proprie accepta** and **castitas metaphorice accepta sive spiritualis,** *chastity properly understood* and *chastity understood metaphorically* or *spiritual chastity.* On the difference between *castitas* and *continentia,* see *continentia* under 4. On **consilium perpetuae castitatis,** see *consilium* under 2. As kinds of *castitas* in this (2) sense are: (a), **castitas communis,** *the general* or *customary purity,* the opposite of *castitas particularis,* i.e., special purity as it is practiced by a virgin.—(b), **castitas coniugalis, castitas virginalis,** and **castitas vidualis,** *marital purity, virginal purity,* and *the purity of widowhood.*—(c), **castitas perfecta,** *perfect purity.*—(d), **castitas vera,** *true purity.*—(e), **castitas vidualis,** see *castitas coniugalis.*—(f), **castitas virginalis,** see *castitas coniugalis.*

castratura, ae, *f., emasculation, castration.*

castro, are, avi, atum, 1, *v. a., to deprive of generative power, emasculate.*

castrum, i, *n.,* (1) *any fortified place, a fort, castle,* (2) *several* soldiers' tents situated together, a military camp, encampment.

castus, a, um, *adj.,* (1) *morally pure, unpolluted, spotless,* (2) *pious, holy, sacred.*—**caste,** *adv., chastely, uprightly.*

casualis, e, *adj., accidental, fortuitous, casual,* in the wider and narrower sense of the word. Cf. *casus.* In the wider sense *casualis* is the synonym of *fortuitus* and the opposite of *provisus* and *per se volitus seu intentus.*—**casualis,** in the narrower sense of the word is the opposite of *fortuitus.* See *fortuitus.* On the difference between *casualis* and *fortuitus* in the narrower sense of the word see *fortuna* under 1. On **actus casualis,** see *actus* under 1; on **effectus casualis,** see *effectus;* on **generatio casualis,** see *generatio* under 1; on **res casualis,** see *res.*—**casualiter,** *adv., accidentally,* a synonym of *fortuito,* also the opposite of it, (see above), also the opposite of *essentialiter.*

casualiter, *adv.,* see *casualis.*

casula, ae, *f., a chasuble.*

Casulanus, i, *m., Casulanus,* a co-presbyter of Saint Augustine to whom the latter addresses a letter which St. Thomas quotes in the S.T.

casus, us, *m.,* (1) *fall, downfall,* (fig.), (2) *occurrence, happening, case, instance,* (3) *chance* in the wider and narrower sense of the word, Aristotle's *automaton,* synonym of *per se vanum;* in the wider sense a synonym also of *fortuna* and signifies each particular cause which produces something toward which it was not directed and so is only incidentally connected with it in operation and effect, and occurs only in rare cases; in its narrower sense *casus* is the opposite of *fortuna* (see under *fortuna*) and signifies blind chance, i.e., an irrational particular cause which produces something toward which it was not inclined by nature and therefore is only incidentally related to its operation and effect and also occurs only in rare cases, (4) *misfortune, mishap,* (5) *case* in the grammatical sense, *case* and *form* in declension and inflexion, (6) *falling away; separation,* (7) *falling away from God, falling into sin.*—On **aequivocus a casu sive per casum,** see *aequivocus* under 1; on **agere a casu,** see *agere* under 1; on **fieri a casu,** see *fieri;* on **generatio a casu,** see *generatio* under 1.—Kinds of *casus* in this (5) sense are: (a), **casus nominis,** and **casus verbi,** *case of a noun* and *form of a verb.*—(b), **casus obliquus** and **casus rectus,** *the oblique* or *dependent case* and *the upright* or *independent case.*—(c), **casus rectus,** see *casus obliquus.*—(d), **casus verbi,** see *casus nominis.*

catalogus, i, *m., a list of names, catalogue.*

Cataphrygae, arum, *m., the Cata-phrygians,* a sect of Montanists, so called because it originated in Phrygia.

cataracta, ae, *f., a flood-gate.*

catechismus, i, *m., religious in-struction, a book of elementary Christian instruction, catechism.*

catechizatio, onis, *f., a systematic oral religious instruction, cate-chization.*

catechizo, are, 1, *v. a., to catechize, instruct in religion.*

catechumenus, i, *m.,* and a, ae, *f., a catechumen,* one who is re-ceiving elementary instruction in religion.

categorematice, *adv.,* see *categore-maticus.*

categorematicus, a, um, *adj., cate-gorical,* i.e., *related to a category,* (see *praedicamentum*), the oppo-site of *syncategorematicus.* On **dictio categorematica,** see *dictio* under 2.—**categorematice,** *adv., in a categorical* or *positive man-ner, in the sense of a category, categorically,* (see *praedicamen-tum* under 2), the opposite of *syncategorematice.* On **sumere categorematice,** see *sumere* un-der 3.

categoria, ae, *f., a predicament, category* or *class of predicables.*

categoricus, a, um, *adj.,* (1) *declar-ing, declarative, declaring un-conditionally, categorical,* a syn-onym of *praedicativus,* the op-posite of *condicionalis,* (2) *de-claring affirmatively, affirming,* a synonym of *praedicativus,* the

opposite of *negativus.*—On **enun-tiatio categorica,** see *enuntiatio* under 2; on **propositio catego-rica,** see *propositio* under 2; on **syllogismus categoricus,** see *syl-logismus.*—**categorica,** sc. *enun-tiatio* or *propositio, the cate-gorical statement,* i.e. that state-ment in which an idea is implic-itly declared by another. On **de-monstratio categorica,** see *de-monstratio* under 3.

catena, ae, *f., a chain* or *closely-linked series,* a series of excerpts especially from the works of the Church Fathers intended to clear up some points of Scrip-tural exegesis.

cathedra, ae, *f., a chair, stool, arm-chair,* used in the proper and improper sense of the word.— Kinds of *cathedra* are: (a), **ca-thedra episcopalis seu pontifi-calis,** *the episcopal chair.*—(b), **cathedra magistralis,** *the profes-sorial chair.*—(c), **cathedra ponti-ficalis,** *the pontifical chair.*

catholice, *adv.,* see *catholicus.*

catholicus, a, um, *adj., orthodox, catholic.*—**catholicus,** i, *m., a Catholic.*—**catholice,** *adv., in the Catholic way, according to the Catholic rite.*

Catilina, ae, *m.* L. *Sergius Catilina, Catiline,* a Roman who was notorious for several times at-tempting insurrections against his country.

Catilinarius, a, um, *adj., Catilina-rian, pertaining to Catiline.*

Cato, onis, *m.*, *Cato,* a cognomen
of several celebrated Romans,
(1) *M. Porcius Cato,* the elder,
distinguished as a rigid judge
of morals; hence called *Censo-*
rius, whose most celebrated
works were the *Origines* and *De*
Re Rustica, (2) *M. Porcius Cato,*
the younger, descendant of the
elder, the enemy of Caesar, who
committed suicide after the battle of Pharsalia, at Utica; hence
the appellation Uticensis, (3)
Dionysius Cato, the author of a
work of unknown date entitled
De Moribus ad Filium, frequently quoted by Chaucer and used
as a manual in the schools of the
Middle Ages.

caulae, arum, *f., a sheep-fold.*

causa, ae, *f., cause* in the wider
sense of the word, the *aitia*
or *aition* of Aristotle, i.e., that
which contributes in a positive
manner to the existence of another, a wide synonym of *prin-*
cipium, the opposite both of
privatio and *effectus,* (2) *oper-*
ating or *producing cause,* (3)
cause or purpose, motive of ac-
tion, reason, a synonym of *ratio,*
(4) *reason in the logical sense of*
the word, (5) *thing, affair,* a synonym of *res,* (6) *affair* in the judicial sense, *affair of the law,*
legal affair, lawsuit.—On the difference between *causa, elemen-*
tum, and *principium,* see *elemen-*
tum and *principium.* On **debitum**
causae finalis et formalis, see
debitus under 1; on **ordo causae,**

causae formalis et materialis,
see *ordo* under 1; on **origo cau-**
sae finalis, see *origo;* on **princi-**
pium secundum causas singulas,
see *principium;* on **ratio causae**
efficientis, finalis et formalis, see
ratio under 4.—Kinds of *causa* in
this (1) sense are: (a), **causa ac-**
tiva seu agens seu cogens seu
effectiva seu efficax seu efficiens
seu movens seu motiva seu ori-
ginans, *the effective* or *compel-*
ling cause or *the producing* or
inducing cause, or *that which*
gives a start; in other words,
that principle which by a so-
called action bestows existence
upon something substantially different from itself.—(b), **causa**
agens, see *causa activa.*—(c),
causa cogens, see *causa activa.*—
(d), **causa communis seu univer-**
salis and **causa propria,** *the gen-*
eral or *universal cause* and *the*
individual or *particular cause.*—
(e), **causa effectiva seu efficax**
seu efficiens, see *causa activa.*—
(f), **causa exemplaris sive forma-**
lis exemplaris, *the exemplary*
cause which consists in a form
to be imitated exteriorly.—(g),
causa extrinseca and **causa in-**
trinseca, *the exterior cause* or
the cause opposite to thing ex-
teriorly produced, and *the inner*
cause or *the cause which be-*
longs to the substance of the
thing produced.—(h), **causa fina-**
lis, *the cause of an end* or *aim,*
final cause. Cf. *finis.*—(i), **causa**
formalis, *the forming* or *shaping*

cause, that principle belonging to the substance of a thing by which it attains and possesses the being and existence peculiar to it. Cf. *principium formale.—* (j), causa **formalis exemplaris,** see *causa exemplaris.—*(k), **causa formalis extra rem** and **causa formalis inhaerens sive intrinseca,** *the forming* or *shaping cause of a thing which lies outside itself,* (cf. *causa exemplaris* above), *the inherent* or *the inner cause of the thing.—*(l), **causa formalis inhaerens,** see *causa formalis extra rem.—*(m), **causa formalis intrinseca,** see *causa formalis extra rem.—*(n), **causa intrinseca,** see *causa extrinseca.* —(o), **causa materialis,** *the material cause* or *the cause that gives matter to a thing;* in other words that principle from which a thing comes or has come into being. Cf. *materia* and *principium materiale.—*(p), **causa motiva,** see *causa activa.—*(q), **causa movens,** see *causa activa.—*(r), **causa originans,** see *causa activa.* —(s), **causa movens directe** and **causa movens indirecte,** *the directly* and *indirectly moving cause.—*(t), **causa posterior** and **causa prior,** *the later* and *the earlier cause.—*(u), **causa prior,** see *causa posterior.—*(v), **causa propria,** see *causa communis.—* (w), **causa universalis,** see *causa communis.—*On **appropriare per causam,** see *appropriare* under 2; on **bonum ex causa,** see *bonus*

under 2; on **cognitio per causam,** see *cognitio* under 2; on **cognoscere ex causa seu per causam,** see *cognoscere* under 2; on **defectus causae,** see *defectus* under 2; on **locus a causa,** see *locus* under 4; on **malum causae,** see *malus* under 2; on **praedicare per causam,** see *praedicare* under 2; on **praedicatio per causam,** see *praedicatio* under 2; on **spirituale per causam,** see *spiritualis* under 3; on **velle in causam,** see *velle* under 1; on **verum in causam,** see *verus* under 1; on **voluntarium secundum causam,** see *voluntarius* under 3.—Kinds of *causa* in this (2) sense are: (a), **causa accidentalis,** *the unessential* or *secondary cause.—*(b), **causa actualis seu in actu** and **causa in potentia,** *the actually producing cause (operans in actu)* and *the cause able to produce (potens operari)* or *the cause in the state of reality* and *that in the state of potentiality.* —(c), **causa adiuvans seu coadiuvans, causa consilians, causa praeparans seu disponens seu dispositiva** and **causa perficiens seu perfectiva seu consummativa,** *the helping* or *assisting cause, the advising cause, the preparing cause, the consummating* or *completing cause.—*(d), **causa aequivoca sive aequivoce agens, causa analogice agens** and **causa univoce sive univoce agens,** *the homonymous, the analogous,* and *the synonymous cause,* (cf. *ana-*

logus and *synonymous*), or *the cause which produces an effect unlike it, that which produces a relatively like effect,* and *that which produces a similar effect.* —(e), **causa aequivoce agens,** see *causa aequivoca.*—(f), **causa altissima,** *the highest cause.*—(g), **causa altissima in aliquo genere** and **causa altissima simpliciter,** *the highest cause in any kind of causes* and *the simply* or *absolutely highest cause.*—(h), **causa altissima simpliciter,** see *causa altissima in aliquo genere.*—(i), **causa animalis** and **causa intellectualis,** *the sensitive cause* or *the cause endowed with senses* and *the intellectual or rational cause.*—(j), **causa appropriata seu propria seu particularis seu singularis** and **causa communis seu universalis,** *the individual* or *particular* or *single cause* and *the general* or *universal cause.*—(k), **causa coadiuvans,** see *causa adiuvans.*—(l), **causa communis,** see *causa appropriata.*—(m), **causa completa** and **causa incompleta seu imperfecta,** *the complete* or *perfect cause* and *the incomplete* or *imperfect cause.*—(n), **causa composita** and **causa simplex,** *the composite cause* and *the simple cause.*—(o), **causa conclusionis,** *the cause of a conclusion* or *of a final sentence.*—(p), **causa concurrens,** *the concurring* or *cooperating cause.*—(q), **causa consilians,** see *causa adiuvans.*—(r), **causa conspecialis,** *the cause*

that belongs to another of the same kind.—(s), **causa consubstantialis,** *the cause of the same substance as that of the effect.*—(t), **causa consummativa,** see *causa adiuvans.*—(u), **causa contingens** and **causa necessaria,** *the cause not operating of necessity* and *that operating of necessity.*—(v), **causa corporalis** and **causa spiritualis,** *the corporal* and *the spiritual cause.*—(w), **causa creatrix sive factrix** and **causa gubernativa,** *the creative* or *producing cause* and *the leading* or *governing cause.*—(x), **causa defectibilis** and **causa defectiva sive deficiens,** *the defective* and *the lacking cause.*—(y), **causa defectiva seu deficiens,** see *causa defectibilis.*—(z), **causa determinata,** and **causa indeterminata,** *the determined* and *the undetermined cause.*—(a²), **causa directiva seu directiva dicta** and **causa indirectiva seu indirecte vel occasionaliter dicta,** *the direct* and *the indirect* or *incidental cause;* in other words, the cause which produces a definite effect aiming directly at it, or the cause which has a share in producing the effect in so far as it prepares the effect or establishes the necessary condition for it production. —(b²), **causa directe dicta,** see *causa directe.*—(c²), **causa disponens,** see *causa adiuvans.*—(d²), **causa dispositiva,** see *causa adiuvans.*—(e²), **causa essendi** and **causa fiendi seu generationis,** *the* *cause of being* and *the cause of becoming* or *coming into existence.*—(f^2), causa essendi hoc and causa essendi simpliciter, *the cause of being such and such, the cause of simply* or *absolutely being.*—(g^2), causa essendi simpliciter, see *causa essendi hoc.*—(h^2), causa exterior seu extrinseca and causa interior, *the exterior* and *the interior cause* or *the cause influencing a thing from the outside* and *the cause active within itself.* Cf. *causa extrinseca* above under (1).—(i^2), causa extrinseca, see *causa exterior* . . . —(j^2), causa factrix, see *causa creatrix.*—(k^2), causa fatalis, *the active cause as blind* and *unavoidable fate.*—(l^2), causa fiendi, see *causa essendi.*—(m^2), causa fortuita, *the cause operating in the manner of an accident.*—(n^2), causa generans prohibens and causa removens prohibens, *the cause which prepares an obstacle* and *the cause which removes an obstacle,* thereby allowing an effect to proceed.—(o^2), causa generationis, see *causa essendi.*—(p^2), causa gubernativa, see *causa creatrix.*—(q^2), causa immediata and causa mediata, *the immediate* and *the mediate cause.*—(r^2), causa immobilis and causa transmutabilis seu variabilis, *the fixed* or *unchangeable cause* and *the transient* or *changeable cause.*—(s^2), causa impediens and causa impedita, *the impending* and *the impeded cause.*—(t^2), causa im-

pedita, see *causa impediens.*—(u^2), causa imperfecta, see *causa completa.*—(v^2), causa in actu, see *causa actualis.*—(w^2), causa incompleta, see *causa completa.*—(x^2), causa indeterminata, see *causa determinata.*—(y^2), causa indirecta, see *causa directa.*—(z^2), causa indirecte dicta, see *causa directa.*—(a^3), causa inferens, *the cause that draws an inference* or *that admits an inference.*—(b^3), causa inferior, causa superior and causa suprema, *the subordinated* or *lower cause, the superior* or *higher* and *the highest cause.*—(c^3), causa influens, *the cause which affects* or *exercises influence.*—(d^3), causa in potentia, see *causa actualis.*—(e^3), causa instrumentalis seu secundaria and causa principalis seu primaria, *the instrumental* or *secondary cause* and *the principal* or *primary cause.*—(f^3), causa intellectualis, see *causa animalis.*—(g^3), causa interior, see *causa exterior.*—(h^3), causa intermedia seu media, *the middle cause* or *the cause that stands between,* so called because it stands between the *causa prima seu suprema* and *the effectus.*—(i^3), causa iustificans, *the vindicating* or *justifying cause.*—(j^3), causa media, see *causa intermedia.*—(k^3), causa mediata, see *causa immediata.*—(l^3), causa meritoria, *the cause which merits something.*—(m^3), causa naturae alicuius in hoc and causa naturae alicuius simpliciter, *the cause of a nature* and *essence as it is realized in this* or *that individual,* and *the simple* or *absolute cause of a nature* and *essence.*—(n³), **causa naturae alicuius simpliciter,** see *causa naturae alicuius in hoc.*—(o³), **causa naturalis causa non naturalis** and **causa praeternaturalis seu violenta,** *the natural cause, the unnatural cause, the cause against nature* or *violent cause.*—(p³), **causa naturalis seu per naturam seu naturaliter agens** and **causa voluntaria seu per voluntatem,** *the natural cause* and *the cause of the will,* in other words, the cause which is directed by the blind force of nature and that which is directed by the free will.—(q³), **causa naturaliter agens,** see *causa naturalis.*—(r³), **causa necessaria,** see *causa contingens.*—(s³), **causa non naturalis,** see *causa naturalis.*—(t³), **causa occasionaliter dicta,** see *causa directa.*—(u³), **causa particularis,** see *causa appropriata.*—(v³), **causa per accidens seu secundum accidens** and **causa per se,** *the cause which is active because of something other than itself according to its nature* and *essence.*—(w³), **causa per aliud seu per alterum** and **causa per se,** *the cause operating through something else* or *by virtue of something else* and *that active through itself* or *through its own power.* Cf. *causa per accidens.*—(x³), **causa per alterum,** see *causa per aliud.*—(y³), **causa per naturam,** see *causa naturalis.*—(z³), **causa perfectiva,** see *causa adiuvans.*—(a⁴), **causa perficiens,** see *causa adiuvans.*—(b⁴), **causa per se,** see *causa per accidens* and *causa per aliud.*—(c⁴), **causa per se entis inquantum huiusmodi** and **causa per se huius entis,** *the cause active by itself of being as such* and *the cause active by itself of this* or *that being.*—(d⁴), **causa per se huius entis,** see *causa per se entis inquantum huiusmodi.*—(e⁴), **causa per se infinita,** *the interminable cause active by itself* or *according to its own nature* and *essence.*—(f⁴), **causa per voluntatem,** see *causa naturalis.*—(g⁴), **causa posterior** and **causa prior,** *the later* and *the earlier cause.*—(h⁴), **causa praeparans,** see *causa adiuvans.*—(i⁴), **causa praeternaturalis,** see *causa naturalis.*—(j⁴), **causa prima** and **causa secunda,** *the first cause by which God is usually to be understood, but at times a produced cause also,* and *the second cause which always represents something created.*—(k⁴), **causa primaria,** see *causa instrumentalis.*—(l⁴), **causa primordialis,** *the primitive cause.*—(m⁴), **causa principalis,** see *causa instrumentalis.*—(n⁴), **causa prior,** see *causa posterior.*—(o⁴), **causa privans,** *the incapacitating cause, the cause that effects a deficiency.*—(p⁴), **causa propria,** see *causa appropriata.*—(q⁴), **causa pro-**

pinqua seu proxima and **causa remota**, *the near* or *next cause* and *the remote cause considered from its effects.*—(r⁴), **causa regitiva**, *the ruling cause.*—(s⁴), **causa remota**, see *causa proxima.*—(t⁴), **causa removens prohibens**, see *causa generans prohibens.*—(u⁴), **causa sacramentalis**, *the sacramental cause.*—(v⁴), **causa secunda**, see *causa prima.*—(w⁴), **causa secundum accidens**, see *causa per accidens.*—(x⁴), **causa seminalis**, *the germinating cause.*—(y⁴), **causa sensibilis**, *the cause realized by the senses.*—(z⁴), **causa simplex**, see *causa composita.*—(a⁵), **causa sine qua non**, *the cause without which no definite effect takes place;* in other words, the cause necessary for the production of a certain effect.—(b⁵), **causa singularis**, see *causa appropriata.*—(c⁵), **causa spiritualis**, see *causa corporalis.*—(d⁵), **causa sufficiens**, *the cause sufficient for producing an effect,* see *causa sufficiens* under 4.—(e⁵), **causa sui esse**, *cause of one's own being.*—(f⁵), **causa superior**, see *causa inferior.*—(g⁵), **causa suprema**, see *causa inferior.*—(h⁵), **causa temporalis**, *the temporal cause.*—(i⁵), **causa transmutabilis**, see *causa immobilis.*—(j⁵), **causa universalis**, see *causa appropriata.*—(k⁵), **causa universalissima**, *the most universal cause,* i.e., *God.*—(l⁵), **causa universaliter prima**, *the universally* or *the absolutely first cause.*—

(m⁵), **causa univoca**, see *causa aequivoca.*—(n⁵), **causa variabilis**, see *causa immobilis.*—(o⁵), **causa violenta**, see *causa naturalis.*—(p⁵), **causa voluntaria**, see *causa naturalis.*—**ad remotionem causae sequitur remotio effectus** seu **remota causa removetur effectus**, *when the cause is removed, so also is the effect.*—**Augmentata causa augmentatur effectus, seu crescente causa crescit effectus, seu multiplicata causa multiplicatur effectus**, *if the cause is strengthened* or *increased, so also is the effect.*—**Causa est potior causato seu effectu, seu, semper in causa est aliquid nobilius quam in causato**, *the cause is always more excellent than its effect.*—**Causa per se est prior ea, quae est per accidens**, *the cause active of itself* and *according to its nature is prior to that which is active because of something else.*—**Causa, quae per se semper est potior ea, quae est per aliud, seu, semper causa, quae est per se, potior seu prior est ea, quae est per aliud seu alterum**, the translation of the Aristotelian passage, *to gar auto kath' hauto on aition aei proteron tou kath' heteron, the cause active through itself* or *by virtue of itself is prior to that which is active by virtue of something else.*—**Causis debent proportionaliter respondere effectus**, see *effectus.*—**Cessante causa cessat effectus, seu deficiente causa ne-**

cesse est et effectum deficere, *if the cause ceases, so also does the effect.*—Contingit aliquid unum commune habere plures causas, secundum quod convenit diversis, see *effectus.*—Contingit unius effectus accipi quasi plures causas in diversis, see *effectus.*—Crescente causa crescit effectus, see *effectus.*—Deficiente causa necesse est effectum deficere, see above.—Diversorum diversi sunt effectus, see *effectus.*—Effectus assimilatur suae causae, see *effectus.*—Effectus deficiens non procedit nisi a causa deficiente, see *effectus.*—Effectus magis denominatur a causa proxima, quam a causa remota, see *effectus.*—Effectus non potest extendi ultra suam causam, see *effectus.*—Effectus suis causis proportionaliter respondent, see *effectus.*—Idem non est causa sui ipsius, seu, nihil est causa sui ipsius, *nothing can bring forth itself.* Cf. Aristotle's *Metaphysics* 1. 3. 984 a. 21. ff.—Manente causa manet seu non tollitur effectus, *as long as the cause remains active, so also does its effect.*—Multiplicata causa multiplicatur effectus, see above.—Nihil est causa sui ipsius, see above.—Non potest esse nisi una causa unius effectus in omnibus, *there can be but one cause for one effect in all things.*—Omne causatum convertitur in suam causam per desiderium, *every*

thing caused turns to its cause through a desire for it. Cf. *effectus.*—Omnis causa per accidens reducitur ad causam per se, *every cause active for the sake of something else is to be traced to a cause which is active of itself and according to its own nature.*—Omnis effectus est posterior sua causa, see *effectus.*—Omnis effectus in sua causa aliqualiter praeexsistit similitudo, see *effectus.*—Posita causa ponitur effectus, seu, posita causa sufficienti ponitur effectus, seu posita causa sufficienti necesse est effectum poni, seu, posita causa sufficienti nihil aliud requiritur ad effectum inducendum seu nihil aliud videtur esse necessarium ad effectum, *with the establishment of the sufficient cause the effect is equally established, or, besides the establishment of the sufficient cause nothing else seems to be necessary for producing the effect* provided that (1) by cause is understood *causa actualis* or *in actu* (see above), (2) this cause represents a *causa naturalis* (see above), and (3) one keeps in mind that effect which is directly inclined to the cause according to nature.—Quanto aliqua causa est altior, tanto ad plura se extendit eius causalitas, or, quanto aliqua causa est superior, tanto ad plura se extendit in causando, or, quanto est causa superior, tanto eius virtus ad plura se extendit, or, quanto fuerit causa universalior, tanto ad plura se extendit et efficacius producit, *the higher a cause stands in the rank of causes, the greater is its sphere of action* and *the more effective is its strength.*—quidquid est causa causae, est causa causati, or, quidquid est causa causae, oportet esse causam effectus, *whatever is a cause of another cause is the cause of the effect.*—Remota causa removetur effectus, see above, *ad remotionem causae* etc.—Semper causa, quae est per se, potior seu prior est ea, quae est per aliud seu alterum, see above: *causa quae est per se* etc.—Semper in causa est aliquid nobilius, quam in causato, see above: *causa est prior etc.*—Ubi est eadem causa, et idem effectus, *where the cause is the same, the effect also is the same.*—Kinds of *causa* in this (3) sense are: (a), causa allegorica, causa anagogica, and causa moralis, *the allegorical, the anagogical* or *mystical,* and *the moral cause.*—(b), causa anagogica, see *causa allegorica.*—(c), causa congruentiae, *the cause of propriety.*—(d), causa conveniens seu rationibilis, *the fitting* or *reasonable cause.*—(e), causa figuralis seu mystica and causa litteralis, *the figurative, the mystic* and *the literal cause.*—(f), causa litteralis, see *causa figuralis.*—(g), causa moralis, see *causa allegorica.*—(h),

causa mystica, see *causa figuralis.*—(i), causa rationabilis, see *causa conveniens.* Liber (liberum) est, qui (quod) sui causa est, see *liber.*—Kinds of *causa* in this (4) sense are: (a), causa apparentiae, and causa exsistentiae, *the cause of appearance* and *the cause of being* or *the apparent* and *the real cause.*—(b), causa cogens and cause sufficiens, *the compelling cause* (see *causa cogens* under 2) and *the sufficient cause* (see *causa sufficiens* under 2).—(c), causa consequentiae, *the cause of necessary sequence.* —(d), causa exsistentiae, see *causa apparentiae.*—(e), causa sufficiens, see *causa cogens.*—On forum causarum, see *forum* under 1; on genus causarum, see *genus* under 2.—Kinds of *causa* in this (5) sense are: (a), causa affinitatis, *the cause of affinity.*—(b), causa contentiosa, *the disputed case* or *the contested legal case.*—(c), causa divortii, *a case of divorce.*—(d), causa favorabilis, *the favorable legal case.*—(e), causa libertatis, *the case dealing with the status of freedom.*—(f), causa matrimonii, *the matrimonial case.*—(g), causa sanguinis, *the case concerning life* and *death.*—(h), causa separationis matrimonii, *the case of matrimonial separation.*

causalis, e, *adj., causal, causative.* On dictio causalis, see *dictio* under 2; on esse causale, see *esse;* on perfectio causalis, see *perfec-*

tio under 2; on **ratio causalis**, see
ratio under 11.—**causaliter**, *adv.*,
after the manner or *in the sense
of the effective cause, causally,
according to cause*, a synonym
of **secundum causam**. On **appropriare causaliter**, see *appropriare*
under 2; on **dicere causaliter**, see
dicere under 3; on **intellegere
causaliter**, see *intellegere* under
3; on **ponere causaliter**, see *ponere* under 2; on **praedicare causaliter**, see *praedicare* under 2;
on **tenere causaliter**, see *tenere*
under 7.

causalitas, atis, *f.*, (1) *causality,
character, that existing relation
of a thing according to which it
is the cause of something*, (2)
cause, synonym of *causa*—On
modus causalitatis, see *modus*
under 3; on **via causalitatis seu
per causalitatem**, see *via* under
3. Cf. PP. Q. 5. Art. 2 (quarter);
PP. Q. 13. Art. 10; PP. Q. 22.
Art. 3; PP. Q. 45. Art. 6 (quinquies); PP. Q. 45. Art. 7; et passim.

causaliter, *adv.*, see *causalis*.

causativus, a, um, adj., *causing, effecting, bringing forth, causative*.

causo, are, avi, atum, 1, *v. a.*, *to
cause, effect, bring forth an effect.*—Kinds of *causare* are: (a),
causare efficienter, *to bring forth
something in the way of the efficient cause.*—(b), **causare per
accidens** and **causare per se**, *to
bring forth something by virtue
of something else*, and *by virtue
of itself* or *according to its own*

nature.—(c), **causare per se**, see
causare per accidens. On **ignorantia causans**, see *ignorantia* under 1; on **prius in causando**, see
prior under 1.—**Causa est prior
causato**, see *causa* under 2. **Omne causatum convertitur in suam
causam per desiderium**, see *causa* under 2. **Quidquid est causa
causae, est causa causati**, see
causa under 2. **Quod est primum
in causando, ultimum est in causato**, *whatever is the first in the
sphere of action is the last in the
sphere of the effect.* **Semper in
causa est aliquid nobilius, quam
in causato**, see *causa* under 2.

cautela, ae, *f.*, *caution, precaution.*

cautio, onis, *f.*, *wariness, precaution, caution, heedfulness, circumspection.*

cautus, a, um, *adj.*, *careful, circumspect, cautious*, as an adjective
found in the S.T., usually in the
comparative degree.— **caute**, *adv.
cautiously.*

caveo, ere, cavi, cautum, 3, *v. n.*
and *a.*, *to be on one's guard, take
heed, beware, guard against,
avoid*, (1) with *in* and *acc.*, (2)
with *a* or *ab* and *abl.*, (3) with
de and *abl.*, (4) with simple *abl.*,
(5) with *ut* (*ne*) and *subj.*, (6)
with *inf.*, (7) as *act.* with the *acc.*
of person or thing, and in *pass.*

caverna, ae, *f.*, *a cavern, cavity,
hole, grotto.*

cavo, are, avi, atum, 1, *v. a.*, *to
make hollow, hollow out.*

cedo, ere, cessi, cessum, 3, *v. n.*
and *a.*, (1) *to happen, result, turn*

out, (2) *concede, yield to, submit to.*

cedrinus, a, um, *adj., of cedarwood, cedar.*

cedrus, i, *f., the cedar, juniper-tree.*

Celantia, ae, *f., Celantia,* a matron to whom St. Jerome addresses a letter on the dangers arising from flattery.

celatio, onis, *f., a seal, secret,* any instrumentality that keeps something close, secret, or unknown, as the seal of confession.—**celatio confessionis,** *the seal of confession,* synonym of *sigillum confessionis.* See above.

celeber, ebris, ebre, *adj., distinguished, celebrated, famous,* honored by a great assembly, procession, train, etc.—**celebriter,** *adv., frequently.*

celebratio, onis, *f., the act, process, time* or *means of celebrating, celebration, something performed with solemn rites.*

celebritas, atis, *f.,* (1) *the act of celebrating, celebration,* synonym of *celebratio,* (2) *Celebrity, fame, renown.*

celebriter, *adv.,* see *celeber.*

celebro, are, avi, atum, 1, *v. a., to celebrate, solemnize, carry out* or *perform in a formal manner.*—**celebrare missam,** *to celebrate mass.*

celeritas, atis, *f., celerity, speed, swiftness, quickness.*

celerrime, *adv., quickly.*

cellarium, ii, *n., pantry, cellar.*

cellula, ae, *f., a small room* or

space used figuratively here for the womb of the Virgin Mary.

celo, are, avi, atum, 1, *v. a., to conceal, to keep secret.*

celsitudo, inis, *f., celsitude, loftiness, altitude, height, exaltation, dignity.*

Celsus, i, *m., Celsus Iuventus,* son of the jurist Celsus and one of the conspirators against Domitian. His *Digestorum libri* XXXIX are arranged in agreement with Hadrian's code of laws.

celsus, a, um, *adj., extending upward, high, lofty.*

Celtae, arum, *m., the Celts,* a great parent-stock of people in the north of Europe.

censeo, ere, ui, censum, 2, *v. a.,* (1) *to deem, consider, think,* (2) *to allow, maintain, approve,* (3) *to incorporate,* (4) *to enroll.*

censura, ae, *f., severity.*

census, us, *m., a census, riches, property, rating, wealth.*

centenarius, a, um, *adj., consisting of a hundred, centenarian.*

centeni, ae, a, *num. adj., a hundred, a hundred each.*

centesimus, a, um, *num. ordin., a hundredfold.*

centies, *adv., a hundred times.*

centiloquium, ii, *n., the Centiloquium,* often called *karpos* or *Fructus Librorum Suorum,* an astrological work containing a hundred aphorisms by Claudius Ptolemaeus, a Greek mathematician, astronomer, and geographer in Upper Egypt in the second century A.D.

centrum, i, *n., the centre, the middle of a circle.*

centum, *indecl. num., a hundred.*

centuplum, i, *n., a hundred-fold, centuple.*

centurio, onis, *m., a centurion, captain, the commander of a century,* occupying a station below the tribune.

Cephas, ae, *Cephas,* a Chaldaic word meaning "rock" and given by Christ to Simon, the son of Jonas, who was thereafter called "Peter".

cera, ae, *f., wax.*

cerebrum, i, *n., the brain, the head.*

Ceres, eris, *f., Ceres,* the daughter of Saturn and Ops, goddess of agriculture, especially of the cultivation of corn.

cereus, i, *m., a candle, a wax taper.*

Cerinthus, i, *m., Cerinthus,* a heretical Jew who came from Egypt into Asia Minor towards the end of the first century and taught a strange mixture of Judaism, Christianity, and paganism, leaning towards Gnosticism.

cerno, ere, crevi, cretum, 3, *v. a., to perceive, see, discern,* used in the S.T. only in quotation.

certamen, inis, *n., a contest, struggle, strife, battle.*

certificatio, onis, *f., an attestation, asseveration, giving of assurance.*

certifico, are, avi, atum, 1, *v. a., to certify as accurate, inform, at-*test, *bear testimony to, assure, make evident, confirm.*

certitudinalis, e, *adj., sure, certain,* synonym of *certus,* not used in S.T. On **cognitio certitudinalis,** see *cognitio* under 2.—**certitudinaliter,** *adv.,* see *certitudo* and *certus, with certainty* or *surety, unfailingly,* a synonym of *certe* and *certo.* On **cognoscere certitudinaliter,** see *cognoscere* under 2.

certitudinaliter, *adv.,* see *certitudinalis.*

certitudo, inis, *f.,* (1) *certainty, surety* in general, (2) *certainty, surety of knowledge,* (3) *certainty, surety* in the striving after and the attainment of an aim, (4) *exact certainty, fast limits.* Cf. *certus.*—Kinds of *certitudo* in the general sense of the word are: (a), **certitudo adhaesionis seu inhaesionis** and **certitudo inclinationis,** *the certainty of assent* and *that of inclination,* a synonym of *certitudo cognitionis* and *certitudo ordinis.*—(b), **certitudo cognitionis** and **certitudo ordinis,** *the certainty of knowledge* and *that of inclination toward something.*—(c), **causa inclinationis,** see *causa adhaesionis.*—(d), **causa inhaesionis,** see *causa adhaesionis.*—(e), **causa ordinis,** see *causa cognitionis.*— On **procedere per certitudinem,** see *procedere* under 2.—Kinds of *certitudo* in this (2) sense are: (a), **certitudo absoluta** and **certitudo condicionata,** *the uncondi-*

tioned (cf. *certitudo absoluta* under 3) and *the conditioned certainty.*—(b), **certitudo condicionata**, see *certitudo absoluta.*—(c), **certitudo demonstrativa seu infallibilis seu fixa** and **certitudo probabilis**, *the apodictic* or *infallible* or *unswerving certainty* and *the moral certainty.*—(d), **certitudo experimentalis seu sensibilis** and **certitudo per demonstrationem**, *the actual* or *apparent certainty* and *certainty based on proof.*—(e), **certitudo fidei, certitudo opinionis, certitudo principiorum,** and **certitudo scientiae,** *the certainty of faith, that of opinion, that of principles,* and *that of knowledge from reason.*—(f), **certitudo fixa,** see *certitudo demonstrativa.*—(g), **certitudo infallibilis,** see *certitudo demonstrativa.*—(h), **certitudo iudicii,** *the certainty of judgment.* —(i), **certitudo omnimoda, seu perfecta,** *the certainty considered from every point of view* or *the perfect certainty.*—(j), **certitudo opinionis,** see *certitudo fidei.*— (k), **certitudo perfecta,** see *certitudo omnimoda.*—(l), **certitudo praescientiae,** *the certainty of divine foreknowledge.*—(m), **certitudo principiorum,** see *certitudo fidei.*—(n), **certitudo probabilis,** see *certitudo demonstrativa.*—(o), **certitudo providentiae,** *the certainty of Divine Providence.*—(p), **certitudo rationis,** *the certainty of reason.*—(q), **certitudo scientiae,** see *certitudo fi-*

dei.—(r), **certitudo sensibilis,** see *certitudo experimentalis.*—(s), **certitudo veritatis,** *the certainty of truth.*—(t), **certitudo visionis,** *the certainty of intuitive perception* or *insight.*—Kinds of *certitudo* in this (3) sense are: (a), **certitudo absoluta** and **certitudo quaedam,** *the unconditioned certainty* (see *certitudo absoluta* under 2), and *a kind of certainty.* —(b), **certitudo praedestinationis** and **certitudo reprobationis,** *the certainty of divine foreknowledge* and *that of divine repudiation.*—(c), **certitudo quaedam,** see *certitudo absoluta.*—(d), **certitudo reprobationis,** see *certitudo praedestinationis.*

certo, are, avi, atum, 1, *v. freq. a.,* to fight, struggle, contend, combat.

certus, a, um, *adj.,* (1), *certain,* both in relation to the knowledge of a thing and in relation to the striving after and attainment of a goal, (2) *exactly, certain, firmly determined.*—On **apprehensio certa,** see *apprehensio* under 2; on **cognitio certa,** see *cognitio* under 2; on **iudicium certum,** see *iudicium* under 3; on **matrimonium certum,** see *matrimonium;* on **scientia certa,** see *scientia* under 1; on **signum certum,** see *signum* under 1.—The following are to be distinguished here: **certus formaliter** and **certus materialiter,** *firmly established formally* or *according to essence* and *firmly established materially* or *in re-*

lation to a single concrete thing.
—certe, *adv., assuredly, really, surely, certainly.*

cervix, icis, *f., the neck, nape.*

cervus, i, *a stag, deer.*

cespito, are, avi, atum, 1, *v. n., to stumble* or *trip while walking.*

cessatio, onis, *f., cessation, omission.*

cessio, onis, *f., a resignation, giving up.*

cesso, are, avi, atum, 1, *v. freq. n* and *a., to be still, be inactive, cease.*

cetus, i, *m.,* (acc. to the Grk. *cetos, m.,* and hence the plural *cete = kete*) *any large sea-animal,* particularly *a species of whale.*

Chalcedonensis, e, *adj., Chalcedonian.* The references are all to the fourth Ecumenical Council convened in 451 at Chalcedon in Bithynia, by Pope Leo I, for the purpose of settling the monophysite controversy raised by the teaching of Dioscurus, Patriarch of Alexandria, and Eutyches, archimandrite of a monastery near Constantinople.

Chaldaei, orum, *m., the Chaldaeans,* a people of Assyria, distinguished in an early age for their knowledge of astrology and astronomy.

Chaldaicus, a, um, *adj., Chaldaean.*

Cham, *m., indecl., Ham,* a son of Noe.

Chanaan, *f., indecl., the land of Chanaan* or *Palestine.*

Chananaeus, a, um, *adj., of Chanan, Chananaean.*

chaos or **chaus,** *abl. chao* (other cases not used in the classical period), *chaos, confusion.*

character, eris, *m.,* (1) *a written character* or *letter, flourish,* (2) *impressed sign, imprinted mark, an indelible quality of soul.—* Kinds of *character* in this (2) sense are: (a), **character baptismalis seu baptismi, character confirmationis** and **character ordinis seu ordinis sacerdotalis, seu sacerdotii,** *the indelible mark of baptism, that of confirmation, and that of holy orders.—*(b), **character bestiae** and **character Christi,** *the mark of the apocalyptic animal* and *the mark of Christ.—*(c), **character Christi,** see *character bestiae.—*(d), **character confirmationis,** see *character baptismalis.—*(e), **character corporalis** and **character spiritualis,** *the physical* and *the spiritual mark.—*(f), **character fidelium,** *the mark of the Christian.—* (g), **character interior,** *interior character, inward mark.—*(h), **character militaris,** *military mark* or *character.—*(i), **character ordinis seu ordinis sacerdotalis,** see *character baptismalis.—*(j), **character sacerdotii,** see *character baptismalis.—*(k), **character sacramentalis,** *the sacramental mark* or *character.—*(l), **character spiritualis,** see *character corporalis.*

characterizo, are, avi, atum, 1, *v. a., to characterize, mark, set forth the character of.*

charadrius, ii, *m., a yellowish bird.*

charitas, atis, *love of God,* as the chief object of our supernatural happiness, an infused theological virtue. Cf. *caritas actualis.* In sense of a *habitus, charitas* is understood as a virtue, i.e., a theological virtue.—Taken in the sense of an act, *charitas* is a fruit of the Holy Ghost; cf. *fructus* under 2.—On the mutual relationship between *charitas, amor,* and *dilectio,* see *dilectio* under 1. On affectio charitatis, see *affectio,* on agens per charitatem, see *agens;* on amor charitatis, see *amor* under 1; on bonum charitatis, see *bonus* under 3; on debitum charitatis, see *debitus* under 1; on dilectio charitatis, see *dilectio* under 1; on donum charitatis, see *donum* under 2; on lex charitatis, see *lex* under 1; on magnitudo charitatis, see *magnitudo* under 3; on perfectio charitatis, see *perfectio* under 2; on praeceptum charitatis, see *praeceptum;* on sacramentum charitatis, see *sacramentum* under 3.—Kinds of *charitas* are: (a), charitas actualis and charitas habitualis, *the actual* and *the habitual love* or *the love in the sense of an act* and *that in the sense of an habitus.*—(b), charitas Christi, *Christ's love or charity.*—(c), charitas creata and charitas increata, *created love* or *that of a creature* and *uncreated love* or *divine love.*—(d), charitas Dei, *the charity of God.*—(e), charitas divina, *divine love or charity.*—

(f), charitas eliciens and charitas imperans, *the eliciting* and *the commanding love;* in other words, the *habitus* of love for God in so far as it reproduces an act of love from itself and in so far as it induces the act of another virtue.—(g), charitas fraterna, *fraternal love* or *charity.*—(h) charitas habitualis, see *charitas actualis.*—(i), charitas imperans, see *charitas eliciens.*—(j), charitas imperfecta and charitas perfecta, *the imperfect* and *the perfect love.* Cf. charitas incipiens.—(k), charitas incipiens, charitas proficiens and charitas perfecta, *the beginning love, the progressing love,* and *the perfect love* or *the love of the beginner, that of the advanced,* and *that of the perfect.*—(l), charitas increata, see *charitas creata.*—(m), charitas patriae and charitas viae, *love in the heavenly fatherland* and *that on the way to it;* in other words, *the heavenly* and *the earthly love.*—(n), charitas perfecta, see *charitas imperfecta* and *charitas incipiens.*—(o), charitas proficiens, see *charitas incipiens.*—(p), charitas viae, see *charitas patriae.* Charitas dicitur esse forma aliarum virtutum, *love is said to be the form of all other virtues.*—Charitas dicitur finis aliarum virtutum, *love is called the aim of all virtues.* Cf. below: *Charitas est motor omnium virtutum.*—Charitas dicitur mater aliarum virtutum, *charity* or *love is called the mother of all virtues.*—**Charitas est motor omnium virtutum,** *charity* or *love is the mover* or *rouser of all virtues.*—**Charitas est radix omnium virtutum,** *charity or love is the root of all virtues.*

charitative, *adv.*, see *charitativus.*

charitativus, a, um, *adj.*, *pertaining to charity, of a charitable nature, charitative, loving.*—charitative, *adv.*, *charitably, in a charitable manner.*

charta, ae, *f.*, *a parchment, letter, document.*

chaunos, i, *m.*, Grk. *chaunos, a blusterer, swaggerer, wind-bag, braggadocio.*

cheir, cheiros, *f.*, Grk. *cheir, the hand.*

chere, Grk. *chaire, hail, welcome,* a synonym of *salve.*

cherub, *m. plur.*, **Cherubim,** (*cherubin*), *the cherubim,* the name of a rank of angels mentioned in the Old Testament.

Chiliastiae, arum, *m.*, *the Chiliasts,* the believers in chiliasm or the doctrine that Christ will reign on earth a thousand years visibly and personally.

chiromantia, ae, *f.*, *chiromancy, palmistry,* the art of predicting events or telling fortunes by inspecting the hand.

chirotheca, ae, *f.*, *the episcopal glove,* a glove forming part of a bishop's official vestments.

chlamys, ydis, *m.*, *a Grecian military cloak, chlamis.*

cholera, ae, *f.*, *bile,* one of the juices of the animal body, one of the humours of ancient psychology, determining the so-called temperaments.—**inflammatio cholerae,** *the rising* and *overflowing of the bile.*

cholericus, a, um, *adj.*, *choleric, bilious, of a bilious temperament, easily provoked to anger, irascible.* On **complexio cholerica,** see *complexio* under 2; on **homo cholericus,** see *homo.*

chorda, ae, *f. a string* of a musical instrument, *cord.*

chorus, i, *m.*, *a chorus, choir.*

chrisma, atis, *n.*, *chrism,* a mixed unguent of oil and balm consecrated by a bishop on Holy Thursday and used for sacramental unctions, and solemn consecrations; hence, that with which one is anointed.

christallinus, a, um, *adj.*, *crystalline, like crystal, transparent, pure, pellucid.*

christianitas, atis, *f.*, *Christianity.*

Christianus, a, um, *adj.*, *Christian.* —**Christianus,** i, *m.*, *a Christian.*

christiformiter, *adv.*, *christiform, in the manner* or *in the person of Christ.*

Christus, i, *m.*, *Christ.*

chronici, (sc. libri), orum, *m.*, *chronicles,* a register of facts and events in the order of time.

Chrysostomus, i, *m.*, *Chrysostom.* Saint and doctor of the Church, bishop of Constantinople, c 347-407. In the S.T., St. Thomas quotes from the *De Compunc-*

tione Cordis, the *De Sacerdotio* and from a large number of his homilies, especially those on the gospels of St. Matthew and of St. John. St. Thomas makes frequent reference to the *Opus Imperfectum in Matthaeum* which he ascribes to John Chrysostom. This work, however, is that of an Arian author of the fifth century.

cibaria, orum, *n.*, *food, nutriment, provisions, victuals.*

cibatio, onis, *f.*, *the act of eating, taking a meal.*

cibo, no *perf.*, atum, 1, *v. a.*, *to give food to someone, to feed.*

cibus, i, *m.*, *food.*

cicatrix, icis, *f.*, *a scar, cicatrice.*

Cicero, onis, *m.*, *Cicero, M. Tullius*, the greatest of the Roman orators, born on the third of January, 106 B.C. at Arpinum; assassinated, at the age of sixty-three years, by the soldiers of Antonius, 43 B.C.

ciconia, ae *f.*, *a stork.*

cidaris, is, *f.*, *a tiara, diadem*, the Pope's triple crown.

cilicinus, a, um, *adj.*, *made of haircloth.*

cilicium, ii, *n.*, *a hair-shirt.*

cingo, ere, nxi, cinctum, 3, *v. a.*, *to surround.*

cingulum, i, *n.*, *a girdle, belt*, used *figuratively* and *literally.*

cinis, eris, *m.*, (1) *ashes*, (2) *the remains of a human body turned to dust.*

circa, = **circum**, *prep.* with *acc.*, *about, around, concerning.* On

materia circa quam, see *materia* under 1; on **principium circa quod**, see *principium.* **Circa esse**, *to belong to something, to concern something, to revolve around something, to have something for an object.*

circuitus, us, *m.*, *a circuit, distance around, compass, a passing around.*

circularis, e, *adj.*, *circular, moving in a circle.* On **deductio circularis**, see *deductio* under 3; on **definitio circularis**, see *definitio* under 2; on **demonstratio circularis**, see *demonstratio* under 3; on **figura circularis**, see *figura* under 1; on **generatio circularis**, see *generatio* under 1; on **linea circularis**, see *linea* under 1; on **magnitudo circularis**, see *magnitudo* under 1; on **motus circularis**, see *motus* under 1; on **probatio circularis**, see *probatio* under 2; on **processus circularis**, see *processus* under 1; on **ratio circularis**, see *ratio* under 13; on **syllogismus circularis**, see *syllogismus.*—**circulariter**, *adv.*, *circularly, in a circular direction, moving in circles.* On **demonstrare circulariter**, see *demonstrare* under 3; on **ferri circulariter**, see *ferre* under 3; on **fieri circulariter**, see *fieri;* on **latio circulariter**, see *latio* under 1; on **movere circulariter**, see see *movere.*

circulariter, *adv.*, see *circularis.*

circulatio, onis, *f.*, *circular course, revolution, circulation.*

circulus, i, *m.,* (1) *circle, circular part* or *orbit, revolution* in literal sense, (2) *circle, circular path* or *orbit, revolution* in figurative sense, (3) *sphere, region,* synonym of *globus* and *orbis.*—On **ferri circulo, circulum et secundum circulum,** see *ferre* under 3; on **generare circulo,** see *generare quadratura circuli, the squaring of a circle,* i.e., *the quadrature of a circle* or *a fourth part of a circle.*—Kinds of *circulus* in this (1) sense are the following: (a), **circulus aequinoctialis,** *the circle that makes day and night equal, the equator.*— (b), **circulus animalium seu zodiacus,** *the animal* or *astronomical circle.*—(c), **circulus lacteus,** *the milky way.*—(d), **circulus lunaris,** *lunar circle, circle of the moon.*—(e), **circulus maximus** and **circulus parvus,** *the largest and a small circle of a sphere;* the latter is also called *epicyclus,* i. e., a small circle having its center on the circumference of a greater circle, an *epicycle.*—(f), **circulus obliquatus seu obliquus,** *the oblique circle* or *the ellipse.* —(g), **circulus parvus,** see *circulus maximus.*—(h), **circulus zodiacus,** see *circulus animalium.*— On **demonstrare circulo,** see *demonstrare* under 3; on **generare circulo,** see *generare.*

circumamictus, a, um, *adj., enveloped, surrounded.*

circumcedo, ere, cessi, cessum, 3, *v. n.* and *a.,* to include.

circumcido, cidi, cissum, 3, *v. a.,* (1) *to circumcize, to perform circumcision upon;* hence, sometimes in Scripture, *to purify from sin,* (2) *to trim, pare, cut short.*

circumcingo, ere, 3, *v. a.,* to surround.

circumcisio, onis, *f., a cutting around, circumcision, spiritual circumcision.*

circumdo, dare, dedi, datum, 1, *v. a.,* to put around, wrap around, encompass.

circumeo, or **circueo,** ire, ivi, or ii or circui, circuitum, 4, *v. n.* and *a.,* to wander around a place, pass through, go the rounds of.

circumferentia, ae, *f., a circumference.*

circumfero, ferre, tuli, latum, 3, *v. a.,* to bear around, move or carry around.

circumfulgeo, ere, 2, *v. n.,* to shine around.

circumfundo, ere, fudi, fusum, 3, *v. a.,* to diffuse, to pour or send out so as to spread in all directions.

circumlino, ere, litum, 3, *v. a.,* to anoint.

circumlocutio, onis, *f., circumlocution, periphasis.*

circumpono, ere, posui, positum, 3, *v. a.,* to surround, clothe.

circumquaque, *adv., on every side, all around.*

circumsaepio, ire, sepsi, septum, 4, *v. a.,* to hedge or fence around with something, to surround, enclose.

circumscribo, ere, psi, ptum, 3, *v. a.*
(1) *to circumscribe, encircle,* (2)
limit, define, (3) *write over, re-*
write in other words.—The following must be distinguished
here: **circumscribere terminis es-**
sentialibus and **circumscribere**
terminis localibus, *to fix an idea*
or *notion* and *to enclose locally.*

circumscriptio, onis, *f., limitation,*
restriction, the state of being lim-
ited or *bounded, limited compre-*
hension.

circumscriptive, *adv., after the*
manner or *in the sense of a cir-*
cumscription, in which the parts
of the circumscription so correspond with those of the cir-
circumscribed that the latter are
measured through the former cir-
cumscriptively, part by part, the
opposite of *definitive.* On **esse**
in loco circumscriptive, see *locus*
under 2; on **significare circum-**
scriptive, see *significare.*

circumspectio, onis, *f., Circum-*
spection, cautious and *careful*
observation with a view to wise
conduct.

circumspicio, ere, exi, ectum, 3,
v. n. and *a.,* (1) *to look around,*
look about, (2) *view something*
mentally, consider.

circumstantia, ae, *f.,* (1) *circum-*
stance, surrounding circumstan-
ces in general, the opposite of
substantia, (2) *circumstance of*
a human action.—Kinds of *cir-*
cumstantia in general are: (a),
circumstantia actus seu actus
seu **actus humani seu actus mo-**
ralis, *the circumstance of hu-*
man action. The entire PS. Q. 7
deals with the topic, *de circum-*
stantiis humanorum actuum.—
(b), **circumstantia litterae,** *the*
circumstance of the context of
a book. The circumstances of a
human action are seven as follows: *quis, quid, ubi, quibus*
auxiliis, cur, quomodo, quando.
On **bonitas circumstantiae seu**
ex circumstantia, see *bonitas*
under 1; on **bonum ex circum-**
stantia, see *bonus* under 2.—
Kinds of *circumstantia* in this
(2) sense are: (a), **circumstantia**
aggravans, *the aggravating cir-*
cumstance.—(b), **circumstantia**
constituens speciem and **circum-**
stantia mutans speciem, *the cir-*
cumstance which determines the
kind of action and that which
changes it.—(c), **circumstantia**
debita, *due circumstance.*—(d),
circumstantia mutans speciem,
see *circumstantia constituens*
speciem.—(e), **circumstantia prin-**
cipalis, *the main circumstance.*

circumsto, are, steti, 1, *v. n.* and *a.,*
to stand around in a circle, take
a station around, stand around a
person or *thing;* with *acc.,* sur-
round, encircle, encompass.

circumvelo, are, 1, *v. a., to cover*
around, envelop.

circumvenio, ire, veni, ventum, 4,
v. a., to circumvent, to gain ad-
vantage over, or *get the better*
of by craft, artifice or *fraud.*

circumventio, onis, *f., circumvention, defrauding, a forestalling by artifice, a circumventing.*

circumvolutio, onis, *f., a circumvolution, a turning around a center.*

circus, i, *m., the circus,* an enclosure used for exhibiting horse-and-chariot-races and gladiatorial combats.

Cisterciensis, e, *adj., Cistercian,* of or belonging to the order of monks founded in 1098 at Cistercium (Citeaux) in France, an offshoot of the Benedictines.

cisterna, ae, *f., a cistern.*

cithara, ae, *f., the cithara, harp.*

citharista, ae, *m., a player on the cithara, a citharist.*

citharizo, are, 1, *v. n., to play on the cithara.*

citharoedus, i, *m., a cithaorus,* on who plays on the cithara accompanying it with the voice.

cito, *adv.,* see *citus.*

cito, are, avi, atum, 1, *v. a.,* (1) *to quote, cite,* used in phrase *loco citato, in a passage already cited,* (2) *called, summoned.*

citra, *prep.* with *acc., without, aside from, without regard to.*

citrinus, a, um, *adj., citrine, having the same color as a lemon, greenish-yellow,* a synonym of *subflavus.*

citrum, i, *n., the citron-tree.*

citus, a, um, *adj., quick, alert.* —**cito,** *adv., quickly, speedily, soon.—comp.* **citius,** *more quickly, sooner.—sup:* **citissime,** *very quickly.*

civilis, e, *adj., civil, civic, concerning* or *pertaining to the citizen, political, social,* synonym of *politicus* and *socialis.* On **animal civile,** see *animal* under 1; on **ars civilis,** see *ars* under 2; on **bonitas civilis,** see *bonitas* under 1; on **communicatio civilis,** see *communicatio* under 3; on **communitas civilis,** see *communitas* under 2; on **conversatio civilis,** see *conversatio* under 1; on **felicitas civilis,** see *felicitas;* on **fortitudo civilis,** see *fortitudo* under 2; on **iudicium civile,** see *iudicium* under 1; on **ius civile,** see *ius* under 1; on **iustitia civilis,** see *iustitia* under 1; on **iustum civile,** see *iustus;* on **lex civilis,** see *lex* under 1; on **malitia civilis,** see *malitia* under 3; on **materia civilis,** see *materia* under 2; on **multitudo civilis,** see *multitudo* under 4; on **operatio civilis,** see *operatio* under 2; on **opus civile,** see *opus* under 4; on **ordinatio civilis,** see *ordinatio* under 2; on **potestas civilis,** see *potestas* under 3; on **scientia civilis,** see *scientia* under 1; on **subiectio civilis,** see *subiectio* under 2; on **theologia civilis,** see *theologia* under 1; on **virtus civilis,** see *virtus* under 1; on **vita civilis,** see *vita* under 3.— Homo est naturaliter seu secundum suam naturam animal civile, see *homo.*

civilitas, atis, *f., the art of government, politics, society.*

civis, is, *comm., a citizen, a fellow citizen.*

civitas, atis, *f.,* *the citizens united in a community, the body-politic, the state, a city,* synonym of *urbs.*—**civitas Dei,** *the city of God;* **De Civitate Dei,** *On the City of God,* St. Augustine's masterpiece dealing with the two cities, the city of the evil and the city of the good as the city of God. The work is named after one city.

clam, *adv., secretly, privately.*

clamo, are, avi, atum, 1, *v. n.* and *a., proclaim, declare, cry out, invoke.*

clamor, oris, *m.,* (1) *a sound, call shout,* (2) *a cry, plea, prayer, turning of the mind to someone,* e.g., *God,* a synonym of *intentio cordis,* (3) *the voice of a crier.* The appearance of Christ on the day of the resurrection, in so far as it has the force of a command, is called His voice (*vox*), and this voice is sometimes called a cry (*clamor*), as of a crier summoning to judgment, (4) *an outcry, a disorderly* and *confused speech, a rising of the voice in anger,* a synonym of *racha.*

clamose, *adv.,* see *clamosus.*

clamosus, a, um, *adj., loud, clamoring, persistent*—**clamose,** *adv., clamorously, noisily.*

clandestinus, a, um, *adj., clandestine, kept secret, concealed, surreptitious.*

clango, ere, *no perf.,* 3, *v. n., to clang, sound, cause to send forth a loud, sharp, and ringing metallic sound.*

clare, *adv.,* see *clarus.*

clareo, ere, 2, *v. n., to become bright, illustrious, renowned, distinguished.*

claresco, ere, clarui, 3, *v. inch. n., to shine forth, become clear, grow bright.*

claria, ae, *f.,* = *kleria, glory,* which is clear knowledge together with praise, a synonym of *gloria.*

clarificatio, onis, *f., a glorification, condition of clarity, state of being glorified, uplifted to celestial honor and blessedness.*

clarifico, are, 1, *v. a.,* (1) *to make bright,* (2) *to glorify, exalt to a state of glory,* a synonym of *glorifico.*

claritas, atis, *f.,* (1) *clearness, brightness,* (2) *clarity, distinctness,* a synonym of *limpiditas,* (3) *gleam of light, radiance splendor,* (4) *fame, prestige, good repute.*—**claritas lactea seu circuli lactei,** *the brightness of the milky way.* On **gloria claritatis,** see *gloria* under 2.—Kinds of *claritas* in this (3) sense are: (a), **claritas corporalis** and **claritas spiritualis,** *the bodily* and *the spiritual splendor.*—(b), **claritas corporis,** *splendor of the body.* —(c), **claritas corporis gloriosi,** *splendor of the glorified body.*— (d), **claritas divina,** *divine splendor.*—(e), **claritas Christi,** *splendor of Christ.*—(f), **claritas Dei,** *splendor of God.*—(g), **claritas gloriae seu gloriosa** and **claritas naturae seu naturalis,** *the splen-*

dor of heavenly glory and natural glory.—(h), **claritas gloriosa,** see claritas gloriae.—(i), **claritas huius vitae** and **claritas patriae,** the splendor of this life and that of the heavenly fatherland, or the earthly and the heavenly splendor.—(j), **claritas imaginaria** and **claritas sensibilis,** the imaginary splendor and that realized by the senses.—(k), **claritas naturae,** see claritas gloriae.—(l), **claritas naturalis,** see claritas gloriae.—(m), **claritas patriae,** see claritas huius vitae.—(n), **claritas sensibilis,** see claritas imaginaria.—(o), **claritas spiritualis,** see claritas corporalis.—(p), **claritas vera,** true splendor.

clarus, a, um, adj., (1) clear, manifest, plain, evident, intelligible, (2) brilliant, celebrated, renowned, famous.

clare, adv, clearly, distinctly.

claudicatio, onis, f., a limping, lameness.

claudico, are, 1, v. a., to limp, be lame, halt, be defective, used lit. and fig.

claudo, ere, si, um, 3, v. a., to shut something that is open, close, shut up, the opposite of aperire. —**clausum,** i, n., an enclosed place, a closed passage.

claudus, a, um, adj., lame, limping, halting.

clausio, onis, f., the act of closing or shutting something, as a door, gate.

claustrum, i, n., (also **claustra,** orum) (1) bar, bolt, barrier, (2) a

place that is shut up, enclosure, cloister, (3) restraint, enclosure, fig.

clavicula, ae, f., dim., a little key, used fig.

clavis, is, f., (1) key in the general sense of the word, (2) key in the spiritual sense of the word, i.e., the power to remit or retain the guilt and the punishment of sin, having the same meaning as potestas or virtus or vis clavium.— **clavis materialis,** the material key. On **actus clavis seu clavium,** see actus under 1; on **potestas clavis,** see potestas under 2; on **virtus clavis,** see virtus under 1; on **vis clavis,** see vis under 1.— Kinds of clavis in this (2) sense of a spiritual key are: (a), **clavis auctoritatis, clavis excellentiae,** and **clavis ministerii seu ecclesiae,** the power of the key of the author or the founder, that of the distinguished in the service, that of the service or of the Church. —(b), **clavis caeli seu regni seu regni caelestis** and **clavis inferni,** the key of the heavenly kingdom and that of hell.—(c), **clavis ecclesiae,** see clavis auctoritatis.— (d), **clavis excellentiae,** see clavis auctoritatis.—(e), **clavis inferni,** see clavis caeli.—(f), **clavis iurisdictionis** and **clavis ordinis,** the power of the key of exterior jurisdiction and that of sacramental consecration.—(g), **clavis ministerii,** see clavis auctoritatis.—(h), **clavis ordinis,** see clavis iurisdictionis.—(i), **clavis**

regni seu regni caelestis, see *clavis caeli.*—(j), **clavis principalis,** *the principal power of the key.*— (k), **clavis scientiae,** *the key of knowledge* or *discernment as to whether or not one is worthy of absolution.*

Cledonius, i, *m., Cledonius,* a trusted friend and correspondent of Gregory Nazianzen. Having spent his early years about the court he devoted himself to the religious life in the diocese of Nazianzus and gave up his property to the service of the poor. Gregory addressed to Cledonius his two celebrated letters against Apollinaris. The second of these was written in answer to one of Cledonius, asking him to declare his faith on the person of Christ which he was accused of dividing. In it Gregory begs Cledonius to assure all that he held the Nicene faith inviolate. These letters were adopted as articles of faith by the councils of Ephesus and Chalcedon.

Clemens, entis, *m., Clement,* generally known as *Clemens Romanus.* According to common tradition, one of the first, if not the first, bishop of Rome after the apostles, and certainly a leading member of that church towards the end of the first century. He was saint and martyr. The only genuine work of Clement is the Epistle to the Corinthians. Other writings ascribed to him are now regarded as spurious. St. Thomas

in the S.T. refers to the so-called second letter to the Corinthians, the *Epitome de Gestis Petri* under the name of *Itinerarium Clementis* and the *Ep. decretal secunda ad Iacobum Fratrem Domini.*

clemens, entis, *adj., mild, merciful.*
clementia, ae, *f., mildness, gentleness,* the opposite of *crudelitas* and *saevitia.* On the difference between *clementia* and *mansuetudo,* see *mansuetudo.*
clericalis, e, *adj., clerical, priestly.*
clericatura, ae, *f., the clerical state.*
clericatus, us, *m., the clerical office.*
clericus, i, *m., cleric, in* St. Thomas all who have been ordained for the ecclesiastical ministry, including *presbyteri, diaconi, subdiaconi, lectores, cantores,* but not *episcopi* or *sacerdotes,* although like many others St. Thomas is not always consistent in his use of the term. *Monachi* and *religiosi* are not regarded ordinarily as in the ministry of the church, i.e., as having care of souls and giving spiritual service to them, but they may be. In the latter case they too would be *clerici.*
clerus, i, *m., the clergy, the clerical order.*
clibanus, i, *m., an oven,* used *lit.* and *fig.*
cloaca, ae, *f., a drain, sewer.*
clypeum, (**clypeus**), i, *n., a shield.*
coacervatio, onis, *f., a heaping together.*

coacervo, are, avi, atum, 1, *v. a.,*
to heap together, heap in a mass.

coacte, *adv.,* see *cogo.*

coactio, onis, *f., force, exterior*
power, a synonym of *violentia*
and *vis,* the opposite of *libertas*
and *persuasio.* On **libertas a**
necessitate coactionis, see *liber-*
tas under 2; on **necessarium ne-**
cessitate coactionis seu per co-
actionem, see *necessarius* under
1; on **necessitate coactionis,** see
necessitas under 1.—Kinds of
coactio are: (a), **coactio com-**
pellens seu sufficiens seu per-
fecta, *the compelling* or *the*
sufficient or *the perfect force.*
—(b), **coactio impellens seu in-**
ducens seu insufficiens seu im-
perfecta, *the inciting* or *induc-*
ing or *insufficient* or *imperfect*
force.

coactivus, a, um, *adj., forcing, in-*
ducing with exterior power. On
potestas coactiva, see *potestas*
under 3; on **virtus coactiva,** see
virtus under 6; on **vis coactiva,**
see *vis* under 2.

coadiutor, oris, *m., an assistant,*
coadjutor.

coadiuvo, are, iuvi, iutum, 1, *v.*
a., to help, help another or each
other.

coadoro, are, 1, *v. a.,* to worship
or *adore along with.*

coaduno, are, avi, atum, 1, *v. a.,*
to unite, add, or join together.

coaequalis, e, *adj., co-equal, of*
like age.

coaequo, are, avi, atum, 1, *v. a.,*
to make one thing equal or even

with another, make something
of the same value as another.

coaeternitas, atis, *f., co-eternity.*

coaeternus, a, um, *adj., coeternal.*

coaevus, a, um, *adj., coeval, of the*
same age, coeternal with something.

coagito, are, *no perf.* atum, 1, *v. a.,*
to discuss together, a synonym
of *cogito.*

coalesco, ere, alui, alitum, 3, *v.*
inch. n., to coalesce, come together, unite.

coaptatio, onis, *f., coaptation, adap-*
tation, aptitude, kinship, bond,
an accurate joining together,
quality of being suited for something.

coapto, are, *no perf.,* atum, 1, *v. a.,*
to fit, join with something, com-
pose of, adjust, adapt.

coarctatio, onis, *f., a contraction,*
a drawing together.

coarcto, are, avi, atum, 1, *v. a.,* to
restrict, contract, confine, com-
press.

coassisto, ere, coastiti, no **sup.,** 3,
v. n., to coassist, aid.

coassumo, ere, sumpsi, sumptum,
3, *v. a.,* to assume together, co-
assume.

coccineus, a, um., *adj., scarlet-*
colored.

coccus, i, *m., scarlet cloth.*

codex, icis, *m.,* (1) *a code of laws,*
(2) *a codex* or *manuscript, a*
book.

coelestis, e, *adj.,* see *caelestis.*

coelum, i, *n.,* see *caelum.*

coena, ae, *f., a supper, the Lord's*
supper.

coenaculum, i, *n.*, (caenaculum), *a dining room,* usually in an upper story, the upper room in which Christ ate the last supper with His disciples.

coeno, are, avi, atum, 1, *v. n.* and *a., to sup, partake of the evening meal, dine, eat.*

coenobium, ii, *n., a cloister, convent, monastery.*

coeo, ire, ivi, or ii, itum, *v. a.* and *n.,* (1) *to unite, to combine, to merge,* (2) *to copulate.*

coepi, isse,——, 3, *v. a.* and *n., to begin, commence, undertake.*

coepiscopus, i, *m., an associate bishop.*

coerceo, ere, cui, citum, 2, *v. a., to restrain, check, coerce, curb.*

coercitio, onis, *f., coercion, restraint, chastisement.*

coessentialis, e, *adj., equally essential with something, coessential.*

coetus, us, see *coitus.*

coexhibeo, ere, ui, itum, 2, *v. a., to show, exhibit, manifest at the same time as something else is being displayed.*

coexistentia, ae, *f., coexistence.*

coexisto, ere, stiti, stitum, 3, *v. n., to coexist, exist together with.*

cogitatio, onis, *f.,* (1) *thinking* or *thought* in the general and broader sense of the word, (2) *thinking* or *thought* in the narrower and proper sense of the word, i.e., *contemplation, reflection.* One kind of *cogitatio* in this sense is: **cogitatio cordis,** *secret thought, the thought of the intellect* or *reason.* On **diver-**sus cogitatione, see *diversus;* on **concupiscentia cogitationis,** see *concupiscentia* under 1.—Kinds of *cogitatio* in this (2) sense are: (a), **cogitatio actualis,** *thought consisting in an action,* i.e., which consists in the use of intellectual representation.—(b), **cogitatio formata** and **cogitatio informis,** *formed* and *formless thinking,* i.e., that thinking which is bound by a *firma assensio* to the recognized truth, and that in which this *firma assensio* is lacking.—(c), **cogitatio honesta** and **cogitatio turpis,** *seemly* and *unseemly, impure* or *vicious thought.*—(d), **cogitatio inform-is,** see *cogitatio formata.*—(e), **cogitatio interior seu intima,** *the inner thought.*—(f), **cogitatio turpis,** see *cogitatio honesta.*—(g), **cogitatio vana,** *vain thought—*(h), **cogitatio volubilis,** *discursive thinking.*

cogitativus, a, um, *adj., thinking, judging,* in the broader and in the narrower sense of the words. Cf. *cogitatio.* On **potentia cogitativa,** see *potentia* under 2; on **virtus cogitativa,** see *virtus* under 1; on **vis cogitativa,** see *vis* under 1.—**Cogitativa sc. potentia seu virtus seu vis,** *the sensible judging power of man,* i.e., that faculty of man by means of which he recognizes on the one hand the individual relations of usefulness and harmfulness in physical or material things not comprehended by the exterior senses, and on the other hand, the phantasms or imaginary representations derived from these material things for the abstraction of general ideas.

cogitatus, us, *m.,* *a thinking, thought.*

cogito, are, avi, atum, 1, *v. a.,* (1) *to think* in the general and broader sense of the word, (2) *to think* in the narrower and proper sense of the word, i.e., *to think backwards* and *forward, think over, consider.*

cognatio, onis, *f., relationship, intimate* or *natural connection, kindred.*—Kinds of *cognatio* are the following: (a), **carnalis cognatio et spiritualis cognatio,** *carnal relationship* and *spiritual relationship.*—(b), **legalis cognatio,** *legal relationship.*—(c), **spiritualis cognatio,** see *carnalis cognatio.*

cognatus, a, um, *adj., kindred, related, like, similar.*—**cognatus,** i, *m.,* and **cognata,** ae, *f., a blood-relation, kinsman.*

cognitio, onis, *f.,* (1) *knowledge* in a wide and general sense, without distinguishing the different faculties by which it is attained, or the product from the process. It is the ability, found in all living beings except plants, of receiving the form of things other than self without losing self-identity, because they possess formally or eminently a sensitive soul. Found on different levels, it may be *sense knowl-edge* or *sense perception; rational knowledge,* i.e., intellectual knowledge which is discursive; *angelic knowledge,* i.e., intellectual knowledge without discursus or reasoning but intuitive; and *divine knowledge.* Thus it includes *sensation,* all the operations of the senses, internal and external, and their products; *apprehension, judgment* and *reasoning, intuition,* all the operations of an intellect, human, angelic or divine, and the habits of wisdom, science, understanding, art, and prudence. To preserve the distinction, as the Romance languages still do, between *cognitio* and *scientia,* it might better be rendered by *perception, awareness,* or *recognition,* (2) *knowledge* in a narrower sense as the function or activity of knowing or perceiving, i.e., psychological knowledge.—Kinds of *cognitio* in this (1) sense are: **cognitio coitus** and **cognitio notitiae,** *knowledge in the manner of cohabitation* or *copulation, carnal knowledge* and *knowledge in the manner of knowing,* i.e., *the knowledge of sexual intercourse and psychological knowledge.* On **certitudo cognitionis,** see *certitudo* under 1; on **cognoscere in cognitionis principio,** see *cognoscere;* on **iudicare per modum cognitionis,** see *iudicare* under 2; on **iudicium cognitionis,** see *iudicium* under 4; on **primum cognitionis,**

seu secundum cognitionem, see *primus;* on **principium cognitionis,** see *principium;* on **prius cognitionis, in cognitione, ordine cognitionis, secundum cognitionem et cognitio intellectiva,** see *prior* under 1; on **quantitas cognitionis,** see *quantitas* under 2; on **veritas cognitionis adquisitae, infusae et naturalis,** see *veritas* under 1.—Kinds of *cognitio* in in this (2) sense are: (a), **cognitio absoluta** and **cognitio collativa seu comparata,** *the absolute knowledge* or *the knowledge considered by itself* and *the comparative* or *compared knowledge.*—(b), **cognitio actualis, conitio habitualis,** and **cognitio virtualis seu potentialis,** *knowledge consisting in an action* or *taking place in reality, the knowledge that has become inactive* and *the knowledge at hand by virtue of power or potentiality.*—(c), **cognitio adquisita** and **cognitio infusa,** *the knowledge acquired by one's own activity and knowledge bestowed* or *infused by God.*—(d), **cognitio ad rem** and **cognitio a re accepta,** *knowledge reduced to a thing as its cause and knowledge derived from a thing.*—(e), **cognitio aenigmatica seu specularis** and **cognitio aperta seu apparens seu manifesta,** *inferred* or *reflected knowledge* and *open* or *manifest knowledge of God,* so called in connection with 1 Cor. 13. 12.—(f), **cognitio affectiva.**—*knowledge connected with love* and *producing love.*—(g), **cognitio angelica seu angeli,** *angelic knowledge* or *angel's knowledge.*—(h), **cognitio aperta,** see *cognitio aenigmatica.*—(i), **cognitio apparens,** see *cognitio aenigmatica.*—(j), **cognitio a re accepta,** see *cognitio ad rem.*—(k), **cognitio beata,** *the blessed* or *enrapturing knowledge of God as shared by the angels and man in heaven.*—(l), **cognitio certa seu certitudinalis, cognitio per verisimilitudinem** and **cognitio coniecturalis,** *certain* or *sure knowledge, probable* and *surmised* or *conjectured knowledge.*—(m), **cognitio certitudinalis,** see *cognitio certa.*—(n), **cognitio collativa,** see *cognitio absoluta.*—(o), **cognitio communis seu generalis seu universalis** and **cognitio propria seu particularis seu specialis,** *the general* and *the proper* and *the particular knowledge.*—(p), **cognitio comparata,** see *cognitio absoluta.*—(q), **cognitio completa seu perfecta seu plena** and **cognitio imperfecta seu defectiva seu deficiens,** *the complete* or *perfect* or *full knowledge* and *the imperfect* or *defective knowledge.*—(r), **cognitio complexorum** and **cognitio incomplexorum,** *the knowledge of that associated with a statement* and *knowledge not so associated,* i.e., *knowledge of a judgment* or *decision* and *that of the idea.*—(s), **cognitio comprehensionis,** *the knowledge of comprehension.*—(t), **co-**

gnitio comprehensoris seu patriae and **cognitio viatoris seu viae seu praesentis vitae seu praesentis status,** *the knowledge of the possessor of God* and *of the heavenly fatherland* (qua Deus per suam essentiam videtur), and *the knowledge of the pilgrim* or *of the way to the heavenly fatherland* or *of the knowledge of the present life or conditions,* (quae est per speculum et aenigma sensibilium creaturarum).— (u), **cognitio confusa seu indistincta seu indeterminata** and **cognitio distincta seu determinata,** *the indistinct* or *indefinite* and *the clear* or *definite knowledge.*—(v), **cognitio coniecturalis,** see *cognitio certa.*—(w), **cognitio coniuncta** and **cognitio remota,** *the knowledge connected with a being* and *that removed from it* or *the knowledge which comes to a being itself and which befits another but directs the activity of that being.*—(x), **cognitio creata** *the created* or *produced knowledge.*—(y), **cognitio defectiva seu deficiens,** see *cognitio completa.*—(z), **cognitio Dei,** *knowledge of God.*—(a²), **cognitio determinata,** see *cognitio confusa.*—(b²), **cognitio discursiva seu ratiocinativa** and **cognitio sine discursu seu intellectus,** *discursive* and *intuitive knowledge,* i.e., knowledge which comes about through a *discursus,* namely, through a progression of reasonings from something known

to something unknown, and that knowledge which comes about without such a *discursus* and which consists of intuition.—(c²), **cognitio distincta,** see *cognitio confusa.*—(d²), **cognitio diurna** and **cognitio nocturna,** *knowledge of the day* and *that of the night,* i.e., *that of the angels* and *that of the devil.*—(e²), **cognitio divina,** *the divine knowledge* or *the knowledge of God.*—(f²), **cognitio divinorum,** *knowledge of divine things.*—(g²), **cognitio essentialis,** *the essential knowledge,* i.e., *of God.*—(h²), **cognitio experimentalis,** *the knowledge of experience.* See *cognitio discursiva.*—(i²), **cognitio explicita** and **cognitio implicita,** *the unfolded* or *developed knowledge* and *the enfolded* or *restricted knowledge.*—(j²), **cognitio fallax,** *the deceiving* or *erring knowledge.*—(k²), **cognitio fidei,** *the knowledge of faith.*—(l²), **cognitio finis imperfecta** and **cognitio finis perfecta,** *the imperfect* and *perfect knowledge of an aim.*— (m²), **cognitio finis perfecta,** see *cognitio finis imperfecta.*—(n²), **cognitio formalis,** *formal knowledge,* i.e., the knowledge of that which is related to something else as its form or the principle that gives form.—(o²), **cognitio generalis,** see *cognitio communis.*—(p²), **cognitio gloriae** and **cognitio gratiae seu gratuita,** *knowledge in the glory of heaven* and *the knowledge which is* *given to man on earth by God as the result of grace.*—(q²), **cognitio gratiae,** see *cognitio gloriae.*—(r²), **cognitio gratuita,** see *cognitio gloriae.*—(s²), **cognitio habitualis,** see *cognitio actualis.*—(t²), **cognitio hominis,** *the knowledge of man* or *possessed by man.*—(u²), **cognitio humana,** *human knowledge.*—(v²), **cognitio imaginaria seu imaginativa,** *the knowledge* or *the power of imagination.*—(w²), **cognitio immaterialis** and **cognitio materialis,** *the knowledge which comes about without bodily organs* and *that which comes with them,* i.e., *spiritual* and *material knowledge.*—(x²), **cognitio imperfecta,** see *cognitio completa.*—(y²), **cognitio implicita,** see *cognitio explicita.*—(z²), **cognitio incomplexorum,** see *cognitio complexorum.*—(a³), **cognitio indeterminata,** see *cognitio confusa.*—(b³), **cognitio indistincta,** see *cognitio confusa.*—(c³), **cognitio infusa,** see *cognitio adquisita.*—(d³), **cognitio inquisitiva seu venativa,** *the investigating* or *searching knowledge,* i.e., *knowledge which depends on an investigation* or *which results from such.* —(e³), **cognitio intellectiva seu intellectualis seu intelligibilis seu intellectus seu rationis** and **cognitio sensitiva seu sensibilis seu sensus,** *intellectual knowledge* or *the knowledge of reason* and *sensitive knowledge* or *the knowledge of the senses.*—(f³),

cognitio intellectualis, see *cognitio intellectiva.*—(g³), **cognitio intellectus,** see *cognitio intellectiva.*—(h³), **cognitio intelligibilis,** see *cognitio intellectiva.*—(i), **cognitio manifesta,** see *cognitio aenigmatica.*—(j³), **cognitio materialis,** see *cognitio immaterialis.* —(k³), **cognitio matutina** and **cognitio vespertina,** *the morning* and *the evening knowledge,* namely of angels, i.e., that knowledge by which the angels know the things of the world in the Divine Word, and that knowledge by which they recognize those things outside the Word in their own nature.—(l³), **cognitio meridiana,** *the midday knowledge of the angels,* which is a kind of morning knowledge. —(m³), **cognitio meritoria,** *the meritorious knowledge.*—(n³), **cognitio naturalis** and **cognitio supernaturalis,** *the natural* and *the supernatural knowledge.*—(o³), **cognitio necessaria,** *the necessary knowledge* or *the knowledge that could not be otherwise.*— (p³), **cognitio nocturna,** see *cognitio diurna.*—(q³), **cognitio obumbrata seu obscuritati admixta,** *the darkened* or *obscure knowledge.*—(r³), **cognitio obscuritati admixta,** see *cognitio obumbrata.* —(s³), **cognitio particularis,** see *cognitio communis.*—(t³), **cognitio patriae,** see *cognitio comprehensoris.*—(u³), **cognitio per causam** and **cognitio per effectum,** *the knowledge of a thing from* *its cause* and *the knowledge of a thing from its effect* or *knowledge a priori,* and *knowledge a posteriori.*—(v^3), **cognitio per effectum,** see *cognitio per causam.* (w^3), **cognitio perfecta,** see *cognitio completa.*—(x^3), **cognitio per verisimilitudinem,** see *cognitio certa.*—(y^3), **cognitio philosophica** and **cognitio theologica,** *philosophical* and *theological knowledge.*—(z^3), **cognitio plena,** see *cognitio completa.*—(a^4), **cognitio potentialis,** see *cognitio actualis.*—(b^4), **cognitio practica** and **cognitio speculativa,** *the practical* and *the speculative* or *theoretical knowledge,* i.e., knowledge directed to an action or effect and that directed to an observation or to contemplation. —(c^4), **cognitio praesentis status seu vitae,** see *cognitio comprehensoris.*—(d^4), **cognitio prima seu primitiva** and **cognitio ultima,** *the first* or *original knowledge* and *the last knowledge.*— (e^4), **cognitio primitiva,** see *cognitio prima.*—(f^4), **cognitio prophetica,** *prophetic knowledge.*— (g^4), **cognitio propria,** see *cognitio communis.*—(h^4), **cognitio prudentiae,** *the knowledge of prudence.*—(i^4), **cognitio ratiocinativa,** see *cognitio discursiva.* —(j^4), **cognitio reflexiva,** *reflexive knowledge.*—(k^4), **cognitio remota,** see *cognitio coniuncta.*— (l^4), **cognitio rerum (humanarum),** *the knowledge of (human) things.*—(m^4), **cognitio**

sensibilis seu sensitiva, see *cognitio intellectiva.*—(n^4), **cognitio sensitiva,** see *cognitio intellectiva.*—(o^4), **cognitio sensus,** see *cognitio intellectiva.*—(p^4), **cognitio simplex,** *the simple knowledge,* i.e. the knowledge which consists of a purely abstract notion, but yet is not composed after the manner of a judgment in which an idea is expressed by another.—(q^4), **cognitio sine discursu,** see *cognitio discursiva.* —(r^4), **cognitio singularium,** *the knowledge of singulars.*—(s^4), **cognitio specialis,** see *cognitio communis.*—(t^4), **cognitio specifica,** *the specific knowledge* or *the knowledge of essence.*—(u^4), **cognitio specularis,** see *cognitio aenigmatica.*—(v^4), **cognitio speculativa,** see *cognitio practica.* —(w^4), **cognitio summaria,** *the knowledge which includes only the chief matter.*—(x^4), **cognitio supernaturalis,** see *cognitio naturalis.*—(y^4), **cognitio supersubstantialis,** *the supersubstantial knowledge.*—(z^4), **cognitio theologica,** see *cognitio philosophica.* —(a^5), **cognitio ultima,** see *cognitio prima.*—(b^5), **cognitio uniformis,** *the uniform* or *homogeneous knowledge.*—(c^5), **cognitio universalis,** see *cognitio communis.*—(d^5), **cognitio venativa,** see *cognitio inquisitiva.*— (e^5), **cognitio veri,** *knowledge of truth.*—(f^5), **cognitio veritatis,** *knowledge of the truth.* —(g^5), **cognitio vespertina,** see *cogni-*

tio matutina.—(h⁵), **cognitio viae,** see *cognitio comprehensoris.* —(i⁵), **cognitio viatoris,** see *cognitio comprehensoris.*—(j⁵), **cognitio virtualis,** see *cognitio actualis.*—(k⁵), **cognitio volubilis,** *fluent knowledge.*—**Aliqua cognitio quanto altior est, tanto est magis unita et ad plura se extendit,** *the higher a knowledge stands according to its rank, the more unified or simple it is in itself and the more it embraces;* cf. *unire.*—**Cognitio contingit seu est, secundum quod cognitum est in cognoscente,** or, **cognitio fit per hoc, quod cognitum est in cognoscente,** or **cognitio non fit, nisi secundum quod cognitum est in cognoscente,** or, **cognitio fit, secundum quod cognitum est in cognoscente,** or, **cognitio fit, secundum quod cognitum aliquo modo est in cognoscente,** *knowledge is effected in as much as the thing known in some way exists in the one who knows.*— **Cognitio est media inter cognoscentem et obiectum,** *knowledge stands midway between him who knows* and *the thing known.* —**Cognitio facientis determinat formam facti,** *the knowledge of him who produces determines the form of what is produced,* i.e., every work is directed in its formation according to the idea of him who produces it.— **Cognitio fit per hoc, quod cognitum est in cognoscente,** see above: *Cognitio contingit etc.*—

Cognitio fit, secundum quod cognitum aliquo modo est in cognoscente, see above: *Cognitio contingit* etc.—**Cognitio non fit, nisi secundum quod cognitum est in cognoscente,** see above: *Cognitio contingit* etc.—**Cognitio omnis fit per assimilationem cognoscentis et cogniti,** or, **omnis cognitio est seu fit per assimilationem cognoscentis ad cognitum,** or, **omnis cognitio fit secundum similitudinem cogniti in cognoscente,** or, **quaelibet cognitio perficitur per hoc, quod similitudo rei cognitae est in cognoscente,** *knowledge comes into being thus: the knower is made to resemble the known in so far indeed as he takes upon himself not physically but intentionally a likeness of the known thing,* see below: *Omnis cognitio est per speciem* etc.—**Omnis cognitio est seu fit per assimilationem cognoscentis ad cognitum,** see above: *Cognitio omnis fit* etc.— **Omnis cognitio est per speciem aliquam, per cuius informationem fit assimilatio cognoscentis ad rem cognitam,** or, **omnis cognitio est per speciem aliquam cognoti in cognoscente,** *every knowledge comes into being thus: a representation or likeness of the known exists in the knower, which impresses upon the knower its form immaterially and makes him similar not physically but cognitively to the known.* See above: *Cognitio omnis fit*

etc.—Omnis cognitio est per uni-
onem rei cognitae ad cognoscentem, *every knowledge comes
into existence as the result of a
union of the known thing with
the knower.*—Omnis cognitio est
secundum aliquam formam, quae
est in cognoscente principium
cognitionis, or, quaelibet cognitio
fit per modum formae, quae est
in cognoscente, *every knowledge
takes place as the result of a
form which in the knower is the
principle of the knowledge.*—
Omnis cognitio est secundum
modum eius quo aliquid cognoscitur, *every knowledge directs
itself according to the manner
and fashion of that whereby
something is known, sicut omnis
operatio est secundum modum
formae, quo aliquis operatur.*—
Omnis cognitio fit secundum
similitudinem cogniti in cognoscente, see above: *Cognitio
omnis fit* etc.—Oportet quod
cognitio fiat secundum modum
cognoscentis, *knowledge must
take place according to the
mode of existence* and *character
of the knower, quod patet ex
hoc, quod eiusdem rei cognitio
est in sensu cum condicionibus
materialibus, quia sensus est potentia in materia, in intellectu
autem, quia immaterialis est,
eiusdem cognitio est sine appen-
ditiis materiae.*—Quaelibet cognitio fit per modum formae, quae
est in cognoscente, see above:
Omnis cognitio est secundum

aliquam formam etc.—Quaelibet
cognitio perficitur hoc, quod
similitudo rei cognitae est in cognoscente, see above: *Cognitio
omnis fit* etc.—

cognitivus, a, um, *adj.*, (1) *knowing,* synonym of *cognoscitivus,*
(2) *belonging 'to knowledge,
concerning knowledge.*—On habitus cognitivus, see *habitus* under 4; on pars cognitiva, see *pars*
under 1; on potentia cognitiva,
see *potentia* under 1; on ratio
cognitiva, see *ratio* under 1; on
virtus cognitiva, see *virtus* under
1; on vis cognitiva, see *vis* under
1.—On conclusio cognitiva, see
conclusio under 2; on intentio
cognitiva, see *intentio* under 4;
on iudicium cognitivum, see *iudicium* under 4.

cognitor, oris, *m., one who knows,
a knower.*

cognominatio, onis, *f., a designation,, title, a distinguishing appellation.*

cognoscibilis, e, *adj., recognizable,
discernible.* On ratio cognoscibilis, see *ratio* under 14.

cognoscibilitas, atis, *f., cognizabili-
ty, perceptibility.*

cognoscitivus, a, um, *adj., cogno-
scitive, knowing,* a synonym of
cognitivus. On habitus cognoscitivus, see *habitus* under 4; on
intellectus cognoscitivus quidditatis rei, see *intellectus* under 4;
on pars cognoscitiva, see *pars*
under 1; on potentia cognoscitiva, see *potentia* under 2; on
principium cognoscitivum, see

principium; on sensus magis seu maxime cognoscitivus, see *sensus* under 3; on substantia cognoscitiva, see *substantia* under 2; on virtus cognoscitiva, see *virtus* under 1; on vis cognoscitiva, see *vis* under 1.—Cognoscitivum, sc. principium, *the principle of knowledge* or *the faculty of knowledge.*

cognosco, ere, gnovi, gnitum, 3, *v. a.,* (cf. *cognitio*), (1) *to know* in the general and broader sense of the word, *to perceive, discern, apprehend,* (2) *to know* in the judicial sense, i.e., *to judge* or *decide* about something, (3) *to know* in the carnal sense, i.e., to exercise the *copula carnalis.*— One kind of *cognoscere* in this sense is cognoscere carnaliter, *to know carnally,* or *associate with some one sexually.* On esse in cognoscente, see *esse;* on intellectus cognoscens quod quid est, see *intellectus* under 4; on principium cognoscendi et principium primum cognoscendi, see *principium;* on ratio cognoscendi, see *ratio* under 12. On substantia cognoscens, see *substantia* under 2. The following are kinds of cognoscere in this (1) sense: (a), cognoscere abstracte seu in abstractione and cognoscere concrete seu in concretione, *to know something in its abstract* or *general form and to know something in its concrete form.*—(b), cognoscere actu seu in actu, cognoscere habitualiter

seu in habitu and cognoscere in potentia, *to know something at the present moment, after the manner of a habit to which we do not presently avert, and according to an as yet unfilled capacity.* Thus a man while reading this, actually reads English bu might habitually know Latin, and undertake at some future date to acquire Sanskirt.—(c), cognoscere affirmative, *to know in the sense of an affirmation,* i.e., to know in the sense that the knower expresses a positive decision of a thing.—(d), cognoscere an est and cognoscere quid est, *to know whether a thing is* or *exists* and *to know what a thing is.*—(e), cognoscere certitudinaliter and cognoscere coniecturaliter, *to know something with sureness* and *certainty* and *to know something in the manner of a conjecture.*—(f), cognoscere coniecturaliter, see *cognoscere certitudinaliter.*—(g), cognoscere concreta, see *cognoscere abstracte.*—(h), cognoscere cum discursu and cognoscere simplici intuitu, *to know something discursively* and *intuitively.* See also *discursus.*—(i), cognoscere demonstrative seu per modum necessitatis and cognoscere probabiliter seu per modum probabilitatis, *to know something in consequence of a demonstrated proof* or *with apodictic certainty* and *to know something with probability, i.e., to know that something must be* or *to know that something can be.*—(j), **cognoscere determinate seu distincte** and **cognoscere indistincte**, *to know something in a certain* and *in an uncertain way.*—(k), **cognoscere directe** and **cognoscere indirecte**, *to know something directly* or *in a straight-forward way* and *to know something indirectly* or *in a round-about way.*—(l), **cognoscere distincte**, see *cognoscere determinate.*—(m), **cognoscere ex causa seu per causam** and **cognoscere ex effectu seu per effectum**, *to know something from* and *through its cause* and *to know something from* and *through its effect.*—(n), **cognoscere ex effectu**, see *cognoscere ex causa.*—(o), **cognoscere explicite** and **cognoscere implicite**, *to know something in an unfolded* or *open way* and *to know something in an enveloped* or *contained way.*—(p), **cognoscere habitualiter**, see *cognoscere actu.*—(q), **cognoscere immaterialiter** and **cognoscere materialiter**, *to know something in an immaterial* or *spiritual manner* and *to do so materially.* Knowledge as such is always immaterial; the objects known may be material.—(r), **cognoscere imperfecte** and **cognoscere perfecte**, *to know something imperfectly* and *to know something perfectly.* —(s), **cognoscere implicite**, see *cognoscere explicite.*—(t), **cognoscere in abstractione**, see *cognoscere*

abstracte.—(u), **cognoscere in actu**, see *cognoscere actu.*—(v), **cognoscere in aenigmate seu in speculo** *to know something in a riddle* or *in a mirror.*—(w), **cognoscere in alio** and **cognoscere in seipso**, *to know something in another* and *to know something in oneself.*—(x), **cognoscere in cognitionis principio** and **cognoscere in obiecto cognito**, *to know in a principle whence something comes* and *in a known object.*—(y), **cognoscere in concretione**, see *cognoscere abstracte.*—(z), **cognoscere in habitu**, see *cognoscere actu.*—(a^2), **cognoscere in obiecto cognito**, see *cognoscere in cognitionis principio.*—(b^2), **cognoscere in particulari seu in speciali** and **cognoscere in universali seu universaliter seu in quadam communitate**, *to know something in general* and *in particular.*—(c^2), **cognoscere in potentia**, see *cognoscere actu.*—(d^2), **cognoscere in quadam communitate**, see *cognoscere in particulari.*—(e^2), **cognoscere in seipso**, see *cognoscere in alio.*—(f^2), **cognoscere in speciali**, see *cognoscere in particulari.*—(g^2), **cognoscere in speculo**, see *cognoscere in aenigmate.*—(h^2), **cognoscere in universali**, see *cognoscere in particulari.*—(i^2), **cognoscere incomplexe**, *to know in a manner not complex,* i.e., intuitively, without formulation of a proposition.—(j^2), **cognoscere indirecte**, see *cognoscere* *directe.*—(k²), **cognoscere indistincte,** see *cognoscere distincte.* —(l²), **cognoscere intellectualiter,** *to know something in an intellectual way.*—(m²), **cognoscere materialiter,** *to know something according to matter.*—(n²), **cognoscere naturaliter,** *to know naturally*—(o²), **cognoscere per abstractionem** and **cognoscere per impressionem,** *to know something as the result of abstraction* or *separation* or *as the result of an imprint* or *impression.*—(p²), **cognoscere per accidens** and **cognoscere per se,** *to know something indirectly through something else* and *to know something directly through oneself.*—(q²), **cognoscere per actum,** *to know through actualization.*—(r²), **cognoscere per causam,** see *cognoscere ex causa.* —(s²), **cognoscere per effectum,** see *cognoscere ex causa.*—(t²), **cognoscere per essentiam,** *to know by one's essence.*—(u²), **cognoscere per excessum seu per modum excellentiae, cognoscere per remotionem seu per modum remotionis,** and **cognoscere ut causam seu secundum habitudinem principii,** *to know something, namely God, in a manner of excess* or *excellence, to know something in a manner of removal* or *negation* and *to know something as a cause* or *in its relationship as a principle,* i.e., *to know something,* namely God, *in that one assigns to Him a*

perfection of an infinitely high degree, in that one utterly denies an imperfection on His part and conceives Him as the effective cause or *principle of visible creation.*—(v²), **cognoscere per impressionem,** see *cognoscere per abstractionem.*—(w²), **cognoscere per intellectum,** *to know through the intellect.*—(x²), **cognoscere per modum excellentiae,** see *cognoscere per excessum.* —(y²), **cognoscere per modum necessitatis,** see *cognoscere demonstrative.*—(z²), **cognoscere per modum probabilitatis,** see *cognoscere demonstrative.*—(a³), **cognoscere per modum remotionis,** see *cognoscere per excessum.*—(b³), **cognoscere per modum speculationis seu speculative,** *to know in the manner* or *in the sense of pure speculation without considering a doing* or *activity in which knowledge can be valued.*—(c³), **cognoscere per modum visionis,** *to know in the manner of direct intuition.*—(d³), **cognoscere per praesentiam suae essentiae in cognoscente, cognoscere per praesentiam suae similitudinis in potentia cognoscitiva** and **cognoscere per praesentiam suae similitudinis resultantis in aliqua re,** *to know something in consequence of the presence of its essence in the knower, to know something in consequence of the presence of its direct image in the knowing faculty* and *to* *know something in consequence of the presence of its reflection in anything.*—(e³), **cognoscere per praesentiam suae similitudinis in potentia cognoscitiva,** see *cognoscere per praesentiam suae essentiae in cognoscente.*—(f³), **cognoscere per praesentiam suae similitudinis resultantis in aliqua re,** see *cognoscere per praesentiam suae essentiae in cognoscente.* —(g³), **cognoscere per rationem,** *to know through reason.*—(h³), **cognoscere per remotionem,** see *cognoscere per excessum.*—(i³), **cognoscere per revelationem, cognoscere per se** and **cognoscere per signa,** *to know something through revelation, to know something through itself,* and *to know something through signs.*— (j³), **cognoscere per scientiam,** *to know by habitual knowledge.*— (k³), **cognoscere per se,** see *cognoscere per accidens* and *cognoscere per revelationem.*—(l³), **cognoscere per sensum,** *to know something through a sense.*—(m³), **cognoscere per signa,** see *cognoscere per revelationem.*—(n³), **cognoscere per similitudinem,** *to know by a reflected likeness.*— (o³), **cognoscere per speciem,** *to know something through cognitive representations.*—(p³), **cognoscere per speciem continentis** and **cognoscere per speciem propriam,** *to know something through a cognitive representation of one who possesses the knowledge and to know some-*

thing through its own cognitive representation.—(q³), **cognoscere per speciem propriam,** see *cognoscere per speciem continentis.*—(r³), **cognoscere perfecte,** see *cognoscere imperfecte.*—(s³), **cognoscere plene,** *to know something fully.*—(t³), **cognoscere primo,** *to know something first and next.*—(u³), **cognoscere probabiliter,** see *cognoscere demonstrative.*—(v³), **cognoscere rem quantum ad ea, quae ipsam consequuntur** and **cognoscere rem secundum id quod est,** *to know a thing with reference to that which is proper to it* and *to know it according to what it is in itself.*—(w³), **cognoscere rem secundum id quod est,** see *cognoscere rem quantum ad ea, quae ipsam consequuntur.*—(x³), **cognoscere secundum habitudinem principii,** see *cognoscere per excessum.*—(y³), **cognoscere secundum quid** and **cognoscere simpliciter,** *to know something with reference to something or in a certain respect* and *to know something simply or absolutely.*— (z³), **cognoscere simplici intuitu,** see *cognoscere cum discursu.*— (a⁴), **cognoscere simpliciter,** see *cognoscere secundum quid.*—(b⁴), **cognoscere speculative,** see *cognoscere per modum speculationis.*—(c⁴), **cognoscere universaliter,** see *cognoscere in particulari.* —(d⁴), **cognoscere ut causam,** see *cognoscere per excessum.*—**cognita sunt in cognoscente secundum**

modum cognoscentis et non secundum modum rerum cogni-
tarum, or, cognoscens continet
species cogniti secundum modum
suum, or, omne cognoscens habet cognitionem de re cognita
non per modum rei cognitae,
sed per modum cognoscentis,
*the known or the representation
of the known is in the knower
after the manner of the knower*
and *not after the manner of
the known.*—Cognoscens continet
species cogniti secundum modum
suum, see above: *cognita sunt in*
etc.—Cognoscentis et cognoscibilis oportet esse aliquam proportionem, *the knower* and *the
knowable must stand in some
kind of relation to each other.*—
Omne cognoscens habet cognitionem de re cognita non per
modum rei cognitae, sed per
modum cognoscentis, see above.
Cognita sunt in etc.—Res non
cognoscitur ab anima nisi per
aliquam sui similitudinem exsistentem vel in sensu vel in intellectu, see *res.*—Unumquodque
cognoscitur, secundum quod est
in actu non secundum quod est
in potentia, *everything is known
only in as far and in as much as
it exists in reality, not however,
in so far as it exists merely in
potentiality.*

cogo, cogere, coegi, coactum, 3,
v. a., to force, induce.—**coacte,**
adv., through force, coercively.

cohabitatio, onis, *f., cohabitation, a
dwelling together.*

cohabito, are, 1, *v. n., to dwell
together, cohabit.*

cohaereo, ere, haesi, haesum, 2,
v. n., to cling together, be united.

cohibeo, ere, ui, itum, 2, *v. a.,
to keep back, hinder, restrain,
check.*

cohibitio, onis, *f., a restraining,
governing, curbing, prohibition,
prevention.*

cohibitivus, a, um, *adj., cohibitive,
curbing, restraining.*

coincido, ere, 3, *v. n., coincide.*

coinquino, are, avi, atum, 1, *v. a.,*
(1) of infectuous diseases, *to
infect,* (2) *to defile, to contaminate.*

cointellego, ere, exi, ectum, 3, *v. a.,
to know with, understand with.*

coitus, us, *m.,* (1) *coition, copulation, sexual intercourse,* (2) *an
assembly, body, collection of
persons considered as a whole.*

collabor, i, collapsus, 3, *v. dep., to
fall, to fall into ruins, sink, stoop,*
used *lit.* and *fig.*

collactaneus, i, *m., a foster-brother,
a brother nourished at the same
breast.*

collatio, onis, *f.,* (1) *a bringing together, collection,* (2) *a placing
together, comparison,* (3) *transmission, participation, bestowal,
distribution.*—On **iudicare ex collatione,** see *iudicare* under 3.—
Kinds of *collatio* in this (3)
sense are: (a), **collatio carnalis**
and **collatio simoniaca** (sc. **alicuius spiritualis rei**), *the carnal
bestowal or one which proceeds
from carnal consideration* and *si-*

moniacal bestowal or *the bestowal of a spiritual thing for the sake of an earthly advantage.*—(b), **collatio liberalis**, *the generous bestowal.*—(c), **collatio simoniaca**, see *collatio carnalis.*

collativus, a, um, *adj., comparing, comparative.* On **motus collativus**, see *motus* under 2; on **ratio collativa**, see *ratio* under 4; on **scientia collativa**, see *scientia* under 2; on **virtus collativa**, see *virtus* under 1; on **vis collativa**, see *vis* under 1.

collaudatio, onis, *f., warm praise, collaudation.*

collaudo, are, avi, atum, 1, *v. a., to praise, commend, extol highly, collaud.*

collecta, ae, *f.,* (1) *a meeting, assemblage, congregation, collection,* (2) *the Collect of the Mass,* i.e., *the Prayer of the Day.*

collectio, onis, *f.,* (1) *a gathering, collection, blending together, assembly* of persons or things, (2) *a series,* as of persons related by blood and descending from a common ancestor in various degrees.

collective, *adv.,* see *collectivus.*

collectivus, a, um, *adj., collective, composing.* On **nomen collectivum**, see *nomen* under 1; on **unitas collectiva**, see *unitas.*—**collective**, *adv., after the manner* or *in the sense of collecting* or *composing, collectively,* synonym of *composite* and *coniunctim,* the opposite of *distributive, divise, divisim,* and *divisive.* On

accipere collective, see *accipere* under 3; on **intellegere collective**, see *intellegere* under 3; on **tenere collective**, see *tenere* under 7.

collegiatus, i, *m., he who is with one in a society, college, corporation,* etc., *a collegian.*

collegium, ii, *m.,* and *n.,* (1) *a college, society, assembly, company, community,* (2) *a chapter* or *body of clergy connected with some collegiate church or cathedral.*

collido, ere, lisi, lisum, 3, *v. a., to bruise, beat, press together, dash against.*

colligatio, onis, *f., a tie, bond, joining, cohesion.*

colligo, ere, legi, lectum, 3, *v. a., to gather, collect.*

colligo, are, avi, atum, 1, *v. a., to unite, connect, tie, fasten, bind,* used *lit.* and *fig.*

collinio, ire, ivi, itum, 4, *v. a., to rub over something.*

collis, is, *m., a hill.*

collocatio, onis, *f.,* (1) *a putting together, erecting, placing, laying,* (2) *a place of rest, stopping* or *halting place, establishment,* a synonym of *mansio.*

colloco, are, avi, atum, 1, *v. a., to place together, arrange, station, set up, place.*

collocutio, onis, *f., a conversation.*

colloquium, ii, *n., a conversation, conference, discourse, colloquy.*

colloquor, i, cutus, 3, *v. dep., to talk together, converse, hold a conversation,* (1) used with *ad* and *acc.*, (2) *cum* and *abl.*, (3) with *dat.*, (4) *absol.*

colludo, ere, si, sum, 3, *v. n.*, *to act collusively, plot secretly with evil design.*

collum, i, *n.*, (1) *the neck,* that part of an animal which connects the head with the trunk, (2) *the shoulders,* (3) *life,* used symbolically.

colluvio, onis, *f.*, *defilement, stain.*

colo, ere, colui, cultum, 3, *v. a.*, (1) *to till, tend, take care of a field,* (2) *honor, revere, reverence, worship.—***colens,** entis, *P. a.*, *honoring, treating respectfully; subst., a reverer, worshipper.*

colo, are, avi, atum, *v. a.*, *to filter, strain, clarify, purify.*

colonus, i, *m.*, *a farmer, husbandman, one who cultivates another's land.*

color, oris, *m.*, (1) *color, hue, tint,* (2) *outward s. w, appearance,* (3) *coloring, style,* especially of diction, (4) *complexion, the natural color of men.*

coloro, are, avi, atum, 1, *v. a.*, *to color, tinge, color reddish* or *brownish.*

Colossenses, ium, *m.*, *the Colossians, the inhabitants of Colossae;* to the Church in Colossae Paul's Epistle to the Colossians was addressed.

columba, ae, *f.*, *a dove, a pigeon.*

columna, ae, *f.*, (1) *a column, pillar,* used *lit.* and *fig.* (2) *objects resembling a pillar,* as the pillar of cloud and fire that guided the exodus of the Israelites from Egypt, (3) on printed matter, *one of the two or more vertical series of lines separated by a rule* or *blank space.*

coma, ae, *f.*, (1) *the hair of the head,* (2) *a tail* or *train,* as the nebulosity surrounding the nucleus of a comet.

comatus, a, um, *adj.*, (1) *decked with something resembling hair;* with **stella,** *a star having a radiant, hairy train; a comet,* (2) *clothed, decked.*

combinatio, onis, *f.*, *a joining two by two, combination.*

comburo, ere, 3, *v. a.*, *to burn up, consume,* used *lit.* and *fig.*

combustibilis, e, *adj.*, *combustible,* that may be set on fire and burned, *susceptible of combustion.—***combustibile,** is, *n.*, *any substance that will readily ignite and burn, a combustible.*

combustio, onis, *f.*, *a burning, consuming.*

comedo, ere, edi, esum, 3, *v. a.*, *to eat entirely up, eat, consume.*

comes, itis, *comm.*, (1) *a companion, associate, comrade, sharer, partner,* used *lit.* and *fig.*, (2) *a prerequisite, an accompanying attendant* or *condition.*

comessatio, onis, *f.*, *rioting, revelling, luxurious* and *profligate living, boisterous festivity.*

comestibilia, ium, *n.*, *eatables, edibles, foods.*

comestio, onis, *f.*, *a consuming, eating of food, a meal.*

cometes, ae, *f.*, *a comet.*

comis, e, *adj.*, *affable, pleasant.*

comitor, ari, atus, 1, *v. dep. a., to accompany, attend, follow as a result.*

commaculo, are, avi, atum, 1, *v. a., to spot, stain, pollute, defile on every side.*

commaneo, ere, 2, *v. n., to remain somewhere constantly, to live together.*

commansio, onis, *f., a living together.*

commassatio, onis, *f., an assemblage of persons that collectively make one unit, an assemblage.*

commater, tris, *f., a co-mater, godmother,* a woman who contracted a spiritual relationship with a man by being sponsor at baptism either for his child or his godchild.

commemoratio, onis, *f., a calling to mind, reminding, commemorating, remembrance.*

commemorativus, a, um, *adj., commemorative, pertaining to or designed for commemoration.*

commemoro, are, avi, atum, 1, *v. a., to recall an object to memory in all its particulars, mention, call to mind, record, present, commemorate.*

commendabilis, e, *adj., commendable, worthy of praise.*

commendatio, onis, *f.,* (1) *praise, commendation, approval,* (2) *a commemorative prayer said during the mass for the souls in purgatory.*

commendo, are, avi, atum, 1, *v. a.,* (1) *to commend* or *recommend, procure favor for, praise,* (2) *commend to one's care for preservation* or *protection, intrust to one's charge, commit to one's care, commend to,* (3) *be sprung* or *derived, take one's origin from,* (4) *betoken, to be a token* or *sign of, give promise* or *evidence of.*

commensuratio, onis, *f., bringing together, adaptation, proportion, commensurateness.* On **unio per modum commensurationis,** see *unio.*—Kinds of *commensuratio* are: (a), **commensuratio debita,** *the commensurateness that ought to be* or *that is proper.*—(b), **commensuratio proportionata,** *the relative* or *proportionate commensurateness.*

commensuro, are, avi, atum, 1, *v. a., to bring into proportion, adapt, make commensurate.*—**commensuratus,** a, um, *P. a., adapted, made commensurate.*

commentarium, ii, *n., a commentary, exposition, brief explanation, annotation.*

commentator, oris, *m.,* (1) *interpreter, commentator,* (2) *the interpreter* or *commentator per eminentiam,* i.e., the interpreter of the writings of Aristotle by whom is understood the Moorish philosopher Ibn Roshd, called in Latin, Averroes. (✝ 1198.)

commercium, ii, *n., compact, agreement, covenant, contract.*

commetior, iri, mensus, 4, *v. dep., to measure, proportion, make proportionate,* used *fig.*

commilito, onis, *m.*, *a comrade,
companion in war, fellow soldier.*

commilito, are, 1, *v. n.*, *to be a
companion in war, to fight side
by side.*

comminatio, onis, *f.*, *a threatening,
menacing, denunciation, commi-
nation, threat.*

comminatorius, a, um, *adj.*, *commi-
natory, threatening punishment
or vengeance.*

comminor, ari, atus, 1, *v. dep.*, (1)
to threaten, (2) *charge, give command, instruction or advice to.—*
comminatus, a, um, *P. a.*, *threatened.*

comminuo, ere, utum, 3, *v. a.*, *to
break, destroy, crush, wear away,
diminish.*

comminutio, onis, *f.*, *a trituration,
breaking, crushing, reducing to
a fine powder*, a synonym of *contritio*, used *fig.*

commisceo, ere, miscui, mixtum, 2,
v. a., (1) *to mix* or *mingle together, intermingle*, (2) *produce by
mingling, mix carnally, have sexual intercourse.*

commiseror, ari, atus, 1, *v. dep.*, *to
commiserate, feel pity for.*

commissio, onis, *f.*, (1) *commit-
ment, assignment, charge*, (2)
perpetration, commission, the opposite of *omissio*. On **potestas per
commissionem**, see *potestas.—*On
peccatum commissionis, see *peccatum* under 2.

committo, ere, misi, missum, 3,
v. a., (1) *to commit to, assign,
charge, entrust*, (2) *perpetrate,*

commit (a sin or a crime), the
opposite of *omitto.—*commissus,
a, um, *P. a.*, *committed, perpetrated.—*commissum, i, *n.*, *a
transgression, offense, sin.*

commixtio, onis, *f.*, (1) *mixture,
composition*, synonym of *complexio, compositio*, and *mixtio*,
(2) *carnal connection, coition.—*
On **temperamentum commixtionis**, see *temperamentum* under 1;
on **unio per modum commixtionis**, see *unio.*

commodatus, a, um, *P. a.*, (1)
leased out for rent, (2) *loaned.
—*If the loan was to be returned
as money, it was called *commo-
datum;* if the thing was to be
consumed as wine or oil, and
returned in kind, the loan was
called *mutuum.*

commode, *adv.*, *duly, properly, fittingly.*

commoditas, atis, *f.*, *advantage, benefit, profit, consideration.*

commodum, i, *n.*, *profit, gain, advantage, benefit, consideration,
recompense.*

commorior, iri, mortuus, 3, *v. dep.
n.*, *to die with* or *at the same
time with one.*

commoror, ari, atus, 1, *v. dep.* and
n. and *a.*, *to dwell, live together,
remain, stay, tarry, abide, so-
journ.*

commotio, onis, *f.*, (1) *a moving,
motion, agitation, disturbance*,
(2) *fig.*, *a rousing, exciting of
the emotions* or *passions*, with
and without *animi.*

commoveo, ere, movi, motum, 2, *v. a., to move, shake, agitate,* used *lit.* and *fig.*

communicabilis, e, *adj., communicable,* the opposite of *incommunicabilis.* On **nomen communicabile,** see *nomen* under 1.—Special uses of *communicabilis* are as follows: (a), **communicabile proprie** and **communicabile secundum similitudinem seu similitudinis participationem,** *communicable in the proper* and *full sense of the word* and *communicable according to analogy or likeness.* —(b), **communicabile secundum opinionem** and **communicabile secundum rei veritatem,** *communicable according to the opinion of someone and according to the truth* and *reality of a thing.*—(c), **communicabile secundum rei veritatem,** see *communicabile secundum opinionem.*—(d), **communicabile secundum similitudinem seu similitudinis participationem,** see *communicabile proprie.*

communicabilitas, atis, *f., communicability,* the opposite of *incommunicabilitas.*—Kinds of *communicabilitas* are: **communicabilitas assumentis** and **communicabilitas assumptibilis,** *communicability of that which accepts* and *communicability of that which can be accepted.*

communicantia, ae, *f., agreement, conformity, a state of correspondence.*

communicatio, onis, *f.,* (1) *communication, participation, the making common, sharing,* synonym of *communio,* (2) *participation, agreement,* (3) *communication, association, intercourse,* synonym of *communio, communitas, congregatio,* and *conversatio.* See *communicare.*—Kinds of *communicatio* in this (1) sense are: (a), **communicatio idiomatum,** *participation in peculiarities.*—(b), **communicatio naturalis,** and **communicatio supernaturalis,** *natural* and *supernatural paticipation.*—(c), **communicatio nominum,** *participation in names.*—(d), **communicatio per modum amoris** and **communicatio per modum naturae,** *participation after the manner of love or through an act of the same* and *participation after the manner of nature or through an act of the same.*—(e), **communicatio per modum naturae,** see *communicatio per modum amoris.*—(f), **communicatio supernaturalis,** see *communicatio naturalis.*—Kinds of *communicatio* in this (2) sense are: (a), **communicatio auctoritate principum** and **communicatio propria voluntate privatarum personarum,** *official* and *private association.*—(b), **communicatio civilis seu civilium operum seu politica, communicatio oeconomica, communicatio divina seu spiritualis,** and **communicatio naturalis,** *civic* or *public association,* i.e., that which consists in civic affairs; *association in domestic* or *family affairs; association in divine* and *spiritual affairs;* and *natural association.* (Cf. *communicatio naturalis*).— (c), **communicatio civilium operum**, see *communicatio civilis.*— (d), **communicatio campsoria,** *association in money-changing* and *banking.*—(e), **communicatio commutativa,** *association in exchange.*—(f), **communicatio divina,** see *communicatio civilis.* —(g), **communicatio naturalis,** see *communicatio civilis.*—(h), **communicatio oeconomica,** see *communicatio civilis.*—(i), **communicatio personalis,** *personal* or *individual association.*—(j), **communicatio politica,** see *communicatio civilis.*—(k), **communicatio propria voluntate privatarum personarum,** see *communicatio auctoritate principum.*—(l), **communicatio spiritualis,** see *communicatio civilis.*

communicativus, a, um, *adj., communicative, permitting participation,* synonym of *diffusivus.*—**Bonum est diffusivum et communicativum sui,** see *bonum* under 1.

communicator, oris, *m., a communicator, one who communicates* or *makes another a partaker of something.*

communico, are, avi, atum, 1, *v. a.,* (1) *to inform, communicate, make generally known, confer,* (2) *participate in, take part* or *share in, have in common, agree, receive Holy Communion,* (3)

have communication with, go about with, associate with. Cf. *communicatio.*—Kinds of *communicare* in this (1) sense are: (a), **communicare per actum naturae** and **communicare per actum voluntatis,** *to communicate something through an act of nature* and *through an act of the free will.*—(b), **communicare per actum voluntatis,** see *communicare per actum naturae.*—(c), **communicare proprie,** *to communicate something in the proper* and *in the full sense of the word.*—(d), **communicare ratione** and **communicare re,** *to communicate something according to its notion or idea and in reality.*— (e), **communicare re,** see *communicare ratione.*

communio, ire, ivi, itum, 4, *v. a., to fortify on all sides, barricade, intrench.*

communio, onis, *f.,* (1) *communication, association,* a synonym of *communicatio, communitas, congregatio,* and *conversatio,* (2) *participation, sharing unity,* likewise a synonym of *communicatio,* (3) *the sacrament of the altar, the Eucharist, Holy Communion.*—Kinds of *communio* in this (1) sense are: **communio domestica** and **communio politica,** *domestic* or *family association* and *public* or *civic association.*

communis, e, *adj.,* (Cf. *communitas*), (1) *common* (i.e., in common), *joint, combined,* the opposite of *proprius, distinctus,* and *individualis,* (2) *general, usual,* synonym of *generalis* and *universalis,* the opposite of *particularis* and *specialis.*—On **accidens commune,** see *accidens* under 2; on **bonum commune,** see *bonum* under 3; on **causa communis,** see *causa* under 1 and 2; on **conceptio communis,** see *conceptio* under 4; on **conceptus communis,** see *conceptus* under 2; on **concupiscentia communis,** see *concupiscentia* under 1; on **defectus communis,** see *defectus* under 2; on **differentia communis,** see *differentia;* on **discretio communis,** see *discretio* under 2; on **dispensatio communis,** see *dispensatio* under 2; on **donum commune,** see *donum* under 2; on **esse commune,** see *esse;* on **essentia communis,** see *essentia* under 1; on **finis communis,** see *finis* under 2; on **forma communis,** see *forma* under 2; on **intentio communis,** see *intentio* under 3; on **instrumentum commune,** see *instrumentum;* on **lex communis,** see *lex* under 1; on **locus communis,** see *locus* under 2; on **materia communis,** see *materia* under 3; on **mensura communis,** see *mensura;* on **modus communis,** see *modus* under 2 and 3; on **motus communis,** see *motus* under 1; on **natura communis,** see *natura;* on **nomen commune,** see *nomen* under 1; on **operatio communis,** see *operatio* under 2; on **oratio communis,** see *oratio* under 3; on

organum commune, see *organum;* on **passio communis,** see *passio* under 1; on **principium commune,** see *principium;* on **propositio communis,** see *propositio* under 2; on **proprietas communis,** see *proprietas* under 1; on **ratio communis,** see *ratio* under 11 and 12; on **sensibile commune,** see *sensibilis* under 3; on **sensus communis,** see *sensus* under 3; on **spiratio communis,** see *spiratio;* on **status communis,** see *status* under 3; on **suffragia communia,** see *suffragium;* on **terminus communis,** see *terminus* under 5; on **usus communis,** see *usus* under 1; on **via communis,** see *via* under 1; on **vita communis,** see *vita* under 3; on **votum commune,** see *votum* under 1.— Kinds of *commune* in this sense are: (a), **commune absolute dictum seu per se acceptum** and **commune quod importat respectum ad creaturas seu acceptum cum respectu ad creaturas,** *the absolutely common* or *the common as such* and *the common with reference to the creature.*— (b), **commune acceptum cum respectu ad creaturas,** see *commune absolute dictum.*—(c), **commune aequivoce, commune analogice seu secundum analogiam seu analogum** and **commune univoce seu univocum,** *the common in the sense of pure homonymity, that in the sense of proportion,* and *that in the sense of homogeneity.*—(d), **commune analogice**

seu analogum, see *commune aequivoce.*—(e), **commune per praedicationem** and **commune secundum participationem,** *the common after the manner of declaration* and *the common after the manner of participation in one* and *the same thing.*—(f), **commune per se acceptum,** see *commune absolute dictum.*—(g), **commune quod importat respectum ad creaturas,** see *commune absolute dictum.*—(h), **commune re seu secundum rem** and **commune secundum rationem,** *the common according to fact* and *the common according to a mental* or *logical consideration.*—(i), **commune secundum analogiam,** see *commune aequivoce.*—(j), **commune secundum participationem,** see *commune per praedicationem.*—(k), **commune secundum rationem,** see *commune re.*—(1), **commune secundum rem,** see *commune re.*—(m), **commune univoce seu univocum,** see *commune aequivoce.*—On **bonitas communis,** see *bonitas* under 1; on **bonum commune,** see *bonus* under 3; on **castitas communis,** see *castitas* under 2; on **cognitio communis,** see *cognitio* under 2; on **conceptio communis,** see *conceptio* under 4; on **desiderium commune,** see *desiderium* under 1; on **differentia communis,** see *differentia;* on **dignitas communis,** see *dignitas* under 2; on **distinctio in communi,** see *distinctio* under 2; on **divisio communis**

analogi seu per analogiam, see *divisio;* on **documentum commune,** see *documentum* under 4; on **eleemosyna communis,** see *eleemosyna;* on **ens communis,** see *ens;* on **esse commune,** see *esse;* on **essentia communis,** see *essentia;* on **finis communis,** see *finis* under 2; on **forma communis,** see *forma* under 2; on **forum commune,** see *forum* under 2; on **genus commune,** see *genus* under 1; on **homo communis,** see *homo;* on **iniustum commune,** see *iniustus;* on **intentio communis;** see *intentio* under 3; on **iudicium commune,,** see *iudicium* under 1; on **ius commune,** see *ius* under 1; on **iustitia communis,** see *iustitia* under 1; on **modus communis,** see *modus* under 2; on **necessitas communis,** see *necessitas* under 3; on **nomen commune,** see *nomen* under 1; on **opinio communis,** see *opinio;* on **origo in communi,** see *origo;* on **perfectio communis,** see *perfectio* under 3; on **praeceptum commune,** see *praeceptum;* on **praedicare in communi,** see *praedicare* under 2; on **propositio communis,** see *propositio;* on **ratio communis,** see *ratio* under 11, 12, and 13; on **resurrectio communis,** see *resurrectio;* on **scientia communis,** see *scientia* under 1; on **species communis,** see *species* under 8; on **unum commune,** see *unus;* on **veritas communis,** see *veritas* under 1; on **verum commune,** see *verus* under 1; on virtus communis, see *virtus* under 1 and 5; on vita communis, see *vita* under 3.—communiter, *adv., together, in common, jointly, in general,* synonym of *in communi.*—in communi, see *communiter;* opposite of *in particulari, in proprio,* and *in speciali.*

communitas, atis, f., (Cf. *communis*), (1) *community, common possession, joint ownership,* (2) *community, social intercourse, association,* a synonym of *communicatio, communio, congregatio,* and *conversatio,* (3) *community, congregation, parish,* (4) *generality,* synonym of *universalitas.*—Kinds of *communitas* in this (1) sense are: (a), communitas analogiae seu analogica and communitas univocationis seu univoca, *the community of proportion* and *that of similarity.* —(b), communitas analogica, see *communitas analogiae.*—(c), communitas assumptibilis, *the community* of the acceptable, i.e., of that which a person can accept or take upon himself.—(d), communitas attributorum, communitas essentiae seu naturae, communitas operationum, communitas relationum essentialium, and communitas negationum, *the community of essential characteristics, that of essences* or *of natures, that of actions, that of essential relations* and *that of negative aspects.*—(e), communitas essentiae, see communitas attributorum.—(f), communitas

generis, communitas speciei and communitas personae, *the community of genus, that of species, that of kind,* and *that of person.* —(g), communitas intentionis seu secundum rationem intentionis and communitas secundum rationem proportionis, *community of relation* or *after the manner of relation,* and *that after the manner of proportions.*—(h), communitas naturae, see *communitas attributorum.*—(i), communitas negationum, see *communitas attributorum.*—(j), communitas operationum, see *communitas attributorum.*—(k), communitas particularis and communitas universalis, *particular* and *general community.*—(l), communitas personae, see *communitas generis.*— (m), communitas rationis and communitas rei, *community of idea* and *that of fact*—(n), communitas rationis fundatae in re, *community of idea based on reality.*—(o), communitas rei, see *communitas rationis.*—(p), communitas relationum essentialium, see *communitas attributorum.*— (q), communitas secundum rationem intentionis, see *communitas intentionis.*—(r), communitas secundum rationem proportionis, see *communitas intentionis.*—(s), communitas speciei, see *communitas generis.*—(t), communitas universalis, see *communitas particularis.*—(u), communitas univoca, see *communitas aequivoce.* —(v), communitas univocationis, see *communitas aequivoce.—* Kinds of *communitas* in this (2) sense are: (a), **communitas civilis seu humana,** *the purely civic* or *universally human association,* quae est hominum ad invicem, the opposite of the *communitas ecclesiastica,* quae est hominum ad Deum.—(b), **communitas humana,** see *communitas civilis.—*(c), **communitas personalis,** *the personal* or *individual association,* quae est personae ad personam.—Kinds of *communitas* in this (3) sense are: (a), **communitas aristocratica, communitas oligarchica,** and **communi. ; democratica,** *the aristocratic, the oligarchic,* and *the democratic community,* i.e., communities presided over by the virtuous, the rich, and the free people.—(b), **communitas civitatis seu politica, communitas domus, communitas vici,** and **communitas universi,** *the state* or *civic community, the family* or *domestic community, the village* or *city community,* and *the world* or *universal community.—*(c), **communitas democratica,** see *communitas aristocratica.—*(d), **communitas domus,** see *communitas civitatis.—*(e), **communitas humana,** *the community of mankind.—*(f), **communitas imperfecta** and **communitas perfecta,** *the imperfect* and *the perfect community.—*(g), **communitas naturalis,** *the natural community.—*(h), **communitas oligarchica,** see

communitas aristocratica.—(i), **communitas perfecta,** see *communitas imperfecta.—*(j), **communitas politica,** see *communitas civitatis.—*(k), **communitas universi,** see *communitas civitatis.—*(l), **communitas vici,** see *communitas civitatis.*

communiter, *adv.,* see *communis.*

commutabilis, e, *adj., mutable, capable* or *liable to change in form, state* or *quality.*

commutatio, onis, *f.,* (1) *change, transformation,* (2) *exchange, barter, commutation,* (3) *conduct at the exchange.—*Kinds of *commutatio* in this (2) sense are: (a), **commutatio campsoria,** *money exchange.—*(b), **commutatio involuntaria** and **commutatio voluntaria,** *voluntary* and *involuntary commutation, the synallagma akousion* and *synallagma hekousion* of Aristotle.—(c), **commutatio naturalis** and **commutatio per seu secundum rationem inventa,** *natural commutation* or *that proceeding from nature* and *that based on human reason.—*(d), **commutatio necessitatis,** *commutation of necessity.—*(e), **commutatio pecunaria,** *commutation by means of money.—*(f), **commutatio per seu secundum rationem inventa,** see *commutatio naturalis.—*(g), **commutatio voluntaria,** see *commutatio involuntaria.—*Ir this sense note **bona commutatio.** *good conduct* or *the virtue of justice in exchange,* the Greek *eusynallaxia.*

commutativus, a, um, *adj., commutable, exchangeable,* in the S.T. used only with *iustitia* and *iustum.* On **iustitia commutativa,** see *iustitia* under 1; on **iustum commutativum,** see *iustus.*

commuto, are, avi, atum, 1, *v. a.,* (1) *to alter, change,* (2) *exchange something with another, exchange, barter.*

comoedia, ae, *f., a comedy.*

compactus, a, um, *P. a.,* of figure or form, *compact, thick-set, firm.*

compagino, are, avi, atum, 1, *v. a., to join together.*

compago, inis, *f., a joint,* a place of union between two bones or separate parts of the skeleton.

compar, paris, *n., comm., a compeer, one having equal rank or standing.*

comparabilis, e, *adj., comparable,* that may be compared, fit to be compared.

comparatio, onis, *f.,* (1) *proportion, relation, direction,* (2) *comparison, comparing.*—Kinds of *comparatio* in this (2) sense are: (a), **comparatio absoluta** and **comparatio respectiva,** *the absolute* and *the respective comparison.*—(b), **comparatio abusiva,** *the abusive comparison.*—(c), **comparatio aequalitatis** and **comparatio similitudinis,** *comparison in the sense of equality* and *that in the sense of resemblance.*—(d), **comparatio respectiva,** see *comparatio absoluta.*—(e), **comparatio similitudinis,** see *comparatio aequalitatis.*

comparative, *adv.,* see *comparativus.*

comparativus, a, um, *adj., of* or *pertaining to comparison, comparative.*—**comparative,** *adv., in the sense of comparison, like a comparison.* On **dicere comparative,** see *dicere* under 3.

compareo, ere, ui, 2, *v. n., to appear, be visible.*

comparo, are, avi, atum, 1, *v. a.,* (1), *to bring into a condition, put oneself in relation to something direct, place in reference, refer,* (2) *compare,* (3) *prepare, procure.*—On **cognitio comparata,** see *cognitio* under 2; on **quantitas comparata,** see *quantitas.*

comparticeps, ticipis, *adj., a partner, one who takes part* or *is associated with another.*

compassio, onis, *f.,* (1) *a natural attraction to something,* (2) *compassion,* a synonym of *misericordia.*

compater, tris, *m., a co-parent, a god-father.*

compaternitas, atis, *f., coparternity,* relationship existing between the godparent and the carnal parent of the same person.

compatior, i, passus, 3, *v. dep.,* (1) *to allow, permit, acknowledge,* used with the *acc.* alone, with the *acc.* followed by the *dat.* or by *secum,* (2) *to feel compassion, suffer pain with, sympathize with, commiserate,* used with the *dat.* and *absol.*—**compatiens,** entis, *P. a., pitying, sympathizing.*

compello, ere, puli, pulsum, 3, *v. a.*, *to drive, move, impel, incite, urge, compel, force, constrain to something*, used with the *acc.*, with the *acc.* and *inf.*, with the *inf.*, with *in* and *acc.*, with *ad* and the *acc.*, and with *ut.*

compendiose, *adv.*, see *compendiosus.*

compendiosus, a, um, *adj.*, *short, brief, compendious.*—**compendiose,** *adv.*, *briefly.*—**compendiosius,** *comp.*, *more quickly.*

compensatio, onis, *f.*, *a balancing, exchange.*

compenso, are, avi, 1; *v. a.*, *to appraise, compensate, set a balance against.*

comperio, ire, peri, pertum, 4, *v. a.*, *to prove, discover, find out, lay open.*

compesco, ere, pescui, 3, *v. a.*, *to hold in check, repress, curb, restrain.*

competo, ere, ivi or ii, itum, 3, *v. a.* and *n.*, (1) *to be appropriate to, suitable to, befit, be attached to, belong to, be due to, be becoming to, be attributable to, be applicable to, correspond to, be competent*, used with the *dat.*, in with the *abl.*, *acc.* and *inf.*, the *inf.*, *quod* and *subj.*, *absol.*, *ad* and *acc.*, (2) *become clear to the mind*, (3) *require, demand, deem necessary, be incumbent on*, used with *ut* and *subj.*

compilo, are, avi, atum, 1, *v. a.*, *to compile, publish, compose a lit-*

erary work from material collected from other works.

complacentia, ae, *f.*, *complacency, satisfaction, delight, the fact or state of being pleased with oneself or others, the manifestation of tranquil pleasure.*

complaceo, ere, ui and placitus sum, 2, *v. n.*, *to be pleasing at the same time, please also, be very pleasing to.*

complantatus, a, um, *P. a.*, *planted along with, planted in.* On **spiritus complantatus,** see *spiritus.*

complector, i, plexus, 3, *v. dep.*, *to embrace, comprise, include as a component part, item or member.*

complementum, i, *n.*, *completion, completeness, termination, perfection, conclusion.* On **perfectio complementi,** see *perfectio* under 2.—Kinds of *complementum* are: (a), **complementum diminutum,** *the diminished completion.*—(b), **complementum formale,** *the formal completion* or *that which refers to form.*—(c), **complementum primum** and **complementum ultimum,** *the first and the last completion.*—(d), **complementum scientiae,** *the completion of knowledge.*—(e), **complementum ultimum,** see *complementum primum.*—(f), **complementum universi,** *the completion of the universe.*—(g), **complementum virtutis,** *the completion of virtue.*—(h), **complementum voluntatis,** *the completion of purpose.*

compleo, ere, evi, etum, 2, *v. a.,*
to fill up, fulfil, make complete
or *perfect, finish, conlude.*—**completus,** a, um, *P. a., filled full,*
full, complete, perfect, synonym
of *perfectus,* the opposite of *incompletus* and *imperfectus.* On
accidens completum, see *accidens* under 2; on **actus completus,** see *actus* under 2; on **beatitudo completa,** see *beatitudo* under 1; on **bonitas completa,** see
bonitas under 2; on **bonum completum,** see *bonus* under 2; on
causa completa, see *causa* under
2; on **cognitio completa,** see *cognitio* under 2; on **definitio completa,** see *definitio* under 2; on
designatio completa, see *designatio;* on **dimensio completa,**
see *dimensio;* on **dominium completum,** see *dominium;* on **ens
completum,** see *ens;* on **esse
completum,** see *esse;* on **essentia
completa,** see *essentia* under 1;
on **forma completa,** see *forma*
under 2; on **generatio completa,**
see *generatio* under 1; on **habitus completus,** see *habitus* under
4; on **individuum completum,**
see *individuum;* on **inductio
completa,** see *inductio* under 4;
on **magnitudo completa,** see *magnitudo* under 1; on **motus completus,** see *motus* under 1; on
natura completa, see *natura;* on
notitia completa, see *notitia* under 2; on **operatio completa,** see
operatio under 2; on **passio completa,** see *passio* under 3; on **potentia completa et non completa,**
see *potentia* under 4; on **quantitas completa,** see *quantitas;* on
scientia completa, see *scientia*
under 2; on **species completa,**
see *species* under 6; on **subsistens completa,** see *subsistens;*
on **substantia completa,** see *substantia* under 2; on **superbia
completa,** see *superbia* under 1;
on **suppositum completum ultima completione,** see *suppositum*
under 2; on **unitas completa,** see
unitas; on **virtus completa,** see
virtus under 1 and 5; on **voluntas completa,** see *voluntas* under
3.—**complete,** *adv., fully, completely, perfectly.*

complete, *adv.,* see *compleo.*

completio, onis, *f., completion,*
achievement, synonym of *consummatio* and *perfectio.*

completive, *adv.,* see *completivus.*

completivus, a, um, *adj., filling up,*
completive completing, achieving, concluding, synonym of *perfectivus.* On **bonum completivum,** see *bonus* under 3; on **differentia completiva,** see *differentia;* on **forma completiva,** see
forma under 2; on **pars completiva,** see *pars* under 1; on **passio
completiva in genere et completiva simpliciter,** see *passio* under
3; on **ratio completiva,** see *ratio*
under 14.—**completive,** *adv., after the manner* or *in the sense of*
completing, of achieving, of concluding, in a complete manner,
completely. On **consistere completive,** see *consistere* under 3.

completorium, ii, *n.*, (= completorium officium), *a service containing prayers at the close of the
day, the compline of the breviary.*

complexe, *adv., after the manner
or in the sense of a composition,
compositionally, compositively;*
synonym of *composite* and *coniunctim,* the opposite of *divise,
divisim, divisive,* and *incomplexe.* On **accipere complexe,** see
accipere under 3.

complexio, onis, *f.,* (1) *construction,
composition,* synonym of *commixtio* and *compositio,* the opposite of *divisio* and *resolutio,* (2)
composition of an animal body,
at times with reference to the
chief humours occurring in it.–
On **aequalitas complexionis,** see
aequalitas under 3; on **temperamentum complexionis,** see *temperamentum* under 1.–Kinds of
complexio in this (1) sense are as
follows: (a), **complexio aequalis,**
the regular or *even temperament.*
–(b), **complexio calida** and **complexio frigida,** *the warm* or *excit-
able* and *the cold or placid temperament.*–(c), **complexio cholerica,** *the choleric temperament.*
–(d), **complexio debita,** *the temperament that should be, the
right temperament, the proper
mixture of the humors.*–(e), **complexio extrema** and **complexio
media seu temperata,** *the extreme* and *the medium* or *moderate temperament.*–(f), **complexio
frigida,** see *complexio calida.*–

(g), **complexio hominis,** see *humana, the temperament of man.*
–(h), **complexio humana,** see
complexio hominis.–(i), **complexio media,** see *complexio extrema.*–(j), **complexio mollis** and
complexio sicca, *the soft* or *tender* and *the dry* or *hard temperament.*–(k), **complexio naturalis,**
the natural temperament or *temperament according to nature.*–
(l), **complexio propria,** *the peculiar temperament.*–(m), **complexio
sicca,** see *complexio mollis.*–(n),
complexio temperata, see *complexio extrema.*–(o), **complexio
terrestris,** *the earthly* or *frigid
temperament.*

complexionatus, a, um, *adj., joined
together, put together.* On **corpus complexionatum,** see *corpus;*
on **qualitas complexionata,** see
qualitas.

complexus, us, *m., embrace, embracing.*

complexus, a, um, *adj., intertwined
with something, joined together,
put together,* the opposite of *incomplexus* and *simplex.* On **conclusio complexa,** see *conclusio*
under 2; on **terminus complexus,** see *terminus* under 5; on
vox complexa, see *vox* under
2.–**Complexa non definiuntur,**
things composed (such as those
that represent *unum per accidens) cannot be defined.*–Discussion about a *complexum* is also with reference to the action of
reason and will. With reference
to the knowledge of reason *com-*

plexum indicates the judgment, because this consists of a twofold composition of expression, i.e., of the expression of one by another. Therefore the more exact term here is *complexum per modum enuntiabilis*. On **apprehendere per modum complexi**, see *apprehendere* under 2; on **cognitio complexio**, see *cognitio* under 2; on **intellectus complexus**, see *intellectus* under 9.—With regard to the will and its desires *complexum* means something brought about in relation to something which is the opposite of the simple and the absolute.

complico, are, avi, atum, (ui, itum), 1, *v. a., to fold together, to join.*

compluit, ere, 3, *v. impers., to rain upon.*

complures, ium, *adj. very many, more than one, not a few, several.*

compono, ere, posui, positum, 3, *v. a.,* (1), *to put together, compound, compose, unite, coalesce,* the opposite of *dividere* and *resolvere,* (2) *arrange, prepare,* (3) *invent, devise.*—On **accidens compositum**, see *accidens* under 2; on **causa composita**, see *causa* under 2; on **corpus compositum**, see *corpus;* on **dictio composita**, see *dictio* under 2; on **enuntiatio composita**, see *enuntiatio* under 2; on **fieri ut compositum**, see *fieri,* on **intellectus compositus**, see *intellectus* under 4 and 9; on **intelligere compositum et dividendo**, see *intellegere* under 1;

on **materia composita**, see *materia* under 3; on **motus compositus**, see *motus* under 1; on **nomen compositum**, see *nomen* under 1; on **numerus compositus**, see *numerus;* on **oratio composita** see *oratio* under 2; on **passio composita**, see *passio* under 1; on **persona composita**, see *persona* under 3; on **propositio composita**, see *propositio* under 2; on **quaestio composita**, see *quaestio;* on **qualitas composita**, see *qualitas;* on **quidditas composita**, see *quidditas;* on **res composita**, see *res;* on **sensus compositus**, see *sensus* under 8; on **substantia composita**, see *substantia* under 2; on **terminus compositus**, see *terminus* under 5; on **verum in composito**, see *verus* under 1.— **componens est causa efficiens compositi,** *that which joins something together is the producing cause thereof.*—**compositum se habet ad simplicia, ut perfectum ad imperfecta,** *the composite is in relation to the simple as the perfect is to the imperfect.*—**in unoquoque genere simplex est prius compositis,** see *simplex.*— **omne compositum est posterius suis componentibus,** *every compound is subsequent to the things that compose it.*—**sensus non componit vel dividit,** see *sensus.*—**simplex est prius composito,** see *simplex.*—**compositus,** a, um, *P. a., arranged, composed, compounded, composite.*—**compositum,** i, *n., a compound, a com-*

posite thing.—**composite,** *adv.,* *in the manner* or *in the sense of compounding, compositely,* synonym of *in sensu composito, collective, complexe,* and *coniunctim,* the opposite of *distributive, divise, divisim, divisive,* and *simpliciter.* On **intellegere composite,** see *intellegere* under 3.

compos, potis, *adj., having the mastery, control,* or *power over a thing, master of.*

composite, *adv.* see *compono.*

compositio, onis, *f.,* (1) *composition, combination,* synonym of *commixtio* and *complexio;* the opposite of *discretio, divisio, resolutio,* and *simplicitas;* as a generic term it is further qualified according to the manner of combination into substantial and accidental. Substantial composition is either physical, if the elements to be combined are physical, or metaphysical, if the elements are metaphysical entities like essence and existence and subsistence, or logical, if the elements are second intentions like genus and difference, (2) *preparation, arrangement.* On **abstrahere per modum compositionis,** see *abstrahere* under 1; on **consonantia compositionis,** see *consonantia* under 2; on **fieri compositione,** see *fieri;* on **ordo compositionis,** see *ordo* under 1; on **processus compositionis,** see *processus* under 2; on **unum compositione,** see *unus;* on **verum in compositione,** see *verus* under 1;

on **via compositionis,** see *via* under 3.—Kinds of *compositio* in this (1) sense are: (a), **compositio accidentalis seu accidentis ad subiectum seu subiecti et accidentis** and **compositio substantialis seu formae ad materiam seu formae et materiae seu ex materia et forma,** *the accidental* and *the substantial composition* or *the combination of an accident with a subject,* and *that of the form with its matter.*—(b), **compositio accidentis ad subiectum,** see *compositio accidentalis.* —(c), **compositio actualis,** *the actual composition.*—(d), **compositio actus et potentia, seu ex actu et potentia,** *the composition of actuality* and *potentiality.*—(e), **compositio enuntiabilium,** *the composition which takes place in statements,* i.e., *the affirmation or negation of a predicate to a subject.*—(f), **compositio ex actu et potentia,** see *compositio actus et potentiae.*—(g), **compositio ex eo quod est et esse seu ex substantia et esse,** *composition of that which is,* or *of substance* or *of person, existence,* and *being.*— (h), **compositio ex materia et forma,** see *compositio accidentalis.*—(i), **compositio ex substantia et esse,** see *compositio ex eo quod est et esse.*—(j), **compositio explicita** and **compositio implicita,** *the unfolded* or *open,* and *the involved* or *contained composition.*—(k), **compositio formae ad materiam seu formae et mate-**

riae, see *compositio accidentalis.* —(l), **compositio generis et differentiae,** *the composition of genus* and *difference, logical composition.*—(m), **compositio humani corporis,** *the composition of the human body.*—(n), **compositio implicita,** see *compositio explicita.*—(o), **compositio intellectus seu rationis** and **compositio rei seu realis,** *composition from the side of reason* and *objective composition.*—(p), **compositio materialis seu quantitativarum partium** and **compositio per receptionem participationum plurium,** *material composition* or *that of material parts,* and *composition through the reception of several participations.*—(q), **compositio naturalis** and **compositio philosophica,** *natural composition* or *that formed in nature* and *that in the sense of philosophy.*—(r), **compositio per receptionem participationum plurium,** see *compositio materialis.*—(s), **compositio philosophica,** see *compositio naturalis.* —(t), **compositio propositionis,** *the composition of a sentence.*—(u), **compositio quantitativarum partium,** see *compositio materialis.*—(v), **compositio quidditatis,** *the composition of quiddity* or *of essence* with personality or subsistence.—(w), **compositio rationis,** see *compositio intellectus.*—(x), **compositio realis,** see *compositio intellectus.*—(y), **compositio rei,** see *compositio intellectus.*—(z), **compositio secundum natu-**ram and **secundum rationem,** *composition in reality* and *that in thought.*—(a^2), **compositio secundum rationem,** see *compositio secundum naturam.*—(b^2), **compositio subiecti et accidentis,** see *compositio accidentalis.*—(c^2), **compositio substantialis,** see *compositio accidentalis.*—(d^2), **compositio verbalis,** *composition expressed in words.*

compositivus, a, um, *adj., suitable for uniting, compositive, putting together, synthetic,* the opposite of *resolutorius.* On **modus compositivus,** see *modus* under 3; on **processus compositivus,** see *processus* under 2.

compossibilis, e, *adj., possible of uniting with something, compossible, compatible,* not found in S.T.

comprehendo, ere, di, sum, 3, *v. a.,* (1) *to take in, include in one's self, comprise,* (2) *comprehend, understand,* (3) *seize, reach, hold fast, apprehend, possess* (the final goal).

comprehensibilis, e, *adj., comprehensible, capable of being comprehended* or *grasped by the mind.*

comprehensio, onis, *f.,* (1) *encompassing, inclusion,* (2) *comprehension, understanding,* (3) *apprehension, holding fast, possession,* (4) *possession of God.* On **cognitio comprehensionis,** see *cognitio* under 2; on **notitia comprehensionis,** see *notitia* under 2; on **visio comprehensionis,** see *vi-*

sio under 1.—Kinds of *comprehensio* in this (2) sense are:
(a), **comprehensio gloriae**, *understanding of the glory of heaven.*
—(b), **comprehensio perfecta**, *the
complete* or *full understanding.*
comprehensivus, a, um, *adj., including within itself, comprehensive.* On **scientia comprehensiva**,
see *scientia* under 2; on **visio
comprehensiva**, see *visio* under 1.
comprehensor, oris, *comm.*, (1) *one
who contains* or *includes*, (2) *one
who comprehends, comprehend-
er, possessor,* especially *the possessor of God* or *of heavenly
glory,* the opposite of *viator.*—
On **cognitio comprehensoris**, see
cognitio under 2; on **gaudium
comprehensoris**, see *gaudium;* on
gratia comprehensoris, see *gratia*
under 2; on **perfectio comprehensoris**, see *perfectio* under 3.
comprimo, ere, pressi, pressum, 3,
v. a., (1) *to restrain, suppress,
withhold, repress, curb,* (2) *to
press* or *squeeze something.*
comprobatio, onis, *f., approbation,
the act of formally* or *authoritatively approving as proper* or
commendable.
comprobo, are, avi, atum, 1, *v. a.*,
*to prove, verify something, put
to the test, approve.*
compromitto, ere, misi, missum, 3,
*v. a., to promise mutually, to
abide by the decision of an arbiter.*
comptus, a, um, *v.* 1. como, *P. a.,
adorned, decked, ornamented.*

compugnatio, onis, *f., an engagement, encounter.*
compulsio, onis, *f., an urging, constraint, compulsion, obligation.*
compunctio, onis, *f., remorse, the
sting of conscience, compunction.*
compungo, ere, nxi, nctum, 3, *v. a.*,
*to feel remorse, be goaded by
the sting of conscience.*
computatio, onis, *f., a computing,
reckoning, a computation.*
computo, are, avi, atum, 1, *v. a., to
sum up, reckon up, compute,
enumerate.*
computresco, ere, trui, 3, *v. inch.
n., to rot, to become wholly
putrid.*
conatus, us, *m., an effort, struggle,
endeavor.*
concateno, are, *no perf.,* atum, 1,
v. a., to link or *bind together,
connect.*
concausa, ae, *f., concurrent cause,*
a synonym of *causa secundaria.*
concavitas, atis, *f., a hollow, cavity.*
concavus, a, um, *adj., hollow, concave, arched, vaulted, curved.*—
concavum, i, *n., a vault, hollow
place.*
concedo, ere, cessi, cessum, 3, *v. n.*
and *a., to grant, allow, concede,
affirm, admit, say, give, permit,*
used with the *inf.,* the *dat.* and
inf., the *acc.* and *inf., ut* and
subj., the *dat.* followed by *ut*
and *subj., quod* and *subj., quod*
and *indic.,* the *acc., ad* and *acc.,
acc.* and *dat., in* and *acc., inter*
and *acc., in* and *abl., de* and *abl.,*
with *dat.*

concelebro, are, avi, atum, 1, *v. a.*, *to concelebrate, to celebrate mass,* as a newly-ordained priest, with the ordaining bishop.

concentus, us, *m.*, *concord, agreement,* used in the S.T. only in quot.

conceptio, onis, *f.*, (1) *conception* in the narrow and proper sense of the word, foecundation, (2) *conception* in the broad sense of the word, anything generated, (3) *comprehension, representation,* (4) *intellectual comprehension, intellectual representation, idea, thought,* synonym of *conceptus intentio,* and *ratio.*—Kinds of *conceptio* in this (1) sense are: conceptio miraculosa and conceptio naturalis, *the miraculous* or *supernatural conception* and *the natural conception.*—Conceptio Beatae Virginis, *the conception of the Blessed Virgin.*—Kinds of *conceptio* in this (2) sense are: conceptio intellectualis seu intelligibilis and conceptio materialis, *the intellectual* or *spiritual conception* and *the material* or *earthly conception,* quae apud nos in animalibus invenitur. See *conceptio intellectualis seu intelligibilis* under 3.—Kinds of *conceptio* in this sense are: (a), conceptio animi seu mentis seu intellectus seu intellectualis seu intellegibilis, *the conception of the spirit* or *of the intellect* or *the intellectual conception.*—(b), conceptio intellectualis, see *conceptio animi.*—(c), conceptio in-

tellectus, see *conceptio animi.*—(d), conceptio intelligibilis, see *conceptio animi.*—(e), conceptio mentis, see *conceptio animi.*—(f), conceptio substantialis, *the essential conception of a thing.*—ratio, quam significat nomen, est conceptio intellectus de re significata per nomen, *the intellectual conception* or *idea* or *aspect which a word signifies of a thing is what our reason has conceived about the thing designated by the word.*—Kinds of *conceptio* in this sense are: (a), conceptio communis, *the general thought by which is understood on the one hand an idea, on the other an opinion.*—(b), conceptio naturalis, *the natural conception* or *that from the nature of reason inherent in man.*—(c), conceptio particularis and conceptio universalis, *the particular* and *the universal conception.*—(d), conceptio prima, *the first conception* or *conception according to time.* —(e), conceptio universalis, see *conceptio particularis.*

conceptus, us, *m.*, (1) *conception, fruit of the womb,* synonym of *conceptio,* (2) *comprehension, conception, thought, concept,* synonym of *conceptio.*—Here belong conceptus naturalis and conceptus miraculosus, *natural* and *miraculous conception.*—Kinds of *conceptus* in this (2) sense are: (a), conceptus communis, *general thought.*—(b), conceptus cordis seu mentis seu interior, *the spir-*

itual or *inner conception.*—(c), **conceptus cordis seu mentis seu interior,** *the spiritual* or *inner conception, idea.*—(d), **conceptus intellectus,** *the concept of the intellect.*—(e), **conceptus interior,** see *conceptus cordis.*—(f), **conceptus mentis,** see *conceptus cordis.*

concerno, ere, crevi, cretum, 3, *v. a., to concern, pertain to.*

concertatio, onis, *f., a contest, striving for something, combat, encounter.*

concessio, onis, *f., an allowing, granting, conceding, permission, leave.*

concha, ae, *f., a shell-fish.*

conchilium, ii, *n., a shell-fish.*

concido, ere, cidi, 3, *v. n., to collapse.*

conciliatio, onis, *f., a conciliating.*

concilio, are, avi, atum, 1, *v. a., to win over, harmonize, unite, bring together, reconcile, blend together.*

concilium, ii, *n., an assembly for consultation, assembly, meeting, union, council.*

concino, ere, cinui, *no sup.,* 3, *v. n.* and *a., to sing in concert or harmoniously.*

concipio, ere, cepi, ceptum, 3, *v. a.,* (1) *to conceive through corporeal* or *intellectual procreation,* (2) *comprehend, conceive, grasp.*

concisio, onis, *f., a cutting.*

concitatio, onis, *f., an emotion of the mind, affection, passion.*

concito, are, avi, atum, 1, *v. freq. a., to rouse, urge, impel one to*

any act, feeling, etc.; *to move strongly, to influence, stir up,* used with *acc.* and *ad,* and *in* with the *abl.*

concivis, is, *m., a fellow citizen.*

conclave, is, *n.,* (1) *a wardrobe,* (2) *a room.*

concludo, ere, si, sum, 3, *v. a.,* (1) *to link together, enclose, include,* (2) *terminate, close, end,* (3) *close, draw a conclusion, infer,* (4) *prove, substantiate.*—Kinds of *concludere* in this (4) sense are: (a), **concludere de necessitate, sive ex necessitate,** *to prove with logical necessity* or *to prove that something is necessarily true.*—(b), **concludere simpliciter,** *to prove simply* or *absolutely,* or *to prove that something is so and so under all circumstances.*

conclusio, onis, *f.,* (1) *closing, conclusion, end,* (2) *course of reasoning, argument, conclusion,* i.e., the proposition derived from at least two other, but frequently more, related propositions by a process of reasoning, the external sign of which is a syllogism.—On **causa conclusionis,** see *causa* under 2; on **habitus conclusionis,** see *habitus* under 4; on **quaestio ad conclusionem,** see *quaestio;* on **scientia conclusionis,** see *scientia* under 2; on **virtus conclusionis,** see *virtus* under 6.—Kinds of *conclusio* in this sense are: (a), **conclusio affectiva** and **conclusio cognitiva,** *the conclusion which comes from an emotion* or *which is bound up with a desire* and *the conclusion which consists of a simple cognition.*—(b), **conclusio cognitiva,** see *conclusio affectiva.*—(c), **conclusio complexa,** *the complex conclusion.*—(d), **conclusio demonstrabilis seu demonstrativa,** *the conclusion which is demonstrable* or *one which has been demonstrated and in both cases proved to be true.*—(e), **conclusio de necessitate seu necessaria,** *the true conclusion of necessity.*—(f), **conclusio falsa** and **conclusio vera,** *the false* and *the true conclusion.* —(g), **conclusio necessaria,** see *conclusio de necessitate.*—(h), **conclusio particularis seu singularis,** *the particular* or *individual conclusion,* i.e., *the conclusion which concerns something particular* and *individual.*—(i), **conclusio singularis,** see *conclusio particularis.*—(j), **conclusio vera,** see *conclusio falsa.*

concoeno, are, 1, *v. freq. ceno, to dine* or *sup together with someone.*

concomitanter, *adv., concomitantly, at the same time with, at the same time,* the opposite of *antecedenter* and *consequenter.*

concomitantia, ae, *f.,* (1) *accompaniment, concomitance, concomitancy,* (2) *collaboration.*— On **praedicatio per concomitantiam,** see *praedicatio* under 2.— Kinds of *concomitantia,* in this (1) sense are: **concomitantia naturalis** and **concomitantia realis,** *natural* and *real concomitance.*

concomitor, ari, atus, 1, *v. dep., to attend, accompany.* On **delectatio concomitans,** see *delectatio;* on **ignorantia concomitans,** see *ignorantia* under 1; on **poena concomitans peccatum,** see *poena;* on **voluntas concomitans,** see *voluntas.*

concordia, ae, *f., harmony, concord,* the opposite of *discordia.* On the difference between *concordia* and *pax,* see *pax* under 1.

concorditer, *adv.,* see *concors.*

concordo, are, avi, atum, 1, *v. n.* and *a.,* of persons and things, *to agree, be of one mind, harmonize, be united* or *concordant with;* used with *cum* and *abl., in* and *abl., ad* and *acc.,* the *dat.,* and *absol.*

concors, cordis, *adj., of the same mind, agreeing, concordant, harmonious.*—**concorditer,** *adv., harmoniously, amicably.*

concreatus, a, um, *adj., concreated, created together* or *contemporaneously.*

concrete, *adv.,* see *concretus.*

concretio, onis, *f.,* (1) *a growing together, concrescence,* synonym of *condensatio, congregatio,* and *inspissatio,* the opposite of *disgregatio* and *rarefactio,* (2) *a growing together, coalescence* with something, the opposite of *discretio,* (3) *specialization,* i.e., coalescence of the general being of a thing with its particular or individual definitions, the opposite of *abstractio* and *separatio.* —On the difference between

concretio and *unitio,* see *unitio.*
animal sumitur a natura sensitiva per modum concretionis, *the
animal* or *the disposition of the
animal in the definition and essence of man is taken from his
sensitive nature and is therefore
considered in the concrete, not
as an abstract idea.*—esse aliarum
formarum non est, nisi in concretione formarum ad materiam,
all other forms (except the human soul) *have their existence
only in that they are united and
developed with matter.*—On cognoscere in concretione, see
cognoscere under 2; on dicere
in concretione, see *dicere* under
3; on modus concretionis, see
modus under 2; on significare
in concretione, see *significare.*

concretive, *adv.,* see *concretivus.*

concretivus, a, um, *adj.,* (1) *making grow together, joining together, concretive,* synonym of
congregativus and *unitivus,* the
opposite of *discretivus* and *disgregativus,* (2) *specializing, making specific, expressing something that has been particularized, concretive,* synonym of *concretus.*—See also *amor.* On praedicatio concretiva, see *praedicatio* under 2; on virtus concretiva, see *virtus* under 1; on vis
concretiva, see *vis* under 1.—
On nomen concretivum, see *nomen* under 1.—concretive, *adv.,
in the manner of particularizing*
or *specifying, concretively.*

concretus, a, um, *adj.,* (1) *grown
together, consolidated,* (2) *grown
together, coalesced with something,* (3) *made specific, specialized, particularized,* i.e., coalesced with special or individual
characteristics, the opposite of
abstractus, (4) *expressing something specialized* or *individualized,* synonym of *concretivus.*—
On elementum concretius, see
elementum under 1.—On esse
concretum, see *esse.*—On forma
concreta, see *forma* under 2; on
ratio concreta, see *ratio* under
11.—concretum, sc. materiae, *the
essence of a thing developed
with particular or individual
characteristics,* the opposite of
abstractum.—in concreto, *in the
concrete,* in a definite subject.
On nomen concretum, see *nomen* under 1.—concrete, *adv.,
concretely.*

concubina, ae, *f., a concubine,* a
woman who cohabits with a
man without marriage.

concubinarius, a, um, *adj., having
a concubine, concubitous.*

concubitor, oris, *m., a bed fellow.*

concubitus, us, *m., copulation, coition.*

conculco, are, avi, atum, 1, *v. a.,
to tread under foot, crush* or
bruise by treading.

concumbo, ere, cubui, cubitum, 3,
v. n., to lie with (for copulation).

concupiscentia, ae, *f.,* (1) *desire,
greed, cupidity* in the broader
sense of the word, synonym of
appetitus and *cupiditas,* (2) *sen-*

sual desire, sensual greed. The natural inclination in every creature with a sensitive nature to seek the good befitting that nature is called appetite or concupiscence. This nature can be related to good in various ways which are called passions from *pati,* because the nature is acted upon by the good—or its absence. Thus, concerning good we have the passion of *love,* whether it be present or absent; *joy,* when it is present; *desire,* when it is absent. This is concupiscence in the restricted sense. Concerning evil, we have *hatred, fear* when it threatens; *sadness,* when it is present to us. These are the concupiscible passions. (3) *inordinate desire, sinful greed, evil covetousness.*—On **amor concupiscentiae,** see *amor* under 1; on **dilectio concupiscentiae,** see *dilectio* under 1.—Kinds of *concupiscentia* in this (1) sense are: (a), **concupiscentia animalis seu sensibilis seu sensualitatis seu quae est passio** and **concupiscentia quae est actus voluntatis,** *the animal* or *sensual desire which consists in a passion properly so called,* and *the desire of the will* or *the transcendental desire.*—(b), **concupiscentia apposita seu non naturalis** and **concupiscentia necessaria seu naturalis,** *the desire which is added to the nature of a thing or which is consequent upon knowledge, and the desire that befits a thing by necessity*

or the desire natural to it.—(c), **concupiscentia bona** and **concupiscentia mala seu prava,** *the morally good* and *the morally evil* or *wicked desire.*—(d), **conpiscentia cogitationis,** *the desire of thought.*—(e), **concupiscentia communis** and **concupiscentia propria,** *the desire common to man and the desire peculiar to man.*—(f), **concupiscentia confusa seu indeterminata** and **concupiscentia determinata,** *the confused* or *indefinite desire* and *the definite desire.*—(g), **concupiscentia cum ratione** and **concupiscentia sine ratione seu irrationalis.**—(h), **concupiscentia determinata,** see *concupiscentia confusa.*—(i), **concupiscentia fomitis,** *the desire of evil concupiscence.*—(j), **concupiscentia illicita,** *unlawful* or *illicit desire.*—(k), **concupiscentia immoderata seu inordinata** and **concupiscentia moderata seu ordinata,** *the immoderate* or *inordinate desire* and *the moderate* or *regulated desire.*—(l), **concupiscentia indeterminata,** see *concupiscentia confusa.*—(m), **concupiscentia inordinata,** see *concupiscentia confusa.*—(n), **concupiscentia irrationalis,** see *concupiscentia cum ratione.*—(o), **concupiscentia mala,** see *concupiscentia bona.*—(p), **concupiscentia moderata,** see *concupiscentia immoderata.*—(q), **concupiscentia naturalis,** see *concupiscentia apposita.*—(r), **concupiscentia necessaria,** see *concu-*

piscentia apposita.—(s), **concupiscentia non naturalis,** see *concupiscentia apposita.*—(t), **concupiscentia ordinata,** see *concupiscentia immoderata.*—(u), **concupiscentia pecuniae,** *desire of money.*—(v) **concupiscentia praecedens** and **concupiscentia quae sequitur,** *the desire that precedes reason* and *that which follows it.* —(w), **concupiscentia prava,** see *concupiscentia bona.*—(x), **concupiscentia propria,** see *concupiscentia communis.*—(y), **concupiscentia quae est actus animalis,** see *concupiscentia animalis.*—(z), **concupiscentia quae est passio,** see *concupiscentia animalis.*—(a²), **concupiscentia quae sequitur,** see *concupiscentia praecedens.*—(b²), **concupiscentia sensibilis,** see *concupiscentia animalis.* (c²), **concupiscentia sensualitatis,** see *concupiscentia animalis.*—(d²), **concupiscentia sine ratione,** see *concupiscentia cum ratione.* —(e²), **concupiscentia superflua,** *the superfluous* or *excessive desire.* On **desiderium concupiscentiae,** see *desiderium;* on **continens concupiscentia,** see *incontinens;* on **incontinentia concupiscentiae,** see *incontinentia;* on **spiritus concupiscentiae,** see *spiritus;* on **vulnus concupiscentiae,** see *vulnus.*—Kinds of *concupiscentia* in this sense are: (a), **concupiscentia accensa,** *the inflamed desire.*—(b), **concupiscentia amens,** *raving desire.*—**adustio concupiscentiae,** *the brand* or

burning of evil desire. On **deformitas immoderatae concupiscentiae,** see *deformitas* under 2; on **fomes concupiscentiae,** see *fomes* under 1; on **lex concupiscentiae,** see *lex* under 1.—Kinds of *concupiscentia* in this (3) sense are: (a), **concupiscentia actualis** and **concupiscentia habitualis,** *the active* and *the habitual evil desire* or *the desire in the sense of an action and that in the sense of a habit.*—(b), **concupiscentia carnalis seu carnis** and **concupiscentia oculorum,** *the desire of the flesh* and *the desire of the eyes.*—(c), **concupiscentia carnis,** see *concupiscentia carnalis.*—(d), **concupiscentia habitualis,** see *concupiscentia actualis.*—(e), **concupiscentia oculorum,** see *concupiscentia carnalis.*—(f), **concupiscentia venereorum,** *sordid lust.*

concupiscibilis, e, *adv.,* (1) *desirable, covetous,* (2) *concupiscent, desiring, desirous.*—**concupiscibilis** sc. *vis seu potentia* usually indicates the capacity of sensual desire or tendency which, taken together with *vis irascibilis,* constitutes the *appetitus sensitivus* in man as well as in animal. On **passio concupiscibilis,** see *passio* under 3. Sometimes, however, the spiritual desire of the will is understood by *concupiscibilis.*

concupiscibilitas, atis, *f., concupiscense, the desire of the senses which seek only its own gratification, undue lustful appetite* or *passion.*

concupisco, ere, cupivi, or cupii, itum, 3, *v. inch. a., to long much for a thing, be very desirous of,* used with the *acc.,* the *inf.,* and *absolutely.*

concurro, ere, curri, cursum, 3, *v. n., to run together, coincide, concur.* On **causa concurrens,** see *causa* under 2.

concursus, us, *m., the coming together, coincidence, concurrence.*

concutio, ere, cussi, cussum, 3, *v. a.,* (1) *to strike, do violence to someone,* (2) *to terrify, trouble, put in fear.*

condecentia, ae, *f., the becoming, the appropriate, fitness.*

condecet, ere, *v. impers., it becomes* or *is becoming, meet, seemly.*

condelectatio, onis, *f., delectation, pleasure.*

condelector, ari, 1, *v. pass., to share pleasure* or *happiness with someone, rejoice, be happy.*

condemnabilis, e, *adj., worthy of condemnation.*

condemnatio, onis, *f., a condemning, condemnation.*

condemno, are, avi, atum, 1, *v. a., to sentence, condemn, convict.*

condenso, are, 1, *v. a., to condense, to press close together, gather together.*

condescendo, ere, *no perf.,* 3, *v. n., to condescend, stoop, let one's self down.*

condictio, onis, *f., a formal claim of restitution.*

condictum, i, *n., an agreement.*

condignativus, a, um, *adj., befitting becoming,* synonym of *condignus* and *dignativus.* On **unio condignativa,** see *unio.*

condignitas, atis, *f., condignity,* the relation of equality between merit of action, conduct, or person, and the value of the award meted out.

condignus, a, um, *adj., worthy, becoming, fitting,* synonym of *condignativus* and *debitus,* the opposite of *congruus.* On **mereri ex condigno,** see *mereri;* on **meritorium ex condigno,** see *meritorius;* on **meritum condignum,** see *meritum* under 1.

condimentum, i, *n., seasoning.*

condio, ire, ivi or ii, itum, 4, *v. a., to embalm a dead body.*

conditio, onis, *f.,* (1) *foundation, establishment, arrangement,* synonym of *creatio* and *institutio,* (2) *situation, position, relation, rank,* (3) *quality, state, condition, nature, peculiarity,* (4) *condition, term.—*conditio servilis, *the position of slave.* On **perfectum secundum conditionem alicuius,** see *perfectus;* on **status primae conditionis,** see *status.—* Kinds of *conditio* in this (2) sense are: (a), **conditio corporalis,** *physical nature* or *condition.—*(b), **conditio essentialis,** *essential condition.—*(c), **conditio generalis,** *general condition.* —(d), **conditio individualis,** *individual condition.—*(e), **conditio materialis,** *material condition.* —(f), **conditio naturalis,** *natural* *condition.*—(g), **conditio particularis,** *particular condition.*—(h), **conditio principalis,** *principal condition.*—(i), **conditio specialis,** *special condition.* On **debitum conditionis,** see *debitus* under 1; on **necessarium ex conditione et ex conditione agentis et finis,** see *necessarius* under 1; on **necessarium sub conditione,** see *necessarius* under 2; on **voluntarium absque et sub conditione,** see *voluntarius* under 3.

conditionalis, e, adj., *conditional, with a condition attached, limiting* or *limited by restrictions or stipulations,* synonym of *conditionatus,* the opposite of *absolutus* and *categoricus.* On **debitum conditionale,** see *debitus* under 1; on **enuntiatio conditionalis,** see *enuntiatio* under 2; on **necessitas conditionalis,** see *necessitas* under 1; on **propositio conditionalis,** see *propositio* under 2; on **syllogismus conditionalis,** see *syllogismus.*—**conditionalis** sc. **propositio,** *the conditional proposition,* i.e., that statement whereby an idea is expressed conditionally by another.—A kind of *conditionalis* sc. *propositio* is *conditionalis necessaria* sc. *propositio, the necessarily true conditional sentence.*—**conditionaliter,** adv. *conditionally,* the opposite of *pure, simpliciter.*

conditionatus, a, um, *adj., conditioned, with a condition attached,* synonym of *conditionalis,* the opposite of *absolutus.* On

certitudo conditionata, see *certitudo* under 2; on **consensus conditionatus,** see *consensus* under 2; on **debitum conditionatum,** see *debitus* under 1; on **impossibilitas conditionata,** see *impossibilitas;* on **libertas conditionata,** see *libertas* under 1; on **meritum conditionatum,** see *meritum* under 1; on **necessitas conditionata,** see *necessitas* under 1-3.

conditive, *adv., operatively, in a manner characterized by operativeness or power* (here, of the Holy Spirit) *to produce effect.*

conditor, oris, *m., a maker, creator, establisher, founder, source.*

condivido, ere, visi, visum, 3, *v. a., to share with something else, distinguish from something else, coordinate.*—**divisum non condividitur dividentibus,** see *dividere* under 1.

condo, ere, didi, ditum, 3, *v. a.,* (1) *to create, establish, make, fashion, produce, form;* used with *acc.; in* and *abl; a* and *abl.; cum* and *abl.,* (2) of written productions, *draw up, write, frame* or *compose,* (3) of the founding of towns or states, *to build, establish, found,* (4) *bury;* (5) with the accessory idea of carefulness, *put away, place away.*

condoleo, ere, 2, *v. n., to suffer with another, feel another's pain, sympathize with,* used with *dat.* —**condolens,** antis, *P. a., sympathizing.*

condonabilis, e, *adj., pardonable, forgivable, that may be pardoned* or *shown clemency* or *indulgence.*

condono, are, avi, atum, 1, *v. a., to pardon, remit an offense.*

conduco, ere, duxi, ctum, 3, *v. a.* and *n., to hire for one's use, rent, employ;* used with *acc.,* and *abl.* of price.

conductio, onis, *f., a hiring, farming.*

conductor, oris, *m., one who hires a thing, a tenant.*

confabulatio, onis, *f., a confab, a conversation, discoursing together.*

confectio, onis, *f., a making, preparing, producing, arranging.*

confero, ferre, contuli, collatum, 3, *v. a.,* (1) *contribute to something, conduce,* synonym of *facere,* (2) *put side by side, compare,* (3) *bestow, confer, judge, contribute.*

confesse, *adv.,* see *confiteor.*

confessio, onis, *f.,* (1) *confession in general,* (2) *confession of sins, confession.*—Kinds of *confessio* in this (1) sense are: **confessio fidei, confessio gratiarum actionis seu laudis, confessio humilitatis seu peccatorum,** and **confessio veritatis,** *the confession of faith, that of thanksgiving* or *of praise, that of humility* or *of sins,* and *the confession of truth.*— **Confessiones Augustini,** *the Confessions of St. Augustine.* On **forum confessionis,** see *forum* under 2.—Kinds of *confessio* in

this (2) sense are: (a), **confessio actualis** and **confessio in proposito exsistens,** *the confession which takes place in reality* and *the intended confession.*—(b), **confessio discreta,** *the confession made with discrimination.*—(c), **confessio exterior** and **confessio interior,** *the exterior* and *the interior confession.*—(d), **confessio generalis** and **confessio particularis seu specialis,** *the general* and *the particular confession.*—(e), **confessio informis,** *the confession not made through love of God.*—(f), **confessio in proposito exsistens,** see *confessio actualis.*—(g), **confessio interior,** see *confessio exterior.*—(h), **confessio particularis,** see *confessio generalis.*—(i), **confessio sacramentalis,** *the sacramental confession,* i.e., *the confession belonging to the sacrament of penance.*—(j), **confessio specialis,** see *confessio generalis.*—**sigillum confessionis,** *the seal of confession.*

confessor, oris, *m.,* (1) *a confessor,* a priest who administers the sacrament of penance, (2) *a confessor,* one who confesses or makes profession of his faith in Christianity, or who avows his faith in the face of persecution; also one who leads an exemplary Christian life and wins a reputation for sanctity.

confestim, *adv., immediately, speedily, without delay, straightway.*

conficio, ere, feci, fectum, 3, *v. a.*,
(1) *to make something from
something*, used with *ex* and *de*,
(2) with reference to the Holy
Eucharist and the Mass, *consecrate, accomplish, effect, perform, perfect, offer up*, (3) *make,
prepare, mix*, (4) *to total up,
amount to*.

confidenter, *adv.*, see *confido*.

confidentia, ae, *f.*, *confidence, trust*.

confido, ere, fisus sum, 3, *v. n.*, *to
trust, trust in, believe, be confident of* with *de* and *abl.*, *be self-
confident;* used with *de* and
abl., in and *abl., ad* and *acc.,
acc.* and *inf.*, and *absolutely.—*
confidenter, *adv., boldly, dar-
ingly, confidently*.

configo, ere, xi, xum, 3, *v. a., to
pierce through, fasten.—*confix-
us, a, um, *P. a., pierced through,
transfixed.*

configuratio, onis, *f., like formation, uniformity*.

configurativus, a, um, *adj., making
similar, making uniform, config-
urative.* On signum configurativum, see *signum* under 1.

configuro, are, avi, atum, 1, *v. a.*,
(1) *to make from* or *after something, make uniform*, (2) *symbolize*.

confingo, ere, finxi, fictum, 3, *v. a.*,
to invent, devise, feign, pretend.

confinium, ii, *n., neighborhood,
nearness, close connection, contiguity*.

confirmatio, onis, *f.*, (1) *fortifica-
tion, strengthening*, (2) *corrob-*

oration, confirmation, (3) *the
sacrament of confirmation*.

confirmativus, a, um, *adj., confirmative, tending to conform, con-
firmatory*.

confirmator, oris, *m., a confirmant*,
one who administers the rite of
confirmation.

confirmo, are, avi, atum, 1, *v. a.*,
(1) *fortify, strengthen, confirm*,
(2) *corroborate, confirm*, (3)
*perform the sacrament of con-
firmation, confirm.—*confirmatus,
a, um, *P. a., strengthened, cor-
roborated, confirmed*.

confiteor, eri, fessus, *v. dep., to acknowledge, reveal, make known,
confess.—*confessus, a, um, *P. a.,
confessed, manifested, made evident.—*confesse, *adv., admitted-
ly, confessedly, conformably*, the
Aristotelian *homologos*. On veritas confesse se habens, see *veritas* under 1.

conflagratio, onis, *f., a burning,
conflagration*.

conflatilis, e, *adj., molten, made of
matter in a state of fusion, cast*.

conflatio, onis, *f.*, (1) *a moulding,
casting in metal*, (2) *a conflagration, burning, kindling*.

conflictus, us, *m., a fight, contest*.

conflo, are, avi, atum, 1, *v. a.*, (1)
to produce, cause, effect, (2)
melt, purge, cleanse.

confluo, ere, xi, ctum, 3, *v. a.* and
n., to flow or *run together*.

confoederatio, onis, *f., compact,
agreement, complicity, alliance,
binding together*.

conformabilis, e, *adj., conformable*.

conformatio, onis, f., *conformity*.

conformis, e, *adj., uniform, conformed,* the opposite of *difformis.*—conformiter, *adv., in conformity, conformably.*

conformitas, atis, f., *conformity,* agreement in respect of some formality, synonym of *uniformitas,* the opposite of *difformitas.*—Kinds of *conformitas* are: (a), conformitas gloriae and conformitas gratiae, *the conformity of heavenly glory* and *that of divine grace.*—(b), conformitas gratiae, see *conformitas gloriae.*—(c), conformitas imaginis and conformitas similitudinis, *conformity according to an image* and *that according to similarity.* (d), conformitas in natura seu secundum convenientiam in natura, *the conformity of nature.*—(e), conformitas secundum convenientiam in nature, see *conformitas in natura.*—(f), conformitas secundum quid and conformitas simpliciter, *the respective conformity* or *the conformity in a certain respect* and *the simple* or *absolute conformity.*—(g), conformitas similitudinis, see *conformitas imaginis.*—(h), conformitas simipliciter, see *conformitas secundum quid.*

conformiter, *adv.,* see *conformis.*

conformo, are, avi, atum, 1, *v. a., to conform, make like in form, bring into harmony* or *correspondence with a model* or *example, to act in accord* or *conformity;*

used with *dat., acc.,* and *dat.; in* with the *abl.*

confortatio, onis, f., *a strengthening, comfort.*

confortativus, a, um, *adj., strengthening, comforting, having the properties for consoling.*

conforto, are, 1, *v. a., to strengthen much.*

confractio, onis, f., *a confraction* or *breaking up.*

confricatio, onis, f., *a rubbing, striking.*

confringo, ere, fregi, fractum, 3, *v. a., to break in pieces.*

confugio, ere, fugi, 3, *v. n.,* (1) *to take refuge in, have recourse to,* (2) *to flee to a place for refuge,* (3) with *ad ecclesiam, change from one creed to another,* (4) with *ad religionem, enter religion, become a member of a religious order.*

confugium, ii, n., *a flight to shelter.*

confundo, ere, fudi, fusum, 3, *v. a., to mingle, confound, confuse,* the opposite of *distinguo.*—confuse, *adv., confusedly, without order, disorderly,* synonym of *indistincte,* the opposite of *distincte* and *ordinate.* On dicere confuse, see *dicere* under 3; on notum confuse, see *notus;* on supponere confuse, see *supponere* under 4.—confusus, a, um, *P. a.,* (1) *poured together, mixed, mingled,* (2) *vague, indistinct, confused,* synonym of *indistinctus, inordinatus,* the opposite of *distinctus, ordinatus.*—On concupiscentia confusa, see *concupis-*

centia under 1; on **imaginatio
confusa,** see *imaginatio* under 1;
on **nomen confusum,** see *nomen*
under 1; on **similitudo confusa,**
see *similitudo* under 1; on **suppositio confusa,** see *suppositio*
under 4.

confuse, *adv.,* see *confundo.*

confusibilis, e, *adj., capable of being confused, embarrassed.*

confusio, onis, *f.,* (1) *mixture,
medley, mingling,* the opposite •
of *discretio, distinctio,* and *mixtio vera,* (2) *confusion, bewilderment, disorder,* the opposite of
distinctio and *ordo,* (3) *indefiniteness, vagueness, ambiguity,*
synonym of *indistinctio,* the opposite of *distinctio,* (4) *conster-
nation, shame.*—On **unio per modum confusionis,** see *unio.*

confusus, a, um, *adj.,* see *confundo.*

confutatio, onis, *f., confusion,
shame, perplexity.*

confuto, are, avi, atum, 1, *v. a.,
to confute, refute successfully,
prove to be wrong, answer
conclusively, put to silence by
words.*

congaudeo, ere, 2, *v. n., to rejoice
with.*

congelatio, onis, *f., a freezing, con-
gealing.*

congelo, are, avi, atum, 1, *v. a.*
and *n., to cause to freeze up,
congeal.*

congemisco, ere, 3, *v. inch. n., to
sigh deeply, groan.*

congero, ere, gessi, gestum, 3, *v. a.,
to amass,* heap something on

something else in an unfriendly
manner.

conglorificatus, a, um, *adj., glorified together with.*

conglutino, are, avi, atum, 1, *v. a.,
to attach, bind closely.*—**conglu-
tinans,** antis, *P. a., binding.*

congratulatio, onis, *f., congratula-
tion, a hearty sympathy in another's joys* or *hopes.*

congregatio, onis, *f.,* (1) *a gathering* or *scraping together, union,*
synonym of *concretio, condensatio* and *inspissatio,* the opposite
of *discretio, disgregatio,* and *rarefactio,* (2) *band, society, association, congregation,* synonym
of *communicatio, communio,* and
communitas.—Kinds of *congregatio* in this (2) sense are: (a),
congregatio corporalis and **congregatio spiritualis,** *the corporeal*
and *the spiritual union.*—(b), **congregatio oeconomica** and **congregatio politica,** *the domestic* and
the political union.—(c), **congregatio politica,** see *congregatio
oeconomica.*—(d), **congregatio
spiritualis,** see *congregatio corporalis.*

congregativus, a, um, *adj., suitable
for uniting, gathering, collecting,*
synonym of *concretivus,* and *unitivus,* the opposite of *disgregativus.* On **amor congregativus,** see
amor under 1.

congrego, are, avi, atum, 1, *v. a.,*
(1) *to collect, assemble, unite,
gather together, bring together,*
used of persons, animals, and
things, (2) *convoke, call togeth-*

er by summons, (3) *condense, bring into a smaller* and *denser state,* (4) *to collect, amass, accumulate something.*

congressus, us, *m., a hostile encounter, conflict.*

congrue, *adv.,* see *congruus.*

congruenter, *adv.,* see *congruo.*

congruentia, ae, *f., congruity, fitness, suitability, becomingness,* synonym of *congruitas.* On **causa congruentiae,** see *causa* under 5; on **medium congruentiae,** see *medium* under 2.

congruitas, atis, *f., congruity, fitness, suitability, becomingness,* synonym of *congruentia.* On **debitum congruitatis,** see *debitus* under 1; on **medium congruitatis,** see *medium* under 2; on **ordo congruitatis,** see *ordo* under 2.

congruo, ere, ui, 3, *v. n., to coincide* or *correspond with a person* or *thing in substance or feeling or time, be suited or adapted to, agree with, accord, fit, be fitting,* used (1) *absl.,* (2) with *dat.,* (3) with *ad* and *acc.,* (4) with *cum* and *abl.*—**congruens,** entis, *P. a., agreeing, fit, appropriate, suitable, consistent, congruous.*—**congruenter,** *adv., agreeably, fitly, suitably,* synonym of *congrue.*

congruus, a, um, *adj., congruous, fitting, becoming, suitable,* as distinguished from *condignus* and *debitus.*—**ex congruo,** *in a fitting manner, becomingly.* On **definitio congrua,** see *definitio*

under 2; on **mereri ex congruo,** see *mereri;* on **meritorum ex congruo,** see *meritorius;* on **meritum congruum,** see *meritum* under 1. —**congrue,** *adv., fittingly, becomingly, suitably,* synonym of *congruenter.*

coniaceo ere, *to lie together.*

conicio, ere, ieci, iectum, 3, *v. a., to conjecture, guess, surmise.*

coniecto, are, avi, atum, 1, *v. freq. a.,* (1) *to conclude* or *infer by conjecture, conjecture,* (2), *aim at, seek.*

coniectura, ae, *f.,* (1) *a conjecture, an opinion founded on a comparison of facts, guess, conjectural inference,* (2) *of the language of augury, a conclusion drawn from signs or omens, a divining, divination, prediction,* (3) *an element of rhetorical representation founded on conjecture.*

coniecturalis, e, *adj., belonging to conjecture or supposition, conjectural.* On **ars coniecturalis,** see *ars* under 2; on **cognitio coniecturalis,** see *cognitio* under 2; on **scientia coniecturalis,** see *scientia* under 2.—**coniecturaliter,** *adv., conjecturally, supposedly by conjecture.* On **cognoscere coniecturaliter,** see *cognoscere* under 2.

coniecturaliter, *adv.,* see *coniecturalis.*

coniecturatio, onis, *f., a conjecture, an inference drawn from probabilities; bona coniecturatio, a guessing well, happy conjecture,* synonymous with *eustochia* (also Greek), one of the parts of *prudence* mentioned by Aristotle and to which *sollertia* (shrewdness) belongs, or the *easy and rapid conjecture in finding the middle term.*

coniecturativus, a, um, *adj.*, *having skill in conjecture or tracing things which are hidden from ordinary and easy perception, skillful in conjecture.*

coniecturo, are, avi, atum, 1, *v. a.*, *to conjecture, surmise, form a tentative opinion regarding.*

coniugalis, e, *adj.*, *relating to marriage, conjugal.* On **actus coniugalis,** see *actus* under 1; on **bonum coniugale,** see *bonus* under 3; on **castitas coniugalis,** see *castitas* under 2; on **continentia coniugalis,** see *continentia* under 4; on **pudicitia coniugalis,** see *pudicitia;* on **status coniugalis,** see *status* under 4; on **vita coniugalis,** see *vita* under 3.—**coniugaliter,** *adv.*, *as a married person.*

coniugaliter, *adv.*, see *coniugalis.*

coniugatio, onis, *f.*, (1) *pairing, connecting, uniting,* synonym of *connexio,* (2) *a pair, yoke.*

coniugium, ii, *n.*, *a connection by marriage, marriage, wedlock,* synonym of *matrimonium.*

coniugo, are, avi, atum, 1, *v. a.*, *to marry, wed.*—**coniugatus,** a, um, *P. a.*, *joined together, united, married.*

coniuncte, *adv.*, see *coniungo.*

coniunctim, *adv.*, *after the manner* or *in the sense of a union* or *joining, jointly, in common,* synonym of *collective, complexe, composite, coniuncte,* the opposite of *distributive, divise, divisim, divisive, disiunctim.*

coniunctio, anis, *f.*, (1) *a union, relation, connection by relationship, affinity, friendship, intimacy,* (2) *a union, the act or state of being united with something, the union of minds, of the soul with God,* (3) *a carnal union, a conjugal connection, wedlock.*

coniunctum, i, *n.*, *a composition, that which is composed or made up of parts, as soul and body in man.*

coniungibilis, e, *adj.*, *capable of being joined.*

coniungo, ere, nxi, nctum, 3, *v. a.*, (1) *to bind together, connect, join, unite, compose, form by uniting,* constr. with *dat.*, the *acc.* alone, with *cum* and *abl.*, with *ad invicem,* and used *absolutely,* (2) *join carnally, copulate.* —**coniunctus,** a, um, *P. a.*, *joined together, united, bound,* the opposite of *separatus.* On **forma coniuncta,** see *forma* under 2; on **intellectus coniunctus,** see *intellectus* under 1; on **locatum coniunctum,** see *locare;* on **malum coniunctum,** see *malus* under 3; on **medium coniunctum,** see *medium* under 2; on **motor coniunctus,** see *motor;* on **occasio coniuncta,** see *occasio;* on operatio coniuncta, see *operatio* under 2; on **organum coniunctum**, see *organum;* on **passio coniuncta**, see *passio* under 2; on **persona coniuncta**, see *persona* under 3; on **potentia coniuncta**, see *potentia* under 2; on **proportionalitas coniuncta**, see *proportionalitas;* on **proprietas coniuncta**, see *proprietas* under 1; on **res coniuncta**, see *res;* on **speculum coniunctum**, see *speculum* under 1; on **spiritus coniunctus**, see *spiritus;* on **substantia coniuncta**, see *substantia* under 2; on **terminus coniunctus**, see *terminus* under 4; on **voluntas coniuncta**, see *voluntas* under 3.— **coniuncte**, *adv., in connection, conjointly, at the same time, in a friendly manner,* found only in the comparative degree in the S.T. and only in quotation.

coniunx, iugis, *comm., one who is united in marriage, a consort, spouse, wife, husband,* in plur. for *married pair.*

coniuratio, onis, *f., a conspiracy, plot.* The *Coniuratio Catilinae* or *Bellum Catilinarium* is a history of the conspiracy of Catiline during the consulship of Cicero, 63 B.C.

connaturalis, e, *adj.,* (1) *of the same nature as someone else,* (2) *agreeing with the nature of a thing, natural,* synonym of *naturalis.*—On **filius connaturalis**, see *filius* under 1; on **forma connaturalis**, see *forma* under 2.— On **actio connaturalis**, see *actio*

under 4; on **apprehensio connaturalis**, see *apprehensio* under 2; on **bonum connaturale**, see *bonus* under 3; on **delectatio connaturalis**, see *delectatio;* on **lumen connaturale**, see *lumen;* on **operatio connaturalis**, see *operatio* under 2; on **qualitas connaturalis**, see *qualitas;* on **scientia connaturalis**, see *scientia* under 2; on **species connaturalis**, see *species* under 5.—**connaturaliter**, *adv., in a manner agreeing with the nature of a thing, naturally,* synonym of *naturaliter,* does not occur in S.T.

connaturalitas, atis, *f.,* (1) *like nature,* (2) *natural relation* or *agreement with something, natural inclination to something, natural attraction to something, natural inclination or attraction.*

connaturaliter, *adv.,* see *connaturalis.*

connecto, ere, nexui, nexum, 3, *v. a., to connect, entwine, link together, join together.* Used with *acc., in* and *abl., dat.,* and *abl.; dat.,* and *ad.*—**connexus**, a, um, *P. a., connected, joined.*

connexio, onis, *f., a tying together, connection, adherence,* synonym of *coniugatio.*

connoto, are, avi, atum, 1, *v. a., to connote, indicate* indirectly by the use of a word or idea.—**connotans**, antis, *P. a., connoting, having a meaning more extensive than the word implies.*— **connotatus**, a, um, *P. a., connoted, signified.*

connubium, ii, *n., marriage, wed-lock.*

connumeratio, onis, *f., a connu-meration, reckoning together.*

connumero, are, 1, *v. a., to number among, reckon among,* used with *per, cum, ad* and *acc., dat., in-ter* and *acc., acc.* and *dat., in* and *abl.—***connumeratus,** a, um, *P. a., reckoned, numbered.*

conor, ari, atus, sum., 1, *v. dep., to undertake, endeavor, attempt, try, strive for.* Used with the *inf.,* with *ad, ad* and *gerundive.*

conpeto, see *competo.*

conplexio, see *complexio.*

conprobo, see *comprobo.*

conqueror, i, questus, 3, *v. dep. a, to complain of a thing, to bewail.*

conquiesco, ere, quievi, quietum, 3, *v. n., to rest, repose, be at rest.*

conquiro, ere, quisivi, quisitum, 3, *v. a., to acquire, seek, ask.*

conregno, are, 1, *v. n., to reign to-gether with someone,* used with the *dative.*

conresuscito, are, avi, atum, 1, *v. a., to raise from the dead to-gether.*

consanguineus, a, um, *adj., con-sanquine, consanguineous, blood relationship resulting from col-lateral or lineal consanguinity and distinguished from affinis or relationship by marriage.—***con-sanguinea,** ae, *f., a kinswoman, a female blood-relation.—***consan-guineus,** i, *m.,* frequently used as *subst.* in *plur.—***consanguinei,**

orum, *m., kinsmen, blood-rela-tions.*

consanguinitas, atis, *f., blood rela-tionship, consanguinity.* On **gra-dus consanguinitatis,** see *gradus* under 1; on **linea consanguini-tatis,** see *linea* under 2.

conscendo, ere, ndi, nsum, 3, *v. a.* and *n., to mount, ascend,* used with *ad* and *acc.,* the *acc.*

conscientia, ae, *f.,* (1) *joint-knowl-edge,* (2) *consciousness,* (3) *conscience,* (4), *matter of con-science, case of conscience.—*On **forum conscientiae,** see *forum* under 2; on **iudicium conscien-tiae,** see *iudicium* under 1 and 3; on **munditia conscientiae,** see *munditia,;* on **scintilla conscien-tiae,** see *scintilla.—***remorsus con-scientiae,** *sting of conscience, remorse of conscience.—***vermis conscientiae,** *the worm of con-science, the remorse of con-science.* See *remorsus conscien-tiae.—*Kinds of *conscientia* in this (3) sense are: (a), **conscien-tia bona** and **conscientia mala seu remordens,** *the good con-science* and *the evil conscience* or *the conscience that has scru-ples.—*(b), **conscientia errans seu erronea** and **conscientia recta,** *the erroneous* and *the right con-science.—*(c), **conscientia immun-da seu inquinata** and **conscientia munda seu pura,** *the impure* or *the polluted conscience* and *the pure conscience.—*(d), **conscientia inquinata,** see *conscientia im-munda.—*(e), **conscientia mala,**

see *conscientia bona.*—(f), **conscientia munda**, see *conscientia immunda.*—(g), **conscientia pura**, see *conscientia immunda.*—(h), **conscientia recta**, see *conscientia errans.*—(i), **conscientia remordens**, see *conscientia bona.*

conscius, a, um, *adj.*, (1) *knowing* or *conscious of something with another*, used with the *gen.*, (2) *knowing something in one's self*, *conscious of*, with *sibi*, used with the *gen.*, *a subj. cl.*, and *de.*

conscribo, ere, psi, ptum, 3, *v. a.*, (1) *to put together in writing, compose, write,* (2) *write together on a roll* or *list, enroll,* so the frequently occurring title of Senators: **Patres Conscripti**, *chosen, elect, assembled fathers,* (3) *draw up a law;* **libellus conscriptus de repudio**, *a bill of divorce,* (4) *draw up a creed,* or *formal summary of fundamental points of religious belief, conscribere fidem,* (5) used *figuratively.*

conscriptio, onis, *f.*, (1) *a conscription, a drawing up in writing;* used *figuratively* of the names of the elect in the book of life, *a knowledge of those chosen for life eternal,* (2) *the drawing up of a brief or bill, libelli conscriptio,* (3) *writings,* used in the plural.

onsecratio, onis, *f.*, (1) *a consecration,* an act by which a thing is separated from a common and profane use to a sacred one, or by which a person or thing is dedicated to the service and

worship of God, (2) *the Consecration at the Holy Sacrifice of the Mass,* the act by which in the celebration of Holy Mass the bread and wine are changed into the body and blood of Christ, the species or outward semblance of bread and wine alone remaining.

consecrativus, a, um, *adj.*, *consecratory, consecrating, pertaining to the consecration of the Mass.*

consecro, are, avi, atum, 1, *v. a.*, (1) *to sanctify, hallow, recognize something as holy,* (2) *dedicate or consecrate a person to God, devote one's life and prerogatives to the service of God,* (3) *set some person or thing apart as sacred or dedicated to sacred things,* (4) *administer, perform the ceremonies of,* (5) *consecrate, exercise the power conferred on a priest at ordination of changing bread and wine into the Body and Blood of Christ at the consecration of the Mass.*

consecutio, onis, *f.*, (1) *an acquiring, obtaining, attainment,* (2) *execution, the act of carrying into effect,* synonymous with *generatio.*

consecutive, *adv.*, *after the manner* or *in the sense of a series, of a succession, consecutively,* the opposite of *causaliter.* On **intellegere consecutive**, see *intellegere* under 3; on **ponere consecutive**, see *ponere* under 2; on

tenere consecutive, see *tenere* under 7.

consecutivus, a, um, *adj., following by succession, consecutive.*

consedeo, ere, sedi, sessum, 2, *v. n., to sit with someone.*

consempiternus, a, um, *adj., coeternal.*

consensio, onis, *f., an agreeing together, consent, unanimity,* only in quotation in the S.T.

consensus, us, *m.,* (1) *consent, assent in the broad sense,* (2) *consent, assent of the will, acquiescence.*—Kinds of *consensus* in this sense (1) are: **consensus rationis** and **consensus voluntatis,** *the consent of the rational appetite* and *the consent of the will.*—Kinds of *consensus* in this (2) sense are: (a), **consensus coactus,** *compulsory consent.*—(b), consensus conditionatus, *the conditioned consent.*—(c), **consensus deliberatus,** *the deliberate consent or the consent based on deliberation.*—(d), **consensus determinatus,** *the determined consent.*—(e), **consensus expressus** and **consensus interpretativus,** *the expressed consent and that existing according to an explanation or the consent as explained by or evident in action.*—(f), **consensus interior seu mentalis seu mentis,** *the inner consent.*—(g), **consensus interpretativus,** see *consensus expressus.* (h), **consensus matrimonialis seu nuptialis,** *the consent to marriage.*—(i), **consensus mentalis,**

see *consensus interior.*—(j), **consensus mentis,** see *consensus interior.*—(k), **consensus mutuus,** *the mutual consent.*—(l), **consensus nuptialis,** see *consensus matrimonialis.*

consentaneus, a, um, *adj., agreeing or in accordance with something,* used with *the dative.*—**consentaneum est,** *it agrees with something, it is fitting, consistent, proper,* used with *ut* and *subj.,* with the *dative.* On **unio consentanea,** see *unio.*

consentio, ire, sensi, sensum, 4, *v. n.* and *a.,* (1) *to concur with, agree with in the broad sense,* opposite of *dissentio,* constr. with *dat.,* and *absl.,* (2) *consent to* constr. with *in* and *acc., ad* and *acc.,* and *absl.*—On the difference between *consentire* and *assentire,* see *assentire.*—**consentire interpretative,** *to consent to something in an explanatory manner,* i.e., *to do* or *omit something which is explained as assent.*

Consentius, ii, *m., Consentius,* a lay theologian of the time of Augustine, who lived on certain islands, probably the Balearic. In Epistle 205 Augustine answers some questions raised by Consentius on the nature of the risen body.

consepelio, ire, *no perf. sepultus,* 4, *v. a., to bury with,* used with the *dative, in* and *abl., cum* and *abl.*

consequens, *P. a.,* see *consequor.*

consequenter, *adv.*, see *consequor.*

consequentia, ae, *f.*, (1) *succession, series,* (2) *logical conclusion, deduction, inference* that derives from the logical form in which the argument is proposed.—On causa consequentiae, see *causa* under 4; on necessitas consequentiae, see *necessitas* under 2; on prius a quo non convertitur consequentia essendi seu subsistendi, see *prior* under 1.

consequor, i, secutus, 3, *v. dep. a.,* (1) *to follow after something, follow after, accompany,* used *absl.* or with *ad* and *acc.,* (2) *result from something, be the consequence of something, follow from something,* used *absl.,* or with *ad* and *acc.* or with *ex* and *abl.,* (3) *attain, obtain,* (4) *be obtained, result.*—consequens, entis, *P. a.,* (1) *following after, following, consequent,* the opposite of *antecedens,* (2) *conclusion of a conditional sentence,* also the opposite of *antecedens,* (3) *logical, conclusive, consequence,* which derives from the nature of things.—On bonum consequens, see *bonus* under 2; on consideratio consequens, see *consideratio;* on ignorantia consequens, see *ignorantia* under 1; on intellegere ex consequente, see *intellegere* under 1; on intentio consequens, see *intentio* under 2; on passio consequens, see *passio* under 3; on poena consequens ex peccata, see *poena;* on privatio consequens ali-

quam potentiam, see *privatio* under 2; on qualitas consequens, see *qualitas;* on sophisma consequens, see *sophisma;* on voluntas consequens, see *voluntas* under 3.—ex consequenti, *in consequence, subsequently.* On significare ex consequenti, see *significare.*—On fallacia consequentis, see *fallacia* under 2; on positio consequentis, see *positio* under 3; on sophisma consequentis, see *sophisma.*—per consequens, *consequently, accordingly.* On necessitas consequentis, see *necessitas* under 1.—consequenter, *adv.,* (1) *subsequently, afterwards, after that, thereupon,* the opposite of *antecedenter* and *concomitanter,* (2) *in direct sequence after something* or *out of something,* the *exhexes* of Aristotle, (3) *consequently, accordingly,* synonym of *per consequens.*—On agere consequenter, see *agere* under 1; on ad beatitudinem pertinere consequenter, see *beatitudo* under 1; on velle consequenter, see *velle* under 1. On dignius est esse continuum, quam consequenter, see *continuus* under 2; on duo puncta non sunt consequenter se habentia ad invicem, see *punctum.*

conservatio, onis, *f.,* (1) *preservation,* (2) *keeping, retention.*

conservative, *adv.,* see *conservativus.*

conservativus, a, um, *adj.,* (1) *preserving,* the opposite of *corruptivus,* (2) *keeping, retaining, conservative.*—On **dicere conservative,** see *dicere* under 3.—On **dicere conservative,** see *dicere* under 3.

conservator, oris, *m., a keeper, preserver, defender.*

conservo, are, avi, atum, 1, v. a., (1) *to preserve,* (2) *keep, retain.* —On **locus conservans,** see *locus* under 2.

conservus, i, *m., a fellow-slave, a companion in servitude.*

consessio, onis, *f., a sitting together, sitting,* synonym of *consessus.*

consessus, us, *m.,* (1) *an assembly,* (2) *a sitting together* or *with,* synonym of *consessio.*

considerabilis, e, *adj., worthy of consideration* or *investigation.*

consideratio, onis, *f., consideration, deliberation,* synonym of *deliberatio.*—Kinds of *consideratio* are: (a), **consideratio absoluta** and **consideratio comparativa,** *the absolute* and *the comparative consideration.*—(b), **consideratio abstracta,** *the abstract* or *general consideration.*—(c), **consideratio actualis,** *the present, conscious advertence as opposed to habitual.*—(d), **consideratio comparativa,** see *consideratio absoluta.*—(e), **consideratio consequens** and **consideratio prima,** *the consequent* and *the first consideration.* —(f), **consideratio contemplata,** *the contemplated consideration.* —(g), **consideratio discursiva seu ratiocinativa seu rationalis** and **consideratio intellectualis,** *the discursive* or *syllogistic consider-*

ation and *the intuitive consideration.*—(h), **consideratio formata,** *the consideration connected with the considered object by firma assensio.*—(i), **consideratio intellectualis,** see *consideratio discursiva.*—(j), **consideratio logica** and **consideratio realis,** *the logical* and *real consideration* or *the consideration of a thing from the standpoint of logic* and *that from the standpoint of metaphysics.* —(k), **consideratio materialis,** *the consideration of a thing on its material side.*—(l), **consideratio moralis** and **consideratio naturalis,** *the moral consideration* and *that of natural science.*— (m), **consideratio naturalis,** see *consideratio moralis.*—(n), **consideratio particularis** and **consideratio universalis,** *the particular* and *the general consideration.*—(o), **consideratio prima,** see *consideratio consequens.*— (p), **consideratio ratiocinativa,** see *consideratio discursiva.*—(q), **consideratio rationalis,** see *consideratio discursiva.*—(r), **consideratio realis,** see *consideratio logica.*—(s), **consideratio simplex seu unita,** *the simple* or *unified consideration.*—(t), **consideratio speculativa,** *the speculative* or *theoretical consideration.*—(u), **consideratio theologica,** *the theological consideration.*—(v), **consideratio unita,** see *consideratio simplex.*—(w), **consideratio universalis,** see *consideratio particularis.*

considerativus, a, um, *adj., considering, contemplative, considera-
tive,* synonym of *contemplativus,*
does not occur in S.T. On **habitus considerativus,** see *habitus*
under 4.

considero, are, avi, atum, 1, *v. a.,
to fix one's eyes upon, take into
consideration, consider, ponder,*
synonym of *delibero.*—Kinds of
considerare are: (a), **considerare
absoluta,** *to consider something
simply,* i.e., without reference
to this or that individual circumstance.—(b), **considerare actualiter,** *to consider in reality.*
—(c), **considerare diligenter,** *to
consider carefully.*—(d), **considerare in particulari** and **considerare in universali,** *to consider in
particular* and *to consider in general.*—(e), **considerare in speciali
seu specialiter,** *to consider in a
special way.*—(f), **considerare in
universali seu universaliter,** see
considerare in particulari.—(g),
considerare logice and **considerare physice,** *to consider something logically,* i.e., *from the
standpoint of a logician,* and *to
consider something physically,*
i.e., *from the standpoint of a
physicist.*—(h), **considerare materialiter,** *to consider in material
aspects, materially.*—(i), **considerare physice,** see *considerare
logice.*—(j), **considerare proprie,**
to consider properly, fittingly.—
(k), **considerare rationabiliter,**
*to consider rationally, reasona-
bly.*—(l), **considerare recte,** *to

consider rightly.*—(m), **considerare simpliciter,** *to consider simply* or *absolutely.*—(n), **considerare ut determinate** and **considerare ut indeterminate,** *to consider something in a definite* and
in an indefinite manner or *to
consider something from the
point of view of a definite end*
and *from the point of view of
an indefinite nature.*—(o), **considerare ut indeterminate,** see
considerare ut determinate.—(p),
considerare ut in facto esse and
considerare ut in fieri, *to consider something in the state of its
becoming* and *of its completion.*
—(q), **considerare ut in fieri,** see
considerare ut in facto esse.

considium, ii, *n., a sitting together.*
consido, ere, sedi, sessum, 3, *v. n.,
to sit down together, take a seat
together.*

consignatio, onis, *f., a sealing,
signing, imprinting,* often synonymous with *character,* or *the
mark* or *seal imprinted, a permanent impress* or *character left
on the soul by a sacrament.*

consignificatio, onis, *f., connotation, signification.*

consignifico, are, avi, atum, 1, *v.
a., to connote, express with.*

consigno, are, avi, atum, 1, *v. a.,*
(1) *to mark, distinguish* or *designate by some outward sign or
mark,* (2) *to mark with a sign,
especially with a cross, to leave
a permanent impress on the
soul.*—**consignatus,** a, um, *P. a.,
marked, signed.*—**consignans,** an-

tis, *P. a., sealing, stamping a likeness of something on something else.*

consiliabilis, e, *adj., to be considered, worthy of consultation or consideration from others.* On **desiderium consiliabile,** see *desiderium* under 1.

consiliarius, ii, *m., a counsellor, adviser.*

consiliatio, onis, *f., counsel, a counselling, advice.*

consiliativus, a, um, *adj., counsel giving, advising, capable of giving counsel or advise,* Aristotelian *bouleutikos.* On **appetitus consiliativus,** see *appetitus* under 1; on **virtus consiliativa,** see *virtus* under 5; on **voluntas consiliativa,** see *voluntas* under 3.

consiliator, oris, *m., a counsellor.*

consilior, ari, atus, 1, *v. dep.,* (1) *to reflect, commune with one's own thoughts, deliberate,* (2) *advise, counsel, give advice.*— On **causa consilians,** see *causa* under 2.

consilium, ii, *n.,* (1) *consideration, reflexion, deliberation,* (2) *counsel, advice.*—On **donum consilii,** see *donum* under 2; on **opus consilii,** see *opus* under 4.—A special kind of **consilium** in this sense is **consilium voluntatis,** *the deliberation of the will or the deliberation which takes place with a free will.*—**consilium est appetitus inquisitivus,** *deliberation is an inquiring appetite or an appetite based on inquiry.* On **perfectio consilii,** see *perfectio* under 3.—Kinds of *consilium* in

this (2) sense are: (a), **consilium bonum** and **consilium malum,** *the good* and *the bad counsel.*—(b), **consilium de continentia seu de continentia perpetua observanda seu de virginitate seu virginitatis seu perpetuae castitatis,** *the counsel of continence* or *of chastity* or *of virginity.*—(c), **consilium de virginitate,** see *consilium de continentia.*—(d), **consilium evangelicum seu Evangelii,** *the evangelical counsel* or *the counsel contained in the Gospel.*—(e), **consilium Evangelii,** see *consilium evangelicum.*—(f), **consilium generale seu perfectum** and **consilium particulare,** *the universal* or *the perfect counsel* and *the particular counsel* or *the counsel concerning a single case.*—(g), **consilium humanum,** *human counsel.*—(h), **consilium malum,** see *consilium bonum.*—(i), **consilium medicinae,** *medicinal counsel.*—(j), **consilium oboedientiae,** *the counsel of voluntary obedience to the superior of an order.*—(k), **consilium particulare,** see *consilium generale.*—(l), **consilium paupertatis perpetuae,** *the counsel of constant* or *perpetual voluntary poverty.*—(m), **consilium perfectum,** see *consilium generale.*—(n), **consilium perpetuae castitatis,** see *consilium de continentia.*—(o), **consilium secundum quid** and **consilium simpliciter,** *the respective* and *the absolute counsel.*—(p), **consilium simpliciter,** see *consilium secun-*

dum quid.—(q), **consilium virginitatis,** see *consilium de continentia.*

consimilis, e, *adj., similar in all respects, like, homogeneous.*—As
subst., only in the phrases: **et
consimilia, et consimiles,** *and the
like, and similar things.*

consistentia, ae, *f.,* (1)*continuance,
consistence, good condition, safe-
ty,* synonym of *incolumitas,* (2)
mass, matter, material.

consisto, ere, stiti, stitum, 3, *v. n.,*
(1) *to continue, last, persevere,*
(2) *exist, be,* (3) *consist in something.* On **actio consistens in agente,** see *actio* under 1.—Kinds
of *consistere* in this (2) sense
are: (a), **consistere instrumentaliter** and **consistere per auctoritatem,** *to exist after the manner of an instrument* and *after
the manner of authorship* or *of
an author.*—(b), **consistere per
auctoritatem,** see *consistere instrumentaliter.*—(c), **consistere radicaliter,** *to exist like a root.*—
Kinds of *consistere* in this (3)
sense are: (a), **consistere essentialiter,** *to consist essentially.*—
(b), **consistere completive** and
consistere originaliter, *to consist
according to completion and according to origin.*—(c), **consistere
formaliter** and **consistere substantialiter,** *to consist in something according to its form* and
according to its essence.—(d),
consistere originaliter, see *consistere completive.*—(e), **consistere principaliter,** *to consist*

*in something according to the
principal matter in substance.*—
(f), **consistere simpliciter,** *to
consist simply.*—(g), **consistere
substantialiter,** see *consistere formaliter.*—(h), **consistere totaliter,**
to consist wholly or *completely.*

consobrinus, i, *m., a cousin, the
child of a mother's sister;* but
more frequently **consobrini** is
used of *all cousins-german, children of brothers* or *sisters.*

consociatio, onis, *f., a union, fellowship, society, association in
social relationship.*

consocio, are, avi, atum, 1, *v. a.,
to unite, associate, join with,*
used with the *dative.*—**consocia-
tus,** a, um, *P. a., united.*

consocius, i, *m., a companion, aid,
fellow, associate.*

consolatio, onis, *f.,* (1) *a consoling,
consolation, comfort, an encouragement, encouraging,* (2) *a
consolatory discourse* or *treatise,*
especially the *Consolatio Philosophiae,* the title of a discourse
on Philosophy written by Boethius while in prison at Pavia.

consolativus, a, um, *adj., comforting, consolatory.*

consolator, oris, *m., one who con-
soles, a comforter.*

consolidativus, a, um, *adj., consol-
idant, having the power of con-
solidating;* especially in medicine, *tending to heal wounds.*

consolido, are, *no perf.,* atum, 1,
v. a., to make firm or *solid, unite into one body* or *system.*

consolo, are, avi, atum, 1, *v. a.*, *to comfort, cheer, console,* synonym of *consolor.*

consolor, ari, atus, 1, *v. dep.*, *to console, encourage, comfort, cheer,* synonym of *consolo.*

consonantia, ae, *f.*, (1) *harmony, agreement, accord* in the real and in the unreal sense of the word, synonym of *convenientia* and *harmonia,* the opposite of *dissonantia,* (2) *the teaching of harmony, the teaching of music, the field of harmony or of music.*—Kinds of *consonantia* in general are: (a), **consonantia compositionis** and **consonantia ordinis,** *the harmony in composing and combining* and *the harmony in order.*—(b), **consonantia musica seu musicalis seu musicae,** *musical harmony* or *the harmony in music.*—(c), **consonantia naturalis,** *natural harmony.*—(d), **consonantia ordinis,** see *consonantia compositionis.*

consono, are, ui, 1, *to agree, be consonant with, be in harmony with.*—**consonans,** antis, *P. a.*, *harmonious,* opposite of *inconsonans.*

consonus, a, um, *adj.*, *harmonious, agreeing with, agreeing in thought* or *purpose, in keeping with something, fit, suitable.*

consopio, ire, *no perf.*, itum, *v. a.*, *to lull to sleep, to bring into an unconscious state.*

consors, sortis, *m.*, *a companion, partaker of something, sharer, partner.*

consortium, ii, *n.*, *a partnership, fellowship, society, participation, association with.*

conspecialis, e, *adj.*, *belonging to the same kind,* not used in S.T. On **causa conspecialis,** see *causa* under 2.

conspectus, us, *m.*, (1) *a seeing, looking at, sight, view, the range of sight, power of vision;* in **conspectu,** *before the eyes of, in the presence of,* (2) *the gaze, attentive observation,* (3) *a particular look or expression as a look of pity* or *favor,* (4) *a mental view, glance.*

conspergo, ere, si, sum, 3, *v. a.*, *to sprinkle, bespatter.*

conspicabilis, e, *adj.*, *evident, plain* or *manifest to the mind* or *senses.*

conspicio, ere, spexi, spectum, 3, *v. a.*, and *n.*, (1) *to gaze upon, observe, contemplate,* (2) *perceive mentally, understand, comprehend.*

conspicuus, a, um, *adj.*, *that is* or *comes in view, visible, conspicuous.*

conspuo, *no perf.*, utum, 3, *v. a.* and *n.*, *to spit upon in contempt, spit upon.*

constans, antis, *part.* and *P. a.*, see *consto.*

constanter, *adv.*, see *consto.*

constantia, ae, *f.*, *firmness, steadfastness, perseverence, constancy.* On the relationship of *constantia* or *perseverantia,* see *perseverantia.* Cf. SS. Q. 137. Art. 3; which deals with the question:

Utrum constantia pertineat ad perseverantiam.

Constantinopolis, is, *f.,* Grk. *Konstantinou polis, the city of Constantinople,* previously called *Byzantium,* Turkish *Stamboul.*

Constantinopolitanus, a, um, *adj., of Constantinople: urbs,* i.e., *Constantinople.*

Constantinus, i, *m.,* C. Flavius Valerius Claudis Constantinus, *Constantine,* emperor of Rome, born A.D. 274, died A.D. 323. The great change which makes the reign of Constantine an epoch in church history is the union between Church and state, and the introduction of the personal interference of the emperor.

constellatio, onis, *f., a collection of stars supposed to exert an influence on human affairs, a constellation.*

constituo, ere, ui, utum, 3, *v. a.,* (1) *to put together, construct,* (2) *produce, achieve, accomplish, make,* (3) *put up, propose, place, arrange,* (4) *appoint, assign, establish.*—Kinds of *constituere* in this (2) sense are: (a), **constituere formaliter,** *to produce something according to its form* and *essence.*—(b), **constituere integraliter,** *to produce something according to its whole.*— (c), **constituere per artem,** *to produce something through art.*

constitutio, onis, *f.,* (1) *a constitution of the whole from parts, disposition, nature,* (2) *appoint-*

ment, establishment, (3) *a body of laws, constitution.*

constitutivus, a, um, *adj., constructive, productive, accompletive,* the opposite of *distinctivus.* On **differentia constitutiva,** see *differentia;* on **forma constitutiva,** see *forma* under 2.—**constitutive,** *adv., in the manner* or *in the sense of founding, building, constructing; constructively,* not used in S.T.

consto, are, stiti, statum, 1, *v. n.,* (1) *to stand firm, be stable* or *steadfast,* (2) *to stand firm, be certain* or *sure, be established,* (3) *exist, be present,* (4) *exist, consist of.*—**constans,** antis, *P. a., standing firm, firm, unchangeable, stable.*—**constanter,** *adv., firmly, steadily, constantly.*

constrictio, onis, *f., a binding* or *drawing together, contraction,* opposite of *dilatatio.*

constrictivus, a, um, *adj., contracting, limiting, constructive.* On **vis constrictiva,** see *vis* under 1.

constrictus, a, um, *adj.,* see *constringo.*

constringo, ere, strinxi, strictum, 3, *v. a.,* (1) *to draw together, bind together, bind, tie up, fetter,* (2) trop., *restrain, hold in check,* (3) *constrain, compel.*—**constrictus,** a, um, *P. a., checked, restrained, bound.*

constructio, onis, *f.,* (1) *a putting* or *placing together, a joining together, building, construction,* opposite of *destructio* and *resolutio,* (2) fig., *erection, construc-*

tion, (3) *in gram., grammatical
connection, construction.*
constructivus, a, um, *adj., productive of, constructive of.*
construo, ere, struxi, structum, 3,
v. a., (1) *to make up by piling
up, construct, build,* used both
lit. and *fig.,* (2) esp. in *gram.
lang., connect grammatically,
construct, construe.*
consubstantialis, e, *adj., of like
substance, of like essence, consubstantial.* On **agens consubstantiale,** see *agens;* on **causa
consubstantialis,** see *causa* under
2; on **principium consubstantiale,** see *principium.*
consubstantialitas, atis, *f., like substance, like essence, consubstantiality.*
consuesco, ere, suevi, suetum, 3,
v. a. and *n., to accustom oneself, be accustomed, be wont,*
constr. regularly with *inf.,* opposite of *dissuescere.*—**consuetus,**
a, um, *P. a., used, accustomed,
usual, ordinary, wonted, customary,* opposite of *inconsuetus.*
consuetudinalis, e, *adj., accustomed, usual, of custom, of use.*
consuetudo, inis, *f.,* (1) *custom,
usage, habit,* synonym of *habitudo, mos,* (2) *state of being conversant, experience.*—With prep.,
**ex consuetudine, per consuetudinem, propter consuetudinem,
secundum consuetudinem,** and
absol., **consuetudine,** *according
to* or *from custom, by* or *from
habit, in a usual* or *customary
manner,* etc. Less frequently,

contra consuetudinem and **praeter consuetudinem,** *contrary to
custom.*
consulo, ere, lui, ltum, *v. n.* and
a., (1) esp. *consulere alicui* or
*alicui rei, to take care for some
person or thing, be mindful of,
take care of, look to, have regard for, counsel* or *consult for,*
(2) *consulere aliquem, consult
with one, ask his opinion* or *advice, take counsel of, consult,
question,* (3) *consulere aliquid,
take counsel* or *deliberate upon
something, consider,* (4) *give advice, advise, counsel* with *acc.,*
and *absol.*—**consultum,** i, *n.,
a decree, decision, resolution,*
(2) *consultation, inquiry.*—**senatus consultum,** *a decree of the
Senate.*—**consulte,** *adv., considerately, deliberately, designedly,
on purpose.*
consultatio, onis, *f., a mature deliberation, consideration, consultation.*
consulte, *adv.,* see *consulo.*
consulto, are, avi, atum, 1, *v. freq.
a., to reflect, consider maturely,
take counsel, deliberate.*
consultorius, a, um, *adj., of consultation, consultatory.*
consultum, i, *n.,* see *consulo.*
consummatio, onis, *f.,* (1) *finish,
termination, conclusion, end,* (2)
*consummation, accomplishment,
fulfilment,* (3) *completeness,
making complete, completion,
perfection,* synonym of *completio* and *perfectio.*—A kind of
consummatio in this (1) sense

is: **consummatio saeculi seu temporum,** *the end of the world* or *of time.*—Kinds of *consummatio* in this (3) sense are: (a), **consummatio gloriae, consummatio gratiae,** and **consummatio naturae,** *the completion of heavenly glory, that of grace,* and *that of nature.*—(b), **consummatio gratiae,** see *comsummatio gloriae.*—(c), **consummatio monastica,** *the monastic perfection,* i.e., *consecration.*—(d), **consummatio naturae,** see *consummatio gloriae.*—(e), **consummatio ultima,** *the last perfection,* which is that of heaven.

consummative, *adv.,* see *consummativus.*

consummativus, a, um, *adj., completing, perfecting, effecting, consummative.* On **causa consummativa,** see *causa* under 2.—**consummative,** *adv., after the manner or sense of completion, consummatively.*

consummator, oris, *m., a completer, finisher.*

consummatus, a, um, *P. a.,* see *consummo.*

consummo, are, avi, atum, 1, *v. a.,* (1) *to finish, bring to an end,* (2) *consummate, accomplish, fulfil,* (3) *complete, make complete, get ready.* On **matrimonium consummatum,** see *matrimonium.*—On **bonum consummatum,** see *bonus* under 2; on **gratia consummata,** see *gratia* under 2; on **perfectio consummata,** see *perfectio;* on **voluntas consummata,**

see *voluntas* under 3.—**consummatus,** a, um, *P. a., brought to the highest degree, perfect, complete, consummate.*

consumo, ere, sumpsi, sumptum, 3, *v. a., consume, squander, annihilate, destroy, bring to naught.*

consumptio, onis, *f.,* (1) *spending, consumption,* (2) *wasting, lavishing, squandering,* synonym of *apirocalia, banausia,* and *prodigalitas,* the opposite of *avaritia, illiberalitas,* and *parvificentia.*

consumptivus, a, um, *adj., tending to consume, destructive, consumptive.*

consumptor, oris, *m., consumer, destroyer, waster,* opposite of *parvificus.*

consuo, ere, sui, sutum, 3, *v. a., sew, stitch* or *join together.*

consurgo, ere, surrexi, surrectum, 3, *v. n.,* (1) of living beings, rare in S.T., constr. *ad* or *in aliquid,* also *absol., to rise* or *stand up* for any action, (2) of inanimate things, common in S.T., constr. *ad* or *in aliquid,* usually *absol., arise.*

contactus, us, *m., a touching, touch, contact,* both in the true and the figurative senses of the word. On **infinitum per contactum,** see *infinitus;* on **unire per contactum virtutis et per modum contactus,** see *unire.*—Kinds of *contactus* in general are: (a), **contactus corporalis seu corporeus** and **contactus spiritualis,** *the physical* and *the spiritual contact.*—(b), **contactus quanti-**

tatis seu molis and **contactus vir-tutis seu virtualis,** *the physical quantitative contact* and *that of power,* or *operation,* both of which are in fact identical with the two mentioned above.—(c), **contactus spiritualis,** see *contactus corporalis.*—(d), **contactus virtualis,** see *contactus quantitatis.*—(e), **contactus virtutis,** see *contactus quantitatis.*—**nullum a gens corporale efficienter agit nisi per contactum,** see *agens.*

contagio, onis, *f., a touching, contact, touch, contagion, infection,* synonym of *contagium,* used in S.T. only in quotation.

contagiosus, a, um, *adj., contagious.*

contagium, ii, *n., a touching, contact, touch, contagion, infection,* synonym of *contagio.*

contaminatio, onis, *f., a polluting, contamination, defilement.*

contamino, are, avi, atum, 1, *v. a., to contaminate, defile, stain,* used in the S.T. only in quote.

contego, ere, texi, tectum, 3, *v. a., to cover up, conceal.*

contemno, ere, tempsi, temptum, 3, *v. a., to consider a person* or *thing as unimportant or of small value, esteem lightly, contemn, despise, disdain.*

contemperantia, ae, *f., equal measure, correct relation,* synonym of *contemperatio,* not in S.T.

contemperatio, onis, *f., equal measure, correct relation,* synonym of *contemperantia.*

contempero, are, avi, atum, 1, *v.*

a., to moderate or *temper by mixing.*

contemplatio, onis, *f., contemplation, meditation* in its strictest use; *contemplation* is the simple gazing of the mind at manifest truth. On the difference between *contemplatio* and *speculatio Dei* we read: nomen contemplationis significat illum actum principalem, quo quis Deum in seipso contemplatur, sed speculatio magis nominat illum actum quo quis divina in rebus creatis quasi in speculo inspicit, 3 Sent. 35. 1. 2. 3 c. On **delectatio contemplationis,** see *delectatio;* on **puritas contemplationis,** see *puritas* under 1; on **votum contemplationis,** see *votum* under 1.—Kinds of *contemplatio,* namely *contemplatio Dei* are the following: (a), **contemplatio beata,** *the blessed contemplation* or *the contemplation of the blessed in heaven.*—(b), **contemplatio deiformis,** *God-like contemplation.*—(c), **contemplatio expedita seu libera,** *the unhindered* or *free contemplation* (quia facile est ea considerare in universali).—(d), **contemplatio explicita,** *the explicit* or *open contemplation.*—(e), **contemplatio imperfecta et contemplatio perfecta,** *the imperfect* (per creaturas) and *the perfect contemplation* (qua videtur Deus immediate per suam essentiam).—(f), **contemplatio intima,** *internal contemplation.*—(g), **contempla-**

tio libera, see *contemplatio expedita.*—(h), **contemplatio mentis,** *contemplation of the mind.*—(i), **contemplatio nuda,** *bare contemplation* or *contemplation separated from all individuals.*—(j), **contemplatio patriae et contemplatio viae,** *the contemplation of God in the heavenly fatherland* and *the contemplation on the way,* or *the heavenly* and *the earthly contemplations.*—(k), **contemplatio perfecta,** see *contemplatio imperfecta.*—(l), **contemplatio philosophica et contemplatio theologorum,** *the philosophical* and *theological contemplations.*—(m), **contemplatio sapientiae,** *the contemplation of wisdom,* (quae est sapientiae actus).—(n), **contemplatio simplex,** *simple contemplation.*—(o), **contemplatio spiritualis,** *spiritual contemplation.*—(p), **contemplatio theologorum,** see *contemplatio philosophica.*—(q), **contemplatio veritatis,** *contemplation of truth.* —(r), **contemplatio viae,** see *contemplatio patriae.*

contemplativus, a, um, *adj., examining, contemplative,* synonym of *considerativus.* On **actio contemplativa,** see *actio* under 1; on **beatitudo contemplativa,** see *beatitudo* under 1; on **felicitas contemplativa,** see *felicitas;* on **inquisitio contemplativa,** see *inquisitio;* on **intellectus contemplativus,** see *intellectus* under 3; on **religio contemplativa,** see *religio* under 2; on **virtus contem-**

plativa, see *virtus* under 5; on vita **contemplativa,** see *vita* under 3.

contemplor, ari, atus, 1, *v. dep., to contemplate, meditate.*

contemptibilis, e, *adj., contemptible.*

contemptibiliter, *adv., contemptibly.*

contemptor, oris, *m., a contemner, despiser.*

contemptus, us, *m., contempt, a despising, contemning.*

contendo, ere, di, tum, 3, *v. a.* and *n.,* (1) *to contend, maintain by argument;* **contendere iudicio,** *go to law,* used with *abl.,* in and *abl., cum* and *abl., contra* and *acc., de* and *abl.,* the *acc.* and *inf.,* (2) *pertain to, apply to,* used with *ad* and *acc.,* (3) *strain eagerly after, strive for, exert one's energies towards some goal,* used with the *abl. of means, pro* and the *abl.,* the *inf.*

contentio, onis, *f., contradiction, disputing, wordy contention, squabble, quarrel.*

contentiose, *adv.,* see *contentiosus.*

contentiosus, a, um, *adj., pertaining to contention, contentious, disputatious.* On **causa contentiosa,** see *causa* under 6.—**contentiose,** *adv., contentiously.*

contentive, *adv., conservatively, tending to conserve* or *hold together;* synonym of *conservative.*

contentus, a, um, *P. a.,* see *contineo.*

contero, ere, trivi, tritum, 3, *v. a.,* (1) *to grind, bruise, crush, sep-*

arate into small pieces, (2) *be broken in spirit* because of a sense of sin, *be bruised, crushed, contrite, conscience-smitten, penitent, sorry,* used frequently in this sense with *de* and *abl.,* and always in the *pass.—*contritus, a, um, *P. a., contrite, penitent.*

conterritus, a, um, *P. a., terrified, frightened.*

contestatio, onis, *f., a contestation, attestation, the act of contesting, disputing, pleading.*

contestor, ari, atus, 1, *v. dep.,* to *call to witness.*

contextus, a, um, *P. a., entwined, interwoven.*

contextus, us, *m., a context, the whole text of a work, the body of matter on a written or printed page as distinguished from notes.*

contiguatio, onis, *f., the immediate contact of two things,* so that their boundaries lie close to each other, *contiguity,* the opposite of *continuatio* and *continuitas,* not in S.T.

contiguus, a, um, *adj., neighboring, bordering on, contiguous, directly touching something,* the *haptomenos* of Aristotle, the opposite of *continuus.* On totum contiguum, see *totus* under 1.

continens, entis, *P. a.,* see *contineo.*

continentia, ae, *f.,* (1) *holding together, coherence,* (2) *containing in itself, inclusion, contents, essence,* (3) *abstinence, restraint* in the broader sense of the word, i.e., *self-control, temperance,* the opposite of *incontinentia,* (4) *re-straint* in the narrower sense of the word, *continence,* likewise the opposite of *incontinentia.—* Kinds of *continentia* in this (2) sense are: (a), continentia localis, *the local content.—*(b), continentia virtualis, *the virtual content.* On the difference between *continentia* and *temperantia,* see *temperantia.—*Kinds of *continentia* in this (3) sense are: continentia simpliciter and continentia secundum quid seu cum additione seu secundum similitudinem, *the simple* or *absolute restraint* and *the so-called restraint with reference to something* or *with reference to a similarity.* On the difference between *continentia* and *castitas* the following is said: haec duo distinguantur per hoc, quod castitas refrenat hominem ab illicitis, continentia vero etiam a licitis, sive per hoc, quod continens, patitur concupiscentias, sed non deducitur, castus autem neque patitur, neque deducitur. Ps. Q. 70. Art. 3 c. *Continentia* is one of the *fructus Spiritus Sancti;* see *fructus.* On bonum continentiae, see *bonus;* on consilium de continentia, see *consilium;* on votum continentiae, see *votum.—*Kinds of *continentia* in this (4) sense are: (a), continentia coniugalis, continentia vidualis, and continentia virginalis, *marital continence, the continence of widowhood,* and *virginal continence.—*(b), continentia **perfecta**, *the perfect conti-nence.*—(c), **continentia perpetua**, *perpetual continence.*—(d), **conti-nentia principalis** and **continen-tia secundaria**, *the principal* or *the most excellent continence* and *the secondary continence.*—(e), **continentia secundaria**, see *continentia principalis.*—(f), **con-tinentia vidualis**, see *continentia coniugalis.*—(g), **continentia virgi-nalis**, see *continentia coniugalis.*

contineo, ere, ui, tentum, 2, *v. a.* and *n.*, (1) *to hold* or *keep to-gether, hold fast, preserve, re-strain*, (2) *bound, limit, enclose, include, contain*, usually with *in* or *sub* and *abl.*, also with *inter* or *intra* and *acc.*, (3) *check, curb, subdue, repress, restrain*, (4) *be contained in something, be composed of, rest upon, be supported by*, in *pass.* and *ali-qua re.*—**continens**, entis, *P. a.*, (1) *holding together, tenacious*, (2) *including, limiting, contain-ing*, (3) *bordering upon, neigh-boring, contiguous, near*, (4) *connected, continuous, uninter-rupted*, (5) *continent, moderate, temperate*, the opposite of *in-continens.*—On **corpus continens et contentum**, see *corpus;* on **lo-cus continens**, see *locus* under 2; on **species continens**, see *spe-cies* under 5.—On the difference between *continens* and *tempera-tus*, see *temperatus* under 5.— Kinds of *continens* in this (5) sense are: **continens simpliciter** and **continens secundum quid**

seu cum aliqua additione, *the simply* or *absolutely restrained* and *the restrained in a certain respect* or *with a certain limita-tion.*—**continens**, entis, *m.*, or *f.*, *who restrains his passions, con-tinent, moderate, temperate.*— **continens**, entis, *n.*, *that which contains, a container.*—**contentus**, a, um, *P. a.*, (1) *contained, en-closed, included*, (2) *contented, satisfied.*—**contenta**, orum, *n.*, *contents.*

contingens, entis, *P. a.*, see *con-tingo.*

contingenter, *adv.*, see *contingo.*

contingentia, ae, *f.*, *not a necessi-ty*, by which may be understood the *logical* as well as the *ontolo-gical necessity, contingency*, the opposite of *necessitas.*

contingo, ere, tigi, tactum, 3, *v. a.* and *n.*, (1) *to happen to one, befall, fall to one's lot, come to pass*, (2) used often impers., *it happens, befalls, comes to pass*, with *inf.*, *ut* and *subj.*, *quod* and *subj.*—**contingens**, entis, *P. a.*, (1) *touching, contacting with*, (2) *ontologically not necessary, not existing of necessity, contin-gent*, that which does not have to be what it is, or even to be at all, the opposite of *necessari-us*, (3) *logically not necessary, not of necessity valid* or *true, contingent*, also the opposite of *necessarius.*—On the difference between *contingens* and *neces-sarius* the following is said: con-tingens a necessario differt, secundum quod unumquodque in sua causa est; contingens enim sic in sua causa est, ut non esse ex ea possit et esse, necessarium vero ex sua causa non potest non esse, secundum id vero, quod utrumque eorum in se est, non differt quantum ad esse, super quod fundatur verum, quia in contingenti secundum id, quod in se est, non est esse et non esse, sed solum esse, licet in futurum contingens possit non esse, C. G. 1. On **causa contingens,** see *causa* under 2; on **effectus contingens,** see *effectus;* on **materia contingens,** see *materia* under 3; on **operabile contingens,** see *operabilis;* on **principium contingens,** see *principium;* on **singulare contingens,** see *singularis* under 1.—Kinds of *contingens* in this (2) sense are: (a), **contingens ad utrumlibet seu ad utrumque seu incertum seu indeterminatum seu infinitum** and **contingens determinatum ad unum,** *unnecessary in two respects,* or *the uncertainly* or *indefinitely unnecessary* and *the definitely necessary in a single respect,* that which is indifferent to various determinations and that which is conceived or regarded as determined, but only contingently, to be this rather than anything else.—(b), **contingens determinatum ad unum,** see *contingens ad utrumlibet.*—(c), **contingens futurum** and **contingens praesens,** *the un-*

necessary in the future and *in the present.*—(d), **contingens incertum,** see *contingens ad utrumlibet.*—(e), **contingens indeterminatum,** see *contingens ad utrumlibet.*—(f), **contingens possibile,** *possibly necessary.*—(g), **contingens praesens,** see *contingens futurum.*—(h), **contingens ut in paucioribus** and **contingens ut in pluribus,** *the possible that may occur in the fewest* and *the most instances.*—(i), **contingens ut in pluribus,** see *contingens ut in paucioribus.*—**Humani actus in singularibus contingentibus consistunt,** *human actions are concerned with affairs that may not take place,* or *take place differently.* **Nihil enim est ideo contingens, quin in se aliquid necessarium habeat,** *nothing is so contingent that it does not have something necessary in itself,* as for example, in the case of a thing of nature, it is necessary that it have a very definite existence and act according to its form.—On **falsum contingens,** see *falsum;* on **minor de contingenti,** see *minor* under 3; on **propositio contingens,** see *propositio* under 2; on **syllogismus contingens,** see *syllogismus;* on **veritas contingens,** see *veritas* under 1; on **verum contingens seu a contingenti,** see *verus* under 1.—**contingenter,** *adv., not of necessity, contingently,* by which may be understood the logical as well as the ontological contingency, the opposite of *necessario, necesse,* and *de* or *ex necessitate.*

continuatio, onis, *f.,* (1) *direct combination, connection,* synonym of *continuitas* and *unio,* the opposite of *contiguatio,* (2) *a following of one thing after another, an unbroken series, continuation, succession,* likewise synonym of *continuitas.*—Kinds of *continuatio* in this (2) sense are: **continuatio actus** and **continuatio habitus,** *the lasting continuation of an action and that of a habitus.*

continue, *adv.,* see *continuus.*

continuitas, atis, *f.,* (1) *a direct combination, connection of two things, so that their exterior boundaries fall together, continuity,* synonym *continuatio* and *unio,* the opposite of *contiguatio,* (2) *a following of one thing after another, an unbroken series, continuation, succession, continuity,* likewise a synonym of *continuatio.*—On **diversitas continuitatis,** see *diversitas;* on **unitas continuitatis,** see *unitas;* on **unum continuitatis,** see *unus.*—Kinds of *continuitas* in this sense are: **continuitas actualis** and **continuitas habitualis,** *the lasting continuation of an action* and *that of an habitus.*

continuo, are, avi, atum, 1, *v. a.* and *n.,* (1) *to combine directly, connect two things, unite,* (2) *continue* or *link without interruption, connect,* frequently in *pass.*—**continuans,** antis, *P. a., continuing*—**continuatus,** a, um, *P. a., continued.*

continuo, *adv.,* see *continuus.*

continuus, a, um, *adj.,* (1) *directly combined, connected with something,* the opposite of *contiguus, discontinuatus, discontinuus,* (2) *connected in itself, uninterruptedly succeeding one another, lasting continually,* Aristotelian *syneches,* the opposite of *intercisus* and *discretus.* (3) *touching something directly,* synonym of *contiguus.*—On **actus continuus,** see *actus* under 1; on **divisio continua,** see *divisio;* on **generatio continua,** see *generatio* under 1; on **magnum continuum,** see *magnus;* on **motus continuus et non continuus,** see *motus* under 1; on **mutatio continua,** see *mutatio;* on **operatio continua,** see *operatio* under 2; on **pars continua et non continua,** see *pars* under 1; on **proportionalitas continua,** see *proportionalitas;* on **quantitas continua,** see *quantitas* under 1; on **tempus continuum et noncontinuum,** see *tempus;* on **totum continuum,** see *totus* under 1; on **unio continua,** see *unio;* on **unitas continua,** see *unitas;* on **visio continua,** see *visio* under 1. —Kinds of *continuum* in this (2) sense are: (a), **continuum fluens** and **continuum permanens,** *the flowing continuum* or *that in motion* and *the permanent* or *static continuum.*—(b), **continuum homogeneum,** *the homogene-*

ous continuum.—(c), **continuum per aliud, seu secundum aliud** and **continuum secundum se,** *the continuum through something else* or *according to something else* and *the continuum existing according to itself.*—(d), **continuum per artem, continuum per violentiam,** and **continuum per seu secundum naturam,** *the continuum brought about by art, that by violence* or *forced,* and *that by itself.*—(e), **continuum permanens,** see *continuum fluens.*—(f), **continuum per naturam,** see *continuum per artem.*—(g), **continuum per violentiam,** see *continuum per artem.*—(h), **continuum secundum aliud,** see *continuum per aliud.*—(i), **continuum secundum naturam,** see *continuum per artem.*—(j), **continuum secundum se,** see *continuum per aliud.*—**dignius est esse continuum, quam consequenter,** *to be connected within self is more worthy and better than to follow indirectly from something, quia plus habet de ratione unitatis et perpetuitatis.*—**ex multis parvis non possunt fieri magna continua,** *great continua cannot arise from many small things.*—**in continuis inter quaelibet duo signa sive inter duo puncta semper est aliquod medium accipere,** or, **inter quaelibet duo indivisibilia est continuum medium,** *between any two signs* or *points of continua there is always a middle member which is like-*

wise a continuum.—**nullum continuum est indivisibile,** *no continuum is indivisible*: cf. *corpus.*—**nullum continuum ex indivisibilibus componitur,** *no continuum is composed of indivisibles.*—**omne continuum est divisibile in divisibilia,** *every continuum can be divided into divisibles.*—**continue,** *adv., continuously, without interruption,* the opposite of *intercise.*—**continuo,** *adv., immediately, forthwith, directly, without delay,* synonym of *statim.*

contra, *adv.* and *prep.,* (1) *adv., the contrary, the opposite, on the contrary,* (2) *prep.* with *acc.,* (a) *against, in opposition to, contrary to,* (b) *in contrast to, in opposition to.*—**e contra,** *on the contrary, the contrary.*

contractio, onis, *f.,* (1) *contraction,* (2) *compression, limitation.*

contractus, us, *m., a contract, agreement, a formal agreement between two parties.*

contractus, a, um, *P. a.,* see *contraho.*

contradico, ere, xi, ctum, 3, *v. n., to contradict, deny directly* or *by implication, gainsay.*

contradictio, onis, *f.,* (1) *contradiction, disagreement,* in the real and narrower sense of the word, the *antiphasis* of Aristotle, the simple denial of that which someone affirms, or, the simple affirmation of that which someone denies, leaving no middle to which both might agree, (cf. contrarietas), (2) *contradiction,* *disagreement* in the broader sense of the word. On **oppositum in contradictione seu secundum contradictionem seu ut contradictio,** see *opponere;* on **oppositio contradictionis seu secundum contradictionem,** see *oppositio* under 2; on **syllogismus contradictionis,** see *syllogismus.*—Kinds of *contradictio* in this (1) sense are: **contradictio absoluta seu absolute seu simpliciter** and **contradictio quaedam seu participata in contrariis,** *the unconditioned* or *absolute contradiction* and *that made with a certain point of view* or *contained in contraries.*

contradictor, oris, *m., an opponent, one who objects,* or *replies.*

contradictorie, *adv.,* see *contradictorius.*

contradictorius, a, um, *adj., contradicting, contradictory, opposing,* simply denying something that anyone affirms, or simply affirming something that anyone denies. On **enuntiatio contradictoria,** see *enuntiatio* under 2; on **oppositio contradictoria,** see *oppositio* under 2. One kind of *contradictoria* in this sense is **contradictoria absolute,** *raising contradictions to questions in an unconditioned* or *absolute manner.*—**contradictorie,** *adv., in the sense* or *after the manner of a contradiction, contradictorily.* On **oppositum contradictorie,** see *opponere.*

contraeo, ire, 4, *v. n., to withstand, oppose, go against, make resistance,* used with the *dative.*

contraho, ere, traxi, ctum, 3, *v. a.,* (1) *to draw together, contract, assemble, gather,* synonym of *congregare,* (2) *confine, restrain, restrict, limit,* synonym of *restringere, coarctare, finire, determinare,* (3) *draw down upon oneself, assume, acquire,* (4) *conclude, enter upon, contract.*—On **agens contractum,** see *agens;* on **bonum contractum,** see *bonus* under 3; on **differentia contracta,** see *differentia;* on **dispositio contracta seu in partem,** see *dispositio* under 1; on **forma contracta,** see *forma* under 2; on **principium contractum,** see *principium;* on **virtus contracta,** see *virtus* under 1.—On **malitia contracta,** see *malitia* under 3.—**contractus,** a, um, *P. a., drawn together into a narrow space, limited, restricted, acquired, concluded, contracted.*

contranitor, i, 3, *v. dep.* and *n., to rebel against, resist, oppose,* used with the *dative.*

contrapassio, onis, *f., requital, compensation,* synonym of *contrapassum,* does not occur in S.T.

contrapassum, i, *n., corresponding requital, due satisfaction, proper reparation, just compensation,* Aristotelian *antipeponthos.*

contrapatior, i, passus, 3, *dep. v., to endure* or *suffer condignly.*

contrapono, ere, posui, positum, 3, *v. a., to contrapose, set over* *against,* *oppose.*—**contrapositus,** a, um, *P. a., contraposed.*

contrapugno, are, avi, atum, 1, *v. n., to oppose, withstand, resist, countervail.*

contrarie, *adv.,* see *contrarius.*

contrarietas, atis, *f.,* (1) *contrariety,* a state of opposition that lies between extremes in the same class or kind. Unlike contradiction which opposes affirmation and negation and leaves no middle ground, contrariety opposes two affirmations or two negations and admits, with a few exceptions, of intermediate degrees, always however under a particular aspect, or within a certain class or genus. Thus *white* and *wet* are neither contraries nor contradictories; white and not-white are contradictories; the contrary of white must be sought in the realm of color, and is *black;* the contrary of *wet* will be found in the realm of physical qualities, and is *dry.* Care is necessary when dealing with these two kinds of opposition, since in another application their notions change somewhat. Contrariety and contradiction are applied not only to the things, but also, less properly, to propositions. Since however the subject of the opposed propositions differs, there is no real opposition; but it is convenient for the logician to designate one statement opposed to another as its contradictory, contrary or subcontrary. Thus, the contradictory of the universal affirmative statement, "every man is just," is the particular negative, "some man is not just," and its contrary is the universal negative, "every man is not just." Thus while the predicates, *just* and *not-just* are contradictory, the statement, men are just and men are not just are contraries, (2) *opposition* of any sort.—On **oppositio contrarietatis seu secundum contrarietatem,** see *oppositio,* under 2; on **oppositum ut contrarietas,** see *opponere.*—Kinds of *contrarietas* in this (1) sense are: (a), **contrarietas, enuntiationum, contrarietas opinionum,** and **contrarietas rerum,** *the diametrical opposite of two statements, that of two ideas* and *that of two things.*—(b), **contrarietas immediata** and **contrarietas quae nata est habere medium,** *the diametrical opposites which do not admit a medium,* e.g., odd and even, and *that which by nature admit such.* —(c), **contrarietas in motu seu motus,** *the diametrical opposites in the sphere of motion.*—(d), **contrarietas in mutationibus seu mutationum,** *the diametrical opposite in changes.*—(e), **contrarietas in passionibus,** *the diametrical opposite in passions.*—(f), **contrarietas loci,** see *locus.*—(g), **contrarietas motus,** see *contrarietas in motu.*—(h), **contrarietas mutationum,** see *contrarietas in* *mutationibus.*—(i,) **contrarietas opinionum,** see *contrarietas enuntiationum.*—(j), **contrarietas quae est secundum actum** and **contrarietas quae est secundum potentiam,** *the diametrical opposite between two existing things according to actuality* and *according to potentiality.*—(k), **contrarietas quae est secundum potentiam,** see *contrarietas quae est secundum actum.*—(l), **contrarietas quae nata est habere medium,** see *contrarietas immediata.*—(m), **contrarietas rerum,** see *contrarietas enuntiationum.*—(n), **contrarietas secundum accessum et recessum ab eodem termino** and **contrarietas terminorum,** *the diametrical opposite according to approach to* or *departure from the same terminus* and *that between two different termini.*—(o), **contrarietas terminorum,** see *contrarietas secundum accessum et recessum ab eodem termino.*—(p), **contrarietas voluntatum,** *the opposite* or *contrariety of acts of the will.* —**non est contrarietas medii ad extrema,** *the middle member which lies between the two extremes of a diametrical opposite does not form an opposite with these two extremes.* On **materia contrarietati subiecta et non subiecta,** see *materia* under 3.— Kinds of *contrarietas* in this (2) sense are: (a), **contrarietas directa,** *the exact* or *direct opposite.* —(b), **contrarietas perfecta,** *the*

perfect or *complete opposite;* in fact, identical with *contrarietas directa.*—(c), **contrarietas prima,** *the primary opposition,* namely, the one which prevails beween the *habitus* and the *privatio.*— (d), **contrarietas tangibilis,** *the tangible opposite* or *that perceptible by the sense of touch.* —**contrarietatis principium est oppositio privationis et habitus,** see *habitus.*—**prima contrarietas est habitus et privatio,** see *habitus.*—**principium contrarietatis est privatio et habitus,** see *habitus.* —**privatio et habitus est prima contrarietas quae in omnibus salvatur,** see *habitus* and cf. *contrarietas prima.*

contrarior, ari, *dep., v.,* 1, *to be contrary to, be opposed in situation, direction, aim, purpose,* or *operation.*

contrarius, a, um, *adj.,* (1) *diametrically opposed, directly opposed, exactly opposed,* Aristotelian *antikeimenos to kata diametron,* i.e., whatever within the same kind are most distant from each other.—(2) *opposed,* i.e., most distant from each other.—On **differentia contraria,** see *differentia,* on **enumeratio contraria,** see *enumeratio* under 2; on **fieri ex contrario,** see *fieri;* on **forma contraria,** see *forma* under 2; on **oppositum ut contrarium,** see *opponere;* on **oppositio contraria,** see *oppositio* under 2; on **species contraria,** see *species* under 8.—Kinds of *contraria* in this (1) sense are: (a), **contraria immediata** and **contraria mediata,** *the diametrically opposed,* which does not admit a middle, e.g., odd and even, and that which does admit such.—(b), **contraria in mente** and **contraria in rerum natura,** *the diametrically opposed in thought* and *that in the reality of things.*—(c), **contraria in rerum natura,** see *contraria in mente.*—(d), **contraria mediata,** see *contraria immediata.*—(e), **contraria posteriora** and **contraria priora,** *the later* and *the primarily diametrically opposed.*—(f), **contraria prima,** *the primary diametrically opposed.*—(g), **contraria primo seu principaliter** and **contraria secundario seu secundario modo,** *the diametrically opposed first* and *foremost* and *that secondarily.*—(h), **contraria principaliter,** see *contraria primo.*—(i), **contraria priora,** see *contraria posteriora.*—(j), **contraria secundario seu secundario modo,** see *contraria primo.*—(k), **contraria secundum formam seu speciem** and **contraria secundum locum,** *the diametrically opposed according to form* and *kind* and *that acccording to place.*—(1), **contraria secundum formam generis** and **contraria secundum formam speciei,** *the diametrically opposed according to the form* or *the essence of its genus* (sicut virtus et vitium), and *that according to the form* and *the essence of its species*

(sicut iustitia et iniustitia).—(m), **contraria secundum formam speciei,** see *contraria secundum formam generis.*—(n), **contraria secundum locum,** see *contraria secundum formam.*—(o), **contraria secundum speciem,** see *contraria secundum formam.*—**contraria iuxta se posita magis elucescunt,** *the diametrically opposed become clearer* and *more distant when they are placed opposite each other.*—**contraria mutuo se expellunt,** *the diametrically opposed expel each other,* in any particular subject.—**contraria nata sunt fieri circa idem,** *the diametrically opposed are disposed by nature to occur in the same subject, quando subiectum aequaliter se habet ad utrumque contrariorum.*—**contrariorum eadem est scientia,** *one* and *the same science treats the diametrically opposed.*—**nihil prohibet contraria eidem inesse non secundum idem,** *in different ways the diametrically opposed can come to one* and *the same subject.*—**non convenit plura esse contraria uni,** *to one* and *the same thing there cannot be several diametrically opposed at the same time.*—**rationes contrariorum in intellectu non sunt contrariae,** *the notions of diametrically opposed things are not diametrically opposed to each other in the intellect.*—**unum contrariorum est quodammodo ratio alterius,** *the conception of one of* *two diametrically opposed things is to a certain degree that of the other, in so far as one is defined by means of the other* and *this is possible, cum se habeant sicut perfectum et imperfectum.*—**utrumque contrariorum est natura quaedam,** *each of two diametrically opposed things is a nature,* i.e., *something positive.*—Kinds of *contrarium* in this (2) sense are: **contrarium proprium seu proprie seu vere** and **contrarium improprium,** *the proper* or *true* and *the improper diametrically opposed.*—**contrarium,** i, *n., the opposite, reverse, contrary, the diametrically opposite.*—**ex (e) contrario,** *on the contrary, on the other hand, vice versa.*—**contrario,** same as *ex (e) contrario* but rarely used.—**in contrarium,** *to the contrary, to the opposite side of a question.*—**contrarie,** *adv., in the manner or sense of contrasting opposites, in an opposite direction, in a different manner, contrarily.*

contratendens, dentis, *m., a contender, one who contends* or *maintains by argument.*

contremisco, ere, mui, 3, *v. inch. n.* and *a., to shake, to tremble all over.*

contribulo, are, no perf., atum, 1, *v. a., to afflict, crush, bruise.*—**contribulatus,** a, um, *P. a. afflicted.*

contristabilis, e, *adj., sad, depressing, gloomy, disagreeable, painful.*

contristatio, onis, *f., an afflicting, affliction, grief.*

contristativus, a, um, *adj., painful, displeasing, saddening, depressing.*

contristo, are, avi, atum, 1, *v. a., to make sad* or *sorrowful, pain, sadden, afflict.*—**contristans,** antis, *P. a., saddening, sorrowing.* —**contristatus,** a, um, *P. a., sorrowful, saddened.*

contritio, onis, *f.,* (1) *grinding, crushing,* (2) as one of the important integrating parts of Penance *compunction of heart, perfect contrition, contrition,* voluntary sorrow for sin with the resolve to confess and satisfy for them.—A kind of *contritio* in this (2) sense is: **contritio generalis,** *the general, the perfect contrition with reference to all sins.*

controversia, ae, *f., a controversy, contention, dispute, debate.*

contubernium, ii, *n., fellowship, the condition of being sharer* or *partaker.*

contueor, eri, uitus, 2, *v. a., to look on, gaze on, consider attentively.*

contuitus, us, *m., an attentive looking at, a view, sight.*

contumacia, ae, *f., contumacy, insolent* and *stubborn perverseness.*

contumaciter, *adv.,* see *contumax.*

contumax, acis, *adj., contumacious, insolent, stubborn, obstinate.*—**contumaciter,** *adv., obstinately, stubbornly.*

contumelia, ae, *f.*, *insult, affront, injury*, in its narrower as well as in its broader sense, a synonym of *contumeliatio*.

contumelians, antis, *P. a.*, *insulting, reviling, abusing by speech*.

contumeliatio, onis, *f.*, *insolence*, synonym of *contumelia*, a kind of *parvipensio*.

contumeliativus, a, um, *adj.*, *contumelious, exhibiting contumely*. On **dispositio contumeliativa,** see *dispositio* under 3.

contumeliosus, a um, *adj.*, *full of abuse, reproachful, insolent*.

conturbans, antis, *P. a.*, *distracting, confusing, causing conturbation*.

conturbatio, onis, *f.*, *disturbance, disorder, conturbation*.

conturbo, are, avi, atum, 1, *v. a.*, *to disturb, throw into confusion.* —**conturbatus,** a, um, *P. a.*, *disturbed, confused, disquieted*.

convalescentia, ae, *f.*, *a regaining of health, convalescence*.

convalesco, ere, ui, 3, *v. inch. n.*, *to recover from a disease, to regain health, to grow strong*.

conveniens, entis, *P. a.*, see *convenio*.

convenienter, *adv.*, see *convenio*.

convenientia, ae, *f.*, (1) *suitability, convenience, fitness,* (2) *agreement, harmony*, synonym of *consonantia* and *harmonia*, the opposite of *differentia* and *contrarietas*. On **debitum convenientiae,** see *debitus* under 1.—Kinds of *convenientia* in this (2) sense

are: (a), **convenientia potentiae ad actum** and **convenientia secundum proprietates naturae,** *the agreement of potentiality with its actualization* and *that with reference to natural characteristics.* —(b), **convenientia proportionalitatis** and **convenientia proportionis,** *the harmony of proportionality* and *that of proportion.* —(c), **convenientia proportionis,** see *convenientia proportionalitatis.*—(d), **convenientia secundum proportionem,** *agreement according to a proportion* or *a similarity.*—(e), **convenientia secundum proprietates naturae,** see *convenientia potentiae ad actum.*

convenio, ire, veni, ventum, 4, *v. n.* and *a.*, (1) *to come together, meet together, assemble,* (2) *agree with in wishes or decisions, accord, harmonzie,* (3) *res convenit* or impers. *convenit, is becoming, seemly, suitable, appropriate, proper.*—**conveniens,** entis, *P. a.*, *agreeing, consistent, harmonious, meet, fit, suitable.* On **desiderium conveniens,** see *desiderium* under 1; on **finis conveniens,** see *finis* under 1; on **proportio conveniens et non conveniens,** see *proportio* under 1.—**convenienter,** *adv.*, *fitly, suitably, conformably, consistently.*

conventiculum, i, *n.*, *an assembly, meeting, conventicle*.

conventio, onis, *f.*, *an agreement, a compact, covenant, fellowship, harmony*.

conventus, us, *m.*, *an assembly, a gathering of people for divine worship, a meeting.*

conversatio, onis, *f.*, (1) *social intercourse, association,* synonym of *communicatio, communio,* and *communitas,* (2) *conduct, way of life.*—As kinds of *conversatio* in this (1) sense are: (a), **conversatio civilis seu politica,** *the civic or public intercourse.*—(b), **conversatio domestica,** *the domestic intercourse.*—(c), **conversatio exterior,** *the exterior association.*—(d), **conversatio politica,** see *conversatio civilis.*—Kinds of *conversatio* in this (2) sense are: (a), **conversatio carnalis,** *carnal conduct.*—(b), **conversatio regularis,** *the religious life.*—(c), **conversatio virtuoso,** *the virtuous conduct.*

conversio, onis, *f.*, (1) *a turning, overturning, turning round, turning point,* (2) *transformation, change,* synonym of *immutatio, mutatio,* and *transmutatio,* (3) *turning to, directing to,* the opposite of *aversio,* (4) *turning to God or Christianity, conversion,* also the opposite of *aversio.*—Kinds of *conversio* in this (2) sense are: (a), **conversio circularis seu mutua,** *the circular or the the mutual change* which takes place, dum a primo generato devenitur ad ultimum et ab ultimo reditur ad primum, non idem numero, sed idem specie.—(b), **conversio formalis** and **conversio substantialis,** *the formal*

and *the substantial change,* i.e., the change in which only the form of a thing, not, however, the matter also is affected, (omnis conversio, quae fit secundum leges naturae, est formalis), and that by which tota substantia huius convertitur in totam substantiam illius.—(c), **conversio miraculosa seu supernaturalis** and **conversio naturalis,** *the miraculous* and *supernatural* and *the natural change.*—(d), **conversio mutua,** see *conversio circularis.*—(e), **conversio naturalis,** see *conversio miraculosa.*—(f), **conversio perfecta,** *the perfect* or *complete change.*—(g), **conversio substantialis,** see *conversio formalis.*—(h), **conversio successiva,** *the change which takes place gradually,* the opposite of *conversio subita seu instantanea,* i.e., *the change which takes place in an instant.*—(i), **conversio supernaturalis,** see *conversio miraculosa.*—Kinds of *conversio* in this (3) sense are: (a), **conversio indebita,** *the improper turning to* or *that which should not be.*—(b), **conversio inordinata,** *the inordinate* or *disreputable turning to.* Under this heading belongs: **conversio meritoria,** *the conversion which is meritorious with God.*

conversivus, a, um, *adj.*, *having a converting quality, transforming.*

converso, ari, atus, 1, *v. freq.*, (1) *to converse with, associate with, live with, be intimately ac-*

quainted with, (2) abide, live, dwell somewhere, (3) pass one's life, live.

convertibilis, e, adj., (1) turnable, convertible, interchangeable, whether in the reality of a thing or in an assertion, (2) changeable, transformable.—On **effectus convertibilis et non-convertibilis,** see effectus; on **ratio convertibilis,** see ratio under 9; on **terminus convertibilis,** see terminus under 4.—**verum et ens sunt convertibilia,** the true and being are convertible terms.—**convertibiliter,** adv., changeably, convertibly, interchangeably, not in S.T. On **praedicare convertibiliter,** see praedicare under 2.

convertibilitas, atis, f., convertibility, changeability, not in S.T.

converto, ere, ti, sum, 3, v. a., (1) to turn around, turn, return in the reality of things, (2) return in statement, interchange, declare in the reverse, speak in reverse, so that the subject of the statement is made the predicate and the predicate of the same is made the subject of the next sentence, (3) change, transform, (4) turn to, direct to, (5) turn to God, convert.—**omnis effectus convertitur in suum principium seu ad causam, a qua procedit,** see effectus.—**unumquodque naturaliter convertitur ad id, quod melius est,** every thing by nature turns toward that which is better for itself.—**conversus,** a, um, P. a., turned around, turned,

changed, directed to, converted. —**e converso,** conversely, in the opposite way, in the other way about.

convexus, a, um, adj., convex, rounded, concave.

convicior, ari, atus, 1, v. dep., to revile, reproach, taunt, rail.— **conviciatus,** a, um, P. a., insulted, reviled.—**convicians,** antis, P. a., used substantively, a reviler, one given to reviling.

conviciosus, a, um, adj., deriding, mocking, scornful, contemptuous.

convicium, ii, n., reproach, insult, railing.

convictio, onis, f., conviction, proof.

convictus, us, m., social intercourse, relationship, companionship, fellowship, society, company.

convinco, ere, vici, victum, 3, v. a., (1) to convict, find guilty after a judicious trial, used with the inf., acc., de, and ex, (2) to convince, satisfy by evidence in respect to a truth or falsity, to prove, used with acc., de and abl.—**convictus,** a, um, P. a., convinced, convicted.

conviva, ae, comm., a guest, one who feasts with another, a table companion.

convivium, ii, n., a banquet, social feast, entertainment.

convivo, ere, vixi, 3, v. n., to live with, dwell with, associate with.

convivor, ari, atus, 1, v. dep., to eat, to feast, to banquet with others.

convoco, are, avi, atum, 1, *v. a., to call together, convoke, assemble.*

convolo, are, avi, atum, 1, *v. n., to come to, come hastily to.*

convolutio, onis, *f., a turning over, reflection, meditation, contemplation.*

convolvo, ere, volvi, volutum, 3, *v. a., to collect, roll together, roll up.*

cooperatio, onis, *f., co-operation.*

cooperator, oris, *m., a cooperator, joint laborer.*

cooperculum, i, *n., a cover, lid.*

cooperio, ire, rui, rtum, 4, *v. a., to cover wholly, cover over, overwhelm.*—**cooperiens,** entis, *P. a., covering over.*

cooperor, ari, atus, sum, 1, *v. dep., to work with* or *together, combine, unite.*—**cooperans,** antis, *P. a., working with, cooperating.*

coopertura, ae, *f., a covering, cover.*

coordino, are, avi, atum, 1, *v. a., to coordinate, make coordinate, place in harmonious* or *reciprocal relations.*—**coordinatus,** a, um, *P. a., coordinated, coordinate.*

copia, ae, *f.,* (1) *abundance, plenty,* (2) of possessions, *riches, wealth,* (3) with reference to action, *ability, opportunity, means of doing a thing.*

copiose, *adv.,* see *copiosus.*

copiosus, a, um, *adj., furnished abundantly with a thing, well supplied, rich, copious.*—**copiose,** *adv., copiously, abundantly, plentifully.*

copula, ae, *f., union;* **copula carnalis, copula coniugalis, copula spiritualis,** *sexual union, conjugal union, spiritual connection.*

copulatim, *adv., in the manner* or *in the sense of combining, condensing, in union,* synonym of *coniunctim,* the opposite of *disiunctim,* not in S.T.

copulatio, onis, *f., copulation, union.*

copulo, are, avi, atum, 1, *v. a., to add, couple, unite, join;* used with the *dat., acc.*—**copulans,** antis, *P. a., uniting.*—**copulatus,** a, um, *P. a., joined together, united, connected.*

coquo, ere, xi, ctum, 3, *v. a., to cook, bake, boil, roast, parch.*—**coctus,** a, um, *P. a., baked.*

coquus, i, *m., a cook.*

cor, cordis, *n.,* (1) *heart* in the general sense of the word, (2) *heart* in the proper sense of the word, (3) *heart* in the figurative sense of the word.—On **infirmitas cordis,** see *infirmitas* under 1; on **ira cordis,** see *ira* under 1.—On **blasphemia cordis,** see *blasphemia;* on **cogitatio cordis,** see *cogitatio* under 1; on **conceptus cordis,** see *conceptus* under 2; on **munditia cordis,** see *munditia;* on **peccatum cordis** see *peccatum* under 2; on **verbum cordis et in corde enuntiatum,** see *verbum* under 1; on **vestigium cordis,** see *vestigium;* on **voluntas cordis,** see *voluntas* under 3.—**duritia cordis,** *hardness of heart,* i.e., *of* the will.—ex (e) **toto corde,** *with one's whole heart.*—**obduratio cordis,** *obduracy of the heart,* i.e., *of the will.*

coram, *adv.* and *prep.,* used only as a *prep.* with *abl.* in the S.T. *in the presence of, before the eyes of, in the face of, before.*

Corinthii, orum, *m., the Corinthians.*

Corinthus, *f., Corinth, a celebrated commercial city in the Peloponnesus.*

corium, ii, *n, hide, leather, skin.*

Cornelius, a, um, *Cornelian,* **lex Cornelia,** *the Cornelian Law,* one of the laws passed in the dictatorship of Sulla.

Cornelius, ii, *Cornelius,* centurion of a cohort called *Italica.* He was a devout and God-fearing man whom the Lord, in a vision, ordered Peter to baptize. This happened in 36 A.D. Cornelius is said to have been bishop of Caesarea after the death of Zachaeus.

cornicula, ae, *f., dim., a little crow.*

cornu, us, *n., a horn, a hard* and *generally crooked growth upon the head of many mammiferous animals,* (2) *the peaks which terminate the miter of a bishop.*

cornupeta, ae, *adj., comm., butting, pushing* or *goring with the horns.*

corona, ae, *f.,* (1) *a crown, reward,* synonymous with **aureola** or *the reward added to the essential bliss of heaven for spiritual victories achieved on earth,* (2) *a wreath, garland,* the **spina-**

rum **corona** or *crown of thorns which Christ wore during His passion, also a garland given as a prize,* (3) *a crown or tonsure, the shaving of the crown of the head of a person entering the priesthood or a monastic order.*

coronatio, onis, *f., the tonsure, the ceremony of shaving the crown of the head, or receiving the priest's tonsure.*

corono, are, avi, atum, 1, *v. a., to do honor to, reward.*

corporalis, e, *adj.,* (1) *corporeal, bodily,* synonym of *corporeus,* the opposite of *incorporalis, incorporeus,* and *spiritualis,* (2) in neut. as noun, *the corporal.*— On **actio corporalis,** see *actio* under 1; on **adoratio corporalis,** see *adoratio* under 1; on **agens corporalis,** see *agens;* on **alteratio corporalis,** see *alteratio;* on **amatio corporalis,** see *amatio;* on **bonum corporale,** see *bonus* under 3; on **caecitas corporalis,** see *caecitas;* on **causa corporalis,** see *causa* under 2; on **character corporalis,** see *character* under 2; on **claritas corporalis,** see *claritas* under 3; on **condicio corporalis,** see *condicio* under 3; on **congregatio corporalis,** see *congregatio* under 2; on **contactus corporalis,** see *contactus;* on **cor corporale,** see *cor* under 1; on **cultus corporalis,** see *cultus* under 2; on **defectus corporalis,** see *defectus* under 4; on **delectatio corporalis,** see *delectatio;* on **dispositio corporalis,** see *dispositio* under 2;

on **divitiae corporales**, see *diviti-ae;* on **dolor corporalis**, see *dolor;* on **donum corporale**, see *donum* under 1; on **eleemosyna corporalis**, see *eleemosyna;* on **elementum corporale**, see *elementum* under 1; on **esse corporale**, see *esse;* on **figura corporalis**, see *figura* under 1; on **forma corporalis**, see *forma* under 2; on **fornicatio corporalis**, see *fornicatio* under 2; on **fortitudo corporalis**, see *fortitudo* under 1; on **fructus corporalis**, see *fructus* under 1; on **fundamentum corporale**, see *fundamentum;* on **generatio corporalis**, see *generatio* under 1; on **gloria corporalis**, see *gloria* under 2; on **habitus corporalis**, see *habitus* under 4; on **ieiunium corporale**, see *ieiunium;* on **immunditia corporalis**, see *immunditia;* on **immutatio corporalis**, see *immutatio* under 2; on **individuum corporale**, see *individuum;* on **integritas corporalis**, see *integritas;* on **locus corporalis**, see *locus* under 1; on **lumen corporale**, see *lumen;* on **lux corporalis**, see *lux;* on **magnitudo corporalis**, see *magnitudo* under 2; on **malum corporale**, see *malus* under 3; on **materia corporalis**, see *materia* under 3; on **matrimonium corporale**, see *matrimonium;* on **miraculum corporale**, see *miraculum* under 1; on **mors corporalis**, see *mors;* on **motus corporalis**, see *motus* under 2; on **munditia corporalis**, see *munditia;* on **natura corporalis**, see *na-*

tura; on **necessitas corporalis**, see *necessitas;* on **oculus corporalis**, see *oculus;* on **operatio corporalis**, see *operatio* under 2; on **opus corporale**, see *opus* under 4; on **organum corporale**, see *organum;* on **passio corporalis**, see *passio* under 2; on **peccatum corporale**, see *peccatum* under 2; on **poena corporalis**, see *poena;* on **potentia corporalis**, see *potentia* under 2; on **potestas corporalis**, see *potestas* under 3; on **praesentia corporalis**, see *praesentia;* on **pulchritudo corporalis**, see *pulchritudo;* on **qualitas corporalis**, see *qualitas;* on **quantitas corporalis**, see *quantitas* under 1; on **res corporalis**, see *res;* on **resurrectio corporalis**, see *resurrectio;* on **sacrificium corporale**, see *sacrificium;* on **scandalum corporale**, see *scandalum* under 1; on **sensus corporalis**, see *sensus* under 2; on **servitus corporalis**, see *servitus* under 1; on **signum corporale**, see *signum* under 1; on **similitudo corporalis**, see *similitudo* under 2; on **species corporalis**, see *species* under 6; on **spiritus corporalis**, see *spiritus;* on **subiectio corporalis**, see *subiectio;* on **substantia corporalis**, see *substantia* under 2; on **tactus corporalis**, see *tactus* under 1; on **transmutatio corporalis**, see *transmutatio* under 1; on **usura corporalis**, see *usura;* on **via corporalis**, see *via* under 1; on **virtus corporalis**, see *virtus* under 1; on **vis corporalis**, see *vis;* on

visio corporalis, see *visio;* on visus corporalis, see *visus;* on vita
corporalis, see *vita* under 1; on
voluptas corporalis, see *voluptas.*
—nullum agens corporale efficienter agit nisi per contactum, *no
corporal cause is active as an effective cause otherwise than by
contact with that upon which it
acts.*—corporaliter, *adv.,* corpo-
rally, bodily, opposite of *spiritualiter.*

corporaliter, *adv.,* see *corporalis.*

corporeitas, atis, *f.,* corporality, ma-
teriality, the opposite of *incorporeitas* and *spiritualitas.* On forma corporeitas, see *forma* under 2.

corporeus, a, um, *adj.,* corporal,
bodily, synonym of *corporalis,*
the opposite of *incorporalis, incorporeus,* and *spiritualis.* On
agens corporeum, see *agens;* on
caelum corporeum, see *caelum;*
on elementum corporeum, see
elementum under 1; on figura
corporea, see *figura* under 1; on
genus corporeum, see *genus* under 1; on habitus corporeus, see
habitus under 4; on locus corporeus, see *locus* under 1; on lux
corporeus, see *lux* under 1; on
motus corporeus, see *motus* under 2; on mundus corporeus, see
mundus under 1; on natura corporea, see *natura;* on organum
corporeum, see *organum;* on passio corporea, see *passio* under 2;
on principium corporeum, see
principium; on qualitas corporea,
see *qualitas;* on quantitas corpor-

ea, see *quantitas* under 2; on res
corporea, see *res;* on spiritus corporeus, see *spiritus;* on substantia corporea, see *substantia* under
2; on tactus corporeus, see *tactus;* on virtus corporea, see *virtus* under 1; on visio corporea,
see *visio* under 1. One kind of
corporeum is corporeum primum,
the first corporal thing, i.e., *the
heavens.*—Omne agens corpore-
um agit per contactum, *every
bodily cause operates through
contact with that upon which it
acts.*

corporo, are, avi, atum, 1, *v. a., to
incorporate, combine together* or
*with something else so as to
form a consistent whole.*—corpo-
ratus, a, um, *P. a.,* embodied.

corpulentia, ae, *f.,* corpulence,
grossness or *fleshiness of body.*

corpulentus, a, um, *adj.,* corpulent,
physically or *bodily large.* On
materia corpulenta, see *materia*
under 3; on substantia corpulenta, see *substantia* under 3.

corpus, oris, *body,* either in physical sense as material, or mathematical as tridimensional, *frame,*
a synonym of *elementum,* the
opposite of *spiritus.* On bonum
corpus et secundum corpus, see
bonus under 3; on dispositio
corporis, see *dispositio* under 4;
on dos corporis, see *dos* under
2; on elementum corporis, see
elementum under 1; on gloria
corporis, see *gloria* under 2; on
habitus corporis, see *habitus* under 4; on immunditia corporis,

see *immunditia;* on **integritas corporis**, see *integritas;* on **macula in corpore**, see *macula;* on **malum corpus**, see *malus* under 3; on **necessitas corporis**, see *necessitas* under 3; on **passio corporis**, see *passio* under 2; on **potentia corporis**, see *potentia* under 2; on **pulchritudo corporis**, see *pulchritudo;* on **quantitas corporis**, see *quantitas* under 2; on **resurrectio corporis**, see *resurrectio;* on **unitas corporis**, see *unitas;* on **virtus corporis**, see *virtus* under 1; on **vita corporis**, see, *vita* under 1.—Kinds of *corpus* are the following: (a), **corpus aereum, corpus aqueum**, and **corpus solidum**, *the airy* or *gaseous body, watery* or *fluid body,* and *solid body.*—(b), **corpus agile**, *the light, agile body.*— (c), **corpus anhomoeomerum** and **corpus homoeomerum seu homogeneum seu uniforme**, *the body that consists of unlike parts and that which consists of like parts.* —(d), **corpus animale** and **corpus spirituale** sc. hominis, *the animal-like body,* and *the spiritual or spiritualized body of man,* of which the first is derived from the fact that *animalibus passionibus subiacet et alimonia indiget,* and the last because *totaliter spiritui subiectum est,* or *spiritibus quantum ad aliquid simile est.*—(e), **corpus animatum seu vivum** and **corpus inanimatum**, *the body with the soul* or *the living body* and *the soulless*

or *lifeless body.*—(f), **corpus aqueum**, see *corpus aereum.*—(g), **corpus artificiale seu non naturale** and **corpus naturale seu physicum**, *the artificial* or *unnatural body* and *the natural body,* i.e., the body which has come into existence with the aid of art and that which has come into existence through nature.—(h), **corpus assumptum**, *the assumed body.* —(i), **corpus bestiale** and **corpus hominis seu humanum**, *the animal and the human body.*—(j), **corpus caeleste** and **corpus terrenum seu terrestre**, *the heavenly* and *the earthly body.*—(k), **corpus carnale seu carneum**, *the carnal body or that consisting of flesh and bone.*—(l), **corpus circulare seu sphaericum** and **corpus rectilineum seu rectum**, *the round* or *spherical body* and *that consisting of a straight line.* —(m), **corpus clarum seu lucidum** and **corpus opacum seu tenebrosum**, *the bright* or *shining body* and *the dark* or *obscured body.*—(n), **corpus commixtum seu mixtum seu complexionatum seu compositum** and **corpus simplex**, *the composed* and *the simple body,* i.e., *that body consisting of two* or *more elements* and *that consisting of one element.*— (o), **corpus complexionatum**, see *corpus commixtum.*—(p), **corpus compositum**, see *corpus commixtum.*—(q), **corpus coniunctum seu proprium** and **corpus exterius seu extraneum**, *the body* *combined* or *joined with action and that outside or a stranger to it.*—(r), **corpus continens** and **corpus contentum**, *the enclosing* and *the enclosed body.*—(s), **corpus contentum**, see *corpus continens.*—(t), **corpus corruptibile** and **corpus incorruptibile**, *the corruptible* and *the incorruptible body*, i.e., the body subject to dissolution and that not so subject.—(u), **corpus determinatum seu terminatum seu finitum**, and **corpus interminatum seu infinitum**, *the determined* or *finite* and *the undetermined* and *infinite body.*—(v), **corpus diaphanum**, *the transparent body.*—(w), **corpus divinum**, *the divine body*, i.e., *heaven.*—(x), **corpus divisibile**, and **corpus indivisible**, *the divisible* and *the indivisible body.*—(y), **corpus Dominicum**, *the body of the Lord.*—(z), **corpus effigiatum seu figuratum**, *the formed body* or *the body cast into a definite form.*—(a²), **corpus elementare**, *the elementary body*, i.e., *the body consisting of one* or *more elements.*—(b²), **corpus exterius**, see *corpus coniunctum.*—(c²), **corpus extraneum**, see *corpus coniunctum.*—(d²), **corpus figuratum**, see *corpus effigiatum.*—(e²), **corpus finitum**, see *corpus determinatum.*—(f²), **corpus firmamenti**, *the body of the firmament* or *the firmament.*—(g²), **corpus formatum**, *the formed body*, i.e., *the body supplied with form.*—(h²), **corpus**

glorificatum seu gloriosum and **corpus non gloriosum seu ignobile**, *the glorified* or *transfigured body* and *the body which is not glorified* or *transfigured.*—(i²), **corpus gloriosum**, see *corpus glorificatum.*—(j²), **corpus grave seu ponderosum** and **corpus leve**, *the heavy* and *the light body.*—(k²), **corpus hominis**, see *corpus bestiale.*—(l²), **corpus homoeomerum**, see *corpus anhomoeomerum.*—(m²), **corpus homogeneum**, see *corpus anhomoeomerum.*—(n²), **corpus humanum**, see *corpus bestiale.*—(o²), **corpus igneum**, *the fiery body.*—(p²), **corpus ignobile**, see *corpus glorificatum.*—(q²), **corpus immortale**, *the immortal* or *everlasting body*, see *corpus divinum.*—(r²), **corpus impalpabile** and **corpus palpabile**, *the impalpable* and *the palpable body.*—(s²), **corpus impassibile** and **corpus passibile**, *the body which is incapable of suffering* (id est, absque passionibus sensibilibus) and *the body that is capable of suffering.*—(t²), **corpus inanimatum**, see *corpus animatum.*—(u²), **corpus incorruptibile**, see *corpus corruptibile.*—(v²), **corpus indivisibile**, see *corpus divisibile.*—(w²), **corpus inferius** and **corpus superius**, *the lower* and *the upper body* or *that which is found below the moon* (*a lunari globo inferius*) and *that which is found above it.*—(x²), **corpus infinitum**, see *corpus determinatum.*—(y²), **corpus intellegibile** and

corpus sensibile, *the body appearing in the imagination,* (*quod est corpus mathematicum*), and *that perceptible through the senses,* (*quod est corpus naturale*).—(z²), **corpus interminatum,** see *corpus determinatum.*—(a³), **corpus leve,** see *corpus grave.* —(b³), **corpus locans,** and **corpus locatum,** *the locating* and *the located body.*—(c³), **corpus locatum,** see *corpus locans.*— (d³), **corpus lucidum,** see *corpus clarum.*—(e³), **corpus materiale,** *the body attached to matter.*—(f³), **corpus mathematicum** and **corpus naturale,** *the mathematical* and *the physical body,* of which the former *nihil est aliud quam dimensiones* (*corporis*) *separatae,* and the latter is the body which exists with a fixed essence *in rerum natura.*— (g³), **corpus minerale,** *the mineral body* or *the mineral.*—(h³), **corpus mixtum,** see *corpus commixtum.* —(i³), **corpus mobile,** *the body which can be moved locally.*— (j³), **corpus mysticum sc. Christi,** *the mystical body of Christ,* i.e., *the Church.*—(k³), **corpus naturale,** see *corpus artificiale* and *corpus mathematicum.*—(l³), **corpus non gloriosum,** see *corpus glorificatum.*—(m³), **corpus non naturale,** see *corpus artificiale.*—(n³), **corpus opacum,** see *corpus clarum.*—(o³), **corpus organicum seu organizatum,** *the organic body* or *the body supplied with organs.*— (p³), **corpus palpabile,** see *corpus*

impalpabile.—(q³), **corpus particulare,** *the particular* or *single body.*—(r³), **corpus passibile,** see *corpus impassible.*—(s³), **corpus phantasticum** and **corpus verum,** *the phantastic* and *the real body.*—(t³), **corpus physicum,** see *corpus artificiale.*—(u³), **corpus ponderosum,** see *corpus grave.*—(v³), **corpus primum,** *the first body, quod est omnium corporum contentivum,* or *one of those of which all other bodies are composed.*—(w³), **corpus primum alterans,** *the first qualitatively changing body,* i.e., *Heaven.*— (x³), **corpus proprium,** see *corpus coniunctum.*—(y³), **corpus quantum,** *the somewhat large body, the tolerably large body.*—(z³), **corpus quintum,** *the fifth body.*— (a⁴), **corpus rectilineum,** see *corpus circulare.*—(b⁴), **corpus rectum,** see *corpus circulare.*—(c⁴), **corpus sensibile,** see *corpus intellegibile.*—(d⁴), **corpus sidereum,** *the body of a star.*—(e⁴), **corpus simplex,** see *corpus commixtum.*— (f⁴), **corpus solidum,** see *corpus aereum.*—(g⁴), **corpus speculare,** *the reflected body.*—(h⁴), **corpus sphaericum,** see *corpus circulare.* —(i⁴), **corpus spirituale,** see *corpus animale.*—(j⁴), **corpus subsistens,** *the subsisting body.*—(k⁴), **corpus substantificatum,** *the body made into a substance.*—(l⁴), **corpus subtile,** *the subtle body.* —(m⁴), **corpus superius,** see *corpus inferius.*—(n⁴), **corpus supremum,** *the supreme body,* quod est omnium corporum contenti-vum.—(o⁴), **corpus tactivum** and **corpus tangibile,** *the touching* and *the tangible body.*—(p⁴), **corpus tangibile,** see *corpus tactivum.*—(q⁴), **corpus tenebrosum,** see *corpus clarum.*—(r⁴), **corpus terminatum,** see *corpus determinatum.*—(s⁴), **corpus terrenum,** see *corpus caeleste.*—(t⁴), **corpus terrestre,** see *corpus caeleste.*—(u⁴), **corpus uniforme,** see *corpus homoeomerum.*—(v⁴), **corpus verum,** see *corpus phantasticum.*—(w⁴), **corpus vivum,** see *corpus animatum.*—corpora naturalia ad certum terminum dividuntur, or, **corpora naturalia in infinitum dividi non possunt,** or, **omnium natura constantium positus est terminus,** *bodies, as they are found in nature can be divided only up to a definite limit, ultra quem species non salvatur, quia quaelibet species determinatam quantitatem requirit et in plus et in minus.*—corpora naturalia in infinitum dividi non possunt, see above.—corpora tangendo agunt, or, **nullum corpus agit nisi tangendo,** *bodies do not effect anything otherwise than by contact with those upon which they exercise an influence.*—nullum corpus agit nisi per motum, *no body is active unless first put into motion.*—nullum corpus agit nisi tangendo, see above.—nullum corpus potest directe agere in id, quod nullo modo est cor-

poreum, *no body can directly influence something spiritual.*—omnium natura constantium positus est terminus, see above.

corpusculum, i, *n. dim., a small, frail body.*

corrado, ere, si, sum, 3, *v. a., to scrape.*

correctio, onis, *f.,* (1) *guidance, instruction, reprimand,* (2) *correction, amendment.*—Kinds of *correctio* in this (1) sense are the following: (a), **correctio divina** and **correctio humana,** *divine guidance* and *human guidance.*—(b), **correctio fraterna,** *brotherly guidance.*—(c), **correctio fraterna simplex** and **correctio praelatorum,** *the simple brotherly guidance which pertains to equals* and *the guidance of superiors which has special reference to their subjects.*—(d), **correctio humana,** see *correctio divina.*—(e), **correctio indebita,** *the improper guidance,* the opposite of *correctio debita,* quae est secundum debitas circumstantias, secundum quod est actus virtutis.—(f), **correctio praelatorum,** see *correctio fraterna simplex.*

corrector, oris, *m., a corrector, improver.*

corregno, are, see *conregno.*

correlativus, a, um, *adj., having, indicating,* or *involving a reciprocal relation, correlative.*

correptio, onis, *f.,* (1) *a reproof, correction, correption,* (2) **"De correptione et gratia,"** *On Correction* and *Grace,* one of the

Anti-Pelagian books of St. Augustine written after 412.

correspondeo, ere, di, sum, 2, *v. a.*, *to correspond, to answer* or *conform to the description of something else, be similar, agree in details.*

corresuscito, are, see *conresuscito.*

corrigia, ae, *f.*, *a girdle, band, belt.*

corrigibilis, e, *adj.*, *corrigible, capable of being corrected* or *set right.*

corrigo, ere, rexi, rectum, 3, *v. a.*, (1) *to make straight, set right,* (2) *to improve, amend, correct, reform, make better.*

corripio, ere, ripui, reptum, 3, *v. a.*, *to correct, rebuke, chide, admonish, reprove.*

corrixor, ari, atus, 1, *v. dep. n.*, *to quarrel, dispute, wrangle.*

corroboro, ari, avi, atum, 1, *v. a.*, *to make strong, strengthen, invigorate.*

corrodo, ere, si sum, 3, *v. a.*, *to gnaw, gnaw to pieces.*

corrosio, onis, *f.*, *corrosion, wasting away, the action of wasting away by slow degrees.*

corrumpo, ere, rupi, ruptum, corrumptum), 3, *v. a.*, (1) *to destroy, cause to disappear* in the general and broader sense of the word, i.e., cause a thing to disappear in any way, the opposite of *generare,* (2) *destroy, cause to disappear* in a particular or narrower sense of the word, i.e., cause a thing to disappear through dissolution or decomposition, also the opposite of *gene-*

rare, (3) *spoil, make worse.*— Kinds of *corrumpere* in this (1) sense are: (a), **corrumpere per accidens** and **corrumpere per se,** *to destroy something along with something else* and *directly through itself.*—(b), **corrumpere per se,** see *corrumpere per accidens.*—(c), **corrumpere proprie,** *to destroy in the real sense.* On **dispositio corrumpens et totaliter corrumpens,** see *dispositio.*— Kinds of *corrumpere* in this (2) sense are: (a), **corrumpere active seu effective** and **corrumpere formaliter,** *to destroy after the manner of activity* or *active cause* and *destroy after the manner of form* or *formal cause.*—(b), **corrumpere effective,** see *corrumpere active.*—(c), **corrumpere formaliter,** see *corrumpere active.*— (d), **corrumpere miraculose** and **corrumpere naturaliter,** *to destroy in a miraculous* or *supernatural way* and *destroy in a natural way.*—(e), **corrumpere naturaliter,** see *corrumpere miraculose.*—(f), **corrumpere secundum quid** and **corrumpere simpliciter,** *to destroy something according to this* or *that* or *in a certain respect* and *destroy something simply* or *absolutely.*—(g), **corrumpere simpliciter,** see *corrumpere secundum quid.*—**non corrumpitur aliquid in omnino non ens,** *that which is corrupted in the proper sense of the word is not annihilated.*—**quae corrumptur, eadem numero iterari**

non possunt, *that which is cor-*
rupted can no more return as
the same according to the indi-
vidual. On **aestimatio corrupta,**
see *aestimatio;* on **habitus cor-**
ruptus, see *habitus* under 4; on
intentio corrupta, see *intentio*
under 2; on **natura corrupta,** see
natura; on **politia corrupta,** see
politia under 1; on **ratio corrup-**
ta, see *ratio* under 6; on **regimen**
corruptum, see *regimen.*—**cor-**
rupte, *corruptly, perversely, in-*
correctly.

corruo, ere, ui, 3, *v. n.* and *a., to*
fall, fall together, send to the
ground, used *lit.* and *fig.*

corrupte, *adv.,* see *corrumpo.*

corruptela, ae, *f., a corrupting, se-*
ducing, misleading, corruption,
that which corrupts.

corruptibilis, e, *adj., destructible,*
extinguishable, perishable, in
the broader and narrower sense
of the word, the opposite of *ge-*
nerabilis and *incorruptibilis.* On
bonum corruptibile, see *bonus*
under 3; on **esse corruptibile,**
see *esse;* on **corpus corruptibile,**
see *corpus;* on **forma corruptibi-**
lis, see *forma* under 2; on **mate-**
ria corruptibilis, see *materia* under 3; on **natura corruptibilis,**
see *natura;* on **substantia corrup-**
tibilis, see *substantia* under 2;
on **virtus corruptibilis,** see *virtus*
under 1; on **vita corruptibilis,**
see *vita* under 1.—**corruptibilia**
per generationem redeunt ad
idem specie, non ad idem nu-
mero, *corruptible things when*

destroyed return to something
which is the same according to
kind but not according to the
individual.

corruptibilitas, atis, *f., destructibil-*
ity, perishableness in the broad-
er sense of the word, opposite
of *incorruptibilitas.*—A kind of
corruptibilitas is: **corruptibilitas**
naturalis, *the natural destructi-*
bility.

corruptio, onis, *f.,* (1) *destruction,*
annihilation, extinction in the
general and broader sense of
the word, i.e., the destruction or
annihilation of a thing as such
in any manner, the opposite of
generatio, (2), *destruction, ex-*
tinction in the special and narrower sense of the word, i.e., the
destruction of a thing through
the dissolution of the matter and
form, and the substitution of a
new form in the same matter.
When both matter and form disappear, it is annihilation; form
alone, corruption, (3) *corruption,*
perversion, deterioration, dege-
neiation, the opposite of perfec-
tio.—On **motus corruptionis,** see
motus under 2; on **status corrup-**
tionis, see *status* under 3.—Kinds
of *corruptio* in this (2) sense are:
(a), **corruptio alicuius seu aliqua**
seu huius seu huiusmodi seu se-
cundum quid and **corruptio sim-**
plex seu simpliciter, *a certain*
kind of destruction or *the de-*
struction of this and *that in a*
thing or *the destruction with*
reference to something and *the*

simple destruction of the same or *the absolute destruction of the same, of which the first destruction signifies now the separation of the accidental form, now the change of an ignoble substance into a noble substance; the second signifies now the separation of the substantial form* and *now the change of a noble substance into an ignoble substance.*—(b), **corruptio artificialium,** *the destruction of works of art.*—(c), **corruptio contra naturam seu extra naturam seu violenta, corruptio secundum naturam seu naturalis** and **corruptio miraculosa,** *forced* or *unnatural destruction, natural destruction* or *that conformable to nature,* and *the miraculous* or *supernatural destruction.*—(d), **corruptio extra naturam,** see *corruptio contra naturam.*—(e), **corruptio huius seu huiusmodi,** see *corruptio alicuius.*—(f), **corruptio miraculosa,** see *corruptio contra naturam.*—(g), **corruptio mutua,** *the mutual destruction,* i.e., a series of destructions, with the last of which the thing destroyed first comes to light again.—(h), **corruptio naturalis,** see *corruptio contra naturam.*—(i), **corruptio propria,** *the destruction proper to a thing* or *the destruction inflicted on oneself.*—(j), **corruptio secundum naturam,** see *corruptio contra naturam.*—(k), **corruptio secundum quid,** see *corruptio alicuius.*—(l), **corruptio simplex,**

see *corruptio alicuius.*—(m), **corruptio simpliciter,** see *corruptio alicuius.*—(n), **corruptio substantialis,** *the substantial destruction through the loss of the substantial form* or *the destruction aimed at the substance of a thing.*—(o), **corruptio violenta,** see *corruptio contra naturam.*—**generationes et corruptiones ex contrariis et in contraria sunt,** see *generatio.*—**generatio huius est corruptio illius et corruptio huius est generatio alterius,** see *generatio.*—**generatio unius est corruptio alterius et corruptio unius est generatio alterius,** see *generatio.*—**primum in generatione est postremum in corruptione,** see *generatione.*—On **malum corruptionis,** see *malus* under 2 and 3.—Kinds of *corruptio* in this (3) sense are: (a), **corruptio carnalis seu carnis,** *the carnal corruption* or *the corruption of the flesh,* by which is meant sometimes the corruption of man's sensible nature, again the destruction of the *signaculum virginalis pudoris,* and again destruction as a result of a voluntary *resolutio seminis delectationem sensibilem causans.*—(b), **corruptio carnis,** see *corruptio carnalis.*—(c), **corruptio culpae** and **corruptio poenae,** *the corruption of men because of a guilt* and *the corruption of man because of punishment.*—(d), **corruptio fomitis,** *corruption of man as a result of concupiscence,* i.e., *evil desire.*—(e), **corruptio moralis,** and **corruptio naturalis,** *the moral* and *the natural corruption.*—(f), **corruptio naturae** and **corruptio personae,** *the corruption of nature* and *that of a person,* i.e., *a man.*—(g), **corruptio naturalis,** see *corruptio moralis.*—(h), **corruptio peccati originalis,** *the corruption of man in consequence of original sin.*—(i), **corruptio personae,** see *corruptio naturae.*—(j), **corruptio poenae,** see *corruptio culpae.*—(k), **corruptio politiae,** *the corruption of a state.*—(l), **corruptio propinqua** and **corruptio remota,** *the proximate* and *the remote corruption.*—(m), **corruptio remota,** see *corruptio propinqua.*—(n), **corruptio sensualitatis,** *the corruption of sensuality* or *the sensual nature of man.*

corruptivus, a, um, *adj., destroying,* in the broader and narrower sense of the word, *corrupting, corruptive,* the opposite of *conservativus, generativus,* and *perfectivus.* On **amor corruptivus,** see *amor* under 1; on **malum corruptivum,** see *malus* under 3; on **passio corruptiva,** see *passio* under 2.

corruptor, oris, *m., a corruptor, seducer.*

cortina, ae, *f., a curtain.*

coruscatio, onis, *f., a coruscation, a flash of brilliant light, lightning.*

corusco, are, 1, *v.* and *n., to gleam, glitter, shine, coruscate.*

corvinus, a, um, *adj., raven-like, of* or *pertaining to the raven.*

corvus, i, *m., a raven.*

costa, ae, *f.,* (1) *a rib,* (2) *the side of the human body.*

crapula, ae, *f., intemperance in the use of food* or *drink.*

cras, *adv., tomorrow.*

crassus, a, um, *adj., gross, fat, dense, thick, solid.*

crastinus, a, um, *adj., of tomorrow, tomorrow's.*—**crastinum,** i, *n., tomorrow, the morrow.*

Crates, is, *m., Crates, a Theban philosopher.*

craticula, ae, *f., a small gridiron.*

creabilis, e, *adj., creatable, that can be made* or *created.*

creatio, onis, *f.,* (1) *production, creation* in the special and narrow sense of the word, i.e., the bringing forth of a thing from absolutely no pre-existent matter, (2) *creation* in the broader and general sense of the word, i.e., the bringing forth from something, making from something, development, synonym of *condicio* and *factio.* On **imago creationis,** see *imago* under 1; on **status creationis,** see *status* under 3.—Kinds of *creatio* in this (1) sense are: **creatio active accepta seu significata** and **creatio passive accepta seu sumpta,** *creation in the active* and *that in the passive sense of the word,* in other words, creation which is an *actio* or activity of God and that being-created which is a kind of *passio,* i.e., expressed by the reception of being on the part of creature.—Kinds of *creatio* in this (2) sense are: **creatio prima** and **creatio secunda seu nova,** *the first* and *the second or new creation.*

creativus, a, um, *adj., creative, having the power to create in any sense.*

creator oris, *m., a creator, founder, the Creator of the world, God.*

creatrix, icis, *f., creatrix, creative.* On **causa creatrix,** see *causa* under 2.

creatura, ae, *f., a creature, something created, the creation.*

creber, bra, brum, *adj., frequent.*

crebescens, entis, *P. a., increasing, growing strong, becoming widespread.*

credibilis, e, *adj., credible, worthy of being believed.*

creditor, oris, *m., a creditor.*

credo, ere, didi, creditum, 3, *v. a.,* (1) *to believe* in the general sense of the word, i.e., to assent not for intrinsic reasons but on the authority of someone, (2) *believe* in the supernatural sense of the word, i.e., to assent firmly to truths on the authority of God revealing. On **scientia credendorum,** see *scientia* under 2. —Kinds of *credere* in this (2) sense are: (a), **credere Deo** or **Deum** or **in Deum,** *to believe God* or *in God with loving devotion.*—(b), **credere explicite** and **credere implicite,** *to believe something explicitly and implicitly.*—(c), **credere implicite,** see

credere explicite.—(d), **credere in Deum,** see *credere Deo.*

credulitas, atis, *f.,* (1) *belief, faith,* synonym of *fides,* the opposite of *incredulitas* and *infidelitas,* (2) *opinion in matters of faith.*

crementum, i, *n., growth, increase.*

cremo, are, avi, atum, 1, *v. a.,* (1) *to burn, consume by fire,* used especially of the burning of victims in sacrifice, (2) *to burn, make suffer pain* as in the case of the souls in purgatory who are made fit for paradise by expiatory suffering, also used to describe the pains of those who suffer eternal punishment in hell.

creo, are, avi, atum, 1, *v. a.,* (1) *produce, create* in the narrower sense of the word, i.e., *to bring forth the whole being of a thing from no pre-existing matter,* (2) *create* in the broader sense of the word, i.e., to make from something, to make into something, promote; synonym of *facere.*—On **agens creatum,** see *agens;* on **beatitudo creata,** see *beatitudo* under 1; on **bonitas creata,** see *bonitas* under 1; on **bonum creatum,** see *bonus* under 3; on **caritas creata,** see *caritas;* on **cognitio creata,** see *cognitio* under 2; on **dilectio creata,** see *dilectio* under 1; on **donum creatum,** see *donum* under 1; on **ens creatum,** see *ens;* on **esse creatum,** see *esse;* on **gloria creata,** see *gloria* under 2; on **gratia creata,** see *gratia* under 2;

on **hypostasis creata,** see *hypostasis* under 3; on **infinitum creatum,** see *infinitus;* on **intellectus creatus,** see *intellectus* under 3; on **lumen creatum,** see *lumen;* on **natura creata,** see *natura;* on **potentia creata,** see *potentia* under 3; on **ratio creata,** see *ratio* under 12; on **regula creata,** see *regula* under 1; on **sapientia creata,** see *sapientia* under 1; on **scientia creata,** see *scientia* under 2; on **similitudo creata,** see *similitudo;* on **species creata inhaerens,** see *species* under 5; on **substantia creata,** see *substantia* under 2; on **suppositum creatum,** see *suppositum* under 2; on **unitas creata,** see *unitas;* on **veritas creata,** see *veritas* under 1; on **virtus creata,** see *virtus* under 1; on **vita creata,** see *vita* under 1; on **voluntas creata,** see *voluntas* under 2.—Kinds of *creans* in this (1) sense are: **creans instrumentale** and **creans primum,** *the instrumental* and *the first* or *chief creator.*

crepido, inis, *f., pedestal, base.*

crepusculum, i, *n., twilight, evening twilight, the dusk of the evening.*

cresco, ere, crevi, cretum, 3, *v. inch. n., to increase, grow, thrive, augment, spread, multiply,* of things abstract and concrete.—**crescens,** entis, *part. n.,* used substantively, *increase.*

crimen, inis, *n., crime, sin, guilt, charge, fault, offense, accusation.*

criminalis, e, *adj., criminal, of* or *pertaining to crime.*—**criminaliter,** *adv., criminally.*

criminaliter, *adv.,* see *criminalis.*

criminator, oris, *m., an accuser, informer, one who charges others publicly with crimes, either by accusing or by railing at them.*

criminosus, a, um, *adj., guilty of crime, full of guilty deeds.*

crisis, is, *f., judgment, decision.*

crispus, a, um, *adj., curled, crimped.*

crocito, are, 1, *v. freq. n., to croak loudly.*

crucesignatio, onis, *f., the sign of the cross.*

cruciatus, us, *m., torture, torment, a torturing, execution, suffering.*

crucifigo, ere, fixi, xum, 3, *v. a.,* (1) *to put to death by fastening on a cross,* (2) *mortify, subdue,* as impulses or desires.

crucifixio, onis, *f., crucifixion,* the act of putting to death by nailing to a cross.

crucifixor, oris, *m., a crucifier.*

crucio, are, avi, atum, 1, *v. a., to torture, torment.*

crudelis, e, *adj., cruel, morally rude* or *unfeeling, unmerciful, severe.*

crudelitas, atis, *f,. harshness, severity, cruelty, barbarity.*

cruditas, atis, *f., crudity, rawness.*

crudus, a, um, *adj., raw, uncooked.*

cruor, oris, *m., blood.*

crus, uris, *n., the leg, shank, shin.*

crux, ucis, *f., a cross, tree, frame* or *other wooden instrument of* *execution,* on which criminals were impaled or hanged.

crystallinus, a, um, *adj., crystalline, made of crystal, crystal.*

crystallus, i, *m., crystal.*

cubiculum, i, *n., an apartment for reclining* or *sleeping, a resting-place.*

cubicus, a, um, *adj., cubic, cubical.*

cubitalis, e, *adj., a cubit long.*

cubitum, i, *n.,* (*cubitus,* i, *m.*), *a cubit, an ell,* the distance from the elbow to the tip of the middle finger.

cuiusmodi = *qualis, of such a kind as, of such a nature as, such as.*

culex, icis, *m., a gnat, midge, fly.*

culmen, inis, *n., the top, summit, height.*

culpa, ae, *f., guilt, fault, blame.* On the difference between *culpa* and *poena,* see *poena.* On **actus culpa,** see *actus* under 1; on **corruptio culpae,** see *corruptio* under 3; on **defectus culpae,** see *defectus* under 2; on **deformitas culpae,** see *deformitas* under 2; on **immunditia culpae,** see *immunditia;* on **impuritas culpae,** see *impuritas* under 1; on **libertas a culpa,** see *libertas* under 3; on **malitia culpae,** see *malitia* under 3; on **malum culpae,** see *malus* under 3; on **purgatio a culpa,** see *purgatio;* on **status culpae,** see *status* under 3.—Kinds of *culpa* are: (a), **culpa actualis** and **culpa originalis,** *the guilt of action* and *the guilt of inheritance,* i.e., the guilt which man has incurred by committing a deed and that which he has inherited through his descent from his first parents.—(b), **culpa criminalis,** *the guilt in consequence of the commission of a crime.*—(c), **culpa mortalis** and **culpa venialis,** *the mortal guilt and the venial guilt.*—(d), **culpa naturae,** *the guilt in the nature of a being.*—(e), **culpa originalis,** see *culpa actualis.*—(f), **culpa praecedens,** and **culpa subsequens,** *the guilt preceding* and *that following an action.*—(g), **culpa subsequens,** see *culpa praecedens.*—(h), **culpa venialis,** see *culpa mortalis.*

culpabilis, e, *adj., culpable, guilty,* opposite of *laudabilis.* On **defectus culpabilis,** see *defectus* under 2.—**culpabiliter,** *adv., culpably.*

culpabiliter, *adv.,* see *culpabilis.*

culpo, are, avi, atum, 1, *v. a., to blame, reprehend, condemn, censure,* opposite of *laudo, probo, commendo.*

cultellus, i, *m., dim., a small knife.*

culter, tri, *m., a knife.*

cultor, oris, *m., a worshipper, reverencer.*

cultura, ae, *f., a cultivating, cultivation.*

cultus, us, *m.,* (1) *care, culture, honor,* (2) *veneration, worship,* (3) *worship of God or a god.*— Kinds of *cultus* in this (2) sense are: (a), **cultus corporalis seu exterior** and **cultus spiritualis seu interior,** *the bodily* or *exterior veneration* and *the spirit-*

ual or *the inner veneration.*—(b), **cultus daemonum,** *the worship of demons.*—(c), **cultus debitus,** and **cultus indebitus,** *due* or *proper worship,* and *improper worship* or *worship that should not exist.*—(d), **cultus Dei seu divinitatis seu divinus,** *the worship of God.*—(e), **cultus divinitatis,** see *cultus Dei.*—(f), **cultus divinus,** see *cultus Dei.*—(g), **cultus exterior,** see *cultus corporalis.*—(h), **cultus indebitus,** see *cultus debitus.*—(i), **cultus interior,** see *cultus corporalis.*—(j), **cultus spiritualis,** see *cultus corporalis.*—On **disparitas cultus,** see *disparitas.*—Kinds of *cultus* in this (3) sense are: **cultus idololatriae** and **cultus latriae,** the worship of a god in the manner of idolatry and that in the manner of the true worship of God.

cum, (1) *prep.* with *abl., with, together with, in connection* or *company with, along with,* sometimes to be translated *and,* (2) *conj.* with *indicative* in purely temporal clauses, with *subjunctive* in mixed temporal clauses, also in causal and concessive clauses, *when, as, while, after, since, although.*

cuminibilis, e, *adj., stingy, niggardly.*

cuminum, i, *n., a cumin, a plant;* **cumini venditor,** *a cumin seller, a niggard, a meanly parsimonious person.*

cumque, *adv., whenever, whenso-*

ever, serves for the generalizing of any action, event, time.

cumulo, are, avi, atum, 1, *v. a., to augment by heaping up, to increase, accumulate.*

cumulus, i, *m.,* (1) *a summit, peak, point, crown, increase, superabundance,* (2) **cumulus ratiocinii,** *the computing of accounts,* a synonym of *acervus Mercurii.* The gentiles ascribed the keeping of accounts to Mercury; the heap of Mercury, **acervus Mercurii,** signifies the computing of accounts.

cunae, arum, *f., a cradle,* used figuratively for *earliest childhood.*

cunctus, a, um, and more frequently in the plural, *cuncti, ae, a, adj., all in a body, all together, the whole, all, entire.*

cupiditas, atis, *f., greediness, desire, covetousness,* synonym of *avaritia* and *concupiscentia.*—Kinds of *cupiditas* are: (a), **cupiditas actualis** and **cupiditas habitualis,** *the desire in action* and *that which consists in a habit.*—(b), **cupiditas aestuans,** *the increased* or *passionate desire.*—(c), **cupiditas generalis,** *the general desire.*—(d), **cupiditas habitualis,** see *cupiditas actualis.*—(e), **cupiditas venialis peccati,** *the desire that consists in a venial sin* in contrast to the desire that consists in a mortal sin.

cupido, inis, *f., desire, wish, longing, eagerness.* In a bad sense, *desire, lust, passion, greed.*

cupidus, a, um, *adj., desirous of, covetous, covetous of money.*

cupio, iri, ivi or ii, itum, 3, *v. a., to long for a thing, desire, wish,* construed with (1) the *acc.,* (2) the *inf.,* (3) the *acc.* and the *inf.*

cupisco, ere, 3, *v. inch., to covet, long much for something, be very desirous of.*

cuprum, i, *n.,* late Latin for *cyprium, copper, bronze.*

cur, *adv.* = **quam ob rem,** *for what reason, wherefore, why, to what purpose, from what motive.*

cura, ae, *f.,* (1) *care, attention, concern, solicitude, thought, welfare,* generally used with the *gen.,* and *de* with *abl.,* (2) *a duty, charge over something, management, jurisdiction;* **cura parentum, cura patris,** *parental jurisdiction;* **cura animarum,** *spiritual direction of souls;* **cura regiminis,** *charge of the government;* **cura pastionis,** *pastoral care;* **cura pastoralis,** *the duty of a parish priest,* or *the district* and *people under his charge, a curacy;* **cura episcopalis,** *a bishopric,* the office of a bishop or the district and people under his charge, *diocese;* **cura rei familiaris,** *charge of a household,* (3) *care, provision against harm* or *need, precaution.*

curabilis, e, *adj., curable,* the opposite of *incurabilis.*

curatio, onis, *f.,* (1) *a healing, cure, the act, process, means by which a cure is effected,* used of

spiritual and physical ailments, (2) **curatio funeris,** *the management* or *care of a funeral.*

curator, oris, *m., superintendent, commissioner, manager, overseer, officer.*

curia, ae, *f., a curia* or *court.*

curialitas, atis, *f., geniality, jocularity, jocoseness, the state of being genial,* a synonym of *iocularitas.*

curiose, *adv.,* see *curiosus.*

curiositas, atis, *f., desire of knowledge, curiosity, inquisitiveness.*

curiosus, a, um, *adj.,* (1) *curious, inquisitive, inquiring eagerly about a thing,* (2) *odd,* of a whimsical appearance.—**curiose,** *adv.,* (1) *with care, carefully,* (2) *inquisitively, curiously.*

curo, are, avi, atum, 1, *v. a.,* (1) *to care for, take* or *have care of, be solicitous for, look or attend to, trouble oneself about,* constr. with *acc., inf., de* and *abl., ut* and *sub.,* and *absl.,* (2) *cure, heal,* of the soul as well as of the body.—**presbyteri curati vel archidiaconi,** *presbyters* or *archdeacons who have benefices to which the care of souls is attached.*

curriculum, i, *n., a period* or *cycle* of *time.*

curro, ere, cucurri, cursum, 3, *v. n., to run, move quickly, hasten, fly.*

currus, us, *m., a chariot, car.*

cursitatio, onis, *f., adv., bustle, care.*

cursor, oris, *m.,* *a courier, a special emissary carrying messages or dispatches.*

cursus, us, *m.,* *a course, progress, direction, way.*—Kinds of *cursus* are: (a), **cursus naturae,** *course of nature.*—(b), **cursus rerum,** *course of events, order of things.* —(c), **cursus spiritualis,** *the spiritual course.*—(d), **cursus temporis,** *course of time.*

curvatio, onis, *f.,* *a curve, bending.*

curvitas, atis, *f.,* *a curve, curvity, curvature.*

curvo, are, avi, atum, 1, *v. a.,* *to make to yield, move.*

curvus, a, um, *adj., crooked, bent.*

custodia, ae, *f.,* (1) *a watching, guardianship, protection, safeguard,* (2) **custodia pecuniae,** *a saving, economy, carefulness in outlay,* (3) *a prison, place of confinement,* (4) **De custodia virginitatis,** *on guarding chastity,* a special admonition on the rules which should regulate the conduct of those who devote themselves to virginity, and contained in Letter twenty-two of St. Jerome to Eustochium.

custodio, ire, ivi or ii, itum, 4, *to watch, protect, keep, defend, guard, preserve.*

custoditivus, a, um, *adj., inclined* or *tending to keep, protect, protective, save, guard.*

custos, odis, *comm., perserver, keeper, protector, defender.*

cycnus, i, *m., the swan.*

cymbalum, i, *n., a cymbal.*

Cyprianus, i, *m., Thascius Caecilius*

Cyprian of Carthage; saint, bishop, and martyr; died 258 A.D. He was the first great organizer of the Church, and a staunch defender of unity under Rome. His systematic habits and powers of business contributed greatly to his success as an administrator. His address was dignified, conciliatory, affectionate; his looks attractive by their grave joyousness. Of his works, St. Thomas in the S.T. quotes chiefly the *De Habitu Virginum;* also the *De Oratione Dominica,* and several letters.

Cyrillus, i, *m., Cyril,* saint and doctor of the Church, archbishop of Alexandria; died on June 9 or 27, 444 A.D. Against Nestorius he taught the use of the term *theotokos* in a letter to the monks of Egypt. He was a man of strong will and vehement nature, tending to be overly vehement and impatient in controversy. He must, however, be praised for his faith, firmness, intrepidity, fortitude, endurance, perseverance. He is quoted on the supremacy of the Roman Pontiff. There are also references to his Epistola Synodica received by the Council of Ephesus and to his commentaries on St. Luke and St. John.

Cyrus, i, *m.,* (1) Cyrus, the founder of the Persian monarchy, (2) *Cyrus,* bishop of Phasia and patriarch of Alexandria, A.D. 630-641.

D

Dacia, ae, *f.,* in classical Latin, *Dacia,* the Roman province of Dacia between the Danube and the Carpathian mountains, but used in medieval times to designate the Scandanavian countries.

daemon, onis, *m.,* (1) in the pre-christian sense, *an intelligent being with an airy body,* dwelling in the upper air, *a spirit,* (2) in the Christian sense, *a fallen angel, an evil spirit,* always so used by St. Thomas, (3) *a ghost, apparition,* (4) *idol,* i.e., evil spirit as the object of false worship.—One kind of *daemon* in this (2) sense is: **daemon incubus,** *the incumbent devil* in the exercise of the connubial act, the opposite of **daemon succubus,** *the succumbing devil.*

daemoniacus, a, um, *adj., devilish, demoniac, pertaining to an evil spirit.*—**daemoniacus,** i, *m., a daemoniac, one possessed by an evil spirit.*

daemonium, ii, *n.,* (1) *a demon, devil,* (2) *idol.*

dalmatica, ae, *f., a dalmatic, a wide-sleeved tunic of silk worn over the alb and cassock by a sacred minister at high mass.*

Damascenus, i, *m., Damascene, a native of Damascus,* esp. St. John, priest and doctor of the Church, born about 677 A.D., and died around the middle of the eighth century. St. Thomas quotes from his *De fide catholica* and *De fide orthodoxa.*

Damasus, i, *m., Damasus, pope.* He is said to have been a Spaniard and to have succeeded Pope Liberius in 366 A.D. He was the principal defender of the orthodoxy of the Church against Arian and other heretics. It was at his urging that St. Jerome prepared the Vulgate. His correspondence with Jerome, his attached and devoted friend and secretary, began A.D. 376 and closed with his death A.D. 384. Six of Jerome's letters to him are expositions of difficult passages of Scripture elicited by letters of Damasus asking the aid of his learning. He died in December 384 A.D. after a pontificate of eighteen years.

damnabilis, e, *adj., damnable, worthy of condemnation.*

damnatio, onis, *f., damnation,* condemnation to punishment in the life to come; the consignment of a person judicially to everlasting perdition, as the damnation of the wicked.

damnifico, are, avi, atum, 1, *v. a., to injure, damnify, to cause injury* or *damage to, in person* or *estate.*

damno, are, avi, atum, 1, *v. a., to condemn, damn, doom, sentence one to any punishment,* constr. with the *acc.* of the person either (1) alone or (2) with the *abl.*

or (3) *de* or (4) *ad.*—**damnatus,** i, *m., the damned, condemned.*

damnosus, a, um, *adj., injurious, hurtful, destructive.*

damnum, i, *n.,* (1) *loss, injury, harm, hurt, damage,* (2) *indemnity,* that which is paid or given as compensation or reimbursement for a loss.

Daniel, elis, *m., Daniel,* the hero and traditional author of the book that bears his name. He belonged to the tribe of Judah and was of noble or perhaps royal descent. He was carried as a prisoner into Babylon by Nebuchadnezzar after the capture of Jerusalem, and was instructed in the learning and tongue of the Chaldeans. At the age of eighty Daniel was one of the chief ministers in the kingdom under Darius the Mede. The Book of Daniel is one of the books of the Old Testament, generally divided into two main parts; the first recounts the events of Daniel's life, and the second contains his prophecies.

Dardanus, i, *m., Dardanus,* a nobleman and devout Christian. He lived in the early part of the fifth century and held the office of governor in the Gallic provinces.

Dathan, *indecl. n., m., Dathan,* the son of Eliab, of the tribe of Reuben. He conspired with his brother Abiron against Moses and Aaron.

datio, onis, *f., the act of giving, giving, donation,* the opposite of *acceptio.*—Kinds of *datio* are: (a), **datio ad iustitiam pertinens** and **datio ad liberalitatem pertinens,** *the giving from justice* and *the giving from generosity.*—(b), **datio ad liberalitatem pertinens,** see *datio ad iustitiam pertinens.* —(c), **datio illicita** and **datio non illicita,** *the giving which is not allowed* and *that which is allowed.*—(d), **datio non illicita,** see *datio illicita.*

dator, oris, *m., a giver.*

David, *m., indecl.* or vidis, (1) *David,* the second and greatest of the Kings of Israel and the youngest of the eight sons of Jesse, the Bethlehemite. He belonged to the tribe of Judah. As a ruler, warrior, and organizer he stands preeminent among the heroes of Israel. He is the principal author of the Book of Psalms, (2) *David,* of Dinant, a pantheistic philosopher who lived in the first decades of the thirteenth century. He was a magister, or teacher at Paris where he wrote Quaternulli (little note books), which was condemned by a provincial council in 1210. Whatever is known of his doctrines is derived chiefly from Albert the Great and St. Thomas.

de, *prep., from, out of, concerning,* constr. with *abl.,* synonym of *ex.* On **materia de qua,** see *materia* under 1.

dea, ae, *f., a goddess.*

dealbatio, onis, *f., a whitewashing, whitening, the act of making white.*

dealbo, are, avi, atum, 1, *v. a., to whiten over, to whitewash.* Pass., *be white.*

dealtero, are, avi, atum, 1, *v. a., to alter* or *change completely.*

deauro, are, avi, atum, 1, *v. a., to gild, gild over.*

Debbora, ae, *f., Debbora,* prophetess of Mt. Ephraim and the wife of Lapidoth who judged Israel, and who with Barac defeated Sisara about 1285 B.C.

debello, are, avi, atum, 1, *v. n.* and *a., to conquer completely, vanquish, subdue.*

debeo, ere, ui, itum, 2, *v. a.,* (1) *to owe, be under obligation to render* or *pay,* commonly in pass., *is due,* (2) with the *inf., be bound, be in duty bound, ought, must, should.*—**debitus,** a, um, *P. a., intended, proper, becoming, due, conformable to duty, required, necessary,* synonym of *iustus* and *necessarius,* the opposite of *indebitus.* On **actio debita,** see *actio* under 1; on **actus debitus,** see *actus* under 2; on **circumstantia debita,** see *circumstantia;* on **commensuratio debita,** see *commensuratio;* on **complexio debita,** see *complexio* under 2; on **dispositio debita,** see *dispositio* under 4; on **finis debitus,** see *finis* under 5; on **forma debita,** see *forma* under 2; on **materia debita,** see *materia*

under 3; on **mensura debita,** see *mensura;* on **modus debitus,** see *modus* under 2; on **movere per modum debitum,** see *movere;* on **operatio debita,** see *operatio;* on **oppositio debita,** see *oppositio* under 1; on **ordo debitus,** see *ordo;* on **perfectio debita,** see *perfectio* under 2; on **petitio debita,** see *petitio* under 1; on **praeparatio debita,** see *praeparatio* under 1; on **proportio debita,** see *proportio;* on **quantitas debita,** see *quantitas.*—**debitum,** i, *n., what is due, debt, duty, obligation.*— Kinds of *debitum* are: (a), **debitum amicabile seu amicitiae,** *the duty of friendship.*—(b), **debitum amicitiae,** see *debitum amicabile.* —(c), **debitum carnale,** *the carnal* or *marital debt.*—(d), **debitum causae finalis** and **debitum causae formalis,** *the influence of the motive* or *intention of a work, that of the formal cause.*— (e), **debitum causae formalis,** see *debitum causae finalis.*—(f), **debitum charitatis** and **debitum iuris seu iustitiae,** *the duty of love* and *that of justice.*—(g), **debitum condicionale seu condicionatum seu condicionis,** *the conditionally necessary.*—(h), **debitum condicionis,** see *debitum condicionale.* —(i), **debitum congruitatis seu convenientiae seu per modum condecentiae seu secundum quandam decentiam** and **debitum necessitatis seu secundum necessitatem,** *the requirement of suitability* or *good form* and *that* *of necessity.*—(j), **debitum coniugii seu matrimonii,** *the marital duty.*—(k), **debitum continentiae,** *the obligation of continency.*—(l), **debitum convenientiae,** see *debitum congruitatis.*—(m), **debitum essendi,** *the necessity of being.*—(n), **debitum ex eo, quod ipse exhibet** and **debitum propter necessitatem,** *that which is due someone because he gives something* and *that which is due because he is in need of it.*—(o), **debitum ex merito proveniens** and **debitum secundum condicionnem naturae,** *that which belongs to someone by reason of merit* and *that which is due him according to the state of his nature.*—(p), **debitum ex ordine alicuius ad aliquem seu propter aliud** and **debitum per se seu secundum se,** *that which is due a thing as a result of its relationship to something else* or *on account of another* and *that which is due it as such* or *in consequence of itself.*—(q), **debitum gratitudinis,** *a debt of gratitude.*—(r), **debitum honestatis seu morale** and **debitum legale,** *duty according to propriety* or *morality* and *that according to a positive law,* i.e., *moral duty* and *legal duty.*—(s), **debitum iuris,** see *debitum charitatis.*—(t), **debitum iustitiae,** see *debitum charitatis.*—(u), **debitum legale,** see *debitum honestatis.*—(v), **debitum matrimonii,** see *debitum coniugii.*—(w), **debitum morale,** see

debitum honestatis.—(x), **debitum mortis,** *the necessity of dying.*—(y), **debitum multitudinis** and **debitum unius,** *the duty of the multitude* or *the crowd as such* and *that of the individual.*—(z), **debitum necessitatis,** see *debitum congruitatis.*—(a²), **debitum obedientiae,** *the duty of obedience.*—(b²), **debitum per se,** see *debitum ex ordine alicuius ad aliquem.*—(c²), **debitum poenae,** *the debt of punishment.*—(d²), **debitum propter aliud,** see *debitum ex ordine alicuius ad aliquem.*—(e²), **debitum propter necessitatem,** see *debitum ex eo, quod ipse exhibet.*—(f²), **debitum secundum conditionem naturae,** see *debitum ex merito proveniens.*—(g²), **debitum secundum necessitatem,** see *debitum congruitatis.*—(h²), **debitum secundum quandam decentiam,** see *debitum congruitatis.*—(i²), **debitum secundum regulam legis determinantis** and **debitum secundum regulam rationis,** *the duty according to the rule of a determining law* and *that according to the guidance of reason,* i.e., the *legal* and *the moral duty.* Cf. *debitum honestatis.*—(j²), **debitum secundum regulam rationis,** see *debitum secundum regulam legis determinantis.*—(k²), **debitum secundum se,** see *debitum ex ordine alicuius ad aliquem.*—(l²), **debitum servitutis,** *the duty arising from servitude.*—(m²), **debitum unius,** see *debitum multitu-*

*dinis.—*ex **debito,** *according to the debt, as due,* often constr. with *gen.—***debite,** *adv., duly, rightly, justly, properly.*

debilis, e, *adj., weak, imperfect, frail, infirm, feeble, lame, wanting in activity;* (1) of inanimate subjects, (2) of animate subjects, (3) used figuratively, *weak in mind.—***debiliter,** *adv., infirmly, lamely, feebly.*

debilitas, atis, *f.,* (1) *weakness, debilitation, weakening,* synonym of *infirmitas,* (2) *weakness of the soul, weakness of the will,* the *astheneia* of Aristotle (Eth. Nic. VII. 8. 1150 b 19).

debilitatio, onis, *f., a laming, weakening.*

debiliter, *adv.,* see *debilis.*

debilito, are, avi, atum, 1, *v. a., to lame, cripple, weaken, disable, maim.—*Kinds of *debilitare* are: **debilitare per accidens** and **debilitare per se,** *to weaken something incidentally* or *because of something else* and *to weaken something as such* or *because of itself.*

debite, *adv.,* see *debeo.*

debitor, oris, *m., a debtor,* one who is indebted or under obligations to someone for something, used with the *genitive* of the thing, and *dative* of the person.

debitum, i, *n.,* see *debeo.*

decalogus, i, *m., the decalogue, the ten commandments, the moral law.*

decanto, are, avi, atum, 1, *v. a., to chant, to sing to a chant.*

decapito, are, avi, atum, 1, *v. a., to behead, execute, decapitate.*

decas, adis, *f., a decade, any group, set* or *arrangement of ten.*

decedo, ere, cessi, cessum, 3, *v. n., to go away, depart, withdraw,* synonym of *linquo, relinquo, desero, destituo, deficio, discedo, excedo,* opposite of *accedo, maneo, succedo;* constr. absol., rarely with *de, ex,* and *a.*

decem, *num., ten.*

decens, entis, *P. a.,* see *decet.*

decenter, *adv.,* see *decet.*

decentia, ae, *f., decency, decorum, becomingness, moral fitness, fitting* and *due regard for propriety.*

deceptio, onis, *f., a deceiving, deception, deceitfulness.*

deceptor, oris, *m., a deceiver.*

decerno, ere, crevi, cretum, 3, *v. a.* and *n., to decide, determine.*

decerto, are, avi, atum, 1, *v. n.* and *a., to contend, fight.*

decet, cuit, 2, *v. impers., it is seemly, comely, becoming, it beseems, behooves, is fitting, suitable, proper.—***decens,** entis, *P. a., seemingly, becoming, decent, proper, fit.*

decibilis, e, *adj., becoming, meet, suitable, proper.*

decido, ere, cidi, 3, *v. n.,* in a figurative sense, *to fall, fall away;* **in peccatum decidere,** *to fall into sin;* **in nihilum decidere,** *to sink into nihility,* used with *a, ab* and *abl., in* and *acc.*

decido, ere, cidi, cisum, 3, *v. a., to cut off, divide, separate.*

decies, *num., adv., ten times.*

decimatio, onis, *f., the taking of a tenth, a tithing.*

decimo, are, avi, atum, 1, *v. a., to cause to pay tithes, pay tithes of* (anything), *tithe.*

decimus, a, um, *adj., the tenth.*

decima, ae, *f.,* (sc. *pars*), *the tenth part, tithe.*

decipio, ere, cepi, ceptum, 3, *v. a., to catch, ensnare, entrap, beguile, elude, deceive, cheat.*

decisio, onis, *f., a separation, loss.*

Decius, ii, *m., Decius,* the name of an eminent plebeian gens at Rome. Its best known members were the two Decii (P. Decius Mus, father and son), who, as consuls, voluntarily devoted themselves to death to save their country, the former at Veseris 340 B.C., the latter at Sentinum 295 B.C.

declaratio, onis, *f., a disclosure, exposition, manifestation, declaration.*

declarativus, a, um, *adj., explanatory, clear, serving for explanation.*

declaro, are, avi, atum, 1, *v. a., to make clear, plain, evident, manifest, to explain, declare,* also in a figurative sense, *to make clear to the mind, show, prove,* used with the *acc.* and *inf.,* with *acc.*

declinatio, onis, *f.,* (1) in the older grammarians, every change of form which a word undergoes, as *declension,* strictly so called, *conjugation, comparison, deriva-* tion, etc.; among the later grammarians, *declension* as distinguished from *coniugatio, comparatio, derivatio,* etc., (2) *a turning away from a thing, an avoiding, avoidance.*

declino, are, avi, atum, 1, *v. a.,* and *n.,* (1) *to avoid, shun* with an object denoting that from which one turns aside, (2) *turn aside* towards something, used with *ad* and *in* with *acc.;* **declinare ad idololatriam,** *fall into idolatry;* **declinare in neutram partem,** *turn neither to this side nor that;* **declinare in alteram partem,** *turn to one side;* **declinare in malum,** *incline to evil;* **declinare in unam partem magis quam in aliam,** *to incline to one side rather than the other;* **declinare ad tyranni dem,** *to degenerate into tyranny,* (3) *turn away from, deviate,* used with *a, ab,* and *abl.,* (4) *decrease, degenerate, dwindle,* used with *in* and *acc.—***declinans,** antis, *P. a., turning aside* to something.

decoctio, onis, *f., a boiling, cooking, a decoction, a boiling out or separation.*

decollatus, a, um, *P. a., beheaded, decapitated.*

decoquo, ere, xi, ctum, 3, *v. a., to boil, cook, prepare food by subjecting it to the action of heat.*

decoctus, a, um, *P. a., cooked.*

decor, oris, *m., what is seemly or becoming, comeliness, elegance, grace, beauty, ornament.*

decoro, are, avi, atum, 1, *v. a., to decorate, adorn, embellish, beautify.*

decorus, a, um, *adj., becoming, fitting, seemly, proper, suitable, decorous.*—**decorum,** i, *n., that which is seemly, suitable, seemliness, fitness, propriety, decorum.*

decrementum, i, *n., decrease, diminution.*

decresco, ere, crevi,, cretum, 3, *v. n., to decrease, grow less.*

decretalis, is, *f., a decretal, a letter* or *rescript* of the pope determining some point in ecclesiastical law.

decretum, i, *n.,* (1) *a decree, a law* or *ordinance of an ecclesiastical ruler, council* or *legislative body,* (2) a book or compilation of decrees, orders or laws, especially the **Decretum Gratiani,** the *Decretal of Gratian* or the papal decrees up to and including those of Innocent II published about 1150 by Gratian, a Camaldolese monk, a master of theology at the University of Bologna.

decurio, onis, *m., a decurion, the head* or *chief of a decuria;* after the extension of the Roman dominion, the members of the senate of the municipia and the colonies were called *decuriones.*

decurrens, entis, *P. a., flowing.*

decursus, us, *m., course, rotation, methodical* or *regular sequence, influence.*

decus, oris, *n., ornament, grace, embellishment, splendor, glory, honor. dignity,* anything that ornaments, embellishes, adorns, honors.

dedecus, oris, *n., disgrace, dishonor, infamy, shame.*

dedicatio, onis, *f., dedication, consecration.*

dedico, are, avi, atum, 1, *v. a., to dedicate, consecrate* a person or thing to God, to His service, or to some sacred purpose.

dedignatio, onis, *f., a disdaining, refusal.*

dedignor, ari, atus, 1, *v. a.,* dep., *to disdain, reject as unworthy,* used with the *infinitive.*

dedo, ere, didi, ditum, 3, *v. a.,* (1) *to apply, devote, dedicate one's self,* used with *se,* with the *dat.,* (2) *to surrender, yield,* used with *acc.* and *dat.*—**deditus,** a, um, *P. a., given up to, addicted, devoted* to something.

deduco, ere, xi, ctum, 3, *v. a.,* (1) *to lead, bring, fetch, draw away, convey,* used with *acc.,* and *ad* and *in* with *acc.,* (2) *derive from, deduce, draw, take,* used with *a* and *ex* with *abl.* and with *acc.,* (3) *mislead, lead astray, seduce.* —Common expressions are: (a), **deducere ad hoc,** *to come to a point or conclusion.*—(b), **deducere conclusiones,** *to draw conclusions.*—(c), **deducere ad notitiam multorum,** *to bring to the notice of many.*—(d), **deducere mentem ad hoc,** *to exercise the mind to this extent, exercise the memory to this extent.*—(e), **deducere in pactum,** *to enter into a compact.*—(f), **deducere recom-**

pensationem, *to draw a recompense.*—(g), **deducere tributa,** *to deduct taxes.* —(h), **deducere expensas,** *to deduct expenses.*—(i), **deduci ad mortis sententiam,** *to face the death penalty.*—(j), **deduci ad successionem,** *to be made successor.*—(k), **deducere senectutem meam ad inferos,** *to bring down my grey hairs to death.*

deductio, onis, *f.*, (1) *leading, guidance,* (2) *leading away, derivation,* (3) *deduction, establishment,* (4) *maintenance,* the Aristotelian *diagoge* (cf. Aristotle, Pol. VIII. 5. 139 a 25 ff).—Kinds of *deductio* in this (3) sense are: **deductio circularis seu reflexa** and **deductio directa,** *the deduction which moves in a circle* or *looks backward* and *that which is direct, by which the last derives something in general from another* and *the first, that from which something was derived, in turn derives from this.*

defatigo or **defetigo,** are, avi, atum, 1, *v. a., to weary out, tire* a person; *to fatigue, exhaust.*

defectibilis, e, *adj., defectible, showing defects, lacking, deficient.* On **causa defectibilis,** see *causa* under 2.

defective, see *defectivus.*

defectivus, a, um, *adj., imperfect, faulty, defective.* On **bonum defectivum,** see *bonus;* on **causa defectiva,** see *causa;* on **cognitio defectiva,** see *cognitio;* on **operatio defectiva,** see *operatio;* on

passio defectiva, see *passio;* on **potentia defectiva,** see *potentia;* on **solutio defectiva,** see *solutio;* on **virtus defectiva,** see *virtus.*—

defective, *adv., in a defective manner, defectively,* synonym of *deficienter,* the opposite of *indeficienter* and *perfecte.*

defectus, us, *m.,* (1) *a failing, lacking, absence* in the general sense of the word, synonym of *negatio,* the opposite of *habitus,* (2) *fault, defect, lack,* i.e., *the nonexistence of that which should exist,* synonym of *deficientia, infirmitas,* and *privatio,* the opposite of *excellentia* and *perfectio.* —Kinds of *defectus* in this sense are: (a), **defectus actionis** and **defectus virtutis,** *the defect of an action* and *that of power.*— (b), **defectus activi principii seu agentis** and **defectus recipientis,** *the defect of the active principle* (cf. *defectus causae*) and *that of the recipient,* i.e., *of that thing which receives the action of the active principle upon itself,* (cf., *defectus ex parte accipientis*).—(c), **defectus agentis,** see *defectus activi principii.*—(d), **defectus causae** and **defectus effectus,** *the defect of cause* (cf. *defectus activi principii*) and *that of effect.*—(e), **defectus communis** and **defectus proprius,** *the common* or *general,* and *the particular* or *true defect.*—(f), **defectus corporalis** and **defectus spiritualis,** *the corporal* and *the spiritual defect.*—(g), **defectus cul-**

pabilis seu culpae and **defectus poenalis seu poenae,** *the defect as a result of a guilt* and *as a result of a punishment, voluntary moral defect which is punishable,* and *defect either moral or physical, which is involuntary or against the will, undergone as a result of guilt.*—(h), **defectus culpae,** see *defectus culpabilis.*—(i), **defectus effectus,** see *defectus causae.*—(j), **defectus ex parte accipientis** and **defectus ex parte dantis,** *the defect on the part of the recipient* and *that on the part of the giver.* Cf. *defectus activi principii.*—(k), **defectus ex parte dantis,** see *defectus ex parte accipientis.*—(l), **defectus naturae seu naturalis** and **defectus voluntarius,** *the defect inherent in the nature of a thing* or *the natural defect* and *the voluntary defect* or *that incurred with a free will.*—(m), **defectus naturalis,** see *defectus naturae.*—(n), **defectus poenalis,** see *defectus culpabilis.*—(o), **defectus poenae,** see *defectus culpabilis.*—(p), **defectus proprius,** see *defectus communis.*—(q), **defectus puerilis** and **defectus senilis,** *the defect of childhood* and *that of old age.* (r), **defectus recipientis,** see *defectus activi principii.*—(s), **defectus senilis,** see *defectus puerilis.*—(t), **defectus spiritualis,** see *defectus corporalis.*—(u), **defectus virtutis,** see *defectus actionis.* —(v), **defectus voluntarius,** see *defectus naturae.*

defendo, ere, di, sum, 3, *v. a.,* (1) *to defend, guard, protect, cover,* with the *acc.* of that from which anything is warded off, rarely with *ab aliquo* and *contra aliquid* or *aliquem,* (2) of speech, *support, defend, maintain, bring forward, allege in defence,* (3) legally, *defend, prosecute.*

defensatrix, icis, *f., she who defends.*

defensio, onis, *f.,* (1) *a defending, defence,* (2) *legal maintenance of a right.*

defensor, oris, *m., a defender.*

defero, ferre, tuli, latum, *v. a.,* (1) *to bring, bear, carry a thing,* (a) not stating the terminus, (b) stating the terminus, used with *adv.* of place, *in* and *ad* with *acc.,* the *dat.,* (2) *carry one thing* to another with the idea of changing or increasing the quality, *to add,* also *carry* in the sense of *wear,* (3) *to report, relate, tell, reveal,* (4) *give, confer upon, bestow,* used with *acc.* and *dat., acc.* alone, and *ad* with *acc.*—**deferens,** entis, *P. a., deferent,* something that carries or conveys.— **delatus,** a, um, *P. a., carried.*

deficienter, *adv.,* see *deficere.*

deficientia, *f.,* (1) *letting off, ceasing,* the opposite of *indeficientia,* not in S.T.

deficio, ere, feci, fectum, 3, *v. a.,* and *n.,* (1) *to fall off, become alienated, be detached from something,* (2) *fall off, leave off, cease,* (3) *fall off, begin to fail,* *vanish, become defective, fall short,* (4) *fall off against another, remain behind something, be defective, permit to fail,* (5) *fail, not to exist,* (6) *remain behind the truth, fail, err.* On **actio deficiens,** see *actio* under 1; on **actus deficiens,** see *actus* under 1; on **agens deficiens,** see *agens;* on **bonitas deficiens,** see *bonitas* under 1; on **bonum deficiens,** see *bonus* under 2; on **causa deficiens,** see *causa* under 2; on **cognitio deficiens,** see *cognitio* under 2; on **effectus deficiens,** see *effectus;* on **imago deficiens,** see *imago* under 1; on **qualitas deficiens,** see *qualitas;* on **similitudo deficiens,** see *similitudo* under 1; on **species deficiens,** see *species* under 6; on **virtus deficiens,** see *virtus* under 1 and 5.—**Natura non deficit in necessariis,** see *natura.* **Natura non deficit nisi in paucioribus,** see *natura.*—**deficienter,** *adv., in the manner of falling off, in a defective* or *deficient manner, deficiently,* synonym of *defective,* the opposite of *indeficienter, perfecte,* and *plenarie.*

defigo, ere, xi, xum, 3, *v. a.,* (1) *to fix, fasten, turn intently,* used figuratively; **defigere intentionem in aliquo,** *to fix the attention on something;* **defigere affectum in aliquo,** *to fix the heart on something,* (2) **manus defigere,** *to strike hands,* i.e., *to close a contract as surety, to*

pledge one's person.—**defixus,** a, um, *P. a., fixed.*

definio, (diffinio), ire, ivi, itum, 4, *v. a.,* (1) *to fix the limits of, bound, limit* in the general sense of the word, (2) *to fix the limits of, bound, limit* in the logical sense of the word, i.e., to set forth or declare that which constitutes the essence of a thing, (3) *determine, dispose.*—On **principium definiens,** see *principium.* —Kinds of *definire* in this (2) sense are: (a), **definire absolute,** and **definire cum dependentia ad subiectum,** *to define something with reference to* and *for itself* and to *define something with an expression of that upon which it is dependent.*—(b), **definire cum dependentia ad subiectum,** see *definire absolute.*—(c), **definire in abstracto** and **definire in concreto,** *to define something in general* and *to define something so taken as it exsists in reality.*—(d), **definire in concreto,** see *definire in abstracto.*—(e), **definire per posterius** and **definire principaliter,** *to define something in the sense of the later* and *in the sense of the essential* and *of the earlier.*—(f), **definire principaliter,** see *definire per posterius.* —**complexa non definiuntur,** see *complexus;* **cuicumque convenit definitio, convenit et definitum,** see *definitio* under 2; **definitio convertitur seu debet converti cum definito,** see *definitio* under 2; **definitio et definitum sunt**

idem, see *definitio* under 2; **multiplicata definitione multiplicatur et definitum,** see *definitio* under 2; **remota definitione aufertur definitum,** see *definitio* under 2.

definitio, (diffinitio), onis, *f.,* (1) *limitation, restriction, definition* in the general sense of the word, (2) *limitation, restriction, definition* in the logical sense of the word, i.e., *the presentation* or *expression* of that which constitutes the essence of a thing, *notional essence, notion,* synonym of *ratio* and *terminus,* (3) *determination, disposition.* On **idem definitione,** see *idem;* on **pars definitionis,** see *pars* under 1; on **primum secundum definitionem,** see *primus;* on **prius definitione seu secundum definitionem,** see *prior* under 1; on **unitas definitionis,** see *unitas;* on **via definitionis,** see *via* under 3.—Kinds of *definitio* in this (2) sense are: (a), **definitio absoluta,** *the definition without reference,* i.e., the definition that takes no consideration of anything else.—(b), **definitio accidentis** and **definitio substantiae,** *the definition of accident* and *that of substance.*—(c), **definitio circularis,** *the definition that turns in a circle,* so called because in it one explains something from another which before was explained from the first.—(d), **definitio competens seu congrua seu sufficiens** and **definitio incompetens seu incon-**grua seu insufficiens, *the definition that proves to be adequate* or *the suitable* or *the sufficient definition* and *the definition that proves to be inadequate* or *unsuitable* or *the insufficient definition.*—(e), **definitio completa seu perfecta** and **definitio incompleta seu imperfecta,** *the perfect* and *the imperfect definition.*—(f), **definitio congrua,** see *definitio competens.*—(g), **definitio dialectica seu logica** and **definitio realis,** *the logical* and *the objective definition.*—(h), **definitio falsa, definitio large sumpta,** and **definitio vera,** *the false* and *the improper definition, the definition in a wide sense* and *the true* or *proper definition.*—(i), **definitio formalis** and **definitio materialis,** *the formal definition* or *that given with respect to form* and *the material definition* or *that given with respect to material.*—(j), **definitio imperfecta,** see *definitio completa.*—(k), **definitio incompetens,** see *definitio competens.*—(l), **definitio incompleta,** see *definitio completa.*—(m), **definitio incongrua,** see *definitio competens.*—(n), **definitio insufficiens,** see *definitio competens.*—(o), **definitio large sumpta,** see *definitio falsa.*—(p), **definitio logica,** see *definitio dialectica.*—(q), **definitio materialis,** see *definitio formalis.*—(r), **definitio mathematica** and **definitio naturalis seu physica,** *the mathematical* and *the scientific definition* or *the definition of the mathematicians* and *that of the natural scientists.*—(s), **definitio naturalis,** see *definitio mathematica.*—(t), **definitio perfecta,** see *definitio completa.*—(u), **definitio physica,** see *definitio mathematica.*—(v), **definitio quae est per causam finalem** and **definitio quae est per causam materialem,** *the definition which is derived from the end* or *purpose of a thing* and *that derived from its material.*—(w), **definitio quae est per causam materialem,** see *definitio quae est per causam finalem.*—(x), **definitio realis,** see *definitio dialectica.*—(y), **definitio remota,** *the remote definition* or *that which lies distant from the essence of a thing.*—(z), **definitio secundum viam compositionis data** and **definitio secundum viam resolutionis data,** *the definition given in a synthetical manner* and *that given in an analytical manner.*—(a²), **definitio secundum viam resolutionis data,** see *definitio secundum viam compositionis data.*—(b²), **definitio substantiae,** see *definitio accidentis.*—(c²), **definitio sufficiens,** see *definitio competens.*—(d²), **definitio universalis,** *the universal definition* or *that universally held.*—(e²), **definitio vera,** see *definitio falsa.*—**cuicumque convenit definitio, convenit et definitum,** *to what a definition is always suitable to this the notion defined by it* and *the*

thing that corresponds to the latter are suitable.—**definitio convertitur cum definito** or **definitio debet converti cum definito,** *the definition must be interchangeable with the thing defined,* i.e., the predicate of a sentence, which forms the definition of a thing, and the subject of the sentence which contains the definition, if the definition is to be correct, must be interchangeable, so that one can just as well say: *homo est animal rationale* as the reverse: *animal rationale est homo.*—**definitio dividit definitum in singularia,** *the definition divides the defined into the individual parts of the substance.*—**definitio et definitum sunt idem,** or, **definitio est idem rei,** *the definition* or *that expressed through the definition is one and the same with the defined* or *the defined thing.*—**multiplicata definitione multiplicatur et definitum,** *if the definition increases by a characteristic, so does the thing define increase,* so that as a result its essence is changed.—**particularium non est scientia nec definitio,** see *particularis.*—**ratio quam significat nomen, est definitio,** *the intellectual presentation of a thing, of which the linguistic sign is a name and not a sentence, is the definition of the same.* Cf. also *conceptio.*—**remota definitione aufertur definitum,** *if a definition is removed through the* *omission of a factor of the same, so also is that which is defined by it.*

definitive, (diffinitive), *adv.,* see *definitivus.*

definitivus, (diffinitivus), a, um, *adj.,* (1) *marking off, definitive, final,* (2) *defining,* i.e., representing or indicating the essence of a thing.—On **sententia definitiva,** see *sententia* under 2. On **ratio definitiva,** see *ratio* under 8.—**definitive,** (diffinitive), *adv.,* (1) *after the manner* or *in the sense of demarcation, limitation, restriction, enclosure,* in which the parts enclosed do not correspond with those of their limitation and on this account cannot be measured by the latter. Spiritual substances are in place *definitive* by their activity there, the opposite of *circumscriptive,* (2) *after the manner* or *in the sense of a definition.* Cf. *definitio* under (2). On **esse in loco definitive,** see *locus* under 2.— On **significare definitive,** see *significare.*

deflecto, ere, xi, ctum, 3, *v. a.* and *n., to turn aside,* or *in another direction,* used *figuratively.*

defleo, ere, evi, etum, 2, *v. a.* and *n., to weep over something, lament, deplore, bewail.*

deflexio, onis, *f., a deflection, turning aside, deviation from the usual* or *proper course.*

defloratio, onis, *f., a defloration; defloratio virginum, a deflower-*

ing of virgins, depriving of virginity.

defloro, are, avi, *v. a., to deflower; deflorare virginem, to ravish, seduce a maiden.*

defluo, ere, xi, 3, *v. n.,* (1) *to flow down,* (2) of things not liquids, used in a figurative sense, *to pass from,* (3) *to fall from a higher to a lower state;* **defluere per peccatum,** *to fall on account of sin,* (4) *to pass away, be lost.*

defluxio, onis, *f., a discharge.*

defluxus, us, *m.,* (1) *a flowing off, issue, efflux,* (2) *a falling downwards,* used figuratively, *a falling into sin.*

defodio, ere, fodi, fossum, 3, *v. a., to dig;* **defodere in terram,** *to bury in the earth,* used here figuratively, meaning *to conceal.*

deforis, *adv., from outside, outside.*

deformis, e, *adj., formless,* synonym of *informis.* On **actus deformis,** see *actus* under 1.

deformitas, atis, *f.,* (1) *formlessness,* synonym of *difformitas* and *informitas,* (2) *deformity, atrociousness, ugliness,* likewise synonym of *informitas.*—A kind of *deformitas* in this (1) sense is: **deformitas actus,** *formlessness of an act,* i.e., the deficiency of a relation befitting it in the circumstances of an activity. Cf. also *actus deformis* under *actus.*— Kinds of *deformitas* in this (2) sense are: (a), **deformitas adulterii,** *the ugliness of adultery.*— (b), **deformitas culpae,** *the ugliness of guilt.*—(c), **deformitas for-**

nicationis, *the ugliness of forni-cation.*—(d), **deformitas gulae,** *the ugliness of gluttony.*—(e), **deformitas immoderatae concupiscentiae,** *the ugliness of immoderate desire.*—(f), **deformitas imprudentiae,** *the ugliness of imprudence.*—(g), **deformitas iniustitiae,** *the ugliness of injustice.* —(h), **deformitas inoboedientiae,** *the ugliness of disobedience.*—(i), **deformitas luxuriae,** *the ugliness of luxury.*—(j), **deformitas peccati,** *the ugliness of sin.*—(k), **deformitas superbiae,** *the ugliness of pride.*

deformo, are, avi, atum, 1, *v. a.,* to *deform, disfigure, spoil, mar.*— **deformatus,** a, um, *P. a.,* de-formed.*

defraudatio, onis, *f.,* (1) *a defrauding, cheating.*

defraudo, are, avi, atum, 1, *v. a.,* *to defraud, overreach, cheat.*

defugio, ere, fugi, 3, *v. a.,* *to flee, shun, avoid.*

defungor, i, functus, 3, *v. dep.,* de-part, die,* synonym of *morior,* opposite of *vivo.*—**defunctus,** i, *m.,* = *mortuus, deceased, defunct;* very commonly in plural, **defuncti** = *mortui, the dead.*

degenero, are, avi, atum, 1, *v. n.* and *a.,* *to degenerate, depart from its race* or *kind.*

dego, ere, degi, 3, *v. a.,* *to live, spend, pass.* sc. time.

degradatio, onis, *f., degradation, the act of lowering* as in rank, or the *deprival of honor* and *power;* **degradatio sacerdotis,** *the*

degradation of a priest, or *the taking away of the use of his sacerdotal prerogatives.*

degrado, are, avi, atum, 1, *v. a., to degrade, lower in rank, standing* or *character, strip of office* or *dignity;* **degradare clericum ab officio,** *to degrade a cleric from office.*—**degradatus,** a, um, *P. a., degraded;* **sacerdos degradatus,** *a degraded priest, a priest deprived of the use of his sacerdotal powers.*

degusto, are, avi, atum, 1, *v. a., to taste,* used in a figurative sense.

dehonestatio, onis, *f., disgrace, dishonor.*

dehonesto, are, 1, *v. a., to dehonestate, disparage, dishonor.*

dehonoratio, onis, *f., a dishonoring, dishonor.*

dehonoro, are, avi, atum, 1, *v. a., to dishonor.*

deicio, ere, ieci, iectum, 3, *v. a.,* (1) *to overthrow, cast down, bring down,* (2) in pass. voice used as middle, *fall,* (3) in the pass., *be dejected, be cast down, be disheartened.*—**deiciens,** entis, *P. a., throwing down.*—**deiectus,** a, um, *P. a., thrown.*

deiectio, onis, *f.,* (1) *downfall, defeat,* (2) *dejection, depression, sadness,* (3) *abasement.*

deiectivus, a, um, *adj., dejectory, having a tendency to cast down* or *depress.*

deifico, are, avi, atum, 1, *v. a., to deify, make one a god.*—**deificatus,** a, um, *P. a., deified.*

deificus, a, um, *adj., sacred, divine.*

deiformis, e, *adj., godlike.* On **contemplatio deiformis,** see *contemplatio;* on **intellectus deiformis,** see *intellectus* under 3.

deiformitas, atis, *f., God-likeness, likeness to God.*

deinceps, *adj.,* and *adv., following, thereafter, next, following.*—In phrases, (1) **ac deinceps,** (2) **et deinceps,** (3) **et sic deinceps,** *and so forth.*

deinde, *adv., thereafter, thereupon, afterwards,* in local succession, *next.*

deitas, atis, *f.,* (1) *deity* in the abstract sense of the word, i.e., *Godhead, Godhood,* (2) *deity* in the concrete sense of the word, i.e., *God.* On **fruitio Deitatis,** see *fruitio.*

delectabilis, e, *adj., enjoyable, entertaining, giving pleasure.* On **amicitia delectabilis,** see *amicitia* under 1; on **bonum delectabile,** see *bonus* under 3; on **sentire aliquid delectabile,** see *sentire* under 1.—Kinds of *delectabile* are: (a), **delectabile carnis,** *that of the flesh which is enjoyable.* —(b), **delectabile ciborum seu in cibis** and **delectabile venereorum seu venereum,** *the enjoyable in eating* and *drinking* and *the enjoyable in sex.*—(c), **delectabile in cibis,** see *delectabile ciborum.*—(d), **delectabile innaturale seu non secundum naturam** and **delectabile secundum naturam,** *the enjoyable that is not natural* or *according to nature* and *that according to nature.*

—(e), **delectabile memoratum,** *the enjoyable that comes from recollection.*—(f), **delectabile non secundum naturam,** see *delectabile innaturale.*—(g), **delectabile secundum naturam,** see *delectabile innaturale.*—(h), **delectabile secundum sensum seu sensus,** *the sensible enjoyment* or *that which gives pleasure to the senses.*—(i), **delectabile secundum tactum,** *the enjoyable through touch.*—(j), **delectabile sensus,** see *delectabile secundum sensum.*—(k), **delectabile venereorum seu venereum,** see *delectabile ciborum.*—**delectabiliter,** *adv., delightfully.*

delectabilitas, atis, *f., delectation, great pleasure* or *enjoyment, delectability.*

delectabiliter, *adv.,* see *delectabilis.*

delectamentum, i, *n., a delight.*

delectatio, onis, *f., amusement, delight, enjoyment* in the broader and narrower senses of the words, synonym of *gaudium* and *laetitia.* On the difference between *delectatio* and *gaudium,* see *gaudium.* On **magnitudo delectationis,** see *magnitudo* under 3.—Kinds of *delectatio* in the more general sense of the word are: (a), **delectatio actualis seu secundum actum, delectatio memoriae seu per memoriam** and **delectatio spei seu per spem,** *the enjoyment that arises in an action of the senses, that produced by remembrance* and *that by hope,* or *the enjoyment of some-*

thing in the present, past, and future.—(b), **delectatio aliena seu extranea** and **delectatio propria seu concomitans,** the enjoyment which is foreign to or outside a habit or that which is proper to or accompanies it.—(c), **delectatio animalis seu spiritualis seu non naturalis** and **delectatio corporalis, seu naturalis seu connaturalis,** the inorganic or suprasensory enjoyment and the physical, organic, sense pleasure.—(d), **delectatio apparenter** and **delectatio vere seu vera,** the apparent or ostensible and the true or real enjoyment.—(e), **delectatio appetitus intellectivi seu delectatio secundum intellectum seu intellectus seu intellectualis seu intelligibilis** and **delectatio appetitus sensibilis seu sensitivi seu delectatio sensus seu secundum sensum seu sensibilis seu sensitiva,** the enjoyment of the intellectual and that of the sensitive part of the soul or the intellectual and the sensual enjoyment.—(f), **delectatio appetitus sensibilis seu sensitivi,** see delectatio appetitus intellectivi.—(g), **delectatio bestialis seu brutorum** and **delectatio humana,** the animal or bestial and the human enjoyment.—(h), **delectatio bona seu eligibilis seu laudabilis** and **delectatio mala seu prava seu perversa seu inhonesta seu probrosa seu turpis,** the good enjoyment or that which is worthy of choice or praise and the evil or

bad or dishonorable or shameful enjoyment.—(i), **delectatio brutorum,** see delectatio bestialis.—(j), **delectatio carnalis seu carnis seu corporalis** and **delectatio spiritualis,** the carnal or physical and the mental or suprasensible enjoyment. Cf. delectatio animalis.—(k), **delectatio carnis,** see delectatio carnalis. —(1), **delectatio cibi,** enjoyment in food.—(m), **delectatio concomitans,** see delectatio aliena.—(n), **delectatio connaturalis,** according to the bodily side of man, see delectatio animalis.—(o), **delectatio contemplationis,** the enjoyment of contemplation or that effected by the contemplation of an object.—(p), **delectatio corporalis,** see delectatio carnalis.—(q), **delectatio diuturna seu morosa,** the lasting or prolonged enjoyment. In morals, a specific kind of internal sin, frequently but not necessarily, against the VI commandment.—(r), **delectatio eligibilis,** see delectatio bona.—(s), **delectatio exterior seu exterioris actus** and **delectatio interior,** the exterior and interior enjoyment, i.e., the enjoyment effected through an exterior act and that through thinking thereon.—(t), **delectatio exterioris actus,** see delectatio exterior.—(u), **delectatio extranea,** see delectatio aliena.—(v), **delectatio humana,** see delectatio bestialis.—(w), **delectatio immixta seu simplex** and **delectatio** mixta, *the unmixed* or *simple* and *the mixed enjoyment*. Cf. 10 Eth. 3 c.—(x), delectatio immoderata seu inordinata, *the immoderate* or *inordinate enjoyment*.—(y), delectatio imperfecta and delectatio perfecta, *the imperfect* and *the perfect enjoyment*.—(z), delectatio inhonesta, see *delectatio bona*.—(a²), delectatio innaturalis, see *delectatio animalis*.—(b²), delectatio inordinata, see *delectatio immoderata*. —(c²), delectatio intellectualis, see *delectatio appetitus intellectivi*.—(d²), delectatio intellectus, see *delectatio appetitus intellectivi*.—(e²), delectatio intelligibilis, see *delectatio appetitus intellectivi*.—(f²), delectatio interior, see *delectatio exterior*.—(g²), delectatio laudabilis, see *delectatio bona*.—(h²), delectatio mala, see *delectatio bona*.—(i²), delectatio memoriae, see *delectatio actualis*.—(j²), delectatio mixta, see *delectatio immixta*.—(k²), delectatio morosa, see *delectatio diuturna*. —(l²), delectatio mortalis and delectatio venialis, *the mortal enjoyment* or *that constituting a mortal sin*, and *the easily pardoned enjoyment* or *that constituting a venial sin*.—(m²), delectatio naturalis, see *delectatio animalis*.—(n²), delectatio non-naturalis, see *delectatio animalis*. —(o²), delectatio perfecta, see *delectatio imperfecta*.—(p²), delectatio per memoriam, see *delectatio actualis*.—(q²), delectatio per

spem, see *delectatio actualis*.— (r²), delectatio perversa, see *delectatio bona*.—(s²), delectatio prava, see *delectatio bona*.—(t²), delectatio probrosa, see *delectatio bona*.—(u²), delectatio propria, see *delectatio aliena*.—(v²), delectatio secundum actum, see *delectatio actualis*.—(w²), delectatio secundum intellectum, see *delectatio appetitus intellectivi*.— (x²), delectatio secundum sensum, see *delectatio appetitus intellectivi*.—(y²), delectatio secundum tactum seu tactus, *the enjoyment in the sense of touch*.— (z²), delectatio sensibilis seu sensitiva, see *delectatio appetitus intellectivi*.—(a³), delectatio sensus, see *delectatio appetitus intellectivi*.—(b³), delectatio servilis, *the servile enjoyment*.—(c³), delectatio simplex, see *delectatio immixta*.—(d³), delectatio spei, see *delectatio memoriae*.—(e³), delectatio spiritualis, see *delectatio carnalis*.—(f³), delectatio superflua, *the excessive* or *immoderate enjoyment*.—(g³), delectatio tactus, see *delectatio secundum tactum*.—(h³), delectatio turpis, see *delectatio bona*.—(i³), delectatio venerea seu veneorum, *the sexual enjoyment*.—(j³), delectatio venialis, see *delectatio mortalis*. —(k³), delectatio vera seu vere, see *delectatio apparenter*.—(l³), delectatio visus, *visual enjoyment*.—(m³), delectatio vitae activae and delectatio vitae contemplativae, *the enjoyment of the active* and *that of the contemplative life.*—(n³), **delectatio vitae contemplativae**, see *delectatio vitae activae.*—**delectatio est quaedam sensibilis generatio in naturam**, *enjoyment is a certain perceptible* or *perceived production, which is directed upon the nature of a thing*, i.e., upon something in conformity with nature; in other words, what is produced by something which befits its nature, taking place perceptibly in a being and felt by it.—**delectatio non est generatio, sed magis consistit in factum esse**, or, **delectatio non in generatione consistit, sed magis in esse generatum**, *enjoyment consists not so much in a coming into existence* or *producing*, as Plato says, *as in an existence* or *production.*

delectativus, a, um, *adj., delectable, giving great pleasure.*

delecto, are, avi, atum, 1, *v. intens. a., to delight, give pleasure, please*, used with *in, ex, de* and *abl., abl.* alone, *acc., inf.*, and *absolutely.*—**delectans**, ntis, *P. a., delighting, pleasing.*—**delectatus**, a, um, *P. a., delighted, pleased.*

delegatus, a, um, *P. a., delegated.*

deleo, ere, evi, etum, 2, *v. a., to abolish, destroy, annihilate.*

deletio, onis, *f., a blotting out, removal, destroying, deletion.*

delibatus, a, um, *P. a., tasted*, used figuratively.

deliberatio, onis, *f., deliberation, consideration, consultation,* syn-

onym of *consideratio.* On **peccatum ex deliberatione**, see *peccatum* under 2.—One kind of *deliberatio* is: **deliberatio inquisitiva**, *the inquiring deliberation* or *the deliberation that proceeds in the manner of an inquiry.*

deliberativus, a, um, *adj., relating to deliberation, deliberative, deliberating, considering.* On **ratio deliberativa**, see *ratio* under 3; on **vis deliberativa**, see *vis* under 1.

delibero, are, avi, atum, 1, *v. a., to deliberate, consider,* synonym of *considero.* On **appetitus deliberatus**, see *appetitus* under 1; on **consensus deliberatus**, see *consensus* under 2; on **finis deliberatus**, see *finis* under 2; on **ratio deliberata**, see *ratio* under 3 and 7; on **voluntas deliberata**, see *voluntas* under 3.

delicatus, a, um, *adj.,* (1) *delicate, fine,* (2) *overnice, fastidious, squeamish.*

deliciae, arum, *f.,* (sing. *delicia*, ae, *f.*), (1) in the singular, *delicacy,* a susceptibility to the inconveniences of labor, resulting from delicacy of health, *tenderness,* (2) in the plural, *pleasure, delight, luxuriousness, voluptuousness.*

deliciosus, a, um, *adj.,* (1) *delicious, choice,* (2) *delightful, affording delight,* (3) *voluptuous, effeminate.*

delictum, i, *n.,* (delinquo), prop. a falling short of the standard of law, especially a transgression against the positive law; while *peccatum* is usually against the natural law; *a sin, crime, transgression, a sin of omission.* Sometimes it is taken strictly for the omission of something concerning God or for a man's intentional derelection of duty.

delinio, ire, ivi, delinitum, 4, *v. a., to daub, besmear, spread* or *rub over;* in the Summa used twice figuratively, *cajole, flatter, blandish, wheedle.*

delinquo, ere, liqui, lictum, 3, *v. n.* and *a., to fail, be wanting* in one's duty, *commit a fault, do wrong, transgress, offend.*—**delinquens,** ntis, *P. a., m.,* or *f.* as subst., *a transgressor, sinner, delinquent.*

deliramentum, i, *n., nonsense, absurdity.*

deliro, are, *v. n., to rave, speak in an incoherent manner.*

delusio, onis, *f., a ridiculing, teasing, joking.*

demando, are, avi, atum, 1, *v. a., to give in charge, intrust, commit.*

dementia, ae, *f., madness, folly.*

demereor, eri, demeritus, 2, *v. a.* dep. used only once in the active voice in the S.T., *to demerit, be worthy of retribution, deserve to lose.*

demergo, ere, si, mersum, 3, *v. a., to plunge into, submerge.*—**demersus,** a, um, *P. a., plunged, submerged.*

demeritorius, a, um, *adj., demeritorious, blameworthy, lacking in merit.*

demeritum, i, *n., demerit, the opposite of meritum.*—One kind of *demeritum* is: **demeritum substantiale,** *the essential demerit* or *demerit according to its essence.*

demissus, a, um, *P. a., brought down, lowered.*

demo, ere, mpsi, mptum, 3, *v. a., to take away, take off, subtract.*

democratia, ae, *f., government by the people, democracy.*

democraticus, a, um, *adj., democratic.* On **communitas democratica,** see *communitas* under 3; on **lex democratica,** see *lex* under 1; on **politia democratica,** see *politia* under 1.

Democritus, i, *m., Democritus,* a celebrated philosopher (fifth century B.C.) born at Abdera, an adherent of the Eleatic school, and the originator of the atomic theory.

demonstrabilis, e, *adj.,* (1) *that can be pointed out, demonstrable, presentable, producible,* (2) *demonstrable* as being necessarily true.—On **conclusio demonstrabilis,** see *conclusio* under 2; on **propositio demonstrabilis,** see *propositio* under 2.

demonstratio, onis, *f.,* (1) *showing, presentation, indication,* (2) *making known, explanation, proof, demonstration,* synonym of *ostensio,* (3) *proof* or *argumentation* in the narrower sense of the word, i.e., *demonstratio* *scientialis seu scientifica,* i.e., that proof which demonstrates something as being necessarily true, an argument productive of certitude, not opinion, also a synonym of *ostensio.*—On **significare cum demonstratione,** see *significare.*—Kinds of *demonstratio* in this (1) sense are: (a), **demonstratio ad intellectum** and **demonstratio ad sensum,** *indication with reference to the intellect* and *indication with reference to the senses.*—(b), **demonstratio ad sensum,** see *demonstratio ad intellectum.*—(c), **demonstratio personalis** and **demonstratio simplex,** *the personal* and *the simple indication* or *the indication with reference to a definite person* and *the general indication.*—(d), **demonstratio simplex,** see *demonstratio personalis.*—Kinds of *demonstratio* in this (2) sense are: (a), **demonstratio exemplaris,** *the exemplified proof* or *that illustrated by an example.*—(b), **demonstratio scientalis seu scientifica,** *the scientific proof* or *that producing a knowledge of something.*—On **ars demonstrationis,** see *ars* under 2; on **elementum demonstrationis,** see *elementum* under 1; on **medium demonstrationis seu in demonstratione,** see *medium* under 2; on **principium demonstrationis,** see *principium;* on **syllogismus demonstrationis,** see *syllogismus;* on **via demonstrationis,** see *via* under 3; on

virtus demonstrationis, see *virtus* under 7; on **vis demonstrationis,** see *vis* under 2.—Kinds of *demonstratio* in this (3) sense are: (a), **demonstratio ad aliquem seu ad hominem (sc. arguentem) seu ad contradicendum** and **demonstratio simpliciter seu vera,** *the proof directed against anyone* or *against a person who maintains something* or *the opposing proof* and *the simple proof* or *that which confirms a truth.*—(b), **demonstratio ad contradicendum,** see *demonstratio ad aliquem.*—(c), **demonstratio ad hominem,** see *demonstratio ad aliquem.*—(d), **demonstratio ad impossibile ducens** and **demonstratio ostensiva,** *the proof which leads to something impossible* or *absurd* and *that which to a certain degree shows a thing to be true* or *the indirect* and *the direct proof.*—(e), **demonstratio affirmativa seu categorica seu praedicativa** and **demonstratio negativa seu privativa,** *the affirmative proof* or *that which expresses something in the affirmative* and *the negative proof,* i.e., the proof which confirms that something is the case and that which confirms that something is not the case.—(f), **demonstratio categorica,** see *demonstratio affirmativa.*—(g), **demonstratio circularis,** *the proof which proceeds in a circle* or *is given in a roundabout way.*—(h), **demonstratio negativa,** see *de-*

monstratio affirmativa.—(i), **demonstratio operativa,** *the proof which produces other knowledge.*—(j), **demonstratio ostensiva,** see *demonstratio ad impossibile ducens.*—(k), **demonstratio particularis** and **demonstratio universalis,** *the particular* and *the general proof.*—(l), **demonstratio physica,** *the physical proof* or *that of natural science.* —(m), **demonstratio positione differens,** *the proof which is different by reason of the position of its premises.*—(n), **demonstratio praedicativa,** see *demonstratio affirmativa.*—(o), **demonstratio privativa,** see *demonstratio affirmativa.*—(p), **demonstratio propter quid** and **demonstratio quia seu signi,** *the proof from the cause* and *that from the effect* or *from the sign* or *the proof a priori* and *that a posteriori.*—(q), **demonstratio quia,** see *demonstratio propter quid.*—(r), **demonstratio signi,** see *demonstratio propter quid.*—(s), **demonstratio simpliciter,** see *demonstratio ad aliquem.*—(t), **demonstratio universalis,** see *demonstratio particularis.*—(u), **demonstratio vera,** see *demonstratio ad aliquem.*

demonstrative, *adv., in the manner of a proof, in a manner that proves something to be necessarily true in the sense of such a proof, demonstratively,* the opposite of *logice* and *probabiliter.* On **cognoscere demonstrative,** see *cognoscere* under 2; on **di-**

cere demonstrative, see *dicere* under 3; on **intellegere demonstrative,** see *intellegere* under 1; on **probare demonstrative,** see *probare;* on **procedere demonstrative,** see *procedere* under 2; on **scire demonstrative,** see *scire* under 2.

demonstrativus, a, um, *adj.,* (1) *showing, indicative, pointing out,* (2) *confirming something as necessarily true, being necessarily true, demonstrative,* (3) *concerning the proof which confirms something as being necessarily true.* On **medium demonstrativum,** see *medium* under 2; on **pronomen demonstrativum,** see *pronomen;* on **signum demonstrativum,** see *signum* under 1.— On **ars demonstrativa,** see *ars* under 2; on **certitudo demonstrativa,** see *certitudo* under 2; on **conclusio demonstrativa,** see *conclusio* under 2; on **disputatio demonstrativa,** see *disputatio;* on **habitus demonstrativus,** see *habitus* under 4; on **materia demonstrativa,** see *materia* under 2; on **medium demonstrativum,** see *medium* under 2; on **principium demonstrativum,** see *principium;* on **probatio demonstrativa,** see *probatio* under 2; on **processus demonstrativus,** see *processus* under 2; on **pronomen demonstrativum,** see *pronomen;* on **propositio demonstrativa,** see *propositio* under 2; on **ratio demonstrativa,** see *ratio* under 13; on **scientia demonstrativa,** see *scientia* under 2; on **syllogismus demonstrativus**, see *syllogismus;* on **veritas demonstrativa**, see *veritas* under 3.

demonstrator, oris, *m., he who proves something as necessary* or *as necessarily true, a demonstrator,* the opposite of *dialecticus.*

demonstro, are, avi, atum, 1, *v. a.,* (1) *to show, present, exhibit,* (2) *make known, explain, substantiate, prove, demonstrate,* (3) *prove something as being necessarily true.*—On **aliquid demonstratum,** see *aliquis;* on **individuum demonstratum,** see *individuum;* on **materia demonstrata,** see *materia* under 3; on **singulare demonstratum,** see *singularis.*—Kinds of *demonstrare* in this sense are: **demonstrare quantum ad intellectum** and **demonstrare quantum ad sensum,** *to show with reference to the intellect* and *to show with reference to the senses.* On **modus demonstrandi,** see *modus* under 2.— Kinds of *demonstrare* in this (3) sense are: (a), **demonstrare argumentative** and **demonstrare redargutive seu elenchice,** *to prove something in the sense of a proof in the wider meaning of the word* and *to prove something in the sense of a refutation.*—(b), **demonstrare circulariter seu circulo,** *to prove by going in a circle.*—(c), **demonstrare circulo,** see *demonstrare circulariter.*— (d), **demonstrare elenchice,** see

demonstrare argumentative.—(e), **demonstrare ostensive,** *to prove manifestly,* i.e., to prove something in such a manner that at the end of the proof one can exhibit it as true in some measure. —(f), **demonstrare redargutive,** see *demonstrare argumentative.* —(g), **demonstrare simpliciter,** *to prove something simply* or *plainly.*—(h), **demonstrare sufficienter,** *to prove something sufficiently.*

Demophilus, i, *m., Demophilus,* a monk, addressed in the eighth letter which appears under the name of Dionysius the Areopagite.

demoror, ari, atus, 1, *v. dep. n.* and *a., to tarry, dwell, remain in the same place for a while.*

demulceo, ere, lsi, mulctum, 2, *v. a., to soothe, please, calm.*

demum, *adv.,* used to give prominence to an idea in opposition to or restriction of another, *at length, at last, at any rate, lastly,* used enclitically with the adverb *tunc.*

denarius, ii, *m.,* (1) the number *ten,* (2) *a coin* of small value, *a penny, a leaden coin.*

denegatio, onis, *f., a refusal, denial.*

denego, are, avi, atum, 1, *v. a.,* (1) *to deny, refuse, to grant* or *give something,* (2) *deny, refuse to admit* or *believe something.*

denigratio, onis, *f., a blackening.*

denigro, are, 1, *v. a., to blacken,* used figuratively.—**denigratus,** a, um, *P. a., blackened.*

denique, *adv.,* (1) in ascending to a higher or more general expression, *even, in fact,* (2) to introduce the last of a series, *finally, lastly.*

denominatio, onis, *f., name, denomination, title, term.* On **praedicare, per modum denominationis,** see *praedicare* under 2; on praedicatio per denominationem, see *praedicatio* under 2.— A kind of *denominatio* is: **denominatio praedicamentalis,** *the name of a thing after one of the ten predicaments* (see *praedicamentum*).—**denominatio fit a forma quae dat speciem rei,** or **omnis denominatio est a forma, quae dat esse et est principium operationis,** or, **omnis denominatio est a forma,** *the name of a thing occurs from the form which endows it with being* and *forms the principle of its activity.*—**denominatio fit a potiori,** *the name of a thing is given after the more eminent part of the same.*—**denominatio fit ex completo et ultimo et manifestiori,** *the name of a thing is given according to its perfect* and *last* and *more manifest form.*—**denominatio proprie est secundum habitudinem accidentis ad subiectum,** *the proper name of a thing is given according to the relation of an accident to its subject.*—**denominatio rei maxime debet fieri a perfectione et fine,** or, **iustum est, quod omnia definiantur et denominentur a fine,**

the translation of the Aristotelian text: *apo tou telous hapanta prosegoreuein dikaion, the name of a thing ought especially to be taken from that which forms its fulfillment* and *end.*—**denominationes consueverunt fieri a perfectiori,** *the names of things are customarily given from that which is the more perfect among them.*—**iustum est, quod omnia definiantur et denominentur a fine,** see above: *denominatio rei,* etc.—**omnis denominatio est a forma, quae dat esse et est principium operationis,** see above: *denominatio fit a forma,* etc. **omnis denominatio fit a forma,** see above: *denominatio fit a forma,* etc.

denominative, *adv., by derivation, after the manner of naming, denominatively.* On **dicere denominative,** see *dicere* under 3; on **praedicare denominative,** see *praedicare* under 2.

denominativus, a, um, *adj., naming, designating, formed by derivation, denominative,* not used in the S.T. On **praedicatio denominativa,** see *praedicatio* under 2.

denomino, are, avi, atum, 1, *v. a.,* to *name, term, designate, denominate,* synonym of *dicere.*— **iustum est, quod omnia definiantur et denominentur a fine,** or **res denominatur a fine et complemento,** or **unumquodque denominatur a fine,** the translation of the Aristotelian text: *apo tou* *telous hapanta prosegoreuein di-kaion, everything is rightly named* and *defined according to that which forms its end or completion.*—omne accidens denominat proprium subiectum, *every accident names its peculiar subject,* i.e., *from every accident is taken a designation of its subject.*—res debet denominari ab eo, quod est de essentia sua, or, unaquaeque res proprie denominatur a sua quidditate, *a thing must be properly named from that which belongs to its essence.*—res denominatur a fine et complemento, see above: *iustum est, quod* etc.— unaquaeque res proprie denominatur a sua quidditate, see above: *res debet denominari ab eo* etc.—unumquodque denominatur a fine, see above: *iustum est, quod omnia* etc.— unumquodque denominatur a sua forma, *everthing is named after its form.*—unumquodque praecipue denominatur et definitur secundum id quod convenit ei primo et per se, non autem secundum id quod convenit ei per aliud, *everything is especially named* and *defined according to that which is first due it* and *through itself,* i.e., *through its own nature* and *essence, not however according to that which is due it through another.*

denoto, are, avi, atum, 1, *v. a., to denote, mark out, indicate, designate.*

dens, dentis, *m.,* (1) *a tooth,* (2) of things resembling a tooth, *a tooth point, spike.*—dolor dentium, *a tooth ache.*—strepitus dentium, *a chattering of the teeth.*—stridor dentium, *gnashing of the teeth.*

densitas, atis, *f., thickness, density.*

denso, are, avi, atum, 1, *v. a., to make thick, press together, thicken.*

densus, a, um, *adj., thick, dense,* i.e., consisting of parts crowded together, opposite of *rarus.*

denudatio, onis, *f., a laying bare, uncovering.*

denudo, are, avi, atum, 1, *v. a., to lay bare, uncover, expose.*—denudatus, a, um, *P. a., stripped of, deprived, divested,* used with *ab* and *abl.*

denuntiatio, onis, *f.,* (1) *announcement, declaration, pronouncement,* (2) *denunciation,* the act of declaring an action or person.

denuntiativus, a, um, *adj., monitory, indicatory, conveying monition, admonitory.*

denuntiator, oris, *m., a denouncer,* one who publicly accuses or declares as deserving of punishment.

denuntio, are, avi, atum, 1, *v. a.,* (1) *announce, declare, name,* (2) *denounce, threaten.*

denuo, *adv.,* (1) of the restoration of things which have been destroyed *anew, afresh,* = *de integro,* (2) for *iterum, a second time, once more,* (3) for *rursus,* of anything that is repeated not precisely a second time, *once again*, *again*, hence often with verbs compounded with *re*.

deordinatio, onis, *f., inordinateness, disorder, deordination,* a departure from or violation of the settled order of things.

deordino, are, avi, atum, *to disorder, put out of order, disarrange, disturb,* synonym of *inordino,* opposite of *ordino.*—**deordinatus,** a, um, *P. a., disordered, disarranged, disturbed,* On **actus deordinatus,** see *actus* under 1; on **voluntas deordinata,** see *voluntas* under 3.

deorsum, adv., (1) *downwards,* opposite of *sursum,* (2) *down, below,* also the opposite of *sursum.*

depaupero, are, avi, atum, 1, *v. a., to depauperate, impoverish, make poor.*

depello, ere, puli, pulsum, 3, *v. a., to expel, remove, displace.*—**depulsus,** a, um, *P. a., expelled, removed.*

dependentia, ae, *f., dependence,* the state of relying on something or someone.

dependeo, ere, 2, *v. a., to be dependent on, be governed by, be derived from,* constr. with *e* (*ex*) or *a* (*ab*).

deperditio, onis, *f., loss.*

deperdo, ere, didi, ditum, 3, *v. a., to lose.*—**deperditus,** a, um, *P. a., lost.*

depereo, ire, ii (fut. deperiet for -ibit) 4, *v. n., to go to ruin, perish, be lost, impaired, dimin-*

ished, often followed by the *dat.* of the person or thing for whom and of which something has been impaired or diminished.

depingo, ere, pinxi, pictum, 3, *v. a., to depict, paint in colors, paint.*

depono, ere, posui, positum, 3, *v. a.,* (1) *to lay down, lay aside, give up, denounce,* (2) *give in charge to, commit to, intrust to,* (3) *take down, depose.*—**depositus,** a, um, *P. a., intrusted, deposited.*

deporto, are, avi, atum, 1, *v. a., to carry,* or *convey down, carry away,* used with *in* and *ad* with *acc.*

deposco, ere, poposci, 3, *v. a., to beseech, request earnestly, require, ask.*

depositarius, ii, *m., a depositary, a person entrusted with anything,* especially money.

depositio, onis, *f.,* (1) *a putting off, laying aside, a parting from, getting rid* of, (2) *a deposition;* the act of deposing from office, dignity or power.

depraedatio, onis, *f., a plundering.*

depraedor, ari, atus, 1, *v. dep. a., to plunder, pillage, ravage.*

depravo, are, avi, atum, 1, *v. a.,* used figuratively, *to pervert, corrupt, spoil, deprave.*—**depravatus,** a, um, *P. a., depraved.*

deprecatio, onis, *f., a prayer for pardon, deprecation, petition,* synonym of *inductio* and *petitio.*

deprecativus, a, um, *adj., tending to remove* or *avert evil by* *prayer, deprecatory,* the opposite of *imperative.*

deprecor, ari, atus, 1, *v. dep. a., to pray, intercede, pray for, intercede in behalf of, beseech in prayer.*

deprehendo, ere, di, sum, 3, *v. a., to catch, overtake, surprise, apprehend, take, find out, discover.—***deprehensus,** a, um, *P. a., caught, apprehended, discovered.*

depressio, onis, *f.,* (1) *depression, a pressing* or *sinking down, lowness of spirits,* (2) *a depression, the act of repressing,* or *the condition of being depressed.*

deprimo, ere, pressi, pressum, 3, *v. a.,* (1) *weigh down, press down, repress, injure,* (2) fig., *depress, dispirit.—***depressus,** a, um, *P. a., deep lying, depressed.*

depromo, ere, prompsi, promptum, 3, *v. a., to bring forth something, bring, fetch.*

depuratio, onis, *f., depuration, purification,* the process of purifying or separating, said of things physical and spiritual.

depuratus, a, um, *adj. made* or *become free from impurities, depurated, purified.*

deputatio, onis, *f.,* (1) *authorization, appointment, deputation,* the act or state of being deputed, the authority so deputed, (2) *an assignment,* a giving or promise to give money or property to someone.

deputo, are, avi, atum, 1, *v. a., to destine, allot* to anyone or any-

thing, *delegate, assign, depute.* —**deputatus,** a, um, *P. a., alloted, assigned, delegated, deputed.*

deratiocinor, ari, atus, 1, *v. dep. a., to conclude badly* or *incorrectly,* does not accur in S.T.

derelictio, onis, *f., abandonment, forsaking.*

derelinquo, ere, liqui, lictum, 3, *v. a.,* (1) *to abandon, forsake, give up, leave, let stand,* (2) *to give over, yield, resign,* (3) *to neglect* or *fail to do something,* (4) *to bequeath.—***delinquere aliquid sub dubio,** *to leave something doubtful.—***derelinquere aliquid intelligentiae,** *to leave something to the intelligence.—***derelinquere aliquem,** *to desert* or *forsake someone,* i.e., to leave them unprotected.—**derelictus,** a, um, *P. a., forsaken, abandoned.*

derideo, ere, si, sum, 2, *v. a., to laugh at, laugh to scorn, scoff at, deride, ridicule,* (2) *to disregard, leave out of consideration, make light of.—***deridens,** ntis, *m., derider.*

derisibilis, e, *adj., ridiculous, absurd, open to derision.*

derisio, onis, *f., derision, the act of deriding* or *the state of being derided* or *put to shame by someone, ridicule, mockery, contempt shown by words* and *laughter. Derisio* and *subsannatio* are similar in motive but differ in the manner of attaining the end, because *derisio* is done by words and laughter while *subsannatio* is done by a sneer or grimace of contempt made by slightly raising the upper lip and nostrils.

derisor, oris, *m.*, *a mocker, derider, scoffer, satirical person.*

derisorie, *adv.*, see *derisorius.*

derisorius, a, um, *adj.*, *ridiculous, serving for laughter.*—**derisorie,** *adv.*, *ridiculously, derisively,* characterized by derision or mockery.

derivatio, onis, *f.*, (1) *derivation, the act of deriving or acquiring from an origin or source, or the condition of being derived,* (2) in gramm. *derivation, etymology of words.*

derivo, are, avi, atum, 1, *v. a.*, (1) *to draw off, deduce, derive,* with *a* (*ab*) or *e* (*ex*) lit and *fig.*, (2) *dispense, distribute* with *ad,* (3) in gramm. *derive,* sc. one word from another.—**derivatus,** a, um, *P. a., drawn, deduced, derived.*

derogatio, onis, *f.*, *derogation, disparagement, the act of injuring or seeking to injure in reputation, detraction, depreciation.*

derogo, are, avi, atum, 1, *v. a. to take away, detract from, diminish, disparage, dishonor,* constr. with *dat.*

descendo, ere, di, sum, 3, *v. n.*, (1) *come down, fall, descend, penetrate deeply,* opposite of *ascendo,* (2) *lower one's self, descend to an evil act,* (3) *descend* or *proceed* from any person, *be in line of descent.*—**descendens,** entis, *m.*, and *f.*, *a descendant;* plur. **descendentes,** *posterity.*

descensio, onis, *f.*, *a going down, descent,* opposite of *ascensio.*

descensus, us, *m.*, *a descent, lineal descent,* opposite of *ascensus.*

describo, ere, psi, 3, *v. a.*, *to represent, delineate, describe.*

descriptio, onis, *f.*, *a description.*

desero, ere, ui, rtum, 3, *v. a.*, *to leave, desert, abandon.*—**desertus,** a, um, *P. a., deserted, left, abandoned.*—**desertum,** i, *n.*, *a desert place, desert, waste.*—**in desertis,** *in desert places.*

desertio, onis, *f.*, *a forsaking, giving up.*—**desertio temporalium bonorum,** *the renunciation of temporal goods.*

desertor, oris, *m.*, *a deserter, one who forsakes an allegiance or duty.*

desertum, i, *n.*, see *desero.*

deservio, ire, 4, *v. n.*, *to serve, be devoted to, subject to, subservient to,* used with the *dat.*, rarely with *ad* and *acc.*

desicco, are, no perf., atum, 1, *v. a.*, *to desiccate, season, remove the moisture from,* used literally and figuratively.—**desiccans,** ntis, *P. a., drying, parching.*—**desiccatus,** a, um, *P. a., seasoned.*

desiderabilis, e, *adj.*, *desirable.*

desideranter, *adv.*, see *desidero.*

desiderativus, a, um, *adj.*, *desiderative, having* or *implying desire.*

desiderium, ii, *n.*, (1) *desire* in the proper sense of the word, i.e., the longing for a thing which one as yet does not possess, (2) *desire* in the broader sense of the word, i.e., the longing for a thing in like measure, whether it is possessed or not.—On **quies desiderii**, see *quies.*—Kinds of *desiderium* in this (1) sense are: (a), **desiderium caeleste**, and **desiderium saeculare**, *the heavenly* and *the worldly* or *earthly desire.*—(b), **desiderium carnale seu carnis**, *the desire of the flesh.*—(c), **desiderium carnis**, see *desiderium carnale.*—(d), **desiderium commune**, *the general desire.*—(e), **desiderium concupiscentiae seu sensus** and **desiderium intellectuale**, *the desire of sensual appetite* or *of the sensual part of the soul* and *the intellectual desire.*—(f), **desiderium consiliabile**, *the deliberating* or *deliberate desire*, the translation of the Aristotelian phrase *bouleutike orexis.*—(g), **desiderium conveniens**, *the suitable* or *proper desire.*—(h), **desiderium intellectuale**, see *desiderium concupiscentiae.*—(i), **desiderium naturae seu naturale**, *the desire of nature* or *the natural desire.*—(j), **desiderium naturale**, see *desiderium naturae.*—(k), **desiderium pium**, *the pious desire* or *the pious wish.*—(l), **desiderium saeculare**, see *desiderium caeleste.*—(m), **desiderium sensus**, see *desiderium concupiscentiae.*—impossibile est naturale desiderium esse inane, or, **naturale desiderium non potest esse inane**, or, **naturale et commune desiderium non potest esse vacuum et inane**, *the natu-*

ral and *the general desire cannot be impossible of fulfillment.*

desidero, are, avi, atum, 1, *v. a.*, *to desire* for the pleasure or enjoyment of something; *wish* or *earnestly long for; covet; crave.* —**desiderans**, ntis, *m., one who desires, a desirer.*—**desideratus**, a, um, *P. a., desired.*

desidia, ae, f., *slothfulness, idleness, indolence, inactivity.*

designatio, onis, f., *designation, determination*, synonym of *determinatio.*—Kinds of *designatio* are: (a), **designatio completa**, *the complete determination.*—(b), **designatio essentialis seu substantialis**, *the essential determination.* —(c), **designatio substantialis**, see *designatio essentialis.*

designativus, a, um, *adj., designating, determining*, synonym of *determinativus.*

designo, are, avi, atum, 1, *v. a.*, (1) *to designate, point out, signify, denote, describe, represent*, (2) *to mark out, trace out.*—**designatus**, a, um, *P. a., designated.*

desino, ere, sii, situm, 3, *v. a.* and *n., to leave off, cease, desist*, the opposite of *incipio.*

desisto, ere, stiti, stitum, 3, *v. a.* and *n., to leave off, cease, desist from*, constr. (1) with *a* or *ab*, (2) with *inf.*, (3) *absol.*

desolatio, onis, f., (1) *a desolating, the act of making desolate, devastation*, (2) *desolation, the state* or *condition of being desolate, loneliness.*

desolo, are, avi, atum, 1, *v. a., to desolate, deprive of inhabitants,* or *to strip of dwellings, goods,* and *products, ravage;* hence to leave lonely and bare.

despectio, onis, *f., a looking down upon,* in a figurative sense, *contempt, despising.*

despector, oris, *m., a despiser. disdainer,* one who treats others with indifference or contempt.

despectus, us, *m., a looking down upon, contempt, a despising.*

desperabilis, e, *adj., incurable, desperate.*

desperatio, onis, *f., hopelessness, despair,* in the narrower and broader senses of the word, opposite of *spes.*—In the narrower sense of the word, *desperatio* is one of the irascible affections (see **passio irascibilis** under *passio.*) With reference to spiritual goods, it is opposed to the theological virtue of hope, it is a *filia acidiae* (see *acidia*) and a sin against the Holy Ghost (see *peccatum in Spiritum sanctum.*)

despero, are, avi, atum, 1, *v. n.* and *a., to be hopeless, have no hope of, despair, give up,* opposite of *spero,* constr. most frequently (1) with *de,* (2) *absol.,* less frequently, (3) with *acc.* and *inf.*—**desperans,** antis, *P. a., despairing.*—As a *subst. a despairing person, despairer.*—**desperatus,** a, um, *P. a., given up, despaired of, irremediable, desperate.*

despicientia, ae, *f., a despising, contempt.*

despicio, ere, exi, ectum, 3, *v. n.* and *a., to look down upon, despise, disdain.*

despondeo, ere, spondi, sponsum, 2, *v. a., to betroth, engage, espouse.*

desponsatio, onis, *f., a betrothing, betrothal.*

desponsator, oris, *m., a fiance, a betrothed person.*

desponso, are, no perf., atum, 1, *v. a., to betroth, promise to marry.* —**desponsata,** ae, *f., betrothed, promised in marriage.*

despoticus, a, um, *adj., imperious, despotic,* synonym of *dominativus,* and *tyrannicus.* On **dominium despoticum,** see *dominium;* on **principatus despoticus,** see *principatus* under 1; on **regimen despoticum,** see *regimen;* on **scientia despotica,** see *scientia* under 2.

destinatio, onis, *f., destination, the predetermined end;* sometimes it is taken for someone's real mission to a given end or for a mission conceived in someone's mind.

destino, are, avi, atum, 1, *v. a.,* (1) *to destine, send to a destined end,* (2) *destine, resolve firmly* on a determined course of action.

destituo, ere, ui, utum, 3, *v. a.,* (1) *to deprive, strip, rob of,* mostly passive in this sense, used with the *abl.* of the thing taken away, opposite of *statuo,* (2) *abandon,* *forsake, impair,* in any way.—**destitutus,** a, um, *P. a., deprived of.*

destitutio, onis, *f., destitution, a forsaking, a failure.*

destructio, onis, *f., a destroying, destruction.*

destructor, oris, *m., a destroyer, one who pulls down.*

destruo, ere, xi, ctum, 3, *v. a.,* (1) *to tear down,* (2) *to destroy, ruin, weaken,* used figuratively, (3) *cause the downfall of; overthrow.*—**destructus,** a, um, *P. a., destroyed.*

desudo, are, avi, atum, 1, *v. n.* and *a., to sweat greatly, exert* or *fatigue one's self.*

desum, esse, fui, *v. n., to be absent, fail, be wanting,* constr. with (1) *dat.,* (2) *in,* (3) *ad,* (4) *quin,* and (5) *absol.*

desumo, ere, mpsi, 3, *v. a., to pick out, choose, take, select.*

desuper, *adv.,* (1) *from above, on high,* that which transcends the merely physical or natural, (2) *from overhead, over one's head, aloft.*

desursum, *adv.,* (1) *from above,* i.e., *from God,* (2) *above,* i.e., a condition superior in quality, degree, rank.

detectio, onis, *f., an uncovering, revealing.*

detego, ere, texi, ctum, 3, *v. a., to disclose, make known, reveal to knowledge, free from secrecy.*—**detectus,** a, um, *P. a., disclosed, revealed.*

detentio, onis, *f., a keeping back, detaining.*

deterior, ius, *adj.,* comp. (*sup.* deterrimus, a, um), *worse, poorer, meaner.*

deterioratio, onis, *f., a mangling,* the act of making torn or jagged wounds, a synonym of *laceratio.*

deteriorativus, a, um, *adj., deteriorating, deteriorative.* On **amor deteriorativus,** see *amor* under 1.

deterioro, are, avi, atum, 1, *v. a., to deteriorate, make worse, reduce in quality, lessen in value, worth,* or the like.

determinabilis, e, *adj., determinable, finite, terminable, that may be terminated,* or *that will in due course come to an end.*

determinate, *adv.,* see *determino.*

determinatio, onis, *f.,* (1) *demarcation, stipulation, determination,* synonym of *designatio,* the opposite of *indeterminatio,* (2) *arrangement, direction, decision, determination.*—Kinds of *determinatio* in this (1) sense are: (a), **determinatio activa** and **determinatio passiva,** *the active* and *the passive determination* or *self-determination* and *the determination of a being* or *faculty coming from something foreign to it.*—(b), **determinatio diminuens,** *the diminishing determination* or *that which includes a diminution.*—(c), **determinatio distinctionis** and **determinatio limitationis,** *the determination of distinction* and *that of limitation* or *the distinguishing* and *the limiting determination.*—(d), **determinatio limitationis,** see *determinatio di-*

stinctionis.—(e), **determinatio passiva,** see *determinatio activa.*

determinative, see *determinativus.*

determinativus, a, um, *adj.*, *limiting, fixing, determining, determinative,* synonym of *designativus.*—**determinative,** adv., *definitively, in the sense* or *in the manner of a stipulation* or *determination, determinatively.* On **dicere determinative,** see *dicere* under 3.

determino, are, avi, atum, 1, *v. a.,* (1) *delimit, fix, determine,* (2) *direct, arrange, order.*—**determinatus,** a, um, *P. a.,* (1) *delimited, fixed, determined,* synonym of *finitus* and *terminatus,* the opposite of *indefinitus, indeterminatus, infinitus,* and *interminatus,* (2) *directed, arranged, ordered,* synonym of *ordinatus.*—On **actio determinata,** see *actio* under 1; on **bonum determinatum,** see *bonus* under 3; on **causa determinata,** see *causa* under 2; on **cognitio determinata,** see *cognitio* under 2; on **concupiscentia determinata,** see *concupiscentia* under 1; on **concensus determinatus,** see *concensus* under 2; on **corpus determinatum,** see *corpus;* on **dispositio determinata,** see *dispositio* under 4; on **distantia determinata,** see *distantia;* on **effectus determinatus,** see *effectus;* on **esse determinatum,** see *esse;* on **forma determinata,** see *forma* under 2; on **iudicium determinatum ad unum,** see *iudicium* under 4; on **linea deter-**

minata, see *linea* under 1; on **locus determinatus,** see *locus* under 2; on **magnitudo determinata,** see *magnitudo* under 1; on **materia determinata,** see *materia* under 3; on **multitudo determinata,** see *multitudo* under 3; on **natura determinata,** see *natura;* on **numerus determinatus,** see *numerus;* on **passio determinata,** see *passio* under 2; on **phantasia determinata,** see *phantasia* under 2; on **proportio determinata,** see *proportio* under 1; on **quantitas determinata,** see *quantitas;* on **ratio determinata,** see *ratio* under 14; on **suppositio determinata,** see *suppositio* under 4; on **suppositum determinatum,** see *suppositum* under 2; on **tempus determinatum,** see *tempus;* on **virtus determinata,** see *virtus* under 1 and 5.—On **iudicium determinatum et non determinatum ad unum,** see *iudicium* under 4. —**determinate,** adv., *in a defined, fixed, determined manner, determinately,* the opposite of *indeterminately.* On **considerare ut determinate,** see *considerare;* on **significare determinate,** see *significare.*

deterreo, ere, ui, itum, 2, *v. a., to deter, prevent, hinder.*

detestabilis, e, *adj., detestable.*

detestatio, onis, *f.,* (1) *a detestation, abhorrence,* (2) *detestation,* a formal expression of condemnation.

detestor, ari, atus, 1, *v. dep. a., to*

hate intensely, abominate, detest, abhor.

detineo, ere, ui, tentum, 2, *v. a., to hold off, keep back, detain.* —**detentus,** a, um, *P. a., kept back, detained.*

detorqueo, ere, si, tum, 2, *v. a.* and *n., to twist out of shape;* in a figurative sense, *to misrepresent, distort.*

detractabilis, e, *adj., dishonorable, characterized by* or *bringing dishonor* or *reproach.*

detractio, onis, *f., detraction, the act of revealing,* directly or indirectly, the real defects and faults of a person in order to blacken his good name.

detractor, oris, *m., a detractor,* one who seeks to diminish the reputation of another; one who reveals the real faults or flaws in the character of another.

detraho, ere, xi, ctum, 3, *v. a.,* (1) *to take away, remove, withdraw, take from, draw,* (2) *disparage, detract from.*

detrimentum, i, *n., an injury,* anything so done as to operate adversely to one in his person, property, rights or attributes; *harm, loss, damage, detriment.*

detrudo, ere, si, sum, 3, *v. a., to thrust down, cast down, to force away.*

deturpo, are, 1, *v. a., to disfigure, defile.*

Deus, i, *God,* the concrete subject of *deitas, divinitas,* and *divina.* "God is God" has been called a a perfect definition, but theology cannot rest satisfied with this definition in the face of the unwarranted demands of science. Accordingly it expresses itself concerning *the capability of knowledge,* concerning *the idea,* and concerning *the attributes of God,* upon the basis of Scriptures. Cardinal Newman, in his "Idea of a University", discourse III, gives an unexcelled description. "I mean then by the Supreme Being, one who is simply self-dependent, and the only Being who is such: moreover, that He is without beginning or Eternal, and the only Eternal; that in consequence He has lived a whole eternity by Himself; and hence that He is all-sufficient, sufficient for His own blessedness, and all-blessed, and ever-blessed. Further, I mean a Being, who, having these prerogatives, has the Supreme Good, or rather is the Supreme Good, or has all the attributes of Good in infinite intenseness; all wisdom, all truth, all justice, all love, all holiness, all beautifulness; who is omnipotent; omniscient; omnipresent; ineffably one, absolutely perfect; and such, that what we do not know and cannot even imagine of Him, is far more wonderful than what we do and can. I mean One who is sovereign over His own will and actions, though always according to the eternal Rule of right and wrong, which is Himself. I mean, moreover, that He created all things out of nothing, and preserves them every moment, and could destroy them as easily as He made them; and that in consequence, He is separated from them by an abyss, and is incommunicable in all His attributes. And further, He has stamped upon all things, in the hour of their creation, their respective natures, and has given them their work and mission and their length of days, greater or less, in their appointed place. I mean, too, that He is ever present with His works, one by one, and confronts every thing He has made by His particular and most loving Providence, and manifests Himself to each according to its needs; and has on rational beings imprinted the moral law, and given them power to obey it, imposing on them the duty of worship and service, searching and scanning them through and through with His omniscient eye, and putting before them a present trail and a judgment to come." St. Thomas in the S.T. proves the existence of God in PP. Q. 2. Art. 3. Cf. also PP. Q. 2. Art. 1 (utrum Deum esse sit per se notum); PP. Q. 2. Art. 2 (utrum Deum esse sit demonstrabile); et passim, especially PP. Q. 1 through PP. Q. 47 pr. On **arbitrium liberum Dei,** see *arbitrium* under 4; on **credere**

Deo, Deum et in Deum, see *credere* under 2; on **cultus Dei,** see *cultus* under 2; on **donum Dei,** see *donum* under 1; on **electio de Deo dicta,** see *electio* under 1; on **esse Dei,** see *esse;* on **genus Dei,** see *genus* under 1; on **gloria Dei,** see *gloria* under 1; on **homo Deus,** see *homo;* on **iudicium Dei,** see *iudicium* under 1; on **lumen Dei,** see *lumen;* on **nomen Dei,** see *nomen* under 1; on **praeceptum Dei,** see *praeceptum;* on **prophetia Dei,** see *prophetia;* on **providentia Dei,** see *providentia;* on **regnum Dei,** see *regnum;* on **sapientia secundum Deum,** see *sapientia* under 1; on **scientia Dei,** see *scientia* under 2; on **servitus Dei,** see *servitus* under 2; on **spiritus Dei,** see *spiritus;* on **tentatio Dei,** see *tentatio* under 1; on **tristitia secundum Deum,** see *tristitia* under 1; on **virtus Dei,** see *virtus* under 1; on **visio Dei, visio Deo per creaturam et visio Dei per essentiam,** see *visio* under 1; on **vita Dei,** see *vita* under 1; on **voluntas Dei,** see *voluntas* under 2.—**amor Dei est congregativus,** see *amor* under 1.—**Deus et natura nihil frustra faciunt,** see *frustra.*—**Deus nihil facit frustra,** see *frustra.*—**in Deo affirmationes sunt incompactae,** see *affirmatio* under 1.—**in operibus Dei et ecclesiae nihil est vanum et frustra,** see *frustra.*—**in operibus Dei non est aliquid frustra,** see *frustra.*—**natura in sua operatione**

Dei operationem imitatur, see *natura.*—natura nihil facit frustra, ita nec Deus, see *frustra.*—deus, i, *m., a god, a deity.*

deuteronomium, ii, *n., deuteronomy, the second* or *repeated Law, the fifth book of the Pentateuch,* so called because it contains a second statement of the Law.

devasto, are, no perf., atum, 1, *v. a., to lay waste, devastate.*

devenio, ire, veni, ventum, 4, *v. n., to reach, arrive at, come to,* in a figurative sense, used with *in* and *ad* with *acc.*

deviatio, onis, *f., a deviation, departing, a straying from, variation* or *deflection from a customary way, rule, method* or *standard.*

devictus, a, um, *P. a., conquered, vanquished, beaten.*

devio, are, avi, 1, *v. n., to turn from the straight road, go aside, deviate.*

devirgino, are, avi, atum, 1, *v. a., to violate, deprive of virginity.*

devitatio, onis, *f., an avoidance.*

devito, are, avi, atum, 1, *v. a., to avoid, go out of the way of, shun.*

devolvo, ere, volvi, volutum, 3, *v. a.,* mid., *to sink down, fall into.*

devoro, are, avi, atum, 1, *v. a.,* of inanimate things, *to swallow up, ingulf.*

devote, *adv.,* see *devoveo.*

devotio, onis, *f.,* the opposite of *indevotio,* (1) *devotion,* state of being devoted, and one of the interior acts of religion; an act of

the appetitive part of the soul and a special movement of the will to give oneself readily to things concerning the service of God; *fervor, ardor, zeal,* (2) *devotion,* observant attention or notice, as when directed towards a particular person or a given object; *consideration, regard,* (3) *devotion,* an expression of devotedness or devoutness; especially an act of religious worship; *a religious exercise, prayer,* usually in the plural, *devotions.*— Some common phrases are: (a), devotio orationis, *fervor in prayer.*—(b), devotio fidelium, *fervor of the faithful.*—(c), devotio fidei Christianae, *devotion of the Christian faith.*

devoveo, ere, vovi, votum, 2, *v. a., to vow, devote.*—devovere se in mortem, *to devote one's self to death.*—devotus, a, um, *P. a.,* (1) *devout, pious,* (2) *devoted* or *attached* to a person or thing.— devote, *adv., devoutly, with reverence* or *solemnity.*

dexter, tera, terum, also tra, trum, (1) *to the right, on the right side, right,* opposite of *sinister,* (2) *favorable, propitious, fortunate.*

dextrorsum, *adv., towards the right side, to the right side.*

diabolicus, a, um, *adj., devilish, proceeding* or *derived from the devil, characteristic of the devil, diabolic, diabolical.*

diabolus, i, *m., the devil, the chief of the apostate angels, enemy* and *tempter of man;* the prince and ruler of the Kingdom of evil, the arch-enemy of God. In the Old Testament he is commonly alluded to as *Satan*, and in the new Testament as *Beelzebub, serpent, dragon,* and is also described as the *god of this world,* the *evil one* and the *prince of devils.*

diaconatus, us, *m., deaconship, diaconate, the office of a deacon.*

diaconissa, ae, *f., a deaconess,* one one who performed some duties analogous to those of a deacon, with regard to the women of the congregation, catechizing, assisting at baptism, etc. They were not, however, the recipient of any order.

diaconus, i, *m., a deacon,* one of a major order ranking next below the priesthood who assists the priests in all the solemn rites of Christ's Church, particularly at Mass, and in the distribution of of Holy Communion, and in solemn baptism. It is the deacon's duty also to read the gospel in Church and to preach it as one catechizing. They were originally chosen (Acts, vi, 1-5) to administer the temporalities of the Church.

diadema, atis, *n., a royal headdress, a diadem.*

diaeta, ae, *f.,* (1) *a diet, prescribed manner of living,* (2) *a day's journey,* or about twenty-five miles.

dialectice, *adv.,* see *dialecticus.*

dialecticus, a, um, *adj.,* (1) *suited to what has been discussed, in dispute, not possible of certain conclusion, probable,* (2) *suited to discussion, causing debate* or *dispute, not bringing to a certain conclusion.*—On **definitio dialectica,** see *definitio* under 2; on **problema dialecticum,** see *problema;* on **propositio dialectica,** see *propositio* under 2.—On **disputatio dialectica,** see *disputatio;* on **locus dialecticus,** see *locus* under 4; on **medium dialecticum,** see *medium* under 2; on **oratio dialectica,** see *oratio* under 1; on **scientia dialectica,** see *scientia* under 2; on **syllogismus dialecticus,** see *syllogismus.*—**dialectica,** sc. **ars seu scientia,** synonym of *scientia dialectica* and *topica, the art* or *science of discussing* or *debating about something in such a way that no real certainty but only a greater* or *less probability is reached.*—Kinds of *dialectica* are: **dialectica docens,** and **dialectica utens,** *the teaching* and *the using dialectic,* i.e., *the dialectic of theory* or *explanation* and *that of practice* or *application.*—**dialecticus,** i, *m., he who possess the art* or *science of making something probable* and *knows how to practice it, a dialectician, a logician,* the opposite of *demonstrator.*—**dialectice,** *adv., dialectically.*

dialogus, i, *m., a dialogue,* a literary work in the form of a conversation between two or more people. St. Thomas quotes freely from the Dialogorum Libri IV of Gregory the Great.

diametrialiter, *adv.*, *diametrically, in a diametrical manner.*

diametros, i, *f.*, *a diameter.*

diaphaneitas, atis, *f.*, *diaphaneity, transparency.*

diaphanus, a, um, *adj.*, *diaphanous, transparent.* On **corpus diaphanum**, see *corpus.*—**diaphanum**, i, *n.*, *diaphanum*, the transparent or translucent medium of the light.

Diares, is, *m.*, *Diares*, a name mentioned in Aristotle's *De Anima* II, 6, 21, and used by St. Thomas in elucidating a point similar to that treated by Aristotle under the foregoing reference.

diastole, es, *f.*, *diastole*, opp. of *systole*, the regular expansion or dilation of the heart and of the arteries in beating.

dicaion, (*dikaios, a, on*) *adj.*, *observant of the rules of right, righteous, right, just.*

dicibilis, e, *adj.*, *that can be said, applicable.*

dico, are, avi, atum, 1, *v. a.*, *dedicate, consecrate, devote.*

dico, ere, xi, ctum, 3, (1) *to say, speak, talk* in the narrower and wider sense of the word, (2) *signify, name, designate,* synonym of *denominare,* (3) *say, relate, state, declare,* synonym of *praedicare.*—On **relativum secundum dici**, see *relativus.*—Kinds of *dicere* in this sense are: (a), **dicere mentis seu rationis** and **di-**

cere oris seu vocis, *the speaking of the mind* or *reason* and *that of the mouth* or *the voice.*—(b), **dicere oris,** see *dicere mentis.*—(c), **dicere per oppositum alicui,** *to say something in opposition.*—(d), **dicere rationis,** see *dicere mentis.* —(e), **dicere sufficienter,** *to say enough.*—(f), **dicere vocis,** see *dicere mentis.*—**actus et potentia ad se invicem dicuntur,** or, **potentia dicitur ad actum,** *we speak of reality with regard to corresponding possibility* and *of possibility with reference to corresponding reality.*—**bonum et malum dicuntur secundum ordinem ad finem vel privationem ordinis,** *the question of the morally good* or *the morally evil is with reference to the ordering of a thing to its last goal* or *with reference to the denial of this ordering.*—**demonstratio ad demonstrabile dicitur,** *proof is mentioned with reference to that which can be proven.*—**potentia dicitur ad actum,** see above: *actus et potentia* etc.—**quod ab omnibus communiter dicitur, impossibile est totaliter esse falsum,** *what is commonly asserted by all cannot possibly be entirely false.*—**simul intenduntur ea, quae dicuntur ad invicem,** *things that are said with reference to one another are known simultaneously.* On **relatio secundum dici ad aliquid,** see *relatio.*—Kinds of *dicere* in this (2) sense are: (a), **dicere ab aeterno seu** aeternaliter and **dicere de tempore seu ex tempore seu temporaliter,** *to say something as existing from eternity* and *something as existing from a definite time;* in other words, *to say something in the sense of the eternal* and *something in the sense of the temporal.*—(b), **dicere absolute seu simpliciter** and **dicere comparative seu relative seu secundum quid,** *to express something without respect to anything* or *simply* or *absolutely* and *to express something with reference to something else* or *in a certain respect.*—(c), **dicere abstractive seu in abstracto seu ut in abstracto seu per abstractionem** and **dicere concretive seu in concertione seu in concreto,** *to express something in the abstract* and *something in the concrete sense* or *to express something thought of as in the state of a generalization* and *something thought of as in the state of the particular.*—(d), **dicere accidentaliter** and **dicere substantialiter seu secundum substantiam,** *to express something in the sense of an accident* and *something in the sense of a substance.*—(e), **dicere adiective** and **dicere substantive,** *to express something in the sense* or *in the form of an adjective* and *something in the sense* or *in the form of a substantive.*—(f), **dicere aequivoce, dicere analogice seu secundum analogiam** and **dicere univoce,** *to express something in the sense of mere homonymy, something in the sense of analogy* or *proportion* and *something in the sense of homogeneity,* that is, to use words which are the same, but the sense of which is totally different, or comparatively the same, or exactly the same.—(g), **dicere aeternaliter,** see *dicere ab aeterno.*—(h), **dicere affirmative seu positive** and **dicere negative seu privative seu remotive,** *to express something in an affirmative* and *something in a negative sense,* i.e., *something in the sense of existence* and *non-existence.*—(i), **dicere analogice,** see *dicere aequivoce.*—(j), **dicere antonomastice,** *to express antonomastically.*—(k), **dicere causaliter seu effective,** *to express something in the sense of a cause* and *in the sense of a producing cause.*—(l), **dicere comparative,** see *dicere absolute.*—(m), **dicere concretive,** see *dicere abstractive.*—(n), **dicere confuse seu indistincte,** *to express something in an indefinite* or *indistinct manner.*—(o), **dicere conservative,** *to express something in the sense of preservation* or *of the preserving cause.*—(p), **dicere demonstrative** and **dicere probabiliter,** *to express something as necessary* or *as being necessarily true* and *to express something as probable.*—(q), **dicere denominative,** *to express something in the sense of a mere name.*—(r), **di-**

cere determinative and dicere opinative, *to express something in the sense of a fixed determination and something in the sense of an opinion.*—(s), dicere de nullo and dicere de omni, *to express something as belonging to no extensive term or notion of a thing and to express something as extensive term or notion of a thing and to express something as belonging to each of the same.* —(t), dicere de omni, see *dicere de nullo.*—(u), dicere de subiecto, *to say something about its ontological subject,* i.e., *of its substance.*—(v), dicere de tempore, see *dicere ab aeterno.*—(w), dicere effective, see *dicere causaliter.*—(x), dicere eminentius, *to express something in an eminent sense.*—(y), dicere essentialiter seu per essentiam seu substantialiter and dicere participative seu participatione seu per participationem, *to express something in the sense of essence or substance and something in the sense of the participated in or shared.*—(z), dicere ex tempore, see *dicere ab aeterno.*—(a²), dicere figurate seu metaphorice seu per metaphoram seu symbolice seu translative seu per similitudinem and dicere proprie seu per proprietatem seu secundum proprietatem, *to express something in the figurative or symbolic sense and something in the proper sense.*—(b²), dicere in abstracto, see *dicere abstractive.*—

(c²), dicere in concretione, see *dicere abstractive.*—(d²), dicere in concreto, see *dicere abstractive.*—(e²), dicere indistincte, see *dicere confuse.*—(f²), dicere metaphorice, see *dicere figurate.*—(g²), dicere multiplicative, *to express something in the sense of a multiplication.*—(h²), dicere negative, see *dicere affirmative.*—(i²), dicere notionaliter and dicere personaliter, *to express something in the sense of a notio and something in the sense of a person.*—(j²), dicere omnino aequivoce seu proprie seu pure aequivoce, *to express something in the sense of proper or bare equivocation.*—(k²), dicere opinative, see *dicere determinative.*—(l²), dicere participatione, see *dicere essentialiter.*—(m²), dicere participative, see *dicere essentialiter.*—(n²), dicere partitive, *to say something in the sense of a division.*—(o²), dicere passive, *to express something in a passive sense.* Illud passive dicitur, quod a verbo passivo derivatur. —(p²), dicere per abstractionem, see *dicere abstractive.*—(q²), dicere per accidens and dicere per se, *to express something about a thing because of something accompanying it and to express something about a thing as belonging to its nature.*—(r²), dicere per essentiam, see *dicere essentialiter.*—(s²), dicere per modum identitatis and dicere per modum informationis, *to express* something *in the sense of identity* and *something in the sense of giving form.*—(t²), **dicere per modum informationis**, see *dicere per modum identitatis.*—(u²), **dicere per participationem**, see *dicere essentialiter.*—(v²), **dicere per posterius** and **dicere per prius**, *to express something in the sense of the later* and *something in the sense of the earlier*, i.e., *to express something as belonging to a thing later* and *something as belonging to it earlier.*—(w²), **dicere per prius**, see *dicere per posterius.*—(x²), **dicere per proprietatem**, see *dicere figurate.*—(y²), **dicere per se**, see *dicere per accidens.*—(z²), **dicere per similitudinem**, see *dicere figurate.*—(a³), **dicere personaliter**, see *dicere notionaliter.*—(b³), **dicere positive**, see *dicere affirmative.*—(c³), **dicere primo**, *to express something of a thing as belonging to it first.* Omne, quod primo praedicatur, praedicatur per se, sed non convertitur.—(d³), **dicere privative**, see *dicere affirmative.*—(e³), **dicere probabiliter**, see *dicere demonstrative.*—(f³), **dicere proprie**, see *dicere figurate.*—(g³), **dicere proprie aequivoce**, see *dicere omnino aequivoce.*—(h³), **dicere pure aequivoce**, see *dicere omnino aequivoce.*—(i³), **dicere relative**, see *dicere absolute.*—(j³), **dicere remotive**, see *dicere affirmative.*—(k³), **dicere secundum analogiam**, see *dicere aequivoce.*—(l³), **dicere secundum**

opinionem and **dicere secundum veritatem**, *to express something in the sense of a mere opinion* and *something in the sense of a decided truth.*—(m³), **dicere secundum proprietatem**, see *dicere figurate.*—(n³), **dicere secundum quid**, see *dicere absolute.*—(o³), **dicere secundum substantiam**, see *dicere accidentaliter.*—(p³), **dicere secundum veritatem**, see *dicere secundum opinionem.*—(q³), **dicere sicut in facto esse** and **dicere sicut in fieri**, *to express something as in the state of having become* and *to express something as existing in the state of becoming.*—(r³), **dicere sicut in fieri**, see *dicere sicut in facto esse.*—(s³), **dicere similitudinarie**, see *dicere metaphorice.*—(t³), **dicere simpliciter**, see *dicere absolute.*—(u³), **dicere substantialiter**, see *dicere accidentaliter* and *dicere essentialiter.*—(v³), **dicere substantive**, see *dicere adiective.*—(w³), **dicere symbolice**, see *dicere figurate.*—(x³), **dicere temporaliter**, see *dicere ab aeterno.*—(y³), **dicere translative**, see *dicere figurate.*—(z³), **dicere universaliter**, *to express something general or common about a thing.*—(a⁴), **dicere univoce**, see *dicere aequivoce.*—(b⁴), **dicere ut in abstracto**, see *dicere abstractive.*—**dictum**, i, *n.*, *something said*, i.e., *a saying, a word.*

dictamen, inis, *n.*, (late Lat. for *dictum*), *utterance, dictum, prescription.*

dictio, onis, *f.*, (1) *saying, talking, speech,* synonym of *locutio,* (2) *figure of speech, idiom, mode of expression,* synonym of *locutio, nomen, terminus,* and *oratio.—* On **fallacia extra dictionem, fallacia in dictione et fallacia figurae dictionis,** see *fallacia* under 2; on **figura dictionis,** see *figura* under 2; on **paralogismus extra dictionem et in dictione,** see *paralogismus.—*Kinds of *dictio* in this (2) sense are: (a), **dictio aequivoca,** *the equivocal* or *ambiguous expression.—*(b), **dictio aliquis sive quidam, dictio omnis, dictio non-omnis,** and **dictio nullus,** *the expression of someone* or *of a certain person, the expression of everyone, the expression of not everyone,* and *the expression of no-one,* i.e., *the particular affirmative, the general affirmative, the particular negative,* and *the general negative.—*(c), **dictio categorematica** and **dictio syncategorematica,** *the categorematical* and *the syncategorematical expression,* or *a restrictive* and *non-restrictive modification.—*(d), **dictio causalis,** *the expression which indicates a cause* or *a reason.—*(e), **dictio composita** and **dictio simplex,** *the composite* and *the simple expression* i.e., *the expression composed of several words* or *that forms a sentence* and *that which consists of a single word.—*(f), **dictio exclusiva,** *the exclusive expression* or *that*

which indicates an exclusion.— (g), **dictio exercens aliquid sive officialis** and **dictio significans aliquam rem conceptam,** *the expression that carries out something* or *that performs a duty* or *that indicates a considered thing.—*(h), **dictio non-omnis,** see *dictio aliquis.—*(i), **dictio nullus,** see *dictio aliquis.—*(j), **dictio officialis,** see *dictio exercens aliquid.—*(k), **dictio omnis,** see *dictio aliquis.—*(l), **dictio per se significans,** *the expression that indicates something by itself alone.* —(m), **dictio quidam,** see *dictio aliquis.—*(n), **dictio significans aliquem rem conceptam,** see *dictio exercens aliquid.—*(o), **dictio simplex,** see *dictio composita.* —(p), **dictio syncategorematica,** see *dictio categorematica.—*(q), **dictio tertia,** *the third expression in a sentence,* i.e., *the copula.*

dicto, are, avi, atum, 1, *v. freq. a.,* to *prescribe, decree, recommend, dictate.—***dictans,** ntis, *P. a., dictating, directing the words* or *substance of.*

Didymus, i, *m., Didymus,* head of the catechetical school of Alexandria in the fourth century, was born in 309 or 314 A.D. The best information about Didymus is derived from Jerome who refers to him as his old teacher and "my seer". Writing in 392, De Viris Illustribus 109, he gives a short biographical account of Didymus. Jerome translated Didymus' treatise on the Holy

Spirit and prefixed a preface to it; this treatise was a protest against Macedonianism.

dies, ei, *m.*, (in sing. sometimes f.,) (1) *day,* the natural day, as opposed to night, the period from dawn to dark, (2) *day,* the twenty-four hours that elapse during one revolution of the earth upon its axis, (3) *day* (a) any period of time occupied by some course of operations, (b) *days* of creation; these were creative days, stages in the process of creation, but not days of twenty-four hours.— Common phrases are: **de die in diem,** *from day to day.*—**in die,** *daily, every day.*—**de die,** *for the day, daily.*—**tota die,** *all the time.* —**dies et noctes,** *day* and *night, unceasingly.*—**dies iudicii,** *the day of judgment.*—**dies mortis,** *day of death.*—**dies sabbati,** *the Sabbath day.*—**dies dominica,** *the Lord's day, Sunday.*—**dies gloriae,** *the day of glory* or *the perfect day.*—**dies festi,** *holy days.*— **dies nativitatis,** *a birthday.*—**dies solemnes,** *days of solemnity.*— **dies fausti vel infausti,** *lucky* or *unlucky days.*—**dies dominicales,** *dominical days,* days relating to Christ as the Lord, or to Sunday as the Lord's Day.—**dies circumcisionis,** *day of circumcision.*— **dies purgationis,** *the day of purification.*—**dies azymorum,** *day of the Azymes, the Passover.*—**dies festus Paschae,** *the festival day of the Pasch.*—**dies passionis,** *the day of the Passion, Good Friday.*

—**novissimus dies,** *the last day, the day of final judgment.*—**dies ascensionis,** *the day of the Ascension, Ascension Day.*—**dies resurrectionis,** *day of the resurrection, Easter Sunday.*—**dierum Antiquus,** *the Ancient of Days, God the Father.*—**dies Pentecostes,** *the day of Pentecost.*—**dies Natalis,** *a birthday,* especially Christ's birthday.

diffamatio, onis, *f., defamation.*

diffamo, are, avi, atum, 1, *v. a., to defame, bring disrepute upon; disgrace, dishonor.*

differenter, *adv.,* see *differo.*

differentia, ae, *f., the difference between two things in this* or *that respect but not in all respects,* not as radical as *diversitas,* but more than *distinctio,* the opposite of *convenientia* and *similitudo,* a quality which distinguishes one class or type from another. In logic, and in philosophy, the concept of *differentia* is a most important one. It is that which makes each thing to be what it is specifically. It is the active, determining element which restricts and confines the potential and determinable extension of a genus to this or that species. Thus the species, "rational animal," is constituted by limiting the genus "animal" by the difference "rational" setting this species off from all other animals which are not-rational. It is the formal element in any definition; the genus is the material element. On the relation of *differentia* to *distinctio* and *diversitas*, see *distinctio* under 2, and *diversitas*. On **nomen differentiae**, see *nomen* under 1.— Kinds of *differentia*, as understood in the general sense of the word, are: (a), **differentia accidentalis** and **differentia substantialis seu essentialis**, *the unessential* and *the essential difference*.—(b), **differentia affirmativa** and **differentia negativa**, *the difference which consists in something positive* and *that which consists in something negative*.— (c), **differentia communis** and **differentia particularis seu propria**, *the universal* or *general difference* and *the special* or *particular difference*.—(d), **differentia completiva sc. speciei**, *the difference that brings about the true nature* or *species of a thing* or *that brings it to a conclusion*, identical with *differentia specifica ultima*.—(e), **differentia constituens speciem seu constitutiva speciei**, *the difference that brings out the true nature of a species*, again identical with *differentia specifica ultima*.—(f), **differentia constitutiva**, see *differentia constituens*.—(g), **differentia contrahens seu determinans**, *the difference that limits* or *defines a genus*.—(h), **differentia contraria seu opposita** and **differentia media**, *the difference opposed to another* and *the middle difference* or *that lying between two opposite differences*. —(i), **differentia determinans**, see *differentia contrahens*.—(j), **differentia diversificans seu dividens seu divisiva**, *the difference that divides* or *separates a kind*. —(k), **differentia dividens**, see *differentia diversificans*.—(l), **differentia divisiva**, see *differentia diversificans*.—(m), **differentia essentialis**, see *differentia accidentalis*.—(n), **differentia formalis** and **differentia materialis**, *the difference which springs from the form* and *that which springs from the material of a thing*.— (o), **differentia generis seu secundum genus**, **differentia speciei seu secundum speciem** and **differentia secundum numerum**, *the difference of genus, that of species*, and *individual difference*.—(p), **differentia immediata**, *the immediate difference* or *that which divides a genus immediately*.—(q), **differentia incompossibilis**, *the difference which is not possible together with another difference*.—(r), **differentia loci**, see *locus*.—(s), **differentia materialis**, see *differentia formalis*.—(t), **differentia media**, see *differentia contraria*.—(u), **differentia negativa**, see *differentia affirmativa*.—(v), **differentia opposita**, see *differentia contraria*. —(w), **differentia particularis**, see *differentia communis*.—(x), **differentia per accidens** and **differentia per se**, *the difference that belongs to a thing as such* and *through its own nature* and *that which belongs to it only incidentally.*—(y), **differentia perfecta**, *the perfect* or *the greatest difference.*—(z), **differentia per se**, see *differentia per accidens.*—(a²), **differentia posterior** and **differentia prior**, *the later* and *the earlier difference* or *that which comes to a thing according to its nature later* and *that which comes to it according to its nature earlier.*—(b²), **differentia prima** and **differentia ultima seu specifica ultima**, *the first* and *the last difference* or *the difference that belongs to a thing according to nature first* and *that which belongs to it according to nature last.*—(c²), **differentia prima contraria**, *the first of the opposite differences in a thing.*—(d²), **differentia prior**, see *differentia posterior.*—(e²), **differentia propria**, see *differentia communis.*—(f²), **differentia realis**, *the objective difference.*—(g²), **differentia secundum genus**, see *differentia generis.*—(h²), **differentia secundum numerum**, see *differentia generis.*—(i²), **differentia secundum speciem**, see *differentia generis.*—(j²), **differentia simplex**, *the simple difference.*—(k²), **differentia speciei**, see *differentia generis.*—(l²), **differentia specifica seu specificans**, *the difference of genus* or *that difference which establishes the species* and *essence.*—(m²), **differentia specifica ultima**, see *differentia*

prima.—(n²), **differentia substantialis**, see *differentia accidentalis.*—(o²), **differentia ultima**, see *differentia prima.*—(p²), **differentia vera**, *the true difference.*—**definitio est ex genere et differentia**, see *definitio.*—**species constituitur ex genere et differentia**, see *species.*

differo, differre, distuli, dilatum, *v. a.* and *n.*, (1) *to put off, defer, delay,* (2) *be different* in the one or the other point but not in all points.—**dilatus**, a, um, *P. a.*, *delayed, deferred.*—On the difference between *differre* and *diversum esse*, see *diversus.*—Kinds of *differre* in this (2) sense are: (a), **differre genere, differre specie seu secundum speciem,** and **differre numero,** *to be different according to genus, according to species* and *according to the individual.*—(b), **differere materialiter** and **differre secundum formam,** *to be different according to matter* and *different according to form.*—(3), **differre numero,** see *differre genere.*—(d), **differre secundum obiectum,** *to be different according to object* or *end.*—(e), **differre per essentiam** and **differre supposito seu secundum hypostasim seu substantiam,** *to be different according to essence* and *according to suppositum* or *to be different according to individual substance.*—(f), **differre ratione seu secundum rationem** and **differre re seu secundum rem seu realiter,** *to be different ac-*

cording to reason and *reality* or *according to idea* and *according to fact.*—(g), **differre re,** see *differre ratione.*—(h), **differre realiter,** see *differre ratione.*—(i), **differre secundum essentiam,** *to differ according to essence.*—(j), **differre secundum formam,** see *differre materialiter.*—(k), **differre secundum hypostasim,** see *differre per essentiam.*—(l), **differre secundum rationem,** see *differre ratione.*—(m), **differre secundum rem,** see *differre ratione.*—(n), **differre secundum speciem,** see *differre genere.*—(o), **differre secundum substantiam,** see *differre per essentiam.*—(p), **differre specie,** see *differre genere.*—(q), **differre supposito,** see *differre per essentiam.*—**differens,** entis, *P. a., different, superior.*—**differenter,** *adv., differently.*

difficilis, e, *adj.,* (1) *hard, difficult, troublesome,* (2) *of character, hard to manage, slow, surly, ill-tempered, morose.*—*Adv.,* in three forms but *difficile* is used most frequently.—(a), **difficile,** *with difficulty.*—(b), **difficiliter,** *with difficulty.*—(c), **difficulter,** *with difficulty.*—*Adv. phrase,* **de difficili,** *with difficulty.*

difficiliter, *adv.,* see *difficilis.*

difficultas, atis, *f.,* (1) *a difficulty, obstacle, hinderance,* the state or quality of being difficult; the condition of a work or task as greatly beset with obstacles or perplexities; the character of a thing as requiring much effort,

wisdom or skill to do or accomplish it, also that which makes a thing hard to do or accomplish, (2) *a difficulty,* an objection rendering a doctrine or statement hard to receive; that which renders something not easy to understand or explain.

difficulter, *adv.,* see *difficilis.*

diffidentia, ae, *f., diffidence, distrust, unbelief.*—**filii diffidentiae,** *sons of despair.*—**sine spei diffidentia,** *with unfailing hope.*

diffinio, see *definio.*

diffinitio, see *definitio.*

diffinitive, see *definitive.*

diffinitivus, see *definitivus.*

difformis, e, *adj., not uniform, manifold,* the opposite of *conformis* and *uniformis.* On **motus difformis,** see *motus;* on **pars difformis,** see *pars.*—**difformiter,** *adv., in an ununiform* or *manifold manner, not uniformly, multifariously,* the opposite of *conformiter* and *uniformiter.*

difformitas, atis, *f., difformity, the state* or *quality of being unlike* or *difformed* or *of irregular form, manifoldness,* the opposite of *conformitas* and *uniformitas.* On **motus difformitatis,** see *motus.*

difformiter, see *difformis.*

diffundo, ere, fudi, fusum, 3, *v. a., to pour out, let run out, let flow over, spread out, impart.*—**diffundens,** entis, *P. a., diffusing, spreading.*—**diffusus,** a, um, *P. a., spread out, extended, diffuse.*—**diffuse,** *adv., in a scattered manner, copiously.*

diffusio, onis, *f.,* *pouring out, spreading out, imparting.*—**summa diffusio voluntatis est per modum amoris,** see *voluntas* under 2.

diffusive, *adv.,* see *diffusivus.*

diffusivus, a, um, *adj., pouring out, spreading, imparting,* synonym of *communicativus.*—**bonum est diffusivum et communicativum,** see *bonus.*—**diffusive,** *adv., in the manner* or *in the sense of pouring out, of spreading out, of imparting, diffusively.*

digero, ere, gessi, gestum, 3, *v. a.,* (1) *to dissolve, clear away, wear away,* (2) *to digest.*—**digerens,** entis, *P. a., digesting, dissolving.*—**digestus,** a, um, *P. a.,* (a) *digested, absorbed,* (b) *seasoned, prepared.*—**digesta,** orum, *n., Digests, the name given to a collection of writings distributed under certain heads, especially of Justinian's code of laws, the Pandects, Digests.*

digesta, orum, *n.,* see *digero.*

digestio, onis, *f.,* (1) *a dividing of food, dissolving, digestion,* the process by which food taken into the body is dissolved and chemically changed so that it can be assimilated by the blood and furnish nutriment to the body; the separation of the nutritious from the waste elements, (2) *fermentation.*

digestivus, a, um, *adj., digestive, pertaining to digestion.*

digitus, i, *m., a finger, any digit of*

the hand.—**pulpae digitorum,** *finger-tips.*

dignativus, a, um, *adj., decent, proper,* synonym of *condignativus* and *condignus.* On **unio dignativa,** see *unio.*

digne, *adv.,* see *dignus.*

dignifico, are, avi, atum, 1, *v. a., to think worthy, dignify,* used with *acc.* of the person and *abl.* of the thing.

dignitas, atis, *f.,* (1) *dignity, worthiness, worth,* (2) *fundamental truth, principle, axiom,* the *axioma* or *koinon legomenon axioma* of Aristotle (cf. Anal. post. 1. 2, 72 a. 17; 10, 76 b. 14). On **iustum secundum dignitatem,** see *iustus;* on **ordo dignitatis et secundum dignitatem,** see *ordo* under 1; on **prius ordine dignitatis,** see *prior* under 1.—A kind of *dignitas* in this (2) sense is: **dignitas communis seu prima,** *the general* or *first principle.*

dignor, ari, atus, 1, *v. dep. a., to deem worthy* or *deserving,* used with the *acc.* of the person and the *abl.* of the thing, (2) *to regard as fit, becoming, worthy of one's self, to deign;* and with a negative, *not to deign, to disdain,* used with the *inf.* as object.

dignoscentia, ae, *f., the power of distinguishing, knowledge.*

dignosco, ere, 3, *v. a., to know apart, distinguish, discern* one thing from another, used *absol.,* with *ab* and *abl.,* the *acc.*

dignus, a, um, *adj., worthy, suitable, fitting, proper.*—**digne,** *adv., worthily, fitly, becomingly.*

digredior, i, gressus, 3, *v. dep. n., to go away, depart.*

diiudicatio, onis, *f., a judging, deciding, determining.*

diiudico, are, avi, atum, 1, *v. a., to judge by discerning* or *distinguishing, to decide, determine.* With the idea of the particle predominating, *to discern by judging, to distinguish between two things.*

dilabor, i, lapsus, 3, *v. dep. n.,* (1) *to go to ruin, be lost, perish, decay,* (2) *to let fall, drop,* (3) *to fall to a lower state, to fall into sin.*

dilanio, are, avi, atum, 1, *v. a., to divide into pieces, tear.*—**dilaniatus,** a, um, *P. a., torn, mangled.*

dilatatio, onis, *f., dilatation, expansion, extension, enlarging, an extending,* the opposite of *constrictio.*—**dilatatio sui,** *self-dilatement, a puffing up of one's self.*

dilatio, onis, *f., a putting off, delaying, deferring, delay, lapse of time.*

dilato, are, avi, atum, 1, *v. freq. a.* and *n.,* (1) *to expand, dilate, spread out, enlarge,* (2) *to swell as* with importance; *assume a pompous air.*

dilectio, onis, *f.,* (1) *love* in the sense of an act of the will, which takes place on the basis of a previous choice of the will, (2) *love* in the sense of a *dos,* (3) *love* in the sense of a title of address.— On **affectus dilectionis,** see *affectus* under 2; on **praeceptum dilectionis,** see *praeceptum.*— Kinds of *dilectio* in this (1) sense are: (a), **dilectio amicitiae** and **dilectio concupiscentiae,** *the love of friendship* and *that of desire.* —(b), **dilectio beata,** *the beatific* and *the beatifying love of angels* and *men in heaven.*—(c), **dilectio charitatis seu charitativa,** *the love that consists in charitas* or *love for God.*—(d), **dilectio charitativa,** see *dilectio charitatis.*— (e), **dilectio concupiscentiae,** see *dilectio amicitiae.*—(f), **dilectio creata** and **dilectio increata,** *the created* and *the uncreated love* or *the love of the creature* and *that of the creator.*—(g), **dilectio electiva** and **dilectio naturalis,** *love by choice* and *love by nature,* i.e., *love that rests upon free choice* and *that which rests on natural impulse.*—(h), **dilectio essentialis** and **dilectio notionalis,** *the essential love* and *that forming a notio.*—(i), **dilectio gloriae** and **dilectio gratuita,** *love in the glory of heaven* and *that bestowed by grace.*—(j), **dilectio gratuita,** see *dilectio gloriae.*— (k), **dilectio imperfecta seu insufficiens** and **dilectio perfecta,** *the imperfect* or *insufficient love* and *the perfect love.*—(l), **dilectio increata,** see *dilectio creata.* —(m), **dilectio insufficiens,** see *dilectio imperfecta.*—(n), **dilectio meritoria,** *the meritorious love.*—

(o), **dilectio naturalis,** see *dilectio electiva.*—(p), **dilectio non recta** and **dilectio recta,** *the wrong* and *the right love.*—(q), **dilectio notionalis,** see *dilectio essentialis.*—(r), **dilectio perfecta,** see *delectio imperfecta.*—(s), **dilectio politica seu politicae virtutis,** *civic love* or *love of political virtue.*—(t), **dilectio politicae virtutis,** see *dilectio politica.*—(u), **dilectio recta,** see *dilectio non recta.*

dilector, oris, *m., a lover.*

dilectus, us, see *delectus.*

diligenter, see *diligo.*

diligentia, ae, *f.,* (1) *diligence, carefulness, proper heed* or *attention, care, caution,* the degree of personal care, attention or effort due from one in a given situation, opposite of *negligentia,* (2) *parsimony, undue sparingness* in the expenditure of money, *extreme economy, closeness, stinginess.*

diligibilis, e, *adj., estimable, amiable, lovable.*

diligibilitas, atis, *f., loveableness.*

diligo, ere, lexi, lectum, 3, *v. a., to value* or *esteem highly, love,* synonym of *amo.*—**diligens,** P. a., *loving, attentive, diligent.*—**diligenter,** adv., *carefully, attentively, diligently.*—**dilectus,** a, um, P. a., *loved, beloved, dear.*

dilucide, adv., *clearly, brightly, plainly.*

diluculum, ii, *n., day-break, dawn.*

diluo, ere, ui, utum, 3, *v. a., to wash away,* used figuratively.

diluvium, ii, *n., a deluge, a great overflowing of the land by water; flood;* specifically, the flood in the time of Noe recorded in Gen. VII.

dimensio, onis, *f., extent, dimension.* On **indivisibile secundum dimensionem,** see *indivisibilis;* on **materia dimensioni subiecta,** see *materia* under 3.—Kinds of *dimensio* are: (a), **dimensio completa** and **dimensio incompleta,** *the complete* and *the incomplete dimension.*—(b), **dimensio imaginaria** and **dimensio realis,** *the imaginary* and *the real dimension.*—(c), **dimensio incompleta,** see *dimensio completa.*—(d), **dimensio indeterminata seu interminata** and **dimensio terminata,** *the undetermined* or *unlimited dimension* and *the limited dimension.*—(e), **dimensio interminata,** see *dimensio indeterminata.*—(f), **dimensio quantitativa,** *dimension of quantity.*—(g), **dimensio realis,** see *dimensio imaginaria.*—(h), **dimensio sacramentalis,** *sacramental dimension.*—(i), **dimensio separata,** *the dimension separated from matter.*—(j), **dimensio terminata,** see *dimensio indeterminata.*

dimensionatus, a, um, *adj., dimensioned, having dimensions, dimensional.*—On **quantitas dimensiva,** see *quantitas* under 1.—**dimensive,** adv., *extensively.*

dimidius, a, um, *adj., half.*—**dimidium,** ii, *n., the half.*

diminuo, ere, —, diminutum, 3, *v. a., to diminish, lessen.* On **complementum diminutum,** see *complementum;* on **determinatio diminuens,** see *determinatio* under 1; on **dispositio diminuens,** see *dispositio* under 4; on **ens diminutum,** see *ens;* on **potentia diminuta,** see *potentia* under 2.— **diminuens,** entis, *P. a., diminishing, lessening.*—**diminutus,** a, um, *P. a., diminished, lessened.*—**diminute,** *adv., diminutely, incompletely.*

diminute, *adv.,* see *diminuo.*

diminutio, onis, *f.,* (1) *the act of diminishing in quality, value, rank, size, reduction, lessening, diminution,* (2) *the condition of being diminished, diminution,* the opposite of *augmentum* and *additio.*

diminutive, *adv.,* see *diminutivus.*

diminutivus, a, um, *adj., diminutive, tending to diminish.*—**diminutive,** *adv., diminutively, as a diminutive.*

dimissio, onis, *f.,* (1) *a remission, the act of remitting, discharge from penalty, pardon, deliverance, absolution,* (2) *a dismissal, leave to depart, divorce,* (3) *a bequeathment.*

dimitto, ere, misi, missum, 3, *v. a.,* (1) *discharge, dismiss, release, let go, divorce,* (2) *discharge from penalty, remit, pardon, absolve.*—**dimissus,** a, um, *P. a., discharged, dismissed, pardoned, absolved.*

Dinandum, i, *n., Dinant,* a town in Namur province, Belgium, supposedly the birthplace of David of Dinant, a pantheistic philosopher of the thirteenth century.

dinotica, (sc. *potentia*), ae, *f., cunningness, cleverness,* the *deinotes* of Aristotle, natural diligence which may be directed to both good and evil.

dioecesanus, a, um, *adj., diocesan, of* or *pertaining to a diocese.*

diocesis, is, *f., a bishop's jurisdiction, diocese, the territory* or *churches under a bishop's jurisdiction.*

Diocletianus, i, *m., Diocletian* (284-305, A.D.), a celebrated Roman emperor born of an obscure family in Dalmatia in the town of Dioclea from which he derived his first name, probably originally Docles, afterwards lengthened to the Greek form Diocles, and after his accession to the Empire to the Roman form Diocletianus.

Dionysius, ii, *m., Dionysius, the Pseudo-Areopagite.* He lived from the very earliest to the latter half of the fifth century, and was in all probability a native of Syria. He was a Christian Platonist and a disciple of Proclus. His writings were translated into Latin about 858 A.D. by Scotus Erigena. St. Thomas quotes abundantly from three principal works of Dionysius: *De Divinis Nominibus, De Coelesti (Angelica) Hierarchia,* and *De Eccle-*

siastica Hierarchia. There are also a few scattered references to the *Theologia Mystica* and various letters—*ad Demophilum, ad Polycarpum, ad Caium monachum, ad Dorotheum,* and *ad Ioannem Evangelistam.*

Dioscorus, i, *m.*, (1) *Dioscorus,* a physician whose conversion and baptism are related by Augustine to Alypius in epistle 227. In all probability this is the same Dioscorus who wrote to Augustine enclosing a number of questions on Cicero and philosophy. Augustine who was just recovering from an illness, and overwhelmed with business, wrote him a long letter (Ep. 118) refusing his request, and telling him that such questions are obsolete. However, he proceeds to give him the principles of his own philosophy in the same way as in his letters to Coelestinus and Consentius, (2) *Dioscorus,* patriarch of Alexandria, succeeded Cyril in the bishopric about midsummer in 444 A.D. After he had involved himself in the Monophysite heresy, he was accused of having greatly misconducted himself in the first year of his episcopate. Already in June 445 Pope Leo the Great wrote him a letter in which he pointed out to Dioscorus the existing abuses in the church at Alexandria. His name is conspicuous on the list of "violent men" in church history.

directe, *adv.,* see *dirigo.*

directio, onis, *f.,* (1) *direction, guidance,* (2) *direction,* act of directing or focusing the attention on a single object, (3) *direction,* the act of directing or aiming something, (4) plural, *directions,* facts of knowledge, *solutions.*

directivus, a, um, *adj., giving direction, directing, guiding, directive.* On **donum directivum,** see *donum* under 1; on **vis directiva,** see *vis* under 2.

directus, a, um, *P. a.,* see *dirigo.*

diremptio, onis, *f., a separation.*

dirigibilis, e, *adj., dirigible, capable of being directed* or *guided.*

dirigo, ere, rexi, rectum, 3, *v. a., to direct, guide, arrange.—***dirigens,** entis, *P. a., directing, guiding, arranging.—***directus,** a, um, *P. a.,* (1) *straight, direct, directed,* opposite of *indirectus,* (2) *perpendicular, vertical,* also the opposite of *indirectus.* On **causa directa,** see *causa;* on **contrarietas directa,** see *contrarietas;* on **deductio directa,** see *deductio;* on **fieri in directum,** see *fieri;* on **infinitum in directum,** see *infinitus;* on **motus directus,** see *motus;* on **movere in directum,** see *movere;* on **oppositio directa,** see *oppositio.—***directe,** *adv.,* (1), *directly to a goal,* either immediately or mediately, i.e., with or without media which lie in the way of the goal to be attained, the opposite of *indirecte* and *oblique,* (2) *in a direct manner,* the opposite of *indirecte* and *mediate*, (3) *vertically*.—On **apprehendere directe**, see *apprehendere* under 2; on **causa movens**, see *causa* under 1; on **causa directe dicta**, see *causa* under 2; on **cognoscere directe**, see *cognoscere* under 2; on **disponere directe**, see *disponere* under 2; on **facere directe**, see *facere* under 1; on **oppositum directe**, see *opponere;* on **syllogismus directe concludens**, see *syllogismus;* on **velle directe**, see *velle;* on **voluntarium directe**, see *voluntarius* under 3.

dirimo, ere, emi, emptum, 3, *v. a.,* to break, off, end by destroying a connection or bond, used figuratively.

diripio, ere, ui, eptum, 3, *v. a.,* to rob, take away, despoil.

dirumpo, ere, rupi, ruptum, 3, *v. a.,* to burst asunder, break.

diruo, ere, rui, rutum, 3, *v. a.,* to tear asunder, demolish, destroy.

dirus, a, um, *adj., fearful, awful, harsh.*

discalceatus, a, um, *adj., unshod, bare-footed.*

discedo, ere, cessi, cessum, 3, *v. n.,* (1) with the notion of *cedere* predominating, *to depart from* any place or person, *to go away from,* (a) used with *ab, ex* and *abl.,* (b) designating the terminus ad quem, (2) *give up, forsake, leave, recede, withdraw,* used figuratively, (3) *cease, vanish, disappear.*

disceptatio, onis, *f.,* (1) *a discussion, debate,* the process of discussing any question, (2) *a disquisition, an examination* or *inquiry.*

discerno, ere, crevi, cretum, 3, *v. a.,* (1) *to separate things according to their qualities, distinguish between, discern,* (2) *to determine, resolve, decide,* (3) *to reveal, indicate distinctly.*—**discernens**, ntis, *P. a., discerning, distinguishing between.*—**discretus**, a, um, *P. a., discrete, made up of distinct parts* or *separate units, discontinuous.*

discerpo, ere, psi, ptum, 3, *v. a.,* to tear to pieces, rend, tear.—**discerpens**, ntis, *P. a., tearing.*

discessus, us, *m., departure, a going away.*

disciplina, ae, *f.,* (1) *instruction* in the passive sense of the word, i.e., *to be instructed,* opposite of *doctrina,* (2) *knowledge, science,* (3) *department of instruction, branch of instruction, science, art,* synonym of *ars, doctrina,* and *scientia,* (4) *mathematics,* Aristotelian *mathema* (Phys. II. 9, 200 a 15; De Cael III. 1, 299 a 4), (5) *discipline, education, schooling, training.*—On **paralogismus disciplinae**, see *paralogismus.*—Kinds of *disciplina* in this (3) sense are: (a), **disciplina agonastica, seu luctativa** and **disciplina exercitiva seu gymnastica,** *the art of wrestling* and *gymnastics.*—(b), **disciplina exercitiva,** see *disciplina agonastica.*

—(c), **disciplina figurativa,** *the forming art.*—(d), **disciplina grammatica seu litterarum** and **disciplina rationalis,** *grammar* and *logic.*—(e), **disciplina illiberalis seu servilis** and **disciplina liberalis,** *the servile* and *the free art* or *the art of the slave* and *that of the free man.*—(f), **disciplina iudicativa** and **disciplina rhetorica,** *the art of judging* and *that of rhetoric.* On **scientia iudicativa,** see *scientia.*—(g), **disciplina liberalis,** see *disciplina illiberalis.*—(h), **disciplina litterarum,** see *disciplina grammatica.*—(i), **disciplina medicativa,** *the art of healing* or *medical science.*—(j), **disciplina musica seu musicae,** *music.*—(k), **disciplina philosophica** and **disciplina theologica,** *the philosophical* and *theological science.*—(l), **disciplina rationalis,** see *disciplina grammatica.*—(m), **disciplina rhetorica,** see *disciplina iudicativa.*—(n), **disciplina servilis,** see *disciplina illiberalis.*—(o), **disciplina theologica,** see *disciplina philosophica.* —Kinds of *disciplina* in this (4) sense are: (a), **disciplina legum,** *the training of the law* or *through the laws.*—(b), **disciplina paterna,** *paternal training.*

disciplinabilis, e, *adj.,* (1) *capable of being learned, capable of being trained, capable of being broken in,* (2) *capable of being taught, producing knowledge, serving the knowledge of reason,* the opposite of *indisciplinabilis.*

—On **sensus disciplinabilis,** see *sensus* under 3.—**disciplinabiliter,** *adv., after the manner* or *in the sense of proof which demonstrates something as being necessarily true, in an instructive manner.*

disciplinabiliter, *adv.,* see *disciplinabilis.*

disciplinalis, e, *adj.,* (1) *instructive,* (2) *producing a certain knowledge,* (3) *mathematical.*—On **syllogismus disciplinalis,** see *syllogismus.*—(3) on **scientia disciplinalis,** see *scientia* under 1.

disciplinatus, a, um, *adj.,* (1) *well trained, brought up,* (2) *instructed, well instructed, scientifically educated,* (3) *mathematically educated.*

discipulatus, us, *m., discipleship, the condition of a disciple.*

discipulus, i, *m.,* (1) *a disciple,* one who believes the teaching of another, or who adopts and follows some doctrine of another, (2) *a disciple,* one who receives instruction, a *pupil* or *learned.*

disco, ere, didici, 3, *v. a., to learn, learn to know, become acquainted with,* used with *acc., acc.* and *inf., rel. cl.,* and *absol.*

discohaerentia, *f., disconnection, incoherence,* does not occur in S.T.

discontinuatio, onis, *f., lack of connection, incoherence,* does not occur in S.T.

discontinuo, are, avi, atum, 1, *v. a.* and *n., to separate, disconnect, make incoherent.*

discontinuus, a, um, *adj., not directly connected, not hanging together, discontinuous,* synonym of *intercisus* and *discretus,* the opposite of *continuous.*

disconvenientia, ae, *f., an inconvenience, want of agreement, inconsistency, disagreement.*

discooperio, ire, perui, pertum, 4, *v. a., to uncover, remove the covering from,* used with the abl.—**discoopertus,** a, um, *P. a., uncovered.*

discordia, ae, *f., disagreement, dissension, discord,* the opposite of *concordia.*

discordo, are, avi, 1, *v. n.,* (1) of animate things, *to disagree, be at variance, differ, quarrel,* (2) of inanimate things, *to be unlike, out of harmony with, to disagree, be inconsistent with, opposed to,* the opposite of *concordo.*—**discordans,** ntis, *P. a., disagreeing, clashing, being at variance.*

discredo, ere, didi, ditum, 3, *v. a., to be incredulous towards, not to believe.*

discrepans, ntis, *P. a., discrepant, varying, different.*

discrepantia, ae, *f., unlike condition,* the state of being disparate or dissimilar, *discordance, discrepancy.*

discrete, *adv.,* (1) *in a separate* or *special manner,* synonym of *discretive,* the opposite of *unite* and *unitive,* (2) *with distinction, with circumspection.*

discretio, onis, *f.,* (1) *growing apart, dilation, loosening,* synonym of *disgregatio and rarefactio,* the opposite of *concretio, condensatio, congregatio* and *inspissatio,* (2) *separation, division, discrimination,* synonym of *distinctio, divisio,* and *separatio,* the opposite of *confusio* and *unitio,* (3) *distinction,* the opposite of *indiscretio,* (4) *the distinction between good* and *evil, discretion, knowledge,* (5) *distinction, difference,* synonym of *distinctio.*—Kinds of *discretio* in this (2) sense are: (a), **discretio communis seu unita** and **discretio propria,** *the common* or *united discrimination* and *the particular* or *peculiar discrimination,* i.e., *the discrimination common to several things* and *therefore being only one* and *that peculiar to each of them.*—(b), **discretio divina seu in divinis,** *the divine discrimination* or *that which takes place in God.*—(c), **discretio in divinis,** see *discretio divina.*—(d), **discretio propria,** see *discretio communis.*—(e), **discretio realis,** and **discretio secundum rationem,** *the real* and *the notional discrimination.*—(f), **discretio secundum rationem,** see *discretio realis.*—(g), **discretio unita,** see *discretio communis.* On **iudicium discretionis,** see *iudicium* under 2 and 3. On *discretio* in this (3) sense, note the following: **discretio sapientiae,** *the discrimination* of *wisdom* or *the discrimination made with wisdom.*

discretive, *adv.,* see *discretivus.*

discretivus, a, um, *adj.,* (1) *separating, dividing, discriminating,* synonym of *disgregativus,* the opposite of *concretivus, congregativus,* and *unitivus,* (2) *distinguishing.*—On **terminus discretivus,** see *terminus;* on **vis discretiva,** see *vis.*—**discretive,** *adv., after the manner* or *in the sense of dividing* or *of discriminating, in a separate* or *special manner, discretively,* synonym of *discrete,* the opposite of *unite* and *unitive.*

discretor, oris, *m., a discerner, he who discerns* or *judges.*

discrimen, inis, *n., chance, risk, hazard, undetermined probability in general.*

discrimino, are, avi, atum, 1, *v. a., to discriminate, distinguish, note* or *set apart as different, perceive the difference between.*

discurro, ere, curri and cucurri, cursum, 3, *v. n.,* (1) *to run to* and *fro, run around, run through something,* (2) *go from one thing to another in thought, think over* and *over, examine, discuss, infer, conclude,* synonym of *ratiocinari;* the opposite of *intellegere.* On **intellegere discurrendo,** see *intellegere* under 1; on **potentia discurrens,** see *potentia* under 2.

discursive, *adv.,* see *discursivus.*

discursivus, a, um, *adj., inferring, concluding, of* or *pertaining to* *the understanding* or *power of connected thinking;* exhibiting the process and method of ratiocination; elaborative as opposed to intuitive, synonym of *ratiocinotivus.* On **cognitio discursiva,** see *cognitio* under 2; on **consideratio discursiva,** see *consideratio;* on **intellectus discursivus,** see *intellectus* under 3; on **motus discursivus,** see *motus* under 2; on **scientia discursiva,** see *scientia* under 2.—**discursive,** *adv., in the manner* or *sense of inferring* or *concluding.*

discursus, us, *m.,* (1) *running here* and *there, rambling, running through, course,* (2) *thoughtful transition from one thing to another, discussion, conference, deduction,* synonym of *ratio* and *ratiocinatio,* the opposite of *cognitio sine discursu, intellectus,* and *simplex intuitus.* On **cognoscere per discursum,** see *cognoscere* under 2; on **intellegere cum et sine discursu,** see *intellegere* under 1.

discussio, onis, *f.,* (1) *a shaking, shock,* (2) *discussion, examination.*—On **dubitatio discussionis,** see *dubitatio.* On **iudicum discussionis,** see *iudicium* under 2.

discutio, ere, cussi, cussum, 3, *v. a., to examine, scrutinize, consider, discuss.*

disgregatio, onis, *f., a putting apart, dispersing, disunion, separation,* synonym of *discretio* and *rarefactio,* the opposite of *concretio,* *congregatio, condensatio,* and *inspissatio.*

disgregativus, a, um, *adj., putting apart, dispersing, loosening, separating,* synonym of *discretivus,* the opposite of *concretivus, congregativus,* and *unitivus.*

disgrego, are, 1, *v. a.,* (1) *to separate, dilate, enlarge in all directions,* (2) *disperse, disunite, separate, scatter, divide.*

disiunctim, *adv., in the manner* or *sense of separating, of putting apart,* synonym of *divisim,* the opposite of *coniunctim* and *copulatim.*

disiunctio, onis, *f., separation, putting apart.* On **accipere sub disiunctione,** see *accipere* under 3; on **inducere sub disiunctione,** see *inducere* under 2; on **ponere sub disiunctione,** see *ponere* under 3.

disiunctivus, a, um, *adj., separating, putting apart,* synonym of *divisivus.* On **enuntiatio disiunctiva,** see *enuntiatio* under 2; on **propositio disiunctiva,** see *propositio* under 2; on **syllogismus disiunctivus,** see *syllogismus.*

disiungo, ere, xi, ctum, 3, *v. a., to separate, disjoin, disunite, sever, divide.*—**disiunctus,** a, um, *P. a., separated, excluded.* On **pars disiuncta,** see *pars* under 1; on **proportionalitas disiuncta,** see *proportionalitas;* on **terminus disiunctus,** see *terminus* under 4.

dispar, aris, *adj., unlike, dissimilar, different, unequal.*

disparatus, a, um, *P. a., unpaired, dissimilar, disparate, having no distinct relation in common,* so different that they cannot be put together in pairs, the opposite of *par.* On **forma disparata,** see *forma* under 2; on **relatio disparata,** see *relatio;* on **scientia disparata,** see *scientia* under 1; on **species disparata,** see *species* under 8.

dispareo, ere, ui, itum, 2, *v. n., to disappear, vanish, vanish out of sight.*

disparitas, atis, *f., impossibility of being paired, complete difference, disparity.*—Kinds of *disparitas* are: (a), **disparitas cultus,** *complete difference in the worship of God as practiced by Christians* and *non-Christians.*—(b), **disparitas fidei,** *complete difference in religious belief as opposed to disparitas cultus which is concerned with the externals of worship.*

dispartior, iri, 4, *v. a., to distribute.*

dispendium, ii, *n.,* (1) *loss, the art* or *state of losing, failure to keep* or *win,* (2) *privation, misfortune.*

dispensabilis, e, *adj., dispensable,* that may be removed by or made the subject of a dispensation.

dispensatio, onis, *f.,* (1) *distribution, dispending, administration,* (2) *apportionment, imposition,* (3) *arrangement, disposition, management,* (4) *freeing, release, dispensation.*—Kinds of *dispensatio* in this (3) sense are: **dispensatio communis** and **dispen-**

satio specialis, *the general* and *the particular management.*

dispensative, *adv.,* see *dispensativus.*

dispensativus, a, um, *adj., distributing, dispensing, managing.* On **iustum dispensativum,** see *iustus.*—**dispensative,** *adv., after the manner* or *in the sense of disengaging, separating, freeing from a precept* or *legal obligation, by way of exception, dispensatively,* synonym of *dispensatorie* or *per dispensationem.*

dispensator, oris, *m., distributer, dispenser, administrator.*

dispensatorie, *adv., after the manner* or *in the sense of a disengaging, a separating, a freeing from a precept* or *legal obligation,* synonym of *dispensative.*

dispenso, are, avi, atum, 1, *v. freq. a.,* (1) *to distribute, dispense, manage,* (2) *allot, impose,* (3) *arrange, dispose, establish,* (4) *lose, disengage, free from a precept* or *a legal obligation.*

disperdo, ere, didi, ditum, 3, *v. a., to disperse, drive in different directions,* used with *de* and *abl.*

dispereo, ire, ii, 4, *v. n., to go completely to ruin, be lost, disappear.*

dispergo, ere, si, sum, 3, *v. a., to scatter on all sides, to divide, disperse,* used lit. and fig.

dispersio, onis, *f., dispersion, the act of scattering* or *the state of being scattered.*

dispertio, ire, ivi or ii, itum, 4, *v. a., to distribute, divide.*

displicentia, ae, *f., displeasure, pain, discomfort.*

displiceo, ere, ui, itum, 2, *v. n., to displease, vex, annoy, offend.*

dispono, ere, posui, positum, 3, *v. a.,* (1) *to take apart, distribute, arrange, dispose,* (2) *prepare, establish, make suitable, affect,* (3) *order, command, decree.*—On **actio disponens,** see *actio* under 1; on **causa disponens,** see *causa* under 2; on **principium disponens,** see *principium;* on **ratio disponens,** see *ratio* under 12.—Kinds of *disponere* in this (2) sense are: **disponere directe** and **disponere removendo prohibens,** *to prepare directly* and *indirectly,* i.e., to prepare something so that one immediately aims at it, or so that one removes the obstacle that stands in the way of it.—**disponens,** entis, *P. a., disposing, preparing, decreasing.*—**dispositum,** a, um, *P. a., disposed, prepared, decreed.*

dispositio, onis, *f.,* (1) *systematic arrangement, management, disposition,* (2) *systematic iuxtaposition, disposal, placing,* (3) *preparation, bent of mind, inclination, condition, suitableness,* synonym of *praeparatio* and *habitus,* the opposite of *indispositio,* (4) *position, site,* synonym of *positio* and *situs,* (5) *order, prescription, ordinance.* In general, according to St. Thomas, matter is the subject of dispositions, as distinguished from the habits of the intellect and the will. Disposition is the more easily changed.—Kinds of *dispositio* in this (2) sense are: **dispositio assistentium** and **dispositio ministrantium,** *the position of an assitant* or *owner* and *that of the serving* or *servants.*—On the difference between *dispositio* and *habitus,* see *habitus.* On **ignorantia dispositionis seu secundum dispositionem seu perversae dispositionis,** see *ignorantia* under 1; on **perfectio dispositionis,** see *perfectio* under 2; on **prius ordine dispositionis,** see *prior* under 1.—Kinds of *dispositio* in this (3) sense are: (a), **dispositio accidentalis,** *the unessential disposition.* —(b), **dispositio activa** and **dispositio passiva,** *the disposition to act* and *that to be acted upon.* —(c), **dispositio actualis,** and **dispositio habitualis,** *the disposition that is explicit, here* and *now,* and *that which is prolonged, continual,* and *implicit.* —(d), **dispositio aegritudinalis** and **dispositio bestialis,** *the sickly disposition* and *the beastly disposition.*—(e), **dispositio animae** and **dispositio corporis seu corporales,** *the condition of the mind* and *that of the body* or *the physical condition.*—(f), **dispositio bestialis,** see *dispositio aegritudinalis.*—(g), **dispositio contrahens seu in partem contrahens˙ seu specificans, dispositio diminuens** and **dispositio corrumpens seu totaliter corrumpens,** *the disposition that limits something*

completely or *partially* or *makes it a species, that diminishes it,* and *that destroys it utterly.*—(h), **dispositio contumeliativa,** *the disposition inclined to insult.*— (i), **dispositio corporalis,** see *dispositio animae.*—(j), **dispositio corporis,** see *dispositio animae.*— (k), **dispositio corrumpens,** see *dispositio contrahens.*—(l), **dispositio debita,** *the disposition that ought to be* or *the proper disposition.*—(m), **dispositio determinata,** *a definite disposition, the disposition determined in this way* or *that.*—(n), **dispositio diminuens,** see *dispositio contrahens.*—(o), **dispositio gratuita** and **dispositio naturalis,** *the disposition bestowed by grace* and *the natural disposition.*—(p), **dispositio habitualis,** see *dispositio actualis.*—(q), **dispositio inordinata** *the disordered* or *inorderly disposition.*—(r), **dispositio in partem contrahens,** see *dispositio contrahens.*—(s), **dispositio mala,** *the bad disposition.*—(t), **dispositio materialis,** *the disposition of a thing according to its matter.*— (u), **dispositio naturalis,** see *dispositio gratuita.*—(v), **dispositio passiva,** see *dispositio activa.*— (w), **dispositio perfecta,** *the perfect* and *the perfectly developed disposition.*—(x), **dispositio propinqua seu proxima** and **dispositio remota,** *the imminent* or *immediate disposition* and *the disposition remote to some act related to it.*—(y), **dispositio pro-**

pria, *the proper* or *particular disposition.*—(z), **dispositio remota,** see *dispositio propinqua.*—(a²), **dispositio specificans,** see *dispositio contrahens.*—(b²), **dispositio totaliter corrumpens,** see *dispositio contrahens.*—(c²), **dispositio ultima,** *the last disposition of a thing towards an action.*

dispositive, *adv.,* see *dispositivus.*

dispositivus, a, um, *adj., preparing, arranging, making suitable, dispositive.* On **causa dispositiva,** see *causa* under 2; on **finis dispositivus,** see *finis* under 2; on **principium dispositivum,** see *principium.*—**dispositive,** *adv., in the manner* or *in the sense of preparation, of arrangement, dispositively.*

disputatio, onis, *f., disputation, scientific discussion,* i.e., *discussion about a thing with a presentation of the arguments which speak for or against it.*—Kinds of *disputatio* are: (a), **disputatio demonstrativa seu doctrinalis seu magistralis,** *the demonstrating disputation* or *the disputation of the teacher* or *the master which shows a thesis to be certain* and *necessary.*—(b), **disputatio dialectica,** *the dialectic disputation* or *that which shows a thing probable.*—(c), **disputatio doctrinalis,** see *disputatio demonstrativa.*—(d), **disputatio litigiosa seu sophistica,** *the quarrelsome* or *subtle disputation.*—(e), **disputatio magistralis,** see *disputatio demonstrativa.*—(f), **disputatio pro-**

pria, *the disputation proper to an object* or *the peculiar disputation* which corresponds to it and its principles.—(g), **disputatio publica,** *the public disputation.*—(h), **disputatio rhetorica,** *the rhetorical disputation* or *the disputation of the orator.*—(i), **disputatio sophistica,** see *disputatio litigiosa.*—(j), **disputatio tentativa,** *the disputation assigned as a test* or *experiment of something.*—(k), **disputatio theologica,** *the theological dispute* or *the dispute assigned to a theological subject.*

disputative, *adv.,* see *disputativus.*

disputativus, a, um, *adj., disputing, disputative,* i.e., *speaking for* or *against a thing for the sake of argument* and *classification.* On **modus disputativus,** see *modus;* on **oratio disputativa,** see *oratio;* on **ratio disputativa,** see *ratio.*—**disputative,** *adv., after the manner* and *in the sense of the disputation, disputatively.*

disputo, are, avi, atum, 1, *v. n.* and *a., dispute, discuss, argue.*

disquiro, ere, 3, *v. a., to penetrate, pierce to the meaning of, discern,*

disrumpo, ere, rupi, ruptum, 3, *v. a.,* (1) *to tear asunder, destroy,* (2) *to break off, sever,* used fig.

dissemino, are, avi, atum, 1, *v. a., to spread abroad, disseminate.*

dissensio, onis, *f., dissension, angry* or *violent difference of opinions, disagreement accompanied by contention, discord, clashing, strife.*

dissensus, us, *m., dissent, the act* or *state of dissenting, refusal of assent, approval* or *agreement,* opposite of *assensus.*

dissentio, ire, si, sum, 4, *v. n.,* (1) *to dissent, disagree in opinion, think* or *feel in a contrary manner, withhold assent,* also *withhold approval* and *consent,* used with *ab, in* and *abl., inter se,* (2) of inanimate things, *dissent, be unlike, dissimilar, differ, be out of harmony with,* (3) *dissent, to refuse adherence to the teaching of the established Church.*

dissero, ere, rui, rtum, 3, *v. a., to discuss, speak, discourse, treat of a thing,* used with *de* and *abl.*

dissideo, ere, edi, essum, 2, *v. n.,* (1) *to be separate, be apart, lack compactness,* used with *inter se,* (2) *contradict, think differently,* used with the *dative.*

dissidium, ii, *n.,* (1) *a dividing, disturbance, disunion, dispute, dissension,* (2) *a separation, divorce.*

dissimilis, e, *adj., dissimilar, unlike, different,* used *absol.,* with *dat., gen., ad* and *acc., in* and *abl., ab* and *abl., de* and *abl.—dissimiliter, adv., differently, in a different manner.*

dissimiliter, *adv.,* see *dissimilis.*

dissimilitudo, inis, *f., unlikeness, difference, dissimilitude,* opposite of *similitudo.*

dissimulatio, onis, *f., dissimulation, a dissembling, concealing, disguising, connivance.*

dissimulo, are, avi, atum, 1, *v. a.,* (1) *to dissemble,* (2) *neglect, leave unnoticed.*

dissipatio, onis, *f., destruction.*

dissipator, oris, *m., a disperser, destroyer.*

dissipo, are, avi, atum, 1, *v. a.,* (1) *to demolish, destroy* by tearing down, (2) *squander, waste profusely,* (3) *dissipate, pursue pleasure* or *indulgence to excess,* (4) *disperse* or *scatter utterly.*

dissolubilis, e, *adj., dissoluble, that may be dissolved.*

dissolutio, onis, *f.,* (1) *dissolution,* the act of dissolving, destroying something or of separating it into parts, (2) *dissolution,* the act of destroying a connection or bond, (3) *dissolution, laxity, want of firmness, a slackening* or *abating,* synonym of *remissio,* (4) *dissolution, the breaking up of a multitude,* (5) *dissolution,* the act of annulling or setting aside.

dissolvo, ere, solvi, solutum, 3, *v. a.,* (1) *dissolve, destroy, separate into parts,* (2) *relax, loosen, dissipate,* (3) *dissolve, annul.—dissolutus,* a, um, *P. a., dissolved, destroyed, relaxed, loosened.*

dissonantia, ae, *f.,* (1) *dissonance, disaccord, discordance, want of accord, state of being inharmonious, a repugnance, incongruousness,* opposite of *consonantia* and synonym of *repugnantia,* (2) *a discrepancy, a disagreement between things which are expected to correspond.*

dissono, are, 1, *v. n., to disagree, differ, be at variance,* used with *ab* and *abl.,* the *dative.*—**dissonans,** ntis, *P. a., disagreeing.*

dissonus, a, um, *adj., discordant, inconsistent, contradictory* or *disagreeing.*

dissuadens, ntis, *P. a., dissuading.* Ideo libellus scribebatur, ut mora interveniente et consilio scribarum dissuadente, vir a proposito repudiandi desisteret, PT S. Q. 67, Art. 7 c.

dissuesco, ere, 3, *v. n., to become unaccustomed to,* opposite of *consuesco.*

dissuetudo, dinis, *f., a becoming unaccustomed, disusing, desuetude.*

distans, antis, *P. a.,* see *disto.*

distantia, ae, *f., distance, remoteness.*—Kinds of *distantia* are: (a), **distantia determinata seu finita** and **distantia infinita,** *the determined* or *finite distance* and *the infinite distance.*—(b), **distantia extrema seu maxima,** *the extreme of greatest distance.*—(c), **distantia finita,** see *distantia determinata.*—(d), **distantia infinita,** see *distantia determinata.*—(e), **distantia maxima,** see *distantia extrema.*

distemperantia, ae, *f., distemperature, bodily derangement, state of disturbance, the absence* or *lack of a relation which ought to exist,* opposite of *temperamentum* and *temperantia.*

distempero, are, avi, atum, 1, *v. a.,* and *n., to distemper, affect with*

disease or *disorder.*—**distemperatus,** a, um, *P. a., distempered, of unequal temperature.*

distillo, are, avi, atum, 1, *v. a.,* and *n., to drop* or *trickle down, distil.*—**distillans,** ntis, *P. a., trickling, dropping.*

distincte, *adv.,* see *distinguo.*

distinctim, *adv., distinctly.*

distinctio, onis, *f.,* (1) *separation, division, distinction, discrimination,* synonym of *discretio* and *divisio,* the opposite of *confusio* and *unitas,* (2) *state of separation, unlikeness, difference,* synonym of *discretio,* the opposite of *identitas* and *unitas.*—Kinds of *distinctio* in this sense are: (a), **distinctio essentialis** and **distinctio personalis seu personae,** *the essential* and *the personal difference* or *the difference in essence* and *that in person.*—(b), **distinctio formae seu secundum formam seu formalis** and **distinctio materiae seu materialis,** *difference according to form,* i.e., *specific,* and *that according to matter,* i.e., *numerical* or *even generic.*—(c), **distinctio formalis,** see *distinctio formae.*—(d), **distinctio in communi** and **distinctio specialis,** *the general* and *the particular difference.*—(e), **distinctio in substantia seu substantiae,** *difference according to substance* or *according to essence.*—(f), **distinctio localis,** *local difference* or *difference according to place.*—(g), **distinctio**

materiae, see *distinctio formae.*
—(h), **distinctio materialis,** see
distinctio formae.—(i), **distinctio
numeralis seu secundum nume-
rum** and **distinctio specei,** *the
difference according to number*
and *that according to species.*
—(j), **distinctio personae,** see
distinctio essentialis.—(k), **distinctio personalis,** see *distinctio essentialis.*—(l), **distinctio quantitativa,** *difference in size.*—(m),
**distinctio realis seu secundum
rem** and **distinctio secundum
rationem tantum,** *the real* and
the merely notional difference.
Things are really distinct when
they lack identity apart from or
independently of the consideration of the mind; things are rationally distinct when that which
is in reality one offers different aspects to the mind, whence
different concepts or ideas are
formed. Every real distinction
is also rationally distinct but not
vice versa.—(n), **distinctio relationis,** *the difference in respect
to something.*—(o), **distinctio secundum formam,** see *distinctio
formae.*—(p), **distinctio secundum
numerum,** see *distinctio numeralis.*—(q), **distinctio secundum
ordinem** and **distinctio secundum originem,** *the difference of
order* or *rank* and *that according
to origin.*—(r), **distinctio secundum rationem tantum,** see *distinctio realis.*—(s), **distinctio secundum res,** see *distinctio realis.*
(t), **distinctio specialis,** see *di-*

stinctio in communi.—(u), **distinctio speciei,** see *distinctio numeralis.*—(v), **distinctio suppositi,**
*difference according to a sin-
gle substance.*—**quanto distinctio
prior est, tanto propinquior est
unitati,** *the earlier a difference
between two things, the closer
is the unity of the same,* i.e., if
several differences prevail between two things, of which one
supports the other, then there
arises a difference in that respect wherein the things are one
or similar, the more closely so,
the sooner it is added to the
series of differences.

distinctivus, a, um, *adj., distinctive,
indicating distinction* or *difference, separating, dividing,* the
opposite of *constitutivus.* On **signum distinctivum,** see *signum*
under 1.

distinguibilis, e, *adj., distinguish-
able, capable of being distinguished, separated* or *recognized
as distinct.*

distinguo, ere, nixi, nctum, 3, *v.
a., to separate, divide, distinguish.* On **cognitio distincta,** see
cognitio under 2; on **effectus
distinctus,** see *effectus;* on **esse
distinctum,** see *esse;* on **forma
distincta,** see *forma* under 2; on
relatio distinguens personam,
see *relatio;* on **subsistens distinctum,** see *subsistens* under 3; on
substantia distinguens, see *substantia* under 1; **on suppositum
distinctum et realiter distinctum,**
see *suppositum* under 2.—Kinds

of *distinguere* are: (a), **distingui accidente** and **distingui substantialiter seu secundum esse substantiale,** *to be distinguished according to accident* and *according to substance.*—(b), **distingui formaliter** and **distingui materialiter,** *to be distinguished according to form* and *according to matter.*—(c), **distingui materialiter,** see *distingui formaliter.*—(d), **distingui per aliud** and **distingui per se seu seipso seu secundum seipsum,** *to be distinguished through something else* and *through itself.*—(e), **distingui per se,** see *distingui per aliud.*—(f), **distingui ratione seu secundum rationem** and **distingui realiter seu secundum rem,** *to be distinguished according to notion* and *according to fact.*—(g), **distingui realiter,** see *distingui ratione.*—(h), **distingui relatione originis seu secundum originem,** *to be distinguished with regard to origin* or *according to origin.*—(i), **distingui secundum ad aliquid** and **distingui secundum aliquid,** *to be distinguished through a relation with something* and *to be distinguished through something absolute.*—(j), **distingui secundum aliquid,** see *distingui secundum ad aliquid.*—(k), **distingui secundum esse substantiale,** see *distingui accidente.*—(l), **distingui secundum originem,** see *distingui relatione originis.*—(m), **distingui secundum rationem,** see *distin-*

gui ratione.—(n), **distingui secundum rem,** see *distingui ratione.*—(o), **distingui secundum seipsum,** see *distingui per aliud.*—(p), **distingui secundum speciem,** *to be distinguished according to species.*—(q), **distingui seipso,** see *distingui per aliud.*—(r), **distingui substantialiter,** see *distingui accidente.*—(s), **distingui supposito,** *to be distinguished according to single substance.*—**distinguens,** entis, *P. a., separating, distinguishing.*—**distinctus,** a, um, *P. a., separated, separate, distinct.*—**distincte,** *adv., distinctly, clearly, in a definite manner,* the opposite of *confuse* and *indistincte.*

disto, are, 1, *v. n., to stand apart, be separated, be distant.*—**distans,** antis, *P. a., standing apart, being removed, distant.*

distortus, a, um, *P. a., distorted, misshapen, deformed.*

distractio, onis, *f.,* (1) *alienation,* the act of alienating or making over the possession of a thing to another so as to make it his property, (2) *distraction,* a drawing off or diversion of the mind from some object claiming attention.

distraho, ere, xi, ctum, 3, *v. a.,* (1) *to distract, divert* or turn aside the mind from concentrating on some particular thing, (2) in mercant. lang., *to sell separately in parcels, to retail,* (3) *to divide, sunder,* (4) *to withdraw, remove.*—**distrahens,** ntis, *P. a., distracting.*

distribuo, ere, ui, utum, 3, *v. a., to divide, distribute, apportion.*

distributio, onis, *f.*, (1) *distribution, disposing,* (2) *partition, separation.*—Kinds of *distributio* in this (1) sense are: (a), **distributio absoluta** and **distributio accommodata**, *simple distribution* or that which includes all that comes into consideration and the accommodated distribution or that which is valid only for some.—(b), **distributio accommodata,** see *distributio absoluta.*—(c), **distributio commensurata**, *commensurate distribution.*—(d), **distributio universalis**, *the common distribution.*

distributive, *adv.*, see *distributivus.*

distributivus, a, um, *adj.*, (1) *disposing, distributive,* (2) *dividing, separating.*—On **iustitia distributiva**, see *iustitia;* on **iustum distributivum**, see *iustus.*—On **signum distributivum**, see *signum* under 1.—**distributive**, *adv., in the manner* or *sense of dividing* or *distributing, distributively,* synonym of *divise, divisim,* and *divisive,* the opposite of *collective, composite,* and *coniunctim.* On **intellegere distributive**, see *intellegere* under 3; on **sumere distributive**, see *sumere* under 3.

distributor, oris, *m., a distributer.*

districte, *adv.*, see *districtus.*

districtio, onis, *f., strictness,* the character of being strict in any sense.

districtus, a, um, *P. a., strict, severe, mortified.* On **vita districta,**

see *vita* under 3.—**districte**, *adv., strictly, severely.*

ditio, onis, *f., sway, power, rule, authority.*

dito, are, avi, 1, *v. a., to enrich, increase the wealth of.*

diu, *adv., a long time, long while, long.*—**diutius**, *comp., longer.* Occasionally there is no comparison intended, and then *diutius* = *a long time, very long.*

dium, i, *n., the open sky, the open air.*

diurnus, a, um, *adj., diurnal, daily, of* or *belonging to the day.*

diutinus, a, um, *adj., of long duration, lasting, long.*

diutius, *adv.*, see *diu.*

diuturne, *adv.*, see *diuturnus.*

diuturnitas, atis, *f., length of time, long duration, durability,* (a) with the *genitive,* (b) *absolutely.*

diuturnus, a, um, *adj., of long duration, lasting, long.*—**diuturne**, *adv., long, a long time.*

divello, ere, velli, velsum, 3, *v. a.,* (1) *to displace, separate, remove,* (2) *tear away from,* used fig.

diverbero, are, *no perf.*, atum, 1, *v. a., to sunder, destroy.*

diversificativus, a, um, *adj., making otherwise* or *different, diversifying.*

diversifico, are, avi, atum, 1, *v. a., to make otherwise* or *different, diversify.*—Kinds of *diversificare* are: **diversificare formaliter** and **diversificare materialiter**, *to make something different according to form* and *to do so according to matter.*

diversimode, *adv., otherwise, in a different manner, in another way, differently.*

diversitas, atis, *f., complete distinction, difference,* synonym of *differentia,* the opposite of *identitas* and *unitas.* On relatio diversitatis, see *relatio;* on relativum diversitatis, see *relativus.*—Kinds of *diversitas* are: (a), diversitas accidentalis seu accidentis, and diversitas substantiae seu secundum substantiam seu essentiae, *the unessential* and *the essential difference.*—(b), diversitas accidentis, see *diversitas accidentalis.*—(c), diversitas actualis and diversitas potentialis, *the real* and *the potential difference.*—(d), diversitas continuitatis, *the difference of the immediate connection,* i.e., *the difference which has resulted from the partition of a continuation.*—(e), diversitas essentiae, see *diversitas accidentalis.*—(f), diversitas formae seu formalis and diversitas materiae seu materialis, *the formal* and *the material difference, the difference according to form* and *according to matter.*—(g), diversitas formalis, see *diversitas formae.*—(h), diversitas generis seu in genere seu secundum genus, diversitas speciei seu in specie seu secundum speciem and diversitas individuii seu in numero seu secundum numerum, *the difference of genus, that of species,* and *that according to the single thing* or *individual.*—(i), diversitas gradus, *difference according to degree.*—(j), diversitas hypostasis seu suppositi seu secundum suppositum and diversitas naturae seu naturalis, *the difference according to the single substance* and *that according to nature.*—(k), diversitas individui, see *diversitas generis.*—(l), diversitas in genere, see *diversitas generis.*—(m), diversitas in numero, see *diversitas generis.*—(n), diversitas in specie, see *diversitas generis.*—(o), diversitas materiae, see *diversitas formae.*—(p), diversitas materialis, see *diversitas formae.*—(q), diversitas naturae, see *diversitas hypostasis.*—(r), diversitas naturalis, see *diversitas hypostasis.*—(s), diversitas potentiae materiae, *the difference in the potentiality* and *in the possibility of matter.*—(t), diversitas rationis and diversitas realis, *the notional* and *the real difference.*—(u), diversitas secundum genus, see *diversitas generis.*—(v), diversitas secundum numerum, see *diversitas generis.*—(w), diversitas secundum speciem, see *diversitas generis.*—(x), diversitas secundum substantiam, see *diversitas accidentalis.*—(y), diversitas secundum suppositum, see *diversitas hypostasis.*—(z), diversitas significationis and diversitas suppositionis, *the difference in the designation* and *that in the meaning.*—(a²), diversitas speciei, see *diversitas generis.*—(b²), **diversitas substantiae,** see *diversitas accidentalis.*—(c²), **diversitas suppositi,** see *diversitas hypostasis.*—(d²), **diversitas suppositionis,** see *diversitas significationis.*—(e²), **diversitas susceptivi,** *the difference of the susceptible principle* or *of the subject.*

diversorium, i, *n., a lodging place, an inn.*

diversus, a, um, *adj., completely* or *absolutely different, diverse, opposite, contrary, conflicting,* synonym of *differens,* antonym of *idem* and *unus.*—Kinds of *diversus* are: (a), **diversus actu** and **diversus cogitatione seu ratione,** *different in reality* and *in thought* or *according to notion.*—(b), **diversus cogitatione,** see *diversus actu.*—(c), **diversus genere, diversus specie seu secundum speciem,** and **diversus numero,** *different according to genus, according to species,* and *according to number* or *according to the single thing.*—(d), **diversus numero,** see *diversus genere.*—(e), **diversus ratione,** see *diversus actu.*—(f), **diversus secundum accidens** and **diversus secundum substantiam,** *different unessentially* and *essentially.*—(g), **diversus secundum speciem,** see *diversus genere.*—(h), **diversus secundum substantiam,** see *diversus secundum accidens.*—(i), **diversus simpliciter,** *different simply* or *absolutely.*—(j), **diversus specie,** see *diversus genere.*

—**diversum,** i, *n., the opposite, the different, the contrary.*

diverto, ere, ti, sum, 3, *v. n., to part, separate, turn aside.*—**diversus,** a, um, *P. a.,* see *diversus, adj.*

dives, itis, and **dis,** dite, *adj., rich.* —*Comp.,* **ditior.**—*Sup.,* **ditissimus.**

divido, ere, visi, visum, 3, *v. a.,* (1) *to divide, separate, distribute,* synonym of *distinguere* and *resolvere,* the opposite of *componere,* (2) *distinguish.*—On **differentia dividens,** see *differentia;* on **intellectus dividens,** see *intellectus* under 4; on **intellegere componendo et dividendo,** see *intellegere* under 1; on **sensus dividens,** see *sensus* under 8. —Kinds of *dividere* in this sense are: (a), **dividere ex opposito,** *to divide in the sense* and *from the point of view of the opposition* or *contrast.*—(b), **dividere per accidens,** and **dividere per se seu proprie,** *to divide something according to something which belongs to it accidently* or *to divide unintentionally* and *to to divide something according to itself* or *according to its nature* and *reality, to divide intentionally.*—(c), **dividere per se,** see *dividere per accidens.*—(d), **dividere proprie,** see *dividere per accidens.*—**divisum non condividitur dividentibus,** *the divided is not divided exactly as the things which divide it* or *into which it is divided,* i.e., *the division of* *the whole is made otherwise than each of its member's division.*—nullum divisibile est sua divisio, qua dividitur, see *divisio.* —sensus non componit vel dividit, see *sensus.*—dividens, entis, P. a., *dividing, separating, distinguishing.*—divisus, a, um, P. a., *divided, separated, distinguished*—divise, adv., *after the manner of division or separation, divisively,* synonym of *distributive, divisim, divisive,* the opposite of *collective, complexe, composite, coniunctim.* On intellegere divise, see *intellegere under* 3; on recipere divise, see *recipere* under 3; on sumere divise, see *sumere* under 3; on tenere divise, see *tenere* under 7.—divisim, adv., *after the manner of division or separation, divisively,* synonym of *distributive, divise, divisive,* the opposite of *collective, complexe, composite,* and *coniunctim.* On intellegere divisim, see *intellegere* under 1.

divinatio, onis, f., (1) *prophecy, divination,* i.e., *any prophecy of a future thing,* (2) *foretelling,* i.e., the forbidden or superstitious prophecy of a future thing, (3) *divine opinion* obtained through divine revelation.—Kinds of *divinatio* in the general sense are: divinatio illicita seu superstitiosa and divinatio licita seu non-superstitiosa, *forbidden* or *superstitious* and *the permitted* or *non-superstitious prophecy.* On superstitio divinationis, see *su-*

perstitio.—One kind of *divinatio* in this (2) sense is: divinatio sortium, *fortune-telling from the casting of lots.*

divinativus, a, um, adj., (1) *prophesying, foretelling,* (2) *divining, guessing.*—On sors divinativa, see *sors* under 1; on superstitio divinativa, see *superstitio.* —On scientia divinativa, see *scientia* under 1.

divinator, oris, m., *a soothsayer, diviner.*

divinatorius, a, um, adj., *divinatory, of* or *pertaining to divination.*

divinitas, atis, f., (1) *deity* in the abstract sense of the word, *divinity,* (2) *deity* in the concrete sense of the word, *God.*—divinitas fontana, *the divine fountainhead.* On cultus divinitatis, see *cultus* under 2.

divinitus, adv., (1) *divinely, by divine providence* or *influence,* (2) *by divine communication, by inspiration, prophetically.*

divino, are, avi, atum, 1, v. a., *to foresee, divine,* also *to foretell, predict, prophesy,* used *absol.*— divinans, ntis, m., *a diviner.*

divinus, a, um, adj., *divine,* i.e., *becoming to God, belonging to God, concerning God, proceeding from God, leading to God, like unto God.* On aeternitas divina, see *aeternitas;* on agens divinum, see *agens under* 4; on amor divinus, see *amor* under 1; on attributum divinum, see *attributum;* on auctoritas divina, see *auctoritas* under 4; on beneficium divinum, see *beneficium;* on bonitas divina, see *bonitas* under 1 and 2; on bonum divinum, see *bonus* under 3; on cognitio divina, see *cognitio* under 2; on communicatio divina, see *communicatio* under 3; on corpus divinum, see *corpus;* on correctio divina, see *correctio;* on cultus divinus, see *cultus* under 1; on discretio divina, see *discretio* under 2; on dogma divinum, see *dogma;* on dominium divinum, see *dominium;* on electio divina, see *electio* under 1; on ens divinum, see *ens;* on esse divinum, see *esse;* on essentia divina, see *essentia;* on forma divina, see *forma* under 2; on fruitio divina, see *fruitio;* on generatio divina, see *generatio* under 1; on gloria divina, see *gloria* under 1; on habitus divinus, see *habitus* under 4; on influxus divinus, see *influxus;* on inspiratio divina, see *inspiratio;* on instinctus divinus, see *instinctus;* on intellectus divinus, see *intellectus* under 1 and 3; on intelligibile divinum, see *intelligibilis* under 2; on iudicium divinum, see *iudicium* under 1 and 2; on ius divinum, see *ius* under 1; on iustitia divina, see *iustitia* under 1; on lex divina, see *lex* under 1; on lumen divinum, see *lumen;* on mandatum divinum, see *mandatum;* on motio divina, see *motio;* on natura divina, see *natura;* on nomen divinum, see *nomen* under 1; on officium divinum,

see *officium* under 2; on opus divinum, see *opus* under 1; on passio divina, see *passio* under 2; on perfectio divina, see *perfectio* under 2; on philosophia divina, see *philosophia;* on potentia divina, see *potentia* under 2; on potestas divina, see *potestas* under 3; on praedicatio divina, see *praedicatio* under 2; on prophetia divina, see *prophetia;* on providentia divina, see *providentia;* on ratio divina, see *ratio* under 8 and 12; on regimen divinum, see *regimen;* on regula divina, see *regula* under 1; on relatio divina, see *relatio;* on res divina, see *res;* on revelatio divina, see *revelatio;* on sapientia divina, see *sapientia* under 1 and 3; on scientia divina, see *scientia* under 1 and 2; on scriptura divina, see *scriptura* under 2; on similitudo divina, see *similitudo* under 1; on spiritus divinus, see *spiritus;* on substantia divina, see *substantia* under 2; on suppositum divinum naturae, see *suppositum* under 2; on trinitas divina, see *trinitas* under 1; on veritas divina, see *veritas* under 1; on virtus divina, see *virtus* under 1, 4, and 5; on visio divina, see *visio* under 1; on vita divina, see *vita* under 1 and 3; on voluntas divina, see *voluntas* under 2 and 3.—divinus, i, *m., diviner, prophet.*—divina, orum, *n., God Himself, divine things, God-like things.*

divise, *adv.,* see *divido.*

divisibilis, e, *adj.*, *divisible, separable*, the opposite of *indivisibilis*. On **corpus divisibile**, see *corpus;* on **locus divisibilis**, see locus under 1; on **passio divisibilis**, see *passio* under 1.—Kinds of *divisibilis* are: (a), **divisibilis in infinitum**, *divisible to infinity.*—(b), **divisibilis in potentia**, *divisible potentially.*—(c), **divisibilis secundum accidens** and **divisibilis secundum speciem**, *divisible with reference to an accident* and *with reference to species* and *essence.*—(d), **divisibilis secundum speciem**, see *divisibilis secundum accidens.*—**nullum divisibile est sua divisio qua dividitur**, see *divisio.*

divisim, *adv.*, see *divido.*

divisio, onis, *f.*, *division, separation, partition, classification*, synonym of *discretio, distinctio*, and *resolutio*, the opposite of *commixtio, complexio, compositio*, and *indivisio*. On **abstrahere per modum divisionis**, see *abstrahere* under 1; on **infinitum divisionis seu per divisionem seu secundum divisionem**, see *infinitus;* on **locus a divisione**, see *locus* under 4; on **verum in divisione**, see *verus* under 1; on **via divisionis**, see *via* under 3.—Kinds of *divisio* are: (a), **divisio actualis seu in actu**, *the division or subdivision taking place or consisting in reality.*—(b), **divisio communis analogi seu per analogiam** and **divisio univoci**, *the division of a common thing after the*

manner of analogy and *that of the homogeneous.*—(c), **divisio communis per analogiam**, see *divisio communis analogi.*—(d), **divisio continui**, *the division of what hangs together.*—(e), **divisio essentiae seu per essentiam seu secundum essentiam seu essentiam seu essentialis** and **divisio quantitatis seu per quantitatem seu secundum quantitatem seu quantitativa**, *the division of a thing according to its essence* and *that according to its matter.*—(f), **divisio essentialis**, see *divisio essentiae.*—(g), **divisio formalis seu secundum formam** and **divisio materialis seu secundum materiam**, *division according to form* and *division according to matter.*—(h), **divisio in actu**, see *divisio actualis.*—(i), **divisio infinita**, *the division that goes into the infinite.*—(j), **divisio intellectus**, *the division taking place on the side of reason* or *the negation.*—(k), **divisio materialis**, see *divisio formalis.*—(l), **divisio per essentiam**, see *divisio essentiae.*—(m), **divisio per quantitatem**, see *divisio essentiae.*—(n), **divisio per se**, *the division of a thing according to itself* or *according to its nature and essence.*—(o), **divisio quantitatis**, see *divisio essentiae.*—(p), **divisio quantitativa**, see *divisio essentiae.*—(q), **divisio recta**, *the correct division.*—(r), **divisio secundum essentiam**, see *divisio essentiae.*—(s), **divisio secundum formam**, see *divisio for-*

malis.—(t), **divisio secundum materiam,** see *divisio formalis.*—(u), **divisio secundum naturam** and **divisio secundum rationem,** *the division that takes place in nature* and *in reason.*—(v), **divisio secundum quantitatem,** see *divisio essentiae.*—(w), **divisio secundum quid** and **divisio simpliciter,** *the division in a certain respect* and *the simple division.*—(x), **divisio secundum rationem,** see *divisio secundum naturam.*—(y), **divisio simpliciter,** see *divisio secundum quid.*—(z), **divisio univoce,** see *divisio communis analogi.*—**nullum divisibile est sua divisio, qua dividitur,** *no subdivision of the whole is its own subdivision,* i.e., *that by which it is divided.*—**omnis divisio debet esse per opposita,** *every division must depend, if it is to be correct* (see *divisio recta*) *on things which are opposed to each other.*—**unumquodque refugit divisionem sui,** *everything struggles against its division.*

divisive, *adv., after the manner* or *in the sense of a division* or *separation, divisively,* synonym of *distributive, divise,* and *divisim,* the opposite of *collective, complexe, composite,* and *coniunctim.*

divisivus, a, um, *adj., dividing, separating, subdividing, classifying, divisive.* On **differentia divisiva,** see *differentia;* on **propositio divisiva,** see *propositio* under

2; on **syllogismus divisivus,** see *syllogismus.*

divisor, oris, *m., a divider.*

divisorius, a, um, *adj., causing* or *expressing division* or *separation, divisory.*

divitiae, arum, *f., riches, wealth.*—Kinds of *divitiae* are: (a), **divitiae artificiales** and **divitiae naturales,** *artificial riches* or *riches obtained through the skill of man* and *natural riches* or *riches offered by nature.*—(b), **divitiae corporales seu exteriores** and **divitiae spirituales,** *the physical* or *material* or *external* and *the spiritual riches.*—(c), **divitiae exteriores,** see *divitiae corporales.*—(d), **divitiae naturales,** see *divitiae artificiales.*—(e), **divitiae non verae** and **divitiae verae,** *the real* and *unreal riches* or *the apparent* and *the true riches.*—(f), **divitiae spirituales,** see *divitiae corporales.*—(g), **divitiae verae,** see *divitiae non verae.*

divortium, ii, *n., a divorce,* the dissolution of the marriage bond, *divortium plenum a vinculo,* or the permament separation of the parties, the bond remaining *divortium semi-plenum.*

divulgatio, onis, *f., a divulgation, the act of divulgating, publishing, spreading abroad.*

divulgo, are, avi, atum, 1, *v. a., to spread among the people, make common, publish, divulge.*—**divulgatus,** a, um, *P. a., revealed, preached, published.*

do, dare, dedi, datum, *v. a.*, (1) *to give,* (2) *to give in, admit, grant,* (3) *state, determine.* On **occasio data,** see *occasio.*—**dare operam,** *to bestow labor* and *pains on anything, devote oneself to.*—**dare intellegere,** *to give to understand.*—**dato per impossibile,** *granted after the manner* or *in the sense of the impossible.*—**dans,** dantis, *P. a., giving, bestowing, one giving.*—**datus,** a, um, *P. a., given, bestowed.*—**datum,** i, *n., gift, present.*

doceo, ere, cui, ctum, 2, *v. a., to teach, instruct, inform, show, tell,* used with (1) *acc.* of person and thing, (2) with *acc.* of the thing, (3) with *acc.* of the person, (4) with *acc.* of the person and de with *abl.*, (5) with *acc.* and *inf.*, (6) with the *acc.* and *abl.*, of means or instrument, (7) with the *inf.*, (8) with a *substantive cl.*, (a) *indic.*, (b) *subj.*, (9) with *ut* and *subj.*, (10) *absol.*—**docens,** ntis, *P. a., teaching, instructing.*—**doctus,** a, um, *P. a., learned, skilled, versed, experienced.*

docilis, e, *adj., easily taught, docile.*

docilitas, atis, *f., docility, quality of being docile, tractableness, aptness for being taught;* an integral part of prudence.

doctor, oris, *m.*, (1) *teacher,* (2) *teacher of the Christian faith.*—Kinds of *doctor* are: (a), **doctor ecclesiae,** *teacher of the Christian Church,* whose authority is greatly venerated; see *doctor Graecorum* below.—(b), **doctor fidei,** *teacher of the Christian faith.*—Kinds of *doctor* in this (2) sense are: (a), **doctor gentium** and **doctor Iudaeorum,** *teacher of the heathen* and *of the Jews.* —(b), **doctor Graecorum** and **doctor Latinus seu noster,** *teacher of the Greek Church* and *teacher of the Latin Church.* The theological writers of the East who enjoyed the greatest authority were St. Basil, St. Gregory Nazienzenus, St. John Chrysostom, St. John Damascene, St. Anthanasius, and the two St. Cyril's. The Latin doctors were St. Ambrose, St. Augustine, St. Jerome, St. Gregory, to which may be added St. Hilary and St. Peter Chrysologos. Various saints have been added in the course of time by the Popes until the number now stands at 29. St. Thomas, St. Albert, St. Bonaventure, and St. Anthony of Padua are the only Scholastics to be declared doctors of the Church.—(c), **doctor Iudaeorum,** see *doctor gentium.* —(d), **doctor Latinus,** see *doctor Graecorum.*—(e), **doctor noster,** see *doctor Graecorum.*

doctrina, ae, *f.*, (1) *instruction* in the active sense of the word, *teaching, informing,* synonym of *doctio* and *doctrinatio,* the opposite of *disciplina,* (2) *instruction* in the passive sense of the word, synonym of *disciplina,* (3) *doctrine, dogma,* (4) *profession* *of teaching, branch of learning, science,* synonym of *disciplina.* —Kinds of *doctrina* to be noted here are: **doctrina privata** and **doctrina publica,** *private* and *public instruction.* On **fundamentum spiritualis doctrinae,** see *fundamentum;* on **veritas doctrinae,** see *veritas.*—Kinds of *doctrina* in this (3) sense are: (a), **doctrina fidei** and **doctrina philosophiae seu philosophica,** *the science of faith* or *theology* and *philosophy.*—(b), **doctrina moralis seu morum,** *moral philosophy* or *ethics.*—(c), **doctrina morum,** see *doctrina moralis.*— (d), **doctrina philosophiae,** see *doctrina fidei.*—(e), **doctrina philosophica,** see *doctrina fidei.* —(f), **doctrina politica,** *political science.*—(g), **doctrina sacra** and **doctrina saecularis,** *sacred* and *worldly science,* or *supernatural theology* and *profane science.*— (h), **doctrina saecularis,** see *doctrina sacra.*

doctrinalis, e, *adj., instructing, teaching, doctrinal.* On **disputatio doctrinalis,** see *disputatio;* on **scientia doctrinalis,** see *scientia* under 1.

doctrinatio, onis, *f., instruction, teaching, indoctrination,* synonym of *doctrina.*

documentum, i, *n.,* (1) *document, voucher, proof,* (2) *doctrine, teaching.*—Kinds of *documentum* in this (2) sense are: (a), **documentum commune,** *common teaching.*—(b), **documentum fidei**

seu **fidei nostrae,** *the teaching of Christianity* or *of our faith.* —(c), **documentum philosophiae seu philosophicum** and **documentum physicum,** *the teaching of philosophy* and *the teaching of physics.*—(d), **documentum philosophicum,** see *documentum philosophiae.*—(e), **documentum physicum,** see *documentum philosophiae.*

dogma, atis, *n., a philosophic tenet,* but more commonly *revealed doctrine, dogma.*—Kinds of *dogma* are: (a), **dogma acroamaticum seu auditionale, dogma syntagmaticum seu coordinale** and **dogma encyclium,** *dogma which is to be heard* or *intended merely for verbal delivery, that which stands in connection with other dogmas* and *that which belongs to the sphere of general knowledge.*—(b), **dogma auditionale,** see *dogma acroamaticum.*—(c), **dogma coordinale,** see *dogma acroamaticum.*—(d), **dogma divinum,** *the divine* or *revealed dogma.*—(e), **dogma ecclesiasticum,** *the ecclesiastical dogma.* The De Ecclesiasticis Dogmatibus, ascribed to St. Augustine, is frequently quoted by St. T.— (f), **dogma encyclium,** see *dogma acroamaticum.*—(g), **dogma fidei,** *the dogma of Christian faith.*—(h), **dogma perplexum,** *the doubtful dogma.*—(i), **dogma perversum,** *the perverted* or *misinterpreted dogma.*

doleo, ere, ui, itum, 2, *v. n.,* and *a.,* (1) mentally *to grieve for, deplore, lament, be sorry for, be afflicted at* or *on account of anything,* used with (a), *acc.,* (b), *acc.* and *inf.,* (c), *inf.,* (d), *pro, ex , in* and *de* with *abl.,* (e), *ad* and *propter* with *acc.,* (f), *quod, si,* (g), *absol.,* (2) corporally *to feel pain, suffer pain, be in pain, ache.*—**dolens,** entis, *P. a., causing pain, affecting with any degree of physical distress.*

dolium, ii, *n., a cask, a very large jar of globular form with a wide mouth.*

dolo, are, avi, atum, 1, *v. a., to chip with an axe, hew, trim.*

dolor, oris, *m., pain, smart, ache,* in the broader and narrower sense of the word, the opposite of *delectatio.* On the difference between *dolor* and *tristitia,* both taken in the narrower sense of the word, see *tristitia.*—Kinds of *dolor* are: **dolor corporalis seu exterior seu sensibilis seu sensitivae partis** and **dolor spiritualis seu interior,** *the physical* or *exterior* or *sensible pain* and *the spiritual* or *inner pain.*

dolorosus, a, um, *adj., painful, full of sorrow.*

dolose, *adv.,* see *dolosus.*

dolositas, atis, *f., deceit, deceitfulness.*

dolosus, a, um, *adj., sly, crafty, cunning, deceitful.*—**dolose,** *adv., craftily, deceitfully.*

dolus, i, *m., an evil, artifice;* hence *evil intent, wrong doing* with a view to the consequences, opp. *culpa, negligence.* In the older and esp. the jurid. lang.: *dolus malus,* a standing expression for *guile, fraud, deceit;* without *malus: guile, deceit, deception. Dolus* denotes a certain execution of craftiness whether this is effected by word or by deeds.

domesticus, a, um, *adj.,* (1) *of* or *belonging to one's house,* or *one's family, domestic, familiar, household,* synonym of *oeconomicus,* (2) *domesticated, trained,* (3) like the Greek *oikeios* = proprius, *proper, personal, one's own.*—On **animal domesticum,** see *animal* under 1 and 2; on **bonum domesticum,** see *bonus* under 3; on **communio domestica,** see *communio* under 1; on **multitudo domestica,** see *multitudo* under 4; on **persona domestica,** see *persona* under 3; on **vita domestica,** see *vita* under 3.— **Homo est naturaliter seu secundum suam naturam animal domesticum,** see *homo.*—**domestici,** orum, *m., inmates of a household, the members of a family.*

domicilium, ii, *n., an abode, dwelling.*

domina, ae, *f., mistress, she who commands* or *rules.*

dominatio, onis, *f.,* (1) *lordship, lord* (degree of rank), in the plural, *dominations, an order of the celestial hierarchy, angels, spiritual powers,* (2) *domination, dominion, control by the exercise of power* or *constituted* *authority* especially that of a master over his slaves, the opposite of *servitus,* (3) *domination, mental control,* or the dominion of the superior over the inferior ability or resources.

dominativus, a, um, *adj.,* (1) *belonging to a sovereign* or *a lord, ruling, dominant,* synonym of *architectonicus* and *principativus,* the opposite of *servilis,* (2) *imperious, dictatorial,* synonym of *despoticus,* the opposite of *servilis.*—(1), on **ratio dominativa,** see *ratio;* on **scientia dominativa,** see *scientia.*—On **ius dominativum,** see *ius* under 1; on **iustum dominativum,** see *iustus;* on **potestas dominativa,** see *potestas* under 3; on **principatus dominativus,** see *principatus* under 1; on **subiectio dominativa,** see *subiectio* under 2.

dominicalis, e, *adj., dominical,* pertaining to Sunday as the Lord's day.

dominicus, a, um, *adj., of* or *belonging to a lord* or *master, lordly* applied here to Christ who is spoken of as the Lord.—Common phrases are: (a), **oratio dominica,** *the Lord's prayer.*—(b), **dominica dies,** *the Lord's day.*—(c), **dominica passio,** *the Lord's passion.*—(d), **dominica coena,** *the Lord's supper.*—(e), **dominicum corpus,** *the Lord's body.*—(f), **resurrectio dominica,** *the Lord's resurrection.*

dominium, ii, *n., dominion, might, power,* synonym of *potestas,*

principatus, and *regimen.* On **auctoritas dominii,** see *auctoritas* under 4; on **ius dominii,** see *ius* under 1; on **relatio dominii,** see *relatio.*—Kinds of *dominium* are: (a), **dominium completum seu perfectum seu plenarium** and **dominium incompletum seu particulare,** *the complete* or *the full power* and *the incomplete* or *the partial power.*—(b), **dominium despoticum seu tyranni,** *the despotic* or *tyrannical power.*—(c), **dominium divinum,** *the divine power.*—(d), **dominium imperiale** and **dominium regale seu regis,** *the imperial* and *the royal power.*—(e), **dominium incompletum,** see *dominium completum.*—(f), **dominium iustum seu legitimum,** *the just* or *the lawful power.*—(g), **dominium legitimum,** see *dominium iustum.*—(h), **dominium monarchicum** and **dominium plurimum seu politicum,** *the monarchial* and *the democratic power* or *that of the individual* and *that of the several.*—(i), **dominium mortis,** *the power* or *might over death.*—(j), **dominium naturale,** *the natural power* or *that which belongs to some one by nature.*—(k), **dominium oeconomicum,** *the domestic power* or *the power of the family.*—(l), **dominium particulare,** see *dominium completum.* —(m), **dominium perfectum,** see *dominium completum.*—(n), **dominium Petri seu summi pontificis,** *the power of Peter* or *of the*

Pope.—(o), **dominium plenarium,** see *dominium completum.*—(p), **dominium plurium,** see *dominium monarchicum.*—(q), **dominium politicum,** see *dominium monarchicum.*—(r), **dominium principale,** *the principal power.*—(s), **dominium regale,** see *dominium imperiale.*—(t), **dominium regis,** see *dominium imperiale.*—(u), **dominium sacerdotale,** *the sacerdotal power.*—(v), **dominium spirituale** and **dominium temporale,** *the spiritual* and *the temporal* or *worldly power.*—(w), **dominium sui actus,** *power over one's own activity.*—(x), **dominium summi pontificis,** see *dominium Petri.*—(y), **dominium supremum,** *the supreme* or *highest power.*—(z), **dominium temporale,** see *dominium spirituale.* —(a²), **dominium tyranni,** see *dominium despoticum.*

dominor, ari, atus, 1, *v. dep. n.,* (1) *to be lord* and *master, to have dominion, bear rule, domineer,* used with *in* and *acc., dat., super* and *acc., gen., in* and *abl.,* and *absol.,* (2) *to reign, rule, govern,* etc., of inanimate and abstract subjects.—**dominans,** antis, *P. a., ruling, bearing sway.*— **dominans,** antis, *m., an absolute ruler.*

dominus, i, *m.,* (1) *lord, ruler, master,* the opposite of *servus,* (2) *the Lord per eminentiam,* i.e., *God.*—On **relatio domini,** see *relatio.*—Kinds of *dominus* are: (a) **dominus gloriae,** *the Lord of*

heavenly glory.—(b), **dominus per accidens,** and **dominus per naturam,** *the Lord in accordance with something which belongs to Him accidently* and *the Lord in accordance with His own nature* and *essence.*—(c), **dominus per naturam,** see *dominus per accidens.*—(d), **dominus sui actus,** *the Lord of His own action.*—(e), **dominus temporalis,** *the temporal* or *worldly lord.* On **homo dominus,** see *homo;* on **spiritus dominus,** see *spiritus.*

domo, are, ui, itum, 1, *v. a., to tame, vanquish, overcome, subdue.*—**domitus,** a, um, *P. a., tame.*

domus, us, and i, 2d and 4th decl., *f.,* (1) *a house, home,* (2) *a household, family, race,* a group of persons descended from the same stock; a family of high rank or an illustrious race, (3) *a house, the dwelling of a religious community.*—Common phrases are: (a), **in domum meam,** *into my house,* of the body as the dwelling of the soul.—(b), **domus regia,** *a royal home, palace.*—(c), **domus Dei,** *the house of God.*—(d), **domus Christi,** *the house of Christ, a church.*—(e), **domus spiritualis,** *a spiritual dwelling.*

donarium, ii, *n., a votive offering.*

donatio, onis, *f., a presenting, gift, donation, the act of giving* or *bestowing.*

Donatista, ae, *m., a Donatist,* one of a sect, named from Donatus, that arose in North Africa in the fourth century and claimed to be the only true church, holding that the church was to be composed only of saints. The sect continued for three centuries and had various divisions, as the Circumcelliones, the Primianists, and the Maximianists.

donec, *conj.*, *until*, *up to the time at which*, used with (1) indic., (2) *subjunctive*.

dono, are, avi, atum, 1, *v. a.*, (1) *to present*, *bestow*, *grant*, *confer*, (2) *to forgive*, *to pardon* an offence or him that committed it, (3) *to present* one with anything, *endow* or *favor* with a gift.

donum, i, *n.*, (1) *gift, present*, (2) *gift of the Holy Ghost*, (3) *Holy Ghost.*—Kinds of *donum* in this sense are: (a), **donum corporale** and **donum spirituale**, *the corporal* and *the spiritual gift, or the gift for the body* and *the gift for the soul of man.*—(b), **donum creatum** and **donum increatum**, *the created* and *the uncreated gift or the Holy Ghost.*—(c), **donum Dei** and **donum hominis**, *the gift of God* and *that of man.*—(d), **donum directivum** and **donum exsequens**, *the gift that guides* and *rules* and *the gift that executes* or *obeys.*—(e), **donum exsequens**, see *donum directivum.*—(f), **donum gloriae**, and **donum gratiae**, *the gift that consists of heavenly glory* and *that consists of divine grace.*—(g), **donum gratiae**, see *donum gloriae.*—(h), **donum gratiae datum seu gratuitum seu su-** pernaturale and **donum naturale**, *the gift bestowed from grace* or *the supernatural* and *the natural gift.*—(i), **donum gratuitum**, see *donum gratis datum.*—(j), **donum hominis**, see *donum Dei.*—(k), **donum increatum**, see *donum creatum.*—(l), **donum naturale**, see *donum gratis datum.*—(m), **donum personale**, *the personal gift.* —(n), **donum spirituale**, see *donum corporale.*—(o), **donum Spiritus sancti**, *the gift of the Holy Ghost* and *also the Holy Ghost Himself* —(p), **donum spontaneum**, *the gift made of itself* or *of its own accord.*—(q), **donum supernaturale**, see *donum gratis datum.*—On the relationship between *donum Spiritus sancti, beatitudo, fructus Spiritus sancti,* and *virtus*, see *fructus* under 2. On **gratia donorum**, see *gratia* under 2.—Kinds of *donum* in this (2) sense are: (a), **donum charitatis**, *the gift of love.*—(b), **donum commune** and **donum speciale**, *the common* and *the special gift.* —(c), **donum consilii**, *the gift of counsel.*—(d), **donum fortitudinis**, *the gift of fortitude* or *strength.* —(e), **donum intellectus**, *the gift of understanding* or *insight.*—(f), **donum intellectus consummatum** and **donum intellectus inchoatum**, *the completed* and *the inceptive gift of understanding* or *the gift of the completed understanding* or *the understanding only begun.*—(g), **donum intellectus inchoatum**, see *donum intel-*

lectus consummatum.—(h), **donum linguarum,** *the gift of languages* or *the gift of speaking in different languages at the same time.*—(i), **donum pietatis,** *the gift of piety.*—(j), **donum primum,** *the first gift (of grace),* i.e., *the Holy Ghost Himself.*—(k), **donum prophetale seu propheticum seu prophetiae,** *the prophesying gift* or *the gift of prophesy.*—(l), **donum prophetiae,** see *donum prophetale.*—(m), **donum sapientiae,** *the gift of wisdom.*—(n), **donum scientiae,** *the gift of knowledge.*—(o), **donum speciale,** see *donum commune.*—(p), **donum timoris,** *the gift of the fear of the Lord.*

dormio, ire, ivi or ii, itum, 4, *v. n.,* (1) *to sleep, rest* or *repose in sleep,* (2) *to sleep, rest in death,* (3) *to sleep, lack watchfulness* or *attentiveness, be careless* or *remiss.*

dormitio, onis, *f., a sleeping.*

Dorotheus, i, *m., Dorotheus,* the deacon addressed in the fifth letter ascribed to Dionysius the Areopagite.

dorsum, i, *n., the back.*

dos, otis, *f.,* (1) *dowry* for marriage, (2) *dowry* of the saints in heaven. —Kinds of *dos* in this sense are: **dos animae** and **dos corporis,** *the dowry of the soul* and *that of the body.*

doto, are, avi, atum, 1, *v. a.,* (1) *to endow, to give a dowry to one's bride,* (2) *to endow, confer something desirable upon.*—**dot-**

atus, a, um, *adj., dowered, endowed.*

draco, onis, *m.,* (1) *a dragon,* (2) *the serpent, the Devil.*

dromedarius, ii, *m., a dromedary.*

dualitas, atis, *f., duality,* the state or character of being composed of two, twoness.

dubie, *adv., doubtfully.*

dubietas, atis, *f., doubt, uncertainty.*

dubitabilis, e, *adj., doubtful, to be doubted.*

dubitatio, onis, *f., doubt, deliberation, timidity, hesitation.*—Kinds of *dubitatio* are: (a), **dubitatio admirationis,** *the doubt of amazement.*—(b), **dubitatio discussionis,** *the doubt of discussion.* Cf. PT. Q. 27. Art. 4 ad 2, quoted above.—(c), **dubitatio incredulitatis seu infidelitatis,** *the doubt of unbelief.*—(d), **dubitatio infidelitatis,** see *dubitatio incredulitatis.*—(e), **dubitatio problematica,** *the hypothetical doubt.* Cf. 1 Anal. 42 e.

dubitativus, a, um, *adj., doubtful, dubitative.* On **oratio dubitativa,** see *oratio.*

dubito, are, avi, atum, 1, *v. freq. n.* and *a., to doubt, waver in opinion, be uncertain, be in doubt, doubt,* used (1) with *acc.* and *inf.,* (2) with *quin,* (3) with *interrog. particles,* (4) *absol.,* (5) with *de* and *abl.*

dubius, a, um, *adj.,* (1) *doubtful, precarious, critical, dubious,* (2) in the *neuter absol.,* **dubium est,** *it is doubtful, uncertain, unde-*

cided, used with *dat.,* with *quin,* with *interrog. cl., a substantive clause* with *quod.*—Common phrases are: (a), **venire in dubium,** *to come into doubt.*—(b), **sine dubio,** *without doubt.*—(c), **dubium habere,** *to regard as uncertain.*—(d), **absque dubio,** *without doubt.*—(e), **vertere in dubium,** *to incline to* or *give rise to doubt.*—(f), **procul dubio,** *beyond question, undoubtedly.*—(g), **sub dubio,** *in doubt, doubtful.*—(h), **dubium,** i, *n.,* (also *pl.* **dubia** as subst.), *a doubt.*

ducatus, us, *m.,* (1) *guidance,* (2) *dukedom,* the dignity, office or rank of duke.

ducenti, ae, a, *num., two hundred.*

ducibilis, e, *adj., ductible, easily led* or *drawn on, ductile.*

duco, ere, xi, ctum, 3, *v. a.,* (1) used *literally,* (a), in gen., *to lead, draw, steer, guide, bring forward,* (b), with *uxorem, to lead a wife home,* i.e., *to marry,* (c), with the accessory idea of creation, formation, *to produce, form, construct, make, fashion, shape, dispose,* (d), *to lead, command an army* or *division,* (e), transferred beyond the military sphere, *to be leader, chief, first in any thing,* (f), a legal technical term, *to lead away, take, drag, carry off a person before court, to death, punishment,* etc. (2) used *fig.,* (a), *to draw, derive* its origin from anything, (b), of time, *to pass, spend, enjoy,* (c), *to lead* or *conduct* as a

way or a road, (d), with regard to time, *to draw out, extend,* (e), *to lead* a person as regards his will or opinions in any directions, *to move, incite, induce,* (f), *to deem, hold an opinion,* (g), *to multiply, to perform the operation of multiplication upon,* a synonym of *multiplicare.*

ductilis, e, *adj., ductile, capable of being drawn* or *hammered out.*

ductio, onis, *f. , guidance, a leading.*

ductivus, a, um, *adj., indicative of leadership, conductive.*

ductor, oris, *m., leader, a guide, one who leads another in any path* or *direction.*

ductrix, icis, *f., a female leader, a guide.*

ductus, us, *m.,* (1) *a guidance, directing,* (2) *multiplication,* the process of finding the sum of a number called the multiplicand repeated as many times as there are units in another number called the multiplier.

duellum, i, *n., a duel,* a combat between two persons, especially one fought with deadly weapons according to prearrangement and in the presence of seconds or witnesses to decide some quarrel or point of honor.

dulcedo, inis, *f.,* (1) *sweetness,* the quality of being sweet, (2) used *fig., pleasantness, agreeableness, delightfulness.*

dulcis, e, *adj.,* (1) of things agreeable to the taste, (a) *sweet,* having a flavor or taste like honey,

(b) *sweet,* having a fresh or mild taste, as opposed to salty, sour, rancid, (2) *sweet,* agreeable to the mind, (3) *kind, gracious,* characterized by kindness or amiability.

Dulcitius, ii, *m., Dulcitius,* a tribune and notary, charged with executing the imperial decrees against the Donatists, 420 A.D., to whom Augustine writes (Ep. 204) blaming him for proclaiming that they were to be given up to the death that they deserved.

dulia, ae, *f.,* = Grk. *douleia,* (1) *servitude, subjection,* (2) *the virtue of subjection* or *of serving,* and first moreover that which the slave practices towards his master and then that which man practices towards any preeminent being.—On **adoratio duliae,** see *adoratio* under 1; on **honor duliae,** see *honor.*

dum, conj., (1) *while, whilst, during the time in which, as long as.* In general, construed with the indicative, except in *oratio obliqua,* where the subjunctive is sometimes used, (2) in conditional relations as a restrictive particle, like *quatenus* and *dumtaxat, so long as, provided that, if only,* (3) *until, until that.* Construed with the subjunctive or the indicative, according as the idea of aim or simply of time predominates, (4) like *cum, when,* and *since* with the indicative or subjunctive.—**dummo-**

do, like (2) above with emphatic *modo.*

dummodo, see *dum.*

duntaxat, *adv.,* (1) *only, simply, merely,* (2) *to this extent, so far, in so far, lit.* as far as it holds good, (3) *provided that,* approaches closely in meaning to *dummodo.*

duo, ae, o, *card. num.,* (1) *two,* (2) *the two, both.*

duodecim, *card. num., twelve.*

duodecimus, a, um, *ord. num., the twelfth.*

duodenarius, a, um, *adj., containing twelve.*

duodeni, ae, a, *distr. num., twelve each, twelve.*

duplatus, a, um, *P. a., doubled.*

duplex, icis, *adj.,* (1) *two-fold, double,* (2) of character, *characterized by ambiguity, deceit,* or *insincerity, double-tongued, double-hearted, deceitful.*—**dupliciter,** *adv., doubly, on two accounts.*

duplicitas, atis, *f.,* (1) *double-dealing, insincerity,* the opposite of *simplicitas,* (2) *ambiguity,* synonym of *multiplicitas.*

dupliciter, *adv.,* see *duplex.*

duplico, are, avi, atum, 1, *v. a.,* (1) *to double,* (2) *to double,* i.e., *to increase, enlarge, augment.*

duplus, a, um *adj., double, twice as large, twice as much.*—**duplum,** i, *n., the double of anything.*

durabilis, e, *adj., lasting, durable.*

durabilitas atis, *f., lastingness, durability.*

duratio, onis, *f.*, (1) *duration, continuance in time;* the period during which anything lasts, (2) *duration, time in general,* especially as the condition of continued existence; one of the seven ultimate categories of being.

duriter, *adv.,* see *durus.*

duritia, ae, (also **durities**) *f.,* (1) *hardness,* the state or quality of being hard, (2) used *fig.,* (a) *hard-heartedness, obduracy, invincible hardness of heart, confirmed* and *wilful insensibility to the claims of God* and *the moral law, stubborn wickedness,* (b) *harshness, severity,* (c) *hardness, frigidity, coldness of feeling, affection* or *manner.*

durities, see *duritia.*

duro, are, avi, atum, 1, *v. a.,* to *hold out, to continue in existence, last, remain,* used *fig.*

durus, a, um, *adj.,* (1) as affecting the sense of feeling, *hard, rough;* solid and firm in substance, (2) used *fig.,* (a) the opposite of morally mild, gentle, *harsh, rude, rough, stubborn, coarse, obstinate,* austere or unfeeling in character or demeanor; unmarked by a kindly disposition, (b) of things, *severe, toilsome, hard, troublesome, disagreeable.* —**dura,** orum, *n., hardships, difficulties.*—**duriter,** *adv., harshly, sternly.*

dux, ducis, *com.,* (1) *a leader, conductor, guide,* (2) in milit. lang., *a general, commander-in-chief, officer, commander, leader,* (3) *transf.,* beyond the milit. sphere, *a leader, chief, head.*

dyscolus, a, um, *adj., of a bad temper, peevish, irritable.*

E

eatenus, *adv., in so far,* designates the limit to which an action or condition extends, followed by *quatenus.*

ebenus, i, *f., the ebon-tree, ebony.*

Ebionitae, arum, *m., the Ebionites,* a group of heretics in the early church, chiefly made up of Pharisees and Essenes, and characterized by denial of the divinity of Christ and the rejection of the Pauline epistles.

ebrietas, atis, *f., ebriety, intoxication produced by liquor, drunkenness.*

ebriosus, i, *m., a drunkard, sot.*

ebrius, a, um, *adj., full of drink, drunk, intoxicated.*—**ebrius,** i, *m., a drunkard.*

ecce, *adv.,* see, *behold,* points out an object with emphasis, used only in quot. in S.T.

ecclesia, ae, *f.,* (1) *the universal Church, the Church,* i.e., the community of all believers in Christ, (2) *an individual church, parish church, church.*—On **bonum ecclesiae,** see *bonus;* on **caput ecclesiae,** see *caput;* on **clavis ecclesiae,** see *clavis;* on

doctor ecclesiae, see *doctor;* on
fides ecclesiae, see *fides;* on
forum ecclesiae, see *forum;* on
fundamentum ecclesiae, see *fundamentum;* on **ieiunium ecclesiae,** see *ieiunium;* on **iudicium ecclesiae,** see *iudicium;* on
ordo ecclesiae, see *ordo;* on
praeceptum ecclesiae, see *praeceptum;* on **praelatus ecclesiae,**
see *praelatus;* on **sacramentum
ecclesiae,** see *sacramentum.—*
Kinds of *ecclesia* in this sense
are: (a), **ecclesia caelestis seu
secundum statum patriae** and
**ecclesia terrena seu secundum
statum viae,** *the heavenly* and
the earthly Church or *the
Church in accordance with its
place in the heavenly fatherland* and *that with reference to
its place on the way to the
same.—*(b), **ecclesia militans** and
ecclesia triumphans, *the Church
militant on earth* and *the
Church triumphant in heaven.*
—(c), **ecclesia moderna** and **ecclesia primitiva,** *the Church* of
today and *the first* or *original
Church.—*(d), **ecclesia primitiva,** see *ecclesia moderna.—*(e),
**ecclesia secundum statum pa-
triae,** see *ecclesia caelestis.—*
(f), **ecclesia secundum statum
viae,** see *ecclesia caelestis.—*(g),
ecclesia terrena, see *ecclesia
caelestis.—*(h), **ecclesia triumphans,** see *ecclesia militans.—*
(i), **ecclesia universalis,** *the universal Church.—*(j), **Ecclesia vera,** see *ecclesia militans.*

Ecclesiastes, ae, *m., Ecclesiastes,*
one of the three canonical books
of the Holy Scripture attributed
by Jewish tradition to King Solomon; apparently a record of the
author's worldly experience, with
reflections on the vanity of human aspirations.
ecclesiasticus, a, um, *adj., ecclesiastical, of* or *belonging to the
Church,* especially considered
as an organized and governing
power.—**Ecclesiasticus,** i, *m., Ecclesiasticus,* one of the books of
the Apocrypha, resembling in
form the Proverbs of Solomon.
eclipsis, is, *f., an eclipse,* the ob-
scuration of a heavenly body
by its entering the shadow of
another body, as when the moon
enters the shadow of the earth.
eclipso, are, avi, atum, 1, *v. a.,
to eclipse, to cause to suffer e-
clipse, to darken* or *hide,* as one
heavenly body to another.
edico, ere, xi, ctum, 3, *v. a., to
order, enjoin,* used with *acc.*
and *inf.*
edictum, i, *n., an order, command.*
editio, onis, *f., an edition* or *published form of some literary
work.*
edo, ere, edi, esum, 3, *v. a., to eat.*
edo, ere, didi, ditum, 3, *v. a., to
bring forth* anything new, *to
produce, beget, form,* (1) of
what is born, *to beget,* (2) of
literary productions, *to put forth,
publish,* (3) tranferred, *to set
forth, publish, relate, tell, declare,* (4) jurid. and polit. tech-

nical term, *to give out, promulgate, proclaim, ordain.*

edoceo, ere, cui, ctum, 2, *v. a., to teach thoroughly, instruct, inform, appraise* one of anything.

edomo, are, ui, itum, 1, *v. a., to conquer, overcome, tame.—* **edomitus,** a, um, *P. a., tamed subdued.*

educatio, onis, *f., education, bringing-up, rearing, training* of men and animals.

educo, are, avi, atum, 1, *v. a., to bring up a child,* physically or mentally, *to rear, educate.*

educo, ere, xi, ctum, 3, *v. a., to lead out, draw out.—***educere de potentia materiae,** *to produce something which was formerly only potential, to reduce from the state of potential existence to actual existence. See materia prima.—*In so far as the effective cause brings out the form which it realizes in the potentiality of matter, it is said *inducere* or *introducere formam.*

eductio, onis, *f., a removal, taking out.*

effective, *adv.,* see *effectivus.*

effectivus, a, um, *adj., producing, effecting, effective.* On **causa effectiva,** see *causa;* on **exemplar effectivum,** see *exemplar;* on **principium effectivum et primum effectivum,** see *principium;* on **virtus effectiva,** see *virtus.—* **effective,** *adv., after the manner or in the sense of the producing cause or effect, effectively.* On **agere effective,** see *agere;* on

corrumpere effective, see *corrumpere;* on **dicere effective,** see *dicere;* on **facere effective,** see *facere;* on **operari effective,** see *operari;* on **verum effective,** see *verus.*

effectus, us, *m., the produced, the created, the accomplished effect,* the opposite of *causa* and *principium.* On **cognitio per effectum,** see *cognitio;* on **cognoscere ex effectu,** see *cognoscere;* on **defectus effectus,** see *defectus;* on **imperfectio effectus,** see *imperfectio;* on **malum effectus,** see *malus;* on **scire per effectum,** see *scire.—*Kinds of *effectus* are: (a), **effectus adaequatus,** *the effect perfectly equal with its cause.—*(b), **effectus aequivocus** and **effectus univocus,** *the homonymous* and *the homogeneous effect,* i.e. *the effect which has the name but not the essence in common with its cause* and *that which has both in common with its cause.—*(c), **effectus alienus seu extraneus** and **effectus proprius,** *the effect which is foreign to its cause* and *only superficially connected with it* and *that which is proper or peculiar to its cause.—*(d), **effectus casualis seu fortuitus,** *the accidental effect.—*(e), **effectus contingens** and **effectus necessarius,** *the uncertain* and *the necessary effect.—*(f), **effectus convertibilis, et non-convertibilis,** *the convertible* and *the un-convertible cause,* i.e., *the effect which is so* connected with its cause that it always presupposes the same exactly as it follows from the same, and *that effect with which this is not the case.*—(g), **effectus deficiens,** *the defective* or *imperfect effect.*—(h), **effectus determinatus seu distinctus,** *the determined* or *distinguished effect.* (i), **effectus distinctus,** see *effectus determinatus.*—(j), **effectus extraneus,** see *effectus alienus.*—(k), **effectus extrinsecus** and **effectus forinsecus,** *the outer* and *the inner effect.*—(l), **effectus forinsecus,** see *effectus extrinsecus.*—(m), **effectus formae,** *the effect of the substantial form of a thing.*—(n), **effectus formalis,** *the effect according to form.*—(o), **effectus fortuitus,** see *effectus casualis.*—(p), **effectus immediatus seu proximus,** *the immediate* or *nearest effect.*—(q), **effectus in actu** and **effectus in potentia,** *the effect in the state of actuality* and *that in the state of potentiality,* or *the actually existent* and *the potential effect.*—(r), **effectus in potentia,** see *effectus in actu.*—(s), **effectus naturalis** and **effectus supernaturalis,** *the natural* and *the supernatural effect.*—(t), **effectus necessarius,** see *effectus contingens.*—(u), **effectus non-convertibilis,** see *effectus convertibilis.*—(v), **effectus particularis** and **effectus universalis,** *the particular* and *the general effect.*—(w), **effectus per accidens** and **effectus per se,** *the effect realized through something else* and *that realized for itself,* also *the indirect* and *the direct effect.*—(x), **effectus per se,** see *effectus per accidens.*—(y), **effectus positivus** and **effectus privativus seu privationis seu remotivus,** *the positive* and *the deprived* or *removed effect,* i.e., *the effect which is something positive in the reality of the thing,* and *the effect which produces an absence* or *lack of something.*—(z), **effectus privationis,** see *effectus positivus.*—(a^2), **effectus privativus,** see *effectus positivus.*—(b^2), **effectus proprius,** see *effectus alienus.*—(c^2), **effectus proximus,** see *effectus immediatus.*—(d^2), **effectus remotivus,** see *effectus positivus.*—(e^2), **effectus supernaturalis,** see *effectus naturalis.*—(f^2), **effectus universalis,** see *effectus particularis.*—(g^2), **effectus univocus,** see *effectus aequivocus.*—**Ad remotionem causae sequitur remotio effectus,** see *causa* under 2.—**augmentata causa augmentatur effectus,** see *causa.*—**causa est potior effectu,** see *causa.*—**causis debent proportionaliter respondere effectus,** or, **effectus causis suis proportionati sunt,** or, **effectus suis causis proportionaliter respondent,** or, **oportet effectum proportionaliter referre ad causam suam,** *effects must always stand in proportion to their causes.* See *causa.*—**cessante causa cessat effectus,** see *causa.*—contingit aliquid unum commune habere plures causas, secundum quod convenit diversis or, contingit unius effectus accipi quasi plures causas in diversis, *it may happen that one* and *the same effect may have several causes.*—crescente causa crescit effectus, see *causa.*—deficiente causa necesse est effectum deficere, see *causa.*—diversorum diversi sunt effectus, *different causes have also different effects.*—effectus assimilatur in forma non quidem instrumento, sed principali agenti, *the effect with respect to its form,* i.e., *its species or kind, is not similar to the instrument by means of which it is brought forth but to the chief cause.*—effectus assimilatur in specie non agenti remoto sed propinquo, *the effect in relation to its species and essence is similar not to the remote but to the nearest cause.*—effectus assimilatur suae causae, *the effect is considered similar to its cause.*—effectus causae secundae reducitur in causam primam, *the effect of a second cause is attributed to the first cause by virtue of which it is active.*—effectus causis suis proportionati sunt, see above: *causis* etc.—effectus deficiens non procedit nisi a causa deficiente, *a deficient effect comes only from a deficient cause.*—effectus magis denominatur a causa proxima, quam a causa remota, *the effect is named more after its nearest cause than after its remote cause.*—effectus non est nisi in termino motus, *the effect does not appear until the activity of its production is finished.*—effectus non potest extendi ultra suam causam, *the effect cannot in its completeness go beyond its cause.*—effectus suis causis proportionaliter respondent, see above: *causis* etc.—manente causa manet seu non tollitur effectus, see *causa.*—multiplicata causa multiplicatur effectus, see *causa.*—non potest esse nisi una causa unius effectus in omnibus, see *causa.*—omnis effectus convertitur in suum principium seu ad causam, a qua procedit, *every effect turns back to its cause.* Cf. *redire.*—omnis effectus est posterior sua causa, *every effect is subsequent to its cause.*—omnis effectus in sua causa aliqualiter praeexsistit similitudo, *there exists beforehand in some manner a likeness of every effect in its cause.*—posita causa seu causa sufficienti ponitur effectus, see *causa.*—posita causa sufficienti necesse est effectum poni, see *causa.*—posita causa sufficienti nihil aliud requiritur ad effectum inducendum, see *causa.*—posita causa sufficienti nihil aliud videtur esse necessarium ad effectum, see *causa.*—quidquid est causa causae, oportet esse causam effectus, see *causa.*—remota causa removetur effectus, see *causa.*—

ubi est eadem causa, est idem effectus, see *causa.*

effemino, are, avi, atum, 1, *v. a.,* *to enervate, weaken.*—**effeminatus,** a, um, *P. a., effeminate.*

effero, efferre, extuli, elatum, 3, *v. a.,* used figuratively, (1) in the *pass.,* to be carried out of one's self by passions, feelings, etc., *to be carried away, hurried away, transported,* (2) *to exalt, elevate,* (3) with *se, to carry one's self high, to lift up one's self* on account of anything; also with *se, to throw one's self into, to enter into with zeal,* (4) *to attain to something.*—**elatus,** a, um, *P. a., exalted, lofty, high.*

effervens, entis, *P. a., boiling with passion, fervent, ardent.*

efficacia, ae, *f., efficacy, efficiency, virtue,* the state or quality of being efficacious; the power to produce an intended effect as shown in the production of it.

efficaciter, *adv.,* see *efficax.*

efficax, acis, *adj., efficacious, powerful, effective, efficient.* On **causa efficax,** see *causa;* on **ratio efficax,** see *ratio.*—**efficaciter,** *adv., efficaciously, effectively, efficiently.*

efficienter, *adv.,* see *efficio.*

efficientia, ae, *f., production, effect, efficient power.* On **agere per modum efficientiae,** see *agere;* on **operari per modum efficientiae,** see *operari.*

efficio, ere, feci, fectum, 3, *v. a.,* *to bring to pass, effect, accomplish, make, form, execute,* used

with *acc., subst. cl. quin* and *subj., ut* and *subj.*—In the *pass. impers., it was brought about,* used with *ut* and *subj.*—**efficiens,** entis, *P. a., efficient, effecting, effective;* **efficiens causa,** *efficient cause,* the force or agent that does the work. On **causa efficiens,** see *causa.*—**effectus,** a, um, *P. a., effected, completed, wrought.*—**effectum,** i, *n., an effect.*—**efficienter,** *adv. efficiently.* On **agere efficienter,** see *agere;* on **causare efficienter,** see *causare.*

effigiatus, a, um, *adj., portrayed, formed.* On **corpus effigiatum,** see *corpus.*

effigies, ei, *f.,* (1) *lit., an image, an artistic copy, imitation* of an object, (2) *fig., form, appearance, visible shape* of anything.

efflagito, are, avi, atum, 1, *v. a., to demand, ask urgently.*

effluo, ere, xi, 3, *v. n.,* (1) *to flow* or *run out, flow forth,* (2) transferred of non-fluid bodies, *to go out, issue forth, flow, proceed, emanate.*

effluxio, onis, *f., an efflux, issue.*

effluxus, us, *m., an efflux, flow, issue, emanation, the act of issuing* or *flowing forth from an origin* or *source.*

effodio, ere, fodi, fossum, 3, *v. a., to dig out, dig up.*

effrenate, *adv.,* see *effrenatus.*

effrenatus, a, um, *P. a., unbridled, without a rein.*—**effrenate,** *adv., unrestrainedly.*

effugio, ere, fugi, 3, *v. n.* and *a.,* *to escape, to avoid, evade,* (1) of personal subjects, (2) of inanimate subjects.

effugo, are, avi, atum, 1, *v. a., to put to flight.*

effulgeo, ere, si, 2, *v. n., to shine, gleam forth, glitter.*

effundo, ere, fudi, fusum, 3, *v. a.,* (1) *to pour out, to pour forth,* (a) *to pour out* a liquid, (b) *to shed, spill blood,* (c) of objects not liquid, *to spread, diffuse, impart, spread.*—**effusus,** a, um, *P. a., poured out, shed.*

effusio, onis, *f.,* (1) *a pouring out, shedding of blood,* (2) *excess, profusion* of anything, (3) used figuratively, *an outpouring,* used of intangible things.

effusor, oris, *m., a prodigal, waster.*

egenus, a, um, *adj.,* (1) *needy, destitute,* (2) *poor, worthless, beggarly.*

egeo, ere, ui, 2, *v. n.,* (1) *to be needy, necessitous, in want, poor,* used absolutely, (2) *to need want, lack, be in need of,* used with *inf.,* as *object;* with *gen.* and *abl.* of the thing needed, (a) with an animate subject, (b) with an inanimate subject.— **egens, entis,** *P. a., needy, necessitous, in want, very poor.*

egestas, atis, *f., want, indigence, necessity, extreme poverty.*

egestio, onis, *f., excrement, feces.*

egredior, i, gressus, 3, *v. dep. n.* and *a.,* (1) *to go* or *come out, come forth* from any place or point, (a) of animate subjects, (b) of inanimate subjects, (2) *to disregard, to go away from,* used with the *acc.,* (3) *to surpass, exceed,* used figuratively.

egregius, a, um, *adj., distinguished, surpassing, excellent, eminent.*— **egregia forma,** *a handsome figure.*

egressio, onis, *f., a going out* or *forth.*

eiectio, onis, *f., a casting* or *throwing out.*

eicio, ere, ieci, iectum, 3, *v. a.,* (1) *to cast, thrust* or *drive out, to eject, send off, expel,* (2) *to cast up, throw up, vomit.*

eiusmodi (is *plus* modus,) *of that kind, of such a kind, such.*

elabor, i, elapsus, 3, *v. dep. n.* and *a., to pass away, escape from the mind,* used figuratively.— **elabi a memoria,** *to slip from the memory, to forget.*

elaboratus, a, um, *P. a., acquired, produced by labor.*

elargior, iri, 4, *v. dep. a., to give out, distribute, bestow.*

elargitio, onis, *f., a giving, bestowing* something.

elatio, onis, *f., elation, a jubilant* or *triumphant state of mind accompanied by boasting, vainglory; pride, glory, vanity, self-congratulation,* a synonym sometimes used for *inanis gloria, gloriatio.*

Eleazarus, i, *m.,* (1) *Eleazar,* the third son of Aaron whom he succeeded as high-priest of the Hebrews; he was buried on Mount Ephraim, (2) *Eleazar* an

ancient scribe who suffered martyrdom at Antioch under Antiochus IV.

electio, onis, *f.*, (1) *selection,
choice,* which falls on means and
hence the opposite of *voluntas,*
(2) *divine selection, electio divina.*—On the difference between
electio and *intentio,* see *intentio.*
On **agere per electionem voluntatis,** see *agere;* on **ignorantia
electionis et malae electionis,** see
ignorantia; on **iudicium electionis,** see *iudicium;* on **libertas
electionis,** see *libertas;* on **mutabilis secundum electionem,** see
mutabilis; on **operari per electionem,** see *operari;* on **peccare ex
electione,** see *peccare;* on **potestas propriae electionis,** see *potestas;* on **velle per electionem,**
see *velle.*—Kinds of *electio* in
this sense are: (a), **electio bona
seu recta** and **electio mala,** *the
good* or *right* and *the bad selection.*—(b), **electio canonica,** *the
choice corresponding to the stat-
utes of the Church.*—(c), **electio
de Deo dicta seu divina,** *the divine choice* or *selection.*—(d),
electio divina, see *electio de Deo
dicta.*—(e), **electio mala,** see *electio bona.*—(f), **electio recta,** see
electio bona.—**electio est appetitus praeconsiliati,** a translation,
not entirely accurate, of Aris-.
totle's words: *he de · proairesis
orexis bouleutike, choice is the
desire for something previously
considered* or *the desire for that
which previously was the object*

of consideration; in this connection **electio** is also called *desiderium consiliabile.*—**electio vel
est intellectus appetitivus vel
appetitus intellectivus,** the translation of the Aristotelian passage:
*e orektikos nous he proairesis
e orexis dianoetike, choice is
either the desiring reason* or *the
intellectual desire.*—Kinds of *electio* in this sense are: (a), **electio
aeterna** and **electio temporalis,**
the eternal and *the temporal
selection* or *the selection from
eternity* and *that taking place
in time.*—(b), **electio gratuita,**
*the selection springing from pure
grace.*—(c), **electio praedestinationis aeternae** and **electio
praesentis iustitiae,** *the selection of eternal predestination* and
of present justice.—(d), **electio
praesentis iustitiae,** see *electio
praedestinationis aeternae.*—(e),
electio temporalis, see *electio
aeternae.*

elective, *adv.,* see *electivus.*

electivus, a, um, *adj., selective,
elective.* On **dilectio electiva,** see
dilectio; on **habitus electivus,**
see *habitus;* on **vis electiva,** see
vis.—**elective,** *adv., electively.*

electuarium, ii, *n., a medicament
that melts in the mouth, an elec-
tuary.*

electus, i, *m.,* used almost always
in the plural in the S.T., **electi,**
orum, (1) *the elect, those who
are called to everlasting life;* also, *the saved* collectively, (2)
bishops-elect, persons not yet

admitted to episcopal consecration but selected.

eleemosyna, ae, *f., alms.*—Kinds of *eleemosyna* are: (a), **eleemosyna communis seu generalis** and **eleemosyna specialis,** *general* and *particular alms.*—(b), **eleemosyna corporalis,** and **eleemosyna spiritualis,** *the corporal* and *the spiritual alms.*—(c), **eleemosyna generalis,** see *eleemosyna communis.*—(d), **eleemosyna specialis,** see *eleemosyna communis.*—(e), **eleemosyna spiritualis,** see *eleemosyna corporalis.*

elegantia, ae, *f., taste, propriety, refinement, grace, elegance.*

eleison (*eleeson*), *be propitious, have mercy.* The second part of the preparation for the celebration of the mass begins with the prayer, Kyrie eleison, Lord have mercy.

elementalis, e, *adj., consisting of an element, belonging to an element, elemental,* synonym of *elementaris.* On **forma elementalis,** see *forma.*

elementaris, e, *adj., consisting of an element, belonging to an element, elementary,* synonym of *elementalis.* On **corpus elementare,** see *corpus;* on **forma elementaris,** see *forma;* on **materia elementaris,** see *materia;* on **principium elementare,** see *principium;* on **qualitas elementaris,** see *qualitas.*

elementatus, a, um, *adj., compounded of the elements of na-*

ture. On **elementum elementatum,** see *elementum* under 2.

elementum, i, *n.,* (1) *element* in the true sense of the word, i.e., primary ingredient, rudiment, the Aristotelian *stocheion,* the opposite of *elementatum,* (2) *element* in the broader sense of the word, i.e., an ingredient of a thing in the sense of its matter, (3) *element* in the figurative sense, i.e., primary cause, principle. On **forma elementi,** see *forma;* on **liber elementorum Euclidis,** see *liber;* on **qualitas elementi,** see *qualitas;* on **virtus elementi,** see *virtus.*—Kinds of *elementum* in this sense are: (a), **elementum concretius,** *the more consolidated* or *denser element.*—(b), **elementum corporale seu corporeum,** *the corporal element* or *the element that forms a body.*—(c), **elementum corporis,** *the element of a body.*—(d), **elementum demonstrationis,** *the essential part* or *element of a proof.*—(e), **elementum extremum** and **elementum medium,** *the extreme element* or *that to be found at the extreme* (i.e., *fire* and *earth*) and *the middle element* (i.e., *air* and *water*).—(f), **elementum grossum** and **elementum subtile seu nobile,** *the thick* or *coarse element* (i.e., *water* and *earth*) and *the fine* or *noble element* (i.e., *fire* and *air*).—(g), **elementum inferius** and **elementum superius,** *the element that is lower according to its natural place* (i.e., water and earth) and *the higher element* (i.e., fire and air). —(h), **elementum inordinatum** and **elementum ordinatum,** *the disordered* and *the ordered element.*—(i), **elementum leve,** *the light element,* i.e., *fire* and *air.*— (j), **elementum locutionis seu vocis,** *the element of speech* or *of the word.*—(k), **elementum medium,** see *elementum extremum.*— (l), **elementum mundi,** *the element of the world.*—(m), **elementum nobile,** *air* or *fire,* see *elementum grossum.*—(n), **elementum ordinatum,** see *elementum inordinatum.*—(o), **elementum scientiae politicae,** *the element of political science.*—(p), **elementum subtile,** see *elementum grossum.*—(q), **elementum superius,** see *elementum inferius.*—(r), **elementum terrestre,** *the earthly element* or *the element consisting of earth.*—(s), **elementum vocis,** see *elementum locutionis.*— Kinds of *elementum* in this sense are: (a), **elementum elementatum** and **elementum simplex,** *matter composed of two* or *more elements* and *the simple matter,* or *the matter consisting of a single element.*—(b), **elementum primum,** *the first element of the world,* according to which is to be understood on the one hand one of the so-called four elements.—(c), **elementum sensibile,** *material perceptible through the senses.*—(d), **elementum simplex,** see *elementum elementatum.*—

Kinds of *elementum* in this (3) sense are: (a), **elementum materiale,** *the principle acting after the manner of material.*—(b), **elementum universale,** *the universal principle of a thing.*

elenchice, *adv.,* *in the manner* or *in the sense of a disproof, elenctically.* On **demonstrare elenchice,** see *demonstrare* under 3.

elenchus, i, *m.,* (Grk. *elenchus*), (1) *an elenchus, an argument of disproof,* or *refutation,* the contradictory opposite of a proposition; that which must be proved in order to refute an opponent.— (2), The Sophistic Elenchi is the appendix to the Topics of Aristotle. This phrase means strictly "sophistic confutations", the sophist being regarded primarily as the negative spirit who sets himself to puzzle the plain man by apparent refutation of his cherished opinions.

elephans, antis, *m., an elephant.*

elevatio, onis, *f., elevation, a lifting up, the condition* or *state of being elevated, exaltation,* said of the mind or of material and spiritual things.

elevo, are, no perf., atum, 1, *v. a.,* (1) *to raise* or *lift* something from a lower to a higher level, *raise aloft,* (2) *to raise* or *lift up* in mind and its faculties, (3) of the voice, *to lift up, raise.*—**elevatus,** a, um, *P. a., elevated, raised, exalted, lofty.*

Eli, or **Heli,** *indecl. n. m., Eli* or *Heli,* the high priest who judged the people of Israel for forty years. He was from the family of Ithamar, son of Aaron.

Elias, ae and *Elia,* ae, *m., Elias,* a prophet of the Jehovah in the time of Ahab, 900 B.C., opposed idolatry and iniquity; carried to Heaven in a chariot of fire.

elicio, ere, licui, licitum, 3, *v. a., to draw out, elicit,* with reference to the activity of a faculty, the opposite of *impero.* On **actus elicitus,** see *actus;* on **charitas elicita,** see *charitas;* on **habitus elicitus,** see *habitus;* on **motus elicitus,** see *motus.*

elicitive, *adv.,* see *elicitivus.*

elicitivus, a, um, *adj., drawing out, eliciting,* the opposite of *imperativus.—***elicitive,** *adv., after the manner* and *in the sense of drawing out* or *eliciting,* the opposite of *imperative.*

Eliezer, *indecl. n. m., Eliezer* (c. 1876 B.C.) was procurator of the house of Abraham.

eligentia, ae, *f., electiveness.*

eligibilis, e, *adj., eligible, fit* or *worthy of choice of adoption, suitable.*

eligo, ere, legi, lectum, 3, *v. a., to select, choose, elect.* On the difference between *eligere* and *velle,* see *velle.—***eligens,** ntis, *P. a., selecting, choosing, electing.—***electus,** a, um, *P. a., selecting, chosen, elected.* For *electus* used as a noun, see under *electus.*

Eliodorus, i, *m., Heliodorus,* bishop of Altinum near Aquileia, c. 400 A.D. He formed one of the

band of friends who were drawn together at Aquileia, about 372, for the study of Scripture and the practice of asceticism, which included St. Jerome, Evagrius, Rufinus, Bonosus, and Chromatius afterwards bishop of Aquileia.

Elisabeth, *indecl. n., f.,* (1) *Elizabeth,* Zachary's wife and mother of John the Baptist; she was the daughter of Aaron and Mary's kinswoman, (2) *Elizabeth,* daughter of Aminadab I of the tribe of Juda and wife of Aaron.

Elisaeus, i, *m., Eliseus,* the son of Saphat, servant of Elias and native of Abelmehula.

elongatio, onis, *f., elongation, recession, removal, withdrawal, separation.*

elongo, are, avi, atum, 1, *v. a.* and *n.,* (1) *act., to remove, withdraw, separate,* (2) *neutr., to withdraw, depart.*

eloquentia, ae, *f., eloquence.*

eloquium, ii, *n.,* (1) in Aug. poets and their imitators among prose writers, for *eloquentia, eloquence,* (2) in late Lat., *declaration, communication,* in religious discourse, *Holy Scripture,* the *Word of God.*

eluceo, ere, xi, 2, *v. n., to shine out, show itself, be apparent, manifest,* used figuratively.

elucesco, ere, 3, *v. inch. n., to shine forth, begin to shine.*

emanatio, onis, *f., discharge, emission, emanation,* a general term for something proceeding from a principle.—Kinds of *emanatio* are: **emanatio affectus** and **emanatio intellectus seu intellectualis seu intellegibilis,** *the emanation which takes place from the appetitive faculty* and *that from the transcendental intellectual power.*—(b), **emanatio intellectualis,** see *emanatio effectus.*—(c), **emanatio intellectus,** see *emanatio effectus.*—(d), **emanatio intelligibilis,** see *emanatio affectus.*—(e), **emanatio simplex,** *the simple* or *absolute emanation.*

emancipo, are, avi, atum, 1, *v. a.,* *to emancipate, free, liberate, to release from authority, power* or *control, mental* or *physical.*

emano, are, avi, atum, 1, *v. n.,* *to emanate, take rise, originate;* used chiefly of intangible things from a material source.

emaresco, ere, marcui, 3, *v. inch. n., to wither away, shrink, shrivel.*

embryum, i, *n.,* or **embryo** (**embrio**), onis, *f., embryo,* the germ of an animal in the first stage of its existence; in the human species the first five weeks afterwards it is usually called a fetus.

emenda, ae, *f., amends, reparation, satisfaction* or *compensation,* as for injury, harm, wrong or loss.

emendabilis, e, *adj., that may be amended, capable of a correction, emendable.*

emendatio, onis, *f., amendment, emendation,* the act of amending or the state of being amended; change for the better; *improve-*

ment, correction, as the amendment of health, manners.

emendo, are, avi, atum, 1, *v. a.,* (1) *to free from faults, to correct, improve, amend,* (2) *to emend, correct,* to alter the form or words of a work or document with a view to improvement; *make corrections in.*

emergo, ere, si, sum, 3, *v. a.* and *n., to present itself suddenly for solution.*

emico, are, cui, 1, *v. n., to shine forth, be prominent* or *conspicuous, to become apparent,* used figuratively.

eminenter, adv., see *emineo.*

eminentia, ae, *f.,* (1) *concr., a prominence, protuberance,* (2) *trop., preeminence, excellence.*—On **praedicare per eminentiam,** see *praedicare;* on **praedictio per eminentiam,** see *praedicatio;* on **via eminentiae seu quae est per eminentiam,** see *via.*

emineo, ere, ui, 2, *v. n., trop., to be prominent, stand out, become conspicuous,* opposite of *deficio.*—**eminens,** ntis, *P. a.,* (1) *lit., projecting, prominent, high, lofty,* (2) *trop., lofty, distinguished, eminent.*—**eminenter,** adv., *in an eminent manner, with excellence, highly, eminently.*

Emissenus, a, um, *adj., Emissenus, of Emesa,* now Hems in Syria. Eusebius, Bishop of Emesa 341-359, is called Eusebius Emissenus.

emissio, onis, *f.,* (1) *an emission,* as of excretive substances, (2) *a*

hurling, throwing with violence.
(3) *a going away, departure,
the act of departing,* (4) *an exhalation, a breathing out* or any
process resembling it, (5) *a
spending, giving away, bestowing,* (a) of some active goodness, charity, or beneficency, (b)
of money, (6) *an emission* or *di-
vergence* as of rays in all directions possible from a common
center.

emissivus, a, um, *adj., ready* or
*inclined to give away, open-
handed, munificent.*

emitto, ere, misi, missum, 3, *v. a.,*
(1) *to emit, send out, send forth,
discharge* anything, (2) *to put
forth, produce, shoot, cause to
grow forth, push out, protrude,*
as of plants, (3) *to emit, throw
out, issue* in circulation, as light,
(4) *to spend, part with* gradually, *use up* for a useless or useful purpose; *squander, waste,* as
money.—Common phrases are:
(a), **emittere lacrymas,** *to shed
tears, weep.*—(b), **emittere spiritum,** *to give up the ghost, soul
or spirit; to die.*—(c), **emittere
vocem,** *to utter, speak.*—(d),
emittere professionem, *to make
profession;* to bind oneself sol-
emnly by vows to a religious
Order or Congregation.—(e), **e-
mittere votum,** *to make a vow,*
especially a vow to surrender
oneself to a higher life of holiness.

Emmanuel, is, *m., Emmanuel,* i.e.,
nobiscum Deus, God with us.

Christ is often called "the Emmanuel", a name designating the
cause of salvation, which is the
union of the Divine and human
natures in the Person of the Son
of God, the result of which union was that God is with us.

Emmaus, *indecl. n., n. Emmaus,* a
village seven and one-half miles
from Jerusalem.

emo, ere, emi, emptum, 3, *v. a.,* (1)
lit., to buy, purchase, (2) *fig., to
buy, buy up, purchase, gain, acquire, procure.*

emollesco, ere, 3, *v. n., to enervate,
weaken, render effeminate* or
feeble.

emollio, ire, ii, itum, 4, *v. a.,* used
figuratively, *to soften, make soft,*
(1) in a good sense, *to make mild*
or *gentle,* (2) in a bad sense, *to
enervate, render effeminate.*

emollitio, onis, *f., a softening, a
making less hard in texture* or
substance.

emolumentum, i, *n., emolument,
gain, profit, general advantage.*

Empedocles, is, *m., Empedocles,* a
famous natural philosopher of
Agrigentum, about 460 B.C.

emphaticus, a, um, *adj., emphatic,
expressive.*

emplastrum, i, *n.,* in medic. lang.,
a plaster, a topical application of
some substance harder than ointment, used to produce a local
effect.

emptio, onis, *f., a buying, a purchase.*

emptor, oris, *m., a buyer, pur-
chaser.*

empyreus, a, um, *adj.*, *empyrean*, i.e., *fiery, of* or *pertaining to the region of pure fire*, so called not from its heat but from its brightness.—**coelum empyreum,** *the empyreum* or *fiery heaven*, *the highest heaven*, hence, the abode of God and the Angels.

emundatio, onis, *f.*, *a cleansing*, the act of freeing from defilement, physical or moral.

emundo, are, no perf., atum, 1, *v. a.*, (1) *to cleanse, to free from sin or its defilement*, (2) *to cleanse ceremonially for sacred service.*

enarratio, onis, *f.*, *a detailed exposition, interpretation.* St. Thomas has a few references to the Enarrationes in Psalmos of St. Augustine.

enarro, are, avi, atum, 1, *v. a.*, *to declare, make known, manifest, explain in detail, set forth the significance of.*

encaenia, orum, *n.*, *a consecration, dedication, festival.*

enchiridion, ii, *n.*, *an enchiridion, a handbook.* St. Thomas quotes freely the Enchiridion of St. Augustine which is a summary of the Christian Faith. The subject matter of the book is concerning Faith, Hope, and Charity; so that the Christian dogmas are really considered, not merely speculatively, but in their relation to these three great Christian virtues.

energumenos, (*energoumenos*), i, *m.*, *an energumen,* one who is possessed by evil spirits; *a demoniac,* a synonym of *arreptitius.*

enim, *conj.*, its position is regularly after the first word, or the first two or more closely connected words in the sentence, (1) to corroborate a preceding assertion like *equidem, certe, vero;* hence frequently connected with these particles, *truly, certainly, to be sure, indeed, in fact,* (2) to prove or show the grounds of a preceding assertion, *for.*—(1), there is no definite example of this usage in the S.T.

Enoch, *indecl.*, *n. m.*, *Enoch II,* the son of Jared and father of Methusalem. He "walked with God," a phrase expressive of constant companionship, and so at the age of three hundred sixty five he was taken up to heaven; he will return at the time of antichrist to give warnings and preach penance to the people.

enormis, e, *adj.*, *enormous, heinous.*

ens, entis, *n.*, *being,* or more properly, *a being, something having esse,* either essential or existential, in some way, not necessarily actual. It is the concrete subject of *esse* (q. v.), the opposite of *nihil* and *non-ens.* Being is the widest and most fundamental concept in the thought of St. Thomas. It is wider even than *reality,* and defies definition since there is nothing prior to it by which it can be defined.

It is an analogical concept, that is, has different meanings when applied to different orders and kinds of beings. A being is either uncaused, i.e., God alone, or caused, i.e., creatures. Created being is either real or rational, according as its objective existence is independent of a created mind or not. Thus certain relations, privations, negations, and chimeras, are not real beings, but *entia rationis*. Both real and rational being can be either potential or actual. Potential being which is *what can be,* although it is not as yet actual, is either possible, if there is no intrinsic incompatibility to the fusion of its constituents as there would be, e. g., to a squared circle, or to an infinite creature, or simply potential, if it exists as a real, though unrealized, capacity either to be something, or to become something. Actual being, not synonymous with real being though often confused with it, is the realization of a capacity. Thus existence is the act of essence, sensation of the sense, writing of the writer. Logical being is *ens rationis*, ontological being is reality. On the difference between *ens* and *res,* see *res.*—Kinds of *ens* in the ontological as well as the logical sense of the word are: (a), **ens absolute seu simpliciter** and **ens hoc seu tale,** *the absolutely* or *simply being,* which is understood without all or any modifications, and *being this* or *that* or *such a being.*—(b), **ens absolutum,** *the independent* or *unconditioned being.*—(c), **ens actu seu in actu** and **ens potentia seu in potentia,** the *on energeia* and *on danamei* of Aristotle, *the actual* and *the potential being,* or *the being that is in the state of actuality* and *that which is in the state of potentiality.*—(d), **ens commune seu universale seu in universali** and **ens particulare,** *the common* or *universal being* or *being in general* and *the particular being.*—(e), **ens completum seu perfectum** and **ens incompletum seu imperfectum,** *the complete* or *the perfect being* and *the incomplete* or *imperfect being.*—(f), **ens creatum** and **ens divinum,** *the created* and *the divine being.*—(g), **ens debilissimum,** *the weakest being.*—(h), **ens diminutum,** *the diminished being* which according to the thing is identical with *ens in anima* and therefore is called diminished, because the reality of the real being of which it is an image is lacking to it.—(i), **ens divinum,** see *ens creatum.*—(j), **ens essentialiter seu per essentiam** and **ens per participationem,** *the being that is essentially so* or *that through its own essence* and *the being by participation in being.*—(k), **ens extra animam seu in rebus extra animam seu naturae seu naturale** and **ens in anima** seu in ratione seu rationis, *the being outside the soul* or *that in things* and *outside the soul* and *the being in the soul* or *in the reason,* i.e., *the thing of nature* and *that of thought.*—(l), ens fixum, *the fixed* or *lasting being.*—(m), ens hoc, see *ens absolute.*—(n), ens immobile and ens mobile, *the immovable* and *the movable being.*—(o), ens imperfectum, see *ens completum.*—(p), ens in actu, see *ens actu.*—(q), ens in actu simpliciter, *the simple* or *absolute being,* the opposite of *ens in actu secundum quid,* i.e., of that which is actual being only respectively or in a certain respect.—(r), ens in alio and ens per se seu subsistens, *the being in another* and *that by itself* or *not in another.*—(s), ens in anima, see *ens extra animam.*—(t), ens incompletum, see *ens completum.*—(u), ens infinitum, *the Infinite Being.*—(v), ens in potentia, see *ens actu.*—(w), ens in potentia secundum quid and ens in potentia simpliciter, *the being which under one aspect is susceptible of further actualization,* or *the being in a certain potential respect* and *the simple* or *the completely potential being, which is primary matter.*—(x), ens in potentia simpliciter, see *ens in potentia secundum quid.*—(y), ens in ratione, see *ens extra animam.*—(z), ens in rebus, see *ens extra animam.*—(a^2), ens inseparabile, and ens separabile, *the*

inseparable and *separable being.*—(b^2), ens in universali, see *ens commune.*—(c^2), ens maxime seu maximum, *the maximum being.*—(d^2), ens mobile, see *ens immobile.*—(e^2), ens naturae, as opposed to logical being, see *ens extra animam.*—(f^2), ens naturale, as opposed to artificial, see *ens extra animam.*—(g^2), ens particulare, see *ens commune.*—(h^2), ens per accidens seu secundum accidens and ens per se seu secundum se, *the on kata symbebekos* and *on kath' hauto* of Aristotle, *the being indirectly because of the being of something else* and *being directly through its own self,* i.e., that which is being through a determination that comes to it incidentally and that which is being through its own nature and essence.—(i^2), ens per essentiam, see *ens essentialiter.*—(j^2), ens perfectum, see *ens completum.*—(k^2), ens per participationem, see *ens essentialiter.*—(l^2), ens per se, *that whose very nature is to be;* see *ens in alio, ens per accidens,* and *ens per aliud.* (m^2), ens positive dictum seu positivum, *being placed in the realm of reality* and *being intended in such a sense.*—(n^2), ens positivum, see *ens positive dictum.*—(o^2), ens potentia, see *ens actu.*—(p^2), ens primo seu primum, *the primary* or *first being,* so called because it deserves the name of being in the first place. —(q^2), ens privatum, *the deprived being* or *the being which lacks something which should not be lacking.*—(r^2), **ens rationis,** that which exists only in the mind; see *ens extra animam.*—(s^2), **ens secundum accidens,** see *ens per accidens.*—(t^2), **ens secundum quid** and **ens simpliciter,** *being in a certain respect,* under which is meant now *ens in potentia,* and now *accident,* and *the simple* or *absolute being,* under which is to be understood now *ens actu,* now *substance.*—(u^2), **ens secundum se,** see *ens per accidens.*—(v^2), **ens separabile,** see *ens inseparabile.*—(w^2), **ens signatum,** *the designated* or *fixed being.*—(x^2), **ens simplicitur,** see *ens absolute* and *ens secundum quid.* —(y^2), **ens subsistens,** see *ens in alio.*—(z^2), **ens tale,** see *ens absolute.*—(a^3), **ens universale,** see *ens commune.*—(b^3), **ens universaliter perfectum,** *the universally* or *entirely perfect being.*—**Actus et potentia dividunt quodlibet genus entium,** see *actus.*—**Bonum convertitur cum ente,** see *convertere.*—**Ens dividitur in seu per seu secundum decem praedicamenta seu genera,** *being is divided into ten categories* or *kinds of being.*—**Ens dividitur per contingens et necessarium,** *being is divided into the necessary* and *the casual.*—**Ens dividitur per potentiam et actum,** *being is divided into potentiality* and *actuality* or *into the possible* and *the actual.*—**Ens et res convertuntur,** see *convertere.*—**Ens et unum convertuntur,** see *convertere.*— **Ens non importat habitudinem causae, nisi formalis tantum, vel inhaerentis vel exemplaris,** *being does not bear the character of any cause except formal, which either dwells in the thing in question* or *is related to it as a model.*—**Ens non potest esse genus,** *being cannot be a kind* or *genus.*—**Illud quod consequitur omne ens, convenit enti, inquantum est ens,** *whatever accompanies every being, belongs to it as such,* i.e., according to its nature and essence.—**Potentia et actus sunt de primis differentiis entis,** see *potentia.*—**Verum cum ente convertitur,** see *convertere.*

ensis, is, *m., a sword.*

entelechia, ae, *f., accomplishment, actuality, substantial form,* the *entelecheia* of Aristotle; does not occur in the S.T.

enthymema, atis, *n., a blunted conclusion,* so called because one of its premises has remained *en thumo,* i.e., in the mind, has not been expressed in words; does not occur in the S.T.

entitas, atis, *f., character of being,* i.e., that relation according to which it can be said of a thing that it is there or it exists. Cf. *ens* and *esse.*

enumeratio, onis, *f., an enumeration, a counting up,* a detailed mention of things in succession; hence a list or catalogue.

enumero, are, avi, atum, 1, *v. a.,* to enumerate, name one by one, specify singly, tell, also count or ascertain the number of.

enuntiabilis, e, *adj., that can be proclaimed* or *announced, enunciable.—Enuntiabile* is the *opinion* or *statement* in which a proclamation is made. Synonym of *enuntiatio.* On **complexum per modum enuntiabilis,** see *complexus;* on **compositio enuntiabilis,** see *compositio;* on **veritas enuntiabilis,** see *veritas;* on **verum enuntiabile,** see *verus* under 1.—Kinds of *enuntiabile* in the sense of *opinion* are the following: (a), **enuntiabile de futuro, enuntiabile de praesenti,** and **enuntiabile de praeterito,** *opinion of the future, that of the present,* and *that of the past.* —(b), **enuntiabile de praesenti,** see *enuntiabile de futuro.*—(c), **enuntiabile de praeterito,** see *enuntiabile de futuro.*—(d), **enuntiabile necessarium** and **enuntiabile possibile,** *the necessarily true* and *the possible* or *not necessarily true opinion* or *statement.*—(e), **enuntiabile possibile,** see *enuntiabile necessarium.*

enuntiatio, onis, *f.,* (1) *expression, publication,* (2) the literal expression of a *statement, opinion,* synonym of *enuntiabile.*—On the relation of *enuntiatio* to *propositio,* see *propositio.*—In every *enuntiatio* there are five points of view according to which it can be considered or divided, namely:—(1), *unitas,* i.e., the unity or uniformity of the statement.—(2), *qualitas,* i.e., the nature of the copula or the form of the statement.—(3), *quantitas,* i.e., the extent to which the conception of the subject is taken. —(4), *tempus,* i.e., determination of the time of the copula.— (5) *habitudo praedicati ad subiectum,* i.e., the relationship of the predicate to the subject according to which it is determined whether a sentence has been constructed in *materia necessaria vel naturali,* or *in materia impossibili seu remota* or *in materia possibili sive contingenti.* On **contrarietas enuntiationis,** see *contrarietas;* on **falsum in enuntiatione,** see *falsus;* on **materia enuntiationis,** see *materia;* on **pluralitas enuntiationis,** see *pluralitas;* on **veritas enuntiationis,** see *veritas;* on **verum in enuntiatione,** see *verus.*—Kinds of *enuntiatio* are the following: (a), **enuntiatio aequipollens,** *the statement of equal power* or *of equal worth.*—(b), **enuntiatio affirmativa** and **enuntiatio negativa,** *the affirmative* and *negative statement.*—(c), **enuntiatio categorica** and **enuntiatio condicionalis seu hypothetica,** *the categorical* or *unconditioned* and *the conditioned* or *hypothetical sentence.*—(d), **enuntiatio composita** and **enuntiatio simplex,** *the composite* and *the simple statement,* i.e., that statement which either in its subject or in its predicate contains several ideas simultaneously, e.g., animal rationale mortale currit, and that which is vox significativa de eo, quod est aliquid, quod pertinet ad affirmationem, vel non est aliquid, quod pertinet ad negationem, e.g., homo est iustus and homo non est iustus. —(e), **enuntiatio condicionalis,** see *enuntiatio categorica.*—(f), **enuntiatio contradictoria, enuntiatio contraria,** and **enuntiatio subcontraria,** *the contradictory, the contrary,* and *subcontrary opposed statement,* i.e., that statement which is related to another as a particular affirmative to a general negative or as a general affirmative to a particular negative sentence; that sentence which is related to another as a general affirmative to a general negative sentence or the reverse; and that sentence which is opposed to another sentence according to the wording because both sentences opposed and contrary are subjected and subordinated to each other as partial statements.—(g), **enuntiatio contraria,** see *enuntiatio contradictoria.*—(h), **enuntiatio copulativa,** *the connective statement,* i.e., that compound statement whose subject as well as the predicate consists of several ideas bound together by particles or which through a connective is composed of two or more complete

sentences, e.g., homo est albus et equus est albus.—(i), **enuntiatio de futuro, enuntiatio de praesenti,** and **enuntiatio de preterito,** *the statement with future tense, that with present tense,* and *that with past tense.*—(j), **enuntiatio de praedicato finito, enuntiatio de praedicato infinito,** and **enuntiatio de praedicato privativo seu privativa,** *the statement with a complete predicate, that with an indefinite predicate,* and *that with a predicate depriving the subject of something,* e.g., homo est iustus, homo est non iustus, homo est iniustus.—(k), **enuntiatio de praedicato infinito,** see *enuntiatio de praedicato finito.*—(l), **enuntiatio de praedicato privativo,** see *enuntiatio de praedicato finito.*—(m), **enuntiatio de praesenti,** see *enuntiatio de futuro.*—(n), **enuntiatio de praeterito,** see *enuntiatio de futuro.*—(o), **enuntiatio de subiecto infinito,** *the statement with an indefinite subject,* e.g., non-homo est iustus, non-homo non est iustus.—(p), **enuntiatio disiunctiva,** *a disjunctive statement.*—(q), **enuntiatio exterior,** *the exterior statement* or *that formed with audible words which is opposed to that formed in thought.*—(r), **enuntiatio hypothetica,** see *enuntiatio categorica.*—(s), **enuntiatio indefinita seu infinita, enuntiatio particularis, enuntiatio singularis** and **enuntiatio universalis,** *the undetermined statement, the particu-*

lar or *special statement, the singular* or *single,* and *the general* or *universal statement.*—(t), **enuntiatio infinita,** see *enuntiatio indefinita.*—(u), **enuntiatio negativa,** see *enuntiatio affirmativa.*—(v), **enuntiatio particularis,** see *enuntiatio indefinita.*—(w), **enuntiationes plures** and **enuntiatio una,** *the plural* and *the single sentence,* i.e., the statement which expresses several opinions and that which expresses only one.—(x), **enuntiatio privativa,** see *enuntiatio de praedicato infinito.*—(y), **enuntiatio prophetica,** *the prophetic statement.*—(z), **enuntiatio simplex,** see *enuntiatio composita.*—(a²), **enuntiatio singularis,** see *enuntiatio indefinita.*—(b²), **enuntiatio subcontraria,** see *enuntiatio contradictoria.*—(c²), **enuntiatio transposita,** the transposed or inverted statements, e.g., *homo est non-iustus* instead of *homo non est iustus.*—(d²), **enuntiatio una,** see *enuntiationes plures.*—(e²), **enuntiatio una absolute seu simplex seu simpliciter** and **enuntiatio una secundum quid seu coniunctione,** *the unconditioned* or *absolutely simple statement* and *the relatively unified statement* or *the uniform statement produced by a connective.*—(f²), **enuntiatio una coniunctione,** see *enuntiatio una absolute.*—(g²), **enuntiatio una secundum quid,** see *enuntiatio una absolute.*—(h²), **enuntiatio una simplex seu simpliciter,** see *enun-*

tiatio una absolute.—(i²), **enuntiatio universalis,** see *enuntiatio indefinita.*

enuntio, are, avi, atum, 1, *v. a.,* (1) *to divulge, reveal, disclose,* (2) *to speak out, say, express, declare.*

eo, ire, ivi, or ii, itum, *v. n.,* (1) *to go,* move from one place, state or station to another, as by walking, riding, flying, (a) of animate things, (b) of inanimate things, (2) used figuratively.

Ephesii, orum, *m., the Ephesians;* the epistle of St. Paul to the church at Ephesus, treating of the redemptive purposes of God as embracing both Jews and Gentiles.

Ephesinus, a, um, *adj., of Ephesus,* an old and celebrated commercial city of Ionia, with a temple to Diana. St. Thomas in the S.T. refers frequently to the Council of Ephesus held in 431, under Pope Celestine, who died before the end of the council. Nestorius, Bishop of Constantinople, who taught the unity of nature in Christ was condemned, and the condemnation was ratified by Pope Sixtus III, the successor of Celestine.

ephod, n. indecl., *an ephod,* a priestly vestment of linen, especially that worn by the Jewish high priest over the tunic and outer garment. It was sleeveless and was divided below the armpits, one part covering the breast, and the other the back. The ephod of the high priest was richly embroidered and bound with a girdle. To each shoulder was fastened an onyx engraved with the six tribes and set in gold ouches; and from these ouches hung the breastplate.

Ephron, n. indecl., m., Ephron, a Hittite who sold Abraham a burying-place.

epi, (Grk. epi) a Greek prep., upon, on.

epicheia, (epiikia), ae, f., the becoming, as opposed to what is just, equity, i.e., virtue, to do what is right and virtuous, synonym of aequitas.

Epictetus, i, m., Epictetus, bishop of Corinth, circ. A.D. 369. He received a celebrated letter from Athanasius in reply to his request for arguments against certain errors then in controversy at Corinth. Some had maintained that the human body of our Lord was consubstantial with His deity; others that he was a man adopted only to be the Son of God. Athanasius blames Epictetus for having even allowed these opinions to be set forth.

Epicurei, orum, m., the Epicureans, the followers of Epicurus, the famous Greek philosopher of Gargettus in Attica, who was the author of a philosophy which assumed pleasure to be the highest good.

epicyclus, i, m., an epicycle, a circle whose center was conceived to move around the earth in a larger circle called the defferent, while a planet moved around its circumference. In the case of the outer planets the motion around the epicycle represents the apparent alternations of the direct and the retrograde motions due to the motion of the earth around the sun.

epiikes, e, adj., = epieikes, (1) proper, right, just, synonym of aequus, (2) acting properly, doing what is right and just.

epiikia, see epicheia.

epilepsia, ae, f., epilepsy, the falling sickness.

epilepticus, i, m., epileptikos, epileptic.

epiphania, orum, n., the Epiphany, a festival in commemoration of the manifestation of Christ to the Gentiles, especially in the visit of the Magi to Bethlehem, celebrated on January 6.

epireasmus, i, m., epereasmos, despiteful treatment, envy, grudge.

episcopalis, e, adj., episcopal, of or pertaining to a bishop or bishops.

episcopatus, us, m., an episcopate, episcopal see, the office or dignity of a bishop, a bishopric.

episcopein = episkopein, pres. inf. of episkopeo, a synonym of superintendere, to watch over.

episcopus, i, m., a bishop, a person admitted by episcopal consecration to the highest order of the ministry, with the power to administer Holy Orders and Confirmation, and exercising authoritative jurisdiction within his diocese.

epistola, ae, *f.*, *an epistle, a written message, communication,* especially applied to ancient epistolary writings of sacred character or of literary excellence. St. Thomas in the S.T. quotes freely from the letters of Augustine and Jerome and occasionally from Cyril, Gregory Nazianzus, Isidore, Cyprian, Athanasius, and the popes. His use of the letters of Saint Basil is negligible. A few references to Seneca's letters occur.

epistolaris, e, *adj.*, *of* or *belonging to a letter, epistolary.*

epulo, onis, *m.*, *a feaster, carouser, glutton.*

epulor, ari, atus, 1, *v. dep. n.* and *a.*, *to feast on, eat.*

equa, ae, *f.*, *a mare.*

eques, itis, *m.*, *a rider, horseman.*

equester, tris, tre, *adj.*, *equestrian, belonging to a horseman, practised in* or *given to horsemanship.*

equinus, a, um, *adj.*, *equine, of* or *belonging to horses.*

equito, are, avi, atum, 1, *v. n.* and *a.*, *to ride.*

equus, i, *m.*, *a horse, steed, charger.*

eradicatio, onis, *f.*, *eradication, the act of rooting out,* or *the condition of being rooted out.*

eradico, are, avi, atum, 1, *v. a.*, (1) *to pluck up by the roots, root out, eradicate,* (2) *transf.*: aliquem, *to root out utterly, destroy.*

erectio, onis, *f.*, (1) *erection, the act* or *process of building* or *constructing, that which is erected,* (2) *erection, the state of being erected,* or *lifted up.*

eremita, ae, *m.*, *an eremite, hermit.*

eremiticus, a, um, *adj.*, *eremitical, living like a hermit, dwelling alone* or *in desert wilds, solitary.* On **religio eremitica,** see *religio;* on **vita eremitica,** see *vita.*

eremus, i, *m.*, *a wilderness, desert.*

ereptio, onis, *f.*, *an ereption, a forcible taking away, a loss.*

erga, *prep.* with *acc.* in general of every kind of mental relation to a person or thing, *to, towards, in respect to.*

ergo, *adv.*, *consequently, accordingly, therefore, then.*

erigo, ere, rexi, rectum, 3, *v. a.*, (1) *to raise, lift anything,* (a) *to erect, build up, put up,* cause to rise as a result of construction, (b) *to lift,* raise by conscious effort, as the eyes, (c) *to set up, cause to assume an upright position,* as a flag pole, (d) *to lift* or *raise something* to an erect position, as the body, (2) *fig.*, (a) *to raise up* something, as one's hopes, (b) *to raise, elevate, advance to some higher state,* (c) *to stir, lift up* to action or emotion, (d) *to lift up* in spirit.— With *se,* **erigere se,** *to arise, to begin, to act mentally* or *physically.*—**animus erigit se in elationem,** *the mind puffs up, swells as with importance.*—**erigere se contra** or **adversus,** *to lift one's* self against, defy, act in disregard of.—**erectus**, a, um, *P. a.*,—(1), *erect, elevated, directed upwards.*—(2), *erect, upright in position.*—(3), *erect, attentive, alert.* —(4), *upright, morally correct.*

eripio, ere, ipui, eptum, 3, *v. a.*, *to snatch away, take away,* used in *a literal* and *figurative* sense.—**eripere aliquem a damnatione**, *to save some one from hell.*

erogatio, onis, *f.*, *a paying out, distribution.*

erogo, are, avi, atum, 1, *v. a.*, *to pay out, disburse, expend.*—With a slight change of meaning, note the following phrases: (a), **erogare corpus Christi**, *to dispense* or *distribute the Body of Christ.* —(b), **erogare sermonem**, *to deliver a sermon.*

erro, are, avi, atum, 1, *v. n.* and *a.*, (1) *to err, leave the right path* or *direction, stray, wander,* (2) *fig.*, (a) *to err, wander from the truth, mistake* as in judgment, *be incorrect,* (b) *to err, depart from the right, go astray morally, sin.* —**errans**, ntis, *P. a.*, *erring, mistaking, understanding wrongly.* —**errantes**, tium, *comm.*, *the perplexed, misguided;* also *the erring,* those in error or who have gone astray from the truth, especially in matters of opinion or belief. The *Dux errantium, the guide of the perplexed* was one of the philosophical works of Maimonides (Rabbi Moyses), a Jewish commentator. It was translated into Hebrew as Mo-

reh Nebukim, and into Latin as Doctor Perplexorum, Dux Dubitantium. The Arabic original was published with a French translation entitled "Guide des egares" by Munk, 1856-66.—**erratum**, i, *n.*, *an error, mistake.*

erronee, *adv.*, see *erroneus.*

erroneus, a, um, *adj.*, *erroneous, marked by error;* characterized by wrong or false views or principles; *not true or just; incorrect; mistaken.*—**erronee**, *adv.*, *erroneously.*

error, oris, *m.*, *error, erring.* On **impuritas erroris**, see *impuritas.* —Kinds of *error* are: **error involuntarius** and **error voluntarius**, *the unwilling* and *the willing error.*—*Parvus error in principio magnus est in fine,* the translation of the Aristotelian expression: *to en arche mikron en te teleute ginetai pammegethes,* an error, small in the beginning, becomes great in the end.

erubescentia, ae, *f.*, *erubescence, shamefacedness,* the manifestation of shame in one's face, one of the six species of fear assigned by St. John Damascene in his *De fide Orthodoxa,* and discussed by St. Thomas in the S.T. Shamefacedness is the fear of disgrace in a deed that is yet to be done; shame is fear of disgrace in a deed already done.

erubescibilis, e, *adj.*, *of which one should be ashamed.*

erubesco, ere, bui, 3, *v. inch.*, *n.* and *a.*, *to redden* or *blush,* as with confusion, modesty or shame, used with the *abl.*, *ab.*, *de* and *ex* with the *abl.*, *absol.*, *acc.*, *inf.*

eructo, are, 1, *v. a., to utter, proclaim, relate.*

erudio, ire, ivi or ii, itum, 4, *v. a.,* (1) *to publish, educate, instruct, teach,* (a) *to educate, inform by teaching, instruct, tell what to believe,* (b) *to enlighten,* bestow spiritual light upon; cause to see clearly; *instruct,* (c) *to educate, bring up* from immaturity, as a child, (2) *transf.,* of objects not personal.

eruditio, onis, *f.,* (1) *erudition,* the act or process of instructing, (2) *erudition,* a high degree of accurate knowledge gained by personal study or by instruction; *accomplished scholarship;* the state of being learned or erudite.

eruditor, oris, *m., an instructor, teacher.*

erumpo, ere, rupi, ruptum, 3, *v. a.,* and *n.,* (1) *lit., to break out, discharge, flow out* from any enclosed source, (2) *fig. fall into,* to enter either accidentally or naturally into some state of mind, course, or association.

eruo, ere, ui, utum, 3, *v. a.,* used *fig.,* (1) *to overwhelm, overcome, to achieve the mastery, conquer,* (2) *to rescue, release.*

eruptio, onis, *f., an outbreak, a sudden breaking forth,* as of something that has been pent up or restrained, used figuratively of manifestations of passion.

Esau, *n. indecl. m., Esau,* the oldest son of Isaac; sold his birthright to Jacob.

esca, ae, *f., food used lit.* and *fig.*

Esdras, ae, *m., Esdras,* Books of. Two canonical books of the Old Testament. In the first of these books it is related that Esdras, or Ezra, "the prince of the Synagogue", revised the Book of the Law and took care that its provisions should be observed. Mention is also made of King Cyrus breaking up the Babylonian captivity by permitting the expatriated Jews to return to Jerusalem and rebuild their temple. Nehemias succeeded Esdras. Jewish tradition regards Esdras as the author of the Books of Esdras.

esse, essendi, *n., to be* or *being* in the ontological as well as in the logical sense of the word, the opposite likewise of *non-esse* and of *fieri; existence.* On **esse in minus,** see *minor;* on **esse in plus,** see *plus.*—On the relationship of *esse to essentia,* see *essentia.* On **analogia secundum esse,** see *analogia;* on **causa esse,** see *causa;* on **debitum esse,** see *debitus;* on **gradus esse,** see *gradus;* on **idem secundum esse,** see *idem;* on **modus esse,** see *modus;* on **necessitas esse,** see *necessitas;* on **possibilitas esse seu ad esse et non esse,** see *possibilitas;* on **potentia ad esse,** see *potentia;* on **potestas esse,** see *potestas;* on **principium esse et primum esse,** see *principium;* on **prius in esse**

seu secundum ordinem in esse, see *prior;* on **quaestio de esse simpliciter,** see *quaestio;* on **relatio secundum esse,** see *relatio;* on **relativum secundum esse,** see *relativus.*—Esse with the preceding or following dative of a word is an imitation of an Aristotelian expression and indicates the being peculiar to a thing, i.e., its essence, not its existence, and furthermore the being of the thing which is indicated by the word in the dative case or the essence or the abstract essence of the same. Cf. *quod quid erat esse seu quod quid est* under *qui.*—Kinds of *esse* in the ontological sense are: (a), **esse ab alio seu per aliud** and **esse per se,** *existence from another* or *through another* and *through itself.* Cf. also *esse per accidens.*—(b), **esse absolute seu simpliciter seu simpliciter acceptum** and **esse secundum quid seu esse aliquid seu aliquo modo seu hoc seu tale seu tantum,** *the absolute* or *simple* or *simply considered being* and *being in a certain respect* or *being something* or *in some manner* or *this* or *such* or *so great being.*—(c), **esse absolutum** and **esse concretum,** *existence in itself, apart from its subject,* (*non dependens a corpore*), and *existence considered in something.*—(d), **esse accidentale seu accidentis** and **esse substantiale seu substantiae,** *the accidental* and *the essential being*

or *the mode of existence of accident* and *that of substance.*—(e), **esse accidentis,** see *esse accidentale.*—(f), **esse actu seu in actu seu actuale** and **esse in potentia,** *being according to act* and *that according to potentiality.*—(g), **esse actuale,** see *esse actu.*—(h), **esse alicuius seu huius,** *being of someone* or *of this.*—(i), **esse aliquo modo,** see *esse absolute.*—(j), **esse animatum seu vitale,** *the animated* or *living being.* Cf. above *esse viventibus.*—(k), **esse causale** and **esse essentiale,** *the causal* and *the essential being.*—(l), **esse commune seu universale** and **esse proprium seu particulatum seu determinatum,** *the common* or *universal being* and *the peculiar* or *particular* or *determined being.*—(m), **esse completum seu perfectum** and **esse incompletum seu imperfectum,** *the complete* or *perfect being* and *the incomplete* or *the imperfect being.*—(n), **esse concretum,** see *esse absolutum.*—(o), **esse corporale** and **esse spirituale,** *the corporal being* and *the spiritual* or *immaterial being.* Cf. also *esse immateriale* and *esse intentionale.*—(p), **esse corruptible** and **esse incorruptible,** *transient being* and *intransient being.*—(q), **esse creatum seu creaturae** and **esse Dei seu divinum,** *the created* or *the produced being* and *the divine* or *uncreated being.*—(r), **esse creaturae,** see *esse creatum.*—(s), **esse debilissimum,** *the* *weakest being,* because it lacks concrete reality, under which is to be understood on the one hand the relationship of one thing to another, on the other esse in anima seu intentionale.— (t), esse Dei, see *esse creatum.* —(u), esse dependens and esse non-dependens, *the being dependent on something* and *the being not dependent on anything.*—(v), esse determinatum, see *esse commune.*—(w), esse discretum and esse unitum, *the separated* and *the united being.* —(x), esse distinctum and esse indistinctum, *the distinguished* or *determined being* and *the not distinguished* or *undetermined being.*—(y), esse divinum, see *esse creatum.*—(z), esse essentiale, see *esse causale.*—(a^2), esse essentialiter and esse participative, *being according to essence* and *being according to participation.*—(b^2), esse ex aliquo, see *ex.*—(c^2), esse finitum seu limitatum and esse infinitum seu non limitatum, *the finite* or *limited being* and *the infinite or unlimited being.*—(d^2), esse firmum seu fixum seu permanens seu stans and esse fluens seu transiens, *the firm* or *fixed* or *permanent being* and *the fluent* or *passing being.*—(e^2), esse fixum, see *esse firmum.*—(f^2), esse fluens, *transient existence.* See *esse firmum.*—(g^2), esse formale, *being corresponding to the form of a thing.*—(h^2), esse gloriae, esse gratiae seu gratuitum and esse naturae seu naturale, *being of the glory in heaven, being of grace, being of nature.*—(i^2), esse gratiae, see *esse gloriae.*— (j^2), esse gratuitum, see *esse gloriae.*—(k^2), esse hoc, see *esse absolute.*—(l^2), esse huius, see *esse alicuius.*—(m^2), esse immateriale and esse materiale, *an essence without matter,* or *a material essence existing in an immaterial state,* i.e., *in an intellect, being not conditioned by a connection with matter* and *that conditioned by a connection with matter.*— (n^2), esse imperfectum, see *esse completum.*—(o^2), esse in actu, *actual existence.* See *esse actu.*— (p^2), esse in alio seu receptum seu non subsistens and esse in se seu in seipso seu non receptum seu subsistens seu per se subsistens seu separatum subsistens, *being in another* or *being received in something* or *existence not by reason of itself* and *being in itself* or *being not in another* or *being not received* or *existent of itself* or *separated existent being.*—(q^2), esse in anima, *real existence in the soul.*— (r^2), esse in aliquo, *being in any one thing.*—(s^2), esse in cognoscente, *existence in the mind.* See *esse in anima.*—(t^2), esse incompletum, see *esse completum.*—(u^2), esse incorruptibile, see *esse corruptibile.*—(v^2), esse indistinctum, see *esse distinctum.*—(w^2), esse in eo quod quid est, the Aristotelian *hyparchein en to ti esti, being contained in the essence of a thing.*—(x^2), esse infinitum, *limitless being,* either casually so, as a mathematical surface, which is strictly *indefinite,* or necessarily so, as the being of God who alone is strictly *infinite,* see *esse finitum.*—(y^2), esse in minus, see *minor.*—(z^2), esse in numero, see *numerus.*—(a^3), esse in parte and esse totaliter seu secundum secundum totum suum posse, *being in part* or *according to a part,* Aristotle's *to epi merous,* Anal. post. II, 1, 89. b. 39, and *being totally, Aristotle's to haplos, idem,* or *according to all its authority.*—(b^3), esse in plus, see *plus.*—(c^3), esse in potentia, *unrealized existence.* See *esse actu.*—(d^3), esse in se, see *esse in alio.*—(e^3), esse in seipso, see *esse in alio.*—(f^3), esse in seipso non primo seu secundum alterum seu secundum partem seu per partem and esse in seipso primo, *being in consequence of another* or *in accordance with a part* and *being primarily in itself.*—(g^3), esse in seipso per partem, see *esse in seipso non primo.*—(h^3), esse in seipso primo, see *esse in seipso non primo.*—(i^3), esse in seipso primo et per accidens seu secundum accidens and esse in seipso primo et per se, *being in the first place* and *according to something else* and *being in the first place* and *according to itself* and *in itself.*—(j^3), esse in seipso pri-

mo et per se, see *esse in seipso et per accidens.*—(k^3), esse in seipso secundum alterum, see *esse in seipso non primo.*—(l^3), esse in seipso secundum partem, see *esse in seipso non primo.*—(m^3), esse in subiecto, *being in a subject* or *being in something as in its subject.*—(n^3), esse intellectuale seu intelligibile and esse sensibile, *the intellectual* and *sensible being.* These are the two great orders of being. Intelligible being is the object of the intellect, is immaterial either of itself or by abstraction from matter by some intellect, and analogously unites God, the angels, and the rational part of man into one order. Sensible being is the object of the senses, is material and corporeal, therefore unintelligible in itself, and unites the lower part of man with all creation below him. *Esse intelligibile* also means a manner of existence, as when the mind considers matter, it is said to exist in *esse intelligibile.*—(o^3), esse intelligibile, see *esse intellectuale.*—(p^3), esse intentionale and esse naturae seu naturale seu reale seu rei, *the mental* or *cognitive existence* and *the natural state as it belongs to a thing existing in reality.* A thing can exist in two different modes or states, one of which is objective, extramental, natural and the other is subjective, intra-sensible or intra-intellectual, intentional. This latter is not the same as rational being, which is such precisely because it has no objective, extra-mental existence, apart from the mind or ratio which engenders it.—(q³), **esse limitatum**, see *esse finitum.*—(r³), **esse locale**, *the local* or *spatial being.*—(s³), **esse materiale**, *either material being*, or *existence in matter*, see *esse immateriale.*—(t³), **esse naturae**, see *esse gloriae* and *esse intentionale.*—(u³), **esse naturale**, see *esse gloriae* and *esse intentionale.*—(v³), **esse non dependens**, *independent existence*. See *esse dependens.*—(w³), **esse non limitatum**, see *esse finitum.*—(x³), **esse non receptum**, *self-existence*. See *esse in alio.*—(y³), **esse non subsistens**, see *esse in alio.*—(z³), **esse participatum seu per participationem** and **esse per essentiam**, *existence which is received from another* and *existence by* and *of the very nature.*—(a⁴), **esse participative**, see *esse essentialiter.*—(b⁴), **esse particulatum**, see *esse commune.*—(c⁴), **esse per accidens** and **esse per se**, *being through something else* and *being in its own self* or *its own nature* and *essence.*—(d⁴), **esse per aliud**, see *esse ab alio.*—(e⁴), **esse per essentiam**, see *esse participatum.*—(f⁴), **esse perfectum**, see *esse completum.*—(g⁴), **esse permanens**, see *esse firmum.*—(h⁴), **esse per participationem**, see *esse participatum.*—(i⁴), **esse perpetuum**, *perpetual being,*—(j⁴), **esse per se**, *substantial existence,*

not dependent on any creature. See *esse ab alio* and *esse per accidens.*—(k⁴), **esse per se subsistens**, *self-subsistent being*. See *esse in alio.*—(l⁴), **esse personale**, *the personal being* or *person-being.*—(m⁴), **esse primitivum seu primordiale** and **esse ultimum seu terminatum**, *the original* or *primitive being* and *the last* or *completed* or *concluded being.* —(n⁴), **esse primordiale**, see *esse primitivum.*—(o⁴), **esse primum** and **esse secundum**, *the first* or *divine being* and *the second* or *created being.*—(p⁴), **esse principale** and **esse secundarium**, *the principal* and *the subordinated being* or *the being in the first* and *that in the second rank.*— (q⁴), **esse proprium**, see *esse commune.*—(r⁴), **esse purum seu tantum**, *pure* or *only being.*—(s⁴), **esse reale**, see *esse intentionale.* —(t⁴), **esse receptum**, see *esse in alio.*—(u⁴), **esse rei**, *existence as foundation for action.* See *esse intentionale.*—(v⁴), **esse secundum**, see *esse primum.*—(w⁴), **esse secundum quid**, *qualified existence.* See *esse absolute.*—(x⁴), **esse secundum totum suum posse**, see *esse in parte.*—(y⁴), **esse sensibile**, see *esse intellectuale, being in the sensible, as distinct from the intellectual order.*—(z⁴), **esse separatum subsistens**, see *esse in alio.*—(a⁵), **esse similitudinarium**, *the being of a likeness.*— (b⁵), **esse simpliciter**, *unqualified being*. See *esse absolute.*—(c⁵), esse simpliciter acceptum, see *esse absolute*.—(d⁵), esse specificum, *the peculiar being of a species*.—(e⁵), esse spirituale, see *esse corporale*.—(f⁵), esse stans, *permanent existence*. See *esse firmum*.—(g⁵), esse subsistens, see *esse in alio*.—(h⁵), esse substantiae, *mode of existence peculiar to substance*. See *esse accidentale*.—(i⁵), esse substantiale, see *esse accidentale*.—(j⁵), esse superadditum, *the added being*. —(k⁵), esse tale, see *esse absolute*.—(l⁵), esse tantum, see *esse purum*.—(m⁵), esse terminatum, see *esse primitivum*.—(n⁵), esse totaliter, see *esse in parte*.—(o⁵), esse transiens, *transient existence*. See *esse firmum*.—(p⁵), esse ultimum, see *esse primitivum*.—(q⁵), esse universale, see *esse commune*.—(r⁵), esse vitale, see *esse animatum*.—Agere sequitur ad esse in actu, see *agere*.—Eius est agere, cuius est esse, see *agere*.—Eo modo aliquid operatur, quo est, or, modus operandi uniuscuiusque rei sequitur modum essendi ipsius, or, similiter unumquodque habet esse et operationem, or, unumquodque operatur, secundum quod est, *the manner of action* and *that of the being of any single thing correspond*.—Esse consequitur seu sequitur formam, or, esse per se consequitur ad formam, or, esse consequitur naturam, *existence arises from the substantial form* or *according to the nature* and *essence of the thing*.—Esse cuiuslibet rei consistit in indivisione, *the being of every single thing is indivisible*. —Esse est prius natura quam agere, see *agere*.—Esse et esse verum convertuntur, see *convertere*.—Esse non convenit formae tantum, nec materiae tantum, sed composito, *in physical things neither form not matter alone exist but rather both combined*.—Esse per se consequitur ad formam, see above: *esse consequitur etc.*—Esse substantiale cuiuslibet rei in indivisibili consistit, *the essence of each thing can neither be added to nor taken away from*.—Illud est unaquaeque res quod operatur operationes illius rei, *each* and *everything is that which produces its proper actions, wherefore* illud est homo, quod operatur operationes hominis.—Illud, quod est ultimum in resolutione, est primum in esse, *what is last in disintegration, this is first in being* or *becoming*.—In iis, quae possunt esse et non esse, prius est non esse, quam esse, *with those things which can be* and *not be, non-being is earlier than being*.— Ipsum esse nihil aliud adiunctum habere potest, *to being as such nothing can be added*.—Modus operandi uniuscuiusque rei sequitur modum essendi ipsius, see above: *eo modo aliquid etc.*— Nihil est formalius aut simplicius quam esse, *nothing is more formal* or *irreducible than being*.— Nulla res habet potestatem supra suum esse, *nothing has power over its own existence, so that it can take away the same or change it in the least.*—Omne, quod est in altero, est in eo per modum eius in quo est, *everything that is in another is in it according to the manner of the same.*—Omne, quod est per accidens, reducitur ad id, quod est per se, *everything that is by accident is to be referred to something which is a being as such and according to itself.*—Omne, quod est per aliud, reducitur ad id quod est per se, *what is always through another is to be referred to that which is itself through itself.*—Omne, quod incipit esse vel desinit, per motum vel mutationem hoc patitur, *all that begins or ceases to be, does so in consequence of a motion or of a change.*—Quod est per accidens, est posterius eo quod est per se, *and the reverse,* quod est per se, prius est eo quod est per accidens, *that which is through accident is posterior to that which is or exists as such and according to itself,* and vice versa.—Similiter unumquodque habet esse et operationem, see above: *eo modo aliquid* etc. —Unumquodque operatur, secundum quod est, see *eo modo aliquid* etc.

essentia, ae, *f.,* (1) *essence,* as distinct from existence, *being,* that whereby, whether it be a substance or an accident, it is what

it is, (2) *being,* that which has an essence. *Essentia, forma, natura, quidditas, quod quid est, quod quid erat esse, species,* and *substantia,* all refer to the same thing but under different aspects. *Forma* is the determining element which makes a thing to be what it is, and constitutes it in its *species.* Thus, e.g., rationality is the *forma* which qualifies animality and constitutes the essence of man as rational animal, which is also his species. The essence conceived of as the principle of characteristic properties and all operations is *natura.* The answer to the question, *what is it? quid sit?* is the *quidditas,* or *whatness,* the *quod quid est,* and the *quod quid erat esse,* the latter two expressions being literal transliterations of Aristotelian expressions. *Substantia* is the essence conceived of as supporting and giving existence to accidents like size, shape, motion, etc. For St. Thomas, essence abstracts from existence; the only essentially existent being is God. Hence existence is related to essence as actuality to potentiality. On the relation of *essentia* to *natura,* see *natura.* On **beatitudo per essentiam,** see *beatitudo;* on **beatus per essentiam,** see *beatus;* on **bonitas de essentia rei, bonitas extra essentiam rei et bonitas per essentiam,** see *bonitas;* on **bonum per essentiam,** see *bonus;* on **communitas essentiae,** see *communitas;* on **dicere per essentiam,** see *dicere;* on **differre per essentiam,** see *differre;* on **diversitas essentiae,** see *diversitas;* on **divisio essentiae seu per essentiam seu secundum essentiam,** see *divisio;* on **ens per essentiam,** see *ens;* on **esse per essentiam,** see *esse;* on **finis quantum ad essentiam,** see *finis;* on **humanus per essentiam,** see *humanus;* on **infinitum essentiae seu secundum essentiam,** see *infinitus;* on **malum per essentiam,** see *malus;* on **ordo essentiae,** see *ordo;* on **pars essentiae,** see *pars;* on **praedicare per essentiam,** see *praedicare;* on **praedicatio per essentiam,** see *praedicatio;* on **principium essentiae,** see *principium;* on **ratio per essentiam,** see *ratio;* on **rationale per essentiam,** see *rationalis;* on **redire ad essentiam suam,** see *redire;* on **relatus per essentiam suam,** see *relatus;* on **spirituale per essentiam,** see *spiritualis;* on **tale per essentiam,** see *talis;* on **terminus quantum ad essentiam,** see *terminus;* on **totalitas essentiae,** see *totalitas;* on **unio secundum essentiam,** see *unio;* on **unitas essentiae,** see *unitas;* on **veritas per essentiam,** see *veritas;* on **visio per essentiam,** see *visio;* on **voluntas per essentiam,** see *voluntas.*—Kinds of *essentia* in this (1) sense are: (a), **essentia communis** and **essentia propria,** *the universal* or *general essence* and *the proper* or *peculiar essence.*—(b),

essentia completa and **essentia quaedam seu secundum quid,** *the complete* or *perfect essence* and *a certain kind of essence* or *relative essence.*—(c), **essentia divina,** *divine essence.*—(d), **essentia finita et infinita,** *the limited* or *finite essence* and *the unlimited* or *infinite essence.*—(e), **essentia infinita,** see *essentia finita.* —(f), **essentia propria,** see *essentia communis.*—(g), **essentia quaedam,** see *essentia completa.* —(h), **essentia secundum quid,** see *essentia completa.*—(i), **essentia separata,** *essence separated from matter.*—(j), **essentia simplex,** *the simple essence,* i.e., *not composed of form* and *matter.*— (k), **essentia visibilis,** *visible essence.*—As a special kind of *essentia* in this (2) sense we have **essentia quinta,** *the fifth essence* or *the fifth (simple) body* (cf. *corpus quintum)* or *the fifth element* (cf. *elementum),* i.e., that element of which the heavenly bodies consist and through the influence of which the elementary parts of earthly bodies are united and held together.

essentialis, e, *adj.,* (1) *essential,* i.e., concerning essence, belonging to it, proceeding from it, synonym of *substantialis,* the opposite of *accidentalis,* (2) *really self-existing,* i.e., determining essence, the opposite of *participatus* (see *participare)* and *per participationem.* On **bonum secundum esse essentiale,** see *bonus;* on **actio**

essentialis, see *actio;* on **actus essentialis**, see *actus;* on **adiectivum essentiale**, see *adiectivus;* on **attributum essentiale**, see *attributum;* on **conditio essentialis**, see *conditio;* on **designatio essentialis**, see *designatio;* on **differentia essentialis**, see *differentia;* on **distinctio essentialis**, see *distinctio;* on **divisio essentialis**, see *divisio;* on **esse essentialis**, see *esse;* on **forma essentialis**, see *forma;* on **gloria essentialis**, see *gloria;* on **immutatio essentialis**, see *immutatio;* on **intentio essentialis**, see *intentio;* on **lumen essentiale**, see *lumen;* on **nomen essentiale**, see *nomen;* on **ordo essentialis**, see *ordo;* on **pars essentialis**, see *pars;* on **perfectio essentialis**, see *perfectio;* on **poena essentialis**, see *poena;* on **potentia essentialis**, see *potentia;* on **praedicatio essentialis**, see *praedicatio;* on **praedicatum essentiale**, see *praedicatum;* on **praemium essentiale**, see *praemium;* on **principium essentiale**, see *principium;* on **proprietas essentialis**, see *proprietas;* on **proprium essentiale**, see *proprius;* on **qualitas essentialis**, see *qualitas;* on **terminus essentialis**, see *terminus;* on **totum essentiale**, see *totum;* on **unitas essentialis**, see *unitas.*—On **bonitas essentialis**, see *bonitas;* on **bonum essentiale**, see *bonus;* on **cognitio essentialis**, see *cognitio;* on **dilectio essentialis**, see *dilectio;* on **rationale essentiale**, see *rationa-*

lis; on **sapientia essentialis**, see *sapientia;* on **verbum essentiale**, see *verbum.*

essentialiter, *adv., after the manner or in the sense of essence, essentially,* synonym of *substantialiter,* the opposite of *accidentaliter* and *participative.*—On **ad beatitudinem pertinere essentialiter**, see *beatitudo;* on **appropriare essentialiter**, see *appropiare;* on **bonum essentialiter**, see *bonus;* on **dicere essentialiter**, see *dicere;* on **ens essentialiter**, see *ens;* on **esse essentialiter**, see *esse;* on **existere essentialiter**, see *existere;* on **infinitum essentialiter**, see *infinitus;* on **praedicare essentialiter**, see *praedicare;* on **rationalis essentialiter**, see *rationalis;* on **sumere essentialiter**, see *sumere;* on **unire essentialiter**, see *unire;* on **veritas essentialiter dicta**, see *veritas;* on **verum essentialiter**, see *verus;* on **voluntas essentialiter dicta**, see *voluntas.*

Estha, ae, *f., Estha,* the name of the wife of Matthan, who afterwards married Melchi.

Esther, *n. indecl., f.,* (1) *Esther,* queen of Persia and wife of Assuerus, who is identified with Xerxes (485-465 B.C.). She was a daughter of Abihail of the tribe of Benjamin, her Jewish name being Edessa. She had been adopted by her father's brother Mardochai, and her beauty caused Assuerus to choose her as his queen instead of his divorced wife Vasthi. In this position she was able to protect her people against the plots of Aman, a royal favorite, (2) *Esther,* Book of, a book of the Bible relating the history of a Jewish orphan girl named Edessa, later Esther. It portrays Persian court life with great exactness of detail and apparently is based upon court annals and written Jewish sources.

esuries, ei, *f.,* (1) *hunger, craving* or *desire for food,* (2) *fig., a hunger, any strong desire; a craving.*

esurio, ire, ii, itum, 4, *v. desid. n.* and *a.,* (1) *to hunger, desire to eat, be hungry, suffer from long abstinence from food; crave food,* (2) used *fig., to hunger; have an eager desire for; long,* as to hunger after righteousness.

esuritio, onis, *f., a hungering, hunger.*

esus, us, *m.,* (1) *an eating,* (2) *food.*

et, *conj.,* (1) *and,* to connect in the most general manner single words or entire sentences, (2) *and indeed, and moreover, and that too,* to subjoin a word or phrase which more accurately defines or more briefly comprehends what goes before, (3) when repeated *et . . . et,* it serves to connect two ideas partitively, *both . . . and, as well . . . as, not only . . . but also.*

etenim, *conj.,* subjoins a corroborative clause, or one which contains the reason of a preceding

statement, *for truly, and indeed, because that, since.*

ethicus, a, um, *adj.,* (1) *customary, occurring frequently, lasting,* (2) *ethical,* synonym of *moralis.—*On **scientia ethica,** see *scientia.—***ethica,** (sc. *scientia* or *philosophia*), ae, *f., moral philosophy.* —*ethica,* orum, *n., the science of right* and *wrong,* or *the science of right conduct, ethics,* the Nicomachean Ethics of Aristotle. The Aristotelian corpus on moral science contains three complete treatises from all of which St. Thomas quotes freely,—the Nicomachean Ethics, the Eudemian Ethics, and the Magna Moralia, the last two of doubtful Aristotelian authorship.

ethnicus, i, *m., a heathen.*

ethos, eos, *n.,* = Grk. *ethos, manner, custom, way, practice,* a synonym of *mos.*

etiam, *conj., and also, and furthermore, also, likewise, besides,* synonym of *quoque.*

etiamsi, a concessive conditional particle, = *kai ei,* more emphatic than *etsi, even if, although, albeit.* Its use with the *indic.* in the S.T. is rare; St. Thomas consistently uses it with the *subj.—* (1), with *indic.—*(2), with *subj.*

etsi, *conj.,* like etiamsi, a concessive conditional particle, *though, although, albeit,* used with (1) the *indic.,* (2) *subj.;* St. Thomas shows preference for the *subj.,* (3) *ellipt.* without a verb.

etymologia, ae, *f.,* (1) *derivation of words, etymology,* (2) *Etymologiae, Book of Etymologies,* a work of St. Isidore of Seville, frequently quoted in the S.T.

eu, *interj.,* = Grk. *eu, well, good,* a synonym of *bene.*

eubulia, ae, *f.,* = *euboulia, aptitude, capacity, talent, the virtue of good counsel, the euboulia* of Aristotle. On the difference between *eubulia* and *synesis,* see *synesis.*

eucharis, is, *adj.,* = Grk. *eucharis, agreeable, grateful, gracious.*

eucharistia, ae, *f.,* (1) *the virtue of thanksgiving* or *thankfulness,* (2) *the Sacrament of the altar.*

Euclides, is, *m., Euclid,* the geometrician of Alexandria under the Ptolemy Philadelphus.

Eudemicus, a, um, *adj., Eudemian,* a body of ethical doctrine, other than Nicomachean, *of* or *pertaining to Eudemus, a pupil of Aristotle.*

Eudoxius, ii, *m., Eudoxius,* a monk, probably abbot of a monastery in the island of Capraria to whom Augustine wrote in affectionate terms, exhorting the brethren not to make their monastic retirement an excuse for declining active service in the Church, but to be strenuous at all times in discharging their conventual duties, and to remember the liability to temptation even within their peaceful abode.

eufortunatus, a, um, *adj., very much favored by luck, very fortunate,* the opposite of *infortunatus,* does not occur in the S.T.

eufortunium, i, *n., good fortune, good luck,* the opposite of *infortunium,* does not occur in the S.T.

euge, *interj.,* an exclamation of joy, applause, admiration, *well done, good.*

eugnomosyne, ae, *f., the capacity* or *virtue of good* or *right judgment over exceptional things,* of the same meaning as Aristotle's *gnome.*

Eugubius, ii, *m., Gubbio,* a city in the province of Perugia, Italy; has Roman ruins.

Eunomianus, a, um, *adj., Eunomian,* a follower of Eunomius.

Eunomius, ii, *m., Eunomius* of Cappadocia, bishop of Cyzicus 360-364 A.D., after the expulsion of Eleusius. As a writer he was more copious than elegant. Basil the Great considered his Apologeticus worthy of an elaborate refutation which we possess in five books.

eunuchus, i, *m.,* (1) *an eunuch,* (2) the *Eunuch,* the name of one of Terence's comedies.

eupathia, ae, *f., eupathy,* the just and temperate mind which the Stoics made the ideal virtue.

Euphemius, ii, *m., Euphemius,* third patriarch of Constantinople, succeeding Fravitta and followed by Macedonius II. He ruled six years and three months,

489-496 A.D., and died 515 A.D.

Euphrates, is, *m.*, *Euphrates*, a well-known river in Syria, which rises in Armenia, and, after its junction with the Tigris, empties into the Persian Gulf.

eupsychia, ae, *f.*, = Grk. *eupsychia*, opp. of *kakapsychia*, *good courage*, *high spirit*, a synonym of *bona animositas*.

eusebia, ae, *f.*, *the virtue of the fear of God, fear of God*, synonym of *latria* and *theosebia*.

Eusebius, ii, *m.*, (1) *Eusebius* of Caesarea or Eusebius Pamphili, Bishop of Caesarea in Palestine (c. 260-c. 341). St. Thomas refers to his *Historia Ecclesiastica*, to his *Oratio de laudibus Constantini*, and to *Quaestiones ad Marinum*, (2) Eusebius, Bishop of Emesa, ob. (360). Author of numerous works (St. Jerome, *De viris illustr.*, XCI), nearly all of which have disappeared. Those published under his name are rather to be ascribed to Eusebius of Alexandria or to Eusebius of Caesarea. St. Thomas quotes as his a Paschal homily, (3) *Eusebius*, pope, succeeded Marcellus as bishop of Rome A.D. 309 or 310. There are three spurious decretal epistles attributed to Eusebius; one to the bishops of Campania and Tuscia, referring to the Invention of the Cross and ordering the celebration of a festival in its honor; containing also a long

lecture on the authority of St. Peter, and directions as to the reconciliation of properly baptized heretics by the imposition of hands of bishops.

eustochia, ae, *f.*, *the capability* or *the virtue of good conjecture* or *guessing in practical things*, the *eustochia* of Aristotle; cf. *ars coniecturalis*.

Eustochium, ii, *f.*, *Eustochium*, third daughter of Paula the friend of Jerome, from whose writings all that is known of her is gathered. Her original name, apparently, was Julia, her father, Toxotius, tracing his ancestry through the Julian family. The Greek name *Eustochion* implying justness of aim, seems to have been added as a term of endearment. The letters which Jerome wrote for her instruction were many. She is reckoned as a saint, her festival being September 28.

eusunetoi, orum, *m.*, *usunetoi*, *men of good sense*, synonym of *sensati*, opposite of *insensati*.

eusynesia, ae, *f.*, *plain understanding, understanding, common sense*, synonym of *synesis*.

eutrapelia, ae, *f.*, *the capacity for* or *virtue of good* or *agreeable teasing* or *joking*, the *eutrapelia* of Aristotle.

eutrapelus, a, um, *adj.*, *joking in a lively* and *agreeable manner, witty;* the *eutrapelos* of Aristotle.

Eutyches, is, *m.*, *Eutyches*, archimandrite of a monastery near

Constantinople in the fifth century A.D., who ascribed to Christ a divine nature only.

Eutychius, ii, *m., Eutychius,* patriarch of Constantinople; born at Theium in Phrygia 512 A.D. Towards the end of his life Eutychius maintained in a book on the resurrection, now lost, that after the resurrection the body will be more subtle than air, and no longer palpable. Gregory the Great, then residing at Constantinople as delegate of the Roman Church, felt himself bound to oppose this opinion.

Eva, ae, *f., Eve,* the first woman.

evacuatio, onis, *f., a voiding, the act of voiding.*

evacuo, are, avi, atum, 1, *v. a.,* (1) *to annul, destroy* the *force* or *validity* or *effect of; to render void* or *declare invalid,* (2) in the *pass., to fail* or *become* or *be found deficient* in faithfulness.

evado, ere, si, sum, 3, *v. n.* and *a.,* (1) *to escape, flee from* so as to get clear of; *obtain security* or *deliverance from; get away from; enjoy immunity from; evade; avoid;* elude something such as punishment, misery, guilt, sickness, death, danger, etc., (2) *to escape, succeed in getting away from, run away; emerge* into safety or freedom, (3) *to evade, elude* mental efforts, as an explanation, etc., (4) *to escape death, survive, live through in spite of.*

evagatio, onis, *f., evagation, wandering of the thoughts.*

evago, are, 1, *v. n.,* (1) *to wander, roam, go about* without or as if without plan or aim, (2) *to wander, stray from the subject,* to have mental evagations, especially in prayer.

evanesco, ere, nui, 3, *v. inch. n.,* (1) *to vanish* or *pass away, die away, disappear,* (2) used figuratively.

evangelicus, a, um, *adj., evangelical, relating to* or *agreeing with the gospel, contained in the gospel.* On **consilium evangelicum,** see *consilium;* on **lex evangelica,** see *lex;* on **paupertas evangelica,** see *paupertas;* on **sacerdos evangelicus,** see *sacerdos;* on **sacramentum evangelicum,** see *sacramentum.*

evangelista, ae, *m., an evangelist, one who brings good news, a preacher of the Gospel.* In the New Testament the term denotes a function rather than an office (Act. 21; Eph., 4; 2 Tim., 4.). Since the third century the term is used exclusively of the writers of the Gospels—Matthew, Mark, Luke, and John.

evangelium, ii, *n., the gospel,* the good tidings of Jesus Christ, as found in any one of the four memoirs of Jesus Christ contained in the New Testament, ascribed to Matthew, Mark, Luke, and John.

evangelizo, are, avi, atum, 1, *v. a., to preach, declare, proclaim,* always with the necessary notion of *bringing good tidings,* proclaiming the Gospel; *to evangelize, to win to the Gospel* by preaching.

Evangelus, i, *m., Evangelus, a presbyter* known through two letters of Jerome to him, 73 and 146. Vallarsi thinks he was from Africa, and was the Evangelus, bishop of Assurae, mentioned in the Gesta Collationis Carthaginensis (Evangelus 2), and also the Evangelus to whom Anianus Celecensis dedicated his translation of Chrysostom's Homilies.

evaporatio, onis, *f., an evaporating, evaporation.*

evaporo, are, 1, *v. a., to disperse in vapor, evaporate.*

evasio, onis, *f., an avoiding, evasion, the act, means* or *result of evading, eluding* or *avoiding* something.

evello, ere, velli, vulsum, 3, *v. a.* (1) *to take away, remove something,* (2) *fig., to root out, eradicate, tear away.*

evenio, ire, veni, ventum, 4, *v. n.,* (1) used *fig.,* (a) *to fall out, come to pass, happen,* (b) with *alicui, to befall, to betide one,* (2) *to proceed, follow, result,* as a consequence from anything, *to turn out, issue,* end in any way used only of things.

eventus, us, *m.,* (1) *event, issue, result, consequence of an action,* (2) *a happening, occurrence, emergency; any unexpected oc-*currence or condition calling for immediate action.

everto, ere, ti, sum, 3, *v. a., to overthrow, overturn, throw down, destroy,* used (1) *lit.,* (2) *fig.*

evidens, entis, *adj., apparent, evident, visible, manifest, plain, clear.—***evidenter,** *evidently, manifestly.*

evidenter, *adv.,* see *evidens.*

evidentia, ae, *f.,* (1) *evidence, manifest correctness, publicity,* (2) *insight to correctness, clear understanding.*

evigilo, are, avi, atum, 1, *v. n.* and *a., to awake, rise up* from the grave, to resume the conscious exercise of the senses which have lain dormant in death.

evitabilis, e, *adj., avoidable.*

evito, are, avi, atum, 1, *v. a., to avoid, shun.*

evoco, are, avi, atum, 1, *v. a., to evoke, call forth.*

Evodius, ii, *m., Evodius,* bishop of Uzalis in proconsular Africa, not far from Utica. Like Augustine, born at Tagaste, he became intimate with him at Milan, 385 or 386 A.D., and the friendship thus begun lasted through life. Four letters of Evodius to Augustine are extant, numbered in the list 158, 160, 161, 163, all written about 414. In number 163, Evodius asks Augustine for his opinion concerning the "spirits in prison," of Pet. III, 18, 19, and on other points. In his reply, Ep. 164, Augustine says that it cannot be denied that our Lord descended "ad inferos", and released some who were there from suffering of some kind.

evolatio, onis, *f., an escaping, rising out of flight.*

evolo, are, avi, atum, 1, *v. n., to go away quickly, fly, pass away* or *disappear quickly,* used *fig.*

evomo, ere, ui, itum, 3, *v. a., to vomit forth, vomit.*

evulsio, onis, *f., a pulling out, extraction, the act of extracting.*

ex or **e,** *prep. with abl., out, out of, out from, on the part of, on account of, through, as a consequence of, according to, by means of.* On **impossibile ex se,** see *impossibile;* on **materia ex qua,** see *materia;* on **principium ex quo,** see *principium;* on **tenere se ex parte,** see *tenere;* on **terminus ex quo,** see *terminus.*—**aliquid esse vel fieri ex aliquo** is possible as follows: (1), **proprie et primo,** i.e., *in the proper manner* and *in the first place,* (2), **proprie sed non primo,** i.e., *in the proper manner but not in the first place,* and (3), **non proprie,** i.e., *in an improper manner.*

exactio, onis, *f.,* (1) *an exaction, demanding, requisition* of anything, as a right, (2) *an exaction, a compulsory levy, fee, payment* or the like, especially when unjustly or oppressively demanded.

exactor, oris, *m., an exactor, one who exacts as by authority* or *insists on as a right.*

exacuo, ere, ui, utum, 3, *v. a., to make very sharp, sharpen, make pointed.*

exaggeratio, onis, *f., an exaggeration, a representation with extravagant* or *untruthful additions; misleading enlargement.*

exaggero, are, avi, atum, 1, *v. a., to enlarge, heap by piling up, exaggerate.*

exaltatio, onis, *f.,* (1) *elevation, raising,* (2) *exaltation, spiritual elevation,* (3) *trop., pride, haughtiness.*

exalto, are, avi, atum, 1, *v. a.,* (1) *to lift* or *raise anything,* (2) used *fig.,* (a) *to raise, elevate, exalt; to pay high honor to; glorify* or *extol; ascribe excellence* or *sublimity to; magnify;* (b) *to raise in pitch* or *strength,* as the voice; *increase the degree, force* or *intensity of,* (c) *to exalt in commendation; to regard* or *comment upon* as worthy of favorable attention, (d) *to exalt, raise,* especially in excellency or some specified particular.—**exaltatus,** a, um, *P. a., exalted, elevated, hence raised in dignity.*

examen, inis, *n., a weighing, consideration, examination, investigation,* used *fig.*

examinatio, onis, *f.,* (1) *a weighing, examination, the act* or *process of examining; careful scrutiny* or *inquiry; investigation,* (2) *examination, a test* or *trial by some special procedure.*—**examinatio sui,** *self-examination.*

examino, are, avi, atum, 1, *v. n.* and *a.*, (1) *to weigh, ponder, consider, examine, try, test; to examine critically* for the purpose of arriving at a conclusion, ascertaining a truth or fact, (2) *to bewilder mentally.*—**examinatus,** a, um, *P. a., tried, reduced to a pure state, separated from other matter by melting.*

exardesco, ere, arsi, arsum, 3, *v. inch. n., to be kindled, break out,* used *fig.*

exaspero, are, avi, atum, 1, *v. a., to exasperate, make bitter; become fierce,* used *fig.*—**exasperans,** ntis, *P. a., exasperating, inciting* or *stirring up by enraging.*

exasperatus, a, um, *P. a., exasperated, irritated, provoked.*

exaudibilis, e, *adj., that may be hearkened to for the purpose of complying with, that may be heard.*

exaudio, ire, ivi or ii, itum, 4, *v. a., to hearken, listen to, regard, grant.*

exauditio, onis, *f., a hearkening to, listening to, granting.*

excaecatio, onis, *f., blindness in spiritual matters; insensibility to the claims of God or of the moral law.*

excaeco, are, avi, atum, 1, *v. a., to blind, render incapable of discernment in spiritual matters, make morally blind,* used *fig.*—**excaecatus,** a, um, *P. a., blinded spiritually.*

excandescentia, ae, *f., irascibility, nascent anger, passionateness.*

excedenter, *adv.,* see *excedo.*

excedo, ere, cessi, cessum, 3, *v. n.* and *a., to go beyond, surpass, exceed a certain limit* or *measure.*—**excedenter,** *adv., to an excessive degree, immoderately, in a high degree.*

excellens, entis, *P. a.,* see *excello.*

excellenter, *adv.,* see *excello.*

excellentia, ae, *f.,* (1) *prominence, precedence, preference,* (2) *excellence, magnificence,* used as title of address, (3) *excess, surplus,* the opposite of *defectus.*— On **clavis excellentiae,** see *clavis;* on **cognoscere per modum excellentiae,** see *cognoscere;* on **potestas excellentiae,** see *potestas;* on **virtus excellentiae,** see *virtus.*—Kinds of *excellentia* in this (1) sense are: (a), **excellentia imaginabilis, excellentia sensibilis,** and **excellentia intellegibilis,** *preference presented in the imagination, preference preceptible through the senses, conceivable imagination.*—(b), **excellentia intellegibilis,** see *excellentia imaginabilis.*—(c), **excellentia propria,** *proper preference.*—(d), **excellentia sensibilis,** see *excellentia imaginabilis.*

excello, ere, cellui, celsum, 3, *v. a.* and *n., to excel, surpass,* used with *in* and *abl., abl.* alone, *acc.,* and *absol.*—**excellens,** entis, *P. a.,* (1) *excellent, superior, surpassing, having a good quality* or *qualities in a high degree; possessing distinguished merit; eminent by reason of worth* or *value,*

(2) *excellent, eminent* or *excelling in rank* or *dignity; of high
estate, exalted.*—**excellenter**, *adv.,
excellently.*—**excelsus**, a, um, *P.
a.,* (1) *elevated, lofty, high,*
(2) used *fig., high, lofty, distinguished, excellent, noble.*—**ex-
celsum**, i, *n., an elevated position* or *station.*—**excelse**, *adv., on
high.*

excelse, *adv.,* see *excello.*

excelsus, a, um, *P. a.,* see *excello.*

excentricus, i, *m., an eccentric, the
circumscribing circle of an ellip-
tic orbit.*

exceptio, onis, *f.,* (1) *an exception,*
that which is not covered by or
is at variance with a rule or
statement, (2) *an exception,* a
formal objection in equity and
admiralty courts to some action
or pleading.

exceptive, *adv., in the sense of an
exception, exceptionally.* Cf. 1
Sent. 21 exp. On **ponere exceptive**, see *ponere* under 1.

excessus, us, *m.,* (1) *a departure,* (a)
*a departure, decease, departure
from this life, death,* (b) used
*fig., a going out, departure, a
leaving of the mental powers,
loss of self possession,* with or
without *mentis,*—**excessus mentis** = *ekstasis,* (2) *excess,* (a)
the amount by which one thing,
quantity or number, is greater
than another, proper, or required limit, measure, or experience, (c) the act or habit of
gratifying inordinately the appetites or desires.

1. **excido**, ere, cidi, 3, *v. n., to
fall from, slip away,* used *fig.,*
(1) *to slip out, escape from the
memory,* (2) *to fall from, depart from rectitude.*

2. **excido**, ere, idi, isum, 3, *v. a.,*
(1) *lit., to cut out* or *off, cut* or
hew. (2) *fig., to extirpate, remove, banish.*

excipio, ere, cepi, ceptum, 3, *v. a.,*
(1) with the notion of "ex" predominating, *to except, make an
exception of, leave out, exclude,*
(2) with the notion of the verb
predominating, (a) *to take a
thing to one's self, catch, receive,*
(b) *to overtake, befall; to fall
out* or *occur to in the course of
events; happen to,* (c) *to support, sustain, give assistance to;
to maintain.*—On **actio excepta,**
see *actio.*

excisio, onis, *f.,* used *fig., an excision, a cutting off* or *out; a doing away with.*

excitatio, onis, *f., a rousing up,
wakening.*

excitativus, a, um, *adj., excitative,
of an exciting nature, tending to
excite.*

excito, are, avi, atum, 1, *v. freq. a.,*
(1) *lit.,* (a) of animate things, *to
rouse, stir up,* (b) of inanimate
things, *to rouse, stir up,* (2) *fig.,*
(a) in gen., *to raise up, arouse,
awaken, excite, stimulate, enliv-
en,* (b) in partic., with the accessory idea of producing, *to
cause, occasion, excite.*—**excita-
tus**, a, um, *P. a., roused, incited.*

exclamo, are, avi, atum, 1, *v. n.* and *a., to call* or *cry aloud, exclaim.*

excludo, ere, si, sum, 3, (1) *to exclude, shut out, cut off, remove, separate,* (2) *to exclude, reject,* as exceptional, inappropriate, illegal or the like.

exclusio, onis, *f., a shutting out, exclusion.*

exclusivus, a, um, *adj., excluding, exclusive.* On **dictio exclusiva,** see *dictio.*

excogitatio, onis, *f., excogitation, a thinking out, contriving, invention, devising* or the result of such operation of the mind, *a determination; formation of a fixed purpose; a firm resolve,* a synonym of Grk. *gnome, sententia, mens, adinventio.*

excogito, are, avi, atum, 1, *v. a., to excogitate, think out carefully* or *ingeniously; to find out by thinking; invent, devise.*

excolo, ere, colui, cultum, 3, *v. a., to work carefully, to tend, cultivate, till,* used *lit.* and *fig.*

excommunicatio, onis, *f., exclusion from a community* especially from the community of the Church, *excommunication.—* Kinds of *excommunicatio* are: **excommunicatio maior** and **excommunicatio minor,** *the greater* and *the less excommunication,* (no longer distinguished).

excommunico, are, avi, atum, 1, *v. a., to excommunicate, to punish by cutting off from church membership.* — **excommunicatus,** a, um, *P. a., excommunicated.*

excruciatio, onis, *f., torment, torture.*

excubiae, arum, *f., persons keeping watch, guard.*

excusabilis, e, *adj., excusable, that may be excused.*

excusatio, onis, *f., an excusing, excuse,* used with *obj.* or *subj. gen., absol.*

excuso, are, avi, atum, 1, *v. a.,* (1) *to excuse, absolve* or *free from imputation* or *fault; pronounce innocent of wrong; acquit of blame,* (2) *to excuse, offer an apology* or *excuse for,* used *reflexively,* (3) *to excuse, to be* or *serve as an excuse* or *a sufficient reason for,* (4) *to excuse, to release from an obligation.*

excutio, ere, cussi, cussum, 3, *v. a., to shake off, cast out, drive out.*

execrabilis, e, *adj., execrable, worthy of execration, accursed, damnable, outrageous, abominable, hateful.*

execratio, onis, *f., a cursing, execration,* the act of binding one's self or something belonging to one's self to punishment if what is alleged be not true.

executio, onis, *f., an accomplishment, execution, performance; a putting into use, action,* or *practice; the active* and *appropriate employment* or *exertion,* as of a power or function. On **ordo executionis,** see *ordo.—***quod est pri-**

mum in intentione, est ultimum in executione, see *intentio.*

executivus, a, um, *adj., executive, having the function of executing* or *performing; carrying into effect,* synonym of *exequens.* On potentia executiva, see *potentia;* on virtus executiva, see *virtus.*

executor, oris, *m., an executor, an accomplisher, performer.*

executrix, icis, *f., an executrix, an accomplisher, performer.*

exemplar, aris, *n.,* (1) *a copy, image,* (2) *pattern, model, example,* a loose synonym of *forma, idea, imago,* and *species.*—Kinds of *exemplar* in this (2) sense are: (a), exemplar effectivum, *the producing* or *effecting example.* Cf. Virt. 2. 3 ad 8.—(b) exemplar exemplatum, *the copied example* or *that produced according to something else.*—(c), exemplar principale, *chief example.*—(d), exemplar separatum, *the separated example* or *the example existing by itself.*—exemplar potius est quam exemplatum, *the example is superior to its copy.* Cf. SS. Q. 26. Art. 4 c.—exemplar prius est exemplato, *the example is prior to its copy.*

exemplaris, e, *adj.,* (1) *pertaining to the pattern* or *model,* usually in a mind, (2) *exemplary.*—On causa exemplaris, see *causa;* on forma exemplaris and forma prima exemplaris, see *forma;* on medium exemplare, see *medium;* on principium exemplare et primum exemplare, see *principium;*

on similitudo exemplaris, see *similitudo;* on species exemplaris, see *species;* on virtus exemplaris, see *virtus.*—On demonstratio exemplaris, see *demonstratio;* on locutio exemplaris, see *locutio;* on ostensio exemplaris, see *ostensio.*—exemplariter, *adv.,* (1) *in a typical manner, in the sense of a typical cause,* (2) *in an exemplary manner.*

exemplaritas, atis, *f., figurativeness, typicalness.*

exemplariter, *adv.,* see *exemplaris.*

exemplifico, are, avi, atum, 1, *v. a.,* and *n., to exemplify, show by example, illustrate.*

exemplo, are, avi, atum, 1, *v. a., to adduce as an example, model, pattern* or *original to be copied* or *imitated.*—exemplatus, a, um, *P. a., cited* or *alleged as pertinent for example, model* or *pattern.*

exemplum, i, *n.,* (1) *model, pattern, standard,* the *paradeigma* of Aristotle (Phys. II, 3, 194. b. 26), (2) *example,* (3) *conclusion* by analogy, likewise the *paradeigma* of Aristotle (Anal. prior. II. 24, 68. b. 38).

exennium, i, *n., a gift, present.*

exeo, ire, ii, itum, 4, *n.* and *a.,* (1) *lit.,* (a), *to go out* or *forth, go away,* (b) *to issue forth, flow,* (c) *ex vita, de corpore, a corpore, exire* alone, *to go away, leave, quit, to depart from life,* (d) *to go out* or *forth in any manner; to issue, escape,* (e) *to go out, surrender influence over,* as of the demon, (2) *fig.*, (a) *to come forth, pass from, proceed, go out from,* (b) *to go beyond* or *pass the limits of anything,* used with the *acc.,* (c) *to escape, evade, depart from,* (d) *to go beyond the bounds, exceed.*—**exire claustrum, exire de claustris** or **exire** used elliptically, *to go from the convent* on some mission or *to leave the convent* entirely and give up the practice of the evangelical counsels.—**exire sorte,** *to go chosen by lot.*—**exiens,** euntis, *P. a.,* with *a corpore, departing, dying.*—**exeuntes,** ium, *c.,* the *dying, those departing from the present life.*—**exire de ventre, exire de vulva, exire per uterum, exire de utero, exire utero,** *to go forth into being, be born.*

exequiae, arum, *f., obsequies, burial services.*

exequor, i, cutus, 3, *v. dep. a., to follow up, prosecute, carry out; to perform, execute, accomplish, fulfill.*—**exequi peccatum,** *to commit sin.*—**exequens,** entis, *P. a., achieving, performing,* synonym of *executivus.* On **ars exequens,** see *ars;* on **donum exequens,** see *donum;* on **potentia exequens,** see *potentia;* on **principium exequens,** see *principium.*

exerceo, ere, ui, itum, 2, *v. a.,* (1) *to engage busily, occupy, employ, exercise* a person or thing in some action, (2) with *se* or *pass.* in mid. force, *exercise* or *train one's self, practise,* (3) *practise, follow, exercise any employ-*

ment, *employ one's self about, make use of anything.*—**exercens,** entis, *P. a., exercising, practising, carrying out.*—**exercitus,** a, um, *P. a., exercised, practised, carried out.*

exercitatio, onis, *f.,* (1) *exercise,* (a) *activity for the benefit or training of body or mind,* (b) *exercise, work,* as of tradesmen, (2) fig., (a) *exercise, struggle, earnest effort* either to accomplish or prevent something, (b) *trouble, hardship, trial, any experience, event* or *thing that puts strength, patience* or *faith to the test,* (c) *exercise, a putting of something into use, action* or *practise,* (3) *an exercise, a devotional act performed,* as in the reception of the sacraments. —**exercitationes ad bella,** *exercises for war,* the practise of the science and arts of military operations.

exercitium, ii, *n.,* (1) *in gen., exercise,* the performance of any activity involving effort, mental or physical, in order to attain proficiency in something, or to maintain a proficiency already acquired by similar activity, (2) *exercise,* activity for the benefit or training of body or mind, (3) *exercise, trial, that which tries one; any experience, event* or *thing that puts strength, patience* or *faith to the test; an affliction* or *temptation that exercises* or *proves character; trouble, hardship,* (4) *practice, a* *repeated exercise*, (5) *a practice*, a customary action regarded as an individual habit, (6) *a use*, the act of using as a means to a purpose, (7) in the *pl.*, *exercitia bellica*, *exercises of arms*, the acts and practices of war employed in maneuvers, duelling or between contesting parties in a tournament.

exercitivus, a, um, *adj.*, *practising*, *exercising*. On **ars exercitiva**, see *ars;* on **disciplina exercitiva**, see *disciplina*.

exercito, are, avi, atum, 1, *v. freq. a., to exercise diligently* and *frequently; practise.*—**exercitatus**, a, um, *P. a., well-exercised, practised, versed, trained.*

exercitus, us, *m., an army; an exercised, disciplined body of men.*

exhalans, antis, *P. a., exhaling, passing off.*

exhalatio, onis, *f., an exhalation, vapor.*

exhaurio, ire, hausi, haustum, 4, *v. a.*, (1) *to exhaust, take away, remove*, (2) *to extirpate, to get rid of by taking out by the roots; eradicate.*

exheredo, are, avi, atum, 1, *v. a., to exheredate, disinherit, cut off from hereditary right.*

exhibeo, ere, ui, itum, 2, *v. a.*, (1) *hold forth, tender, offer, present, deliver*, (2) *show, display, exhibit*, (3) *confer, bestow*, (4) *maintain, support, provide*, (5) *procure, occasion, cause.*—**exhibens**, entis, *adj., offering, presenting, showing, displaying.*—

exhibitus, a, um, *P. a., offered, presented, produced, displayed, exhibited.*

exhibitio, onis, *f.*, (1) *a giving, presentation, bestowal, an offering* or *the act of presenting something for acceptance*, (2) *an exhibition, the act of exhibiting; manifestation, display*, (3) *the act of administering* or *the state of being administered*, as, *the administration of the sacraments.*

exhilaro, are, avi, atum, 1, *v. a., to gladden, cheer, rejoice, delight.*

exhonoratio, onis, *f., a dishonoring, dishonor.*

exhorreo, ere, 2, *v. a., to tremble at* or *shudder exceedingly at any thing; to dread.*

exhorresco, ere, rui, 3, *v. inch., n.* and *a., to tremble* or *shudder exceedingly, to be terrified.*

exhortatio, onis, *f., an exhorting, exhortation.*

exhortatorius, a, um, *adj., belonging to* or *containing exhortation, hortatory.*

exhortor, ari, atus, 1, *v. dep. a., to exhort, to incite to some good deed* or *course of conduct by appeal* or *argument; address* or *appeal to earnestly;* hence, *to admonish, warn, advise.*

exigentia, ae, *f., an exigency, pressing necessity; pressing need* or *demand.*

exigo, ere, egi, actum, 3, *v. a.*, (1) *demand, require, exact, enforce*, (2) *examine, try, measure, weigh.*

exiguus, a, um, *adj., small, little, mean.*—**exiguum,** i, *n., a little, a trifle.*

exilium, ii, *n.,* (1) *banishment, exile,* (2) *a place of exile.*

eximius, a, um, *adj., distinguished, extraordinary, uncommon, great.*

eximo, ere, emi, emptum, 3, *v. a., to exempt, free, release,* used with *a, ab,* and *abl.*—**exemptus,** a, um, *P. a.,* (1) *exempt, free, clear* or *released* as from some liability, restriction or burden affecting other persons or things; *exempted,* (2) *exempt* by a regulation in canon law making persons or places subject to the Holy See instead of to the diocesan bishop.

exinanio, ire, ivi or ii, itum, 4, *v. a.,* (1) *to destroy, raze, to level* with the ground or foundation by overthrowing or demolishing, (2) *to empty, lay aside one's glory.*

exinanitio, onis, *f.,* (1) *a voiding, emptying,* a removing all of something contained from that which contains it, (2) *exinanition, an emptying, a passing* from a higher to a lower scale of dignity; becoming of a subject class or living in the condition of servitude; a laying aside of glory, *renunciation.*

exinde, *adv., from there, from that place, thence, hence, accordingly.*

existentia, (exsistentia), *f., existence,* that by which an essence becomes actual, or is placed out-side of its potential state in its causes. On the relationship between *existentia* and *essentia,* which is the same as that between *esse* and *essentia, see essentia.* On **causa existentiae,** see *causa.*

existimatio, onis, *f., estimation, valuation, opinion, idea, notion,* synonym of *aestimatio.* On **iudicium naturalis existimationis,** see *iudicium.*—Kinds of *existimatio* are: (a), **existimatio falsa,** *false evaluation.*—(b), **existimatio intellectualis** and **existimatio naturalis,** *the evaluation of reason* and *the natural evaluation* or *that with consideration* and *that without consideration.*—(c), **existimatio naturalis,** see *existimatio intellectualis.*—(d), **existimatio practica** and **existimatio speculativa,** *the evaluation aiming at the practical* or *practice* and *that directed toward speculation* or *knowledge.*—(e), **existimatio recta,** *the right* or *true evaluation.*—(f), **existimatio speculativa,** see *existimatio practica.*—(g), **existimatio vera,** see *existimatio recta.*

existimo, are, avi, atum, 1, *v. a., to judge, consider, suppose, think, esteem,* used with *acc.* and *inf., subst. cl.*

existo, ere, stiti, stitum, 3, *v. n., to be, exist,* i.e., to be actual, to be outside of one's causes, to be in a higher state than potentiality, Aristotelian *exo einai,* a synonym of *esse actuale,* as opposed both to *non-esse* and *esse potentiale*. Subsistence, with which existence might be confused, is quite another concept. Subsistence is existence of itself, not in some subject; it is the abstract quality which is peculiar to substance precisely as distinct from accident. Accidents have existence but not subsistence, because they exist by reason of the substance in which they inhere, not in themselves. Existence, then, is a wider concept than subsistence, and is the actualization of any potency to be.—The relationship between *existere* and *essentia* is the same as that between *esse* and *essentia*. Cf. *essentia*. On **actus existendi**, see *actus;* on **forma per se existens**, see *forma;* on **sapientia existens**, see *sapientia;* on **species per se existens**, see *species*.—Kinds of *existere* are: (a), **existere actu**, *to exist in reality* or *in the state of reality, not in the state of potentiality*.—(b), **existere essentialiter** and **existere radicaliter**, *to exist according to essence* and *according to the root* or *the beginning*.—(c), **existere incommunicabiliter**, *to exist in a manner not mediate* or *communicable*.—(d), **existere per se**, *to exist by itself, not in another*.—(e), **existere radicaliter**, see *existere essentialiter*.—**ubi unum sufficit, aliud superflue existit,** *where one cause is sufficient, every other is superflu-*

ous. Cf. *fieri, natura,* and *plus.*—**existens,** *P. a., being, existing.*

exitium, ii, *n., destruction, ruin, hurt.*

exitus, us, *m.,* (1) *lit., a going out* or *forth, egress, departure,* (2) *fig., end, conclusion, issue, result.*

Exodus, i, *f., Exodus,* the second book of the Old Testament, usually called Shemoth by the Hebrews. It describes the giving of the divine law and establishment of Jehovah's dwelling place in the tabernacle, and opens with the account of the Exodus of Israel from Egypt. St. Thomas refers frequently to the Book of Exodus.

exopto, are, avi, atum, 1, *v. a., to desire greatly, long for.*

exorbito, are, avi, atum, 1, *v. n.* and *a., to turn aside, turn out of the right track,* used *fig.*

exorcismus, i, *m., exorcism,* the act of exorcising evil spirits; also a solemn ceremony or formula of adjuration used in such exorcising.

exorcista, ae, *m., an exorcist, one who exorcises* or *who practises exorcism,* the third minor order in the Latin Church. This office confers on the recipient the spiritual power of expelling demons from persons possessed, whether the persons are baptized or catechumens, by the imposition of hands.

exorcizo, are, avi, 1, *v. a., to exorcise, to cast* or *drive out evil* *spirits by religious ceremonies.*

exordium, ii, *n., the beginning, outset, commencement, source* of anything.

exorior, iri, ortus, 3 and 4, *v. dep. n.,* (1) *to originate, be the origin* or *producing cause of; create.* (2) *fig., to arise, proceed, originate, begin.*

exoro, are, avi, atum, 1, *v. a., to pray, address devoutly* or *earnestly,* as God or any object of worship in petition, adoration or thanksgiving.

exorsus, us, *m., a beginning, commencement.*

exortus, us, *m., a coming forth, growth, rising.*

expando, ere, pandi, pansum or passum, 3, *v. a., to extend, spread out, put forth,* as to extend the hands in prayer.—**expansus,** a, um, *adj., extended, stretched out.*

expansus, a, um, *adj.,* see *expando.*

expavesco, ere, pavi, 3, *v. inch. n.* and *a., to be* or *become greatly terrified, to be very much afraid; to be greatly frightened at* or *afraid of, to fear greatly.*

expectatio, onis, *f.,* (1) *an awaiting, expectation, expecting,* (2) *the object of expectation* or *longing.*

expecto, are, avi, atum, 1, *v. a., to expect, await* something that is to come or take place, *to be waiting for;* also *to await* with hope, fear, desire, expectation.

expediens, entis, *P. a.,* see *expedio.*

expello, ere, puli, pulsum, 3, *v. a.,* (1) *res expedit* or *impers., expedit*

alicui = *lit., it helps out, furthers, promotes;* hence, *it is serviceable, profitable, advantageous, useful, expedient,* used with *ad* and *acc., dat., ut* and *subj., absol.,* (2) *to dispatch, dispose of quickly.*—**expediens,** entis, *P. a., expedient, serving to promote a desired end* or *interest; suitable under the circumstances; advisable.*—**expeditus,** a, um, *P. a., unimpeded, unincumbered, disengaged, free, easy.* On **contemplatio expedita,** see *contemplatio;* on **operatio expedita,** see *operatio;* on **potestas expedita,** see *potestas.*—**expedite,** *adv., readily, promptly, quickly.*

expedite, *adv.,* see *expedio.*

expeditus, a, um, *adj.,* see *expedio.*

expedio, ire, ivi or ii, itum, 4, *v. a., to expel, drive out, thrust out* or *away, eject,* used *lit.,* and *fig.*

expendo, ere, di, sum, 3, *v. a., to expend, pay out* or *lay out; use up; spend,* as to spend money, labor, thought, or time.

expensa, ae, *f., a disbursement, expense.*

experientia, ae, *f.,* (1) *learning through experience, becoming acquainted with a thing,* synonym of *experimentum,* (2) *experience,* synonym of *experimentum,* opposite of *inexperientia.*— On **scientia experientiae,** see *scientia.*

experimentalis, e, *adj., concerned with experience, experimental.* On **certitudo experimentalis,** see *certitudo;* on **cognitio experimen-**

talis, see *cognitio;* on **notitia experimentalis**, see *notitia;* on **scientia experimentalis**, see *scientia;* on **visio experimentalis**, see *visio.* —experimentaliter, *adv., in the manner of an experiment, experimentally.*

experimentaliter, *adv.,* see *experimentalis.*

experimentum, i, *n.,* (1) *trial, test, experiment,* (2) *learning through experience, becoming acquainted with a thing,* synonym of *experientia,* (3) *experience,* synonym of *experientia.*

experior, iri, pertus, 4, *v. dep. a.,* (1) *to try* a thing, either by way of testing it or attempting it; *to probe, put to the test, to try* a thing, (2) *to experience, to know by experience, become acquainted with* by personal trial, feeling, and the like, *undergo personally, feel.*—**expertus,** a, um, *P. a., expert, tried, proved, known by experience.*

expers, tis, *adj., destitute* or *devoid of, free from, deprived of, without,* used with the *gen.*

expertus, a, um, *P. a.,* see *experior.*

expeto, ere, ivi or ii, itum, 3, *v. a.,* and *n., to long for, seek after, covet, wish for, ask, beseech* something, used with *acc.* and *inf., acc.* with *a* and *abl.*

expiabilis, e, *adj., expiable, that may be expiated* or *atoned for.*

expiatio, onis, *f., satisfaction, atonement, expiation,* the active means of expiating or the making repa-ration or satisfaction as for offense or sin; the removing of guilt by suffering punishment; *atonement* or *an atonement.*— **Festus Expiationis,** *the Feast of Expiation.* Under the old Law there were seven temporal solemnities and one continual solemnity. One of these, the Feast of Expiation, was celebrated once a year in memory of the blessing whereby at the prayer of Moses, God forgave the people's sin of worshipping the calf; the Feast of Expiation signified the cleansing of the Christian people from sins.—**sacrificium expiationis,** *the sacrifice of expiation,* a sacrifice having the power or character of an expiation, as the sacrifice of the Cross, the sacrifice of the Mass.

expiativus, a, um, *adj., expiative, pertaining to, of the nature of,* or *for the purpose of expiation.*

expiator, oris, *m., an atoner, expiator.*

expio, are, avī, atum, 1, *v. a.,* (1) *to make satisfaction, amends, atonement* for a crime or a criminal; *to purify anything defiled with crime; to atone for, to expiate, purge by sacrifice,* (2) *to atone for, make amends for, repair, make good.*

explanatio, onis, *f., an explanation, interpretation.*

explano, are, avi, atum, 1, *v. a., to explain, make plain* or *clear; cause to be understood.*

expleo, ere, evi, etum, 2, *v. a.*, (1) *lit., to fill up, fill full*, (2) *fig.*, (a) *to fulfill, discharge, execute, perform a duty*, (b) *to fill up, complete, finish*, (c) *to satisfy, sate, glut, appease a longing.*

expletio, onis, *f., a fulfillment, accomplishment.*

explicatio, onis, *f., an unfolding, uncoiling*, used *fig.*; *of speech, an unfolding, expounding, an explication, explanation*, especially of a passage in any text, or definition, as of a word, by unfolding what is implied in it.

explicativus, a, um, *adj., explicative, serving to unfold or explain.*

explicite, see *explico.*

explicitus, a, um, *P. a.*, see *explico.*

explico, are, avi and ui, atum and itum, *v. a.*, (1) *lit., to unfold, spread open, reveal itself*, (2) *fig., of speech, to unfold, explain, treat, state, explain, express.*—**explicitus,** a, um, *P. a., unfolded, explained, clear, plain,* the opposite of *implicitus.* On **cognitio explicita,** see *cognitio;* on **compositio explicita,** see *compositio;* on **contemplatio explicita,** see *contemplatio;* on **fides explicita,** see *fides.*—**explicite,** *adv., in the manner or in the sense of explaining or unfolding, explicitly,* the opposite of *implicite.* On **appetere explicite,** see *appetere;* on **cognoscere explicite,** see *cognoscere;* on **credere explicite,** see *credere;* on **ponere explicite,** see *ponere;* on **scire explicite,** see *scire.*

explorator, oris, *m., a spy,* (1) *a spy, one who watches others secretly; a person who spies,* (2) *an explorer, one who subjects something to examination.*

exploro, are, avi, atum, 1, *v. a.*, (1) *to explain, examine, subject to search* or *examination; look over in order to examine; search through the parts of,* (2) *to explore, test, try by subjecting to some experiment.*

expolio, are, avi, atum, 1, *v. a., to despoil, to strip* or *deprive of something.*

expono, ere, posui, positum, 3, *v. a.*, (1) *lit.*, (a) *to expose, to lay open, place in a perilous* or *unprotected situation,* (b) *to expose, bring out of concealment, show openly, exhibit,* (2) *fig., to explain, expound, interpret.*

exposco, ere, poposci, 3, *v. a., to ask earnestly, beg, request, demand.*

expositio, onis, *f., exposition, an explanation* or *interpretation of the meaning of something,* as of a passage or work; also, any work containing an analysis or interpretation; *commentary.*

expositive, *adv.*, see *expositivus.*

expositivus, a, um, *adj., interpreting, explaining, expositive.* On **propositio expositiva,** see *propositio;* on **ratio expositiva ipsius rei nominatae, nominis et significationis nominis,** see *ratio;* on **syllogismus expositivus,** see *syllogismus.*—**expositive,** *adv., in the manner* or *in the sense of inter-*

preting or *explaining exposi-
tively.*

expositor, oris, *m., an expounder,
interpreter, commentator,* one
who expounds or makes explanatory notes upon a text.

expresse, *adv.,* see *exprimo.*

expressio, onis, *f.,* (1) *expression,
the act of uttering, declaring* or
representing by written or *spok-
en language* or *by gesture* or
look; hence, any act or object by
which some truth or idea is con-
veyed, (2) *expression,* the visible
and outward aspect; the significant or characteristic features or
appearance; *look, attitude,* especially, the ensemble of the face
as indicating feelings, mood, or
character.

expressive, *adv.,* see *expressivus.*

expressivus, a, um, *adj., expressing,
expressive.* Quia vel est expressivum, Eph. 3. 4. On **verbum expressivum,** see *verbum.*—**expressive,** *adv., in the manner of expressing, in a marked manner,
expressively.*

expressus, a, um, *P. a.,* see *exprimo.*

exprimo, ere, pressi, pressum, 3, *v.
a.,* (1) *to press* or *squeeze out,
force out,* (2) *represent, portray,
describe, express.*—**exprimens,**
entis, *P. a., representing, describing, expressing.*—**expressus,**
a, um, *P. a., expressed, explicit,
distinct, clear,* the opposite of
interpretativus. On **consensus expressus,** see *consensus;* on **oratio
expressa,** see *oratio;* on **pactum
expressum,** see *pactum;* on **re-**

praesentatio expressa, see *repraesentatio;* on **signum expressum,**
see *signum;* on **similitudo expressa,** see *similitudo.*—**expresse,**
adv., in a pronounced or *decided manner, expressly, distinctly,
clearly,* the opposite of *interpretative.* On **tentare expresse,** see
tentare.

exprobrabilis, e, *adj., worthy of reproach.*

exprobratio, onis, *f., a reviling, disgrace, reproach.*

exprobro, are, avi, atum, 1, *v. a.,
to rebuke, upbraid, reproach.*

expugno, are, avi, atum, 3, *v. a.,*
(1) *lit.,* (a) of place, *to take by
assault, storm, capture, reduce,*
(b) *transf.,* of persons, *to subdue,
overcome, vanquish,* (2) *fig., to
expel, drive out.*

expuitio, onis, *f., exspuition, a spit-
ting out, expectoration.*

expulsio, onis, *f., expulsion, a driv-
ing out.*

expulsivus, a, um, *adj., expulsive,
tending* or *serving to expel.*

expuo, ere, ui, utum, 3, *v. n., to
spit.*

expurgo, are, avi, atum, 1, *v. a.,
to clear from censure, justify, excuse, exonerate.*

exquiro, ere, sivi, situm, 3, *v. a.,
to search out diligently, seek for;
make inquiry, inquire, ask.*—**ex-
quisitus,** a, um, *P. a., exquisite,
carefully sought out.*—**exquisite,**
*adv., carefully, accurately, par-
ticularly, excellently.*

exquisite, *adv.,* see *exquiro.*

exsaturo, are, avi, atum, 1, *v. a.,* to satisfy completely, to satiate, sate.

exsecutio, see *executio.*

exsecutivus, a, um, see *executivus.*

exsequens, see *exequor.*

exsicco, are, avi, atum, 1, *v. a.,* to exsiccate; to dry up or out; remove moisture from.

exsistentia, see *existentia.*

exsistere, see *existere.*

exsolvo, ere, solvi, solutum, 3, *v. a.,* to discharge, pay a debt or obligation.

exsufflatio, onis, *f., exsufflation, exorcism* by blowing or breathing upon the one possessed by an evil spirit.

exsufflo, are, 1, *v. a.,* to exsufflate, breathe upon; to dispel an evil spirit by blowing; a form of exorcism, used only as an Ecclesiastical term.

exsurrectio, onis, *f., an arising.*

extasis, acc. im, abl. i, *f., rapture, ecstasy.*

extendo, ere, di, sum, 3, *v. a.,* (1) *lit.,* to extend, spread out, stretch out, (2) *fig.,* (a) to extend so as to include, comprise, embrace, (b) to extend, exaggerate, cause to appear larger or more important than is warranted by facts, (c) to extend, accord or concede as proper; grant; to bring before one for acceptance or rejection, (d) of time, to extend, prolong. —**extensus,** a, um, *P. a.,* (1) extended, stretched, used literally and figuratively.

extensibilis, e, *adj., extensible, capable of extension* or *expansion; expansive.*

extensio, onis, *f., extension,* the act or process of extending, or the state of being extended, a reaching or stretching out, as in space, time, or scope, used (1) *lit.,* (2) *fig.,* especially in a logical context, for the applicability of a concept to a greater or lesser number of particulars. Thus, e.g., animal has greater extension than man. It has a quantitative connotation, while *intensio* is qualitative.

extensive, *adv., according to expansion, in the manner of expansion, extensively, quantitatively more* or *greater,* the opposite of *intensive.* On **frui extensive,** see *frui;* on **infinitum extensive,** see *infinitus;* on **maior extensive,** see *maior.*

extensivus, a, um, *adj., extensive, expansive, what may be extended,* the opposite of *intensivus.* On **infinitas extensiva,** see *infinitas;* on **quantitas extensiva,** see *quantitas.*

extensus, a, um, *P. a.,* see *extendo.*

extenuo, are, avi, atum, 1, *v. a.,* to diminish, dispel.

extergeo, ere, si, sum, 2, *v. a.,* to wipe off, wipe dry.

exterior, exterius, *adj., outer, exterior,* synonym of *extrinsecus,* the opposite of *interior, intraneus,* and *intrinsecus.* On **accidens exterior,** see *accidens;* on **actio exterior,** see *actio;* on **actus ex-**

terior, see *actus;* on **adoratio exterior**, see *adoratio;* on **affectio exterior**, see *affectio;* on **agens exterior**, see *agens;* on **apprehensio exterior**, see *apprehensio;* on **blasphemia exterior**, see *blasphemia;* on **bonum exterior**, see *bonus;* on **causa exterior**, see *causa;* on **confessio exterior**, see *confessio;* on **conversatio exterior**, see *conversatio;* on **corpus exterius**, see *corpus;* on **cultus exterior**, see *cultus;* on **delectatio exterior**, see *delectatio;* on **divitiae exteriores**, see *divitiae;* on **dolor exterior**, see *dolor;* on **enuntiatio exterior**, see *enuntiatio;* on **factio exterior**, see *factio;* on **finis exterior**, see *finis;* on **forma exterior**, see *forma;* on **homo exterior**, see *homo;* on **immunditia exterior**, see *immunditia;* on **inspiratio exterior**, see *inspiratio;* on **instrumentum exterius**, see *instrumentum;* on **iudicium exterius**, see *iudicium;* on **locus exterior**, see *locus;* on **locutio exterior**, see *locutio;* on **malum exterius**, see *malus;* on **materia exterior**, see *materia;* on **missio exterior**, see *missio;* on **necessarium ex aliquo exteriori**, see *necessarius;* on **operatio exterior**, see *operatio;* on **opus exterius**, see *opus;* on **oratio exterior**, see *oratio;* on **passio exterior**, see *passio;* on **perfectio exterior**, see *perfectio;* on **poenitentia exterior**, see *poenitentia;* on **principatus exterior**, see *principatus;* on **principium exterius**, see *princi-*

pium; on **pulchritudo exterior**, see *pulchritudo;* on **ratio exterior**, see *ratio;* on **res exterior**, see *res;* on **sacrificium exterius**, see *sacrificium;* on **sensibile exterius**, see *sensibilis;* on **sensus exterior**, see *sensus;* on **tentatio exterior**, see *tentatio;* on **verbum exterius**, see *verbum;* on **vis exterior**, see *vis;* on **visio exterior**, see *visio;* on **vita exterior**, see *vita;* on **vox exterior**, see *vox.—***exterius**, *adv., on the outside, externally.—***extremus**, a, um, *sup. adj., extreme, last,* synonym of *ultimus.* On **complexio extrema**, see *complexio;* on **distantia extrema**, see *distantia;* on **elementum extremum**, see *elementum;* on **iudicium extremum**, see *iudicium;* on **necessitas extrema**, see *necessitas;* on **terminus extremus**, see *terminus;* on **unctio extrema**, see *unctio.—*In the *neutr. absol.* and as *subst.* = **extremum**, i, *n.,* (1) *extreme boundary, final point, final member, extreme,* synonym of *extremitas, finis, terminus,* and *ultimum,* (2) *extreme idea* or *notion,* i.e., *one of two ideas, the expression of which is chiefly concerned with a conclusion,* synonym of *extremitas* and *terminus.* The major and minor terms of a syllogism which are united in the mean or middle term.—Kinds of *extremum* in this (1) sense are: (a), **extremum ignobilius seu vilius** and **extremum nobilius**, *the ignoble* or *weaker* and *the more noble term* *of a syllogism.* Cf. Opp. 1 and 2. —(b), **extremum nobilius,** see *extremum ignobilius.*—(c), **extremum relationis,** *the final member of a relation.*—(d), **extremum vilius,** see *extremum ignobilius.*

exterminator, oris, *m., a destroyer.*

exterminium, ii, *n., extermination.*

extermino, are, avi, atum, 1, *v. a.,* (1) *to exterminate; to remove* by either death or banishment, (2) *to destroy, dispel, mar,* used fig.

externus, a, um, *adj., outward, external.*

exterreo, ere, ui, itum, 2, *v. a., to strike with terror, frighten, affright.*

extersio, onis, *f., extersion, the act of effacing* or *expunging.*

extinctio, onis, *f., extinction,* used *fig.*

extinguo, ere, nxi, nctum, 3, *v. a.,* (1) *lit.,* (a) *to put out what is burning; to quench, extinguish,* (b) *transf., to deprive of life* or *strength, to kill, destroy,* (2) *fig., to abolish, destroy, annihilate.*

extirpatio, onis, *f., extirpation, a rooting out.*

extirpo, are, avi, atum, 1, *v. a.,* (1) *lit., to extirpate, pluck up by the stem* or *root, to root out,* (2) *fig., to root out, eradicate, extirpate.*

exto, are, 1, *v. n.,* (1) *to appear, show* or *present itself,* used with *dat.,* (2) *to exist, be; to be seen* or *found* at the present time.

extollentia, ae, *f., a lifting* or *raising;* with *oculorum, superciliousness, haughtiness.*

extollo, ere, 3, *v. a., to raise, elevate, exalt, lift up, extol,* used *fig.*

extorqueo, ere, si, tum, 2, *v. a., to extort, obtain by force, violence, threats,* or the subjection of another to some necessity, used *lit.,* and *fig.*

extra, (1) *adv.,* and (2) *prep.,* with *acc., on the outside, without, outside of, beyond, except,* the opposite of *intra, intus.*—**ab extra,** *from without, from outside.* —**ad extra,** *toward the outside, outward.* For the *adv., exterius,* see *exterior.*—**Extra,** an abbreviation for Extra Decretum Gratiana and stands here for the Decretals of Gregory IX.

Extra, see *extra* under 2.

extraho, ere, xi, ctum, 3, *v. a., to draw out* or *forth, drag out.*

extraneus, a, um, *adj., apparent, extraneous, strange,* synonym of *exterior* and *extrinsecus,* the opposite of *interior, intraneus,* and *intrinsecus.* On **accidens extraneum,** see *accidens;* on **corpus extraneum,** see *corpus;* on **effectus extraneus,** see *effectus;* on **imaginatio extranea,** see *imaginatio;* on **materia extranea,** see *materia;* on **medium extraneum,** see *medium;* on **natura extranea,** see *natura;* on **operatio extranea,** see *operatio;* on **opinio extranea,** see *opinio;* on **persona extranea,** see *persona;* on **positio extranea,** see *positio;* on **principium extraneum,** see *principium;* on **qualitas extranea,** see *qualitas;* on **ratio**

extranea, see *ratio.*—extraneus,
i, *m.*, *a stranger.*

extraordinarius, a, um, *adj.*, *extraordinary*, being beyond or out of
the common order, course, or
method; exceeding the ordinary
degree.

extravagantes, ium, *m.*, *extravagantes*, (*Lat.*, extra, beyond; va-
gare, to go,) certain collections
of papal decretals not contained
in the Decree of Gratian or the
three early collections of the Corpus Iuris, namely the Decretals
of Gregory IX, the sixth book
of the Decretals and the Clemen-
tines.

extremitas, atis, *f.*, (1) *the extremity, end of a thing*, synonym of
extremum, finis, terminus, and
ultimum, (2) *extreme, term,* one
of two ideas for whose expression it is chiefly a question of a
conclusion, a synonym of *extremum* and *terminus.*—Kinds of.
extremitas in this (2) sense are:
extremitas maior and extremitas
minor, *the extreme term with
the larger extent* and *that with
the smaller extent,* or the major
and the minor term of a syllogism.

extremus, a, um, see *exterior.*

extrinsece, see *extrinsecus.*

extrinsecus, *adv.*, *from without,
from abroad, in an exterior manner, outwardly,* synonym of *extrinsece,* the opposite of *intranee, intrinsece* and *intrinsecus.*
On relatio extrinsecus affixa, see
relatio.

extrinsecus, a, um, *adj.*, *outer, exterior,* synonym of *exterior,* the
opposite of *interior, intraneus,*
and *intrinsecus.* On accidens extrinsecum, see *accidens;* on agens extrinsecus, see *agens;* on
bonum extrinsecum, see *bonus;*
on causa extrinseca, see *causa;*
on effectus extrinsecus, see *effectus;* on finis extrinsecus, see
finis; on forma extrinseca, see
forma; on instrumentum extrinsecum, see *instrumentum;* on medium extrinsecum, see *medium;*
on mensura extrinseca, see *mensura;* on motor extrinsecus, see
motor; on movens extrinsecum,
see *movere;* on multitudo extrinseca, see *multitudo;* on necessitas ex aliquo extrinseco, see *necessitas;* on organum extrinsecum, see *organum;* on passio ab
extrinseco illata, see *passio;* on
perfectio extrinseca, see *perfectio;* on principium extrinsecum,
see *principium;* on res extrinseca,
see *res;* on veritas extrinseca, see
veritas.—ab or ex extrinseco,
*from without, from an outside
source.*—extrinsece, *adv.*, *outwardly, extrinsically,* synonym
of *extrinsecus,* the opposite of
intranee, intrinsece, and *intrinsecus.*

exuberantia, ae, *f.*, *superabun-
ance, exuberance.*

exultatio, onis, *f.*, (1) *lit., a springing up, leaping, frisking,* (2) *ex-
ultation,* the act or state of exulting; triumphant joy; elevation of spirit over victory, suc-

cess, or any advantage gained, so called fom the exterior signs of inward delight breaking forth from its bounds.

exulto, are, avi, atum, 1, *v. n.,* (1) *lit., to leap* or *jump up,* (2) *fig., to exult, rejoice exceedingly.*

exuo, ere, ui, utum, 3, *v. a., to free from, divest one's self of any-thing.—***exutus,** a, um, *adj., P. a., freed from.*

exupero, (exsupero), are, avi, atum, 1, *v. n.* and *a., to overcome, get the upper hand.*

exurgo, (exsurgo), ere, surrexi, 3, *v. n., to rise up, get up.*

exuro, ere, ussi, ustum, 3, *v. a., to burn out, consume, burn up.—***exustus,** a, um, *P. a., burned, devastated by fire.*

Ezechias, ae, *m., Ezechias,* King of Juda, son and successor of Achaz. The events of his reign are related in the Fourth Book of Kings, and also in the paral-lel account in the Second Book of Paralipomenon.

Ezechiel, is, *m.,* (1) *Ezechiel,* son of Buzi, one of the priests who in the year 598 B.C. had been deported together with Joachim as prisoners from Jerusalem. With the other exiles he settled in Till-Abid near the Chobar in Babylonia and seems to have spent the rest of his life there, (2) *Ezechiel,* a prophetical Book of the Old Testament by Eze-chiel who was one of the proph-ets of the captivity. It foretold the destruction of Jerusalem and prepared the Jews for the res-toration.

F

faber, bri, *m., a worker in wood, stone, metal,* etc., *a forger, smith, artificer, carpenter, joiner.*

Fabianus, i, *m., Fabian,* saint, pope, 236-250. During his reign of fourteen years there was a lull in the storm of persecution. Under him considerable work was done in the catacombs. Fabian died a martyr Jan. 20, 250 at the beginning of the De-cian persecution and was bur-ied in the Crypt of the Popes in the catacomb of St. Callistus.

Fabiola, ae, *f., Fabiola,* a rich Roman matron who took St. Jerome for her spiritual guide. She divorced her first husband and then married again, but did penance for this error and visit-ed the Holy Land. When the Huns invaded Palestine she re-turned to Rome, and in con-junction with Pammachius, the widowed husband of the rich Paulina, established a hostel for travellers at Ostia just before her death.

fabrica, ae, *f.,* (1) *a building, fab-ric,* any skilful production, (a) *lit.,* (b) *fig.,* (2) *fabric, texture, tissue, substance.*

fabricatio, onis, *f.*, *a making, fram-ing, constructing.*

fabrico, are, avi, atum, 1, *v. a.,* also, in quot., *fabricor,* ari, atus, 1, *v. a.,* (1) *to make out of wood, stone, metal* etc., *to frame, forge, construct, build,* (2) *transf.*, *to make, form, fashion.*

fabrilis, e, *adj.*, *of* or *belonging to an artificer.*

fabula, ae, *adj.*, *a fable, narrative.*

fabularis, e, *adj.*, *fabulous.*

fabulor, ari, atus, 1, *v. dep. a.,* (1) *to speak, converse, talk, chat,* (2) *to say, utter.*

fabulosus, a, um, *adj.*, *fabulous, in-credible.*

facetia, ae, *f.*, *a jest, witticism.*

facies, ei, *f.*, (1) *lit.*, (a) *the face,* the anterior portion of the head, in which the eyes, nose, and mouth are situated, (b) *the fea-tures, shape, form, appearance* or *characteristics* of persons or things, (c) *form, kind, state;* the nature of a thing as perceived by the senses or intellect, (d) *the face* or *surface of anything; that side presented to view,* the exte-rior part of anything that has length, breadth, and thickness, (2) (a) *a mental* or *moral vision,* or *a way of viewing; estimation, mind,* as according to the mind of the Church, (b) *face, personal presence,* (c) *face, countenance,* especially as indicative of dispo-sition or state of mind, (d) *face, advent, act of appearing* or *com-ing into view,* (e) with *prima.*: prima facie, *at first sight.*—facie

ad faciem, *face to face,* so as to face or be in the actual presence of each other.—**resistere alicui in faciem,** *to withstand someone to the face,* as an equal.

facilis, e, *adj.*, *easy to do, easy, without difficulty,* opposite of *difficilis.*—**facile,** *adv.*, *easily, without trouble* or *difficulty.*—**fa-ciliter,** *adv.*, *easily.*—**de facili,** *easily.*

facilitas, atis, *f.*, *facility, the quality of being easy to accomplish* or *to be accomplished; freedom from difficulty; ease; readiness; dex-terity.*

faciliter, *adv.*, see *facilis.*

facinus, oris, *n.*, *a crime, outrage,* not used in S.T. except in quot.

facio, ere, feci, factum, 3, *v. a.* and *n.*, (1) *to make, do,* a loose syno-nym of *agere,* the opposite of *pati,* (2) *create, produce, effect, achieve,* an effect outside the maker, the opposite of *agere,* (3) *do something, contribute,* syno-nym of *conferre.* See *fio.*—On **bonum facienti,** see *bonus.*—Kinds of *facere* in this (1) sense are: **facere directe** and **facere in-directe seu per accidens,** *to do something directly* and *to do something indirectly* or *acciden-tally.*—Kinds of *facere* in this (2) sense are: **facere effective** and **facere formaliter,** *to produce something in the manner of the effective cause* and *in the man-ner of form.*—**cognitio facientis determinat formam facti,** see *co-gnitio.*—faciens est honorabilius facto, *that effecting is nobler* or *more excellent than that effected.* The maker is greater than the thing made, because the latter depends on the former. Cf. *agens est honorabilius patiente* under *agens.*—faciens, entis, *P. a., making, creating, contributing.*—factus, a, um, *P. a., made, created, contributed.*—factum, i, *n., that which is done, deed, act, exploit, achievement, a fact.*—de facto, *actually, in fact.*

factibilis, e, *adj., possible of being made, producible, achievable in a work, feasible, practicable,* the opposite . of *agibilis.*—factibilia, ium, *n., things to be made.* On ratio factibilium, see *ratio;* on ars est recta ratio factibilium, see *ars.*

factio, onis, *f., a making, doing, preparing, accomplishment, achievement,* as distinguished from *actio.* On principium factionis, see *principium.*—Kinds of *factio* are: (a), factio exterior, *the exterior invisible production.*—(b), factio momentanea and factio successiva, *the immediate* or *sudden* and *the gradual production.*—(c), factio naturalis, *the natural production,* or *that according to nature.*—(d), factio particularis, *the partial production* or *that in part.*—(e), factio successiva, see *factio momentanea.*

factivus, a, um, *adj., having the power to make, factive, producing, accomplishing an effect,* as distinguished *from activus.* On ars factiva, see *ars;* on forma activa, see *forma;* on habitus factivus, see *habitus;* on operatio factiva et operatio factiva finis, see *operatio;* on organum factivum, see *organum;* on ratio factiva, see *ratio;* on scientia factiva, see *scientia;* on species factiva, see *species;* on verbum factivum, see *verbum;* on vis factiva, see *vis.*

factor, oris, *m.,* factrix, icis, *f., the producer, accomplisher, maker,* the opposite of *actor.* On causa factrix, see *causa.*

factrix, icis, *f., an artificer, one who produces new constructions out of existing material.*

factum, i, *n.,* see *facio.*

facultas, atis, *f.,* (1) *facility of a power* in passing over to its activity, (2) *capacity to do* or *become something, a potency, power,* (3) *possession, property.*

facundia, ae, *f., eloquence, fluency,* used in the S.T. only in quot.

faeculentia, ae, *f., fecal matter.*

faeculentus, a, um, *adj., feculent, turbulent, thick, muddy.*

faex, faecis, *f., dregs, refuse.*

Falcidius, a, um, *adj., of Falcidius, Falcidian*: lex, *the law of Falcidius respecting bequests, which provided that no Roman citizen should by testament divert more than three-fourths of his estate from his legal heirs.*

falco, onis, *m., a falcon.*

fallacia, ae, *f.,* (1) *deception, fraud, deceit,* (2) *false conclusion, fallacy, false inference,* synonym of *paralogismus* and *sophisma.*— Kinds of *fallacia* in this (2) sense are: (a), **fallacia accidentis,** *the false conclusion from an accident* which takes place when someone concludes from that which is only accidental to a thing as though it were essential and belonged to it—(b), **fallacia aequivocationis,** *the false conclusion of equivocation* or *ambiguity,* into which one falls when in the syllogism or the proof he uses a word now in its proper meaning and then in its improper or transferred meaning. This is one of the six fallacies in word. See below.— (c), **fallacia consequentis,** *the fallacy of the conclusion,* the error into which one falls by confusing the order between the antecedent and consequent parts of a conditional sentence. When the antecedent is verified, the consequent is true; but verifying the consequent does not verify the antecedent. It is fallacious to argue that if the consequent be verified, the antecedent becomes true. For example, if X is a man, a fortiori he is an animal; but if Y is an animal, he is not necessarily a man.—(d), **fallacia extra dictionem** and **fallacia in dictione,** the *paralogismos exo tes lexeos* and the *paralogismos para ten lexin* of Aristotle, fallacy in the subject-matter and in the word, *the dialectic* or *objective false conclusion* and *the grammatical* or *linguistic false con-*

clusion, of which the first is suited to lead into error through extending a partial likeness or difference in the matter of the argument to complete similarity or difference and the latter through grammatical likeness of expression or of a word.—(e), **fallacia figurae dictionis,** *the false conclusion of a figure of speech,* which consists in this, that the same linguistic expression, which according to grammar admits of several interpretations is understood otherwise in the major premise than in the minor premise. —(f), **fallacia in dictione,** see *fallacia extra dictionem.*

fallaciter, *adv.,* see *fallax.*

fallax, acis, *adj., deceitful, deceptive, fallacious; of, pertaining to, embodying* or *involving a fallacy; deceptive, as in quality* or *appearance.*—**fallaciter,** *adv., deceitfully, fallaciously.*

fallo, ere, fefelli, falsum, 3, *v. a., to deceive, trick, dupe, cheat, disappoint.*

falsarius, ii, *m., a falsifier, forger of money,* written documents, wills, etc.

false, *adv.,* see *falsus,* a, um.

falsifico, are, 1, *v. a., to tamper with, make alterations* in a letter or manuscript to pervert or vitiate.

falsiloquus, a, um, *adj., (falsus* plus *loquor), that speaks falsehoods, speaking falsehoods.*

falsitas, atis, *f.,* (1) *falseness, falsity, falsehood, untruth,* the opposite of *veritas*, (2) *falseness against God, godlessness.*—On **spiritus falsitatis**, see *spiritus;* on **syllogismus falsitatis**, see *syllogismus.*

falso, are, avi, atum, 1, *v. a., to falsify, forge, counterfeit; endow with an appearance contrary to truth.*

falsus, a, um, *adj., false, untrue, incorrect, not genuine,* the contrary of *verus.* On **aestimatio falsa**, see *aestimatio;* on **beatitudo falsa**, see *beatitudo;* on **conclusio falsa**, see *conclusio;* on **definitio falsa**, see *definitio;* on **felicitas falsa**, see *felicitas;* on **intellectus falsus**, see *intellectus;* on **iudicium falsum**, see *iudicium;* on **locutio falsa**, see *locutio;* on **negatio falsa**, see *negatio;* on **opinio falsa**, see *opinio;* on **opus falsum**, see *opus;* on **oratio falsa**, see *oratio;* on **praedicare falsum**, see *praedicare;* on **praedicatio falsa**, see *praedicatio;* on **principium falsum**, see *principium;* on **propositio falsa**, see *propositio;* on **prudentia falsa**, see *prudentia;* on **ratio falsa**, see *ratio;* on **ratiocinatio falsa**, see *ratiocinatio;* on **res falsa**, see *res;* on **res falsa secundum quid et falsa simpliciter**, see *res;* on **scientia falsa**, see *scientia;* on **syllogismus falsus**, see *syllogismus;* on **vox falsa**, see *vox.*— Kinds of *falsus* are: (a), **falsum absolute seu absolutum seu simpliciter seu secundum se** and **falsum secundum quid seu ex**

suppositione, *the absolutely* or *simply* or *essentially false* and *the false in a certain respect.*— (b), **falsum absolutum**, see *falsum absolute.*—(c), **falsum contingens** and **falsum impossibile**, *that which is false under certain conditions,* and *that which is false because intrinsically impossible* or *the necessarily false.* —(d), **falsum ex suppositione**, *false according to the concrete object to which a word refers.*— (e), **falsum formaliter** and **falsum materialiter**, *false according to form and matter.*—(f), **falsum impossible**, see *falsum contingens.* —(g), **falsum in enuntiatione**, **falsum in mente**, and **falsum in re seu natura**, *the false in the statement, the wrong in the thought,* and *the false in reality outside the mind* or *in the nature of the thing.*—(h), **falsum in mente**, see *falsum in enuntiatione.*—(i), **falsum in natura**, see *falsum in enuntiatione.*—(j), **falsum in re**, see *falsum in enuntiatione.*—(k), **falsum in se** and **falsum quantum ad radicem**, *the false in itself,* and *the false in its roots* or *fundamentally false.*—(l), **falsum in se** and **falsum respectu alicuius rei**, *false in itself* and *false with reference to something else.* —(m), **falsum materialiter**, see *falsum formaliter.*—(n), **falsum quantum ad radicem**, see *falsum in se.*—(o), **falsum respectu alterius rei**, see *falsum in se.*—(p), **falsum secundum quid**, see *falsum* *absolute.*—(q), **falsum secundum se,** see *falsum absolute.*—(r), **falsum simpliciter,** see *falsum absolute.*—(s), **falsum totaliter,** *totally* or *entirely false.*—**falso,** *adv., falsely, wrongly, by mistake.*—**false,** *adv., wrongly, falsely, untruly,* opposite of *vere.*

falx, falcis, *f., a sickle, scythe.*

fama, ae, *f.,* (1) *report, rumor, saying,* that which people say or tell; *the common talk,* (2) *fame, renown, celebrity,* the widely disseminated knowledge or report of a man's character, deeds or abilities; *public* or *general reputation,* especially when favorably, a synonym of *gloria,* (3) *reputation,* the estimation in which a person is held by others; especially the popular opinion whether favorable or the reverse.—**bona fama,** *a good name.*

famelicus, i, *m., a hungry* or *famished person, one suffering from hunger.*

fames, is, *f.,* (1) *lit., hunger,* (2) *transf., famine.*

familia, ae, *f.,* (1) *in gen., a family; the members of a household,* (2) **paterfamilias,** *the proprietor of an estate; the head of a family;* **filius familias,** *a son under the father's power, a minor.*

familiaris, e, *adj.,* (1) *of* or *belonging to the house, household,* or *family,* (2) *transf., intimate, friendly, familiar.*—**familiaris res,** *the household, household interests, family affairs, property.*—**familiaris instinctus,** *inward* or

interior instinct.—**familiaris revelatio,** *interior revelation.*—**familiaris,** is, *m., a friend, a familiar acquaintance, companion.*—**familiariter,** *adv., familiarly, intimately, on friendly terms.*

familiaritas, atis, *f., familiarity, intimacy, familiar intercourse, friendship, intimate acquaintance.*

familiariter, *adv.,* see *familiaris.*

famosus, a, um, *adj., famous, much talked of, famed, celebrated.*

famula, ae, *f., a maid-servant, handmaid.*

famulatus, us, *m., service,* in religion; *that devotion of heart* and *life which is due to God; obedience to the divine commands.*

famulor, ari, atus, 1, *v. dep. n., to be a servant, to serve, attend, wait on.*

famulus, i, *m., a servant, attendant,* found in the S.T. only in quot.

fantasmagoria, ae, *f., fantasmagoria, trickery,* a changing incoherent series of apparitions, appearances or phantasms, a synonym of *praestigium.*

far, farris, *n., maize,* a grain produced from the maize plant, used as a food by men and animals.

farina, ae, *f., ground corn, meal, flour.*

fas, *indecl., n.,* (1) *orig.* belonging to the relig. lang., *the divine law,* (2) *transf.,* (a) *in gen. justice, equity,* but usually to be translated as an adjective, *right,* *proper, allowable, lawful, fit, permitted,* hence *possible.*

fascinans, antis, *P. a., bewitching, charming.*—**fascinans oculus,** *the evil eye;* the supposed faculty of harming by spiteful looks, superstitiously attributed to certain persons as a natural endowment. It is much dreaded in Mediterranean Europe, the Levant, and the East in general, where charms are used against its influence, as for the protection of children, cattle, etc.

fascinatio, onis, *f., enchantment* or *spell through evil glance.*

fascis, is *m., a burden, load.*

fastidio, ire, ivi or ii, itum, 4, *v. n., to loathe, dislike, despise, feel disgust for; to shrink* from anything unpleasant to the senses.

fastidiosus, a, um, *adj., that creates disgust, disgusting, loathsome, distasteful, disagreeable.*

fastidium, ii, *n.,* (1) *lit., a loathing distaste,* (2) *fig., disgust, distaste, weariness, tediousness.*

fastigatio, onis, *f., fastigation, sloping to a point,* used *fig.,* here with *sine,* meaning *without wearing down,* hence *untiringly.*

fastigium, ii, *n., top, height, summit,* used in the S.T. only in quot.

fastus, us, *m., pride, haughtiness, ostentation.*

fatalis, e, *adj., concerning fate, belonging to fate, fatal.* On **causa fatalis,** see *causa.*

fateor, eri, fassus, 2, *v. dep. a., to confess, declare, maintain, own,*

grant, acknowledge, used (1) with *acc.* and *inf.,* (2) *acc.* alone, (3) with ellips. of *acc.,* (4) with a *quod s*ubst. cl. in the indic., (5) *absol.*

fatigatio, onis, *f., weariness, fatigue.*

fatigo, are, avi, atum, 1, *v. a., to weary, tire, fatigue,* used in the *passive.*

fatuitas, atis, *f., fatuity, entire privation of the spiritual sense.*

fatum, i, *n., fate, destiny.*

fatuus, a, um, *adj., foolish, silly, fatuous.*—**fatuus,** i, *m., a fool, idiot.*

fauces, ium, *f., jaws.*

Faunus, i, *m., Fauns,* one of a class of deities of the woods and herds represented as half human, with pointed ears, a tail, short horns, and goats' feet. The fauns are often grouped with the satyrs, who were said to be in some respects similar.

faustus, a, um, *adj., lucky, favorable, auspicious.*

Faustus, i, *m., Faustus,* a Manichaean doctor, who visited Carthage in 383 A.D. Augustine, who had then been a Manichaean for nine years, placed himself under his direction. The only effect which he produced upon his gifted pupil, however, was to loosen the snare in which he had been so long entangled, and to dissatisfy him with Manichaeism. (Augustine, *contr. Faust. Manich.* 1). Many years later a book which Faustus had written was put into the hands of Augustine by some of his brethren and at their request he wrote a reply to it, a copy of which he sent to Jerome A.D. 400. St. Thomas gives numerous references to the *Contra Faustum*.

fautor, oris, *m.*, *a favorer, furtherer, promoter, maintainer.*

faveo, ere, favi, fautum, 2, *v. n.*, *to favor, look upon* or *behave towards with favor* or *kindness; countenance; befriend; try to please; gain the favor of,* used with the *dative.*

favilla, ae, *f.*, *hot cinders* or *ashes.*

favor, oris, *m.*, (1) *favor, good will, inclination, partiality,* (2) *benefit, profit, advantage,* (3) *approbation, applause, popularity.*

favorabilis, e, *adj.*, (1) *favored, in favor, popular, beloved,* (2) *pleasing, agreeable.*

favorabilitas, atis, *f.*, *favorableness.*

fax, facis, *f.*, *a torch, firebrand*

febricitantes, ium, *c.*, *fever-patients, those who have fever.*

febris, is, *f.*, (1) *prop., fever,* (a) *sing.,* (b) *plur.,* (2) *fig.*

fecundatio, onis, *f.*, *fruitfulness, fecundity,* synonym of *fecunditas.*

fecunditas, atis, *f.*, (1) *fruitfulness, fecundity,* synonym of *fecundatio,* (a) in a material sense, (b) with a spiritual signification, (2) *transf., abundance, plenty.*

fecundo, are, 1, *v. a.*, (1) *to fecundate, render capable of development,* as the ovum of an animal or plant, by union with the sper-

matozoa; *impregnate; fertilize,* (2) *fig., to fecundate, made fecund, render fruitful.*

fecundus, a, um, *adj.*, *fruitful, fertile.*

fel, fellis, *n.*, (1) *gall,* the viscid, bitter fluid secreted by the liver, *bile,* (2) *gall,* a bitter substance mixed with the wine preferred to Christ on the cross. The word *fel* as used in the Gospel of St. Matthew is a rendering of the Greek word *chole,* which in turn renders the Hebrew word signifying "poison". The Hebrews considered all bitter herbs as poisonous, and so the translators were induced to express all bitter substances by the Greek *chole,* gall. Myrrh also fell under the category of poisons, on account of its bitterness; hence the "gall" or "poison" of St. Matthew's gospel is identical with the myrrh of St. Mark's, (3) *fig., wrath, bitter anger.*

Felicianus, i, *m.*, *Felicianus,* the name of a person either real or imaginary, but of whom really nothing is known, though he is called by Alcuin an Arian Bishop. He is represented as one of the interlocutors in a dialogue carried on with St. Augustine on the nature of the Trinity. The treatise which contains this is entitled Contra Felicianum, Arianum, de Unitate Trinitatis, and was formerly ascribed to Augustine.

felicitas, atis, *f.*, *happiness, bless-edness*, synonym of *beatitudo.—* Kinds of *felicitas* are: (a), **felici-tas activa** and **felicitas contem-plativa seu speculativa**, *the hap-piness of active* and *of contem-plative living.—*(b), **felicitas civ-ilis seu politica**, *the happiness of the civic* or *public life.—*(c), **felicitas contemplativa**, see *felic-ita activa.—*(d), **felicitas falsa seu secundum opinionem** and **felicitas vera seu secundum veri-tatem**, *the false* or *supposed hap-piness* and *the true* or *real hap-piness.—*(e), **felicitas futura**, *the future happiness.—*(f), **felicitas imperfecta** and **felicitas perfecta**, *the imperfect* and *the perfect happiness*, of which the former consists of an indirect knowledge of God and the latter of a direct contemplation of Him.—(g), **feli-citas perfecta**, see *felicitas im-perfecta.—*(h), **felicitas politica**, see *felicitas civilis.—*(i), **felicitas secundum opinionem**, see *felici-tas falsa.—*(j), **felicitas secundum veritatem**, see *felicitas falsa.—* (k), **felicitas speculativa**, see *feli-citas activa.—*(l), **felicitas terre-na**, *the earthly happiness.—*(m), **felicitas ultima**, *the last* or *high-est happiness.*

feliciter, *adv.*, see *felix.*

Felix, Felicis, *m.*, (1) *Felix*, Felix of Nola in Campania. He was of Syrian extraction but born at Nola, where his father Hermias had settled. The date of his death is uncertain, but many miracles are said to have been wrought around the place of his interment, over which a church was built. Augustine speaks of an apparition of Felix at the time of the barbarian invasion as attested by trustworthy wit-nesses, (2) *Felix*, bishop of Rome, probably from Jan. 5, 269 A.D. to Dec. 30, 274 A.D. He appears in the Roman Calendar as a saint and Martyr, his day being May 30. St. Thomas quotes a letter of his on the sub-ject of the Hypostatic Union.

felix, icis, *adj.*, *happy, joyous, blessed.—***feliciter**, *adv.*, *blissful-ly, happily.*

felleus, a, um, *adj.*, *of gall, full of gall, like gall.*

femina, ae, *f.*, (1) *lit.*, (a) of human beings, *a female, woman,* (b), of beasts, *a female, she,* (2) *transf.*, in the lang. of nat. hist., of plants and animals, *female.*

feminalia, ium, *n.*, *loin-cloths, bandages for the upper part of the thigh.*

femineitas, atis, *f.*, *femineity, wom-anliness; womanly nature* or *character.*

femineus, a, um, *adj.*, *of* or *be-longing to a woman, woman-ly, feminine.—***femineum genus**, *womankind.—***femineus sexus**, *the female sex.*

femininus, a, um, *adj.*, (1) *female*, characterized by organs for con-ceiving and bringing forth young or producing *ova;* of or pertain-ing to sex so characterized, (2) in *gram., of the feminine gender, feminine,* applicable to females only, or to objects classified with them.

femoralia, ium, *n.,* used in the pl., *femoralia, breeches* worn as a part of his pontifical vestment by the Jewish high priest.

femur, oris, *n., the thigh.*

feneror, ari, atus, sum, 1, *v. dep., to fenerate, lend upon usury.*

fenestra, ae, *f., a window, an opening* in the wall or roof of a building or other structure including architecturally, the casement, sash, panes, shutters, etc.; hence the name is often applied to one of its parts.

fenus, oris, *n., interest, the proceeds from capital lent out,* in a broad sense, *a lending.*

fere, *adv.,* with the idea of approach predominant, *nearly, almost, well-nigh,* especially with words of number, quantity, multitude.

feria, ae, *f., a week-day,* used with ordinals for the names of the days of the week, as *quinta feria, the fifth day, Thursday.*

feriatus, a, um, *P. a., unoccupied, disengaged.* The *feriatum tempus, holy season,* is a designation for any season of the ecclesiastical year, such as advent and lent, during which time there is a turning away or leisure from worldly amusements and a greater concentration on spiritual things.

ferio, ire, 4, *v. a.,* (1) *to strike, beat, hit,* (2) used *fig., to punish, inflict punishment.*

feritas, atis, *f., fierceness, brutality, the state* or *quality of being brutal; coarse, cruelty.*

fermento, are, avi, atum, 1, *v. a., to leaven, to produce fermentation in; make light by fermentation,* as dough.—**fermentatus,** a, um, *P. a., fermented, leavened,* that in which fermentation has been produced.

fermentum, i, *n., leaven, fermenting dough,* used to raise or lighten other dough.

fero, ferre, tuli, latum, 3, *v. a.* and *n.,* (1) *to carry, conduct,* (2) *deliver, arrange,* (3) *carry forward, move on,* (4) *carry to, turn towards, move towards,* (5) *endure, bear.*—On **sphaera ferens,** see *sphaera.*—Kinds of *ferre* in this sense are: **ferre circulariter seu circulo** and **ferre circulum seu secundum circulum,** the Aristotelian *kuklo kai kuklon pheresthai, circular moving* or *moving in a circle* and *returning to itself after the manner of a circle.*—One kind of *ferre* in this sense is **ferre universaliter,** *to turn toward in general.*

ferox, ocis, *adj., cruel, fierce, savage.*

ferramentum, i, *n., a sharp-edged, iron tool.*

ferreus, a, um, *adj., made of iron, iron.*

ferrum, i, *n.,* (1) *lit., iron,* (2) *transf.,* anything made of iron, *a sword.*—**iudicium ferri candentis,** *trial by hot iron.* St. Thomas quotes a decree of Pope Stephen V in which he condemns inquisition by torture.

fertilitas, atis, *f., fertility, fruitfulness.*

ferus, a, um, *adj., brutal,* characteristic of a brute; *inhuman, cruel, vindictive.*—**fera,** ae, *f., a wild beast.*

fervefacio, ere, feci, factum, 3, *v. a., to enkindle, stir to action, excite, incite.*

fervens, entis, *P. a.,* see *ferveo.*

ferventer, *adv.,* see *ferveo.*

ferveo, ere, 2, *v. n.,* used *fig., to glow, to be animated* with strong emotion, as zeal, love.—**fervens,** entis, *P. a.,* (1) *lit., boiling hot, burning,* (2) *fig., fervent, ardent in feeling.*—**ferventer,** *adv., fervently.*

fervesco, ere, 3, *v. inch. n.,* used *fig., to boil, to be stirred by violent emotion.*

fervor, oris, *m.,* used *fig., fervor, heat, vehemence, ardor, passion, intensity of feeling.*

festinanter, *adv.,* see *festino.*

festinantia, ae, *f., haste, necessity for hurry.*

festinatio, onis, *f., a hastening, haste, hurry, dispatch, speed.*

festine, *adv.,* see *festinus.*

festino, are, avi, atum, 1, *v. n.* and *a.,* (1) *to make haste, move with celerity, be quick,* (2) *transf., to make haste with a thing, hurry, do speedily,* used with an *object clause.*—**festin-** anter, *adv., hastily, speedily, quickly.*

festinus, a, um, *adj., hastening, hasty, in haste, quick, speedy.*—**festine,** *adv., hastily.*

festivitas, atis, *f., a festival, a feast.*

festivus, a, um, *adj., festival, festive, of* or *pertaining to,* or *suitable to* a feast or to an anniversary or set time of religious celebration, used with *dies* and *tempus;* **festivus dies,** *a festival day, feast-day, holy day,* a day consecrated or set apart for religious observance, usually in commemoration of some important event.—**festivum tempus,** *festal time, a time of festive celebration, an anniversary* or season designated for giving special honor to God, to the saints or to important events.

festuca, ae, *f.,* (1) *lit., a straw, stalk, stem,* (2) *transf., a mote, an exceedingly small particle,* as of dust, *a speck; mite.*

festus, a, um, *adj., of* or *belonging to a feast* or *feast day* or *holy day,* that is, a day consecrated or set apart to honor God, His saints or some important mystery of religion, *solemn, festive, festal.*—**festum,** i, *n., a feast, holy day,* (1) an ecclesiastical feast or holy day celebrates the commemoration of the sacred mysteries and events of our redemption as well as the memory of the Mother of Christ, His apostles, martyrs, and saints, by special services and rest from work, (2) in the Old Law there were several feasts and one continual feast, namely the sacrifice of the lamb every morning and evening, signifying the perpetuity of divine bliss. The temporal feasts included the solemnity of the sabbath, the feast of the new moon, the feast of the passover, the feast of pentecost, the feast of trumpets, the feast of expiation, the feast of tabernacles, the feast of assembly and congregation.

feto, are, 1, *v. n.*, and *a.*, *to breed*, *bring forth*, used in S.T. only in quot.

fetus, us, *m.*, the young in the womb; the unborn offspring of animals after it has attained definite characteristics.

feudum, i, *n.*, *a feud, fee, fief*, a landed estate held under feudal tenure. In the feudal system an ecclesiastical fief followed all the laws laid down for the temporal fiefs. The system of feudal tenure was not always restricted to lands, as church revenues and tithes were farmed out to secular persons as a species of ecclesiastical fief.—Common phrases are: **tenere in feudum,** *to hold in fee* or as a feud on condition of feudal homage.—**dare in feudum,** *to give in fee,* to give as a feud or fief under the laws of feudal tenure.

fibra, ae, *f.*, *entrails, the internal parts of an animal; viscera.*

ficte, *adv.,* see *fingo.*

fictilis, e, *adj.;* *fictile, earthen, made of clay,* used in the S.T. only in quot.

fictio, onis, *f.*, (1) *pretence, insincerity, dissimulation, a feigning,* that which is advanced or displayed for the purpose of concealing or misrepresenting the reality, a synonym of *simulatio,* (2) *fiction,* an imaginary fictitious statement, account etc.

fictitius, a, um, *adj.*, *fictitious, not genuine,* created or formed by the imagination.

fictor, oris, *m.*, (1) *a maker, former,* (2) *a feigner, one who uses false appearances.*

fictus, a, um, *P. a.*, see *fingo.*

ficulnea, ae, *f.*, *a fig-tree.*

ficus, i, and us, *a fig-tree,* used in the S.T. only in quot.

fideiubeo, ere, iussi, iussum, 2, *v. n.*, *to be surety* or *bail, to give* or *go bail* for anyone.

fideiussor, oris, *m.*, *a fidejussor,* a person bound as security for another.

fidelis, e, *adj.*, (1) *believing, believing religiously, believing as a Christian,* the opposite of *infidelis,* (2) *faithful, loyal,* likewise the opposite of *infidelis.* On **character fidelium,** see *character;* on **homo fidelis,** see *homo.* —**fideliter,** *adv., faithfully, surely, honestly.*

fidelitas, atis, *f.*, *faithfulness, trustiness, firm adherence, fidelity.*

fideliter, *adv.,* see *fidelis.*

fidenter, *adv., confidently, boldly,* used in the S.T. only in quot.

fides, ei, *f.,* (1) *faith in the sense of an act, to believe,* (2) *faith in the sense of a habitus,* a theological virtue, infused by God, by which we firmly assent to what God has revealed, solely on His authority, the opposite of *infidelitas,* (3) *faith in the* sense of the object believed, (4) *faithfulness, loyalty,* also the opposite of *infidelitas,* (5) *assurance, promise, pledge.—***actus fidei,** *the act of faith.* On **certitudo fidei,** see *certitudo;* on **cognitio fidei,** see *cognitio;* on **confessio fidei,** see *confessio;* on **gratia fidei,** see *gratia;* on **iustitia fidei,** see *iustitia;* on **lumen fidei,** see *lumen;* on **meritum fidei,** see *meritum;* on **quantitas fidei,** see *quantitas;* on **ratio fidei informata,** see *ratio;* on **via fidei,** see *via;* on **visio fidei,** see *visio.—*Kinds of *fides* in this (2) sense are: (a), **fides adquisita** and **fides infusa,** *the acquired faith* and *that infused by God.* —(b), **fides communiter accepta** and **fides proprie accepta,** *faith in the wider* and *the narrower* and *the improper sense of the word.—*(c), **fides ficta,** *feigned* or *fictitious faith.—*(d), **fides formata seu vivens** and **fides informis seu mortua,** *the formed faith* or *that pervaded by charity* or *the living faith in one in the state of grace* and *the unformed faith (because deprived of charity)* or *the dead faith in one in mortal sin.—*(e), **fides in-**forms, *faith without sanctifying grace.* See *fides formata.—*(f), **fides mortua,** see *fides informis.* —(g), **fides oculata,** *faith supplied* or *illuminated by the eyes.* —(h), **fides proprie accepta,** *assent on the authority of God,* see *fides communiter accepta.—* (i), **fides recta,** *the right* or *true faith.—*(j), **fides vivens,** see *fides formata.—***fides est fundamentum virtutum,** *faith is the foundation of all supernatural virtues.* On **apostasia a fide,** see *apostasia;* on **articulus fidei,** see *articulus;* on **doctor fidei,** see *doctor;* on **doctrina fidei,** see *doctrina;* on **documentum fidei nostrae,** see *documentum;* on **dogma fidei,** see *dogma;* on **lex fidei,** see *lex;* on **professio fidei,** see *professio;* on **sacramentum fidei,** see *sacramentum;* on **sententia fidei,** see *sententia;* on **veritas fidei,** see *veritas.—*Kinds of *fides* in this (3) sense are: (a), **fides Catholica seu Christiana seu ecclesiae seu nostra,** *the Catholic* or *Christian* or *our faith* or *the faith of the Catholic Church,* i.e., Catholic doctrine.—(b), **fides Christiana,** see *fides Catholica.—*(c), **fides ecclesiae,** see *fides Catholica.—* (d), **fides explicita** and **fides implicita,** *the explicit* or *unfolded faith* and *the implicit* or *unexplained faith.—*(e), **fides implicita,** see *fides explicita.—*(f), **fides nostra,** see *fides Catholica.—* Faith is one of the twelve fruits of the Holy Ghost. Cf. *fructus.*

fiducia, ae, *f., a confidence, reliance, assurance.*

fiducialiter, *adv., confidently.*

figmentum, i, *n.,* (1) *a figure, anything made, a production, creation, device,* (2) *fiction,* that which is feigned or imagined, as opposed to that which is true.

figo, ere, xi, xum, 3, *v. a.,* (1) *lit., to fix, fasten, drive* or *thrust in, attach, affix,* (2) *fig., to fix, fasten, direct,* used with *in* and *abl.* —**fixus,** a, um, *P. a., fixed, fast, immovable.*—**fixe,** *adv., fixedly, attentively.*

figulus, i, *m., a potter, one who makes earthenware, stoneware,* or *porcelain.*

figura, ae, *f.,* (1) *figure, form* in the narrow and proper sense of the word, the quantitative size and shape of material things, as distinct from *forma,* (2) *figure, form,* in the wider sense of the word, a synonym of *forma,* (3) *figure,* in the improper sense of the word, *picture, symbol, model.*—On the difference between *figura* and *forma,* see *forma.*— Kinds of *figura* in this (1) sense are: (a), **figura acuta,** *the acute figure.*—(b) **figura circularis seu rotunda** and **figura rectilinea,** *the circular* and *the rectilinear figure.*—(c), **figura corporalis seu corporea seu solida** and **figura plana seu superficialis,** *the corporeal* or *tri-dimensional figure* and *the plane* or *surface figure.*— (d), **figura helica,** *the spiral figure.*—(e), **figura lenticularis** and

figura ovalis, *the lens-shaped* and *the egg-shaped figure* or *oviform.*—(f), **figura ovalis,** see *figura lenticularis.*—(g), **figura perfecta,** *the perfect figure,* i.e., *the circle* or *globe.*—(h), **figura plana,** see *figura corporalis.*—(i), **figura rectilinea,** see *figura circularis.*— (j), **figura rotunda,** see *figura circularis.*—(k), **figura solida,** see *figura corporalis.*—(l), **figura sphaerica,** *the spherical figure.*— (m), **figura superficialis,** see *figura corporalis.*—(n), **figura triangularis,** *the triangular figure, the triangle.*—Kinds of *figura* in this (2) sense are: (a), **figura dictionis,** *the figure of speech.*— (b), **figura praedicamenti,** *the form of expression,* i.e., *the predicate.*—(c), **figura syllogismi,** *the pattern of terms in a syllogism.* Kinds of *figura* in this (3) sense are: (a), **figura legalis,** *the example of the Old Testament; the legal figure.*—(b), **figura sensibilis,** *the sensible picture* or *figure.*

figuralis, e, *adj.,* (1) *figurative,* opposite of *litteralis,* (2) *symbolical, typical,* also the opposite of *litteralis,* synonym of *mysticus.*— On **actus figuralis,** see *actus;* on **causa figuralis,** see *causa;* on **intellectus figuralis,** see *intellectus;* on **praeceptum figurale** see *praeceptum;* on **ratio figuralis,** see *ratio;* on **sacerdos figuralis,** see *sacerdos;* on **sacerdotium figurale,** see *sacerdotium;* on **sacrificum figurale,** see *sacrificium.* —**figuraliter,** *adv.,* (1) *in a pic-*

torial manner or *illustrative way,*
figuratively, (2) *in a symbolic* or
allegorical manner, in a typical
way.

figuraliter, *adv.,* see *figuralis.*

figurate, *adv.,* see *figuro.*

figuratio, onis, *f., formation, form,*
shape, figure.

figurative, see *figurativus.*

figurativus, a, um, *adj.,* (1) *form-*
ing, shaping, (2) *figurative,* synonym of *figuralis,* (3) *symbolical,*
typical, also synonym of *figura-*
lis.—On **disciplina figurativa,** see
disciplina.—On **locutio figurativa,**
see *locutio;* on **significatio figur-**
ativa, see *significatio.*—**figurati-**
ve, *adv., in an allegorical* or
symbolic manner, allegorically,
symbolically, synonym of *figur-*
ate.

figuro, are, avi, atum, 1, *v. a.,* (1)
to configure, form, shape, (2) *ex-*
press in figurative language, (3)
symbolize, exemplify. On **ars fig-**
urandi, see *ars;* on **corpus figur-**
atum, see *corpus.*—On **locutio**
figurata, see *locutio.*—**figuratus,**
a, um, *Part.* and *P. a., symbol-*
ized, typified.—**figurate,** *adv.,*
figuratively, symbolically, typi-
cally, synonym of *figurative.*

filia, ae, *f.,* (1) *a daughter,* (2) *fig.,*
an offshoot, daughter, something
conceived as feminine and regarded in connection with its
origin.

filialis, e, *adj., filial, becoming to a*
child in relation to its parents.

filiatio, onis, *f., filial relationship,*
sonship, filiation. Cf. *genitus.* On

relatio filiationis, see *relatio.*—
Kinds of *filiatio* are: (a), **filiatio**
adoptionis seu adoptiva and **fili-**
atio naturalis, *filial relationship*
depending on adoption or *the*
adoptive filial relationship and
the natural filial relationship
or *that depending on nature.*—
(b), **filiatio adoptiva,** see *filiatio*
adoptionis.—(c), **filiatio aeterna**
and **filiatio temporalis,** *the eter-*
nal filial relationship or *that ex-*
isting from eternity and *the tem-*
poral filial relationship or *that*
arising in time.—(d), **filiatio na-**
turalis, see *filiatio adoptionis.*—
(e), **filiatio rationis tantum,** and
filiatio realis, *the filial relation-*
ship that would exist only in the
mind and *real filial relationship.*
—(f), **filiatio realis,** see *filiatio ra-*
tionis tantum.—(g), **filiatio sub-**
sistens, *the subsistent filial rela-*
tionship, which constitutes the
second Person of the Trinity.—
(h), **filiatio temporalis,** see *filia-*
tio aeterna.

filius, i, *m.,* (1) *son, daughter, child,*
in the proper sense of the word
(cf. *filiatio*) synonym of *genitus*
and *natus,* the opposite of *pater,*
(2) *son, daughter, child* in the
improper sense of the word, i.e.,
descendant, offspring.—Kinds of
filius in this (1) sense are: (a),
filius adoptatus, et filius natura-
lis, *the adopted child* or *that*
taken in place of one's own and
the natural child or *the child re-*
sulting through procreation.—(b),
filius adoptionis, see *filius adop-*

tatus.—(c), **filius adoptivus**, see *filius adoptatus.*—(d), **filius caelestis et filius terrenus**, *the heavenly* and *the earthly son.*—(e), **filius connaturalis**, *the son of like nature.*—(f), **filius corporalis** and **filius spiritualis**, *the corporal* and *the spiritual son*, or *the son after the body* and *after the spirit.*—(g), **filius illegitimus** and **filius legitimus**, *the unlawful* or *illegitimate son* and *the lawful* or *legitimate son.*—(h), **filius legitimus**, see *filius illegitimus.*—(i), **filius naturalis**, see *filius adoptatus.*—(j), **filius per gratiam adoptationis**, see *filius adoptatus.*—(k), **filius per naturam**, see *filius adoptatus.*—(l), **filius spiritualis**, see *filius corporalis.*—(m), **filius spurius**, *the unnatural son* or *bastard.*—(n), **filius terrenus**, see *filius caelestis.* On **filiae acidiae**, see *acidia;* on **filiae avaritiae**, see *avaritia;* on **filiae inanis gloriae**, see *gloria;* on **filiae gulae**, see *gula;* on **filiae invidiae**, see *invidia;* on **filiae irae**, see *ira.*

filum, i, *n.*, *a thread.*

fimbriae, arum, *f.*, *fibres, threads, shreds, fringes.*

fimus, i, *m.*, *dung, excrement, ordure.*

finalis, e, *adj.*, (1) *of* or *pertaining to the end, finally, concluding, final*, (2) *of* or *relating to the purpose, purposeful.*—On **beatitudo finalis**, see *beatitudo;* on **bonum finale**, see *bonus;* on **gloria finalis**, see *gloria;* on **impoenitentia finalis**, see *impoeniten-*

tia; on **iudicium finale**, see *iudicium;* on **passio finalis in genere et finalis simpliciter**, see *passio.*—On **causa finalis**, see *causa;* on **principium finale et primum finale**, see *principium.*—**finaliter**, *adv.*, (1) *in the end, at the close, in a final manner*, (2) *until the end, until the close.*

finaliter, *adv.*, see *finalis.*

findo, ere, fidi, fissum, 3, *v. a.*, *to separate, part, divide.*—**fissus**, a, um, *P. a.*, *cloven, parted.*

fingo, ere, finxi, fictum, 3, *v. a.*, (1) *lit.*, *to fashion, make form*, (2) *fig.*, (a) *to form mentally*, or *in speech, imagine, think, suppose, stretch out*, (b) *to feign, pretend, counterfeit.*—**fictus**, a, um, *P. a.*, *insincere, feigned, false.*—**ficte**, *adv.*, *insincerely.*

finio, ire, ivi, itum, 4, *v. a.*, (1) *to limit, bound*, (2) *to put an end to, finish, terminate.*—**finitus**, a, um, *P. a.*, *bounded, limited, ended*, synonym of *determinatus* and *terminatus*, the opposite of *indefinitus, indeterminatus, infinitus*, and *interminatus.* On **corpus finitum**, see *corpus;* on **distantia finita**, see *distantia;* on **esse finitum**, see *esse;* on **essentia finita**, see *essentia* under 1; on **generatio finita**, see *generatio* under 1; on **gratia finita**, see *gratia* under 2; on **linea finita**, see *linea* under 1; on **magnitudo finita**, see *magnitudo* under 1; on **nomen finitum**, see *nomen* under 1; on **poena finita**, see *poena;* on **potentia finita**, see *po-*

tentia under 2; on **praedicatum finitum**, see *praedicatum* under 1; on **principium finitum**, see *principium;* on **proportio finita,** see *proportio* under 1; on **quantitas finita,** see *quantitas* under 1; on **substantia finita,** see *substantia* under 2; on **tempus finitum,** see *tempus;* on **verbum finitum,** see *verbum* under 2; on **virtus finita,** see *virtus* under 1. —**finite,** *adv., to a certain extent, within limits, finitely.*

finis, is, *m.,* (1) *end, limit, conclusion,* synonym of *extremitas, extremum, terminus,* and *ultimum,* (2) *aim, purpose,* synonym of **causa finalis** and **terminus.**— Kinds of *finis* in this (1) sense are: (a), **finis intentionis,** *the intended purpose.* Cf. Pot. 1. 2 ob. 8.—(b), **finis magnitudinis seu quantitatis,** *the limit of size.* —(c), **finis motus,** *the limit of motion.*—(d), **finis perfectionis,** *the limit of perfection.*—(e), **finis quantitas,** see *finis magnitudinis.*—(f), **finis quantum ad essentiam,** *the limit of a thing according to essence.*—(g), **finis relationis,** *the terminal member of a relation.*—**finis honorabilius est quam finitum,** (2 Cael. 20 g), *the limit is more honorable than the limited.*—On **bonitas ex fine,** see *bonitas;* on **bonum ex fine,** see *bonus;* on **cognitio finis imperfecta et perfecta,** see *cognitio;* on **movere per modum finis,** see *movere;* on **necessarium ex necessitate seu ex suppositione**

seu respectu finis, see *necessarius;* on **necessitas finis seu ex fine,** see *necessitas;* on **operatio adquisitiva seu factiva et operatio meritoria finis,** see *operatio;* on **ordo finis,** see *ordo;* on **perfectio finis seu ex ratione finis,** see *perfectio;* on **ratio finis,** see *ratio.*—**propter finem agere seu operari seu moveri,** *to wish to be active* or *to be moved for a purpose*—Kinds of *finis* in this sense are: (a), **finis agentis seu operantis seu intentionis** and **finis operis seu operationis,** *the purpose of the doer* or *that of his intention* and *the purpose of the work* or *the purpose achieved.* Cf. *finis exterior.*—(b), **finis alteri applicatus** and **finis in se consideratus,** *the purpose applied to something* and *the purpose considered in itself.*—(c), **finis bonus** and **finis malus,** *the good* and *the evil purpose.*—(d), **finis communis seu universalis** and **finis proprius seu particularis,** *the general* or *the common purpose* and *the specific* or *proper purpose.*—(e), **finis conveniens,** *the suitable purpose.*—(f), **finis cuius seu ut cuius** and **finis quo seu ut quo,** *the hou heneka hois* and *hou heneka ho* of Aristotle, *the purpose according to which* and *the purpose through* or *by which,* whereby to obtain it; the former consists in the desired thing itself and the latter either in the possession and the enjoyment of the thing or in the means.—(g), **finis debitus,** *the due* or *proper purpose.*—(h), **finis deliberatus seu per rationem praestitutus** and **finis imaginatus,** *the deliberate* and *the imagined purpose* or that based on reason and that on the imagination.—(i), **finis dispositivus,** *the disposing* or *dispositive purpose.* Cf. Quodl. 5. 10. 19 c.— (j), **finis exterior seu extrinsecus** and **finis interior,** *the exterior* and *the interior aim,* or *the purpose of the agent in working* and *the purpose of the work itself.* Cf. *finis agentis.*—(k), **finis extrinsecus,** see *finis exterior.*— (l), **finis imaginatus,** see *finis deliberatus.*—(m), **finis in se consideratus,** see *finis alteri applicatus.*—(n), **finis intellegibilis** and **finis sensibilis,** *the intelligible* and *the sensible purpose.*— (o), **finis intentionis,** see *finis agentis.*—(p), **finis interior,** see *finis exterior.*—(q), **finis malus,** see *finis bonus.*—(r), **finis moralis** and **finis naturalis,** *the moral purpose* and *the purpose of nature.*—(s), **finis naturalis** and **finis supernaturalis,** *the natural* (cf. *finis moralis*) and *the supernatural purpose.*—(t), **finis operantis,** *the purpose of the agent,* see *finis agentis.*—(u), **finis operationis,** *the purpose which the work directly serves,* see *finis agentis.*—(v), **finis operis,** see *finis agentis* and *finis operantis.* —(w), **finis particularis,** see *finis communis.*—(x), **finis per ratio-**

nem praestitutus, see *finis deliberatus.*—(y), **finis posterior** and **finis praecedens,** *the posterior* or *following* and *the anterior* or *preceding purpose.*—(z), **finis postremus seu remotus seu ultimus** and **finis propinquus seu proximus,** *the last* or *ultimate* and *the closer* or *proximate purpose.*— (a²), **finis praecedens,** see *finis posterior.*—(b²), **finis praeexistens,** *the purpose of an activity which precedes in the order of time,* and *is the cause of the thing produced.*—(c²), **finis principalis** and **finis secundarius,** *the principal* and *the secondary purpose.*—(d²), **finis propinquus,** see *finis postremus.*—(e²), **finis proprius,** see *finis communis.*—(f²), **finis proximus,** see *finis postremus.*—(g²), **finis quo,** see *finis cuius.*—(h²), **finis remotus,** see *finis postremus.*—(i²), **finis secundarius,** see *finis principalis.*—(j²), **finis sensibilis,** see *finis intelligibilis.*—(k²), **finis spiritualis,** *the spiritual* or *religious purpose.*—(l²), **finis supernaturalis,** see *finis naturalis.*— (m²), **finis ultimus,** see *finis postremus.*—(n²), **finis ultimus quoad aliquem seu hunc** and **finis ultimus simpliciter,** *the final purpose with reference to someone* or *to this one* and *that one, who is striving after the same,* or *the purpose final in every respect which is the same for all men.*—(o²), **finis ultimus secundum rationem ultimi finis seu finis ultimus simpliciter** and **finis**

ultimus secundum id, in quo finis ultimi ratio invenitur, *the last purpose as it is considered according to its essence* or *the ultimate purpose* and *the last purpose with reference to that in which the essence of the last purpose appears to be realized.* Cf. *finis ultimus quoad aliquem.* —(p²), **finis ultimus secundum id, in quo finis ultimi ratio invenitur,** see *finis ultimus secundum rationem ultimi finis.*—(q²), **finis ultimus simpliciter,** see *finis ultimus secundum rationem ultimi finis* and *finis ultimus quoad aliquem.*—(r²), **finis universalis,** see *finis communis.*—(s²), **finis ut cuius,** see *finis cuius.*—(t²), **finis ut quo,** see *finis cuius.*— **agens omne propter finem agit,** see *agens.*—**cessante fine cessare debet id quod est ad finem,** *with the cessation of the purpose striving for it must also cease.*— **denominatio rei maxime debet fieri a perfectione et fine,** see *denominatio.*—**ex fine sumitur ratio eorum, quae sunt ad finem,** *the distinctive nature of those things which lead to the purpose depends upon the purpose.*—**finis est prior in intentione, sed est posterior in executione,** or **finis, etsi sit postremus in executione, est tamen primus in intentione,** or, **finis qui est ultimus in consecutione est primus in intentione,** in the sphere of the achievment or attainment the purpose is last (and the means

to the purpose first); in the sphere of the intention the purpose is first (and the means to the purpose last).—**iustum est, quod omnia definiantur et denominentur a fine,** see *denominare.*—**principium intentionis est ultimus finis, principium autem exsecutionis est primum eorum, quae sunt ad finem,** *the beginning of the intention is the last purpose, but the beginning of the accomplishment is the first of those things which lead to the purpose.*—**qualis unusquisque est, talis finis videtur ei,** the translation of the Aristotelian expression *hopoios poth' hekastos esti, toiouto kai to telos phainetai auto, as each one is conditioned* and *disposed, so does he choose the purpose of his striving.*— **quod est optimum in unoquoque, est finis eius,** *the best in everything is its purpose.*—**ratio cuiuslibet rei factae sumitur ex fine quem faciens intendit,** *the purpose toward which the worker strives determines the nature of the work done.*—**remoto fine frustra reparatur illud quod est ad finem,** *when the purpose is removed, the reconstruction of the means to the purpose is in vain.*—**res denominatur a fine; unumquodque denominatur a fine,** see *denominare.*

finitas, tatis, *f., finite state, finity, limitation,* the opposite of *infinitas.*

finite, *adv.,* see *finio.*

finitimus, a, um, *adj., neighboring.*
fio, fieri, factum, 3, *v. a.* and *n.,*
to be made, be done, become,
arise, happen, synonym of *gen-*
erari, the opposite of *esse* and
factum esse. Cf. *facio.* On **causa**
fiendi, see *causa;* on **considerare**
ut in fieri et in facto esse, see
considerare; on **dicere sicut in**
fieri et in facto esse, see *dicere;*
on **ignorantia facti,** see *ignoran-*
tia; on **lex factorum,** see *lex;* on
principium fiendi et facti, see
principium; on **rixa factorum,**
see *rixa;* on **significare ut in fi-**
eri, see *significare;* on **tentare**
factis, see *tentare.*—Kinds of *fi-*
eri are: (a), **fieri ab arte, fieri**
ab fortuna, fieri a casu, and **fieri**
ab natura, *to come into existence*
through art, through fortune,
through chance, and *through*
nature. Cf. *naturale.*—(b), **fieri**
abstractione, fieri alteratione,
abstractione fieri alteratione, fi-
eri appositione, fieri compositi-
one, and **fieri transfiguratione,**
to come about by abstraction
from matter, or *by alteration, by*
addition, by combination, and
by reorganization.—(c), **fieri a**
casu, see *fieri ab arte.*—(d), **fieri**
a fortuna, see *fieri ab arte.*—(e),
fieri aliud and **fieri alterum,** *to*
become something else accord-
ing to substance and *condition.*
—(f), **fieri alteratione,** see *fieri*
abstractione.—(g), **fieri alterum,**
see *fieri aliud.*—(h), **fieri a natu-**
ra, see *fieri ab arte.*—(i), **fieri**
appositione, see *fieri abstracti-*

one.—(j), **fieri circulariter seu se-**
cundum generationem circula-
rem and **fieri in directum seu**
in rectum, *to come into exist-*
ence like a circular course and
in a straight line, i.e., *to come*
into existence in such a way
that the process of becoming in
a certain way describes a circle
in so far as a thing in its con-
tinued change finally again be-
comes that which it was in the
beginning, and *to come into*
existence in such a way that the
process of becoming from one
product to another goes farther
and *farther like a straight line*
from one point to another.—(k),
fieri compositione, see *fieri ab-*
stractione.—(l), **fieri ex alio** and
fieri ex altero, *to become from*
another substance and *from an-*
other condition.—(m), **fieri ex ali-**
quo and **fieri ex nihilo,** *to be-*
come from something and *to*
become from nothing.—(n), **fieri**
ex altero, see *fieri ex alio.*—(o),
fieri ex contrario seu opposito
and **fieri ex medio,** *to become*
out of the opposite and *to be-*
come out of the mean between
two opposites.—(p), **fieri ex me-**
dio, see *fieri ex contrario.*—(q),
fieri ex nihilo, see *fieri ex aliquo.*
—(r), **fieri ex opposito,** see *fieri*
ex contrario.—(s), **fieri ex per-**
manente and **fieri ex permutato,**
to become from a constant and
from a changed thing, i.e., to
become from something which,
in the process of becoming and

after it, remains, and to become from something which in this process and through it is changed and to this extent disappears.— (t), fieri ex permutato, see *fieri ex permanente.*—(u), fieri ex privatione and fieri ex subiecto, *to become out of a lack* or *privation which befalls a thing* and *to become from the subject of this privation.*—(v), fieri ex subiecto, see *fieri ex privatione.*—(w), fieri in directum seu in rectum, see *fieri circulariter.*—(x), fieri naturale seu naturaliter seu secundum naturam and fieri secundum artem, *the natural* and *the artistic production* or *the becoming according to nature* and *that according to art.* Cf. *fieri ab arte.* —(y), fieri per accidens seu secundum accidens and fieri per se, *to become through something else* and *to become of itself* or *of its own nature* and *essence.*—(z), fieri per modum inhaerentiae, *to become after the manner of adhesion.*—(a²), fieri per se, see *fieri per accidens.*—(b²), fieri secundum accidens, see *fieri per accidens.*—(c²), fieri secundum artem, see *fieri naturale.*—(d²), fieri secundum esse accidentale and fieri secundum esse substantiale seu substantialiter, *to become after the manner of the accidental* and *to become after that of the substantial existence.*—(e²), fieri secundum esse substantiale, see *fieri secundum esse accidentale.*—(f²), fieri secundum quid

and fieri simpliciter, *to become respectively* or *in a certain respect* and *to become simply* or *absolutely.*—(g²), fieri simpliciter, see *fieri secundum quid.*—(h²), fieri substantialiter, see *fieri secundum esse accidentale.*—(i²), fieri transfiguratione, see *fieri abstractione.*—(j²), fieri ut compositum and fieri ut simplex, *to become as something composed* and *to become as something simple.*—(k²), fieri ut simplex, see *fieri ut compositum.*—ad id, quod potest fieri per unum, superfluum est plura ponere, or, non est faciendum per plura, quod bene potest fieri per unum, or, quod fieri potest per pauciora, superfluum est, si fiat per plura, or, quod potest compleri per pauciora, non fit per plura, or, quod potest fieri per unum, superflue fit per multos, or, quod potest sufficienter fieri per unum, superfluum est, quod fiat per multa, or, quod sufficienter fit uno posito, melius est per unum fieri, quam per multa, or, quod sufficienter potest fieri unum non oportet quod per aliquid aliud inducatur, *where a single cause suffices for the formation of something, a multiplicity of causes is superfluous.* Cf. *exsistere, natura,* and *plus.*—ex nihilo nihil fit, see *nihil.*—factum esse est indivisibile, *to have been done is something indivisible.*— fieri non potest esse consequenter se habens et contiguum cum hoc, quod est factum esse, *the becoming* and *the having become cannot immediately follow each other* and *moreover cannot touch each other.*—impossibile est fieri illud, quod non potest esse factum, *it is impossible to become what cannot be made.*— in omni factione, in qua est successio, fieri est ante factum esse, *in every making in which there is a succession, becoming is earlier than having been made.*—in omni factione naturali oportet esse subiectum, *every making in nature embraces a subject of the making.*—in quolibet fieri sunt tria, scilicet subiectum et terminus factionis et oppositum eius, *in every becoming three things are to be distinguished, namely, the subject* and *what it has become,* and *what it was not before becoming.*—non est faciendum per plura, quod bene potest fieri per unum, see above: *ad id, quod potest fieri* etc.—non est fieri, nisi aliquid factum sit prius, neque est aliquid factum esse, nisi fiat prius, *there is a becoming only when a having become preceded, nor does a thing come to be, unless it became so previously.*—omne quod fit, ad hoc fit, *the purpose of every becoming is being or existence.*—omnia, quae fiunt, fiunt ab aliquo agente et ex aliquo sicut ex materia et iterum fiunt aliquid, quod est terminus, *all that is made, is made by some*

agent, and *from something as from material,* and *again is made something which is the end* or *purpose.*—quod fieri potest per pauciora, superfluum est, si fiat per plura; quod potest compleri per pauciora principia, non fit per plura; quod potest fieri per unum, superflue fit per multos; quod potest sufficienter fieri per unum, superfluum est, quod fiat per multa; quod sufficienter fit uno posito, melius est per unum fieri, quam per multa; quod sufficienter potest fieri per unum, non oportet, quod per aliquid aliud inducatur; see above: *ad id, quod potest fieri* etc.

firmamentum, i, *n.*, (1) *lit, the firmament, sky above the earth,* (2) *fig.,* (a) in *gen., a support, prop, stay* (b) in *partic.* a rhet. t.t., *the chief support of an argument.*

firme, *adv.* see *firmus,* a, um.

firmitas, atis, *f. power, strength, force, steadiness, stability, firmness, steadfastness, durability,* used *figuratively.*

firmiter, *adv.,* see *firmus.*

firmo, are, avi, atum, 1, *v. a.,* (1) *lit., to make firm, fast,* (2) *fig.,* (a) *to fix, fasten, secure firmly,* (b) *to confirm, ratify, condition,* (c) *to strengthen, increase the courage* or *resolution of; encourage, animate,* (d) *to establish, found, ordain,* (e) *to confirm, show, prove; to affirm, assent, declare, promise the correctness* or *truth of a circumstance* or *statement,* (f) in the *pass., to be strengthened in something; be made callous, hard.*—firmare **nomen**, *to establish* or *adopt a name.*—firmatus, a, um, *P. a.*, (1) *condensed, solidified*, (2) *established, settled* or *fixed firmly*, (3) *hardened in sin.*

firmus, a, um, *adj.*, (1) *lit.*, *firm*, (in opp. to frail, destructible), *steadfast, stable, strong, powerful*, (2) *fig.*, *firm* in strength or durability, also in opinion, affection, etc., *fast, constant steadfast, immovable, powerful, strong, true, faithful.*—firme, and **firmiter**, *adv.*, *firmly, steadily, lastingly, powerfully.*

fissio, onis, *f.*, *a division, dividing.*

fissura, ae, *f.*, *a cleft, fissure, crack* or *crack-like depression; a cleft, slit* or *furrow.*

fistula, ae, *f.*, (1) *a reed-pipe, flute*, (2) *a water-pipe.*

fixe, *adv.*, see *figo.*

fixio, onis, *f.*, *a fastening, fixing, attaching firmly* or *immovably; a piercing.*

fixus, a, um, *P. a.*, see *figo.*

flagellatio, onis, *f.*, *a flagellation, scourging, whipping.*

flagello, are, avi, atum, 1, *v. a.*, *to whip, scourge, lash.*—flagellans, antis, *P. a.*, *lashing, punishing.* —flagellatus, a, um, *P. a.*, *whipped, scourged.*

flagellum, i, *n.*, *dim.*, (1) *lit.*, *a whip, scourge*, (2) *fig.*, *scourge, severe punishment*, any instrumentality for causing suffering or death.

flagitiosus, a, um, *adj.*, *shameful, disgraceful, infamous, flagitious, profligate, dissolute, scandalous.*

flagitium, ii, *n.*, *a crime*, a grave offence against morality or the social order; flagrant violation of law or morality in general; *wickedness, iniquity.*

flagito, are, avi, atum, 1, *v. freq. a.*, *to entreat, solicit* a thing, *demand, ask.*

flamen, inis, *n.*, *a breeze, breath of air*, a synonym of *spiritus*. The principle of life often represented under the figure of a breath of air. Accordingly the word *spiritus*, a synonym of *flamen*, has been used to signify a living, intelligent, incorporeal being, such as the soul. In the New Testament, it signifies the Holy Ghost, the spirit of truth. The term *flamen* has been likewise used as a name for the Holy Spirit, whose special office is to move the heart to love God and to conceive penitence for sin. **baptismus flaminis**, *baptism of the Holy Spirit* or *baptism of desire*, is a phrase employed in the third century by the anonymous author of the book "De rebaptismate," and is defined as a movement of the Holy Spirit which produces in the soul faith, charity, and sorrow, in consequence of which there arises an implicit desire to receive the sacrament of baptism.

flamma, ae, *f.*, (1) *lit. a flame, blaze, fire* in aerial matter, a stream of vapor or gas made luminous by heat, usually by the heat of its own combustion, (2) *fig.*, (a) *the flame* or *fire of passion* such as of love, or the condition proceeding from rage, striving, or earnest desire, (b) *a flame,* any raging evil.

flammeus, a, um, *adj., flaming, fiery-red.*

flatus, us, *m., a breath, breeze,* a synonym of *spiritus.*

Flavianus, i, *m., Flavian,* saint, bishop of Constantinople, date of birth unknown; died at Hypaepa in Lydia, August 449. At a council of bishops convened at Constantinople by Flavian, November 8, 448 to settle a dispute which had arisen among his clergy, the Archimandrite Eutyches was accused of heresy and excommunicated by Flavian. Eutyches appealed to pope St. Leo, who investigated the disputed question, and then sent his sublime dogmatic letter (epistle xxviii), called the Tome, to Flavian concisely setting forth and confirming the doctrine of the incarnation and the union of the divine and human natures in the one person of Christ.

flavus, a, um, *adj., golden yellow, reddish yellow, flaxen-colored.*

flecto, ere, xi, xum, 3, *v. a.* and *n.,* (1) *lit., to bend, bow, curve, turn around,* (2) *fig.,* in *gen., to bend, turn, direct,* (b) in *partic., to move, persuade, prevail upon, soften, appease.*

fleo, ere, flevi, fletum, 2, *v. n.* and *a., to weep, cry, shed tears,* a synonym of *ploro, lugeo, lacrimo.*

fletus, us, *m., a weeping, wailing, lamenting.*

flexibilis, e, *adj., flexible, pliant, tractable,* used *fig.*

flexibilitas, atis, *f., flexibility.*

floreo, ere, ui, 2, *v. n., to flower,* used *lit.* and *fig.*

floridus, a, um, *adj., full of* or *abounding with flowers, flowery.*

floritio, onis, *f., a blossoming, flowering.*

flos, oris, *m., a flower, blossom,* (1) *lit.,* (2) *fig.*

flosculus, i, *m., a floweret, a little flower.*

fluctuo, are, avi, atum, 1, *v. n., to fluctuate, waver, hesitate; to be restless, unquiet,* used *fig.*—**fluctuans,** antis, *P. a., restless, undulating, stormy,* used *lit.* and *fig.*

fluctus, us, *m., a wave, billow, surge,* esp. of the sea.

fluentum, i, *n., a stream, running water, river.*

fluidus, a, um, *adj., flowing, fluid, moist.*

flumen, inis, *n., a flowing of water, flood, stream,* (1) in *partic., a river,* (2) *transf.,* of other things which flow in streams or like streams, as *a stream of fire.*

fluo, ere, xi, xum, 3, *v. n.,* (1) *lit.,* (a) *to issue, flow out, to pass away* from any enclosed place, (b) *to flow from anything, pro-*

ceed from, be due to, as a cause, (c) of animal fluid, *to flow, rise* in daily movement; *pass along* the vessels of the body, the opposite of *refluere* and used with it in the phrase, **fluere et refluere,** *to flow* and *ebb,* (2) *fig., to flow, go, proceed, come forth,* (a) of time, *to flow, pass* (b) *to flow, proceed* or *emanate,* as from a source.—**fluere et refluere,** *to flow back* and *forth, come* and *go, appear* and *disappear,* move from one place to another. —**fluens,** entis, *P. a.,* (1) *lit., flowing,* as a liquid, (2) *fig., transient, passing.*—**fluxus,** a, um, *P. a., flowing.*

fluvius, ii, *m.,* (1) *lit.,* (a) *a river,* (b) *transf.,* in *gen.* like flumen, for *running water, a stream,* (2) *fig.*

fluxibilitas, atis, *f., fluxibility, the quality of being fluxible; flowing.*

fluxus, us *m.,* (1) *a flowing, flow,* the act of flowing, or what flows; the movement of a fluid or anything analogous in a continuous current, (2) of a number, series of moving objects, *a flow, flux, passing,* (3) of time, *a flow, passing,* (4) of delineation or construction by drawing, *a flow, issue of a line,* by drawing a pencil from a given point across a paper.—**fluxus et refluxus,** *the flow* and *ebb,* alternate advance and recession, as of the tide.

fodio, ere, fodi, fossum, 3, *v. n.* and *a., to dig, dig up, dig out.*

foederatus, a, um, *P. a., leagued together, confederated, allied.*

foeditas, atis, *f., foulness, filthiness, horridness, deformity.*

foedo, are, avi, atum, 1, *v. a., to disfigure, mar, deform.*

foedus, a, um, *adj., disgraceful, base, shameful, foul, detestable.*

foedus, eris, *n.,* (1) *a covenant, pledge, agreement* between two or more persons, (2) *a bond, a uniting force* or *influence* by which a union of any kind is maintained, (3) *a treaty, a settlement* arrived at by treating or negotiation; a contract between groups of people or nations relating to peace, truce, alliance, commerce or other national or international relations; *a covenant, compact.*—**coniugale foedus,** *the marriage bond.*

foenum, i, (**fenum,** i), *n., hay.*

foetens, entis, *P. a., stinking, fetid, giving forth an offensive odor.*

foetidus, a, um, *adj., fetid, stinking, that has an ill smell.*

foetor, oris, *m., an offensive smell, stench.*

folium, ii, *n., of plants, a leaf.*

folliculus, i, *m.,* (1) *a follicule, a small bag, sack,* (2) *transf., a husk,* the outer covering of certain seeds.

fomentum, i, *n.,* (1) *lit.,* (a) *kindling wood, fuel,* combustible matter used to kindle or sustain fire or produce heat, as wood, (b) *nutriment,* that which nourishes; that which promotes the growth or repairs the natural waste of animal or vegetable organisms; *aliment;* a synonym of *nutrimentum,* (2) fig., (a) *an incentive,* that which incites or tends to incite to action, serves as a stimulus; that which moves the mind or inflames the passions, (b) *abetment, the act of abetting, aid, instigation, countenance,* (c) *comport,* anything that contributes to the ease or satisfaction of the mind or body.

fomes, itis, *m.,* (1) *kindling, tinder, spark* in the general sense of the word, (2) *the spark* or *the incitement of evil desire.*—(1), not used in the literal sense in the *Summa Theologica.*—**incendium fomitis,** *the fire* or *the intensive act of evil desire.* On **concupiscentia fomitis,** see *concupiscentia;* on **corruptio fomitis,** see *corruptio;* on **lex fomitis,** see *lex;* on **virtus fomitis,** see *virtus.*

fons, fontis, *m.,* (1) *lit.,* (a) *a spring, fountain, well-source,* (b) with or without *baptismi, the fountain of baptism,* i.e., *the waters of baptism,* the application, as the name of the vessel, being secondary, (2) *fig., a fountain-head, source, origin, cause.*—Common phrases are: **suscipere de sacro fonte,** *to take* or *receive from the sacred waters of baptism,* said of sponsors, who in the case of baptism by immersion, do not hold the child while it is being immersed, but receive it from the hands of the priest after it has been immersed.—**levare de sacro fonte,** *to raise from the waters of baptism.*—**recipere de sacro fonte,** *to receive from the waters of baptism.*

fontalis, e, *adj., lending authority, of good authority, fontal,* synonym of *fontanus.* On **principium fontale,** see *principium.*

fontalitas, atis, *f., authority, origin, authorship.*

fontanus, a, um, *adj., lending authority, of good authority, fontal,* synonym of *fontalis.*

for, fari, fatus, 1, *v. defect., to speak, say.*—**fans,** antis, *P. a., speaking.*—**fandus,** a, um, *P. a., that may be spoken* or *uttered, speaking.*

foramen, inis, *n., an opening, hole, cave, cavity.*—**foramen formicarum,** *an ants' nest* or *hill.*—**foramen acus,** *the eye of a needle.*

foras, *adv.,* (1) *forth, out, abroad,* (2) like a preposition, with the *acc., outside of, beyond.*

forensis, e, *adj., forensic, pertaining to courts of justice; relating to* or *used in legal proceedings,* as in the phrase **forenses causae,** *lawsuits,* used in S.T. only in quot.

forinsecus, *adv., outwardly, from without, on the outside,* used in S.T. only in quot.

foris, *adv., out of doors, abroad, without.*

forma, ae, *f.,* (1) *form, shape,* synonym of *figura,* (2) *form,* a species of quality as distinct from *figura,* the configuration of an artificial thing as distinct from figure which is the configuration of natural things, (3) *form*, the actualizing principle that makes a thing to be what it is, the opposite of *materia*. In the ontological order it is the formal cause, the form-giving principle, and is very much the same as *essentia, natura, quod quid erat esse, quidditas, species,* and *substantia;* in the logical order it is *species, idea, exemplar,* and *imago.* In the thought of St. Thomas, it is a concept of great variety and fecundity, and generally signifies actuality in contrast to the potentiality of matter, or determination of quality or kind in contrast to the indeterminacy of matter. It is not something preexisting, but is conceived of as being united with primary matter to constitute the substance of a thing. Other forms, called accidental, then appear to clothe the substance with its predicamental accidents. Some forms, the angels and human souls, exist independently of matter; but most forms disappear when the composite of which they are the principle of actual existence is dissolved, (4) *mode, manner,* (5) *formula.*—dator formarum, *the giver of forms, of visible things,* namely, one of the intelligences which Avicenna accepts.—intensio formae and remissio formae, *the extension* or *increase* and *the remission* or *decrease of form.*— perfectio seu quantitas formae,

the perfection or *size of the form.* On abstractio formae a materia, see *abstractio;* on abstrahere formam a materia, see *abstrahere;* on actus formae, see *actus;* on contraria secundum formam, see *contrarius;* on differre secundum, see *differre;* on distinctio formae seu secundum formam, see *distinctio;* on diversitas formae, see *diversitas;* on divisio secundum formam, see *divisio;* on educere formam de potentia materiae, see *educere;* on idem secundum formam, see *idem;* on inchoatio formae, see *inchoatio;* on infinitum ex parte formae seu secundum formam seu secundum rationem formae, see *infinitus;* on intensio formae, see above; on magnitudo formae, see above; on motus ad formam, see *motus;* on necessitas formae, see *necessitas;* on ordo formae, see *ordo;* on pars secundum formam, see *pars;* on quantitas formae, see *above;* on remissio formae, see above; on significare per modum formae seu ut forma supposti, see *significare;* on similitudo per participationem eiusdem formae, see *similitudo;* on substantia formae sacramentalis, see *substantia;* on transmutatio secundum formam, see *transmutatio.*—Kinds of *forma* in this second sense are: (a), forma absoluta and forma relativa, *form in thought* or *in reality separated from matter* or *from that which gives existence to a thing without reference to matter* and *from that which gives existence to a thing with reference to something else.*—(b), **forma absolute seu absolute accepta seu per se seu secundum se considerata seu abstracta** and **forma concreta seu in materia,** *form taken* or *considered in* and *for itself* or *that abstracted from matter either in reality* or *in thought* and *that coalesced with matter* or *in its existence.*—(c), **forma abstracta,** see *forma absolute.*—(d), **forma accidentalis** and **forma accidentalis seu substantialis,** *the accidental* and *the substantial* or *essential form,* i.e., the form which determines an already existing subject, on which it depends for its existence and that form which in connection with the potency of matter constitutes the substance and essence of the thing.—(e), **forma activa seu factiva seu operativa,** *the effective* or *producing form,* namely, what tends to produce its likeness in other things.—(f), **forma adaequata** and **forma proportionata,** *the balanced* or *equal form* and *the analogous form* or *that brought into proportion.*—(g), **forma adquisita, forma influxa,** and **forma concreata seu innata,** *the form gained by one's own efforts, the infused form,* and *the inborn form.*—(h), **forma apprehensa** and **forma in natura existens,** *the apprehended form* or *that acquired by a cognitive faculty* and *that existing in na-*

ture or *in the things of nature.*—(i), **forma artificialis seu artis seu artificiati** and **forma naturalis,** *the artistic form* or *that of art* or *that of a work of art* and *the natural form* or *the form of a thing of nature.*—(j), **forma artificiati,** *the form of a thing made by man.* See *forma artificialis.*—(k), **forma artis,** see *forma artificialis.*—(l), **forma communis seu indeterminata** and **forma determinata seu distincta,** *a general* or *indefinite form* (which is a contradiction in terms) and *the definite form.*—(m), **forma communis** and **forma propria,** *the general* and *proper* or *peculiar form.*—(n), **forma completa seu perfecta** and **forma incompleta seu imperfecta,** *the complete* or *perfect form* and *the incomplete* and *imperfect form.*—(o), **forma completiva,** *the accomplishing form,* i.e., that form which the nature and essence of a thing bring into complete existence.—(p), **forma concreata,** see *forma adquisita.*—(q), **forma concreta,** see *forma absolute.*—(r), **forma coniuncta seu participata** and **forma separata,** *the form connected with matter,* and *the form separated from matter.* Cf. *forma absoluta* and *forma absolute.*—(s), **forma connaturalis,** *the form of like nature.*—(t), **forma constitutiva,** *the form which in conjunction with matter produces the substance and essence of a thing.*—(u), **forma contracta,** *the form limited in its power* and *control over matter.*—(v), **forma contraria,** *the form opposed to a privation* or *to another form.*—(w), **forma corporalis,** and **forma spiritualis,** *the corporeal* and *the spiritual* or *spirit-like form.* Cf. *forma immaterialis.*—(x), **forma corporeitatis,** *the form of an extended body,* i.e., that in a thing upon which depend its corporal nature and essence.—(y), **forma corruptibilis** and **forma incorruptibilis,** *the corruptible* and *the incorruptible form.*—(z), **forma corruptibilium** and **forma generabilium,** *the form of the corruptible thing* and *that of the generable thing.*—(a²), **forma debita,** *the necessary* or *proper form.*—(b²), **forma Dei seu divina** and **forma servilis,** *the divine* or *God's form* or *nature,* and *the form* or *nature of the servant.*—(c²), **forma determinata,** see *forma communis.*—(d²), **forma disparata,** *the disparate form* or *that form which is so unlike another form that it cannot be paired with it.*—(e²), **forma distincta,** see *forma communis.*—(f²), **forma divina,** see *forma Dei.*—(g²), **forma elementalis seu elementaris seu elementi, forma mixti seu mixti corporis seu mixtionis, forma vegetabilis, forma sensitiva** and **forma humana seu intellectiva,** *the elementary form* or *the form of one of the four elements, the form of the mixed* or *composed body* or *the form of*

the mixture of composition of a body, the vegetative form or *the vegetative soul, the sensitive* or *animal soul* and *the intellectual form* or *man's soul.*—(h²), **forma elementi,** see *forma elementalis.* —(i²), **forma essentialis,** *that which constitutes a thing as what it is* and *not something else,* see *forma accidentalis.*—(j²), **forma exemplaris seu idealis,** *the exemplary form.*—(k²), **forma extrinseca** and **forma intrinseca,** *the outer form* or *the form corresponding to a thing which is identical with the forma exemplaris* or *the exemplar,* and *the inner form* or *the form abiding in a thing.* Cf. *causa formalis extra rem* under *causa.*—(l²), **forma factiva,** see *forma activa.*—(m²), **forma fixa stans seu manens seu quiescens seu habitualis,** *the form that stands firm* or *the abiding* or *resting form* or *the form that has become fixed,* the opposite of *passio* or *impressio transiens.*—(n²), **forma generalis seu generis, forma specialis seu specifica seu speciei seu secundum speciem** and **forma individua seu individualis, seu individuata seu secundum numerum,** *the generic form* or *the form of genus, the special form* or *that of species,* and *the individual* or *numerical form,* i.e, the form under which a thing is put in a genus or kind, that under which it is in a species or class, and that which gives it its individual character.—(o²), **forma generabilium**, see *forma corruptibilium.* —(p²), **forma generis**, see *forma generalis.*—(q²), **forma habitualis**, see *forma fixa stans.*—(r²), **forma humana**, see *forma elementalis.*—(s²), **forma idealis**, see *forma exemplaris.*—(t²), **forma imaginabilis seu imaginaria seu imaginata, forma intellecta seu intellectus seu intellegibilis** and **forma sensata seu sensibilis,** *the sensibly imaginable* or *imagined form, the intellectually recognized* or *recognizable form* and *the sensibly perceptive* or *perceived form,* i.e., the form in the faculty of the imagination, that in the faculty of the intellect, and that perceptible or perceived by an exterior sense in the form of a thing.—(u²), **forma immaterialis** and **forma materialis,** *the spiritual form completely independent of matter,* and *that designed solely for matter,* i.e., that form which in its own being is independent of matter and any connection with it, and also, if it is united with matter, is not entirely immerged in it and encompassed by it, and that form which in its being is wholly and completely bound to matter and on that account only through the connection with it possesses existence. Cf. *forma corporalis* and *forma inhaerens.*—(v²), **forma immediata sc. materiae primae,** *the immediate form of primary matter* or *that form which comes to*

primary matter without the instrumentality of another form. Cf. *forma intermedia.*—(w²), **forma imperfecta,** see *forma completa.*—(x²), **forma incompleta,** see *forma completa.*—(y²), **forma incorruptibilis,** see *forma corruptibilis.*—(z²), **forma indeterminata,** see *forma communis.*—(a³), **forma individua seu individualis seu individuata,** see *forma generalis.*—(b³), **forma indivisibilis seu simplex,** *the indivisible* or *simple form.*—(c³), **forma inducenda** and **forma obicienda,** *the form to be introduced* and *that to be displaced.*—(d³), **forma inferior** and **forma nobilior,** *the inferior form* and *the nobler form.*—(e³), **forma influxa,** see *forma adquisita.*—(f³), **forma inhaerens seu non subsistens** and **forma subsistens seu per se subsistens seu per existens seu per se stans,** *the form inherent in a matter* or *a subject* or *not existing by itself* and *that existing by itself alone* and *consisting of itself alone.*—(g³), **forma in materia,** *concrete form,* see *forma absolute.*—(h³), **forma innata,** see *forma adquisita.*—(i³), **forma in natura existens,** see *forma apprehensa.*—(j³), **forma intellecta,** see *forma imaginabilis.*—(k³), **forma intellectiva,** see *forma elementalis.*—(l³), **forma intellectus,** see *forma imaginabilis.*—(m³), **forma intellegibilis,** see *forma imaginabilis.*—(n³), **forma intermedia seu media, forma prima,** and **forma ultima,** *the* *intermediate* or *transitional form, the first* and *the last form of a thing in the process of its gradual development* or *cessation of it.* —(o³), **forma intrinseca**, see *forma extrinseca.*—(p³), **forma manens**, see *forma fixa stans.*—(q³), **forma materialis**, see *forma immaterialis.*—(r³), **forma media**, see *forma intermedia.*—(s³), **forma mixti seu mixti corporis**, see *forma elementalis.*—(t³), **forma mixtionis**, see *forma elementalis.*— —(u³), **forma naturalis**, see *forma artificialis.*—(v³), **forma nobilior**, see *forma inferior.*—(w³), **forma non-subsistens**, *a form which exists only in union with matter,* see *forma inhaerens.*—(x³), **forma obicienda**, see *forma inducenda.* (y³), **forma operativa**, see *forma activa.*—(z³), **forma participata**, *a form that is a likeness of a form existing elsewhere independently,* see *forma coniuncta.*—(a⁴), **forma particularis** and **forma universalis**, *the particular* and *the general form of a thing.* Cf. *forma generalis.*—(b⁴), **forma perfecta**, see *forma completa.*—(c⁴), **forma permanens**, see *forma fixa stans.*—(d⁴), **forma per se**, see *forma absolute.*—(e⁴), **forma per se existens**, see *forma inhaerens.*— (f⁴), **forma per se stans**, see *forma inhaerens.*—(g⁴), **forma per se subsistens**, see *forma inhaerens.* —(h⁴), **forma prima**, see *forma intermedia.*—(i⁴), **forma prima exemplaris**, *the first exemplary form,* i.e., the idea of things in

the mind of God.—(j⁴), **forma primordialis** and **forma seminalis**, *the primordial* and *the fertile form.*—(k⁴), **forma principalis** and **forma secundaria**, *the principal* and *the subordinate form.*—(l⁴), **forma pura**, *the simple* or *pure form,* i.e., *the form that is only form.*—(m⁴), **forma quiescens**, see *forma fixa stans.*—(n⁴), **forma relativa**, see *forma absoluta.*—(o⁴), **forma sacramenti**, *the form of the sacrament,* i.e., the words which accompany the exterior sign of the sacrament and give it its meaning.—(p⁴), **forma secundaria**, see *forma principalis.*— (q⁴), **forma secundum numerum**, see *forma generalis.*— (r⁴), **forma secundum se considerata**, see *forma absolute.*—(s⁴), **forma secundum speciem**, see *forma generalis.*—(t⁴), **forma seminalis**, see *forma primordialis.*—(u⁴), **forma sensata**, see *forma imaginabilis.* —(v⁴), **forma sensibilis**, see *forma imaginabilis.*—(w⁴), **forma sensitiva**, see *forma elementalis.*—(x⁴), **forma separata**, see *forma coniuncta.*—(y⁴), **forma servilis**, see *forma Dei.*—(z⁴), **forma signata seu significata**, *the form signified thus.*—(a⁵), **forma significata**, see *forma signata.*—(b⁵), **forma simplex**, see *forma indivisibilis.*— (c⁵), **forma situalis**, *the form which establishes a local situation.*—(d⁵), **forma specialis**, see *forma generalis.*—(e⁵), **forma speciei**, see *forma generalis.*— (f⁵), **forma specifica**, see *forma* *generalis.*—(g⁵), **forma spiritualis,** see *forma corporalis.*—(h⁵), **forma subsistens,** see *forma inhaerens.* —(i⁵), **forma substantialis,** *that form which united to primary matter, constitutes the substance of a thing,* see *forma accidentalis.*—(j⁵), **forma substrata,** *the underlying* or *fundamental form.* —(k⁵), **forma superanturalis,** *the supernatural form.*—(l⁵), **forma syllogismi seu syllogistica,** *the form of the conclusion,* i.e., the necessity of the deduction of the conclusion from the premises. Cf. *forma syllogismi* above.—(m⁵), **forma syllogistica,** see *forma syllogismi.*—(n⁵), **forma ultima,** see *forma intermedia.*—(o⁵), **forma universalis,** see *forma particularis.*—(p⁵), **forma vegetabilis,** *the soul of plants,* see *forma elementalis.*—(q⁵), **forma virtutis,** *the form of virtue,* i.e., *grace.*—a **forma sumitur differentia** (1 Perih. 8 c), *the proper* or *essential difference of a thing from another is taken from its substantial form.*—**agit unumquodque ratione formae,** see *agere.*—**denominatio fit a forma, quae dat speciem ·rei,** *the name of a thing is taken from the form to which it owes its species* and *essence.*— **forma est finis generationis, non ipsius generati,** *the form is the goal of generation but not of the generated.* Cf. *generatio.*—**forma est finis materiae,** *the form is the purpose of matter.*—**forma est quo agens agit** or, **forma est**

principium agendi in unoquoque or, **illud, quo primo aliquid operatur, est forma eius, cui operatio attribuitur** or, **unumquodque agens agit per suam formam,** *the form of a thing is the first inner principle of its activity.*—**quanto aliqua forma est nobilior et simplicior tanto est maioris virtutis,** *the nobler* and *simpler the form is, the greater is the sphere of its efficacy.*—**unumquodque agens agit per suam formam,** see above: *forma est, quod* etc.—**unumquodque denominatur a sua forma,** see *denominare.*—A kind of *forma* in this (3) sense is: **forma syllogismi,** *the form of the syllogism.* Cf. also *forma syllogismi* under *syllogismus.*

formabilis, e, *adj., that may be formed* or *fashioned.*

formalis, e, *adj., relating to the form of a thing, referring to the form of a thing, relating after the manner of form, formal,* the opposite of *materialis.* On **causa formalis, causa formalis exemplaris, causa formalis extra rem et inhaerens seu intrinseca,** see *causa;* on **cognitio formalis,** see *cognitio;* on **complementum formale,** see *complementum;* on **conversio formalis,** see *conversio;* on **definitio formalis,** see *definitio;* on **differentia formalis,** see *differentia;* on **distinctio formalis,** see *distinctio;* on **diversitas formalis,** see *diversitas;* on **divisio formalis,** see *divisio;* on **effectus formalis,** see *effectus;*

on **esse formale**, see *esse;* on **infinitum formale**, see *infinitus;* on **intentio formalis**, see *intentio;* on **medium formale**, see *medium;* on **multiplicatio formalis** see *multiplicatio;* on **multitudo formalis**, see *multitudo;* on **mutatio formalis**, see *mutatio;* on **obiectum formale**, see *obiectum;* on **origo formalis**, see *origo;* on **pars formalis**, see *pars;* on **perfectio formalis**, see *perfectio;* on **primum formale**, see *primus;* on **principium formale et primum formale**, see *principium;* on **ratio formalis seu formalis obiecti**, see *ratio;* on **significatio formalis**, see *significatio;* on **similitudo formalis**, see *similitudo;* on **terminatio formalis**, see *terminatio;* on **transmutatio formalis**, see *transmutatio;* on **utilitas formalis**, see *utilitas.*—**formaliter**, *adv., after the manner of form, in the sense of form, with reference to form, formally.* On **actus formaliter bonus**, see *actus;* on **agere formaliter**, see *agere;* on **bonum formaliter seu formaliter dictum**, see *bonus;* on **certus formaliter**, see *certus;* on **consistere formaliter**, see *consistere;* on **constituere formaliter**, see *constituere;* on **distingui formaliter**, see *distinguere;* on **divisificare formaliter**, see *divisificare;* on **facere formaliter**, see *facere;* on **falsus formaliter**, see *falsus;* on **intellegere formaliter**, see *intellegere;* on **obiectum formaliter**, see *obiectum;* on **operari formaliter**, see

operari; on **operatio formaliter**, see *operatio;* on **oppositum formaliter**, see *opponere;* on **significare formaliter**, see *significare;* on **tenere formaliter**, see *tenere;* on **unum formaliter**, see *unum;* on **verum formaliter**, see *verus;* on **volitum formaliter**, see *volitus.*

formalitas, atis, *f., formality, form relation,* i.e., that which is peculiar to form as such and constitutes its essence.

formaliter, *adv.,* see *formalis.*

formatio, onis, *f.,* (1) *formation, fashioning, moulding,* i.e., the bestowal of a visible form or shape, synonym of *informatio,* the opposite of *infiguratio,* (2) *granting form,* i.e., providing with an inner form, likewise the synonym of *informatio,* the opposite of *informitas.*—Kinds of *formatio* in this (2) sense are: (a), **formatio intellectus**, *granting form to reason.*—(b), **formatio naturae spiritualis**, *granting form to spiritual nature* or *creature.*—(c), **formatio ultima**, *the final granting of form.*

formativus, a, um, *adj., forming, shaping, formative,* synonym of *informativus.* On **virtus formativa**, see *virtus;* on **vis formativa**, see *vis.*

formica, ae, *f., an ant, pismire.*

formido, inis, *f., fearfulness, fear, terror, dread, trepidation.*

formido, are, avi, atum, 1, *v. a.* and *n., to fear, dread anything; to be *afraid, terrified, frightened,* used with the *inf., acc.,* and *ne.*

formidolosus, a, um, *adj., fearful, full of fear, producing fear.*

formo, are, avi, atum, 1, *v. a., to form, put form into, shape,* i.e., *to provide an outer* or *inner form,* synonym of *informare.—* **formatus,** a, um, *P. a., formed, shaped.* On **cogitatio formata,** see *cogitatio;* on **corpus formatum,** see *corpus;* on **fides formata,** see *fides;* on **genus formatum,** see *genus;* on **spes formata,** see *spes;* on **subiectum formatum,** see *subiectum.*

formositas, atis, *f., beauty.*

formula, ae, *f.,* (1) *a fine form, beauty, gracefulness,* (2) *a form, rule, method, formula* for regulating judicial proceedings.

fornax, acis, *f., a fire, furnace.*

fornicaria, ae, *f., an adultress.*

fornicarie, *adv., after the manner of a fornicator, through fornication.*

fornicarius, a, um, *adj., fornicating,* pertaining to the illicit intercourse of unmarried persons, also, loosely, of persons married or unmarried.—**fornicarius,** ii, *m.,* or **fornicaria,** ae, *f., a fornicator; prostitute.*

fornicatio, onis, *f.,* (1) *fornication* in the narrower sense of the word, (2) *fornication* in the broader sense of the word.—One kind of *fornicatio* in this sense is: **fornicatio simplex,** *simple fornication.*—Kinds of *fornicatio* in this (2) sense are: **fornicatio cor-**

poralis and **fornicatio spiritualis,** *the corporal* and *the spiritual* or *immaterial fornication.*

fornicator, oris, *m., a fornicator.*

fornicor, ari, atus, 1, *v. dep. n.,* (1) *lit., to fornicate, commit whoredom* or *fornication,* (2) *fig., to fornicate, prostitute,* devote to unworthy uses, as to prostitute one's gifts.

forsan, *adv.,* ellipt. for *fors sit an,* and *forsitan, perhaps, perchance,* used (1) with *sub.,* (2) *indic.*

forsitan, *adv.,* contr. from *fors sit an, perhaps, peradventure,* used with the indic.

fortasse, also **fortassis,** *adv., perhaps, possible, probably, peradventure.*

forte, *adv.,* (1) *by accident, casually, accidentally,* (2) *trans.,* to denote uncertainty corresponding to the Gr. *an, perhaps, perchance, peradventure,* used with (a) *nisi,* (b) *si,* (c) *ne,* (d) in *relat. clauses.*

fortificatio, onis, *f., a strengthening, fortifying.*

fortifico, are, 1, *v. a., to make strong, strengthen, fortify.*

fortis, e, *adj.,* (1) physically, *powerful, strong,* (2) mentally, *strong, powerful, vigorous, firm, steadfast, courageous, brave, manly,* (a) of human beings, (b) of inanimate and abstract things. —**fortiter,** *adv.,* (1) physically, *strongly, powerfully, vigorously,* (2) mentally, *strongly, powerful-*

ly, boldly, intrepidly, valiantly, bravely, manfully.

fortiter, adv., see fortis.

fortitudo, inis, f., (1) strength, firmness, (2) strength, firmness of soul, in the sense of a general virtue, (3) fortitude, courage of soul, in the sense of a particular virtue, (4) feat of strength, trial of strength.—Kinds of fortitudo in this (1) sense are: **fortitudo corporalis** and **fortitudo spiritualis,** the corporal and the spiritual fortitude or the fortitude of the soul.—**actus fortitudinis,** an act of valour.—**actus principalis fortitudinis,** the main or principal act of valour. On **donum fortitudinis,** see donum.—Kinds of fortitudo in this (3) sense are: (a), **fortitudo civilis seu politica,** civil valour or the valour of citizens of the state.—(b), **fortitudo gratuita,** the valour or courage bestowed by the grace of God, such that one is ready to suffer martyrdom in behalf of his faith. —(c), **fortitudo militaris,** the valour of soldiers in war.—(d), **fortitudo non vera** and **fortitudo vera,** false or untrue valour and true or real valour.—(e), **fortitudo politica,** see fortitudo civilis.—(f), **fortitudo quae est per ignorantiam,** the valour from ignorance.— (g), **fortitudo quae est per iram,** the valour of anger.—(h), **fortitudo quae est per spem,** the valour which comes through hope.—(i), **fortitudo vera,** see fortitudo non vera. Cf. virtus.

fortuito, adv., see fortuitus.

fortuitus, a, um, adj., fortuitous, accidental in the wider and in the narrower sense of the word. Cf. fortuna. In the wider sense, fortuitus is a synonym of casualis, the opposite of provisus and per se volitus seu intentus, and signifies that which in an unforeseen and in an unexpected manner and thus quite incidentally is connected with the activity and the effect of a particular cause and therefore occurs in rare cases. In the narrower sense, fortuitus is the opposite of casualis and signifies that which in an unforeseen and in an unexpected manner and thus quite incidentally is connected with the activity and the effect of a particular rational cause, and therefore occurs but seldom. On **causa fortuita,** see causa; on **effectus fortuitus,** see effectus.—**fortuito,** adv. fortuitously, accidentally, synonym of casualiter, when applied to natural events, and the opposite of it when applied to rational affairs. See fortuitus.

fortuna, ae, f., (1) chance, accident in the wider and in the narrower sense of the word, the tuche of Aristotle, (2) good fortune, good luck, fortune, luck.—(1), in the wider sense of the word, fortuna is a synonym of casus and per se vanum and signifies that particular cause which produces something toward which it did not aim, and which accordingly is only incidentally connected with its action and its effect and therefore also occurs only in rare cases. On **aequivocus per fortunam,** see *aequivocus;* on **agere a fortuna,** see *agere;* on **bonum fortunae,** see *bonus;* on **fieri a fortuna,** see *fieri.*—Kinds of *fortuna* in this (1) sense are: **fortuna bona** and **fortuna mala,** *the good* or *lucky chance* and *the evil* or *unlucky chance.*—a **fortuna nihil fit,** *nothing happens through accident.*—**scientia non est eorum, quae sunt a fortuna,** *there is no knowledge of the things that are from accident.*

Fortunatus, i, *m., Fortunatus,* Bishop of Cirta or Constantinia, chief town of Numidia, associated with St. Augustine on several occasions. He appears as one of the seven Catholic managers at the Carthaginian Conference A.D. 411, but took no prominent part in the proceedings, except to remark on the delays caused by the Donatists. He also appears to have joined in a letter concerning Pelagianism, sent to Pope Innocent by the Council of Milevum, A.D. 416. Cf. Augustine, Epp. 53 and 176.

fortunatus, a, um, *adj.,* (1) *visited by chance, exposed to chance,* (2) *visited by good fortune, favored by fortune, fortunate,* the opposite of *infortunatus,* (3) *lucky.*—Kinds of *fortunatus* in this sense are: **bene fortunatus** and **mala fortunatus,** *he who is*

visited by good luck and *he who is visited by bad luck,* or *the lucky person* and *the unlucky person.* Cf. *infortunatus.*

fortunium, i, *n., happy fortune, lucky chance,* synonym of *bona fortuna.*

forum, i, *n.,* (1) *a forum, a market,* as a place for buying and selling, (1 a) *lit.,* (1 b) *fig.,* (2) *a forum, court, tribunal;* either the place of trials or the exercise itself of civil or ecclesiastical authority, used *literally* and *figuratively.* In the S.T. St. Thomas refers mainly to *iurisdictio fori interni et externi.* The *iurisdictio fori interni, the jurisdiction of the internal forum,* refers primarily and directly to the private utility of the faithful and is exercised chiefly in the administration of the sacraments. Hence it is called **forum conscientiae,** *the forum of conscience.* The **iurisdictio fori externi,** *the jurisdiction of the external court* relates to the public good of the faithful taken as a body. To make laws, decide controversies on faith, morals or discipline, punish criminals and the like are acts of the external court.—The following phrases indicate jurisdiction belonging to the internal forum: —(1), **forum conscientiae,** *the forum of conscience.*—(2), **forum confessionis,** *the tribunal of confession.*—(3), **forum poenitentiae,** *the tribunal of Penance.*—(4), **forum poenitentialis,** *the tribu-*

nal of Penance.—The following phrases refer to the external forum: (1), **forum contentiosum, forum iudiciale,** *a contentious court,* one that is exercised *cum forma iudicii,* i.e., according to the forms prescribed for trials or judicial acts.—(2), **forum publicum exterioris iudicii,** *the public tribunal of external judgment.*—(3), **exterius forum,** *the external forum.*—(4), **forum Ecclesiae,** *the tribunal of the Church.*—(5), **forum causarum,** *a court of causes, public tribunal.*

fossa, ae, *f., a trench, hole in the ground,* used in the S.T. only in quot.

fovea, ae, *f., a pit,* used *figuratively* and *literally.*

foveo, ere, fovi, fotum, 2, *v. a.,* (1) *lit., to warm, keep warm,* (2) *tansf.,* (a) physically, *to cherish, foster, nourish with care, provide with nourishment,* (b) mentally, *to cherish, caress, love, favor, support, assist, encourage.*

fractio, onis, *f.,* (1) *lit., a breaking,* (2) *fig., a breaking, transgression,* a failing to carry out or act in accordance with.

fractor, oris, *m., a breaker, breaker in pieces.*

fragilis, e, *adj.,* (1) *easily broken, brittle, fragile,* (2) *transf.,* in gen., *weak, perishable, frail,* physically or mentally.

fragilitas, atis, *f., frailty, weakness, frailness;* the state or condition of being frail; liability to be broken or destroyed; hence, *moral* or *intellectual weakness; infirmity of the will.*

fragrans, antis, *P. a., emitting a smell, sweet-scented, fragrant.*

fragrantia, ae, *f., scent, odor, fragrance.*

Franci, orum, *m., the Franks,* Germanic tribes who settled on the Rhine under this title early in the Christian era.

Francia, ae, *f., France.*

frangibilis, e, *adj., frangible,* capable of being broken; *fragile.*

frangibilitas, atis, *f., breakableness, frangibility, fragility.*

frango, ere, fregi, fractum, 3, *v. a.,* (1) *lit., to break, break in pieces; dash to pieces, shiver, break in two,* (2) *fig.,* (a) *to break down, weaken, subdue, violate; to soften, move, touch,* (b) *to transgress, violate, fail to keep* or *observe an oath, the seal of confession, a vow, one's faith,* etc.—Note the following phrases: **frangere claustra pudoris,** *to break the barriers of modesty* or *the hymenal membrane.*—**frangere crura,** *to break the legs.*—**frangere os,** *to break a bone.*—**frangere ecclesiam,** *to break into a church.*—**fractus,** a, um, *P. a.,* (1) *lit.,* (a) *broken, separated forcibly into parts,* (b) *broken, wrecked,* as a ship, (2) *fig., broken, transgressed,* as a vow, promise, etc.

frater, tris, *m.,* (1) *a brother,* a male person having the same parent or parents as another or others, (a) **frater uterinus,** *an uterine brother,* one born of the same mother but not of the same father, (b) plural, **fratres consanguinei,** *brothers by relationship, blood relations, those who are descended from the same ancestor,* (2) *a brother,* one of those among whom exists some sympathy or common or family bond; one of the same race, descent, association, class or company, (a) *a brother, fellow-man, fellow-creature,* entitled to the consideration due to neighbor, (b) plural, *the brethren;* in the New Testament, the members of the early Christian Church, (c) *a brother,* a member of a religious order.— **Fratres Praedicatores,** *Friars Preachers,* or *the Preaching Friars.* St. Dominic founded this Order in 1215, and Pope Honorius III approved the society in 1216 under the title of Preaching Friars.

fraternitas, atis, *f., brotherhood, fraternity,* the state, condition, or relation of brotherhood; hence, that sympathy and affection which should characterize the brotherly relation.

fraternus, a, um, *adj., brotherly, fraternal; of, pertaining to,* or *befitting a brother* or *brethren; like brothers.* There are numerous occurrences of the following phrases in the S.T.: **fraterna correctio,** *fraternal correction* or the exercise of fraternal charity

in which brother reproves brother. It supposes serious fault, its object being the offender's correction, not the satisfaction of the offended. In various orders and congregations it is a recognized means of perfection.—**fraterna charitas,** *fraternal charity, brotherly love, the love of one's neighbor.* When human relations are so intimate as to become similar to natural brotherhood, the law is termed the law of fraternal charity.

fraudo, are, avi, atum, 1, *v. a., to deprive one of anything,* used with the *abl.*

fraudulenter, *adv.,* see *fraudulentus.*

fraudulentia, ae, *f., fraud, cheating,* an act of deliberate deception practised with the object of securing something to the prejudice of another.

fraudulentus, a, um, *adj., fraudulent, cheating; practising, planning* or *addicted to fraud.*— **fraudulenter,** *adv., fraudulently.*

fraus, fraudis, *f.,* (1) *fraud, criminal deception;* the using of false representations to obtain an unjust advantage or to injure the rights or interests of another. Fraud and guile are often practised in buying and selling, (2) *fraud,* an act or instance of deception, an artifice by which the right or interest of another is injured, a dishonest trick, used in the *sing.* and *plur.,* (3) *in a passive sense, state of be-*

ing defrauded or *cheated,* (4) *fraud,* (a) *prevarication, a stepping out of the line of duty, a violation of duty;* especially of an advocate who has a secret understanding with the opposite party; *the making up of a sham accusation* or *defense, collusion,* (b) *fraud,* misrepresentation by shaping or turning statements, *equivocation.*— Phrases in which *fraus* is used with the general idea of cheating are: **absque fraude,** *without employing deceit.*—**in fraudem,** *for the purpose of cheating, with a fraudulent intention.*— **pia fraus,** *a pious fraud,* a deception practised for the furtherance of what is considered a good object; especially for the advancement of religion. It is not approved by St. Thomas.

freno, are, avi, atum, 1, *v. a., to restrain,* used in the S.T. only in quot., used *fig.*

frenum, i, *n.,* (1) *lit., a bridle,* (2) *transf.,* like our terms *bridle* and *curb,* i.e., *means of guiding* or *governing, restraint, check, limit.*

frequens, entis, *adj.,* of inanim. and abstr. things, *repeated, often, frequent, common, usual.*— Common phrases are: **frequens fama,** *consistent report.* Gloria est frequens de aliquo fama cum laude, SS. Q. 132. Art. 1 ob. 3, in quot.—**frequens cibus,** *food served frequently.*—**frequens min-**

isterium, *much serving.*—**frequenter,** *adv., often, frequently.*

frequenter, *adv.,* see *frequens.*

frequentia, ae, *f., frequency,* the property of being frequent or of repeated occurrence, used (1) with the *gen.,* (2) *absol.*

frequento, are, avi, atum, 1, *v. a.,* (1) *to visit* or *resort to frequently, frequent,* (2) *to do* or *make use of frequently, repeat.*

fretus, a, um, *adj., relying* or *depending upon, trusting to,* used with the *abl.*

frico, are, fricui, ctum, 1, *v. a., to rub, rub down.*

frigeo, ere, 2, *v. n.,* (1) *lit., to be cold, chilly, to freeze,* (2) *fig.,* to be *inactive* or *at a standstill; to be lifeless, languid, frigid.*

frigesco, ere, fixi, 3, *v. inch. n.,* (1) *lit., to become* or *grow cold, to be chilled,* (2) *fig., to become inactive, languid, faint.*

frigiditas, atis, *f.,* (1) *the cold, frigidity,* the state or condition of *being frigid; coldness; lack of warmth,* (2) *frigidity, want of generative heat; impotency.*

frigido, are, 1, *v. a., to make cold, to cool.*

frigidus, a, um, *adj.,* (1) *lit., cold, cool, chill, chilling,* (2) *fig., frigid,* lacking in generative warmth or vigor; *impotent.*—**frigidum,** i, *n., the cold.*

frigus, oris, *n., cold, coldness, coolness,* a relative term implying a condition of the atmosphere or of a body which produces to the human touch a sensation of cold or absence of heat, (1) in gen., (2) in partic., *the cold of winter, cold weather.*

frivolus, a, um, *adj., frivolous, audacious, mischievous.*

frondesco, ere, ui, 3, *v. inch. n., to become leafy, to put forth leaves, to shoot out.*

frons, frondis, *f., foliage, a growth of leaves,* used only in the plural in the S.T.

frons, frontis, *f.,* (I) *lit., the forehead, brow, front,* the part of the face which reaches upward from the eyebrows to the natural line of the hair, (II), *fig.,* (1) *the first appearance, the beginning, principle,* a synonym of *prima pars,* (2) *the character* or *feeling expressed by the brow,* used in two opposite applications, (a) a *capacity of blushing, sense of shame* or *decency; modesty,* (b) *command of countenance, unblushing front; assurance, impudence, audacity.*

Frontinus, i, *m., Frontinus,* Sex. Iulius, superintendent of the Roman aqueducts under Nerva, in the latter half of the first century of the Christian era.

fructeta, orum, *n., bushes, thickets,* used in the S.T. only in quot.

fructifer, era, erum, *adj., fruit-bearing, fruitful,* used *lit.* and *fig.*

fructificatio, onis, *f., a bearing of fruit.*

fructifico, are, 1, *v. n., to bear fruit,* used *lit.* and *fig.*

fructuosus, a, um, *adj., abounding in fruit, fruitful, productive,* *profitable, advantageous,* used *fig.*

fructus, us, *m.,* (1) *fruit* in the proper and in the transferred sense of the word, (2) *fruit of the Holy Spirit,* a good act, or an act of virtue, done through the grace of the Holy Ghost, in which man takes pleasure. PS. Q. 70. is devoted to these acts. Cf. *fructus Spiritus sancti.*— Kinds of *fructus* with reference to man are to be distinguished as follows: (a), **fructus adeptus seu adquisitus** and **fructus productus,** *the fruit already existing* and *the fruit gained* or *acquired* and *the fruit first brought into existence.*—(b), **fructus adquisitus,** see *fructus adeptus.*—(c), **fructus corporalis seu sensibilis** and **fructus spiritualis,** *the physical* or *sensible fruit* and *the spiritual* or *supersensible fruit.*—(d), **fructus productus,** see *fructus adeptus.*—(e), **fructus rationis** and **fructus Spiritus sancti,** *the fruit of human reason* and *the fruit of the Holy Spirit.*—(f), **fructus sensibilis,** see *fructus corporalis.*—(g), **fructus spiritualis,** see *fructus corporalis.*—(h), **fructus Spiritus sancti,** see *fructus rationis.*—The *fructus Spiritus sancti* are as follows: *amor Dei seu caritas* (see *amor* and *caritas*), *gaudium* (see the article), *pax* (see the article); *patientia* (see the article), *longanimitas* (see the article), *bonitas* (see the article), *benignitas* (see the article), *mansuetudo* (see the article), *fides seu fidelitas* (see *fides*), *modestia* (see the article), *continentia* (see the article), *castitas* (see the article).

fruibilis, e, *adj., amusing, enjoyable* in the wider and the narrower senses of the word. Cf. *frui* and *fruitio.* In its narrower sense *fruibilis* is the opposite of *utilis* and *utibilis.*

fruitio, onis, *amusement, enjoyment* in the wider and narrower senses of the word. Cf. *fruor.* Taken in its narrower sense, *fruitio* is the opposite of *usus. Fruitio* is the activity of an appetitive faculty and consists in the delightful enjoyment of a thing striven for as the ultimate goal. Since then among the things of nature man alone is able to recognize a thing, in so far as it is the goal of his striving and is able to set it up for himself as a goal, because he alone of all the things of nature possesses the gift of reason, while beasts can only recognize the object which is the recurring object of their desire and all other things of nature are able to recognize nothing at all, it is clear that *fruitio* in the proper and full sense of the word can be ascribed only to man. But in so far as the beast by means of his sensible power is able in a slight degree to comprehend that which serves as the object and the goal of his desire, with

reference to it also can mention be made of a *fruitio* but only in the improper and wider sense of the word. The *fruitio* of man has its chief object in his *finis ultimus,* i.e., in God, because only in Him are the two substantially identical moments of that which is called *fructus* in the perfect sense of the word united.—The **fruitio** of the blessed in heaven is *una de tribus dotibus animae* (see *dos*) *quae respondet caritati.*—On **gaudium fruitionis,** see *gaudium.*—Kinds of *fruitio* are: (a), **fruitio aeterna** and **fruitio temporalis,** *the eternal enjoyment* (*of God*) and *the temporal enjoyment of a temporal good.*—(b), **fruitio beata,** *the blessed enjoyment* or *the enjoyment of the blessed in heaven.*—(c), **fruitio Deitatis seu divina,** *the enjoyment of God* or *the divine enjoyment.*—(d), **fruitio divina,** see *fruitio Deitas.*—(e), **fruitio imperfecta** and **fruitio perfecta,** *the imperfect* and *the perfect enjoyment.*—(f), **fruitio perfecta,** see *fruitio imperfecta.*—(g), **fruitio temporalis,** see *fruitio aeterna.*

frumentum, i, *n.,* (1) *sing., any grain,* especially *wheat,* (2) plural, *kinds of grain,* used (a) *lit.,* (b) *fig.*

fruor, i, fructus, 3, *v. dep. n., to enjoy* in the wider and narrower sense of the word. *Frui* in the narrower sense of the word, the

opposite of *uti,* is not the action
of a faculty of knowledge but
that of a faculty of desire, and
that precisely not an action of
desire which is directed towards
a goal not yet attained, but rather the cessation of striving in the
quiet enjoyment of possession.
Yet not with every faculty of desire is there an action striving for
a goal, which deserves the name
of *frui* in its proper meaning, but
only with the will of man who
by means of his reason can not
only recognize the thing striven
for as a goal, in so far as it is a
goal, but also can be conscious
that he is striving for it as a goal
of his desire and eventually that
he has attained it as his goal.
Wherefore it is said: frui non est
actus potentiae pervenientis ad
finem sicut exsequentis (which
is possible likewise with animals
and with unintelligent and inanimate beings), sed potentiae imperantis exsecutionem (i.e., of
the will). The proper object of
frui is the *finis ultimus* of man,
i.e., God. On the difference between *frui* and *uti,* see *uti.—*
Kinds of *frui* are: (a), **frui extensive** and **frui intensive,** *to enjoy
something according to its ex-
panse or greatness* and *to enjoy
something to a high degree.—*(b),
frui intensive, see *frui extensive.*
—(c), **frui sicut habitu, frui sicut
instrumento,** and **frui sicut obiecto,** *to enjoy something as habitus which calls forth the act of*

*fruitio, to enjoy something as
means of fruitio* and *to enjoy
something as object.—*(d), **frui
sicut instrumento,** see *frui sicut
habitu.—*(e), **frui sicut obiecto,**
see *frui sicut habitu.*

frustatim, *adv., piecemeal, in
pieces.*

frustra, *adv., in vain, useless, aimless, superfluous,* synonym of
inanis, vacuus, and *vanus.—***per
se frustra,** synonym of *per se
vanum* (see *vanus*), *aimless in
itself* or *as such.—***Deus et natura nihil frustra faciunt,** or, **Deus nihil facit frustra . . . similiter etiam natura nihil facit frustra,** or, **in operibus Dei non est
aliquid frustra, sicut nec in operibus naturae, natura nihil
facit frustra, ita nec Deus,** the
translation of the Aristotelian
passage: *ho theos kai he physis
ouden maten poiousin, God and
nature do nothing to no purpose.—***impossibile est, appetitum naturalem esse frustra,** *the
natural desire of a thing cannot
be in vain.—***in operibus Dei non
est aliquid frustra, sicut nec in
operibus naturae,** see above:
Deus et natura etc.—**natura nihil facit frustra,** or, **nihil frustra
natura facit,** or, **nihil est frustra
in natura,** or, **rerum naturalium
actiones non sunt frustra,** the
translation of the Aristotelian
passage: *outhen maten he physis
poiei, nature* or *the things of
nature do nothing in vain.—***natura nihil facit frustra, ita nec**

Deus, see above: *Deus et natura* etc.—natura nihil facit frustra, neque deficit in necessariis, see *natura.*—nihil est frustra in natura, see above: *natura nihil facit frustra.*—nihil frustra natura facit, see above: *natura nihil facit frustra.*—nulla virtus datur alicui rei frustra, *no power is given to something without purpose.*—rerum naturalium actiones non sunt frustra, see above: *natura nihil facit frustra.*

frustror, ari, atus, 1, *v. dep.;* also: **frustro,** are, avi, 1, *v. a.,* (1) *in the act. form,* (a) *to deceive, trick,* a synonym of *decipere,* (b) *to void, nullify, annul,* (2) *pass.,* (a) *to thwart, defeat, frustrate, baulk, to prevent the accomplishment of,* as *by interposing an obstacle,* (b), *to cheat, defraud,* used with the *ablative,* (3) *transf.,* in *dep.,* form, *to make vain, of no effect, or useless.*

frux, frugis, *f.,* (1) *lit.,* plur., *fruits,* (*grain, tree-fruits,* etc.), (2) *fig., ad frugem, to moral worth, excellence, virtue, fruit.*

fucatio, onis, *f., fucation, coloring, painting; the act of painting the face.*

fuco, are, avi, atum, 1, *v. a., to color, paint, dye, powder,* used in the S.T. only in quot.

fuga, ae, *f.,* (1) *lit., a fleeing, flight, a running away, the act of fleeing* or *running away from ·danger,* etc., *hasty departure* or *retreat,* (2) *fig., flight, an abhorrence* or *avoidance of; a detestation, avoidance, abhorrence, aversion.*—Common phrases are: **fuga mali,** *the shunning of evil.*—**fuga doloris,** *flight from sorrow.*—**fuga tristitiae,** *the shunning of sorrow.*—**fuga appetitus,** *avoidance in the appetite.*—**fuga boni,** *the avoidance of good.*

fugibilis, e, *adj.,* with a passive signification; *to be avoided.*

fugio, ere, fugi, fugitum, 3, *v. n.* and *a.,* (I) *neutr., to take flight, run away,* (1) *lit.,* (2) *fig.,* (II) act., (1) *to flee from, seek to avoid, to shun anything,* (a) *lit.,* (b) *fig.,* (2) *to discard, cast away,* as no longer required or fit for a particular purpose.—**fugiens,** entis, *P. a.,* (1) *lit., fleeing, running away,* (2) *shunning, avoiding, shirking,* (a) *lit.,* (b) *fig.*

fugitans, antis, *P. a., avoiding, shunning,* used in S.T. only in quot.

fugitivus, a, um, *adj., fleeing, fugitive, runaway.*—**fugitivum** sc. **principium,** the translation of the Aristotelian word *pheutikon, the fleeing principle* or the totality of the appetitive faculty of an animal being considered in so far as they flee evil; the opposite of *appetitivum.*

fugo, are, avi, atum, 1, *v. a., to put to flight; drive* or *chase away, to rout,* used *fig.*

fulcimentum, i, *n., support,* used *fig.*

fulcio, ire, fulsi, fultum, 4, *v. a.*, *to support, sustain, uphold,* used *fig.*—**fultus,** a, um, *P. a.*, *supported, upheld, sustained.*

Fulgentius, ii, *m.*, *Fulgentius,* Fabius Claudius Gordianus, bishop of Ruspe was born in 468 A.D. and died 533 A.D. His life was spent for the most part in the provinces of north-western Africa which were brought under the cruel tyranny of the Vandal Kings, Genseric, Hunneric, and Thrasimund. St. Thomas mentions his dissertation Ad Monimum, libri tres. I. De duplice praedestinatione Dei, and De Fide ad Petrum Diaconum. The Liber de Fide is inserted in Augustine's works. Many of his writings reveal his strong sympathy with the opinions of Augustine on the doctrines of predestination, of grace, and of the remission of sin.

fulgeo, ere, fulsi, 2, *v. n.*, *lit.*, *to flash, lighten,* (1) *transf.*, *to flash, glitter, gleam, shine,* (2) *fig.*, *to shine, gleam, be illustrious, conspicuous.*—**fulgens,** entis, *P. a.*, *shining, glittering;* in a *fig.* sense, *illustrious.*

fulgor, oris, *m.*, (1) *lightning,* (2) *transf.*, (a) *flash, brightness, splendor,* (b) *fig.*, *brightness, splendor, glory.*

fumalis, e, *adj.*, *volatile,* characterized by a natural tendency to dispersion in fumes or vapour.

fumo, are, 1, *v. n.*, *to smoke, reek.*

fumositas, atis, *f.*, *volatility, exhalation, fume, vapor.*

fumosus, a, um, *adj.*, *full of smoke, smoky, reeky.*

fumus, i, *m.*, *smoke,* used *lit.* and *fig.*

functio, onis, *f.*, *a function, an office properly belonging* or *assigned to a person in a particular station* or *character; one's proper business, duty, office.*

fundamentum, i, *m.*, *foundation, groundwork, basis,* synonym of *hypostasis.*—Kinds of *fundamentum* in the general sense of the word are: (a), **fundamentum corporale seu materiale** and **fundamentum in spiritualibus seu spiritualis aedificii,** *the physical* and *the spiritual foundation* or *the foundation of a material* and *that of a spiritual structure.*—(b), **fundamentum ecclesiae,** *the foundation of the Catholic Church.*—(c), **fundamentum in intellectu** and **fundamentum in re,** *the foundation in reason* or *in the thinking of reason* and *the foundation in the thing* or *outside reason.*—(d), **fundamentum in re,** see *fundamentum in intellectu.*—(e), **fundamentum in spiritualibus,** see *fundamentum corporale.*—(f), **fundamentum materiale,** see *fundamentum corporale.*—(g), **fundamentum principale** and **fundamentum secundarium,** *the chief foundation* and *the secondary foundation.*—(h), **fundamentum proximum** and **fundamentum remotum,** *the proximate founda-*

tion and *the remote foundation.*
—(i), **fundamentum relationis,**
the basis or *basis of relation.*—
(j), **fundamentum remotum,** see
fundamentum proximum.—(k),
fundamentum secundarium, see
fundamentum principale.—(l),
**fundamentum spiritualis aedific-
ii,** see *fundamentum corporale.*
—(m), **fundamentum spiritualis
doctrinae,** *the foundation of
spiritual teaching.*

fundatio, onis, *f.,* *a founding, foundation.*

funditus, *adv.,* used *fig., utterly,
entirely, totally, completely.*

fundo, are, avi, atum, 1, *v. a.,* (1)
lit., to establish, to locate or
place in a particular situation or
spot, (2) *fig., to base, to place
upon a foundation* or *basis;
ground; establish.*

fundo, ere, fudi, fusum, 3, *v. a.,* (1)
lit., of fluids, *to shed, spill.* (2)
fig., in particular of speech, *to
pour forth, utter.*—**fusus,** a, um,
P. a., poured forth.

fundus, i, *m., a definitely defined
portion of land.*

funestus, a, um, *adj., fatal, deadly,*
used in the S.T. only in quot.

fungor, fungi, functus, *v. dep., to
busy one's self with* or *be engaged in something; to perform,
exercise, execute, discharge, observe,* used with the *ablative.*

funis, is, *m., a rope, a thick cord.*

funus, eris, *n., a funeral,* the formal
conveyance of a dead person to
the grave or tomb and the final

disposal of the body; more especially, the preceding and accompanying rites and ceremonies;
obsequies.

fur, furis, *comm.,* (1) *a thief,* one
who steals, especially one who
steals furtively or without violence, a burglar, as distinguished
from a robber, (2) *transf.,* as a
term of vituperation applied to
anyone, *thief, rogue.*

furia, ae, *f., madness, mental derangement, insanity, dementia,
lunacy.*

furibundus, a, um, *adj., raging,
mad, furious.*

furiosus, a, um, *adj., full of madness* or *rage, fierce.*—**furiosus,** i,
m., a furiosus, madman, lunatic,
an *insane person.*

furnus, i, *m., a furnace, oven.*

furor, ari, atus, 1, *v. dep. a.,* (1)
lit., to steal, purloin, pilfer, (2)
transf., in *gen., to take away by
stealth, remove secretly, cozen.*

furor, oris, *m., a raving, rage, madness, fury, quickness to anger
with a desire to revenge.*

furtim, *adv., by stealth, secretly,
privily.*

furtive, *adv., stealthily, secretly,
furtively.*

furtum, i, *n.,* (1) *a theft,* the secret
and wilfully wrongful appropria-
tion of a movable thing not one's
own whether such appropriation
is coupled with an actual removal of the thing from the custody
of another or not, (2) *a theft, the
thing which has been stolen.*

furvus, a, um, *adj., dark, dusky, black,* used in the S.T. only in quot.

fuscus, a, um, *adj., dark, dusky,* used in the S.T. only in quot.

futuritio, onis, *f., futurity,* the state or quality of being future.

futurus, a, um, *P. a., future,* such as will or may be hereafter; that will be or occur at any time to come later than the present; pertaining to or expressing time to come.—**futurum,** i, *n., the future,* the time yet to come; time later than the present; that which will be or occur in time subsequent to the present, (1) *the future, time to come,* (2) *the future,* that which is already determined in its cause to happen in the future, (3) in the plural, *future events.* —Common phrases are: in futuro, in futurum, *in the future life, in the world to come, in the life to come.*—One kind of *futurum* in this (2) sense is: **futurum contingens,** an event which is contingent because from one point of view it may or may not take place since it depends upon contigent cause, but which is a future event since from another point of view it is already determined in its causes. Otherwise it would not differ from mere possibility.

G

Gabaon, onis, *f., Gabaon* or *Gibeon,* a city of Judea.

Gabriel, is, *m., Gabriel,* an arch-angel sent with a message from God, as to Daniel and the Blessed Virgin Mary.

Gaianitae, arum, *m., the Gaianites* or incorruptibilists, also called the Phantasiastae, a sect of Monophysites who held that Christ was always incorruptible, and that he died only phantasmally. The Gaianites received their name from Gaianus, monophysite patriarch of Alexandria.

Gaianus, i, *m., Gaianus,* monophysite patriarch of Alexandria, chosen by the party of the Incorruptibilist, whilst the party of the Corruptibilists put forward Theodosius, 537, A.D. Gaianus, having held the see for three hundred days, was banished by order of the empress Theodora. From this Gaianus the sect of Incorruptibilists at Alexandria received the name Gaianites.

Galatae, arum, *m., the Galatians,* a Celtic people who migrated into Phrygia. The *Epistle to the Galatians,* quoted so frequently in the S.T., is a letter written by the Apostle Paul about 56 A.D. to the churches of Galatia, showing the impossibility of salvation by the ceremonial law.

Galenus, i, *m., Galen, Claudius (Galenus),* (131-201), a Greek medical writer and philosopher.

galerum, i, *n.*, *a miter*, a head dress worn by church dignitaries, as popes, archbishops, bishops, and abbot; at one time it resembled a hat but it has undergone many changes of shape during the centuries until the present shape was evolved.

Galilaea, ae, *f.*, *Galilee*, a province in northern Palestine.

Gallia, ae, *f.*, *Gaul*, the country of the Gauls, which embraced what is now Northern Italy, France, Belgium, and parts of Holland, Switzerland, and Germany.

Gallicus, a, um, *adj.*, *Gallic* of or belonging to the Gauls.

gallina, ae, *f.*, *a hen*.

Gallus, i, *m.*, *a Gaul*.

Garizim, *indecl. n.*, *Garizim*, a very high mountain in Samaria.

garritus, us, *m.*, *a chattering, chirping*.

garrulus, a, um, *adj.*, *chattering, prattling*.

gaudenter, *adv.*, see *gaudeo*.

Gaudentius, ii, *m.*, *Gaudentius*, bishop of Constance who was succeeded by Joannes I. His death took place in 616. St. Thomas quotes a letter of Pelagius II to Gaudentius on a question about the form of baptism and on triple immersion.

gaudeo, ere, gavisus, 2, *v. n.* and *a.*, (1) in gen., *to rejoice, be glad* or *joyful respecting anything, to take pleasure in, be pleased with, delight in* (of inward joy, opp. *laetari*, to show one's self glad, exhibit joy), used (a) with

acc. and *inf.*, (b) the *abl.*, (c) *in, cum, de, ex,* and *abl.*, (d) *absol.*, (2) in partic., *to feel joy in, enjoy, have the use* or *benefit of something* as a good, used with the *abl.*—**gaudens,** entis, *P. a.*, *rejoicing.*—**gaudenter,** *adv.*, *joyfully, rejoicingly.*

gaudium, ii, *n.*, *joy, gladness, delight*, a special kind of *delectatio*, namely, that *delectatio* which springs from the knowledge or the performance of a good, the actual possession and enjoyment of good, the opposite of *tristitia*. —Kinds of *gaudium* are: (a), **gaudium comprehensoris** and **gaudium viatoris,** *the joy of the possessor* (of heavenly blessedness) and *the joy of the pilgrim* (to heaven).—(b), **gaudium fruitionis,** *the pleasure of enjoyment.* —(c), **gaudium rei** and **gaudium spei,** *the joy of reality* and *that of hope* or the joy which springs from a good held in possession according to reality and that which springs from the hope for the possession of this good.—(d), **gaudium spei,** see *gaudium rei.*— (e), **gaudium spirituale,** *the spiritual joy* or *the joy in a spiritual good*, to which the *gaudium corporale*, i.e, the bodily joy or the joy in a sensible good on the one hand and *acedia* on the other, form the contrasts.—(f), **gaudium viatoris,** see *gaudium comprehensoris.*—**gaudium spirituale,** in so far as it relates to God and divine things, is one of the *fructus*

Spiritus sancti (see *fructus*) and consists in an *effectus seu actus consequens caritatis* (see *caritas*) *actum principalem, qui est dilectio* (see *dilectio*), and indeed in an *effectus interior*.

Gaza, ae, *f., Gaza,* the name of several cities; the most celebrated is the ancient city of Gaza in Palestine.

Gazer, *indecl., f., Gazer,* a city in the Province of Judea below Lydda.

gazophylachium, ii, *n., a gazophylacium, a treasury, offertory box.*

Gedeon, onis, *m., Gedeon,* also called Jerobaal and Jerubesheth, was one of the Greater Judges of Israel. He belonged to the tribe of Manasses and to the family of Abiezer. Gedeon's father was Joas and lived in Ephra.

gehenna, ae, *f., hell.*

gehennalis, e, *adj., of hell, hellish.*

Gelasius, ii, *Gelasius* I, Saint (492-496). He insisted on the Primacy of the Pope being derived from Christ himself and not from secular or ecclesiastical sanction. St. Thomas quotes from his decrees.

Gelboe, *indecl. n., Gelboe,* a mountain extending from Jezrahel to the Jordan where Saul and the Israelites fled before the face of the Philistines.

Gellius, ii, *m., Gellius, Aulus Gellius,* a grammarian of the first half of the second century of the Christian era, author of the *Noctes Atticae.*

geminatio, onis, *f., a doubling.*

gemino, are, avi, atum, 1, *v. a.* and *n., to double.—*germinatus, a, um, *adj., doubled.*

geminus, a, um, *adj., paired, double, two-fold, both, two.—*gemini, orum, *m., twins.*

gemitus, us, *m., a sighing, sigh, moan, a groan, lamentation, complaint.*

gemma, ae, *f., a precious stone, a gem.*

gemo, ere, ui, itum, 3, *v. n.* and *a.,* (1) act, *to sigh over, bemoan, bewail,* (2) neutr., of beasts, *to make a mournful noise, to cry.*

genealogia, ae, *f., a genealogy.*

generabilis, e, *adj., that has the power of generating, generative, creative, that may be generated or produced,* the opposite of *corruptibilis.* Cf. *genero* and *generatio.* On **forma generabilium,** see *forma;* on **materia generabilis,** see *materia;* on **natura generabilis,** see *natura;* on **substantia generabilis,** see *substantia.*

generalis, e, *adj.,* (1) *of* or *belonging to a kind* or *species, generic, relating to the manner of a kind,* the opposite of *specialis,* (2) *of* or *relating to all,* general synonym of *communis* and *universalis,* the opposite of *particularis* and *specialis.—*On **forma generalis,** see *forma.—*On **cognitio generalis,** see *cognitio;* on **confessio generalis,** see *confessio;* on **consilium generale,** see *consilium;* on **contritio generalis,** see *contritio;* on **cupiditas generalis,** see *cupiditas;* on **eleemosyna generalis,** see *eleemosyna;* on **genus generale,** see *genus;* on **iudicium generale,** see *iudicium;* on **iustitia generalis,** see *iustitia;* on **oppositum in generali,** see *opponere;* on **passio generalis,** see *passio;* on **peccatum generale,** see *peccatum;* on **praeceptum generale,** see *praeceptum;* on **resurrectio generalis,** see *resurrectio;* on **virtus generalis,** see *virtus.*—**generaliter,** *adv., in general, generally,* opposite of *specialiter.*—**in generali,** *in general, generally,* synonym of *generaliter,* opposite of *specialiter, in speciali,* and *in singulari.*

generalitas, atis, *f.,* (1) *generality, the bulk* or *main body, the principal position; extent,* (2) *generality,* the state or quality of being general or generalized, opposite of *specialitas* and *singularitas.*

generatio, onis, *f.,* (1) *procreation, generation* in the proper sense of the word, i.e., *bringing forth, origination, coming into being out of some pre-existent,* the opposite of *corruptio,* (2) *procreation, generation* in the improper sense of the word, i.e., *bringing forth, coming into being out of nothing;* likewise the opposite of *corruptio,* (3) *species, genus,* synonym of *genus.*—On **causa generationis,** see *causa;* on **ordo generationis seu secundum viam generationis,** see *ordo;* on **posterius generationis,** see *posterior;*

on **principium generationis,** see *principium;* on **prius generationis seu in generationem seu ordine generationis seu secundum ordinem generationis seu in via generationis seu secundum viam generationis,** see *prior;* on **relatio generationis,** see *relatio;* on **status generationis,** see *status.*— Kinds of *generatio* in this (1) sense are: (a), **generatio absoluta seu simplex seu simpliciter** and **generatio aliqua seu quaedam seu alicuius seu huius secundum partem seu secundum quid,** *the simple* or *absolute* and *the respective* or *partial generation,* or *a certain generation,* i.e., *a generation which has a substance and that which has an accident as a result,* or *the generation which consists in the changing of an ignoble to a noble substance* and *that which consists in the reverse.*—(b), **generatio a casu seu casualis seu per accidens** and **generatio per se seu per se intenta,** *the generation that arises by accident* or *the accidental generation* or *that which takes place accidentally* and *generation as such* or *aimed at by itself.* —(c), **generatio activa seu active sumpta** and **generatio passiva seu passive sumpta seu accepta,** *the active* and *the passive generation* or *generation in the active* and *in the passive sense of the word.*—(d), **generatio active sumpta,** see *generatio activa.*— (e), **generatio aequivoce seu non** univoca and **generatio univoca,** *the homonymous but not homogeneous generation* and *the homogeneous generation* or *the generation of a dissimilar* and *that of similar being.*—(f), **generatio aeterna** and **generatio temporalis,** *the eternal generation* or *that taking place in eternity* and *the temporal generation* or *that happening in time.*—(g), **generatio alicuius seu aliqua,** see *generatio absoluta.*—(h), **generatio animalis seu carnalis seu corporalis** and **generatio spiritualis,** *the animal* or *carnal* or *corporal generation* and *the spiritual generation.*—Cf. also *generatio intelligibilis.*—(i), **generatio animalis** and **generatio inanimati,** *the generation of a being endowed with senses* and *that of a soulless* or *lifeless being.*—(j), **generatio artificialis seu secundum artem** and **generatio naturalis seu secundum naturam,** *artificial generation* or *that according to art* and *the natural generation* or *that according to nature.* Cf. also *generatio contra naturam.*—(k), **generatio artificialium,** *the production of works of art.*—(l), **generatio carnalis,** see *generatio animalis.*—(m), **generatio casualis,** see *generatio a casu.*—(n), **generatio circularis seu in circuitu seu mutua** and **generatio recta seu in rectum,** *the circular* or *reciprocal production* and *the rectilinear* or *the production ever going forward in the manner of* *a straight line.*—(o), **generatio completa,** *the complete production.*—(p), **generatio continua seu perpetua,** *the uninterrupted* or *everlasting production.*—(q), **generatio contra naturam seu extra naturam seu violenta, generatio secundum naturam seu naturalis** and **generatio miraculosa,** *the unnatural* or *violent production, the natural production* or *that according to nature,* and *the miraculous* or *supernatural production.*—(r), **generatio corporalis,** see *generatio animalis.*—(s), **generatio divina** and **generatio humana,** *the divine production* or *that taking place in God* and *the human production* or *that accomplished by man.*—(t), **generatio extra naturam,** see *generatio contra naturam.*—(u), **generatio finita** and **generatio infinita,** *the limited production* or *that having an end* and *the infinite production* or *that continued without end.*—(v), **generatio huius,** see *generatio absoluta.*—(w), **generatio humana,** see *generatio divina.*—(x), **generatio inanimati,** see *generatio animalis.*—(y), **generatio in circuitu,** see *generatio circularis.*—(z), **generatio infinita,** see *generatio finita.*—(a²), **generatio intellegibilis** and **generatio materialis,** *the intellectual* or *immaterial production* and *the material* or *physical production.* —(b²), **generatio intermedia seu media generatio prima,** and **generatio ultima,** *the intermediate* *production,* that which lies between the first and the last production, as if a thing must pass through a series of productions before it reaches completion, *the first* and *the last production.*— (c^2), generatio legalis, *the legal production,* i.e., the production that corresponds to the law of the Old Testament.—(d^2), generatio materialis, see *generatio intellegibilis.*—(e^2), generatio media, see *generatio intermedia.*— (f^2), generatio miraculosa, see *generatio contra naturam.*—(g^2), generatio momentanea, *the momentary production* or that accomplished in an instant.—(h^2), generatio mutua, see *generatio circularis.*—(i^2), generatio naturalis, see *generatio artificialis* and *generatio contra naturam.*— (j^2), generatio non-univoca, see *generatio aequivoca.*—(k^2), generatio occulta, *the production hidden from the eyes.*—(l^2), generatio passiva, see *generatio activa.* —(m^2), generatio passive accepta seu sumpta, see *generatio activa.*—(n^2), generatio per accidens, see *generatio a casu.*—(o^2), generatio perpetua, see *generatio continua.*—(p^2), generatio per se seu per se intenta, see *generatio a casu.*—(q^2), generatio prima, see *generatio intermedia.*—(r^2), generatio quaedam, see *generatio absoluta.*—(s^2), generatio recta, see *generatio circularis.*—(t^2), generatio secundum artem, see *generatio artificialis.*—(u^2), generatio se-

cundum naturam, see *generatio artificialis* and *generatio contra naturam.*—(v^2), generatio secundum partem, see *generatio absoluta.*—(w^2), generatio secundum quid, see *generatio absoluta.*— (x^2), generatio secundum rectum, see *generatio circularis.*—(y^2), generatio simplex, see *generatio absoluta.*—(z^2), generatio simpliciter, see *generatio absoluta.*— (a^3), generatio spiritualis, see *generatio animalis.*—(b^3), generatio spontanea, *the production which takes place of itself* (i.e., *sine semine*).—(c^3), generatio substantialis, *the production of a substance.*—(d^3), generatio temporalis, see *generatio aeterna.*—(e^3), generatio ultima, see *generatio intermedia.*—(f^3), generatio univoca, see *generatio aequivoca.*— (g^3), generatio violenta, see *generatio contra naturam.*—actus generatione et tempore est posterior potentia, see *actus.*—alterationis terminus est generatio, see *alteratio.*—communium non est generatio, sed particularium, *there is no production of common things but only of particular things.*—forma est finis generationis non ipsius generati, see *forma.*—generatio est propter formam, or, terminus generationis est natura rei, *the production of a thing aims at its form* or *nature,* i.e., *at the introduction of form into matter, whereby the nature* and *essence of a thing are established.* Cf. below: *omnis ge-*

neratio est etc.—**generationes et corruptiones ex contrariis et in contraria sunt,** *those things which for the processes of production as for those of dissolution form the terminus a quo* and *the terminus ad quem are mutually opposed to each other.* —**generationis non est generatio,** *for the production there is no production.*—**generationis subiectum non est id quo generatur, sed materia eius,** *generation takes place not in the form by which a thing is generated but in matter.* Cf. below: *omnis generatio* etc.—**generatio recipit speciem a termino,** *production receives its species* and *essence from its terminus ad quem, i.e., from that towards which it aims.* —**generatio significat ut in fieri,** *production signifies the process of becoming.*—**generatio unius est corruptio alterius** and **corruptio unius est generatio alterius,** or both together, **generatio huius est corruptio illius et corruptio huius est generatio alterius,** the translation of the Aristotelian passage: *to auto esti genesis men toudi phthora de toudi, kai phthora men toudi genesis de toudi, the generation of a thing implies the disappearance of another* and *vice versa.*—**impossibile est per generationem reiterari idem numero,** *in the process of production it is impossible to reproduce the same numerical individual as existed before.*—**in om-**

ni **generatione, quod est in potentia est prius tempore et posterius natura, quod autem est completum in actu est prius natura et posterius tempore,** or, in via generationis semper incompletum est prius completo, licet in via perfectionis sit totum e contrario, or, **quae sunt posteriora in generatione, sunt priora secundum substantiam et speciem, id est, perfectione,** or, **quod est posterius in generatione, est prius secundum naturam,** *in every generation, the imperfect* and *incomplete is first in the order of time, although the complete* and *actual thing which is the aim of generation is first according to the order of nature.*—**omnis generatio est ex aliquo, scilicet ex materia, et ad aliquid scilicet ad formam,** *every production presupposes something in which it is produced, namely, matter* (cf. above: **generationis subiectum non est,** etc.), and *aims at something,* namely, *at form* (cf. above: **generatio est propter** etc.).—**primum in generatione est postremum in corruptione,** and the reverse, **ultimum in generatione est primum in resolutione,** *that which is the first in the origin of a thing is the last in the disappearance of the same* and *the reverse.*—**quae sunt posteriora in generatione, sunt priora secundum substantiam et speciem, id est, perfectione,** see above: *in omni generatione* etc.—**quod** est posterius in generatione, est prius secundum naturam, see above: *in omni generatione* etc. —terminus generationis est natura rei, see above: *generatio est propter* etc.—ultimum in generatione est primum in resolutione, see above: *primum in generatione* etc.—ultimum in generatione est primum in intentione, *what is last in the process of generation is the first thing intended.*

generativus, a, um, *producing, procreating, generative.*—On actus generativus, see *actus;* on anima generativa, see *anima;* on motio generativa, see *motio;* on potentia generativa, see *potentia;* on species generativa, see *species;* on virtus generativa, see *virtus;* on vis generativa, see *vis.*

genero, are, avi, atum, 1, *v. a., to beget, procreate, engender, produce, create, originate from something,* the opposite of *corrumpo.* On causa generans prohibens, see *causa;* on habitus generans, see *habitus;* on potentia generans, see *potentia.*—Kinds of *generare* are: (a), generare ad invicem seu circulo, *to produce in a cycle, in other words, so to produce that two things are alternately produced from each other.*—(b), generare circulo, see *generare ad invicem.*—(c), generare naturale, *the natural production or the production found in nature.*—(d), generare per accidens and generare per se, *to produce something accidentally*

or *by reason of something else,* and *to produce something as such* or *by reason of itself.*—(e), generare per artem and generare per naturam, *to produce something in the manner of art and in that of nature.*—(f), generare per naturam, see *generare per artem.*—(g), generare per se, see *generare per accidens.*—(h), generare secundum quid and generare simpliciter *to produce something with reference to* or *according to something else* and *to produce something simply* or *absolutely,* whereby the first relates to the accident and the last to the substance.—(i), generare simpliciter, see *generare secundum quid.*—(j), generare univocum, *to generate something specifically like the generator.*—de ratione generantis est, quod generet sibi simile secundum formam, *it is of the essence of that which generates that it generates something which is similar to it according to the form through which it generates.*—non generatur aliquid ex omnino non ente, or, omne quod generatur, generatur ex materia, *nothing arises from nothing; whatever arises, arises from a previously existing matter.*—omne quod generatur oportet esse compositum ex materia et forma, *whatever comes into existence by generation must be composed of form and matter, because it comes into existence by the fact that a*

*form is introduced into previous-
ly existing matter.*—**in rebus inferioribus oportet quod generans
non sit forma tantum, sed compositum ex materia et forma,**
*that which produces something
in material things, cannot be
form alone, but rather composed
of material* and *form.*—**simile
generat sibi simile,** *everything
produces something similar to
itself.*—**unumquodque generatur
ex his, in quae resolvitur,** *everything is generated from those elements into which it is resolved.*
—**generans,** antis, *P. a., begetting, generating, producing.*—**generatus,** a, um, *P. a., begotten,
generated, produced.*

generositas, atis, *f., generosity,
goodness.*

genesis, is, *f., Genesis,* the name of
the first book of Moses (the
story of creation).

genethliacus, i, *m., a genethliatic,
a calculator of nativities.*

genetrix, icis, *f., she that has borne
anyone,* or *produced anything, a
mother.*

genitalis, e, *adj., of* or *pertaining to
generation* or *birth, causing generation* or *birth, fruitful, generative, genital.*—**genitalia,** ium, *n.,*
(sc. *membra*), *genitals, the external organs of generation.*

genitivus, a, um, *adj., genitive,* indicating source, origin, possession or the like; applied to a case
in grammar with *casus* understood, the *genitive case.*

genitor, oris, *m., a genitor, beget-
ter, father, creator.*

genitus, a, um, *P. a.,* see *gigno.*

Genovefa, ae, *f., Genevieve,* patron
saint of Paris and France, born
424 and died 512 A.D.

gens, gentis, *f.,* (1) *a race, nation,
people,* (2) opp. to Jews and
Christians, *pagan nations, heathen, gentiles,* (3) *a tribe,* in ancient states an ethnical, hereditary, or political division of a
united people, as the tribe of
Israel.

gentilis, e, *adj., gentile, pagan,* belonging to a people not Jewish
nor Christian.—**gentilis,** is, *m.,*
(1) *a gentile, heathen, pagan;*
among the Jews, a person of a
non-Jewish race or faith, one not
a Jew; among the Christians, one
who is neither Jew nor Christian, (2) plural, *the Gentiles.*

gentilitas, atis, *f.,* (1) in eccl. Lat.,
heathenism, paganism, (2) *concr.,
the heathen, pagan.*

genu, us, *n., the knee.*

genuflecto, ere, flexi, xum, 3, *v. a.*
and *n., to genuflect, kneel* as in
worship.

genuflexio, onis, *f., a genuflection,*
a bending of the knee in wor-
ship.

genus, eris, *n.,* (1) *genus, kind* in
the general sense of the word,
synonym of *generatio,* (2) *genus,
kind* in the narrower and proper
sense of the word, the opposite
of *species,* (3) *the highest genus,
category.*—Kinds of *genus* in this
(1) sense are: (a), **genus Dei,** *the*

genus of God.—(b), **genus femininum**, **genus masculinum**, and **genus neutrum**, *the masculine, the feminine,* and *the neuter gender.*—(c), **genus formatum** and **genus informe**, *the restricted genus* or *that provided with a form* and *the unrestricted* or *formless genus.*—(d), **genus humanum**, *the human genus.*—(e), **genus informe**, see *genus formatum.*—(f), **genus masculinum**, see *genus femininum.*—(g), **genus neutrum**, see *genus femininum.* —(h), **genus substantivatum**, *the genus made substantial.*—in **genere esse**, *to belong to a genus, fall under a genus.* On **alter genere**, see *alter;* on **bonitas ex genere**, see *bonitas;* on **bonum ex genere**, see *bonus;* on **communitas generis**, see *communitas;* on **differentia generis seu secundum genus**, see *differentia;* on **differre genus**, see *differre;* on **diversitas generis seu in genere seu secundum genus**, see *diversitas;* on **diversus generis**, see *diversus;* on **forma generis**, see *forma;* on **idem genere seu in natura generis**, see *idem;* on **intentio generis**, see *intentio;* on **malum ex genere**, see *malus;* on **negatio extra genus, in genere et in genere determinatio**, see *negatio;* on **nomen generis**, see *nomen;* on **oppositio in genere**, see *oppositio;* on **pars generis**, see *pars;* on **passio generis**, see *passio;* on **primum in genere aliquo**, see *primus;* on **principium primum**

in **genere**, see *principium;* on **problema de genere**, see *problema;* on **propinquitas generis**, see *propinquitas;* on **propositio prima in genere**, see *propositio;* on **prudens in aliquo genere**, see *prudens;* on **quidditas generis**, see *quidditas;* on **ratio generis**, see *ratio;* on **relatio generis**, see *relatio;* on **sapientia in aliquo genere**, see *sapientia;* on **similitudo generis**, see *similitudo;* on **unum genere seu in genere**, see *unus.*— Kinds of *genus* in this (2) sense are: (a), **genus attinentiae**, *the genus of relationship.*—(b), **genus causarum**, *the four kinds of causes.*—(c), **genus commune** and **genus speciale**, *the general* or *common genus* and *the special genus.*—(d), **genus corporeum**, *the genus of body.*—(e), **genus generalissimum** and **genus quodlibet**, *the most general genus* and *any genus whatsoever.*—(f), **genus inferius seu subalternatum** and **genus superius**, *the inferior* and *the superior genus.*—(g), **genus innominatum** and **genus nominatum**, *an unnamed* and *the named genus.*—(h), **genus intermedium seu medium, genus primum seu supremum seu remotissimum** and **genus proximum**, *the intermediate, the first* or *highest* or *most remote,* and *the genus closest to the species.*—(i), **genus logice sumptum seu logicum** and **genus naturaliter sumptum seu naturale seu physicum**, *the logical* and *the physical genus* or *the* *genus in the mind as a universal,* and *in reality.* Cf. *genus naturae.* —(j), **genus logicum,** see *genus logice sumptum.*—(k), **genus medium,** see *genus intermedium.*—(l), **genus morale seu moralium seu moris** and **genus naturae,** *the genus of morals* and *that of nature;* cf. *genus naturale.*—(m), **genus moris,** *moral matters,* see *genus morale.*—(n), **genus naturae,** see *genus morale.*—(o), **genus naturale,** see *genus logice sumptum.*—(p), **genus naturaliter sumptum,** one of the kinds of substance, corporeal, organic, etc., . . . , as in the tree of Porphyry. See *genus logice sumptum.*—(q), **genus nominatum,** see *genus innominatum.*—(r), **genus physicum,** see *genus logice sumptum.*—(s), **genus praedicabile** and **genus praedicamentale,** *predicable genus,* i.e., *a being of reason,* and *predicamental genus of real beings, like substance, quality, quantity,* etc.—(t), **genus primum,** see *genus intermedium.* —(u), **genus propinquum** and **genus remotum,** *the proximate* and *the remote genus,* calculated from individual things.—(v), **genus proximum,** see *genus intermedium.*—(w), **genus quodlibet,** see *genus generalissimum.*—(a²), **genus remotissimum,** see *genus intermedium.*—(b²), **genus remotum,** see *genus propinquum.*— (c²), **genus speciale,** see *genus commune.*—(d²), **genus subalternum,** see *genus inferius.*—(e²),

genus subiectum, *generically one subject.*—(f²), **genus superius,** see *genus inferius.*—(g²), **genus supremum,** see *genus intermedium.*—(h²), **genus univocum,** *univocal genus.* All genera are univocal because they are predicated in the same sense of their species.—**in quolibet genere quanto aliquid est prius tanto est simplicius et in paucioribus consistens,** *the higher something is reckoned in an ontological series of things belonging to the same genus, so much the simpler is it* and *so much the fewer in number.*—**non est descensus neque transitus de genere in genus,** *a descent* or *transition from one to another (metabasis eis allo genos) is not allowed.*—**actus et potentia dividunt quodlibet genus entium,** see *actus* under (2).—**unumquodque genus dividitur per potentiam et actum,** see *actus* under (2).

geomantia, ae, *f.*, *geomancy,* divination by means of some aspect of the earth, particularly by the observation of points and lines on the earth, or on paper, or by means of the figures formed by pebbles or particles of earth thrown at random.

geometer, tri, (also **geometra,** ae), *m.*, *a geometer, a geometrician.*

geometra, ae, *m.*, see *geometer.*

geometria, ae, *f.*, *geometry,* the mathematics of continuous quantity.

geometricalis, e, *adj., geometrical, of* or *pertaining to geometry, according to the rules* or *principles of geometry.*

geometricus, a, um, *geometric, geometrical, of* or *belonging to geometry.* On **aequalitas geometrica,** see *aequalitas;* on **medium geometricum,** see *medium;* on **proportio geometrica,** see *proportio.*

Germani, orum, *m., the Germans.*

Germanus, i, *m., Germanus,* bishop of Capua, sent with other legates in 519 to Constantinople by Pope Hormisdas. They were instructed to hold communion with no one who would not sign the Libellus, which contained the condemnation of the patriarch Acacius and his successors, Euphemius and Macedonius, on the ground of their unorthodoxy in the matter of Monophysitism. Hormisdas wrote several letters to Germanus and his companions.

germen, inis, *n.,* (1) in the plural, *crops, fruits,* (2) *a sowing,* the act or process of scattering or depositing, as seed, on or in the ground for reproduction, used *fig.*

germinatio, onis, *f., a germination, bringing forth, sprouting.*

germinativus, a, um, *adj., shooting forth, sprouting, germinative.*

germino, are, avi, atum, 1, *v. n.* and *a.,* (1) *neutr.,* to sprout, germinate, (2) *act.,* to beget, produce, (a) *lit.,* (b) *fig.*

gero, ere, gessi, gestum, 3, *v. a.,* (1) *lit., to bear about with one, to bear, carry, to wear, have,* (2) *fig.,* (a) *to bear, cherish, entertain,* (b) *to portray, represent,* (c) *gerere se, to deport, bear, behave* or *conduct one's self* in any manner, (d) with the accessory idea of activity or exertion, to sustain the charge of any undertaking or business, *to administer, manage, regulate, rule, govern, conduct, carry on, wage, transact, accomplish, perform* (cf. facio, ago)—in *pass.* also in gen., *to happen, take place, be done.*—Common phrases are: **gerere vicem baptismatis,** *to take the place of baptism.*—**gerere in proposito,** *to have the intention.* —**gerere vicem Dei,** *to take the place of God.*—**gerere personam,** *to sustain the character, play the part, impersonate.*—**gerere vicem apostolorum,** *to take the place of the apostles.*—**gerere figuram Christi,** *to take the place of Christ.*—**gerere typum Christi,** *to represent Christ.*—Common phrases are: **gerere bellum,** *to wage war.*—**gerere curam reipublicae,** *to have charge of the commonwealth.*—**gerere providentiam,** *to exercise providence.*—**gerere curam boni communis,** *to take care of the common good.*—**gerere sollicitudinem de custodia alicuius,** *to be guardian to someone.*—**gerere procurationem alicuius,** *to sustain the charge of anything.*—**ge-**

rere saecularia negotia, *to transact secular business.*—gerere curam alicuius, *to take care of,*
or *have charge of some person*
or *thing.*—res gesta, *a deed.*—
res gestae, *events, occurrences,
deeds.*—gestum, i, *n., an occurrence, happening, a fact.*—gesta,
orum, *n., deeds, acts, accom-
plishments.*

gerundium, ii, *n.,* in *gram., a ger-
und.*

gesta, orum, *n.,* see *gero.*

gesticulatio, onis, *f., a gesticulation, a motion of the body* or
limbs.

gestio, ire, ivi, or ii, itum, 4, *to
exult, rejoice.*—gestiens, entis, *P.
a., exulting, rejoicing.*

gesto, are, avi, atum, 1, *v. freq. a.*
and *n., to bear, carry, have,* (1)
lit., (2) *fig.*

gestus, us, *m., the bearing,* i.e.,
motion of the body, esp. of the
hand or arm, *carriage, posture,
attitude, motion, gesture.*

Geth, *indecl. n., Geth,* one of the
five strongest towns of the Philistines in the plain of Sephela,
the others being Gaza, Azot, As-
calon, and Accaron.

gibbus, i, *m., a hump, a protuberance,* especially that caused by a
curved spine or a fleshy growth
on the back.

Giezi, *indecl., n., m., Giezi,* the
servant of Eliseus who received
money from the leper who had
been healed.

Giezitae, arum, *m., the Giezites,* a
synonym of *simonists,* the sellers

of spiritual things. The word is
derived from Giezi, the disciple
of Eliseus (4 Kings V. 20-24),
who received money from the
leper who had been healed.

gigas, antis, *m., a giant.*

gigno, ere, genui, genitum, 3, *to
beget, bear, bring forth, produce.*—genitus, a, um, *P. a., produced, born;* used substantively,
son or *daughter,* synonym of *filius* and *natus;* the opposite of *ingenitus.* On sapientia genita, see
sapientia.

Gilbertus, i, *m., Gilbertus Porretanus, Gilbert de la Porree,* bishop
of Poitiers, philosopher, theologian, and general scholar; born
at Poitiers in 1076. He studied
under Hilary in Poitiers, under
Bernard of Chartres and finally under Anselm at Laon. His
teaching regarding the Blessed
Trinity involved him in trouble
for a time; the dispute, however, ended amicably without
any very definite issue. Gilbert
died universally regretted in
1154.

glacialis, e, *adj., icy, frozen, full
of ice.*

glacies, ei, *f., ice.*

gladius, ii, *m., a sword,* used (1)
lit., (2) *fig.*

globus, i, *m., globe, sphere, region,* synonym of *circulus, orbis,* and *sphaera.*

gloria, ae, *f.,* (1) *glory, renown,
splendor, glorification,* the opposite of *ignominia,* (2) *heavenly
splendor, supernatural glorifica-*

tion. On the difference between *gloria* and *honor,* see *honor.—* Kinds of *gloria* in this (1) sense are: (a), **gloria caelestis seu patriae,** *the heavenly splendor* or *the splendor of the heavenly fatherland.—*(b), **gloria Dei seu divina** and **gloria mundana,** *the splendor of God* and *that of the world* or *the divine* and *the worldly splendor.—*(c), **gloria divina,** see *gloria Dei.—*(d), **gloria inanis seu vana** and **gloria vera,** *the vain* and *the true glory.—*(e), **gloria mundana,** see *gloira Dei.* —(f), **gloria naturalis** and **gloria spiritualis** (Ps. 7 b), *the natural* and *the spiritual glory of man,* namely, his likeness with God and his good conscience.—(g), **gloria patriae,** see *gloria caelestis.—*(h), **gloria spiritualis,** see *gloria naturalis.—*(i), **gloria supererogationis,** *the glory of having accomplished something above the required* or *the necessary.—*(j), **gloria vana,** see *gloria inanis.—*(k), **gloria vera,** see *gloria inanis.—*(l), **gloria vitae aeternae,** *the glory of eternal life.—* The offspring (*filiae*) of *inanis gloria,* which is one of the seven capital sins and is distinguished from *superbia* are: inoboedientia, iactania, hypocrisis, contentio, pertinacia, discordia, novitatum praesumptio. On **bonum gloriae,** see *bonus;* on **claritas gloriae,** see *claritas;* on **cognitio gloriae,** see *cognitio;* on **comprehensio gloriae,** see *com-*

prehensio; on **dilectio gloriae,** see *dilectio;* on **dominus gloriae,** see *dominus;* on **donum gloriae,** see *donum;* on **esse gloria,** see *esse;* on **imago gloriae,** see *imago;* on **immortalitas gloriae,** see *immortalitas;* on **impassibilitas gloriae,** see *impassibilitas;* on **incorruptibile secundum gloriam,** see *incorruptibilis;* on **libertas gloriae,** see *libertas;* on **lumen gloriae seu divinae gloriae,** see *lumen;* on **lux gloriae,** see *lux;* on **operatio gloriae,** see *operatio;* on **perfectio gloriae,** see *perfectio;* on **potestas gloriae,** see *potestas;* on **retributio gloriae,** see *retributio;* on **similitudo gloriae,** see *similitudo;* on **status gloriae seu gloriae consummatae,** see *status;* on **visio gloriae,** see *visio;* on **vita gloriae,** see *vita.—*Kinds of *gloria* in this sense are: (a), **gloria accidentalis** and **gloria essentialis,** *the accidental* or *unessential* and *the essential glory in heaven.—*(b), **gloria animae seu spiritualis** and **gloria corporis seu corporalis,** *the heavenly glorification of the soul* and *that of the body* or *the spiritual* and *the physical heavenly glorification.—* (c), **gloria claritatis,** *the heavenly glorification that consists of the brightness* and *radiance of the body.—*(d), **gloria corporalis,** see *gloria animae.—*(e), **gloria corporis,** see *gloria animae.—*(f), **gloria creata,** *the created heavenly glory.* Cf. Verit. 29. 1 a.—(g), **gloria essentialis,** see *gloria acci-*

dentalis.—(h), **gloriae finalis seu futura,** *the final* or *future glory.* —(i), **gloria futura,** see *gloria finalis.*—(j), **gloria perfecta,** *the complete* or *perfect heavenly glory.*—(k), **gloria spiritualis,** see *gloria animae.*

gloriatio, onis, *f., a boasting, vaunting.*

glorificatio, onis, *f., glorification, glory.*

glorifico, are, avi, atum, 1, *v. a.,* (1) *to glorify, magnify* and *honor* as in worship; *exalt in thought* and *speech; give* or *ascribe glory to; adore, worship,* (2) *to glorify, to exalt to a state of glory, raise to power* and *happiness; uplift to celestial honor* and *blessedness.*—**glorificatus,** a, um, *P. a., glorified,* used in the phrase, **glorificatum corpus,** *a glorified body,* a revivified body in its new state of existence after it has risen from the dead. It is distinguished by four transcendent qualities, viz. *impassibility,* which places it beyond the reach of pain and inconvenience; *brightness* or *glory,* by which it shines like the sun; *agility,* the capability of the body to move with the utmost facility and quickness wherever the soul pleases; and *subtility* by which the body becomes subject to the absolute dominion of the soul. St. Thomas speaks of **glorificatus oculus, glorificata anima, glorificatus homo, glorificata na-**

tura, **glorificata caro,** all synonyms of **glorificatum corpus.**

glorior, ari, atus, 1, *v. dep. a.* and *n., to glory, rejoice, boast, pride one's self* on anything, used with (1) *de, in* and *abl.,* (2) *abl.* alone, (3) and *ad* with the *acc.*

gloriosus, a, um, *adj.,* (1) *famous, glorious, renowned,* (2) *elevated to heavenly glory, celestially glorified.*—On **claritas gloriosa,** see *claritas;* on **corpus gloriosum,** see *corpus;* on **incorruptibilitas corporis gloriosa,** see *incorruptibilitas;* on **resurrectio gloriosa,** see *resurrectio;* on **virgo gloriosa,** see *virgo;* on **visio gloriosa,** see *visio;* on **vita gloriosa,** see *vita.*

glossa, ae, *f., a gloss,* a note or comment especially a marginal or interlinear note explanatory of something obscure, obsolete or foreign in the text. The Glosses to which St. Thomas makes frequent references are Scriptural Commentaries. Chief among them are the *Glossa Ordinaria* of Walafrid Strabo (ob. 849), and the *Glossa Interlinearis* of Anselm of Laon (ob. 1117). The Glossa Ordinaria is so called from its common use during the Middle Ages; it was known as "the tongue of the Scripture." The Glossa Interlinearis derives its name from the fact that it was written over the words in the text of the Vulgate.—**Glossa Ordinaria,** *the Ordinary Gloss,* the one commonly used.—**Glossa Interlinearis,** *an interlinear gloss.*

gluten, inis, *n.* and **glutinum,** i, *n.,* (1) *lit., gluten,* an albuminoid or protein compound substance found in animal matter; *coagulable, lymph,* (2) *transf., a bond, connecting tie.*

glutinum, i, *n.,* see *gluten.*

gnome, es, *f., aptitude* or *ability to judge rightly over the extraordinary things of life,* synonym of *eugnomosyne.*

Godolias, ae, *m., Godolias,* the son of Ahicam, slain by Ismahel and his followers in Masphath.

Golgotha, *indecl. n., Golgotha,* the place outside Jerusalem where Christ was crucified. The Latin *calvaria* is a translation of the Greek *kranion* of the Evangelists, which is an interpretation of the Hebrew Gulgoleth meaning skull.

Gonsaldus, i, *m., Gonsaldus,* a priest mentioned in the Decretals of Gregory IX (XVII, qu. ii. can. Gonsaldus) who under pressure of sickness and emotional fervor promised to become a monk but when restored to health refused to keep his promise. St. Thomas uses this instance in discussing the obligation following such promises.

gradatim, *adv., by degrees, step by step, little by little, gradually.*

gradior, i, gressus, 3, *v. dep. n., to step, walk go.*

graduale, is, *n., the Gradual,* the response and versicle to the Epistle, so called because formerly at High Mass it was sung on the step (gradus) of the altar. It ordinarily accentuates something in the Epistle, and is taken, except in rare cases, from Scripture, mostly from the Psalms.

gradus, us, *m.,* (1) *grade, degree* in the narrower and in the wider sense of the word, *step,* (2) *grade* in the mathematical and in the astronomical sense.—On **diversitas gradus,** see *diversitas.* —Kinds of *gradus* are: (a), **gradus affinitatis** and **gradus consanguinitatis,** *the degree of affinity by marriage* and *that of blood relationship.*—(b), **gradus attinentiae seu propinquitatis,** *the degree of propinquity* or *relationship.*—(c), **gradus consanguinitatis,** see *gradus affinitatis,* —(d), **gradus ecclesiasticus,** *the ecclesiastical grade.* Cf. Eph. 4. 4.—(e), **gradus essendi,** *degree of existence.*—(f), **gradus in bonitate,** *the grade of good.*—(g), **gradus propinquitatis,** see *gradus attinentiae.*—(h), **gradus vitae,** *the degree of life.*—(i), **gradus viventium,** *the degree of living beings.*

Graece, *adv.,* see *Graeci.*

Graeci, orum, *m., the Grecians, Greeks.*—**Graecus,** a, um, *adj., of* or *belonging to the Greeks, Greek, Grecian.*—**Graecum,** i, *n., the Greek language, Greek.*— **Graece,** *adv., in the Greek language, in Greek.*

Graecum, i, *n.,* see *Graeci.*

Graecus, a, um, *adj,.* see *Graeci.*

grammatica, ae, *f., grammar.*

grammaticalis, e, *adj., of* or *pertaining to grammar, grammatical.*

grammatice, *adv., grammatically, according to the rules of grammar.*

grammaticus, i, *m., a grammarian.*

granatum, i, *n., a pomegranate.*

grandis, e, *adj., full-grown, large, big, great.*

grandiusculus, a, um, *adj., dim., fairly well grown up.*

grando, inis, *f., hail, a hail-storm.*

granum, i, *n., grain, seed.*

grassor, ari, atus, 1, *v. dep. n.* and *a., to rage against, attack, proceed against.*

grate, *adv.,* see *gratus.*

gratia, ae, *f.,* (1) in the wide sense, a quality which renders the recipient pleasing or favorable, *favor,* or that which is freely given, *grace,* (2) in a restricted sense, any gift of God, whether due to nature, or above it, and usually and most properly *a supernatural gift of God to a rational creature for the purpose of eternal salvation.* The notion of grace is an analogical one and has many applications in St. Thomas. Created grace is either ˙granted for the sanctification of the individual or for the sanctification of others. This latter, called *gratia gratis data,* comprehends the charismatic gifts described by St. Paul and com-

mon in the early Church, the gift, or grace, of tongues, interpretation, miracles, healing, prophecy, etc., treated by St. Thomas in SS. Q. 171, ff. The former, called *gratia gratum faciens,* is either habitual or actual. Habitual or *sanctifying grace* is a permanent quality inherent in the essence of the soul giving it a share in the divine nature. This grace brings with it other permanent qualities which supernaturalize the faculties of the soul, like the infused theological and moral virtues, the gifts of the Holy Ghost, and the sacramental characters in the practical intellect. *Actual grace* is a supernatural and transient quality conferred by God to elicit supernatural acts. This is sufficient grace if its effect is the capacity to act; efficacious if its effect is the act itself. Grace is also variously called *exciting* or *assisting,* from its relation to some good object; *operating* and *cooperating,* from its relation to some effect; *prevenient* and *concomitant,* according to the effect of grace in us; *internal* or *external; healing* and *elevating.* All grace after the fall of Adam is the *grace of Christ* as distinct from the *grace of God* which the Angels and Adam enjoyed, (3) *grace per eminentiam,* uncreated grace, God Himself, or the Holy Ghost, (4) *thanks, gratitude.*—On **agens per gratiam,** see *agens;* on **revelatio gratiae,** see *revelatio.*—**plenitudo gratiae,** *the fullness of sanctifying grace.* On **bonum gratiae,** see *bonus;* on **cognitio gratiae,** see *cognitio;* on **donum gratiae,** see *donum;* on **esse gratiae,** see *esse;* on **habitus gratiae,** see *habitus;* on **imago gratiae,** see *imago;* on **incorruptibile per donum gratiae,** see *incorruptibilis;* on **invidia fraternae gratiae,** see *invidia;* on **iustitia gratiae,** see *iustitia;* on **lex gratiae,** see *lex;* on **lumen gratiae,** see *lumen;* on **perfectio gratiae,** see *perfectio;* on **puritas per gratiam,** see *puritas;* on **radix gratiae,** see *radix;* on **sacramentum gratiae et plenitudinis gratiae,** see *sacramentum;* on **similitudo gratiae,** see *similitudo;* on **spiritus gratiae,** see *spiritus;* on **status gratiae,** see *status;* on **veritas gratiae,** see *veritas;* on **vita gratiae,** see *vita.*—Kinds of *gratia* in this (2) sense are: (a), **gratia adoptionis,** *the grace of adoption.*—(b), **gratia capitis** and **gratia personalis,** *the grace of the head* and *personal grace,* i.e., the grace which Jesus possesses as Head of the Church and the grace which He possesses in His human nature.—(c), **gratia comprehensoris** and **gratia viatoris,** *the grace of one who enjoys the goal attained* and *that of the pilgrim on earth.*—(d), **gratia consummata seu perfecta** and **gratia imperfecta,** *the complete or perfect grace, which consists in the glory of heaven* and *the imperfect grace.*—(e), **gratia cooperans,** *the cooperating* and *the operating grace.*—(f), **gratia creata,** *the created grace,* the opposite of God, *the uncreated grace.* Cf. *gratia* under (3).—(g), **gratia curationum seu sanitatum,** *the charismatic grace of healing the sick.*—(h), **gratia donorum, gratia sacramentalis seu sacramentorum** and **gratia virtutum,** *the grace of the gifts of the Holy Ghost, the grace of the sacraments* and *the grace of the virtues,* i.e., the grace which consists in the infusion of the gifts of the Holy Ghost, that which is dispensed through the sacraments, and that which consists in the infused virtues. Cf. *donum* under (2), and *virtus* under (4). —(i), **gratia fidei,** *the grace of faith* or *that which consists of faith.*—(j), **gratia finalis,** *the grace bestowed at the end of life* or *that lasting until the end of life.* —(k), **gratia finita** and **gratia infinita,** *the finite* and *the infinitely great grace.*—(l), **gratia gratis data** and **gratia gratum faciens,** *the undeservedly* (for the use of others) *given grace* and *the grace that makes the man who receives it pleasing to God,* charismatic and personal grace.—(m), **gratia gratum faciens,** see *gratia gratis data.*—(n), **gratia habitualis,** *the habitual* or *sanctifying grace,* which is opposed to **gratia actualis** or **auxilium gratiae,** i.e., the permanent quality of soul rendering it pleasing to God.—(o), gratia **imperfecta**, *the grace of this life*. See *gratia consummata*. —(p), gratia **infinita**, see *gratia finita*.—(q), gratia **iustificans seu sanctificans seu reparans**, *the justifying* or *sanctifying grace* or *the grace that restores all different effects of grace*.—(r), gratia **linguarum seu locutionis**, *the charismatic grace of languages* or *speech*, of like meaning with *donum linguarum*.—(s), gratia **locutionis**, see *gratia linguarum*.—(t), gratia **miraculorum seu signorum**, *the charismatic grace of miracles* or *of the working of miracles*.—(u), gratia **operans**, *operative grace*, the source of justification. See *gratia cooperans*.—(v), gratia **patriae** and gratia **viae**, *the grace of the heavenly fatherland* and *that on the way to the same*.—(w), gratia **perfecta**, see *gratia consummata*. —(x), gratia **personalis**, see *gratia capitis*.—(y), gratia **plenissima seu gratia plenitudinis**, *the fullest grace* or *grace in its entire fullness*. Cf. *plenitudo gratiae*.—(z), gratia **plenitudinis**, see *gratia plenissima*.—(a²), gratia **praeveniens** and gratia **subsequens**, *the antecedent* and *the subsequent grace*.—(b²), gratia **privilegiata**, *grace in the manner of a privilege*.—(c²), gratia **prophetalis seu prophetiae**, *the charismatic grace of prophecy*, of the same meaning as *donum prophe-*

tale.—(d²), gratia **reparans**, *sanctifying grace restoring man to God's favor*. See *gratia iustificans*.—(e²), gratia **sacramentalis seu sacramentorum**, *sacramental grace*. See *gratia donorum*.—(f), gratia **sanctificans**, *sanctifying* or *habitual grace viewed from its primary effect of rendering man holy*. See *gratia iustificans*.—(g²), gratia **sanitatum**, see *gratia curationum*.—(h²), gratia **sermonis sapientiae et scientiae**, *the charismatic grace of the speech of wisdom* and *of the speech of science*, of like meaning with a certain kind of *donum sapientiae et scientiae*.—(i²), gratia **signorum**, see *gratia miraculorum*. —(j²), gratia **singularis**, *the singular* or *special grace*.—(k²), gratia **spiritualis**, *the spiritual grace* or *the grace given to man*, which forms the opposite of *gratia corporalis*, *the grace bestowed upon the body*—(l²), gratia **subsequens**, see *gratia praecedens*.— (m²), gratia **unionis**, *the grace of the union of the human* and *the divine nature of Christ in one person*.—(n²), gratia **viatoris**, see *gratia comprehensoris*.—(o²), gratia **virtutum**, *the infused virtues of faith, hope* and *charity*, and *the infused moral virtues*. See *gratia donorum*. On **confessio gratiarum actionis**, see *confessio*. —**gratis**, *adv.*, *out of favour* or *kindness*, without recompense or reward, *for nothing, gratuitously, gratis*, synonym of *gratuito*.

Gratianopolitanus, a, um, *adj., of Gratianopolis,* a city in Gallia Narbonensis, now Grenoble in Dauphine.

Gratianus, i, *m., Gratian.*—(1) Roman Emperor, son of Valentinian I; born at Sermium, 359; died at Lyons, 383. Before he had attained his ninth year he received the purple robe and diadem with the title of Augustus, and on the death of his father, he became Emperor of the West. Gratian's reign marks a distinct epoch in the transition of the empire from paganism to Christianity. At the time of his accession (375) he refused the insignia of pontifex maximus, which even Constantine and the other emperors had accepted. At the instance of St. Ambrose, who became his chief adviser, he caused the statue of Victory to be removed from the senate house at Rome (382). It was for Gratian that St. Ambrose wrote his great treatise.—(2) *Gratian,* John, a monk and professor at the University of Bologna, c. 1150. The **Decretum Gratiani,** *the Decretal of Gratian* was a collection of canonical decrees and excerpts from the Fathers and from Roman Law published by Gratian on his private authority. Before his time there were many decrees of particular councils in the East, in Africa, Spain, and Gaul. Gratian sought to bring order into these various collections, adding brief comments and intending it as a text for the great law school at Bologna. It forms part of the Corpus Iuris Canonici.

gratificatio, onis, *f., a showing kindness, doing favors, bestowing grace* on anyone.

gratifico, are, avi, atum, 1, *v. n.* and *a., to make pleasing, gratify.*

gratiositas, atis, *f., agreeableness, graciousness.*

gratiosus, a, um, *adj., pleasing, agreeable, in favor, beloved, popular, regarded.*

gratis, *adv.,* see *gratia.*

gratitudo, inis, *f., gratitude, a sense of appreciation of favors received, an emotion* or *sentiment of thankfulness, the state of being grateful,* a synonym of *gratia.*

gratuito, *adv.,* see *gratuitus.*

gratuitus, a, um, *adj., that is done without pay* or *reward* or *profit, free, spontaneous, voluntary, gratuitous.*—**gratuito,** *adv., without pay* or *profit, for naught, gratis,* synonym of *gratis.* On **accidens gratuitum,** see *accidens;* on **amor gratuitus,** see *amor;* on **cognitio gratuita,** see *cognitio;* on **dilectio gratuita,** see *dilectio;* on **dispositio gratuita,** see *dispositio;* on **donum gratuitum,** see *donum;* on **electio gratuita,** see *electio;* on **esse gratuitum,** see *esse;* on **fortitudo gratuita,** see *fortitudo;* on **habitus gratuitus,** see *habitus;* on **iustitia gratuita,** see *iustitia;* on **lumen gratui-**

tum, see *lumen;* on **prudentia gratuita,** see *prudentia;* on **virtus gratuita,** see *virtus;* on **voluntas gratuita,** see *voluntas.*

gratus, a, um, *adj.,* (1) *pass., beloved, dear, acceptable, pleasing, agreeable,* (2) *act., thankful, grateful; thankworthy, deserving* or *procuring thanks.*—Numerous instances occur in the *Summa* of phrases containing *gratum,* **gratia gratum faciens,** *ingratiating grace, sanctifying grace, the grace which renders the possessor pleasing to God.*— **grate,** *adv., with pleasure, agreeably, willingly.*

gravamen, inis, *n., trouble, burden, physical inconvenience.*

gravedo, inis, *f., weight, heaviness of the limbs.*

gravidus, a, um, *adj., pregnant,* used *lit.* and *fig.*

gravis, e, *adj.,* (1) *lit.,* with respect to weight, *heavy, weighty, ponderous, burdensome,* (a) in *gen.,* (b) in *partic.,* for the usual *gravidus, with young, pregnant,* (c) of the state of bodily sickness, *grave, serious, dangerous,* (2) *fig.,* (a) in a bad sense, *grave,* used to delineate the character of things, *burdensome, grievous, painful, severe,* (b) in a good sense, with respect to character, *serious-minded, grave* in disposition, manner or character.—Common phrases are: **gravis poena,** *severe punishment.*—**grave peccatum,** *a grave sin, of a serious nature, grievous.*—**gravis cu-**

ra, *a grave responsibility.*—**grave nocumentum,** *a grave injury.*— **gravis turbatio,** *a grave disturbance.*—**grave crimen,** *an enormous crime.*—**gravis populus,** *a serious-minded people.*—**graviter,** *adv., grievously, severely, deeply,* used *lit.* and *fig.*

gravitas, atis, *f.,* (1) *lit.,* (a) *weight, heaviness,* (b) *gravity,* the degree of intensity with which one body is affected by the attraction of gravitation exercised by another body, (2) *fig.,* (a) *gravity,* the quality of being charged with or involving great consequences; *atrocity, seriousness; enormity,* (b) *seriousness, solemnity, dignity of character, sobriety of demeanor,* used of persons and things, (c) *labor, care, trouble, annoyance.*

graviter, *adv.,* see *gravis.*

gravo, are, avi, atum, 1, *v. a.,* (1) *lit., to load, burden, weigh down, oppress,* (2) *fig., to burden, oppress, incommode, aggravate.*

gregalis, e, *adv., gregarious, not habitually living alone.*

gregatim, *adv., in flocks* or *herds.*

Gregorius, ii, (1) *Gregory I* (the Great), Saint, Pope, and Doctor of the Church, born at Rome in 540. The Pontificate of this Pope (590-604) presents one of the most imposing features in the history of the Church. He adopted the title "servus servorum" which his successors have retained. Though a member of a wealthy family, Gregory, following the call of God, exchanged his costly vesture for the habit of St. Benedict, and relinquished his palace for a cloister, in which he lived with some monks until Pope Pelagius sent him as apocrisiarius to Constantinople, a position he occupied for six years, after which he became Abbot of his monastery, from which the voice of the clergy and of the people alike called him forth to occupy the chair of St. Peter. St. Thomas quotes freely from his *Moralium* Libri XXXV, or Commentary on the Book of Job, and also from his *Regulae Pastoralis Liber; Dialogorum Libri II; Homiliarum in Evangelia Libri II; Registrum Epistolarum,* and *Libri duo in Ezechielem.* St. Thomas also quotes from the *Gregorian Sacramentary* which is not entirely the work of Gregory, (2) *Gregory II,* Saint, Pope (715-731), born at Rome and died there. He is the first papal almoner or librarian known to us by name. As pope, he upheld the primacy of the Holy See, and opposed the iconoclastic edicts of Leo the Isaurian, while at the same time giving him the allegiance due to a temporal sovereign. His opposition to the Byzantine Empire brought the Lombards in union with the papacy. He sent St. Boniface to Germany, and re-

paired Monte Cassino and the walls of Rome, (3) *Gregory III,* Saint, Pope, born at Syria and died at Rome. A renowned ecclesiastical administrator, he continued the struggle against Iconoclasm, opposed the Lombards, aided foreign missions, and completed the restoration of the walls of Rome. St. Thomas quotes a letter of his to St. Boniface which is ascribed to *Gregory II,* (4) *Gregory VII* (Hildebrand), Saint, Pope (1073-1085), born at Saona, Italy and died at Salerno. He entered the Benedictine Order. He strove to stamp out clerical simony and incontinence and enacted decrees against these abuses at his first Lenten Synod (1074). St. Thomas refers to his *Registri sive Epistolarum libri* (S.T., SS. Q. 100 Art. 1 ob. 1), (5) *Gregory of Nazianzus,* Saint, Doctor of the Church, was born at Nazianzus, Asia Minor about 325, and died there in 369 A.D. He was bishop of Constantinople at the time of the First General Council held at that place. St. Thomas quotes three of his orations 17, 39, 40, one of his epistles *ad Cledonium,* and his *Carmen XXXVIII de Genealogia Christi,* (6) *Gregory of Nyssa,* Saint, Confessor, Father of the Church was born at Sebaste, Asia Minor in 331. He was the brother of SS. Basil and Macrina. St. Thomas quotes from *De Hominis Opificio* (*De*

Homine), *De Occursu Domini,
De Christi Resurrectione oratio
I; De iis qui in fide dormierunt,*
ascribed to St. John Damascene.
St. Thomas ascribed to him, *De
Providentia, De Anima,* and *De
Natura Hominis,* works of Nemesius, probably Bishop of
Emesa, an author imbued with
Neoplatonic ideas.

gremium, ii, *n., the lap, bosom,*
used *lit.* and *fig.*

gressibilis, e, *adj., ambulatory, having the power of walking* or *moving about.*

gressivus, a, um, *adj., gressorial, adapted for walking.*

gressus, us, *m., a stepping, going, step, course, way.*

grex, gregis, *m.,* (1) *lit., a flock, herd, a company* or *collection of animals,* particularly of small animals, as sheep, goats, etc., (2) *fig.,* (a), *a flock,* the persons belonging to a congregation, church, parish or diocese as under the care of their special guide or pastor, (b) *a flock, multitude, great numbers of anything.*

grossities, ei, *f.,* (1) *grossness, bigness, as of matter,* (2) *coarseness,* the state of being formed of coarse particles.

grossus, a, um, *adj.,* (1) *lit.,* (a) *gross, thick, big, bulky,* (b) *gross,* wanting in fineness, coarse in composition, (c) *thick,* closely compacted so as to be thick or dense, as smoke, (2) *fig.,* (a) *stupid,* wanting in delicacy of

perception, (b) *gross,* not specific or detailed, *general.*

grus, gruis *f., a crane.*

gryps, gryphis, *m., a griffin, a fanciful creature,* half lion and half eagle reputed to be the offspring of a lion and an eagle.

gubernaculum, i, *n., a helm, rudder,* used *fig.*

gubernatio, onis, *f.,* (1) *directing, guidance, governing, government,* (2) *divine guidance* of the world.

gubernativus, a, um, *leading guiding, governing, directing.* On **ars gubernativa,** see *ars;* on **causa gubernativa,** see *causa.*

gubernator, oris, *m.,* (1) *lit., a steersman, pilot, captain of a ship,* (2) *transf., a director, ruler, governor.*

gubernatorius, a, um, *adj., gubernatorial, of* or *pertaining to the office of guiding* or *directing anything.*

guberno, are, avi, atum, 1, *v. a.,* (1) *lit., to steer* or *pilot a ship,* (2) *trans.,* in *gen., to direct, manage, conduct, govern, guide.*

Guilisarius, ii, (**Belisarius,** ii), *m., Guilisarius* or *Belisarius,* a Byzantine general who in 537 caused the exile of Pope Silverius. Cf. article Silverius, Pope, in Cath. Encyc., also letter II of Pope Silverius in Migne, P.L. Cf. SS. Q. 108. Art. 1 ad 4.

gula, ae, *f., gluttony, gormandizing,* the opposite of *abstinentia* and *temperantia. Gula* is one of the seven capital sins. Cf. SS. Q.

148. Art. 5 c. Cf. also vitium under (2). Its *filiae* are the following: *inepta laetitia, scurrilitas, immunditia, multiloquium,* and *hebetudo circa intelligentiam.* Cf. SS. Q. 148. Art. 6 c and ad 1-3; Mal. 14. 4 c. On **deformitas gulae,** see *deformitas.*

gulose, *adv.,* see *gulosus.*

gulosus, a, um, *adj., gluttonous.—* **gulose,** *gluttonously.*

gurges, itis, *m., transf., a stream.*

gustabilis, e, *adj., appetizing, exciting appetite.*

gusto, are, avi, atum, 1, *v. a., to taste, partake of, enjoy,* used *fig.* —**gustans,** antis, *P. a., tasting of food,* used *lit.*

gustus, us, *m.,* (1) *taste,* the particular sensation excited when a soluble substance is brought in contact with certain parts of the mouth, particularly the tongue, used (a) *lit.,* (b) *fig.,* (2) *taste* that one of the senses which responds to its adequate stimulus with gustatory sensations and which thus gives the perception of the savors and flavors of different things. Since the adequate stimulus of taste is chemical, only soluble substances, as far as known, have any taste. The specific end-organs or receptors of this sense are the so-called gustatory buds or taste buds situated chiefly on the upper surface and edges of the tongue, but also to some extent on the soft palate and larynx. The sensory nerve fibers which supply these organs come from three of the cranial nerves, (3) *taste, liking,* a preference for anything, (4) *taste,* the act of perceiving the flavor of by the sense of taste.

gutta, ae, *f., a drop of a fluid, a drop.*

guttur, uris, *n., the throat.*

gyrus, i, *m., a circle.*

H

Habacuc, *indecl. n., m., Habacuc,* the eighth of the minor Prophets who probably flourished towards the end of the seventh century B.C. He foretold the captivity of the Jews and the fall of the Assyrian empire. The Book of Habacuc in the Old Testament contains the prophecies of Habacuc, foretelling, as a thing incredible to Juda, the invasion of the Chaldeans.

habeo, ere, ui, itum, 2, *v. a.* and *n., to have* in the widest sense of the word, *hold, keep, possess, cherish, entertain, say, occupy, enclose, contain.—***habens,** entis, *P. a., having, possessing, enclosing, containing.—***habitus,** a, um, *P. a.,* (1) *held* or *kept* in a certain condition, *had* or *possessed,* (2) *following something immediately* or *touching it,* the *echomenos* of Aristotle.—On **bonum habi-**

tum, see *bonus.*—On **medium ha-bitum**, see *medium.*

habilis, e, *adj., apt, fit, expert, skillful.*

habilitas, atis, *f., ability, skill, aptitude,* synonym of *habilitatio.*

habilitatio, onis, *f., skillfulness, facility,* synonym of *habilitas,* not used in the S.T.

habilito, are, avi, 1, *v. a., to habilitate, make fit* or *suitable.*

habitabilis, e, *adj., habitable, fit to be inhabited* or *dwelt in, inhabitable.*

habitaculum, i, *n., a dwelling place, habitation.*

habitatio, onis, *f., dwelling, inhabiting, habitation.*

habitator, oris, *m.,* (1) *a dweller in a house, an occupant, tenant* (2) *transf., an inhabitant of a country.*

habito, are, avi, atum, 1, *v. freq. a.* and *n.,* (1) *act., to have possession of, to inhabit a place,* (2) *neutr., to dwell, abide, reside, live anywhere.*

habitualis, e, *adj., being neutral, not active,* but strongly disposed to a particular activity, *that which has assumed the character of a habitus,* i.e., *of a lasting state, habitual,* the opposite of *actualis* and *virtualis.* On **caritas habitualis**, see *caritas;* on **cognitio habitualis**, see *cognitio;* on **concupiscentia habitualis**, see *concupiscentia;* on **continuitas habitualis**, see *continuitas;* on **cupiditas habitualis**, see *cupiditas;* on **dispositio habitualis**, see

dispositio; on **forma habitualis**, see *forma;* on **gratia habitualis**, see *gratia;* on **intellectus habitualis**, see *intellectus;* on **intentio habitualis**, see *intentio;* on **libido habitualis**, see *libido;* on **lumen habituale**, see *lumen;* on **malitia habitualis**, see *malitia;* on **ordinatio habitualis**, see *ordinatio;* on **paupertas habitualis**, see *paupertas;* on **perfectio habitualis**, see *perfectio;* on **potentia habitualis**, see *potentia;* on **respectus habitualis**, see *respectus;* on **scientia habitualis**, see *scientia;* on **voluntas habitualis**, see *voluntas.* —**habitualiter**, *adv., according to the state* or *condition, in an habitual manner,* in a state not actual, nor yet purely potential, but potentially determined, the opposite of *actualiter* and of *virtualiter.* On **cognoscere habitualiter**, see *cognoscere.*

habitualiter, *adv.,* see *habitualis.*

habitudinalis, e, *adj., proportional, relative, respective.*

habitudo, inis, *f., condition, plight, habit, appearance, relation, respect,* synonym of *intentio, ratio,* and *relatio.* On **cognoscere secundum habitudinem principii**, see *cognoscere.*—Kinds of *habitudo* are: (a), **habitudo accidentalis**, *the accidental* or *unessential relation.*—(b), **habitudo innaturalis** and **habitudo naturalis**, *the unnatural* and *the natural relation.*—(c), **habitudo naturalis**, see *habitudo innaturalis.*—(d), **habitudo necessaria**, *the neces-*

sary relation that cannot be otherwise.—(e), **habitudo realis,** *the real relation* or *the relation that occurs outside the mind.*—(f), **habitudo relativa,** *the relation that presents something relative.*—(g), **habitudo universalis,** *the general relation.*—(h), **habitudo violenta** and **habitudo voluntaria,** *the forced* and *the voluntary relation.*—(i), **habitudo voluntaria,** see *habitudo violenta.*

habitus, us, *m.*, (1) *dressing, clothing, garment,* (2) *having, possession,* a form or an act, synonym of *habere* (5 Phys. 3 b), one of the so-called *postpraedicamenta* of Aristotle, the opposite of *defectus, negatio,* and *privatio,* (3) *having on, wearing, dressed, clothed,* likewise synonym of *habere,* one of the ten categories of Aristotle, (4) *habit* in the proper sense of the word, a kind of predicamental quality in that it is a modification of the substance not easily changed. In this sense it is opposed to mere disposition which is easily changed. Such a habit is either a modification of the nature, as health, or, more commonly of some faculty rendering it more prompt to act well or badly. Both habit and disposition are in turn contradivided with *potentia,* potency, (5) *habit* in the narrower sense of the word, i.e., *peculiarity, inclination,* fitness of a thing for something, synonym of *dispositio, habilitas,* and *habi-*

tudo, (6) *habitus* in the figurative sense of the word, i.e., the object of a *habitus.*—On **oppositum secundum habitum et privationem,** see *opponere.*—One kind of *habitus* in this sense is, **habitus quiescens,** *the possession which results in rest.*—**contrarietatis principium est oppositio privationis et habitus,** or, **prima contrarietas est habitus et privatio,** or, **principium contrarietatis est privatio et habitus,** or, **privatio et habitus est prima contrarietas,** *the foundation of all contrary opposition is the opposition of possessing* and *being deprived of a thing.*—**habitus naturaliter prior est privatione,** *naturally the possession of a thing is prior to being deprived of it.*—**prima contrarietas est habitus et privatio,** see above: *contrarietatis principium* etc.—**principium contrarietatis est oppositio privationis et habitus,** see above: *contrarietatis principium* etc.—**privatio et habitus est prima contrarietas,** see *contrarietatis principium* etc.—**intensio habitus** and **remissio habitus,** *the increase* and *the diminution of habit.*—**magnitudo seu quantitas habitus,** *the magnitude* or *perfection of a habit.* On **bonitas ex forma habitus,** see *bonitas;* on **cognoscere in habitu,** see *cognoscere;* on **continuatio habitus,** see *continuatio;* on **frui sicut habitus,** see *frui;* on **inchoatio habitus,** see *inchoatio;* on **intellectus in habitu,** see *intellectus;*

on **intensio habitus**, see *intensio;* on **magnitudo habitus**, see *magnitudo;* on **quantitas habitus,** see *quantitas;* on **radix habitus,** see *radix;* on **remissio habitus,** see *remissio;* on **scientia in habitu,** see *scientia;* on **scire in habitu,** see *scire;* on **substantia habitus,** see *substantia;* on **voluntas secundum habitum,** see *voluntas.* —Kinds of *habitus* in this sense are: (a), **habitus activus sive practicus, habitus factivus,** and **habitus cognitivus seu cognoscitivus seu considerativus seu speculativus,** *habit of activity, without reference to work performed, productive habits directed to useful activity which results in some exterior work, practical habits which direct means to an end,* and *cognitive* or *speculative habits of mind which determine the abstract consideration of truth.*—(b), **habitus adquisitus seu consuetudinalis, habitus gratuitus seu infusus** and **habitus innatus seu naturalis,** *the habit acquired by exercise* or *accomplished by habit, that bestowed* or *infused by the grace of God,* and *the inborn habitus* or *that inherent by nature.* Cf. *habitus naturalis.*—(c), **habitus animae seu animalis seu spiritualis** and **habitus corporis seu corporalis seu corporeus,** *the habit of the soul* and *that of the body* or *the immaterial* or *spiritual* and *the physical habit.*—(d), **habitus animalis,** see *habitus animae.*—(e),

habitus athleticus, *the habit of an athlete.*—(f), **habitus bonus,** and **habitus malus,** *the morally good* and *the morally bad habits.* —(g), **habitus cognitivus seu cognoscitivus,** see *habitus activus.* —(h), **habitus completus,** *the complete* or *the completely formed habitus.*—(i), **habitus conclusionum seu scientiae seu scientiarum** and **habitus principiorum seu intellectus,** *the habit of knowledge consisting of conclusions rigidly deduced from principles of knowledge* and *the habit of the immediate insight into the principles of knowledge.*—(j), **habitus considerativus,** see *habitus activus.*—(k), **habitus consuetudinalis,** see *habitus adquisitus.* —(l), **habitus corporalis sive corporeus,** see *habitus animae.*—(m), **habitus corporis,** see *habitus animae.*—(n), **habitus corruptus** and **habitus generatus,** *the corrupted* or *vanished habit* and *the produced* or *generated habit.*—(o), **habitus demonstrativus,** the translation of the Aristotelian expression *hexis spodeiktike, the habit of demonstration* or *that accomplished through demonstration,* i.e., *science.*—(p), **habitus divinus seu heroicus,** *the divine* or *the heroic habit,* because of its passing beyond human measure.—(q), **habitus electivus seu voluntarius,** *the translation of the Aristotelian expression hexis proairetike, the habit of correct choice,* i.e., faciens bonam electionem, or *the habit of proper free will,* omnis virtus in libera voluntate consistit, unde dicitur habitus electivus vel voluntarius.—(r), **habitus eliciens** and **habitus imperans,** *the habit eliciting an act* and *the habit commanding to elicit it.*— —(s), **habitus factivus,** see *habitus activus.*—(t), **habitus feralis,** *the destructive* or *wild habit.*— (u), **habitus generatus,** see *habitus corruptus.*—(v), **habitus gratiae seu iustitiae,** *the habit of sanctifying grace* or *of jusification.*—(w), **habitus gratuitus,** see *habitus adquisitius.*—(x), **habitus heroicus,** see *habitus divinus.*— (y), **habitus imperans,** see *habitus eliciens.*—(z), **habitus infusus,** see *habitus adquisitus.*—(a^2), **habitus innatus,** see *habitus adquisitus.*—(b^2), **habitus intellectivus seu intellectualis,** and **habitus moralis,** *the habit of knowledge in the intellect* and *the habit of moral act in the will.*—(c^2), **habitus intellectus,** *the habitual knowledge of first principles,* called *understanding.* See *habitus conclusionum.*—(d^2), **habitus iustitiae,** *the moral virtue of rendering to each his due, justice.* —(e^2), **habitus ligatus** and **habitus solutus,** *the bound* and *loosed habit.*—(f^2), **habitus malus,** see *habitus bonus.*—(g^2), **habitus moralis,** *a habit in the appetitive faculties, either prudence, justice, fortitude* or *temperance.* See *habitus intellectivus.*—(h^2),

habitus naturalis, habitus non naturalis and **habitus supernaturalis,** *the natural* (cf. *habitus adquisitus*) and *the non-natural* and *the supernatural habit.*—(i^2), **habitus non-naturalis,** see *habitus naturalis.*—(j^2), **habitus operativus,** *the habit of action* which on the one hand forms the opposite of *habitus factivus,* and on the other is identical with it, as opposed to entitative habit.—(k^2), **habitus opinativus,** *the habit of opinion,* i.e., *that considers something as probable.*—(l^2), **habitus personalis,** *the personal habit,* or *the habit belonging to a person as such.*—(m^2), **habitus politicus,** *the political habit* or *that of the actions of public life.*—(n^2), **habitus practicus,** see *habitus activus.*—(o^2), **habitus principiorum,** same as habit of understanding. See *habitus conclusionum.*—(p^2), **habitus scientiae seu scientiarum,** see *habitus conclusionum.*— (q^2), **habitus speculativus,** see *habitus activus.*—(r^2), **habitus virtuosus seu virtutis** and **habitus vitiosus,** *the virtuous* and *the vicious habit,* and *the habit of virtue* and *that of vice.*—(s^2), **habitus virtutis,** see *habitus virtuosus.*—(t^2), **habitus vitiosus,** see *habitus virtuosus.*—**cuius est habitus, eius est actus,** or the reverse, **eius est habitus, cuius est operatio,** *habit* and *activity which correspond to each other have the same subject.*—**cuiuslibet habitus mensura quaedam**

est id, ad quod habitus ordinatur, *the measure* and *norm of any habit is that toward which it is directed.*—eius est habitus, cuius est operatio, see above: *cuius est habitus* etc.—habitus alicuius potentiae distinguuntur specie secundum differentiam eius quod est per se obiectum potentiae, or, habitus distinguuntur secundum obiecta, or, omnes habitus distinguuntur per obiecta, ex quibus speciem habent, *the habits of a faculty are distinguished as to species according to that which is the primary object of the power* or *faculty in question,* or more commonly, *habits are differentiated according to their objects from which they derive their species* and *essence.*—habitus in sui ratione non includit indivisibilitatem, *habit does not include in its essential concept indivisibility so that as a result it can be increased* or *lessened,* or *added to* or *taken from.*—habitus per actus cognoscuntur, *habits are known from the activities which come forth from them.*—habitus propter actus sunt, *habits exist for the sake of the actions which come from them.*—in repentinis signum interioris habitus praecipue accipi potest, *those actions which are performed instantly,* i.e., *without further deliberation, serve especially as countersigns for the existence* and *being of an inner habit.*—materialis diversitas obi

ecti non diversificat habitum, sed solum formalis, *not material but formal difference of the object establishes a difference of habit.*—omnes habitus distinguuntur per obiecta, ex quibus speciem habent, see above: *habitus alicuius potentiae* etc.—quales sunt habitus, tales actus reddunt, *acts are such according to the habits whence they emanate.* —A kind of *habitus* in this (5) sense is: habitus prophetiae, *the habit of prophecy* or *the prophetic habit.*

hactenus, *adv.,* *in time,* to indicate a limit, *up to this time, thus far, so far, till now, hitherto.*

haereo, ere, haesi, haesum, 2, *v. n.,* (1) *lit., to hang* or *hold fast, to hang, stick, cleave, cling, adhere, be fixed, sit fast, remain close* to anything or in any manner, used with the *abl., in* with *abl.,* (2) *fig.,* with the idea of duration in time predominating, *to remain fixed, to abide* or *continue anywhere.*

haeresiarcha, ae, *m., a leader of a sect, heresiarch.*

haeresis, *f., special teaching, erroneus doctrine* in matters of faith that is obstinately adhered to, *heresy,* synonym of *secta.* On the difference between *haeresis* and *schisma,* see *schisma.*

haereticus, a, um, *adj., of* or *belonging to heretical religious doctrine, heretical.*—haereticus, i, *m., a teacher of false doctrine, a heretic.* On the difference be tween *haereticus* and *schismaticus*, see *schisma*. On **infidelitas haereticorum**, see *infidelitas*.

hagiographa, orum, *n.*, *hagiographa, sacred writings,* the last of three principal divisions of the Old Testament Scriptures.

hagiographus, i, *m.*, *a hagiographer, sacred writer,* especially one who writes by the inspiration of the Holy Ghost, such as Job, David, and Solomon.

Hai, *indecl. n.*, *Hai,* a town in the land of Chanaan; two miles east of Bethel.

halyaetus, i, *m.*, *the haliaetus, osprey,* a widely distributed pandionoid bird of prey, dark-brown above, with head, neck, and lower parts mostly white; *the fish-hawk.* It preys on fish which it captures in its talons.

harmonia, ae, *f.*, *harmony, concord, agreement, consonance,* synonym of *consonantia* and *convenientia*. On **passio harmoniae**, see *passio*.

harmonizatus, a, um, *P. a.*, *harmonized, brought into harmony.*

haurio, ire, hausi, haustum, 4, *v. a.*, (1) *lit.*, *to draw water,* (2) *fig.*, *to draw, originate, proceed.*

haustus, us, *m.*, *a drink, draught.*

Haymo, onis, *m.*, *Haymo,* or *Haimo,* or *Aimo,* a Benedictine Bishop of the Ninth century; died March 26, 853. When a youth he entered the Order of St. Benedict at Fulda, where the celebrated Rabanus Maurus

was one of his fellow students. He was a prolific writer; most of his genuine works are commentaries on Holy Writ.

hebdomada, ae, *f.*, *a hebdomad; the number seven; any seven things;* especially *a period of seven days; a week.*

hebdomas, adis, *f.*, *the number seven, seven days,* used in the S.T. only for a work of Boethius, the *De Hebdomadibus* or *An omne quod est sit bonum.*

hebes, etis, *adj.*, (1) *lit.*, *blunt, dull,* (2) *fig.*, *dull, stupid, heavy.*

hebesco, ere, *v. inch.*, *n.*, *to grow dull,* used *fig.*, only in quod. in S.T.

hebeto, are, avi, atum, 1, *v. a.*, (1) *lit.*, *to make blunt* or *dull, to blunt,* (2) *fig.*, *to blunt, make stupid, dull.*

hebetudo, inis, *f.*, *bluntness, dullness, hebetude,* the condition or state of being blunt or dull.

Hebraei, orum, *m.*, *Hebrews, Jews, Israelites* or descendants of Jacob (Israel) in contrast to the Gentile races. In his epistle to the Hebrews, St. Paul, making use of the authority of the Old Testament, describes under the most sublime traits the divinity of Jesus Christ, His quality as Mediator and Redeemer, His eternal priesthood, the superiority of the New Covenant over the Old, and the intimate relation of both. St. Paul wrote this epistle to the Christians in Palesine; most of them had been

Jews before.—**Hebraeus,** a, um, *adj., Hebrew,* of or belonging to the Hebrews.—**Hebraicus,** a, um, *adj., Hebraic, relating to* or *characteristic of the Hebrews, Hebrew.*

Hebraeus, a, um, *adj.,* see *Hebraei.*

Hebraicus, a, um, see *Hebraei.*

Hebron, *indecl. n., Hebron,* called Cariah-Arbe, a city in Palestine, situated on a hill among the mountains of Juda, about twenty miles south of Jerusalem. It is one of the oldest existing Biblical towns.

hecticus, a, um, *hectic, habitual* or *constitutional;* characterized by or denoting a wasting habit or condition of body.

Hector, oris, *m., Hector,* son of *Priam* and *Hecuba,* husband of *Andromache,* the bravest of the Trojans.

Hedibia, ae, *m., Hedibia,* a lady of Gaul, who corresponded with St. Jerome, then at Bethlehem about 405 A.D. She was of a remarkable family descended from the Druids, and holding the hereditary office of priests of Belen, who was identified with Apollo, at Bayeux. Hedibia was a diligent student of Scripture, and, finding no one in her neighborhood who could assist her, she sent a list of questions to Jerome, begging him to answer her. He did so in a long letter, epistle 120.

Helcana (Elcana) III, *m., Helcana,* a man of Ramah, a Zuphite of the hill-country of Ephraim; he was the husband of Anna and father of Samuel.

Heli, *indecl. n., m.,* (1) *Heli I,* a judge and high-priest whose history is related in I Kings, 1-4. He lived at Silo where the ark of the Lord was kept at that time. The Bible represents him as weak and indulgent to his sons Ophni and Phinees, whose crimes brought ruin on their country and on their father's house, (2) *Heli II,* is evidently the same as the preceding. In Luke he is said to be the father of Joseph, while in Matth. 1, 16, Jacob was Joseph's father. The most probable explanation of the seeming contradiction is afforded by having recourse to the levirate law among the Jews, which prescribes that when a man dies childless his widow shall not marry to another; but his brother shall take her and raise up seed for his brother (Deut. XXV, 5). The child, therefore, of the second marriage is legally the child of the first. Heli having died childless, his widow became the wife of his brother Jacob, and Joseph was the offspring of the marriage, by nature the son of Jacob, but legally the son of Heli. It is likely that Matthew gives the natural, and Luke the legal descent.

Helias, ae, *m., Elias,* the most wonderful prophet of the Old Testament. Of his origin nothing is known except that he was a Thesbite; whether from Thisbe of Nephtali or from Thesbon is not absolutely certain. According to IV. Kings, 3, Elias's career ended before the death of Josephat. As he was conversing with Eliseus on the hills of Moab, "a fiery chariot and fiery horses parted them asunder and Elias went up by a whirlwind to Heaven".

Heliodorus, i, *m., Heliodorus,* bishop of Altinum near Aquileia about 400 A.D. He had served originally as a soldier, but had left that calling and was ordained priest. He formed one of the band of friends who were drawn together at Aquileia, about the year 372, for the study of Scripture and the practice of asceticism, which included St. Jerome, Evagrius afterwards bishop of Antioch, Rufinus, Bonosus, and Chromatius afterwards bishop of Aquileia. When St. Jerome resolved to go into the solitude of the desert of Chalcis, Heliodorus, who had accompanied Jerome to the East, returned to Aquileia. Letter XIV of Jerome to Heliodorus reproaches him for having gone back from the perfect way of the ascetic life. St. Thomas quotes this letter and also letter XL of Jerome to Heliodorus, Bishop of Altinum, consoling him for the loss of his nephew, Nepotian who had died of fever.

Helisaeus, ei, *m., Eliseus,* son of Saphat. After learning on Mount Horeb that Eliseus had been selected by God as his successor in the prophetic office, Elias set out to make known the divine will. This he did by casting his mantle over the shoulders of Eliseus, whom he found among those that were ploughing with twelve yoke of oxen. Eliseus delayed only long enough to kill the yoke of oxen, whose flesh he boiled with the very wood of the plough. After he had shared this farewell repast with his father, mother, and friends, the newly chosen Prophet followed Elias and ministered to him (Kings 3. 19-19).

Helvidius, ii, *m., Helvidius,* heresiarch of the fourth century, disciple of Auxentius, Bishop of Milan. He pretended that Mary had, after the birth of Jesus Christ, several children with St. Joseph, and declared that the state of marriage is as meritorious as that of virginity. St. Jerome refuted him.

hemisphaerium, ei, *a half-globe, hemisphere.*

Hemor, *indecl. n., m., Hemor,* prince of the Sichemites and father of Sichem. Sichem humiliated Dina the daughter of Jacob and was slain together with Hemor by her enraged brothers, Simeon and Levi (Gen. 34).

hepar, atis, *n., the liver.*

Heptateuchos, i, *m., the Hepta-teuch,* the first seven books of the Old Testament.

Heraclitus, i, *m., Heraclitus,* a Greek philosopher (535-475 B.C.); he taught that all things are in a continual state of flux.

herba, ae, *f., a herb, springing vegetation, grass, green stalks* or *blades, green crops, herbage.*

Hercules, is, *m., Hercules,* son of Jupiter and Alcmena.

hereditas atis, *f.,* (1) *an inheritance,* that which is or is to be inherited, whether property or physical, mental or family characteristics, whatever is transmitted by descent or succession; *heritage,* (a) *abstr.,* (b) *concr.,* (2) *fig., an inheritance, a possession* or *blessing,* blessing bestowed by divine gift.

Herennius, i,, *m., Herennius,* used in the S.T. only in the title *Rhetorica ad Herennium,* a work, probably falsely, ascribed to Cicero.

heres, edis, *comm., an heir, heiress.*

heri, *adv., yesterday.*

Heribaldus, i, *m., Heribaldus* (829-57), saint, bishop of Auxerre, first chaplain of Louis the Pious and several times given ambassadorial charges.

Hermes, etis, *m., Hermes* Trismegistus, the Greek name for the Egyptian god Thoth, regarded as the author of civilization, the inventor of writing, art, science, and religion. The sacred canon of the Egyptians in forty-two books divided in six sections, constituting an encyclopaedia of general learning was ascribed to him under the name of the Hermetic Books.

Hermogenes, is, *m., Hermogenes,* a magician who was converted with Philetes by St. James the Greater.

herniosus, a, um, *adj., ruptured, having a rupture.*

Herodes, is, *m.,* (1) *Herod I,* a King of Judea, surnamed the Great, was the son of Antipater, an Idumaean. In 40 B.C. Octavian and Antony obtained for him from the Roman senate the crown of Judea, and between these two powerful friends he went up to the temple of Jupiter to thank the gods of Rome. The eclipse mentioned by Josephus fixed the date of Herod's death in the spring 750 A.U.C. or 4 B.C. Christ was born before Herod's death but how long before is uncertain; the possible dates lie between 746 and 750 A.U.C., (2) *Herod III* (Antipas) was the son of Herod the Great after whose death he became ruler of Galilee. He married the daughter of Aretas, King of Arabia, but later lived with Herodias, the wife of his own half-brother Philip. John the Baptist rebuked Antipas for the adulterous union and Herodias took vengeance by having John beheaded.

herodio, onis, *m., an unknown bird,* perhaps *the heron* whose voracity is insatiable.

heroicus, a, um, *adj., of* or *relating to heroes, heroic, lordly.* On **habitus heroicus,** see *habitus;* on **virtus heroica,** see *virtus.*

Hesperus, i, *m., Hesperus, the evening star.*

hesternus, a, um, *adj., of yesterday, yesterday's.*

Hesychius, ii, *m.,* (1) *Hesychius* of Jerusalem, a most prolific exegete of the fifth century. The *commentary on Leviticus* quoted by St. Thomas is the work of a later and unknown author, (2) *Hesychius,* bishop of Salona in Dalmatia, not, as has been supposed, an African bishop. He succeeded John IV in 405 and died about 429. He wrote to St. Augustine asking him about the true interpretation of Daniel's prophecy of the seventy weeks. This letter is not extant. St. Augustine's replies are interesting, revealing the thoughts and ideas entertained at this period by Christians, and the view which some of them took of the passing events of the age, and their relation to the prophecies both of the Old and New Testament (Aug. Ep. 199).

heterogeneus, a, um, *adj., heterogeneous,* unlike in character or quality, structure or composi-

tion; consisting of dissimilar elements.

Heu! *interj., alas!* an exclamation of grief or pain.

Hexaemeron, i, *n., the Hexaemeron* (*of* or *in six days*), (1) the account in Genesis I of the formation of the world. On three days God separates light from darkness; water above from water below; water from dry land. On three more days God peoples the world with living beings, (2) *hexaemeron,* the name of the works made by various authors such as Bede, Basil, and Ambrose, on the first chapters of Genesis and the first six days of creation.

hic, haec, hoc, *pron. demonstr., this.* On **bonum quoad hunc,** see *bonus;* on **corruptio huius seu huiusmodi,** see *corruptio;* on **ens hoc,** see *ens;* on **esse hoc et esse huius,** see *esse;* on **generatio huius,** see *generatio;* on **impossibile huic,** see *impossibile;* on **malum huic seu quantum ad hoc,** see *malus;* on **transmutatio ex hoc in hoc,** see *transmutatio.* —Sometimes *haec* stands elliptically for *haec propositio.—Hoc aliquid,* translation of the Aristotelian expression *tode ti, this determined substance, this individual substantial non-accidental thing,* synonym of *hoc signatum,* and *aliquid monstratum seu demonstratum.—***huiusmodi,** *such, such like.* On **corruptio**

huiusmodi, see *corruptio;* on inquantum huiusmodi, see *quantus.*

hiems, emis, *f., the winter, winter
season.*

hierarcha, ae, *m., hierarch, bishop,*
synonym of *episcopus,* found in
S.T. only in quotation.

hierarchia, ae, *f., holy authority,
hierarchy.* On ordo hierarchiae,
see *ordo.*—Kinds of *hierarchia*
are: (a), hierarchia angelica seu
angelorum and hierarchia humana seu hominum, *the angelic*
and *the human hierarchy* or *the
hierarchy of angels* and *that of
men.*—(b), hierarchia angelorum, see *hierarchia angelica.*—
(c), hierarchia caelestis, hierarchia subcaelestis, and hierarchia
supercaelestis, *the heavenly* (i.e.,
the angelic), *the subheavenly*
(i.e., *the human*), and *the super-
heavenly hierarchy.*—(d), hierarchia ecclesiastica seu nostra and
hierarchia veteris testamenti, *the
ecclesiastical* or *our hierarchy*
and *the hierarchy of the Old
Testament.*—(e), hierarchia hominum, see *hierarchia angelica.*—
(f), hierarchia humana, see *hierarchia angelica.*—(g), hierarchia
infima seu ultima seu tertia, hierarchia media seu secunda and
hierarchia prima, *the lowest* or
the last or *third hierarchy, the
middle* or *second* and *the first
hierarchy, namely of the angels.*
—(h), hierarchia media, see *hierarchia infima.*—(i) hierarchia nostra, see *hierarchia ecclesiastica.*

—(j), hierarchia prima, see *hierarchia infima.*—(k), hierarchia secunda, see *hierarchia infima.*—(l),
hierarchia subcaelestis, see *hierarchia caelestis.*—(m), hierarchia
supercaelestis, see *hierarchia
caelestis.*—(n), hierarchia tertia,
see *hierarchia infima.*—(o), hierarchia ultima, see *hierarchia infima.*—(p), hierarchia veteris testamenti, see *hierarchia ecclesiastica.*

hierarchicus, a, um, *adj., hierarchical,* i.e., concerning a holy authority or hierarchy, belonging
to it, coming from it. On actio
hierarchica, see *actio;* on actus
hierarchicus, see *actus;* on operatio hierarchica, see *operatio;*
on ordo hierarchicus, see *ordo;*
on potestas hierarchica, see *potestas;* on virtus hierarchica, see
virtus.

Hieronymus, i, *m., Jerome,* Saint,
Confessor, Doctor of the Church
(c 340-420), was born at Stridon,
Dalmatia and died at Bethlehem. From 374 to 379 he led a
life of seclusion and prayer in
the desert of Chalcis. Returning
to Antioch he was ordained
priest. He was a friend of St.
Gregory Nazianzen and through
him came to study the Scriptures. After visiting Rome and
journeying through the Holy
Land he retired to a monastery
in Bethlehem. There he prayed,
fasted, and labored on the Vulgate edition of the Bible. St.
Thomas quotes from many of his

writings especially the *De Viris Illustribus, Adversus Iovinianum, Contra Vigilantium, Adversus Helvidium,* from many of his Biblical commentaries, and from many of his letters. *The Expositio Fidei ad Damascum,* ascribed by St. Thomas to Jerome, is the work of Pelagius. St. Jerome's correspondence, after his works of translation and exegesis, is the most important part of his literary output. *The Epistola ad Paulinum et Eustochium,* or Sermon on the Assumption, quoted by St. Thomas is spurious. St. Thomas quotes also from the spurious *Symboli Explanatio ad Damasum* (*Expositio Catholicae Fidei*), and the *Prologus in Ioannem Evangelistam.*

Hierosolyma, orum, *n., Jerusalem, a city in Palestine.*—Also *fem. acc.:* **Hierosolymam.**—In *neutr., indecl.,* **Hierusalem.**

Hierosolymita, ae, *m., a Jerusalemite, an inhabitant of Jerusalem.*

Hierotheus, ei, *m., Hierotheus,* a writer whose works are quoted by the Pseudo-Dionysius, who styles him his teacher. Hierotheus, according to the legend which makes him the teacher of Dionysius, the Areopagite, was born during the reign of Augustus, of a distinguished family at Athens. He was a Platonic philospher and a member of the council of nine who composed the Areopagite senate. Upon his conversion to Christianity he was appointed by St. Paul to be bishop at Athens.

Hierusalem, see *Hierosolyma.*

hilaris, e, *adj., cheerful, glad, joyous.*

hilaritas, atis, *f., hilarity, joyousness, cheerfulness, gladness.*

Hilarius, i, *m., Hilary,* Saint, Bishop of Poitiers, was born in that city at the beginning of the fourth century and died there November 1, 368. Belonging to a noble and, very probably, pagan family, he was instructed in all the branches of profane learning, but, having also taken up the study of the Holy Scriptures and finding there the truth which he sought so ardently, he renounced idolatry and was baptized. The S.T. contains references to his *De Synodis, De Trinitate,* and his *Commentary on St. Matthew.*

hinc, *adv.,* (1) *in space, from this place, hence,* (2) *transf.,* with reference to the origin or cause of anything, *from this source, from this cause, hence.*

Hipponensis, e, *adj., of* or *belonging to Hippo.*

Hiram, *indecl. n., m., Hiram III,* son of a woman of the daughters of Dan, a skilled artificer in metals, wood, and stone, was sent by Hiram, King of Tyre, to Solomon when the latter was building his temple and palace in order that Solomon might use his skill and prudence.

hircus, i, *m., a he-goat, buck.*

hirundo, inis, *f.*, *a swallow*, used in the S.T. only in quot.

Hispania, ae, *f.*, *Spain*, the country of the Spaniards.

hispidus, a, um, *adj.*, *hairy*, used in the S.T. only in quot.

historia, ae, *f.*, (1) *lit.*, *a narrative of past events, history, a written narrative* constituting a continuous methodical record in order of time, of important or public events, especially those connected with a particular country, or people, (2) *transf.*, *a narrative, account, tale, story.*—**ecclesiastica historia**, *ecclesiastical* or *church history.*—**histora animalium**, *the history of animals*, a very important work of Aristotle, in which he treats of all the peculiarities of this division of the natural kingdom, according to genera, classes, and species.

historice, *adv.*, see *historicus*.

historicus, a, um, *adj.*, *of* or *belonging to history, historical.*—**historice**, *adv.*, *historically*.

historiographus, i, *m.*, *a writer of history, historiographer*.

histrio, onis, *m.*, *a stage-player, actor, buffoon, comedian*.

histrionatus, us, *m.*, *stage-playing*.

hodie, *adv.*, (1) *lit.*, *today*, (2) *tranf.*, in gen., *today, at the present time, at this time, now, in these times*.

hodiernus, a, um, *adj.*, *of this day, today's*.

hoedus, i, *m.*, *a kid, young goat*.

holocaustum, i, *n.*, *a holocaust*, a sacrificial offering burnt whole or wholly consumed; a form of oblation practised by the Jews as well as by pagan nations of antiquity; hence, the complete surrender of anything as an act of atonement or consecration to God.

Holofernus, i, *m.*, *Holofernes*, an Assyrian general killed by Judith (Judith 13).

homicida, ae, *comm.*, *a man-slayer, homicide, a murderer, murderess*.

homicidium, ii, *n.*, *man-slaughter, homicide, murder*, the destroying of human life, taking the life of another unjustly. Its malice consists in interfering with God's rights over life as its author and owner and with the God-given right of man to life.

homilia, ae, *f.*, *a homily*, primitively it signifies a discourse held with one or more individuals, but in ecclesiastical use it means a discourse held in the Church and addressed by the bishop or priest to the congregation. These discourses were of the most simple character. The early Christian homily may be described as a popular exposition of a portion of Scripture accompanied by moral reflections and exhortations. The name homily is frequently used as a synonym for sermon.

homo, inis, *comm.*, *a human being, man*. On **actio hominis**, see *actio;* on **actus hominis**, see *actus;* on **anima hominis**, see *anima;* on beatitudo hominis, see *beatitudo;* on bonum hominis, see *bonus;* on complexio hominis, see *complexio;* on corpus hominis, see *corpus;* on demonstratio ad hominem, see *demonstratio;* on donum hominis, see *donum;* on hierarchia hominum, see *hierarchia;* on intellectus hominis, see *intellectus;* on irascibilis homo, see *irascibilis;* on iudicium hominis, see *iudicium;* on lex hominis, see *lex;* on ostensio ad hominem, see *ostensio;* on perfectio hominis, perfectio prima et ultima hominis, see *perfectio;* on per se homo, see under *homo abstractus;* on regimen hominis, see *regimen;* on sapientia hominis, see *sapientia;* on servitus hominis, see *servitus;* on solutio ad hominem, see *solutio;* on virtus hominis, see *virtus;* on vita hominis, see *vita.*—Kinds of *homo* are: (a), homo abstractus seu separatus, seu extra materiam seu communis seu per se homo and homo materialis seu naturalis seu realis seu sensibilis seu singularis, *the idea of man withdrawn* or *separated in thought from the individual man* or *the general man* or *man without matter* or *man by* or *for himself* and *man supplied with matter* or *man in nature* and *existing outside the mind* or *the sensibly realized man* or *the individual man.*—(b), homo animalis and homo spiritualis, *the sensual man* or *the man given over to sensual lust*

(cf. *homo carnalis*) and *the spiritual* or *spiritually minded man.* —(c), homo apparens seu similitudinarius and homo verus, *the apparent* and *the true man.*—(d), homo bestialis, *the bestial* or *brutalized man.*—(e), homo bonus simpliciter, *the simply* or *absolutely good man,* i.e., morally. —(f), homo caelestis and homo terrenus, *the heavenly* or *heavenly-minded man* and *the earthly* or *earthly minded man.*—(g), homo carnalis, *the carnal* or *carnally conceived man* (cf. *homo abstractus*) and *the man having flesh* and *bone* (cf. *homo animalis*).—(h), homo cholericus and homo phlegmaticus, *the choleric* and *the phlegmatic man* or *the man with a choleric* and *the man with a phlegmatic temperament.* —(i), homo communis, see *homo abstractus.*—(j), homo Deus seu dominus seu dominicus and homo purus, *the God-man* or *the man who is Lord per eminentiam,* and *the pure man* or *the man who is nothing other than man.*—(k), homo dominicus, see *homo Deus.*—(l), homo dominus, see *homo Deus.*—(m), homo exterior and homo interior, *the exterior man, by which is meant on the one hand a man as opposed to another man* and *again the sensible-physical side* or *nature of man* and *the inner man,* i.e., *the spiritual side* or *nature of man.*—(n), homo extra materiam, see *homo abstractus.*—(o), homo fidelis and homo infidelis, *the believing* and *the unbelieving man.*—(p), homo idealis, *the ideal man,* synonym of the *homo per se* of *Plato.* Cf. *homo abstractus.*—(q), homo infidelis, see *homo fidelis.*—(r), homo interior, see *homo exterior.*—(s), homo materialis, see *homo abstractus.*—(t), homo naturalis, see *homo abstractus.*—(u), homo phlegmaticus, see *homo cholericus.*—(v), homo plebeius seu vulgaris, *the man of the people* or *the common man.*—(w), homo privatus, *the private man* or *private being.*—(x), homo purus, see *homo Deus.*—(y), homo realis, see *homo abstractus.*—(z), homo saeculi, *the man of the world* or *worldling.*—(a²), homo sensibilis, see *homo abstractus.* (b²), homo separatus, see *homo abstractus.*—(c²), homo silvestris, *the man of the forest,* id est, in silvis commorans.—(d²), homo similitudinarius, see *homo apparens.*—(e²), homo singularis, see *homo abstractus.*—(f²), homo solitarius, *the man who lives for himself alone, the hermit.*—(g²), homo spiritualis, see *homo animalis.*—(h²), homo terrenus, see *homo caelestis.*—(i²), homo verus, see *homo apparens.*—(j²), homo vulgaris, see *homo plebeius.*—homo est naturaliter seu secundum suam naturam animal domesticum et civile seu politicum seu sociabile seu sociale, the translation of the Aristotel-

ian passage: *anthropos physei politikon zoon, man is by nature a domestic, civic,* and *social animal being.*—homo malus est pessimum omnium animalium, *the morally evil man is the evilest of animal beings.*—homo naturaliter desiderat beatitudinem, see *beatitudo.*

homoeomerus, a, um, *adj.,* *consisting of like* or *similar parts,* not found in the S.T. On corpus homoeomerum, see *corpus;* on totum homoeomerum, see *totus.*

homogeneus, a, um, *adj., of like kind, homogeneous.* On continuum homogeneum, see *continuus;* on corpus homogeneum, see *corpus;* on magnitudo homogenea, see *magnitudo;* on mensura homogenea, see *mensura;* on regula homogenea, see *regula.*

homousion, (Grk. *homousion*), *of one essence, consubstantial.*

honestas, atis, *f.,* (1) *noble bearing, exterior behavior, politeness,* (2) *the virtue of exterior politeness* or *decency,* (3) *decent property, wealth.*—On debitum honestatis, see *debitus;* on iustitia publicae honestatis, see *iustitia.*

honesto, are, avi, atum, 1, *v. a.,* *to dignify, to cause to appear honest* or *honorable; to justify, defend, excuse.*

honestus, a, um, *adj., honorable, polite, decent.* On amicitia honesti, see *amicitia;* on bonum honestum, see *bonus;* on cogita-

tio honesta, see *cogitatio;* on **vita honesta,** see *vita.—***honeste,** *adv., honorably, politely, decently.*

honor, oris, *m., public repute, honor,* esteem paid to someone because of his virtue.—Kinds of *honor* are: (a), **honor duliae** and **honor latriae,** *the honor of submission* and *that of adoration.*—(b), **honor latriae,** see *honor duliae.*—(c), **honor mundanus,** *the worldy honor.*

honorabilis, e, *adj., honorable, that procures honor* or *esteem.—***honorabiliter,** *adv., respectably, honorably.*

honorabilitas, atis, *f., honorability,* the state of being honorable or entitled to respect, esteem or reverence, used in the S.T. only in quot.

honorabiliter, *adv.,* see *honorabilis.*

honorarius, a, um, *adj., honorary; honorarium ius* or *praetorium ius, honorary* or *praetorian law,* the law of the praetors and the edicts of the aediles.

honoratio, onis, *f., a mark of respect, honor.*

Honoratus, i, *m., Honoratus,* bishop of Thiabe, in Numidia, c. A.D. 428. Possidius, who calls him "vir sanctus", states that he consulted Augustine at the time of the Vandal invasion respecting the duty of clergy and bishops to retire before the danger. Augustine in reply sent him a letter he had written to Quodvultdeus. Honoratus was not satisfied by Augustine's reasoning. Augustine then addressed him expressly on the subject in epistle 228. St. Thomas quotes from ep. 228 in the S.T.

honorificatio, onis, *f., the doing of honor, honoring,* synonym of *honorificentia.*

honorifice, *adv.,* see *honorificus.*

honorificentia, ae, *f., the doing of honor, honoring,* synonym of *honorificatio.*

honorifico, are, avi, atum, 1, *v. a., to do honor to, to honor,* used in the S.T. only in quot.

honorificus, a, um, *adj., that does honor, honorable.—***honorifice,** *adv., honorably, with honor* or *respect.*

honoro, are, avi, atum, 1, *v. a.,* in *gen., to do honor to, pay worthy respect to by some outward action; to worship; perform one's devotions to,* (1) *to honor God* and *His saints,* (2) *to honor persons* and *things.*

hora, ae, *f.,* (1) *an hour,* a space of time containing sixty minutes; the twenty-fourth part of a civil day, (2) *the hour,* each of those points of time at which the twelve successive divisions after noon or midnight, as shown by a dial or time piece, are completed; by extension, any definite point or time of the day, (3) *the hour,* a stated time of occupation or duty, an appointed time; an occasion, (4) used somewhat indefinitely for a short or limited space of time, more or less than *an hour,* especially in the phrase, **ad ho-ram,** *for the time being, now and then, for a time, for the moment,* (5) with canonica, *the canonical hour,* the fixed portion of the Divine Office which the Church appoints to be recited at the different hours of the day.—Common phrases are: **aliqua hora,** *at some time.*—**hora serotina,** *the evening hour.* —**aliis horis,** *at other times.*—**omnibus horis,** *at all hours, con-tinually.*—**brevis hora temporis,** *a short space of time.*

Horatius, ii, *m., Horace,* whose full name was Quintus Horatius Flaccus, was born at Venusia, December 8, 65 B.C. His liter-ary works are divided into Odes, Epodes, Satires, and Epistles. St. Thomas quotes from the first book of his Epistles.

hordeaceus, a, um, *adj., hordea-ceous, pertaining to, resembling* or *characteristic of barley.*

hordeum, i, *n., barley.*

horologium, ii, *n., a clock, horo-loge.*

horreo, ere, ui, 2, *v. n.* and *a.,* (1) *to tremble, shudder, quake with fright,* used with *de* and *abl.,* with the *inf.,* (2) more freq. as a *verb act.,* with an object.

horresco, ere, ui, 3, *v. a., to be-gin to shake, shudder,* or *trem-ble for fear, to become fright-ened, terrified,* used with the *acc.*

horreum, i, *n., a barn, storehouse,* esp. for preserving grain, used in the S. T. only in quot.

horribilis, is, *adj., terrible, dread-ful, horrible.*

horror, oris, *m., horror, a painful* emotion compounded of loathing and fear; strong aversion min-gled with dread; the feeling ex-cited by something shocking or frightful; intense dislike or re-pugnance.

hortatorius, a, um, *adj., persua-sive, encouraging.*

hortatus, us, *m., exhortation, en-couragement.*

hortor, ari, atus, 1, *v. dep., to exhort, encourage, urge one strongly to do a thing,* used with the *inf., ut* and *subj.,* and *acc.*

hortus, i, *m., a garden.*

hosanna, *hosanna,* (Heb. ho shi a na, *save me*), an exclamation of joy; its origin is traced to the 117th Psalm which was recited daily by a priest in the proces-sion around the altar during the Feast of Tabernacles, when the people were commanded to re-joice before the Lord. Ho shi a na was repeated so often that it became abbreviated into ho-sanna.

hospes, itis, *m., a sojourner, visi-tor, guest, friend.*

hospitalitas, atis, *f., hospitality.*

hospitiolum, i, *n., a little inn, a small dwelling-place.*

hospitium, ii, *n.,* (1) *a hospitable reception, entertainment, hospi-*

tality, (2) *a place of entertainment for strangers, a lodging, inn, guest-chamber*, used *lit.* and *fig.*

hostia, ae, *f.*, (1) in the Old Testament, *an animal sacrificed, a victim, sacrifice.* Bloody sacrifices consisted in the slaying of certain animals. The offering to God of a victim entirely consumed by fire was in use among the Jews and some pagan nations of antiquity and was regarded as the highest and most complete expression of man's reverence to God, (2) in Christian sacrifice, *a victim.* On the Cross Christ offered Himself as victim (hostia) and in a bloody manner; in the Mass through His ministers in an unbloody manner. The Mass is identical with the sacrifice of the cross in the victim (hostia) and the priest (sacerdos) which is Christ, (3) *a host*, the sacred host or the bread after the consecration when it has been changed into the body of Christ, Victim of sacrifice, (4) *a sacrifice, offering, the act of surrendering* or giving something for the attainment of some higher advantage. —This word is used frequently in the following phrases: **hostia pro peccato,** *the sin offering* which was offered for great sin, sins of the whole nation or individual trespasses.—**hostia pacifica,** *the peace-offering.* This kind of sacrifice was prescribed for certain occasions and was offered by the whole nation or by individuals in thanksgiving for blessings or as a means to obtain grace. The *peace-offerings* were subdivided into the sacrifice of thanksgiving or praise, the sacrifice in fulfillment of a vow and entirely voluntary offerings.—**hostia pacifica pro gratiarum actione,** *a peace-offering of thanksgiving.*— **hostia pacifica ex voto,** *a peace offering in fulfillment of a vow.*

hostilis, e, *adj., hostile, of* or *belonging to an enemy.*—**hostiliter,** *adv., hostilely, in a hostile manner, like an enemy.*

hostiliter, *adv.,* see *hostilis.*

hostis, is, *comm.,* (1) *an enemy* (a) *an unfriendly* or *hostile person,* one who is arrayed or enlisted in antagonism against another or who opposes a cause, custom or state of things, (b) *the devil* and *the evil spirits,* (c) *fig., anything that operates prejudicially upon, counteracts the action of,* (2) *the enemy* (a) *sing., a soldier of a nation at war with another; one of a hostile army* or *nation,* (b) *plur., an army* or *military force hostile to another army in the field.*

Hugo, onis, *m., Hugh,* Canon Regular of the Monastery of St. Victor (1096-1141), was probably born in Saxony. He was the eldest son of Conrad, Count of Blankenburg. In 1133 he became head of the School of St.

Victor, Paris, which under him acquired great celebrity. His writings cover the whole range of the arts and sacred science of his age. St. Thomas quotes from his *De Sacramentis, De Potestate ligandi et solvendi*, which forms part of that work, *De Contemplatione et eius speciebus*, or *De Modo Orandi*. Reference is also made in the S.T. to the *Summa Sententiarum*.

humanatio, onis, *f.*, *the making human*, *incarnation*, a synonym of *incarnatio*, the word used to express the union of the divine nature of the Son of God with human nature in the person of Jesus Christ.

humanitas, atis, *f.*, (1) in gen., *humanity*, *quality* or *condition of being human*, *manhood;* the human faculties or attributes collectively; *human nature; man in the abstract*, (2) in partic., **humanitas Christi**, *the humanity* or *human nature of Christ*, which the Son of God assumed when he was conceived and made man by the power of the Holy Ghost in the womb of the Blessed Virgin Mary, (3) *humanity, humaneness*, the disposition to treat human beings with consideration and compassion, and to relieve their distresses; *kindness* as shown in courteous acts, *benevolence*.

humanitus, *adv.*, *humanly*, *after the manner of men*.

humano, are, avi, atum, 1, *to make human;* used only in the *pass.* of the incarnation of Christ.

humanus, a, um, *adj.*, *human*, i.e., belonging to man as such, concerning him as such, proceeding from man as rational, the opposite of *animal, angelic*, and *divine*. On **actio humana**, see *actio;* on **actus humanus**, see *actus;* on **anima humana**, see *anima;* on **appetitus humanus**, see *appetitus;* on **bonum humanum et bonum naturae humanae**, see *bonus;* on **communitas humana**, see *communitas*; on **complexio humana**, see *complexio;* on **corpus humanum**, see *corpus;* on **correctio humana**, see *correctio;* on **delectatio humana**, see *delectatio;* on **forma humana**, see *forma;* on **generatio humana**, see *generatio;* on **genus humanum**, see *genus;* on **hierarchia humana**, see *hierarchia;* on **incontinentia humana**, see *incontinentia;* on **intellectus humanus**, see *intellectus;* on **iudicium humanum**, see *iudicium;* on **ius humanum**, see *ius;* on **iustitia humana**, see *iustitia;* on **iustum humanum**, see *iustus;* on **lex humana**, see *lex;* on **nativitas humana**, see *nativitas;* on **natura humana**, see *natura;* on **operatio humana**, see *operatio;* on **passio humana**, see *passio;* on **peccatum humanum**, see *peccatum;* on **potestas humana**, see *potestas;* on **proprietas humana**, see *proprietas;* on **providentia humana**, see *provi-*

dentia; on **ratio humana,** see *ra-tio;* on **regimen humanum,** see *regimen;* on **res humana,** see *res;* on **sapientia humana,** see *sa-pientia;* on **sensualitas humana,** see *sensualitas;* on **stultitia hu-mana,** see *stultitia;* on **timor hu-manus,** see *timor;* on **virtus humana,** see *virtus;* on **vita hu-mana et vita proprie humana,** see *vita;* on **voluntas humana,** see *voluntas;* on **vox humana,** see *vox.*—Kinds of *humanus* are: **humanus per essentiam** and **humanus per participationem,** *human according to essence* and *human according to participa-tion.*

humecto, are, avi, atum, 1, *v. a.* and *n., to moisten, make wet.*

humerus, i, *m., the shoulder,* used (1) *lit.,* (2) *fig.*

humiditas, atis, *f.,* (1) *humidity,* the condition of being humid or pervaded with moisture or water, (2) *humidity,* any fluid matter in the body, such as blood, digestive juices, etc.

humidus, a, um, *adj., moist, fluid, humid, damp.*—**humidum,** i, *n., moisture, humidity, dampness.*—Kinds of *humidum* are: (a), **hu-midum naturale,** *natural mois-ture.*—(b), **humidum nutrimen-tale** and **humidum seminale,** *the nourishing moisture* and *the seed-cultivating moisture.*—(c), **humidum radicale,** *the root* or *orginal moisture of a thing.*—(d), **humidum seminale,** see *hu-midum nutrimentale.*

humiliatio, onis, *f., an humbling, humiliation, the act of humili-ating* or *the condition of being humiliated.*

humilio, are, avi, atum, 1, *v. a., to humble, abase, humiliate.*

humilis, e, *adj.,* (1) *low, low-ly, small, slight,* (2) *lowly mind-ed, obscure, humble.*—**humiliter,** *adv., abjectly, humbly.*

humilitas, atis, *f.,* (1) *abasement, humiliation,* (2) *self-abasement,* (3) *humility,* the opposite of *superbia.*

humiliter, *adv.,* see *humilis.*

humor, oris, *m.,* (1) *humor, mois-ture, damp, exhalation, vapor* used (a) *lit.,* (b) *fig.,* (2) *humor,* any fluid or juice of an animal or plant, either natural or mor-bid, (a) in *gen.,* (b) in *partic., hu-mor,* in ancient and medieval physiology, one of the four kinds of fluids (cardinal humors) of the body: blood, phlegm, choler, and melancholy or black choler, by the relative proportions of which a person's physical and mental qualities and dispositions were held to be determined.

humus, i, *f., the earth, ground, soil.*

hyacinthinus, a, um, *adj., hyacin-thine, like* or *characteristic of the hyacinth,* especially in point of color, *hyacinth-colored, purple, violet.*

hyacinthus, i, *m., transf., the pur-ple* or *violet color.*

hydromantia, ae, *f., hydromancy, divination by water.*

hydropisis, is, *f., the dropsy.*

hymnus, i, *m., a song of praise, a hymn.*

hyperbolicus, a, um, *adj., hyperbolical, excessive.*

hyperdulia, ae, *f., the virtue of deep submission,* i.e., of veneration, of special reverence.

hypo, from Grk. *hypo* and a synonym for *falsum* here, used in S.T. only in quot.

hypocrisis, is, *f., hypocrisy, pretended sanctity.*

hypocrita, ae, *m., a hypocrite,* one who acts a false part or assumes a character other than the real, with the design of gaining commendation; especially, one who makes false profession of his virtues, views, or beliefs.

hypognosticon, i, *n., a response,* a synonym of *subnotatio.* The Hypognosticon, among the spurious works of St. Augustine, is directed against the dogma of the Pelagians.

hypostasis, is, *f.,* (1) *basis, foundation,* synonym of *fundamentum, basis, subiectum,* and *substantia,* (2) *single substance,* a concrete individualized nature, (3) *rational single substance, person.*—On **differre secundum hypostasim,** see *differre;* on **diversitas hypostasis,** see *diversitas;* on **unio in**

hypostasi secundum hypostasim, see *unio;* on **unire secundum hypostasim,** see *unire;* on **unitas hypostasis,** see *unitas.*—Kinds of *hypostasis* in this (3) sense are: **hypostasis creata** and **hypostasis increata,** *the created* and *the uncreated person.*

hypostaticus, a, um, *adj., pertaining to the person, hypostatic.* On **proprietas hypostatica,** see *proprietas.*—**hypostatice,** *adv.,* (1) *according to substance,* synonym of *substantialiter,* (2) *according to person,* synonym of *personaliter.*

hypothesis, is, *f., an hypothesis,* that which is laid as the foundation of an argument, *a supposition.*

hypotheticus, a, um, *adj., conditioned, containing a condition, hypothetic,* not found in S.T. On **enuntiatio hypothetica,** see *enuntiatio;* on **syllogismus hypotheticus,** see *syllogismus.*

hypotyposis, is, *f., portrait, picture,* not found in S.T.

hyssopus, i, *f., hyssop,* a plant which is often mentioned in Scripture (Ex. XII, 22; Hebr. IX, 19), the twigs of which were used for sprinkling in the ceremony of purification.

I

ibi, *adv., in that place, there.*

ibidem, *adv., in the same place, in that very place, just there.*

ibis, is and dis, *f., the ibis,* a bird held sacred by the Egyptians, which lived on water-animals.

ictus, us, *m., a blow, stroke, thrust.*

idcirco, *adv.,* (1) *on that account, for that reason, therefore,* (2) *relatively,* (a) corresp. to causal sentences with *quia,* (b) with a clause denoting *purpose,* with *ut.*

idea, ae, *f., intellectual representation, notion, conception, idea,* synonym of *exemplar, forma, imago, ratio,* and *species.*—Kinds of *idea* are: (a), **idea indeterminata,** *the undetermined notion.*—(b), **idea separata,** *the notion separated from the nature of a thing* or *existing separately.*—(c), **idea simplex,** *the simple representation.*

idealis, e, *adj., existing in idea, representative, ideal,* synonym of *exemplaris.* On **forma idealis,** see *forma;* on **homo idealis,** see *homo;* on **infinitum ideale,** see *infinitus;* on **ratio idealis,** see *ratio;* on **relatio idealis,** see *relatio;* on **similitudo idealis,** see *similitudo;* on **species idealis,** see *species.*

ideatio, onis, *f., representation, imagination of an exemplar, ideation.*

idem, eadem, idem, *pron., the same,* the opposite of *diversus.*—**eiusdem est,** *it is the same according to the fact.*—**eiusdem rationis est,** *it is the same according to idea* and *essence.*—Kinds of *idem* are: (a), **idem definitione,** *the same according to definition.*—(b), **idem genere seu in natura generis, idem specie seu in natura speciei seu per speciem suppositi** and **idem numero seu in numero seu secundum numerum,** *the same according to genus, according to species,* and *according to the individual* or *number.*—(c), **idem materia seu secundum materiam** and **idem secundum formam,** *the same according to matter* and *according to form.*—(d), **idem natura seu per naturam suppositi** and **idem ratione seu per rationem suppositi seu secundum suppositum seu supposito,** *the same according to the nature* and *essence of a single substance* and *according to the single substance.*—(e), **idem in natura generis,** see *idem genere.*—(f), **idem in natura speciei,** see *idem genere.*—(g), **idem numero,** see *idem genere.*—(h), **idem per naturam suppositi,** see *idem natura.*—(i), **idem per rationem suppositi,** see *idem natura.*—(j), **idem per speciem suppositi,** see *idem genere.*—(k), **idem ratione seu secundum rationem** and **idem re seu secundum rem seu secundum esse,** *the same according to the idea* and *according to the thing* or *being.*—(l), **idem re,** see *idem ratione.*—(m), **idem secundum analogiam** and **idem secundum univocationem,** *the same according to analogy* or *relation* and *according to similar terminology* or *univocation.*—(n), **idem secundum esse,** see *idem ratione.*—(o), **idem secundum formam,** see *idem materia.*—(p), **idem secundum materiam,** see *idem materia.*—(q), **idem,**

secundum numerum, see *idem genere.*—(r), idem secundum quid and idem simpliciter seu totaliter, *respectively the same or in a certain respect and entirely or aboslutely the same.*—(s), idem secundum rationem, see *idem ratione.*—(t), idem secundum rem, see *idem ratione.*—(u), idem secundum suppositum, see *idem natura*—(v), idem secundum univocationem, see *idem secundum analogiam.*—(w), idem simpliciter, see *idem secundum quid.*—(x), idem specie, see *idem genere.*—(y), idem subiecto, *the same according to the support or bearer,* whether it is taken in its logical or in its ontological sense.—(z), idem supposito, see *idem natura.*—(a²), idem totaliter, see *idem secundum quid.*—idem eidem idem, or, quodlibet sibi ipsi est idem, *everything is like itself.*—idem semper facit idem, or, idem eodem modo se habens semper facit idem, *one* and *the same always do the same,* i.e., *same thing always acts in the same manner.*—quaecumque uni et eidem sunt eadem, sibi invicem sunt eadem, *all things that are like one* and *the same thing are alike to each other.*—quodlibet sibi ipsi est idem, see above: *idem eidem idem.*

identitas, atis, *f., sameness, identity.* On dicere per modum identitatis, see *dicere;* on praedicatio per identitatem, see *praedi-*

catio; on relatio identitatis, see *relatio;* on relativum identitatis, see *relativus.*—Kinds of *identitas* are: (a), identitas absoluta, *the unconditioned* or *absolute identity.*—(b), identitas naturae, *the identity of nature* and *of essence.*—(c), identitas realis seu rei seu secundum rem, *the objective identity* or *the identity according to the object.*—(d), identitas rei, see *identitas realis.*—(e), identitas secundum rem, see *identitas realis.*

ideo, *adv., for that reason, on that account, therefore,* (1) *relatively,* (a) with causal particle, *quia,* (b) with intentional particles, *ut, ne,* (2) absol.

ideo, are, avi, atum, 1, *v. a. and n., to conceive an idea, imagine, ideate,* not found in S.T.

idiognomones, um, *comm., the self-opinionated.*

idioma, atis, *n.,* (1) *peculiarity,* (2) *peculiarity of speech, peculiar manner of speech, idiom, dialect,* not found in the S.T.—On communicatio idiomatum, see *communicatio.*

idiota, ae, *m., an uneducated, ignorant, inexperienced, common person.*

idolium, ii, *n., an idol-temple.*

idololatres, ae, *f., an idol-worshipper, idolator.*

idololatria, ae, *f., idol-worship, idolatry.* On cultus idolatriae, see *cultus;* on superstitio idololatriae, see *superstitio.*

idololatro, are, avi, *v. n., to idola-
trize, practice idolatry, worship
idols.*

idolum, i, *n.,* (1) *image, picture,* (2)
idol.

idonee, *adv.,* see *idoneus.*

idoneitas, atis, *f., fitness, meetness,
usefulness.*

idoneus, a, um, *adj., meet, proper,
fit, becoming, suitable, apt, capable, convenient, sufficient* (of
persons and things), used with
(a) *ad,* (b) *erga,* (c) the *dat.,*
(d) the *inf.,* (e) *absol.*—**idonee,**
adv., fitly, suitably, properly.

Idumaei, orum, *m., the Idumeans,
the descendants of Esau,* who inhabited Idumea, the name given
by the Greeks to the land of
Edom, which extended originally from the Dead Sea to the Elanitic gulf of the Red Sea. Afterwards it extended more into the
south of Juda towards Hebron.

igitur, *conj.,* used in introducing an
inference or deduction, or in
drawing a logical conclusion,
*then, therefore, accordingly, con-
sequently.*

ignarus, a, um, *adj., ignorant of a
thing, not knowing, unacquainted with, inexperienced, unaware,*
used *absol.,* and with the *gen.*

Ignatius, ii, *m., Ignatius,* Saint,
Bishop of Antioch. He was born
in Syria about the year 50 and
died at Rome between 98 and
117. He was a disciple of St.
John the Evangelist and occupied the episcopal chair at Antioch for thirty-seven years as suc-

cessor of St. Peter and Evodius.
According to his own ardent de-
sire he suffered martydom for
Christ.

ignavia, ae, *f., inactivity, laziness,
negligence, weakness.*

ignavus, a, um, *adj., slothful, idle,
bad, lazy, cowardly, dastardly,*
used in the S.T. only in quot.

ignesco, ere, *v. inch. n.,* used *fig.,
to burn with passion, glow,* used
in the S.T. only in quot.

igneus, a, um, *adj.,* (1) lit., *of fire,
fiery, flaming,* (2) transf., of col-
or, *fiery, flaming, resplendent.*

ignio, ire, ivi or ii, itum, 4, *v. a., to
ignite, set on fire, make red-hot,*
used lit and fig.—**ignitus,** a, um,
P. a., ignited, fiery, glowing.

ignis, is, *m.,* (1) *fire,* (a) lit., *the
natural agency or active princi-
ple in combustion,* popularly
conceived as a substance visible
in the form of a ruddy glow, (b)
as one of the four elements, (c)
with reference to hell or purgatory, (2) *a fire,* fuel in the state
of combustion, a mass of burning
material, as on a hearth, or in a
furnace, (3) fig., *fire,* (a) *great
afflictions, trials,* (b) *liveliness* or
intensity of thought, feeling, or
action; ardor, passion, esp. of
love.

ignitio, onis, *f., ignition, the act of
igniting,* or *the state of being
ignited.*

ignitus, a, um, *P. a.,* see *ignio.*

ignobilis, e, *adj.,* (1) *ignoble, of inferior kind, less honorable, less
perfect, less excellent, mean,* (2)

of lowly origin, base-born, ig-noble.

ignobilitas, atis, *f.*, (1) lit., *low birth, mean origin,* (2) transf., of things, *inferior quality, badness.*

ignominia, ae, *f.*, (1) in gen., *igno-miny, dishonor, disgrace, shame,* (2) *ignominy, public disgrace,* as the result of civil punishment.

ignominiosus, a, um, *adj., ignomini-ous, shameful, disgraceful.*

ignoranter, *adv.,* see *ignoro.*

ignorantia, ae, *f.*, (1) *ignorance, want of knowledge* or *informa-tion* in the general sense of the word, synonym of *nescientia,* the opposite of *scientia,* (2) *igno-rance, want of knowledge* or *in-formation* in the proper and the narrower sense of the word. On **fortitudo, quae est per ignoran-tiam,** see *fortitudo;* on **involun-tarium per ignorantiam,** see *in-voluntarius;* on **peccare ex igno-rantia,** see *peccare;* on **purgatio a tenebris ignorantiae,** see *pur-gatio;* on **syllogismus ignorantiae seu secundum ignorantiam,** see *syllogismus.*—Kinds of *ignorantia* in this (1) sense are: (a), **ignoran-tia antecedens seu praecedens seu causans, ignorantia concomi-tans** and **ignorantia consequens,** *the ignorance preceding an act of the will* and *causing an action. that accompanying it* and *that following upon* or *from an act of the will.*—(b), **ignorantia causans,** see *ignorantia antecedens.*—(c), **ignorantia concomitans,** see *igno-rantia antecedens.*—(d), **ignoran-**

tia **consequens,** see *ignorantia antecedens.*—(e), **ignorantia di-recte volita seu voluntaria** and **ignorantia indirecte volita seu voluntaria,** *the directly* or *indi-rectly desired* or *voluntary igno-rance.*—(f), **ignorantia dispositio-nis seu secundum dispositionem seu perversae dispositionis** and **ignorantia negationis seu secun-dum negationem seu secundum simplicem negationem,** the Aris-totelian *agnoia kata diathesin* and *agnoia kat' apophasin, the ignorance in consequence of a bad aptitude for knowledge* and *that of a simple negation of knowledge.*—(g), **ignorantia elec-tionis** and **ignorantia malae elec-tionis,** *the ignorance of choice* and *that of bad choice.* The first of these prevails with him who does not know what he should chose, and the latter with him who does not consider, while choosing, what he can and should choose.—(h), **ignorantia facti** and **ignorantia iuris,** *igno-rance in relation to a fact,* and *that in relation to a law,* i.e., ig-norance of this or of that circum-stance of an action and igno-rance of that which in a stated case is right.—(i), **ignorantia in-directe volita seu voluntaria,** see *ignorantia directe volita seu vo-luntaria.*—(j), **ignorantia in non attingendo,** *the ignorance which consists in the failure to attain knowledge* or *in the failure to comprehend the object of knowl-*

edge, which is identical with *ignorantia negationis seu negative accepta.*—(k), ignorantia invincibilis and ignorantia vincibilis, *invincible* and *vincible ignorance.*—(l), ignorantia involuntaria and ignorantia voluntaria, *the involuntary* and *the voluntary ignorance.*—(m), ignorantia iuris, see *ignorantia facti.*—(n), ignorantia iuris in particulari and ignorantia universalium iuris, *ignorance of a particular law* and *ignorance of the common legal precepts.*—(o), ignorantia malae electionis, see *ignorantia electionis.*—(p), ignorantia negationis, see *ignorantia dispositionis.*—(q), ignorantia negative accepta and ignorantia privative accepta, *ignorance in the negative* and *in the positive sense of the word,* i.e., ignorance of a thing in general and ignorance of that which one ought to know.—(r), ignorantia negligentiae, *ignorance as the result of negligence.* Cf. *ignorantia indirecte volita.*—(s), ignorantia particularis and ignorantia universalis seu quae est in universali, *the particular* or *partial ignorance* and *the general ignorance.*—(t), ignorantia per accidens voluntaria and ignorantia per se voluntaria, *ignorance because of something accidental* and *ignorance voluntary of itself* and *as such.*—(u), ignorantia per se voluntaria, see *ignorantia per accidens voluntaria.*—(v), ignorantia perversae dispositionis,

see *ignorantia dispositionis.*—(w), ignorantia praecedens, see *ignorantia antecedens.*—(x), ignorantia privative accepta, see *ignorantia negative accepta.*—(y), ignorantia quae est per syllogismum and ignorantia quae non est per syllogismum, *ignorance in which is the result* and *that which is not the result of a conclusion.*—(z), ignorantia quae est in universali, see *ignorantia particularis.*—(a²), ignorantia quae non est per syllogismum, see *ignorantia quae est per syllogismum.*—(b²), ignorantia secundum dispositionem, see *ignorantia dispositionis.*—(c²), ignorantia secundum negationem seu simplicem negationem, see *ignorantia dispositionis.*—(d²), ignorantia universalis, see *ignorantia particularis.*—(e²), ignorantia universalium iuris, see *ignorantia iuris in particulari.*—(f²), ignorantia vincibilis, see *ignorantia invincibilis.*—(g²), ignorantia voluntaria, see *ignorantia involuntaria.*—Kinds of *ignorantia* in this (2) sense are: (a), ignorantia affectata seu vitiosa, *the intentional* or *sinful ignorance.*—(b), ignorantia excusans and ignorantia non excusans, *ignorance excusing from sin* and *that not excusing from sin.*—(c), ignorantia infidelitatis, *ignorance which consists in unbelief.*—(d), ignorantia non excusans, see *ignorantia excusans.*—(e), ignorantia vitiosa, see *ignorantia affectata.*

ignoro, are, avi, atum, 1, *v. a.* and n., (1) *not to know a person or thing, to have no knowledge of, to be unacquainted with, to be ignorant of, to mistake, misunderstand,* (2) *to take no notice of, ignore, disregard.*—**ignorans,** antis, *P. a., not knowing, unaware, ignorant of a thing.*—**ignoranter,** *adv,. ignorantly, without knowing; unknowingly, in the manner of one untaught or uninformed.* —**ignoratus,** a, um, *P. a., not known, misunderstood.*

ignosco, ere, novi, notum, 3, *v. a.,* (1) *to pardon, forgive,* used (a) *absol.,* (b) with the *dat.,* (2) *pass. impers.*

ignotus, a, um, *adj., pass., unknown.*—**ignotum,** i, *n., that which is unknown, the unknown.*

Ilerdensis, e, *adj., of* or *pertaining to Ilerda* or *Lerida,* the second city in Catalonia, built on the right bank of the River Segra, about 100 miles from Barcelona.

illabor, i, illapsus, 3, *v. dep.,* (1) *to obsess, exert influence over; harass,* or *beset,* as of an evil spirit, (2) *to penetrate, enter* and *diffuse itself through, to permeate,* used fig.

illac, *adv., that way, on that side.*

illaesus, a, um, *adj., unhurt, unharmed, uninjured, unimpaired.*

illapsus, us, *m., a falling, gliding,* or *flowing in,* used in S.T. only in quot.

illaqueo, are, avi, atum, 1, *v. a., to entangle,* used fig., and in S.T. only in quot.

illatio, onis, *f.,* (1) *bringing in, introducing,* (2) *infliction,* (3) *inference, conclusion.*

illativus, a, um, *adj., inferring, concluding, illative.*

ille, illa, illud, *pron. demonstr., that; he, she, it.* In the S.T. there are no instances of the use of any of the various adverbial forms of *ille,* e.g., *illa* (*in that way, in that direction, there*), *illo* (*to that place, thither*); etc.

illecebra, ae, *f., an enticement, attraction, charm, allurement, bait, lure.*

illecebrosus, a, um, *adj., attractive, very enticing,* used in S.T. only in quot.

illegalis, e, *adj., not lawful, unlawful,* opposite of *legalis.* On **iniustitia illegalis,** see *iniustitia;* on **iniustum illegale,** see *iniustus.*

illegitime, *adv.,* see *illegitimus.*

illegitimitas, atis, *f., illegitimacy,* the state of being born out of lawful wedlock.

illegitimus, a, um, *adj., unlawful, not permitted, illegal, illegitimate,* opposite of *legitimus.* On **filius illegitimus,** see *filius;* on **matrimonium illegitimum,** see *matrimonium;* on **persona illegitima,** see *persona.*—**illegitime,** *adv., unlawfully, illegitimately.*

illibatus, a, um, *adj., unspotted.*

illiberalis, e, *adj.,* (1) *not free, dependent,* synonym of *servilis* and *servus,* the opposite of *liber* and *liberalis,* (2) *ungenerous, stingy, miserly, niggardly,* the synonym of *avarus,* the opposite of *libera-*

lis and *prodigus.*—On **disciplina illiberalis,** see *disciplina.*

illiberalitas, atis, *f., conduct unworthy of a freeman, ignoble* or *ungenerous behavior, meanness, stinginess,* synonym of *avaritia,* the opposite of *liberalitas* and *prodigalitas.*

illic, *adv., in that place, yonder, there.*

illicio, ere, lexi, lectum, 3, *v. a., to allure, entice,* used in S.T. only in quot.

illicite, *adv.,* see *illicitus.*

illicitus, a, um, *adj., not allowed, forbidden, unlawful, illegal, illicit,* the opposite of *licitus.* On **actus illicitus,** see *actus;* on **concupiscentia illicita,** see *concupiscentia;* on **iudicium illicitum,** see *iudicium;* on **iuramentum illicitum,** see *iuramentum;* on **observantia illicita,** see *observantia;* on **observatio illicita,** see *observatio.*—**illicite,** *adv., unlawfully, illegally, illicitly.*

illico, *adv., of time, immediately, directly,* used in S.T. only in quot.

illigo, are, avi, atum, 1, *v. a., to fasten.*

illinc, *adv., from that person* or *thing, from that quarter,* used in S.T. only in quot.

illitteratus, a, um, *adj., unlettered, illiterate, uneducated, unlearned.*

illuc, *adv., to that place, thither.*

illucesco, ere, luxi, 3, *inch. n.* and *a., to shine,* used fig.—**illucescens,** entis, *P. a., dawning,* be-

ginning to grow light in the morning.

illudo, ere, si, sum, 3, *v. a.,* (1) *to deceive, impose upon,* (2) *to deride, make the object of mockery* or *ridicule, mock.*

illuminatio, onis, *f.,* (1) *illumination, the act of illuminating; a lighting up, a diffusion of light* used (a) lit., (b) fig., (2) *illumination; mental enlightenment; imparted light;* especially in theology, *spiritual enlightenment* in connection with divine truth; the manifestation of what is conceived by the mind as depending directly on primal truth, that is, on God, (3) *illumination, light, power of vision, eyesight.*

illuminativus, a, um, *adj., enlightening, illuminative.* On **ordo illuminativus,** see *ordo;* on **virtus illuminativa,** see *virtus;* on **vis illuminativa,** see *vis.*

illumino, are, avi, atum, 1, *v. a.,* (1) lit., *to light up, give light to, shine* (2) fig., (a) in gen., *to enlighten spiritually,* (b) in partic., *to illuminate, enlighten the intellect,* a term used by theologians in defining the method of intellectual communication by illumination carried on between the angels or of the manifestation of angelic concepts derived from primal truth, that is from God, to other angels, (c) with *caecus,* **illuminare caecum,** *to give light* or *sight to the blind.*

illusio, onis, *f., an illusion,* (1) *the fact* or *condition of being de-*

ceived; a false conception or idea, (2) something that deceives or deludes by producing a false impression; a deceptive or illusive appearance, statement, belief, (3) derision; mockery, the act of deriding or mocking.

illusor, oris, m., a mocker, derider.

illustratio, onis, f., an illustration, lighting up, illumination, enlightenment, (1) a spiritual or intellectual enlightenment, (2) physical, an illumination, lighting up.

illustris, e, adj., (1) lit., clear, bright, lustrous, (2) fig., distinguished, illustrious, famous, honorable.—De viris illustribus, On Famous Men, a work of St. Jerome's, in which he gives sketches of the lives of Christian writers as Suetonius in his work of the same title had given of the lives of the old Roman authors.

illustro, are, avi, atum, 1, v. a., (1) lit., to light up, make light, illuminate, (2) fig., (a) to light up, throw the light of intelligence on, (b) to illuminate, light up the mind with a supernatural light.

imaginabilis, e, adj., sensibly conceivable, conceivable, imaginable. On **bonum imaginabile,** see bonus; on **forma imaginabilis,** see forma.—**imaginabiliter,** adv., imaginatively, in imagination.

imaginabiliter, adv., see imaginabilis.

imaginaliter, adv., imaginatively.

imaginarius, a, um, adj., of or belonging to images, imaginary, belonging to a sensible conception, sensibly conceiving, sensibly conceivable. On **apprehensio imaginaria,** see apprehensio; on **bonum imaginarium,** see bonus; on **claritas imaginaria,** see claritas; on **cognitio imaginaria,** see cognitio; on **dimensio imaginaria,** see dimensio; on **forma imaginaria,** see forma; on **revelatio imaginaria,** see revelatio; on **tempus imaginaria,** see tempus; on **virtus imaginaria,** see virtus; on **vis imaginaria,** see vis; on **visio imaginaria,** see visio.—**imaginarie,** adv., in a sensibly conceivable manner, according to imagination.

imaginatio, onis, f., (1) a mental image, fancy, imagination, conception, phantasm, synonym of phantasia, phantasma, and theorema, (2) power of imagination, phantasy, imaginative faculty, synonym of phantasia.—Kinds of imaginatio in this (1) sense are: (a), **imaginatio confusa seu indeterminata,** the confused or indefinite image which has as its opposite imaginatio distincta seu determinata, i.e., the distinct or definite image.—(b), **imaginatio extranea,** the foreign or strange image.—(c), **imaginatio falsa,** the false imagination.—(d), **imaginatio indeterminata,** see imaginatio confusa.—(e), **imaginatio particularis,** the *particular image.*—(f), **imaginatio per intellectum,** *the intellectual conception* or *idea.* On the difference between *imaginatio* and *memoria,* see *memoria.* On **apprehendere per imaginationem,** see *apprehendere;* on **apprehensio imaginationis,** see *apprehensio;* on **visio imaginationis,** see *visio.*

imaginativus, a, um, *adj., imagining through the senses, imaginative.*—**imaginativa** sc. **potentia seu virtus seu vis,** *the sensible power of imagination* or *the sensible imaginative faculty.* On **potentia imaginativa,** see *potentia;* on **virtus imaginativa,** see *virtus;* on **vis imaginativa,** see *vis;* on **visio imaginativa,** see *visio.*

imaginatus, a, um, *P. a., imagined, conceived in the mind, supposed, fancied.*

imagino, are, avi, atum, 1, *v. a.,* used as a deponent verb except in p.p. part., *to conceive sensibly, picture to one's self, fancy, imagine.* On **affirmatio imaginata,** see *affirmatio;* on **bonum imaginatum,** see *bonus;* on **finis imaginatus,** see *finis;* on **species imaginata,** see *species.*

imago, inis, *f.,* (1) *copy, image, picture,* (2) *idol, carving,* (3) *pattern, model,* synonym of *exemplar, forma, idea,* and *species.*—On the difference between *imago* and *vestigium,* see *vestigium.* On **repraesentatio imaginis seu per modum imaginis,** see *repraesentatio;* on **similitudo**

imaginis, see *similitudo.*—Kinds of *imago* in this (1) sense are: (a), **imago astronomica,** *the astronomic image* or *constellation.* —(b), **imago creationis seu naturae, imago recreationis seu gratiae** and **imago similitudinis seu gloriae,** *the image of creation* or *nature, that of restoration* or *of grace,* and *that of analogy* or *of glory,* i.e., the image of God which every one according to creation and as a result of nature carries within himself, that which the just man as the result of his inner sanctification possesses through grace, and that dwelling in the blessed of heaven as a result of the glory of God and their similar glory.—(c), **imago deficiens seu imperfecta** and **imago perfecta,** *the deficient* or *the imperfect image* and *the perfect image.*—(d), **imago gloriae,** see *imago creationis.*—(e), **imago gratiae,** see *imago creationis.*— (f), **imago imperfecta,** see *imago deficiens.*—(g), **imago naturae,** see *imago creationis.*—(h), **imago perfecta,** see *imago deficiens.*— (i), **imago recreationis,** see *imago creationis.*—(j), **imago representiva,** *the representative* or *vicarious image.*—(k), **imago similitudinis,** see *imago creationis.*

imbecille, *adv.,* see *imbecillis.*

imbecillis, e, *adj., weak, feeble.*— **imbecille,** *adv., weakly, feebly.*

imbecillitas, atis, *f.,* (1) *weakness, debility, feebleness,* (a) of the body, (b) transf., of condition as regards ability, *incompetency* or *incapacity* to do something, (2) of the mind, *intellectual weakness*, (3) fig., (spiritual) *weakness*.

imber, bris, *m., rain, heavy* or *violent rain, a rain-storm, shower of rain.*

imbuo, ere, ui, utum, 3, *v. a., to imbue, to inspire* or *impress early, to accustom, inure, initiate, instruct.—***imbutus,** a, um, *P. a., somewhat instructed, imbued, initiated, trained.*

imbutus, a, um, *P. a.,* see *imbuo.*

imitabilis, e, *adj., that may be imitated, imitable.*

imitatio, onis, *f., imitation, the action* or *practice of imitating* or *copying.*

imitator, oris, *f., an imitator,* used with the *gen.*

imitor, ari, atus, 1, *v.* freq. *a.* dep., *to imitate, act like, copy after, seek to resemble, to do* or *try to do after the manner of, follow as an example in conduct* or *action.*

immaculatus, a, um, *adj.,* (1) lit., *immaculate, unblemished, free from physical defect* or *disfigurement,* (2) fig., *immaculate, undefiled, unsullied, holy, unspotted, free from the taint of sin* or *evil.*

immaneo, ere, 2, *v. n., to remain in, hold to, cling to.—***immanens,** entis, *P. a., immanent, abiding, indwelling, remaining within.*

immanis, e, *adj.,* (1) of inanimate and abstract things, *immense, enormous, heinous,* (2) *monstrous in character, fierce, savage, wild.*

immanitas, atis, *f., enormity, heinousness, savagery,* used in S.T. only in quot.

immaterialis, e, *adj., immaterial, not being of the nature of material, not connected with any material, not existing in any material,* the opposite of *materialis.* On **cognitio immaterialis,** see *cognitio;* on **esse immateriale,** see *esse;* on **forma immaterialis,** see *forma;* on **immutatio immaterialis,** see *immutatio;* on **potentia immaterialis,** see *potentia;* on **principium immateriale,** see *principium;* on **processio immaterialis,** see *processio;* on **qualitas immaterialis,** see *qualitas;* on **res immaterialis,** see *res;* on **substantia immaterialis,** see *substantia;* on **virtus immaterialis,** see *virtus.—***immaterialiter,** *adv., in an immaterial manner, immaterially,* the opposite of *materialiter.* On **cognoscere immaterialiter,** see *cognoscere;* on **intellegere immaterialiter,** see *intellegere;* on **recipere immaterialiter,** see *recipere;* on **scire immaterialiter,** see *scire.*

immaterialitas, atis, *f., immateriality, freedom from material,* synonym of *spiritualitas,* opposite of *materialitas.*

immaterialiter, see *immaterialis.*

immediate, see *immediatus.*

immediatio, onis, *f., immediateness, immediacy.*

immediatus, a, um, *adj., not interposed by anything else, underived, direct, adjacent to, immediate,* the opposite of *mediatus.* On **agens immediatum,** see *agens;* on **auctoritas immediata,** see *auctoritas;* on **causa immediata,** see *causa;* on **contrarietas immediata,** see *contrarietas;* on **contraria immediata,** see *contrarius;* on **differentia immediata,** see *differentia;* on **effectus immediatus,** see *effectus;* on **forma immediata,** see *forma;* on **movens immediatum,** see *movens;* on **oppositum immediatum,** see *opponere;* on **praedicatio immediata,** see *praedicatio;* on **principium immediatum,** see *principium;* on **propositio immediata,** see *propositio;* on **visio immediata,** see *visio.*—**immediatus in determinato susceptivo** is distinguished from *immediatus omnino seu simpliciter* thus: oppositio contradictionis omnino est immediata, oppositio vero privationis est immediata in determinato susceptivo, non autem est immediata simpliciter.—**immediate,** *adv., in a direct manner without interference of something else, immediately,* synonym of *directe,* the opposite of *mediate* or *mediante aliquo.* On **movens immediate,** see *movens;* on **movere immediate,** see *movere;* on **procedere immediate,** see *procedere;* on **unire immediate,** see *unire.*

immediocriter, *adv., in no moderate degree.*

immensitas, atis, *f.,* (1) *immeasurableness, boundlessness, greatness, infinity,* (2) *immensity, the attribute of God by which we understand Him to be uncircumscribable by any place, even before place existed.* Subsequent to creation, He is omnipresent because by His substance He is in every place, and He permeates all things, in heaven and on earth.

immensus, a, um, *adj.,* (1) lit., *immense, very great in degree, extent, size,* or *quantity,* (2) fig., *immense, immeasurably large, of boundless extent, infinite, unfathomable.*—**in immensum,** *to an immeasurable degree.*

immergo, ere, si, sum, 3, *v. a.,* (1) *to dip* or *plunge into water,* esp. *to baptize by immersion,* (2) transf., *to plunge into, bury,* as the soul plunged into hell, (3) fig., (a) *to merge, cause to enter, enclose, as to merge the soul into the body,* (b) *to plunge* or *sink* into a particular state of body or mind; *to involve deeply, absorb* in some action or activity.

immerito, *adv., undeservedly, without cause,* used in the S.T. only in quot.

immersio, onis, *f., immersion,* (1) in partic., the act of dipping or plunging into the water used in the administration of Baptism; called triple or trine immersion when the candidate is dipped three times, in the name of each Person of the Holy Trinity, (2) fig., *immersion, the state of being overwhelmed* or *deeply engaged; absorption.*

imminentia, ae, *f.,* *imminence, nearness.*

immineo, ere, 2, *v. a.,* (I) lit., *to threaten, menace,* (II) fig., (1) *to be incumbent upon,* (2) of an event, almost always of evil or danger, *to be near at hand, to impend threateningly, to overhang; to be ready, to befall* or *overtake one; to be close at hand in its incidence, to come on shortly,* (a) in gen., (b) in partic.—**imminens,** entis, *P. a., pending, coming on shortly, imminent.*

imminuo, ere, ui, utum, 2, *v. a.,* *to lessen, diminish a thing.*

immisceo, ere, ui, xtum, 2, *v. a.,* (1) lit., *to intermingle, mix in, intermix,* (2) fig.—Common phrases are: *se immiscere alicui rei, to take part in, concern oneself with, meddle with something.*—*immiscere se, to obtrude itself.*—*immiscere mendacia veritati, to mix the false with the true.*—*immiscere prohibitionem caeremonialibus, to insert a prohibition among the ceremonial observances.*

immisericordia, ae, *f.,* *mercilessness, unmercifulness.*

immissio, onis, *f.,* (1) *a letting in, infusion,* (2) *intervention, interposition, interference with the acts of others,* (3) *immission,* in

Eucharistic use it is equal to *commixtio* or the putting of a small particle of the Host into the chalice at the communion of the Mass, typifying the reunion of body and soul at the resurrection.

immissor, oris, *m.,* *a sender, one who sends,* used in the S.T. only in quot.

immitigabilis, e, *immitigable, that cannot be softened* or *allayed,* used in S.T. only in quot.

immitis, e, *adj., harsh, rough, cruel, pitiless.*

immitto, ere, isi, issum, 3, *v. a.,* *to put in, insert, inject, infuse; to let in, admit, introduce things material* or *immaterial.*

immixtio, onis, *f.,* *admixture, the ingredient added to the principal substance in forming a mixture.*

immixtus, a, um, *adj., unmixed.*

immobilis, e, *adj., immovable,* the opposite of *mobilis.* On **animal immobile,** see *animal;* on **causa immobile,** see *causa;* on **corpus immobile,** see *corpus;* on **movens immobile,** see *movens;* on **substantia immobilis,** see *substantia.* —**immobiliter,** *adv., immovably.*

immobilitas, atis, *f.,* (1) lit., *immobility, the condition of being immobile; incapacity of moving,* or *of being moved,* (2) fig., *unchangeableness, immutability,* one of the attributes of God. God is absolutely immutable, in every sense; in His substance, His knowledge, His will; His decrees; one simple eternal act is His essence.

immobiliter, *adv.,* see *immobilis.*

immobilito, are, 1, *v. a.,* (1) *to immobilize, paralyze, render incapable of movement,* (2) *decide definitely, fix, settle, determine.*

immoderantia, ae, *f., want of moderation, intemperance, immoderation.*

immoderate, *adv.,* see *immoderatus.*

immoderatio, onis, *f., want of moderation, excess.*

immoderatus, a, um, *adj., immoderate, unrestrained, unbridled.—immoderate, adv., immoderately, in an immoderate manner* or *degree; beyond reasonable limits; excessively, extravagantly, too much.*

immodicus, a, um, *adj., excessive, beyond bounds, immoderate.*

immodificatus, a, um, *adj., unmodified, unchanged.*

immolatio, onis, *f.,* (1) *immolation, the action of immolating* or *offering in sacrifice; sacrificial slaughter of a victim; sacrifice,* (2) applied to the sacrifice of the mass, *immolation,* the commemoration of Christ's death and passion in the mass is called a sacrifice, oblation or immolation of Christ.

immolatitius, a, um, *adj., of* or *for a sacrifice, sacrificial.*

immolo, are, avi, atum, 1, *v. a.,* (1) *to immolate, to bring as an offering, sacrifice,* (2) fig., *to present as an offering, sacrifice,*

give up for the sake of something else.

immoror, ari, atus, 1, *v. dep. n., to tarry* or *remain, to abide in, to dwell upon.*

immortalis, e, *adj., undying, immortal* in the narrower and in the wider sense of the word.— On **caro immortalis,** see *caro;* on **vita immortalis,** see *vita.*

immortalitas, atis, *f., exemption from death, immortality* in the narrower and in the wider sense of the word.—Kinds of *immortalitas* in the general sense of the word are: (a), **immortalitas gloriae,** *immortality in the glory of heaven.*—(b), **immortalitas naturalis,** *natural immortality.*—(c), **immortalitas perfecta,** *the perfect immortality.*—(d), **immortalitas spiritualis,** *spiritual immortality,* qualis est resurgentium.

immunde, *adv.,* see *immundus.*

immunditia, ae, *f., impurity, uncleanness, filth,* synonym of *impuritas,* and *pollutio, the* opposite of *munditia.* On **passio immunditiae,** see *passio;* on **servitus immunditiae,** see *servitus.*—Kinds of *immunditia* are: (a), **immunditia corporalis seu corporis seu exterior** and **immunditia mentis,** *the physical* or *exterior impurity* and *the mental* or *inner impurity.*—(b), **immunditia corporis,** see *immunditia corporalis.*—(c), **immunditia culpae seu peccati** and **immunditia irregularitatis,** *impurity consisting of a sin* or *guilt* and *that consisting of an irregularity.*—(d), **immunditia exterior,** see *immunditia corporalis.*—(e), **immunditia irregularitatis,** see *immunditia culpae.*—(f), **immunditia luxuriae,** *the impurity arising from lust,* quae potest attendi sive secundum inordinatam emissionem quarumcumque superfluitatum vel specialiter quantum ad emissionem seminis.—(g), **immunditia mentis,** see *immunditia corporalis.*—(h), **immunditia peccati,** see *immunditia culpae.*—(i), **immunditia spiritualis,** *spiritual impurity.*

immundo, are, avi, 1, *v. a.,* *to defile, render unclean.*

immundus, a, um, *adj.,* (1) lit., *unclean, filthy,* (2) fig., *unclean, impure,* (a) of persons, as the result of sin, or by contact with any legal or ceremonial uncleanness, (b) of speech and thought, (c) *the unclean spirit; a wicked spirit; a demon,* (3) ceremonially *unclean,* (a) *constituting a source of defilement,* said specifically in Jewish law of certain animals forbidden for use in sacrifice or for food, (b) *everything of the harvest before the first fruits had been offered was considered unclean in the Old Testament,* (c) *certain states* or *conditions of the human body wherein the influence* and *consequences of sin appear more clearly* and *more forcibly, were in the Mosaic Law considered*

to defile a man. He became thereby unclean before the Lord, and was deprived of the benefit and privileges of the covenant. Those states were: death, leprosy, some normal and abnormal physiological functions, and childbirth.—**immunde,** *adv., impurely, uncleanly, filthily.*

immunis, e, *adj.,* (1) lit. (a) *free* or *exempt from a public burden* or *charge* as in the case of ecclesiastical persons exempt from taxation, (b) transf. *immune, free from,* as physical unsightliness, (2) fig. *not sharing* or *partaking in, free from, devoid of, without something,* used with *a, ab* and the *abl.*

immunitas, atis, *f.,* (1) lit., *immunity, freedom* or *exemption from anything,* as the exemption of ecclesiastical persons and things from secular or civil liabilities, burdens, or duties, (2) fig., *immunity, freedom* or *exemption from anything evil* or *injurious.*

immutabilis, e, *adj.,* (1) in gen., *immutable, not subject* or *susceptible to change; changeless,* (2) in partic., *immutable, unchangeable,* an attribute of God, the same forever and ever, in whom there is no change, nor the shadow of alteration.

immutabilitas, atis, *f.,* (1) in gen., *immobility, fixedness, stability,* (2) in partic., an attribute of God, *immutability, the quality of being immutable; unchange-*

*ableness, invariableness, unal-
terableness.*—immutabiliter, *adv.,
unchangeably.*

immutabiliter, *adv.,* see *immutabilis.*

immutatio, onis, *f.,* (1) *lack of
change, immutability, unchangeableness,* (2) *change,* i.e., passing from one state to another,
synonym of *conversio, mutatio,*
and *transmutatio.*—Kinds of *immutatio* in this (2) sense are:
(a), immutatio accidentalis and
immutatio essentialis, *the unessential* and *the essential change.*
—(b), immutatio animalis seu
sensibilis seu immaterialis seu
spiritualis and immutatio corporalis seu materialis seu naturalis
sc. organi animae, *the spiritual*
or *sensible* or *immaterial* or *intellectual change* and *the physical change* or *the change that
affects the nature of an organ
of the soul.*—(c), immutatio corporalis, see *immutatio animalis.*
—(d), immutatio essentialis, see
immutatio accidentalis.—(e), immutatio immaterialis, see *immutatio animalis.*—(f), immutatio
materialis, see *immutatio animalis.*—(g), immutatio naturalis, see
immutatio animalis.—(h), immutatio sensibilis, see *immutatio
animalis.*—(i), immutatio spiritualis, see *immutatio animalis* and
immutatio naturalis.

immutativus, a, um, *adj., changing.*
On vis immutativus, see *vis.*

immutatus, a, um, *adj., unchanged.*

immuto, are, avi, atum, 1, *v. a., to
change, alter, transform.*

imo, *adv.,* introduces a sentence
rectifying a mistake, implied
doubt, or understatement in a
question, *nay, nay but, nay
rather.*

impacatus, a, um, *adj., not peaceable, unquiet, unpacific,* used
in the S.T. only in quot.

impactio, onis, *f., a striking against,
concussion, an impact.*

impalpabilis, e, *adj., impalpable,
intangible,* the opposite of *palpabilis.* On corpus impalpabile,
see *corpus.*

impar, aris, *adj.,* (1) in gen., *uneven, unequal, dissimilar,* (a) in
number, *odd, uneven,* not divisible by two, (b) in quality, (2)
in partic., (with the accessory
idea of smaller, inferior), *inferior, weaker.*

imparatus, a, um, *adj., unprepared, not ready, unprovided.*

impartibilis, e, *adj., indivisible,
without parts.*

impartior, iri, 4, dep. *v. a.,* (also
in the *dep.* from *impertior*) *to
impart, give, offer.*

impassibilis, e, *adj., incapable of
suffering, passionless,* synonym
of *insensibilis,* the opposite of
passibilis. On caro impassibilis,
see *caro;* on corpus impassibile,
see *corpus;* on intellectus impassibilis, see *intellectus.*

impassibilitas, atis, *f.,* (1) *incapacity for suffering, impassibility,*
the opposite of *passibilitas,* (2)
apathy, synonym of *insensibili-*

tas.—One kind of *impassibilitas* is: **impassibilitas gloriae seu gloriosorum,** *impassibility of glory* or *of the glorified in heaven* which is the opposite of *impassibilitas naturae,* i.e., of natural impassibility.

impatiens, entis, *adj., that cannot bear, will not endure* or *suffer, impatient of anything.*

impatientia, ae, *f., impatience, unwillingness* or *inability to bear anything, want of endurance.*

impaviditas, atis, *f., impavidity, fearlessness.*

impavidus, a, um, *adj., impavid, fearless, undaunted.*

impeccabilitas, atis, *f., impeccability, the quality* or *character of being impeccable, freedom from liability to sin, wrongdoing* or *error.*

impedimentum, i, *n.,* (1) *an impediment, hindrance, that by which something is entangled,* (a) in gen., (b) in particular, *an impediment* to marriage, a condition or circumstance which under natural, Divine, or Church law, renders a marriage unlawful or invalid. Some impediments are merely forbidding, *impedimenta impedientia;* others are annulling, *impedimenta dirimentia.* The former make the marriage illicit; the latter render it also invalid, (2) *an impediment,* something that impedes the functions or health of the body.

impedio, ire, ivi, or ii, itum, 4, *v. a., to hamper, impede, hinder,*

prevent, constr., with (1) *acc.,* (2) *ab.,* (3) *ne, quin, quominus,* (4) the *inf.,* (5) *absol.*—**impediens,** entis, *P. a., hindering, preventing.* On **causa impediens,** see, *causa.*—**impeditus,** a, um, *P. a., hindered, prevented.* On **causa impedita,** see *causa;* on **operatio impedita,** see *operatio.*

impeditio, onis, *f., impedition, the action of impeding* or *fact of being impeded; hindering.*

impeditivus, a, um, *adj., impeditive, tending to impede* or *obstruct; of the nature of an impediment; obstructive, hindering.*

impeditor, oris, *m., a hinderer, obstructer.*

impello, ere, puli, pulsum, 3, *v. a.,* (1) lit., (a) *to strike against a thing,* (b) in partic. with the accessory idea of motion, *to set in motion, impel,* (2) fig., *to impel, incite, urge;* esp. *to instigate, stimulate, persuade,* used with (a) *in* or *ad* and *acc.,* (b) *ut* with *subj.,* (c) the simple *acc.,* (d) *absol.,* (e) in *pass.*

impendo, ere, di, sum, 3, *v. a., to give, bestow, vouchsafe, expend, discharge, impart, devote,* used with *acc.* alone, and with *acc.* and *dat.*—**impensus,** a, um, *P. a., bestowed, rendered.*—**impensa,** ae, *f., fee, charge, cost.*

impensus, a, um, *Part.* and *P. a.,* see *impendo.*

imperativus, a, um, *adj.,* (1) *commanding* in the proper sense of the word, (2) *commanding* in the broader sense of the word. —On modus imperativus, see *modus;* on oratio imperativa, see *oratio;* on verbum imperativum, see *verbum;* on virtus imperativa, see *virtus;* on vis imperativa, see *vis.*—imperative, *adv., in the sense of a commanding, imperatively,* setting subordinates to work, the opposite of *permissive* and *elicitive,* the latter in relation to the activity of a faculty.

imperator, oris, *m.,* (1) *emperor;* in Roman History a word generally meaning commander, under the Republic conferred by salutation of the soldiers on a victorious general; afterwards under the Empire, confined to the head of the State, in whose name all victories were won, and thus the equivalent of its English representative, emperor, (2) applied to Christ as *commander-in-chief, absolute ruler.*

imperceptibilis, e, *adj., imperceptible.*

imperfecte, *adv.,* see *imperfectus.*

imperfectio, onis, *f., imperfection,* the opposite of *perfectio.*—Kinds of *imperfectio* are: (a), imperfectio actus, *the imperfection of an action.*—(b), imperfectio agentis and imperfectio effectus, *the imperfection of a cause* and *that of an effect.*—(c), imperfectio effectus, see *imperfectio agentis.* —(d), imperfectio moralis, *the moral imperfection.*—(e), imperfectio virtutis, *the imperfection of a virtue.*

imperfectus, a, um, *adj., unfinished, incomplete, imperfect,* synonym of *incompletus,* the opposite of *completus* and *perfectus.* On actus imperfecti et imperfectus, see *actus;* on agens imperfectus, see *agens;* on amicitia imperfecta, see *amicitia;* on amor imperfectus, see *amor;* on animal imperfectum, see *animal;* on beatitudo imperfecta, see *beatitudo;* on bonitas imperfecta, see *bonitas;* on bonum imperfectum, see *bonus;* on caritas imperfecta, see *caritas;* on causa imperfecta, see *causa;* on coactio imperfecta, see *coactio;* on cognitio imperfecta, see *cognitio;* on communitas imperfecta, see *communitas;* on contemplatio imperfecta, see *contemplatio;* on definitio imperfecta, see *definitio;* on delectatio imperfecta, see *delectatio;* on dilectio imperfecta, see *dilectio;* on ens imperfectum, see *ens;* on esse imperfectum, see *esse;* on felicitas imperfecta, see *felicitas;* on forma imperfecta, see *forma;* on fruitio imperfecta, see *fruitio;* on gratia imperfecta, see *gratia;* on inductio imperfecta see *inductio;* on ira imperfecta, see *ira;* on linea imperfecta, see *linea;* on magnitudo imperfecta, see *magnitudo;* on matrimonium imperfectum, see *matrimonium;* on motus imperfectus, see *motus;* on numerus imperfectus, see *numerus;* on oboedientia imperfecta, see *oboedientia;* on operatio imperfecta, see *operatio;* on **oratio imperfecta,** see *oratio;* on **pax imperfecta,** see *pax;* on **praedicatio imperfecta,** see *praedicatio;* on **prudentia imperfecta,** see *prudentia;* on **perfectio imperfecta,** see *perfectio;* on **potentia imperfecta,** see *potentia;* on **qualitas imperfecta,** see *qualitas;* on **quantitas imperfecta,** see *quantitas;* on **ratio imperfecta,** see *ratio;* on **regimen imperfectum,** see *regimen;* on **resurrectio imperfecta,** see *resurrectio;* on **scientia imperfecta,** see *scientia;* on **similitudo imperfecta,** see *similitudo;* on **species imperfecta,** see *species;* on **status imperfectus,** see *status;* on **virtus imperfecta,** see *virtus;* on **visio imperfecta,** see *visio;* on **vita imperfecta,** see *vita.—* **imperfectum est prius quam perfectum, in fieri,** *in the sphere of becoming* or *beginning, the imperfect is prior to the perfect.* —**in omnibus generibus contingit aliquid esse dupliciter, vel sicut perfectum, vel sicut imperfectum,** see *perfectus.*—**naturali ordine perfectum praecedit imperfectum,** see *perfectus.*—**omne, quod est imperfectum, sub eodem genere cadit cum perfecto, non quidem sicut species, sed per reductionem,** *everything that is imperfect falls under the same genus as the perfection that corresponds to it not as a species but as ultimately reducible to it.* —**perfecta naturaliter sunt priora imperfectis,** see *perfectus.—*

perfectum est prius imperfecto et natura et tempore, see *perfectus.*—**perfectum est prius imperfecto in rerum naturalium ordine,** see *perfectus.*—**perfectum naturaliter est prius imperfecto,** see *perfectus.*—**perfectum natura prius est imperfecto,** see *perfectus.* —**perfectum secundum substantiam prius est imperfecto,** see *perfectus.*—**veniente perfecto evacuatur imperfectum, quod scilicet ei opponitur,** see *perfectus.*— **opus imperfectum,** the title of a work included among works of St. John Chrysostom, is the work of an Arian author of the fifth century. St. Thomas makes frequent reference to the *Opus imperfectum.*—**imperfecte,** *adv., imperfectly, incompletely,* the opposite of *perfecte.* On **cognoscere perfecte,** see *cognoscere;* on **velle imperfecta,** see *velle.*

imperialis, e, *adj., imperial,* found only in quot. in S.T. On **dominium imperiale,** see *dominium.*

imperiose, *adv., imperiously, tyrannically,* used in the S.T. only in quot.

imperitia, ae, *f., inexperience, ignorance, unskilfulness.*

imperitus, a, um, *adj., unskilled, unlettered, ignorant, without experience,* used in the S.T. only in quot.

imperium, ii, *n.,* (1) *command, the intellectual act directing the activity of the will,* (2) *command* in the wider sense of the word, (3) *chief command, imperial power,*

(4) *empire, kingdom.*—Kinds of *imperium* in this (1) sense are: **imperium intellectus** and **imperium voluntatis,** *the command* or *power of reason* and *that of the will.* A kind of *imperium* in this (4) sense is: **imperium mundanum,** *the worldly kingdom.*

impermixtus, a, um, *adj., unmixed.*

impero, are, avi, atum, 1, *v. a.,* and *n.,* (1) *to command, order* in the proper and narrower sense of the word, *to direct the activity of another faculty,* the opposite of *elicere,* (2) *to command* in the broader sense of the word.—On **actus imperatus,** see *actus;* on **ars imperans,** see *ars;* on **caritas imperans,** see *caritas;* on **habitus imperans,** see *habitus;* on **motus imperans,** see *motus;* on **potentia imperans et imperata,** see *potentia;* on **principium imperans,** see *principium;* on **virtus imperans,** see *virtus.*—**imperans,** antis, *P. a., commanding, ordering.*—**imperatus,** a, um, *P. a., commanded, ordered.*

impersonalis, e, *adj., impersonal.*

impersuasibilis, e, *adj., impersuasible, not to be persuaded, unyielding.*

impertransibilis, e., *adj., impertransible, that cannot be passed through* or *crossed.*

imperturbatus, a, um, *adj., undisturbed,* used in the S.T. only in quot.

impetigo, onis, *f., a scabby eruption of the skin, impetigo.*

impeto, ere, 3, *v. a., to accuse.*

impetrabilis, e, *adj., pass., easy to be obtained, attainable.*

impetratio, onis, *f., impetration, the action of obtaining* or *procuring by request* or *entreaty.*

impetrativus, a, um, *adj., obtained by entreaty,* or *vows, impetrative.*

impetro, are, avi, atum, 1, *v. a., to get, obtain, procure, accomplish, bring to pass,* used *absol.,* with a *subst. cl.,* the *acc.,* and *ut.*

impetuositas, atis, *f., impetuosity,* the quality of being impetuous; sudden or violent energy of movement, action, etc., *vehemence,* especially of feeling, temper, disposition.

impetuosus, a, um, *adj., impetuous, violent.* On **appetitus impetuosus,** see *appetitus.*

impetus, us, *m., assault, attack, impetuosity, impulse.*—Kinds of *impetus* are: (a), **impetus irae,** *the impulse of anger.*—(b), **impetus naturae seu naturalis,** *the natural impulse.*—(c), **impetus naturalis,** see *impetus naturae.*—(d), **impetus passionis,** *the impulse of passion.*—(e), **impetus sensualitatis,** *the impulse to sensuality* or *to carnal desire.*

impie, *adv.,* see *impius.*

impietas, atis, *f., impiety, ungodliness, want of reverence for God* and *religion.*

impignoro, are, avi, atum, 1, *v. a., to impignorate, to pledge, mortgage.*

impingo, ere, pegi, pactum, 3, *v. a.,* (1) lit., *to fall, strike against, trip,* *stumble against,* (2) fig., (a) *to stumble,* (b) *to bring a charge against someone,* used with the *dat.* of the person accused.

impinguo, are, no perf., 1, *v. a., to make fat, fatten.*

impius, a, um, *adj.,* (1) of persons, or things personified, *impious, ungodly, without piety* or *reverence for God* and *His ordinances; presumptuously irreligious, wicked, profane,* (2) *irreverent, undutiful, wanting in reverence* or *dutifulness towards parents.* —**impii,** orum, *m., the wicked, the damned.*—**impie,** *adv., irreligiously, impiously, wickedly.*

implacabilis, e, *adj., unappeasable, implacable,* used in the S.T. only in quot.

impleo, ere, evi, etum, 2, *v. a.,* (I) lit., *to fill, fill up,* (II) fig., (1) in gen., *to fill, make full,* (2) in partic., (a) *to resemble exactly, be correlative to, correspond to,* (b) *to satisfy, to cause to have enough, to meet the desire,* or *fulfill the expectation of,* used with the *abl.,* (c) *to fill, infuse something into the mind; to awaken in the mind* or *heart a feeling, idea, impulse, purpose,* (d) with *vicem,* **implere vicem alicuius,** *to fill* or *take the place of someone,* (3) with the accessory idea of activity, *to fulfill, discharge, execute, satisfy.*

impletio, onis, *f.,* (1) *impletion, the action of filling,* (2) *fulfillment, accomplishment.*

impletivus, a, um, *adj., impletive, having the quality of fulfilling* or *discharging.*

implicatio, onis, *f., implication, the action of implying; the fact of being implied* or *involved, without being plainly expressed; that which is involved* or *implied in something else.*

implicite, *adv.,* see *implico.*

implicitus, a, um, *P. a.,* see *implico.*

implico, are, avi, atum, or ui, itum, 1, *v. a., to entangle, implicate, involve, envelop, engage.*—**implicitus,** a, um, *P. a., contained, involved, confused, intricate,* the opposite of *explicitus.* On **cognitio implicita,** see *cognitio;* on **compositio implicita,** see *compositio;* on **fides implicita,** see *fides;* on **malitia implicita,** see *malitia.*—**implicite,** *adv., in a contained manner, intricately, in an envolved way,* the opposite of *explicite.* On **appetere implicite,** see *appetere;* on **cognoscere implicite,** see *cognoscere;* on **credere implicite,** see *credere;* on **ponere implicite,** see *ponere.*

imploratio, onis, *f., a beseeching for help, imploring.*

imploro, are, avi, atum, 1, *v. a.,* (1) with personal objects, *to invoke, call to one's assistance, call upon for aid; to beseech, entreat, implore,* (2) with inanimate or abstract subjects, *to pray earnestly for, to beseech, entreat, implore, appeal to.*

impoenitens, entis, *adj., not repenting, impenitent.*

impoenitentia, ae, *f.*, *impenitence, unrepenting spirit,* i.e., the intention to persevere in sin, as well as being guilty, the opposite of *poenitentia.*—**impoenitentia finalis,** *impenitence until the end,* a sin against the Holy Ghost. Cf. *peccatum in Spiritum sanctum* under *peccatum.*

impono, ere, posui, positum, 3, *v. a.*, (1) lit., (a) *to place, put, set* or *lay into, upon* or *in a place,* (b) eccl. use, *to impose, to lay hands* in blessing, or in ordination, confirmation, etc., used with *acc., acc.* and *dat.,* (2) fig., (a) *to impose, bestow, apply authoritatively a name upon, on, to,* (b) *to impose, lay on as something to be borne, endured, submitted to; to inflict something on* or *upon; to enforce authoritatively,* (c) *to impose, lay a crime,* charge statement to the account of someone; *to impute, charge.*—**imponere vinum cum aqua,** *to mix wine with water.*—**imponere terminum,** *to set a limit* to something.—**imponere modum,** *to prescribe the mode* for something.

importabilis, e, *adj., that cannot be borne, insupportable, unbearable, unendurable.*

importo, are, avi, atum, (1) *to carry into, bring into, import,* (2) *carry within oneself, grasp within oneself, include, express, mean.*—Kinds of *importare* in this (2) sense are: **importare in obliquo** and **importare in recto,** *to signify something in an ob-*lique or *slanting* and *in a straight line,* i.e., to signify something indirectly and directly.

importune, *adv.,* see *importunus.*

importunitas, atis, *f., solicitude, uneasiness of mind* occasioned by desire, anxiety, or fear.

importunus, a, um, *adj., importune, inopportune, untimely.*—**importune,** *adv.,* (1) *pertinaciously, persistently,* with urgent, persistent sollicitation, (2) *inopportunely, out of season.*

impos, potis, *adj., without power of, not master of,* used in the S.T. only in quot.

impositio, onis, *f.,* (1) lit., *imposition,* (a) *the action of putting* or *adding something,* (b) *a placing upon* or *laying on* of hands in blessing, ordination, confirmation, etc. Christ sometimes used this gesture in working miracles; the Apostles in conferring the sacraments of confirmation and holy orders. Catholic liturgy employs it in the sacraments of baptism, confirmation, extreme unction, and holy orders, (2) fig., (a) *imposition,* the action of imposing or laying on as a burden or duty, (b) *the action of attaching, affixing* or *ascribing; bestowal of a name,* (c) *the application, meaning, signification* of a name to a thing.—**sacramentum manus impositionis,** *the sacrament of the imposition of the hand,* i.e., *confirmation.*

impossibilis, e, *adj., impossible,* i.e., that which is not and cannot be;

opposite of *possibilis.* On demonstratio ad impossibile ducens, see *demonstratio;* on falsum impossibile, see *falsus;* on
materia impossibilis, see *materia;* on processus ad impossibile,
see *processus;* on propositio de
impossibili, see *propositio;* on
ratio ducens seu deducens ad
impossibile, see *ratio;* on syllogismus ad impossibile, de impossibili, et ducens ad impossibile,
see *syllogismus.*—Kinds of *impossibile* are: (a), impossibile
absolute and impossibile ex suppositione seu suppositis quibusdam seu aliquo posito, *the unconditionally impossible* and *the
conditionally impossible.*—(b),
impossibile alicui seu huic seu
in ordine ad aliquid and impossibile simpliciter, *the impossible
under some aspect either for this
or of that or respectively* and *the
the simply or absolutely impossible.*—(c), impossibile aliquo posito, see *impossibile absolute.*—
(d), impossibile ex se seu per se
seu secundum se seu secundum
seipsum seu secundum nullam
potentiam and impossibile per
respectum ad aliquam potentiam, *the impossible of or in itself.*
(cf. *impossibile per accidens*) or
without reference to any power
and *with reference to some power,* i.e., *the intrinsically* and *extrinsically impossible.*—(e), impossibile ex suppositione, *hypothetically impossible.* See *impossibile absolute.*—(f), impossibile

huic, see *impossibile alicui.*—(g),
impossibile in natura seu naturae
and impossibile rationalis philosophiae, *the impossible in the
realm of nature* and *that in the
realm of logic.*—(h), impossibile
in ordine ad aliquid, see *impossibile alicui.*—(i), impossibile naturae, see *impossibile in natura.*—
(j), impossibile per accidens and
impossibile per se, *the impossible because of something outside
itself* and *the impossible because
of itself* (cf. *impossibile ex se*)
or *the impossible as such.*—(k),
impossibile per respectum ad aliquam potentiam, see *impossibile
ex se.*—(l), impossibile per se, see
impossibile ex se and *impossibile
per accidens.*—(m), impossibile
rationalis philosophiae, see *impossibile in natura.*—(n), impossibile secundum aliquam potentiam, see *impossibile ex se.*—(o),
impossibile secundum aliquam
potentiam activam and impossibile secundum aliquam potentiam passivam, *the impossible according to an active power* and
that according to a passive power.—(p), impossibile secundum
aliquam potentiam passivam, see
*impossibile secundum aliquam
potentiam activam.*—(q), impossibile secundum causam inferiorem and impossibile secundum
causam superiorem, *the impossible according to a lower or secondary cause* and *that according
to a higher or superior cause.*—
(r), impossibile secundum cau-

sam superiorem, see *impossibile secundum causam inferiorem.*—(s), impossibile secundum nullam potentiam, see *impossibile ex se.*—(t), impossibile secundum se, see *impossibile ex se.*—(u), impossibile secundum seipsum, see *impossibile ex se.*—(v), impossibile simpliciter, see *impossibile alicui.*—(w), impossibile suppositis quibusdam, see *impossibile absolute.*—ex falso contingenti non sequitur falsum impossibile, *from a false unnecessary or contingent no false impossibility follows.*—sublato impossibili tollitur necessarium, *if one denies the impossible, so also is the corresponding necessary denied.*

impossibilitas, atis, *f., impossibility,* that which cannot exist because it is either self-contradictory or contradictory to the established order of efficient and final causality, the opposite of *possibilitas.* —Kinds of *impossibilitas* are: (a), impossibilitas absoluta and impossibilitas condicionata, *the unconditioned* and *the conditioned impossibility.*—(b), impossibilitas aestimata, *the supposed* or *pretended impossibility.*—(c), impossibilitas conditionata, see *impossibilitas absoluta.*—(d), impossibilitas per se, *the impossibility of a thing through itself* or *in itself.*

impotens, entis, *adj.,* (1) *impotent, having no power* or *ability to accomplish anything; powerless, helpless, ineffective,* said of persons and things, (2) *impotent,*

physically weak; without bodily strength, (3) *impotent, incapable of copulation.*

impotentia, ae, *f., inability* or *incompetence* in the proper and in the improper sense of the word, synonym of *impotentialitas,* the opposite of *potentia, potentialitas,* and *potestas.—Impotentia* belongs to the second kind of *qualitas.* Cf. *qualitas.*—Kinds of *impotentia* are: (a), impotentia activa and impotentia passiva, *the active* and *the passive inability* or *incompetence.*—(b), impotentia coeundi, *the inability* or *incompetence for carnal intercourse.*—(c), impotentia naturalis, *natural inability* or *incompetence* or *that existing through nature.*—(d), impotentia passiva, see *impotentia activa.*

impotentialitas, atis, *f., impotentiality, inability,* or *incapacity,* synonym of *impotentia,* the opposite of *potentia, potentialitas,* and *potestas,* does not occur in S.T.

impraegnatio, onis, *f., impregnation, fertilization.*

impraegno, are, avi, atum, 1, *v. a.,* to *impregnate, make pregnant.*

impraemeditatus, a, um, *adj., unprepared, unpremeditated*

imprecatio, onis, *f., imprecation, invoking of evil.*

imprecor, ari, atus, 1, *v. dep. a.,* to *invoke* on a person, *to call down upon, to imprecate.*

impressio, onis, *f.,* (I) lit., *impression,* the action involved in the pressure of one thing upon or into the surface of another, (1) in gen., (a) *the imprint* of form on formless matter, (b) of light upon air, (c) *influence*, the effective action of one thing upon another; the effect of such action, a change produced in some passive subject by the operation of an external cause, (2) in partic., (a) *an impression, trail* of any thing, a synonym of *vestigium*, (b) *a mark, impression* produced on any surface by the application of a seal, stamp, etc., (c) *a form, shape*, (d) plural, *impressions, atmospheric conditions*, (e) *an impression*, the impact or shock of any physical force, (f) *a reproduction of something*, (II) fig., *impression*, (1) in gen., *the effect produced by external force* or *influence on the senses* or *mind*, (2) in partic., *an impression*, (a), *a notion, remembrance, belief* impressed upon the mind; a somewhat vague or indistinct notion remaining in the mind as a survival from some distinct knowledge, (b), *the action of stamping a character on something*, (c), *a likeness, image of something in the mind.*

imprimo, ere, pressi, pressum, 3, *v. a.*, (1) lit., *to impress, stamp, imprint*, (2) fig., *to impress, stamp, mark*, used with *acc.* and *dat., in* and *acc., acc.* alone, *acc.* with *in* and *acc.*, with *in* and *abl.*

improbabilitas, atis, *f., improbability*, the opposite of *probabilitas.*

improbe, *adv.*, see *improbus.*

improbitas, atis, *f.*, (1) *dishonesty*, (2) pl., *reproaches, the words of one who reproaches.*

improbo, are, avi, atum, 1, *v. a.*, (1) *to disapprove, condemn, reject* an opinion, explanation, solution, theory, etc., (2) *to censure, reprove, condemn, express disapproval* of an act.

improbus, a, um, *adj., morally bad, wicked, base, impious, shameless*, used in the S.T. only in quot.—**improbe,** *adv., wrongly, wickedly.*

improcessibilis, e, *adj., unproceeding.*

improhibitus, a, um, *adj., unforbidden, permitted.*

improperium, ii, *n., a taunt, a bitterly sarcastic remark; insulting reproach.*

impropero, are, avi, atum, 1, *v. n.* and *a., to reproach, upbraid, taunt.*

improportionabilis, e, *adj., unproportionate.* — **improportionabiliter,** *adv., not proportionally, unproportionately.*

improportionabiliter, *adv.*, see *improportionabilis.*

improportionaliter, *adv.*, see *improportionatus.*

improportionatus, a, um, *adj., unproportionate, not proportionate, out of proportion, disproportionate.*—**improportionaliter,** *adv., not proportionally, out of proportion.*

improprie, *adv.*, see *improprius.*

improprius, a, um, *adj.*, (1) *improper, unsuitable, unfit, not in accordance with the nature of the case* or *purpose in view*, (2) *inaccurate, incorrect, inexact, not in accordance with truth, fact, reason* or *rule*, said of a meaning given to a word or phrase which is not the *proper* or *literal* one, but *metaphorical.*—**improprie**, *adv.*, *improperly*

improvidentia, ae, *f.*, *want of foresight, improvidence.*

improvisio, onis, *f.*, *improvision, want of prevision.*

improvisum, i, *n.*, see *improvisus.*

improvisus, a, um, *adj.*, *unforeseen.*—**improvisum**, i, *n.*, *that which is unforeseen, an emergency*, used *adverbially* with *ex* and the *abl.*, *unexpectedly, suddenly.*

imprudens, entis, *adj.*, *imprudent, wanting in prudence* or *discretion; the reverse of prudent; rash, heedless, indiscreet.*

imprudentia, ae, *f.*, *imprudence, shamelessness*, the opposite of *prudentia.*—The chief kinds of *imprudentia* are: *inconsideratio, inconstantia, negligentia*, and *praecipitatio*. On **deformit**as **prudentiae,** see *deformitas.*

impubes, eris, *com.*, *a minor*, one below the age when full civil and personal rights can be exercised.

impudens, entis, *adj.*, *shameless, without shame,* used in the S.T. only in quot.—**impudenter**, *adv.*, *impudently.*

impudenter, *adv.*, see *impudens.*

impudentia, ae, *f.*, *impudence, offensive forwardness with disregard of the opinions of others*, used in the S.T. only in quot.

impudice, *adv.*, see *impudicus.*

impudicitia, ae, *f.*, *shameful conduct short of fornication, immodesty, lewdness*, the opposite of *pudicitia. Impudicitia* belongs to the *opera carnis.* Cf. *caro.*

impudicus, a, um, *adj.*, *immodest, impure.*—**impudice**, *adv.*, *unchastely, lewdly.*

impugnatio, onis, *f.*, *an attack, assault*, (1) *the action of attacking* or *assaulting a person;* esp. spiritual *assault, temptation*, (2) *impugnment, the action of impugning an opinion* etc.; *calling in question, disputing.*

impugnativus, a, um, *adj.*, *capable of resisting* something.

impugnator, oris, *m.*, *an impugner, assailant, one who impugns* or *assails an enemy.*

impugno, are, avi, atum, 1, *v. a.*, *to fight against a person* or *thing, to attack, assail*, (1) lit., in the milit. sphere, (2) transf., beyond the milit. sphere, *to attack, assail, oppose, resist.*

impulsio, onis, *f.*, (1) lit., *impulsion, the action* of striking upon or pushing against, (2) fig., (a) *impulsion*, that which impels or constrains a person to do something, (b) *an impulse, incitement, instigation.*

impulsivum, i, *n.*, *an impulsive, an impelling agent* or *cause.*

impulsus, us, *m.,* (1) lit., *impulse, motion* caused by the sudden application of force, (2) fig., *impulse, incitement* or stimulus to action arising from some state of mind or feeling.

impune, *adv., without punishment, without fear of punishment, with impunity.*

impunitas, atis, *f., freedom* or *safety from punishment, impunity.*

impunitus, a, um, *adj., unpunished.*

impuritas, atis, *f.,* (1) *impurity* in the proper sense, i.e., not being free from a stain, synonym of *immunditia,* the opposite of *munditia* and *puritas,* (2) *impurity* in the improper sense of the word, i.e., not being free of admixture.—With reference to the rational creature and especially as regards the soul of man, the following are kinds of *impuritas* in this (1) sense: (a), **impuritas culpae,** *the impurity which consists of the guilt of sin.*—(b), **impuritas erroris,** *the impurity which results from an error.*—(c), **impuritas intellectus,** *the impurity of the mind.*—(d), **impuritas peccati,** *impurity as a result of sin.*

impurus, a, um, *adj.,* (1) lit., *impure,* (a) *containing offensive matter, dirty, unclean,* (b) *mixed with* or *containing some extraneous* or *foreign matter,* especially an inferior or baser kind, *adulteration,* (2) fig., *not pure morally; defiled by sin.*

imputo, are, avi, atum, 1, *v. a., to impute,* (1) *to bring a fault* or *the like into the reckoning against; to lay to the charge of; to attribute* or *assign as due* or *owing to,* (2) less frequently in a good sense, *to ascribe* or *reckon to.*

imputribilis, e, *adj., not liable to decay, incorruptible.*

imus, a, um, *adj.,* see *inferus.*

in, *prep.* with *abl.* and *acc.,* denotes either rest or motion within or into a place or thing, the opposite of *ex,* (1) *in, within, on, upon, among, at;* (2) *into, to, towards.*

inaccessibilis, e, *adj., unapproachable, inaccessible.*

inadorabilis, e, *not to be adored, unadorable.*

inaequalis, e, *adj., unequal, uneven, unlike, of different sizes, irregular,* the opposite of *aequalis.* On **amicitia inter inaequales,** see *amicitia;* on **iniustum inaequale,** see *iniustus;* on **motus inaequalis,** see *motus;* on **proportio inaequalis,** see *proportio.*—Kinds of *inaequale* are: **inaequale excedens** and **inaequale excessum,** *the unequal surpassing another* or *the greater* and *the unequal surpassed by another* or *the smaller.*—Each of these two kinds of *inaequale* has five subspecies. Thus *inaequale excedens* includes: *numerus multiplex, superparticularis, superpartiens, multiplex superparticularis, multiplex superpartiens;* and *inaequale excessum* includes: *numerus submultiplex, subparticularis, subpartiens, submultiplex subparticularis, submultiplex subpartiens.* Cf. *numerus.*— **inaequaliter,** *adv., unequally, unevenly, irregularly, disproportionately.*

inaequalitas, atis, *f.,* (1) *unevenness, unlikeness, inequality* in the sense of physical size, the opposite of *aequalitas,* (2) *unevenness, unlikeness, inequality* in the figurative sense of size, likewise the opposite of *aequalitas.*— On **proportio inaequalitatis,** see *proportio.*

inaequaliter, see *inaequalis.*

inaestimabiliter, *adv.,* see *inaestimabilis.*

inaestimabilis, e, *adj., inestimable, inconceivable.*—**inaestimabiliter,** *adv., inestimably, incalculably.*

inalterabilis, e, *adj., unchangeable, unalterable.*—**inalterabiliter,** *adv., unchangeably, unalterably.*

inalterabiliter, *adv.,* see *inalterabilis.*

inamissibiliter, *adv., inamissibly, in a manner that cannot lose.*

inanimatus, a, um, *adj.,* (1) *lifeless, inanimate,* the opposite of *animalis* and *animatus,* (2) *not sensitive, not knowing through the senses,* the opposite of *animalis, animatus,* and *sensitivus.*—On **corpus inanimatum,** see *corpus;* on **generatio inanimata,** see *generatio;* on **instrumentum inanimatum,** see *instrumentum;* on

iustitia inanimata, see *iustitia;* on **res inanimata,** see *res.*

inanis, e, *adj.,* (1) *empty, void,* synonym of *vacuus,* the opposite of *plenus;* (2) *vain, useless,* synonym of *frustra, vacuus,* and *vanus,* the opposite of *efficax.*—On **gloria inanis,** see *gloria;* on **signum inane,** see *signum.*—**naturale desiderium non potest esse inane,** see *desiderium.*—**inaniter,** *adv., vainly, idly, uselessly.*

inaniter, *adv.,* see *inanis.*

inappellatio, onis, *f., unsocialness, want of intercourse* or *neglect to call upon* or *speak to one's friends,* used in the S.T. only in quot.

inardesco, ere, arsi, 3, *v. inch. n., to kindle, glow, burn,* used fig., *to long for ardently.*

inassumptibilis, e, *adj., unassumable,* used in the S.T. only in quot.

inassumptus, a, um, *adj., not assumed* or *taken on, unassumed,* used in S.T. only in quot.

inauditus, a, um, *adj., unheard,* on account of its novelty or strangeness.

incalesco, ere, calui, 3, *v. inch. n., to glow, kindle with passion,* used fig.

incantatio, onis, *f., incantation,* the use of a formula of words, spoken or chanted, to produce a magical effect.

incarceratio, onis, *f., incarceration, imprisonment.*

incarcero, are, avi, atum, 1, *v. a., to incarcerate, shut up in prison;*

imprison.—**incarceratus,** a, um, *P. a., incarcerated, imprisoned.*

incarnatio, onis, *f., the incarnation,* the action or the fact of being incarnate or made flesh; a becoming incarnate; assumption of, or existence in, a human nature; a word used to express the union of the Divine nature of the Second Person of the Trinity with human nature in the person of Jesus Christ. The Apostle, St. John, says: The Word was made Flesh. The Word is the Son of God; by Flesh in Scripture is meant mankind, human nature, man, body and soul, as in Luke 3: "And all flesh shall see the salvation of God."

incarno, are, avi, atum, 1, *v. a.,* orig. *to make flesh,* hence in the *pass. incarnari, incarnatus,* as used by St. Thomas, *to be made flesh, to become incarnate,* especially when used of Christ. The Son of God assumed our flesh and dwelt among us like one of us in order to redeem us. His Divine nature was substantially united to a human nature like ours.

incassum, *adv., in vain, uselessly, to no purpose,* used in the S.T. only in quot.

incaute, *adv.,* see *incautus.*

incautela, ae, *f., incautiousness, want of foresight, carelessness.*

incautus, a, um, *adj., incautious, thoughtless, careless, heedless, rash.*—**incaute,** *adv., incautiously, imprudently.*

incedo, ere, cessi, cessum, 3, *v. n., to go, walk, step, approach to, proceed to,* (1) lit., (2) fig.

incendiarius, ii, *m., an incendiary,* one who maliciously sets on fire a building or other property, especially a dwelling; one who commits arson.

incendium, ii, *n.,* (1) lit., *fire,* (2) fig., *fire, flame, heat, glow, vehemence.*

incendo, ere, di, sum, 3, *v. a.,* (1) lit., *to set fire to, to kindle, burn,* (2) fig., *to kindle, inflame, set on fire; to fire, rouse, incite, excite, stir up.*—**carbones incensi,** *burning coals.*—**totum incensum,** *all burnt.*

incensio, onis, *f., a lighting up, emitting of light.*

incensor, oris, *m., an inciter, instigator.*

incensum, i, *n., incense.*

incentivum, i, *n., an incentive.*

incentor, oris, *m., an inciter, exciter.*

inceptio, onis, *f., a beginning.*

incertitudo, inis, *f., incertitude, uncertainty, uncertain* or *insecure condition; insecurity.*

incertus, a, um, *adj.,* (1) of things whose external or internal qualities are not firmly established, *uncertain, unsettled, doubtful, untrustworthy, not fast, not firm,* (2) as regards one's perceptions or convictions, *not firmly established, uncertain, undetermined, doubtful, dubious,* used with an *interrog. cl.*—**incertum,** i, *n., an uncertainty.*

incessus, us, *m.*, *deportment, gait.*

incestuose, *adv.*, see *incestuosus.*

incestuosus, a, um, *adj.*, *incestuous.*
—**incestuose,** *adv.*, *incestuously.*

incestus, us, *m.*, *incest,* carnal intercourse with relatives of blood or affinity, whom the Church forbids one to marry.

inchoatio, onis, *f.*, (1) *beginning, germ,* (2) *first element, origin, principle, cause,* the *arche* of Aristotle (cf. De Divin. per Somnum c. 2, 463. b. 28), synonym of *principium* and *causa.*— Kinds of *inchoatio* in this (1) sense are: (a), **inchoatio formae,** *the beginning of a form.*—(b), **inchoatio habitus,** *the beginning of a habit.*—(c), **inchoatio naturalis,** *the natural beginning* or *that resting in the nature of a thing.* —(d), **inchoatio virtutis,** *the beginning of a virtue.*

inchoo, are, avi, atum, 1, *v. a.* and *n.*, (1) *act.*, *to lay the foundation of a thing, to begin, commence,* used with the *acc., inf.*, (2) *neutr.*, *to begin; commence, take a beginning.*—**inchoatus,** a, um, *P. a.*, *inchoate, just begun, in an imperfect stage;* hence *imperfect.*

incido, ere, cidi, casum, 3, *v. n.*, (1) *lit.*, (a) *to fall among people,* used with *in* and *acc.*, (b) *to meet, encroach upon something,* used with *dat.*, (c) *to fall upon a person,* used with *in* and *acc.*, (2) *fig.*, (a) in gen., *to fall into any condition,* sin, error, passion, calamity, sickness, etc., used

with *in* and *acc.*, (b) *to fall in with, coincide with, agree with, be identical with,* (c) *to fall out, happen, occur.*

(2) **incido,** ere, cidi, cisum, 3, *v. a.*, *to cut, cut into, cut through.*

incineratio, onis, *f.*, *incineration,* the action or process of reducing to dust.

incinero, are, 1, *v. a.*, *to incinerate, reduce to ashes.*

incipio, ere, cepi, ceptum, 3, *v. a.* and *n.*, (1) *act.*, with the accessory idea of action, *to begin to do something,* used with *inf. ab., acc.*, (2) *neutr.*, *to begin to be, to begin, commence,* used absol., with *ab.*

incircumcisus, a, um, *adj.*, *uncircumcised.*

incircumscripte, *adv.*, see *incircumscriptus.*

incircumscriptibilis, e, *adj.*, *incircumscriptible,* incapable of being circumscribed by place or limited; *boundless.*

incircumscriptus, a, um, *adj.*, *infinite, uncircumscribed by location in place; incomprehensible, beyond the reach of intellect* or *research, unfathomable to the mind.*—**incircumscripte,** *adv.*, *without limitation.*

incircumspectio, onis, *f.*, *incircumspection.*

incisio, onis, *f.*, (1) *lit.*, (a) *incision, an engraving, the action of cutting* into something, (b) *a lopping off* of something superfluous, as the hair, (2) *fig.*, *a divi-*

sion, the effect produced by dividing.

incisura, ae, *f., a cutting into, incision.*

incitamentum, i, *n., an incentive, inducement,* used with the *gen.* or *ad.*

incito, are, avi, atum, 1, *v. a., to incite, encourage, instigate, rouse, spur on,* used fig.—**incitatus,** a, um, *adj., incited, roused.*

inclinatio, onis, *f., an inclination,* (1) fig., the condition of being mentally inclined or disposed to something, or an instance of such condition; *a tendency* or *bent of the mind, will,* or *desires towards* a particular object; *disposition, propensity, learning,* (2) of things inanimate, *the natural tendency* or *affinity of inorganic substances,* which impel them towards what is suitable to their nature.

inclino, are, avi, atum, 1, *v. a.* and *n.,* (I) *act, to cause to lean, bend, incline, turn a thing* in any direction; *to bend down, bow a thing,* (1) *lit.,* (a) with *caput, to incline, bow* or *bend* the head toward a person, and hence downward, (b) with **seipsum,** *to bend one's self, to bow* or *bend* the body as a gesture of respect, (c) with **aurem,** *to bend* or *turn one's ear toward a speaker; to give ear, listen favorably, attend to,* (d) *to tend towards* some condition; to have some attribute in an incipient degree, (2) *fig.,* (a) *to incline, bend the mind, heart, will,* etc.,

towards some course or action, (b) *to decree, ordain,* used with *ut* and *subj.,* (c) **inclinare caput,** *to bow the head, to obey, be subject* to a person, (II) neutr., *to incline to, be favorably disposed* towards a thing.

includo, ere, si, sum, 3, *v. a.,* (1) lit., (a) *to shut* or *close in; to inclose* within material limits: *to shut up, confine,* used with *in* and *acc., acc., abl., in* and *abl.,* (b) fig., *to include;* the limits, object, or inclusion being non-material, used with *acc., in* and *abl.,* (2) transf., *to contain, comprise, embrace,* to contain as a constituent part of a whole.

inclusio, onis, *f., inclusion, the fact* or *condition of being included.*

incoactus, a, um, *adj., untrammelled,* used in the S.T. only in quot.

incoepio, ere, coepi, coeptum, 3, *v. a.* and *n., to begin, commence, undertake,* used with (a) *inf. act.,* (b) *acc.,* (c) *absol.,* (d) with an ellipsis for dicere coepi.

incognitus, a, um, *adj., not known, unknown.*

incola, ae, *comm., an inhabitant of a place, a resident.*

incolatus, us, *m., a residing, a dwelling in a place.*

incolo, are, 1, *v. a.* and *n., to dwell* or *abide in a place, to inhabit.*

incolorabilis, e, *adj., uncolored, without color.*

incolumitas, atis, *f., good condition, soundness, safety, well being.*

incommensurabilis, e, *adj., not having a common measure, incommensurable*. On quantitas incommensurabilis, see *quantitas*.

incommensuratus, a, um, *adj., incommensurate*.

incommoditas, atis, *f., injury, affliction, damage*.

incommodum, i, *n., inconvenience, trouble, disadvantage, detriment, injury*.

incommunicabilis, e, *adj., incommunicable*, the opposite of *communicabilis*. On nomen incommunicabile, see *nomen;* on substantia incommunicabilis, see *substantia.—*Kinds of *incommunicabile* are: incommunicabile ratione seu secundum rationem and incommunicabile re seu secundum rem seu secundum rei veritatem, *incommunicable according to notion* or *conception* and *incommunicable according to reality.—*incommunicabiliter, *adv., incommunicably*. On existere incommunicabiliter, see *existere*.

incommunicabilitas, atis, *f., incommunicability*, the opposite of *communicabilitas.—*Kinds of *incommunicabilitas* are: incommunicabilitas assumptibilis, incommunicabilitas partis and incommunicabilitas universalis, *the incommunicability of the acceptable* and *of the admissable, i.e., the impossibility of the being accepted,* or *admitted, the incommunicability of a part* or *the particular incommunicability* or *the*

incommunicability *according to the whole*.

incommunicabiliter, see *incommunicabilis*.

incommutabilis, e, *adj., unchangeable, immutable, incommutable*.

incommutabilitas, atis, *f., unchangeablenes, immutability*.

incompactus, a, um, *adj., incompact, loosely put together, vague,* used *fig*.

incomparabilis, e, *adj., incomparable, that cannot be equalled.—*incomparabiliter, *adv., incomparably*.

incomparabiliter, *adv.,* see *incomparabilis*.

incompetens, entis, *adj.,* (1) of persons, *incompetent, unfit* for something, (2) applied to things in general not measuring up to the standard of accuracy, suitableness, capability, competency, propriety and the like, hence, *inaccurate, faulty, incorrect, unfit, unsuitable, unbecoming, improportionate to*.

incompositus, a, um, *adj.,* (1) *lit.,* (a) *shapeless, out of order, wanting in orderly arrangement,* (b) used in describing the earth before God filled it with herbs and plants, hence *unadorned,* that is, without the comeliness which the earth owes to the plants that clothe it, as it were, with a garment, (2) *fig., wild, riotous*.

incomprehensibilis, e, *adj., incomprehensible,* (1) *that cannot be grasped by the understanding;*

beyond the reach of the intellect; unfathomable by the mind, (2) *that cannot be contained* or *circumscribed within limits; illimitable, boundless, immense.—* **incomprehensibiliter,** *adv., incomprehensibly, beyond mental comprehension.*

incomprehensibilitas, atis, *f., incomprehensibility, incapability* of being comprised or circumscribed within limits; *boundlessness, infinity,* used in S.T. only in quot.

incomprehensibiliter, *adv.,* see *incomprehensibilis.*

incomprehensus, a, um, *adj., incomprehended.*

inconcusse, *adv.,* see *inconcussus.*

inconcussus, a, um, *adj., immovable, constant, firm,* used *fig.—***inconcusse,** *adv., firmly.*

inconfuse, *adv.,* see *inconfusus.*

inconfusus, a, um, *adj., unconfused.—***inconfuse,** *adv., inconfusedly, without confusion.*

incongrue, *adv.,* see *incongruus.*

incongruenter, *adv., inconsistently, incongruently,* used in the S.T. only in quot.

incongruitas, atis, *f., unfittingness, unsuitableness.*

incongruus, a, um, *adj., incongruous, unsuitable, unfit, unseemly, inconsistent.—***incongrue,** *adv., incorrectly, unbecomingly.*

inconsiderate, *adv., inconsiderately.*

inconsonans, antis, *adj., inconsonant, discordant, not consonant* or *agreeable to.*

inconstans, antis, *adj., inconstant,* (1) of persons or their character, actions etc.; *not steadfast, fickle, changeable,* failing to persevere in what one has proposed to do, (2) of things, *irregular, variable, disagreeing.*

inconsuetus, a, um, *adj., unwonted, unusual, unaccustomed.—***inconsueti,** orum, *comm., strangers.*

inconsummatus, a, um, *adj., not consummated* or *completed.*

incomsumptibilis, e, *adj., inconsumptible,* incapable of being consumed; *incorruptible.*

incontaminabilis, e, *adj., incontaminable,* incapable of being contaminated.

incontaminatus, a, um, *adj., uncontaminated, undefiled, unaffected* by any corruption, *spotless,* used in the S.T. only in quot.

incontinens, tis, *adj., incontinent, immoderate, intemperate.—***incontinenter,** *adv., incontinently, immoderately, intemperately.*

incontinenter, *adv.,* see *incontinens.*

inconveniens, entis, *adj.,* (1) in gen., *unfitting, unsuitable, unseemly, unbecoming,* (2) of persons, *disagreeable,* (3) of statements, facts or theories, *unreasonable, incongruous, inadmissible, absurd, insufficient.—* **inconveniens,** entis, *n.,* (1) *an inconvenience, a troublesome* or *untoward circumstance,* (2) *that which is inconvenient; something inconsistent with reason; an absurdity, incongruity.—***habe-**

re pro inconvenienti, *to con-*
sider ridiculous, impossible, un-
*fitting.—*inconvenienter, *adv., un-*
suitably.

inconvenienter, *adv.,* see *incon-*
veniens.

inconvenientia, ae, *f., unbecoming-*
ness, unfittingness, incongruity.

inconvertibiliter, *adv., unchange-*
ably, unalterably.

incorporalis, e, *adj., incorporeal,*
synonym of *incorporeus* and *spi-*
ritualis, the opposite of *corpora-*
lis and *corporeus.* On res incorporalis, see *res;* on substantia
incorporalis, see *substantia.—*in-
corporalia, ium, *n., incorporeal*
things, things that are insubstan-
tial, immaterial.

incorporatio, onis, *f., incorporation,*
the action of incorporating two
or more things, or one thing with
another; the process or condition
of being so incorporated; union
in or into one body, used *fig.*

incorporeitas, atis, *f., incorporeal-*
ity, immateriality, synonym of
spiritualitas, the opposite of *cor-*
poreitas, found once in the S.T.
and in quot.

incorporeus, a, um, *adj., incorpore-*
al, without a body, synonym of
incorporalis and *spiritualis,* the
opposite of *corporalis* and *corpo-*
reus. On agens incorporeum, see
agens; on potentia incorporea,
see *potentia;* on principium incorporeum, see *principium;* on
substantia incorporea, see *sub-*
stantia; on virtus incorporea, see
virtus.

incorporo, are, avi, atum, 1, *v. a.,*
(1) *lit.,* (a) *to incorporate, furnish*
with a body, give shape to, (b)
to incorporate, accumulate; to
add as one thing to another, (2)
fig., to unite so as to form one
body; *to grow into each other, to*
*form an intimate union.—*incor-
poratus, *P. a., incorporated,* used
lit. and *fig.*

incorrigibilis, e, *adj.,* of persons,
their habits, etc., *incorrigible, in-*
capable of being corrected or
*amended.—*incorrigibiliter, *adv.,*
incorrigibly, in an incorrigible
manner, beyond the power of
amendment.

incorrigibiliter, *adv.,* see *incorrigi-*
bilis.

incorruptela, ae, *f., imperishable-*
ness, incorruption.

incorruptibilis, e, *adj., imperisha-*
ble, incorruptible in the proper
and in the general sense of the
word, the opposite of *corrupti-*
*bilis.—*On corpus incorruptibile,
see *corpus;* on esse incorruptibile, see *esse;* on forma incorruptibilis, see *forma;* on substantia
incorruptibilis, see *substantia;* on
veritas incorruptibilis, see *veri-*
tas; on virtus incorruptibilis, see
virtus; on vita incorruptibilis, see
*vita.—*Kinds of *incorruptible* in
the proper sense of the word
are: incorruptibile per donum
gratiae, incorruptibile secundum
gloriam, and incorruptibile secundum naturam, *the incorrupti-*
ble as the result of a gift of grace
sent by God, that in accordance

with heavenly glorification, and *that according to nature.*—incorruptibile est prius corruptibili et natura et tempore, *the incorruptible is prior to the corruptible both by nature and by time.*

incorruptibilitas, atis, *imperishableness, incorruptibility,* the opposite of *corruptibilitas.*—Kinds of *incorruptibilitas* are: incorruptibilitas corporis gloriosi and incorruptibilitas naturalis, *the incorruptibility of the glorified body* and *natural incorruptibility.*

incorruptio, onis, *f.,* (1) *imperishableness, incorruptibility,* the opposite of *corruptio,* (2) *innocence, soundness,* i.e., the state of being uninjured or undamaged.—On status incorruptionis, see *status.*—Kinds of *incorruptio* in this (2) sense are: incorruptio carnis and incorruptio spiritus, *carnal innocence* with reference to the *signaculum virginale,* having the same meaning as *virginity,* and *spiritual innocence* or *sinlessness.*

incorruptus, a, um, *adj.,* (1) *lit., unspoiled, uncorrupted,* (2) *fig., uncorrupted, pure.*

increabilis, e, *adj., uncreatable, incapable of being created, self-existent, uncreated.*

increatus, a, um, *adj., uncreated, unmade,* the opposite of *creatus.* On beatitudo increata, see *beatitudo;* on bonitas increata, see *bonitas;* on bonum increatum, see *bonus;* on caritas increata, see *caritas;* on dilectio increata,

see *dilectio;* on donum increatum, see *donum;* on hypostasis increata, see *hypostasis;* on intellectus increatus, see *intellectus;* on lumen increatum, see *lumen;* on regula increata, see *regula;* on sapientia increata, see *sapientia;* on scientia increata, see *scientia;* on speculum increatum, see *speculum;* on suppositum increatum, see *suppositum;* on Trinitas increata, see *Trinitas;* on unitas increata, see *unitas;* on veritas increata, see *veritas;* on vita increata, see *vita.*

incredibilis, e, *adj., pass., not credible, incredible, that cannot be believed* or *trusted.*

incredulitas, atis, *f., religious disbelief, incredulity,* synonym of *infidelitas,* the opposite of *credulitas* and *fides.* On dubitatio incredulitatis, see *dubitatio.*

incredulus, a, um, *adj., unbelieving, incredulous, without faith.*

incrementum, i, *n.,* (1) *lit., growth, increase,* (2) *increase, increment, addition.*

increpabilis, e, *adj., blameworthy, reprehensible.*

increpatio, onis, *f., a chiding, reproof, rebuke.*

increpo, are, ui, itum, 1, *v. n.* and *a., to upbraid, chide, reprove, rebuke,* used *absol.,* with *acc.*

incresco, ere, evi, 3, *v. n.,* (1) in gen., *to grow, increase, to become greater* in size, amount, duration or degree; *to be enlarged, extended* or *intensified,*

(2) pregn., *to increase in fortune; grow more prosperous.*

incubans, ntis, *P. a., incubating, hatching eggs* by sitting on them or by some equivalent process.

incubus, i, *m., an incubus,* a feigned evil spirit or demon, originating in personified representations of the nightmare, supposed to descend upon persons in their sleep, and especially to seek carnal intercourse with women.

inculpabilis, e, *adj., inculpable, blameless,* used in S.T. only in quot.

inculpatus, a, um, *adj., blameless.*

inculpo, are, avi, atum, 1, *v. a., to blame, find fault with.*

incultus, a, um, *adj.,* (1) *lit., uncultivated,* in a natural state of wildness, (2) *transf., coarse, homely, rough.*

incumbo, ere, cubui, cubitum, 3, *v. n., fig.,* (1) *to press upon, threaten,* used *absol.,* (2) *to be incumbent upon one as a duty,* used with the *dat., in* and *abl.,* and *absol.*

incurabilis, e, *adj.,* (1) *incurable;* incapable of being cured by medicine or medical skill, (2), *transf.,* and *fig., not admitting of remedy, correction* or *reformation.*

incuria, ae, *f., carelessness, want of care, negligence.*

incurro, ere, curri, cucurri, cursum, 3, *v. n.* and *a., to incur,* used *fig.,* (1) *to meet* or *fall in* with something inconvenient,

harmful, onerous; *to become liable* or *subject to;* to bring down upon one's self, (2) *to commit, become guilty of perjury, falsehood, guilt, sacrilege, sin, crime,* etc., (3) *to enter into,* used with *in* and *acc.*

incursus, us, *m., an incursion, a sudden attack,* used *lit.* and *fig.*

incutio, ere, cussi, cussum, 3, *v. a., to inspire with, excite, produce terror, disturbance,* etc.

inde, *adv.,* (1) of place, *from that place, from there, thence,* (2) of things, *thence, from that thing; from that matter, circumstance,* etc.

indebite, *adv.,* see *indebitus.*

indebitus, a, um, *adj., not due, improper, unseemly,* the opposite of *debitus.* On **affectio indebita,** see *affectio;* on **conversio indebita,** see *conversio;* on **correctio indebita,** see *correctio;* on **cultus indebitus,** see *cultus;* on **materia indebita,** see *materia;* on **modus indebitus,** see *modus;* on **superstitio indebita cultus veri Dei,** see *superstitio.* —**indebite,** *adv., without just cause, unduly.*

indecens, tis, *adj.,* (1) *unbecoming, highly unsuitable* or *inappropriate; contrary to the fitness of things,* (2) *indecent,* offending against the recognized standards of propriety and delicacy; *highly indelicate; suggesting* or *tending to obscenity.*— **indecenter,** *adv., unbecomingly, unworthily.*

indecenter, *adv.,* see *indecens.*

indecentia, ae, *f.,* (1) *unbecomingness,* (2) *indecency, an indecent act.*

indeclinabiliter, *adv., inflexibly, firmly.*

indefectibilis, e, *adj., indefectible, unfailing.*

indefective, *adv., indefectibly,* without capability of failure.

indeficiens, entis, *adj., unfailing, incessant, continual.*—**indeficienter,** *adv.,* (1) *unfailingly, incessantly, continually,* (2) *faultlessly,* synonym of *perfecte,* the opposite of *defective* and *deficienter.*

indeficientia, ae, *f., an unfailing supply, continuousness,* the opposite of *deficientia.*

indefinitus, a, um, *adj., unlimited, endless, indefinite,* synonym of *indeterminatus, infinitus,* and *interminatus,* the opposite of *determinatus, finitus,* and *terminatus.*—On **enuntiatio indefinita,** see *enuntiatio;* on **propositio indefinita,** see *propositio.*

indelebilis, e, *adj.,* of the spiritual character impressed or conferred by some of the sacraments, *indelible, permanent.*—**indelebiliter,** *adv., indelibly,* so as not to be blotted out or effaced.

indelebiliter, *adv.,* see *indelebilis.*

indemnis, e, *adj., free from loss.*

indemnitas, atis, *f., indemnity,* security against loss.

indemonstrabilis, e, *adj., indemonstrable,* incapable of being demonstrated or proved, said especially of primary or axiomatic truths, principles, etc.

indesinenter, *adv., indesinently, without ceasing* or *interruption, continuously, incessantly,* used in the S.T. only in quot.

indeterminate, *adv.,* see *indeterminatus.*

indeterminatio, onis, *f., boundlessness, indefiniteness,* the opposite of *determinatio.*

indeterminatus, a, um, *adj., undefined, unlimited,* synonym of *indefinitus, infinitus,* and *interminatus.* On **agens indeterminatum,** see *agens;* on **causa indeterminata,** see *causa;* on **cognitio indeterminata,** see *cognitio;* on **concupiscentia indeterminata,** see *concupiscentia;* on **dimensio indeterminata,** see *dimensio;* on **forma indeterminata,** see *forma;* on **idea indeterminata,** see *idea;* on **imaginatio indeterminata,** see *imaginatio;* on **phantasia indeterminata,** see *phantasia;* on **quantitas indeterminata,** see *quantitas;* on **ratio indeterminata,** see *ratio.* —**indeterminate,** *adv., undefinedly, unlimitedly,* the opposite of *determinate* and *distincte.* On **considerare ut indeterminate,** see *considerare;* on **significare indeterminate,** see *significare.*

indetractibilis, e, *adj., indetractible.* —**indetractibiles passiones,** *passions without defect* or *knowledge* or *grace.*

indevote, *adv.,* see *indevotus.*

indevotio, onis, *f., lack of devotion, irreverence, irreligion, impi-*

ety, the opposite of *devotio,* does not occur in S.T.

indevotus, a, um, *adj., profane, irreligious,* occurs in the S.T. only in quot.—**indevote,** *adv., indevoutly, without devotion.*

index, dicis, *com.,* (1) lit., of things, *the forefinger, index-finger,* (2) in gen., (a) *a sign, mark,* (b) of persons, *an informer, herald.*

indicativus, a, um, *adj., announcing, declaring, indicative.* On **oratio indicativa,** see *oratio.*

indifferens, entis, *adj.,* (1) *not distinguishing itself, not differing,* (2) *neither good nor evil, indifferent, inconsequent,* (3) *indiscriminate, indefinite, indifferent.*—On **species indifferens,** see *species.*—Kinds of *indifferens* in this sense are: (a), **indifferens secundum speciem,** *not different according to species.*—(b), **indifferens secundum substantiam,** *not different according to substance.* On **actus indifferens ad vitam,** see *actus.*—On **actio indifferens,** see *actio;* on **actus indifferens,** see *actus.*—**indifferenter,** *adv., without distinction, indiscriminately, indifferently.*

indicium, ii, *n.,* in gen., *a sign, mark, token, proof, indication.*

indico, are, avi, atum, 1, *v. a.,* in gen., *to show, declare, disclose, make known, reveal, betray,* (1) of persons, used with *acc., acc.* and *dat., dat.* alone, (2) of things, concr. and abstr., *show, indicate,* used with *acc., rel. cl.,*

dat.—**indicare iustitiam,** *to show* or *bestow justice.*

indico, ere, xi, ctum, 3, *v. a.,* (1) *to declare publicly, to proclaim, publish, announce,* used *lit.* and *fig.,* (2) esp., *to impose, enjoin, inflict, to lay upon* as an order or command; *to prescribe* as a guide, direction or rule of action. —**indicere bellum,** *to declare war,* used *lit.* and *fig.*

indictio, onis, *f., a declaration, proclamation.*

indifferentia, ae, *f., want of distinction* or *difference, similarity, equivalence.*—One kind of *indifferentia* is: **indifferentia speciei,** *the want of distinction* or *difference in species.*

indigena, ae, *m., a native.*

indigentia, ae, *f., need, want, indigence.*

indigeo, ere, ui, 2, *v. n., to need, want, to stand in need* or *want of anything,* (1) lit., used with (a) the *abl.,* (b) *gen.,* (2) in gen., *to need, require,* used with (a) the *abl.,* (b) *inf.,* (c) *ut* with *subj.*—**indigens,** entis, *P. a., in want of, needing anything,* used with the *gen.,* the *abl.*—**indigens,** entis, *comm., a needy* or *indigent person.*

indigestio, onis, *f., indigestion.*

indignatio, onis, *f., indignation, wrath, displeasure.*

indigne, *adv.,* see *indignus.*

indignitas, atis, *f., unworthiness.*

indignor, ari, atus, 1, *v. dep. a., to be angry* or *displeased, to be in-*

dignant, used *absol.,* with the *dat.*

indignus, a, um, *adj., unworthy, undeserving,* (I) of persons, (1) in gen., *unworthy,* used (a) with *inf.,* (b) *absol.,* (c) *ut* and *subj.,* (d) *abl.,* (e) *ad* and *acc.,* (f) *gen.,* (II) of inanimate and abstract things, (1) *unworthy, offensive, unfitting,* used with (a) *gen.,* (b) *absol.,* (c) *dat.*—**indigne,** *adv.,* (1) *unworthily, undeservedly,* (2) *indignantly.*

indigus, a, um, *adj., needing.*

indirectus, a, um, *adj.,* (1) *moving sideways, on a bypath,* the opposite of *directus,* (2) *oblique, sloping,* likewise the opposite of *directus.*—On **actus indirectus,** see *actus;* on **causa indirecta,** see *causa.*—**indirecte,** *adv.,* (1) *in a side direction, sideways, obliquely, indirectly,* synonym of *ex latere* and *oblique,* the opposite of *directe,* (2) *in an indirect manner, indirectly,* the opposite of *directe* and *immediate.*—On **causa indirecte dicta,** see *causa;* on **causa movens indirecte,** see *causa;* on **cognoscere indirecte,** see *cognoscere;* on **facere indirecte,** see *facere;* on **oppositum indirecte,** see *opponere;* on **syllogismus indirecte concludens,** see *syllogismus;* on **velle indirecte,** see *velle;* on **voluntarium indirecte,** see *voluntarius.*

indisciplinabilis, e, *adj., incapable of being taught, undisciplinable,* the opposite of *disciplinabilis,* does not occur in the S.T.

indiscrete, *adv.,* see *indiscretus.*

indiscretio, onis, *f., lack of discernment, indiscretion, lack of discrimination,* the opposite *of discretio.*

indiscretus, a, um, *adj.,* (1) *unseparated, undivided,* the opposite of *discretus,* (2) *undistinguished, without distinction,* likewise the opposite of *discretus,* (3) *undistinguishable, not endowed with distinctiveness.*—On **actio indiscreta,** see *actio;* on **oboedientia indiscreta,** see *oboedientia.*—**indiscrete,** *adv., without distinction, alike, indiscriminately.*

indispensabilis, e, *adj., indispensable,* (1) not subject to Ecclesiastical dispensation; that cannot be permitted, allowed or condoned; by suspension or relaxation of law or canon, (2) of a law, obligation, duty, *that cannot be dispensed with, remitted, set aside* or *neglected.*

indispositio, onis, *f., lack of preparation* or *of inclination* or *of aptitude, indisposition,* the opposite of *dispositio.*

indispositus, a, um, *adj., indisposed, unfitted, unqualified.*

indissolubilis, e, *adj.,* (1) *lit., indissoluble,* that cannot be dissolved into its elements or particles; incapable of being decomposed or disintegrated, (2) *fig., indissoluble,* that cannot be dissolved, undone or broken, *firm, stable, perpetually binding.*—**indissolubiliter,** *adv., indissolubly, in an indissoluble manner, firmly.*

indissolubilitas, atis, *f., indissolubility,* used *fig.,* (1) *incapability of being dissolved, undone* or *broken,* (2) of an obligation or connection, *indissolubility, perpetuity of binding force.*

indissolubiliter, *adv.,* see *indissolubilis.*

indissolutus, a, um, *adj., unbroken, entire.*

indistincte, see *indistinctus.*

indistinctio, onis, *f., indistinctness, lack of distinction, indefiniteness,* synonym of *confusio,* the opposite of *distinctio,* not used in the S.T.

indistinctus, a, um, *adj.,* (1) *not separated, not divided,* the opposite of *distinctus,* (2) *not distinct, indiscriminate, not definite,* synonym of *confusus,* the opposite of *distinctus.*—On **cognitio indistincta,** see *cognitio;* on **esse indistinctum,** see *esse;* on **suppositum indistinctum,** see *suppositum.*—**indistincte,** *adv., without distinction, indiscriminately,* synonym of *confuse,* the opposite of *distincte.* On **cognoscere indistincte,** see *cognoscere;* on **dicere indistincte,** see *dicere;* on **scire indistincte,** see *scire;* on **supponere indistincte,** see *supponere.*

inditus, a, um, *P. a., put* or *place into, thrown upon, implanted.* On **scientia indita,** see *scientia;* on **species indita,** see *species.*

individualis, e, *adj., not divided, indivisible, individual,* i.e., concerning or belonging to a single thing, the ultimate unit of division, synonym of *individuus,* the opposite of *universalis.* On **accidens individuale,** see *accidens;* on **conditio individualis,** see *conditio;* on **forma individualis,** see *forma;* on **intentio individualis,** see *intentio;* on **materia individualis,** see *materia;* on **principium individuale,** see *principium;* on **proprietas individualis,** see *proprietas;* on **species individualis,** see *species.*—**individualiter,** *adv., in the manner* or *in the sense of an individual, individually.*

individualitas, atis, *f., individuality,* i.e., the relation of a thing according to which it is an individual, not found in the S.T. On **intentio individualitatis,** see *intentio.*

individuatio, onis, *f., the formation of an individual* as such, *individuation,* the quality that makes anything *this* singular thing, and distinguishes it from everything else of its kind or class. On **principium individuationis,** see *principium.*

individuo, are, avi, atum, 1, *v. a., to form an individual, grant being to an individual, individuate,* to distinguish from everything else in the same species or genus.—**individuans,** antis, *P. a., forming an individual, individuating.* On **accidens individuans,** see *accidens;* on **forma individuans,** see *forma;* on **materia individuans,** see *materia;* on **principium individuans,** see *prin-*

cipium; on **proprietas individu-ans,** see *proprietas.—***individua-tus,** a, um, *P. a., made an individual, individuated.*

individuus, a, um, *adj., not divided, indivisible, individual, concerning* or *belonging to an individual,* synonym of *individualis,* the opposite of *universalis.* On **actus individuus,** see *actus;* on **forma individua,** see *forma;* on **propositio non individua,** see *propositio;* on **species individua,** see *species;* on **substantia individua,** see *substantia.—***individuum,** i, *an individual thing;* that which is not only indivisible in itself but also because incommunicable to others, exists apart for itself; *an atom;* the opposite of *species.* On **accidens individui,** see *accidens;* on **bonum individui, unius individui et proprii individui,** see *bonus;* on **diversitas individui,** see *diversitas;* on **natura individui,** see *natura;* on **necessarium individui,** see *necessarius;* on **pars individui,** see *pars;* on **quidditas individui,** see *quidditas;* on **unire in individuum,** see *unire.—*Kinds of *individuum* are: (a), **individuum completum,** *the complete* or *perfect individual,* the opposite of *individuum incompletum,* i.e., *the incomplete* or *imperfect individual,* which forms only a part of the former.—(b), **individuum corporale seu sensibile** and **individuum spirituale,** *the corporal* or *sensibly perceptible individual*

and *the spiritual* or *supersensibly perceptible individual.—*(c), **individuum demonstratum seu designatum** and **individuum vagum,** *the proven* or *designated* or *defined individual* and *the undefined individual.—*(d), **individuum designatum,** see *individuum demonstratum.—*(e), **individuum per se subsistens seu substantiae,** *the individual existing for itself* or *forming a substance,* the opposite of *individuum accidentis,* i.e., the individual needing a subject or forming an accident.—(f), **individuum sensibile,** see *individuum corporale.—*(g), **individuum spirituale,** see *individuum corporale.—*(h), **individuum substantiae,** see *individuum per se subsistens.—*(i), **individuum vagum,** see *individuum demonstratum.—***individua non cadunt sub consideratione artis,** *individuals do not fall under the treatment of science,* i.e., not as the objects of scientific treatment.—**individua sunt propter speciem,** *individuals exist for their own species.*

indivise, *adv.,* see *indivisus.*

indivisibilis, e, *adj., indivisible,* that which of its nature cannot be divided, the opposite of *divisibilis.* On **corpus indivisibile,** see *corpus;* on **forma indivisibilis,** see *forma;* on **intelligentia indivisibilis,** see *intelligentia;* on **locus indivisibilis,** see *locus;* on **res indivisibilis,** see *res;* on **terminus indivisibilis,** see *terminus.—*Kinds of *indivisibile* are: (a), **indivisibile quantitatis, seu secundum quantitatem**, *indivisible according to quantity.*—(b), **indivisibile secundum dimensionem** and **indivisibile secundum successionem**, *indivisible according to dimension* and *that according to succession.*—(c), **indivisibile secundum quantitatem**, see *indivisibile quantitatis.*—(d), **indivisibile secundum speciem**, *indivisible according to essence.*—(e), **indivisibile secundum successionem**, see *indivisibile secundum dimensionem.*—**esse substantiale cuiuslibet rei in indivisibili consistit**, see *esse.*—**factum esse est indivisibile**, see *fieri.*—**indivisibile est quod quid est ipsius boni**, *the very essence of the good is the fact that it is indivisible.*—**ratio cuiuslibet speciei substantiae consistit in indivisibili**, see *species.*—**indivisibiliter**, *adv.*, *indivisibly.*

indivisibilitas, atis, *f.*, *indivisibility, inseparability,* synonym of *inseparabilitas.* On **participare secundum rationem indivisibilitatis**, see *participare;* on **unum indivisibilitate**, see *unus.*—**habitus in sui ratione non includit indivisibilitatem**, see *habitus.*—**ratio unius consistit in indivisibilitate**, see *ratio.*

indivisibiliter, *adv.*, see *indivisibilis.*

indivisio, onis, *f.*, *entirety, completeness, indivision,* the opposite of *divisio.*

indivisus, a, um, *adj.*, *undivided,* synonym of *unus,* the opposite of *divisus.*—**indivisum**, i, *n.*, *the undivided,* the opposite of *divisum.*—Kinds of *indivisum* are: (a), **indivisum per accidens** and **indivisum per se**, *the undivided by accident* and *that by itself* and *by its own nature.*—(b), **indivisum per se**, see *indivisum per accidens.*—(c), **indivisum respectu alicuius** and **indivisum simpliciter**, *the undivided in a certain respect* and *the simply* or *plainly undivided.*—(d), **indivisum simpliciter**, see *indivisum respectu alicuius.*—**indivise**, *adv.*, *undividedly, in common.*

indo, ere, didi, ditum, 3, *v. a.*, *to impart, give to, apply to, impose on, attach to.*—**inditus**, a, um, *P. a.*, *put* or *placed into, thrown upon.* See under *inditus.*

indoctus, a, um, *adj.*, *ignorant.*

indoles, is, *f.*, *disposition, native quality.*

indubitanter, *adv.*, *indubitably, without doubt.*

indubitatus, a, um, *adj.*, *without doubt, certain, sure.*

induciae, arum, *f.*, *a truce in a lover's quarrel, a cessation of hostilities.*

induco, ere, xi, ctum, 3, *v. a.*, (1) *to lead into, introduce,* synonym of *introducere,* (2) *lead on, conduct towards, cause to appear,* (3) *conduct, lead,* (4) *incite, impel, cause,* (5) *lead up to* in the sense of proof, i.e., *to conclude from the individual to the gener-*

al, the opposite of *syllogizare.*—
On **forma inducenda**, see *forma.*
—**inducere sub disiunctione**, *to
bring in separately.* On **coactio
inducens**, see *coactio.*—**inducens,
ntis**, *P. a.*, *leading, bringing forward, introducing, inducing.*—
inductus, a, um, *P. a.*, *lead into,
brought forward, introduced, induced.*

inductio, onis, *f.*, (1) *a leading in,
introduction*, (2) *a bringing in,
leading, production*, (3) *inciting,
impelling, inducing*, (4) *induction* in the sense of a proof, the
apagoge of Aristotle, i.e., that
process in which a general conclusion is drawn from individual
things.—Kinds of *inductio* in this
sense are: **inductio necessaria**
and **inductio persuasoria**, *the
necessary inducing* and *persuasive inducing.* On **via inductionis**, see *via.*—Kinds of *inductio* in
this (4) sense are: **inductio completa** and **inductio imperfecta**,
the complete and *the incomplete
induction*, i.e., that induction in
which all individuals belonging
to a species are taken into consideration and that with which
this is not the case.

inductive, *adv.*, see *inductivus.*

inductivus, a, um, *adj.*, (1) *impelling, inducing, causing, inducive*,
(2) *leading up* in the sense of
a proof, *inductive, concluding*
from the single to the general,
belonging to induction.—On **propositio inductiva**, see *propositio;*
on **ratio inductiva**, see *ratio.*—**in-**

ductive, *adv.*, *after the manner
of induction, inductively.*

induitio, onis, *f.*, *induition, putting
on* (of a garment).

indulgentia, ae, *f.*, (1) *remission, release, acquittal*, (2) *indulgence*,
i.e., the remission of punishment
due to sin.

indulgeo, ere, si, tum, 2, *v. n.* and
a., (1) *neutr.*, *to be indulgent to,
to favor, pardon*, used with *dat.*,
(2) *act.*, (a) *to grant, give, allow,
bestow* as a favor, used with
acc., (b) *ut* and *subj.* (c) in the
passive.—**Deo indulgente**, *by
God's mercy.*—**indulgere poenam
alicui**, *to remit the punishment
of someone.*

indumentum, i, *n.*, (1) lit., (a) in
gen., *clothing*, (b) in partic. *garment, robe*, (2) fig., *a garment.*

induo, ere, ui, utum, 3, *v. a.*, (1)
lit., *to put on an article of dress,
to clothe*, used with the *abl.*, the
acc., (2) fig., (a) *to put on, assume*, (b) *to clothe* with abstract
things.—**induere hominem**, *to put
on the new man.* It is not enough
to put off the old man (Ephes.
IV. 23); we must put on the virtues of the new man, Jesus
Christ. As Adam was the principle or the beginning of the old
corruption, and through him sin
has entered into us all; so the
first principle and beginning of
the new life and renovation is
Christ, for "as in Adam, all die,
so also in Christ all shall be
made alive." (I Cor. XV. 22; Gal.
VI. 15).—**induere Christum**, *to*

put on Christ (Gal. III. 27). To put on Christ means to assume the character of Christ, to clothe one's self with Christ's dispositions and qualities.

induratio, onis, *f.,* (1) lit., *induration, the action of hardening;* the process of being hardened or becoming hard; also *hardened condition,* (2) fig., *a hardening of character* or *feeling.*

induro, are, avi, tum, 1, *v. a.,* and *n.,* (1) *lit., to make hard, to harden,* (2) *fig., to harden, steel.*

industria, ae, *f.,* (1) *diligence, activity, assiduity, industry,* (2) *purpose, intention, premeditation,* (3) *adroitness, skill.* On **peccare ex industria,** see *peccare;* on **peccatum industriae,** see *peccatum.* —One kind of *industria* in this (3) sense is: **industria saecularis,** *the worldly* or *purely human skill.*

inebriatio, onis, *f., inebriation.*

inebrio, are, avi, atum, 1, *v. a.,* (1) lit., *to make drunk, to inebriate,* (2) fig.—The following phrases occur occasionally: **potus ebrians,** *an inebriating draught,* and **potus valens inebriare,** *a draught strong enough to make one intoxicated.*—**inebriatus,** a, um, *P. a., inebriated, intoxicated, drunken.*

inedia, ae, *f., want of food, hunger, fasting.*

ineffabilis, e, *adj., ineffable, unutterable, unpronounceable.*—**ineffabiliter,** *adv. ineffably.*

ineffabiliter, *adv.,* see *ineffabilis.*

inefficacia, ae, *f., inefficacy.*

inefficax, cacis, *adj., ineffectual, inefficient.*

inenarrabilis, e, *adj., indescribable, that cannot be related* or *described.*

ineo, ire, ivi, and ii, itum, 4, *v. a.* and *n.,* used fig., *to enter upon, take part in.*—The following phrases are of frequent occurrence.—**inire pactum cum aliquo,** *to enter into* or *form an agreement with someone.*—**inire societatem cum aliquo,** *to form an association with a person.*—**inire consortium,** *to enter partnership.* —**inire matrimonium,** *to enter marriage, to marry.*

ineptitudo, inis, *f., ineptitude, want of aptitude, inaptness, unfitness for something.*

ineptus, a, um, *adj., unsuitable, inept, unfit.*

inestimabilis, e, *adj., inestimable, too great, profound* or *intense to be estimated.*

inevitabilis, e, *adj., unavoidable, inevitable.*

inexcusabilis, e, *adj., inexcusable, that cannot be excused,* used in the S.T. only in quot.

inexperientia, ae, *f., inexperience.*

inexpertus, a, um, *adj., inexperienced, having no* or *little experience,* used with *gen.*

inexpiabilis, e, *adj., that cannot be atoned for* or *expiated, inexpiable.*

inexterminabilis, e, *adj., incorruptible, imperishable, everlasting, eternal,* used in the S.T. only in quot.

inextinguibilis, e, *adj.*, *inextinguish-able, that cannot be put out.*

infallibilis, e, *adj.*, *infallible, not liable to err,* or *lead into error,* applied to the field of knowledge as well as to that of desire or aspiration, and in no sense synonymous with *impeccable.* On **certitudo infallibilis**, see *certitudo*; on **probatio infallibilis**, see *probatio.*—infallibiliter, *adv.*, *infallibly, in an unfailing manner, inevitably.*

infallibilitas, atis, *f.*, *infallibility* in knowledge as well as in the desire or aspiration of a thing.

infallibiliter, see *infallibilis.*

infamatio, onis, *f.*, *a calumny, defamation.*

infamia, ae, *f.*, (1) *ill fame, ill report* of a person or thing; *bad repute, dishonor, disgrace, infamy,* (2) *irreverent speech,* a synonym of *blasphemia,* in the plural, *infamies.*

infamis, e, *adj.*, *infamous,* of ill fame or repute; famed or notorious for badness of any kind; *notoriously evil, wicked* or *vile; held in infamy* or *public disgrace,* (1) of persons, (2) of things.

infamo, are, avi, atum, 1, *v. a.*, *to bring into ill repute, to brand with infamy, to disgrace, dishonor, defame.*

infans, fantis, *comm.*, *a young* or *little child, an infant, babe.*

infantia, ae, *f.*, (1) *an infant,* (2) transf., (a) *infancy, early child-*hood, (b) collect., *the young, children.*

infantilis, e, *adj.*, *of* or *belonging to infants* or *little children, infantile.*

infaustus, a, um, *adj.*, *unlucky.*

infectio, onis, *f.*, (1) lit., *infection,* (2) fig., *infection, stain,* that which taints or corrupts morally.

infelix, icis, *adj.*, *unhappy, miserable, unfortunate,* used in the S.T. only in quot.

inferior, ius, see *inferus.*

inferioritas, atis, *f.*, *inferiority, the quality* or *condition of being inferior.*

infernalis, e, *adj.*, *infernal, like that of hell; hellish.*—infernalia, ium, *n.*, *the infernal regions, hell.*

infernus, i, *m.*, *the lower world, hell,* the opposite of *paradisus* and *caelum.* On **clavis inferni**, see *clavis*; on **limbus inferni**, see *limbus*; on **poena inferni**, see *poena.*—inferni, orum, *m.*, *the inhabitants of hell, the people of the lower regions.*

infero, inferre, intuli, illatus, 3, *v. a.*, (1) *to carry in, bring in, put on, add on, cause, inflict,* (2) *infer, conclude.* On **causa inferens**, see *causa*; on **virtus inferens**, see *virtus.*—illatus, a, um, *P. a.*, *brought in, put on, caused, inflicted.*

inferus, a, um, *adj.*, *that is below, underneath, lower,* not found in the S.T. in the positive degree except in the form, **inferi**, orum, *m.*, *the inhabitants of the infernal regions, hell.*—Comp.: **infer-**

ior, ius, (1) *lower, inferior,* the opposite of *superior,* (2) *a lower body, a body of the sublunary region,* (3) *subordinate, inferior, insignificant,* (4) *a distant member of a species.*—On **animal inferius,** see *animal;* on **causa inferior,** see *causa;* on **corpus inferius,** see *corpus;* on **elementum inferius,** see *elementum;* on **motus inferior,** see *motus;* on **mundus inferior,** see *mundus;* on **orbis inferior,** see *orbis;* on **ordo inferior,** see *ordo;* on **ratio inferior,** see *ratio;* on **sphaera inferior,** see *sphaera.*—On **agens inferius,** see *agens;* on **appetitus inferior,** see *appetitus;* on **ars inferior,** see *ars;* on **forma inferior,** see *forma;* on **genus inferius,** see *genus;* on **intellectus inferior,** see *intellectus;* on **natura inferior,** see *natura;* on **ordo inferior,** see *ordo;* on **potestas inferior,** see *potestas;* on **providentia inferior,** see *providentia;* on **scientia inferior,** see *scientia;* on **spiritus inferior,** see *spiritus;* on **status inferior,** see *status;* on **substantia inferior,** see *substantia;* on **virtus inferior,** see *virtus;* on **vis inferior,** see *vis;* on **visio inferior,** see *visio.*—in **superiori semper includitur virtus inferioris,** see *superior.*—**perfectiones quae attribuuntur inferiori per multa superiori attribuuntur per unum,** *the perfections which are attributed to the inferior on the basis of many principles are attributed to the superior on the*

basis of one.—**semper inferior participat aliquid de perfectione superioris,** *the inferior always participates in some measure in the perfection of the superior.*—Sup.: **infimus** and **imus,** a, um, *lowest, last,* opposite of *primus, summus,* and *supremus.*—**infime,** *adv., at the bottom, least of all.*

infestatio, onis, *f., an assault* or *attack of any kind.*

infesto, are, avi, atum, 1, *v. a., to attack, assail, annoy,* or *trouble* a person or thing in a persistent manner.

infestus, a, um, *adj., hostile, troublesome.*

inficio, ere, feci, fectum, 3, *v. a., to put* or *dip into any thing;* (1) lit., (a) *to stain, dye, color, tinge with,* (b) transf., in a bad sense, *to taint, infect, spoil, pollute,* (c) *to infect* with any disease-producing germs, (2) fig., (a) *to stain, corrupt, infect,* (b) transf., *to infect, bewitch,* gain ascendancy over to such a degree as to take away the power of resistance, (c) *to undervalue, depreciate.*

inficior, ari, atus, 1, *v. dep. a., to deny.*

infidelis, e, *adj.,* (1) *incredulous, disbelieving,* also *an infidel, one who rejects the true faith,* understood with reference to religion, the opposite of *fidelis,* (2) *faithless, perfidious,* likewise the opposite of *fidelis.*—On **homo infidelis,** see *homo.*—**infideliter,** *adv., faithlessly, perfidiously.*

infidelitas, atis, *f.*, (1) *disbelief, infidelity,* used with reference to religion, synonym of *incredulitas,* the opposite of *credulitas* and *fides.*—On dubitatio infidelitatis, see *dubitatio;* on ignorantia infidelitatis, see *ignorantia.*—Kinds of *infidelitas* are: infidelitas gentilium seu paganorum, infidelitas haereticorum, and infidelitas Iudaeorum, *the disbelief of the heathens* or *pagans, that of the heretics,* and *that of the Jews.*

infideliter, *adv.,* see *infidelis.*

infidus, a, um, *adj., untrustworthy, not to be trusted,* used in the S.T. only in quot.

infigo, ere, xi, xum, 3, *v. a.,* (1) lit., (a) *to fix, fasten in,* (b) *to inflict, to lay on,* as a stroke, blow, wound, (2) *to infix, impress, imprint.*

infigurabilis, e, *adj., shapeless; ill-shaped, deformed.*

infiguratio, onis, *f., deformity, shapelessness,* synonym of *informitas,* the opposite of *figuratio* and *formatio,* not found in S.T.

infiguratus, a, um, *unformed, shapeless,* opposite of *figuratus,* not found in S.T.

infime, see *inferus.*

infimus, a, um, see *inferus.*

infinitas, atis, *f., boundlessness, endlessness, infinity,* the opposite of *finitas.* On via infinitatis, see *via.*—Kinds of *infinitas* are: (a), infinitas extensiva and infinitas intensiva, *the extensive* and *the intensive infinity,* i.e., *the boundlessness of extensiveness* or *size* and *that of intensity* or *power.*—(b), infinitas intensiva, see *infinitas extensiva.*—(c), infinitas materiae seu materialis, *the material infinity* or *the infinity of matter,* which is opposed to *infinitas formalis,* i.e., formal infinity or infinity according to form. Since matter is the source of potentiality, material infinity is only potentially boundless, being actually finite.—(d), infinitas materialis, see *infinitas materiae.*—(e), infinitas multitudinis, *the infinity of plurality* or *number.*—(f), infinitas secundum aliquid seu quid and infinitas simpliciter, *the respective infinity* or *that in a certain respect,* and *the simple* or *absolute infinity.*—(g), infinitas simpliciter, see *infinitas secundum aliquid.*

infinities, *adv., an infinite number of times, infinitely.*

infinitivus, i, *m.,* gram., *the infinitive,* the name of that form of a verb which expresses simply the notion of the verb without predicating it of any subject, usually classed as a mood.

infinitus, a, um, *adj., indefinite, unlimited, boundless,* synonym of *indefinitus, indeterminatus,* and *interminatus,* the opposite of *determinatus, finitus,* and *terminatus.* On bonum infinitum, see *bonus;* on corpus infinitum, see *corpus;* on distantia infinita, see *distantia;* on divisio infinita, see *divisio;* on ens infinitum, see *ens;* on **esse infinitum,** see *esse;* on **essentia infinita,** see *essentia;* on **generatio infinita,** see *generatio;* on **gratia infinita,** see *gratia;* on **linea infinita,** see *linea;* on **magnitudo infinita,** see *magnitudo;* on **modus infinitus,** see *modus;* on **multitudo infinita,** see *multitudo*; on **negativa infinita,** see *negativus;* on **nomen infinitum,** see *nomen;* on **poena infinita,** see *poena;* on **potentia infinita,** see *potentia;* on **praedicatum infinitum,** see *praedicatum;* on **principium infinitum,** see *principium;* on **quantitas infinita,** see *quantitas;* on **spatium infinitum,** see *spatium;* on **subiectum infinitum,** see *subiectum;* on **substantia infinita,** see *substantia;* on **tempus infinitum,** see *tempus;* on **terminus infinitus,** see *terminus;* on **verbum infinitum et infiniti modi,** see *verbum;* on **virtus infinita,** see *virtus.*—Kinds of *infinitum* are: (a), **infinitum ablatione seu divisione seu per divisionem seu secundum divisionem** and **infinitum appositione seu per appositionem seu in ultimis,** *the endless through removal of limits or division into infinite parts* and *that through endless addition of parts or through the lack of termination.*—(b), **infinitum actu seu in actu** and **infinitum potentia seu infinitum potentia,** *the actually* and *the potentially infinite* or *the infinite in the state of actuality and that in the state of*

potentiality.—(c), **infinitum appositione,** see *infinitum ablatione.*—(d), **infinitum creatum** and **infinitum primum,** *the created* and *the first* or *uncreated infinity.*—(e), **infinitum divisione,** see *infinitum ablatione.*—(f), **infinitum duratione seu secundum durationem** and **infinitum quantitate seu quantitatis seu in quantitate seu secundum quantitatem,** *the endless according to time* and *that according to quantity,* i.e., the indefinite.—(g), **infinitum essentiae seu secundum essentiam,** *the boundless according to essence.*—(h), **infinitum essentialiter** and **infinitum participative seu participatum seu participatione seu per participationem seu per adquisitionem,** *the essential infinity* and *the endless through participation in the essential* or *through the appropriation* or *the acquisition of the same.*—(i), **infinitum ex parte formae seu secundum formam seu secundum rationem formae seu formale** and **infinitum ex parte materiae seu secundum materiam seu secundum rationem materiae seu materiale,** *the endless on the part of the form* and *that on the part of the matter of a thing,* or *the endless with reference to form* and *that with reference to matter.*—(j), **infinitum ex parte materiae,** see *infinitum ex parte formae.*—(k), **infinitum ex parte post,** *the endless on the part of thereafter* or *with reference to* *what follows.*—(l), **infinitum extensive** and **infinitum intensive,** *the endless of extension* and *that according to intensity* or *exertion.*—(m), **infinitum formale,** see *infinitum ex parte formae.*—(n), **infinitum ideale,** *the model infinity.*—(o), **infinitum in actu,** see *infinitum actu.*—(p), **infinitum in directum,** *the endless proceeding in a straight line.*—(q), **infinitum in magnitudine seu magnitudine seu secundum magnitudinem** and **infinitum multitudine seu multitudinis seu secundum multitudinem seu secundum numerum seu in numero,** *the endless according to size* or *dimension* and *that according to number.*—(r), **infinitum in numero,** see *infinitum in magnitudine.*—(s), **infinitum in potentia,** see *infinitum actu.*—(t), **infinitum in quantitate,** see *infinitum duratione.* Cf. PT. Q. 10. Art. 3 ad 1.—(u), **infinitum intensive,** see *infinitum extensive.* —(v), **infinitum in ultimis,** see *infinitum ablatione.*—(w), **infinitum magnitudine,** see *infinitum in magnitudine.*—(x), **infinitum materiale,** see *infinitum ex parte formae.*—(y), **infinitum multitudine seu multitudinis,** see *infinitum in magnitudine.*—(z), **infinitum negative dictum seu sumptum** and **infinitum privative dictum seu sumptum,** *the infinity in the sense of simple negation of limitation* and *that in the sense of a privation of limitation*

that is ordinarily present.—(a²), **infinitum omnino seu secundum totum seu simpliciter** and **infinitum quo seu secundum quid,** *the endlessness which is entire* or *simple* or *absolute* and *that which is boundless only in a certain respect.*—(b²), **infinitum participatione,** see *infinitum essentialiter.*—(c²), **infinitum participative,** see *infinitum essentialiter.* —(d²), **infinitum participatum,** see *infinitum essentialiter.*—(e²), **infinitum per accidens** and **infinitum per se,** *the endless according to something else* and *that according to its own self* and *its own nature.*—(f²), **infinitum per adquisitionem,** see *infinitum essentialiter.*—(g²), **infinitum per appositionem,** see *infinitum ablatione.*—(h²), **infinitum per contactum,** *the endless resulting from direct contact.*—(i²), **infinitum per divisionem,** see *infinitum ablatione.*—(j²), **infinitum per participationem,** see *infinitum essentialiter.*—(k²), **infinitum per se,** see *infinitum per accidens.*—(l²), **infinitum potentia,** see *infinitum actu.*—(m²), **infinitum primum,** see *infinitum creatum.*—(n²), **infinitum privative dictum seu sumptum,** see *infinitum negative dictum seu sumptum.*—(o²), **infinitum purum,** *the pure infinity,* not mixed with anything finite.— (p²), **infinitum quantitate seu quantitatis,** see *infinitum duratione.*—(q²), **infinitum quo,** see *infinitum omnino.*—(r)², **infinitum** secundum divisionem, see *infinitum ablatione.*—(s²), infinitum secundum durationem, see *infinitum duratione.*—(t²), infinitum secundum essentiam, see *infinitum essentiae.*—(u²), infinitum secundum formam, see *infinitum ex parte formae.*—(v²), infinitum secundum magnitudinem, see *infinitum in magnitudine.*—(w²), infinitum secundum materiam, see *infinitum ex parte formae.*—(x²), infinitum secundum multitudinem, see *infinitum in magnitudine.*—(z²), infinitum secundum numerum, see *infinitum in magnitudine.*—(a³), infinitum secundum quantitatem, see *infinitum duratione.*—(b³), infinitum secundum quid, see *infinitum omnino.* —(c³), infinitum secundum rationem formae, see *infinitum ex parte formae.*—(d³), infinitum secundum rationem materiae, see *infinitum ex parte formae.*—(e³), infinitum secundum speciem, *the endless according to species.*— (f³), infinitum secundum totum, see *infinitum omnino.*—(g³), infinitum separatum, *the separated infinity* or *that existing for itself.* —(h³), infinitum simpliciter, see *infinitum omnino.*—(i³), infinitum virtualiter, *the endless according to power.*—infinitum, i, *n., an infinitude, an indefinite amount* or *number, infinity,* synonym of *infinitas.*—in or ad infinitum, or infinita, *to infinity, without end.*— impossibile est infinitum pertransire or infinita non contingit tran-

sire or infinita non est transire seu pertransire or infinitum non potest transiri or non est infinita transire, the translation of the Aristotelian passage: *ta d'apeira me esti dielthein, infinity cannot be measured by man either in reality* or *in thoughts.* Cf. below: *infinitum nec cognosci* etc.—infinita cognosci non possunt or infinita inquantum huiusmodi non sunt scibilia or infinitorum non est scientia, *the endless as such is neither discernible nor knowable to man.* Cf. below: *impossibile est* etc.—infinita non contingit transire, see above: *impossibile est* etc.—infinita non est transire seu pertransire, see above: *impossibile est* etc.—infiniti ad finitum nulla est proportio, *between the infinite* and *finite there is no proportion.*—infinitorum non est scientia, see above: *infinita cognosci* etc.—infinitum nec cognosci nec transiri potest, *the endless can neither be known nor measured by man.*—infinitum non potest transiri, see above: *impossibile est* etc.—non est infinita transire, see above: *impossibile est* etc.—infinite, *adv., without bounds, without end, infinitely.*

infirmitas, atis, (1) *want of strength, weakness, feebleness,* synonym of *debilitas,* (2) *want of spirit, want of courage, timidity,* the opposite of *fortitudo.*—On peccare ex infirmitate, see *pec-*

care; on **peccatum ex infirmitate,** see *peccatum;* on **vulnus infirmitatis,** see *vulnus.*—Kinds of *infirmitas* in this (1) sense are: (a), **infirmitas animae,** *the weakness of soul* or *of fervour.*—(b), **infirmitas cordis,** *weakness of the heart.*

infirmo, are, avi, atum, 1, *v. a.* and *n.,* (1) lit., *to weaken, deprive of strength; to make physically infirm,* (2) fig., (a) *to weaken morally,* (b) *to weaken* or *impair* the force of an argument, reason, proof etc.; *to render doubtful* or *questionable.*

infirmus, a, um, *adj.,* (1) of persons, with reference to physical condition, (a) *not strong, sick, physically weak* or *feeble,* (b) of persons with reference to the mind, *not firm* in character or purpose; *weak, frail, irresolute,* (c) of parts of the body, *unhealthy, diseased,* (2) of animals, *sick, unhealthy,* (3) of things, *weak, feeble, of no weight* or *consequence,* (a) abstract things, (b) arguments, laws, opinions.

inflammatio, onis, *f.,* (1) lit., (a) *brightness, a blazing appearance,* (b) transf., of the body, *a heating, inflammation,* (2) fig., *a kindling, inflaming.*

inflammo, are, avi, atum, 1, *v. a.,* (1) *to set on fire, light up, enkindle,* (2) fig., *to rouse, excite, enkindle.*

inflatio, onis, *f., inflation,* the condition of being puffed up with vanity, pride, or baseless notions.

inflativus, a, um, *adj., inflative, of inflating quality* or *tendency; flatulent.*

inflecto, ere, exi, exum, 3, *v. a.,* (1) *lit., to bind, contort,* (2) *fig., to change, alter, affect, pervert.*

inflexibilis, e, *adj., inflexible, unchangeable.*

inflictio, onis, *f., infliction,* the action of inflicting pain, punishment, annoyance, etc.

inflictivus, a, um, *adj., inflictive, tending to inflict.*

inflictor, oris, *m., an inflicter,* one who inflicts or causes something to be suffered or endured.

infligo, ere, ixi, ictum, 3, *v. a., to inflict, lay on* as a stroke, blow or wound; *to impose* or *lay upon* a person as something that must be suffered or endured, (1) corporal or spiritual punishment, (2) punishment after death, (3) to impose the law of excommunication, (4) evil of any kind.

inflo, are, avi, atum, 1, *v. a., to swell, puff up, inflate,* used *fig.* —**inflatus,** a, um, *P. a., puffed up, inflated.*

influentia, ae, *f.,* (1) in gen., *influence,* the action or fact of flowing in; *inflowing, influx, inflow,* said of the action of light and of immaterial things conceived of as flowing in, (a) *the inflow of light,* (b) *influence, inflow, influx,* the exertion of action of which the operation is unseen or insensible, or perceptible only in its object, by one thing upon another; the action thus exer-

cised, (2) *influence, the inflowing, immission* or *infusion* into a
person or thing, of any kind of
divine, spiritual, moral, immaterial or secret power of principle;
that which flows in or is infused,
(3) *influence,* the capacity of
producing effects by insensible
or invisible means, without the
employment of material force or
the exercise of formal authority;
moral power over a person.

influo, ere, xi, xum, 3, *v. n., to flow
in, exercise an influence over,
influence.* On **causa influens,** see
causa; on **forma influxa,** see
forma.

influxio, onis, *f., a discharge, a
flowing in.*

influxus, us, *m., influence.*—Kinds
of *influxus* are: (a), **influxus divinus,** *the divine influence.*—(b),
influxus intelligibilis, *the intellectual* or *spiritual influence.*

informatio, onis, *f.,* (1) *formation,*
i.e., providing with a form, synonym of *formatio,* (2) *arrangement, management.* On **dicere
per modum informationis,** see
dicere; on **praedicare per informationem,** see *praedicare;* on
praedicatio per informationem,
see *praedicatio.*—One kind of *informatio* in this sense is: **informatio intellectus,** *the formation
of reason* or *the intellectual presentation.*

informativus, a, um, *adj.,* (1) *formative,* i.e., *furnishing something
with a form,* synonym of *formativus,* (2) *arranging, shaping.*

informis, e, *adj., formless, unformed, misshapen,* synonym of
deformis, the opposite of *formatus.* On **cogitatio informis,** see
cogitatio; on **confessio informis,**
see *confessio;* on **fides informis,**
see *fides;* on **genus informe,** see
genus; on **materia informis,** see
materia; on **natura informis,** see
natura; on **spes informis,** see
spes; on **subiectum informe,** see
subiectum; on **virtus informis,**
see *virtus.*—**informiter,** *adv., hid-
eously, horribly, in a manner
without form,* found in the S.T.
only in quotation.

informitas, atis, *f.,* (1) *formlessness,
matter in a primitive state,* synonym of *infiguratio,* the opposite
of *figuratio* and *formatio,* (2)
*that which has an unbecoming
form and is misshapen, deformity,* the opposite of *formositas,*
the synonym of *deformitas.*

informo, are, avi, atum, (1) *to give
to a thing its essential* or *substantial form,* or *its accidental
fashion,* synonym of *formare,* (2)
establish, prepare, inform.

infortunatus, a, um, *adj.,* (1) *struck
by an unfortunate accident, unfortunate,* the opposite of *fortunatus,* (2) *struck by a great misfortune, severely afflicted,* opposite of *eufortunatus,* not found
in the S.T.

infortunium, i, *n., a very unfortunate accident, a great tragedy,
misfortune,* the opposite of *eufortunium,* and *fortunium.*

infra, (I) *adv.,* of a following place in a writing, *below,* (II) *prep.,* (1) *lit.,* (a) of place, *below, beneath, a given point,* (b) of time, *within a given limit,* (c) of age, *below,* (d) of number, *less than,* (2) *fig., below, beneath* in rank, honor, esteem.

infrangibilis, e, *adj., infrangible, that cannot be broken; indissoluble.*

infrigidatio, onis, *f., infrigidation, the action of cooling; a cooling.*

infrigido, are, avi, atum, 1, *v. a., to infrigidate, to make cold* or *frigid; to chill, cool.*—**infrigidatus,** a, um, *P. a., made cold, cooled.*

infrigidus, a, um, *adj., cold.*

infringo, ere, fregi, fractum, 3, *v. a., to break, check, infringe, weaken* in any way.—**infractus,** a, um, *P. a.,* of speech, *effeminate, subdued.*

infructuosus, a, um, *adj.,* (1) *lit., unfruitful,* (2) *fig., useless, barren, fruitless.*

infundo, ere, fudi, fusum, 3, *v. a., to pour into* or *upon, infuse,* opposite of *transfundo.*—**infusus,** a, um, *P. a., poured over* or *into, infused,* the opposite of *innatus.* On **habitus infusus,** see *habitus;* on **iustitia infusa,** see *iustitia;* on **potestas infusa,** see *potestas;* on **prudentia infusa,** see *prudentia;* on **sapientia infusa,** see *sapientia;* on **scientia infusa,** see *scientia;* on **species infusa,** see *species;* on **temperantia infusa,** see *temperantia;* on **virtus infusa,** see *virtus.*

infusio, onis, *f., infusion,* the action of pouring in; the action of infusing some principle or quality or idea into the mind or soul or heart, esp., of the work of God in the imparting of grace, virtue; the infusion of the soul into the body; of knowledge, science, etc. —Common phrases are: **infusio virtutis,** *infusion of virtue.* Infused virtue is not acquired by repeated acts but poured into the soul directly by God.—**infusio fidei,** *the infusion of faith.*—**infusio charitatis,** *the infusion of charity.*—**infusio gratiae,** *infusion of grace.*

ingeminatio, onis, *f., ingemination,* the action of repeating or reiterating a word or statement; *a repetition, reiteration.*

ingemisco, ere, ui, 3, *v. a.* and *n., to groan* or *sigh over a thing,* used with *acc.* and *inf., absol.*

ingenerabilis, e, *adj., not producible, not producible, ingenerable,* the opposite of *generabilis.*

ingeneratio, onis, *f., ingenerability,* used in the S.T. only in quot.

ingeniose, *adv., ingeniously,* used in the S.T. only in quot.

ingeniositas, atis, *f., keenness, ingenuity, inventiveness,* not found in the S.T.

ingenitus, a, um, *P. a., ungenerated, unborn, unproduced,* the opposite of *genitus.* It is a property of the First Person of the Trinity. On **sapientia ingenita,** see *sapientia.*

ingenium, ii, *n.,* (1) *genius, talent, inventive power,* (2) *a clever idea, a work of art.*

ingens, tis, *adj., of immoderate size, vast, huge, prodigious, enormous; great, mighty, remarkable.*

ingenuus, a, um, *adj., ingenuous, of free* or *honorable birth, noble.* —ingenuus, i, *m., a free-born man.*

ingero, ere, gessi, gestum, 3, *v. a.,* (1) *lit.,* (a) in gen., *to bring, carry something,* (b) ingerere se, *to betake one's self to,* (2) *fig.,* (a) in gen., *to carry, bring, convey something immaterial,* (b) of language, *to pour forth, pour out against,* (c) *to heap up,* (d) ingerere se, *to betake one's self* to anything, *busy one's self with, interfere with.*—The following phrases show some of the uses of *ingerere se.*—**ingerere se negotiis lucrativis,** *to occupy one's self with money-making trades.*—**ingerere se aspectui et auditui,** *to present one's self to human sight* and *hearing.*—**ingerere se ad maiores ordines,** *to present one's self for higher Orders.*—**ingerere se ad divina,** *to attend divine services.* The following are numerous uses of phrases containing *ingerere se.*—**ingerere se molestiis,** *to fight against trouble.*—**ingerere se pravis concupiscentiis,** *to give way to wicked desires.*—**ingere se ad tentationes,** *to expose one's self to temptation.*—**ingerere se gaudium sibi,** *to gather joy for one's self.*

ingestio, onis, *f., a prompting, uttering, dictating.*

inglorians, antis, *P. a., being without glory.*

ingloriatio, onis, *f., ingloriousness,* the condition or quality of being inglorious; *ignominy, disgrace.*

ingloriosus, a, um, *adj., of actions, mode of life,* etc., bringing no glory or honor to a person; hence conferring disgrace; *shameful; ignominious.*

inglorius, a, um, *adj., inglorious.*

ingluvies, ei, *f., gluttony,* used in the S.T. only in quot.

ingratitudo, inis, *f., ingratitude, unthankfulness; want* or *absence of gratitude;* indisposition to acknowledge or reciprocate benefits received.

ingratus, a, um, *adj., unthankful, ungrateful,* not feeling or showing gratitude.

ingredior, i, essus, 3, *v. dep. n.* and *a.,* (I) *lit.,* (1) *to make entry into lands as a formal assertion of ownership,* used with *acc.,* (2) *to go* or *come into a closed space,* e.g., *a house, room,* etc., used with *acc., in* and *acc.,* and *absol.,* (a) of persons, (b) of things, (II) *fig.,* (1) in gen., *to enter, come in, penetrate,* (2) *to enter a monastery, to enter religion; to become a monk* or *nun,* used with *acc.,* (3) *to enter a state* or *condition with the additional notion of place,* used with *in* and *acc.*

ingressus, us, *m.,* (1) *lit.,* (a) *a going into, entering something,*

(b) *a walk, step, gait,* (c) in a bad sense *an advance,* (2) *fig.,* (a) *a going into; entering religion* or *a monastery,* i.e., *becoming a monk* or *nun,* (b) with a spiritual signification, *an entering,* or *going into the hearts of men,* said of Christ.

ingrosso, are, avi, atum, 1 *v. a.* and *n., to thicken.*

ingruens, entis, *P. a.,* used *fig., ingruent, assailing, attacking, coming on,* used in the S.T. only in quot.—**febris ingruens tempore praestituto,** *a fever coming on at an appointed time, an intermittent fever.*

ingruentia, ae, *f., ingruence, a coming on, onset, attack.*

inhabilis, e, *adj.,* used *fig., unfit, incapable, unable.*

inhabitabilis, e, *adj., uninhabitable.*

inhabitatio, onis, *f., inhabitation,* (1) the act of inhabiting or occupying as a dwelling, (2) *spiritual indwelling.*

inhabito, are, avi, atum, 1, *v. a., to dwell in, to inhabit,* used *lit.* and *fig.*

inhaerentia, ae, *f., inherence.* On **fieri modum inhaerentiae,** see *fieri;* on **praedicare per modum inhaerentiae,** see *praedicare;* on **praedicatio per inhaerentiam,** see *praedicatio;* on **propositio simplicis inhaerentiae,** see *propositio.*

inhaero, ere, haesi, haesum, 2, *v. n., to cling to, cleave to, adhere to,* used both *lit.* and *fig.*—**inhaerens,** ntis, *P. a., inherent.* On

forma inhaerens, see *forma;* on **relatio inhaerens,** see *relatio;* on **species concreata inhaerens,** see *species;* on **veritas inhaerens,** see *veritas.*

inhaesio, onis, *f., a hanging* or *adhering to,* (1) *a firm attachment, fidelity* to something, i.e. a truth, (2) with *mutua, mutual indwelling,* said esp. of the inhabitation of a soul by God because of union with Christ through sanctifying grace.

inhibeo, ere, ui, itum, 2, *v. a., to restrain, hinder, prevent, inhibit,* used with *acc., inf.*

inhibitio, onis, *f., an inhibition, a prohibition,* especially one formally issued by a person of ecclesiastical authority.

inhio, are, avi, atum, 1, *v. n.,* and *a.,* (1) *to regard with longing, yearn for something,* used with *inf., ad* and *acc.,* (2) *to hear eagerly, attend closely to,* used with *abl.*

inhonestas, atis, *f., dishonor, disgrace, unbecomingness, indecency.*

inhoneste, *adv.,* see *inhonestus.*

inhonestus, a, um, *adj., dishonorable, shameful, disgraceful; indecent, vile.*—**inhoneste,** *adv., indecently, disgracefully.*

inhonoratio, onis, *f., a dishonoring,* used in the S.T. only in quot.

inhonoro, are, avi, atum, 1, *v. a., to dishonor.*—**inhonoratus,** a, um, *P. a., unhonored, disregarded.*

inhumanitas, atis, *f., inhuman conduct, savageness, barbarity, inhumanity. Inhumanitas* is a *filia* or offspring of *avaritia.* Cf. *avaritia.*

inhumanus, a, um, *adj., inhuman,* used in the S.T. only in quot.

inhumatus, a, um, *P. a., buried in the ground,* used in the S.T. only in quot.

inhumatus, a, um, *adj., unburied.*

inicio, ere, ieci, iectum, 3, *v. a.,* (1) *lit., to throw* or *put on* or *upon, to throw at* or *over* anything, (a) **inicere manum sibi,** *to lay hands on one's self, to commit suicide,* (b) **inicere manus in aliquem,** *to lay hands on someone,* (c) **inicere vincula alicui,** *to put chains on someone,* (2) *fig.,* (a) *to infuse, inspire,* used with *acc.* and *dat.,* (b) **inicere se periculo,** *to expose one's self to danger,* (c) **inicere laqueum alicui,** *to lay a snare for someone.*

inimicitia, ae, *f., enmity, hostility, hatred, unfriendliness.*—**capitales inimicitiae,** *a deadly feud.* Octavus, si habeat inimicitias capitales, PTS. Q. 24. Art. 1 c.

inimico, are, 1, *v. a., to make enemies, to set at variance,* used in the S.T. only in quot.

inimicus, a, um, *adj., unfriendly, inimical, hostile.*—**inimicus,** i, *m., an enemy.*

inique, *adv.,* see *iniquus.*

iniquitas, atis, *f.,* used *fig.,* (1) sing., *iniquity, unrighteousness, wickedness, sin,* (2) plur., *crimes,*

unrighteous act or *doings, sins,* (3) *want* or *violation of equity; injustice, unfairness.*

iniquus, a, um, *adj.,* (1) of things in gen., *wrong, bad, wicked, sinful,* (2) of a law, precept, statute, statement, *unfair, unjust,* (3) temperament of mind, *unwilling, impatient, discontented,* (4) of people, *wicked, unjust, evil.*—**iniqui,** orum, *m., the wicked.*—**inique,** *adv., unjustly.*

initialis, e, *adj., initial, of* or *pertaining to a beginning;* existing at, or constituting the beginning of some action or process; existing at the outset; *primary.*

initio, are, avi, atum, 1, *v. a.,* (1) *to begin, commence, enter upon, give rise to, start,* (2) *to initiate, inaugurate, introduce* into acquaintance with something.—**initiatus,** a, um, *P. a., commenced, begun.*

initium, ii, *n., a beginning, commencement,* (1) the commencement of an action or state, entrance into being or upon a course; also that which originates something; the *origin; source,* (2) *an initial point of time;* the first part or initial stage of anything.

iniaceo, ere, cui, citum, 2, *v. n., to be at hand, lie near.*

iniunctio, onis, *f., an injunction, command, order, precept* or *direction.*

iniungo, ere, iunxi, ctum, 3, *v. a.,* used *fig.,* (1) *to adhere* or *cling* with strong attachment, (2) *to* *lay on* or *upon* as a burden; *to charge, enjoin,* used with *dat.,* followed by *ut* and *subj., quod* and *subj.,* the *acc.*

iniuria, ae, *f., an injury,* anything that is done contrary to justice and equity, (1) *lit.,* harm or loss caused to or sustained by a person or thing; *harm, detriment, damage,* (2) *transf.,* (a) *wrongful treatment* or *action;* violation or infringement of another's rights; suffering or mischief wilfully or unjustly inflicted; an *insult, wrong,* (b) an *injustice,* (c) intentionally hurtful or offensive speech or words; *reviling, insult, calumny.*

iniuriator, oris, *m., an injurer, one who injures,* used in the S.T. only in quot.

iniurior, ari, atus, 1, *v. dep., to do an injury, to injure,* used *absol.,* with *dat., acc.*

iniuriose, *adv.,* see *iniuriosus.*

iniuriosus, a, um, *adj., injurious, wrongful.*—**iniuriose,** *adv., injuriously, wrongfully.*

iniuste, *adv.,* see *iniustus.*

iniustificatio, onis, *f., injustice* in the sense of an act, *unjust action,* the *adikema* of Aristotle, i.e., that action which proceeds from the *habitus* of *iniustitia,* the opposite of *iustificatio.*—One kind of *iniustificatio* is: **iniustificatio particularis,** *the particular injustice.*

iniustitia, ae, *f.,* (1) *injustice* in the proper sense of the word, i.e., in the sense of a *habitus,* a *bad*

habit, a vice, the opposite of iustitia, (2) *injustice* in the transferred sense of the word, i.e., the lack of probity, likewise the opposite of *iustitia.*—Kinds of *iniustitia* in this sense are: (a), **iniustitia illegalis** and **iniustitia secundum inaequalitatem quandam ad alterum seu quae dicitur inaequalitas,** *the unlawful* or *illegal injustice* and *the injustice which is called inequality,* because it aims at an unequal measure of good and bad.—(b), **iniustitia particularis seu specialis seu quae est particularis malitia** and **iniustitia quae est omnis seu tota malitia,** *the particular* and *the general injustice,* or the injustice which is malicious in part and that which is wholly malicious.—(c), **iniustitia quae dicitur inaequalitas,** see *iniustitia illegalis.*—(d), **iniustitia quae est omnis seu tota malitia,** see *iniustitia particularis.*—(e), **iniustitia quae est particularis malitia,** see *iniustitia particularis.*—(f), **iniustitia inaequalitatem quandam ad alterum,** see *iniustitia illegalis.*—(g), **iniustitia specialis,** see *iniustitia particularis.*

iniustus, a, um, *adj., that is contrary to right* and *justice, unjust, wrongful, unfair,* the opposite of *iustus.* On **iudicium iniustum,** see *iudicium;* on **iuramentum iniustum,** see *iuramentum;* on **lex iniusta,** see *lex;* on **politia iniusta,** see *politia;* on **regimen iniustum,** see *regimen;* on **vindicta**

iniusta, see *vindicta.*—Kinds of
iniustus are: iniustus avarus, iniustus illegalis, and iniustus inaequalis, the *adikos pleonektes,
adikos paranomos* and *adikos
anisos* of Aristotle, *the unjust
in the sense of the avaricious,
the unjust who has broken a law,
the unjust who desires an unequal measure* or *an inequality
of good* and *evil.*—iniustum, i, *n.,
injustice.*—Kinds of *iniustum* are:
(a), iniustum comune and iniustum particulare seu particulariter dictum, *the general* and *the
particular unjust thing* or *injustice.*—(b), iniustum illegale and
iniustum inaequale, the *adikon
paranomon* and *adikon anison* of
Aristotle, *the illegal unjust thing*
or *injustice* and *the unjust thing*
or *injustice that consists in a desire for inequality* or *for an unequal measure of good* and *bad.*
Cf. also *iniustitia illegalis* under
iniustitia.—(c), iniustum inaequale, see *iniustum illegale.*—(d),
iniustum particulare seu particulariter dictum, see *iniustum commune.*—(e), iniustum per se, *the
unjust thing* or *injustice in* or *for
itself.*—iniuste, *adv., wrongfully,
unfairly, unjustly,* synonym of
male, the opposite of *iuste.*

inlocalis, e, *adj., illocal, having no
place* or *location in space.*

innascibilis, e, *adj., innascible, that
cannot be born; not subject to
the condition of birth.*

innascibilitas, atis, *f., incapability
of being born, innascibility,* one

of the notions characteristic of
the First Person of the Trinity.

innascor, i, natus, 3, *v. dep., to be
born in, arise in, originate in, be
produced in.*—innatus, a, um, *P.
a., inborn, innate, inherent, natural.* See under *innatus.*

innaturalis, e, *adj.,* (1) *not natural,
not normal,* the opposite of *naturalis,* (2) *contrary to nature, unnatural,* the opposite of *naturalis.*
—On accidens innaturale, see *accidens;* on delectatio innaturalis,
see *delectatio.*—On delectabile
innaturale, see *delectabilis;* on
habitudo innaturalis, see *habitudo;* on motus innaturalis, see
motus; on quies innaturalis, see
quies; on transmutatio innaturalis, see *transmutatio.*

innatus, a, um, *P. a., inborn, innate,
inherent, natural,* the opposite of
infusus and *adquisitus.* On forma
innata, see *forma;* on habitus innatus, see *habitus;* on iustitia innata, see *iustitia;* on principium
innatum, see *principium;* on scientia innata, see *scientia;* on similitudo innata, see *similitudo;*
on species innata, see *species.*

innecto, ere, nexui, nexum, 3, *v. a.,*
used *fig.,* (1) *to connect, join,
mingle with,* (2) *to implicate, involve.*

innitor, i, nixus, or nisus, 3, *v. dep.,*
(1) *lit., to lean* or *rest upon, to
support one's self by anything,*
used with *dat.,* (2) *fig., to lean
upon, rely on, rest on, depend
on,* used with the *dat.*

innocens, entis, *adj., that harms no one, blameless, guiltless, innocent.*—**innocens,** entis, *m., the guiltless man.*—**Sancti Innocentes,** *the Holy Innocents, martyrs,* male children slain by Herod.— **innocenter,** *adv., harmlessly, blamelessly, innocently.*

innocenter, *adv.,* see *innocens.*

innocentia, ae, *f., innocence, the quality of being innocent,* (1) *freedom from sin,* guilt or moral wrong in general; *without stain,* the state of being untainted with or unacquainted with evil which was the condition of Adam, and consequently the human race, before the Fall; *moral purity,* (2) freedom from specific guilt; the fact of not being guilty of that with which one is charged; *guiltlessness,* (3) freedom from cunning or artifice; *guilelessness, simplicity,* (4) *collect. concr.*

Innocentius, ii, *m.,*—(1) *Innocent* I, bishop of Rome after Anastasius, from May 402 to March 417 A.D. He was a native of Albano. Rome was sacked by Alaric during his pontificate. He took measures against the Manichaeans, Montanists, and Priscillianists, corresponded with St. John Chrysostom in the latter's exile, and confirmed the condemnation of Pelagius by African synods. St. Thomas quotes his authority in three places in the S.T.—(2) *Innocent* III, Pope (Lotario de Conti), one of the greatest popes of the Middle Ages, son of Count Trasimund of Segni and nephew of Clement III, born in 1160 at Anagni and died June 16, 1216 at Perugia. He expounded the relations between the Empire and the Papacy in a decree afterwards embodied in the *Corpus Iuris.* He is author of a work entitled *De Sacro Altaris Mysterio,* to which St. Thomas frequently refers, sometimes, however, ascribing his quotation to Hugh of St. Victor,—(3) *Innocent* IV, pope, (Sinibaldo de Fieschi), count of Lavagna, born at Genoa, date unknown; died at Naples, December 7, 1254. He is the author of *Apparatus in quinque libros decretalium.*

innominabilis, e, *adj., innominable, unmentionable, not fit to be named.*

innominatus, a, um, *adj., unnamed, without a name.*

innotesco, ere, tui, 3, *v. inch., n., to become known,* used *absol.,* with *dat.*

innovabilis, e, *adj., subject to change.*

innovatio, onis, *f., a renewing, an alteration, innovation, renewal.*

innovo, are, avi, atum, 1, *v. a., to renew, alter.*—**innovatus,** a, um, *P. a., renewed, made new.*

innoxius, a, um, *adj., innocent, that does harm to none, not guilty, blameless.*

innumerabilis, e, *adj., countless, innumerable.*

innumerus, a, um, *adj., countless, innumerable.*

innuo, ere, ui, utum, 3, *v. n., to intimitate, to make known formally, to notify, announce, state,* used with *acc., ut* and *subj.*

innuptus, a, um, *adj., unmarried.*

inobediens, entis, *P. a., disobedient.*

inobedientia, ae, *f., disobedience.*

inolesco, ere, levi, olitum, 3, *v. n.* and *a.,* used *fig., to prevail, be in force, have effect* or *power.*

inopia, ae, *f.,* (1) *in gen., want, lack, scarcity of anything,* (2) *in partic.,* (a) *want,* esp. of *necessaries, need,* (b) *transf.,* of a speaker, *poverty of words.*

inopinabiliter, *adv., without doubt,* used in the S.T. only in quot.

inopinatus, a, um, *adj., not expected, unexpected.*—**inopinatum,** i, *n., something unexpected,* hence, **ex opinato,** adverbially, *unexpectedly.*

inops, opis, *adj.,* (1) of persons, *poor, helpless through poverty, indigent,* (2) of things inanimate, *poor, characterized by poverty.*

inordinate, *adv.,* see *inordinatus.*

inordinatio, onis, *f., inordination, disorder,* the condition of being inordinate in conduct, affections, etc.; *inordinateness.*

inordinatus, a, um, *adj., not arranged, disordered, irregular,* synonym of *deordinatus,* the opposite of *ordinatus.* On **actus inordinatus,** see *actus* under 1; on **affectio inordinata,** see *affectio;* on **amor inordinatus,** see *amor*

under 1; on **concupiscentia inordinata,** see *concupiscentia* under 1; on **conversio inordinata,** see *conversio* under 3; on **delectatio inordinata,** see *delectatio;* on **dispositio inordinata,** see *dispositio* under 4; on **elementum inordinatum,** see *elementum* under 1; on **ira inordinata,** see *ira* under 1; on **libido inordinata,** see *libido* under 1; on **motus inordinatus,** see *motus* under 1; on **passio inordinata,** see *passio* under 3; on **phantasma inordinatum,** see *phantasma* under 2.—**inordinate,** *adv., irregularly, without order, inordinately, excessively.*

inquam, 3, *v., defect.,* the only forms found are inquam, inquit, inquiunt; *I say, he says, they say.*

inquantum, see *quantus.*

inquieto, are, avi, atum, 1, *v. a., to disquiet, disturb.*

inquietudo, inis, *f., disquietude, uneasiness, restlessness of mind* or *body.*

inquietus, a, um, *adj., restless, unquiet.*

inquinatio, onis, *f., a defiling,* used *fig.*

inquino, are, avi, atum, 1, *v. a.,* (1) *lit., to defile, stain, befoul, pollute,* (2) *fig., to pollute, defile, corrupt, contaminate.*

inquiro, ere, sivi, situm, 3, *v. a., to search, pry, examine, inquire into.*

inquisitio, onis, *f., a searching into* or *inquiring into, examination,* *investigation.*—Kinds of *inquisitio* are: (a), **inquisitio consiliativa**, *the reflecting consideration.* —(b), **inquisitio contemplativa**, *the contemplating* or *contemplative consideration.*—(c), **inquisitio studiosa**, *the zealous* or *earnest consideration.*

inquisitive, *adv.*, see *inquisitivus.*

inquisitivus, a, um, *adj., examining, investigating, inquisitive.*—**inquisitive**, *adv., in an investigating way, inquisitively*, synonym of *inquirendo;* the opposite of *assertive* and *determinando.*

inquisitor, oris, *m., examiner, investigator*, used in S.T. only in quot.

insanabilis, e, *adj.*, (1) *lit., incurable*, that cannot be cured or healed, (2) *fig., incurable, without remedy.*

insanabilitas, atis, *f., insanability, the quality of being insanable; incurableness.*

insania, ae, *f.*, (1) *as a disease, insanity*, (2) as a personal quality, *madness, senselessness, folly*, (3) *fig., excess, extravagance* in anything.

insanio, ire, ivi, itum, 4, *v. n.*, (1) *to be mad, insane*, (2) *to be foolish, silly.*

insanus, a, um, *adj.*, of persons, also of the mind, *insane, not of sound mind, mad; unsound.*

insatiabilis, e, *adj., insatiable, that cannot be satisfied.*

inscius, a, um, *adj., not knowing, ignorant of a thing*, used in the S.T. only in quot.

inscribo, ere, psi, ptum, 3, *v. a., to inscribe, to write, mark* or *delineate words, a name, characters,* etc., *in* or *on something.*

inscriptio, onis, *f., inscription*, an accusation or challenge at law made under the condition that if it were false, the accuser would undergo the same punishment that would have been inflicted on the accused if found guilty.

insectator, oris, *m., a persecutor.*

insectus, a, um, *adj., unhewn.*

insecutio, onis, *f., pursuit, a pursuing*, a following with a view to reach or obtain.

insensatus, a, um, *adj., senseless*, lacking sense or understanding; *unintelligent, stupid, foolish, insensate.*

insensibilis, e, *adj.*, (1) *not perceptible to the senses, that cannot be felt*, the opposite of *sensibilis*, (2) *senseless, devoid of the senses, belonging to a senseless being*, likewise the opposite of *sensibilis*, (3) *unsentient, senseless, deadened*, the synonym of *impossibilis*, the Aristotelian *anaisthetos.*—On **natura insensibilis**, see *natura;* on **potentia insensibilis**, see *potentia.*—**insensibiliter**, *adv., imperceptibly.*

insensibilitas, atis, *f.*, (1) *senselessness, irrationality*, (2) *insensibility, insentiency, deadness*, synonym of *impassibilitas*, the *anaisthesia* of Aristotle.

insensibiliter, *adv.*, see *insensibilis.*

inseparabilis, e, *adj., that cannot be separated, inseparable.* On **acci-**

dens inseparabile, see *accidens* under 2; on **ens inseparabile,** see *ens.*—**inseparabiliter,** *adv., inseparably.*

inseparabilitas, atis, *f., inseparableness,* incapable of being separated, said of two or more united things or persons, or of their connection or relation.—**inseparabilitas matrimonii,** *the indissolubility of matrimony,* or the incapability of its being annulled.

inseparabiliter, *adv.,* see *inseparabilis.*

insepultus, a, um, *adj., unburied.*

insequor, i, cutus, 3, *v. dep. n.* and *a.,* (1) *lit., to pursue, follow up, press upon, attack,* (2) *fig., to pursue, proceed along with a view to some end.*

1. **insero,** ere, sevi, situm, 3, *v. a., to implant,* used *fig.*—**insitus,** a, um, *P. a., implanted, infixed, ingrafted,* used *lit.* and *fig.*

2. **insero,** ere, sevi, sertum, 3, *v. a.,* (1) *lit.,* (a) *to insert,* used with the *dat.,* (b) *to ingraft,* used *absol.* (2) *fig.,* (a) *to implant, ingraft,* used with the *dat., acc.* and *dat.,* (b) with *se, to insert, introduce into; insinuate itself.*

inservio, ire, ivi, itum, 4, *v. n.* and *a., to be devoted* or *attached to, to be submissive to, obey, serve,* used with the *dat.*

insidiae, arum, *f., plur.,* (1) in *gen., an artifice, crafty device, snare,* used *lit.* and *fig.,* (2) *military term, an ambush, a disposition* or *arrangement of troops for attacking an enemy from a concealed*

station, hence, *unseen peril; device to entrap, snare.*

insidiator, oris, *m., a lurker, plotter.*

insidiatrix, icis, *adj., insidious, cunning, deceitful.*

insidior, ari, atus, 1, *v. dep., to lie in ambush, lie in wait for,* used with the *dat.,* (1) *lit.,* (2) *fig.*

insidiose, *adv.,* see *insidiosus.*

insidiosus, a, um, *adj., cunning, deceitful.*—**insidiose,** *adv., cunningly, treacherously.*

insigne, is, *n.,* (1) *lit.,* (a) *a sign, trace* of anything, (b) *a sign* or *trophy of honor,* (c) *a badge, insignia* of a military leader, (2) *fig., a mark* or *token* indicative of anything.

insignio, ire, ivi, itum, 4, *v. a., to put a mark upon, to mark; to distinguish* with a mark, used *lit.* and *fig.*—**insignitus,** a, um, *P. a., marked, branded, sealed.*

insignis, e, *adj., remarkable, noted, extraordinary.*

insilio, ere, ui, 4, *v. n., to attack, strike at, revolt against,* used with *in* and *acc.*

insimul, *adv., at the same time, at once,* used in the S.T. only in quot.

insinuatio, onis, *f.,* (1) *insinuation,* the suggestion or hunting of anything indirectly, covertly, or by allusion or implication, (2) *notification, publication.*

insinuo, are, avi, atum, 1, *v. a.* and *n., to insinuate, to signify,* or *express indirectly, to give, to understand; to hint, suggest, imply.*

insipiens, entis, *adj., foolish, igno-rant.*—**insipienter,** *adv., foolishly.*

insipienter, *adv.,* see *insipiens.*

insipientia, ae, *f., insipience, the quality of being insipient; lack of wisdom; unwisdom; foolishness.*

insisto, ere, stiti, 3, *v. n.,* (1) *to follow up, pursue an object* or *enterprise; to press vigorously, apply* or *devote one's self to,* used with the *dat.,* (2) *to insist* on something, *persist,* continue steadfastly in a course of action, used with *ad* and *acc.,* the *dat.*

insolitus, a, um, *adj., unwonted, unusual.*

insolubilitas, atis, *f., insolubility, indissolubility,* (1) *incapable of being terminated,* (2) *incapable of being annulled; perpetually binding.*

insolutus, a, um, *adj., not solved.*

insomnietas, atis, *f., sleeplessness.*

insomnis, e, *adj., sleepless.*

insomnium, ii, *n., sleeplessness.*

insono, are, ui, 1, *v. n., to sound, resound.*

inspectio, onis, *f.,* (I) *lit.,* (1) *an inspection,* (a) *a looking on, watching, seeing, beholding* something, (b) *plural, spectacles, sights,* (c) *the action of looking in* something as a mirror, (d) in a bad sense, *a staring at,* (2) in *partic., a looking through, examination,* the action of inspecting or looking narrowly into; careful scrutiny or survey; close or critical examination, (II) *fig., consideration, contemplation.*

inspector, oris, *m., an examiner,* one who inspects or looks carefully at or into.

inspicio, ere, spexi, spectum, 3, *v. a., to look at, see, look into, inspect; examine,* (1) *lit.,* (a) *in gen.,* (b) *in partic., to examine* something with a view to finding out its condition, character, nature, etc., (2) *fig., to consider, examine, become acquainted with, comprehend, perceive.*

inspiratio, onis, *f., infusion, inspiration,* in particular, the divine motion by which the Holy Scriptures were written.—Kinds of *inspiratio* are: (a), **inspiratio actualis,** *the inspiration taking place in reality.*—(b), **inspiratio divina seu supernaturalis,** *the divine* or *supernatural inspiration.*—(c), **inspiratio exterior** and **inspiratio interior seu interna,** *the exterior* and *the interior inspiration.*—(d), **inspiratio interior seu interna,** see *inspiratio exterior.*—(e), **inspiratio supernaturalis,** see *inspiratio divina.*

inspirator, oris, *m., an inspirer, one who* or *that which inspires.*

inspiro, are, avi, atum, 1, *v. a.* and *n.,* (1) *lit., to breathe life, a soul into,* (2) *fig.,* (a) *to inspire, to infuse* some thoughts or feeling into a person, to animate by some spiritual influence, said of God or the Holy Spirit, or of a divinity or supernatural agency, (b) *to infuse* something into the mind; *to enkindle, arouse, awaken* in the mind or heart, a feeling, impulse, purpose.—**inspirare in faciem hominis spiraculum vitae,** *to breathe the breath of life into the face of man.*

inspissatio, onis, *f., inspissation,* the action of becoming thick or dense; *condensation.*

inspissatus, a, um, *adj., thickened.*

instabilis, e, *adj.,* (1) *lit., instable, lacking stability; unstable,* (2) *fig., inconstant, changeable.*

instabilitas, atis, *f., instability,* the quality of being unstable; lack of stability in regard to position, condition, or moral qualities; want of steadiness, fixity, or firmness of purpose or character.

instans, antis, *n., instant, moment,* synonym of *nunc,* the indivisible of time, which is not time. On **unitas instantis,** see *unitas.*— Kinds of *instans* are: (a), **instans nunc,** *the moment of now.*—(b) **instans signatum,** *the designated* or *determined instant.*

instantaneus, a, um, *adj., sudden, instantaneous,* synonym of *momentaneous* and *subitus,* the opposite of *successivus.* On **actio instantanea,** see *actio;* on **motus instantaneus,** see *motus;* on **mutatio instantanea,** see *mutatio.*

instantia, ae, *f.,* (1) *a stand, objection,* (2) *force, vehemence, insistence* in speaking.—Kinds of *instantia* in this (1) sense are: (a), **instantia propria,** *the proper* or *special objection.*—(b), **instantia rationabilis** and **instantia sophistica,** *the rational* and *the sophistic objection.*—(c), **instantia rea-**

lis, *the real objection.*—(d), **instantia sophistica,** see *instantia rationabilis.*—(e), **instantia universalis,** *the universal objection* or *that expressed through a universal opinion.*

instar, n. indecl., used with *ad* and followed by the *gen., like.*

instauro, are, avi, atum, 1, *v. a., to restore, re-establish.*

instigatio, onis, *f., instigation, incitement.*

instigo, are, avi, atum, 1, *v. a., to urge, stimulate, stir up, incite, excite,* to bring about by incitement or persuasion.

instinctus, us, *m., instigation, impulse,* springing from the nature, and anticipating deliberation. On **iudicare ex naturalis instinctu,** see *iudicare;* on **operari naturali instinctu,** see *operari;* on **velle naturalis instinctu,** see *velle.*—Kinds of *instinctus* are: (a), **instinctus daemonis seu diaboli,** *the instigation of the devil.*—(b), **instinctus diaboli,** see *instinctus daemonis.*—(c), **instinctus divinus,** *the divine impulse.*—(d), **instinctus interior,** *the inner impulse.*—(e), **instinctus naturae seu naturalis,** *the impulse of nature* or *the natural impulse.*—(f), **instinctus naturalis,** see *instinctus naturae.*

instituo, ere, ui, utum, 3, *v. a.,* (I) (1) *lit., to establish, create; put,* or *place something* some place, (2) *to lay out something* (3) *to erect, set up* an altar, image, temple, etc., (II) *fig.,* (1) in gen.,

to set up, establish, found, ordain; to introduce or bring into
use, (2) to institute a sacrament,
(3) to initiate, start something,
(4) to establish in an office,
charge, or position, (a) to institute, consecrate someone for divine service, (b) to place one in
spiritual charge, (c) to appoint
as instructor, king, heir, etc., (5)
to enjoin, ordain, command, order, used with ut, quod and
subj., (6) to teach, instruct; to
establish in principles, (7) to
determine; to fix in the mind,
resolve upon.—The following
phrases show a varied use of instituere: instituere nomen, to
coin a name.—instituere verbum,
to vary a word by using it in a
particular mood.—instituere religionem, to establish a religious
order.—instituere indulgentiam,
to put an indulgence on something connected with divine worship.—institutere vestes ministrorum in Ecclesia, to prescribe
certain vestments for the ministers of the Church.

institutio, onis, f., (1) an arrangement, placing, the action of placing or setting something in some
place, as the erection of a statue,
(2) institution, the action of in-
stituting or establishing; setting
on foot or in operation; foundation, ordainment; the fact of being instituted, (3) the establishment or ordination of a sacrament, esp. of the Holy Eucharist
by Christ, (4) a preparation, the
action of fitting someone beforehand for a particular service; a
making ready, induction, a synonym of consecratio, (5) instruction, education, teaching, training, (6) authorization, precept,
decree, commandment, ordinance, (7) an institute, elements
of instruction; a book of first
principles, an elementary treatise.—institutio nominis, the signification or meaning of a name.

institutor, oris, m., (1) a founder,
creator, institutor, one who institutes or establishes, (2) a teacher, instructor.

institutum, i, n., a precept, rule,
command, or a collection or rules
constituting a prescribed guide
for conduct or action.

insto, are, stiti, statum, 1, v. n., (1)
lit., to draw nigh, approach, (2)
fig., (a) to follow eagerly, pursue,
used with the dat., (b) to demand earnestly, insist upon, used
with subj., (c) to assail, attack
morally with a view to produce
changes in the feelings, character, conduct, used absol., with
ad and the gerund.

instructio, onis, f., instruction, (1)
the action of instructing or
teaching; the imparting of
knowledge, information, (2) a
making known to a person what
he is required to do; a direction,
order, mandate, oral or written.

instructor, oris, m., an instructor,
one who instructs; a teacher.

instructus, a, um, P. a., see instruo.

instrumentalis, e, *adj.*, *instrumental,* operative only by power conferred by another, the opposite of *principalis.* On **agens instrumentale,** see *agens;* on **causa instrumentalis,** see *causa;* on **creans instrumentale,** see *creare;* on **virtus instrumentalis,** see *virtus.* —**instrumentaliter,** *adv.,* *in the manner or the sense of an instrument, instrumentally,* synonym of *ministerialiter,* the opposite of *auctoritative* and *principaliter.* On **operari instrumentaliter,** see *operari;* on **tentare instrumentaliter,** see *tentare;* on **movere instrumentaliter,** see *movere.*

instrumentaliter, *adv.,* see *instrumentalis.*

instrumentum, i, *n.,* *an implement, instrument,* synonym of *organum,* the opposite of *agens principale, causa principalis,* and *movens principale.* Although an instrument makes a specific contribution to the production of an effect, it operates only in virtue of motion or power given it from the principal cause; otherwise it would not be an instrument. On **frui sicut instrumento,** see *frui.*— Kinds of *instrumentum* are: (a), **instrumentum animatum** and **instrumentum inanimatum,** the Aristotelian *organon empsychon* and *organon apsychon, the animated* or *living instrument* and *the inanimate* or *lifeless instrument.*—(b), **instrumentum assumptum seu exterius seu extrinsecum seu separatum** and **instrumentum coniunctum seu unitum,** *the instrument assumed by an active being* or *externally joined to it* or *separated from it* and *the instrument naturally bound* or *joined with a substance.*—(c), **instrumentum commune** and **instrumentum proprium,** *the common* and *the proper instrument.* —(d), **instrumentum coniunctum,** *an instrument that is naturally united to the agent.* See *instrumentum assumptum.*—(e), **instrumentum exterius seu extrinsecum,** see *instrumentum assumptum.*—(f), **instrumentum inanimatum,** see *instrumentum animatum.*—(g), **instrumentum naturale,** *the natural instrument.*—(h), **instrumentum necessarium** and **instrumentum propter bene esse,** *the necessary* and *the advantageous instrument.*—(i), **instrumentum proprium,** see *instrumentum commune.*—(j), **instrumentum propter bene esse,** see *instrumentum necessarium.*—(k), **instrumentum rationis,** *the instrument of reason.*—(l), **instrumentum regulans** and **instrumentum regulatum,** *the regulating* or *ordering* and *the regulated* or *ordered instrument.*—(m), **instrumentum regulatum,** see *instrumentum regulans.*—(n), **instrumentum separatum,** see *instrumentum assumptum.*—(o), **instrumentum unitum,** see *instrumentum assumptum.*—(p), **instrumentum vocale,** *the instrument of voice* or *of speech.*— **effectus assimilatur in forma non** quidem instrumento, sed principali agenti, see *effectus.*—non est procedere in infinitum in instrumentis, *there is no unending succession of instrumental causes.*

instruo, ere, xi, ctum, 3, *v. a.*, (1) *lit., to build, construct,* (2) *fig., to provide with information, to teach, instruct.*—instructus, a, um, *P. a., instructed, taught, informed.*

insufficiens, entis, *adj., inadequate, insufficient,* the opposite of *sufficiens.* On **agens insufficiens,** see *agens;* on **coactio insufficiens,** see *coactio;* on **definitio insufficiens,** see *definitio;* on **dilectio insufficiens,** see *dilectio;* on **principium insufficiens,** see *principium.*—insufficienter, *adv., inadequately, insufficiently.*

insum, esse, fui, futurus, *v. n., to exist in* or *upon* (*something else*), *be indwelling.* On **minor de inesse,** see *minor;* on **propositio de inesse et de inesse impliciter,** see *propositio;* on **syllogismus de inesse,** see *syllogismus.*—Kinds of *inesse* are: (a), **inesse naturaliter,** *indwelling in a natural manner* or *according to nature.*—(b), **inesse per accidens et inesse per se,** *to be present not directly but in consequence of something,* and *to be present directly of itself* or *according to its nature.*—(c), **inesse per se,** see *inesse per accidens.*—(d), **inesse primo,** *indwelling* or *inherent in the first place.*

insurgo, ere, surrexi, rectum, 3, *v. n., to rise, rise up, rise against,* (1) *to rise* or *come into existence, originate,* (2) *to rise from an inactive state,* (3) *to rise against, break forth in active opposition* or *for the purpose of assailing.*

insurrectio, onis, *f., a recrimination,* the action of recriminating or making a countercharge against an accuser.

intactus, a, um, *adj.,* (1) in *gen., untouched,* (2) of virgins, *untouched, chaste, inviolate.*

integer, tegra, tegrum, *adj., untouched, unhurt, unchanged,* (1) *lit.,* (a) in *gen., whole, entire, complete,* (b) of physical condition, *sound, healthy,* (c) of age, with *aetas aetatis integrae, of full age* or *in the flower of age,* (2) *fig.,* (a) in *gen., entire, whole, complete,* (b) in *partic., blameless, perfect,* (c) of the judgment, reason, disposition, *unbiased, unimpaired, honest,* (d) of the moral virtues, *sound, unimpaired,* (e) of female chastity, *spotless, pure.* —The following phrases occur: **ex integro,** *in its entirety.*—**in integrum,** *to a former state* or *condition.*—integre, *adv., wholly, entirely, perfectly.*

integralis, e, *adj., undamaged, intact, composing a whole, integral,* synonym of *integer.* On **pars integralis,** see *pars.*—integraliter, *adv., in the manner* or *sense of entirety, integrally.*

integraliter, see *integralis.*

integritas, atis, *f., the undiminished* or *unimpaired condition of a thing, completeness, soundness,*

integrity. On status integritatis
naturae, see *status.*—Kinds of *integritas* are: (a), **integritas carnis
seu corporis seu corporalis** and
integritas mentis, *integrity of the
flesh* or *of the body* and *that of
the spirit with reference to the
virtue of purity.*—(b), **integritas
corporalis,** see *integritas carnis.*—
(c), **integritas corporis,** see *integritas carnis.*—(d), **integritas
mentis,** see *integritas carnis.*—(e),
integritas naturae and **integritas
personalis,** *integrity of nature*
and *that of person.*—(f), **integritas personalis,** see *integritas naturae.*—(g), **integritas speciei,** *the
integrity of essence.*—(h), **integritas virginalis,** *the virginal integrity.*

integro, are, avi, atum, 1, *v. a.,* *to
set forth* or *present something
in its entirety, make whole, renew.* On **principium integrans,**
see *principium.*

intellectivus, a, um, *adj.,* (1) *intellectual,* i.e., belonging to the
intellectual or rational part of
man, synonym of *cognitivus, rationalis* and *intellegibilis,* the opposite of *appetitivus, voluntarius, sensibilis,* and *sensitivus,* (2)
knowing intellectually, as distinct from discursively, *capable
of intellectual knowledge, intellectual,* synonym of *intellectualis,* the opposite of *rationalis.*—
On **affectio intellectiva,** see *affectio;* on **appetitus intellectivus,**
see *appetitus;* on **apprehensio
intellectiva,** see *apprehensio;* on

cognitio intellectiva, see *cognitio;* on **forma intellectiva,** see
forma; on **operatio intellectiva,**
see *operatio;* on **potentia intellectiva,** see *potentia;* on **visio intellectiva,** see *visio;* on **vita intellectiva,** see *vita.*—On **anima intellectiva,** see *anima;* on **habitus
intellectivus,** see *habitus;* on
memoria intellectiva, see *memoria;* on **natura intellectiva,** see
natura; on **pars intellectiva,** see
pars; on **potentia intellectiva,**
see *potentia;* on **principium intellectivum,** see *principium;* on
ratio intellectiva, see *ratio;* on
substantia intellectiva, see *substantia;* on **virtus intellectiva,** see
virtus; on **vis intellectiva,** see
vis.—**intellectivum** sc. **principium
seu genus potentiarum animae,**
the translation of Aristotle's
terms, *noetikon* and *dianoetikon,
the intellectual cognitive principle* or *the intellectual faculties of
the human soul.*

intellectualis, e, *adj.,* (1) *supersensual, immaterial, transcendental,
intellectual,* i.e., belonging to
the immaterial part of the human substance, being of an
order transcending matter and
sensation, synonym of *intellegibilis* and *rationalis,* the opposite
of *sensibilis, animalis,* and *sensitivus,* (2) *knowing transcendentally in the broader sense of
the word,* i.e., knowledge higher
than sense, whether intuitive or
discursive, abstractive knowledge of universals, synonym of

intellectivus and *rationalis,* the opposite of *sensibilis* and *sensitivus,* (3) *knowing transcendentally in the narrower sense of the word,* i.e., the act of the suprasensible cognitive faculty arriving at truth directly and immediately, intuitively, and not indirectly and through the medium of some other truth, the opposite of *rationalis.*—On actio intellectualis, see *actio;* on amor intellectualis, see *amor;* on appetitus intellectualis, see *appetitus;* on apprehensio intellectualis, see *apprehensio;* on bonum intellectuale, see *bonum;* on caelum intellectuale, see *caelum;* on cognitio intellectualis, see *cognitio;* on conceptio intellectualis, see *conceptio;* on delectatio intellectualis, see *delectatio;* on desiderium intellectuale, see *desiderium;* on emanatio intellectualis, see *emanatio;* on esse intellectuale, see *esse;* on existimatio intellectualis, see *existimatio;* on habitus intellectualis, see *habitus;* on intentio intellectualis, see *intentio;* on locutio intellectualis, see *locutio;* on lumen intellectuale, seu intellectualis naturae, see *lumen;* on lux intellectualis, see *lux;* on modus intellectualis, see *modus;* on motus intellectualis, see *motus;* on notio intellectualis, see *notio;* on oculus intellectualis, see *oculus;* on operatio intellectualis, see *operatio;* on perfectio intellectualis, see *perfectio;* on potentia intellectualis, see *potentia;* on puritas intellectualis, see *puritas;* on intellectualis cognitio, see *cognitio;* on ratio intellectualis, see *ratio;* on revelatio intellectualis, see *revelatio;* on scientia intellectualis, see *scientia;* on signum intellectuale, see *signum;* on species intellectualis, see *species;* on virtus intellectualis, see *virtus;* on visio intellectualis, see *visio;* on vita intellectualis, see *vita.*—On agens intellectuale, see *agens;* on anima intellectualis, see *anima;* on causa intellectualis, see *causa;* on natura intellectualis, see *natura;* on principium intellectuale, see *principium;* on substantia intellectualis, see *substantia.*—On consideratio intellectualis, see *consideratio;* on substantia intellectualis, see *substantia.*—intellectualiter, *adv.,* (1) *intellectually* in the broader sense of the word, i.e., in a general discernible manner of the intellect, synonym of *intelligibiliter,* the opposite of *sensibiliter,* (2) *intellectually* in the narrower sense of the word, i.e., in a discernible manner of the non-discursive intuition of the intellect, likewise a synonym of *intelligibiliter,* the opposite of *rationabiliter.*—On cognoscere intellectualiter, see *cognoscere.*

intellectualitas, atis, *f.,* (1) a faculty of knowledge that transcends the material and the singular, *intellectuality,* i.e., immaterial or rational knowledge, the opposite of *sensibilitas*, (2) *immaterial discernability* or *cognoscibility*.

intellectualiter, *adv.*, see *intellectualis*.

intellectus, us, *m.*, (1) an immaterial intelligent substance, the *nous* or the *logistikon* of Aristotle, synonym of *substantia, separata, angelus, intelligentia* and *ratio*, the opposite of *corpus*, (2) *reason, intellect* in the sense of a faculty, i.e., of a faculty of perception, but both of an organic or sentient and an inorganic or transcendental faculty of perception, synonym of *sensus*, rarely used by St. Thomas in this sense, (3) *reason, intellect* in the sense of an immaterial, inorganic faculty of knowledge, synonym of *ratio*, the opposite of *sensus*, (4) *activity of the reason, intellectual knowledge*, likewise a synonym of *intelligentia* and *ratio*, (5) *intuition, intellect* in the sense of a transcendental intuitive faculty of knowledge or of a spiritual faculty of contemplation, which arrives at truth non-discursively, directly and immediately, synonym of *oculus intellectualis seu spiritualis*, the opposite of *ratio*, (6) *intellectual discernment of first principles* in the sense of an habitual, direct discernment and assent to the highest principles of knowledge, thus also called *intellectus principiorum*, Aristotle's *nous*

ton archon, the opposite on the one hand of *ars, prudentia, sapientia*, and *scientia*, and on the other hand of *ratio* and *synteresis*, (7) *intellectual discernment, discernment*, i.e., immediate intellectual knowledge, synonym of *intellegentia*, the opposite of *ratio* and *scientia*, (8) *understanding, intellectual comprehension*, synonym of *intellegentia*, (9) *intellectual representation, transcendental representation*, synonym of *ratio*, (10) *signification, sense, meaning*, synonym of *ratio, sensus, significatio, virtus, vis*.—On **delectatio intellectus, seu secundum intellectum**, see *delectatio*.—Kinds of *intellectus* in this sense are: (a), **intellectus caelestis,** *the heavenly intellect* or *that of the angels*.—(b), **intellectus coniunctus** and **intellectus immixtus seu separatus,** *the intellect joined with a body* and *that not naturally united to a body*.—(c), **intellectus divinus,** *the divine* or *God-like intellect*.—(d), **intellectus immixtus,** see *intellectus coniunctus*.—(e), **intellectus impassibilis** and **intellectus passibilis,** *the impassive intellect* or *that unsusceptible to change* and *the passible intellect* or *that susceptible to change*.—(f), **intellectus passibilis,** see *intellectus abstrahens* under (3).—(g), **intellectus primus** and **intellectus secundus,** *the first* and *the second intellect* in the ontological order of the intellects.—(h), intellectus secundus, see *intellectus primus*.—(i), intellectus separatus, see *intellectus coniunctus*.—(j), intellectus superior, *the superior intellect*.—voluntas proprie in intellectu, the translation of the Aristotelian passage: *en to logistiko he boulesis ginetai, volition has its origin in intellectual knowledge*. One kind of *intellectus* in this (2) sense is intellectus passivus, the *nous pathetikos* of Aristotle, i.e., the enduring or possible intellect under which is to be understood on the one hand a complexity of several internal sense faculties, and on the other hand only a single faculty but different on different occasions. —On abstractio intellectus seu per intellectum, see *abstractio;* on abstrahere per intellectum, see *abstrahere;* on agens per intellectum, see *agens;* on agere per intellectum, see *agere;* on apprehendere per intellectum, see *apprehendere;* on apprehensio intellectus, see *apprehensio;* on bonum intellectus seu secundum intellectum, see *bonus;* on cognitio intellectus, see *cognitio;* on compositio intellectus, see *compositio;* on conceptio intellectus, see *conceptio;* on demonstrare quantum ad intellectum, see *demonstrare;* on demonstratio ad intellectum, see *demonstratio;* on divisio intellectus, see *divisio;* on emanatio intellectus,

see *emanatio;* on forma intellectus, see *forma;* on formatio intellectus, see *formatio;* on fundamentum in intellectu, see *fundamentum;* on habitus intellectus, see *habitus;* on imaginatio per intellectum, see *imaginatio;* on imperium intellectus, see *imperium;* on impuritas intellectus, see *impuritas;* on informatio intellectus, see *informatio;* on intentio intellectus, see *intentio;* on iudicium intellectus, see *iudicium;* on lumen intellectus, see *lumen;* on malum intellectus, see *malus;* on motus intellectus, see *motus;* on movere per intellectum, see *movere;* on opus intellectus, see *opus;* on passio intellectus seu intellectus possibilis, see *passio;* on perfectio intellectus seu secundum intellectum, see *perfectio;* on perfectus intellectus seu secundum intellectum, see *perfectus;* on principium intellectus practici et speculativi et secundum intellectum, see *principium;* on prius secundum intellectum, see *prior;* on procedere per modum intellectus, see *procedere;* on processio per modum intellectus seu secundum intellectum, see *processio;* on puritas intellectus, see *puritas;* on verbum intellectus, see *verbum;* on veritas intellectus, see *veritas;* on verum intellectus seu in intellectu, verum intellectus practici et speculativi, see *verus;* on vitium intellectus, see *vitium*.—Kinds of *intellectus* in this (3) sense are:

(a), **intellectus abstrahens seu depurans seu agens** and **intellectus possibilis seu potentialis,** the *nous poietikos* and *nous dunamei* of Aristotle, *the abstracting* or *clarifying* or *active intellect* and *the potential* or *passible intellect*. These are two distinct faculties. One is called abstracting and clarifying intellect, because it withdraws from the *phantasmata*, i.e., the sensible representations of things present in the phantasy or imagination, the *species intellegibiles*, i.e., the intellectually cognitive content which are the universal, common or general notes of extramental reality (quia intellectus illud quod intellegit abstrahit a sensu, oportet quod lapis prius cognoscatur a virtute imaginativa sive phantastica, quae abstractior est reliquis virtutibus sensitivis, Univ. 2), by neglecting the singular, material, concrete qualities of the phantasms, and it is also called active or effective intellect, because it effects or produces from the purely sensible species, i.e., *phantasmata*, the purely intelligible species which inform and determine the operation of the *intellectus possibilis*. The other is called potential or passible intellect, because it is in the state of potentiality as regards the reception of any and all intellectual cognitive representations, the *species intellegibiles*, which

reduce it from potentiality to act, and determine it to know this rather than that, like a note book in which to be sure something can be written but in reality contains no writing as yet, and is indifferent to what is to be written.—(b), **intellectus activus seu operativus seu practicus** and **intellectus contemplativus seu speculativus seu theoricus,** the *nous praktikos kai theoretikos* of Aristotle, *the active* or *operating* or *producing intellect* and *the speculative* or *contemplative intellect*, i.e., the intellect according as it puts its knowledge to use in making or doing and the intellect according as it seeks knowledge merely for the sake of knowledge and contemplation.—(c), **intellectus acutus sive perspicax,** *the sharp* or *penetrating intellect*.—(d), **intellectus adeptus, seu in actu, intellectus habitualis seu in habitu** and **intellectus in potentia,** *a mind actively using knowledge, a mind furnished with knowledge but not using it at the moment,* and *a mind devoid of knowledge but capable of acquiring it*. Thus, for example, a man might be actually considering the meaning of intellectus, habitually aware of his name and address, and a potential student of theology.—(e), **intellectus aeternus seu divinus, intellectus angelicus** and **intellectus animae seu hominis seu humanus,** *the eternal* or *divine* *intellect, that of the angels,* and *that of the human soul* or *of man.*—(f), **intellectus agens,** see *intellectus abstrahens.*—(g), **intellectus angelicus,** see *intellectus aeternus.*—(h), **intellectus animae,** see *intellectus aeternus.*—(i), **intellectus beatus,** *the intellect of the blessed in heaven.*—(j), **intellectus captivatus,** *the captivated intellect.*—(k), **intellectus contemplativus,** see *intellectus activus.*—(l), **intellectus creatus** and **intellectus increatus,** *the created* and *the uncreated intellect.*—(m), **intellectus deiformis,** *the God-like intellect.*—(n), **intellectus depurans,** see *intellectus abstrahens.*—(o), **intellectus discursivus seu ratiocinativus,** *the intellect that infers* or *draws conclusions, ratio* as opposed to *intellectus.*—(p), **intellectus divinus,** see *intellectus aeternus.*—(q), **intellectus habitualis,** see *intellectus adeptus.*—(r), **intellectus hominis,** see *intellectus aeternus.*—(s), **intellectus humanus,** see *intellectus aeternus.*—(t), **intellectus hylealis seu materialis,** *the intellect acting like material.*—(u), **intellectus in actu,** see *intellectus adeptus.*—(v), **intellectus increatus,** see *intellectus creatus.*—(w), **intellectus inferior** and **intellectus infimus,** *the lower* or *inferior intellect* and *the lowest* or *most inferior intellect* as a species of the genus, intellectual substance.—(x), **intellectus infimus,** see *intellectus inferior.*—(y),

intellectus in habitu, see *intellectus adeptus.*—(z), **intellectus in potentia,** see *intellectus adeptus.*—(a^2), **intellectus inquisitivus,** *the investigating* or *searching intellect.*—(b^2), **intellectus materialis,** see *intellectus hylealis.*—(c^2), **intellectus obumbratus,** *the overshadowed* or *darkened intellect.*—(d^2), **intellectus operativus,** see *intellectus activus.*—(e^2), **intellectus perspicax,** see *intellectus acutus.*—(f^2), **intellectus possibilis,** see *intellectus abstrahens.*—(g^2), **intellectus potentialis,** see *intellectus abstrahens.*—(h^2), **intellectus practicus,** see *intellectus activus.*—(i^2), **intellectus ratiocinativus,** see *intellectus discursivus.*—(j^2), **intellectus simplex,** *the simple intellect* (of God and of angels), called "simple" because it attains truth in one uncomplicated glance, the intuitive intellect, whereas the human intellect on the other hand usually also employs the discursive intellect, proceeding from premises that are better known to conclusions and thus is not only called *intellectus* but also *ratio.*—(k^2), **intellectus speculativus,** see *intellectus activus.*—(l^2), **intellectus supernaturalis,** *the supernatural intellect.*—(m^2), **intellectus theoricus,** see *intellectus activus.*—(n^2), **intellectus velatus,** *the veiled intellect.*—**actio intellectus consistit in hoc quod ratio rei intellectae est in intellegente** (PP. Q. 82. Art. 3

c), or, **intellectus est in actu per hoc quod res intellecta est in intellectu secundum suam similitudinem,** *the action of the intellect consists in this,* or *rather the intellect is discovered in the state of activity by reason of the fact that the thing known* or *better the essence of the same is received according to its species in him who knows in his intellect.*—intellectum in actu non est aliquid ab intellectu intellegente actu, sed idem, or, intellectus est quodammodo ipsa intellegibilia, or, intellectus et intellegibile in actu sunt unum, or, intellectus in actu et intellegibile in actu sunt unum, or, intellegibile in actu et intellectus in actu sunt unum, or, intellectus in actu dicitur esse intellectum in actu, or, intellectus in actu fit intellectum in actu, or, intellectus in actu quodammodo est intellectum in actu, or, intellectus in actu est intellegibile in actu, or, intellegibile in actu est intellectus in actu, or, intellectus in actu est res intellecta, the translation of the Aristotelian passage: *ho nous estin ho kat'energeian noon ta pragmata,* the intellect found in the state of activity or actually knowing is really the same as the object which according to its intelligible species is received into the intellect and thereby is actually known intellectually. The intellect becomes, in the act of knowledge, the object known since the same form which makes the object actual also makes the passible intellect actual, being present not physically but mentally in the intelligible species.—**intellectus est in actu per hoc, quod res intellecta est in intellectu secundum suam similitudinem,** see above: *actus intellectus consistit* etc.—**intellectus est naturaliter universalium apprehensivus,** or, **intellectus est universalium et non singulorum,** *the intellect has the universal* and *not the individual as its object.*—**intellectus est quodammodo ipsa intellegibilia,** see above: *intellectum in actu* etc.—**intellectus est universalium et non singularium,** see above: *intellectus est naturaliter* etc.—**intellectus et intellegibile in actu sunt unum,** see above: *intellectus in actu* etc.—**intellectus in actu dicitur esse seu est intellectum in actu,** see above: *intellectus in actu* etc.—**intellectus in actu est intellegibile in actu,** see above: *intellectus in actu* etc.—**intellectus in actu est res intellecta,** see above: *intellectus in actu* etc.—**intellectus in actu et intellegibile in actu sunt unum,** see above: *intellectus in actu* etc.—**intellectus in actu quodammodo est intellectum in actu,** see above: *intellectus in actu* etc.—**intellectus speculativus extensione fit practicus,** *the speculative intellect through extension, i.e., through* *the relation of its object becomes practical in the sphere of doing* and *acting.*—intellegibile in actu est intellectus in actu, see above: *intellectum in actu* etc.—intellegibile in actu et intellectus in actu sunt unum, see above: *intellectum in actu* etc.—Kinds of *intellectus* in this (4) sense are: (a), intellectus appetitivi seu appetitivus, the *nous oretikos* according to Aristotle, *the act of desire of an intellectual creature,* or *the appetite for good presented by an intellect,* i.e., the choice of the will.—(b), intellectus cognoscens quod quid est seu cognoscitivus quidditatem rei seu quidditatem rei apprehendens, intellectus componens et dividens and intellectus discursivus seu ratiocinans seu ratiocinando discurrens, *the act of the intellect that simply apprehends the essence of a thing,* (simple apprehension), *an act of the intellect that unites* or *separates a predicate of a subject* (judgment) or *the act of the intellect that from several judgments infers* and *draws conclusions* (reasoning).—(c), intellectus cognoscitivus quidditatem rei, *simple apprehension*. See *intellectus cognoscens quod quid est.*—(d), intellectus componens, *affirmative judgment.* See *intellectus cognoscens quod quid est.*—(e), intellectus discursivus, *reasoning.* See *intellectus cognoscens quod quid est.*—(f), intellectus

dividens, *negative judgment.* See *intellectus cognoscens quod quid est.*—(g), intellectus quidditatem rei apprehendens, *simple apprehension.* See *intellectus cognoscens quod quid est.*—(h), intellectus ratiocinans seu ratiocinando discurrens, see *intellectus cognoscens quod quid est.* —On donum intellectus, see *donum;* on habitus intellectus, see *habitus.*—Kinds of *intellectus* in this (8) sense are: (a), intellectus affirmativus and intellectus negativus, *the affirmative* and *the negative understanding* or *the intellectual perception in the affirmative* or *negative sense.*— (b), intellectus falsus seu perversus and intellectus verus seu rectus, *the false* or *wrong* and *the true* or *right understanding.*— (c), intellectus negativus, see *intellectus affirmativus.*—(e), intellectus perversus, see *intellectus falsus.*—(e), intellectus rectus, see *intellectus falsus.*—(f), intellectus verus, see *intellectus falsus.*—On modus intellectus, see *modus;* on veritas intellectus, see *veritas.*— Kinds of *intellectus* in this (9) sense are: (a), intellectus complexorum seu compositus and intellectus incomplexorum seu incomplexus seu simplex, *the rational conception of a composite reality* or *the composite intellectual conception* and *the rational conception of an incomposite reality* or *the simple intellectual conception,* i.e., *judgment* and *idea.*—(b), **intellectus compositus,** see *intellectus complexorum.*—(c), **intellectus incomplexorum,** see *intellectus complexorum.*—(d), **intellectus incomplexus,** see *intellectus complexorum.*—(e), **intellectus mathematicus** and **intellectus naturalis,** *the mathematical* and *the natural scientific conception of the intellect* or *the mathematical* and *the natural scientific idea.*—(f), **intellectus naturae speciei,** *the intellectual conception* or *the idea of a nature as a common class.*—(g), **intellectus naturalis,** see *intellectus mathematicus.*—(h), **intellectus principalis,** *the chief rational conception* or *the main idea.*—(i), **intellectus simplex,** see *intellectus complexorum.*—Kinds of *intellectus* in this (10) sense are: **intellectus figuralis seu mystica** and **intellectus litteralis,** *the prefigurative* or *mystical* and *the literal significance.*

intellegentia, ae, *f.,* (1) *an intelligence,* an incorporeal, immaterial substance, *an angel,* synonym of *intellectus,* the opposite of *corpus* and *homo,* (2) *rational activity, rational comprehension,* likewise a synonym of *intellectus* (see 4) and *ratio,* (3) *rational insight, insight,* i.e. immediate apprehension, synonym of *intellectus,* (4) *understanding, intellectual conception,* synonym of *intellectus.*—On **speculum intellegentiarum,** see *speculum.*—Kinds of *intellegentia* in this (1) sense are: (a), **intellegentia agens,** *the active intelligence* as it was taught by Avicenna.—(b), **intellegentia prima** and **intellegentia secunda,** *the first* and *the second intelligence,* likewise according to the teachings of Avicenna.—(c), **intellegentia secunda,** see *intellegentia prima.*—**intellegentiae sunt finitae superius et infinitae inferius,** *intellectual substances in an upward direction,* i.e., *according to their being* or *essence, are considered within limits; in a downward direction,* i.e., *with reference to material they are considered without limits.* On **notitia simplicis intellegentiae,** see *notitia;* on **puritas intellegentiae,** see *puritas;* on **relatio secundum rationem intellegentiae tantum,** see *relatio;* on **scientia simplicis intellegentiae,** see *scientia.*—Kinds of *intellegentia* in this (2) sense are: (a), **intellegentia actualis,** *rational comprehension actually taking place.*—(b), **intellegentia incomplexorum seu indivisibilium,** the Aristotelian *noesis ton adiaireton, the rational comprehension* or *the intellectual comprehension of the non-composite* or *indivisible,* i.e., *of essence of things.*—(c), **intellegentia indivisibilium,** see *intellegentia incomplexorum.*—(d), **intellegentia simplex,** *the simple rational comprehension,* which consists of the mere notion of a thing.

intellegibilis, e, *adj.,* (1) *supersensual, rational,* i.e., belonging to the transcendental or rational part of the soul, synonym of *intellectualis* and *rationalis,* the opposite of *sensibilis,* (2) *supersensually perceptible,* or *cognoscible, perceptible* or *cognoscible through reason,* the opposite of *sensibilis,* (3) *imaginable, conceivable* either through reason or through imagination. On **actio intellegibilis,** see *actio;* on **actus intellegibilis,** see *actus;* on **appetitus intellegibilis,** see *appetitus;* on **cognitio intellegibilis,** see *cognitio;* on **conceptio intellegibilis,** see *conceptio;* on **delectatio intellegibilis,** see *delectatio;* on **emanatio intellegibilis,** see *emanatio;* on **generatio intellegibilis,** see *generatio;* on **locutio intellegibilis,** see *locutio;* on **lumen intellegibile,** see *lumen;* on **lux intellegibilis,** see *lux;* on **operatio intellegibilis,** see *operatio;* on **potentia intellegibilis,** see *potentia;* on **ratio intellegibilis,** see *ratio;* on **spiritus intellegibilis,** see *spiritus;* on **virtus intellegibilis,** see *virtus.*—On **bonum intellegibile,** see *bonus;* on **corpus intellegibile,** see *corpus;* on **esse intellegibile,** see *esse;* on **finis intellegibilis,** see *finis;* on **influxus intellegibilis,** see *influxus;* on **intentio intellegibilis,** see *intentio;* on **modus intellegibilis,** see *mo-*

dus; on **natura intellegibilis,** see *natura;* on **nomen intellegibile,** see *nomen;* on **processio intellegibilis,** see *processio;* on **processus intellegibilis,** see *processus;* on **ratio intellegibilis,** see *ratio;* on **relatio intellegibilis,** see *relatio;* on **res intellegibilis,** see *res;* on **saeculum intellegibile,** see *saeculum;* on **similitudo intellegibilis,** see *similitudo;* on **species intellegibilis,** see *species;* on **speculum intelligibile,** see *speculum;* on **spiritus intellegibilis,** see *spiritus;* on **totum intellegibile,** see *totus;* on **verbum intellegibile,** see *verbum;* on **veritas intellegibilis,** see *veritas;* on **via intellegibilis,** see *via;* on **visio intellegibilis,** see *visio.*—Kinds of *intellegibile* in this (2) sense are: (a), **intellegibile actu seu in actu** and **intellegibile in potentia,** *the intelligible in the state of actuality* and *that in the state of potentiality.*—(b), **intellegibile altissimum seu summum seu divinum,** *the highest intelligible, according to rank* or *the divine intelligible,* i.e., *God.*—(c), **intellegibile divinum,** see *intellegibile altissimum.*—(d), **intellegibile excellens seu maximum seu maxime seu vade** and **intellegibile minus seu infimum,** *the intelligible that according to its nautre excels* or *is greatest* and *the lesser* or *least intelligible.*—(e), **intellegibile incomplexum,** *the noncompounded intelligible* or *the* *idea.*—(f), **intellegibile in actu**, see *intellegibile actu.*—(g), **intellegibile infimum**, see *intellegibile excellens.*—(h), **intellegibile in potentia**, see *intellegibile actu.*—(i), **intellegibile maxime sive maximum**, see *intellegibile excellens.*—(j), **intellegibile minus**, see *intellegibile excellens.*—(k), **intellegibile optimum**, see *intellegibile perfectissimum, the best* or *most perfect intelligible*, i.e., *God.*—(l), **intellegibile perfectissimum**, see *intellegibile optimum.*—(m), **intellegibile per se sive secundum se sive secundum naturam suam**, *the intelligible according to* or *for itself* or *according to its nature.*—(n), **intellegibile primum**, *the first intelligible, be it first according to itself* and *according to rank*, or *be it first with reference to our perception.*—(o), **intellegibile secundum naturam suam**, see *intellegibile per se.*—(p), **intellegibile secundum se**, see *intellegibile per se.*—(q), **intellegibile speculatum**, *the speculated* or *contemplated* or *perceived intelligible.*—(r), **intellegibile universalius**, *the more general intelligible.*—(s), **intellegibile valde**, see *intellegibile excellens.*—**intellectus est quodammodo ipsa intellegibilia**, see *intellectus.*—**intellectus in actu est intellegibile in actu**, see *intellectus.*—**intellectus in actu et intellegibile in actu sunt unum**, see *intellectus.*—**intellegibile in actu et intellectus in actu sunt**

unum, see *intellectus.* On **materia intellegibilis, materia intellegibilis communis et individualis**, see *materia.*—**intellegibiliter**, *adv.*, (1) *intelligibly* in the wider sense of the word, i.e., in a manner, chiefly discernible, of the intellect, synonym of *intellectualiter*, the opposite of *sensibiliter*, (2) *intelligibly* in the narrower sense of the word, i.e., in a discernible manner of the intuitively active intellect, likewise a synonym of *intellectualiter*, the opposite of *rationaliter.*

intellegibilitas, atis, *f.*, *intelligibility, perceptibility* by an intellect, the opposite of *sensibilitas.*

intellego, ere, exi, ectum, 3, *v. a.*, (1) *to perceive intellectually, perceive with an intellect, understand*, (2) *perceive immediately with the intellect, realize*, the opposite of *discurrere* and *ratiocinari*, (3) *understand, grasp, comprehend.* On **affirmatio intellecta**, see *affirmatio;* on **forma intellecta**, see *forma;* on **intentio intellecta**, see *intentio;* on **ordo secundum modum intellectus**, see *ordo;* on **ratio intellecta**, see *ratio;* on **relatio intellecta**, see *relatio;* on **species intellecta**, see *species;* on **substantia intellecta**, see *substantia.*—With reference to *intellegere* there is to be distinguished **id quo sive id ut quo intellegitur** and **id quod sive id quod intellegitur**, *that whereby a thing is perceived intellectually* and *that which is so perceived,* i.e., species intellegibilis and the object of knowledge.—*id quod intellegitur* is twofold: **primum seu principale intellectum** and **secundum seu secundarium seu accessorium intellectum**, *the first* or *principal* and *the second* or *subordinate* or *subsidiary intellectually known.* —Kinds of *intellegere* in this (1) sense are: (a), **intellegere actualiter**, *to perceive actually.*—(b), **intellegere componendo et dividendo, intellegere discurrendo seu ratiocinando** and **intellegere quod quid est**, *to perceive by composing* and *dividing* or *forming a judgment, by inferring* or *drawing a conclusion* and *to perceive the essence of a thing notionally.*—(c), **intellegere cum discursu** and **intellegere sine discursu**, *to perceive by means of a process of reasoning* and *to do so without one.*—(d), **intellegere demonstrative**, *to perceive on the basis of a proof concluded of necessity.*—(e), **intellegere discurrendo**, see *intellegere componendo et dividendo.*—(f), **intellegere divisim**, *to perceive one aspect apart from another of the same object.*—(g), **intellegre ex consequenti** and **intellegere primo**, *to perceive as a consequence* and *as a premise.*—(h), **intellegere formaliter per aliquid**, *to perceive precisely as understanding through something.*—(i), **intellegere immaterialiter**, *to perceive in an immaterial way.*—(j), **intellegere per modum necessitatis**, *to perceive of necessity.*—(k), **intellegere primo**, see *intellegere ex consequenti.*—(l), **intellegere principaliter**, *to perceive principally.*—(m), **intellegere quod quid est**, see *intellegere componendo et dividendo.*—(n), **intellegere ratiocinando**, see *intellegere componendo et dividendo.*—(o), **intellegere universaliter**, *to perceive universally.* Cf. *intellegere per modum necessitatis.*—anima intellectiva **non potest intellegere sine phantasmatibus**, or, anima non potest intellegere sine phantasmate, or, **nequaquam sine phantasmate intellegit**, or, **nihil sine phantasmate intellegit anima**, or, quamdiu est anima in corpore, non potest intellegere sine phantasmate, or, ratione naturali sine phantasmate nihil intellegit anima, or intellegere nostrum non est sine phantasmate, or, non contingit intellegere sine phantasmate, the translation of the Aristotelian passage, *oudepote noei aneu phantasmatos he psyche*, also *noein ouk estin aneu phantasmatos, the human soul while in union with the body cannot with its natural intellect perceive anything without imaginative representations, because it obtains all its notions through abstraction from phantasms and furthermore, if it wishes to renew them, it must refer them back and com-*

pare them with the original phantasms.—intellegere nostrum est pati quoddam, the translation of the Aristotelian passage, to noein paschein ti estin, intellectual perception is a kind of receptivity.—intellegere nostrum non est sine phantasmate, see above: anima intellectiva non potest etc.—nequaquam, sine phantasmate intellegit anima, see above: anima intellectiva non potest etc.—nihil sine phantasmate intellegit anima, see above: anima intellectiva non potest etc. — non contingit intellegere sine phantasmate, see above: anima intellectiva non potest etc. — quamdiu est anima in corpore, non potest intellegere sine phantasmate, see above: anima intellectiva non potest etc.—ratione naturali sine phantasmate nihil intellegit anima, see above: anima intellectiva non potest etc.— Kinds of intellegere in this (3) sense are: (a), intellegere affirmative, intellegere negative, and intellegere privative, to understand something in the sense of an affirmation, in the sense of a pure negation, and in the sense of a deficiency that ought not to exist.—(b), intellegere causaliter and intellegere consecutive, to understand something in the sense of a cause and in the sense of a consequence.—(c), intellegere collective seu composite and intellegere distributive seu divise, to understand something universally after the manner of collection or combination and individually after the manner of separation or division.— (d), intellegere composite, see intellegere collective.—(e), intellegere consecutive, see intellegere causaliter.—(f), intellegere distributive, see intellegere collective.—(g), intellegere divise, see intellegere collective.—(h), intellegere metaphorice and intellegere proprie, to understand something in its figurative or metaphorical sense and to understand something in its proper sense.—(i), intellegere negative, see intellegere affirmative. —(j), intellegere privative, see intellegere affirmative.—(k), intellegere proprie, see intellegere metaphorice.—intellegens, entis, P. a., that has understanding, that understands (a thing); intelligent, acquainted with.—intellectus, a, um, P. a., understood, known.

intelligentia, see intellegentia.
intelligibilis, see intellegibilis.
intelligibilitas, see intellegibilitas.
intelligo, see intellego.
intemperantia, ae, f., immoderateness, intemperateness, intemperance, the opposite of temperantia.
intemperatus, a, um, adj., (1) not temperate, tending to excess, inclement, immoderate, the opposite of temperatus, (2) not observing moderation, immod-

erate, likewise the opposite of *temperatus.*

intemperies, ei, *f., unsettledness* or *inclemency of the weather; intemperateness, excess of heat* or *cold.*

intendo, ere, di, tum and sum, 3, *v. a.,* (1) *to stretch, increase, become stronger* or *more deeply settled, strain,* the opposite of *remittere,* (2) *aspire after, aim at, strive after something, tend, endeavor, intend,* (3) *mean, maintain, have in mind.—* On **motus intensus,** see *motus;* on **passio intensa,** see *passio.—* On the difference between *intendere* and *velle,* see *velle.—* **intendens,** entis, *P. a., aspiring after, endeavoring, intending.—* **intentus, (intensus),** a, um, *P. a., strained, bent, attentive to, intent upon, intent.—***intense,** *adv., with tension, with increase, with exertion, intensely, with strength, with ardor,* synonym of *intensive.*

intensio, onis, *f., stretching out, straining, effort, tension, increase, ardor,* the opposite, of *remissio.* On **intensio formae,** see *forma;* on **intensio habitus,** see *habitus;* on **intensio intentionis,** see *intentio.*

intensivus, a, um, *adj., in the state of tension, of strength, of exertion, of strength, of ardor, intensive,* the opposite of *extensivus.* On **infinitas intensiva,** see *infinitas;* on **magnitudo intensiva,** see *magnitudo;* on **quan-**

titas intensiva, see *quantitas.—* **intensive,** *adv., with tension, with exertion, with strength, with ardor, intensely,* synonym of *intense,* the opposite of *extensive.* On **frui intensive,** see *frui;* on **infinitum intensive,** see *infinitus;* on **maior intensive,** see *maior.*

intentio, onis, *f.,* (1) *attention,* (2) of the will, *aspiration, intention, purpose,* (3) *aspect, notion, relation,* synonym of *habitudo, ratio,* and *relatio,* (4) *resemblance, image, impression,* synonym of *similitudo* and *species,* (5) *intellectual cognitive representation, presentation of the intellect, conception;* synonym of *conceptio intellegibilis* and *ratio.—* On **bonitas intentionis,** see *bonitas;* on **finis intentionis,** see *finis;* on **ordo intentionis et intentio naturae,** see *ordo;* on **quantitas intentionis,** see *quantitas;* on **rectitudo in intentione,** see *rectitudo.—* Kinds of *intentio* in this (2) sense are: (a), **intentio absoluta,** *the unconditional* or *unrelated intention.—* (b), **intentia actualis** and **intentio habitualis,** *the active* and *the habitual intention* and *attention,* or *the intention to which one actually attends* and *that in the sense of a state,* or *general attitude.—* (c), **intentio animalis,** *the sentient intention* or *the intention of a being endowed with senses.—* (d), **intentio bona** and **intentio prava,**

the good and *the bad intention.* —(e), **intentio carnalis,** *the carnal intention suggested by regard for the physical.*—(f), **intentio consequens** and **intentio praecedens,** *the intention subsequent to an action* and *that preceding an action.*—(g), **intentio corrupta,** *the corrupted* or *depraved intention.*—(h), **intenio formalis,** *the intention acting after the manner of form, the formal intention.*—(i), **intentio habitualis,** see *intentio actualis.*—(j), **intentio mentalis,** *the intention existing only in the mind* or *in the thought.*—(k), **intentio praecedens,** see *intentio consequens.*—(l), **intentio prava,** see *intentio bona.*—(m), **intentio prima naturae** and **intentio secunda naturae,** *the first* or *universal* and *the second* or *particular intention of nature.*—(n), **intentio simoniaca,** *the intention that establishes simony* or *a spiritual usury.*—**quod est primum in intentione, est ultimum in exsecutione,** *what is first in time according to intention is last in time according to execution.*—**ultimum in generatione est primum in intentione,** see *generatio.* On **communitas intentionis,** see *communitas;* on **nomen intentionis seu intentionem significans,** see *nomen.*—Kinds of *intentio* in this (3) sense are: (a), **intentio communis seu universalis seu universalitatis** and **intentio particularis seu individualis**

seu **individualitatis,** *the common* or *general* and *the particular* or *single aspect* or *relation* or *an aspect perceived by the mind as found in many things,* or *in one* or *a few.* See *intentio logica.*— (b), **intentio essentialis** and **intentio superaddita,** *the essential* and *the added relation* or *the unessential relation.*—(c), **intentio generis** and **intentio speciei,** *the notion of the genus* and *that of the species,* i.e., the purely mental aspect under which the mind views (intends) a thing according to which it constitutes or falls into a genus and that according to which it constitutes or falls under a species. See *intentio logica.*—(d), **intentio individualis,** see *intentio communis.*—(e), **intentio individualitatis,** see *intentio communis.*—(f), **intentio logica,** *the logical relation* or *that coming under the consideration of logic.* Logical intentions are the *entia rationis,* the beings of reason, the whole area in which thought, not things, is the object of knowledge. After the mind has perceived (intended) reality it reflects on its own operations and ideas, and the results of this second intention are the logical intentions. Thus the concepts of genus, species, and certain kinds of universality are aspects which the mind considers (intends) not in reality but in its own thought and ideas. Terms as the expression of concept, propositions as the expression of judgments, and syllogisms as the expression of reasoning are also logical intentions. Humanity as such does not exist outside the mind but the mind can view (intend) particular men under this common aspect or intention.—(g), **intentio naturae communis,** *the relation* or *aspect of common nature,* i.e., the purely mental relationship which the mind perceives in things which have a common nature, and which it handles as an object of knowledge.—(h), **intentio necessitatis essendi,** *the idea* or *the concept of the necessary being of a thing.*—(i), **intentio particularis,** see *intentio communis.*—(j), **intentio secundae substantiae,** *the idea* or *concept of second substance,* i.e., the aspect of a substantial thing according as it is concrete and individual, *substantia secunda.*—(k), **intentio speciei,** see *intentio generis,* and *intentio logica.*—(l), **intentio superaddita,** see *intentio essentialis.*—(m), **intentio universalis,** see *intentio communis* and *intentio logica.*—(n), **intentio universalitatis,** see *intentio communis,* and *intentio logica.*—Kinds of *intentio* in this (4) sense are: (a), **intentio animae seu cognitiva,** *the image of a thing in the soul* or *the cognitive representation.*—(b), **intentio cognitiva,** see *intentio animae.*—(c), **intentio intellecta, seu intellectus seu intellectualis seu intel-**

legibilis, *the aspect* or *the idea known by the intellect* or *knowable to it.*—(d), **intentio intellectualis,** see *intentio intellecta.*—(e), **intentio intellectus,** see *intentio intellecta.*—(f), **intentio intellegibilis,** see *intentio intellecta.*—(g), **intentio spiritualis,** *the spiritual image.*—Kinds of *intentio* in this (5) sense are: **intentio prima** and **intentio secunda,** *the first* and *the second conception of a thing,* i.e., the intellectual representation of a thing in the direct and that in the reflexion or the reflective recognition of the same, i.e., the representation of a thing according to its general nature and essence, and the representation precisely of this general nature and essence according to the relation of their generality.

intentionalis, e, *adj., figurative, mentally, existent, intentional, immaterial,* the opposite of *realis.* On **esse intentionale,** see *esse;* on **virtus intentionalis,** see *virtus.*

inter, *prep,* with the *acc.,* not used as an *adv.* in the S.T., (1) referring to more than two places or objects, *among, in the midst of, amid, surrounded by,* (2) referring to two places or objects, *between.*

intercedo, ere, cessi, cessum, 3, *v. n.,* (1) *lit., to occur, happen,* (2) *fig.,* (a) *to intercede for* or *in behalf* of someone, (b) *to be, exist.*

intercessio, onis, *f.*, *intercession*, the action of pleading in behalf of another; *entreaty, mediation, solicitation* or *prayer* for another.

intercessor, oris, *m.*, *an intercessor*, one who intercedes or interposes in behalf of another; in religious use, *one that intercedes* with God for man; *a mediator*.

intercido, ere, idi, isum, 3, *v. a.*, *to cut through*.

intercipio, ere, cepi, ceptum, 3, *v. a.*, *to interrupt, cut off*.

intercludo, ere, usi, usum, 3, *v. a.*, *to shut out, shut off*.

interdico, ere, dixi, ctum, 3, *v. a.*, *to forbid, prohibit, interdict, to restrain authoritatively,* (1) *aliquid alicui,* (2) *ne* and *subj.*, (3) *alicui* with *inf.*, (4) *quin* and *subj.*

interdictor, oris, *m.*, *a forbidder, interdicter,* used in the S.T. only in quot.

interdictum, i, *n.*, *a prohibition,* (1) in *gen.*, *a prohibition, interdict, a prohibitive order; restraining decree; authoritative act of prohibition,* (2) *eccl.*, *an interdict,* a censure or prohibition excluding the members of the Church from participation in its rites.

interdum, *adv.*, *sometimes, occasionally, now and then.*

interea, *adv.*, *meanwhile, in the meantime.*

interemptio, onis, *f.*, *destruction.*

intereo, ire, ii, itum, 4, *v. n.*, *to perish, go to ruin* or *decay, die.*

interesse, see *intersum.*

interfectio, onis, *a killing, murdering.*

interfector, oris, *m.*, *a slayer, murderer.*

interficio, ere, feci, fectum, 3, *v. a.*, (1) in *gen.*, *to slay, murder, kill,* (2) with *se, to commit suicide.*

internim, *adv.*, *meanwhile, in the meantime, the interval* between two times; the intervening time.

interimo, ere, emi, emptum, 3, *v. a.*, (1) in *gen.*, *to do away with, abolish; to destroy, kill,* (2) with *se, to kill one's self, commit suicide.*

interior, ius, *gen.* oris, *(comp.* from inter, whence also *sup.* intimus), *inner, interior, nearer,* synonym of *intraneus* and *intrinsecus,* the opposite of *exterior, extraneus,* and *extrinsecus.* On **actus interior,** see *actus;* on **adoratio interior,** see *adoratio;* on **affectio interior,** see *affectio;* on **agens interior,** see *agens;* on **apprehensio interior,** see *apprehensio;* on **blasphemia interior,** see *blasphemia;* on **causa interior,** see *causa;* on **cogitatio interior,** see *cogitatio;* on **conceptus interior,** see *conceptus;* on **confessio interior,** see *confessio;* on **consensus interior,** see *consensus;* on **cultus interior,** see *cultus;* on **delectatio interior,** see *delectatio;* on **dolor interior,** see *dolor;* on **finis interior,** see *finis;* on **forum interius,** see *forum;* on **homo interior,** see *homo;* on **inspiratio interior,** see *inspiratio;* on **instinctus interior,**

see *instinctus;* on **iudicium interius,** see *iudicium;* on **locutio interior,** see *locutio;* on **malum interius,** see *malus;* on **memoria interior,** see *memoria;* on **missio interior,** see *missio;* on **opus interius,** see *opus;* on **pars interior,** see *pars;* on **passio interior,** see *passio;* on **perfectio interior,** see *perfectio;* on **poenitentia interior,** see *poenitentia;* on **principium interius,** see *principium;* on **processio interior,** see *processio;* on **pulchritudo interior,** see *pulchritudo;* on **ratio interior,** see *ratio;* on **sensus interior,** see *sensus;* on **spiritus interior,** see *spiritus;* on **tentatio interior,** see *tentatio;* on **verbum interius,** see *verbum;* on **vis interior,** see *vis.*—*interiora, um, n., the inner parts* or *places, the more hidden* or *more secret.* —*interius, adv., in the inner part, within, more inwardly* or *deeply, internally.*

interitus, us, *m., destruction, death.*

interiacens, entis, *P. a., intervening, coming between.*

interiectio, onis, *f., interjection, the act of ejaculating; exclamation.*

interlinearis, e, *adj., interlinear, situated* or *occurring between the lines;* with *glossa,* a gloss inserted between the lines of the text.

intermedius, a, um, *adj., that is between, intermediate.* On **causa intermedia,** see *causa;* on **forma intermedia,** see *forma;* on **generatio intermedia,** see *gene-*

ratio; on **genus intermedium,** see *genus.*

interminabilis, e, *adj., interminable, endless.*

interminabilitas, atis, *f., interminability, the state* or *quality of being interminable.*

interminatus, a, um, *adj., unbounded, endless, undetermined,* synonym of *indefinitus, indeterminatus,* and *infinitus,* the opposite of *determinatus, finitus,* and *terminatus,* used only once in the S.T. On **corpus interminatum,** see *corpus;* on **dimensio interminata,** see *dimensio.*

intermisceo, ere, scui, xtum, or stum, 2, *v. a., to mingle, mix among,* used in S.T. only in quot.

intermissio, onis, *f., intermission, discontinuance.*

intermitto, ere, misi, missum, 3, *v. a.* and *n.,* (1) *act., to leave off, omit, neglect,* (2) *neutr., to cease, leave off,* used with *quin* and *subj.*

internuntius, i, *m., an internuncio, go-between;* messenger between two parties.

internus, a, um, *adj., inward, interior.*

interpellatio, onis, *f., interpellation, the act of interceding; interposition, mediation.*

interpellator, oris, *m., an interpellator, advocate.*

interpello, are, avi, atum, *v. a.,* (1) in *gen.,* (a) *to speak to,* used with *ad* and *acc.,* (b) *to intercede for someone* or *with someone,* used with *pro* and *abl., apud* and *acc.,*

(c) *to ask, beseech* someone for something, used with *acc., absol.*, (2) *to intervene, to interpose* in a lawsuit so as to become a party to it.

interpolate, *adv., intermittently.*

interpolatio, onis, *f., alteration, change,* the action of inserting as new and authorized, (1) *change of pronunciation,* (2) *of moral character.*

interpolo, are, avi, atum, 1, *v. a., to interpolate, to put* or *place* something between or among other things so as to interrupt the continuity of that thing.

interpono, ere, posui, positum, 3, *v. n.*, (I) *lit.*, (1) in *gen., to put, lay* or *set between* or *among, to interpose, insert between,* (2) in *partic., to insert, interpose, intervene, introduce,* (a) of time, (b) of words or lang., (2) *fig., to interpose, introduce, put in the way, put forward.*

interpositio, onis, *f., interposition, a putting between,* the action or state of interposing.

interpres, etis, *comm., an interpreter,* (1) in *gen., an explainer,* (2) in *partic.,* one who translates orally; especially one who makes intelligible the communications of person speaking different languages.

interpretatio, onis, *f.*, (1) *explanation, interpretation, exposition,* (2) a work of Aristotle, i.e., the *De Interpretatione.*

interpretativus, a, um, *adj.*, (1) *interpreting, explaining, interpre-*

tative, (2) *allowing this* or *that interpretation, being according to the interpretation, interpreted as this* or *that.*—On **potentia interpretativa**, see *potentia;* on **ratio interpretativa**, see *ratio;* on **virtus interpretativa**, see *virtus.*— On **consensus interpretativus**, see *consensus;* on **mors interpretativa**, see *mors;* on **oratio interpretativa**, see *oratio;* on **petitio interpretativa**, see *petitio;* on **praeceptum interpretativum**, see *praeceptum;* on **ratio interpretativa nominis**, see *ratio;* on **signum interpretativum**, see *signum;* on **tentatio interpretativa**, see *tentatio;* on **voluntas interpretativa**, see *voluntas;* on **votum interpretativum**, see *votum.*—**interpretative**, *adv., in an interpretative manner, interpretatively, in the sense of interpretation,* the opposite of *expresse.*

interpretatrix, tricis, *f., an interpretess.*

interpretor, ari, atus, 1, *v. dep.*, (1) in *gen., to interpret, translate, explain,* (2) in *pass.* sense.

interremptio, onis, *f., destruction,* used in the S.T. only in quot.

interrogatio, onis, *f., a questioning, inquiry, examination, interrogation.*

interrogo, are, avi, atum, 1, *v. a., to ask, question, inquire, interrogate.*

interrumpo, ere, rupi, ruptum, 3, *v. a., to interrupt, to hinder* by breaking in upon the course, progress or continuity of, used *lit.* and *fig.*

interruptio, onis, *f., an interruption.*

interscissio, onis, *f., a discontinuance.*

interseco, are, secui, sectum, 1, *v. a., to intersect.*

intersero, ere, sevi, situm, 3, *v. a., to put* or *place between, interpose, add.*

interstitium, i, *n., a space between, interstice, interval.*

intersum, esse, fui, futurus, *v. n.,* (1) *to be between, lie between, be different, differ,* (2) *be present at, take part in, attend.*—**interest,** *impers, it makes a difference, interests, concerns, is of interest, is of importance, const.* with *gen. pers,* or *mea, tua, sua.* and with a *subj.* or *rel-clause, ut* or *ne,* or with *ad.*—**interesse,** indecl. noun, *n., interest,* synonym of *usura.*

intervallum, i, *n.,* (1) in *gen., space between, interval, distance,* (2) *transf., interval of time, intermission, respite.*—**lucidum intervallum,** *a lucid interval,* short space of time between similar states or conditions and their recurrence, a period of mental soundness.

intervenio, ire, veni, ventum, 4, *v. n., to come between, intervene, to come in during,* (1) *lit.,* of things, *to come, be,* or *lie between,* (2) *transf.,* (a) *to take place meanwhile* or *among other things, to happen, occur,* (b) *to*

intervene, to interfere for some end; *interpose.*

interventus, us, *m., a coming between;* transf., *assistance.*

intestato or **ex intestato,** *adv., without a will, intestate.*

intestina, orum, *n., the intestines, entrails.*

intimatio, onis, *f., intimation,* the act of intimating, or that which is intimated; *a declaration* or *notification; specif., a declaration,* or *notification; a hint.*

intimativus, a, um, *adj., significative, manifested.* On **motio intimativa,** see *motio.*

intime, *adv.,* see *intimus.*

intimiditas, atis, *f., intimidity, fearlessness.*

intimidus, a, um, *adj., fearless.*

intimo, are, avi, atum, 1, *v. a., to make known; declare; give notice, hint, intimate.*

intimus, a, um, *adj., inmost, innermost, most secret, most profound, most intimate.*—**intima,** orum, *n., the inmost parts.*—**intime,** *adv., innermostly, intimately.*

intinctio, onis, *f., a moistening, dipping.*

intinctus, a, um, *P. a.,* see *intingo.*

intingo, ere, nxi, nctum, 3, *v. a., to dip in.*—**intinctus,** a, um, *P. a.,* (1) *steeped, soaked* in a liquid till the liquid has had a certain action on the substance, (2) *dipped,* immersed for a short time in any liquid.

intitulo, are, avi, 1, *v. a., to entitle, give a name to.*

intolerabilis, e, *adj., pass., intolerable, insupportable, that cannot be borne.*

intono, are, ui, 1, *v. n., to cry out vehemently.*

intorqueo, ere, torsi, tortum, 3, *v. a., to distort, change* from a normal or proper state.

intra, *adv.* and *prep., adv., on the inside, within.*—**ad intra,** *within.* —(2) prep. used *lit.* and *fig.,* (a) in gen., *within,* (b) of time, *within,* (c) with *acc.* of *pron.,* **intra se,** *inwardly, to one's self.*

intranee, *adv.,* see *intraneus.*

intraneus, a, um, *adj., inner, interior,* synonym of *interior* and *intrinsecus,* the opposite of *exterior, extraneus,* and *extrinsecus.* On **proprietas intranea,** see *proprietas;* on **virtus intranea,** see *virtus.*—**intranee,** *adv., in an interior manner, from within,* synonym of *intrinsece* and *intrinsecus,* the opposite of *extrinsece* and *extrinsecus.*

intransmutabilis, e, *adj., intransmutable, unchangeable.*—**intransmutabiliter,** *adv., intransmutably.*

intransmutabilitas, atis, *f., intransmutability, unchangeableness.*

intransmutabiliter, *adv.,* see *intransmutabilis.*

intrepidus, a, um, *adj., unshaken, undaunted, intrepid.*

intrinsece, see *intrinsecus, adj.*

intrinsecus, *adv., on the inside, inwardly, in an interior manner, from within,* synonym of *intranee* and *intrinsece,* opposite of *extrinsecus* and *extrinsece.* On **movens intrinsecus,** see *movens.*

intrinsecus, a, um, *adj., inner, interior, inward,* synonym of *interior* and *intraneus,* the opposite of *exterior, extraneus,* and *extrinsecus.* On **actus intrinsecus,** see *actus;* on **causa intrinseca,** see *causa;* on **forma intrinseca,** see *forma;* on **mensura intrinseca,** see *mensura;* on **motor intrinsecus,** see *motor;* on **multitudo intrinseca,** see *multitudo;* on **operatio intrinseca,** see *operatio;* on **passio intrinseca et ab intrinseco,** see *passio;* on **perfectio intrinseca,** see *perfectio;* on **principium intrinsecum,** see *principium.*—**intrinsece,** *adv., in an interior manner, from within, intrinsically,* the synonym of *intranee* and *intrinsecus,* the opposite of *extrinsece* and *extrinsecus.*

intro, are, avi, atum, 1, *v. a.* and *n., to go into, to enter into,* (1) *lit.,* used with (a) *acc.,* (b) *in* and *acc.,* (c) *ad* and *acc.,* (d) *per* and *acc.,* (e) *absol.,* (2) *fig.*—The following phrases occur frequently: **intrare religionem** or **intrare monasterium,** *to enter religion, to embrace a monastic life.*—**intrare in religionem christianam,** *to join the Christian religion.*—**intrare scholas,** *to enter the schools, to become a member of an organized body, as a university.*—**intrare in possessionem hereditatis,** *to enter into the possession of an inheritance.*

introduco, ere, duxi, ductum, 3, *v. a., to lead* or *bring into a place, to conduct into* or *within,* (1) *lit.,* (2) *fig.,* (a) in *gen., to bring in, introduce,* (b) *esp.* in speaking or writing, *to introduce a person* or *subject,* (c) *to bring forward, maintain,* (d) *to institute, originate* (e) **introducere in exemplum,** *to set an example.*

introductio, onis, *f., a leading in, introduction.*

introeo, ire, ivi or ii, itum, 4, *v. n., to go in* or *into, to enter,* used with *acc., in* or *ad* with *acc.,* (1) *lit.,* (2) *fig.*

introitus, us, *m., a going in* or *into, an entering, entrance,* (1) in *gen.,* used *lit.* and *fig.,* (2) in *partic., the introit* or *entrance of the Mass, the entrance chant,* the introduction of which is ascribed to Pope Celestine I. The modern introit consists of four parts, the Antiphon, the middle part, the Gloria Patria, and the repeated antiphon.

intromitto, ere, misi, missum, 3, *v. a.,* (1) *to let in, send in, admit,* (2) with *se* followed by *de, to busy oneself about something, to interfere, meddle.*

introrsum and **introrsus,** *adv., inwardly, within, on the inside.*

introspicio, ere, spexi, spectum, 3, *v. a., to look at,* used in the S.T. only in quot.

intueor, eri, itus, 2, *v. dep., to look at, upon* or *towards,* (1) *lit.,* used with *acc.,* (2) *fig.,* of the mind, *to regard, observe, contemplate, consider, give attention to.*—**intueri seipsum,** *to look into* or *at one's self* as a guide of conduct.

intuitus, us, *m.,* (1) *a look, view,* (2) *transf., respect, consideration, regard.*—One kind of *intuitus* in this (1) sense is: **intuitus simplex,** *the simple view,* called simple, because it is not connected with any kind of discursive action.

intumesco, ere, mui, 3, *v. n. inch., to swell up,* used *fig.*

intus, *adv., within, on the inside, inwardly.*

inunctio, onis, *f., an anointing.*

inundatio, onis, *f., an overflowing, deluge, inundation,* used in the S.T. only in quot.

inungo, ere, unxi, unctum, 3, *v. a.,* (1) in *gen., to anoint, to touch* any part of the body with oil, (2) in *partic., to apply* or *pour on oil as a religious ceremony,* e.g., in baptism, confirmation, holy orders, extreme unction; at the coronation of monarchs or at the consecration of the sacred vessels.

inusitatus, a, um, *adj., unusual, unwonted, uncommon.*

inutilis, e, *adj., useless, unserviceable, unprofitable,* used *absol.,* and with *dat.,* (1) of persons, (2) of things, inanim. and abstr.—**inutiliter,** *adv., uselessly, unprofitably.*

inutiliter, *adv.,* see *inutilis.*

invado, ere, vasi, vasum, 3, *v. n.* and *a.,* (1) *lit.,* (a) in *gen., to* *enter, penetrate,* used with acc., (b) *transf., to assail, attack, invade,* used *absol.,* with *acc.,* (2) *fig.,* (a) *to seize, take possession of, usurp,* used with *acc.,* (b) *to lay hold of, press upon,* used with *acc.*

invaleo, ere, 2, *v. n., to be strong against, prevail.*

invalesco, ere, valui, 3, *v. n. inch., to increase, prevail, predominate.*

invaletudo, inis, *f., infirmity, indisposition, sickness.*

invalidus, a, um, *adj., weak, feeble,* (1) *lit,.* (2) *transf.,* (a) *weak, useless,* (b) *invalid, null, not good, having no force.*

invariabilis, e, *adj., invariable,* that does not or can not vary or be varied; *always uniform, unchangeable.—*invariabiliter, *adv., invariably.*

invariabiliter, *adv.,* see *invariabilis.*

invasio, onis, *f., an assailing, attack.*

invasor, oris, *m., invader, intruder.*

inveho, ere, vexi, vectum, 3, *v. a., to carry, bear* or *bring,* used in the S.T. only in quot.

invenditus, a, um, *adj., unsold,* used in the S.T. only in quot.

invenio, ire, veni, ventum, 4, *v. a.,* (1) *lit., to find, discover, come* or *light upon* a thing, *to meet with,* (2) *fig.,* (a) *to find; to discover* through the perception or feelings, *learn by experience; to perceive, ascertain,* (b) *to invent, discover,* (c) *to acquire, get, earn.*

inventio, onis, *f.,* (1) *invention,* the action of coming upon or finding; the action of finding out; *discovery* whether accidental or the result of effort, (2) *De inventione,* one of the earliest of Cicero's efforts in prose composition consisting of four books giving lessons in rhetoric. It was supposed to have been translated from the Greek; two books have come down to us.

inventivus, a, um, *adj., finding, inventive, discovering.—*Inventiva sc. **pars logicae,** *the inventive part of logic,* so called because it has the discovery of truth as its object, i.e., that part of logic which treats the *rationis processus* and which is divided into dialectics or topics, rhetoric, and poetics.

inventor, oris, *m., a finder, one that finds something.*

inverecundia, ae, *f., shamelessness.*

inverecundus, a, um, *adj., shameless, immodest.*

invertibilis, e, *adj., irrevocable.*

investigabilis, e, *adj., investigable, that may be searched into.*

investigatio, onis, *f., a searching* or *inquiring into, investigation.*

investigo, are, avi, atum, 1, *v. a., to trace out, find out, discover, investigate, search into.*

investio, ire, ivi, itum, 4, *v. a., to invest, to clothe* as with office, authority or dignity, used in the S.T. only in quot.

inveterabilis, e, *adj., inveterable.*

invetero, are, avi, atum, 1, *v. a., to grow old.*—**inveteratus,** a, um, *P. a., inveterate, old, of long standing.*

invicem, *adv., one another, mutually, reciprocally.*—Common phrases are:—**ad invicem,** *mutually.*—**in invicem.**—**de invicem.**—**ab invicem.**—**per invicem.**—**pro invicem.**—**contra invicem.**

invictus, a, um, *adj., unconquered.*

invidentia, ae, *f., an envying, envy.*

invideo, ere, vidi, visum, 2, *v. a.,* (1) *to envy* or *grudge* one anything, used with the *dat.,* of the person and *acc.* of the thing exciting the feeling, (2) *to envy, long after* something, used with the *dat.,* (3) *to feel* or *show envy* at a person or thing, used with the *dat., acc.*

invidia, ae, *f., envy, grudge, jealousy.* On **zelus invidiae,** see *zelus.*—Kinds of *invidia* are: **invidia fratris** and **invidia fraternae gratiae,** *jealousy with respect to a brother* and *with respect to the grace of a brother.*—**filiae invidiae,** i.e., *the offspring of envy,* are these five: *afflictio in prosperis proximi, detractio, exsultatio in adversis proximi, odium,* and *susurratio.*

invidus, a, um, *adj., envious.*—**invidus,** i, *m., envious person.*

invigilo, are, avi, atum, 1, *v. n., to watch over* or *on account of anything; to be watchful over* or *on account of,* used with *dat., super,* and *acc.*

invincibilis, e, *adj., invincible, unconquerable, not to be conquered, subdued* or *overcome; insuperable,* as invincible power, invincible ignorance.

inviolabilis, e, *adj.,* (1) *inviolable,* (2) *inviolate.*—**inviolabiliter,** *adv., inviolably.*

inviolabiliter, *adv.,* see *inviolabilis.*

inviolatus, a, um, *adj., inviolate, intact, unprofaned.*

invisibilis, e, *adj., invisible, unseen,* (1) that cannot be seen; that by its nature is not an object of sight, (2) not in sight, not to be seen at a particular time.—**invisibiliter,** *adv., invisibly.*

invisibilitas, atis, *f., invisibility.*

invisibiliter, *adv.,* see *invisibilis.*

invitatio, onis, *f., an invitation.*

invito, are, avi, atum, 1, *v. a., to invite, to treat, entertain,* (1) *lit.,* used with *ad* and the *acc.,* (2) *transf.,* (a) *to incite, allure, attract* (b) *to invite,* ask to do some act or go some place; *request* the presence or the action of, *to ask, request,* used with *ut* and *subj.*

invitus, a, um, *adj., against one's will, unwilling, reluctant,* (1) of persons, (2) *abl., absol.*—**me invito,** *against my will.*

invius, a, um, *adj.,* (1) *lit., impassible,* (2) *transf., in accessible.*

invocatio, onis, *f., an invocation,* (1) the action or the act of invoking or calling upon God in prayer or attestation; *supplication,* or the act or form of supplication for aid or protection, (2) the action

or an act of conjuring or summoning a devil or spirit by incantation.

invoco, are, avi, atum, 1, *v. a.*, *to
invoke, call upon*, esp. as a witness or for aid, (1) with God,
persons, demons as the object,
(2) with things as the object.

involo, are, avi, atum, 1, *v. n.* and
a., *to come upon*, used with *in*
and the *acc.*

involumentum, i, *n.*, *a covering,
wrapping*, used in the S.T. only
in quot.

involuntarie, *adv.*, see *involuntarius.*

involuntarius, a, um, *adj.*, *unintentional, involuntary*, the opposite
of *voluntarius.* On **commutatio
involuntaria**, see *commutatio;* on
ignorantia involuntaria, see *ignorantia;* on **passio involuntaria**,
see *passio;* on **paupertas involuntaria**, see *paupertas;* on **subiectio involuntaria**, see *subiectio.*—
Kinds of *involuntarium* are: (a),
**involuntarium absolute seu sim-
pliciter** and **involuntarium secundum quid**, *the involuntary which
is unconditioned* or *simple* and
that which is so relatively or *in a
certain respect.*—(b), **involuntarium per ignorantiam** and **involuntarium per violentiam**, *the involuntary as the result of ignorance*
and *that as the result of force.*—
(c), **involuntarium per violentiam**, see *involuntarium per ignorantiam.*—(d), **involuntarium secundum quid**, see *involuntarium
absolute.*—(e), **involuntarium sim-**

pliciter, see *involuntarium absolute.*—**involuntarie**, *adv.*, *in an
unintentional manner, involun-
tarily*, the opposite of *voluntarie.*

involutio, onis, *f.*, *a wrapping* or
enfolding someone with something.

involvo, ere, vi, utum, 3, *v. a.*, (1)
lit., *to roll about, wrap up, envelop*, (2) *fig.*, (a) *to enwrap*, (b)
to entangle or *involve* one's self
in something.

ipse, a, um, *pron. demonstr.*, *self,
in person, he* (emphatic), *himself,
herself, itself*, used both substantively and adjectively to denote
that person or thing of which
something is eminently or exclusively predicated.

ira, ae, *f.*, (1) *anger, wrath, rage,
ire*, in the proper sense of the
word, synonym of *iracundia*, (2)
anger in the improper sense of
the word.—On **fortitudo quae est
per iram**, see *fortitudo;* on **incontinens ira**, see *incontinens;* on **incontinentia irae**, see *incontinentia.*—Kinds of *ira* are: (a), **ira
acuta seu fellea**, *sudden anger.*—
(b), **ira bona** and **ira mala**, *the
morally good* and *the morally
bad anger.*—(c), **ira cordis**, *the
anger of the heart* or *interior anger.*—(d), **ira fellea**, see *ira acuta.*
—(e), **ira imperfecta seu immoderata**, *the imperfect* or *immoderate anger.*—(f), **ira inordinata** and
ira ordinata, *the unordered, excessive*, and *the ordered anger.*
Cf. also *ira bona.*—(g), **ira mala**,
see *ira bona.*—(h), **ira moderata**,

see *ira imperfecta.*—(i), **ira ordinata,** see *ira inordinata.*—(j), **ira per vitium seu vitiosa** and **ira per zelum seu virtuosa,** *anger according to vice* or *sin* and *that according to zeal* or *the virtuous anger.*—(k), **ira per zelum,** see *ira per vitium.*—(l), **ira virtuosa,** see *ira per vitium.*—(m), **ira vitiosa,** see *ira per vitium.*—**filiae irae,** i.e., *the offspring of anger* are as follows: *blasphemia, clamor, contumelia, indignatio, rixa,* and *tumor mentis.*

iracundia, ae, *f.,* (1) *a proneness to anger, anger,* synonym of *ira,* (2) *violence of anger, wrath, rage, passion.*

iracundus, a, um, *adj., irascible, irritable, passionate, angry, ireful.*

irascibilis, e, *adj., choleric, irascible,* a kind of passion, including fear, despair, hope, boldness, and anger. On **potentia irascibilis,** see *potentia;* on **vis irascibilis,** see *vis.*—**irascibilis** sc. **potentia seu vis,** *the faculty* or *irascible tendency in the proper* or *narrower* and *in the improper* or *wider sense of the word,* i.e., *the faculty of the sensual desire, which has as its object difficulty in obtaining sensible good* and *avoiding evil.* On **passio irascibilis,** see *passio.*—Kinds of *irascibilis* in the proper sense of the word are: **irascibilis brutalis** and **irascibilis humana,** *the irascible faculty of desire on the part of the brute* and *that on the part of man.*

irascibilitas, atis, *f., irascibility, anger.*

irascitivus, a, um, *adj., angry, irascible.*

irascor, irasci, iratus, 3, *v. dep., to be angry, to be in a rage,* used with (1) *contra* and *acc.,* (2) *absol.,* (3) *dat.*—**iratus,** a, um, *P. a., angered, enraged, violent, furious.*

Irena, ae, *f., Irene,* empress, wife of Leo III (the Isaurian) 716-741 A.D., and mother of Constantine V or VI.

iris, is or iridis, *f., a rainbow.*

ironia, ae, *f., irony,* the *eironeia* of Aristotle, the opposite of *iactantia.*

irones, um, *comm., dissemblers,* those who say less than they think.

irradiatio, onis, *f., irradiation,* the action of irradiating or emitting beams of light, a ray, reflection, used *lit.* and *fig.*

irrationabilis, e, *adj., without reason, irrational,* synonym of *irrationalis,* the opposite of *rationalis* and *rationabilis.* On **pars irrationabilis,** see *pars;* on **res irrationabilis,** see *res.*—**irrationabiliter,** *adv., in a manner without reason, irrationally.*

irrationabilitas, atis, *f., irrationality,* the opposite of *rationabilitas* and *rationalitas,* does not occur in the S.T.

irrationabiliter, *adv.,* see *irrationabilis.*

irrationalis, e, *adj.,* (1) *without reason, irrational,* synonym of *irra-*

tionabilis, the opposite of *ratio-nibilis* and *rationalis,* (2) *unthink-able, unimaginable,* the opposite of *rationalis.*—On **animal irratio-nale,** see *animal;* on **anima irra-tionalis,** see *anima;* on **appetitus irrationalis,** see *appetitus;* on **concupiscentia irrationalis,** see *concupiscentia;* on **natura irratio-nalis,** see *natura;* on **pars irratio-nalis,** see *pars;* on **passio irratio-nalis,** see *passio;* on **potentia ir-rationalis,** see *potentia;* on **res irrationalis,** see *res;* on **vis irra-tionalis,** see *vis.*—**irrationalia ma-gis aguntur ad operandum, quam seipsa agunt,** see *agere.*—**omnia irrationalia agunt ex solo naturae impetu,** *all irrational beings are active as a result purely of a force of nature.*—On **linea irratio-nalis,** see *linea.*

irreddibilis, e, *adj., unreturnable.*

irrefrenate, *adv.,* see *irrefrenatus.*

irrefrenatus, a, um, *adj., unbridled.*—**irrefrenate,** *adv., unbridledly, freely, without restraint.*

irregularis, e, *adj., irregular,* the op-posite of *regularis.* On **magnitu-do irregularis,** see *magnitudo;* on **motus irregularis,** see *motus.*

irregularitas, atis, *f.,* (1) *irregularity* in the proper sense of the word, (2) *irregularity* in the transferred sense of the word, an ecclesias-tical defect impeding Holy Or-ders.—On **immunditia irregulari-tas,** see *immunditia.*—One kind of *irregularitas* in this sense is: **irregularitas legalis,** *irregularity*

in the sense of the law of the Old Testament.

irreligiositas, atis, *f., irreligion, im-piety.*

irremediabilis, e, *adj., irremediable, beyond cure.*

irremissibilis, e, *adj., irremissible, unpardonable, for* or *of which there is no remission.*

irremuneratus, a, um, *adj., unre-warded.*

irreparabilis, e, *adj., irreparable, ir-retrievable.*—**irreparabiliter,** *adv., irreparably,* so as to be beyond reparation or remedy.

irreparabilitas, atis, *f., irreparabili-ty,* the quality of being irrepara-ble.

irreparabiliter, *adv.,* see *irrepara-bilis.*

irrepo, ere, repsi, reptum, 3, *v. n., to creep in* or *into a place.*

irreprehensibilis, e, *adj., unblama-ble, blameless,* used in the S.T. only in quot.

irrequisitus, a, um, *adj., unsought for, unnecessary.*

irretio, ire, ivi or ii, itum, 4, *v. a., to catch, entangle, ensnare,* used *fig.*

irretitus, a, um, *P. a.,* see *irretio.*

irreverenter, *adv., disrespectfully, irreverently.*

irreverentia, ae, *f., want of due re-spect* or *reverence, irreverence, disrespect.*

irrevocabiliter, *adv., irrevocably, beyond recall.*

irrideo, ere, risi, risum, 2, *v. n.* and *a.,* (1) *neutr., to laugh at* a per-son or thing, *to joke, jeer,* (2) *act., to mock, ridicule, laugh to scorn.*

irrisio, onis, f., *a deriding, mocking, mockery.*

irrisor, oris, m., *a derider, mocker, joker, scoffer.*

irrisorius, a, um, adj., *scornful, having the character of deriding or mocking.*

1. **irrito,** are, avi, atum, 1, v. a., *to provoke.*

2. **irrito,** are, 1, v. a., *to make void, invalidate, cancel.*

irritus, a, um, adj., *vain, useless, without effect, ineffectual.*

irrogo, are, avi, atum, 1, v. a., *to impose, appoint, ordain, inflict,* used with the *acc.* of the thing inflicted and the *dat.* of the person receiving the punishment.

irruens, entis, P. a., *rushing into, seizing upon.*

irrumpo, ere, rupi, ruptum, 3, v. n. and a., *to break, violate.*

is, ea, id, pron. demonstr., *he, she, it; this* or *that* man, woman, thing.

Isaac, m., indecl., (1) *Isaac,* the son of Abraham and Sara, (2) *Isaac,* an eastern writer, son of Honanus, whose book, *De definitionibus,* was translated from Arabic into Latin, (3) *Isaac,* a holy monk mentioned by Gregory Dial. lib. 3, 14.

isagoge, es, f., *an isagoge, introduction,* as Porphyry's Isagoge to the Categories of Aristotle.

Isaias, ae, m., *Isaias,* the first of the four great Jewish prophets; died in the year 700 B.C. He must have been of the kingdom of Juda, because in his prophecies he has in view only this kingdom, and Jerusalem seems to have been the theatre of his prophetic activity. The Book of Isaias may be divided into two parts. The first occupies itself especially with the present and a near future, although sometimes the prophet casts a glance into the most remote future and foresees the time of the Messias. The second part occupies itself entirely with the captivity of the Jews, the deliverance of the people, the restoration and glorification of the theocracy by the Messias.

Iscariota, ae, n., *Iscariot,* the surname of Judas, the disciple who betrayed Christ for thirty pieces of silver.

Ischyrognomones, (*ischyrognomones*), *headstrong.*

Isidorus, i, m., *Isidore,* saint, confessor, doctor of the Church and bishop of Seville. He was born in 560 at Cartagena, Spain and died at Seville. During his episcopacy he devoted his energies to promoting science, establishing convents and schools. He is important for his literary work. St. Thomas quotes abundantly from (1) the *Libri Etymologiarum;* (2) references are made to the *Libri Synonymorum, Libri tres Sententiarum, De Summo Bono, De officiis ecclesiasticis,* and to a few epistles.

Ismael, elis, or *indecl., m., Ismael* (Ishmael), (1) the son of Abraham and Agar, the Egyptian and the ancestor of the Ismaelites. He became the father of the twelve chiefs whose names are given in Gen. XXV, 12-16, (2) the son of Nathan and the most wicked of men, who slew Godolia, Jerem. XLI. 8.

Israel, elis, *m., Israel,* (he that striveth with God), (1) the name given to Jacob after wrestling with the angel, (2) the descendants of Jacob called themselves Sons of Israel, and spoke of their nation as Israel.—**Israelitae,** arum, *m., the Israelites.*—**Israelita,** ae, *m.,* an Israelite.—**Israeliticus,** a, um, *adj., Israelitish.*

Israelitae, arum, *m.,* see *Israel.*

Israeliticus, a, um, *adj.,* see *Israel.*

iste, a, ud, *pron. demonstr., this, that man, woman, thing,* (1) in gen. *that thing* near you in place or thought, *that of yours, that of which you speak* or *with which you are connected,* (2) with a general reference, *that, this, the very, that particular person* or *thing, he, she, it,* (a) alone as a *pron.,* (b) with *subst.*

ita, *adv., in this manner, in this wise, in such a way, so, thus.*

Italia, ae, *f., Italy.*

itaque, *conj., and so, therefore, for that reason, consequently.*

item, *adv.,* (1) implying comparison, *just, so, in like manner, likewise, also,* (2) introducing something additional without comparison, *likewise, besides, also, moreover.*

iter, itineris, *n.,* (1) *lit.,* (a) *a going to a distant place, a journey,* (b) of the place to which one goes, travels, etc., *a course, way, path, road,* (2) *fig., a way, path, course.*—**in promptu itineris,** *on the point of starting on a journey.*—**arripere iter,** *to set out on a journey.*

iterabilis, e, *adj., capable of being iterated* or *repeated.*

iteratio, onis, *f., a repetition,* the action of iterating or repeating, often said of readministering a sacrament.

itero, are, avi, atum, 1, *v. a.,* (1) *to do a thing a second time, to repeat, renew,* (2) *to say, mention,* or *assert again, to repeat.*—Also *pleonastically.*—**iterato,** *adv., again, once more.*

iterum, *adv.,* (1) *lit., a second time, once more, anew, again,* (2) *transf., in turn, again, on the other hand.*

itinerarium, ii, *n., an itinerary, an account of a journey.*—**Itinerarium Clementis,** *the itinerary of Clement of Rome.* Among the spurious writings attributed to Clement the chief is one which purported to contain a record made by Clement of discourses of the apostle Peter together with an account of the circumstances under which Clement came to be Peter's travelling companion and other details of Clement's history. The work has come down to us in three principal forms: the *Homilies,* the *Recognitions* or the *Itinerarium St. Clementis,* and the *Epitome.* St. Thomas quotes the *Epitome* *de Gestis Petri* under the name of *Itinerarium Clementis.*

itineror, ari, 1, *v. n.,* and *itinero,* are, *to travel.*

J

iaceo, ere, cui, citum, 2, *v. n.,* (I) lit., (a) in gen., *to lie,* (b) in partic., (1) of sick persons, *to lie ill, to be sick,* (2) *to lie dead, to have fallen,* (3) geographically, *to lie, be situated,* (II) fig., *to lie, be inactive.*—**sub regula iacere,** *to lie under, be oppressed by the rule.*

iacio, ere, ieci, iactum, 3, *v. a.,* (1) *to throw, cast, fling, hurl,* (2) *to lay, set, establish, found, construct.*

Iacob, *m., indecl., Jacob,* (1) the son of Isaac and Rebecca, third patriarch of the chosen people, and the immediate ancestor of the twelve tribes of Israel. He secured through a ruse the blessing which Isaac intended for Esau, and thus was confirmed his possession of the birthright, his struggles for which had begun before his birth, (2) son of Mathan, and father of Joseph spouse of the Blessed Virgin, Matt. 1-16.

Iacobus, i, *m.,* (1) *James I,* (the Greater), saint, apostle, martyr (44 A.D.), son of Zebedee and Salome, elder brother of John the Evangelist, called the Great-er to distinguish him from James the Less who was probably shorter, (2) *James II,* (the Less). One of the twelve apostles, born at Cana, cousin of our Lord and son of Alpheus and Mary, the sister of the Blessed Virgin. The Epistle of St. James, written about the year 59, principally combats the error of those who taught that faith without good works was sufficient, and vigorously protests against the love of riches.

iactans, *P. a.,* see *iacto.*

iactanter, *adv.,* see *iacto.*

iactantia, ae, *f., a boasting, bragging; display, ostentation.*

iactatio, onis, *f., a boasting.*

iactator, oris, *m., a boaster, braggart.*

iacto, are, avi, atum, 1, *v. freq. a* (1) *lit., to throw, cast, hurl.* (2) *fig.,* (a) *to boast,* (b) with *se, to talk boastfully of one's self, to boast, make an ostentatious display.*—**iactans,** antis, *P. a., boasting, bragging, vainglorious.*—**iactanter,** *adv., boastfully.*

iactura, ae, *f., loss,* the act or state of losing, failure to keep or win; *privation.*

iaculatus, a, um, *P. a.,* in eccl. Lat., *uttered rapidly, ejaculated,* used in the S.T. only in quot.

iaculum, i, *n., a dart, javelin,* used in the S.T. only in quot.

iam, *adv.,* (I) of time, denoting a point or moment of time as coinciding with that of the action, etc., described, (A) of present action, (1) as opp. to past or future, *at this time, now, just now,* at present, (2) in contrast with the time at which something was expected, of that which occurs sooner, *already,* (3) as continued from the past, *already, by this time,* (B) of past time, (C) in the time just past, *a little while ago, just,* (2) *by this time, already,* (3) of a time succeeding another time referred to, *from that time, thenceforth,* (C) of future time, prior to some future time, *already,* (D) with negatives, denoting cessation of previous conditions; **iam non,** *no longer,* (II) in other relations, (A) to denote that something will certainly, properly, or easily occur, under certain circumstances, (1) in a conclusion, to emphasize its relations to the condition, *then surely, then,* (2) in a consequence, to denote that it is conceived as immediate, *now, then, therefore.*

ianua, ae, *f.,* (1) *lit.,* (a) *a door, house-door,* (b) *transf., an entrance* of any sort, (2) *fig., an entrance, approach.*

Ianuarius, i, *m.,* (sc. *mensis*) *January.*

Ianuarius, ii, *m., Januarius,* (1) St. Augustine in reply to the queries of Januarius addresses Letters 54 and 55 to him; nothing more is known of him than is contained in these letters, (2) Bishop of Calaris (Cagliari), in Sardinia. He appears to have been a contemporary of Gregory the Great through nearly the whole of his pontificate, and he received a great number of letters from him on a variety of topics.

Iason, onis, *m., Jason III,* a highpriest of the Jews, brother of Onias, whom he robbed of the high-priesthood by buying his dignity from King Antiochus Epiphanes; was supplanted in the same manner two years later by his brother Menelaus.

iaspis, idis, *f., jasper, a green-colored precious stone.*

Iechonias, ae, *m., Jechonias,* King of Juda, nephew of Josias, and son of Joakim, King of Juda, who associated him to the throne at the age of eight years. After the death of his father he reigned alone only three months and ten days. Nabuchodonosor, having taken Jerusalem, led him away captive to Babylon. Jeremias says that he incurred the indignation of the Lord through his crimes, and called him *barren,* because none of his children reigned over Jerusalem.

iecur, iecoris, *n., the liver.*

Iehu, *m., indecl., Jehu,* King of Israel from 884 to 856 B.C. At first, officer in the army of Joram; anointed King by order of the prophet Eliseus; destroyed the whole family of the impious Achab. He had for successor his son Joachaz.

ieiunabilis, e, *adj., fasting, abstaining from food;* going without food.

ieiunium, ii, *n., a fast, fasting.* (1) a natural fast before eating, or the fast before receiving Holy Communion, (2) the fast by which the Church commands us to mortify the body by going without food for a time; at present observed by taking only one full meal in the day, (3) the act of abstaining from food or going hungry, especially as a religious observance.—**ieiunium ieiunii,** *the natural fast.*—**ieiunium ieiunantis,** *the faster's fast,* or the fast for a purpose.

ieiuno, are, 1, *v. n., to fast, to abstain* from food beyond the usual time; especially to go without food, wholly or in part voluntarily, or according to precept, or as a token of grief.

ieiunus, a, um, *adj., fasting, not partaking of food.*

Iephte, *m., indecl., Jephte,* a chieftain and judge of Israel whose history is given in Judges (XI-XII). When he went to battle against the Ammonites, he vowed that whosoever should come forth first from his home to meet him on his return in peace from the children of Ammon

should be offered as a burnt offering. The Ammonites were routed, and as Jephte returned, the first to come out to meet him was his daughter and only child, whom he immolated. However, according to the most probable opinion, he only consecrated her to the Lord.

Ieremias, ae, *m., Jeremias,* one of the four great prophets of the Old Testament, born in the city of Anathoth, in the tribe of Benjamin. Jeremias composed prophecies and lamentations. The Book of Prophecies, divided into 52 chapters, is interesting history from the political, religious, and moral points of view; it is a faithful picture of the unfortunate times in which he lived.

Iericho, *f., indecl., Jericho;* in the Old Testament history, a city of Palestine, situated west of the Jordan, and fourteen miles northeast of Jerusalem. It was destroyed by Josue and rebuilt by Achab; was destroyed by Vespasian, rebuilt by Hadrian, and again destroyed by the Crusaders.

Ieroboam, *m., indecl., Jeroboam I,* King of Israel (953-927 B.C.). Minister of Solomon and disgraced by this prince, he organized a revolt of the ten northern tribes against Roboam, and founded the Kingdom of Israel.

Ierosolyma, ae, *f.,* see *Ierusalem.*

Ierosolymitanus, a, um, *adj., of Je-rusalem,* used in the S.T. only in quot.

Ierusalem, *f., indecl.,* and **Ierosoly-ma,** ae, *f.,* (1) *Jerusalem,* the celebrated metropolis of Pales-tine, called by the Turks Koud-sembarich or Koudsderif, and by the Arabs El Khods, the Holy. It is situated near the center of the country, among the mountains, about thirty-seven miles from the Mediterranean, and about twen-ty-three miles from the Jordan, (2) *the heavenly Jerusalem.*

Iesus, u, *m., Jesus,* (1) the appella-tive name of Our Lord, by com-mand of the angel, Matt. 1, 21, (2) *Jesus* Ben Nave or *Josue,* son of Nun, of the tribe of Ephraim, Moses' successor, the commander of the army of Israel in its battle with Amalec, and one of the spies into Chanaan.

Iezabel, *f., indecl., Jezebel,* the wife of Achab, King of Israel, whom she married before his ac-cession, and by whom she be-came the mother of Athalia, queen of Juda, and of Achaz and Joram, Kings of Israel.

Ioab, *m., indecl., Joab,* general and nephew of David. He command-ed in the war against Isboseth, the son of Saul, as well as against the Gentiles. He treacherously slew Abner, Saul's former cap-tain, after he had become recon-ciled with David, and dispatched Absalon.

Ioachim, *m., indecl.,* (1) *Joachim,* Saint, husband of St. Ann and father of the Blessed Virgin Mary of the tribe of Juda and the family of David, (2) *Joachim,* (also *Joakim*), father of Jechoni-as, King of Juda, who associated his son to the throne at the age of eight, (3) *Joachim* of Flora, Cistercian Abbot and mystic (1132-1202). Certain doctrines of his concerning the mystery of the Blessed Trinity were con-demned in the Lateran Council of 1213.

Ioannis and **Ioannes,** is, *m., John.* (1) *John,* the evangelist, the youngest of the Apostles, son of Zebedee and Salome, and the brother of James the Elder. He labored first in Judea and Sama-ria. He was banished to the is-land of Patmos, in the Grecian archipelago, where about the year 96, he wrote the Apoca-lypse. Returning to Ephesus, he wrote, at the request of the Asi-atic bishops, his Gospel to op-pose the errors of Cerinthus and Ebion about the year 97. His three epistles were written at a later period, (2) *John* the Baptist was the son of Zachary who was a priest in the course of Abia, the eighth of the twenty-four courses into which the priests were di-vided. Elizabeth, the Precursor's mother, was the daughter of Aa-ron according to St. Luke I, 5, (3) *John* Damescene, saint, con-fessor, doctor of the Church

676-c.770). He was born at Damascus, Syria, and was the last of the Greek Fathers, (4) *John* of Egypt and of Lycopolis, an anchoriate of Lycopolis in the Thebaid, in the latter half of the fourth century. His reputation for prophecy reached the court, and he foretold to the Emperor Theodosius himself the success of his arms against Maximus, A.D. 388, (5) *John* Abbot, who gave up the life of an anchorite for that of a coenobite. He discusses the aims of the anchorite and coenobite life in the conferences of the Fathers (Coll. XIX), (6) the Evangelist *John*, mentioned in the Conferences of the Fathers XXIV, 21, (7) John, mentioned in the Decretals of Gregory IX, Lib. III. tit. III. Cap. 7.

Ioas, *m., indecl., Joas,* King of Juda 837-797 B.C., son of Ochozias.

Ioatham, *m., indecl., Joatham,* King of Juda, (748-752) B.C., son and successor of Ozias.

Iob, *m., indecl., Job,* a Biblical personage of whom we know very little. He was an Arabian, remarkable for a holy life. The fact of his riches, consisting in flocks and pasturage, and his acting as priest in his own family, places him, certainly, in the patriarchal times, though there are some who think that he was a contemporary of Moses about 1520 B.C. Job prophesied the coming of the Messias and the

resurrection of the body (XIX. 25, 26). The author of the book is supposed to be Job himself.

iocor, ari, atus, 1, *v. dep. n.* and *a., to joke, jest.*

iocose, *adv.,* see *iocosus.*

iocosus, a, um, *adj., full of jesting, jocose, humorous, facetious,* used here of inanimate and abstract things.—**iocose,** *adv., jestingly, jocosely.*

iocularitas, atis, *f., jocularity,* jocular speech or behavior, *jesting,* a synonym for *scurrilitas* and sometimes for *curialitas.*

ioculator, oris, *m., a jester, joker.*

iocus, i, (plur. also **ioca, iocorum**), *n., a jest, joke.*

Ioel, is, *m., Joel,* the twelfth of the minor prophets. He lived under the reigns of Ezechias and Manasses. His prophecies contain three chapters in which he foretells the Babylonian captivity, the coming of the Messias, and the Last Judgment.

Ionas, ae, *m., Jonas,* one of the twelve minor prophets. He appeared under the reigns of Joas and of Jeroboam II., Kings of Israel, and, under the reigns of Ozias and Azrias, Kings of Juda, and consequently more than 800 years before Christ. The Lord ordered him to foretell to the Ninivites the destruction of their city; but Jonas, being afraid of the dangers of such a mission, embarked for Tarsus, just in the opposite direction. Thrown into the sea by superstitious sailors, he was swallowed by a whale and lived in it for three days. The word of the Lord a second time directed him to visit Ninive. He went thither and accomplished his mission.

Ionathas, ae, *m., Jonathan,* a Jewish warrior, son of Saul, died in 1055 B.C.

Ioram, *m., indecl., Joram,* King of Israel, son of Achab, brother and successor of Ochozias.

Iordanis, is, *m., the Jordan, the principal river of Palestine.*

Iosaphat, *m., indecl., Josaphat,* (1) King of Juda, 904-889 B.C., son of Asa, a pious and enlightened prince, enlarged and fortified several cities of his kingdom; won brilliant victories over the Ammonites, Moabites, and Arabs, (2) *the Valley of Josaphat,* famous valley in Palestine situated between Jerusalem and the Mountain of Olives, through which the Cedron flows. According to a prophecy of Joel the last judgment will take place in this Biblical valley.

Ioseph, *m. indecl. Joseph,* (1) patriarch, eleventh son of Jacob, first-born of Rachel, immediate ancestor of the tribe of Manasses and Ephraim. His father's favorite, he was hated by his brothers, who sold him into bondage to the Ismaelites. Taken into Egypt, he was kindly treated and became the personal attendant of his Egyptian master, Putiphar, eunuch of Pharao. His skill in in-

terpreting dreams brought him to the notice of Pharo who made him keeper of the royal seal and second in power in Egypt, (2) *Saint, Joseph,* spouse of the Blessed Virgin Mary and foster-father of our Lord, born probably at Bethlehem; died at Nazareth, (3) *Joseph of Arimathea,* saint, born at Arimathea, Palestine. He was a wealthy Israelite and a disciple of Christ. He requested from Pilate the body of Jesus and with the help of Nicodemus placed it in the tomb, (4) *Joseph,* son of Mary wife of Alphaeus. His brother was James the Less, Matt. XXVII, 55-56.

Iosephus, i, *m., Josephus* Flavius, born 37 A.D., died about 95. A celebrated Jewish historian. He was of an illustrious priestly descent and related to the Machabean house. He has valuable information concerning Christ in his *Antiquities of the Jews.*

Iosias, ae, *m., Josias,* King of Juda 641-610 B.C. Son of Amon. He was defeated and slain by Pharao Nechao at the battle of Mageddo in the valley of Esdraelon IV. Ki. XXII-XXXIII. 30; Par. XXXIV-XXXV. It was under his reign that the high-priest Helcias found the Book of the Law.

Iosue, *m., indecl., Josue,* the successor of Moses as leader of the Israelites. He was the son of Nun, of the tribe of Ephraim, and was one of the two spies who favorably reported Chanaan. He was an attendant of Moses, who designated him his successor. The book that bears his name, consists, mainly, of an account of the settlement of the Israelites in Chanaan.

Iovinianus, i, *m., Jovinian,* an heretical monk of the fourth century. Our fullest information about him is derived from St. Jerome, who wrote two books, *Adversus Iovinianum.* He opposed celibacy, maintaining that virginal life is no better than the married state in the sight of God, and denied that Mary remained a virgin after she gave birth to Christ.

iubeo, ere, iussi, iussum, 2, *v. a.,* (1) in gen., *to order* one to do something, *to bid, tell, command,* used with *ut,* the *acc.,* with an *object clause,* with the *dat.* followed by an *inf.,* by an *ut clause,* (2) in polit. lang., *to decree.*

iubilaeus, i, *m., the year of Jubilee among the Jews,* in which all the slaves were set free and all lands reverted to their former possessors; it took place every fifty years.

iucunditas, atis, *f., agreeableness, pleasantness, delight, enjoyment.*

iucundus, a, um, *adj., pleasant, agreeable, delightful, pleasing.*

Iuda, *n., indecl., Juda,* (Kingdom), one of the two Jewish states, formed after the schism of Jeroboam (962 B.C.); capital, Jerusalem. Comprising only the two tribes of Juda and Benjamin and only about the sixth part of Judea, it was more powerful and more populated than the Kingdom of Israel.

Iudaea, ae, *f., Judea,* the country of the Jews, Palestine. The name Judaea was applied in different ages either to the whole or part of Palestine. In the time of David, the name Juda denoted that portion of the country which belonged to the tribes of Juda and Benjamin. After the secession of the ten tribes, the territory of the Kingdom of Juda was called Judea, including the tracts belonging to Juda and Benjamin, and also part of that which appertained to the tribes of Dan and Simeon.

Iudaeus, a, um, *adj.,* of or belonging *to Judea, Jewish.*—**Iudaeus,** i, *m., a Jew.*—**Iudaei,** orum, *m., the Jews.*—**Iudaea,** ae, *f., a Jewess.*—**Iudaicus,** a, um, *adj., Jewish.*

Iudaismus, i, *m., Judaism.*

iudaizo, are, 1, *v. n., to live in the Jewish manner.*

Iudas, ae or **Iuda,** *indecl., m.,* (1) *Jude,* saint, one of the twelve apostles, also called Thaddeus. He was the brother of James the Less and one of the Brethren or cousins of Jesus. He is said to have suffered martyrdom in Phoenicia. General tradition regards this apostle as the author of the Catholic epistle of St. Jude in the New Testament, (2) *Juda* (tribe of), the largest of the tribes of Israel. In the desert of Sinai it numbered 74,600 fighting men, and in the plain of Moab, 76,500, (Num. 26, 22), (3) *Juda,* patriarch, reputed forefather of the tribe of Juda. The story of his life is contained in Gen. 29-49. He was the son of Iacob by Lia, (4) *Judas Machabeus,* son of the priest Mathathias and leader of the Jewish army, who waged war of independence against Antiochus of Syria, (5) *Judas* Iscariot, so called from Kerioth, the place of his birth, a city of Juda or Benjamin. He betrayed the Savior into the hands of the Pharisees, for the paltry bribe of thirty pieces of silver or about fifteen dollars.

iudex, icis, *com.,* (1) *lit.,* (a) *a judge,* a public officer who is invested with authority to determine litigated questions or who gives a judgment, (b) **iudex ecclesiasticus,** *an ecclesiastical judge,* a person who possesses ecclesiastical jurisdiction either in general or in the strict sense, (c) *plural,* **Liber iudicum,** the Book of Judges, the seventh book of the Old Testament. This Book, which the Church acknowledges as authentic and canonical, is attributed to Phinees, Esdras, Ezechias, Samuel, or even to all the Judges, each of whom would have written the history of his own judicature, (2) *fig., a judge, decider.*

iudicatio, onis, *f., a judging.*

iudicativus, a, um, *adj., having power to judge, judicative.* On **disciplina iudicativa,** see *disciplina;* on **scientia iudicativa,** see *scientia;* on **virtus iudicativa,** see *virtus.—***iudicativa,** sc. *pars logicae, the judicative part of logic,* i.e., the so-called analytics.

iudicatorium, i, *n., judgment place, court of justice, court.*

iudicialis, e, *adj., of* or *belonging to the courts of justice; judicial.* —**iudicialia praecepta,** *judicial precepts,* precepts which regulate man's relations to other men, and are binding because of their divine institution.

iudiciarius, a, um, *adj., judiciary, judicial.*

iudicium, i, *n.,* (1) *a judicial investigation* to determine what is just, *a trial, a court,* and spec., (2) *the judgement of men* and *angels by God,* both at the moment of death, and at the end of the world, (3) *the act of reason discerning* and *judging,* the second act of the mind, consisting in the affirmation or negation of a predicate to some subject. Also called, in St. Thomas, composition (affirmation of predicate to subject) and division (negation of predicate to subject), (4) any result of such an act of the mind, *an estimate, a judgement,* the expression of which is proposition, just as the expression of an idea is a term, (5) spec., a decision of a judge, *a sentence,* the act of the virtue of justice, (6) in a wide sense, *any datum of knowledge.*—On **forum iudicii,** see *forum.*—Kinds of *iudicium* in this (1) sense are: (a), **iudicium aquae ferventis, iudicium ferri candentis,** and **iudicium ignis,** *trial by boiling water, trial by red-hot iron,* and *trial by fire.*—(b), **iudicium civile seu saeculare seu temporale** and **iudicium ecclesiae seu ecclesiasticum seu spirituale,** *the civil* or *secular* or *temporal court* and *the ecclesiastical* or *church court.*—(c), **iudicium ecclesiasticum,** see *iudicium civile.*—(d), **iudicium ferri candentis,** see *iudicium aquae ferventis.*—(e), **iudicium ignis,** see *iudicium aquae ferventis.*—(f), **iudicium publicum,** *public trial.*—(g), **iudicium spirituale,** see *iudicium civile.*—(h), **iudicium temporale,** see *iudicium civile.*—(2) This judgement is variously called: (a), **iudicium commune seu generale seu universale** and **iudicium singulare,** *the general judgement on the last day* and *the particular judgement.*—(b), **iudicium discussionis** and **iudicium retributionis,** *the investigation into which of man's actions are good* and *bad* and *the meting out of reward* and *punishment.*—(c), **iudicium extremum seu finale seu ultimum,** *the last* or *general judgement.*—(d), **iudicium finale,** see *iudicium extremum.*—(e), **iudicium generale,** see *iudicium commune.*—(f), **iudicium retributionis,** see *iudicium discussionis.*—(g), **iudicium singulare,** *the particular judgement* which takes place at the moment of death. See *iudicium commune.*—(h), **iudicium ultimum,** see *iudicium extremum.*—(i), **iudicium universale,** see *iudicium commune.* On **libertas iudicii,** see *libertas* under (1).—Kinds of *iudicium* in this (3) sense are: (a), **iudicium a natura determinatum ad unum seu a natura inditum seu naturalis existimationis seu naturale seu non-liberum** and **iudicium a natura non determinatum ad unum seu liberum,** *the act of decision* or *choice which is determined by the nature of a being* or *directed by its nature* or *that consisting in a natural valuation* and *not free* and *that not determined by nature but free.*—(b), **iudicium a natura inditum,** see *iudicium a natura determinatum ad unum.*—(c), **iudicium a natura non determinatum ad unum,** see *iudicium a natura determinatum ad unum.*—(d), **iudicium cognitionis seu cognitivae seu iudicium electionis seu liberi arbitrii,** *the last practical judgement of the mind of the desirability of some particular,* which immediately precedes and causes the act of the will.—(e), **iudicium cognitivae,** see *iudicium cognitionis.*—(f), **iudicium electionis,** see *iudicium cognitionis.*—(g), **iudicium exterius** and **iudicium interius,** *the external manifestation* of the judgement of the mind, and *the interior act of judgement itself.*—(h), iudicium illicitum seu vitiosum and iudicium licitum, *the illicit* or *sinful judgement,* e.g., an unkind thought, and *a licit judgement.*—(i), iudicium iniustum, *unjust judgement,* the affirmation or negation of a predicate to a subject to which it does not rightly belong.—(j), iudicium intellectus seu rationis and iudicium sensus, *the judgement of the intellect* and *that of a sense faculty.*—(k), iudicium interius, see *iudicium exterius.*—(l), iudicium liberi arbitrii, see *iudicium cognitionis.*—(m), iudicium liberum, see *iudicium a natura determinatum ad unum.*—(n), iudicium licitum, see *iudicium illicitum.*—(o), iudicium naturale, see *iudicium a natura determinatum ad unum.*—(p), iudicium naturalis existimationis, see *iudicium a natura determinatum ad unum.*—(q), iudicium non-liberum, see *iudicium a natura determinatum ad unum.*—(r), iudicium rationis, see *iudicium intellectus.*—(s), iudicium suspiciosum seu temerarium, *the malicious* or *rash* or *suspicious judgement.*—(t), iudicium temerarium, *rash judgement,* see *iudicium suspiciosum.*—(u), iudicium usurpatum, *the arrogated judgement.*—(v), iudicium vitiosum, see *iudicium illicitum.* On certitudo iudicii, see *certitudo;* on via iudicii, see *via.*—Kinds of *iudicium* in this

(4) sense are: (a), iudicium absolutum seu simpliciter and iudicium secundum quid, *the unconditioned* or *simple judgement* and *that passed conditionally* or *in a certain respect.*—(b), iudicium certum, *the sure* or *certain judgement.*—(c), iudicium conscientiae and iudicium synteresis, *the judgement of conscience* and *the conclusion of synteresis,* which is the habit of first principles of the practical order. The decision of conscience is particular, refers to the lawfulness of this or that particular action; the decision of synteresis is universal, refers to the universal principles of right and wrong.—(d), iudicium de agendis seu operandis, *the judgement of what is to be done, the practical judgement.*—(e), iudicium de operandis, see *iudicium de agendis.*—(f), iudicium de personis, and iudicium de rebus, *the judgement of a person's conduct* or *character* from which we should refrain, and *the judgement of things.*—(g), iudicium de rebus, see *iudicium de personis.*—(h), iudicium Dei seu divinum and iudicium humanum, *the divine* and *the human estimation.*—(i), iudicium discretionis, *discretion* or *consideration.*—(j), iudicium divinum, see *iudicium Dei.*—(k), iudicium ecclesiae, *the judgement of the Church.*—(l), iudicium erroneum seu falsum and iudicium verum seu rectum, *the erroneous* or *false*

judgement and *the true* or *correct judgement.*—(m), **iudicium falsum**, see *iudicium erroneum.*—(n), **iudicium humanum**, see *iudicium Dei.*—(o), **iudicium perfectum**, *the perfect judgement.*—(p), **iudicium rectum**, see *iudicium erroneum.*—(q), **iudicium secundum quid**, see *iudicium absolutum.*—(r), **iudicium simpliciter**, see *iudicium absolutum.*—(s), iudicium supernaturale, *the supernatural judgement.*—(t), **iudicium synteresis**, see *iudicium conscientiae.*—(u), **iudicium universale**, *the general* or *universal judgement.*—(v), **iudicium verum**, see *iudicium erroneum.*—Kinds of *iudicium* in this (5) sense are: (a), **iudicium absolutionis seu purgationis** and **iudicium condemnationis seu reprehensionis**, *the sentence of absolution* or *acquittal* or *purgation* and *that of condemnation* and *censure.*—(b), **iudicium aequum seu iustum** and **iudicium iniustum seu iniquum seu perversum**, *the just* and *the unjust judgement.*—(c), **iudicium condemnationis**, see *iudicium absolutionis.*—(d), **iudicium perversum**, see *iudicium aequum.*—(e), **iudicium purgationis**, see *iudicium absolutionis.*—(f), **iudicium reprehensionis**, see *iudicium absolutionis.*—(g), **iudicium sanguinis**, *the judgement of blood,* or *condemnation to death.*

iudico, are, avi, atum, 1, *v. a.,* (1) *to judge, pass final judgement, pronounce sentence,* (2) *judge,*
decide, to affirm or deny some predicate of a subject. Synonymous with *composition* and *division of predicates.* In composition, the mind affirms a predicate to the thing it is considering; in division, the mind negates the predicate. Also, to assent to the truth of a proposition.—Kinds of *iudicare* in this (1) sense are: **iudicare absolvendo, iudicare discutiendo**, and **iudicare puniendo seu reprehendendo,** *to pronounce sentence by absolving, by examining,* and *by punishing* or *by censuring.* On **sensus iudicandi,** see *sensus* under (2).— Kinds of *iudicare* in this (2) sense are: (a), **iudicare ex collatione** and **iudicare ex naturali instinctu,** *to decide on the basis of a definite comparison* and *as the result of a natural instinct.*—(b), **iudicare ex naturali instinctu**, see *iudicare ex collatione.*—(c), **iudicare iudicio libero seu libere** and **iudicare iudicio non-libero seu naturali,** *to decide with a free judgement* or *with freedom* and *to do so with a non-free* or *natural judgement,* i.e., *as the result of natural instinct.*—(d), **iudicare iudicio naturali**, see *iudicare iudicio libero.*—(e), **iudicare iudicio non-libero**, see *iudicare iudicio libero.*—(f), **iudicare libere**, see *iudicare iudicio libero.*—(g), **iudicare per modum cognitionis** and **iudicare per modum inclinationis,** *to judge something after the manner of the knowledge of the*

same and *after the manner of the inclination toward it.*—(h), **iudicare per modum inclinationis,** see *iudicare per modum cognitionis.*—(i), **iudicare secundum quid** and **iudicare simpliciter,** *to pass judgement on something in a certain respect* or *with reference to something* and *to do so simply* or *absolutely.*—(j), **iudicare simpliciter,** see *iudicare secundum quid.*

Iudith, *f., indecl., Judith,* a Jewish widow who rescued her countrymen, beseiged by the Assyrians, by gaining the affection of their general, Holofernes, and slaying him. The Book of Judith is an Old Testament chronicle which takes its name from this valiant woman, Judith.

iugis, e, *adj., continual, perpetual.* —**iugiter,** *adv., continually, perpetually.*

iugiter, *adv.,* see *iugis.*

iugulatio, onis, *f., a cutting of one's throat, a killing, murdering.*

iugum, i, *n.,* (1) lit., *a yoke,* a frame or cross-bar with attachments used for coupling draft-animals, as oxen, (2) fig., *a yoke, bond.*

Iulianus, i, *m., Julian,* (1) *Julian,* bishop of Eclane, Eclanum, Eculanum, or more properly Aeclanum or Aeculanum, afterwards known as Quintodecimum, near Beneventum. He was a native of Apulia and a distinguished leader of the Pelagians of the fifth century. St. Thomas quotes St.

Augustine's *Contra Iulianum,* (2) bishop of Toledo at the end of the seventh century. He is the last eminent churchman of West Gothic Spain, and, next to Isidore of Seville, perhaps the most eminent. St. Thomas refers to his *Prognosticon,* (3) *Iulianus* Flavius Claudius, the emperor, often called Julian the Apostate. He was born A.D. 331; appointed Caesar, November 6, 355; proclaimed Augustus, April 360; succeeded Constantius as sole emperor, November 3, 361; died in Persia, June 27, 363, (4) *Iulianus,* count of the East, previously viceroy of Egypt. He is called the uncle of the emperor Julian, and is said to have apostatized with him, (5) *Iulianus,* bishop of Cos, the friend and frequent correspondent of Leo the Great, among whose letters a large number are addressed to him. He was by birth an Italian, and had been educated at Rome. St. Thomas quotes from Leo's letter 35 to Julianus. This letter contains an elaborate dogmatic statement against Eutyches, (6) *Iulianus,* bishop of Halicarnassus in the province of Caria, one of the leaders of the Monophysites. In 511, he was active together with Severus and others in instigating the emperor Anastasius to depose Macedonius, the patriarch of Constantinople. On the accession of Justin I in 518, severe measures were taken against the Monophysites, and Julian was driven from his see. By some means he recovered his see, of Halicarnassus, but in the council of Constantinople A.D. 536 under Agapetus bishop of Rome, he was again deposed. After this date he disappears but his opinions continued to spread long afterwards.

Iulius, a, um, *adj.*, (1) **Iulius mensis** (or *absol. Iulius*), *the month of July* which was previously called *Quinctilis,* (2) **Iuliae leges,** *Julian laws,* laws passed in the time of Julius Caesar and C. Iulius Caesar Octavianus. St. Thomas mentions the *Lex Iulia de adulteriis.* This law first made adultery an indictable offence, and deprived the husband of the right of killing his wife taken in adultery, but left the father, under strict limitations, the power of killing his daughter. A woman convicted of adultery was mulcted in half of her *dos* and the third of her separate property, and was banished to some island. The adulterer forfeited half his property, and was banished in like manner, but to a different place.

Iulius, ii, *m.*, (1) *Julius I,* pope, saint, (337-352). He intervened in the Arian controversies; held a synod at Rome, and sent his representatives to the Council of Sardica (342-343), at which St. Athanasius was acquitted of his enemies' accusations, (2) *Iulius,* the name of a Roman gens, especially the celebrated C. *Julius* Caesar, distinguished as general, orator, statesman, and author, assassinated by Brutus and Cassius, B.C. 44, (3) *Iulius,* Sextus Iulius Frontinus, praetor in 70 A.D., consul several times, was appointed *Curator Aquarum* or overseer of the water supply of Rome in 97 A.D. His writings belong rather to the history of technical studies than to that of literature. St. Thomas refers to his *Strategemata.*

iumentum, i, *n., a beast used for drawing* or *carrying, draught-cattle, a beast of burden,* esp. a *horse, mule* or *ass.*

iunctim, *adv., contiguously, side by side.*

iunctura, ae, *f., a joining, uniting.*

iungo, ere, iunxi, iunctum, 3, *v. a.,* (1) lit., (a) in gen., *to join* or *unite together, connect, attach, fasten,* used with the *dat.* of the *indirect object,* (b) *to join* or *bring together,* as to join the hands, used with the *acc.,* (2) transf., (a) in gen., of abstr. things, *to bring together, unite,* (b) esp. of persons, *to join, unite, bring together, associate,* (c) of words, *to add, append* as a statement, *to say.*—**iungere aliquid ad aliud opus,** *to use something in another work.*—**iunctus,** a, um, *P. a.,* (1) of numbers, *added,* (2) of persons, *joined, united* in relationship, marriage, etc.

iunior, see *iuvenis.*

Iuppiter, Iovis, *m., Jupiter* or *Jove, a son of Saturn, brother* and *husband of Juno, the chief god among the Romans.*—Carcer Iovis, *the prison-house of Jupiter,* or *hell.* According to Pythagoras this place of punishment is situated in the middle of the whole world.

iuramentum, i, *n., oath, vow.*— Kinds of *iuramentum* are: (a), **iuramentum assertorium** and **iuramentum promissorium,** *the oath of confirmation* and *that of promise.*—(b), **iuramentum fidelitatis,** *the oath of loyalty.*— (c), **iuramentum illicitum seu iniustum** and **iuramentum licitum,** *the unlawful* or *unjust oath* and *the lawful oath.*—(d), **iuramentum incautum,** *the imprudent oath.*—(e), **iuramentum iniustum,** see *iudicium illicitum.*—(f), **iuramentum licitum,** see *iuramentum illicitum.*—(g), **iuramentum mendax seu perversum,** *the deceitful* or *false oath,* i.e., *perjury.*—(h), **iuramentum perversum,** see *iuramentum mendax.*—(i), **iuramentum promissorium,** see *iuramentum assertorium.*—(j), **iuramentum solemne,** *the solemn oath* or *vow.*

iuratio, onis, *f., a swearing, oath.*

iuratorius, a, um, *adj., of* or *confirmed by an oath, iuratory.*

iurgium, i, *n., a quarrel, strife, dispute, altercation, contention.*

iurisconsultus, i, *m., one skilled in the law, a lawyer, jurist, attorney-at-law.*

iurisdictio, onis, *f., administration of justice, jurisdiction, official authority, judicial power.* On **clavis iurisdictionis,** see *clavis;* on **potestas iurisdictionis,** see *potestas.*—Kinds of *iurisdictio* are: (a), **iurisdictio aequalis** and **iurisdictio superior,** *the equal* and *the higher jurisdiction.*—(b), **iurisdictio limitata,** *the limited jurisdiction.*—(c), **iurisdictio ordinaria,** *the ordinary* or *the usual jurisdiction.*—(d), **iurisdictio superior,** see *iurisdictio aequalis.*

iurisdictionalis, e, *adj., jurisdictional, of* or *pertaining to jurisdiction.*

iurisperitus, i, *n., a jurist, one skilled* or *learned in the law.*

iurista, ae, *m., a jurist.*

iuro, are, avi, atum, 1, *v. n.* and *a., to swear, to take an oath,* used with *acc.* and *inf., acc.* alone, with *per.*

ius, iuris, *n.,* (1) *the right, prerogative, jurisprudence, knowledge of law, law-court, law,* the foundation of *iustitia* and *iustum,* (2) *canonical dicision, ecclesiastical statute.*—On **debitum iuris,** see *debitus;* on **ignorantia iuris, iuris in particulari et universalium iuris,** see *ignorantia;* on **necessitas iuris,** see *necessitas;* on **principium iuris naturalis,** see *principium;* on **praeceptum iuris naturalis et iuris postivi,** see *praeceptum;* on **scientia iuris,** see *scientia.*—Kinds of *ius* (*synonym of iustum*) in the sense of *law* are: (a) **ius canonicum** and **ius**

civile, *the canon* or *church law*
and *the civil* or *secular law.*—(b),
ius civile, see *ius canonicum.*—
(c), ius commune and ius privatum, *the common* or *general law*
and *the private* or *special law.*—
(d), ius divinum and ius humanum, *the divine* and *the human
law.*—(e), ius dominativum seu
dominii seu regni and ius paternum seu patriae potestatis, *the
right of the master over his servants* or *the ruler over his subjects*
or *of the father over his children.*
—(f), ius dominii, see *ius dominativum.*—(g), ius gentium, *the
right of people.*—(h), ius honorarium and ius praetorium, *the law
arising from the decrees of mag-
istrates* and *that from the decrees of a praetor.*—(i), ius humanum, see *ius divinum.*—(j), ius
legale seu positivum and ius naturae seu naturale, *legal* or *positive law* and *the natural law* or
that of nature.—(k), ius matrimonii seu matrimoniale, *the law of
matrimony.*—(l), ius militare and
ius publicum, *the military* and
the public or *civil law.*—(m), ius
naturae, see *ius legale.*—(n), ius
naturale, see *ius legale.*—(o), ius
paternum, see *ius dominativum.*
—(p), ius patriae potestatis, see
ius dominativum.—(q), ius positivum, see *ius legale.*—(r), ius praelationis, *the right of a principalship* or *of a head.*—(s), ius praetorium, see *ius honorarium.*—(t),
ius privatum, see *ius commune.*—

(u), ius publicum, see *ius militare.*—(v), ius regni, see *ius dominativum.*—(w), ius tyrannicum,
the right assumed by a tyrant.

iusiurandum, i, *n., an oath.*

iussio, onis, *f., an order, command.*

iussus, us, *m., an order, command,
decree.*

iuste, see *iustus.*

iustificatio, onis, *f.,* (1) *justification*
in the proper sense of the word,
i.e., *the process of being cleansed
of injustice* and *the resultant performance of a just act* or *doing
right,* the *dikaioma* of Aristotle,
synonym of *iustitia,* the opposite of *iniustificatio,* (2) *justification* in the improper sense of the
word, i.e., as preparatory to or
productive of justice as the state
of friendship with God.—Kinds
of *iustificatio* in this (1) sense
are: (a), iustificatio impii and iustificatio simpliciter, *the justification of the godless* or *sinners
which includes the remission of
the guilt of sin* and *the simple* or
*absolute justification which con-
sists in the infusion of sanctifying
grace.*—(b), iustificatio passive
accepta, *justification in the passive sense of the word.*—(c), iustificatio simpliciter, see *iustificatio
impii.*—(d), iustificatio voluntaria, *voluntary right doing* or *right
doing not prescribed by law.*

iustificativus, a, um, *adj., justifica-
tive, serving to justify.*

iustificator, oris, *m., a justifier, one
who justifies.*

iustifico, are, 1, *v. a.*, *to justify, make just*, to transform a sinner from the state of unrighteousness to the state of holiness and sonship of God. To justify is the work of God alone, in as far as He is merciful. According to the Council of Trent the required dispositions, in order to obtain the grace of being justified, are: Faith, by which man believes all that has been revealed, and, in particular, that the sinner is justified by the grace and merits of Jesus Christ; the fear of Divine justice; hope in the mercy of God; a more or less explicit act by which we commence to love God as the source of all justice; hatred and detestation of sin, with the desire to receive the sacrament of baptism or penance, to lead a new life, and to obey the commandments of God.

Iustinianus, i, *m.*, *Justinian*, a Roman emperor in the sixth century of the Christian era, who caused the compilation of the Corpus Iuris.

iustitia, ae, *f.*, (1) *justice* in the proper sense of the word, i.e., *the moral virtue of justice*, which disposes to render to every man what is rightly due him, the opposite of *iniustitia*, (2) *justice* in the tranferred sense of the word, (iustitia metaphorica seu metaphorice dicta, 3, Sent. 33. 3. 4. 5 ob. 1 and c; 5 Eth. 1 a and 17 a) i.e., *the moral state of justice*, likewise the opposite of *iniustitia*, (3) *justice* in the sense of an action, i.e., *justification* or *a just deed*, synonym of *iustificatio*, (4) *justice* in the sense of the just, privilege, right, synonym of *ius* and *iustum*, (5) *propriety, decorum*, (6) *truth* in the transferred sense of the word, i.e., the conformity of an action with the will which serves it as a guide or rule.—On **debitum iustitiae**, see *debitus;* on **medium iustitiae**, see *medium;* on **necessitas iustitiae**, see *necessitas;* on **ordo iustitiae**, see *ordo;* on **perfectio iustitiae**, see *perfectio;* on **rectitudo iustitiae**, see *rectitudo;* on **servitus iustitiae**, see *servitus;* on **signum publicae iustitiae**, see *signum;* on **veritas iustitiae**, see *veritas;* on **zelus iustitiae**, see *zelus.*—Kinds of *iustitia* in this (1) sense are: (a), **iustitia aequalis seu aequalitatis** and **iustitiae legalis**, *the justice aiming at equality* or *at an equal measure of good* and *bad,* and *legal justice* or *the justice that corresponds to the prescriptions of the law.* Cf. *iustus aequalis* under *iustus.*—(b), **iustitia aequalitatis**, see *iustitia aequalis.*—(c), **iustitia civilis seu politica seu politica simpliciter** and **iustitia oeconomica**, *civil* or *political justice* and *domestic justice* or *that pertaining to family life.*—(d), **iustitia communis seu generalis seu quae est omnis seu tota virtus** and **iustitia particula-**

ris seu specialis seu quae est particularis virtus seu pars totius virtutis, *the general* (cf. *iustitia generalis* under (2)) and *the special justice,* or *the justice which comprises all virtue* and *that which comprises a special virtue.* —(e), **iustitia commutativa** and **iustitia distributiva**, *the mutual justice among equals* and *the justice of a superior to inferiors.*— (f), **iustitia distributiva**, see *iustitia commutativa.*—(g), **iustitia divina** and **iustitia humana**, *the divine* and *the human justice.*—(h), **iustitia humana**, see *iustitia divina.*—(i), **iustitia legalis**, the debt of the inferior to the superior as the community. See *iustitia aequalis.*—(j), **iustitia oeconomica,** *domestic* or *family justice,* see *iustitia civilis.*—(k), **iustitia particularis**, see *iustitia communis.*—(l), **iustitia politica**, see *iustitia civilis.*—(m), **iustia praemians** and **iustitia puniens seu vindicans seu vindicativa**, *the rewarding* and *the punishing* or *avenging justice.*—(n), **iustitia puniens**, see *iustitia praemians.*—(o), **iustitia quae est omnis seu tota virtus,** see *iustitia communis.*—(p), **iustitia quae est pars totius virtutis,** see *iustitia communis.*—(q), **iustitia quae est particularis virtus**, see *iustitia communis.*—(r), **iustitia regiminis**, *the justice of government.*—(s), **iustitia specialis**, see *iustitia communis.*—(t), **iustitia vindicans seu vindicativa,** see

iustitia praemians.—On **habitus iustitiae**, see *habitus;* on **libertas iustitiae**, see *libertas;* on **status iustitiae**, see *status;* on **vita iustitiae**, see *vita.*—Kinds of *iustitia* in this (2) sense are: (a), **iustitia adquisita, iustitia gratias seu gratuita seu infusa** and **iustitia innata seu naturalis,** *justice acquired through one's own practice* and *that bestowed by the grace of God* or *infused* and *justice that is inherent* or *natural.*—(b), **iustitia fidei seu generalis,** *justice from faith* or *general justice,* i.e., the state of sanctifying grace.— (c), **iustitia generalis**, see *iustitia fidei.*—(d), **iustitia gratiae**, see *iustitia adquisita.*—(e), **iustitia gratuita**, see *iustitia adquisita.*—(f), **iustitia infusa**, see *iustitia adquisita.*—(g), **iustitia innata**, see *iustitia adquisita.*—(h), **iustitia legalis** and **iustitia moralis**, *the legal* and *the moral* or *virtuous justice.* Cf. *iustitia legalis* under (1).—(i), **iustitia moralis**, see *iustitia legalis.*—(j), **iustitia naturalis**, see *iustitia legalis.*—(k), **iustitia originalis**, *the original justice.*— (l), **iustitia praesens**, *the present justice* or *that taking place in the present.*—(m), **iustitia publica**, *public justice.*—(n), **iustitia salutaris**, *the salutary justice* or *that promoting health.*—(o), **iustitia vera**, *true justice.*—Kinds of *iustitia* in this (3) sense are: (a), **iustitia animata** and **iustitia inanimata**, *the animate* or *living justice,* i.e., the judge (cf. *iustum anima-tum* under *iustum*), and *the inan-imate* or *lifeless justice.*—(b), **iu-stitia inanimata,** see *iustitia ani-mata.*—(c), **iustitia naturalis,** *the natural justice.*—One kind of *iu-stitia* in this (4) sense is: **iustitia publicae honestatis,** *the proprie-ty of public decorum.*

iusto, are, 1, *v. a., to make just, adjust.*

iustus, a, um, *adj., just, right, up-right, righteous,* synonym of *de-bitus, ius,* and *iustitia,* the oppo-site of *iniustus.* On **aestimatio iusta,** see *aestimatio;* on **domini-um iustum,** see *dominium;* on **lex iusta,** see *lex;* on **politia iusta,** see *politia;* on **regimen iustum,** see *regimen;* on **vindicta iusta,** see *vindicta.*—Kinds of *iustus* are: **iustus aequalis** and **iustus legalis,** the *dikaios isos* and *dikaios nomimos* of Aristotle, *the just striving after equal* or *equal measure of good* and *bad,* and *the just conformable to law* and *existing on conformity with the laws.*—**iustum,** i, *n., that which is right* or *just, justice, right,* syno-nym of *ius.*—Kinds of *iustum* in the sense of the *just* or *justice* are: (a), **iustum aequale** and **iu-stum legale,** the *dikaion ison* and the *dikaion nomimon* of Aristotle, *the just containing like* or *an equal measure of good* and *bad* and *that corresponding to the positive law.* Cf. *iustum legale,* and *iustus aequalis* above.

—(b), **iustum aliqualiter seu se-cundum quid seu quoddam** and **iustum simpliciter,** *justice in a certain way* or *according to something* or *certain species of justice* and *the simple* or *abso-lute justice.*—(c), **iustum anima-tum,** the *dikaion empsyshon* of Aristotle, *the animate* or *living justice,* i.e., *the judge.*—(d), **iu-stum apparens, iustum similitu-dinarium,** and **iustum verum,** *the apparent, the improper,* and *the true justice.*—(e), **iustum civile seu politicum seu politicum pro-prie dictum seu politicum simpli-citer** and **iustum oeconomicum,** *the proper* or *simple civic* or *po-litical justice* and *the domestic justice* or *that current in the family.*—(f), **iustum commutati-vum** and **iustum distributivum,** *the justice that guides exchange* or *trade among equals* and *that guides distribution by the supe-rior to his inferiors* or *the justice in exchange* and *that in distribu-tion of rewards* and *punishment.* —(g), **iustum dispensativum seu dominativum, iustum paternum** and **iustum uxorium,** *the right of the master* or *administrator, the right of the father* and *that of the husband,* i.e., the right which belongs to a master or superior over his servants, to a father over his children, and to a husband over his wife.—(h), **iustum distri-butivum,** see *iustum commutati-vum.*—(i), **iustum dominativum,** see *iustum dispensativum.*—(j), **iustum humanum**, *human right* or *justice.*—(k), **iustum legale**, see *iustum aequale.*—(l), **iustum legale seu secundum legis positionem** and **iustum naturale seu secundum naturam**, *the legal right* or *that determined by law* or *given in words* and *the natural right.*—(m), **iustum morale**, *the moral right.*—(n), **iustum naturale**, see *iustum legale.*—(o), **iustum oeconomicum**, see *iustum civile.*—(p), **iustum particulare seu particulare dictum**, *the particular right,* i.e., that right which applies to individual persons.—(q), **iustum paternum**, see *iustum dispensativum.*—(r), **iustum politicum seu politicum proprie dictum seu politicum simpliciter**, see *iustum civile.*—(s), **iustum populare**, *the right of the people.*—(t), **iustum positivum**, see *iustum legale.*—(u), **iustum quoddam**, see *iustum aliqualiter.*—(v), **iustum secundum dignitatem**, *the right according to dignity.*—(w), **iustum secundum legis positionem**, see *iustum legale.*—(x), **iustum secundum naturam**, see *iustum legale.*—(y), **iustum secundum quid**, see *iustum aliqualiter.*—(z) **iustum sententiale**, *the judicial right.*—(a²), **iustum similitudinarium**, see *iustum apparens.*—(b²), **iustum simpliciter**, see *iustum aliqualiter.*—(c²), **iustum verum**, see *iustum apparens.*—(d²), **iustum vindicativum**, *the*

avenging right or *the right of punishment.*—**iuste**, *adv., rightly, justly, equitably, duly.*

iuvamen, inis, *n., help, aid, assistance.*

iuvamentum, i, *n., help, aid, assistance.*

iuvenilis, e, *adj., of* or *belonging to youth, youthful, juvenile.* The fourth of the six ages of man, between adolescence and maturity.

iuvenis, is, *adj.,* (comp. iunior) *young.*—**iuvenis**, is, *comm., one who is in the flower of his* or *her age* (mostly of persons older than *adolescentes* and younger than *seniores,* i.e., between twenty and forty), *a young person, a young man.*

iuventas, atis, *f., the age of youth, youth.*

iuventus, utis, *f., the age of youth* (from the twentieth to the fortieth year), *youth,* (2) transf., *young persons, youth.*

iuvo, are, iuvi, iutum, 1, *v. a.* and *n., to help, aid, assist, support, benefit.*

iuxta, *adv.* and *prep.,* (I) *adv., near, nigh to,* (II) *prep.,* (1) lit. of place, *very near, close to, near to, hard by,* (2) transf., (a) *about, close to,* (b) *next to, beside,* (c) *like, almost the same,* (d) *according to,* (e) *along with, together with.*—The following phrase is frequently used: **ponere aliquid iuxta se,** *to put something side by side* or *in juxtaposition.*

K

Kalendae, arum, *f.*, *the Calends, the first day of the month.*

kumibilis, e, *adj.*, *niggardly.*

Kyrie, used with *eleison, Kyrie eleeson, Lord have mercy,* an ancient ejaculation used in the Roman rite before the Gloria of the Mass as triple formula before and after triple *Christe eleison,* in hours of Divine Office, in the litany of the Saints, and elsewhere; frequently in other rites without *Christe eleison.*

L

Laban, *m.*, *indecl.*, *Laban,* Biblical Patriarch, son of Bathuel, lived at Haran, Mesopotamia, in the eighteenth century B.C. He gave successively two daughters, Lia and Rachel, in marriage to his nephew Jacob, under condition to serve him during fourteen years.

labes, is, *f.*, *a stain, deformity, blemish, downfall,* used *fig.*

labilitas, atis, *f.*, *lability, frailty,* the state of being labile, or liable to slip, fall or apostatize.

labiliter, *adv.*, *glidingly,* used in the S.T. only in quot.

labium, ii, *n.*, (1) *a lip,* (2) *a laver,* a large vessel of bronze in which the priests washed their hands and feet before sacrifices.

labor, i, lapsus, 3, *v. dep. n.*, used *fig.*, (1) *to fall* into heresy, sin, lying, hypocrisy, avarice, error, etc., used with *in* and *acc.*, and *absol.*, (2) *to slip,* or *fall away from* a thing.

labor, oris, *m.*, (1) *lit., labor, toil, exertion,* (2) *in partic., fatigue, distress, trouble, pain, toil.* (3) plural, (a) with *bonis, good works,* works by which we satisfy God for our sins, like prayer, alms and fasting, especially designated in Scripture and recommended by the Holy Fathers, (b) *labours, work done,* that which requires effort or exertion.

laboriosus, a, um, *adj.*, (1) *attended with much labor, laborious, toilsome, wearisome, difficult, irksome, troublesome,* (2) *inclined to labor, laborious, industrious.*

laboro, are, avi, atum, 1, *v. n.* and *a.*, (1) *to labor, take pains, exert one's self, strive,* (2) *to suffer, to labor under, to be oppressed; afflicted,* or *troubled with.*—**laborans,** antis, *P. a.*, *laboring.*—**laborans agricola,** *the husbandman that labors.*

lac, lactis, *n.*, (1) *lit., milk,* (2) *fig.,* for something used as spiritual nutriment.

lacero, are, avi, atum, 1, *v. a.*, *to tear to pieces, mangle, rend, lacerate,* (1) *lit.,* (2) *fig.*

lacerta, ae, *f.*, *a lizard.*

lacessitus, a, um, *P. a., attacked, assailed, tormented.*

lacrima (lacryma), ae, *f., a tear,* (1) *lit.,* (2) *fig.*—The following phrases are used occasionally: **pro-rumpere in lacrimas,** *to burst into tears.*—**fundere in lacrymas,** *to shed tears.*—**emittere lacrymas,** *to pour forth tears.*

lacrimabilis, e, *adj., tearful.*—**lacri-mabiliter,** *adv., with tears, mournfully.*

lacrimabiliter, *adv.,* see *lacrimabilis.*

lacrimor, ari, atus, 1, *v. dep., to weep, shed tears.*

lacrimula, ae, *f., a little tear, a crocodile-tear,* used in the S.T. only in quot.

lacticinia, orum, *n., a milk-food, a dish prepared with milk* and *eggs.*

lacto, are, avi, atum, 1, *v. a.* and *n., to nourish* at the breast.

lactuca, ae, *f., lettuce.*

lacuna, ae, *f., a pool, pond.*

lacus, us, *m., the pit, the place of the dead.*

laedo, ere, si, sum, 3, *v. a.,* (1) *lit., to wound, injure, damage,* synonym of *saucio, vulnero,* (2) *trop., to trouble, annoy, injure, offend, grieve, hurt.*—**laesa maiestas,** *treason.*

laesio, onis, *f., a leison, hurt, injury.*

laesivus, a, um, *adj., injurious, offensive, harmful.* On **amor laesivus,** see *amor;* on **passio laesiva,** see *passio.*

Laeta, ae, *f., Laeta,* daughter-in-law of Paula, the friend of St. Jerome. She was the daughter of Albinus, a heathen priest. She had one daughter, named Paula after her grandmother. Her husband Toxotius appears to have left the education of the child to his wife who invited the advice of St. Jerome. St. Jerome addresses epistle 107 to her, prescribing the training suitable to form a virgin of Christ.

laetabundus, a, um, *adj., greatly rejoicing, joyful,* used in the S.T. only in quot.

laetifico, are, avi, atum, 1, *v. a., to gladden, cheer, delight.*

laetitia, ae, *f., joy, gladness, cheerfulness,* the opposite of *tristitia.*

laetor, ari, atus, 1, *v. dep. n., to rejoice, feel joy, be joyful* or *glad* at any thing, used with *de, in* and *abl.*

laetus, a, um, *adj., joyful, cheerful, glad.*

Laetus, i, *m., Laetus,* a Christian who quit the monastery of Hippo Regius to resume his position in the world. He wrote to the brethren of the monastery in much doubt and distress of mind, and expressed a wish to hear from Augustine. Augustine addressed epistle 243 to Laetus exhorting him to return to the monastery.

laeva, ae, *f.,* (sc. *manus aut pars*), *the left hand, the left part.*

laicalis, e, *adj., laical, laic,* of or pertaining to a layman, as opposed to clerical.

laicatus, us, *m., laity, laicality, the state* or *condition of a laymen.*

laicus, a, um, *adj., lay, belonging to the laity, not clerical,* i.e., one who has not received ecclesiastical tonsure.—**laicus,** i, *m., a layman, laic,* one not belonging to the clergy.

lambo, ere, bi, bitum, 3, *v. a., to lick, lap,* used in the S.T. only in quot.

Lamech, *m., indecl., Lamech,* descendant of Cain. He had two wives, Ada, mother of Jabel and Jubal, and Sella, mother of Tubalcain and Noema.

lamentum, i, *n., a weeping, lamentation, moaning, sorrowing.*

lamina, ae, *f., a lamina, plate, thin piece of metal, wood, marble,* etc.

lampas, adis, *f., a lamp,* used *fig.* in the S.T.

lana, ae, *f.,* (1) *wool,* (2) *transf.,* **facere lanam,** *to spin wool* or *work in wool.*

lancea, ae *f., a lance, spear.*

lanceatus, a, um, *adj., lanced, pierced with a lance.*

lanceola, ae, *f., dim., a small lance.*

laneus, a, um, *adj., woolen, of wool.*

languens, entis, *P. a., languishing, weak.*

languesco, ere, gui, 3, *v. inch. n., to languish.*

languide, *adv.,* see *languidus.*

languidus, a, um, *adj., sick, feeble, weak.*—**languide,** *adv., delicately.*

languor, oris, *m.,* (1) *lit., sickness, infirmity,* (2) *fig., inactivity, infirmity, apathy, languor, torpor.*

lapidatio, onis, *f., a throwing of stones, stoning,* used *lit.* and *fig.*

lapideus, a, um, *adj.,* (1) *lit., of stone, stony, made* or *consisting of stone,* (2) *fig., stony, hard* and *cold as stone, unfeeling.*

lapido, are, avi, atum, 1, *v. a.* and *n., to throw stones* at a person, *to stone.*

lapillus, i, *m., a little stone, pebble.*

lapis, idis, *m., a stone.*—**lapides pretiosi,** *precious stones, gems* and the non-oxidizable metals having ornamental or market value. **lapis politus,** *a polished stone.*—**lapides secti,** *hewn stones.*—**lapis offensionis,** *a stone of collision,* used fig., and mentioned in Isaias VIII, 14, "He shall become a sanctuary and a stone of collision." God's intervention is always an occasion for the self-manifestation of two classes, the faithful and the faithless (John III, 18-21). As to the latter Jehovah will be a stone against which the foot strikes, and a rock to cause stumbling, so that they will stumble, fall, and break.—**unctio lapidis,** *the anointing of the stone.*

lapsus, us, *m.,* used *fig.,* (1) *a fall, failing, error, fault,* (2) *a slip* in speech.

laqueus, i, *m., a snare,* any trick or allurement by which one is brought into trouble or difficulty or caused to fall into sin.

large, *adv.,* see *largus.*

largior, iri, itus, 4, *v. dep.,* (1) *lit.,* in gen., *to bestow, distribute, lavish,* used with *acc.,* the *acc.* and *dat.,* (2) *fig., to confer, bestow, grant, yield.*

largitas, atis, *f., abundance, plenty, liberality.*

largiter, *adv.,* see *largus.*

largitio, onis, *f., a giving freely, a granting, bestowing, dispensing, imparting.*

largitor, oris, *m., a liberal giver, bestower.*

largus, a, um, *adj., abundant, plentiful, large, much,* (1) in gen., (2) in *particular, liberal, giving abundantly.—***larga vestis,** *a full garment,* a garment having a large amount of material.—**largo modo,** *in a broad sense.—*

large, *adv.,* (1) *abundantly, plentifully, bountifully, liberally,* (2) *widely,* in a broad sense.—**sumere aliquid large,** *to take something in a broad sense,* also in the same sense with *accipere, uti, dicere, ponere, loqui.—***largiter,** *adv., generously.*

larus, i, *m.,* (Grk. *larus*), a long-winged web-footed larine swimming bird. It enjoys strong powers of flight, is a good swimmer, and spends much time in the water.

larvalis, e, *adj., ghostly.*

lascivia, ae, *f., lewdness, moral depravity.*

lascivio, ire, ii, itum, 4, *v. n., to be wanton.*

lascivus, a, um, *adj., lustful, licentious.*

lassitudo, inis, *f., lassitude,* a state of body or mind in which there is a strong disinclination to exertion; *languor, weariness.*

lasso, are, avi, atum, 1, *v. a., to tire, weary.—***lassans,** antis, *P. a., fatiguing.*

latebra, ae, *f., a lurking place, hidden recess,* used *fig.*

latenter, *adv.,* see *lateo.*

latentia, ae, *f., hiddenness, secrecy.*

lateo, ere, ui, 2, *v. n., to lurk, be* or *lie hid,* or *concealed,* used *absol.,* (2) *fig.,* (a) *to be concealed from, be unknown to one,* used with *acc.,* (b) *to lie hid, concealed,* used *absol.—***latens,** entis, *P. a., hiding, lying low, lying hid, lurking,* used *lit.* and *fig.—***latenter,** *adv., in secret, secretly, privately.*

later, eris, *m., a brick.*

Lateranus, a, um, *adj., of* or *belonging to the Lateran,* a palace in the eastern part of Rome, named from the family to which it belonged. It was given by Constantine to the Bishop of Rome, Pope Melchiades. The basilica of St. John in Laterano is the catherdal of the Pope. Eleven Church councils were held in the Lateran Palace.

latibulum, i, *n., a hiding place,* used *fig.*

Latine, *adv.,* see *Latinus.*

Latinus, a, um, *adj., Latin.—***Latini doctores,** *the Latin doctors,* men who have rendered eminent service to ecclesiastical science. The most illustrious of the Fathers of the Church who wrote in Latin are: St. Ambrose, St. Jerome, St. Augustine, and St. Gregory the Great.—**Latine**, *adv., in Latin.*—**Latini**, orum, *m., the Latins.*—**Latinus**, i, *m., a Latin, one who speaks Latin.*

latio, onis, *f.,* (1) *a bearing, a bringing, locomotion,* (2) *proposal, proposition, proclamation.*—On **motus lationis secundum locum**, see *motus.*—Kinds of *latio* in this (1) sense are: (a), **latio circularis**, *circular locomotion.*—(b), **latio prima**, *the first locomotion,* i.e., *motus diurnus.*

latitatio, onis, *f., a hiding, lurking.*

latito, are, avi, atum, 1, *v. freq. n., to be hid* or *concealed, to lie hid, hide.*—**latitans**, antis, *P. a., hiding.*

latitudo, inis, *f.,* (1) *breadth, width* in the literal and in the figurative sense of the word, opposite of *longitudo,* (2) *extent, size, elbowroom.*

lator, oris, *m., a bearer,* i.e., *a mover* or *proposer of a law.*

latrabilis, e, *adj., barking.*

latria, ae, *f.,* (1) *the act of adoration,* i.e., the veneration of God as the highest Lord of heaven and earth, (2) *the virtue of the adoration* or *the veneration of God,* synonym of *eusebia, religio,* and *theosebia,* (3) *manner* or *material of the adoration* or *the veneration of God.*—On **adoratio latriae**, see *adoratio;* on **cultus latriae**, see *cul-*

tus; on **honor latriae**, see *honor;* on **servitus latriae**, see *servitus.*

latro, onis, *m., a robber, thief.*

latrocinium, i, *n., robbery.*

latrocinor, ari, atus, 1, *v. dep., to practice robbery.*

latus, a, um, *adj., broad, wide,* (1) *lit.,* (2) *fig.,*

latus, eris, *n.,* (1) *the side, flank* of men, (2) *the side, flank,* lateral surface of a thing.—**ex latere**, *indirectly.*

laudabilis, e, *adj., to be praised, praiseworthy, lovable.* On **actus laudabilis**, see *actus;* on **bonum laudabile**, see *bonus;* on **delectatio laudabilis**, see *delectatio;* on **passio laudabilis**, see *passio.*—**laudabiliter**, *adv., in a praiseworthy manner, praiseworthily, laudably.*

laudabilitas, atis, *f., laudability, praiseworthiness.*

laudabiliter, *adv.,* see *laudabilis.*

laudative, *adv., in a laudatory manner, praiseworthily,* used in the S.T. only in quot.

laudator, oris, *m., a flatterer.*

Laudefredus, i, *m., Ludfrid,* bishop of Cordova, at the fourth and fifth councils of Toledo (633, 636). His vicar, Valentinianus, represented him at the sixth council. To him was addressed a letter of Isidore's on certain points of church organization.

laudo, are, avi, atum, 1, *v. a., to praise, laud, commend, extol, eulogize.*

Laurentius, ii, *m., Lawrence,* saint, deacon, and martyr, born near

Huesca, Spain. He was chief among the seven deacons of the Roman church. Cyprian mentions the rescript of Valerian directing that bishops, presbyters, and deacons should forthwith be punished, and records the martyrdom of Xystus, bishop of Rome, in accordance with it on August 6. Laurentius, the first of the traditional seven deacons of Rome, suffered four days afterwards.

laus, laudis, *f., praise, commendation.* On the difference between *laus, gloria,* and *honor,* see *gloria* under (1) and *honor.* On **confessio laudis,** see *confessio.—* Kinds of *laus* are: **laus mentalis** and **laus vocalis,** *praise in thought* and *praise in words.*

laute, *adv.,* see *lavo.*

lavacrum, i, *n., a laver,* that which laves or washes.

lavo, are, lavi, lautum, and lotum, 1, *v. a.* and *n., to wash, bathe, lave,* used *lit.* and *fig.—***lautus,** a, um, and **lotus,** a, um, *P. a.,* (1) *lit., washed,* (2) *transf., sumptuous, luxurious.—***laute,** *adv., sumptuously.*

laxativus, a, um, *adj., laxative, gently purgative.*

laxe, *adv.,* see *laxus.*

laxus, a, um, *adj., less strict, more indulgent, easy.—***laxe,** *adv., laxly, in a lax manner, without strictness.*

Lazarus, i, *m., Lazarus,* (1) brother of Martha and Mary, dwelt with his sisters at Bethania, near Je-

rusalem. While Jesus was beyond the Jordan with his apostles, Lazarus fell sick and died. Jesus came to Bethania immediately, and raised him to life again, (2) the beggar in the parable set forth by Christ (Luke 16).

Leander, i, *m., Leander,* Saint, Archbishop of Seville, born at Carthagena, friend of Pope Gregory the Great who dedicated to him his *Commentaries on Job.*

lectio, onis, *f.,* (1) *lit., reading,* the practice of perusing reading matter and considering its contents or meaning, (2) *transf.,* (a) *that which is read, reading,* (b) *a lesson, text,* a designated portion of the Scripture read at Mass from the Old or New Testament, more frequently from the Epistles in the latter, and therefore called Epistle, (c) *a lecture, a discourse* read or pronounced on any subject, (d) *a section,* a subdivision of a chapter.

lector, oris, *m., lector, a reader, one who reads,* (1) in *gen.,* (2) *transf., a clerk in minor orders,* second in the Roman Rite.

lectoratus, us, *m., the lectorate, the office of lector,* used in the S.T. only in quot.

lectus, i, *m., a bed, couch.*

legalis, e, *adj., of* or *belonging to the law, legal,* i.e., conforming to the positive law or determined by the same, in a special sense, pertaining to the Mosaic code.

By law is meant above, (1) **the law in general,** when for example there is a question of **debitum legale** (see *debitus* under 1), **iniustitia legalis** (see *iniustitia* under 2), **iniustum legale** (see *iniustus*), **ius legale** (see *ius* under 1), **iustitia legalis** (see *iustitia* under 1 and 2), **iustum legale** and **iustus legalis** (see *iustus*), **lex legalis** (see *lex* under 1) **servitus legalis** (see *servitus* under 1), **utilitas legalis** (see *utilitas* under 2); (2), **the civil** or **secular law** in opposition to canonical or ecclesiastical law when it is said: legalis computatio attendit descensum a communi radice ex utraque parte; (3), **the law of the Old Testament,** when for example mention is made of **figura legalis** (see *figura* under 3), **generatio legalis** (see *generatio* under 1), **irregularitas legalis** (see *irregularitas* under 2), **observantia legalis** (see *observantia* under 3), **pontifex legalis, sacerdos legalis,** (see *sacredos*), **sacerdotium legale** (see *sacerdotium*), **sacramentum legale** (see *sacramentum* under 2).

legatus, i, *m.,* a *legate.*

legio, onis, *f., a legion,* a great number.

legisconsultus, i, *m., a jurist,* one versed in the science of law.

legislatio, onis, *f., the framing* of a law.

legislator, oris, *m., a legislator, lawgiver.*

legisperitus, i, *m., one learned in the law, a lawyer.*

legispositivus, a, um, *adj., legislative, law-making.* On **ars legispositiva,** see *ars;* on **scientia legispositiva,** see *scientia.*

legitime, see *legitimus.*

legitimo, are, avi, atum, 1, *v. a., to legitimize.*

legitimus, a, um, *adj., fixed* or *appointed by law, lawful, legal, legitimate,* the opposite of *illegitimus.* On **actus legitimus,** see *actus;* on **assumptio legitima,** see *assumptio;* on **dominium legitimum,** see *dominium;* on **filius legitimus,** see *filius;* on **matrimonium legitimum,** see *matrimonium.*–**legitime,** *adv., according to law, lawfully, legally, legitimately.*

lego, ere, legi, lectum, 3, *v. a.,* (1) *to read, peruse,* (2) *lecture.*

legumen, inis, *n., pulse, any leguminous plant.*

lenia, ae, *f., fortitude, patient* and *constant courage,* a synonym of *patientia* vel *tolerantia.*

lenio, ire, ivi, or ii, itum, 4, *v. a.,* and *n., to soothe, alleviate.*

lenis, e, *adj., soft, smooth, mild, gentle, easy, calm.*

lenitas, atis, *f., mildness, tenderness, gentleness, lenity.*

lenitivus, a, um, *adj., lenitive, soothing, emollient.*

lenocinans, antis, *P. a., flattering, deceiving,* used in the S.T. only in quot.

lentus, a, um, *adj.,* of character,

easy, calm, indifferent, uncon- cerned, sluggish.

leo, onis, *m., a lion,* (1) *lit.,* (2) *transf.,* to denote *a courageous person.*

Leo, onis, *m.,* (1) *Leo I,* the Great, Saint and Doctor of the Church. On account of his eminent learning, sanctity, and great achievements, he is called the "Great". Rejecting the false Council of Ephesus, Leo, in 451, summoned the General Council of Chalcedon over which he presided by his legates and in which his Dogmatic Epistle was accepted as the expression of true Catholic Faith. St. Thomas quotes from his Letters to Proterius, Bishop of Alexandria; to Julian, Bishop of Aquileia; to Flavian, Bishop of Constantinople; to the Emperor Leo; to Dioscorus, Bishop of Alexandria; to Theodoret, Bishop of Cyprus; and ad Palaestinos; also from several of his sermons, (2) *Leo I,* emperor, surnamed the Great. He was born about 400 A.D. in the country of the Bessi, in Thrace. He was proclaimed emperor, February 7, 457 and crowned by Anatolius, patriarch of Constantinople, being the first sovereign who received his crown from the hands of a priest. A letter (146) of Pope Leo the Great, addressed to the Emperor Leo urges him to active measures against the heretics.

leoninus, a, um, *adj., of* or *belonging to a lion, a lion's.*

lepra, ae, *f., the leprosy.*

leprosus, a, um, *adj., leprous.—* **leprosus,** i, *m., a leper.—***leprosa,** ae, *f., a leprous woman.*

lepus, oris, *m., a hare,* a short-tailed and long-eared rodent of the *genus lepus,* proverbial for its timidity and swift progression by long leaps.

lethalis, e, *adj., deadly, lethal.—* **lethaliter,** *adv., lethally, in a deadly manner.*

lethaliter, *adv.,* see *lethalis.*

lethargicus, i, *m., a lethargic person.*

Leudefredus, i, *m., Leudefredus,* a bishop of Cordova, at the fourth and fifth councils of Toledo (633, 636). His vicar, Valentinianus, represented him at the sixth council (638). To him was addressed a letter of Isidore's on certain points of church organization.

levatio, onis, *f., a lifting up, raising, elevating.*

Levi, *m., indecl. n., Levi,* third son of Jacob, by Lia. With his brother Simeon he cruelly avenged the humiliation of their sister Dina, for which they were severely rebuked by Jacob. He was head of the tribe set apart for the service of the Lord.

Leviathan, *m., indecl., the Leviathan,* an enormous beast. The term is found in the Latin Vulgate.

levis, e, *adj.,* (1) *lit., light* in weight, *not heavy,* (2) *fig.,* (a) *light, without weight,* i.e., *of no consequence,* hence, in gen., *light, trivial, unimportant, inconsiderable, slight, little, petty,* (b) in disposition or character, *light, light-minded, capricious, inconstant,* without dignity or substantial character, (c) *light, lacking in intensity* or *effect.*—**leviter,** *adv., lightly, easily, without difficulty.*

Levitae, arum, *m., the Levites,* the *Levites,* the descendants of Levi, third son of Jacob by Lia. The whole tribe of Levi by the command of God was set apart for the service of the sanctuary. Therefore in apportionment of the Land of Chanaan, the tribe of Levi received no tribal territory. In lieu of land they received the tithes and also four cities with suburban pasture lands from each of the other tribes of Israel.—**Leviticus,** a, um, *adj., of* or *belonging to the Levi* or *to the Levites, Levitical.* —**Leviticus,** i, *m., Leviticus,* the third Book of the Bible, named from its contents, as it deals exclusively with the series of God and the religious ceremonies of the Old Testament as carried out by the members of the tribe of Levi, both priests and Levites.

levitas, atis, *f.,* (1) *lit., lightness,* as to weight, (2) *fig., levity, light-mindedness, fickleness, inconstancy.*—**levitas animi,** *levity of mind.*

leviter, *adv.,* see *levis.*

levo, are, avi, atum, 1, *v. a.,* (1) *lit., to lift up* something to a higher point, (2) *fig.,* **levare se ad Deum,** *to raise one's self to God,* to lift one's thoughts to God in love and prayer.—**levare oculos in coelum,** *to raise the eyes to heaven,* fix the attention on God the Father.—**levare aliquem baptizatum de sacro fonte,** *to raise someone from the baptismal font,* to act as godparent. See *fons.*

lex, legis, *f.,* an ordinance according to reason to the common good, promulgated by the head of the community, (1) *law* in general, understood as a body of laws as well as a single law, (2) *the secular* or *civil law,* (3) *the law of the Old Testament.* On **bonum secundum legis positionem,** see *bonus* under 2; on **disciplina legis,** see *disciplina* under 3; on **iustum secundum legis positionem,** see *iustus;* on **malum secundum legis positionem,** see *malus* under 2; on **observantia legis,** see *observantia* under 3; on **praeceptum legis et legis naturae seu naturalis,** see *praeceptum;* on **prudentia legis positiva,** see *prudentia;* on **sacerdos novae et veteris legis,** see *sacerdos;* on **sacerdotium veteris legis,** see *sacerdotium;* on **sacramentum legis Mosaicae, novae et veteris legis,** see *sacramentum* under 2; on **status legis,** see *status* under 3; on **substantia legis,** see *substantia* under 8.—Kinds of *lex* in this (1) sense are: (a), **lex aeterna,** *the eternal law,* i.e., the plan of the divine regulation of the world as it exists in God's mind from eternity.—(b), **lex amoris seu caritatis** and **lex timoris,** *the law of love* and *that of fear* or the law based on the love of God and that on the fear of Him, i.e., the law of the New and that of the Old Testament.—(c), **lex caritatis,** see *lex amoris.*—(d), **lex carnis seu fomitis seu membrorum seu concupiscentiae,** *the law of the flesh* or *the emotions* or *of the members* or *of wicked desire.*—(e), **lex civilis,** *the civil law* as opposed to ecclesiastical law.—(f), **lex communis** and **lex privata,** *the common* or *general law* (cf. *lex particularis*) and *the private law* or *privilegium.*—(g), **lex concupiscentiae,** see *lex carnis.*—(h), **lex democratica** and **lex tyrannica,** *the law established by a democracy* or *by a rule of the people* and *that established by a tyrant.*—(i), **lex Dei seu divina** and **lex hominis seu humana,** *the law given to man by God* or *divine law* and *that given by man to his equals* or *human law.*—(j), **lex divina,** see *lex Dei.*—(k), **lex evangelica seu evangelii seu nova** and **lex vetus,** *the law of the Gospel* or *of the New Testament* and *of the Old Testament.*—(l), **lex evangelii,** see *lex evangelica.*—(m), **lex factorum seu mandatorum,** *the law of deeds* and *of*

commands.—(n), **lex fidei seu gratiae,** *the law of faith* or *of grace,* i.e., the law of the New Testament.—(o), **lex fomitis,** see *lex carnis.*—(p), **lex gratiae,** see *lex fidei.*—(q), **lex hominis,** see *lex Dei.*—(r), **lex humana,** see *lex Dei.*—(s), **lex iniusta** and **lex iusta,** *the unjust law* and *the just law.*—(t), **lex iusta,** see *lex iniusta.* —(u), **lex legalis,** *the legitimate law,* i.e., that law which corresponds with the idea of a law.— (v), **lex libertatis** and **lex servitutis,** *the law of freedom* and *that of servitude.*—(w), **lex mandatorum,** see *lex factorum.*—(x), **lex Maurorum seu Saracenorum,** *the law current among the Moors* and *the Saracens.*—(y), **lex membrorum,** see *lex carnis.*—(z), **lex mundana,** *the law of the world.* —(a^2), **lex naturae seu naturalis** and **lex scripta seu scripturae,** *the law of nature* or *the natural law* and *the written law* of God. —(b^2), **lex nova,** see *lex evangelica.*—(c^2), **lex particularis** and **lex universalis,** *the particular* and *the general law.* Cf. *lex communis.*—(d^2), **lex praeparatoria,** *the law preparing for the reception of Christ* or *the law of the Old Testament.*—(e^2), **lex privata,** see *lex communis.*—(f^2), **lex Saracenorum,** see *lex Maurorum.*—(g^2), **lex scripta,** see *lex naturae.*—(h^2), **lex scripturae,** see *lex naturae.*— (i^2), **lex servitutis,** see *lex libertatis.*—(j^2), **lex Spiritus Sancti,** *the law* or *the guidance of the Holy*

S*pirit.*—(k²), **lex timoris,** see *lex amoris.*—(l²), **lex tyrannica,** see *lex democratica.*—(m²), **lex universalis,** see *lex particularis.*—(n²), **lex vetus,** see *lex evangelica.*

Lia, ae, *f., Lia* or *Leah,* elder daughter of Laban, married by stratagem to Jacob who had no love for her; mother of Ruben, Simeon, Levi, Juda, Issachar, Zabulon, and Dina. She was buried in the cave of Malchpelah, beside Sara and Rebecca.

libellus, i, *m., dim.,* (1) in gen., *a little book, pamphlet,* (2) in partic., (a) *a bill, petition,* used with *repudium,* **libellus repudii,** *a bill of divorce,* a formal petition filed in the proper court by either a husband or wife praying for a decree of divorce, (b) *a section of a book.*

libens, entis, *P. a.,* see *libet.*

liber, bri, *m.,* (1) *book* in the general sense of the word, (2) *book* in the figurative sense of the word, (3) *book* in the sense of metonymy, i.e., that which is written in a book.—One kind of *liber* in this (1) sense is: **liber materialis,** *the material* or *physical book,* i.e., the book in the sense of a physical thing. On **repraesentatio libri,** see *repraesentatio.* —Kinds of *liber* in this (2) sense are: (a), **liber mortis** and **liber vitae,** *the book of death* and *the book of life*—(b), **liber praescientiae divinae,** *the book of divine foreknowledge.*—(c), **liber vitae,** see *liber mortis.*—Kinds of *liber*

in this (3) sense are: (a), **liber apocryphus** and **liber authenticus,** *the book falsely attributed to an author* or *the apocryphal book* and *that written by one's own hand* or *the genuine book.* —(b), **liber authenticus,** see *liber apocryphus.*—(c), **liber canonicus,** *the book admitted to the canon of Holy Scriptures.*—(d), **liber originalis,** *the original book.*

liber, a, um, *adj.,* (1) *free, unrestricted, unrestrained, unimpeded,* that acts under no outside necessity, synonym of *voluntarius,* the opposite of *ligatus* and *necessarius,* (2) *free,* from a social point of view, *not a slave, freeborn,* synonym of *liberalis,* the opposite of *illiberalis, servilis* and *servus.*—On **arbitrium liberum et non liberum,** see *arbitrium* under 1, 3, and 4; on **contemplatio libera,** see *contemplatio;* on **iudicium liberum et non liberum,** see *iudicium* under 4; on **opus liberum,** see *opus* under 4; on **potentia libera,** see *potentia* under 2; on **potestas libera,** see *potestas* under 3. On **scientia libera,** see *scientia* under 1.—**Liber est causa sui** or **liber est, qui sui causa est** or **liber est, qui est causa sui** or **ille homo proprie dicitur liber, qui non est alterius causa, sed est causa sui ipsius** or **liberum est quod sui causa est,** the translation of the Aristotelian passage: *anthropos phamen eleutheros ho hautou heneka kai me allou on, free is the man who* controls himself and is not under another.—**liber**, eri, m., a child, always in the plural in the S.T.—**libere**, adv., freely, unrestrictedly, frankly, openly, boldly, the opposite of serviliter. On **iudicare libere**, see iudicare under 3.

Liber, eri, m., an old Italian deity who presided over planting and fructification, afterwards identified with the Greek Bacchus, used in the S.T. only in quot.

liberalis, e, adj., (1) free, befitting a free person, independent, not serving another, synonym of liber, the opposite of illiberalis, servilis, and servus, (2) generous, liberal, the mean between illiberalis and prodigus.—On **actio liberalis**, see actio under 1; on **amicitia liberalis**, see amicitia, on **ars liberalis**, see ars; on **disciplina liberalis**, see disciplina; on **scientia liberalis**, see scientia. —On the difference between liberalis and magnificus, see magnificentia. On **collatio liberalis**, see collatio under 3; on **utilitas liberalis**, see utilitas under 2.— **liberaliter**, adv., (1) in a manner befitting a free man, nobly, kindly, graciously, synonym of libere, the opposite of serviliter, (2) bountifully, profusely, generously, liberally, the mean between illiberaliter and prodige.

liberalitas, atis, f., a way of thinking befitting a freeman, a noble or kind or friendly disposition, noble spirit, kindness, affability, the opposite both of illiberalitas

and prodigalitas.—On the difference between liberalitas and magnificentia, see magnificentia.

liberaliter, see liberalis.

liberatio, onis, f., (1) in gen., a freeing or becoming free, a delivering, release, liberation, (2) in partic., a discharge, a release, remission from sin, fault etc.

liberator, oris, m., a liberator, deliverer.

liberatorius, a, um, adj., liberative, favoring liberty.

libere, see liber.

liberi, orum, m., see liber.

libero, are, avi, atum, 1, v. a., to make or set free, to free, liberate, (1) lit., to release from slavery, manumit, (2) transf., to free, release, extricate, deliver, used with acc., and abl. with a, ab, de, (a) with personal object, (b) with inanim. and abstr. objects.

libertas, atis, f., (1) freedom or liberty in general, i.e., being free from some particular restraint, (2) freedom of the will (cf. libertas arbitrii under 1), the indifference to particular goods precisely because they are particular which enables the will to choose among particular means always in the light of the ultimate goal, (3) free action of the will, (4) freedom, independence, the opposite of servitus.—Kinds of libertas in this (1) sense are: (a), **libertas a culpa** and **libertas a miseria**, freedom from guilt and freedom from misery.—(b), **libertas a iustitia seu iustitiae** and libertas a peccato seu peccati, *the freedom from justice* and *the freedom from sin.*—(c), libertas a miseria, see *libertas a culpa.*—(d), libertas animi, *the liberty of the spirit.*—(e), libertas a peccato, see *libertas a iustitia.*— —(f), libertas apparens and libertas vera, *the apparent* or *supposed liberty* and *the true* or *real liberty.*—(g), libertas arbitrii, *the freedom of arbitration* or *of the will.*—(h), libertas condicionata, *the conditioned* or *conditional liberty.*—(i), libertas gloriae, *freedom from misery in the glory of heaven.*—(j), libertas iudicii, *the liberty of opinion determined by a direction toward something.*—(k), libertas iustitiae, see *libertas a iustitia.*—(l), libertas naturalis, *natural liberty.* —(m), libertas peccati, see *libertas a iustitia.*—(n), libertas secundum quid and libertas simpliciter, *freedom in a certain respect* and *absolute freedom.*—(o), libertas simpliciter, see *libertas secundum quid.*—(p), libertas vera, see *libertas apparens.*—Kinds of *libertas* in this (2) sense are: (a), libertas a coactione and libertas a necessitate, *freedom from exterior force* and *freedom from inner necessity.*—(b), libertas ad bonum and libertas ad malum, *freedom for good* and *freedom for evil.* Cf. *libertas quantum ad ordinem finis.*—(c), libertas ad malum, see *libertas ad bonum.*— (d), libertas a necessitate, see *li-*

bertas a coactione.—(e), libertas electionis, *the freedom of choice.* —(f), libertas quantum ad actum, libertas quantum ad obiectum and libertas quantum ad ordinem finis, *freedom with reference to the decision of the will's activity, freedom with reference to the object of the will's activity,* and *freedom with reference to the direction of the will's activity toward the final aim of man,* i.e., *libertas exercitii seu contradictionis, libertas disparitatis seu specificationis* and *libertas moralitatis seu contrarietatis.* —(g), libertas quantum ad obiectum, see *libertas quantum ad actum.*—(h), libertas quantum ad ordinem finis, see *libertas quantum ad actum.*—On causa libertatis, see *causa;* on lex libertatis, see *lex;* on status libertatis, see *status* under 4.

libet, libuit and libitum, 2, *v. n.,* imper., *it pleases, is pleasing, is agreeable.*—The following phrases occur: ad libitum, *at will.*— —pro libito, *at will.*—libens, entis, *P. a., voluntary, willingly.*— libenter, *adv., willingly, cheerfully, gladly, with pleasure.*

libidinose, see *libidinosus.*

libidinosus, a, um, *adj., sensual, lustful, libidinous.* On amor libidinosus, see *amor* under 1; on appetitus libidinosus, see *appetitus* under 1; on voluptas libidinosa, see *voluptas.*—libidinose, *adv., sensually, lustfully, wantonly.*

libido, inis, *f.*, (1) *desire, enjoyment*, (2) *inordinate desire, sordid enjoyment*, (3) *inordinate sensual appetite.*—Kinds of *libido* in this (1) sense are: (a), **libido inordinata,** *the inordinate* or *unregulated desire.*—(b), **libido privata,** *the desire of the individual as such.*—Kinds of *libido* in this (2) sense are: (a), **libido actualis** and **libido habitualis,** *the inordinate desire in the sense of an action* and *that in the sense of a state.*—(b), **libido appetitus sensitivi** and **libido voluntatis,** *the inordinate desire of the sensual appetitive faculty* and *that of the will.*—(c), **libido habitualis,,** see *libido actualis.*—(d), **libido voluntatis,** see *libido appetitus sensitivi.*

libo, are, avi, atum, 1, *v. a.*, *to take a taste* of a thing.

libra, ae, *f.*, (1) *a pound*, a variable unit of weight or mass used as a standard in several countries for the measurement of any commodity bought and sold by weight, (2) *a pound*, a monetary unit of weight.

licenter, *adv.*, see *licet.*

licentia, ae, *f.*, (1) *leave to do as one pleases, permission*, (2) *unrestrained liberty, unbounded license.*

licentio, are, avi, atum, 1, *v. a.*, *to permit, to allow to be done.*

licet, cuit, and citum est, 2, *v. n.* and *impers.*, *it is lawful, it is allowed*, or *permitted; one may* or *can, one is at liberty* to do so

and so, used (1) with *neutr.* of the *rel. pron.* as a subject without a *dat.*, (2) with the *inf.* or a *subject-clause* with or without a *dat.*, (3) with *ut*, (4) with *inf.* and *subject acc.*—(II). *transf.*, when *licet* introduces a subordinate proposition which makes a concession without abandoning the main proposition, it is used as a conjunction corresponding to *quamquam, quamvis, etsi.* In late Latin it is, like these, connected with the indicative. St. Thomas uses it consistently with the subjunctive. It is often opposed to *tamen* in the main clause. As an *adv.*, with *adj.*, or *part.*, *although.*—**licenter,** *adv.*, *freely, according to one's own pleasure* or *fancy;* and in a bad sense, *without restraint, boldly, imprudently, licentiously.*

licitator, oris, *m.*, (an old erroneous reading for illicitator) *one who bids at an auction to make others bid higher, a sham-bidder, mock-purchaser*, used in the S.T. only in quot.

licite, see *licitus.*

licitor, ari, atus, 1, *v. dep.*, *to offer a price, to bid* for any thing, used in the S.T. only in quot.

licitus, a, um, *P. a.*, *permitted, allowed, lawful, licit*, the opposite of *illicitus.* On **iudicium licitum,** see *iudicium* under 2; on **iuramentum licitum,** see *iuramentum.*—**licite,** *adv.*, *rightfully, lawfully, licitly.*

ligamen, inis, *n.*, *a ligament, bond,* an existing marriage bond which is a diriment impediment to another marriage. It is often known as the impediment of previous marriage.

ligamentum, i, *n.*, *a band, tie,* used here figuratively with *sensus*, **ligamentum sensus,** *suspension of the senses,* or a temporary ceasing of operation on the part of the senses.—**ligamentum rationis,** *the fettering of the reason.*

ligatio, onis, *f.*, *a binding, fettering,* used *lit.*, and *fig.*

ligneus, a, um, *adj.*, *of wood, wooden.*

lignum, i, *n.*, *that which is gathered,* i.e., for firewood, (1) *lit.,* (a) *wood, firewood,* (b) *in gen., timber, wood,* the hard substance of a tree cut for use, as for building, manufacturing purposes, etc., (2) *transf.,* (a) *wood,* something made of wood, (b) *a rod, staff,* (c) *a tree,* (d) *a beam,* a long horizontal piece of wood. —The following are some of the numerous phrases in which *lignum* is used.—**ligna paradisi,** *the trees of Paradise,* or the trees in the Garden of Eden whose fruit Adam and Eve were permitted to eat.—**ligna fructifera,** *fruit-trees.*—**lignum densarum frondum,** *trees of dense foliage.* The following phrases refer to that particular tree in the Garden of Paradise, of whose fruit, by God's formal and clearly understood protest,

Adam and Eve were forbidden to eat.—**lignum scientiae boni et mali,** *the tree of knowledge of good and evil.*—**lignum vitae,** *the tree of life.*—**lignum vetitum,** *the forbidden tree.*—**lignum** (alone), *the particular tree,* or *the forbidden tree.*

ligo, are, avi, atum, 1, *v. a.*, (1) *lit.,* (a) *to bind, tie, fetter* a person, (b) *to tie, bind, fasten* something together, (2) *fig.,* (a) *to fetter* a person with a non-material bond, (b) *to fetter, suspend* the action of, as of the reason, sense, etc., (c) *to bind, unite* persons in matrimony, (d) *to unite, bring together* abstract objects, (e) *to restrain, hold in check* potential qualities of a substance, (f) **ligare et solvere,** *to bind* and *loose,* a phrase signifying the power promised by Christ to the rulers of His Church when He said to the Apostles: Whatsoever you shall bind upon earth, shall be bound also in Heaven; and whatsoever you shall loose upon earth, shall be loosed also in Heaven (Matth., 18). By this Christ conferred upon the rulers of His Church the power to bind the faithful to the observance of the laws and to loose them from impediments to eternal happiness, especially from sin and its consequent debt of punishment, (g) *to bind, oblige, constrain* with authority to do or not to do something.—**ligatus,** a, um, *P. a.,* (1) *lit., bound, tied,* (2) *fig., fettered.*

ligo, onis, *m.*, *a mattock, grub-axe, hoe,* used in the S.T. only in quot.

lilium, ii, *n.*, *a lily,* used in the S.T. only in quot.

limatio, onis, *f.*, *limation,* the act of filing or polishing.

limbus, i, *m.*, *Limbo,* a special place of detention for souls who are not worthy of admission to heaven. On **poena limbi,** see *poena.*—Kinds of *limbus* in this latter sense are: (a), **limbus inferni seu patrum,** *the limbo of hell,* or *of the Patriarchs* where the souls of the just awaited the redemption of Christ. This limbo no longer exists.—(b), **limbus patrum,** see *limbus inferi.*—(c), **limbus puerorum,** *the limbo for children,* i.e., the place where the souls of children who died without baptism are kept. It is a place of perpetual happiness on the level of nature.

limen, inis, *n.*, (1) *a threshold,* (2) *entrance porch,* (3) *a shrine* or *church* erected in honor of some saint.—**carere ecclesiasticis liminibus,** *to be cut off from the Church.*

limes, itis, *m.*, (1) lit., *a boundary, limit* between two fields or estates, (2) fig., *a boundary, limit.*

limito, are, avi, atum, 1, *v. a.*, *to fix, limit, determine, settle,* used fig.—**limitatus,** a, um, *P. a.*, *limited.*

limpide, *adv.*, see *limpidus.*

limipiditas, atis, *f.*, *lucidity, clearness,* synonym of *claritas.*

limipidus, a, um, *adj.*, *clear,* used fig.—**limpide,** *adv.*, *clearly.*

limus, i, *m.*, *slime, mud.*

linea, ae, *f.*, (1) *a line* in the proper sense of the word, (2) *a line* in the improper sense of the word, *descent* (of blood relationship).— Kinds of *linea* in this (1) sense are: (a), **linea abstracta seu mathematica** and **linea naturalis,** *the abstract* or *mathematical line,* and *the natural line* or *that occurring in the things of nature.* —(b), **linea circularis** and **linea helica,** *the circular* and *the spiral line.*—(c), **linea curva, linea reflexa,** and **linea recta,** *the crooked* or *curved line, the bent* or *broken line,* and *the straight line.* —(d), **linea determinata seu finita** and **linea infinita,** *the determined* or *limited line* and *the unlimited line.*—(e), **linea finita,** see *linea determinata.*—(f), **linea helica,** see *linea circularis.*—(g), **linea imperfecta** and **linea perfecta,** *the imperfect* and *the perfect line.*—(h), **linea infinita,** see *linea determinata.*—(i), **linea irrationalis** and **linea rationalis,** *the inconceivable* and *the conceivable line.*—(j), **linea mathematica,** see *linea abstracta.*—(k), **linea mixta** and **linea simplex,** *the mixed* and *the simple line.*—(l), **linea naturalis,** see *linea abstracta.*—(m), **linea perfecta,** see *linea imperfecta.*—(n), **linea rationalis,** see *linea irrationalis.*—(o), **linea recta,** see *linea curva.*—(p), **linea reflexa,** see *linea curva.*—(q), **linea sim-**

plex, see *linea mixta.*—(r), **linea visualis,** *the visual line.*—Kinds of *linea* in this (2) sense are: (a), **linea adscendentium, linea descendentium,** and **linea transversalis,** *ascending, descending,* and *collateral blood relationship.*—(b), **linea consanguinitatis,** *the line of blood relationship.*—(c), **linea descendentium,** see *linea adscendentium.*—(d), **linea transversalis,** see *linea adscendentium.*

linealiter, *adv., in the manner of lines.*

lineamentum, i, *n.,* (1) *lit., a line,* (2) *transf., a feature, lineament,* any part or lineament of the human face; one of the several projections, depressions, outlines, etc., of the face that give it expression and character; in the plural, *the whole face, countenance.*

linearis, e, *adj., linear, of* or *belonging to lines.*

lineus, a, um, *adj., linen, of flax* or *lint.*—**linea** (**vestis**), ae, *f., a linen garment.*

lingua, ae, *f.,* (1) *lit., the tongue,* (2) *transf.,* (a) since the tongue is an organ of speech, *a tongue, utterance, speech, language,* (b) *the tongue* or *language* of a people, (c) *dialect, idiom, mode of speech,* (d) of tongue-shaped things as fiery *tongues.*—The following phrases are of frequent occurrence: **corrigere linguam,** *to hold one's tongue.*—**linguae detrahentium,** *the tongues of backbiters.*—**lingua pruriens,** *an itch-*

ing tongue, a detracting tongue.—**loqui duplici lingua,** *to speak with a double tongue* or with duplicity of speech.—**praeceps lingua,** *a hasty tongue, hasty words.*—**labilitas linguae humanae,** *the lability* or *inconstancy of the human tongue* often called, *the frailty of the human tongue.*—**rea lingua,** *a guilty tongue.*—**munus a lingua,** *oral remuneration,* praise expressed in order to procure human favor, or a request whereby favor is obtained.—**lingua adulatoris,** *the tongue of the flatterer.*—**astuta lingua,** *a cunning tongue.*—**lingua eucharis,** *a gracious tongue.*—**linquae vipereae,** *vipers' tongues, slanderers' tongues.*—**lingua foetida,** *a corrupt tongue,* the language of a perverted character.—**lapsus linguae,** *a slip of the tongue, a lapse in speech.*—**usus linguae,** *the use of speech.*—**donum linguarum,** *the gift of tongues,* a miraculous power of preaching in unknown tongues with which the apostles were endowed.

linio, ire, ivi, itum, 4, *to daub, besmear, anoint, to spread* or *rub over.*

linitio, onis, *f., an anointing.*

linteamen, inis, *n., a linen cloth.*

linteum, i, *n., a linen cloth.*

linum, i, *n.,* (1) *lit., flax,* (2) *transf.,* (a) *a thread,* (b) *linen.*

Linus, i, *m., Linus,* Pope, first bishop of Rome after the apostles, and identified by Irenaeus (III, 2) with the Linus from whom St.

Paul sent greetings to Timothy (2 Tim. IV. 21).

lippitudo, inis, *f.*, *lippitude, chronic ophthalmia, blearedness of the eye;* gummy eyelids due to profuse secretion of the sebaceous humor.

lippus, a, um, *adj.*, *blear-eyed, bleared, inflamed.*

liquefacio, ere, feci, factum, 3, *v. a.*, *to make liquid, to melt, dissolve, liquefy.*—**liquefactus,** a, um, *P. a.*, (1) *lit.*, *molten*, (2) *fig.*, *weakened.*

liquefactio, onis, *f.*, *a melting,* used *lit.* and *fig.*

liquefactivus, a, um, *adj.*, *liquefactive,* pertaining to or productive of liquefaction.

liqueo, ere, liqui or licui, 2, *v. n.*, *to be clear, manifest, apparent, evident,* used in the third person sing., used in the S.T. only in quot.

liquidum, i, *n.*, *clearness, certainty.*

liquor, oris, *m.*, *a liquid, fluid,* (1) in *gen.*, (2) in *partic.*, *liquor, any alcoholic liquor.*—**liquor olivae,** *liquid extract of olives.*

lis, litis, *f.*, (1) in *gen.*, *strife, angry contention, hostile struggling, fighting,* (2) in *partic.*, (a) *a lawsuit, an action* or *process at law,* (b) *strife, disunion* or the lack of harmony and agreement between things inanimate.

litania, ae, *f.*, *a litany,* a liturgical form of prayer in which the clergy lead and the people respond, the same form of response

being repeated in a number of successive clauses.

litigans, antis, *m.*, see *litigo.*

litigiosus, a, um, *adj.*, *fond of disputes, contentious, litigious.* On **disputatio litigiosa,** see *disputatio;* on **ratio litigiosa,** see *ratio;* on **syllogismus litigiosus,** see *syllogismus.*

litigium, i, *n.*, (1) *a dispute, quarrel, strife,* (2) *litigation.*

litigo, are, avi, atum, 1, *v. n.*, *to dispute, quarrel, strive.*—**litigare inter se,** *to contradict one another.*—**litigans,** antis, *m.*, *a litigant.*

littera, ae, *f.*, (1) *a letter* (of the alphabet, *word* (spoken as well as written), (2) *a reading, passage from a book, text,* (3) *a document, letter,* i.e., *epistle, book, scientific work, science.*—On **disciplina litterarum,** see *disciplina* under 3.—**ad seu secundum litteram,** *according to the letter of the text* or *word, literal, word for word.* On **circumstantia litterae,** see *circumstantia* under 1.

litteralis, e, *adj.*, *literal, word for word,* opposite of *figuralis* and *mystica.* On **causa litteralis,** see *causa* under 3; on **intellectus litteralis,** see *intellectus;* on **ratio litteralis,** see *ratio;* on **sensus litteralis,** see *sensus.*—**litteraliter,** *adv.*, *literally, word for word.*

litteraliter, *adv.*, see *litteralis.*

litteratura, ae, *f.*, *letters, learning.*

litteratus, a, um, *adj.*, (1) *marked by letters, separated by letters,* (2) *lettered, learned.*

Livius, i, *m., Livius* (Livy), Titus Patavinus, (59 B.C.-17 A.D.) a Roman historian; of his *History of Rome,* 35 out of 142 books are extant.

livor, oris, *m., envy, spite, malice, ill-will.*

lixatus, a, um, *P. a., boiled.*

lixivium, i, *n., a lixivium, lye,* an infusion of ashes in water.

localis, e, *adj., of* or *belonging to a place, local.* On **approximatio localis,** see *approximatio;* on **continentia localis,** see *continentia* under 2; on **distinctio localis,** see *distinctio* under 2; on **esse locale,** see *esse;* on **motus localis,** see *motus* under 1; on **mutatio secundum esse locale,** see *mutatio;* on **ordo localis,** see *ordo* under 1; on **processio localis,** see *processio.*—**localiter,** *adv., locally.*

localiter, *adv.,* see *localis.*

locatio, onis, *f., a contract of letting* or *hiring, a lease.*

locativus, a, um, *adj., making spacious, making local.* On **virtus locativa,** see *virtus.*

locellus, i, *m., dim., a chest* or *small box* for money, trinkets, etc.

loco, are, avi, atum, 1, *v. a., to make spacious, make room, place, dispose.*—**locatus,** a, um, *P. a., placed, disposed, located.* On **corpus locans et locatum,** see *corpus.*—**locatum coniunctum,** *the located connected with its place,* the opposite of *locatum divisum,* i.e., *the located torn from its place* or *the locat-*

ed *existing in its place but considered as something distinct from it.*

loculi, orum, *m. dim., plural., a purse, a bag.*

locuples, etis, *adj.,* (1) *in gen., rich, wealthy, opulent,* (2), *transf., that which is able to answer for a thing, that is a good surety, responsible, trustworthy,* used in the S.T. only in quot.

locus, i, *m., plur.,* loca, orum, (1) *space, location,* in the wider sense of the word, i.e., that where something is, (2) *space, place, spot* in the proper sense of the word, i.e., the surfaces of the surrounding medium or body, e.g., air, water, etc., (*to tou periechontis peras akineton proton tout'estin ho topos* of Aristotle), (3) *space, place, spot, seat,* in the improper sense of the word, (4) *quotation adduced for sake of proof,* synonym of *argumentum.*—Kinds of *locus* in this (1) sense are: (a), **locus carceralis** and **locus poenalis,** *the place of imprisonment* and *that of punishment.*—(b), **locus corporalis seu corporeus** and **locus spiritualis,** *the physical* and *the spiritual place.* Physical place requires the contact and extension of quantity; spiritual place requires merely the presence of operation, or the application of power.—(c), **locus divisibilis** and **locus indivisibilis seu punctualis,** *the divisible* and *the indivisible* or *punctiform place.*—(d), **locus exterior,** *the outer* or *exterior place.*—(e), **locus indivisibilis,** see *locus divisibilis.*—(f), **locus metaphorice dictus** and **locus proprie dictus,** *the place in the transferred* and *in the proper sense of the word.*—(g), **locus poenalis,** see *locus carceralis.*—(h), **locus proprie dictus,** see *locus metaphorice dictus.*—(i), **locus punctualis,** see *locus divisibile.*—(j), **locus specierum,** *the place where the intellectual species of things are kept,* i.e., *the intellect,* the *topos eidon* of Aristotle.—(k), **locus spiritualis,** see *locus corporalis.* On **contrarius secundum locum,** see *contrarius* under 1; on **motivum secundum locum,** see *motivus;* on **motus secundum locum seu lationis secundum locum,** see *motus* under 1; on **movere secundum locum,** see *movere;* on **mutatio loci,** see *mutatio;* on **ordo secundum locum,** see *ordo* under 1; on **prius secundum locum,** see *prior* under 1; on **simul secundum locum,** see *simul;* on **species loci,** see *species* under 8; on **totalitas loci,** see *totalitas;* on **transmutatio secundum locum,** see *transmutatio* under 1.— **in loco esse** or **mensurari loco et contineri a loco,** i.e., *to be in one space* or *at one place* is possible in several ways: (a), **circumscriptive seu localiter** and **definitive seu operative,** *completely* or *quantitatively* and *definitely* or *operatively,* i.e., in such a way

that the located is entirely surrounded by the locating medium and one part of the delimited corresponds to each part of the limit, which can be verified only of things having quantitative extension, or on the other hand, if this is not the case, that which is operating in a space or place is definitely there because it cannot at the same time be operating somewhere else, at the same time.—(b), **definitive,** see *circumscriptive.*—(c), **localiter,** see *circumscriptive.*—(d), **metaphorice,** *in a metaphorical* or *improper manner.*—(e), **per accidens** and **per se,** *indirectly by reason of something else* and *directly according to itself* or *its own nature.*—(f), **per se,** see *per accidens.*—(g), **secundum quid** and **simpliciter,** *in a certain respect* or *according to something* and *simply* or *absolutely.*—(h), **simpliciter,** see *secundum quid.*—(i), **ut in loco, ut operans in operato, ut pars** and **ut terminus,** *as in the space* or *place* or *as in such, as effecting in the effected* or *as a part* or *as a terminus.*—(j), **ut operans in operato,** see *ut in loco.*—(k), **ut pars,** see *ut in loco.*—(l), **ut terminus,** see *ut in loco.*—Kinds of *locus* in this (3) sense are: (a), **locus communis seu universalis** and **locus proprius seu determinatus,** *the common* or *universal place of all bodies* and *the proper place for each one of them* or *designated for each.*—

(b), **locus conservans** and **locus continens,** *the preserving* and *enclosing place.*—(c), **locus continens,** see *locus conservans.*—(d), **locus determinatus,** see *locus communis.*—(e), **locus naturalis** and **locus non-naturalis,** *the natural* and *the unnatural place.*—(f), **locus non-naturalis,** see *locus naturalis.*—(g), **locus per accidens** and **locus per se,** *the place through another body* and *the place through itself,* i.e., that which is the place of a thing from something outside and which is the place of a thing as such.—(h), **locus per se,** see *locus per accidens.*—(i), **locus primus,** *the first* or *the place that belongs to a body first.*—(j), **locus proprius,** see *locus communis.*—(k), **locus universalis,** see *locus communis.*—(l), **locus vacuus,** *the empty space.*—Kinds of *locus* in this (4) sense are: (a), **locus ab auctoritate,** *the proof of authority.*—(b), **locus a causa,** *the proof deduced from the cause* or *a priori proof.* —(c), **locus a divisione,** *the proof derived from division* or *inductive proof.*—(d), **locus affirmativus** and **locus negativus,** *the affirmative* and *the negative proof.* —(e), **locus a maiori** and **locus a minori,** *the proof concluding from the greater to the smaller* and *from the smaller to the greater.*—(f), **locus a minori,** see *locus a maiori.*—(g), **locus apparens seu sophisticus** and **locus verus,** *the apparent* or *sophistic*

and *the true proof.*—(h), **locus a simili,** *the proof derived from a similarity* or *from an analogy.*— (i), **locus negativus,** see *locus affirmativus.*—(j), **locus dialecticus,** *the dialectic proof* or *the proof from probability.*—(k), **locus sophisticus,** see *locus apparens.*

locusta, ae, *f., a locust.*

locutio, onis, *f.,* (1) *speech, language, discoursing, speaking* in the narrower sense, i.e., the communication of a thought through word of mouth, synonym of *dictio* and *loquela,* (2) *speech, language, speaking* in the wider sense, i.e., the communication of a thought, (3) *speech, utterance, expression,* (4) *a mode of speech, linguistic expression,* synonym of *dictio, nomen, oratio,* and *terminus.*—On **elementum locutionis,** see *elementum* under 1; on **gratia locutionis,** see *gratia* under 2; on **suppositum locutionis,** see *suppositum* under 2.—Kinds of *locutio* in this (1) sense are: (a), **locutio exterior seu vocalis** and **locutio interior seu spiritualis seu intellegibilis seu intellectualibus signis expressa,** *the exterior* or *spoken word* and *the interior* or *spiritual* or *intellectual word* or *speech through intellectual signs.* —(b), **locutio intellectualibus signis expressa,** see *locutio exterior.*—(c), **locutio intellegibilis,** see *locutio exterior.*—(d), **locutio interior,** see *locutio exterior.*—(e), **locutio similitudinaria** and **locutio vera,** *the apparent* and *the* *real speaking.*—(f), **locutio spiritualis**, see *locutio exterior.*—(g), **locutio vera**, see *locutio similitudinaria.*—Kinds of *locutio* in this (2) sense are: (a), **locutio exterior**, *the exterior speech,* or *expression for those standing outside.*—(b), **locutio falsa** and **locutio vera**, *the false* and *the true speech.*—(c), **locutio vera**, see *locutio falsa.*—Kinds of *locutio* in this (3) sense are: (a), **locutio abusiva**, *the abusive expression.*—(b), **locutio emphatica**, *the emphatic expression* or *the expression containing special emphasis.*—(c), **locutio exemplaris**, *the exemplary expression* or *that indicating an example.*—(d), **locutio figurata seu figurativa seu symbolica seu tropica seu metaphorica seu transumptiva seu impropria** and **locutio propria**, *the figurative* or *symbolic* or *the improper* and *the proper expression.*—(e), **locutio hyperbolica**, *the immoderate* or *exaggerating expression.*—(f), **locutio impropria**, see *locutio figurata.*—(g), **locutio metaphorica**, see *locutio figurata.*—(h), **locutio metonymica**, *the expression that forms an exchange of names.*—(i), **locutio propria**, see *locutio figurata.*—(j), **locutio symbolica**, see *locutio figurata.*—(k), **locutio synedochica**, *the expression that designates something by something else.*—(l), **locutio transumptiva**, see *locutio figurata.*—(m), **locutio tropica**, see *locutio figurata.*

locutor, oris, *m., a speaker, orator,* used in the S.T. only in quot.

logicalis, e, *adj., logical,* i.e., belonging to logic, referring to it, synonym of *logicus.* On **scientia logicalis**, see *scientia* under 1.

logice, *adv.*, see *logicus.*

logicus, a, um, *adj., reasonable, logical,* i.e., belonging to or concerning logic, synonym of *logicalis.* On **consideratio logica**, see *consideratio;* on **definitio logica**, see *definitio* under 2; on **genus logicum**, see *genus* under 2; on **intentio logica**, see *intentio* under 3; on **pars logica**, see *pars* under 1; on **probatio logica**, see *probatio* under 2; on **ratio logica**, see *ratio* under 13 and 14.—**logica** sc. **ars**, *the art of logic.*—Kinds of "logica" are: **logica docens** and **logica utens**, *didactic* or *pure logic* and *the practical* or *applied logic,* i.e., logic taken by itself as science and the application of its rules and laws within the sciences.—**logicus**, i, *m.,* sc. *philosophus, the logician.*

logica, orum, *n., logic,* synonym of *logica* sc. *ars sive scientia.*—**logice**, *adv., in a logical manner, in a logical respect, in the sense of logic, logically,* the opposite of *naturaliter* and *physice.* On **considerare logice**, see *considerare;* on **genus logice sumptum**, see *genus* under 2; on **unum logice**, see *unus.*

longaevitas, atis, *f., long life, longevity.*

longanimitas, atis, *f., long-suffer-
ing, patience, forbearance, long-
animity.—longanimitas* is one of
the *fructus Spiritus Sancti.* Cf.
fructus under 2.

longe, *adv.,* see *longus.*

longinquus, a, um, *adj.,* (1) *lit.,*
in space, *far removed, far off,
remote, distant,* (2) *transf.,* of
time, *long, of long duration* or
continuance, prolonged, lasting.
—*a longinquo, from a great distance.*

longitudo, inis, *f.,* (1) *lit., length,*
(2) *transf.,* of time, *length, long
duration.*

Longobardi, orum, *m., the Lombards.*

longus, a, um, *adj., long,* (1) *lit.,
long,* (2) *transf.,* of time, *long,
of long duration* or *continuance,
tedious.—longior via, a more
tedious way.—causa longioris vitae, for prolonging life.—longe,
adv.,* (1) *lit., a long way off,
far off, at a distance,* (2) *fig.,*
(a) of time; *long, for a long
period,* (b) *much, very much,
by far,* esp. with comp., (c)
far, remote from the purpose.—
a longe, from afar, at a distance.
—*valde longe, very far off.—de
longe, from afar.*

loquacitas, atis, *f., talkativeness,
loquacity,* used in the S.T. only
in quot.

loquax, acis, *adj., talkative, loqua-
cious.*

loquela, ae, *f., speech, words,
language, discourse.*

loquor, loqui, locutus, 3, *v. dep.
n.* and *a.,* (1) *neutr., to speak,
tell, say,* used *absol.* and with
dat., (2) *act., to speak, mention.*

Loth, *m., indecl., Lot, son of
Haran* and *nephew of Abraham.*

lotio, onis, *f., a washing.*

lubricus, a, um, *adj., uncertain.—
lubricum, i, n., a slippery* or *hazardous state, period,* or *season;
inconstancy.*

Lucas, ae, *m., Luke,* Saint, the
third Evangelist, and a disciple
of St. Paul whom he joined at
Troas in the year 53. He was
a native of Antioch in Syria, a
physician by profession, and a
painter of no mean skill. Luke
is the author of the third Gospel and of the Acts of the Apostles. He wrote both works in
Greek.

luceo, ere, xi, 2, v. n., (1) *lit., to
shed* or *cause light to shine,
gleam, glitter, to be light* or
clear, (2) *fig.,* (a) *to shine
upon,* (b) *to show through,
shine, be discernible.—lucens*
entis, *P. a., shining, resplendent,*
used *fig.*

lucerna, ae, *f., a lamp, a lantern,*
used *lit.* and *fig.*

Lucia, ae, *f., Lucy,* a virgin and
martyr of Syracuse in Sicily,
whose feast is celebrated on
December 13.

lucidativus, a, um, *adj., light-giving.*

lucidus, a, um, *adj.,* (1) *lit., containing light, full of light, clear,
bright, shining,* (2) *transf., lucid,*

bright, lightsome, said of the bodies of the just after resurrection, (3) *fig.,* (a) of persons, *enlightened,* (b) of statements, *lucid, clear, intelligible.*—**lucida intervalla,** *lucid intervals,* periods of temporary sanity occurring between attacks of lunacy.

lucifer, feri, *m., the morning star,* used in the S.T. only in quot.

Lucinius, ii, *m., Lucinius,* a wealthy Spaniard of Baetica in the end of the fourth century. He opposed the Zoroastrian opinions, which had been introduced into Spain from Africa by Marcus and propagated by Priscillian, Agape, and others. This tendency brought him into relations with St. Jerome, who was then living at Bethlehem. In 397 he sent several scribes to Bethlehem to copy the scriptural works of Jerome; and they returned in Lent 398, having fulfilled their task and bringing with them a letter from Jerome (71), in which Jerome describes the works which had been copied out and thanks him for presents which he had sent, and answers questions about fasting on Saturdays. St. Thomas quotes letter seventy-one.

Lucius, ii, *m.,* (1) *Lucius,* praepositus of the church of St. Juventius at Ticinum, to whom Urban II addresses a letter (P.

L., 151, CCLXXIII), (2) *Lucius III,* pope from 1181 to 1185. Successor of Alexander III. Held the Council of Verona, which the Emperor Frederick Barbarossa likewise attended, and published edicts against the Cathari and Waldenses.

lucrativus, a, um, *adj., lucrative, profitable.*

lucrifacio, ere, feci, factum, 3, *v. v., to lucrify, gain, win* (for Christ).

lucror, ari, atus, i, *v. dep. a.,* (1) *lit.,* (a) in *gen., to gain, get, acquire, make* (as profit), (b) in *partic., to gain* valuable results, useful consequences, (2) *fig., to acquire, win.*

lucrosus, a, um, *adj., lucrative, profitable,* used in the S.T. only in quot.

lucrum, i, *n.,* (1) *lit., gain, profit, advantage,* (2) *transf.,* (a) *love of gain, avarice, greed,* (b) *wealth, riches,* (3) fig., *advantage.*

lucta, ae, *f., a wrestling.*

luctuosus, a, um, *adj., causing sorrow, sorrowful, mournful.*

luctus, us, *m., sorrow, mourning, grief, affliction.*

luculenter, *adv., luculently, clearly,* used here in the *sup.*—**luculentissime,** *very clearly.*

ludibrium, ii, *n., a mockery.*

ludicrus, a, um, *adj., that serves for a sport* or *a past time, amusing, sportive.* On **actio ludrica,** see *actio* under 1.

ludificator, oris, *m.*, *a mocker, one who makes game* of another, used in the S.T. only in quot.

ludifico, are, avi, atum, 1, *v. a.*, and *n.*, *to delude.*

ludo, ere, si, sum, 3, *v. a.*, and *n.*, (1) *lit.*, *to play, play at a game of some kind, to engage in sport* or *lively recreation*, (2) *fig.*, (a) *to jest*, (b) *to play a part on the stage.*

ludus, i, *m.*, (1) *lit.*, (a) in *gen.*, *a play, game, diversion, pastime,* a contest, physical or mental, conducted according to set rules and undertaken for amusement or recreation or winning a stake, (b) in *partic.*, *ludi, public games, spectacles*, (c) *stage plays*, (d) *a school* for elementary instruction and discipline, (2) *transf.*, *game, sport* of any kind; *play, frolic, fun, playful action; joke, jest.*

Lugdunum, i, *n.*, *a city of Gaul, at the confluence of the Arar* and *Rhodanus,* now Lyons.

lugeo, ere, xi, ctum, 2, *v. n.*, and *a.*, *to mourn, lament, bewail.*

lumbare, is, *n.*, *an apron for the loins.*

lumbus, i, *m.*, *a loin.*

lumen, inis, *n.*, *light* in the general sense of the word, but always derived or produced, the effect of *lux.* It is a quality produced by a self-luminous body which is differentiated from its effect by the name *lux.*—On the difference between *lumen* and *lux,* see *lux.*—Kinds of *lumen* in general are: (a), **lumen angelicum,** *the light of knowledge given to the angels.*—(b), **lumen connaturale seu naturale seu naturae seu naturalis rationis** and **lumen supernaturale seu intellectuale excedens lumen naturalis rationis,** *the natural* and *the supernatural light of human reason.*—(c), **lumen corporale** and **lumen spirituale,** *the physical* or *material* and *the spiritual* or *immaterial light.*—(d), **lumen creatum** and **lumen increatum,** *the created* and *the uncreated light.*—(e), **lumen Dei seu divinum,** *the light of God* or *the divine light.*—(f), **lumen divinae gloriae seu gloriae** and **lumen gratiae seu gratuitum,** *the light bestowed in the divine* or *heavenly glory* and *that bestowed on man on earth by grace.*—(g), **lumen divinae revelationis seu fidei,** *the assistance given to the created intellect consisting in divine revelation* or *the supernatural virtue of faith.*—(h), **lumen divinum,** see *lumen Dei.*—(i), **lumen essentiale** and **lumen naturali lumini rationis superadditum,** *the essential* and *the added* or *non-essential light of human reason.*—(j), **lumen fidei,** see *lumen divinae revelationis.*—(k), **lumen gloriae,** see *lumen divinae gloriae.*—(l), **lumen gratiae,** see *lumen divinae gloriae.*—(m), **lumen gratuitum,** see *lumen divinae gloriae.*—(n), **lumen habituale,** *the light that has a permanent disposition* or *the* *static light.*—(o), **lumen increatum**, see *lumen creatum.*—(p), **lumen intellectuale seu intelligibile seu intellectus seu intellectualis naturae seu rationis**, *the intellectual light* or *the light of reason* or *that of a rational nature which belongs to man as well as to angels.*—(q), **lumen intellectuale excedens lumen naturalis rationis**, see *lumen connaturale.*—(r), **lumen intellectualis naturae**, see *lumen intellectuale.*—(s), **lumen intellectus**, see *lumen intellectuale.*—(t), **lumen intellectus agentis**, *the power of the agent intellect to abstract species from phantasms.*—(u), **lumen intelligibile**, see *lumen intellectuale.*—(v), **lumen naturae**, see *lumen connaturale.*—(w), **lumen naturale**, see *lumen connaturale.*—(x), **lumen naturalis rationis**, see *lumen connaturale.*—(y), **lumen prophetiae seu propheticum**, *the light of prophecy* or *the prophetic light.*—(z), **lumen propheticum**, see *lumen prophetiae.*—(a²), **lumen rationis**, see *lumen intellectuale.*—(b²), **lumen solare seu lumen solis**, *the light of the sun.*—(c²), **lumen spirituale**, see *lumen corporale.*—(d²), **lumen supernaturale**, see *lumen connaturale.*

luminare, aris, *n., a luminary, a heavenly body*, used *lit.* and *fig.*

luminositas, atis, *f., luminosity*, the quality or condition of being luminous.

luminosus, a, um, *adj., full of light, light, luminous.*

luna, ae, *f., the moon.*—The following phrases refer to the phases of the moon. These phases or appearances are presented according to the amount of the moon's illumination.—**certa augmenta lunae**, *certain increase*, or *growth* or *phases of the moon.*—**nova luna**, *the new moon*, i.e., when the moon is in conjunction with the sun and therefore invisible.—**luna plena** and **luna plenissima**, *the full moon*, when the earth is between the moon and the sun (disc wholly illuminated).—**diminutio lunae**, *waning of the moon*, periodical decrease in apparent size.—The following phrases consisting of *luna* with an ordinal numeral denote a particular day after the new moon.—**decima luna**, *the tenth moon* or the tenth day after the new moon.—**quarta decima luna**, *the fourteenth day of the moon.*

lunaris, e, *adj., of* or *belonging to the moon, lunar.*

lunaticus, i, *m., a crazy person, lunatic.*

lupanar, aris, *n., a brothel, a house of ill-repute.*

lupus, i, *m., a wolf*, used *lit.* and *fig.*

lusivus, a, um, *adj., lusive, playful, fond of entertainment.*

lutum, i, *n.*, (1) in *gen., mud, clay*, (2) in *partic.*

lux, lucis, *f.*, (1) *light* in the general sense of the word, whatever makes things perceptible or manifest, (2) *light* in the proper

sense of the word, the same as
lux corporalis under (1), (3)
lamp, a light-giving body.—
Kinds of *lux* in this (1) sense
are: (a), **lux angelica,** *the angelic light* or *that emanating from
an angel.*—(b), **lux corporalis seu
corporea** and **lux spiritualis,** *the
physical* or *material* and *the spiritual* or *immaterial light.*—(c), **lux
gloriae,** *the light of heavenly
glory.*—(d), **lux intellectualis seu
intellegibilis** and **lux sensibilis,**
the intellectual and *the sensible
light* or *the light of reason* and
that of the eyes.—(e), **lux intellegibilis,** see *lux intellectualis.*—(f),
lux sensibilis, see *lux intellectualis.* (g), **lux spiritualis,** see *lux
corporalis.*—One kind of *lux* in
this (2) sense is: **lux incorporata,**
light received in a body.

luxuria, ae, *f., voluptuousness,* the
opposite of *castitas,* inordinate
venereal pleasure, under the general virtue of *temperantia.* On
immunditia luxuriae, see *immunditia;* on **macula luxuriae,** see
macula; on **mollities luxuriae,** see
mollities under 2. *Luxuria* is one
of the seven capital sins; its *filiae,* i.e., offspring are: *caecitas*

*mentis, stultitia, inconsideratio,
praecipitatio, inconstantia, amor
sui, odium Dei, affectus saeculi,*
and *horror futuri.* Species luxuriae, i.e., the true kinds, are six:
*fornicatio simplex, adulterium,
incestus, stuprum, raptus,* and
vitium contra naturam.

luxuriose, *adv.,* see *luxuriosus.*

luxuriosus, a, um, *adj., voluptuous,
impure, excessive.* On **vita luxuriosa,** see *vita* under 3.—**luxuriose,** *adv., in a voluptuous* or *impure manner, voluptuously.*

luxus, us, *m., excess, luxury,* used
in the S.T. only in quot.

lymphatus, a, um, *P. a., diluted,
mixed with water.*

ly, *the,* a substitute for the missing
definite article in Latin. Some
consider the word *ly* as the old
Italian article *li* (modern il); others believe it to be the Arabic
article *al* read backwards, which
during the period of medieval
scholasticism was pronounced in
popular Arabic as ul or yl. Most
scholars favor the latter explanation for which parallel develop-
ments can be cited, e.g., *pipi*
as a name of God in the time of
Origen.

M

Macarius, ii, *m., Macarius* of Antioch, Patriarch, deposed in 681.
Macarius's dignity seems to have
been a purely honorary one, for
his patriarchate lay under the

dominion of the Sarcens, and he
himself resided at Constantinople. Nothing is known of him
before the Sixth General Council
which deposed him on account

of his Monothelitism; and after the council he disappeared in a Roman Monastery.

Macedonius, ii, *m., Macedonius,* (1) *heresiarch,* named patriarch of Constantinople by the Arians in 342, he was replaced in 347 by the Catholic Bishop Paulus. Replaced on the patriarchal see in 350, he remained thereon only until 360, at which time the Arians themselves deposed him. Then he became the head of a sect which denied the divinity of the Holy Ghost, (2) a friend of St. Augustine to whom he addresses letter 153. St. Thomas quotes from section 20 of this letter. This Macedonius was vicar of Africa in 414 A.D. and was charged with the duty of enforcing the imperial decrees against the recusant Donatists.

macellum, i, *n., a meat-market.*

maceratio, onis, *f., maceration,* the process of wasting or wearing away the body, flesh, etc.; *mortification.*

maceria, ae, *f., a wall.*

macero, are, avi, atum, 1, *v. a., to weaken, in body* or *mind,* (1) of the mind, *to torture, torment,* (2) of the body, *to chastise, afflict.*

Machabaeus, i, *m., Machabeus,* (1) *Judas Machabeus,* the third son of Mathathias. He drove the Syrians and the Hellenists out of Jerusalem, rededicated the Temple, and begun an offensive and defensive alliance with the Romans. Before the treaty was con-

cluded, however, Judas with 800 men risked battle at Laisa with an overwhelming army of Syrians under Bacchides and was slain. He was succeeded in command by his youngest brother Jonathan (161 B.C.), (2) **Machabaei,** orum, *m., the Machabees.* The story of the Machabees is written in two books of the Old Testament which bear that name. These books are so called because they contain the history of the people of God under the command of Judas Machabeus and his brethren.

Macharius, ii, *m., Macarius* the Elder, born in Upper Egypt about 300. He lived for sixty years in the desert of Skete, and for twenty of these years he said he had never once eaten, drunk or slept as much as nature required. A subtle heretic of the sect of the Hieracites, called so from Hierx, who in the reign of Diocletian denied the resurrection of the dead, had by his sophisms caused some to be unsettled in their faith. St. Macarius, to confirm them in the truth, raised a dead man to life. St. Thomas quoting from the Lives of the Fathers states that Macarius found a human skull and after praying asked whose skull it was. The head confessed that it belonged to a pagan priest who was condemned to hell.

machina, ae, *f., battering-ram, a military machine.*

machinatio, onis, *f.*, *a trick device,* used *fig.*

machinor, ari, atus, 1, *v. dep. a.*, *to contrive artfully, to scheme, plot.*

macies, ei, *f.*, of living beings and the parts of their bodies, (1) *leanness*, (2) *weakness*.

Macrobius, ii, *m.*, *Macrobius*, Ambrosius Theodosius. A grammarian probably of Greek extraction, since he says in the preface to his *Saturnalia* that Latin was to him a foreign tongue. He lived in the fourth century A.D., and was probably a pagan. He wrote on Cicero's *Somnium Scipionis* a commentary quoted by St. Thomas.

macto, are, avi, atum, 1, *v. freq. a.*, *to immolate, sacrifice,* used *fig.*, used in the S.T. only in quot.

macula, ae, *f.*, *a spot, mark, stain.*— Kinds of *macula* are: (a), **macula actualis** and **macula originalis**, *the stain as the result of an activity* and *the stain obtained by inheritance through origin.*—(b), **macula animae** and **macula in corpore**, *the stain of the soul* and *that of the body.*—(c), **macula culpae**, *the stain of blame* or *sin.* —(d), **macula homicidii**, *the sin of homicide.*—(e), **macula in corpore**, see *macula animae.*—(f), **macula luxuriae**, *the stain of sensuality.*—(g), **macula originalis**, see *macula actualis.*—(h), **macula peccati**, *the stain of sin.*

maculo, are, avi, atum, 1, *v. a.*, *to spot, stain, pollute, defile,* used *lit.* and *fig.*—**maculatus,** a, um, *P. a.*, *stained.*

maculosus, a, um, *adj.*, (1) *lit.*, *defective* in some way, (2) *fig.*, *defiled* with sin.

Madiantis, idis, c., *a Madianite*, or a descendant of Madian, son of Cetura (Gen. XXV. 2). The Madianites dwelt originally to the east of the Gulf of Akaba. Later, the Madianites allied themselves with the Moabites against Israel in war (Num. XXII) and in evil seduction (Num. XXV) for which a terrible vengeance was inflicted upon them (Num. XXXI).

madidans, antis, *P. a.*, *moistening, wetting,* used in the S.T. only in quot.

maenianum, i, *n.*, *a balcony, a projecting gallery* (first made use of by Maenius); commonly used in the plural.

Magdalena, ae, *f.*, also **Magdalene**, *indecl.*, *Magdalen, Magdalene*, of Magdala a town on the sea of Galilee. Mary of Magdala or Mary Magdalen is the appellation of a disciple of Christ named Mary, out of whom went seven devils.

Magi, orum, *m.*, *the Magi*, a proper name applied to members of the priestly caste of the Medes, used with specific reference to the wise men from the East who brought gifts to Jesus in Bethlehem. The appearance of a miraculous star caused them to leave the East in search of the King of whose birth the star was a sign.

The star guided them to the house of the Holy Family in Bethlehem where they offered to the child Jesus the choicest of Arabian gifts; gold, frankincense, and myrrh.

magicus, a, um, *adj.*, *of* or *belonging to magic, magic, magical.*

magister, tri, *m.*, (1) *teacher, master*, (2) *the teacher, the master per eminentiam*, i.e., the teacher of the sentences, Peter Lombard. —Kinds of *magister* in this (1) sense are: (a), **magister domus**, *the master* or *head of the house.* —(b), **magister gentium**, *the teacher of the gentiles*, i.e., the Apostle St. Paul.—(c), **magister sententiarum**, *the author of the Sentences*, i.e., Peter Lombard.

magisterium, ii, *n.*, (1) *lit.*, the highest form of teaching, imparting knowledge not only acquired from others, but authoritatively as well, *professorship*, (2) *fig.*, *teaching instruction, advice.*

magistralis, e, *adj.*, (1) *of* or *belonging to a master* or *teacher, masterly*, (2) *belonging to the teacher per eminentiam.*—On **cathedra magistralis**, see *cathedra*; on **disputatio magistralis**, see *disputatio.*

magistratus, us, *m.*, (1) *lit.*, *a magisterial office*, (2) *transf.*, *a magistrate.*

magnalia, ium, *n.*, *great things, glorious things, mighty works.*

magnanimitas, atis, *f.*, *magnanimity, high-mindedness, greatness of soul*, i.e., that virtue by the strength of which man strives after high honors which are difficult to obtain, the opposite of *pusillanimitas.*

magnanimiter, *adv.*, see *magnanimus.*

magnanimus, a, um, *adj.*, *great-souled, magnanimous, high-minded, high-spirited, generous*, the opposite of *pusillanimus.*—**magnanimiter**, *adv.*, *magnanimously, high-mindedly, courageously.*

magnas, atis, *m.*, *a great man, important person, magnate.*

magnes, etis, *m.*, *a magnet.*

magnificatio, onis, *f.*, (1) *glorification*, (2) *boasting.*

magnificentia, ae, *f.*, *grandeur, the virtue of expending money proportionately to the importance of the need, love of splendour*, i.e., the virtue of accomplishing something grand with money for a high purpose, the opposite of *parvificentia.*

magnifico, are, avi, atum, 1, *v. a.*, (1) *to make much of, to value greatly, to esteem highly, set a high value on*, (2) *transf.*, (a) *to magnify, praise highly*, (b) *to honor, exalt*, (c) *to enlarge, magnify.*

magnificus, a, um, *adj.*, *fond of grandeur* or *display, high-minded, great in soul*, the opposite of *parvificus.*—On the difference between *magnificus* and *liberalis*, see *magnificentia.*—**magnifice**, *adv.*, *grandly, sumptuously, gloriously.*

magnipendo, see *pendo*.

magnitudo, inis, *f.*, (1) *extent, magnitude,* size of continuous quantity, in the proper and narrow sense of the word, same as *magnitudo corporalis* under 2, (2) *greatness, magnitude,* in the general and wider sense of the word, (3) *greatness, magnitude* in the improper or figurative sense of the word, same as *magnitudo spiritualis* under 2, synonym of *quantitas,* (4) *greatness, magnitude,* in the metonymical sense of the word, i.e., *the great, something great.* On esse magnitudini, see *esse;* on finis magnitudinis, see *finis* under 1; on infinitum magnitudinis, in magnitudine et secundum magnitudinem, see *infinitus;* on posterius in magnitudine, see *posterior* under 2; on potentia in magnitudine, see *potentia* under 2; on principium magnitudinis, see *principium;* on transmutatio circa magnitudinem, see *transmutatio* under 1.—Kinds of *magnitudo* in this (1) sense are: (a), magnitudo circularis and magnitudo recta, *the circular* and *the straight magnitude.*—(b), magnitudo completa seu perfecta and magnitudo imperfecta, i.e., *the completed* or *perfected magnitude,* by which is meant chiefly the tridimensional object, and also the body fully developed in its own species, and *the uncompleted* or *unperfected magnitude,* by which is meant the line or the surface, and the still uncompleted body in its own species.—(c), magnitudo determinata seu finita and magnitudo infinita, *the limited* or *finite* and *the unlimited* or *infinite magnitude.*—(d), magnitudo finita, see *magnitudo determinata.* —(e), magnitudo heterogenea and magnitudo homogenea, *the heterogeneous* and *homogeneous magnitude* or *the magnitude consisting of dissimilar* and *similar parts.*—(f), magnitudo homogenea, see *magnitudo heterogenea.* —(g), magnitudo imperfecta, see *magnitudo completa.*—(h), magnitudo infinita, see *magnitudo determinata.*—(i), magnitudo irregularis and magnitudo regularis, *the irregular magnitude.*—(j), magnitudo mathematica and magnitudo naturalis, *the mathematical* or *abstract* and *the natural* or *physcial magnitude.*—(k), magnitudo naturalis, see *magnitudo mathematica.*—(l), magnitudo perfecta, see *magnitudo completa.*—(m), magnitudo recta, see *magnitudo circularis.*—(n), magnitudo regularis, see *magnitudo irregularis.*—(o), magnitudo simplex, *the simple* or *uncompounded magnitude.* Cf. also *magnitudo recta et circularis.*—Kinds of *magnitudo* in this (2) sense are: magnitudo corporalis seu sensibilis and magnitudo spiritualis, *the physical* or *sensible magnitude* and *the spiritual* or *intellectual magnitude.*—Kinds of *mag-*

nitudo in this (3) sense are: (a), **magnitudo affectus**, *the magnitude* or *strength of affection* or *attachment.*—(b), **magnitudo amoris seu caritatis**, *the magnitude* or *strength of love.*—(c), **magnitudo caritatis**, see *magnitudo amoris.*—(d), **magnitudo Dei**, *the magnitude* or *perfection of God.*—(e), **magnitudo delectationis**, *the magnitude of pleasure* or *delight.*—(f), **magnitudo habitus**, see *habitus* under 4.—(g), **magnitudo intensive**, *the magnitude of strain* and *exertion.*—(h), **magnitudo passionis**, *the magnitude* or *strength of emotion.*—(i), **magnitudo peccati**, *the magnitude* or *weight of sin.*—(j), **magnitudo perfectionis**, *the magnitude of perfection.*—(k), **magnitudo personae**, *the magnitude* or *grandeur of a person.*—(l), **magnitudo virtutis**, *the magnitude* or *greatness of power.*

magnopere, *adv.*, *earnestly*, used in the S.T. only in quot.—**maximopere**, *most particularly*, *especially*.

magnus, a, um, *adj.*, *great, large*, the opposite of *parvus.*—Kinds of *magnus* with respect to *magnum* are: (a), **magnus absolute seu secundum quantitatem absolutam** and **magnus ad aliquid seu quantitate proportionis seu secundum relationem**, *the simply great* or *great according to simple greatness* and *the proportionately* or *the relatively great.*—(b), **magnus ad aliquid**, see *magnus absolute.*

—(c), **magnum applicatum alicui rei** and **magnum communiter acceptum**, *great as applied to some one thing* or *as expressed of it* and *great in the general* or *usual sense of the word.*—(d), **magnum communiter acceptum**, see *magnum applicatum alicui rei.*—(e), **magnum continuum**, *the continuously great.*—(f), **magnum quantitate proportionis**, see *magnum absolute.*—(g), **magnum secundum quantitatem absolutam**, see *magnum absolute.*—(h), **magnum secundum relationem**, see *magnum absolute*. On **ex multis parvis non possunt fieri magna continua**, see *continuus* under 2.—**maior**, us, *comp. adj.*, (1) *greater* in the general sense of the word, (2) *greater* according to extent, (3) *greater* according to space of time, i.e., *older*, (4) *greater* according to intellectual extent, *more general* or *universal*, hence the *major premise* of a syllogism, (5) *greater* according to perfection, *higher in rank, more important.*—Kinds of *maior* in this (1) sense are: **maior extensive** and **maior intensive**, *greater in expansion* and *greater in exertion* or *effort*. On **mundus maior**, see *mundus* under 1; on **terminus in maiore**, see *terminus* under 1.—On **extremitas maior**, see *extremitas* under 2; on **propositio maior seu maxima**, see *propositio* under 2; on **terminus maior**, see *terminus* under 4.—One kind of *maior* in this (2) sense is: **maior de necessitate,** *the true major premise, that is, true of necessity.* Cf. C.G. 3. 86; 1 Sent. 38. 1. 5 ob. 5.—On **abstractio maior,** see *abstractio* under 3; on **locus a maiore,** see *locus* under 4; on **ordo maior,** see *ordo* under 4; on **persona maior,** see *persona;* on **religio maior,** see *religio* under 2; on **status maior,** see *status* under 4.—*Sup.,* **maximus,** a, um, *greatest, grandest, most important.*—*Comp.,* **magis,** *adv., in a higher degree, more completely, more.*—*Sup.,* **maxime,** *in the highest degree, most of all, most particularly, especially, exceedingly, very.*

magus, i, *m., a magician.*

Magus, i, *m., Magus,* Simon. He was a native of Gitton, in Samaria. By his skill in magic he attained great influence among his countrymen and gained many followers. When St. Peter and St. John came to Samaria, Simon, seeing the miraculous gifts bestowed by these Apostles, offered money to them to obtain the power of conferring the Holy Spirit, whence the sin of Simony is named. He became founder of a sect named after him "Simonians."

Mahumetus, i, *m., Mahomet* or *Mohammed.* He was born in the holy city of Mecca in the year 570, and in his early youth was subject to fits. Having passed a long and mysterious retreat in a cave near Mecca he began to preach religion, declaring that he had received from God through the angel Gabriel, the commission to re-establish the religion of Abraham, Islam, i.e., submission to God. Mohammed died in 632.

maiestas, atis, *f., greatness, grandeur, dignity, majesty.*

maioritas, atis, *f., majority,* the state or fact of being greater; *superiority, pre-eminence, excellence.*

Malachias, ae, *m., Malachias,* the last of the twelve minor Prophets, of the tribe of Zabulon, born at Sophia. He was a contemporary of Nehemias, and prophesied, it is believed, from 412 to 408 B.C. We have from him three chapters, wherein he reproaches the Jews on account of their corruption; he also announces the Messias.

male, *adv.,* see *malus* at end.

maledico, ere, xi, ctum, 3, *v. n.* and *a.,* (1) *to speak ill of, to slander,* used *absol.,* (2) *to curse,* used with *acc., dat.,* and *absol.*—**maledicens,** entis, *P. a., cursing.*—**maledictus,** a, um, *P. a., cursed.*—**maledictum,** i, *n., a curse, oath, imprecation.*

maledictio, onis, *f.,* (1) *evil speaking,* (2) *esp., a curse, malediction.*

maledicus, a, um, *adj., slanderous, of evil tongue.*

malefacio, ere, feci, factum, 3, *v. n., to do evil, harm, mischief* to anyone, *to injure.*

malefactor, oris, *m., an evil-doer, malefactor.*

maleficiatus, a, um, *P. a., maleficiate, rendered impotent by spells.*

maleficium, i, *n.,* (1) *an evil deed, misdeed, wickedness, offence, crime,* the opposite of *beneficium,* (2) *enchantment, witchery, sorcery.*

maleficus, i, *m.,* (1) *an evil-doer,* (2) *a sorcerer, wizard.*

malevolentia, ae, *f., ill-will, evil disposition towards anyone, dislike, hatred, envy, malevolence.* **malevolus,** a, um, *adj., malicious.* —**malevolus,** i, *m., an ill-disposed person, an enemy.*

malignitas, atis, *f., spite, malevolence, malice.*

malignor, ari, atus, 1, *v. dep., to do* or *contrive maliciously, to malign.*

malignus, a, um, *adj., wicked, malignant.*

malitia, ae, *f.,* (1) *badness, baseness, malice,* in the general sense of the word, the opposite of *bonitas,* (2) *badness, baseness, malice,* in the physical sense of the word, (3) *badness, baseness, malice,* in the moral sense of the word, the disposition to moral evil in the will, opposed to the goodness of virtue, (4) *abhorrence of spiritual goods.*—Kinds of *malitia* in this (1) sense are: **malitia moralis** and **malitia naturalis,** *the moral* or *ethical* and *the physical* or *natural badness.* On **peccare ex certa malitia,** see

peccare under 2; on **peccatum malitiae seu ex certa malitia,** see *peccatum* under 2; on **perfectio in malitia,** see *perfectio* under 2; on **status malitiae,** see *status* under 3; on **vulnus malitiae,** see *vulnus.*—Kinds of *malitia* in this (2) sense are: (a), **malitia acta** and **malitia contracta,** *malice committed* and *malice contracted* or *inherited* from someone else.—(b), **malitia actualis** and **malitia habitualis,** *the actual* and *the habitual malice,* or *that consisting of an action* and *that of a state.*—(c), **malitia aegritudinalis** and **malitia bestialis,** *the baseness of sickness* and *the bestial baseness of man.*—(d), **malitia bestialis,** see *malitia aegritudinalis.*—(e), **malitia civilis,** *the civil baseness* or *the baseness of a man with reference to his civic life.*—(f), **malitia contracta,** see *malitia acta.*—(g), **malitia culpae** and **malitia poenae,** *the baseness consisting in guilt* and *that in punishment.*—(h), **malitia cum additione** and **malitia simpliciter,** *baseness with a so-called addition* and *simple baseness.*—(i), **malitia habitualis,** see *malitia actulis.*—(j), **malitia implicita,** *the envolved* or *included baseness.* —(k), **malitia particularis seu specialis seu quaedam** and **malitia tota,** *the partial* or *particular* or *a certain baseness* or *the complete baseness.*—(l), **malitia poenae,** see *malitia culpae.*—(m), **malitia quaedam,** see *malitia parti-*

cularis.—(n), **malitia simpliciter,** see *malitia cum additione.—*(o), **malitia specialis,** see *malitia particularis.—*(p), **malitia tota,** see *malitia particularis.*

malitiosus, a, um, *adj., full of wickedness, wicked.—***malitiose,** *adv., wickedly.*

malleus, i, *m., a hammer, mallet, maul.*

malo, malle, malui, *v. a., to choose rather, prefer.*

malus, a, um, *adj.,* (1) *wicked, bad, evil,* in the general sense of the word, the opposite of *bonus,* (2) *wicked, bad, evil in itself,* or *objectively so,* the same as *malum in se,* that which and in so far as it does not agree with a (divine) will placed over it, i.e., that which lacks the being, goodness, or perfection that it should have, also the opposite of *bonus* (3) *wicked, bad, evil for something, subjectively so,* the same as *malum alicui,* that which should be avoided by a created being, especially by man, because it is harmful; likewise the opposite of *bonus;* used frequently in neuter as a noun in all meanings to signify *not the mere absence of good, but the deprivation of a good in a particular subject in which it ought to be found.—* Kinds of *malum* in this (1) sense are: **malum alicui seu alicuius seu huic seu quantum ad hoc seu secundum quid** and **malum in se seu secundum se seu secundum seipsum seu secun-**

dum **suam naturam seu simpliciter,** *that which is bad for something* or *with respect to this* or *that* or *respectively* and *that which is bad in itself* or *in its nature* or *the simply* and *absolutely bad,* i.e., *the subjectively* and *the objectively bad.* On **actio mala,** see *actio* under 1; on **actus malus,** see *actus* under 1; on **concupiscentia mala,** see *concupiscentia* under 1; on **conscientia mala,** see *conscientia* under 3; on **delectatio mala,** see *delectatio;* on **dispositio mala,** see *dispositio* under 4; on **electio mala,** see *electio* under 1; on **finis malus,** see *finis* under 2; on **habitus malus,** see *habitus* under 4; on **ira mala,** see *ira* under 2; on **libertas ad malum,** see *libertas* under 2; on **mos malus,** see *mos* under 3; on **opus malum,** see *opus* under 4; on **passio mala,** see *passio* under 3; on **ratio mala,** see *ratio* under 14; on **sapientia mala,** see *sapientia* under 1; on **spiritus malus,** see *spiritus;* on **voluntas mala,** see *voluntas* under 3.—Kinds of *malum in this* (2) sense are: (a), **malum absolute seu abstracte accipiendo seu sumptum** and **malum concrete acceptum seu concretive sumptum,** *evil in* and *for itself* or *taken in general* or *the essence of evil* and *evil so comprehended as connected with a thing in which it occurs in reality.—*(b), **malum abstracte accipiendo seu sumptum,** see *malum absolute.—*

(c), **malum actionis seu in actione seu inordinationis in actione** and **malum corruptionis seu in substantia,** *evil attached to an action* and *that attached to a substance,* moral evil and physical evil, i.e., that which consists of the disorder of an action and that which consists of the deterioration or corruption of a substance.—(d), **malum causae** and **malum effectus,** *the evil attached to a cause* and *that attached to an effect.*—(e), **malum concrete acceptum,** see *malum absolute.*—(f), **malum concretive sumptum,** see *malum absolute.*—(g), **malum corruptionis,** see *malum actionis.*—(h), **malum effectus,** see *malum causae.*—(i), **malum ex genere seu secundum speciem suam,** *evil according to its genus* or *(moral) species.*—(j), **malum in actione,** see *malum actionis.*—(k), **malum in actionibus moralibus seu in moralibus seu morale seu moris seu in rebus voluntariis** and **malum in rebus naturalibus seu naturae seu rei naturalis,** *the moral* or *ethical* and *the natural* or *physical evil.*—(l), **malum in moralibus,** see *malum in actionibus moralibus.*—(m), **malum inordinationis,** see *malum actionis.*—(n), **malum in rebus naturalibus,** see *malum in actionibus moralibus.*—(o), **malum in rebus voluntariis,** see *malum in actionibus moralibus.*—(p), **malum in substantia,** see *malum actionis.*—(q,) **malum integre seu integrum seu perfecte seu perfectum seu summe seu summum seu totaliter,** *the perfect* or *highest* or *complete evil.*—(r), **malum morale,** see *malum in actionibus moralibus.*—(s), **malum moris,** see *malum in actionibus moralibus.*—(t), **malum naturae,** see *malum in actionibus moralibus.*—(u), **malum naturaliter seu secundum naturalem ordinem seu per se** and **malum quia prohibitum seu secundum legis positionem,** *evil according to the natural order* or *through itself* or *its own nature* (see *malum per accidens*) and *evil according to a positive law.*—(v), **malum per accidens** and **malum per se,** *that which is an evil accidentally,* and *that which is so through itself, an evil as such by its own nature.*—(w), **malum per essentiam, malum per participationem,** and **malum per privationem participationis,** *essentially evil, that by participation in something bad,* and *that by the deprivation of participation in something good.*—(x), **malum perfecte seu perfectum,** see *malum integre.*—(y), **malum per participationem,** see *malum per essentiam.*—(z), **malum per privationem participationis,** see *malum per essentiam.*—(a²), **malum per se,** see *malum naturaliter* and *malum per accidens.*—(b²), **malum primum,** *the first evil according to time* and *according to nature.*—(c²), **malum quia** prohibitum, see *malum naturaliter.*—(d²), malum secundum legis positionem, see *malum naturaliter.*—(e²), malum secundum naturalem ordinem, see *malum naturaliter.*—(f²), malum secundum quid and malum simpliciter, *that which is evil only relatively to something* and *that which is simply an evil.* Cf. *malum alicui* under 1 and *malum ex suppositione alterius* under 3.—(g²), malum secundum speciem suam, see *malum ex genenere.*—(h²), malum simpliciter, see *malum secundum quid.*—(i²), malum summe seu summum, see *malum integre.*—(j²), malum totaliter, see *malum integre.*—bonum est vehementius in agendo, quam malum, see *bonus* under 2.—bonum fortius est ad movendum quam malum, see *bonus* under 2.—id quod est malum non est aliquid, *evil as such is nothing.*—malum causatur seu contingit ex singularibus defectibus, see *bonus* under 2.—malum contingit multifariam seu multipliciter, see *bonus* under 2.—malum est ex particularibus seu singularibus defectibus, see *bonus* under 2.—malum nominat non ens, *the word evil does not indicate a real being.*—malum non est effectivum aut salvativum alicuius, *an evil is neither the producing nor the maintaining cause of anything.*—malum non est exsistens neque in exsistentibus, *an evil as such exists*

neither for itself nor for anything else.—malum non est nisi in bono ut in subiecto, *an evil can exist only in something good as its subject.*—malum non habet causam efficientem, sed deficientem, *evil has no cause that produces it but a cause deficient in its activity.*—malum omnifariam contingit ex particularibus defectibus, see *bonus* under 2.—quilibet singularis defectus causat malum, see *bonus* under 2.—On fortuna mala, see *fortuna* under 1.—Kinds of *malum* in this (3) sense are: (a), malum absolute acceptum seu absolutum seu simpliciter acceptum seu simpliciter and malum arctum seu arduum seu cum arduitate et elevatione seu sub ratione ardui seu difficile, *evil* or *harmful apprehended simply as such,* and *evil apprehended as difficult to avoid.*—(b), malum absolutum, see *malum absolute acceptum.* —(c), malum animae seu spirituale and malum corporis seu corporale, *the evil of the soul* and *that of the body* or *the spiritual* and *the physical evil.*—(d), malum apparens, and malum verum, *the apparent* and *the true evil.*—(e), malum arctum, see *malum absolute acceptum.*—(f), malum arduum, see *malum absolute acceptum.*—(g), malum coniunctum seu iniacens, *the evil connected with a particular good* and *resting in it.*—(h), malum contristans seu contristativum seu laesivum and malum corruptionis seu corruptivum seu nocivum, *the kakon luperon* and *kakon phthartikon* of Aristotle, *the saddening* or *damaging evil* and *the evil of destruction* or *the destructive evil, of which the former is merely an inclination proceeding from a sensible perception but the latter opposes the nature* and *the inclination arising from the nature of a being.*—(i), malum corporale, see *malum animae.*—(j), malum corporis, see *malum animae.*—(k), malum corruptionis, see *malum contristans.*—(l), malum corruptivum, see *malum contristans.*—(m), malum culpae, and malum poenae seu poenale, *the evil that is constituted by deliberate fault* or *guilt,* and *that consisting of punishment.*—(n), malum cum arduitate et elevatione, see *malum absolute acceptum.*—(o), malum difficile, see *malum absolute acceptum.*—(p), malum ex suppositione alterius and malum secundum se seu simpliciter, *that which is an evil according to the supposition of some one thing* and *that which is evil in itself* or *simply.*—(q), malum exterius and malum interius, *the exterior* and *interior evil.*—(r), malum miacens, see *malum coniunctum.*—(s), malum intellectus, *the evil of reason,* i.e., falsehood or error.—(t), malum interius, see *malum exterius.*—(u), malum laesivum,

see *malum contristans.*—(v), malum nocivum, see *malum contristans.*—(w), malum particulare, *the particular* or *single evil.*—(x), malum poenae, see *malum culpae.*—(y), malum poenale, see *malum culpae.*—(z), malum secundum se, see *malum ex suppositione alterius.*—(a²), malum secundum sensum, *the sensibly perceivable evil.*—(b²), malum simpliciter, see *malum absolute acceptum* and *malum ex suppositione alterius.*—(c²), malum simpliciter acceptum, see *malum absolute acceptum.*—(d²), malum spirituale, see *malum animae.*—(e²), malum sub ratione ardui, see *malum absolute acceptum.*—(f²), malum temporale, *the temporal evil.*—(g²), malum totius multitudinis civilis and malum unius hominis, *the evil of the entire state* and *that of a single individual.*—(h²), malum unius hominis, see *malum totius multitudinis civilis.*—(i), malum verum, see *malum apparens.*— Comp.: peior, peius, *worse.*— Sup., pessimus, a, um, *worst.*— male, *adv., badly, ill, wrongly, wickedly, unfortunately, erroneously, improperly,* etc.—*Comp.,* peius, *in a worse way, worse.*— Sup., pessime, *in the worst way, worst.* Does not occur in the S.T. of St. Thomas.

mamma, ae, *f., a breast, pap,* esp. of females, used in the S.T. only in quot.

mammona, ae, *f.*, *mammon, riches,* used in the S.T. only in quot.

Manasses, is, *m.*, (1) *Manasses,* Jewish patriarch, eldest son of Joseph, born in Egypt, was blessed by Jacob on his death-bed, and became chief of one of the twelve tribes of Israel, (2) *Manasses* (706-639 B.C.), King of Juda, died at Jerusalem. He was the son and impious successor of the good Ezechias. He began to reign when twelve years old. On account of his impiety and cruelty God suffered him to be carried as prisoner to Babylon. Manasses repented, did penance, and was restored to his throne. He tried to repair the evil which he had caused. We have under the name of Manasses, a prayer filled with sentiments of piety which it is believed he composed during his captivity.

mancipatio, onis, *f.*, *a making over, delivery, transfer of a thing to another.*

mancipo, are, avi, atum, 1, *v. a.*, (1) *to devote* or *consecrate to,* used with *acc.* of person or thing devoted or consecrated, and the *dative* of the end to which the person or thing is consecrated, (2) *to make subject to, enslave,* (3) *to bind over, to give the right to another.*—filii non mancipati, *the children not being major* or *of full age.*

mandatum, i, *n.*, *charge, order, commission, injunction, com-mand, mandate.* On lex mandatorum, see *lex* under 1.—Kinds of *mandatum* are: (a), mandatum affirmativum and mandatum prohibitorium, *the affirmative* or *commanding* and *the forbidding* or *preventing mandate.*—(b), mandatum divinum, *the divine mandate.*—(c), mandatum maximum, *the greatest mandate.*—(d), mandatum prohibitorium, see *mandatum affirmativum.*

mandibula, ae, *f.*, *a jaw.*

mando, are, avi, atum, 1, *v. a.*, (1) *lit.*, *to commit to one's charge, to enjoin, order, command,* used (a) *impers. pass.*, (b) with *ut,* (c) *object clause,* (d) *acc.* and *dat.*, (2) transf., *to commit, consign, commend.*

manducatio, onis, *f.*, *manducation, the action of eating,* (1) in *gen.*, (2) in *partic.*, the term applied, usually with qualification as spiritual or sacramental to the act of participation in the Eucharist.

manduco, are, avi, atum, 1, *v. a.*, *to eat by chewing.*

mane, indecl., *the morning, morn.* —(2), as *adv.*, *in the morning, early in the morning.*—de mane, *in the morning.*

maneo, ere, nsi, nsum, 2, *v. n.* and *a.*, (1) neutr., *to stay, tarry, stop, continue, abide,* (2) *remain, last, endure, adhere, abide by* (with *in* and *abl.*).—manens, entis, *P. a.*, *remaining, abiding,* synonym of *permanens,* the opposite of *transiens, pertransiens,* and *transiti-*

vus.—**manentia,** ium, *n., abiding or permanent things.* On **accidens manens,** see *accidens* under 2; on **actio manens,** see *actio* under 1; on **forma manens,** see *forma* under 2; on **operatio manens,** see *operatio* under 2.

mania, ae, *f., mania,* all the phases of general excitement bearing the features of lack of control are loosely called mania. (1) in *gen., madness, insanity,* (2) in *partic., ill-will* or *anger* that continues for a long time and grows old in the memory causing *menis* (ill will) which is derived from *menein* (to dwell).

manicatus, a, um, *adj., manicated, sleeved, furnished with long sleeves.*

Manichaeus, i, *m., Mani,* or *Manes,* but always in St. Augustine, *Manichaeus,* "the illustrious", a Persian religious teacher, (215-276 A.D.). His teaching mingled Zoroastrian dualism with Gnostic Christian elements, and flourished in the West under different forms, counting even the young Augustine among its adherents for a time, until its ultimate phase, the Cathari or the Albigensian heresy, was crushed by the foundation of the Order of Friars Preachers by St. Dominic.—**Manichaei,** orum, *m., Manichaeans.*

manifestatio, onis, *f., a manifesting, manifestation,* (1) in *gen.,* the action or the fact of being manifested; the demonstration, reve-lation, or display of the existence, presence, qualities or nature of some person or thing, (2) in *partic.,* applied to the action of making known to another the state of one's conscience.

manifestative, see *manifestativus.*

manifestativus, a, um, *adj., revealing, manifesting, demonstrative, manifestative.* On **ratio manifestativa ipsius rei nominatae,** see *ratio* under 8; on **verbum manifestativum,** see *verbum* under 1; on **virtus manifestativa,** see *virtus* under 1; on **visio manifestativa,** see *visio* under 1.—**manifestative,** *adv., revealingly, demonstratively.*

manifestator, oris, *m., a manifester, shower, discoverer.*

manifeste, *adv.,* see *manifestus.*

manifesto, are, avi, atum, 1, *v. a., to manifest, make public, discover, show clearly, exhibit.*

manifestus, a, um, *adj.,* (1) in *gen., palpable, clear, plain, apparent, evident, manifest,* (2) in *neutr. sing.* with a subject-clause, *it is manifest that.*—**manifesta,** orum, *n., obvious facts, palpable things.*—**manifestum,** i, *n., openness,* only in adverbial phrases, **in manifesto,** *openly.*—**manifeste,** *adv., manifestly, evidently, clearly.*

manipulus, i, *m.,* (1) pl., *maniples, handfulls, sheaves,* (2) *a maniple,* (a little bundle, because originally a folded handkerchief) a silk embroidered band, about a yard long and three inches wide,

worn on the left arm of subdeacons, deacons, priests, and
bishops during mass, so that it
falls in equal lengths on both
sides.

manna, neutr., *indecl.*, *manna*, a
miraculous food sent by God to
the Hebrews in the Exodus, described in Exodus, 16, and Numbers, 11. The etymology of the
name is given clearly in Exodus,
16: *man hu*, "what is it"?

mano, are, avi, atum, 1, *v. n.*, and
a., *to flow, spring, emanate, have
its origin, originate* from any
thing, used *fig.*

mansio, onis, *f.*, (1) in *gen.*, a
*place of abode, a dwelling, habi-
tation*, (2) plural, (a) used to
translate the Greek *monai;* in
Vulg., *mansions*, i.e., *rooms*,
(John XIV, 2), where *multae
mansiones* means there is room
enough in heaven for the multi-
tudes of the children of God.
Eastern hotels for travellers were
called mansions or abiding places. Some explain the "many mansions" as setting forth different
degrees of holiness. These words
do not convey this sense literally,
except inasmuch as numbers
generally convey some notion of
variety, (b) used for the abodes
of hell.

mansuetudo, inis, *f.*, *mildness, gentleness*, the opposite of *ira*. *Mansuetudo* is one of the fructus Spiritus Sancti. Cf. *fructus* under 2.

mansuetus, a, um, *P. a.*, *mild, gentle, quiet.*

manteia, (Grk. *manteia*) ae, *f.*, *divination*, used in the S.T. only in
quot.

mantile, is, *n.*, *a towel.*

manualis, e, *adj.*, *manual, done,
made*, or *operated by* or used
with the hand or hands.

manubrium, ii, *n.*, *a handle.*

manuduco, ere, xi, ctum, 3, *v. a.*,
*to lead by the hand, to lead,
guide, direct.*

manuductio, onis, *f.*, *manuduction*,
the action of leading, guiding or
introducing, *guidance, introduction, direction.*

manufactus, a, um, *adj.*, *handmade,
made by hand.*

manumissio, onis, *f.*, *manumission,
the freeing of a slave.*

manumissus, a, um, *P. a.*, *manumit-
ted.*

manus, us, *f.*, *a hand.*—The following phrases are of frequent occurrence: **in manu consilii sui,**
in the hand of, or *subject to his
own counsel.* Many explain this
of Adam, before his fall, when
he apparently stood not in such
need of asking continually for
God's assistance.—**per manus sa-
cerdotum,** *by the hands of the
priest*, i.e., *by the act of; from
the hands of.*—**manus gubernato-
ris,** *a governing hand.*—**mori in
manu alicuius verberantis,** *to
die while* or *at the immediate
moment of being beaten.*—**cohi-
bere manum,** *to restrain the
hand* or *to prevent a person
from some course of action.*—**imponere manus,** *to impose hands,*

to place or *lay on the hands.* A perfectly natural gesture signifying the communication of some favor, blessing, power or duty; mentioned in the Old Testament in connection with the patriarch's blessing, their children, the consecration of priests and sacrifice. Christ used it in working miracles; the Apostles made it an essential rite in conferring the sacraments of Confirmation and Holy Orders.—**mittere manum ad aratrum** and **ponere manum ad aratrum,** *to put his hand to the plough,* a proverb and metaphor to signify that nothing must hinder a man from God's service.—**divinatio manus,** *divination of the hands,* i.e, *chiromancy* or *palmistry.*—**in manibus tuis sortes meae,** *my destiny is in your hands.* All the vicissitudes of life are at God's disposal.—**tradere in manus hostium,** *to deliver into the power of the enemy.*—**inferre manus Deo,** *to lay hands on God, attack God.*—**inicere manus sibi,** *to lay hands on himself, to commit suicide.*

manutergium, ii, *n., a towel.*

marca, ae, *f.,* (marcha), *a mark,* a denomination of weight formerly employed for gold and silver throughout Western Europe; its actual weight varied considerably but it was usually regarded as equivalent to eight ounces.

Marcellinus, i, *m., Marcellinus,* Flavius, a tribune and notary, i.e., an officer who having held in the army the rank of tribune, was afterwards employed in the civil capacity of notary, an office of high position. He was a Christian and a man of high character, taking much interest in theological questions. He was a brother to Apringius, afterwards proconsul of Africa, and appears to have usually resided in that country. St. Jerome in a letter to him recommends him to consult St. Augustine, as his bishop, on the subject on which he desires information. An intimate friendship existed between Augustine and Marcellinus.

Marcellus, i, *m., Marcellus,* bishop of Rome probably from May 24 A.D. 307 to Jan. 15, A.D. 309. This pope appears as a martyr in the Roman Martyrology. He was beaten with cudgels for refusing to sacrifice, by order of Maxentius, and afterwards condemned by him to tend the imperial horses as a slave.

marcesco, ere, *v. inch. n., to shrivel, shrink, form corrugation, become old.*

Marcus, i, *m., Mark,* (1) one of the Evangelists. He was probably the same as John Mark, mentioned in the Acts (XII, 25). He was the nephew or cousin of St. Barnabas; he became the favorite companion and disciple of St. Peter in Rome. Mark wrote his Gospel in Greek. His life was ended by martyrdom in the year 68, (2) an anchorite mentioned in the *Prologus super Marcum* which has been falsely ascribed to St. Jerome.

Mardochaeus, ei, *m., Mardochai,* the uncle of Esther, Queen of Persia and wife of Assuerus, who is identified with Xerxes (485-465 B.C.). Mardochai lived in Susan, the capital of Persia.

mare, is, *n., the sea,* (1) in gen., (2) in partic., *the Red Sea.*—**fluxus et refluxus maris,** *the ebb* and *flow of the sea.*

margarita, ae, *f., a pearl,* used in the S.T. only in quot.

Maria, ae, *f.,* (1) *Mary,* the Blessed Virgin. She was the mother of Jesus Christ, daughter of St. Joachim and St. Anna, of the tribe of Juda and of the royal race of David, (2) *Mary* of Bethany; she is mentioned as the sinner (Luke 7), who bathed the feet of Christ; as Mary the sister of Martha and Lazarus and later as Mary Magdalen (Luke 8) who ministered to Christ, by Whom she was freed from seven devils. She was the first witness of the Resurrection, (3) *Mary,* the Mother of James and Joseph. In the narrative of the resurrection she is named Mary of James (Mark, XVI, 1). Her relationship to the Blessed Virgin is obscure. James is termed "of Alpheus," i.e., presumably "son of Alpheus". St. Jerome identifies this Alpheus with Cleophas, who according to Hegesippus, was brother of St. Joseph. Mary of Cleophas, in

that case, would be the sister-in-law of the Blessed Virgin.

marinus, a, um, *adj., of* or *belonging to the sea, marine.*

maritalis, e, *adj., marital, pertaining* or *relating to married people, conjugal.*

maritata, ae, *f., a wife, a married woman.*

maritimus, a, um, *adj., of* or *belonging to the sea, maritime,* used in the S.T. only in quot.

maritus, i, *m., a married man, husband.*

Mars, Martis, *m., Mars, who as father of Romulus, was the primogenitor of the Roman people, the god of war, of husbandry, of shepherds* and *seers.*

marsupium, ii, *n., a purse,* used in the S.T. only in quot.

martellus, i, *m., a hammer, mallet.*

Martha, ae, *f., Martha,* saint, virgin. She was the sister of Lazarus and Mary of Bethany, and shared the honor of Christ's friendship when He stayed as their guest in Bethany. She also served Him in the house of Simon the Leper.

Martianus, i, *m.,* see under *Augustus.*

Martinus, i, *m.,* (1) in gen., *Martin,* a male Christian name common in Western Europe and taken from St. Martin, bishop of Tours, (2) in *partic., Martinus* Bracarensis, Martin, metropolitan bishop of Braga. According to Gregory of Tours, Martin was a native of Pannonia. In 561 he attended the first council of Braga, presided over by Lucretius, metropolitan bishop of Braga. The Acts of the Council were probably compiled by Martin, the person of the greatest literary pretensions then in Gallicia. The *capitula Martini Bracarensis* contain 84 canons which had great vogue and influence in the Middle Ages. These "capitula sive canones orientalium antiquorum patrum synodis a venerabili Martino episcopo, vel ab omni Bracarensi synodo excerpti," were incorporated in the earlist form of the Spanish *Codex Canonum*.

Martyrs, yris, *comm., a witness;* esp. *one who by his death bears witness to the truth of the Christian religion, a martyr.*

martyrium, ii, *n., a testimony, sealed with one's blood, to the truth of the Christian religion, martyrdom.*

mas, maris, *m., a male.*

masculine, *adv.,* see *masculinus.*

masculinus, a, um, *adj.,* (1) *lit., male, masculine,* (2) *transf., in gram., masculine gender.*—**masculine,** *adv., in the masculine gender.*

masculus, i, *m., a male.*

massa, ae, *f., the mass, the generality of mankind, the main body of a race or nation.*

Masso, (**Maso**), onis, *m., Masso,* Bishop. His identity as quoted by S.T. is very uncertain; ad Massonam, likewise ad Massa-

num, likewise Missianum, likewise Massianum.

mastico, are, 1, *v. a., to masticate.*

mater, tris, *f.,* (1) *lit., a mother,* (a) of persons, (b) of animals, (2) *in partic., the Mother of God,* (3) *fig., mother,* applied to things more or less personified, with reference either to a metaphorical giving birth, to the protecting care exercised by a mother, or to the affectionate reverence due to a mother.

materia, ae, *f.,* (1) *matter* in the general sense of the word, the fundamental substratum of all bodies; the permanent subject of generation and corruption, (2) *matter, affair, object* or *objective of an action* or *of a habit* or *of a faculty,* synonym of *obiectum* and *subiectum,* (3) *matter, substance, material cause,* the potential and determinable part of a composite, i.e., that from which something arises or of which it consists, synonym of *subiectum ex quo,* the opposite of *forma.*— Kinds of *materia* in this (1) sense are: **materia circa quam seu de qua, materia in qua,** and **materia ex qua,** *the matter around or about which,* and *the matter from which,* i.e., that about which an action or a faculty with its action moves, or the object of an action and of the faculty belonging to it, that in which an action and the corresponding faculty has its bearer and possessor, or the subject of an action and of the faculty belonging to it, and that from which something arises or of which it consists or the material or the material cause of a thing, the same as *causa materialis*. On **bonitas ex materia**, see *bonitas* under 1.— Kinds of *materia* in this (2) sense are: (a) **materia artis**, see *ars* under 2.—(b), **materia civilis**, *the civic objective* or *the objective that consists of the deeds of civic life.*—(c), **materia demonstrativa**, *the subject matter which permits proof with apodictic certainty.*— (d), **materia exterior seu extranea**, *the exterior* or *extraneous matter.*—(e), **materia extranea**, see *materia exterior.*—(f), **materia moralis**, *the object of moral philosophy.*—(g), **materia principalis**, *the principal object* or *objective.*—(h), **materia propinqua seu proxima** and **materia remota**, *the neighboring* or *proximate* and *the remote matter.* Cf. *materia propinqua* under 3.—(i), **materia propria**, *the proper object* or *objective.*—(j), **materia proxima**, see *materia propinqua.* —(k), **materia remota**, see *materia propinqua.*—On **abstractio a materia, a materia individuali, sensibili et intellegibili**, see *abstractio* under 3; on **abstrahere a materia, a materia communi et a materia individuali seu signata, a materia intellegibili et a materia sensibili**, see *abstrahere* under I 3; on **appetitus materiae**, see *appetitus* under 2; on **distinctio**

materiae, see *distinctio* under 2; on **diversitas materiae**, see *diversitas;* on **divisio secundum materiam**, see *divisio;* on **forma in materia**, see *forma* under 2; on **homo extra materiam**, see *homo;* on **idem materiae seu secundum materiam**, see *idem;* on **infinitas materiae**, see *infinitas;* on **infinitum ex parte materiae seu secundum materiam seu secundum rationem materiae**, see *infinitus;* on **motus ad materiam**, see *motus* under 2; on **ordo materiae**, see *ordo* under 1; on **pars materiae**, see *pars* under 1; on **potentia materiae**, see *potentia* under 4; on **praeparatio materiae**, see *praeparatio* under 1; on **ratio in materia**, see *ratio* under 11; on **transmutatio secundum materiam**, see *transmutatio* under 1; on **vita materia mixta**, see *vita* under 1.—Kinds of *materia* in this (3) sense are: (a), **materia aerea** and **materia terrae seu terrestris**, *the aerial* and *the earthly matter.*— (b), **materia aliena** and **materia propria**, *the foreign* and *the proper matter.* Cf. *materia communis.*—(c), **materia communis** and **materia particularis seu propria seu individualis seu individuans**, *the common* or *general matter*, i.e., the general aspect of all bodies, and *the particularized* or *definite matter.* Cf. *materia aliena.*—(d), **materia composita** and **materia simplex**, *the compounded* and *the simple matter.*—(e), **materia contingens, materia na-**

turalis seu necessaria, materia possibilis, and materia remota seu impossibilis, *the contingent, the natural* or *necessary, the possible* and *the remote* or *impossible subject matter of a proposition.*—(f), materia contrarietati subiecta and materia contrarietati non subiecta, *the matter susceptible of contrary states* or *forms* and *the matter not so subject.*—(g), materia corporalis seu corpulenta seu corporalium and materia spiritualis seu spiritualium, *the corporal* and *the spiritual matter* or *the matter of corporeal* and *that of spiritual things,* (which latter is, of course, a contradiction in terms for St. Thomas).—(h), materia corporalium, see *materia corporalis.*—(i), materia corpulenta, see *materia corporalis.*—(j), materia corruptibilium and materia generabilium, *the matter of corruptible things* and *of things that can be produced.*—(k), materia debita and materia indebita, *the proper* or *suitable* and *the improper* or *unsuitable matter.*—(l), materia demonstrata seu designata seu signata seu determinata and materia non signata, *the designated* or *specified* or *determined matter* and *that not specified by quantity,* or *quantitative dimensions.*—(m), materia designata, see *materia demonstrata.*—(n), materia determinata, see *materia demonstrata.*—(o), materia dimensioni subiecta seu quantitati subiecta, *the matter subjected to extension* or *size,* i.e., *corporal matter.* Cf. *materia corporalis.*—(p), materia elementaris, *the elementary matter* or *the matter of the elements,* i.e., that out of which all composite things have originated.—(q), materia enuntiationis and materia syllogismi, *the subject matter of a single statement* or *proposition* (namely, the conception of the subject and of the predicate) and *that of the whole argumentation* (i.e., the subject, the middle, and the predicate terms, in other words, *the major* and *minor premises).*—(r), materia generabilium, see *materia corruptibilium.*—(s), materia impossibilis, see *materia contingens.*—(t), materia indebita, see *materia debita.*—(u), materia individualis seu individuans, see *materia communis.*—(v), materia informis, *the formless matter* or *matter lacking form,* i.e., matter which lacks either a definite form or any form in general.—(w), materia intellegibilis and materia sensibilis, the Aristotelian *hule noete kai aisthete,* i.e., the immaterial matter or that perceptible only through imagination and the material apprehended through the senses, in which are understood the so-called five sensibly perceived qualities, (cf. *qualitas).*—(x), materia intellegibilis communis seu non signata and materia intellegibilis individualis, *the general intelligible matter* or *that not definitely specified as of this* or *that individual* and *the individual* and *the individual intelligible matter* or *that definitely specified.* (cf. *materia intellegibilis*).—(y), **materia naturalis**, *the natural matter* or *that belonging to nature.* Cf. *materia contingens*.—(z), **materia necessaria**, see *materia contingens*.—(a²), **materia non signata**, see *materia demonstrata*.—(b²), **materia particularis**, see *materia communis*.—(c²), **materia necessaria**, see *materia contingens*.—(d²), **materia possibilis**, see *materia contingens*.—(e²), **materia praeiacens**, *pre-existent material*.—(f²), **materia prima seu pura**, *primary matter*, which is purely material, i.e., without any form or actuality whatever. Primary matter is not sensible or secondary matter; it is perceptible only by reasoning. As pure potentiality it is not intelligible except under the actualization of some substantial form. Although it has not existence of itself, and does not exist actually except in a composite, it is the fundamental stuff of all corporeal things, being the permanent subject in which the generation and corruption of substantial forms takes place. Matter is the potential and determinable part; form is the actual and determining part; the union of both constitutes an actually existent ma-

terial thing. Strictly speaking, neither matter nor form exists, the composite of matter and form exists. There is no matter of any kind in a *spiritual* being, not even primary matter.—(g²), **materia privationi subiecta**, *the matter subjected to a privation* or *a lack* or *the accidental matter*.—(h²), **materia propinqua seu proxima** and **materia remota**, *the proximate* or *next matter* and *the remote matter.* Cf. *materia propinqua* under 2.—(i²), **materia propria**, see *materia aliena* and *materia communis*.—(j²), **materia proxima**, see *materia propinqua*.—(k²), **materia pura**, see *materia prima*.—(l²), **materia quantitati subiecta**, see *materia dimensioni subiecta*.—(m²), **materia remota**, see *materia contingens* and *materia propinqua*.—(n²), **materia sacramenti**, *the matter of the sacrament*, which consists of the sensible things used in the dispensing of the same.—(o²), **materia sanctificata**, *the sanctified matter*.—(p²), **materia sensibilis**, see *materia intellegibilis*.—(q²), **materia sensibilis communis seu in communi** and **materia sensibilis individualis seu signata**, *the general* and *the special* or *individual matter perceived by the senses*.—(r²), **materia sensibilis individualis seu signata**, see *materia sensibilis communis*.—(s²), **materia signata**, see *materia demonstrata.* —(t²), **materia simplex**, see *ma-

teria composita.—(u²), **materia situata**, *the matter provided with a local place.*—(v²), **materia spiritualis seu spiritualium**, see *materia corporalis.*—(w²), **materia syllogismi**, see *materia enuntiationis.*—(x²), **materia terrea seu terrestris**, see *materia aerea.*—(y²), **materia transiens**, *the transient matter.*—(z²), **materia ultima**, *sensible matter.*— **forma est finis materiae**, see *forma* under 2.—**materia est individuationis principium**, or, **materia sensibilis signata est individuationis et singularitatis principium**, *matter*, i.e., *matter that can be perceived by the senses* and *definitely defined matter is the principle of individuality.*— **materia est propter formam**, *matter exists for the sake of form.*— **materia sensibilis signata est individuationis et singularitatis principium**, see above: *materia est individuationis principium.*

materialis, e, *adj.*, (1) *material*, i.e., belonging to the matter, substance, source (*materia ex qua*, see *materia* under 1) of a thing, acting after the manner of the matter of a thing, the opposite of *formalis*, (2) *material*, i.e., being of a material nature, belonging to matter, infected with a matter, existing in a matter, cf. *materia ex qua* under *materia* under 1, the opposite of *immaterialis* and *spiritualis.*—On **causa materialis**, see *causa* under 1; on **consideratio materialis**, see *consideratio;* on **definitio materialis**, see *definitio* under 2; on **differentia materialis**, see *differentia;* on **distinctio materialis**, see *distinctio* under 2; on **diversitas materialis**, see *diversitas;* on **divisio materialis**, see *divisio;* on **elementum materiale**, see *elementum* under 3; on **infinitas materialis**, see *infinitas;* on **infinitum materiale**, see *infinitus;* on **intellectus materialis**, see *intellectus* under 3; on **multitudo materialis**, see *multitudo* under 3; on **mutatio materialis**, see *mutatio;* on **obiectum materiale**, see *obiectum;* on **perfectio materialis**, see *perfectio* under 2; on **primum materiale**, see *primus;* on **principium materiale**, see *principium;* on **processio materialis**, see *processio;* on **significatio materialis**, see *significatio* under 1; on **transmutatio materialis**, see *transmutatio* under 1.—Kinds of *materiale* in this (1) sense are: **materiale signatum fluens et refluens** and **materiale signatum permanens**, *the matter that flows out* and *flows back* or *the passing* and *returning matter* or *the abiding* or *lasting definitely designated matter.* On **agens materiale**, see *agens;* on **cognitio materialis**, see *cognitio* under 2; on **compositio materialis**, see *compositio* under 1; on **conceptio materialis**, see *conceptio* under 2; on **condicio materialis**, see *condicio* under 3; on **corpus materiale**, see *corpus;* on **dispositio**

materialis, see *dispositio* under
4; on **esse materiale,** see *esse;*
on **forma materialis,** see *forma*
under 2; on **fundamentum materiale,** see *fundamentum;* on **generatio materialis,** see *generatio*
under 1; on **homo materialis,** see
homo; on **immutatio materialis,**
see *immutatio* under 2; on **liber
materialis,** see *liber* under 1; on
linea materialis, see *linea* under
1; on **multiplicatio materialis,**
see *multiplicatio;* on **natura materialis,** see *natura;* on **organum
materiale,** see *organum;* on **potentia materialis,** see *potentia*
under 1; on **principium materiale,** see *principium;* on **processio
materialis,** see *processio;* on **qualitas materialis,** see *qualitas;* on
quidditas materialis, see *quidditas;* on **res materialis,** see *res;* on
speculum materiale, see *speculum* under 1; on **substantia materialis,** see *substantia* under 2;
on **virtus materialis,** see *virtus*
under 1.—**materialiter,** *adv.,* (1)
after the manner and *in the
sense of matter, with reference
to the matter of a thing* (cf. *materia ex qua* under *materia* under
1), *materially,* the opposite of
formaliter, (2) *in a material way*
(cf. *materia ex qua* under *materia* under 1), *materially,* the opposite of *immaterialiter.*—On **actus materialiter bonus,** see *actus*
under 1; on **bonum materialiter
dictum,** see *bonus* under 2; on
certus materialiter, see *certus*
under 2; on **differre materialiter,**

see *differre* under 2; on **distingui materialiter,** see *distinguere;*
on **diversificare materialiter,** see
diversificare; on **falsus materialiter,** see *falsus;* on **obiectum materialiter acceptum,** see *obiectum;* on **operatio materialiter bona,** see *operatio* under 2; on **scire materialiter,** see *scire* under
2; on **significare materialiter,** see
significare; on **sumere materialiter,** see *sumere* under 3; on **tenere materialiter,** see *tenere* under 7; on **volitum materialiter,**
see *volitus.*—On **cognoscere materialiter,** see *cognoscere* under
2; on **recipere materialiter,** see
recipere; on **scire materialiter,**
see *scire* under 2.

materialitas, atis, *f., the quality* or
*state of being material, corpore-
ity, materiality.*

materialiter, *adv.,* see *materialis.*

materies, ei, see *materia.* The form
materies is used only once in the
S.T. and then in quotation.

maternitas, atis, *f., motherhood,*
the quality or condition of being
a mother; the character or relation of a mother.

maternus, a, um, *adj., of* or *belonging to a mother, maternal,* (1)
lit., (a), *maternal,* (b) related
through a mother or on the
mother's side, (2) *fig.*

matertera, ae, *f., a mother's sister,*
an aunt by the mother's side,
used in the S.T. only in quot.

Mathathias, ae, *m., Mathathias,* a
priest of the Hasmonean family
mentioned in I Machab. 2.

mathematice, *adv.*, see *mathematicus.*

mathematicus, a, um, *adj., of* or *belonging to mathematics, mathematical.* On **corpus mathematicum,** see *corpus;* on **definitio mathematica,** see *definitio* under 2; on **intellectus mathematicus,** see *intellectus* under 9; on **linea mathematica,** see *linea* under 1; on **magnitudo mathematica,** see *magnitudo* under 1; on **medium mathematicum,** see *medium* under 2; on **modus mathematicus,** see *modus* under 3; on **philosophia mathematica,** see *philosophia;* on **philosophus mathematicus,** see *philosophus* under 1; on **potentia mathematica,** see *potentia* under 1; on **principium mathematicum,** see *principium;* on **processus mathematicus,** see *processus* under 2; on **quantitas mathematica,** see *quantitas* under 1; on **ratio mathematica,** see *ratio* under 13; on **scientia mathematica et pure mathematica,** see *scientia* under 1; on **species mathematica,** see *species* under 8.—**mathematica** sc. **philosophia seu scientia,** *mathematics,* that branch of philosophy that treats of quantity. It stands between natural philosophy or physics, which treats of movable bodies, and metaphysics, which treats of being. Since there are two species of quantity, there are two kinds of mathematics, namely, *arithmetica,* the science of discrete quantity or number and *geometrica,* the science of continuous quantity.—**mathematicus** sc. **philosophus,** *mathemetician.* —**mathematice,** *adv., after the manner* and *in the sense of mathematics, mathematically.*

matrimonialis, e, *adj., of* or *belonging to marriage, matrimonial.* On **actus matrimonialis,** see *actus* under 1; on **consensus matrimonialis,** see *consensus* under 2.—**matrimonialiter,** *adv., in a manner relating to marriage, matrimonially.*

matrimonialiter, *adv.*, see *matrimonialis.*

matrimonium, ii, *n., wedlock, marriage, matrimony.* On **actus matrimonii,** see *actus* under 1; on **bonum matrimonii,** see *bonus* under 3; on **causa matrimonii et separationis matrimonii,** see *causa* under 6; on **debitum matrimonii,** see *debitus* under 1; on **ius matrimonii,** see *ius* under 1; on **status matrimonii,** see *status* under 4.—Kinds of *matrimonium* are: (a), **matrimonium carnale seu corporale seu materiale** and **matrimonium spirituale,** *the carnal* or *physical marriage* and *the immaterial* or *spiritual marriage.* —(b), **matrimonium certum,** *the certain* or *the truly existing matrimony.*—(c), **matrimonium clandestinum,** *the secret marriage* or that not blessed by a priest. Although strongly forbidden, such a marriage was valid, until the Council of Trent, sess, 24, Cap. I. de Refor., decreed the present form of marriage under pain of invalidity.—(d), **matrimonium consummatum** and **matrimonium inconsummatum**, *the marriage completed* or *consummated* (by the *copula carnalis*), and *the marriage not so completed* or *consummated;* cf. *matrimonium initiatum.*—(e), **matrimonium contractum** and **matrimonium contrahendum**, *the marriage already contracted* and *the marriage which is to be contracted* or *agreed upon.*—(f), **matrimonium corporale**, see *matrimonium carnale.*—(g), **matrimonium firmum**, *the firm* or *indissoluble marriage.*—(h), **matrimonium illegitimum** and **matrimonium legitimum**, *the illegitimate* or *invalid marriage* and *the legitimate* or *valid marriage.*—(i), **matrimonium imperfectum** and **matrimonium perfectum**, *the imperfect, unsacramental* and *the perfect sacramental marriage,* or *that of unbelievers* and *that of Christians.*—(j), **matrimonium inconsummatum**, see *matrimonium consummatum.*—(k), **matrimonium initiatum**, *the marriage initiated,* which is opposed to the marriage completed (per carnalem copulam). Cf. *matrimonium consummatum.*—(l), **matrimonium legitimum**, see *matrimonium illegitimum.*—(m), **matrimonium perfectum**, see *matrimonium imperfectum.*—(n), **matrimonium praesumptum seu reputatum** and **matrimonium verum**, *the sup-*

posed or *pretended marriage* and *the true* or *real marriage.*—(o), **matrimonium ratificatum seu ratum**, *the marriage ratified by the Church.*—(p), **matrimonium ratum**, see *matrimonium ratificatum.*—(q), **matrimonium reputatum**, see *matrimonium praesumptum.*—(r), **matrimonium spirituale**, see *matrimonium corporale.*—(s), **matrimonum verum**, see *matrimonium praesumptum.*

Matthaeus, i, *m., Matthew,* Apostle and Evangelist. St. Matthew is the same as Levi, mentioned in the Gospel of St. Luke (V. 27). Matthew was the first of the Evangelists who wrote a Gospel which appeared between the years 64 and 67, or according to others, in the year 42, about the time of the dispersion of the Apostles.

Matthias, ae, *m., Matthias,* Saint, Apostle, was elected to fill the place of the traitor Judas. He died in the year 63.

maturitas, atis, *f., maturity,* the full or proper time for anything.

maturus, a, um, *adj.,* (1) *ripe, ready for,* (2) *mature,* having the powers of mind and body fully developed.

matutinalis, e, *adj., of* or *belonging to the morning, early morning.*

matutinus, a, um, *adj., of* or *belonging to the early morning, dawn, morning,* used fig. here.— **cognitio matutina et vespertina angelorum,** *the morning* and *evening knowledge of the angels,* i.e., knowledge of creatures in God and in themselves, an expression devised by St. Augustine who interprets the six days wherein God made all things as one day, namely the day of angelic knowledge as directed to six classes of things. As in the ordinary day, morning is the beginning, and evening the close of the day, so their knowledge of the primordial being of things to be created but still existent only in the mind of God whom they see directly is called morning knowledge; their knowledge of the very being of the things created, as they stand in their own nature, is termed evening knowledge.—**matutinae,** arum, *f., Matins,* the first part of the Divine Office said towards the break of day in monasteries; it is also called *Nocturn* or *Vigils,* because formerly it was chanted during the night. Lauds are said after Matins. The custom today is to anticipate and to recite these parts on the eve of the feast or *feria* to which they belong.

Maximinus, i, *m., Maximinus,* Arian bishop of Hippo Regius, who had come with the Gothic soldiers into Africa A.D. 427, 428, and held a discussion with St. Augustine on the subject of the Trinity. Augustine replied to his arguments in two books, *Contra Maximinum.*

maximopere, *adv.,* see *magnopere.*

Maximus, i, *m.,* (1) *Maximus,* Valerius, a Roman historian. Of his life we know only that he accompanied the proconsul Sextus Pompeius to Asia in A.D. 27. On his return he composed between A.D. 29 and 32 a collection of historical anecdotes in nine books, *Factorum et Dictorum Memorabilium Libri* which he dedicated to the Emperor Tiberius. St. Thomas gives frequent references to this work. (2) *Maximus,* saint, bishop of Turin, born at Vercelli, died in 466. He was a great Christian orator. The works of Maximus consist of 116 sermons, three treatises on baptism, two treatises respectively entitled *Contra Paganos* and *Contra Iudaeos,* besides a collection of expositions, *De Capitulis Evangeliorum.* St. Thomas quotes from his sermons. (3) *Maximus* of Constantinople (580-662). He was a scion of a noble family and was secretary to the Emperor Heraclius; he resigned his office at court and retired to a monastery near Constantinople of which he became abbot. He wrote commentaries on divers books of Scripture and on the works attributed to Dionysius the Areopagite.

meatus, us, *m.,* (1) *a passing, going, course of a stream,* hence *channel,* used *lit.* and *fig.,* (2) *transf., a passage, opening.*

mechanicus, a, um, *adj., of* or *belonging to mechanics, mechanical.*

medela, ae, *f., a remedy, means of redress,* used *fig.*

medeor, eri, 2, *v. dep. n., to heal, remedy, relieve,* used with the *dat.,* used in the S.T. only in quot.

medians, antis, *P. a., mediating,* acting or serving as an intermediate agent, instrument, means, etc., used with a noun in the *abl. abs., through the medium of.*

mediate, *adv.,* see *mediatus.*

mediator, oris, *m., a mediator.*

mediatus, a, um, *adj., mediated through another, derived, intermediary,* the opposite of *immediatus.* On **causa mediata,** see *causa* under 1; on **contraria mediata,** see *contrarius* under 1; on **oppositum mediatum,** see *opponere;* on **principium mediatum,** see *principium;* on **processio mediata,** see *processio;* on **propositio mediata,** see *propositio* under 1; on **visio mediata,** see *visio* under 1.—**mediate,** *adv., in an indirect way, through the mediacy of another, mediately,* synonym of *indirecte,* the opposite of *directe* and *immediate.* On **movere mediate,** see *movere;* on **procedere mediate,** see *procedere* under 4.

medicamen, inis, *n.,* (1) *lit., a medicament, a healing substance* used in curative arts, (2) *transf., a paint, wash, cosmetic,* (3) *fig., a remedy, antidote.*

medicamentum, i, *n.,* (1) *lit.,* (a) *a drug, remedy, physic, medicine, medicament,* (b) *a condiment, seasoning,* (2) *fig., a remedy, relief, antidote.*

medicatio, onis, *f., a healing, cure* used (1) *lit.,* (2) *fig.*

medicativus, a, um, *adj. medicative,* having the function or power of curing; *curative.*

medicina, ae, *f.,* (1) *lit.,* (a) *the healing* or *medical art, medicine, surgery,* often used as a synonym for *medicus,* (b) *a remedy, medicine,* (2) *fig., a remedy, antidote.*

medicinalis, e, *adj., of* or *pertaining to medicine, designed to improve* or *heal, medicinal.*—**medicinaliter,** *adv., medicinally.*

medicinaliter, *adv.,* see *medicinalis.*

medicor, ari, atus, 1, *v. dep. a., to heal, cure.*—**medicans,** antis, *P. a., healing.*

medicus, i, *m., a medical man, physician, surgeon.*—**omnipotens medicus,** *the all powerful physician, God.*—**spiritualis medicus,** *the spiritual physician, the physician of souls,* i.e., Christ.

medie, *adv.,* see *medius.*

medietas, atis, *f., the middle, place in the middle, midst.*—One kind of *medietas* is: **medietas arithmetica,** *the arithmetical mean.* Cf. *medium arithmeticum* under *medium* under 1.—**virtus moralis est habitus electivus, in medietate exsistens, ut sapiens determinabit,** see *virtus* under 5.—**virtus moralis est quaedam medietas et**

est medii **coniectatrix,** see *virtus* under 5.

mediocris, e, *adj., in a middle state* between too much and too little, *middling, moderate, tolerable, ordinary, common, trivial;* sometimes also *not remarkable, indifferent, mediocre,* (1) in gen., (a) of size, quantity, quality, degree, etc., in material things (b) of abstract things, *ordinary, moderate, weak,* (2) *esp.,* of the mind, *per litoten,* with *non.*—**mediocriter,** *adv., moderately, with moderation.*

mediocritas, atis, *f., a middle state, a medium, a mean.*

mediocriter, *adv.,* see *mediocris.*

Mediolanensis, e, *adj., Milanese, of* or *belonging to Milan.*

meditatio, onis, *f., a thinking over a thing, contemplation, meditation.*

meditor, ari, atus, 1, *v. dep. a.* and *n.,* (1) *to meditate, reflect upon something,* (2) *think of something.*

medium, ii, *n.,* see *medius.*

medius, a, um, *adj., that is in the middle* or *midst, mid, middle.* On **causa media,** see *causa* under 2; on **complexio media,** see *complexio* under 2; on **differentia media,** see *differentia;* on **elementum medium,** see *elementum* under 1; on **forma media,** see *forma* under 2; on **generatio media,** see *generatio* under 1; on **genus medium,** see *genus* under 2; on **hierarchia media,** see *hierarchia;* on **orbis medius,** see *or-*

bis; on **scientia media,** see *scientia* under 1; on **species media,** see *species* under 8; on **substantia media,** see *substantia* under 1; on **terminus medius,** see *terminus* under 4.—**media** sc. **propositio,** *the minor premise of a conclusion,* so called because it holds the middle place between the *propositio maior* (see *propositio* under 2) and the *conclusio* under 2.—**medie,** *adv., in a middle way, moderately, tolerably.*—**medium,** ii, *n.,* (1) *the medium, the middle, the mean,* (2) *means, instrument,* (3) *the middle term,* that notion which by its extent holds the middle between the subject and the predicate of a conclusion and composes or divides them by serving as the predicate of one and the subject of the other. On **fieri ex medio,** see *fieri.*—Kinds of *medium* in this (1) sense are: (a), **medium arithmeticum, medium geometricum,** and **medium harmonicum seu musicum,** *the arithmetical* or *numerical medium, the geometrical* or *proportionate medium* and *the harmonic* or *musical medium.*—(b), **medium geometricum,** see *medium arithmeticum.*—(c), **medium harmonicum,** see *medium arithmeticum.*—(d), **medium in mensuratis et regulatis,** *the medium in things that have a measure* and *a rule.*—(e), **medium iustitiae,** *the medium of justice* or the medium which seeks to determine what must be rendered another, which is the characteristic of the virtue of justice. —(f), **medium musicum**, see *medium arithmeticum*.—(g), **medium proportionis**, *the medium of proportion* or *the proportionate medium.* Cf. *medium arithmeticum*, and *medium iustitiae*.—(h), **medium rationis seu secundum rationem** and **medium rei**, *the medium in accordance with reason* and *that in accordance with reality*.—(i), **medium rei**, see *medium rationis*.—(j), **medium secundum rationem**, see *medium rationis*.—(k), **medium virtutis**, *the medium of virtue*, i.e., *that medium toward which virtue aims*.—**non est contrarietas medii ad extrema**, see *contrarietas* under 1.—**virtus in medio seu in mediocritate consistit**, see *virtus* under 5.—**virtus moralis est quaedam medietas et est medii coniectatrix**, see *virtus* under 5.— **virtus moralis in medio consistit quoad nos determinato ratione**, see *virtus* under 5.—On **unire per medium et sine medio**, see *unire*. —Kinds of *medium* in this (2) sense are: (a), **medium agens** and **medium formale**, *the effective* and *the formative means*, or *the means after the manner of the agent cause* and *that after the manner of form*.—(b), **medium congruentiae seu congruitatis** and **medium necessitatis**, *the means of the fitting* or *the congruous* and *that of necessity* or *that fitting for the attainment of a purpose* and *the means necessary for it*.—(c), **medium coniunctum** and **medium extraneum seu extrinsecum**, *a medium contiguous with a sense organ* and *a separate medium*.—(d), **medium demonstrationis seu in demonstrationibus seu demonstrativum seu necessarium** and **medium dialecticum seu probabile**, *the necessarily true means* or *the means for proving something as necessarily true* and *the probable proof* or *the proof that shows something as probable*.—(e), **medium demonstrativum**, see *medium demonstrationis*.—(f), **medium dialecticum**, see *medium demonstrationis*.—(g), **medium exemplare**, *the exemplary means.* —(h), **medium extraneum**, see *medium coniunctum*.—(i), **medium extraneum seu extra positum** and **medium proprium**, *the outer means of proof* or *the means of proof brought in from the outside* (cf. *medium coniunctum*) and *the proper* or *peculiar means of proof*.—(j), **medium extrapositum**, see *medium extraneum*.— (k), **medium extrinsecum**, see *medium coniunctum*.—(l), **medium formale**, see *medium agens*.— (m), **medium habitum**, *the means touching something directly*, (*id est immediate sequens*).—(n), **medium in demonstrationibus**, see *medium demonstrationis*.—(o), **medium in quo**, **medium quo**, and **medium sub quo sc. cognitionis seu visionis**, *the means*

in which, the means by which,
and *the means under which* or
through which a thing is known
or *seen.*—(p), **medium mathematicum** and **medium naturale,**
the mathematical and *physical
means of proof* or *the means of
proof of a mathematician* and
that of a scientist.—(q), **medium
naturale,** see *medium mathematicum.*—(r), **medium necessarium,**
see *medium demonstrationis.*—
(s), **medium necessitatis,** see *medium congruentiae.*—(t), **medium
probabile,** see *medium demonstrationis.*—(u), **medium proprium,** see *medium extraneum.*—
(v), **medium quo,** see *medium in
quo.*—(w), **medium sensibile,** *the
means of proof perceived by the
senses.*—(x), **medium sub quo,**
see *medium in quo.*—(y), **medium
syllogismi seu syllogisticum,** *the
middle term of a syllogism,* i.e.,
that by means of which a conclusion is made.—(z), **medium syllogisticum,** see *medium syllogismi.*
—**medie,** *adv., in a middling degree, moderately,* does not occur
in the S.T. except as a question-
ble reading.

medulla, ae, *f., the marrow of
bones,* (1) *lit.,* (b) *transf., the
pith, inside, kernel,* (2) *fig., the
marrow, innermost part.*

megalokindynos, a, on, (Grk. *megalokindynos) adj., braving great
dangers, adventurous.*

mel, mellis, *n., honey.*

melancholia, ae, *f., melancholy.*

melancholicus, a, um, *adj., melancholy, atrabilious, having black
bile.*

Melchi, *n., indecl., m., Melchi,* an
ancestor of Christ.

Melchiades, is, *m., Melchiades* or
Miltiades, Saint. He was born in
Africa and reigned as pope from
311 to 314. He presided over
the Council of Rome (313), and
condemned the Donatists. His
Epistola ad episc. Hispaniae is
quoted by St. Thomas.

Melchisedech, *indecl., m., Melchisedech,* King of Salem, a poetic
name for Jerusalem. Abraham returning from his pursuit of Cho-
dorlahomor, was blessed by him,
and in return received the tenth
part of the spoils. The Epistle to
the Hebrews (VI. 20) represents
him as a prototype of Christ; his
charge would have been superior
to the priesthood of that of Aaron's family.

Meldensis, e, *adj., of Meldis* or
Meaux, a town in Northern
France, capitol of an arrondisse-
ment in the department of Seine-
et-Marne, and chief town in the
agricultural region of Brie. In the
Roman period Meldis or Meaux
was the capitol of the Meldi, a
small Gallic tribe, and in the
Middle Ages of Brie. A council
was held at Meaux (Concilium
Meldense) in the year 1082.

melior, melius, see *bonus.*

melioratio, onis, *f., a bettering, improvement, melioration.*

meliorativus, a, um, *adj.*, *making better*, *improving*, *meliorative.* On **amor meliorativus**, see *amor* under 1.

melioro, are, avi, tum, 1, *v. a.*, *to make better*, *to better*, *to improve.*

melius, *comp. adj.*, and *adv.*, see *bonus.*

melodia, ae, *f.*, *a pleasant song*, *melody.*

melota, ae, *f.*, *a sheepskin* (with the wool on).

membrana, ae, *f.*, *a skin* prepared for writing etc., *parchment.*

membrum, i, *n.*, *a limb*, *member of a body*, (1) *lit.*, (2) *transf.*, (a) in *gen.*, in inanimate and abstr. things, *a division*, *head*, (b) of the Church of Christ, (3) *fig.*, with reference to a metaphorical body, chiefly in members of Christ, of Satan.

memini, isse, *v. n.*, (1) *to remember*, *recollect*, *to think of*, *be mindful of* a thing; not to have forgotten a person or thing, *to bear in mind*, used with (a) *gen.*, (b) *acc.*, (c) *acc.* and *inf.*, (d) with *perf. inf.*, (e) *absol.*, (f) the future imper., *memento* used with *ut.* (2) *transf.*, *to make mention of*, *to mention a thing.*

memor, oris, *adj.*, *mindful of a thing*, *remembering*, used with *gen.*—**memoriter**, *adv.*, *from memory*, *by personal recollection.*

memorabilis, e, *adj.*, *memorable*, *remarkable*, *worthy of being re-* membered, *worthy to be mentioned.*

memorativus, a, um, *adj.*, *keeping remembrance*, *holding in memory*, *recollecting*, *memorative.* On **potentia memorativa**, see *potentia* under 2; on **virtus memorativa**, see *virtus* under 1; on **vis memorativa**, see *vis* under 1.— **memorativa** sc. **potentia seu virtus seu vis**, *the faculty of memory.*—**memorativum** sc. **principium**, *the principle* or *faculty of memory*, having the same meaning as *memorativa* above.

memoria, ae, *f.*, (1) *memory* in the sense of an action, *involuntary remembrance*, the opposite of *reminiscentia*, (2) *organic memory* in the sense of a faculty in the narrower sense of the word, i.e., the sense faculty of preserving the relations which the *vis aestimativa* has conceived in things perceived by the senses, as well as the involuntary remembrance of formerly perceived things whose presentations the memory preserves in itself (cf. *memorativa*), (3) *inorganic memory* in the sense of a faculty in the wider sense of the word, i.e., the faculty of preserving within itself the images or presentations of things formerly recognized through the intellect as well as through the senses, (4) *memory* in the improper sense, *token of memory* or *remembrance*, *memorial*, *remembrance.*—**ex memoria multo-**

ties facta circa eandem rem in diversis tamen singularibus fit experimentum or ex mutis memoriis fit unum experimentum or experientia fit ex multis memoriis, the translation of the Aristotelian passage: *ek de mnemes pollakis tou autou ginomenes empeiria, experimental knowledge arises from many remembrances of different examples.*— On **delectatio memoriae seu per memoriam**, see *delectatio.*—One kind of *memoria* in this (3) sense is: **memoria intellectiva seu interior**, *the intellectual* or *inner memory.*

memoriale, is, *n., memorial, that which is kept in remembrance.*

memoriter, *adv.*, see *memor.*

memoro, are, avi, atum, 1, *v. a., to bring to remembrance, remind of, recall.* On **delectabile memoratum**, see *delectabilis.*— **memoror**, ari, atus, sum, 1, *v. dep., to remember, be mindful of.*

memoror, see *memoro.*

mendaciter, *adv.*, see *mendax.*

mendacium, ii, *n., a lie, untruth, falsehood.* On **signum mendacii**, see *signum* under 3; on **spiritus mendacii**, see *spiritus.*—Kinds of *mendacium* are: (a), **mendacium iocosum**, *the pleasing lie, the white lie.*—(b), **mendacium officiosum**, *the lie of necessity, the officious lie.*—(c), **mendacium perniciosum**, *the harmful* or *pernicious lie.*

mendax, dacis, *adj., given to lying, mendacious.*—**mendax**, dacis, *m., a liar.*—**mendaciter**, *adv., falsely, mendaciously.*

mendicatio, onis, *f., a begging, obtaining by begging.*

mendicitas, atis, *f., beggary, mendicity*, the state or condition of being a beggar; the habit or practice of begging.

mendico, are, avi, atum, 1, *v. n.*, and *a., to beg, ask for alms, go a-begging, to beg for something, solicit, obtain by begging*, used with *acc., absol.*

mendicus, i, *m., a beggar, mendicant.*

Menon, onis, *m., Menon*, a Thessalian adventurer, one of the generals of the mercenaries in the army of Cyrus the Younger when the latter marched into Upper Asia against his brother Artaxerxes, B.C. 401. He is the same as the Menon introduced in the dialogue of Plato which bears his name.

mens, mentis, *f.*, (1) *intellect, mind, spirit, intellectual being*, the opposite of *corpus*, and *sensus*, (2) *intellect, intellectual faculty of perceiving* or *desiring*, (3) *remembrance, memory.* On **caecitas mentis**, see *caecitas;* on **conceptus mentis**, see *conceptus* under 2; on **consensus mentis**, see *consensus* under 2; on **immunditia mentis**, see *immunditia;* on **integritas mentis**, see *integritas;* on **oratio mentis**, see *oratio* under 3; on **speculum mentis**, see *speculum* under 1; on **tumor mentis,** see *ira* under 1.—On **contraria in mente,** see *contrarius* under 1; on **dicere mentem,** see *dicere* under 1; on **falsum in mente,** see *falsus;* on **notitia mentis,** see *notitia* under 1; on **verbum mentis,** see *verbum* under 1; on **verum in mente,** see *verus* under 1.

mensa, ae, *f., a table for any purpose,* (1) in *partic.,* **mensa propositionis,** *the table of proposition.* In the Tabernacle which God commanded Moses to build stood the Table of Proposition or the Table of the Shewbreads (Ex. XXV, 23) on which twelve loaves of unleavened bread were placed before the Lord (Lev. XXIV 5-7); hence they were called the Breads of Proposition and the Breads of the Face, being always before the face of the Lord, (2) *transf., food; a table, a meal, eating, support.*—The following phrases are used frequently: **ire ad mensam alicuius,** *to dine with someone.*—**intrare ad mensam alicuius,** *to eat with someone.*—**sacrata mensa,** *a consecrated table, an altar.*—**mensa Domini,** *the table of the Lord, the altar, the communion table.*

mensis, is, *m., a month.*

menstruatus, a, um, *P. a.,* (1) *neutr., menstruous, having the catamenia,* (2) act., fig., *polluted.*

menstruus, a, um, *adj., menstruous.* —**menstruum,** i, *n.,* and **men-** strua, orum, *n., menses, catamenia.*

mensura, ae, *f., a measuring, measure.*—Kinds of *mensura* in the broader sense of the word are: (a), **mensura coaequata seu homogenea** and **mensura excedens,** *the measure equal* or *similar to the measured* and *that exceeding* or *excelling its nature.*—(b), **mensura communis,** *the common measure.*—(c), **mensura debita,** *the proper* or *due measure.*—(d), **mensura excedens,** see *mensura coaequata.*—(e), **mensura extrinseca** and **mensura intrinseca,** *the outer* or *extrinsic* and *the inner* or *intrinsic measure.*—(f), **mensura homogenea,** see *mensura coaequata.*—(g), **mensura intrinseca,** see *mensura extrinseca.*—(h), **mensura prima seu suprema seu remota** and **mensura secunda seu proxima,** *the first* or *highest* or *remote measure* and *the second* or *immediate measure,* i.e., measure in the highest and in the secondary instance.—(i), **mensura proportionata,** *the measure standing in relation to the measured.*—(j), **mensura proxima,** see *mensura prima.*—(k), **mensura quantitativa,** *the measure of physical size.*—(l), **mensura remota,** see *mensura prima.*—(m), **mensura secunda,** see *mensura prima.*—(n), **mensura suprema,** see *mensura prima.*

mensurabilis, e, *adj., that can be measured, measurable.*

mensurate, *adv.,* see *mensuro.*

mensuratio, onis, *f., measure, moderation.*

mensuro, are, avi, atum, 1, *v. a.,* (1) *lit., to measure,* (2) *fig., to measure, estimate.*—**mensurate,** *adv., by measurement.*

mentalis, e, *adj., mental, intellectual.* On **consensus mentalis,** see *consensus* under 2; on **intentio mentalis,** see *intentio* under 2; on **laus mentalis,** see *laus;* on **oratio mentalis,** see *oratio* under 3; on **verbum mentale,** see *verbum* under 1; on **visio mentalis,** see *visio* under 1.—**mentaliter,** *adv., in the mental* or *intellectual manner, in the mental* or *intellectual sense, mentally, intellectually.*

mentaliter, *adv.,* see *mentalis.*

mentio, onis, *f., a calling to mind, a cursory speaking of, a making mention, mentioning, naming, mention.* Numerous examples of the following phrases occur: **facere mentionem de aliquo,** *to make mention of something, to speak about something.*—**audire mentionem alicuius,** *to hear mention of something.*—**habere mentionem de,** *to make mention of something.*

mentior, iri, itus, 4, *v. dep. n.* and *a., to lie, deceive.*—**mentiens,** entis, *m., a liar.*

mercatio, onis, *f., mercantile, dealing.*

mercator, oris, *m., a trader, merchant.*—**lex mercatorum,** *the mercantile law.*

mercenarius, a, um, *adj., paid, hired, mercenary.* On **actus mer-**cenarius, see *actus* under 1; on **amor mercenarius,** see *amor* under 1.

merces, edis, *f.,* (1) *lit., hire, pay, wages, salary, fee, reward,* (2) *transf., a reward,* recompense which is given in return for good done, especially the eternal reward.

Mercurius, ii, *m., Mercury; the son of Jupiter and Maia, the messenger of the gods; as a herald the god of dexterity; in speaking, the god of eloquence; the bestower of prosperity; the god of traders* and *thieves; the presider over roads,* and *conductor of departed souls to the Lower World.*—**acervus Mercurii,** *the heap of Mercury.* St. Thomas explains this passage from the Book of Proverbs, XXVI, 8. Since the gentiles ascribed the keeping of accounts to Mercury, *the heap of Mercury* signifies the reckoning up of an account, when a merchant sometimes substitutes a pebble for one hundred marks.

mereor, eri, itus, 2, *v. dep., merui,* active form always in perfect system, *to deserve, merit,* (cf. *meritum*). On **status merendi,** see *status* under 3.—Kinds of *mereri* are: (a), **mereri aliquo sicut ipso merito** and **mereri aliquo sicut principio merendi,** *to merit through the meritorious work itself,* and *through possession of something which is the principle of merit.* Cf. also *mereri primo* below.—(b), **mereri aliquo sicut**

principio merendi, see *mereri aliquo sicut ipsi merito.*—(c), **mereri
ex condigno** and **mereri ex congruo**, *to merit strictly* and *properly, from justice* or *a contract,*
and *to merit loosely* and *by way
of largesse.*—(d), **mereri ex congruo**, see *mereri ex condigno.*—
(e), **mereri improprie** and **mereri
proprie**, *to merit in the improper*
and *in the proper sense of the
word.*—(f), **mereri primo** and **mereri secundario**, *through something to merit in the first place*
and *in the second place.* Cf. *mereri aliquo sicut ipso merito.*—(g),
mereri proprie, see *mereri improprie.*—(h), **mereri secundario**, see
mereri primo.—**meritum**, i, *n.,* see
meritum.

meretricor, ari, atus, 1, *v. dep. to
deal with harlots, to prostitute.*

meretricius, a, um, *adj., meretri-
cious, of* or *pertaining to harlots*
or *prostitutes.*—**meretricium**, ii,
*n., whoredom, the art of a cour-
tesan.*

meretrix, icis, *f., a prostitute, harlot, courtesan.*

mergo, ere, si, sum, 3, *v. a.,* (1) *lit.,*
(a) *to plunge into water, to sink;
to dip, dip in, immerse,* (b)
transf., to sink in, penetrate, (2)
fig., to plunge into.

mergulus, i, *m., a cormorant, kind
of bird.*

meridianus, a, um, *adj., noon-day,
mid-day.*

meridies, ei, *m., mid-day, noon,* (1)
lit., (2) *transf., the south.*

meritorie, *adv.,* see *meritorius.*

meritorius, a, um, *adj., meritorious,
deserving,* the opposite of *demeritorius.* Cf. *mereri* and *meritum.*
On **actio meritoria**, see *actio* under 1; on **actus meritorius**, see
actus under 1; on **bonum meritorium**, see *bonus* under 2; on **causa meritoria**, see *causa* under 2;
on **cognitio meritoria**, see *cognitio* under 2; on **conversio meritoria**, see *conversio* under 4; on
dilectio meritoria, see *dilectio*
under 1; on **operatio meritoria et
meritoria finis**, see *operatio* under 2; on **opus meritorium et
non-meritorium**, see *opus* under
4; on **oratio meritoria**, see *oratio*
under 3.—Kinds of *meritorius*
are: (a), **meritorium ex condigno**
and **meritorium ex congruo**, *meritorius according to worthiness*
and *according to appropriateness*
or *the properly* and *the suitably
meritorious.* The first is due in
strict justice; the second is given
from liberality.—(b), **meritorium
ex congruo**, see *meritorium ex
condigno.*—(c), **meritorium per
se**, *meritorious through itself* or
as such.—(d), **meritorium primo**,
meritorious in the first place.—
meritorie, *adv., in the sense of
merit, with merit, meritoriously.*

meritum, i, *n., cf., mereri,* (1) *reward, merit* in the proper sense
of the word, i.e., meritorious
work, meritorious action, the opposite of *demeritum,* (2) *merit* in
the improper sense of the word,
i.e., worthiness or fitness for
something. On **agere per modum**

meriti, see *agere* under 1; on **de-bitum ex merito proveniens**, see *debitus* under 1; on **movere per modum meriti**, see *movere;* on **operari per modum meriti**, see *operari;* on **radix meriti**, see *radix;* on **status meriti**, see *status* under 3; on **via meriti**, see *via* under 1.—As kinds of *meritum* in this (1) sense we have the following: (a), **meritum actuale**, *the merit consisting in an action.*— (b), **meritum beatitudinis**, *the merit of happiness* or *the work meriting eternal happiness.* Cf. *meritum vitae aeternae.*—(c), **meritum condicionatum**, *the conditioned* or *subordinated merit.*— (d), **meritum condigni seu condignum** and **meritum congrui**, *the merit of the worthy* or *proper* and *that of the appropriate* or *suitable.*—(e), **meritum congrui**, see *meritum condigni.*—(f), **meritum fidei**, *the merit of supernatural faith.*—(g), **meritum interpretatum**, *apparent merit.*—(h), **meritum mortificatum**, *the killed merit* or *the work deprived of its merit.*—(i), **meritum praecedens**, *the preceding merit* (of divine grace).—(j), **meritum vitae aeternae**, *the merit of eternal life, i.e.,* the work of man by which he merits eternal life. Cf. *meritum beatitudinis.*

merus, a, um, *adj., nothing but, only, mere.*

merx, cis, *f., merchandise, wares, commodities.*

messis, is, *f., the harvest,* used *lit.* and *fig.*

meta, ae, *f., a boundary, limit, measure,* used *fig.*

metalepsis, is, *f., metalepsis, assumption,* the act of assuming or taking for granted.

metallum, i, *n., a metal,* as gold, silver or iron.

metaphora, ae, *f., a rhetorical figure, a metaphor, a transferring of a word from its proper signification to another.*

metaphorice, *adv.*, see *metaphoricus.*

metaphoricus, a, um, *adj., metaphorical, figurative, understood in the metaphorical sense,* synonym of *translativus* and *transumptivus.* On **iustitia metaphorica**, see *iustitia* under 2; on **locutio metaphorica**, see *locutio* under 4; on **modus metaphoricus**, see *modus* under 2.—**metaphorice**, *adv., after the manner* or *in the sense of transfer, metaphorically; figuratively,* synonym of *translative* and *transumptive.* On **accipere metaphorice**, see *accipere* under 3; on **dicere metaphorice**, see *dicere* under 3; on **esse in loco metaphorice**, see *locus* under 2; on **intellegere metaphorice**, see *intellegere* under 3; on **iustitia metaphorice dicta**, see *iustitia* under 2; on **locus metaphorice dictus**, see *locus* under 1; on **nomen metaphorice dictum**, see *nomen* under 1; on **perfectum metaphorice**, see *perfectus* under 1; on **praedicare metapho-**

rice, see *praedicare* under 2; on **sumere metaphorice**, see *sumere* under 3.

metaphysicus, a, um, *adj.*, (1) *metaphysical, concerning* or *belonging to metaphysics*, (2) *the Metaphysics* of Aristotle, i.e., *Metaphysica*, or a commentary on it, e.g., Metaphysics of Avicenna.— On **ratio metaphysica**, see *ratio* under 13; on **scientia metaphysica**, see *scientia* under 1.—**metaphysica** sc. **scientia**, *metaphysics.* —**metaphysicus**, i, *m., the metaphysician.*

meteora, orum, *n., meteors*, used in the S.T. only in referring to Aristotle's *de Meteoris*, (*meteorologika*), *Meteorology.*

methodus, i, *f., mode of proceeding, scientific procedure*, not used in the S.T.

metior, iri, mensus, 4, *v. dep., to measure*, used *fig.*

meto, ere, messui, messum, 3, *v. a.* and *n., to reap, mow, crop*, used *lit.* and *fig.*

metonymia, ae, *f., a figure by which one name is changed for another, a change of names, metonymy.*

metonymicus, a, um, *adj., pertaining to* or *involving metonymy, metonymical*, not used in the S.T. On **locutio metonymica**, see *locutio* under 4.

metrum, i, *n., a measure*; in *partic., a poetical measure, metre; a verse.*

metuo, eri, ui, utum, 3, *v. a.* and *n., to fear, be afraid of a person* or *thing*, used with the *inf., acc., absol.*

metus, us, *m., fear, dread, apprehension, anxiety.*

meus, a, um, *pron., possess., my, mine, belonging to me, my own.*

Michaeas, ae, *m., Micheas* of Morasti, a little town in the tribe of Juda, was contemporary with the prophet Isaias, whom he resembles in his spirit and his style. He is different from the prophet Micheas mentioned in the Third Book of Kings XXII.

Michael, eis, *m., a Hebrew* name, esp. *Michael, the archangel.*

microkindynos, a, on, *adj.*, (*mikrokindynos*), *exposing oneself to danger for trifles.*

migro, are, avi, atum, 1, *v. n.* and *a.*, (1) *lit., to remove from one place to another, to depart, flit, migrate*, (2) *fig., to change, pass over* to something else, used with *in, ad.*

miles, itis, *m.*, (1) in *gen., a soldier*, (2) *Eccl. Lat., a soldier*, said of a servant of God struggling against sin and striving after perfection. —**scribere milites**, *to enlist soldiers.*

militaris, e, *adj., of* or *belonging to a soldier.*

militia, ae, *f.*, (1) *lit., military service, soldiering, warfare*, (2) *fig., warfare, any work of special difficulty requiring a great effort*, used in a spiritual sense.—**liber militiae**, *a book of war*, a book which contains either the names of those chosen for military service; or treats of the art of war; or relates the deeds of soldiers. —**character militiae,** *the mark of enlistment.*—**corporalis nota militiae,** *a bodily mark of military service.*

milito, are, avi, atum, 1, *v. n.,* (1) *lit., to militate, serve as a soldier, take part in warfare,* (2) *transf.,* and *fig., to contend, make war; to strive.*—**Ecclesia militans,** *the Church militant,* the Church on earth is called the Church Militant because of its ceaseless struggle with its three enemies, the world, the devil, and the flesh.

milium, ii, *n., millet, the grain of the millet plant.*

mille, *a thousand,* (1) *lit.,* (a) *sing., an indecl. num. adj.,* (b) *plural.* as *subst.,* rare in the *sing.,* with and without the *gen.,* (2) *transf.,* like the *Gr. myria, a thousand,* for *innumerable, infinite.*

millenarius, a, um, *adj., containing a thousand, millenary.*

milliarius, a, um, *adj., milliary,* per-ˌtaining to the ancient Roman mile of a thousand paces; *making a mile.*—**lapis milliarius,** *a milestone,* used in the S.T. only in quot.

millies, *adv., a thousand times.*

milvus, i, *m., a bird of prey, a kite.*

mimus, i, *m., a jester, mimic actor.*

minae, arum, *f., threats.*

minax, acis, *adj., high-handed, overbearing,* used in the S.T. only in quot.

mineralis, e, *adj., mineral,* having the nature of a mineral; obtained from the bowels of the earth.

mineralia, ium, *n., minerals.*

Minervius, ii, *m., Minervius,* a monk of the diocese of Toulouse in the beginning of the fifth century. He and his brother Alexander in the year 406 hearing that their bishop Exuperius and two presbyters of the diocese, Riparius and Desiderius, were sending their friend Sisinnius to Jerome at Bethlehem, wrote him a letter with many questions on passages of Scripture. Jerome answered (Ep. 119) their two principal questions, on the meaning of "We shall not all sleep, but we shall all be changed" and "We shall be caught up into the clouds".

minister, tri, *m.,* (1) in *gen.,* (a) *an attendant, waiter, servants,* (b) *a minister,* one who acts under the authority of another and carries out executive duties as the representative of such authority, (2) esp. (*eccl. Lat.*) *a minister* of religion, a preacher of Christ. —**familiaris minister,** *a servant of the household.*—**minister artificis,** *craftman's labor.*—**minister legis,** *administrator of the law,* an officer entrusted with the administration of the law.—**minister iudicis,** *the minister of the judge, executioner.*—**ministri Dei,** *the ministers of God,* i.e., *the angels.* —**ministri Dei,** *ministers of God,* i.e., *secular power.*—**minister**

principis, *a minister of a sovereign.*

ministerialis, e, *adj., ministering,* synonym of *instrumentalis.*—**ministerialiter,** *adv., in the manner* or *sense of a servant,* synonym of *instrumentaliter,* the opposite of *per auctoritatem, auctoritative,* and *principaliter.*

ministerialiter, *adv.,* see *ministerialis.*

ministerium, ii, *n., service, employment, performance, ministry.* On **clavis ministerii,** see *clavis* under 2; on **potestas ministerii seu ministerii principalis,** see *potestas* under 3.

ministratio, onis, *f., ministration, service, assistance,* (1) in *gen., the action of rendering aid* or *service to someone,* (2) in *partic., the action of administering the sacraments.*—**ministratio mortis,** *the ministration of death,* i.e., if the ministration performed by Moses in giving the Israelites the Law, which was written on Tables of stone and led to death, was glorious, i.e., accompanied by a glorious manifestation which so shone in the face of Moses that the recipients of that Law could not steadfastly look upon his countenance (Exod. XXXIV. 29-35), how much more glorious is the ministration of the apostles through whom is given to us the Holy Ghost.—**ministratio damnationis,** *the ministration of condemnation.* The law referred to by metonymy as death

in V. 7 is referred to as a condemnation in V. 9, the sense being that it was the occasion while man's corrupt nature was the cause (Rom. VII. 8-11) of death and condemnation.—**ministratio Spiritus,** *the ministration of the Spirit,* i.e., the preaching of the Gospel through which the Holy Ghost is given to men.—The New Law is **ministratio iustitiae,** *a ministration of justice,* i.e., *of justification,* because through it are given the Holy Ghost, sanctifying grace, and glory.

ministrative, *adv., administratively.*

ministrator, oris, *m., an attendant, one who ministers.*

ministro, are, avi, atum, 1, *v. a.,* (1) *lit., to minister, to serve food* or *drink,* (2) *transf.,* (a) *to furnish,* supply something necessary or helpful, used *lit.* and *fig.,* (b) *to minister to the wants* or *comforts of another; to render aid, assist,* (c) *to minister, dispense a sacrament,* (d) *to minister, to serve* or *officiate* in worship, *to act as a minister of the Church.*—**ministrans,** antis, *P. a.,* (1) *administering, guiding, directing, managing affairs,* (2) *ministering, serving officially in worship.*

minor, ari, atus, 1, *v. dep., to threaten.*

minoratio, onis, *f., diminution, reduction, lessening, degrading.*

minoritas, atis, *f., minority, smallness, state* or *condition of being smaller.*

minoro, are, no *perf.*, atum, 1, *v. a.*,
(1) *make smaller, lessen the guilt
of*, (2) *to belittle, disparage, to
lessen one's good name.*—minoratus, a, um, *P. a.*, (1) *diminished,
lessened*, (2) *slighted, dishonored.*—The following Biblical
phrase (Heb. II. 9) occurs: **Christus minoratus est ab angelis,**
*Christ was made lower than the
angels*, on account of the suffering of death.

minuo, ere, ui, utum, 3, *v. a.* and
n., (1) *lit.*, *to diminish, lessen*, (2)
fig., *to lessen, diminish, lower,
reduce.*—minutus, a, um, *P. a.*,
little, small, minute, slight.—minutum, (aes), i, *n.*, *a mite, the
smallest piece of money.*

minutio, onis, *f.*, *a lessening, diminishing.*

minutus, a, um, *P. a.*, see *minuo.*

mirabilis, e, *adj.*, *to be wondered
at, wonderful, marvellous, extraordinary, admirable, singular.*
—mirabile, is, *n.*, *a miracle, won-
drous deed.*—mirabiliter, *adv.*,
(1) *wonderfully, wondrously*, (2)
miraculously.

mirabiliter, *adv.*, see *mirabilis.*

miraculose, *adv.*, see *miraculosus.*

miraculosus, a, um, *adj.*, *miraculous, wonderful, marvellous.* On
actus miraculosus, see *actus* under 1; on **conceptio miraculosa,**
see *conceptio* under 1; on **conceptus miraculosus,** see *conceptus* under 1; on **conversio miraculosa,** see *conversio* under 2; on
corruptio miraculosa, see *corruptio* under 2; on **generatio miracu-**

losa, see *generatio* under 1; on
mutatio miraculosa, see *mutatio;*
on **operatio miraculosa,** see *operatio* under 2; on **opus miraculosum,** see *opus* under 4; on **resurrectio miraculosa,** see *resurrectio;* on **transmutatio miraculosa,**
see *transmutatio* under 1;—miraculose, *adv.*, *miraculously, wonderfully.*

miraculum, i, *n.*, (1) *a miracle* in
the proper sense of the word, *an
effect produced by God, beyond
the power of created nature.* (2)
marvel, miracle in the wider
sense of the word, i.e., *the wonderful* or that which is worthy of
being admired.—On **gratia miraculorum,** see *gratia* under b; on
operatio miraculorum, see *operatio* under 1; on **spiritus miraculorum,** see *spiritus;* on **usus miraculorum,** see *usus* under 1.—
Kinds of *miraculum* in this sense
are: (a), **mirculum contra naturam, miraculum praeter naturam** and **miraculum supra naturam,** *the relative, the modal,*
and *the absolute miracle.* They
are all supernatural, but in different degrees. Nature is utterly
incapable of producing the effect
in the third; in the first and second, the effect of nature is extraordinary relative to this subject in which it occurs, or in the
manner in which it occurs. Cf.
*miraculum quantum ad id in quo
fit.*—(b), **miraculum corporale**
and **miraculum spirituale,** *the
corporal* and *the spiritual mira-*

cle, i.e., the miracle which is worked in a body and that which is worked in the spirit or soul of man.—(c), **miraculum mendax** and **miraculum verum,** *the delusive* or *false* and *the true* or *real miracle.*—(d), **miraculum praeter naturam,** see *miraculum contra naturam.*—(e), **miraculum quantum ad id in quo fit, miraculum quantum ad id quod fit seu quantum ad substantiam facti** and **miraculum quantum ad modum et ordinem faciendi,** *the miracle with respect to that in which it takes place,* or *the miracle according to its subject,* (contra naturam), *the miracle with respect to that which takes place* or *the miracle according to its substance,* (supra naturam), and *the miracle with respect to the act* and *manner of its accomplishment,* (praeter naturam). Cf. also *miraculum contra naturam.* —(f), **miraculum quantum ad id quod fit,** see *miraculum quantum ad id in quo fit.*—(g), **miraculum quantum ad modum et ordinem faciendi,** see *miraculum quantum ad id in quo fit.*—(h), **miraculum quantum ad substantiam facti,** see *miraculum quantum ad id in quo fit.*—(i), **miraculum quoad nos** and **miraculum simpliciter seu simpliciter loquendo,** *the miracle with respect to ourselves* and *the simple miracle,* i.e., that which is so called with reference to our knowledge and that which is really a miracle.—

(j), **miraculum simpliciter seu simpliciter loquendo,** see *miraculum quoad nos.*—(k), **miraculum spirituale,** see *miraculum corporale.*—(l), **miraculum supra naturam,** see *miraculum contra naturam.*—(m), **miraculum verum,** see *miraculum mendax.*

mirificus, a, um, *adj., marvelous, extraordinary.*

miror, ari, atus, 1, *v. dep., a.* and *n., to wonder* or *marvel at, to be astonished* or *amazed at* a thing; *to admire,* used with *quod, acc., si, quia.*

mirus, a, um, *adj., wonderful, marvelous, astonishing, extraordinary.*—**mira,** orum, *n., wonders, marvels.*

misceo, ere, ui, mixtum, 2, *v. a., mix, compound.* See *mixtus,* a, um.

miscibilis, e, *adj., miscible, capable of being mixed* with something.

miser, era, erum, *adj.,* (1) of persons, *unhappy, miserable, unfortunate, needy, poor,* (2) of things, *wretched, unhappy, compassionate, sorrowful.*—**subvenire miseris,** *to succour the needy.*

miserabilis, e, *adj., worthy of pity, pitiable, miserable, deplorable, unhappy, sad.*

miseratio, onis, *f.,* (1) *pity, compassion,* (2) *mercy.* God loves all men. When man is in dire need and misery because he has offended his Creator, God showers His benefits upon him; he is willing to forgive him. This love and goodness of God we call His mercy.

misereor, eri, itus, 2, *v. dep., to have mercy, to pardon, to have pity,* used *absol.,* with the gen., the *dat.,* (1) in gen., (2) esp., of God's forbearance towards His creatures.

miseria, ae, *f., misery, unhappiness, distress, anxiety, unhappy condition.*

misericordia, ae, *f., tenderheartedness, pity, compassion, mercy,* synonym of *compassio.* It is found in God effectively, inasmuch as God's love for men is the cause of the merciful benefits He bestows upon them, but He does not suffer the sorrow which is the formal notion of mercifulness.— *Misericordia,* a kind of *tristitia* (cf. *tristitia* under 1). According to its essence *misericordia* is above all a movement (*motus*) or a stirring of the sensitive and intellective appetite (cf. SS. Q. 30. Art. 3 c), wherefore it is called *affectus misericordiae,* i.e., a sensitive as well as an intellective emotion of compassion; secondly *misericordia* represents a virtue of that *qua homo perficitur ad rationabiliter miserendum.* In the latter sense *misericordia* is one of the eight *beatitudines.* See *beatitudo* under 2.

misericorditer, *adv.,* see *misericors.*

misericors, cordis, *adj., merciful, compassionate, pitiful.*—**misericorditer,** *mercifully, pitifully, tender-heartedly.*

miseror, ari, atus, 1, *v. dep., to have* or *feel compassion, to pity, to have mercy.*

missa, ae, *f., the mass.*

missio, onis, *f., a sending away, sending, mission.*—Kinds of *missio* are: (a), **missio aeterna** and **missio temporalis,** *the eternal mission* or *that existing from eternity* and *the temporal mission* or *that existing in time.*—(b), **missio exterior seu visibilis** and **missio interior seu invisibilis,** *the exterior* or *visible* and *the interior* or *invisible mission.*—(c), **missio interior,** see *missio exterior.*—(d), **missio invisiblis,** see *missio exterior.*—(e), **missio temporalis,** see *missio aeterna.*—(f), **missio visibilis,** see *missio invisibilis.*

mistura, ae, *f.,* see *mixtura.*

mistus, (mix), a, um, *P. a.,* see *mixtus.*

mitesco, ere, *v. inch. n., to grow mild, gentle.*

mitigatio, onis, *f., a soothing, mitigating, mitigation.*

mitigativus, a, um, *adj., soothing, mitigative.*

mitigo, are, avi, atum, 1, *v. a., to make mild* or *gentle, to pacify, soothe, calm, assuage, mitigate.*

mitis, e, *adj., mild, gentle, meek, lenient,* (1) of persons, (2) of things.

mititas, atis, *f., meekness,* a synonym of *mansuetudo.*

mitra, ae, *f., mitre,* a liturgical head-dress worn by bishops and abbots, a form of *tiara.*

mitto, ere, misi, missum, 3, *v. a.,* (1) in gen., *to send, send off, dispatch,* (2) in partic., (a) *to send, throw, cast, hurl,* used lit. and fig., (b) with *manus, to lay hands on someone,* (c) *to put* or *place* something somewhere.— **mittere aliquid in loco alicuius,** *to put* or *substitute one thing for another.*

mixtio, onis, *f., mixture,* synonym of *commixtio* and *complexio.* On **forma mixtionis,** see *forma* under 2; on **unire per modum mixtionis,** see *unire.—Mixtio* is of two kinds: **mixtio vera** and **mixtio ad sensum,** *the true* and *the apparent mixture,* i.e., the mixture after the manner of a chemical compound, in which the component parts (miscibilia) no longer exist in reality according to their nature and essence (mixtione iam perfecta non manent actu, sed virtute, nam si actu manerent, non esset mixtio, sed confusio tantum), and the mixture after the manner of a chemical hodge-podge (cf. *confusio* under 1), in which the component parts continue to exist actually with their nature and essence and not according to power and potentiality. In short if it is a question of *mixtio* as opposed to *confusio, mixtio vera* is in this case to be understood.

mixtura, ae, *f., a mixture,* a preparation of various sorts mixed together.

mixtus, a, um, *adj., mixed, compounded.* On **actio mixta,** see *actio* under 1; on **corpus mixtum,** see *corpus;* on **delectatio mixta,** see *delectatio;* on **forma mixta,** see *forma* under 2; on **motus mixtus,** see *motus* under 1.—**mixtum,** i, *n., a mixed thing, a mixture.*

Moabites, ae, *m., an inhabitant of Moab, a Moabite.*

Moabitis, tidis, *f., a Moabitish woman,* Vulg. Ruth, 1, 22.

mobilis, e, *adj.,* (1) *easy to be moved, movable,* the opposite of *immobilis,* (2) *movable property* or *possessions.* On **corpus mobile,** see *corpus;* on **ens mobile,** see *ens;* on **natura mobilis,** see *natura;* on **substantia mobilis,** see *substantia* under 2.—Kinds of *mobile* in this (1) sense are: (a), **mobile per accidens** and **mobile per se,** *movable indirectly through something outside itself* and *movable directly* or *according to itself.*—(b), **mobile per se,** see *mobile per accidens.*—(c), **mobile primum,** *the first movable,* i.e., *that heavenly body through whose movement all local movement begins.*—**mobiliter,** *adv., with motion, with rapid motion, with mobility,* opposite of *immobiliter.*

mobilitas, atis, *f.,* (1) lit., *mobility,* (2) fig., *changeableness.*

mobiliter, *adv.,* see *mobilis.*

modalis, e, *adj., with reference to mood in connection with grammar, modal, qualified,* not used

in the S.T. On **propositio modalis,** see *propositio* under 2; on
syllogismus de modalibus, see
syllogismus.

moderamen, inis, *n.,* (1) lit., *management, direction, control,* (2)
fig., *moderation, a means of
moderating.*

moderantia, ae, *f., moderation.*

moderate, *adv.,* see *modero.*

moderatio, onis, *f., moderation, the
act of moderating,* (1) *guidance,
control, governance, rule,* (2) the
quality of being moderate with
reference to conduct, desires or
their indulgence; avoidance of
extremes; *temperance.*

moderativus, a, um, *adj., moderating, serving to curb* or *temper.*

moderatus, a, um, *P. a.,* see *modero.*

modernus, a, um, *adj., modern.—*
moderni, orum, *m., moderns,
contemporaries,* opposite of *an-
tiqui.*

modero, are, avi, atum, 1, *v. a., to
regulate.—***moderatus,** a, um, *P.
a., keeping within due bounds,
observing moderation, modera-
tive,* (1) of persons, (2) of things.
*—***moderate,** *adv., with moderation, moderately.*

moderor, ari, atus, 1, *v. dep., to
manage, regulate, to exercise a
controlling influence over; to restrain, control, rule.*

modeste, *adv.,* see *modestus.*

modestia, ae, *f., moderateness,
moderation, modesty.—Modestia*
is one of the fructus *Spiritus
sancti.* Cf. *fructus* under 2.

modestus, a, um, *adj., keeping due
measure, moderate;* esp. in behavior, *modest.—***modeste,** *adv.,
with moderation.*

modicus, a, um, *adj., middling, ordinary, mean, scanty, small,
slight.* The following phrases
show the various uses of
the word.—**modica consideratio,**
*a slight consideration.—***modica
eleemosyna,** *a small alms.—***modicum tempus,** *a short time.—***modica additio,** *a slight addition.--*
**modicum augmentum vel etiam
modicus defectus,** *a little more*
or *a little less.—***modicus excessus,**
*a slight excess.—***modicum,** i, *n.,
a little.—***modico,** *adv., moderately, slightly.*

modificativus, a, um, *adj., modifi-
cative, modifying.*

modifico, are, 1, *v. n.* and *a., to
regulate, control, keep within the
limits, moderate.—***modificatus,** a,
um, *P. a., modified, limited.*

modius, ii, *m., a modius,* a Roman
corn-measure equal to about one
peck; also in the Middle Ages, a
measure of capacity dry and liquid of varying size commonly
rendered by *bushel.*

modulatio, onis, *f., melody, singing,*
used in the S.T. only in quot.

modulus, i, *m., a rhythmical measure, melody,* used in the S.T.
only in quot.

modus, i, *m.,* (1) *measure, quantity,*
(2) *a way, manner, method,* according to which something is or
happens, synonym of *ratio* and
processus, (3) *scientific manner*

or *method, scientific procedure, modus sciendi seu procedendi in scientiis,* see under 1, synonym of *processus, ratio,* and *via,* (4) *mood* or *mode* in the grammatical sense, e.g., a form of the verb, (5) *manner* in the realm of logic.—Kinds of *modus* in this (1) sense are: **modus accidentalis** and **modus substantialis,** *the manner of accidents* and *that of a substance* and *essence of a thing.* Cf. *modus accidentalis* under 2.—Kinds of *modus* in this (2) sense are: (a), **modus abstractionis** and **modus concretionis,** *the manner of abstraction* or *abduction* and *that of putting into the concrete,* i.e., *the manner of generalization* and *that of particularization.*—(b), **modus accidentalis,** *the manner* or *state of accident as opposed to substance.* Cf. *modus accidentalis* under 1.—(c), **modus accipiendi principia,** *the manner* or *method of comprehending the principles of science.*—(d), **modus adquirendi scientiam seu modus procedendi in scientiis seu modus sciendi seu scientiae,** *the scientific method.* Cf. *modus artificialis.*—(e), **modus argumentativus** and **modus narrativus,** *the argumentative* and *the narrative manner.*—(f), **modus artificialis,** *the artistic* or *scientific manner.* Cf. *modus adquirendi scientiam.*—(g), **modus carnalis, modus intellectualis seu intelligibilis** and **modus spiritualis,** *the carnal* or *corporal man-*

ner, the intellectual and *the spiritual manner.*—(h), **modus comminatorius** and **modus promissivus,** *the threatening manner* and *the promising manner.*—(i), **modus communis** and **modus specialis,** *the general* and *the particular manner.* Cf. *modus communis* under 3.—(j), **modus concretionis,** see *modus abstractionis.*—(k), **modus confirmationis** and **modus demonstrandi seu manifestandi veritatem seu veritatis manifestandae,** *the manner of confirmation* and *of attestation,* and *the manner of proving a truth apodictically.*—(l), **modus consignificandi** and **modus significandi,** *the manner of consignification* and *signification* or *connotation* and *denotation.*—(m), **modus debitus** and **modus indebitus,** *the proper* and *the improper manner.*—(n), **modus demonstrandi,** see *modus confirmationis.*—(o), **modus disputativus,** *the arguing kind* or *manner.*—(p), **modus essendi** and **modus operandi,** *the manner of being* and *that of acting.*—(q), **modus indebitus,** see *modus debitus.*—(r), **modus intellectus** and **modus voluntatis,** *the manner of thinking* and *that of willing.*—(s), **modus intellectualis seu intelligibilis,** see *modus carnalis.*—(t), **modus loquendi,** *the manner of speaking.*—(u), **modus manifestandi veritatem,** see *modus confirmationis.*—(v), **modus metaphoricus seu symbolicus** and **modus parabolicus,** *the* *metaphorical* or *symbolical* and *the parabolical manner.*—(w), **modus multorum** and **modus unius**, *the manner of many* or *the manifold manner* and *the manner of one* or *the single manner.*—(x), **modus narrativus**, see *modus argumentativus.*—(y), **modus operandi**, see *modus essendi.*—(z), **modus orativus** and **modus praeceptivus**, *the entreating* and *the commanding manner.* Cf., also *modus deprecativus* under 4.—(a²), **modus parabolicus**, see *modus metaphoricus.*—(b²), **modus praeceptivus**, see *modus orativus.*—(c²), **modus praedicandi**, *manner in which a predicate is said of a subject.*—(d²), **modus procedendi**, *the manner of proceeding* or *of procedure.*—(e²), **modus procedendi in scientiis**, see *modus adquirendi scientiam.*—(f²), **modus promissivus**, see *modus comminatorius.*—(g²), **modus revelativus**, *the revealing manner.*—(h²), **modus sciendi**, see *modus adquirendi scientiam.*—(i²), **modus scientiae**, see *modus adquirendi scientiam.*—(j²), **modus significandi**, see *modus consignificandi.*—(k²), **modus sophisticus**, *the sophistic manner* or *the manner of the sophists.*—(l²), **modus specialis**, see *modus communis.*—(m²), **modus spiritualis**, see *modus carnalis.*—(n²), **modus syllogismi**, *the kind of premises in a syllogism which qualifies the conclusion.*—(o²), **modus symbolicus**, see *modus metaphoricus.*

—(p²), **modus unius**, *unified manner*, see *modus multorum.*—(q²), **modus veritatis manifestandae**, see *modus confirmationis.*—(r²), **modus virtutis**, see *virtus* under 5.—(s²), **modus voluntatis**, see *modus intellectus.*—Kinds of *modus* in this (3) sense are: (a), **modus causalitatis** and **modus negationis**, *the method of causality* or *on a basis of causality* and *the method of negation.*—(b), **modus communis** and **modus proprius**, *the common* and *the proper method.* Cf. *modus communis* under 2.—(c), **modus compositivus** and **modus resolutorius seu resolutionis**, *the compositive* or *synthetic manner* and *the resolving* or *analytic method*, i.e., the method based on combination and that on analysis.—(d), **modus mathematicus**, *the mathematical method.*—(e), **modus negationis**, see *modus causalitatis.*—(f), **modus proprius**, see *modus communis.*—(g), **modus resolutionis**, see *modus compositivus.*—(h), **modus resolutorius**, see *modus compositivus.*—Kinds of *modus* in this (4) sense are: (a), **modus deprecativus seu optativus** and **modus imperativus**, *the optative* and *the imperative mood.* Cf. *modus orativus* under 2.—(b), **modus imperativus**, see *modus deprecativus.*—(c), **modus indicativus**, *the proclaiming* or *indicating mood*, i.e., *the indicative mood.*—(d), **modus infinitus**, *the*

unlimited or undetermined mood,
i.e., the infinitive.—(e), **modus
optativus**, see modus deprecativus. On **syllogismus de modo**,
see syllogismus.

moechia, ae, f., adultery.

moechor, ari, atus, 1, v. dep., to
commit adultery.

moechus, i, m., an adulterer, used
in the S.T. only in quot.

moenia, ium, n., city walls, defensive walls, used in the S.T. only
in quot.

moeror, oris, m., a mourning, sadness, grief, sorrow.

moestus, a, um, adj., sad, sorrowful, melancholy.

Moguntinus, a, um, adj., Mogun-
tine, or or pertaining to Mogun-
tia, now Mainz, (Mayence), in
Germany.

moles, is, f., (1) lit., bulk, mass,
substance. (2) fig., greatness,
strength.

molestia, ae, f., trouble, trouble-
someness, annoyance, molesta-
tion, vexation, disgust, used for
physical and mental annoyances.

molesto, are, 1, v. a., to trouble,
annoy, molest.

molestus, a, um, adj., troublesome,
irksome, grievous, annoying, (1)
of persons, burdensome, oppressive, (2) of things, offensive,
troublesome, importunate.—**molestus perscrutator,** a keen or
sharp critic; critic or examiner
of something.

molimen, inis, n., effort, attempt,
endeavor.

molior, iri, itus, 4, v. dep. n. and
a., to endeavor to do; to undertake, attempt, set about anything.

molliculus, a, um, adj., soft, tender, delicate, used in the S.T.
only in quot.

mollificatio, onis, f., mollification,
something that softens or miti-
gates harshness.

mollio, ire, ivi and ii, itum, 4, v. a.,
to restrain, check.

mollis, e, adj., (1) it., (a) in gen.,
soft, not hard, easily movable,
etc., easily yielding to physical
pressure, (b) of texture or of a
textile, smooth, delicately woven, fibered or grained, (2) fig.,
(a) effeminate, soft, voluptuous,
(b) refined, characterized by refinement or delicacy, high-bred.

mollities, ei, f., and **mollitia,** ae,
f., (1) softness, gentleness, (2)
weakness, effeminacy, the opposite of perseverantia.—One kind
of mollities in this (2) sense is:
mollities luxuriae, the weakness
consisting of voluptuousness.

momentaneus, a, um, adj., short, of
brief duration, momentary, synonym of instantaneus and subitus,
the opposite of successivus. On
factio momentanea, see factio;
on **generatio momentanea,** see
generatio under 1; on **mutatio
momentanea,** see mutatio.

momentum, i, n., (1) a slight movement, the smallest part of motion, (2) a short time, brief
space, moment, (3) weight, influence, importance, moment.

monachalis, e, *adj., monachal, monastic, pertaining to* or *characteristic of monastic life.*

monachatus, us, *m., monachate,* the period of life passed as a monk.

monachus, i, *m., a monk, a cenobite* or *a member of a community of men living apart from the world, under the vows of poverty, chastity, and obedience, in accordance with the rule of a particular order.*

monas, adis, *f., unity; a unit, monad.*

monasterium, ii, *n., a monastery.*

monasticus, a, um, *adj.,* (1) *pertaining to the individual* or *to living alone,* (2) *monastic.*—On **prudentia monastica,** see *prudentia* under 1; on **scientia monastica,** see *scientia* under 1.—On **ordo monasticus,** see *ordo* under 3; on **professio monastica,** see *professio* under 1; on **regula monastica,** see *regula* under 1; on **religio monastica,** see *religio* under 2; on **status monasticus,** see *status* under 4; on **vita monastica,** see *vita* under 3.

moneo, ere, ui, itum, 2, *v. a., to remind, put in mind of, bring to one's recollection; to admonish, advise, warn, instruct, teach.*

monetatus, a, um, *adj., monetized, put into circulation as money.*

monile, is, *n., a necklace, a collar,* used in the S.T. only in quot.

Monimus, i, *m., Monimus,* an intimate friend of Fulgentius of Ruspe with whom he carried on an extensive correspondence on theological questions. The main trouble on the mind of Monimus had been awakened by perusing Augustine's *de Perfectione Iustitiae Hominis,* in which he thought that the great African Father had taught predestination to sin as well as to virtue. The three books "Ad Monimum" written by Fulgentius in Sardinia are addressed to Monimus on this question. Fulgentius assured Monimus that God does not predestine men to sin, but only to the punishment they have merited by their sins.

monitio, onis, *f., advice, admonition, warning.*

monitum, i, *n., admonition, advice, counsel.*

monocolus, a, um, *adj., one-eyed.*

Monologium, ii, *n., the Monologium* sive Exemplum Meditandi de Ratione Fidei, a philosophical and religious work by Anselm, Archbishop of Canterbury, on the essential nature of God.

monomachia, ae, *f., monomachy, a single combat.*

mons, tis, *m., a mountain, mount.*—The following phrases refer to particular mountains.—**Mons Gelboe,** *the mountains of Gelboe,* a small chain of mountains in Manasses west of the Jordan where Saul and Jonathan were slain.—**Mons Garizim,** *Mount Garizim.*—**Mons Oreb,** *Mount Horeb,* also called *Sinai,* the mountains in the peninsula between the Gulf of Suez and Elanitic Gulf. The northern part was called Mount Horeb.—**Mons Sinai**, *Mount Sinai*.—**Mons Oliveti**, *the mountain of Olivet*, east of Jerusalem.

monstro, are, avi, atum, 1, *v. a.*, *to show, point out, to indicate, intimate, inform, teach, instruct, tell anything.*

monstrum, i, *n.*, *a monster, monstrosity*, used lit. and fig.

monstruosus, a, um, *adj.*, *monstrous, deformed.*

Montanus, i, *m.*, *Montanus*, a native of Arabia in Mysia and founder of the Montanists in the middle of the second century A.D. Priscilla and Maximilla, two women of distinction, joined the heretics under Montanus.

monumentum, i, *n.*, *a sepulchral monument, a sepulchre, tomb.*

Mopsuestenus, a, um, *adj.*, *of Mopsuestia*, a titular see of Cilicia Secunda in Asia and suffragan of Anazarbus. Christianity was introduced very early into Mopsuestia, and during the third century there is mention of a bishop Theodorus, the adversary of Paul of Samosata.

mora, ae, *f.*, (1) lit., *a delay*, the fact of being kept waiting or delayed for a time, (2) transf., (a) a space of time between any two events, (b) *time* in an indefinite sense.—**mora temporis**, *a space of time.*

moralis, e, *adj.*, (1) *of* or *belonging to manners* or *morals, moral*, synonym of *ethicus*, (2) *moral philosopher* or *moralist.*—On ac-

tio moralis, see *actio* under 1; on **actus moralis**, see *actus* under 1; on **aequitas moralis**, see *aequitas;* on **bonitas moralis**, see *bonitas* under 1; on **bonum morale, seu in moralibus** seu in actionibus moralibus, see *bonus* under 2; on **causa moralis**, see *causa* under 3; on **consideratio moralis**, see *consideratio;* on **corruptio moralis**, see *corruptio* under 3; on **debitum morale**, see *debitus* under 1; on **doctrina moralis**, see *doctrina* under 3; on **finis moralis**, see *finis* under 2; on **genus morale**, see *genus* under 2; on **habitus moralis**, see *habitus* under 4; on **imperfectio moralis**, see *imperfectio;* on **iustitia moralis**, see *iustitia* under 2, on **iustum morale**, see *iustus;* on **malitia moralis**, see *malitia* under 1; on **malum morale seu in moralibus seu in actionibus moralibus**, see *malus* under 2; on **operatio materia moralis**, see *materia* under 2; on **operatio moralis**, see *operatio* under 2; on **peccatum morale seu in moralibus**, see *peccatum* under 1; on **philosophia moralis**, see *philosophia;* on **philosophus moralis**, see *philosophus* under 1; on **praeceptum morale**, see *praeceptum;* on **quaestio moralis**, see *quaestio;* on **scientia moralis**, see *scientia* under 1; on **sensus moralis**, see *sensus* under 8; on **significatio moralis**, see *significatio* under 1; on **utilitas moralis**, see *utilitas* under 2; on **virtus moralis**, see

virtus under 5; on **vita moralis,**
see *vita* under 3; on **vitium morale,** see *vitium* under 1.—**moraliter,** *adv., in a manner pertaining
to morals, morally.*

moralitas, atis, *f., morality.*

moraliter, *adv.,* see *moralis.*

morbidus, a, um, *adj.,* (1) *sickly,
diseased,* (2) of opinions, *mischievous, unsound.*

morbosus, a, um, *adj., diseased.*

morbus, i, *m., a sickness, disease,
disorder, ailment, illness, malady,*
(1) corporeal, (2) mental.—The
following phrases are frequent:
morbus contagiosus, *a contagious
disease.*—**morbus abominabilis,** *a
loathsome disease.*—**incidere** in
leviorem morbum, *to contract a
less dangerous sickness.*—**morbus
caducus,** *falling sickness, epilepsy.*

mordacitas, atis, *f., mordacity, the
power of biting* or *stinging.*

mordeo, ere, momordi, morsum, 2,
v. a., (1) lit., *to bite,* said of the
teeth, (2) transf., of taste, *to
bite, sting, make the mouth
smart,* (3) fig., (a) *to vex, sting,*
(b) *to injure, hurt* the reputation
of someone.—**momordisse infer-
num,** *to have tasted hell.* The
reference is to Osee XIII, 14.
When Christ by His descent, delivered the Fathers from limbo,
He is said to have tasted hell
and to have descended into hell,
in so far as hell and limbo were
the same as to location.

mordicativus, a, um, *adj., pungent.*

morigeratus, a, um, *adj., cultured,
polished, civilized.*

morio, onis, *m., an arrogant fool,
half-wit.*

morior, mori, mortuus, 3, *v. dep.,*
(1) of man, (a) in gen., *to die,
to cease to live, to expire, to
lose life,* (b) *to die* in a particular state or condition, (c) *to
die unto, to cease* to be under
the power of, to become dead
unto, (d) theol., *to die, to suffer* spiritual death, (2) of abstract
things, *to cease.*—**mortuus,** a,
um *P. a.,* (1) lit., *dead, having
ceased to live, lifeless, inanimate,*
(2) fig., *dead, destitute of religious spirit* and *life.*—**opera
mortua,** *dead works,* those done
without charity, inasmuch as
they fail to proceed from the
principle of life. A work, i.e., a
moral act, is said to be dead in
two ways, first because it is a
cause of death; in this way sinful
works are said to be dead. Secondly, works are dead because
they lack spiritual life which is
founded on charity, whereby the
soul is united to God.—**mortuus,**
i, *m., a dead man.*

moror, ari, atus, 1, *v. dep. n.* and
a., to stay, remain, to continue in
one place, condition or character; *to abide, dwell.*

morositas, atis, *f., a lingering, slowness.*

morosus, a, um, *adj., lingering,
slow, slow in coming.* On **delectatio morosa,** see *delectatio.*

mors, tis, *f.*, *death,* the opposite of *vita.* On **debitum mortis,** see *debitus* under 1; on **dominium mortis,** see *dominium*; on **liber mortis,** see *liber* under 2; on **poena mortis,** see *poena.*—Kinds of *mors* are: (a), **mors aeterna** and **mors temporalis,** *the eternal* or *the everlasting death* and *the temporal death* or *the death that lasts only for a time,* i.e., man's death according to his soul and that according to his body. Cf. *mors carnalis.*—(b), **mors carnalis seu corporalis** and **mors spiritualis,** *the physical* and *the spiritual death of man..* Under the latter may be understood the separation of man's soul from God and man's separation from the world occasioned by his entering a monastery.—(c), **mors corporalis,** see *mors carnalis.*—(d), **mors interpretativa,** *death according to interpretation* or *the interpreted death.*—(e), **mors naturalis** and **mors violenta,** *the natural* and *the violent death.*—(f), **mors spiritualis,** see *mors carnalis.*—(g), **mors temporalis,** see *mors aeterna.*—(h), **mors violenta,** see *mors naturalis.*

morsus, us, *m.,* (1) lit., *a bite,* (2) fig., *sting, pain, vexation.*

mortalis, e, *adj.,* (1) *subject to death, liable to die, mortal,* (2) *causing death, deadly.*—On **caro mortalis,** see *caro* under 1; on **vita mortalis,** see *vita* under 1.—On **culpa mortalis,** see *culpa;* on **delectatio mortalis,** see *delectatio;*

on **peccatum mortale,** see *peccatum* under 2; on **poenitentia mortalis,** see *poenitentia* under 1. —**mortaliter,** *adv., mortally,* used in the S.T. only with peccare.

mortalitas, atis, *f., mortality, the state of being subject to death.*

mortaliter, *adv.,* see *mortalis.*

morticinus, a, um, *adj., dead,* only of animals.

mortifer, fera, erum, *adj.,* (1) lit., *death-bringing, deadly,* (2) transf., *bringing spiritual death.*

mortificatio, onis, *f.,* (1) in gen., *a devitalization,* the act of depriving of vital power or of the power to sustain life, (2) in religious sense, *mortification,* the action of mortifying the flesh or its lusts, the denial of one's appetites and passions by the practice of austere living, for a supernatural motive.

mortifico, are, avi, atum, 1, *v. a.,* (1) lit., *to kill, destroy,* (2) transf., *to deaden, destroy, reduce to weakness.*

mortuus, a, um, *P. a.,* see *morior.*

morum, i, *n., a mulberry.*

mos, moris, *m.,* (1) *custom, usage, habit,* (2) *mode* or *practice* in the wider sense of the word, *natural disposition,* (3) *mode* or *practice* in the narrower sense of the word, (4) *good practice.*—On **bonum moris,** see *bonus* under 2; on **doctrinam morum,** see *doctrina* under 2; on **genus moris,** see *genus* under 4; on **malum moris,** see *malus* under 2; on **peccatum in moribus,** see *peccatum* under

1; on **unitas morum,** see *unitas;* on **via morum** see *via* under 1; on **vitium moris,** see *vitium* under 1.—Kinds of *mos* in this (1) sense are: **mos bonus** and **mos malus,** *good* and *bad practice* or *custom.*

Mosaicus, a, um, *adj., Mosaic, of* or *relating to Moses, the lawgiver of the Hebrews,* or *the writings* and *institutions attributed to him.*

Moses, see *Moyses.*

motio, onis, *f., a moving, motion, impulse, stimulus.*—Kinds of *motio* in this sense are: (a), **motio actualis,** *the real motion* or *that taking place in reality.*—(b), **motio divina,** *the divine impulse.*—(c), **motio generativa,** *the productive motion.*—(d), **motio intimativa,** *the demonstrated* or *suggested motion.*—(e), **motio vitalis,** *the vital motion* or *the motion of life.*

motivus, a, um, *adj., moving, stimulating.* On **anima motiva,** see *anima* under 1; on **causa motiva,** see *causa* under 1; on **potentia motiva,** see *potentia* under 2; on **principium motivum,** see *principium;* on **virtus motiva,** see *virtus* under 1 and 5; on **vis motiva,** see *vis* under 1.—By *motivum* sc. *principium* is to be understood (1) the main stimulating principle, (2) the **motivum secundum locum** sc. **genus potentiarum animae** (= *to kineton kata topon*). —Kinds of *motivum,* as understood in the first instance, are: **motivum primum** and **motivum**

proximum, *the first* and *the next stimulus.*

motor, oris, *m., that which keeps a thing in motion, a mover,* synonym of *movens.*—Kinds of *motor* are: (a), **motor coniunctus seu intrinsecus** and **motor separatus seu extrinsecus,** *the mover connected with the moved* or *the inner mover* and *the mover separated from the moved* or *the outer* or *external mover.*—(b), **motor extrinsecus, sic motor coniunctus,** see *motor coniunctus.*—(c), **motor intrinsecus,** see *motor coniunctus.*—(d), **motor primus,** *the first mover,* namely *God.*—(e), **motor remotus,** *the remote mover,* calculated from that which is moved.—(f), **motor separatus,** see *motor coniunctus.*

motus, us, *m.,* (1) *moving, movement, motion* in the proper sense of the word, as the constant transition from potentiality to act, a kind of *mutatio,* the opposite of *quies,* (2) *action, movement, motion* in the broader and improper sense of the word, synonym of *mutatio* and *operatio,* the opposite of *passio.*—On the difference between *motus* in the proper sense of the word and *mutatio,* see *mutatio.* On **abstrahere a motu,** see *abstrahere* under 1; on **bonum adquisitum per motum et sine motu,** see *bonus* under 3; on **contrarietas motus,** see *contrarietas* under 1; on **finis motus,** see *finis* under 1; on **movere motus recto et secundum motum**

circularem, see *movere;* on posterius motus seu in motu, see
posterior under 2; on **prius in
motu, seu secundum motum seu
secundum ordinem in motu,** see
prior under 1; on **quies motus,**
see *quies;* on **terminus motus,** see
terminus under 1; on **unitas motus,** see *unitas;* on **virtus motus,**
see *virtus* under 7.—Kinds of *motus* in this (1) sense are: (a),
**motus alterationis seu secundum
qualitatem, motus augmenti et
decrementi seu diminutionis seu
in quantitate seu motus secundum quantitatem** and **motus secundum locum seu lationis secundum locum seu localis,** *the
qualitative, the quantitative,* and
the local movement, i.e., alteration, which is movement in the
genus of quality; growth and
shrinkage, which is movement in
the genus of quantity, and local
motion, which is movement from
place to place.—(b), **motus augmenti et decrementi,** see *motus
alterationis.*—(c), **motus caelestis
seu caeli seu in caelo,** *the movement of heaven* or *of the heavenly bodies.*—(d), **motus caeli,** see
motus caelestis.—(e), **motus circularis seu sphaericus, motus obliquus,** and **motus rectus,** *the
circular, the oblique,* and *the
straight movement.*—(f), **motus
commixtus seu mixtus seu compositus** and **motus simplex,** *the
mixed movement* or *the movement composed of two* or *more
movements* and *the simple move-*

ment.—(g), **motus communis** and
motus proprius, *the general* and
the particular or *the proper
movement.*—(h), **motus completus seu perfectus** and **motus imperfectus,** *the complete* or *perfect* and *the imperfect motion.*—
(i), **motus compositus,** see *motus
commixtus.*—(j), **motus constrictionis** and **motus dilationis,** *the
movement of contraction* and
that of expansion.—(k), **motus
continuus** and **motus non-continuus seu interpolatus,** *the connected* or *continued movement*
and *the disconnected* or *broken
movement.*—(l), **motus contra naturam seu extra seu praeter naturam** and **motus secundum naturam,** *the unnatural* and *the
natural movement.* Cf. *motus naturalis* under 2; also *motus innaturalis.*—(m), **motus decrementi,**
see *motus alterationis.*—(n), **motus difformis seu difformitatis**
and **motus uniformis seu uniformitatis,** *the unconformable* or *irregular movement* and *the conformable movement.* Cf. *motus
irregularis.*—(o), **motus difformitatis,** see *motus difformis.*—(p),
motus dilatationis, see *motus
constrictionis.*—(q), **motus diminutionis,** see *motus alterationis.*—
(r), **motus directus, motus retrogradus,** and **motus stationarius,**
*the movement that proceeds
straight on, that moves backward*
or *recurrent,* and *the movement
that takes place in a restricted
locality.*—(s), **motus diurnus,** *the*

daily movement, quo totum caelum revolvitur per motum primi
mobilis ab oriente usque in occi-
dentem.—(t), **motus epicycli** and
motus excentrici, *the movement
of a secondary circle* or *epicycle*
and *that of an eccentric circle.—*
(u), **motus excentrici,** see *motus
epicycli.—*(v), **motus extra naturam,** see *motus contra naturam.*
—(w), **motus imperfectus,** see
motus completus.—(x), **motus in
caelo,** see *motus caelestis.—*(y),
motus inaequalis, see *motus difformis.—*(z), **motus inferior,** *the
lower* or *inferior movement,* i.e.,
the movement of a sublunary
body.—(a²), **motus innaturalis seu
violentus** and **motus naturalis,**
the unnatural or *violent* and *the
natural movement.* Cf. *motus naturalis* under 2; also *motus contra naturam.—*(b²), **motus inordinatus,** *the inordinate* or *disorderly movement,* qui est contra naturam.—(c²), **motus in quantitate,**
see *motus alterationis.—*(d²), **motus intensus** and **motus remissus,**
the intensified and *the retarded
movement.—*(e²), **motus interpolatus,** see *motus continuus.—* (f²),
motus irregularis and **motus regularis,** *the irregular movement.*
—(g²), **motus lationis secundum
locum,** see *motus alterationis.—*
(h²), **motus localis,** see *motus
alterationis.—*(i²), **motus mixtus,**
see *motus commixtus.—*(j²), **motus naturalis,** see *motus innaturalis,* and *motus voluntarius.—*(k²),
motus non-continuus, see *motus*

continuus.—(l²,) **motus obliquus,**
see *motus circularis.—*(m²), **motus
per accidens, motus secundum
partem,** and **motus per se,** *the
movement that belongs incidentally, a movement that belongs
to a thing according to one of
its parts,* and *the movement that
belongs to a thing as such.—*
(n²), **motus perfectus,** see *motus
completus.—*(o²), **motus perpetuus seu sempiternus,** *the perpetual* or *everlasting movement.—*(p²),
motus per se, see *motus per accidens.—*(q²), **motus praeter naturam,** see *motus contra naturam.*
—(r²), **motus primus** and **motus
secundus,** *the first movement*
under which is to be understood
chiefly on the one hand the local
movement but on the other hand
also the daily movement of the
heavens, and the *second movement* which is in opposition to
the first movement in the latter
sense of the word the ecliptic
movement of the heavens in the
path of the zodiac.—(s²), **motus
processivus,** *the forward movement,* secundum quem animalia
moventur de loco ad locum.—(t²),
motus progressivus, see *motus
processivus.—*(u²), **motus proprius,** see *motus communis.—*(v²),
motus rectus, see *motus circularis.* Cf. *motus rectus* under 2.—
(w²), **motus reflexivus seu reflexus,** *the turning* or *bending movement.—*(x²), **motus regularis,** see
motus irregularis.—(y²), **motus remissus,** see *motus intensus.—*(z²),

motus retrogradus, see *motus directus.*—(a³), motus secundum locum, see *motus alterationis.*—(b³), motus secundum naturam, see *motus contra naturam.*—(c³), motus secundum partem, see *motus per accidens.*—(d³), motus secundum qualitatem, see *motus alterationis.*—(e³), motus secundum quantitatem, see *motus alterationis.*—(f³), motus secundum situm, *the movement according to local position.*—(g³), motus secundus, see *motus primus.*—(h³), motus simplex, see *motus commixtus.*—(i³), motus sphaericus, see *motus circularis.*—(j³), motus stationarius, see *motus directus.*—(k³), motus transitivus, *the passing movement.*—(l³), motus uniformis, see *motus difformis.*—(m³), motus uniformitatis, see *motus difformis.*—(n³), motus unus; *uniform or consistent movement.*—(o³), motus unus genere seu secundum genus, motus unus specie seu secundum speciem, and motus unus numero seu secundum substantiam, *generically one motion,* i.e., substantial or accidental, and *specifically one,* i.e., *in the same predicament of quantity, quality,* or *place,* and *numerically one motion according to the time and the individual or the substance in which it occurs.*—(p³), motus unus numero, see *motus unus genere.*—(q³), motus unus secundum genus, see *motus unus genere.*—(r³), motus unus secundum quid* and motus unus

simpliciter, *the movement uniform in a certain respect* and *the simply* or *absolutely uniform movement.*—(s³), motus unus secundum speciem, see *motus unus genere.*—(t³), motus unus secundum substantiam, see *motus unus genere.*—(u³), motus unus simpliciter, see *motus unus secundum quid.*—(v³), motus videntis, and motus visibilis, *the movement of the one who sees* and *that of the visible.*—(w³), motus violentus, see *motus innaturalis.* —(x³), motus visibilis, see *motus videntis.*—(y³), motus voluntarius and motus naturalis, *the voluntary* or *free movement* (cf. *motus voluntarius* under 2) and *the movement of a thing of nature which is not free.*—in instanti non est motus or motus sunt successivi, *movement is not carried out in an instant but only in a succession of instants,* quia semper exspectat aliquid in futurum ad perfectionem suae speciei.— in motu necesse est considerare prius et posterius, *in movement one must distinguish between an earlier* and *a later.*—motus non est ex motibus, sed ex momentis, *movement does not consist of the accretion of many movements but of movements which are related to motion as points to a line.*—motus non accipit speciem a termino a quo sed a termino ad quem, *movement does not receive its species* and *essence* and *accordingly its name from its starting point but from its term.* —motus proprie acceptus est corporum, *movement properly understood belongs to bodies.*—motus sunt successivi, see above: *in instanti* etc.— non potest esse quod aliquis motus sit alicuius motus (5 Phys. 3 d), *a movement cannot itself be the subject of another.*—proprium est modus tempore mensurari, *the proper measure of movement is time.*— On via motus, see *via* under 3.— Kinds of *motus* in this (2) sense are: (a), motus absolutus appetitus and motus appetitus in ordine ad alterum, *the irrelative or unconditioned movement* and *the relative or conditioned movement of the inclination toward something.*—(b), motus ad formam and motus ad privationem, *the movement of a thing towards a form* and *the movement of a thing towards the privation* or *the lack of a form,* i.e., the production and the destruction of a thing.—(c), motus ad privationem, see *motus ad formam.*—(d), motus affectus, *the movement of affection.* Cf. C. G. 3. 151.—(e), motus animalis seu sensibilis seu sensualis seu sensualitatis, motus intellectualis seu rationis and motus naturalis, *the sensible, the rational,* and *the natural movement* or *the movement proceeding on the basis of past knowledge from a sensible* or *ratioinal appetitive faculty* and *the movement proceeding from the nature*

of an appetitive faculty without past knowledge.—(f), motus animi, *emotion, excitement.*—(g), motus appetitivus, *the appetitive movement* or *inclination.*—(h), motus appetitus in ordine ad alterum, see *motus absolutus appetitus.*—(i), motus collativus, *the comparative movement* or *the action of reason.*—(j), motus corporalis seu corporeus and motus spiritualis, *the corporal* and *the physical movement.*—(k), motus corruptionis and motus generationis, *the movement of corruption* and *that of generation.* Cf. *motus ad formam.*—(l), motus discursivus, *the discursive* or *the concluding movement of reason.* —(m), motus elicitus and motus imperatus, *the movement elicited from a faculty* and *that enjoined upon it.*—(n), motus imperatus, see *motus elicitus.*—(o), motus instantaneus seu subitus and motus successivus, *the instantaneous* or *sudden* and *the gradual movement* or *change.*—(p), motus intellectualis, see *motus animalis.*—(q), motus intellectus and motus voluntatis, *the movement of reason* and *that of the will* or *thinking* and *willing.*—(r), motus liberi arbitrii, *the movement of the free will.*—(s), motus naturalis, see *motus animalis.*—(t), motus phantasticus, *the movement* or *action of the imagination.*—(u), motus primo primus and motus secundo primus, *the movement of the appetites which is so fundamental as to be involuntary,* and *that which follows yet remains purely sensual.*–(v), **motus rationis,** see *motus animalis.*–(w), **motus rectus,** *the right* or *correct movement.* Cf. *motus rectus* under 1. –(x), **motus secundo primus,** see *motus primo primus.*–(y), **motus sensibilis seu sensualis,** see *motus animalis.*–(z), **motus sensualitatis,** see *motus animalis.*–(a²), **motus sensus,** *the movement of the sensible perceptive faculties* or *that resulting from sensible experience.*–(b²), **motus spiritualis,** see *motus corporalis.*–(c²), **motus subitus,** see *motus instantaneus.*–(d²), **motus subrepticius,** *the suddenly arising movement.* –(e²), **motus successivus,** see *motus instantaneus.*–(f²), **motus virtutis imperantis** and **motus virtutis imperatae,** *the movement of the commanding power* and *that of the power that is commanded.*–(g²), **motus vitalis,** *the vital movement* or *the movement of life.*–(h²), **motus voluntarius,** *the movement of the will.* Cf. also *motus voluntarius* under 1.– (i²), **motus voluntatis,** see *motus intellectus.*–**appetitivus motus circulo agitur,** *the appetitive movement moves in the manner of a circle.*

movens, entis, Part. and *P. a.,* see *moveo.*

moveo, ere, movi, motum, 2, *v. a.,* *to move,* in the narrow and in the broad senses of the word,

stir, set in motion, shake, disturb. On **causa movens,** see *causa* under 1; on **movens motum,** see *movens;* on **principium movens** and **primum movens,** see *principium;* on **punctus movens et nonmovens,** see *punctus;* on **res movens,** see *res;* on **substantia movens,** see *substantia* under 2.– Kinds of *movere* in the general sense are: (a), **movere circulariter seu secundum motum circularem** and **movere motu recto seu indirectum,** *to move in a circular manner* and *to move in a straight line.*–(b), **movere extra naturam seu per violentiam** and **movere per naturam seu secundum naturam seu naturaliter,** *to move unnaturally* or *by force* and *to move according to nature* or *naturally.*–(c), **movere immediate et movere mediate,** *to move directly* and *indirectly.*–(d), **movere indirectum,** see *movere circulariter.*–(e), **movere instrumentaliter** and **movere principaliter,** *to move in the manner of an agent* and *in the manner of a main cause.*–(f), **movere localiter seu secundum locum,** *to move locally.*–(g), **movere mediate,** see *movere immediate.*–(h), **movere motu recto,** see *movere circulariter.*–(i), **movere naturaliter,** see *movere extra naturam.*–(j), **movere per accidens seu secundum accidens, movere secundum partem** and **movere primo et per se,** *to move something through something else, indirectly, in* *consequence of one of its parts,* and *to move something primarily through itself.*—(k), **movere per intellectum,** *to move with reason* (and *free will*), the opposite of *agere per necessitatem naturae.*— (l), **movere per medium agentis** and **movere per modum finis,** *to move after the manner of an efficient* or *agent cause* and *after the manner of the causal end.*— (m), **movere per modum debiti seu secundum debitum** and **movere per modum meriti,** *to move after the manner of what is necessary* and *after the manner of what is merited.*—(n), **movere per modum finis,** see *movere per modum agentis.*—(o), **movere per modum meriti,** see *movere per modum debiti.*—(p), **movere per naturam,** see *movere extra naturam.*—(q), **movere per se,** see *movere per accidens.*—(r), **movere per violentiam,** see *movere extra naturam.*—(s), **movere primo,** see *movere per accidens.*—(t), **movere principaliter,** see *movere instrumentaliter.*—(u), **movere secundum accidens,** see *movere per accidens.*—(v), **movere secundum debitum,** see *movere per modum debiti.*—(w), **movere secundum locum,** see *movere localiter.*—(x), **movere secundum motum circularem,** see *movere circulariter.*—(y), **movere secundum naturam,** see *movere extra naturam.*—(z), **movere secundum partem,** see *movere per accidens.*— **movere uniformiter,** *to move uni-*

formly.—**moveri accidit moventi et non per se ei competit** (3 Phys. 4 d), *to be moved happens to that which moves not as such but only as an accident.*—**omne motum movetur ab alio,** or, **omne, quod movetur ab alio movetur,** or, **omne quod movetur oportet ab alio moveri,** *all that is moved must be moved by another.*—**movens,** entis, *Part.* and *P. a., that which moves the mover,* synonym of *causa movens* and *motor.*—Kinds of *movens* are: (a), **movens extrinsecum** and **movens intrinsecum,** *the exterior* and *the interior mover.*—(b), **movens immediate seu immediatum** and **movens remotum,** *the immediate* and *the remote* or *mediate mover.*—(c), **movens immobile** and **movens motum,** *the mover immovable by another* and *the mover which is moved by another.*—(d), **movens intrinsecum,** see *movens extrinsecum.*— (e), **movens motum,** see *movens immobile.*—(f), **movens naturale seu physicum,** *a natural physical thing which moves another.*—(g), **movens per accidens** and **movens per se,** *that which produces motion indirectly* or *by accident,* and *that which produces motion directly.* See *movere per accidens.*—(h), **movens per se,** see *movens per accidens.*—(i), **movens physicum,** see *movens naturale.*—(j), **movens primum, movens secundum,** and **movens ultimum,** *the first, the second,* and *the last mover calculated on the one hand from the moved* and *on the other hand from that which is first in a series of movers.*—(k), **movens principale,** *the chief mover.*—(l), **movens remotum,** see *movens immediate.* —(m), **movens secundum,** see *movens primum.*—(n), **movens seipsum,** *the mover that moves itself.* —(o), **movens ultimum,** see *movens primum.*—**motum et movens oportet esse simul,** *the moved* and *the mover must co-exist precisely as such,* i.e., they must stand in immediate contact with each other, whether this be after the manner of a *continuitas* or of a *contiguatio.*—**movens,** entis, *Part.* and *P. a.,* see *moveo.*

mox, *adv., soon, directly, presently.* —The following are some of the phrases showing further use of *mox.*—**mox ut,** *as soon as.*—**mox natus,** *immediately after birth.*— **nominatum mox,** *as soon as mentioned, the very mention.*—**mox factum,** *as soon as made.*—**mox,** *later* in a written discourse.

Moyses, is or i, *m., Moses* (1) the younger son of Amram and Jochebed, who led the Jewish people out of Egypt and gave them the law on Mount Sinai, (2) *Moses Maimonides,* quoted by St. Thomas under the name of Rabbi Moses. He was born of Spanish Jewish parents at Cordova in 1135. His writings include Commentaries, philosophical works, medical and as-

tronomical works. St. Thomas quotes from his Doctor Perplexorum, Dux Dubitantium (or Dux Errantium), and Commentary on the Prophets, (3) *Moses Abbas,* one of the monks in the desert of Scete in Egypt with whom Cassian discusses the science of sanctity in Collatio I and II.

Moysis, see *Moyses.*

mugiens, entis, *P. a., bellowing, roaring.*

mula, ae, *f., a she-mule.*

mulcens, entis, *P. a., delighting.*

muliebris, e, *adj.,* (1) *of* or *belonging to a woman, female,* (2) in a reproachful sense, *womanish, effeminate.*—**muliebria,** ium, *n.,* only in the phrase, **pati muliebria,** *to let one's self be used as a woman, to yield to unnatural vice.*

mulier, eris, *f., a woman, a female,* whether married or not, (1) in *gen.,* (2) *in partic., a wife.*

muliercula, ae, *f., a mere woman, a little woman.*

multifariam, *adv., in many ways.*

multifarie, *adv., in many ways,* used in the S.T. only in quot.

multiformis, e, *adj., multiform, various, diverse, manifold.*—**multiformiter,** *adv., in many ways, variously.*

multiformitas, atis, *f., multiformity.*

multiformiter, *adv.,* see *multiformis.*

multiloquium, ii, *n., much speaking, talkativeness, use of many words, loquaciousness.*

multiplex, icis, *adj., manifold, that has many parts, many, numerous, various.—***multipliciter,** *adv., in manifold* and *various ways.*

multiplicabilis, e, *adj., multiplicable, capable of being multiplied, multipliable.*

multiplicatio, onis, *f., a making manifold, increasing, multiplying, multiplication,* does not occur in the S.T.—Kinds of *multiplicatio* are: (a), **multiplicatio formalis,** and **multiplicatio materialis,** *multiplication according to form* and *that according to matter.*—(b), **multiplicatio materialis,** see *multiplicatio formalis.*—(c), **multiplicatio spiritualis,** *spiritual multiplication.*

multiplicative, *adv., in a multiple manner, in the manner of multiplicity, multiplicatively.* On **dicere multiplicative,** see *dicere* under 3.

multiplicitas, atis, *f.,* (1) *multiplicity, manifoldness, a great quantity,* the opposite of *singularitas* and *unitas,* (2) *many significations, ambiguity,* synonym of *duplicitas.*

multipliciter, *adv.,* see *multiplex.*

multiplico, are, avi, atum, 1, *v. a., to multiply, increase, augment.*

multitudo, inis, *f.,* (1) *multiplicity* in the wider sense of the word, (2) *multitude* in the sense of transcendental multiplicity, the opposite of *unum,* (3) *multiplicity* in the mathematical sense, *multitude,* the opposite of *singularitas* and *unitas,* (4) *a multitude of people, a mass of people.*—Kinds of *multitudo in this* (1) sense are: **multitudo absoluta seu transcendens** and **multitudo numeralis seu mensurata per unum seu quantitatis discretae,** *the absolute notion of plurality not confined to any single category of being* and *the multiplicity of number, measured by a unit,* i.e., *the multiude opposed to unity,* and *the multitude which is number.*—Kinds of *multitudo* in this (2) sense are: **multitudo extrinseca** and **multitudo intrinseca,** *the outer* and *the inner multiplicity.* On **infinitas multitudinis,** see *infinitas;* on **infinitum multitudinis seu secundum multitudinem,** see *infinitus.*—Kinds of *multitudo* in this (3) sense are: (a), **multitudo determinata** and **multitudo infinita,** *the limited* or *finite multiplicity* and *the unlimited* or *endless multiplicity.*—(b), **multitudo formalis** and **multitudo materialis,** *multiplicity according to form* and *that according to matter.*—(c), **multitudo infinita,** see *multitudo determinata.*—(d), **multitudo infinita actu** and **multitudo infinita in potentia,** *the actually infinite number of things* and *that in potentiality.*—(e), **multitudo infinita in potentia,** see *multitudo infinita actu.*—(f), **multitudo infinita per accidens** and **multitudo infinita per se,** *the multitude which is endlessly great by accident* and *that which is so of necessity.*—(g), **multitudo**

per se, see *multitudo infinita per accidens.*—(h), **multitudo materialis,** see *multitudo formalis.*—(i), **multitudo ordinata,** *the organized multiplicity.* On **agibile circa bona vel mala totius multitudinis civilis,** see *agibilis;* on **bonum multitudinis seu totius multitudinis,** see *bonus* under 3; on **debitum multitudinis,** see *debitus* under 1; on **malum totius multitudinis civilis,** see *malus* under 3; on **perfectio multitudinis,** see *perfectio* under 2; on **regimen multitudinis,** see *regimen;* on **unitas multitudinis,** see *unitas.*—Kinds of *multitudo* in this (4) sense are: (a), **multitudo bestialis,** *the bestial* or *brutalized mass of people.*—(b), **multitudo civilis seu civitatis** and **multitudo domestica,** *the civic* and *the domestic mass of people* or *the state* and *the family.*—(c), **multitudo civitatis,** see *multitudo civilis.*—(d), **multitudo domestica,** see *multitudo civilis.*

multoties, *adv., many times, oftentimes, often.*

multus, a, um, *adj., comp. plus,* sup. *plurimus, adj.,* (1) *much* or *many,* in the absolute sense of the word, i.e., *much* not in comparison with anything else, the opposite of *singularis* and *unus,* (2) *much* or *many* in the relative sense of the word, i.e., *much* or *many* in comparison with something else, the opposite of *paucus.* On **modus multorum,** see *modus* under 2; on **regimen mul-**

torum, see *regimen.*—Kinds of *multum* in this (1) sense are: (a), **multum correspondens uni quod convertitur cum ente** and **multum quod pertinet ad genus quantitatis seu quod est in genere quantitas discretae,** *the many in a transcendental* and *numerical sense.* Cf. *multitudo* under 1.—(b), **multum numero seu secundum numerum** and **multum specie,** *much according to number* or *the individual* and *that according to species.*—(c), **multum partibus seu secundum partes,** *much* or *many according to its parts.*—(d), **multum quod est in genere quantitatis discretae,** see *multum correspondens uni quod convertitur cum ente.*—(e), **multum quod pertinet ad genus quantitatis,** see *multum correspondens uni quod convetitur cum ente.*—(f), **multum secundum accidentia** and **multum secundum substantiam,** *much* or *many according to accidents* and *that according to substance.*—(g), **multum secundum numerum,** see *multum numero.*—(h), **multum secundum partes,** see *multum partibus.*—(i), **multum secundum quid** and **multum simpliciter,** *many respectively* or *in a certain respect* and *many simply* or *absolutely.*—(j), **multum secundum substantiam,** see *multum secundum accidentia.*—(k), **multum simpliciter,** see *multum secundum quid.*—(l), **multum specie,** see *multum numero.*—**multo,** *by* *much, much, a great deal, far, by far.—***multum,** *much, very much, greatly, very, often, far.—**Comp.:* **plus,** pluris, *in the plur.,* plures, plura, *more.—Sup.:* **pluri-mus,** a, um, *most, very much, many.—Adv.:* **plurimum,** *very much indeed, exceedingly, at the most.—***ut plurimum,** *for the most part, commonly, usually,* synonym of *plerumque.*

mulus, i, *m., a mule.*

mundanus, a, um, *adj.,* (1) *worldly, belonging to the world,* synonym of *mundialis,* the opposite of *spiritualis,* (2) *worldly-minded, worldly,* synonym of *saecularis,* the opposite of *spiritualis* and *su-permundanus.—*On **potentia mun-dana,** see *potentia* under 3; on **res mundana,** see *res;* on **sub-stantia mundana,** see *substantia* under 2.—On **amor mundanus,** see *amor* under 1; on **gloria mun-dana,** see *gloria* under 1; on **ho-nor mundanus,** see *honor;* on **im-perium mundanum,** see *imperi-um* under 4; on **lex mundana,** see *lex* under 1; on **potestas munda-na,** see *potestas* under 4; on **sa-pientia mundana,** see *sapientia* under 1 and 3; on **stultitia mun-dana,** see *stultitia;* on **timor mun-danus,** see *timor.—***astutia mun-dana,** *the cunning of the children of the world.*

mundatio, onis, *f., a cleansing.*

mundator, oris, *m., a cleanser.*

mundialis, e, *adj., worldly, belong-ing to the world,* synonym of *mundanus,* not in S.T.

munditia, ae, *f., cleanliness, purity* in the general sense of the word, synonym of *puritas,* the opposite of *immunditia* and *impuritas.—* Kinds of *munditia* in the general sense of the word are: (a), **mun-ditia conscientiae,** *purity of con-science,* quae non-nisi per pecca-tum tollitur.—(b), **munditia cor-dis,** *purity of heart.—*(c), **mundi-tia corporalis,** *purity of body, corporal purity.—*(d), **munditia immaculata** and **munditio per-fecta,** *the immaculate* and *the perfect purity.—*(e), **munditia perfecta,** see *munditia immacu-lata.*

mundo, are, 1, *v. a.,* (1) *lit., to cleanse,* make clean from lepro-sy, (2) spiritually from sin.

mundus, i, *m.,* (1) *world* in the proper sense of the word, *uni-verse,* synonym of *universum,* (2) *world* in the improper sense of the word, *child of the world,* synonym of *saeculum.* On **aeter-nitas mundi,** see *aeternitas;* on **anima mundi,** see *anima* under 2; on **bonum huius mundi,** see *bo-num* under 3; on **elementum mundi,** see *elementum* under 1; on **status mundi,** see *status* under 3; on **tentatio mundi seu a mun-do,** see *tentatio* under 2.—Kinds of *mundus* in this (1) sense are: (a), **mundus corporeus seu sensi-bilis,** *the physical world* or *the world perceptible through the senses.—*(b), **mundus inferior,** *the lower world,* qui est circa ter-ram.—(c), **mundus magnus, seu**

maior and **mundus parvus seu minor,** the *kosmos* of Aristotle, *the great* and *the small world, the macrocosm* and *the microcosm.*—(d), **mundus maior,** see *mundus magnus.*—(e), **mundus minor,** see *mundus magnus.*—(f), **mundus parvus,** see *mundus magnus.*—(g), **mundus sensibilis,** see *mundus corporeus.*—On **prudentia mundi,** see *prudentia* under 1; on **sapientia mundi,** see *sapientia* under 1.

munia, ium, *n., gifts,* a synonym of *dona.*

municipium, ii, *n., franchise.*

munio, ire, ivi, or ii, itum, 4, *v. a., to guard, secure, strengthen, support,* used *fig.*

munium, ii, *n., duty.*

munus, eris, *n., present, gift, favor.*—Kinds of *munus* are: **munus linguae seu a lingua, munus a manu** and **munus ab obsequio sc. exhibitum,** *the gift of the tongue, the gift of the hand,* and *the gift of the service.*

munusculum, i, *n., dim., a small gift, a present.*

murmur, uris, *n., a murmuring.*

murmuro, are, avi, atum, 1, *v. n., to murmur.*

murus, i, *m., a wall,* especially *a city wall.*

mus, muris, *comm., a mouse.*

musca, ae, *f., a fly.*

muscipula, ae, *f., a mouse-trap,* used *fig., a snare.*

musica, ae, *f., music.*

musicus, a, um, *adj., of* or *belonging to music, musical.*—**musicus,** i, *m., a musician.*—**musicus,** i, *m., music.*

mustum, i, *n., new* or *unfermented wine, must.*

mutabilis, e, *adj., changeable, mutable,* opposite of *immutabilis.*—Kinds of *mutabile* are: (a), **mutabile per potentiam, quae in ipso est** and **mutabile per potentiam, quae in altero est,** *changeable as a result of a potentiality in itself* and *changeable as a result of a power outside of itself.*—(b), **mutabile per potentiam, quae in altero est,** see *mutabile per potentiam, quae in seipso est.*—(c), **mutabile quia removetur vel abicitur in mutatione** and **mutabile quia subicitur mutationi,** *that which is changeable because it is removed* or *thrown off* and *that which is changeable because it is subject to change.*—(d), **mutabile quia subicitur mutationi,** see *mutabile quia removetur vel abicitur in mutatione.*—(e), **mutabile secundum esse,** *changeable according to its being.*—**mutabiliter,** *adv., changeably.*

mutabilitas, atis, *f., changeableness, mutability.*—Kinds of *mutabilitas* are: (a), **mutabilitas secundum electionem,** *changeableness with reference to choice.*—(b), **mutabilitas secundum potentiam ad esse,** *changeableness with reference to potentiality for being.*—(c), **mutabilitas veritatis,** *the changeableness of truth.*

mutabiliter, *adv.,* see *mutabilis.*

mutatio, onis, *f.*, *changing, mutation*, the most general notion which embraces *generatio, conversio, immutatio, transmutatio, alteratio, motio,* and *augmentatio*. On **contrarietas in mutationibus seu mutationum,** see *contrarietas* under 1; on **terminus mutationis,** see *terminus* under 1.— Kinds of *mutatio* are: (a), **mutatio continua seu successiva** and **mutatio instantanea seu momentanea,** *the change that takes place gradually* or *continuously* and *the change that takes place suddenly* or *instantly.*—(b), **mutatio de seu ex non-subiecto in subiectum, mutatio de seu ex subiecto in non-subiectum** and **mutatio de seu ex subiecto in subiectum,** *generation, the change from a non-subject* or *non-being to a subject* or *being, corruption, the change from a subject* or *being to a non-subject* or *non-being,* and *motion, the change from one subject* or *being to another,* whereby movement in the proper sense of the word is to be understood.—(c), **mutatio de seu ex subiecto in non-subiectum,** see *mutatio ex non-subiecto in subiectum.*—(d), **mutatio de seu ex subiecto in subiectum,** see *mutatio ex non-subiecto in subiectum.* —(e), **mutatio formalis** and **mutatio materialis,** *the change* (of a thing) *according to its form* and *according to its matter.*—(f), **mutatio instantanea,** see *mutatio continua.*—(g), **mutatio loci seu**

secundum esse locale, mutatio substantialis seu secundum esse substantiale seu secundum substantiam, mutatio secundum qualitatem and **mutatio secundum quantitatem,** *the local, the substantial, the qualitative,* and *the quantitative change.*—(h), **mutatio materialis,** see *mutatio formalis.*—(i), **mutatio miraculosa,** *the miraculous change.*—(j), **mutatio momentanea,** see *mutatio continua.*—(k), **mutatio naturalis,** see *mutatio violenta, the natural* and *the violent change.*—(l), **mutatio secundum applicationem virtutis ad diversa** and **mutatio secundum ordinem ad finem,** *change with reference to the application of a power to different things* and *change with reference to the direction towards the end or goal.*—(m), **mutatio secundum esse locale,** see *mutatio loci.*—(n), **mutatio secundum esse substantiale,** see *mutatio loci.*—(o), **mutatio secundum modum intellegendi tantum,** *change according to thinking alone.*—(p), **mutatio secundum qualitatem,** see *mutatio loci.*—(q), **mutatio secundum quantitatem,** see *mutatio loci.*—(r), **mutatio secundum substantiam,** see *mutatio loci.*—(s), **mutatio substantialis,** see *mutatio loci.*—(t), **mutatio successiva,** see *mutatio continua.*—(u), **mutatio violenta,** see *mutatio naturalis.*—**mutationes accipiunt speciem et dignitatem non a termino a quo, sed a termino ad quem,** *changes* *receive their species* and *value not from their source but from their end* or *goal.*—mutationis non potest esse mutatio, *change itself is not subject to another change.*—omnis mutatio est ex opposito aut ex mediis, *every change comes either from the opposite of the thing which forms the result of the change or from something which lies between the two extremes.*—omnis mutatio reducitur ad illud genus, ad quod terminatur, *every change is to be reduced as to its genus to the goal at which it ends.*

mutilatio, onis, *f., a maiming, mutilating, mutilation.*

mutilator, oris, *m., a mutilator, one who maims.*

mutilo, are, avi, atum, 1, *v. a., to mutilate, maim.*—mutilatus, a, um, *P. a., maimed, deformed.*

muto, are, avi, atum, 1, *v. a., to change, alter.*

mutuatio, onis, *f., a loan.*

mutuo, are, avi, atum, 1, *v. a., borrow, take for one's use.*

mutus, a, um, *adj.,* (1) *dumb, mute, destitute of the power of speech,* (2) *of things which utter no sound, speechless, silent.*

mutuus, a, um, *adj., mutual, recip-*

rocal.—mutuum, i, *n., a loan.*—mutuo, *adv., in return, reciprocally, mutually.*

myrrha, ae, *f., myrrh.*

myrtus, i and us, *f., a myrtle.*

mysterium, ii, *n., divine mystery, that which is so hidden that it cannot be understood, secret rites.*—Common phrases are: (a), mysterium Christi, *the mystery of Christ.*—(b), mysterium divinum, *divine mystery.*—(c), mysterium fidei, *the mystery of faith.* —(d), mysterium Incarnationis, *the mystery of the Incarnation.* —(e), mysterium sacrum, *the sacred mystery.*—(f), mysterium Trinitatis, *the mystery of the Trinity.*—(g), mysterium gratiae, *the mystery of grace.*

mystice, *adv.,* see *mysticus.*

mysticus, a, um, *adj., secretive, secret, mystic, mystical.* On causa mystica, see *causa* under 3; on corpus mysticum, see *corpus;* on intellectus mysticus, see *intellectus* under 11; on ratio mystica, see *ratio* under 17; on significatio mystica, see *significatio* under 1; on theologia mystica, see *theologia* under 2.—mystice, *adv., mystically,* opposed to *realiter,* and *physice.*

N

Naaman, *n., indecl., Naaman* III, general of the army of Benadad, King of Syria, a great man in the eyes of his master, rich, but a leper. He was cured by Eliseus the prophet who ordered him to wash seven times in the river Jordan.

Naboth, *n., indecl., Naboth,* inhabitant of Jezrael, Judea; refused to sell his vineyard to King Achab. Queen Jezabel, irritated on this account, caused him to be stoned on a false accusation of having blasphemed God and the King.

Nabuchodonosor, *n.*, *indecl.*, *Nabuchodonosor* II, surnamed the Great. He was King of Babylon and of Ninive (605-562 B.C.); was son and successor of Nabopolassar, and one of the most famous princes of Chaldea.

Nahum, *n.*, *indecl.*, *Nahum*, the seventh of the twelve minor prophets. He lived in the time of Ezechias, about the eighth century B.C. His prophecy in three chapters forms one sole discourse, wherein he announces the second destruction of Ninive by Cyaxares and Nabopolassar.

nam, *conj.*, *for*, used to introduce a confirmation or explanation or reason for a previous statement.

namque, *conj.*, an emphatic confirmative particle, ·a strengthened *nam*, closely resembling that particle in its uses, but introducing the reason or explanation with more assurance; Gr. *kai gar,* *for indeed*, *for truly*, *for.*

nanciscor, i, nactus and nanctus, 3, *v. dep. a.*, *to get, obtain, receive.*

nanus, i, *m.*, *a dwarf.*

naris, is, *f.*, used entirely in the plural, *nares*, ium, *f.*, *the nostrils, the nose.*

narratio, onis, *f.*, *a relating, narrative, story.*

narro, are, avi, atum, 1, *v. a.*, *to tell, relate, narrate, report, recount, set forth*, used with ·*de, quod.*

nascor, i, natus, 3, *v. dep.*, *to be born, be begotten.*—natus est seu aptus natus est used with an infinitive, *to be fitted by birth* or *designed by nature* for that which is expressed by the infinitive.—**nascens**, entis, *P. a.*, *arising, beginning, nascent, infant, immature.*—**natus**, a, um, *P. a.*, *born;* hence as *subst.;* **natus,** i, *m.*, *a son;* and **nata,** ae, *f.*, *a daughter;* and *in plur.* nati, orum, *children, offspring.*—**bene natus** and **male natus,** *to be gifted well* or *badly by nature.*

nasus, i, *m.*, *the nose.*—**nasus curvus,** *a snub-nose.*—**nasus rugatus,** *a wrinkled nose.*

natalis, e, *adj.*, *of* or *belonging to one's birth, birth—, natal.*—**natalis,** is, *m.*, *a birthday.*—**natales,** um, *m.*, *birth, origin, lineage, extraction.*

Nathan, *n.*, *indecl.*, *Nathan*, (1) a son of David and Bethsabee, (2) a prophet in the time of David about the eleventh century B.C. He declared to David that his son would build the temple, reproached him for the crime of which he had rendered himself guilty by killing Uri, in order to possess his wife, Bethsabee, and advised him to acknowledge Solomon as his successor.

natio, onis, *f.*, (1) *a race of people, nation, people,* (2) in eccl. Lat.

like *gens*, and the Gr. *ethnos*, opp. to Christians, *the heathen*.

nativitas, atis, *f.*, *birth*, *nativity*, infrequently a synonym of *natura*. On **relatio nativitatis**, see *relatio*. —Kinds of *nativitas* are: (a), **nativitas aeterna** and **nativitas temporalis**, *the eternal* and *the temporal birth*, or *the birth from eternity* and *that in time.*—(b), **nativitas animalis seu carnalis**, *the animal* or *carnal birth*, the opposite of *nativitas spiritualis*, i.e., *the spiritual birth.*—(c), **nativitas carnalis**, see *nativitas animalis.*—(d), **nativitas ex utero** and **nativitas in utero**, *the birth from the mother's womb*, or *the proper birth* and *the birth in the mother's womb* or *conception*. Cf. *nativitas carnalis.*—(e), **nativitas humana**, *the human birth* or *the birth proper to man.*—(f), **nativitas in utero**, see *nativitas ex utero.*—(g), **nativitas miraculosa** and **nativitas naturalis**, *the miraculous* and *the natural birth.*—(h), **nativitas naturalis**, see *nativitas miraculosa.*—(i), **nativitas temporalis**, see *nativitas aeterna*.

nato, are, avi, atum, 1, *v.* freq. *n.* and *a.*, *to swim, float*.

natura, ae, *f.*, (1) *nature, birth*, synonym of *nativitas*, (2) *nature, the inner principle of the generation of a living thing*, (3) *nature, every inner principle of an activity*, (4) *nature, the form* and *the matter of a physical being*, (5) *nature*, commonly, *the essence of a thing precisely as it is the source of its operations* and *activity*. Cf. *essentia, forma, quidditas, quod quid est, quod quid erat esse, species*, and *substantia*, (6) *nature, an entity, anything viewed in its basic aspect*, be it a substance or an accident, (7) *nature, substance*, (8) *nature, the realm of reality*, (9) *nature, the realm of irrational things.*—On **actio naturae**, see *actio* under 1; on **actus naturae**, see *actus* under 1; on **agens naturae**, see *agens;* on **agere per naturam**, see *agere* under 1; on **assumptio in natura**, see *assumptio* under 1; on **bonitas naturae**, see *bonitas* under 1; on **bonum naturae seu ad naturam communem pertinens, bonum naturae humanae et naturae singularis**, see *bonus* under 2 and 3; on **causa naturae alicuius in hoc, causa naturae alicuius simpliciter et causa per naturam**, see *causa* under 2; on **claritas naturae**, see *claritas* under 3; on **communicatio per modum naturae**, see *communicatio* under 1; on **communitas naturae**, see *communitas* under 1; on **compositio secundum naturam**, see *compositio* under 1; on **continuum per seu secundum naturam**, see *continuus* under 2; on **corruptio naturae, corruptio contra, extra et secundum naturam**, see *corruptio* under 2 and 3; on **culpa naturae**, see *culpa;* on **debitum secundum condicionem naturae**, see *debitus* under 1; on **defectus naturae**, see *defectus* under 2; on **delectabile**

secundum naturam et non secundum naturam, see *delectabilis;* on desiderium naturae, see *desiderium* under 1; on diversitas naturae, see *diversitas;* on divisio secundum naturam, see *divisio;* on dominus per naturam, see *dominus;* on esse naturae, see *esse;* on falsum in natura, see *falsus;* on fieri a natura, see *fieri;* on filius per naturam, see *filius* under 1; on forma in naturae existens, see *forma* under 2; on formatio naturae spiritualis, see *formatio* under 2; on generare per naturam, see *generare;* on generatio contra, extra et secundum naturam, see *generatio* under 1; on genus naturae, see *genus* under 2; on idem natura, in natura generis, in natura speciei et per naturam suppositi, see *idem;* on identitas naturae, see *identitas;* on ieiunium naturae, see *ieiunium;* on imago naturae, see *imago* under 1; on impetus naturae, see *impetus;* on impossibile naturae seu in natura, see *impossibilis;* on incorruptibile secundum naturam, see *incorruptibilis;* on instinctus naturae, see *instinctus;* on integritas naturae, see *integritas;* on intellectus naturae speciei, see *intellectus* under 9; on intellegibile secundum naturam suam, see *intellegibilis* under 2; on intentio naturae communis, see *intentio* under 3; on iudicium a natura determinatum ad unum seu a natura inditum, see *iudicium* under 4; on

ius naturae, see *ius* under 1; on iustum secundum naturam, see *iustus;* on lex naturae, see *lex* under 1; on lumen naturae, see *lumen;* on malum naturae, see *malus* under 2; on miraculum contra, praeter et supra naturam, see *miraculum* under 1; on motus contra seu extra seu praeter et secundum naturam, see *motus* under 1; on movere extra naturam et per seu secundum naturam, see *movere;* on necessarium secundum sui naturam, see *necessarius* under 1; on necessitas naturae, see *necessitas* under 1; on nomen naturae, see *nomen* under 1; on notum naturae seu quoad naturam seu secundum propriam naturam seu secundum sui naturam, see *notus;* on operatio naturae, see *operatio* under 2; on opus naturae, see *opus* under 4; on ordo naturae, see *ordo* under 1; on passio naturae, see *passio* under 2; on peccatum naturae, contra naturam, humanae naturae et totius naturae, see *peccatum* under 1 and 2; on perfectio naturae, see *perfectio* under 2; on perfectus secundum naturam, see *perfectus* under 1; on posterius natura seu secundum naturam, see *posterior* under 2; on potestas naturae, see *potestas* under 2; on principium naturae, see *principium;* on prius natura seu secundum naturam seu in ordine seu ordine naturae seu secundum ordinem naturae, see *prior* under 1; on processio naturae seu secundum naturam seu per modum naturae, see *processio* under 4; on **puritas naturae,** see *puritas* under 1; on **quies extra naturam et secundum naturam,** see *quies;* on **ratio ut natura,** see *ratio* under 3; on **res naturae,** see *res;* on **sanctificatio naturae,** see *sanctificatio* under 1; on **similitudo secundum convenientiam in natura,** see *similitudo* under 1; on **singularitas naturae seu subsistentis in natura,** see *singularitas* under 1; on **status naturae, naturae conditae, naturae corruptae et naturae integrae,** see *status* under 3; on **unio naturae seu in seu secundum naturam,** see *unio;* on **unire in natura seu secundum naturam,** see *unire;* on **unitas naturae, in rerum natura et per naturam,** see *unitas;* on **veritas naturae,** see *veritas* under 1; on **via naturae,** see *via* under 1; on **vis naturae,** see *vis* under 1 and 3; on **vita naturae,** see *vita* under 1; on **vitium naturae et contra naturam,** see *vitium* under 1 and 2; on **voluntabile secundum naturam,** see *voluntabilis;* on **voluntas per modum naturae seu ut natura,** see *voluntas* under 3.—**contra naturam,** *para physin* of Aristotle (Phys. V. 6, 230. a. 20), *against nature* or *unnatural,* i.e., either that which militates against the nature of a definite thing or that which militates against the general order or course of nature.— **extra seu praeter naturam,** *out-*

side nature or *unnatural,* i.e., either that which is beyond the nature of a single thing or that which is beyond the natural order of all things, and both include that which is *contra naturam* and that which is *supra naturam.*—**secundum naturam,** the *kata physin* of Aristotle, *according to nature* or *natural,* i.e., either that which corresponds to the nature of a single thing or that which corresponds in general to the course of nature.—**supra naturam,** *supernatural,* i.e., either that which goes beyond the nature of a single thing and its natural powers or that which in general goes beyond the usual order and customary course of things.—Kinds of *natura* as understood in the general sense of the word are: (a), **natura absoluta,** *the essence of a thing freed or stripped of its individual characteristics.*—(b), **natura angelica, natura humana,** and **natura divina,** *the angelic, the human,* and *the divine nature* or *essence.*—(c), **natura caelestis** and **natura terrestris,** *the heavenly and the earthly nature* or *the nature* and *essence of heavenly bodies which for St. Thomas was generically different from that of earthly or sublunary bodies. Cf. corpus inferius* under *corpus.*—(d), **natura communis seu speciei** and **natura propria seu individui,** *the common essence* or *that common to all things of its kind* and *the es-*

sence peculiar to each one of them, or *the essence of the species* and *that of the individual*.—(e), **natura completa**, *the complete essence of a thing which is opposite to natura incompleta, the incomplete essence of a thing*. Cf. *species completa* under *species* under 6.—(f), **natura condita** and **natura glorificata**, *the created* and *the glorified nature* or *the nature of a being as created, i.e., without grace* and *that in the state of its glorification*.—(g), **natura corporalis seu corporea** and **natura spiritualis**, *the physical* and *the spiritual nature*, understood in the sense of a single being or a number of things as well as in the sense of the essence of a thing.—(h), **natura corrupta** and **natura integra**, *the nature of man after the Fall, corrupted by original sin*, and *the nature before the Fall when reason was in perfect control of all faculties and emotions, and perfectly subject to God*.—(i), **natura corruptibilis et generabilis** and **natura sempiternae permanentiae**, *the corruptible* and *the generable nature* and *the nature of eternal duration*.—(j), **natura creata** and **natura increata**, *the created* and *the uncreated nature* or *substance*.—(k), **natura determinata**, *the determined nature* or *substance*.—(l), **natura divina**, see *natura angelica*.—(m), **natura extranea**, *the extraneous* or *foreign nature of a being* or *the nature*

that comes upon a being from the outside.—(n), **natura generabilis**, see *natura corruptibilis*.—(o), **natura glorificata**, see *natura condita*.—(p), **natura humana**, see *natura angelica*.—(q), **natura increata**, see *natura creata*.—(r), **natura individui**, see *natura communis*.—(s), **natura inferior** and **natura superior**, *the lower* or *inferior* and *the higher* or *superior nature* in the sense of a being or a multiplicity of beings.—(t), **natura informis**, *nature at time of creation, not yet developed into kinds and classes*.—(u), **natura insensibilis**, **natura sensibilis seu sensitiva seu sensualis** and **natura intellegibilis seu intellectiva seu intellectualis**, *the insensible nature* or *that not endowed with sense, the sensible nature*, or *that endowed with sense*, and *that endowed with intellect* or *that which is knowable only by intellect, namely, being* and *the essence of a thing*.—(v), **natura integra**, see *natura corrupta*.—(w), **natura intellectiva seu intellectualis seu intellegibilis**, see *natura insensibilis*.—(x), **natura irrationalis** and **natura rationalis seu rationabilis**, *the irrational* and *the rational nature*, the word being understood in the sense of a substance as well as in that of the essence of a substance.—(y), **natura materialis**, *the material* or *physical nature*.—(z), **natura mobilis**, *the movable nature* or *the movement accessible to sub-*

stance.—(a²), natura naturans, *the nature that serves as the cause of everything that happens according to nature, by which is meant God.*—(b²), natura particularis and natura universalis, *the particular* and *the general nature,* by which is meant a substance, an essence, a power.—(c²), natura prima, *the first essence.*—(d²), natura primaeva, the *primeval substance* or *God.*—(e²), natura propria, see *natura communis.*—(f²), natura rationabilis seu rationalis, see *natura irrationalis.*—(g²), natura sempiternae permanentiae, see *natura corruptibilis.*—(h²), natura sensibilis seu sensitiva seu sensualis, see *natura insensibilis.*—(i²), natura simplex subsistens, *a simple nature, that existing not in union with some other element, but in itself as an independent being,* which is in contrast to *natura rei compositae,* i.e., the nature or essence of a composite thing.—(j²), natura speciei, see *natura communis.*—(k²), natura spiritualis, see *natura corporalis.* —(l²), natura summa, *the highest nature* or *the highest being.*—(m²), natura superior, see *natura inferior.*—(n²), natura terrestris, see *natura caelestis.*—(o²), natura universalis, see *natura particularis.*—ars imitatur naturam, see *ars* under 2.—constitui in propriam naturam, cum sentitur, causat delectationem, *coming into possession of that which*

corresponds to it causes pleasure and *joy when it is received.*—Deus et natura nihil frustra faciunt, see *frustra.*—inferior natura attingit in sui supremo ad aliquid quod est proprium superioris naturae imperfecte illud participans, or, supremum inferioris naturae attingit in quod est infimum superioris, or, natura superior in suo infimo contingit naturam inferiorem in eius supremo, *a nature of a lower order under the aspect of that which is highest in it reaches that which is lowest in a superior nature,* and *vice-versa.*—inter ea quae contingit fieri, natura semper facit id quod est optimum, or, natura semper facit id quod melius est, the translation of the Aristotelian passage: *he physis aei poiei tou endechomenon to beltiston,* de Cael. II. 5; 288. a. 2 f., *nature always does the best possible.*— natura communis determinatur et contrahitur in unoquoque secundum proprietates inventas in illo, *the general nature* or *essence of a thing is determined more closely and restricted more narrowly through its peculiarities.*—natura consequitur suum effectum vel semper vel ut in pluribus, or, natura non deficit nisi in paucioribus, *the nature of a thing in its actions always reaches its goal* or *attains it in most cases; it misses its goal only in a very few instances.*—natura determinata est ad unum, or, natura unius rei est determinata ad unum, or, natura semper ordinatur ad unum, or, natura semper tendit ad unum, *the nature of a thing always tends toward a single object* and *always strives after a single object;* cf. *naturalis* under 1.—natura in sua operatione Dei operationem imitatur, *nature in its operation always imitates the operation of God.*—natura in se recurva est, or, natura semper in se curva est, *the nature of a thing always bends* or *curves back upon itself.* —natura neque deficit in necessariis neque abundat in superfluis, or, natura non abundat in superfluis, sicut nec deficit in necessariis, or, natura nihil facit frustra, neque deficit in necessariis, the translation of the Aristotelian passage: *he physis mete poiei maten methen mete apolipei ti ton amenkeion, nature does nothing that is superfluous* and *likewise fails in nothing that is necessary.*—natura nihil facit frustra, see *frustra.* —natura nihil facit frustra, neque deficit in necessariis, see above: *natura neque deficit,* etc.—natura non abundat superfluis, *nature possesses and does nothing superfluous;* cf. above: *natura neque deficit* etc.—natura non deficit in necessariis, or, natura nulli deficit in necessariis ad propriam operationem explendum, *nature permits a lack in none of the things necessary for the perform-*

ance of its proper activity; cf. above: *natura neque deficit* etc.— natura non deficit, nisi in paucioribus, see above: *natura consequitur* etc.— natura non facit per duo, quod per unum potest facere, *what nature can bring forth by one means, it does not do by two;* cf. above: *natura neque deficit* etc.—natura nulli deficit in necessariis ad propriam operationem explendam, see above: *natura non deficit* etc.—natura quaedam facit propter finem, *nature does certain things for the sake of a goal.*—natura semper facit id quod melius est, see above: *inter ea, quae* etc.—natura semper in se curva est, see above: *natura in se recurva est.*—natura semper ordinatur ad unum, see above: *natura determinata est* etc.—natura semper tendit ad unum, see above: *natura determinata est* etc.—natura superior in suo infimo contingit naturam inferiorem in eius supremo, see above: *inferior natura* etc.—natura uniuscuiusque rei ex eius operatione ostenditur, *the nature of everything is revealed by its activity.*—natura unius rei est determinata ad unum, see above: *natura determinata est* etc.—natura uno et eodem modo operatur, nisi impediatur, *unless the nature of a thing is interfered with, it operates in one and the same way.*—nulla natura potest supra seipsam, *no nature can surpass itself;* cf. *species* under

6.—opus naturae est opus intellegentiae, *every work of nature is the work of an intellect,* i.e., the intellect of God.—quod est praeter naturam, non potest esse sempiternum, *that which is outside nature* or *unnatural cannot last forever.*—ratio contra naturam dividitur, see *ratio* under 3.—supremum inferioris naturae attingit ad id quod est infimum superioris, see above: *inferior natura* etc.

naturalis, e, *adj.,* (1) *natural* in the general sense of the word, i.e., (a) that which a thing has from birth or from its beginning without always flowing from its essence, (b) that which is according to the essence of a thing and therefore belongs to it as such, (c) that to which a thing is inclined as a result of its nature, (d) that which possesses a nature and an essence, (e) that which is a thing of reality and not of thought, (f) that which belongs to the material order, (g) that influence which is ordinarily exerted on a thing by another thing superior to it, (h) that which a sensitive being does as a result of its nature and not on the basis of knowledge, (i) physical, that which exists in the region of physical things with sensibly cognitive qualities, (2) *physical,* pertaining to the philosophy of nature, synonym of *physicus,* (3) *scientific by nature, (naturalia) natural science,* the scientific

writings on nature by Aristotle.— On **accidens naturale,** see *accidens* under 2; on **actio naturalis,** see *actio* under 1; on **activum naturale,** see *activus;* on **actus naturalis,** see *actus* under 1; on **aequitas naturalis,** see *aequitas;* on **aestimativa naturalia,** see *aestimativus;* on **agens naturalis,** see *agens;* on **amicitia naturalis,** see *amicitia* under 1; on **amor naturalis,** see *amor* under 1; on **animal naturale,** see *animal* under 1; on **appetitus naturalis,** see *appetitus* under 4; on **auctoritas naturalis,** see *auctoritas* under 4; on **bonitas naturalis et rei naturalis,** see *bonitas* under 1; on **bonum naturale,** see *bonus* under 2; on **caput naturale,** see *caput;* on **causa naturalis et non-naturalis,** see *causa* under 2; on **claritas naturalis,** see *claritas* under 3; on **cognitio naturalis,** see *cognitio* under 2; on **communicatio naturalis,** see *communicatio* under 1 and 3; on **communitas naturalis,** see *communitas* under 3; on **commutatio naturalis,** see *commutatio* under 2; on **complexio naturalis,** see *complexio* under 2; on **compositio naturalis,** see *compositio* under 1; on **conceptio naturalis,** see *conceptio* under 1 and 4; on **concomitantia naturalis,** see *concomitantia* under 1; on **concupiscentia naturalis et non-naturalis,** see *concupiscentia* under 1; on **conversio naturalis,** see *conversio* under 2; on **corpus naturale et non-natu-**

rale, see *corpus;* on **corruptibilitas naturalis**, see *corruptibilitas;* on **corruptio naturalis**, see *corruptio* under 2 and 3; on **defectus naturalis**, see *defectus* under 2; on **delectatio naturalis et nonnaturalis**, see *delectatio;* on **desiderium naturale**, see *desiderium* under 1; on **dilectio naturalis**, see *dilectio* under 1; on **dispositio naturalis**, see *dispositio* under 4; on **diversitas naturalis**, see *diversitas;* on **divitiae naturales**, see *divitiae;* on **dominium naturale**, see *dominium;* on **donum naturale**, see *donum* under 1; on **effectus naturalis**, see *effectus;* on **ens naturale**, see *ens;* on **esse naturale**, see *esse;* on **existimatio naturalis**, see *existimatio;* on **factio naturalis**, see *factio;* on **facultas naturalis**, see *facultas* under 1; on **fieri naturale**, see *fieri;* on **filiatio naturalis**, see *filiatio;* on **finis naturalis**, see *finis* under 2; on **forma naturalis**, see *forma* under 2; on **generans naturale**, see *generare;* on **generatio naturalis**, see *generatio* under 1; on **genus naturale**, see *genus* under 2; on **gloria naturalis**, see *gloria* under 1; on **habitudo naturalis**, see *habitudo;* on **habitus naturalis et non-naturalis**, see *habitus* under 4; on **homo naturalis**, see *homo;* on **immortalitas naturalis**, see *immortalitas;* on **immutatio naturalis**, see *immutatio* under 2; on **impetus naturalis**, see *impetus;* on **impotentia naturalis**, see *impotentia;* on **inchoatio naturalis**, see *inchoatio* under 1; on **incorruptibilitas naturalis**, see *incorruptibilitas;* on **instinctus naturalis**, see *instinctus;* on **instrumentum naturale**, see *instrumentum;* on **intellectus naturalis**, see *intellectus* under 9; on **iudicium naturale seu naturalis existimationis**, see *iudicium* under 4; on **ius naturale**, see *ius* under 1; on **iustitia naturalis**, see *iustitia* under 2 and 4; on **iustum naturale**, see *iustus;* on **lex naturalis**, see *lex* under 1; on **libertas naturalis**, see *libertas* under 1; on **linea naturalis**, see *linea* under 1; on **locus naturalis et non-naturalis**, see *locus* under 2; on **lumen naturale**, see *lumen;* on **magnitudo naturalis**, see *magnitudo* under 1; on **malitia naturalis**, see *malitia* under 1; on **malum in rebus naturalibus et secundum naturalem ordinem**, see *malus* under 2; on **materia naturalis**, see *materia* under 3; on **medium naturale**, see *medium* under 1 and 2; on **mors naturalis**, see *mors;* on **motus naturalis**, see *motus* under 1 and 2; on **movens naturale**, see *movens;* on **mutatio naturalis**, see *mutatio;* on **nativitas naturalis**, see *nativitas;* on **necessitas naturalis seu naturalis inclinationis seu naturalis ordinis**, see *necessitas* under 1; on **notitia naturalis**, see *notitia* under 2; on **odium naturale et non-naturale**, see *odium;* on **operatio naturalis, operatio naturalis secundum quid et simpliciter**, see *operatio* under 2; on ordo naturalis, see *ordo* under 1; on **origo naturalis**, see *origo;* on **passio naturalis**, see *passio* under 2 and 4; on **peccatum naturale seu in naturalibus**, see *peccatum* under 1 and 2; on **perfectio naturalis**, see *perfectio* under 2 and 4; on **potentia naturalis**, see *potentia* under 2 and 4; on **potestas naturalis**, see *potestas* under 2; on **principium naturale**, see *principium;* on **prophetia naturalis**, see *prophetia;* on **propinquitas naturalis**, see *propinquitas* under 2; on **proprietas naturalis**, see *proprietas* under 1; on **providentia naturalis**, see *providentia;* on **prudentia naturalis**, see *prudentia* under 2; on **qualitas naturalis**, see *qualitas;* on **quantitas naturalis**, see *quantitas* under 1; on **quies naturalis**, see *quies;* on **ratio naturalis**, see *ratio* under 3; on **rectitudo naturalis**, see *rectitudo* under 3; on **regimen naturale**, see *regimen;* on **res naturalis**, see *res;* on **resurrectio naturalis**, see *resurrectio;* on **scientia naturalis et pure naturalis**, see *scientia* under 1 and 2; on **servitus naturalis**, see *servitus* under 1; on **subsistentia naturalis**, see *subsistentia* under 2; on **substantia naturalis**, see *substantia* under 2; on **suppositio naturalis**, see *suppositio* under 4; on **theologia naturalis**, see *theologia* under 1; on **timor naturalis et non-naturalis**, see *timor;* on **transmutatio naturalis**, see *transmutatio;* on **umidum naturale**, see *umidus;*

on **unio naturalis et non-naturalis**, see *unio;* on **unitas naturalis**, see *unitas;* on **veritas naturalis speciei**, see *veritas* under 1; on **virtus naturalis**, see *virtus* under 1; on **vis naturalis**, see *vis* under 1; on **vita naturalis**, see *vita* under 1; on **voluntas naturalis**, see *voluntas* under 3; on **vox naturalis**, see *vox* under 1.–**pura naturalia**, *the purely natural,* created beings possessing no properties or powers of the supernatural.– **naturalia tendunt in fines determinatos**, *the irrational things of nature are ever striving after definite goals.* Cf. *natura.*–On **consideratio naturalis**, see *consideratio;* on **definitio naturalis**, see *definitio* under 2; on **philosophia naturalis**, see *philosophia;* on **philosophus naturalis**, see *philosophus;* on **quaestio naturalis**, see *quaestio;* on **ratio naturalis**, see *ratio* under 13; on **scientia naturalis**, see *scientia* under 2.–**naturalis**, (sc. **philosophus**), synonym of *physicus,* the Aristotelian *physikos* (Phys. II. 2, 193. b. 23), *the nature philosopher, the investigator of nature, the naturalist.*–**naturaliter**, *adv.*, (1) *naturally, conformably to nature, by nature, in a manner corresponding to the natural order,* synonym of *connaturaliter,* the opposite of *supernaturaliter, miraculose,* and *violenter,* (2) in the sense of *natural science, after the manner of natural science,* synonym of *physice,* the opposite of *logice.*–On causa naturaliter agens, see *causa* under 2; on **corrumpere naturaliter**, see *corrumpere* under 2; on **fieri naturaliter**, see *fieri;* on **inesse naturaliter**, see *inesse;* on **malum naturaliter**, see *malus* under 2; on **movere naturaliter**, see *movere;* on **motum naturaliter**, see *motus;* on **principium naturaliter notum**, see *principium;* on **prius naturaliter**, see *prior* under 1; on **procedere naturaliter**, see *procedere;* on **significare naturaliter**, see *significare;* on **simul naturaliter**, see *simul;* on **velle naturaliter**, see *velle* under 1.—On **sumere naturaliter**, see *sumere* under 3.

naturalitas, atis, *f.*, *naturalness, natural condition, natural character* or *disposition.*

naturaliter, *adv.*, see *naturalis.*

naturans, antis, *P. a.*, (of *naturare*) *generating, creating,* used chiefly in the scholastic phrase, *natura naturans, the nature which makes nature.*

natus, i, *m.*, see *nascor.*

natus, us, *m., birth,* used in the phrase **maiores natu**, *the elders.*

naufragium, ii, *n.*, (1) lit., *a shipwreck,* (2) fig., *shipwreck, ruin, loss, destruction.*

nauta, ae, *m., a sailor, seaman, mariner.*

nauticus, a, um, *adj., nautical, of* or *belonging to ships* or *sailors.*

Nave, *n., indecl., Nave,* same as Nun, father of Josue or Jesus Ben Nave.

navicula, ae, *f., a small vessel, a boat, skiff.*

navifactiva, ae, *f., shipwrightry, the art* or *occupation of a shipwright.*

navifactor, oris, *m., a ship-builder.*

navigatorius, a, um, *adj., of* or *pertaining to navigation.*

navigo, are, avi, atum, 1, *v. a., to sail, set sail.*

navis, is, *f., a ship.*—**dirigere navem**, *to steer a ship.*—**compaginare navem**, *to rivet the ship* or *the planks of the ship.*—**gubernare navem**, *to govern* or *guide a ship.* **deserere navem**, *to desert the ship.*

Nazaraei, orum, *m., the Nazarites,* among the ancient Hebrews, religious devotees, set apart to the Lord by a special vow the terms of which are carefully described in Num. VI. They included entire abstinence from wine and intoxicating liquors; they never cut their hair nor approached a dead body. The vow might be taken for a limited period or for life. They first appear in the time of the Philistine oppression.

Nazaraei, orum, *m., the Nazarenes,* heretics of the first century of the Church. They held to the law of Moses, but did not insist on its observance as essential to salvation. They believed in the divinity of Christ, His Incarnation, and His miraculous birth of the Virgin Mary, and also recognized St. Paul as the apostle of the Gentiles. The Nazarenes disappeared from history about the middle of the fifth century.

Nazarenus, i, *m.*, see *Nazareth.*

Nazareth, *n. indecl., Nazareth, a city in Palestine.*—**Nazarenus,** i, *m., the Nazarene.*

Nazianzenus, a, um, *adj., Nazianzene,* of Nazianzus, a titular metropolitan see of Cappadocia Tertia. Nazianzus was a small town the history of which is unknown. It is the modern village of Nenizi east of Ak-Serai in the villayet of Koniah. Its name is inseparably connected with its illustrious doctor and poet-bishop St. Gregory.

ne, *adv.* and *conj.*, the primitive negative Latin particle, *no, not,* (I) *adv.*, in imperative sentences to signify that something must be done, (1) with *subj.*, (2) in purpose clauses, (II) in some of the uses described in (I) the transition to its use to connect clauses is clearly seen. In intentional clauses, and after verbs of fearing and avoiding, *ne* becomes a conjunction (1) after verbs signifying *to fear; to frighten,* (2) after verbs signifying *to avoid, warn, hinder, forbid,* etc.

Nebridius, ii, *m., Nebridius,* a fellow countryman and friend of St. Augustine.

nebula, ae, *f.*, (1) *a cloud,* (2) fig., *darkness, obscurity.*

nebulosus, a, um, *adj., cloudy, misty, foggy.*

nec, *adv.* and *conj.*, see *neque.*

necdum, see *neque.*

necessarius, a, um, *adj.*, (1) *ontologically necessary,* i.e., that which exists in the realm of real being and which cannot fail to exist or cannot exist in a different way, synonym of *debitus* and *necesse,* the opposite of *contingens* and *liber,* (2) *logically necessary, of necessity true* or *right,* i.e., that which in the realm of studied thought or thinking cannot be otherwise, likewise the opposite of *contingens.*—On the difference between *necessarius* and *contingens,* see *contingens* under 2. On **actus necessarius ad vitam,** see *actus* under 1; on **bonum necessarium,** see *bonus* under 2; on **causa necessaria,** see *causa* under 2; on **cognitio necessaria,** see *cognitio* under 2; on **concupiscentia necessaria,** see *concupiscentia* under 1; on **effectus necessarius,** see *effectus;* on **habitudo necessaria,** see *habitudo;* on **inductio necessaria,** see *inductio* under 3; on **instrumentum necessarium,** see *instrumentum;* on **materia necessaria,** see *materia* under 3; on **propositio de necessario,** see *propositio* under 2; on **spiritualitas necessaria,** see *spiritualitas* under 3; on **voluntas necessaria et non-necessaria,** see *voluntas* under 3.—Kinds of *necessarium* in this (1) sense are: (a), **necessarium absolute seu simpliciter** and **necessarium ex conditione seu suppositione seu secundum quid,** *the absolute* or *without condition* or *simply necessary* or *the neces-*

sary with a specified condition or *conditional* or *hypothetical necessity.*—(b), necessarium a priori, *the necessary a priori* or *the necessary from the beginning.*—(c), necessarium ex aliquo exteriori and necessarium secundum sui naturam, *the extrinsically necessary* and *the intrinsically necessary* or *the natural.* Cf. *necessarium per aliud.*—(d), necessarium ex condicione, see *necessarium absolute.*—(e), necessarium ex conditione agentis seu per violentiam seu per coactionem seu necessitate coactionis and necessarium conditione seu ex necessitate seu suppositione seu respectu finis, *the necessary springing from the action of an effective cause* or *of a physical power, which may be violence,* and *the necessary springing from the goal* or *final cause.*—(f), necessarium ex conditione finis, see *necessarium ex conditione agentis.*—(g), necessarium ex necessitate coactionis, see *necessarium ex conditione agentis.*—(h), necessarium ex necessitate finis, see *necessarium ex conditione agentis.*—(i), necessarium ex suppositione, see *necessarium absolute.*—(j), necessarium ex suppositione finis, see *necessarium ex conditione agentis.*—(k), necessarium individui and necessarium personae, *the necessary as an individual* and *as a person,* i.e., that which is necessary to anyone as an individual. and that which is

necessary to him as a person of rank.—(l), necessarium per aliud and necessarium per se, *the necessary from extrinsic causes* and *that from intrinsic causes.* Cf. *necessarium ex aliquo exteriori.*—(m), necessarium per coactionem, see *necessarium ex conditione agentis.*—(n), necessarium per se, see *necessarium per aliud.*—(o), necessarium personae, see *necessarium individui.*—(p), necessarium primum, *the first necessary,* namely God.—(q), necessarium respectu finis, see *necessarium ex conditione agentis.*—(r), necessarium secundum quid, see *necessarium absolute.*—(s), necessarium secundum sui naturam, see *necessarium ex aliquo exteriori.*—(t), necessarium simpliciter, see *necessarium absolute.*—nihil est adeo contingens, quin in se aliquid necessarium habeat, see *contingens* under 2.—On conclusio necessaria, see *conclusio* under 2; on conditionalis necessaria, see *conditionalis;* on enuntiabile necessarium, see *enuntiabilis;* on medium necessarium, see *medium* under 2; on principium necessarium, see *principium;* on propositio necessaria, see *propositio* under 2; on ratio necessaria et non-necessaria, see *ratio* under 13; on syllogismus necessarius seu de necessario, see *syllogismus;* on veritas necessaria, see *veritas* under 1; on verum necessarium et non-necessarium, see *verus* under 1.—Kinds of *necessa-*

rium in this (2) sense are: **necessarium absolute** and **necessarium ex suppositione seu sub conditione**, *the absolutely necessary truth* and *the conditionally necessary truth*. Cf. *necessarium absolute* under 1.—**ex necessariis numquam contingit syllogizare nisi necessarium**, *from necessarily true premises only the necessarily true can be concluded.*—**omnis conditionalis, cuius antecedens est necessarium absolute, consequens est necessarium absolute**, *if in a conditional sentence the protasis (the antecedent) is necessarily true, then so is the apodosis (the consequent).*

necesse, *indecl.*, usually used with *esse*, (1) *necessarily, with necessity*, (2) *necessary*, synonym of *necessarius.*—**absolute seu simpliciter necesse**, *with unconditional or absolute necessity.*

necessitas, atis, *f.*, (1) *ontological necessity*, i.e., necessity in the sphere of real being, such that it cannot be other than it is, the opposite of *contingentia* and *supererogatio*, (2) *logical necessity*, i.e., necessity in the sphere of thought or thinking, such a connection between subject and predicate or between propositions that it cannot be otherwise, the opposite of *contingentia*, (3) *need, want, necessity.*—**necessitatis articulus**, *a case of urgency* or *necessity.*—**de necessitate** and **ex necessitate**, *of necessity, necessarily*. On **agere a seu ex seu in necessitate et per necessitatem naturae**, see *agere* under 1; on **debitum necessitatis et propter seu secundum necessitatem**, see *debitus* under 1; on **intellegere per modum necessitatis**, see *intellegere* under 1; on **libertas a necessitate**, see *libertas* under 2; on **medium necessitatis**, see *medium* under 2; on **operari per necessitatem**, see *operari*; on **ordo necessitatis**, see *ordo* under 2; on **poena ex necessitate inflicta**, see *poena*; on **praeceptum primae, secundae, tertiae, et quartae necessitatis**, see *praeceptum*; on **sacramentum necessitatis**, see *sacramentum* under 3; on **velle ex necessitate**, see *velle* under 1. —Kinds of *necessitas* in this (1) sense are: (a), **necessitas absoluta** and **necessitas conditionalis seu conditionata seu suppositionis seu ex suppositione**, *the simple* or *unconditioned necessity* and *the conditional* or *hypothetical necessity*. Cf. *necessitas absoluta* under 2 and 3.—(b), **necessitas a posteriori** and **necessitas a priori**, *the a posteriori necessity* or *the necessity apparent from consequences* and *the a priori necessity* and *the necessity from the outset.*—(c), **necessitas a priori**, see *necessitas a posteriori.*—(d), **necessitas coactionis seu violentiae seu violenta** and **necessitas finis seu ex fine seu ex conditione seu suppositione finis**, *the necessity of force* and *that of purpose*, i.e., the necessity which comes from an exteriorly exercised power, and that which one imposes on himself by the fixing of and the striving for a goal, both being kinds of *necessitas ex alio seu ex aliquo extrinseco.*—(e), **necessitas conditionalis seu conditionata,** see *necessitas absoluta.*—(f), **necessitas consequentis,** *the necessity of the consequent.* The *consequent* is the proposition which is either the conclusion of a syllogism of which the premises are called the antecedent, or the apodosis of a conditional (hypothetical) proposition. The connection between conclusion and premises or between protasis and apodosis is the *consequence.* The consequent may be a necessary proposition, i.e., one the predicate of which cannot but be found with this subject, even though its connection (consequence) with the antecedent may not be necessary. And conversely, not-necessary propositions may be related by a necessity of consequences. Cf. *necessitas consequentia* under 2.—(g), **necessitas ex alio seu ex aliquo extrinseco** and **necessitas naturae seu naturalis seu naturalis inclinationis seu naturalis ordinis,** *the necessity that arises from something else* or *the exterior necessity* and *the inner* or *natural necessity.* Cf. *necessitas coactionis.*—(h), **necessitas ex aliquo extrinseco,** see *necessitas ex alio.*—(i), **necessitas ex conditione finis,**

see *necessitas coactionis.*—(j), **necessitas ex fine,** see *necessitas coactionis.*—(k), **necessitas ex obligatione praecepti,** *the necessity that arises from the imposition of a precept.*—(l), **necessitas ex suppositione,** see *necessitas absoluta.*—(m), **necessitas ex suppositione finis,** see *necessitas coactionis.* —(n), **necessitas finis,** see *necessitas coactionis.*—(o), **necessitas formae,** and **necessitas materiae,** *the necessity of form* and *that of material,* or the necessity that arises from the form and that from the material of a thing. Cf. *necessitas naturae.*—(p), **necessitas immutabilitatis,** *necessity as the result of immutability.*—(q), **necessitas iuris seu iustitiae,** *the necessity of right* or *of justice,* i.e., *the duty which is imposed by justice.*—(r), **necessitas iustitiae,** see *necessitas iuris.*—(s), **necessitas liberae voluntatis,** *the necessity of free will,* or *the necessity which one imposes on himself of his own accord.*—(t), **necessitas materiae,** see *necessitas formae.*—(u), **necessitas mortis seu moriendi,** *the necessity of death* or *of dying.*—(v), **necessitas moriendi,** see *necessitas mortis.*— (w), **necessitas naturae,** see *necessitas ex alio.*—(x), **necessitas naturalis,** see *necessitas ex alio.*— (y), **necessitas naturalis inclinationis seu necessitas naturalis ordinis,** see *necessitas ex alio.*—(z), **necessitas oboedientiae seu oboedientiam consequens** and **neces-**

sitas voti, *the necessity of willing obedience* and *that of the vow,* i.e., the necessity which the vow of willing obedience imposes on a subject and that which a vow in general imposes.—(a²), **necessitas ordinis,** *the necessity of arrangement with reference to something.* Cf. *necessitas ordinis* under 2.—(b²), **necessitas principii,** *the necessity of principle* or *the necessity which dwells within the effective cause* and *controls it in its effect* or *action.* (c²), **necessitas principiorum essentialium,** *the necessity originating from within* or *the essential principle of a thing.*—(d²), **necessitas scientiae** and **necessitas voluntatis,** *the necessity which is imposed on the action of a being by its knowledge* and *that which is imposed upon it by its will.*—(e²), **necessitas suppositionis,** see *necessitas absoluta.*—(f²), **necessitas violenta seu violentiae,** see *necessitas coactionis.*—(g²), **necessitas voluntatis,** see *necessitas scientiae.*—(h²), **necessitas voti,** see *necessitas oboedientiae.* On **cognoscere per modum necessitatis,** see *cognoscere* under 2; on **concludere de necessitate,** see *concludere* under 4; on **conclusio de necessitate,** see *conclusio* under 2; on **intellegere per modum necessitatis,** see *intellegere* under 1; on **maior de necessitate,** see *maior* under 4; on **propositio necessitatis,** see *propositio* under 2; on **scire ex**

necessitate, see *scire* under 2; on **verum ex necessitate,** see *verum* under 1.—Kinds of *necessitas* in this (2) sense are: (a), **necessitas absoluta** and **necessitas conditionata,** *the unconditional* and *the conditional necessity.* Cf. *necessitas absoluta* under 1 and 3. —(b), **necessitas conditionata,** see *necessitas absoluta.*—(c), **necessitas consequentiae,** *the necessity of the deduction* or *the conclusion,* i.e., the necessity by which the conclusio of a syllogism results from its premises or the apodosis of a conditional sentence from its protasis. Cf. *necessitas consequentis* under 1. —(d), **necessitas ordinis,** *the necessity of order* or *arrangement,* i.e., the predicate with reference to the subject of a sentence. Cf. *necessitas ordinis* under 1. On **commutatio necessitatis,** see *commutatio* under 2.—Kinds of *necessitas* in this (3) sense are: (a), **necessitas absoluta** and **necessitas conditionata,** *the absolute* or *unconditioned* and *the relative necessity* or *need.* Cf. *necessitas absoluta* under 1 and 2.—(b), **necessitas communis** and **necessitas specialis,** *the general* and *the particular needs.*— (c), **necessitas conditionata,** see *necessitas absoluta.*—(d), **necessitas corporalis seu corporis,** *the physical needs.*—(e), **necessitas corporis,** see *necessitas corporalis.*—(f), **necessitas extrema seu ultima,** *the extreme need* or *want.*—(g), **necessitas rei famili-aris,** *the domestic need.*—(h), **necessitas specialis,** see *necessitas communis.*—(i), **necessitas ultima,** see *necessitas extrema.*—(j), **necessitas vitae seu vitae humanae seu vitae temporalis,** *the needs of life,* i.e., of human life in this world.—(k), **necessitas vitae humanae,** see *necessitas vitae.*—(l), **necessitas vitae temporalis,** see *necessitas vitae.*

necessitudo, inis, *f., a close connection* in which one person stands to another as relative or friend, *relationship, friendship, intimacy, bond,* etc.

neco, are, avi, atum, 1, *v. a., to kill, slay, put to death.*

necromantia, ae, *f., necromancy,* the pretended art of revealing future events by means of communication with the dead.

necromanticus, a, um, *adj., necromantic; of, belonging to,* or *used in necromancy* or *magic; performed by necromancy.*—**necromanticus,** i, *m., a necromancer,* one who practices necromancy; one who claims to carry on communication with the dead.

necros, (*nekros*), *dead.*

necto, ere, xui, xum, 3, *v. a., to bind, connect,* used fig.

nedum, *conj., still less,* used to indicate that whereas a certain thing is not, another thing can still less be.

nefandus, a, um, *adj., impious.*

nefarius, a, um, *adj., wicked, nefarious.*

nefas, *n., indecl., something contrary to divine law, sinful, unlawful, abominable; an impious* or *wicked deed.*

negatio, onis, *f.,* (1) *negation, a negative expression, a negative assertion,* a simple denial not to be confused with *privatio* and *remotio,* the opposite of *affirmatio,* (2) *the negative determination of a thing,* synonym of *privatio,* the opposite of *affirmatio.*—On **ignorantia negationis,** see *ignorantia* under 1; on **modus negationis,** see *modus* under 3; on **via negationis,** see *via* under 1; on **virtus negationis,** see *virtus* under 6.—Kinds of *negatio* in this (1) sense are: (a), **negatio de praedicato finito, negatio de praedicato infinito,** and **negatio de praedicato privativo seu privativa,** *the denial of a finite, an infinite,* and *a privative predicate to some subject.*—(b), **negatio falsa** and **negatio vera,** *the false* and *the true negation.* —(c), **negatio privativa,** see *negatio de praedicato finito.*—(d), **negatio una,** *a single negation.*—(e), **negatio vera,** see *negatio falsa.*—ad plura sese extendit negatio, quam affirmatio, see *affirmatio* under 1.—affirmatio et negatio non sunt simul vera, see *affirmatio* under 1.—affirmatio naturaliter est prior negatione, see *affirmatio* under 1.—si affirmatio est causa affirmationis, et negatio est causa negationis, see *affirmatio* under 1.—si negatio est causa negationis, **affirmatio est causa affirmationis**, see *affirmatio* under 1.—On **communitas negationis**, see *communitas* under 1; on **nomen negationis**, see *nomen* under 1; on **oppositio affirmationis et negationis**, see *oppositio* under 2.—Kinds of *negatio* in this (2) sense are: (a), **negatio absoluta seu absolute seu pura seu simplex seu simpliciter seu extra genus** and **negatio in genere seu in genere determinato seu in subiecto seu privativa seu per modum privationis seu secundum privationem**, *the absolute* or *pure* or *simple negation* or *the negation outside of a determined genus* and *the negation within a determined genus* or *with respect to a determined subject* or *in the sense of privation.*—(b), **negatio extra genus**, see *negatio absoluta.*—(c), **negatio in genere**, see *negatio absoluta.*—(d), **negatio in genere determinato**, see *negatio absoluta.*—(e), **negatio in subiecto**, see *negatio absoluta.*—(f), **negatio per modum privationis**, see *negatio absoluta.*—(g), **negatio privativa**, see *negatio absoluta.*—(h), **negatio pura**, see *negatio absoluta.*—(i), **negatio rationis tantum** and **negatio realis**, *the purely mental* and *the objectively negative decision.*—(j), **negatio realis**, see *negatio rationis tantum.*—(k), **negatio secundum privationem**, see *negatio absoluta.*—(l), **negatio simplex seu simpliciter**, see *negatio abso-*

luta.—ex negatione in negationem non est mutatio per se, *a change of a negative statement as such to another negative statement cannot be.*—negatio neque ponit aliquid, neque determinat sibi aliquod subiectum, *a negative statement is nothing positive and does not require a subject for itself.*

negative, see *negativus.*

negativus, a, um, *adj., negating, denying, negative,* synonym of *remotivus,* the opposite of *affirmativus* and *positivus.* On **demonstratio negativa** see *demonstratio* under 3; on **differentia negativa**, see *differentia;* on **enuntiatio negativa**, see *enuntiatio* under 2; on **intellectus negativus**, see *intellectus* under 8; on **locus negativus**, see *locus* under 4; on **nomen negativum**, see *nomen* under 1; on **praeceptum negativum**, see *praeceptum;* on **propositio negativa**, see *propositio* under 2; on **syllogismus negativus**, see *syllogismus;* on **verbum negativum**, see *verbum* under 2;—**negativa**, sc. enuntiatio seu propositio, *the negative expression* or *negation.*—Kinds of *negativa* are: (a), **negativa de praedicato finito** and **negativa de praedicato infinito seu infinita**, *negation of a finite* and *that of an infinite predicate.* Cf. *praedicatum.*—(b), **negativa infinita**, see *negativa de praedicato finito.*—(c), **negativa privativa seu secundum quid** and **negativa simplex seu simpliciter,**

the negation containing a privation or *made in a certain respect*, e.g., homo non est iniustus, and *the simple* or *simply asserted negation*, e.g., homo non est iustus. —(d), **negativa secundum privationem**, see *negativa privativa.*— (e), **negativa secundum quid**, see *negativa privativa.*—(f), **negativa simplex seu simpliciter**, see *negativa privativa.*—**negative**, *adv., in the sense of a negation, after the manner of a negation, negatively,* synonym of *remotive,* the opposite of *affirmativa* and *positive.* On **accipere negative**, see *accipere* under 3; on **dicere negative**, see *dicere* under 3; on **ignorantia negative accepta**, see *ignorantia* under 1; on **infinitum negative dictum, seu sumptum,** see *infinitus;* on **intellegere negative**, see *intellegere* under 3; on **oppositum negative**, see *opponere;* on **praedicare negative**, see *praedicare* under 2; on **significare negative**, see *significare;* on **sumere negative**, see *sumere* under 3.

negligenter, *adv.,* see *negligo.*

negligentia, ae, *f., carelessness, heedlessness, negligence.*

negligo, ere, exi, ectum, 3, *v. a., not to heed, not trouble one's self about, not attend to, to slight, neglect, be regardless of, indifferent to,* used with an *object clause,* with *acc.,* (1) in gen., the opposite of *curare,* (2) in partic., *to make light of, to disregard, contemn, neglect,* a synonym of *dispicere, contemnere, spernere.*

—**negligens**, entis, *P. a., negligent.*—**negligenter**, *adv., negligently, carelessly.*

nego, are, avi, atum, 1, *v. n.* and *a., to say no, to deny, refuse,* (1) in gen., *to say yes* or *no,* used with (a) *acc.* and *inf., to say* or *affirm that not, to deny that* etc., (b) in *pass.* with *inf.,* (2) in partic., (a) *to deny a thing,* really with *quin,* (b) *to deny,* or *refuse,* (c) in eccl. Latin, *to deny any knowledge of, to reject,* used with *acc.* of person.

negotiatio, onis, *f., trading, commercial enterprises, any business* or *traffic.*

negotiativus, a, um, *adj., negotious, involving* or *given to occupation* or *business.*

negotiator, oris, *m., a tradesman.*

negotior, ari, atus, 1, *v. dep. n.* and *a.,* (1) lit., *to conduct business, to trade, traffic,* (2) fig., *to negotiate, to be busy with.*

negotium, ii, *n., a business, employment, occupation, affair,* (2) transf., like *res, matter, affair.*— **theologicum negotium,** *a theological work.*

Nembroth, is, *m., Nembroth* or *Nemrod* or *Nimrod,* the name of a descendant of Chus, son of Cham represented in Gen., X, 8-12 as the founder of the Babylonian empire.

nemesicus, i, *m., one prone to sorrow over the good of the undeserving, a nemesic,* to be distinguished from *invidus;* cf. *nemesiticus.*

nemesis, is, *f., joy at the misfortune of another, malicious joy, jealousy.*

nemesiticus, a, um, *adj., rejoicing in the trouble of others, envious.*

Nemesius, ii, *m., Nemesius,* Bishop of Emesa at the end of the fourth century, of whom nothing is known except that he was author of a rather remarkable treatise, *De natura hominis,* of which chapters II and III appear as a separate work, *de Anima,* among the writings of Gregory Nyssene; being erroneously ascribed to that father. St. Thomas quotes the *De natura hominis,* referring it, however, to Gregory of Nyssa.

nemo, inis, *m.* and *f., no one, no man.*—**nemo alius,** *no one else, no other man.*

nempe, *conj.,* (1) *namely,* (2) in stating an obvious fact, *without doubt.*

Neomenia, ae, *f., the neomenia* or *new moon;* in Greek and Jewish antiquities, the time of the new moon, the beginning of the lunar month, also the festival held at that time.

neophytus, i, *m., a neophyte, a new convert;* one newly admitted to a church or religious body; applied also to a priest or to a novice of a religious order.

nepos, otis, *m.* and *f.,* (1) *a grandson,* (2) *a brother's* or *sister's son, a nephew.*

Nepotianus, i, *m., Nepotianus,* a presbyter at Altinum, under his uncle Heliodorus, the bishop of that place. His death in 396 elicited an interesting letter from Jerome to Heliodorus. It relates his relinquishment of a military life in favor of voluntary poverty and monachism, which he intended to pursue in Egypt, Mesopotamia, or the solitudes of the Dalmatian islands.

neptis, is, *f., a niece.*

nequam, *adj., indecl.,* of character, *worthless, vile, bad.*—**nequiter,** *adv., wickedly.*

nequaquam, *adv., in nowise, by no means, not at all.*

neque, (nec), *adv.* and *conj., not, and not, also not.*—**neque** (nec) . . . **neque** (nec), *neither . . . nor.* —**necdum,** *and not yet, not yet.*

nequeo, ire, ivi and ii, itum, 4, *v. n., not to be able, to be unable, cannot,* used with *inf.*

nequissimus, a, um, *adj.,* see *nequam.*

nequiter, *adv.,* see *nequam.*

nequitia, ae, *f., wickedness, vileness, worthlessness.*

nervosus, a, um, *adj., nervous, full of sinews, sinewy.*

nervus, i, *m., a sinew, tendon, nerve.*

nescientia, ae, *f., ignorance, of what one is not expected to know, nescience.*

nescio, ire, ivi or ii, itum, 4, *v. a., not to know,* the opposite of *scire.*

Nesteros, otis, *m., Nesteros,* a cenobite of the Egyptian desert whom Cassian visited in 395. Two of the *Conferences,* the fourteenth and fifteenth, are held with him, the subjects being *De Spirituali Scientia* and *De Charismatibus Divinis*. St. Thomas quotes Coll. XIV. 4, 5.

Nestoriani, orum, *m.*, see *Nestorianus*.

Nestorianus, a, um, *adj.*, *Nestorian*, of or belonging to Nestorius who was condemned as a heretic at the Council of Ephesus.—**Nestorius,** ii, *m.*, *Nestorius*, Patriarch of Constantinople (428) a vain orator without depth of thought or piety, objected to the title of "Mother of God" as applied to the Blessed Virgin. He maintained that the Blessed Virgin had given birth to the man Jesus, in whom the Son of God dwelt as in a temple; that there are two persons in Christ really distinct, the man Jesus and the Son of God, and that between them, there exists only an external union. The chief adversary of Nestorius was Cyril, Bishop of Alexandria.—**Nestoriani,** orum, *m.*, *the Nestorians, the followers of Nestorius*.

Nestorius, ii, *m.*, see *Nestorianus*.

neuter, tra, trum, *adj.*, (1) in gen., *neither the one nor the other, neither of two*, (2) in partic., of gender, with *genus, neuter*, neither masculine nor feminine.

neutraliter, *adv.*, *as a neuter, in a neuter sense, neutrally*.

nex, necis, *f.*, (1) *a violent death, murder, slaughter*, (2) *death, a natural death*.

nexus, us, *m.*, *a bond, tie, link*, (1) lit., *a link, bond*, a system by which the adjacent parts of a structure are bound together, (2) fig., (a) *a bond*, a binding force or influence, a cause of union, (b) *a tie, bond*, a binding agreement or covenant, (c) *a bond, a moral duty* or *obligation*.

Nicaea, ae, *f.*, *Nicaea*, a city of Bithynia on Lake Ascanius, the modern *Isnik* or *Nice*. The First Council of Nicaea was held in 325 on the occasion of the heresy of Arius. The Second Council of Nicaea was held in 787 to deal with Iconoclasm.—**Nicaenus,** a, um, *adj.*, *Nicene*.

Nicaenus, a, um, *adj.*, see *Nicaea*.

Nicetas, ae, *m.*, *Nicetas*, one of the interlocutors in the *Itinerarium Clementis*, a work attributed to St. Clement of Rome and regarded as of little reliability.

Nicodemus, i, *m.*, *Nicodemus*, saint, martyr. He was a Pharisee mentioned in St. John's Gospel, 7 and 19, as speaking in behalf of Jesus in the Sanhedrin, and assisting at His burial.

Nicolaus, i, *m.*, *Nicholas I*, saint, pope (857-867). He was born at Rome and died there. Elected after the disintegration of the empire of Charlemagne, he found Christianity threatened by laxity in the observance of moral and civil law. To uphold divine and Church law against princes and worldly bishops, he protected the minor clergy and suffragan bishops against their exactions. He upheld the right of appealing to Rome against the decisions of Hincmar of Rheims; defended the integrity of the marriage bond against Lothair II; and supported Ignatius, Patriarch of Constantinople, against the intruder, Photius (2) *Nicholas of Myra*, saint, confessor. He was born at Potara, Lycia, Asia Minor and died at Myra about 352. Although he is popular in the Greek as well as in the Latin Church, nothing is historically certain about him except that he was born at Myra in the fourth Century. In Germany, Switzerland, and the Netherlands it is the custom to make him the secret purveyor of gifts to children on Dec. 6.

nidifico, are, 1, *v. n., to build a nest.*

nidor, oris, *m., a smell.*

nidus, i, *m., a nest,* used fig.

niger, gra, grum, *adj., black, dark.*

nigredo, inis, *f., blackness, black color.*

nigromanticus, a, um, *adj., nigromantic,* of or belonging to, or used in nigromancy or magic.

nihil, (nihilum), *n., indecl., nothing,* the opposite of *ens.*—**ex nihilo nihil concluditur** (Pot. 3. 1 ob. 6), *from nothing, nothing can be concluded.*—**nihil fit proper vilius se,** *nothing is made because of the will of something that is less than it is itself.*—**omne, quod est ex nihilo, vertibile est in nihilum,** *what has arisen from nothing is convertible to nothing, not because it has a positive capacity not to be, but rather in so far as the creator can cease to support it in existence.*—**quod cedit in nihil, non resumitur idem numero,** *what disappears into nothing, no more returns as the same individual.*—**quod autem parum est, quasi nihil accipit ratio,** *what is only a little, reason holds as nothing.*—**nihilominus,** *adv., none the less, no less, nevertheless, notwithstanding.*

nihilominus, *adv.,* see *nihil.*

nimirum, *adv., surely, without doubt, doubtless,* used in the S.T. only in quot.

nimis, *adv.,* (1) lit., *too much, excessively, beyond measure,* (2) transf., *beyond measure, exceedingly.*

nimius, a, um, *adj.,* (1) lit., *beyond measure, excessive,* (2) transf., *beyond measure, exceedingly.*—**nimium,** ii, *n., too much, excess.*—**nimium,** *adv., too much, too.*

Ninive, es, *f., Nineveh,* the ancient capital of Assyria.—**Ninivitae,** arum, *m., the Ninevites, the inhabitants of Nineveh.*

Ninivitae, arum, *m.,* see *Ninive.*

Ninus, i, *m., Ninus,* the son of Belus, the first king of Assyria, husband of Semiramis, and builder of Nineveh.

nisi, *conj., if not, unless,* (1) (a) in gen., (b) with interrogatives and negatives, usually in a different clause, (c) after nihil, *save, but,* *than,* (d) nisi ut, *except that, unless,* (e) nisi quod, *except that which, save only that,* (f) nisi quia, *except because,* i.e., *until that,* (2) in combinations like nisi forte, *unless perhaps,* sometimes ironical.

niteo, ere, 2, *v. n., to shine, look bright,* (1) transf., (a) of persons, *to shine, look bright* or *beautiful,* (b) of wealth, *to shine,* (2) fig., *to shine, look* or *be beautiful.*

nitidus, a, um, *adj.,* (1) in gen., *bright, shining,* (2) of persons, *comely, handsome.*

nitor, i, nisus and nixus, 3, *v. dep. n.,* (1) lit., *to struggle, put forth great efforts,* (2) fig., (a) *to rely* or *depend on,* used with the *abl.,* (b) *to endeavor, strive.*

nitor, oris, *m., brightness, splendor, lustre, sheen,* (1) of body, *comeliness,* (2) of things in gen., *beauty,* (3) of soul, *comeliness, beauty,* (4) of conscience, *brightness.*

nix, nivis, *f., snow.*

nobilis, e, *adj.,* (1) in gen., *noble,* (a) having qualities or properties of a very high or admirable kind, (b) of parts of the body, (c) of places, *excellent,* distinguished by excellence of appearance or by renown, (d) characterized by moral superiority or dignity, (2) in particular, (a) *renowned, famous,* (b) *noble,* illustrious by rank, birth, title.—**nobilis,** is, *m., a nobleman.*—**nobiliter,** *adv., famously, excellently, nobly.*

nobilitas, atis, *f.,* (1) *rank, nobility, birth,* (2) *noble or excellent quality, excellence, superiority, dignity.*

nobiliter, *adv.,* see *nobilis.*

nobilito, are, avi, atum, 1, *v. a., to ennoble, improve.*

noceo, ere, ui, citum, 2, *v. n.* and *a., to do harm, do hurt to, inflict injury,* used (1) with *dat.,* (2) impers. pass., (3) absol., (4) act.—**nocens,** entis, *P. a.,* (1) *that commits a wicked action, guilty,* (2) *harmful, injurious.*

nocivus, a, um, *adj., hurtful, injurious, noxious.*

noctua, ae, *f., an owl.*

nocturnus, a, um, *adj., of* or *belonging to the night, nocturnal.*

nocumentum, i, *n., harm, damage, evil.*

nodus, i, *n., a knot* or *fold* on a lash; by met., for *scourges,* used in *pl.*

Noe, *indecl., Noe.*

Nolanus, a, um, *adj., of* or *belonging to Nola, Nolan.* Nola is a city of remote antiquity in Campania, founded by the Ausonians.

nolens, see *nolo.*

nolo, nolle, nolui, *v. irreg., not to wish, to be unwilling* in the sense of an action, the opposite of *velle.* On the difference between *nolle* and *non velle,* see *velle.*—**nolens,** entis, *P. a., unwilling,* opposite of *volens.*

noluntas, atis, *f., unwillingness,* in the sense of an action, the opposite of *voluntas.* Cf. **nolle.**

nomen, inis, *n.,* (1) *name, noun,* the *onoma* of Aristotle, which is opposed to verb, the *rema* of Aristotle, and in conjunction with it forms a sentence; synonym of *dictio, locutio,* and *terminus,* (2) *first name.*—On **casus nominis,** see *casus* under 4; on **communicatio nominis,** see *communicatio* under 1; on **prius secundum nominis rationem,** see *prior* under 1; on **qualitas nominis,** see *qualitas;* on **substantia nominis,** see *substantia* under 8.—Kinds of *nomen* in this (1) sense are: (a), **nomen absolutum** and **nomen relativum,** *the name with no reference to anything* and *that which expresses such,* i.e., the name that designates a thing in so far as it stands in no relationship to another, and that which designates it according to one or another relationship to another. (b), **nomen abstractum** and **nomen concretum seu concretivum,** *the name which indicates simply the nature* and *essence of a thing is abstracted in thought from its individual characterizations,* and *that name which so designates a thing as it exists in reality;* thus it expresses not simply its general nature and essence but also the individual characterizations which are connected with the same in reality.—(c), **nomen adiectivum** and **nomen substantivum,** *the name of the adjective* and *that of the substantive.*—(d), **nomen aequivocum seu pure ae-** quivocum, **nomen analogum,** and **nomen synonymum,** *the equivocal name,* indicating something dissimilar which stands in no relation to anything else and *that which signifies something similar* or *the same.*—(e), **nomen analogum,** see *nomen aequivocum.*—(f), **nomen appellativum** and **nomen proprium,** *family name* or *surname* and *proper name.*—(g), **nomen collectivum** and **nomen singularis designati,** *the collective noun* or *name* and *that of the specific individual thing.*—(h), **nomen commune** and **nomen speciale,** *the common* or *the general name* and *the particular name.*—(i), **nomen communicabile,** and **nomen incommunicabile,** *the communicable* and *the incommunicable name.*—(j), **nomen compositum** and **nomen simplex,** *the composite* and *the single* or *simple name.*—(k), **nomen concretivum seu concretum,** see *nomen abstractum.*—(l), **nomen confusum** and **nomen distinctum,** *the confused* or *indefinite name* and *the definite name.*—(m), **nomen Dei seu divinum,** *the name of God.*—(n), **nomen differentiae, nomen generis,** and **nomen speciei,** *the name of difference in essence, the name of the genus,* and *that of the species of a thing.*—(o), **nomen diminutivum,** *the diminutive name.*—(p), **nomen divinum,** see *nomen Dei.*—(q), **nomen essentiale seu naturae** and **nomen personale seu**

personae, *the name of essence* and *that of the person* or the name which designates the nature and essence of a thing and that which designates a person. —(r), **nomen finitum** and **nomen infinitum,** *the name which is limited* or *definite in its meaning.*—(s), **nomen generis,** see *nomen differentiae.*—(t), **nomen incommunicabile,** see *nomen communicabile.*—(u), **nomen infinitum,** see *nomen finitum.*—(v), **nomen intellegibile,** *the intelligible name.*—(w), **nomen intentionis seu intentionem significans** and **nomen rei seu rem significans,** *the name that signifies the relation* or *conception of a thing* and *that which signifies the thing itself.*—(x), **nomen intentionem significans,** see *nomen intentionis.*—(y), **nomen metaphorice dictum seu symbolicum seu translativum,** *the name used in the metaphorical* or *symbolical sense.*—(z), **nomen naturae,** see *nomen essentiale.*—(a²), **nomen negationis seu negativum** and **nomen privativum,** *the name that indicates a simple negation* and *that which signifies a privation* or *lack.*—(b²), **nomen negativum,** see *nomen negationis.*—(c²), **nomen notionale,** *the name that expresses a divine notion.*—(d²), **nomen obliquum,** *the inflected noun.*—(e²), **nomen partitivum,** *the partitive noun,* or *the noun expressing a part.*—(f²), **nomen personae,** see *nomen essentiale.*—(g²), **no-**

men **personale,** see *nomen essentiale.*—(h²), **nomen potestatis,** *the name that indicates the might* or *power of a being.*—(i²), **nomen primae impositionis seu intentionis** and **nomen secundae impositionis seu intentionis,** *the name of the first attribution* or *of a first notion which is the concrete singular subject* and *the name of the second attribution* or *of a second notion* which signifies the aspect of individuality of the singular subject.—(j²), **nomen primae intentionis,** see *nomen primae impositionis.*—(k²), **nomen privativum,** see *nomen negationis.*—(l²), **nomen proprium,** see *nomen appellativum.*—(m²), **nomen rei,** see *nomen intentionis.*—(n²), **nomen relationis,** *the name for the relation of one thing to another.*—(o²), **nomen relativum,** see *nomen absolutum.*—(p²), **nomen relativum secundum dici** and **nomen relativum secundum esse,** *the name which indicates a relation which the mind applies to things* and *that which indicates a relation which is present by the very nature of the thing, independent of the mind,* i.e., the name which designates directly a person or thing, and indirectly an accompanying relation to something like "father" is secundum esse; and that word which designates directly the relation of a person or a thing and indirectly this person or thing itself like "mover" is secundum dici.—(q²), nomen rem significans, see *nomen intentionis*.—(r²), nomen secundae impositionis, see *nomen primae impositionis*.—(s²), nomen secundae intentionis, see *nomen primae impositionis*.—(t²), nomen simplex, see *nomen compositum*.—(u²), nomen singularis designati, see *nomen collectivum*. —(v²), nomen speciale, see *nomen commune*.—(w²), nomen speciei, see *nomen differentiae*.— (x²), nomen substantivum, see *nomen adiectivum*.—(y²), nomen symbolicum, see *nomen metaphorice dictum*.—(z²), nomen synonymum, see *nomen aequivocum*.—(a²), nomen tetragrammaton, *the Hebrew name of Jahweh* or *Jehovah which consists of four letters*.—(b³), nomen translativum, see *nomen metaphorice dictum*.—(c³), nomen verbale, *the verb*, actionem et passionem consignificans.—nomen et verbum magis interpretationis principia esse videntur, quam interpretationes, *the noun* and *the verb seem to be principles of interpretation* and *explanation rather than the interpretations* and *principles themselves*.—nominibus utendum est, ut plures seu secundum quod plures utuntur, the translation of the Aristotelian passage: *tais men onomasiais ta pragmata prosagoreuteon kathaper hoi polloi* (Top. II, 2, 110 a. 16 f), *the nouns* or *names of things should be used as the majority use*

them.—ratio quam significat nomen est conceptio intellectus de re significata per nomen, see *conceptio* under 3.—ratio quam significat nomen est definito, see *definitio* under 2.

nominabilis, e, *adj.*, *nominable, capable* or *worthy of being named*.

nominalis, e, *adj.*, *belonging to a name, nominal*.—nominalis, is, *m.*, *a nominalist*.—nominaliter, *adv.*, *by name, expressly*.

nominaliter, *adv.*, see *nominalis*.

nominatio, onis, *f.*, *name, designation*.

nomino, are, avi, atum, 1, *v. a.*, *to call by name, name, nominate*. On genus nominatum, see *genus* under 2.—Kinds of *nominare* are: (a), nominare metaphorice, *to name something metaphorically*. —(b), nominare positive, *to name something in the positive sense*, i.e., in the sense that it appears as something definite in the reality of things.—(c), nominare proprie and nominare symbolice, *to name something in the proper* and *in the symbolic sense*.— (d), nominare secundum quid and nominare simpliciter, *to name something in a certain respect* or *with reference to something* and *to name something simply* or *absolutely*.—(e), nominare simpliciter, see *nominare secundum quid*.—(f), nominare symbolice, see *nominare proprie*.

non, *adv.*, *not*.—non solum ... sed etiam, *not only ... but also*.—A weak negative before adverbs of emphatic assertion.—**non quod,** *not that.*—**non nisi,** *only.*—The negative force of *non* is not destroyed by a following *nec . . . nec.*

nonaginta, *num, adj., ninety.*

nondum, *adv., not yet.*

non-ens, *non-entis, n., non-being, something that is not,* both in the logical and in the ontological senses, the opposite of *ens.*—Kinds of *non-ens* in the ontological sense of the word are: (a), **non-ens omnino seu purum seu simpliciter,** *non-being in general* or *the pure* or *simple non-being.* —(b), **non-ens per se** and **non-ens secundum accidens,** *non-being in itself* and *non-being with respect to something else.*—(c), **non-ens purum,** see *non-ens omnino.*—(d), **non-ens secundum accidens,** see *non-ens per se.*—(e), **non-ens secundum quid,** *non-being with reference to something.*—(f), **non-ens simpliciter,** see *non-ens omnino.*

nongenti, *ae, a, adj., card., ninehundred.*

nonne, *adv.,* the interrogative *non,* expecting an affirmative answer, *not,* used in a direct interrogation.

nonnisi, *conj.,* see *non* and *nisi.*

nonnullus, *a, um, adj., some, several.*

nonumquam, *adv., sometimes.*

nono, *adv.,* see *nonus.*

nonus, *a, um, adj., ord., the ninth.*— **nona,** *ae, f.,* (sc. hora), *the ninth hour of the day,* i.e., the third before sunset.—**nono,** *adv., ninthly.*

norma, *ae, f., a rule, pattern.*

nos, *nostrum, etc., we,* the plur. of *ego.*

nosco, *ere, novi, notum, 3, v. a., to get a knowledge of, become acquainted with, come to know, know;* in perf., *to have become acquainted with, have learned, know.*

noster, *stra, strum, pron. poss., our, our own; ours, of us.*

nota, *ae, f.,* (1) *note, sign, mark* (of distinction), synonym of *notio,* (2) *musical note* or *character.* Not found in the S.T. of St. Thomas.

notabilis, *e, adj., notable, capable of being noted* or *observed; noticeable, perceptible.*—**notabiliter,** *adv., notably, perceptibly.*

notabiliter *adv.,* see *notabilis.*

notarius, *ii, m., a secretary.*

notificatio, *onis, f., a notification, the action of making known, a notice, definition.*

notifico, *are, avi, atum, 1, v. a., to make known, explain.*

notio, *onis, f.,* (1) *note, sign, mark,* synonym of *nota,* (2) *note, sign, mark, distinguishing characteristic* of a divine person, (3) *notion, idea, conception.*—Kinds of *notio* in this (1) sense are: (a), **notio intellectualis,** *the intellectual notion.*—(b), **notio personae seu personalis,** *the mark of a divine person.*—(c), **notio personalis,** see *notio personae.*—One kind of *notio* in this (2) sense is: **notio ac-**

tiva, *the active mark of a divine person* or *the mark of such which consists of some activity.*

notionalis, e, *adj., consisting of* or *conveying ideas, expressing abstract conceptions, characterizing, notional, forming a distinguishing mark* especially with reference to the Divine Persons. On **actus notionalis**, see *actus* under 1; on **adiectivum notionale**, see *adiectivus;* on **dilectio notionalis**, see *dilectio* under 1; on **nomen notionale**, see *nomen* under 1; on **praedicatum notionale**, see *praedicatum;* on **verbum notionale**, see *verbum* under 1.—**notionaliter**, *adv., in the manner* or *sense of a notio, notionally.* On **dicere notionaliter**, see *dicere* under 3; on **sumere notionaliter**, see *sumere* under 3.

notionaliter, *adv.*, see *notionalis.*

notitia, ae, *f.*, (1) *a being known, celebrity, note, fame,* (2) *a knowing, knowledge, information, notion,* synonym of *scientia.*—On **cognitio notitiae**, see *cognitio* under 1; on **scientia simplicis notitiae**, see *scientia* under 2.—Kinds of *notitia* in this (1) sense are: (a), **notitia actualis**, *knowledge consisting in an action,* the opposite of *notitia habitualis,* i.e., *knowledge that has become static.*—(b), **notitia approbationis, notitia simplex seu simplicis intellegentiae** and **notitia visionis,** (a division of the Knowledge of God), *knowledge connected with an approval or consent of the will,*

simple knowledge or *knowledge after the manner of simple intellectual presentation* the object of which is all possible things and *knowledge after the manner of vision,* the object of which is all actual things.—(c), **notitia architectonica seu dominativa seu principativa,** *the governing* or *dominating* or *superior knowledge.*—(d), **notitia completa,** *the complete knowledge.*—(e), **notitia comprehensionis,** *the knowledge of comprehension* or *understanding.*—(f), **notitia dominativa,** see *notitia architectonica.*—(g), **notitia experimentalis,** *experimental knowledge.*—(h), **notitia mentis** and **notitia sensitiva,** *the intellectual knowledge* and *knowledge through the senses.*—(i), **notitia naturalis,** *natural knowledge.*—(j), **notitia praedestinationis,** *the knowledge of predestination,* i.e., the knowledge of God connected with predestination.—(k), **notitia principativa,** see *notitia architectonica.*—(l), **notitia privilegiata,** *the privileged knowledge* or *that forming a privilege.*—(m), **notitia sensitiva,** see *notitia mentis.*—(n), **notitia simplex,** see *notitia approbationis.*—(o), **notitia simplicis intellegentiae,** see *notitia approbationis.*—(p), **notitia visionis,** see *notitia approbationis.*

noto, are, avi, atum, 1, *v. a.*, (1) *to signify, to indicate, note,* (2) *to observe, note,* (3) *to mark* or *brand with infamy.*

notorius, a, um, *adj.*, (1) of facts, *well-known, common* or *generally known* (2) *notorious,* noted for some bad practice, quality etc.; *unfavorably known.*—**notoria ars,** *the notorious art* or *magic art.*

notus, a, um, *adj., known, noted, known as true, true,* synonym of *verus.*—Kinds of *notus* or *notum* are: (a), **notum confuse,** *known confusedly* or *indefinitely.*—(b), **notum in se seu secundum se seu naturae seu quoad naturam seu secundum propriam seu sui naturam seu naturaliter seu simpliciter** and **notum nobis seu quoad nos seu secundum nos,** *known in itself* or *according to itself* or *according to its nature* or *from nature* or *simply* or *absolutely* and *known by us* or *with reference to us.*—(c), **notum naturae,** see *notum in se.*—(d), **notum naturaliter,** see *notum in se.*—(e), **notum per accidens** and **notum per se,** *known by accident* and *by itself* or *as such.* Cf. *notum per aliud.* —(f), **notum per aliud** and **notam per se seu propter se,** *known through something else* and *known through itself.* Cf. *notum per accidens.*—(g), **notum per se,** see *notum per accidens* and *notum per aliud.*—(h), **notum propter se,** see *notum per aliud.*—(i), **notum quoad naturam,** see *notum in se.*—(j), **notum quoad nos,** see *notum in se.*—(k), **notum rationi seu secundum rationem** and **notum sensui seu secundum sensum,** *known to the intellect* and *to the senses* or *known with reference to our intellectual* and *sense knowledge.*—(l), **notum secundum nos,** see *notum in se.*—(m), **notum secundum propriam naturam,** see *notum in se.*—(n), **notum secundum rationem,** see *notum rationi.*—(o), **notum secundum se,** see *notum in se.*—(p), **notum secundum sensum,** see *notum rationi.*—(q), **notum secundum sui naturam,** see *notum in se.*—(r), **notum sensui,** see *notum rationi.*—(s), **notum simpliciter,** see *notum in se.*

Novatiani, orum, *m.,* see *Novatianus.*

Novatianus, i, *m., Novatian,* a schismatic of the third century and founder of the Novatians; he was a Roman priest, and made himself antipope. His name is given as Novatus by Greek writers and also in the verses of Damasus and Prudentius, on account of the metre.—**Novatiani,** orum, *m., the Novatians,* a sect which contended that the Church had no authority either to absolve those who had lapsed through fear of persecution or who had fallen into gross sin after baptism, or to admit them to Holy Communion.

novem, *num., adj., card., nine.*

novitas, atis, *f.,* (1) in gen., *a being new, newness, novelty,* (2) in particular, *rareness, strangeness, unusualness,* (3) fig., *newness, reformation.*

noviter, *adv.,* see *novus.*

novitius, ii, *m., a novice,* (1) *a new-ly-converted person,* (2) *an inex-perienced person;* one who is new to the circumstances in which he is placed.

novo, are, avi, atum, 1, *v. a., to re-new, make new.*

novus, a, um, *adj., new, not old, fresh, recent,* (I) lit., (A) *in gen.,* (1) not existing before, now made or brought into existence for the first time, (2) not previously known; now known for the first time, (a) of things heard or inspired, (b) of feelings, (c) of persons or things, (d) *strange, unfamiliar,* (B) *in partic.,* (1) restored after disappearance, *new,* (2) other than the former or old, (3) morally or spiritually changed, *new,* (II) transf., in *sup. novissimus,* a, um, *last, latest.*—de novo, *anew, afresh.*—**noviter,** *adv., newly.*

nox, noctis, *f., night,* used (1) lit., (2) fig.—media nox, *midnight.*—de nocte, *by night.*—de nocte profunda, *late at night.*

noxius, a, um, *adj.,* (1) *hurtful, harmful, injurious, noxious,* (2) *guilty, culpable, criminal.*—**noxia,** ae, *f., harm, hurt, injury, damage.*

nubes, is, *f., a cloud,* (1) lit., (2) fig., Christian baptism is through water and the Holy Ghost, as instrumental and principal efficient causes, John III. 5. In the case of the Jews of the Exodus, the Holy Ghost was typified by the cloud, the water of baptism by the sea.—lucida nubes, *a bright cloud, the glory-cloud* or *Shechinah,* i.e., dwelling or presence of God. The bright cloud was an indication of the presence of the Divine Majesty; God was accustomed to appear to Israel in a cloud.

nubilosus, a, um, *adj., cloudy, over-cast, lowering.*

nubo, ere, psi, ptum, 3, *v. a.* and *n., to marry, wed,* used *absol.,* and with the *dat.*—nuptus, a, um, *P. a., married, wedded.*—**nupta,** ae, *f., a wife.*

nude, *adv.,* see *nudus.*

nuditas, atis, *f., nakedness, nudity.*

nudius, *num.* (i.e. *nunc*) and *dius* = *dies;* the ending accommodated to that of the following numeral; *it is now the ... day since;* always in connection with ordinal numerals; as *nudius tertius, three days ago, the day before yesterday.*

nudo, are, avi, atum, 1, *v. a.,* (1) *to strip, lay bare, expose to view, uncover,* (2) fig., *to deprive of, strip of.*

nudus, a, um, *adj.,* (1) lit., (a) of the human figure or those parts of it which are usually clothed, *naked, uncovered,* (2) in partic., *poor, needy, destitute, forlorn,* (2) transf., (a) in gen., *bare, mere, pure, simple,* (b) of a truth, fact, statement, *naked, undis-guised, unveiled, simple, bare.*—**nude,** *adv., nakedly, openly, simply.*

nugae, arum, *f., jokes, nonsense, idle speeches,* used in the S.T. only in quot.

nugatio, onis, *f., nugatoriness, the fact of being nugatory.*

nugatorie, *adv.,* see *nugatorius.*

nugatorius, a, um, *adj., trifling, worthless, useless.*—**nugatorie,** *adv., triflingly.*

nullatenus, *adv., in nowise, by no means.*

nullus, a, um, *adj., not any, none, no one,* the opposite of *omnis.* On **dicere de nullo,** see *dicere* under 3; on **dictio nulla,** see *dictio* under 2.

num, *adv.,* an interrog. particle, usually implying that a negative answer is expected.

numen, inis, *n., godhead, divinity, deity, divine majesty.*

numerabilis, e, *adj., numerable.*

numeralis, e, *adj., of* or *belonging to number, numeral.* On **distinctio numeralis,** see *distinctio* under 2; on **multitudo numeralis,** see *multitudo* under 1; on **proportio numeralis,** see *proportio* under 1; on **quantitas numeralis,** see *quantitas* under 1; on **terminus numeralis,** see *terminus* under 5; on **unitas numeralis,** see *unitas.*

numeratio, onis, *f., numeration, numbering, reckoning.*

numeratus, a, um, *P. a.,* see *numero.*

numero, are, avi, atum, 1, *v. a.,* (1) lit., *to count, number, reckon,* (2) fig., *to account, reckon, es-*

teem, consider as a thing.—**numeratus,** a, um, *P. a., numbered.*

numerosus, a, um, *adj., numerous.*

numerus, i, *m., a number,* synonym of *multitudo.* Cf. *multitudo* under 3. On **alius numero,** see *alius;* on **differentia secundum numerum,** see *differentia;* on **differre numerum,** see *differre* under 2; on **distinctio secundum numerum,** see *distinctio* under 2; on **diversitas in numero seu secundum numerum,** see *diversitas;* on **diversus numerus,** see *diversus;* on **forma secundum numerum,** see *forma* under 2; on **idem numerus seu in numero seu secundum numerum,** see *idem;* on **infinitum in numero seu secundum numerum,** see *infinitus;* on **multum numero seu secundum numerum,** see *multus* under 1; on **passio numero,** see *passio* under 1; on **plures numero,** see *plus;* on **ponere in numero,** see *ponere* under 1; on **principium numero,** see *principum;* on **quaestio in numero ponens et non ponens in numero,** see *quaestio;* on **qualitas numero,** see *qualitas;* on **quantitas numero,** see *quantitas* under 1; on **substantia numero,** see *substantia* under 8; on **unitas secundum numerum,** see *unitas;* on **unum numero seu secundum numerum,** see *unus.*—**in numero esse,** *to be present in number.*— Kinds of *numerus* are: (a), **numerus absolute acceptus seu absolutus seu abstractus seu separatus seu simplex seu simpliciter seu**

simpliciter prolatus seu extra numeratum existens seu unitatum and numerus applicatus ad res seu numeratus seu in numerato seu in sensibilibus exsistens seu rerum, *the number abstracted* or *separated in thought* or *the simply comprehended* or *expressed number* or *the number existing outside the numbered* or *the number existing outside mathematical unity* and *the number applied to things* or *the number actually counting* or *the number existing in counted things.*—(b), numerus absolutus, see *numerus absolute acceptus.*—(c), numerus abstractus, see *numerus absolute acceptus.*—(d), numerus applicatus ad res, see *numerus absolute acceptus.*—(e), numerus compositus and numerus incompositus, *the compound* and *the uncompounded number.* Cf. *numerus primus.*—(f), numerus cubicus, and numerus quadratus, *the cubic* (to the third degree) and *the square number* (to the second degree).—(g), numerus determinatus and numerus indeterminatus, *the determined* and *the undetermined number.*—(h), numerus discretus, *the separated* or *special number.*—(i), numerus duplex sesquitertius and numerus duplex sesquiquartus, *the number which is 2⅓ times larger* and *that which is 2¼ times larger than another.*—(j), numerus duplus sesqualter, numerus triplus sesqualter, and numerus quad-

ruplus sesqualter, *the number which contains another within itself 2½ times, that which contains another 3½ times,* and *that which contains another 4½ times.*—(k), numerus duplus superbipartiens and numerus duplus supertripartiens, *the number which is twice as large as another* and *which when divided by the latter remains two* and *three respectively.*—(l), numerus extra numerum exsistens, see *numerus absolute acceptus.*—(m), numerus impar and numerus par, *the uneven* and *the even number.*—(n), numerus imperfectus and numerus perfectus, *the imperfect* and *the perfect number.* In the latter, the sum of the factors equals the product of the factors. Cf. *numerus superfluus.*—(o), numerus incompositus, see *numerus compositus.*—(p), numerus indeterminatus, see *numerus determinatus.*—(q), numerus in sensibilibus existens, see *numerus absolute acceptus.*—(r), numerus multiplex and numerus submultiplex, *the number which is a multiple of another* and *in which the latter is contained several times.*—(s), numerus multiplex superparticularis and numerus multiplex superpartiens, *the number which includes another number several times* and *still exceeds this by a fraction whose numerator is one* and *greater than one respectively.*—(t), numerus multiplex superpartiens, see *numerus multiplex superparticularis.*—(u), **numerus numeratus**, see *numerus absolute acceptus.*—(v), **numerus par**, see *numerus impar.*—(w), **numerus perfectus**, see *numerus imperfectus.*—(x), **numerus pluralis** and **numerus singularis**, *the plural* and *the singular number.*—(y), **numerus primus**, *the first* or *prime number.* Cf. *numerus compositus.*—(z), **numerus quadratus**, see *numerus cubicus.*—(a²), **numerus quadruplus sesquialter**, see *numerus sesquialter.*—(b²), **numerus qualis**, *the number conditioned in such a way* or *a number with a quality.* Cf. *qualitas numeri* under *qualitas.*—(c²), **numerus rerum**, see *numerus absolute acceptus.*—(d²), **numerus separatus**, see *numerus absolute acceptus.*—(e²), **numerus separatus**, see *numerus absolute acceptus.*—(f²), **numerus sesquialter, numerus sesquitertius**, and **numerus sesquiquartus**, *the number which is 1½ times greater, that which is 1⅓ times greater* and *that which is 1¼ times greater than another.*—(g²), **numerus sesquiquartus**, see *numerus sesquialter.*—(h²), **numerus sesquitertius**, see *numerus sesquialter.*—(i²), **numerus simplex seu simpliciter seu simpliciter prolatus**, see *numerus absolute acceptus.*—(j²), **numerus singularis**, see *numerus pluralis.*—(k²), **numerus solidus** and **numerus superficialis**, *the tri-dimensional* or *the two-dimensional number.*—(l²), **nume-

rus submultiplex**, see *numerus multiplex.*—(m²), **numerus submultiplex subparticularis** and **numerus submultiplex subpartiens**, *the number which is contained in a numerus multiplex superparticularis* and *that which is contained in a numerus multiplex superpartiens.*—(n²), **numerus submultiplex subpartiens**, see *numerus submultiplex subparticularis.*—(o²), **numerus subparticularis**, see *numerus superparticularis.*—(p²), **numerus subpartiens**, see *numerus superpartiens.*—(q²), **numerus superficialis**, see *numerus solidus.*—(r²), **numerus superbipartiens, numerus supertripartiens**, and **numerus superquadripartiens**, *the number which when divided by another exceeds it by a fraction whose numerator is respectively* 2, 3, and 4.—(s²), **numerus superfluus**, the translation of the Aristotelian expression *to peritton, the superfluous* or *excessive number,* i.e., the sum of the factors exceeds the product of the factors. Cf. *numerous imperfectus.*—(t²) **numerous superparticularis** and **numerous subparticularis**, *the number which exceeds another number divided within it by a fraction whose numerator is one,* and *the number exceeded in this case.*—(u²), **numerus superpartiens** and **numerus subpartiens**, *the number which exceeds another number divided in it by a fraction whose numerator is greater* *than one* and *the number exceed-ed in this case.*—(v²), **numerus superquadripartiens,** see *numerus superbipartiens.*—(w²), **numerus supertripartiens,** see *numerus superbipartiens.*—(x²), **numerus triplus sesquialiter,** see *numerus duplus sesquialter.*—(y²), **numerus unitatum,** see *numerus absolute acceptus.*—**nullus numerus est infinitus,** *there is no infinite number,* i.e., it is a contradiction in terms, since number implies definite limit.

numisma, atis, *n., money, coin, a piece of money.*

nummus, i, *m., a coin, a piece of money, money.*

numquam, or **nunquam,** *adv., at no time, never.*

numquid, *adv., interrog.,* used in a direct interrogation where there is no corresponding term in English.

nunc, *adv., now, at present, at this time,* synonym of *instans,* the opposite of *tunc.*—Kinds of *nunc* are: (a), **nunc aeternitatis seu stans, nunc aevi** and **nunc temporis seu fluens,** *the present of eternity* or *the static present, the present of everlasting duration* and *the present of time* or *the fleeting present.*—(b), **nunc aevi,** see *nunc aeternitatis.*—(c), **nunc fluens,** see *nunc aeternitatis.*—(d), **nunc per aliquid sui seu secundum aliquid sui seu secundum alterum** and **nunc primo et per se seu secundum seipsum,** *that*

which is called present secondarily with reference to something else or *according to a part of it,* and *that which is called present in the first place* and *completely according to itself.*—(e), **nunc primo et per se,** see *nunc per aliquid sui.*—(f), **nunc secundum aliquid sui,** see *nunc per aliquid sui.*—(g), **nunc secundum alterum,** see *nunc per aliquid sui.*—(h), **nunc secundum seipsum,** see *nunc per aliquid sui.*—(i), **nunc signatum,** *the signified* or *determined present.*—(j), **nunc stans,** see *nunc aeternitatis.*—(k), **nunc temporis,** see *nunc aeternitatis.*

nuncupatio, onis, *f., a name, appellation,* used in the S.T. only in quot.

nuncupo, are, avi, atum, 1, *v. a., to name, designate, mention.*

nundinae, arum, *f., trade, traffic, marketing,* used in the S.T. only in quot.

nuntio, are, avi, atum, 1, *v. a., to announce, declare, report, inform, make known,* used (1) absol., (2) with *acc.* of thing and *dat.* of person, (3) *acc.* alone, (4) in the pass.

nuntium, i, *n., an announcement, message, news.*

nuntius, ii, *m., a messenger.*

nuper, *adv., newly, lately, recently, not long ago.*

nupta, ae, *f.,* see *nubo.*

nuptiae, arum, *f., a marriage, wedding nuptials.*

nuptialis, e, *adj., of* or *belonging to*

a wedding, nuptial.—**nuptialiter,** *adv., as at a wedding, nuptially.*

nuptialiter, *adv.,* see *nuptialis.*

nusquam, *adv., nowhere, in no place.*

nutrimentalis, e, *adj., nourishing, nurturing,* synonym of *nutritivus.* On **humidum nutrimentale,** see *humidus.*

nutrimentum, i, *n.,* (1) lit., *nourishment, nutriment,* (2) fig., *support, nourishment.*

nutrio, ire, ivi, and ii, itum, (I) lit., (1) *to nourish, feed, rear, bring up,* (2) transf., *to support, maintain, nourish,* (a) of persons, (b) of plants, (c) of parts of the body, (d) of inanimate things, (II) fig., *to nourish, cherish, rear, bring up.*

nutritio, onis, *f.,* (1) *nourishment, food,* (2) *nutrition,* the sum of the processes by which an animal or plant absorbs, or takes in and utilizes food substances, (3) the action of *bringing up, rearing.*

nutritius, ii, *m., a bringer up, foster father.*

nutritivus, a, um, *adj.,* (1) *nourishing, nurturing,* synonym of *nutrimentalis,* (2) *vegetative, vegetatively active,* synonym of *vegetativus.*—On **potentia nutritiva,** see *potentia* under 2; on **virtus nutritiva,** see *virtus* under 1.—On **anima nutritiva,** see *anima* under 1; on **operatio nutritiva,** see *operatio* under 2; on **pars nutritiva,** see *pars* under 1; on **vita nutritiva,** see *vita* under 1.—**nutritivum sc. genus, potentiarum animae,** the translation of Aristotle's *threptikon, the vegetative genus of the soul's potentialities.*

nutrix, icis, *f., a nurse,* used lit. and fig.

nutus, us, *m.,* (1) lit., *a nod, gesture,* (2) fig., *command, will, pleasure.*

nux, nucis, *f., a nut.*

Nyssenus, a, um, *adj., Nyssene, of Nyssa* in Cappadocia.

O

o, *interj.,* the commonest exclamation of joy, astonishment, desire, grief, indignation, etc.; *O!, Oh!* used with the *voc.,* used in the S.T. only in quot.

ob, *prep.* with *acc.,* (1) to indicate the object or cause, *on account of, for, because of, by reason of,* (2) with *id* and *hoc, on that account, for this reason, therefore,* (a) with *id,* (b) with *hoc.*

obcaeco, are, avi, atum, 1, *v. a., to blind, make blind,* used fig., used in the S.T. only in quot.

obdormio, ire, ivi, itum, 4, *v. n.* and *a., to fall asleep.*

obduco, ere, xi, ctum, 3, *v. a., to draw* or *spread over* or *draw,* used in the S.T. only in quot.

obduratio, onis, *f., a hardening;* of the mind, *obduration, obduracy, hardness* of the heart.

obduro, are, avi, atum, 1, *v. a.* and *n., to render hard, to harden,* used fig.

obedibilis, e, *adj., capable of obedience, docile.*

obedienter, *adv.,* see *obedio.*

obedientia, ae, *f.,* see *oboedientia.*

obedientialis, e, *adj., obediential; of, pertaining to, of the nature of,* or *characterized by obedience.*

obedio, ire, ivi or ii, itum, 4, *v. n., to obey, yield obedience to, to be subject to,* used with the *dat.* and *absol.*—**obediens,** entis, *P. a., obedient, pliant,* used with the *dat.*—**obedienter,** *adv., obediently.*

obeo, ire, ii, itum, 4, *v. n.* and *a., to die.*

oberro, are, avi, atum, 1, *v. n., to go astray, to miss intellectual truth,* used fig.

obex, icis, *m.* and *f., a hindrance, impediment, obstacle.*

obfirmatus, a, um, *P. a., firm, resolute, fixed.*

obicio, ere, ieci, iectum, 3, *v. a.,* (1) in gen., *to object,* (a) *to bring forward* or *state in opposition;* to adduce as a reason against something, to urge as an objection, used with *in contrarium,* (b) to bring forward as a reason, ground, instance, *to adduce, say, remark, point out,* used with *de,* with *quod,* (2) in partic., (a) to bring as a charge against anyone; to attribute to anyone as a fault or crime, *cast in one's teeth, accuse one of, reproach*

with, used with *acc.* of the thing and *dat.* of the person, with the *acc.* alone, (b) *to impart aliquid alicui.*

obitus, us, *m., death.*

obiectio, onis, *f., an objection,* that which is or may be presented in opposition; *an adverse reason* or *argument.*

obiectum, i, *n., subject matter, subject, object* of an action or of a faculty or of a *habitus,* synonym of *materia circa quam, oppositum,* and *subiectum.* On **cognoscere in obiecto cognito,** see *cognoscere* under 2; on **frui sicut obiecto,** see *frui;* on **libertas quantum ad obiectum,** see *libertas* under 2.—**ratio seu ratio formalis obiecti,** *the formal relationship of a thing to a faculty* or *the precise aspect under which it is object.*—Kinds of *obiectum* are: (a), **obiectum formale seu formaliter acceptum** and **obiectum materiale seu materialiter acceptum,** *the formal object* or *the object formally considered,* i.e., precisely as object, and *the material object* or *the object materially considered as underlying many formalities,* i.e., that manner of being or relationship of being on the part of a thing whereby it is made the object of this or that action, which serves as regards the thing itself as form to matter, and this thing in relation to or for itself taking no account of that manner of being or relationship of being.—(b), **obiectum ma-**

teriale seu materialiter acceptum, see *obiectum formale.*—(c), **obiectum per accidens**, and **obiectum per se**, *an object indirectly through something else* and *an object directly* and *through itself*, i.e., that which is accidentally and that which is itself the object of an action or a faculty.—(d), **obiectum per se**, see *obiectum per accidens.*—(e), **obiectum primo seu principale** and **obiectum secundarium**, *the primary* or *principal object* (*formal*) and *the secondary object* (*formal*) *which is consequent upon the first.*—(f), **obiectum principale**, see *obiectum primo.*—(g), **obiectum proprium**, *the proper* or *characteristic object*, which is identical according to the subject with *obiectum primo seu principale* and is the opposite of *obiectum commune*, i.e., the object common to several actions and faculties.—(h), **obiectum secundarium**, see *obiectum primo.*—(i), **obiectum virtutis**, see *virtus* under 5.

obiurgatio, onis, *f.*, *a chiding, reproof.*

obiurgo, are, avi, atum, 1, *v. a.*, *to chide, upbraid, rebuke.*

oblatio, onis, *f.*, *an offering, presenting, a giving* or *bestowing gratuitously, gift.*—On the difference between *oblatio* and *sacrificium*, see *sacrificium.*

oblectamentum, i, *n.*, *a delight, pleasure*, used in the S.T. only in quot.

oblectatio, onis, *f.*, *a delighting, delight;* **oblectatio carnis**, *the lust of the flesh;* used in the S.T. only in quot.

oblecto, are, avi, atum, 1, *v. a.*, *to delight, to please.*

obligatio, onis, *f.*, (1) in gen., *a binding*, used fig., *a bond* by which one is held captive, (2) in partic., *an obligation*, (a) *an agreement*, a concurrence in an engagement that something shall be done or omitted, (b) *an obligation*, a formal and binding agreement or acknowledgement of a liability to pay a certain sum, (c) that which obligates or constrains; the binding power of a vow, oath, promise, etc., (d) that which a person is bound to do or forbear; any duty imposed by law, promise or contract, (e) the state of being obligated or placed under obligation because of a favor received.

obligativus, a, um, *adj.*, *impeding, restraining.*

obligatorius, a, um, *adj.*, *binding, obligatory.*

obligo, are, avi, atum, 1, *v. a.*, (1) in gen., *to bind, to restrain,* or *hold* by authority, law, duty, promise, vow or other moral tie, (2) in partic., (a) *to bind* or *devote* something to a particular use, (b) *to plight, to put* something in danger of forfeiture, (3) *pass.*, (a) *to be obliged* to do something by a legal or moral tie, (b) *to be bound* or *attached* to someone by allegiance or duty, (c) *to be bound* by the ties of gratitude; *to be indebted to a person for something*, (4) reflex., *to pledge, lay one's self* under constraint or obligation with respect to performance, (5) Jurid. t.t., *to pledge* something as security.—The following phrases are of frequent occurrence: **obligare aliquem ad peccatum mortale**, *to bind someone under pain of mortal sin.*—**obligare ad peccatum**, *to bind under pain of sin.*—**obligare se ad poenam**, *to bind oneself to punishment.*—**obligare ad mortale**, *to bind under pain of mortal sin.*—**obligatus**, a, um, *P. a.*, (1) *bondaged, enslaved, reduced to slavery*, (2) *bound, fettered*, (3) *bound, under obligation.*

oblique, *adv.*, see *obliquus*.

obliquitas, atis, *f.*, *obliqueness*.

obliquo, are, avi, atum, 1, *v. a.*, *to turn aside in an oblique direction*, used fig.—**obliquatus**, a, um, *P. a.*, *deflected*.

obliquus, a, um, *adj.*, (1) *sidelong, slanting, awry, oblique, collateral, parabolic*, when applied to motion as opposed to rectilineal, (2) *oblique case* in declension, the grammatical sense.—On **circulus obliquus**, see *circulus* under 1; on **motus obliquus**, see *motus* under 1; on **nomen obliquum**, see *nomen* under 1.—On **casus obliquus**, see *casus* under 5.—**in obliquo**, *in the grammatical case of an inflection or declension*, the opposite of *in recto*.

On **importare in obliquo**, see *importare* under 2; on **ponere in obliquo**, see *ponere* under 1; on **praedicare in obliquo**, see *praedicare* under 2; on **significare in obliquo**, see *significare*.—**oblique**, *adv.*, *in an indirect manner, in a round-about way, obliquely*, synonym of *indirecte*, the opposite of *directe*.

oblitus, a, um, *P. a.*, see *obliviscor*.

oblivio, onis, *f.*, (1) *lit.*, *a being forgotten, oblivion, forgetfulness*, (2) transf., *a forgetting, forgetfulness*.

obliviosus, a, um, *adj.*, *forgetful*.

obliviscor, i, litus, 3, *v. dep.*, *to forget*, used with (1) *acc.* of the thing, (2) *gen.* of the thing, (3) the *inf.*—**oblitus**, a, um, *adj.*, *forgotten*.

oblongus, a, um, *adj.*, *longish, protruding*.

obloquor, i, locutus, 3, *v. dep.*, *to speak evil about someone*.

obmutesco, ere, tui, 3, *v. inch.*, *n.*, *to be speechless, mute, silent*.

obnoxio, are, 1, *v. a.*, *to render subject* or *obnoxious to any thing*, used in the S.T. only in quot.

obnoxius, a, um, *adj.*, (1) *lit.*, (a) *subject, liable to punishment, obnoxious to punishment, punishable*, (b) *obnoxious, reprehensible, blameworthy*, (c) *subject to, liable, exposed* to sin, death etc., (2) transf., (a) *answerable, responsible, the occasion of*, (b) *subject* to the authority of, *answerable* to some authority, (c) *subject to* or *influenced by*.

obnubilo, are, avi, atum, 1, *v. a.*, *to darken, cloud, obscure.*

oboedientia, ae, *f.*, (1) *obedience* in general, opposite to *inoboedientia*, (2) voluntary *obedience* to an ecclesiastical superior.—On **debitum oboedientiae**, see *debitus* under 1; on **potentia oboedientiae**, see *potentia* under 4.—On **consilium oboedientiae**, see *consilium* under 2; on **necessitas oboedientiae seu oboedientia consequens**, see *necessitas* under 1; on **servitus oboedientiae**, see *servitus* under 2; on **votum oboedientiae**, see *votum* under 1.— Kinds of *oboedientia* in this (2) sense are: (a), **oboedientia discreta** and **oboedientia indiscreta**, *the discrete obedience* and *the indiscrete obedience*, or *the obedience connected with discretion* and *that with indiscretion.*—(b), **oboedientia imperfecta** and **oboedientia perfecta**, *the imperfect* and *the perfect obedience.*—(c), **oboedientia indiscreta**, see *oboedientia discreta.*—(d), **oboedientia perfecta**, see *oboedientia imperfecta.*

oboedientialis, e, *adj.*, *obeying, obedient*, not found in the S.T. of St. Thomas. On **potentia oboedientialis**, see *potentia* under 4; on **ratio oboedientialis**, see *ratio* under 11 and 12.

obolus, i, *m.*, *an obol, a small Greek coin, the sixth part of a drachma*, equivalent to three and a half cents.

obrepo, ere, psi, ptum, 3, *v. n.*, *to steal upon*, used with the *dat.*

obruo, ere, rui, utum, 3, *v. a.*, *to overcome, overpower, eclipse.*

obscoenitas, atis, *f.*, *moral impurity, obscenity, unchastity.*

obscoenus, a, um, *adj.*, *obscene.*

obscuratio, onis, *f.*, (1) lit., *a being dark, darkness*, (2) fig., *obscurity, indistinctness, uncertainty.*

obscure, *adv.*, of speech, *obscurely, indistinctly.*

obscuritas, atis, *f.*, (1) lit., *a being dark, darkness, obscurity*, (2) fig., *obscurity, indistinctness, uncertainty.*

obscuro, are, avi, atum, 1, *v. a.*, (1) lit., (a) *to render dark, to darken, obscure*, (b) transf., *to bedim, diminish, lessen*, (2) fig., (a) *to obscure, darken, becloud*, (b) *to obscure, render unknown.*

obscurus, a, um, *adj.*, (1) lit., (a) of places, *dark*, (b) of a body or surface not reflecting or emitting light, *opaque*, (c) of violence, *harmful, derogatory*, (d) of lowly things, *hidden, obscure*, (2) fig., (a) of knowledge, words, speech, *obscure, unintelligible*, (b) of God's image in the sinner's soul, *dim.*

obsecratio, onis, *f.*, *obsecration, supplication, earnest entreaty.*

obsecro, are, avi, atum, 1, *v. a.*, *to pray, supplicate, implore*, used with the *acc.* of the *person* or *thing.*

obsequium, ii, *n.*, (I) in gen., (1) *obsequiousness, compliance to excess*, (2) *obedience, compli-*

ance, deference, (II) in partic., *service, duty, occupation, employment,* the performance of labor for the benefit of another or at another's command or in fulfillment of duty, (1) *service* to God and to the Church, spiritual serving as shown by obedience, good works and love, (2) *service* to creatures, (a) of a servant or slave, (b) of a child to its parents, *help* of a material nature, *assistance, service* of any kind, (c) of a mother to its child, *care, attention,* (d) to a neighbor, (e) to authority,· (3) *service, occupation, employment,* that set of duties upon which one is regularly employed.—**corporale obsequium,** *bodily homage* or *courtesy rendered.*

obsequoi, i, cutus, 3, *v. dep., to accommodate one's self* to the will of a person; *to comply with, yield to, submit to,* (1) *to submit* to something, *discharge* the duty of, (2) *to obey* someone, (3) *to wait on* someone, serve, (4) *to help, aid* someone, used with the *dat.* of the *person* or *thing.*—**obsequens,** entis, *P. a., obedient, yielding, compliant.*

observantia, ae, *f.,* (1) *observance, attentive consideration,* synonym of *observatio,* (2) as a potential part of the virtue of justice, *the esteem* and *respect due to authority,* (3) *observance, following, performance,* (4) *observance, exercise, performance, practice,* esp. the magical arts of discovering secrets and foretelling the future.—On the difference between *observantia* and *pietas,* see *pietas* under 1. On **pars observantiae,** see *pars* under 1.—Kinds of *observantia* in this (3) sense are: (a), **observantia caeremonialis,** *observance of a ceremonial prescription of the Old Testament,*—(b), **observantia legalis seu legis,** *the observance of the Mosaic law,* by which is understood first law in general, then the law of the Old Testament.— (c), **observantia legis,** see *observantia legalis.*—On **superstitio observantiarum,** see *superstitio.*— Kinds of *observantia* in this (4) sense are: (a), **observantia carnalis,** and **observantia spiritualis,** *the bodily* or *physical* and *the immaterial* or *spiritual performance.*—(b), **observantia illicita,** *fortune-telling.*—(c), **observantia regularis,** *regular observance,* i.e., living according to rule.— (d), **observantia spiritualis,** see *observantia carnalis.*—(e), **observantia vana,** *fortune-telling.*

observatio, onis, *f.,* (1) *observance, attentive consideration,* synonym of *observantia,* (2) *observance, following, performance,* (3) *observance, exercise, performance, use.*—On **superstitio observationum,** see *superstitio.*—Kinds of *observatio* in this (3) sense are: (a), **observatio illicita,** *fortune-telling.*—(b), **observatio legalis,** *the observance of the prescriptions of the Old Testament.*—(c),

observatio superstitiosa, *the superstitious exercise.*—(d), **observatio vana,** *fortune-telling.*

observator, oris, *m., an observer;* **observator legis,** *an observer of the law,* i.e., *one who obeys it.*

observo, are, avi, atum, 1, *v. a.,* (I) *to observe, to attend to* in practice; *to keep, follow,* (1) *to observe* a law, command, custom, practice, covenant or anything prescribed or fixed, (2) *to follow* a principle or rule of action, (3) *to observe, celebrate duly, to solemnize* in the prescribed way a religious rite, ceremony, etc., (4) *to follow the practice, be in the habit of doing something,* (II) *to observe, to attend to* with the mind, *to mark, perceive, observe,* (1) *to give close attention to* with the purpose of hearing, (2) *to inspect* or *regard with attention* for the purpose of divination, (3) *to watch for* in order to take advantage of a proper time or opportunity, (4) *to consider, take into consideration,* (5) *to take notice of* any astronomical feature, (III) *to observe, utter* by way of remark, (IV) by catachresis, *to keep, hold, retain* something.

obsessus, a, um, *P. a.,* (1) lit., of a city, *beseiged,* (2) of an evil spirit, *obsessed, assailed* or *harassed* by an evil spirit.

obsidio, onis, *f., a siege, blockade* of a place, used in the S.T. only in quot.

obsisto, ere, stiti, stitum, 3, *v. n., to set one's will against; to oppose, resist, withstand.*

obsolesco, ere, levi, letum, 3, *v. inch. n., to grow dim, fall into disuse, lose value.*—**obsoletus,** a, um, *P. a., obsolete.*

obsoletus, a, um, *P. a.,* see *obsolesco.*

obstaculum, i, *n., an obstacle, hindrance,* used lit and fig.

obstetrix, icis, *f., a midwife.*

obstinate, *adv.,* see *obstinatus.*

obstinatio, onis, *f., determination, stubbornness, obstinacy.*— One kind of *obstinatio* is: **obstinatio imperfecta,** *the imperfect obstinacy.*

obstinatus, a, um, *P. a., firmly set, fixed,* in a bad sense, *stubborn, obstinate.*—**obstinate,** *adv., wilfully.*

obsto, are, stiti, atum, 1, *v. n.,* (1) lit., *to stand before* or *against* anything, (2) in partic., *to withstand, thwart, hinder, oppose,* used with the *dat.,* absol.—*impers.,* **nec obstat,** *it doesn't matter.*

obstrictus, a, um, *P. a.,* see *obstringo.*

obstringo, ere, strinxi, strictum, 3, *v. a., to bind, fetter, hamper; to oblige, lay under obligation.*—**obstrictus,** a, um, *P. a., bound, obliged.*

obstupescibilis, e, *adj., possible of being confounded, amazed, benumbed,* used in the S.T. only in quot.

obstupesco, ere, ui, 3, *v. inch. n.*
and *a.*, (1) lit., *to become sense-*
less, lose feeling, (2) fig., *to be*
astonished, amazed.

obsum, obesse, obfui or offui, *v. n.*,
to injure, hurt, be prejudicial to,
used with the *dative.*

obtego, ere, xi, ctum, 3, *v. a.*, (1)
lit., *to cover over*, for concealment, (2) fig., *to veil, conceal*,
keep secret.

obtempero, are, avi, atum, 1, *v. a.*,
to comply with, attend to, sub-
mit to, obey, used with the *dat.*

obtenebratio, onis, *f.*, *darkness*,
used fig.

obtenebresco, ere, *v. inch. n.*, *to*
become or *grow dark.*

obtenebro, are, avi, atum, *v. a.*, *to*
make dark, to darken, used lit.
and fig.

obtentus, us, *m.*, *a pretext, pre-*
tence.

obtestans, antis, *P. a.*, *imploring*,
supplicating.

obtineo, ere, tinui, tentum, 2, *v. a.*
and *n.*, (1) *act.*, (a) *to hold, have,*
possess; to preserve, keep, main-
tain, (b) *to get possession of; to*
gain, acquire, obtain something,
(2) *neutr.*, *to obtain, prevail,*
stand.

obtundo, ere, tudi, tusum, 3, *v. a.*,
to weaken, dull.—**obtusus**, a, um,
P. a., *dull, blunt.*

obtusio, onis, *f.*, *bluntness, dullness.*

obtusus, a, um, *P. a.*, see *obtundo.*

obtutus, us, *m.*, (1) *the eye*, (2) fig.,
act of viewing attentively, con-
templation.

obumbrate, see *obumbro.*

obumbratio, onis, *f.*, *a shadow,*
darkness, used fig., used in the
S.T. only in quot.

obumbratus, a, um, see *obumbro.*

obumbro, are, avi, atum, 1, *v. a.*,
to overshadow, shade, obscure,
darken.—**obumbratus**, a, um, *P.*
a., *obscured, darkened.* On **co-**
gnitio obumbrata, see *cognitio*
under 2; on **ratio obumbrata**, see
ratio under 3.—**obumbrate**, *adv.*,
obscurely, under a veil.

obvenio, ire, veni, ventum, 4, *v. n.*,
to fall to one's lot.

obviam, *adv.*, *in the way*, hence,
with verbs of motion (in a good
or bad sense) *towards, against, to*
meet.

obviatio, onis, *f.*, *a saluting, a salu-*
tation.

obvio, are, avi, 1, *v. n.*, (1) in gen.,
to meet, (2) in partic., (a) in a
hostile sense, *to withstand, re-*
sist, oppose, (b) *to obviate.*—(1),
quia superiores caeteris apparebunt in iudicio obviantes Christo in aera, PTS. Q. 89. Art. 1 c.

obvius, a, um, *adj.*, *in the way so*
as to meet, meeting.

obvolvo, ere, vi, utum, 3, *v. a.*, *to*
entangle, used fig.

occasio, onis, *f.*, *occasion, occasion-*
al cause, accidental cause, in-
ducement.—Kinds of *occasio* are:
(a), **occasio accepta** and **occasio**
data, *the accepted* and *the given*
occasion.—(b), **occasio coniuncta**
and **occasio praecedens**, *the oc-*
casion connected with an action
and that preceding it.—(c), **occa-**
sio data, see *occasio accepta.*—

(d), **occasio praecedens**, see *occa-sio coniuncta*.

occasionaliter, *adv.*, *as occasions arise, occasionally, after the man-ner* or *in the sense of an occa-sional* or *accidental cause* or *in-ducement*. On **causa occasionali-ter dicta**, see *causa* under 2.

occasionatus, a, um, see *occasiono*.

occasiono, are, avi, atum, 1, *v. a.*, *to occasion, cause accidentally, induce.*—**occasionatus**, a, um, *P., a., occasioned, induced.*

occasus, us, *m.*, (1) *a falling down, going down, a setting of the heavenly bodies*, esp., the sun, (2) *that quarter of the heavens in which the sun sets, the west.*

occidens, entis, *P. a.*, see *occido*, (2).

occidentalis, e, *adj.*, *western, west-erly.*

occido, (1), ere, cidi, cisum, 3, *v. a.*, (1) lit., *to kill, slay, deprive of life, put to death*, (2) fig., *to kill the soul, to kill spiritually.*

occido, (2), ere, cidi, casum, 3, *v. n.*, of the heavenly bodies, *to go down, set.*—**occidens**, entis, *m.*, *the quarter of the setting sun, the occident, the west.*

occiduus, a, um, *adj.*, *fleeting, per-ishable.*

occisio, onis, *f.*, *a killing, slaying, murder.*

occisor, oris, *m.*, *a slayer, murderer.*

occultatio, onis, *f.*, *concealment*, (1) *cover* or *protection* from obser-vation, (2) *hidden knowledge.*

occulte, *adv.*, see *occultus.*

occulto, are, avi, atum, 1, *v. freq. a.*, *to hide, to conceal, secrete*, (1) with a *pers. pron.*, (2) the place of concealment expressed by (a) *adv. of place*, (b) *sub* with the *abl.*, (c) *in* with the *abl.*, (d) the *abl. alone.*

occultus, a, um, *P. a.*, *hidden, con-cealed, secret.*—**occulta**, orum, *n., plur., secret things, secrets.*—**oc-cultum**, i, *n., secrecy.*—*in adverb. phrase*, **in occulto**, *in secret, se-cretly.*—**occulte**, *adv.*, *in secret, secretly, privately.*

occupatio, onis, *f.*, (1) *a care*, an object of watchful attention, (2) *consideration*, continuous and careful thought, (3) *business, employment, occupation*, the be-ing occupied or employed with, or engaged in something; that in which one is engaged.

occupo, are, avi, atum, 1, *v. a.*, (I) lit., (1) *to possess, take pos-session of, seize anything*, (2) transf., (a) *to fill, occupy, use up space*, (b) of disease, *to possess, occupy; cover the body, over-whelm, oppress*, (II) fig., *to en-gross, employ, busy, engage* the mind, attention, person, often in *pass.*; also *refl.*

occurro, ere, curri, cursum, 3, *v. n.*, (1) lit., of persons, (a) *to go* or *come to, to meet* someone, (b) *to come upon, attack*, (2) transf., (a) *to alight on, fall in with*, (b) *to occur, to appear* in any place, (c) *to come to* any place, (3) fig., (a) *to lie in way of, meet* as an obstacle, (b) *to obviate* or *seek* to *obviate, to meet, counteract,* (c) *to remedy,* (d) *to offer* or *pre-sent* itself; *appear, occur.*

occursus, us, *m., a meeting, falling in with, approach.*

Oceanus, i, *m., the great sea* that encompasses the land, *the ocean.*

Oceanus, i, *m., Oceanus,* a Roman of noble birth in the fourth and fifth centuries, connected by birth with Fabiola and the Julian family, and by friendship with Jerome, Augustine, and Pampmachius. Jerome speaks of him as his son in letter 77; he probably became known to Jerome during his stay in Rome in 383-5.

Ochozias, ae, *m., Ochozias,* son and successor of Joram in the kingdom of Juda.

octavae, arum, *f.,* (rarely sing.) *an octave.* Octaves are made up of a feast-day and the seven days following it. Only certain feasts, and those of higher rank, are celebrated by the Church with an octave.

octavus, a, um, *adj., the eighth.—* **octavo,** *adv., eighthly.*

octo, *num. adj., eight.*

October, bris, *adj., of* or *belonging to the eighth month, the eighth, October,* originally the eighth month of the year, reckoning from March; usually connected with *mensis.*

oculatus, a, um, *adj., furnished with* or *having eyes, seeing.—*videre aut inspicere aliquid oculata fide, *to see something from*

the testimony of the eyes of faith.

oculus, i, *m., eye* in the general sense of the word. On **concupiscentia oculorum,** see *concupiscentia* under 2.—**ictus oculi,** *a twinkling of an eye, an instant.—* Kinds of *oculus* in the general sense of the word are: (a), **oculus carnis seu corporalis** and **oculus in anima seu intellectualis, seu spiritualis,** *the bodily* or *physical eye* and *the eye of the soul* or *the intellectual* and *spiritual eye.*—(b), **oculus corporalis seu corporeus,** see *oculus carnis.* —(c), **oculus in anima,** see *oculus carnis.*—(d), **oculus intellectualis,** see *oculus carnis.*—(e), **oculus intellegentiae** and **oculus rationis,** *the eye of the intuitive perception,* and *that of discursive perception.*—(f), **oculus rationis,** see *oculus intellegentiae.*—(g), **oculus spiritualis,** see *oculus carnis.*

odi, odisse, also **odio,** ire, *v. a., defect.,* perf. as pres., *to hate,* used (1) with the *acc.* of the person or thing, (2) *absol.,* (3) *pass.*

odibilis, e, *adj., that deserves to be hated, hateful, odious.*

odiosus, a, um, *adj., hateful, offensive, annoying, troublesome, odious,* (1) of persons, (2) of things.

oditor, oris, *m., a hater, one who hates* or *dislikes* someone.

odium, i, *n., hatred, grudge, ill-will, animosity, aversion,* the opposite of *amor.*—Kinds of *odium* are: (a), **odium Dei** and **odium proximi,** *hatred toward God* and *hatred toward neighbor.* —(b), **odium naturale** and **odium non-naturale,** *the natural hate* or *that coming from the nature of a being* and *the unnatural hate* or *that not springing from the nature of the being,* i.e., the hate against *id quod est* (*in fact*) *repugnans et corruptivum* (cf. *malum corruptivum* under *malus* under 2), and hate against *id quod apprehenditur ut repugnans et nocivum* (without it actually being so).—(c), **odium non-naturale,** see *odium naturale.* —(d), **odium proximi,** see *odium Dei.—Odium Dei is filia luxuriae.* Cf. *luxuria.*

odor, oris, *m.,* (1) lit., *odor,* that property of a substance that is perceptible by the sense of smell; *scent, smell,* (2) fig., *odor, fragrance.*

odoratus, us, *m.,* (1) *scent,* the odor left by an animal on the ground or the surface passed over, (2) *the sense of smell.*

odorifer, era, erum, *adj., odoriferous, fragrant.*

odoro, are, avi, atum, 1, *v. a.,, to smell out, to detect by the scent.*

oeconomice, see *oeconomicus.*

oeconomicus, a, um, *adj., of* or *relating to domestic economy, domestic,* i.e., concerning the house or the family, synonym of *domesticus.* On **ars oeconomica,** see *ars* under 2; on **communicatio oeconomica,** see *communicatio* under 3; on **congregatio oeconomica,** see *congregatio* under 2; on **do-**minium **oeconomicum,** see *dominium;* on **iustitia oeconomica,** see *iustitia* under 1; on **iustum oeconomicum,** see *iustus;* on **principatus oeconomicus,** see *principatus* under 1; on **providentia oeconomica,** see *providentia;* on **prudentia oeconomica,** see *prudentia* under 1; on **regimen oeconomicum,** see *regimen;* on **scientia oeconomica,** see *scientia* under 1; on **societas oeconomica,** see *societas;* on **subiectio oeconomica,** see *subiectio* under 2.—**oeconomice,** *adv., economically, in a manner relating to domestic economy, with reference to the family.*

offendiculum, i, *n., cause of offence, scandal, something that causes spiritual stumbling; an occasion of sin,* used in the S.T. only in quot.

offendo, ere, di, sum, 3, *v. a.* and *n., to offend, strike against, stumble, commit a fault, displease, annoy, vex, hurt, injure,* etc., (I) lit., (1) *to strike against something* with the foot; *to trip;* (2) *to strike* so as to give physical pain, (II) fig., (1) of persons, (a) *to stumble morally, to do amiss, to transgress,* (b) *to sin against God,* (c) *to offend* someone, *to harm, to hurt* or *wound* the feelings or susceptibilities of anyone; *to vex, annoy, displease* anyone, (d) *pass., to be offended by someone, to take offense,* (2) in Biblical usage, *to be a stumbling block, to cause spiritual* or *moral difficulty* to a person; *to shock,*

(3) of things, *to disturb, annoy, displease*.

offensa, ae, *f.*, *an offence, hurt, injury, wrong, disfavor, hatred*, used fig., (1) *displeasure, disfavor, hatred*, (2) *prejudice, harm*, (3) *a stumbling block; a cause of spiritual* or *moral stumbling; an occasion of stumbling*, or *sin*, (4) *an offending against* or *violating a law; an offence, sin, crime*, (5) *an injury received, an offence, affront, wrong*.

offensio, onis, *f.*, (1) *offence, vexation, displeasure*, (2) *an offence, a stumbling block; a cause of spiritual* or *moral stumbling*.

offero, offerre, obtuli, oblatum, *v. a.*, *to bring before; to present, offer; show, exhibit*, (1) in gen., (a) to present something to God as an act of worship or devotion or to obtain a favor, *to give, offer up*, (b) *to offer, to present* or *give* something to someone for acceptance or refusal, used with the *dat* and *acc.*, (2) in *partic.*, (a) *to offer, present* someone to be baptized, (b) *to offer* someone to the court of the emperor, (c) *to offer* in marriage, *betroth*, (d) **offerre se**, *to offer one's self*, (e) *to offer, to present* to the senses, imagination, sight, notice.

offertorium, ii, *n.*, *the offertory*, (1) that part of the Mass in which the unconsecrated bread and wine are offered to God; the oblation itself; (2) the prayers that accompany this offering; (3) the verse or antiphon that forms a prayer of the proper of the Mass which is sung by the choir while the priest is making the offering.

officialis, e, *adj.*, *official, performing some service* or *duty*. **Officiale membrum,** *official member*, a bodily organ that serves the needs or purposes of a higher one.

officina, ae, *f.*, *a workshop*.

officio, ere, eci, ectum, 3, *v. n.*, *to stand in the way of, to be detrimental* or *hurtful to*.

officiosus, a, um, *adj.*, (1) *officious, doing* or *ready to do kind offices; eager to serve* or *please*; **officiosum mendacium,** *an officious lie, a lie* told as an act of kindness to further another's interests, (2) *dutiful*; active or zealous in doing one's duty.

officium, ii, *n.*, (1) *an obligatory service, duty, obligation, office*, (2) *an official duty, a service, employment, business*, (3) *the prayers of the breviary, the divine office.*—Kinds of *officium* in this (2) sense are: (a), **officium divinum,** the official liturgy of the Church, *the divine office* or the office of God, i.e., the breviary and also the celebration of Holy Mass.—(b), **officium ecclesiasticum** and **officium saeculare,** *the ecclesiastical* and *the secular office.*—(c), **officium episcopale seu pontificale** and **officium sacerdotale,** *the episcopal* and *the sacerdotal office.*—(d), **officium mortuorum,** *the office of the service for the dead.*—(e), **offici-**

um pontificale, see *officium epis-copale.*—(f), **officium proprium,** *the proper service.*—(g), **officium sacerdotale,** see *officium episco-pale.*—(h), **officium saeculare,** see *officium ecclesiasticum.*—(i), **officium scholasticum,** *the scholastic office.*—(j), **officium spirituale,** *the spiritual office.*

offusco, are, 1, *v. a., to darken, ob-scure, dim,* used lit. and fig.

oleum, i, *n., oil, olive oil.* Olive oil, *oleum olivarum,* is obtained from the pulp of olives. It is mixed with balsam in the making of chrism, which is used in the ad-ministering of certain sacra-ments. It represents the copious outpouring of sacramental grace which gives strength to the soul as oil does to the body.

olfacio, ere, eci, actum, 3, *v. a., to smell, scent* something.

olfactus, us, *m., the organ* or *sense of smell.*

oligarchia, ae, *f., a government by a few rich, oligarchy.*

oligarchicus, a, um, *adj., pertaining to an oligarchy, oligarchical.* On **politia oligarchica,** see *politia* under 1.

olim, *adv., once, formerly, in times past.*

oliva, ae, *f.,* (1) *an olive,* (2) lit., *an olive tree.*—**oleum olivarum,** *oil of olives, oil obtained from the pulp of olives.* It is mixed with balsam in the making of chrism which is used in the administra-tion of certain sacraments.—**ra-mus olivae,** *an olive branch.*

Olivetum, i, *n., a place planted with olive trees, an olive grove,* hence, **mons Oliveti,** *the moun-tain of Olivet,* or *of the olive-grove,* east of Jerusalem.

olla, ae, *f., a pot* or *caldron.*

olus, eris, *n., vegetables, garden herbs* of any kind.

Olympius, a, um, *adj., Olympian, of* or *belonging to Olympus; heavenly, celestial.*

Olympus, i, *m., Olympus,* the name of several mountains, the most celebrated of which is one on the borders of Macedonia and Thes-saly, of great height and conse-quently regarded as the seat of the gods.

omissio, onis, *f., an omission,* the non-performance or neglect of action or duty.

omitto, ere, isi, issum, 3, *v. a.,* (1) *to disregard, lay aside,* (2) *to omit, neglect to say something,* (3) of an action, *to leave off, give over, cease* doing anything.

omnifariam, *adv., on all sides, in every way.*

omnimodo, *adv., entirely, altogeth-er,* used in the S.T. only in quot.

omnimodus, a, um, *adj., of all sorts* or *kinds.*

omnino, *adv., altogether, wholly, entirely, absolutely, utterly, at all.*

omnipotens, ntis, *adj., all-powerful, almighty, omnipotent.*—**omnipo-tens,** ntis, *m., the Almighty.*

omnipotentia, ae, *f., almighty pow-er, omnipotence.*—Kinds of *omni-potentia* are: **omnipotentia activa**

and **omnipotentia passiva,** *the active* and *passive omnipotence,* i.e., the faculty of doing or creating anything that does not contain a contradiction within itself, or the omnipotence that is proper only to God, and the faculty of becoming anything that belongs to *materia prima.*

omnis, e, *adj., all, every,* synonym of *perfectus* and *totus.* On **dicere de omni,** see *dicere* under 3; on **dictio omnis,** see *dictio* under 2; on **praedicare de omni,** see *praedicare* under 2.—**omne,** is, *n., the all, the universe.*

omnitenens, ntis, *adj., holding all things, all-swaying,* not found in the S.T.

onero, are, avi, atum, 1, *v. a., to burden, weary, oppress, load,* used fig.

onerosus, a, um, *adj., troublesome, irksome, burdensome.*

Onias, ae, *m., Onias,* great-great-grandson of Onias, high priest of the Jews shortly after the death of Alexander the Great.

onocrotalus, i, *m., the pelican.*

onus, eris, *n.,* (1) lit., *a load, burden,* (2) fig., (a) *a burden* in respect of debts, (b) in gen., *a load, burden, trouble, difficulty* of any kind.

onychinus, i, *m., the onyx.*

opacitas, atis, *f., opacity, opaqueness, darkness.*

opacus, a, um, *adj., opaque, not reflecting* or *emitting light; dull dark.*

opera, ae, *f.,* (1) lit., *a service, a rendering of service,* (2) transf., **operam dare,** *to give attention to anything, to bestow care* or *pains on,* used with (a) *subj.,* (b) *ut,* (c) *dat.*—**locare operas,** *to hire out one's services.*

operabilis, e, *adj., practicable, feasible,* i.e., possible of being carried out through a work or deed, presentable in acting and in doing, synonym of *factibilis* and *agibilis.* On **bonum operabile,** see *bonum* under 3; on **principium operabile,** see *principium;* on **syllogismus operabilis,** see *syllogismus.*—Kinds of *operabile* are: (a), **operabile contingens,** *the contingently practicable,* ie., that which does not of necessity have to be carried out in word or in deed.—(b), **operabile particulare,** *the particularly practicable,* i.e., that which can be presented in a single work, in a single action.

operamentum, i, *n., operation, work, deed.*

operarius, ii, *m., a laborer, workman.*

operatio, onis *f.,* (1) *performing, production,* (2) *activity* or *operation* in the general sense of the word, synonym of *actio, actus,* and *opus,* (3) *immanent operation* or *activity,* the same as *operatio manens in operante* (see under 2), and in this sense distinct from *actio.*—On **communitas operationis,** see *communitas* under 1; on **finis operationis,** see *finis* under 2; on **principium**

operationis, see *principium;* on unitas operationis, see *unitas.—* perfectio operationis, *the perfection of an activity.—*unitas operationis, *the unity of an activity.* —Kinds of *operatio* in this (2) sense are: (a), operatio activa, see *operatio factiva* and *operatio receptiva.—*(b), operatio actualis, *actual action* or *that taking place in reality.—*(c), operatio adquisitiva finis seu factiva finis and operatio meritoria finis, *the action that efficiently acquires a goal* or *that deserves one.—*(d), operatio animalis, *the sensitive action.—*(e), operatio artificialis seu artis and operatio naturalis, *the artistic* and *the natural action,* (cf. *operatio connaturalis, operatio gloriae,* and *operatio violenta*), or *the activity of art* (cf. *ars* under 2) and *that of nature.* —(f), operatio artis, see *operatio artificialis.—*(g), operatio bestialis and operatio humana, *the bestial* or *animal* and *the human action.—*(h), operatio civilis, *the civic action* or *that of a citizen as such.—*(i), operatio communis and operatio propria, *the action common to many things* and *that proper to each of them.—*(j), operatio completa seu perfecta and operatio defectiva seu imperfecta, *the complete* or *perfect* and *the defective* or *imperfect action.—*(k), operatio coniuncti, *the combined* or *united operation of body* and *soul,* the opposite of *operatio solius animae,* i.e., that

operation which has its subject in the soul alone.—(l), operatio connaturalis seu naturalis and operatio miraculosa seu supernaturalis, *the action which corresponds to the nature of a thing* or *is according its nature* (cf. *operatio artificialis, operatio gloriae,* and *operatio violenta*) and *the miraculous* or *supernatural action.—*(m), operatio continua and operatio intercisa, *the continuous* or *uninterrupted* or *interrupted action.—*(n), operatio corporalis, *the physical action.—* (o), operatio debita, *the fitting* or *due action.—*(p), operatio defectiva, see *operatio completa.—*(q), operatio exiens ab ipso operante seu exterior seu transiens and operatio manens in operante seu intrinseca, *the action that goes forth from the active thing, a transitive action, the outer action* and *that which remains within the thing, the immanent action, the inner action.—*(r), operatio expedita seu non-impedita and operatio impedita, *the free* or *unimpeded action* and *the impeded action.—*(s), operatio exterior, see *operatio exiens.—*(t), operatio extranea, *the extraneous* or *foreign action.—*(u), operatio factiva and operatio activa, *the action that consists in effecting* or *producing something* and *that which consists merely in a deed* or *an act.—*Cf. also *operatio receptiva.—*(v), operatio factiva finis, see *operatio adquisitiva fi-*

nis.–(w), **operatio formaliter bona** and **operatio materialiter bona**, *the action that is good because directed to a good purpose*, i.e., *formally good* and *that which is good because it is consonant with the faculty whence it springs*, i.e., *materially good.* –(x), **operatio gloriae** and **operatio naturae**, *action in the glory of heaven* and *that in the condition of nature or of the natural being.* Cf. *operatio artificialis, operatio connaturalis,* and *operatio violenta.*–(y), **operatio hierarchica**, *hierarchical action* or *the action performed by a member of the hierarchy.* Cf. *actio hierarchica* under *actio* under 1.–(z), **operatio humana**, see *operatio bestialis.*–(a²), **operatio impedita**, see *operatio expedita.*–(b²), **operatio imperfecta**, see *operatio completa.*–(c²), **operatio intellectiva seu intelligibilis** and **operatio sensitiva seu sensibilis**, *the immaterial action* and *action through the senses.* See *operatio intellectualis.*–(d²), **operatio intellectualis**, *intellectual action.*–(e²), **operatio intercisa**, see *operatio continua.*–(f²), **operatio intrinseca**, see *operatio exiens.*–(g²), **operatio manens**, see *operatio exiens.*–(h²), **operatio manualis seu manuum**, *handwork, handling, manual work.*–(i²), **operatio manuum**, see *operatio manualis.*–(j²), **operatio materialiter bona**, see *operatio formaliter bona.*–(k²),

operatio meritoria, *meritorious action.*–(l²), **operatio meritoria finis**, see *operatio adquisitiva finis.*–(m²), **operatio miraculosa**, see *operatio connaturalis.*–(n²), **operatio moralis**, *moral action.*– (o²), **operatio naturae**, see *operatio gloriae.*–(p²), **operatio naturalis**, see *operatio artificialis, operatio connaturalis, operatio gloriae,* and *operatio violenta.*–(q²), **operatio naturalis secundum quid** and **operatio naturalis simpliciter**, *action natural in a certain respect* or *with respect to something* and *the simply* or *absolutely natural action.*–(r²), **operatio naturalis simpliciter**, see *operatio naturalis secundum quid.*–(s²), **operatio non recta** and **operatio recta**, *the action which is not rightly ordered* and *that which is right.*–(t²), **operatio nutritiva**, *the vegetative* or *nutritive action.*– (u²), **operatio perfecta**, see *operatio completa.*–(v²), **operatio personalis**, *the personal action* or *that performed by a person.*– (w²), **operatio propria**, see *operatio communis.*–(x²), **operatio receptiva** and **operatio activa**, *the action which consists in accepting* or *receiving* and *that which consists in giving.*–(y²), **operatio recta**, see *operatio non recta.*– (z²), **operatio sensibilis seu sensitiva**, see *operatio intellegibilis.*– (a³), **operatio simplex**, *the simple action*, i.e., that effected without the cooperation of a physical organ.–(b³), **operatio studiosa**, *the* *serious* or *zealous action,* the opposite of *actio ludicra,* (see *actio* under 1).—(c³), **operatio supererogationis,** *action over* and *above what is demanded.*—(d³), **operatio supernaturalis,** see *operatio connaturalis.*—(e³), **operatio theandrica,** *the action of the God-man.*—(f³), **operatio transiens,** see *operatio exiens.*—(g³), **operatio violenta** and **operatio naturalis,** *the violent* or *unnatural action* and *the natural* or *that according to nature.*—(h³), **operatio virtualis,** *the virtuous action.*—(i³), **operatio vitae seu vitalis,** *the vital action.*—(j³), **operatio vitalis,** see *operatio vitae.*—**cuiuslibet rei finis est sua perfectissima operatio,** or, **omnis res est propter suam operationem,** or, **quaelibet res est propter suam operationem,** or, **res unaquaeque dicitur esse propter suam operationem,** or, **unumquodque, quod habet propriam operationem, est propter suam operationem,** the translation of Aristotle's expression: *hekaston estin, hon estin ergon, heneka tou ergou, everything which has a proper action exists for performing this action* and *has its aim therein,* i.e., *in its most perfect action.*—**eius est habitus, cuius est operatio,** see *habitus* under 4.—**modus operationis consequitur formam, quae est operationis principium,** *the mode of the action directs itself according to the form which is the principle of the action.*—**omnis**

operatio est individuorum distinctorum, *every action brings into being fixed individual traits.*—**omnis operatio specificatur per formam, quae est principium operationis,** or, **operatio non recipit speciem a operante, sed a principio operationis,** or, **operationes distinguuntur ad invicem penes terminos et principia,** *every action receives its special species through the form which is the principle of the action, so that actions are distinguished from one another according to their objects* and *according to the faculties which are their proximate principles, not according to the subject operating.*—**omnis potentia reducitur ad operationem sicut ad perfectionem propriam,** see *potentia* under 2.—**omnis res est propter suam operationem,** see above: *cuiuslibet rei finis* etc.—**operatio est in particularibus,** or, **operationes circa singularia sunt,** *actions are concerned with concrete individual things.*—**operationes distinguuntur ad invicem penes terminos et principia,** see above: *omnis operatio specificatur* etc.—**operatio non recepit speciem ab operante, sed a principio operationis,** see above: *omnis operatio specificatur* etc.—**operatio rei demonstrat substantiam et esse ipsius,** *the action of a thing reveals the substance* and *the proper being of the same.*—**operatio rei sequitur formam ipsius,** or, **propria opera-**

tio rei sequitur seu consequitur propriam ipsius naturam, or, operatio substantiam sequitur, *the proper action of a thing is according to its nature* and *essence.* —operatio substantiam sequitur, see above: *operatio rei sequitur* etc.—oportet quod eius sit potentia sicut subiecti, cuius est operatio, see *potentia* under 2.—propria operatio rei sequitur seu consequitur propriam ipsius naturam, see above: *operatio rei sequitur* etc.—quaelibet res est propter suam operationem, see above: *cuiuslibet rei finis* etc.— res unaquaeque dicitur esse propter suam operationem, see above: *cuiuslibet rei finis* etc.— unumquodque, quod habet propriam operationem, est propter suam operationem, see above: *cuiuslibet rei finis* etc.

operativus, a, um, *adj., creative, formative, active, belonging to* or *concerning the operative* and *the active,* the opposite of *speculativus* and *theoricus,* also of *practicus.* On **ars operativa,** see *ars* under 1; on **demonstratio operativa,** see *demonstratio* under 3; on **forma operativa,** see *forma* under 2; on **habitus operativus,** see *habitus* under 4; on **intellectus operativus,** see *intellectus* under 3; on **potentia operativa,** see *potentia* under 1 and 2; on **principium operativum,** see *principium;* on **ratio operativa,** see *ratio* under 3; on **scientia operativa,** see *scientia* under 1; on

syllogismus operativus, see *syllogismus;* on **verbum operativum,** see *verbum* under 1; on **virtus operativa,** see *virtus* under 3.

operator, oris, *m., a worker, workman, operator.*

operatorius, a, um, *adj., effectual.*

operatrix, icis, *f., she that works, a worker.*

operimentum, i, *n., a covering, cover.*

operio, ire, ui, ertum, 4, *v. a.,* (1) lit., (a) *to cover, cover over anything,* (b) *to shut, imprison,* (c) *to clothe,* (2) fig., of sin, *to atone for, cover, cause to be forgotten.* —operte, *adv., covetly.*

operor, ari, atus, *v. dep., n., to operate, be active, do.* On **finis operantis,** see *finis* under 2; on **gratia operantis,** see *gratia* under 2; on **esse in loco ut operans in operato,** see *locus* under 2; on **modus operantis,** see *modus* under 2; on **opus operantis et opus operatum,** see *opus* under 4; on **scientia operantis,** see *scientia* under 2.—Kinds of *operari* are: (a), **operari effective** and **operari formaliter,** *to operate after the manner of the effective cause* and *after the manner of the formal cause* or *of the form.*—(b), **operari formaliter,** see *operari effective.*—(c), **operari instrumentaliter** and **operari principaliter,** *to be active after the manner of the instrumental* and *of the chief cause.*—(d), **operari naturali instinctu,** *to be active instinctively.* —(e), **operari per electionem** and operari per necessitatem, *to be active on the basis of free will* or *by freedom* and *to be active by natural necessity.*—(f), **operari per modum efficientiae** and **operari per modum meriti**, *to operate after the manner of effecting* or *producing* and *after the manner of deserving.*—(g), **operari per modum meriti**, see *operari per modum efficientiae.*—(h), **operari per necessitatem**, see *operari per electionem.*—(i), **operari principaliter**, see *operari instrumentaliter.* (j), **operari supernaturaliter**, *to be active in a supernatural manner.* —**eo modo aliquid operatur, quo est**, see *esse.*—**modus operandi uniuscuiusque rei sequitur modum essendi ipsius**, see *esse.*—**unumquodque operatur secundum quod est**, see *esse.*—**operans**, antis, *P. a.*, *active, efficient, effectual.*—**operatus**, a, um, *P. a.*, *performed, effected.*

operte, *adv.*, see *operio.*

opifex, icis, *comm.*, lit., *a worker, maker, fabricator,* (a) in gen., (b) in partic., *a workman, mechanic, artist.*

opificium, ii, *n.*, *a working, the doing of work, a work.*

opinabiles, e, *adj.*, *that rests on opinion* or *conjecture, likely, probable,* synonym of *probabilis,* the opposite of *scibilis.*

opinative, *adv.*, see *opinativus.*

opinativus, a, um, *adj.*, *meaning, intending,* synonym of *ratiocinativus.* Cf. *opinio.*—**opinativum** sc. **principium animae**, the transla-

tion of the Aristotelian expression *doxastikon,* the principle of opinion, i.e., the activity of the mind concerning variable things, as distinct from invariable and necessary things which are .the object of science.—**opinative**, *adv., according to the principle of opinion, opinatively.*

opinio, onis, *f.*, *opinion, supposition, conjecture,* the sort of assent that falls short of certainty. —On the difference between *opinio* and *suspicio,* see *suspicio* under 1. On **certitudo opinionis**, see *certitudo* under 2; on **communicabile secundum opinionem**, see *communicabilis;* on **dicere secundum opinionem**, see *dicere* under 3; on **felicitas secundum opinionem**, see *felicitas;* on **veritas opinionis**, see *veritas* under 1.— Kinds of *opinio* are: (a), **opinio communis**, *the general opinion* or *that generally accepted.*—(b), **opinio erronea seu falsa** and **opinio recta seu vera**, *the erroneous* or *false* and *the right* or *true opinion.*—(c), **opinio extranea**, *the strange opinion.*—(d), **opinio falsa**, see *opinio erronea.*—(e), **opinio particularis** and **opinio universalis**, *the opinion that refers to something in particular* and *that which refers to something in general.*—(f), **opinio recta**, see *opinio erronea.*—(g), **opinio speculativa**, *the theoretical opinion* or *that referring only to the sphere of knowledge.*—(h), **opinio universalis**, see *opinio particula-*

ris.—(i), **opinio vehemens,** *the strong opinion* or *the belief.*—(j), **opinio vera,** see *opinio falsa.*

opinor, ari, atus, 1, *v. dep., to be of an opinion, to suppose, imagine, conjecture, believe, think, judge,* used with *de,* an *object clause, absol., acc.*—**opinatus,** a, um, *P. a., supposed, imagined, fancied.*

opitulatio, onis, *f., a helping, assisting, help, assistance.*

opitulor, ari, atus, 1, *v. dep. n., to help, aid, assist, succor.*

oportet, ere, uit, 2, *v. impers., it is necessary, needful, proper, becoming* or *reasonable; it behooves; I* (thou, he, etc.) *must* or *ought,* used with (1) *quod clause* in the *subj.,* (2) *ut* and the *subj.,* (3) *inf.* and *subj. acc.,* (4) *absol.*

oppidum, i, *n., a town.*

oppono, ere, posui, situm, 3, *to set* or *place against, oppose, contrast.*—On **dicere per oppositum,** see *dicere* under 1; on **differentia opposita,** see *differentia;* on **dividere ex opposito,** see *dividere* under 1; on **fieri ex opposito,** see *fieri.*—Kinds of *opponere* are: (a), **opponere contradictorie seu ut contradictio seu in contradictione seu secundum contradictionem, opponere contrarie seu ut contrarietas seu ut contrarium seu diametraliter, opponere privative seu ut privatio seu secundum privationem et habitum** and **opponere relative seu ut ad aliquid,** *to oppose contradictorily, contrarily, privatively,* and *relatively,* i.e., to oppose after the manner

of contradiction, to oppose after the manner of the greatest difference between two extremes within the same genus or species, to oppose after the manner of being deprived of something usually present, to oppose after the manner of the extremes of a relationship.—(b), **opponere contrarie,** see *opponere contadictorie.*—(c), **opponere diametraliter,** see *opponere contadictorie.*—(d), **opponere directe** and **indirecte,** *to oppose directly* and *indirectly.*—(e), **opponere formaliter,** *to oppose according to form* or *essence.*—(f), **opponere immediatum** and **opponere mediatum,** *to oppose directly* and *to oppose indirectly.*—(g), **opponere in contradictione,** see *opponere contradictorie.*—(h), **opponere indirecte,** see *opponere directe.*—(i), **opponere in generali** and **opponere in speciali,** *to oppose in general* and *to oppose in particular.*—(j), **opponere in speciali,** see *opponere in generali.*—(k), **opponere mediatum,** see *opponere immediatum.*—(l), **opponere negative,** *to oppose negatively.* This and *opponere affirmative* form the species of *opponere contradictorie,* see above.—(m), **opponere per se,** *to oppose through itself* or *according to itself.*—(n), **opponere privative,** see *opponere contradictorie.*—(o), **opponere relative,** see *opponere contradictorie.*—(p), **opponere secundum contradictionem,** see *opponere contradicto-*

rie.—(q), **opponere secundum privationem et habitum,** see *opponere contradictorie.*—(r), **opponere ut ad aliquid,** see *opponere contradictorie.*—(s), **opponere ut contradictio,** see *opponere contradictorie.*—(t), **opponere ut contrarietas,** see *opponere contradictorie.*—(u), **opponere ut contrarium,** see *opponere contradictorie.* —(v), **opponere ut privatio,** see *opponere contradictorie.*—**oppositus,** a, um, *P. a., placed* or *standing against* or *opposite, opposed to, opposite.*—**oppositum,** i, *n., an opposite.*—**ex opposito,** *contrariwise, oppositely, on the contrary, on the other hand.*—**impossibile est opposita esse simul,** *opposite states cannot occur in the same subject at the same time.*—**oportet opposita esse circa idem,** *opposites must always relate to the same thing.*—**opposita iuxta se posita magis sentiuntur,** or, **oppositum per oppositum manifestatur,** *opposites are made manifest by contrast.*—**opposita non possunt esse in eodem,** or, **opposita non possunt inesse eidem secundum idem,** *opposites cannot be found in the same thing according to the same aspect.*—**oppositum per oppositum manifestatur,** see above: *opposita iuxta* etc.—**quae non sunt opposita, possunt simul esse,** or, **quae non sunt opposita, possunt simul existere in eodem,** *what are not opposites can co-exist in the same thing.*

opporto, are, avi, atum, 1, *v. a., to bring.*

opportune, *adv.,* see *opportunus.*

opportunitas, atis, *f., opportunity, fitness, convenience,* (1) in gen., (a) *a convenience,* that which is convenient or which gives ease or comfort, (b) *adaptability, suitableness,* (2) in partic., *a fit, opportune,* or *favorable time; a favorable occasion.*

opportunus, a, um, *adj.,* (1) in gen., of time, adapted to an end or purpose or circumstance of the case; *fit, suitable, appropriate, convenient,* (2) in partic., (a) *fit, suitable, adapted to anything,* (b) *advantageous, serviceable, useful.*—**opportune,** *adv., fitly, seasonably, opportunely.*

oppositio, onis, *f.,* (1) *opposition* (in place), (2) *opposition, contrast.*—Kinds of *oppositio* in this (1) sense are: (a), **oppositio debita,** *due* or *proper opposition.*—(b), **oppositio directa,** *direct opposition.*—Kinds of *oppositio* in this (2) sense are: (a), **oppositio absoluta,** *the absolute contrast.*—(b), **oppositio affirmationis et negationis,** *the contrast of affirmation* and *negation.*—(c), **oppositio contradictionis seu secundum contradictionem seu contradictoria, oppositio contrarietatis seu contraria, oppositio privationis et habitus seu secundum privationem seu privativa,** and **oppositio relationis seu relativa,** *the contradictory, the contrary, the privative,* and *relative opposition* or *the* contrast in the manner of a contradiction (i.e., of the affirmation and denial of something), *the contrast after the manner of the greatest difference between two things within the same genus or species, the contrast between a lack in something* and *that which it is expected to have,* and *the contrast after the manner of mutual relationship.*—(d), **oppositio contradictoria,** see *oppositio contradictionis.*—(e), **oppositio contraria,** see *oppositio contradictionis.*—(f), **oppositio contrarietatis,** see *oppositio contradictionis.*—(g), **oppositio directa,** *the direct contrast.*—(h), **oppositio in adiecto,** *the contrast of the added with that to which it is added.*—(i), **oppositio in genere seu secundum speciem,** *contrast within a genus* or *the specific contrast.*—(j), **oppositio maxima** and **oppositio minima,** *the greatest* and *the smallest contrast,* of which the former consists of *oppositio contradictionis* and the latter of *oppositio relationis.*—(k), **oppositio minima,** see *oppositio maxima.*—(l), **oppositia negationis,** see *oppositio affirmationis.*—(m), **oppositio prima,** *the first opposite* after its nature, which consists of *oppositio contradictionis.*—(n), **oppositio prima in genere** and **oppositio prima simpliciter,** *the first contrast within a genus* and *the simply* or *absolutely first contrast.*—(o), **oppositio privativa,** see *oppositio contradictionis.*—

(p), **oppositio privationis et habitus,** see *oppositio contradictionis.*—(q), **oppositio relativa,** see *oppostio contradictionis.*—(r), **oppositio secundum contradictionem,** see *oppositio contradictionis.*—(s), **oppositio secundum contrarietatem,** see *oppositio contradictionis.*—(t), **oppositio secundum privationem,** see *oppositio contradictionis.*—(u), **oppositio secundum speciem,** see *oppostio in genere.*

oppressio, onis, *f., oppression,* (1) the exercise of authority or power in a burdensome, harsh or wrongful manner, (2) *violent seizure,* e.g., **daemonum oppressiones,** *diabolical possession,* (3) the action of weighing down, or bearing heavily on a person, the mind, feelings, grief, etc.; pressure of outward circumstances, or of grief, pain or trouble, *a burden.*

oppressor, oris, *m., an oppressor, one who oppresses,* especially one who harrasses with unjust or cruel treatment.

opprimo, ere, essi, essum, 3, *v. a.,* (1) lit., (a) *to crush,* (b) *to press against,* (2) fig., (a) *to oppress,* to keep under by wrongful exercise of authority; to load or burden with cruel or unjust impositions or restraints, (b) *to press* or *bear down, overwhelm, load with debt, fatigue, pain,* inconvenience of any kind, (c) *to check, suppress, quash,* used of persons and things, (d) *to*

thwart, (e) *to force, violate, rav-*
ish.—**oppressus,** a, um, *P. a.,* (1)
oppressed, treated unjustly, (2)
oppressed, weighed down phys-
ically, (3) *oppressed, raped.*

opprobriosus, a, um, *adj., oppro-*
brious, attended by or *involving*
shame or *infamy.*

opprobrium, i, *n., opprobrium, the*
disgrace or *evil reputation at-*
tached to conduct considered
shameful; the imputation or *ex-*
pression of this disgrace; in-
famy, reproach.

oppugno, are, avi, atum, 1, *v. a.,*
(1) lit., *to besiege, war with,* (2)
fig., *to quarrel, resist, attack.*

ops, opis, *f.,* (1) *means* of any
kind that one possesses; *prop-*
erty, substance, wealth, riches,
treasure, (2) *assistance, aid,*
help.

optatio, onis, *f., a wish, a wishing.*

optativus, a, um, *adj., of* or *be-*
longing to a wish, expressing a
wish, optative.

optimates, um, *comm., the nobles,*
the adherents of the best men, in
a political sense, i.e., *the aristo-*
cratic party, the aristocrats.

Optimus, i, *m., Optimus,* bishop
of Antioch, in Pisidia. We have
a very long letter of Basil's addressed to Optimus in A.D. 317,
expounding at his request the
passages relating to Cain (Gen.
IV. 15), Lamech (ib. 23-25), and
the words of Simeon (Lu. II,
34, 35), (Basil Ep. 260).

optio, onis, f., *option, power* or
liberty of choosing.

opto, are, avi, atum, 1, *v. a.,*
to wish, wish for, desire, esp.,
to wish one anything, in a good
or bad sense, used with *acc.,*
absol., and with *ut* and the
subj.—**optatus,** a, um, *P. a.,*
wished, desired.

opulentia, ae, *f., wealth, riches,*
opulence.

opulentus, a, um, *adj., rich,*
wealthy in some respect.

opus, eris, *n.,* (1) *work, product, ac-*
complishment, (2) *literary work,*
a writing, a work, (3) *necessary*
work, necessary, (4) *work, activ-*
ity, labor, synonym of *operatio.*—
On **peccatum operis,** see *pecca-*
tum under 2; on **protestatio ope-**
ris, see *protestatio;* on **rectitudo**
in opere, see *rectitudo* under 3;
on **substantia operis,** see *substan-*
tia under 8.—Kinds of *opus* in
this (1) sense are: (a), **opus divi-**
num, *the divine work.*—(b), **opus**
falsum and **opus verum,** *the false*
or *wrong work* and *the true* or
right work.—(c), **opus verum,** see
opus falsum.—On **finis operis,** see
finis under 2; on **veritas operis,**
see *veritas* under 1.—Kinds of
opus in this (4) sense are: (a),
opus amicabile, *the friendly ac-*
tivity or *the service of friendship.*
—(b), **opus animae** and **opus cor-**
porale, *the activity of the soul*
and *that of the body.*—(c), **opus**
appropriatum, *the appropriate* or
suitable activity.—(d), **opus arti-**
ficiale seu artis and **opus naturae,**
the work of art and *that of na-*
ture.—(e), **opus artis,** see *opus ar-*

tificiale.—(f), **opus bonum** and **opus malum**, *the morally good* and *the morally bad activity.*—(g), **opus carnale seu carnis** and **opus spirituale**, *the carnal* and *immaterial* or *spiritual activity,* i.e., the activity which springs from man's sense appetites in the material part of his nature and that which springs from the spiritual side of his nature.—(h), **opus carnis**, see *opus carnale.*—(i), **opus civile**, *the civic* or *public activity.*—(j), **opus consilii** and **opus praecepti**, *the counseled* and *the prescribed activity.*—(k), **opus corporale**, see *opus animae.*—(l), **opus exterius** and **opus interius**, *the outer activity* or *that which becomes visible* and *the inner activity* or *that which takes place within a being.*—(m), **opus intellectus**, and **opus voluntatis**, *the action of reason* and *that of the will.*—(n), **opus interius**, see *opus exterius.*—(o), **opus liberum** and **opus servile**, *the free* and *the servile activity* or *the activity of the freeborn* and *that of the slave.*—(p), **opus magicum**, *the activity of magic.*—(q), **opus malum**, see *opus bonum.*—(r), **opus manuale seu manuum**, *manual activity* or *activity of the hands.*—(s), **opus manuum**, see *opus manuale.*—(t), **opus meritorium** and **opus non meritorium**, *the meritorious* and *the unmeritorious activity.*—(u), **opus miraculosum**, *miraculous work.*—(v), **opus mortificatum** and **opus vivifica-**

tum, *the profitless* and *the revived work,* i.e., the meritorious work which has been deprived of its merit by a subsequent mortal sin and the once-dead activity which has regained its merit through subsequent penance.—(w), **opus mortuum** and **opus vivum**, *the work of death,* so called, *quia causa est mortis (animae),* or *quia caret vita spirituali, quae est ex caritate,* and *the work of life,* because it is performed in the state of grace.—(x), **opus naturae**, see *opus artificiale.*—(y), **opus non meritorium**, see *opus meritorium.*—(z), **opus operantis** and **opus operatum**, *the work of the performer* and *of the work produced,* i.e., the action considered as it appears with reference to him who performs it and the same action as it appears in itself. In suffragiis quae per malos fiunt, duo possunt considerari: primo ipsum opus operatum, sicut sacrificium altaris.—(a²), **opus operatum**, see *opus operantis.*—(b²), **opus peccati** and **opus virtuosum**, *the sinful* and *the virtuous activity.*—(c²), **opus perfectionis seu supererogationis**, *the work of perfection* and *that of supererogation* or *which exceeds the required.*—(d²), **opus poenale**, *the work imposed as punishment.*—(e²), **opus praecepti**, see *opus consilii.*—(f²), **opus rectum**, *the right work.*—(g²), **opus satisfactionis seu satisfactorium**, *the work that pays the* *debt incurred by sin.*—(h²), **opus satisfactorium**, see *opus satisfactionis.*—(i²), **opus sensus**, *the activity of the senses* or *the sensible acts.*—(j²), **opus servile**, see *opus liberum.*—(k²), **opus spirituale**, see *opus carnale.*—(l²), **opus supererogationis**, see *opus perfectionis.*—(m²), **opus virtuosum**, see *opus peccati.*—(n²), **opus vivificatum**, see *opus mortificatum.*—(o²), **opus vivum**, see *opus mortuum.*—(p²), **opus voluntarium**, *the voluntary activity* or *that performed of one's accord.*—(q²), **opus voluntatis**, see *opus intellectus.*

ora, ae, *f.*, *the extremity of a thing; the edge, hem, fringe* of a garment.

oraculum, i, *n.*, *a divine announcement, an oracle.*

oratio, onis, *f.*, (1) *speech*, in the general sense of the word, (2) *speech* or *sentence*, in the sense of grammar and logic, synonym of *dictio*, *locutio*, and *ratio*, (3) *prayer.*—Kinds of *oratio* in this (1) sense are: (a), **oratio dialectica seu disputativa**, *the speech which discusses something* or *brings out the pros* and *cons.*—(b), **oratio disputativa**, see *oratio dialectica.*—(c), **oratio rhetorica**, *the rhetorical speech.*—Kinds of *oratio* in this (2) sense are: (a), **oratio composita** and **oratio simplex**, *the compound* and *the simple sentence*, the latter of which consists merely of a noun and a verb.—(b), **oratio deprecativa**, **oratio optativa**, **oratio enuntia-**

tiva seu iudicativa seu suppositiva, **oratio imperativa**, **oratio interrogativa**, **oratio dubitativa**, and **oratio vocativa**, *the imploring, the wishing, the declaratory* or *the indicating* or *the imputing, the imperative, the interrogative,* and *the vocative sentence.*—(c), **oratio dubitativa**, see *oratio deprecativa.*—(d), **oratio enuntiativa**, see *oratio deprecativa.*—(e), **oratio falsa** and **oratio vera**, *the false* and *the true speech.*—(f), **oratio imperativa**, see *oratio deprecativa.*—(g), **oratio imperfecta** and **oratio perfecta**, *the imperfect* or *the perfect speech* or *sentence.*—(h), **oratio indicativa**, see *oratio deprecativa.*—(i), **oratio interrogativa**, see *oratio deprecativa.*—(j), **oratio optativa**, see *oratio deprecativa.*—(k), **oratio perfecta**, see *oratio imperfecta.*—(l), **oratio significans quod quid est res**, *the phrase that indicates the essence of a thing.*—(m), **oratio simplex**, see *oratio composita.*—(n), **oratio suppositiva**, see *oratio deprecativa.*—(o), **oratio vera**, see *oratio falsa.*—(p), **oratio vocativa**, see *oratio deprecativa.* On **via orationis**, see *via* under 1; on **votum orationis**, see *votum* under 1.—Kinds of *oratio* in this (3) sense are: (a), **oratio bona seu perfecta**, *the good* or *perfect prayer.*—(b), **oratio communis** and **oratio singularis**, *the common* or *general* and *the single prayer.*—(c), **oratio dominica**, *the Lord's Prayer.*—(d), **oratio expressa** and **oratio** interpretativa, *that expressed as prayer in words* and *that accepted as prayer.*—(e), **oratio exterior seu vocalis** and **oratio interior seu mentalis seu mentis,** *the exterior or vocal* and *the interior or mental prayer.*—(f), **oratio impetrativa, oratio meritoria,** and **oratio satisfactoria,** *the prayer which supplicates, the prayer which merits,* and *the prayer which satisfies for sin.*—(g), **oratio interior,** see *oratio exterior.*—(h), **oratio interpretativa,** see *oratio expressa.*—(i), **oratio mentalis,** see *oratio exterior.*—(j), **oratio mentis,** see *oratio exterior.*—(k), **oratio meritoria,** see *oratio impetrativa.*—(l), **oratio perfecta,** see *oratio bona.* —(m), **oratio privata** and **oratio publica,** *the private* and *the public prayer.* Cf. *oratio communis.* —(n), **oratio publica,** see *oratio privata.*—(o), **oratio satisfactoria,** see *oratio impetrativa.*—(p), **oratio singularis,** see *oratio communis.*—(q), **oratio vocalis,** see *oratio exterior.*

orator, oris, *m., an orator, speaker.*

orbatus, a, um, *P. a., deficient, wanting, defective, incapable.*

orbis, is, *m., circle, sphere, orbit, sky,* synonym of *circulus, globus,* and *sphaera.* On **anima orbis,** see *anima* under 2; on **substantia orbis,** see *substantia* under 2.— Kinds of *orbis* are: **orbis inferior, orbis medius,** and **orbis primus,** *the lower, the middle,* and *the upper sphere of heaven.*

orbitas, atis, *f., a deprivation* or *loss of something.*

ordinabilis, e, *adj., capable of being ordained, ordered,* or *directed to an end, purpose* or *destiny.* —**ordinabiliter,** *adv., in orderly manner.*

ordinabiliter, *adv.,* see *ordinabilis.*

ordinarie, *adv.,* see *ordinarius.*

ordinarius, a, um, *adj., of* or *belonging to order, orderly, according to the usual order.* On **auctoritas ordinaria,** see *auctoritas* under 4; on **iurisdictio ordinaria,** see *iurisdictio.*—**ordinarie,** *adv., in order, orderly, methodically.*

ordinate, *adv.,* see *ordinatus.*

ordinatio, onis, *f.,* (1) *decree, edict, ordinance,* (2) *order, disposition, gradation, order of rank,* synonym of *ordo,* (3) *direction, relation, relating, referring,* likewise a synonym of *ordo,* (4) *sphere of order, degree of rank,* likewise a synonym of *ordo,* (5) *spiritual consecration, sacred ordination,* likewise a synonym of *sacer ordo.*—Kinds of *ordinatio* in this (3) sense are: **ordinatio actualis** and **ordinatio habitualis,** *direction in the sense of an action* and *that in the sense of a state.*—A kind of *ordinatio* in this (4) sense is: **ordinatio praedicamentalis,** the *systoichia tes kategorias* of Aristotle, *the sphere of order of the category.*

ordinativus, a, um, *adj., ordinative,* having the character or function of ordaining, ordering, determining or regulating.

ordinator, oris, *m.*, (1) *an orderer,
ordainer, regulator, arranger,* (2)
an ordainer, one who ordains to
the ministry.

ordinatrix, icis, *f., she that orders*
or *arranges.*

ordinatus, a, um, *P. a., well ordered, orderly, ordained, appointed, ordered.* On actus ordinatus, see *actus* under 1; on affectio ordinata, see *affectio;* on
elementum ordinatum, see *elementum* under 1; on ira ordinata,
see *ira* under 1; on phantasma
ordinatum, see *phantasma* under
2; on poena ordinata, see *poena;*
on potentia ordinata, see *potentia* under 3.—ordinate, *adv., in an
orderly manner, in order, methodically,* opposite of *inordinate.*

ordino, are, avi, atum, 1, *v. a.,* (1)
*to order, set in order, arrange,
adjust, dispose,* (2) *ordain, appoint to office,* especially in a religious sense. On ordinatus and
ordinate, see *ordinatus.*

ordo, inis, *m.,* (1) *order, disposition,
gradation, order of rank,* synonym of *ordinatio,* (2) *direction,
relation, relating, referring,* likewise synonym of *ordinatio,* (3)
sphere of order, degree of rank,
synonym of *ordinatio,* (4) *the
sacrament of Holy Orders, spiritual consecration, ordination,* synonym of *ordinatio,* (5) *religious
order, religious society.*—On bonum secundum naturalem ordinem, see *bonus* under 2; on consonantia ordinis, see *consonantia*
under 2; on distinctio secundum

ordinem, see *distinctio* under 2;
on necessitas naturalis ordinis,
see *necessitas* under 1; on primum in ordine aliquo, see *primus;* on prius ordine seu in ordine seu secundum ordinem, see
prior under 1; on unitas ordinis,
see *unitas;* on unum ordine seu
secundum ordinem, see *unus.*—
per ordinem, *in accordance with
order, by turns.*—Kinds of *ordo*
in this (1) sense are: (a), ordo
agentium seu causarum and ordo
finium, *the order of the effective
causes* or *agents* and *that of the
final purpose.*—(b), ordo apprehensionis, *the order of apprehension* or *comprehension.*—(c), ordo
caelestis hierarchiae and ordo ecclesiae seu ecclesiasticae hierarchiae, *the order of the heavenly
hierarchy* and *that of the ecclesiastical hierarchy.*—(d), ordo causae formalis seu formae and ordo
causae materialis seu materiae,
the order of the formal cause or
of the form and *that of the material cause* or *of the material,*
i.e., the order which passes for
the form and that which passes
for the material of a thing.—(e),
ordo causae materialis, see *ordo
causae formalis.*—(f), ordo causarum, see *ordo agentium.*—(g), ordo compositionis and ordo resolutorius, *the order of composition*
and *that of dissolution* or *the order of synthesis* and *of analysis.*
—(h), ordo consecutionis seu exsecutionis and ordo intentionis,
the order in accomplishment or

execution and *that in intention.*—(i), **ordo debitus,** *the due* or *appropriate order.*—(j), **order dignitatis seu secundum dignitatem, ordo durationis,** and **ordo secundum locum seu localis,** *order according to dignity; that according to duration,* and *that according to place.*—(k), **ordo durationis,** see *ordo dignitatis.*—(l), **ordo ecclesiae,** see *ordo caelestis hierarchiae.*—(m), **ordo ecclesiasticae hierarchiae,** see *ordo caelestis hierarchiae.*—(n), **ordo ecclesiasticus** and **ordo politicus,** *the ecclesiastical* and *the political part.*—(o), **ordo essentiae seu essentialis,** *the order of essence* or *the essential order.*—(p), **ordo essentialis,** see *ordo essentiae.*—(q), **ordo exsecutionis,** see *ordo consecutionis.*—(r), **ordo finium,** see *ordo agentium.*—(s), **ordo formae,** see *ordo causae formalis.*—(t), **ordo generationis et temporis seu secundum viam generationis et temporis** and **ordo naturae seu intentionis naturae seu perfectionis,** *order according to generation* and *according to time* or *according to temporal originating,* and *order according to nature* or *the intention of nature* or *the perfection of a being.*—(u), **ordo hierarchicus,** *the hierarchical order.*—(v), **ordo intentionis,** see *ordo consecutionis.*—(w), **ordo intentionis naturae,** see *ordo generationis.*—(x), **ordo iustitiae,** *the order that corresponds with justice.*—(y), **ordo localis,** see *ordo*

dignitatis.—(z), **ordo materiae,** see *ordo causae formalis.*—(a²), **ordo naturae,** see *ordo generationis, ordo naturalis,* and *ordo originis formalis.*—(b²), **ordo naturalis,** see *ordo naturae* and *ordo rationis rectae; the natural order* or *the order of nature* and *the order of right reason.*—(c²), **ordo originis seu secundum originem seu naturae,** *order according to birth* or *origin.*—(d²), **ordo particularis** and **ordo universalis,** *the particular* and *the universal order.*—(e²), **ordo per accidens seu secundum accidens** and **ordo per se,** *the order of a thing with reference to something incidental to it* and *that which takes place with reference to itself* and *its own nature.*—(f²), **ordo perfectionis,** see *ordo generationis.*—(g²), **ordo per se,** see *ordo per accidens.*—(h²), **ordo politicus,** see *ordo ecclesiasticus.*—(i²), **ordo praeposterus** and **ordo rectus,** *the reversed* or *contrary order* and *the right order.*—(j²), **ordo quem ratio considerando facit in exterioribus rebus quarum ipsa est causa, ordo quem ratio considerando facit in operationibus voluntatis, ordo quem ratio considerando facit in proprio actu** and **ordo quem ratio non facit sed solum considerat,** the various orders which reason either imposes or discovers, namely, *the prudential, the moral, the logical,* and *the ontological order.*—(k²), **ordo quem ratio considerando facit in operationi-**

bus voluntatis, *the moral order,* see *ordo quem ratio considerando facit in exterioribus rebus.—* (l^2), **ordo quem ratio considerando facit in proprio actu,** *the logical order,* see *ordo quem ratio considerando facit in exterioribus rebus.*—(m^2), **ordo quem ratio non facit sed solum considerat,** *the ontological order,* see *ordo quem ratio considerando facit in exterioribus rebus.*—(n^2), **ordo rationis rectae,** see *ordo naturalis.*—(o^2), **ordo realis seu secundum rem,** and **ordo secundum modum intellegendi tantum,** *the real order* or *the order that takes place in things outside thought* and *the order that is realized in thought,* i.e., *the ontological* and *the logical order.*—(p^2), **ordo rectus,** see *ordo praeposterus.*—(q^2), **ordo resolutorius,** see *ordo compositionis.*—(r^2), **ordo retrogradus,** *the retrograding order.*—(s^2), **ordo secundum accidens,** see *ordo per accidens.*—(t^2), **ordo secundum dignitatem,** see *ordo dignitatis.*—(u^2), **ordo secundum locum,** see *ordo dignitatis.*—(v^2), **ordo secundum modum intellegendi tantum,** see *ordo realis.*—(w^2), **ordo secundum originem,** see *ordo originis.*—(x^2), **ordo secundum rem,** see *ordo secundum modum intellegendi tantum.*—(y^2), **ordo secundum viam generationis,** see *ordo generationis.*—(z^2), **ordo secundum temporis,** see *ordo generationis.*—(a^3), **ordo sustentationis,** *the order of maintenance* or *support.*—(b^3), **ordo temporis,** see *ordo generationis.*—(c^3), **ordo universalis,** see *ordo particularis.*—(d^3), **ordo universi,** *the order of the universe.* On **appetibile in ordine ad aliud,** see *appetibilis;* on **bonum ordinis seu quantum ad ordinem in finem,** see *bonus* under 2; on **debitum ex ordine alicuius ad aliquem,** see *debitus* under 1; on **impossibile in ordine ad aliquid,** see *impossibilis;* on **libertas quantum ad ordinem,** see *libertas* under 2; on **potentia in ordine ad aliquid,** see *potentia* under 3.—Kinds of *ordo* in this (2) sense are: **ordo congruitatis** and **ordo necessitatis,** *the direction* or *relation which is befitting* and *that which is necessary.*—Kinds of *ordo* in this (3) sense are: (a), **ordo angelorum,** *order of rank among the angels.*—(b), **ordo diaconi, ordo sacerdotis seu sacerdotalis seu presbyteri** and **ordo episcopi seu episcopalis,** *the order* or *sacred rite by which one becomes a deacon, a priest,* and *a bishop.* Cf. **ordo diaconi** under 4.—(c), **ordo episcopalis,** see *ordo diaconi.*—(d), **ordo episcopi,** see *ordo diaconi.*—(e), **ordo illuminandorum seu illuminativus, ordo immundorum seu purgativus,** and **ordo perfectorum seu perfectivus,** *in the degrees of the spiritual life, the highest is that of the illuminative way, then that among the relatively impure or of purification,* and *that among the perfect or of perfection.*—(f), ordo illuminativus, see *ordo illu-minandorum.*—(g), ordo immun-dorum, see *ordo illuminandorum.* —(h), ordo inferior and ordo su-perior, *the lower* or *inferior order of rank* and *the higher* or *supe-rior order of rank.* Cf. *inferior* under 4.—(i), ordo leviticus, *the Levitical order of rank.*—(j), ordo monachi seu monasticus, *the or-der of rank among monks.*—(k), ordo monasticus, see *ordo mona-chi.*—(l), ordo perfectivus, see *or-do illuminandorum.*—(m), ordo perfectorum, see *ordo illuminan-dorum.*—(n), ordo presbyteri, see *ordo diaconi.*—(o), ordo purgati-vus, see *ordo illuminandorum.*— (p), ordo sacerdotalis, see *ordo diaconi.*—(q), ordo sacerdotis, see *ordo diaconi.*—(r), ordo superior, see *ordo inferior.* On apostasia ordinis, see *apostasia;* on charac-ter ordinis seu ordo sacerdotalis, see *character* under 2; on clavis ordinis, see *clavis* under 2; on potestas ordinis, see *potestas* un-der 3; on sacramentum ordinis, see *sacramentum* under 3.—Kinds of *ordo* in this (4) sense are: (a), ordo diaconi, ordo subdiaconi, and ordo sacerdotis seu sacerdo-talis, *the ordination of deacons, that of subdeacons,* and *that of priests.* Cf. ordo diaconi under 3. —(b), ordo inferior seu minor and ordo superior seu maior, *the in-ferior* or *minor* (Porter, Reader, Exorcist, and Acolyte) and *the superior* or *major order* (Subdea-con, Deacon, and Priest). Cf.

ordo inferior under 3.—(c), ordo maior, see *ordo inferior.*—(d), or-do ministrantium and ordo prin-cipalis, *the order of those who serve the priesthood* and *the chief order,* i.e., those who conse-crate and offer Mass.—(e), ordo minor, see *ordo inferior.*—(f), or-do non-sacer and ordo sacer, *the not holy* and *the holy ordination.* —(g), ordo principalis, see *ordo ministrantium.*—(h), ordo sacer, see *ordo non-sacer.*—(i), ordo sa-cerdotalis, see *ordo diaconi.*—(j), ordo sacerdotis, see *ordo diaconi.* —(k), ordo subdiaconi, see *ordo diaconi.*—(l), ordo superior, see *ordo inferior.*

Oreb, *n.,* indecl., *Horeb,* a moun-tain in the peninsula of Sinai, Arabia.

organice, *adv.,* see *organicus.*

organicus, a, um, *adj., organic, me-chanical, instrumental, supplied with instruments.* On agens or-ganicum, see *agens;* on corpus organicum, see *corpus;* on pars organica, see *pars* under 1.—or-ganice, *adv., after the manner of an instrument, organically.*

organizatus, a, um, *P. a., furnished with organs, fashioned.*

organum, i, *n., organ, implement, instrument, engine,* synonym of *instrumentum.* On potentia affixa organo corporali seu materiali seu utens corporali organo et po-tentia non utens organo corpora-li, see *potentia* under 1; on virtus organi seu organum utens, see *virtus* under 1.—Kinds of *orga-*

num are: (a), **organum activum**
and **organum factivum**, *the active* or *the using instrument* and
the productive instrument.—(b),
organum animatum and **organum
inanimatum**, *the animated* or *living* and *the inanimate* or *lifeless
organ*, the *organon empsychon*
and *organon apsychon* of Aristotle.—(c), **organum commune**
and **organum proprium seu particulare**, *the instrument common
to several* and *the proper* or *particular instrument.*—(d), **organum
coniunctum seu unitum** and **organum extrinsecum seu separatum**, *the instrument connected*
or *united with the being that
uses it*, and *the instrument external to it* or *separable from it.*
—(e), **organum corporale seu corporeum seu materiale**, *the corporal* or *material organ.*—(f), **organum extrinsecum**, see *organum
coniunctum.*—(g), **organum factivum**, see *organum activum.*—(h),
organum materiale, see *organum
corporale.*—(i), **organum musicum**, *the musical instrument.*—(j),
organum particulare, see *organum commune.*—(k), **organum
principale**, *the chief* or *principal
instrument.*—(l), **organum proprium**, see *organum commune.*—
(m), **organum separatum**, see *organum coniunctum.*

oriens, entis, *m.*, see *orior.*

orientalis, e, *adj.*, *of* or *belonging
to the East, Eastern, Oriental.*—
Orientales, ium, *m.*, *the Orientals.*

originalis, e, *adj.*, *primitive, original.* On **culpa originalis**, see *culpa;*
on **iustitia originalis**, see *iustitia*
under 2; on **liber originalis**, see
liber under 3; on **macula originalis**, see *macula;* on **peccatum originale**, see *peccatum* under 2; on
potentia originalis, see *potentia*
under 2; on **principium originale**, see *principium.*—**originaliter**,
adv., *according to the source, in
the sense of the source, as a result of the source, originally*, synonym of *principaliter.* On **consistere originaliter**, see *consistere*
under 3.

originaliter, *adv.*, see *originalis.*

Origines, is, *m.*, *Origen*, a famous
Christian exegete, theologian,
and philosopher of the early part
of the third century. He exercised a very great influence both
in the East and in the West. The
chief tenets of the school which
takes its name from him, and to
which reference is made in the
Summa were the eternity of
Creation and the original equality of created spirits. St. Thomas
quotes from *De Principiis*, to
which he always gives the Greek
title *Peri Archon*, from his commentaries on the *Canticles*, *Matthew*, *John*, and the *Epistle to
the Romans*, and from several
homilies.

origino, are, avi, atum, 1, *v. a.*, *to
give origin to, originate*, synonym
of *principo.* On **causa originans**,
see *causa* under 1; on **principium
originans**, see *principium.*

origo, inis, *f.*, *earliest beginning, source, origin.* On **distinctio secundum originem**, see *distinctio* under 2; on **distingui relatione originis seu secundum originem**, see *distinguere;* on **ordo originis seu secundum originem**, see *ordo* under 1; on **peccatum originis**, see *peccatum* under 2; on **principium originis et secundum originem**, see *principium;* on **processio originis**, see *processio;* on **relatio originis**, see *relatio;* on **vitium originis**, see *vitium* under 1.—Kinds of *origo* are: (a), **origo activa seu active significata** and **origo passiva seu passive significata**, *source in the active* and *in the passive sense of the word,* i.e., *the giving* or *lending* and *the taking* or *receiving.*—(b), **origo active significata**, see *origo activa.*—(c), **origo causae finalis**, and **origo formalis**, *the origin in relation to final cause* and *that in relation to the form* or *essence of a thing.*—(d), **origo declinationis**, *the beginning of (grammatical) inflexion* or *declension* and *conjugation.*—(e), **origo formalis**, see *origo causae finalis.*—(f), **origo in communi** and **origo in speciali**, *source considered in general* and *source considered in particular.*—(g), **origo in speciali**, see *origo in communi.*—(h), **origo naturalis**, *the natural source* or *source according to nature.*—(i), **origo passiva**, see *origo activa.*—(j), **origo passiva significata**, see *origo activa.*—(k), **origo primordialis**, *the original* or *primordial source.*—(l), **origo vitiata**, *the source made faulty* or *the source found fault with.*

orior, iri, ortus, 4, *v. dep.*, (1) in gen., of the heavenly bodies, *to rise, become visible, appear,* (2) transf., in gen., *to come forth; to have one's origin* or *descent, to spring, descend from; to grow* or *spring forth; to rise, take its origin; arise, proceed, originate,* (a) *to rise, proceed from, take its origin,* (b) of plants, *to shoot up, spring from seed,* (c) of persons, *to be born,* (3) fig., *to arise, spring from, rise, become visible.* —**ortus**, a, um, *P. a., born.* —(1) lit., **oriens**, entis, *m., the quarter where the sun rises, the East, the Orient.*—(2) fig., *the Orient, Christ.*

ornamentum, i, *n., ornament, adornment, decoration, embellishment,* etc., (I) lit., (1) plural, (a) in gen., anything used to impart outward beauty to something, *a decoration, embellishment, jewel, trinket, coiffure,* extreme modishness, dress, etc., (b) in partic., *ornaments,* the ritual garments of a church dignitary, esp., a bishop, (2) sing., *ornament,* any part of the body, primarily for use, but which also adds grace and beauty to the human form, (II), fig., *an ornament,* a quality of mind that confers beauty, honor or grace.

ornatus, us, *m.*, (I) lit., (A) *ornament, splendor, display, adorn-*

ment resulting from some adjunct or accessory, primarily for use, but not excluding decoration or embellishment, (1) in gen., (2) in partic., of the world corresponding to the Gr. *kosmos*, (B) something employed to adorn, beautify, embellish; *a decoration, ornament,* (1) *embellishment* of style in speech, (2) *ornaments* of women, (II) fig., (A) in the abstract or as a quality, anything that lends beauty or renders more pleasing, (1) *ornament,* (2) *refinement, polish, good taste.—ornatus vestium, elegance* or *splendor of apparel.*

orno, are, avi, atum, 1, *v. a.,* (1) in gen., *to provide, furnish* with something, (2) in partic., *to ornament, adorn, embellish, deck, set off,* (a) lit., (b) fig., *to adorn, decorate.—ornatus,* a, um, *P. a., adorned,* used lit. and fig.

oro, are, avi, atum, 1, *v. a.* and *n., to pray, supplicate* God, to lift up the mind and heart to God, to adore, praise, thank Him and ask Him for aid, used (a) *absol.,* (b) with *pro* and *abl.,* (c) *ut* and *subj.,* (d) *ne* and *subj.,* (e) *acc.,* (f) *dat.,* (g) *acc.* and *inf.,* (h) *quod* and *subj.*

Orosius, ii, *m., Orosius,* an ecclesiastic of Tarragona who flourished about 500 A.D.; he wrote on the advice of St. Augustine, and to confute the pagans, a history from the beginning of the world to his own times. St. Thomas refers to the *Dialogus*

Quaestionum LXV *sub titulo Orosii percontantis et Augustini respondentis,* which is included in the writings of Augustine but is not a work of Augustine.

orphanus, i, *m., an orphan.*

orthodoxus, a, um, *adj., orthodox.* St. Thomas quotes freely from the *De Fide Orthodoxa,* the Orthodox Faith, of John Damascene.

ortus, us, *m.,* (1) *a rising of the heavenly bodies,* the opposite of *occasus,* (2) *a rise, beginning, origin.—ab ortu nativitatis, from birth.—in ortu, at birth.*

os, oris, *n., the mouth.* The following phrases are of frequent occurrence:—**peccatum oris,** *a sin of word.*—**proferre aliquid ore,** *to reveal something in words.*—**corde, ore, opere,** *in thought, word, and deed.*—**peccare ore,** *to sin by word.*—**confessio oris,** *confession in words, oral confession.*—**ore tenus,** *only so as to talk, orally.*

os, ossis, *n.,* (1) lit., *a bone,* (2) transf., *the stone* of fruit, i.e., fruit stones.

osculatio, onis, *f., a kissing,* used in the S.T. only in quot.

osculor, ari, atus, 1, *v. dep., to kiss.*

osculum, i, *n., a kiss.*

Oseas, ae, *m., Osee* or *Hosea,* one of the minor prophets whose career is known only by his prophecy. The introductory verses record that he carried on his ministry during the reigns of the Judean Kings Ozias, Joathan, Achaz, and Ezechias; and in the

nemesis, is, *f.*, *joy at the misfortune of another, malicious joy, jealousy*.

nemesiticus, a, um, *adj.*, *rejoicing in the trouble of others, envious*.

Nemesius, ii, *m.*, *Nemesius*, Bishop of Emesa at the end of the fourth century, of whom nothing is known except that he was author of a rather remarkable treatise, *De natura hominis*, of which chapters II and III appear as a separate work, *de Anima*, among the writings of Gregory Nyssene; being erroneously ascribed to that father. St. Thomas quotes the *De natura hominis*, referring it, however, to Gregory of Nyssa.

nemo, inis, *m.* and *f.*, *no one, no man.*—**nemo alius**, *no one else, no other man*.

nempe, *conj.*, (1) *namely*, (2) in stating an obvious fact, *without doubt*.

Neomenia, ae, *f.*, *the neomenia* or *new moon;* in Greek and Jewish antiquities, the time of the new moon, the beginning of the lunar month, also the festival held at that time.

neophytus, i, *m.*, *a neophyte, a new convert;* one newly admitted to a church or religious body; applied also to a priest or to a novice of a religious order.

nepos, otis, *m.* and *f.*, (1) *a grandson*, (2) *a brother's* or *sister's son, a nephew*.

Nepotianus, i, *m.*, *Nepotianus*, a presbyter at Altinum, under his uncle Heliodorus, the bishop of that place. His death in 396 elicited an interesting letter from Jerome to Heliodorus. It relates his relinquishment of a military life in favor of voluntary poverty and monachism, which he intended to pursue in Egypt, Mesopotamia, or the solitudes of the Dalmatian islands.

neptis, is, *f.*, *a niece*.

nequam, *adj.*, *indecl.*, of character, *worthless, vile, bad.*—**nequiter**, *adv.*, *wickedly*.

nequaquam, *adv.*, *in nowise, by no means, not at all*.

neque, (nec), *adv.* and *conj.*, *not, and not, also not.*—**neque** (nec) . . . **neque** (nec), *neither . . . nor.* —**necdum**, *and not yet, not yet*.

nequeo, ire, ivi and ii, itum, 4, *v. n.*, *not to be able, to be unable, cannot*, used with *inf*.

nequissimus, a, um, *adj.*, see *nequam*.

nequiter, *adv.*, see *nequam*.

nequitia, ae, *f.*, *wickedness, vileness, worthlessness*.

nervosus, a, um, *adj.*, *nervous, full of sinews, sinewy*.

nervus, i, *m.*, *a sinew, tendon, nerve*.

nescientia, ae, *f.*, *ignorance, of what one is not expected to know, nescience*.

nescio, ire, ivi or ii, itum, 4, *v. a.*, *not to know*, the opposite of *scire*.

Nesteros, otis, *m.*, *Nesteros*, a cenobite of the Egyptian desert whom Cassian visited in 395. Two of the *Conferences*, the fourteenth and fifteenth, are held with him, the subjects being *De Spirituali Scientia* and *De Charismatibus Divinis*. St. Thomas quotes Coll. XIV. 4, 5.

Nestoriani, orum, *m.*, see *Nestorianus*.

Nestorianus, a, um, *adj.*, *Nestorian*, of or belonging to Nestorius who was condemned as a heretic at the Council of Ephesus.—**Nestorius,** ii, *m.*, *Nestorius*, Patriarch of Constantinople (428) a vain orator without depth of thought or piety, objected to the title of "Mother of God" as applied to the Blessed Virgin. He maintained that the Blessed Virgin had given birth to the man Jesus, in whom the Son of God dwelt as in a temple; that there are two persons in Christ really distinct, the man Jesus and the Son of God, and that between them, there exists only an external union. The chief adversary of Nestorius was Cyril, Bishop of Alexandria.—**Nestoriani,** orum, *m.*, *the Nestorians, the followers of Nestorius*.

Nestorius, ii, *m.*, see *Nestorianus*.

neuter, tra, trum, *adj.*, (1) in gen., *neither the one nor the other, neither of two*, (2) in partic., of gender, with *genus, neuter*, neither masculine nor feminine.

neutraliter, *adv.*, *as a neuter, in a neuter sense, neutrally*.

nex, necis, *f.*, (1) *a violent death, murder, slaughter*, (2) *death, a natural death*.

nexus, us, *m.*, *a bond, tie, link*, (1) lit., *a link, bond*, a system by which the adjacent parts of a structure are bound together, (2) fig., (a) *a bond*, a binding force or influence, a cause of union, (b) *a tie, bond*, a binding agreement or covenant, (c) *a bond, a moral duty* or *obligation*.

Nicaea, ae, *f.*, *Nicaea*, a city of Bithynia on Lake Ascanius, the modern *Isnik* or *Nice*. The First Council of Nicaea was held in 325 on the occasion of the heresy of Arius. The Second Council of Nicaea was held in 787 to deal with Iconoclasm.—**Nicaenus,** a, um, *adj.*, *Nicene*.

Nicaenus, a, um, *adj.*, see *Nicaea*.

Nicetas, ae, *m.*, *Nicetas*, one of the interlocutors in the *Itinerarium Clementis*, a work attributed to St. Clement of Rome and regarded as of little reliability.

Nicodemus, i, *m.*, *Nicodemus*, saint, martyr. He was a Pharisee mentioned in St. John's Gospel, 7 and 19, as speaking in behalf of Jesus in the Sanhedrin, and assisting at His burial.

Nicolaus, i, *m.*, *Nicholas I*, saint, pope (857-867). He was born at Rome and died there. Elected after the disintegration of the empire of Charlemagne, he found Christianity threatened by laxity in the observance of moral and civil law. To uphold divine and Church law against princes and worldly bishops, he protected the minor clergy and suffragan bishops against their exactions. He upheld the right of appealing to Rome against the decisions of Hincmar of Rheims; defended the integrity of the marriage bond against Lothair II; and supported Ignatius, Patriarch of Constantinople, against the intruder, Photius (2) *Nicholas of Myra*, saint, confessor. He was born at Potara, Lycia, Asia Minor and died at Myra about 352. Although he is popular in the Greek as well as in the Latin Church, nothing is historically certain about him except that he was born at Myra in the fourth Century. In Germany, Switzerland, and the Netherlands it is the custom to make him the secret purveyor of gifts to children on Dec. 6.

nidifico, are, 1, *v. n., to build a nest.*

nidor, oris, *m., a smell.*

nidus, i, *m., a nest,* used fig.

niger, gra, grum, *adj., black, dark.*

nigredo, inis, *f., blackness, black color.*

nigromanticus, a, um, *adj., nigromantic,* of or belonging to, or used in nigromancy or magic.

nihil, (nihilum), *n., indecl., nothing,* the opposite of *ens.*—**ex nihilo nihil concluditur** (Pot. 3. 1 ob. 6), *from nothing, nothing can be concluded.*—**nihil fit proper vilius se,** *nothing is made because of the will of something that is less than it is itself.*—**omne, quod est ex nihilo, vertibile est in nihilum,** *what has arisen from nothing is convertible to nothing, not because it has a positive capacity not to be, but rather in so far as the creator can cease to support it in existence.*—**quod cedit in nihil, non resumitur idem numero,** *what disappears into nothing, no more returns as the same individual.*—**quod autem parum est, quasi nihil accipit ratio,** *what is only a little, reason holds as nothing.*—**nihilominus,** *adv., none the less, no less, nevertheless, notwithstanding.*

nihilominus, *adv.,* see *nihil.*

nimirum, *adv., surely, without doubt, doubtless,* used in the S.T. only in quot.

nimis, *adv.,* (1) lit., *too much, excessively, beyond measure,* (2) transf., *beyond measure, exceedingly.*

nimius, a, um, *adj.,* (1) lit., *beyond measure, excessive,* (2) transf., *beyond measure, exceedingly.*—**nimium,** ii, *n., too much, excess.*—**nimium,** *adv., too much, too.*

Ninive, es, *f., Nineveh,* the ancient capital of Assyria.—**Ninivitae,** arum, *m., the Ninevites, the inhabitants of Nineveh.*

Ninivitae, arum, *m.,* see *Ninive.*

Ninus, i, *m., Ninus,* the son of Belus, the first king of Assyria, husband of Semiramis, and builder of Nineveh.

nisi, *conj., if not, unless,* (1) (a) in gen., (b) with interrogatives and negatives, usually in a different clause, (c) after nihil, *save, but,* *than,* (d) nisi ut, *except that, unless,* (e) nisi quod, *except that which, save only that,* (f) nisi quia, *except because,* i.e., *until that,* (2) in combinations like nisi forte, *unless perhaps,* sometimes ironical.

niteo, ere, 2, *v. n., to shine, look bright,* (1) transf., (a) of persons, *to shine, look bright* or *beautiful,* (b) of wealth, *to shine,* (2) fig., *to shine, look* or *be beautiful.*

nitidus, a, um, *adj.,* (1) in gen., *bright, shining,* (2) of persons, *comely, handsome.*

nitor, i, nisus and nixus, 3, *v. dep. n.,* (1) lit., *to struggle, put forth great efforts,* (2) fig., (a) *to rely* or *depend on,* used with the *abl.,* (b) *to endeavor, strive.*

nitor, oris, *m., brightness, splendor, lustre, sheen,* (1) of body, *comeliness,* (2) of things in gen., *beauty,* (3) of soul, *comeliness, beauty,* (4) of conscience, *brightness.*

nix, nivis, *f., snow.*

nobilis, e, *adj.,* (1) in gen., *noble,* (a) having qualities or properties of a very high or admirable kind, (b) of parts of the body, (c) of places, *excellent,* distinguished by excellence of appearance or by renown, (d) characterized by moral superiority or dignity, (2) in particular, (a) *renowned, famous,* (b) *noble,* illustrious by rank, birth, title.—**nobilis,** is, *m., a nobleman.*—**nobiliter,** *adv., famously, excellently, nobly.*

nobilitas, atis, *f.,* (1) *rank, nobility, birth,* (2) *noble or excellent quality, excellence, superiority, dignity.*

nobiliter, *adv.,* see *nobilis.*

nobilito, are, avi, atum, 1, *v. a., to ennoble, improve.*

noceo, ere, ui, citum, 2, *v. n.* and *a., to do harm, do hurt to, inflict injury,* used (1) with *dat.,* (2) impers. pass., (3) absol., (4) act.—**nocens,** entis, *P. a.,* (1) *that commits a wicked action, guilty,* (2) *harmful, injurious.*

nocivus, a, um, *adj., hurtful, injurious, noxious.*

noctua, ae, *f., an owl.*

nocturnus, a, um, *adj., of* or *belonging to the night, nocturnal.*

nocumentum, i, *n., harm, damage, evil.*

nodus, i, *n., a knot* or *fold* on a lash; by met., for *scourges,* used in *pl.*

Noe, *indecl., Noe.*

Nolanus, a, um, *adj., of* or *belonging to Nola, Nolan.* Nola is a city of remote antiquity in Campania, founded by the Ausonians.

nolens, see *nolo.*

nolo, nolle, nolui, *v. irreg., not to wish, to be unwilling* in the sense of an action, the opposite of *velle.* On the difference between *nolle* and *non velle,* see *velle.*—**nolens,** entis, *P. a., unwilling,* opposite of *volens.*

noluntas, atis, *f., unwillingness,* in the sense of an action, the opposite of *voluntas.* Cf. **nolle.**

nomen, inis, *n.,* (1) *name, noun,* the *onoma* of Aristotle, which is opposed to verb, the *rema* of Aristotle, and in conjunction with it forms a sentence; synonym of *dictio, locutio,* and *terminus,* (2) *first name.*—On **casus nominis,** see *casus* under 4; on **communicatio nominis,** see *communicatio* under 1; on **prius secundum nominis rationem,** see *prior* under 1; on **qualitas nominis,** see *qualitas;* on **substantia nominis,** see *substantia* under 8.—Kinds of *nomen* in this (1) sense are: (a), **nomen absolutum** and **nomen relativum,** *the name with no reference to anything* and *that which expresses such,* i.e., the name that designates a thing in so far as it stands in no relationship to another, and that which designates it according to one or another relationship to another. (b), **nomen abstractum** and **nomen concretum seu concretivum,** *the name which indicates simply the nature* and *essence of a thing is abstracted in thought from its individual characterizations,* and *that name which so designates a thing as it exists in reality;* thus it expresses not simply its general nature and essence but also the individual characterizations which are connected with the same in reality.—(c), **nomen adiectivum** and **nomen substantivum,** *the name of the adjective* and *that of the substantive.*—(d), **nomen aequivocum seu pure ae-**

quivocum, **nomen analogum,** and **nomen synonymum,** *the equivocal name,* indicating something dissimilar which stands in no relation to anything else and *that which signifies something similar* or *the same.*—(e), **nomen analogum,** see *nomen aequivocum.*—(f), **nomen appellativum** and **nomen proprium,** *family name* or *surname* and *proper name.*—(g), **nomen collectivum** and **nomen singularis designati,** *the collective noun* or *name* and *that of the specific individual thing.*—(h), **nomen commune** and **nomen speciale,** *the common* or *the general name* and *the particular name.*—(i), **nomen communicabile,** and **nomen incommunicabile,** *the communicable* and *the incommunicable name.*—(j), **nomen compositum** and **nomen simplex,** *the composite* and *the single* or *simple name.*—(k), **nomen concretivum seu concretum,** see *nomen abstractum.*—(l), **nomen confusum** and **nomen distinctum,** *the confused* or *indefinite name* and *the definite name.*—(m), **nomen Dei seu divinum,** *the name of God.*—(n), **nomen differentiae, nomen generis,** and **nomen speciei,** *the name of difference in essence, the name of the genus,* and *that of the species of a thing.*—(o), **nomen diminutivum,** *the diminutive name.*—(p), **nomen divinum,** see *nomen Dei.*—(q), **nomen essentiale seu naturae** and **nomen personale seu**

personae, *the name of essence*
and *that of the person* or the
name which designates the nature and essence of a thing and
that which designates a person.
—(r), **nomen finitum** and **nomen
infinitum,** *the name which is
limited* or *definite in its meaning.*—(s), **nomen generis,** see *nomen differentiae.*—(t), **nomen incommunicabile,** see *nomen communicabile.*—(u), **nomen infinitum,** see *nomen finitum.*—(v),
nomen intellegibile, *the intelligible name.*—(w), **nomen intentionis seu intentionem significans**
and **nomen rei seu rem significans,** *the name that signifies the
relation* or *conception of a thing*
and *that which signifies the thing
itself.*—(x), **nomen intentionem
significans,** see *nomen intentionis.*—(y), **nomen metaphorice dictum seu symbolicum seu translativum,** *the name used in the metaphorical* or *symbolical sense.*—
(z), **nomen naturae,** see *nomen
essentiale.*—(a²), **nomen negationis seu negativum** and **nomen
privativum,** *the name that indicates a simple negation* and *that
which signifies a privation* or
lack.—(b²), **nomen negativum,** see
nomen negationis.—(c²), **nomen
notionale,** *the name that expresses a divine notion.*—(d²), **nomen
obliquum,** *the inflected noun.*—
(e²), **nomen partitivum,** *the partitive noun,* or *the noun expressing a part.*—(f²), **nomen personae,**
see *nomen essentiale.*—(g²), **no-**

men **personale,** see *nomen essentiale.*—(h²), **nomen potestatis,** *the
name that indicates the might* or
power of a being.—(i²), **nomen
primae impositionis seu intentionis** and **nomen secundae impositionis seu intentionis,** *the name
of the first attribution* or *of a
first notion which is the concrete
singular subject* and *the name of
the second attribution* or *of a
second notion* which signifies the
aspect of individuality of the
singular subject.*—(j²), **nomen primae intentionis,** see *nomen primae impositionis.*—(k²), **nomen
privativum,** see *nomen negationis.*—(l²), **nomen proprium,** see
nomen appellativum.—(m²), **nomen rei,** see *nomen intentionis.*—
(n²), **nomen relationis,** *the name
for the relation of one thing to
another.*—(o²), **nomen relativum,**
see *nomen absolutum.*—(p²), **nomen relativum secundum dici**
and **nomen relativum secundum
esse,** *the name which indicates a
relation which the mind applies
to things* and *that which indicates a relation which is present
by the very nature of the thing,
independent of the mind,* i.e.,
the name which designates directly a person or thing, and indirectly an accompanying relation to something like "father"
is secundum esse; and that word
which designates directly the relation of a person or a thing and
indirectly this person or thing itself like "mover" is secundum di-

ci.—(q²), **nomen rem significans,** see *nomen intentionis.*—(r²), **nomen secundae impositionis,** see *nomen primae impositionis.*—(s²), **nomen secundae intentionis,** see *nomen primae impositionis.*—(t²), **nomen simplex,** see *nomen compositum.*—(u²), **nomen singularis designati,** see *nomen collectivum.* —(v²), **nomen speciale,** see *nomen commune.*—(w²), **nomen speciei,** see *nomen differentiae.*— (x²), **nomen substantivum,** see *nomen adiectivum.*—(y²), **nomen symbolicum,** see *nomen metaphorice dictum.*—(z²), **nomen synonymum,** see *nomen aequivocum.*—(a²), **nomen tetragrammaton,** *the Hebrew name of Jahweh or Jehovah which consists of four letters.*—(b³), **nomen translativum,** see *nomen metaphorice dictum.*—(c³), **nomen verbale,** *the verb,* actionem et passionem consignificans.—**nomen et verbum magis interpretationis principia esse videntur, quam interpretationes,** *the noun* and *the verb seem to be principles of interpretation* and *explanation rather than the interpretations* and *principles themselves.*—**nominibus utendum est, ut plures seu secundum quod plures utuntur,** the translation of the Aristotelian passage: *tais men onomasiais ta pragmata prosagoreuteon kathaper hoi polloi* (Top. II, 2, 110 a. 16 f), *the nouns* or *names of things should be used as the majority use*

them.—**ratio quam significat nomen est conceptio intellectus de re significata per nomen,** see *conceptio* under 3.—**ratio quam significat nomen est definito,** see *definitio* under 2.

nominabilis, e, *adj., nominable, capable* or *worthy of being named.*

nominalis, e, *adj., belonging to a name, nominal.*—**nominalis,** is, *m., a nominalist.*—**nominaliter,** *adv., by name, expressly.*

nominaliter, *adv.,* see *nominalis.*

nominatio, onis, *f., name, designation.*

nomino, are, avi, atum, 1, *v. a., to call by name, name, nominate.* On **genus nominatum,** see *genus* under 2.—Kinds of *nominare* are: (a), **nominare metaphorice,** *to name something metaphorically.* —(b), **nominare positive,** *to name something in the positive sense,* i.e., in the sense that it appears as something definite in the reality of things.—(c), **nominare proprie** and **nominare symbolice,** *to name something in the proper* and *in the symbolic sense.*—(d), **nominare secundum quid** and **nominare simpliciter,** *to name something in a certain respect* or *with reference to something* and *to name something simply* or *absolutely.*—(e), **nominare simpliciter,** see *nominare secundum quid.*—(f), **nominare symbolice,** see *nominare proprie.*

non, *adv., not.*—**non solum ... sed etiam,** *not only ... but also.*—A weak negative before adverbs of emphatic assertion.—**non quod,** *not that.*—**non nisi,** *only.*—The negative force of *non* is not destroyed by a following *nec ... nec.*

nonaginta, *num, adj., ninety.*

nondum, *adv., not yet.*

non-ens, *non-entis, n., non-being, something that is not,* both in the logical and in the ontological senses, the opposite of *ens.*—Kinds of *non-ens* in the ontological sense of the word are: (a), **non-ens omnino seu purum seu simpliciter,** *non-being in general* or *the pure* or *simple non-being.* —(b), **non-ens per se** and **non-ens secundum accidens,** *non-being in itself* and *non-being with respect to something else.*—(c), **non-ens purum,** see *non-ens omnino.*—(d), **non-ens secundum accidens,** see *non-ens per se.*—(e), **non-ens secundum quid,** *non-being with reference to something.*—(f), **non-ens simpliciter,** see *non-ens omnino.*

nongenti, *ae, a, adj., card., nine-hundred.*

nonne, *adv.,* the interrogative *non,* expecting an affirmative answer, *not,* used in a direct interrogation.

nonnisi, *conj.,* see *non* and *nisi.*

nonnullus, *a, um, adj., some, several.*

nonumquam, *adv., sometimes.*

nono, *adv.,* see *nonus.*

nonus, *a, um, adj., ord., the ninth.*— **nona,** *ae, f.,* (sc. hora), *the ninth*

hour of the day, i.e., the third before sunset.—**nono,** *adv., ninthly.*

norma, *ae, f., a rule, pattern.*

nos, *nostrum,* etc., *we,* the plur. of *ego.*

nosco, *ere, novi, notum, 3, v. a., to get a knowledge of, become acquainted with, come to know, know;* in perf., *to have become acquainted with, have learned, know.*

noster, *stra, strum, pron. poss., our, our own; ours, of us.*

nota, *ae, f.,* (1) *note, sign, mark* (of distinction), synonym of *notio,* (2) *musical note* or *character.* Not found in the S.T. of St. Thomas.

notabilis, *e, adj., notable, capable of being noted* or *observed; noticeable, perceptible.*—**notabiliter,** *adv., notably, perceptibly.*

notabiliter *adv.,* see *notabilis.*

notarius, *ii, m., a secretary.*

notificatio, *onis, f., a notification, the action of making known, a notice, definition.*

notifico, *are, avi, atum, 1, v. a., to make known, explain.*

notio, *onis, f.,* (1) *note, sign, mark,* synonym of *nota,* (2) *note, sign, mark, distinguishing characteristic* of a divine person, (3) *notion, idea, conception.*—Kinds of *notio* in this (1) sense are: (a), **notio intellectualis,** *the intellectual notion.*—(b), **notio personae seu personalis,** *the mark of a divine person.*—(c), **notio personalis,** see *notio personae.*—One kind of *notio* in this (2) sense is: **notio ac-**

tiva, *the active mark of a divine person* or *the mark of such which consists of some activity.*

notionalis, e, *adj., consisting of* or *conveying ideas, expressing abstract conceptions, characterizing, notional, forming a distinguishing mark* especially with reference to the Divine Persons. On **actus notionalis,** see *actus* under 1; on **adiectivum notionale,** see *adiectivus;* on **dilectio notionalis,** see *dilectio* under 1; on **nomen notionale,** see *nomen* under 1; on **praedicatum notionale,** see *praedicatum;* on **verbum notionale,** see *verbum* under 1.—**notionaliter,** *adv., in the manner* or *sense of a notio, notionally.* On **dicere notionaliter,** see *dicere* under 3; on **sumere notionaliter,** see *sumere* under 3.

notionaliter, *adv.,* see *notionalis.*

notitia, ae, *f.,* (1) *a being known, celebrity, note, fame,* (2) *a knowing, knowledge, information, notion,* synonym of *scientia.*—On **cognitio notitiae,** see *cognitio* under 1; on **scientia simplicis notitiae,** see *scientia* under 2.—Kinds of *notitia* in this (1) sense are: (a), **notitia actualis,** *knowledge consisting in an action,* the opposite of *notitia habitualis,* i.e., *knowledge that has become static.*—(b), **notitia approbationis, notitia simplex seu simplicis intellegentiae** and **notitia visionis,** (a division of the Knowledge of God), *knowledge connected with an approval or consent of the will,*

simple knowledge or *knowledge after the manner of simple intellectual presentation* the object of which is all possible things and *knowledge after the manner of vision,* the object of which is all actual things.—(c), **notitia architectonica seu dominativa seu principativa,** *the governing* or *dominating* or *superior knowledge.*—(d), **notitia completa,** *the complete knowledge.*—(e), **notitia comprehensionis,** *the knowledge of comprehension* or *understanding.*—(f), **notitia dominativa,** see *notitia architectonica.*—(g), **notitia experimentalis,** *experimental knowledge.*—(h), **notitia mentis** and **notitia sensitiva,** *the intellectual knowledge* and *knowledge through the senses.*—(i), **notitia naturalis,** *natural knowledge.*—(j), **notitia praedestinationis,** *the knowledge of predestination,* i.e., the knowledge of God connected with predestination.—(k), **notitia principativa,** see *notitia architectonica.*—(l), **notitia privilegiata,** *the privileged knowledge* or *that forming a privilege.*—(m), **notitia sensitiva,** see *notitia mentis.*—(n), **notitia simplex,** see *notitia approbationis.*—(o), **notitia simplicis intellegentiae,** see *notitia approbationis.*—(p), **notitia visionis,** see *notitia approbationis.*

noto, are, avi, atum, 1, *v. a.,* (1) *to signify, to indicate, note,* (2) *to observe, note,* (3) *to mark* or *brand with infamy.*

notorius, a, um, *adj.,* (1) of facts, *well-known, common* or *generally known* (2) *notorious,* noted for some bad practice, quality etc.; *unfavorably known.*—**notoria ars,** *the notorious art* or *magic art.*

notus, a, um, *adj., known, noted, known as true, true,* synonym of *verus.*—Kinds of *notus* or *notum* are: (a), **notum confuse,** *known confusedly* or *indefinitely.*—(b), **notum in se seu secundum se seu naturae seu quoad naturam seu secundum propriam seu sui naturam seu naturaliter seu simpliciter** and **notum nobis seu quoad nos seu secundum nos,** *known in itself* or *according to itself* or *according to its nature* or *from nature* or *simply* or *absolutely* and *known by us* or *with reference to us.*—(c), **notum naturae,** see *notum in se.*—(d), **notum naturaliter,** see *notum in se.*—(e), **notum per accidens** and **notum per se,** *known by accident* and *by itself* or *as such.* Cf. *notum per aliud.* —(f), **notum per aliud** and **notam per se seu propter se,** *known through something else* and *known through itself.* Cf. *notum per accidens.*—(g), **notum per se,** see *notum per accidens* and *notum per aliud.*—(h), **notum propter se,** see *notum per aliud.*—(i), **notum quoad naturam,** see *notum in se.*—(j), **notum quoad nos,** see *notum in se.*—(k), **notum rationi seu secundum rationem** and **notum sensui seu secundum sensum,** *known to the intellect* and *to the senses* or *known with reference to our intellectual* and *sense knowledge.*—(l), **notum secundum nos,** see *notum in se.*—(m), **notum secundum propriam naturam,** see *notum in se.*—(n), **notum secundum rationem,** see *notum rationi.*—(o), **notum secundum se,** see *notum in se.*—(p), **notum secundum sensum,** see *notum rationi.*—(q), **notum secundum sui naturam,** see *notum in se.*—(r), **notum sensui,** see *notum rationi.*—(s), **notum simpliciter,** see *notum in se.*

Novatiani, orum, *m.,* see *Novatianus.*

Novatianus, i, *m., Novatian,* a schismatic of the third century and founder of the Novatians; he was a Roman priest, and made himself antipope. His name is given* as Novatus by Greek writers and also in the verses of Damasus and Prudentius, on account of the metre.—**Novatiani,** orum, *m., the Novatians,* a sect which contended that the Church had no authority either to absolve those who had lapsed through fear of persecution or who had fallen into gross sin after baptism, or to admit them to Holy Communion.

novem, *num., adj., card.,* nine.

novitas, atis, *f.,* (1) in gen., *a being new, newness, novelty,* (2) in particular, *rareness, strangeness, unusualness,* (3) fig., *newness, reformation.*

noviter, *adv.,* see *novus.*

novitius, ii, *m., a novice*, (1) *a new-ly-converted person*, (2) *an inex-perienced person;* one who is new to the circumstances in which he is placed.

novo, are, avi, atum, 1, *v. a., to re-new, make new.*

novus, a, um, *adj., new, not old, fresh, recent,* (I) lit., (A) *in gen.,* (1) not existing before, now made or brought into existence for the first time, (2) not previ-ously known; now known for the first time, (a) of things heard or inspired, (b) of feelings, (c) of persons or things, (d) *strange, unfamiliar,* (B) *in partic.,* (1) re-stored after disappearance, *new,* (2) other than the former or old, (3) morally or spiritually changed, *new,* (II) transf., in *sup. novissimus,* a, um, *last, latest.*—de novo, *anew, afresh.*—**noviter**, *adv., newly.*

nox, noctis, *f., night,* used (1) lit., (2) fig.—**media nox**, *midnight.*—**de nocte**, *by night.*—**de nocte profunda**, *late at night.*

noxius, a, um, *adj.,* (1) *hurtful, harmful, injurious, noxious,* (2) *guilty, culpable, criminal.*—**noxia**, ae, *f., harm, hurt, injury, dam-age.*

nubes, is, *f., a cloud,* (1) lit., (2) fig., Christian baptism is through water and the Holy Ghost, as instrumental and principal effi-cient causes, John III. 5. In the case of the Jews of the Exodus, the Holy Ghost was typified by the cloud, the water of baptism by the sea.—**lucida nubes**, *a bright cloud, the glory-cloud* or *Shechinah,* i.e., dwelling or pres-ence of God. The bright cloud was an indication of the presence of the Divine Majesty; God was accustomed to appear to Israel in a cloud.

nubilosus, a, um, *adj., cloudy, over-cast, lowering.*

nubo, ere, psi, ptum, 3, *v. a.* and *n., to marry, wed,* used *absol.,* and with the *dat.*—**nuptus**, a, um, *P. a., married, wedded.*—**nupta**, ae, *f., a wife.*

nude, *adv.,* see *nudus.*

nuditas, atis, *f., nakedness, nudity.*

nudius, *num.* (i.e. *nunc*) and *dius* = *dies;* the ending accommo-dated to that of the following numeral; *it is now the . . . day since;* always in connection with ordinal numerals; as *nudius ter-tius, three days ago, the day be-fore yesterday.*

nudo, are, avi, atum, 1, *v. a.,* (1) *to strip, lay bare, expose to view, uncover,* (2) fig., *to deprive of, strip of.*

nudus, a, um, *adj.,* (1) lit., (a) of the human figure or those parts of it which are usually clothed, *naked, uncovered,* (2) in partic., *poor, needy, destitute, forlorn,* (2) transf., (a) in gen., *bare, mere, pure, simple,* (b) of a truth, fact, statement, *naked, undis-guised, unveiled, simple, bare.*—**nude**, *adv., nakedly, openly, sim-ply.*

nugae, arum, *f., jokes, nonsense, idle speeches,* used in the S.T. only in quot.

nugatio, onis, *f., nugatoriness, the fact of being nugatory.*

nugatorie, *adv.,* see *nugatorius.*

nugatorius, a, um, *adj., trifling, worthless, useless.*—**nugatorie,** *adv., triflingly.*

nullatenus, *adv., in nowise, by no means.*

nullus, a, um, *adj., not any, none, no one,* the opposite of *omnis.* On **dicere de nullo,** see *dicere* under 3; on **dictio nulla,** see *dictio* under 2.

num, *adv.,* an interrog. particle, usually implying that a negative answer is expected.

numen, inis, *n., godhead, divinity, deity, divine majesty.*

numerabilis, e, *adj., numerable.*

numeralis, e, *adj., of* or *belonging to number, numeral.* On **distinctio numeralis,** see *distinctio* under 2; on **multitudo numeralis,** see *multitudo* under 1; on **proportio numeralis,** see *proportio* under 1; on **quantitas numeralis,** see *quantitas* under 1; on **terminus numeralis,** see *terminus* under 5; on **unitas numeralis,** see *unitas.*

numeratio, onis, *f., numeration, numbering, reckoning.*

numeratus, a, um, *P. a.,* see *numero.*

numero, are, avi, atum, 1, *v. a.,* (1) lit., *to count, number, reckon,* (2) fig., *to account, reckon, es-*

teem, consider as a thing.—**numeratus,** a, um, *P. a., numbered.*

numerosus, a, um, *adj., numerous.*

numerus, i, *m., a number,* synonym of *multitudo.* Cf. *multitudo* under 3. On **alius numero,** see *alius;* on **differentia secundum numerum,** see *differentia;* on **differre numerum,** see *differre* under 2; on **distinctio secundum numerum,** see *distinctio* under 2; on **diversitas in numero seu secundum numerum,** see *diversitas;* on **diversus numerus,** see *diversus;* on **forma secundum numerum,** see *forma* under 2; on **idem numerus seu in numero seu secundum numerum,** see *idem;* on **infinitum in numero seu secundum numerum,** see *infinitus;* on **multum numero seu secundum numerum,** see *multus* under 1; on **passio numero,** see *passio* under 1; on **plures numero,** see *plus;* on **ponere in numero,** see *ponere* under 1; on **principium numero,** see *principium;* on **quaestio in numero ponens et non ponens in numero,** see *quaestio;* on **qualitas numero,** see *qualitas;* on **quantitas numero,** see *quantitas* under 1; on **substantia numero,** see *substantia* under 8; on **unitas secundum numerum,** see *unitas;* on **unum numero seu secundum numerum,** see *unus.*—**in numero esse,** *to be present in number.*— Kinds of *numerus* are: (a), **numerus absolute acceptus seu absolutus seu abstractus seu separatus seu simplex seu simpliciter seu**

simpliciter prolatus seu extra numeratum existens seu unitatum and **numerus applicatus ad res seu numeratus seu in numerato seu in sensibilibus exsistens seu rerum,** *the number abstracted* or *separated in thought* or *the simply comprehended* or *expressed number* or *the number existing outside the numbered* or *the number existing outside mathematical unity* and *the number applied to things* or *the number actually counting* or *the number existing in counted things.*—(b), **numerus absolutus,** see *numerus absolute acceptus.*—(c), **numerus abstractus,** see *numerus absolute acceptus.*—(d), **numerus applicatus ad res,** see *numerus absolute acceptus.*—(e), **numerus compositus** and **numerus incompositus,** *the compound* and *the uncompounded number.* Cf. *numerus primus.*—(f), **numerus cubicus,** and **numerus quadratus,** *the cubic* (to the third degree) and *the square number* (to the second degree).—(g), **numerus determinatus** and **numerus indeterminatus,** *the determined* and *the undetermined number.*—(h), **numerus discretus,** *the separated* or *special number.*—(i), **numerus duplex sesquitertius** and **numerus duplex sesquiquartus,** *the number which is* 2⅓ *times larger* and *that which is* 2¼ *times larger than another.*—(j), **numerus duplus sesquialter, numerus triplus sesquialter,** and **numerus quad-**ruplus sesquialter, *the number which contains another within itself* 2½ *times, that which contains another* 3½ *times,* and *that which contains another* 4½ *times.*—(k), **numerus duplus superbipartiens** and **numerus duplus supertripartiens,** *the number which is twice as large as another* and *which when divided by the latter remains two* and *three respectively.*—(l), **numerus extra numerum exsistens,** see *numerus absolute acceptus.*—(m), **numerus impar** and **numerus par,** *the uneven* and *the even number.*—(n), **numerus imperfectus** and **numerus perfectus,** *the imperfect* and *the perfect number.* In the latter, the sum of the factors equals the product of the factors. Cf. *numerus superfluus.*—(o), **numerus incompositus,** see *numerus compositus.*—(p), **numerus indeterminatus,** see *numerus determinatus.*—(q), **numerus in sensibilibus existens,** see *numerus absolute acceptus.*—(r), **numerus multiplex** and **numerus submultiplex,** *the number which is a multiple of another* and *in which the latter is contained several times.*—(s), **numerus multiplex superparticularis** and **numerus multiplex superpartiens,** *the number which includes another number several times* and *still exceeds this by a fraction whose numerator is one* and *greater than one respectively.*—(t), **numerus multiplex superpartiens,** see *numerus multiplex* *superparticularis.*—(u), **numerus numeratus,** see *numerus absolute acceptus.*—(v), **numerus par,** see *numerus impar.*—(w), **numerus perfectus,** see *numerus imperfectus.*—(x), **numerus pluralis** and **numerus singularis,** *the plural* and *the singular number.*—(y), **numerus primus,** *the first* or *prime number.* Cf. *numerus compositus.*—(z), **numerus quadratus,** see *numerus cubicus.*—(a²), **numerus quadruplus sesquialter,** see *numerus sesquialter.*—(b²), **numerus qualis,** *the number conditioned in such a way* or *a number with a quality.* Cf. *qualitas numeri* under *qualitas.*—(c²), **numerus rerum,** see *numerus absolute acceptus.*—(d²), **numerus separatus,** see *numerus absolute acceptus.*—(e²), **numerus separatus,** see *numerus absolute acceptus.*—(f²), **numerus sesquialter, numerus sesquitertius,** and **numerus sesquiquartus,** *the number which is* 1½ *times greater, that which is* 1⅓ *times greater* and *that which is* 1¼ *times greater than another.*—(g²), **numerus sesquiquartus,** see *numerus sesquialter.*—(h²), **numerus sesquitertius,** see *numerus sesquialter.*—(i²), **numerus simplex seu simpliciter seu simpliciter prolatus,** see *numerus absolute acceptus.*—(j²), **numerus singularis,** see *numerus pluralis.*—(k²), **numerus solidus** and **numerus superficialis,** *the tri-dimensional* or *the two-dimensional number.*—(l²), **nume-**

rus submultiplex, see *numerus multiplex.*—(m²), **numerus submultiplex subparticularis** and **numerus submultiplex subpartiens,** *the number which is contained in a numerus multiplex superparticularis* and *that which is contained in a numerus multiplex superpartiens.*—(n²), **numerus submultiplex subpartiens,** see *numerus submultiplex subparticularis.*—(o²), **numerus subparticularis,** see *numerus superparticularis.*—(p²), **numerus subpartiens,** see *numerus superpartiens.*—(q²), **numerus superficialis,** see *numerus solidus.*—(r²), **numerus superbipartiens, numerus supertripartiens,** and **numerus superquadripartiens,** *the number which when divided by another exceeds it by a fraction whose numerator is respectively* 2, 3, and 4.—(s²), **numerus superfluus,** the translation of the Aristotelian expression *to peritton, the superfluous* or *excessive number,* i.e., the sum of the factors exceeds the product of the factors. Cf. *numerous imperfectus.*—(t²) **numerous superparticularis** and **numerous subparticularis,** *the number which exceeds another number divided within it by a fraction whose numerator is one,* and *the number exceeded in this case.*—(u²), **numerus superpartiens** and **numerus subpartiens,** *the number which exceeds another number divided in it by a fraction whose numerator is greater* *than one* and *the number exceeded in this case.*—(v²), **numerus superquadripartiens**, see *numerus superbipartiens.*—(w²), **numerus supertripartiens**, see *numerus superbipartiens.*—(x²), **numerus triplus sesqualiter**, see *numerus duplus sesquialter.*—(y²), **numerus unitatum**, see *numerus absolute acceptus.*—**nullus numerus est infinitus**, *there is no infinite number*, i.e., it is a contradiction in terms, since number implies definite limit.

numisma, atis, *n., money, coin, a piece of money.*

nummus, i, *m., a coin, a piece of money, money.*

numquam, or **nunquam**, *adv., at no time, never.*

numquid, *adv., interrog.*, used in a direct interrogation where there is no corresponding term in English.

nunc, *adv., now, at present, at this time*, synonym of *instans*, the opposite of *tunc.*—Kinds of *nunc* are: (a), **nunc aeternitatis seu stans**, **nunc aevi** and **nunc temporis seu fluens**, *the present of eternity* or *the static present, the present of everlasting duration* and *the present of time* or *the fleeting present.*—(b), **nunc aevi**, see *nunc aeternitatis.*—(c), **nunc fluens**, see *nunc aeternitatis.*—(d), **nunc per aliquid sui seu secundum aliquid sui seu secundum alterum** and **nunc primo et per se seu secundum seipsum**, *that*

which is called present secondarily with reference to something else or *according to a part of it*, and *that which is called present in the first place* and *completely according to itself.*—(e), **nunc primo et per se**, see *nunc per aliquid sui.*—(f), **nunc secundum aliquid sui**, see *nunc per aliquid sui.*—(g), **nunc secundum alterum**, see *nunc per aliquid sui.*—(h), **nunc secundum seipsum**, see *nunc per aliquid sui.*—(i), **nunc signatum**, *the signified* or *determined present.*—(j), **nunc stans**, see *nunc aeternitatis.*—(k), **nunc temporis**, see *nunc aeternitatis.*

nuncupatio, onis, *f., a name, appellation*, used in the S.T. only in quot.

nuncupo, are, avi, atum, 1, *v. a., to name, designate, mention.*

nundinae, arum, *f., trade, traffic, marketing*, used in the S.T. only in quot.

nuntio, are, avi, atum, 1, *v. a., to announce, declare, report, inform, make known*, used (1) absol., (2) with *acc.* of thing and *dat.* of person, (3) *acc.* alone, (4) in the pass.

nuntium, i, *n., an announcement, message, news.*

nuntius, ii, *m., a messenger.*

nuper, *adv., newly, lately, recently, not long ago.*

nupta, ae, *f.*, see *nubo.*

nuptiae, arum, *f., a marriage, wedding nuptials.*

nuptialis, e, *adj., of* or *belonging to*

a wedding, nuptial.—**nuptialiter,** *adv., as at a wedding, nuptially.*

nuptialiter, *adv.,* see *nuptialis.*

nusquam, *adv., nowhere, in no place.*

nutrimentalis, e, *adj., nourishing, nurturing,* synonym of *nutritivus.* On **humidum nutrimentale,** see *humidus.*

nutrimentum, i, *n.,* (1) lit., *nourishment, nutriment,* (2) fig., *support, nourishment.*

nutrio, ire, ivi, and ii, itum, (I) lit., (1) *to nourish, feed, rear, bring up,* (2) transf., *to support, maintain, nourish,* (a) of persons, (b) of plants, (c) of parts of the body, (d) of inanimate things, (II) fig., *to nourish, cherish, rear, bring up.*

nutritio, onis, *f.,* (1) *nourishment, food,* (2) *nutrition,* the sum of the processes by which an animal or plant absorbs, or takes in and utilizes food substances, (3) the action of *bringing up, rearing.*

nutritius, ii, *m., a bringer up, foster father.*

nutritivus, a, um, *adj.,* (1) *nourishing, nurturing,* synonym of *nutrimentalis,* (2) *vegetative, vegatatively active,* synonym of *vegetativus.*—On **potentia nutritiva,** see *potentia* under 2; on **virtus nutritiva,** see *virtus* under 1.—On **anima nutritiva,** see *anima* under 1; on **operatio nutritiva,** see *operatio* under 2; on **pars nutritiva,** see *pars* under 1; on **vita nutritiva,** see *vita* under 1.—**nutritivum sc. genus, potentiarum animae,** the translation of Aristotle's *threptikon, the vegetative genus of the soul's potentialities.*

nutrix, icis, *f., a nurse,* used lit. and fig.

nutus, us, *m.,* (1) lit., *a nod, gesture,* (2) fig., *command, will, pleasure.*

nux, nucis, *f., a nut.*

Nyssenus, a, um, *adj., Nyssene, of Nyssa* in Cappadocia.

O

o, *interj.,* the commonest exclamation of joy, astonishment, desire, grief, indignation, etc.; *O!, Oh!* used with the *voc.,* used in the S.T. only in quot.

ob, *prep.* with *acc.,* (1) to indicate the object or cause, *on account of, for, because of, by reason of,* (2) with *id* and *hoc, on that account, for this reason, therefore,* (a) with *id,* (b) with *hoc.*

obcaeco, are, avi, atum, 1, *v. a., to blind, make blind,* used fig., used in the S.T. only in quot.

obdormio, ire, ivi, itum, 4, *v. n.* and *a., to fall asleep.*

obduco, ere, xi, ctum, 3, *v. a., to draw* or *spread over* or *draw,* used in the S.T. only in quot.

obduratio, onis, *f., a hardening;* of the mind, *obduration, obduracy, hardness* of the heart.

obduro, are, avi, atum, 1, *v. a.* and *n., to render hard, to harden,* used fig.

obedibilis, e, *adj., capable of obedience, docile.*

obedienter, *adv.,* see *obedio.*

obedientia, ae, *f.,* see *oboedientia.*

obedientialis, e, *adj., obediential; of, pertaining to, of the nature of,* or *characterized by obedience.*

obedio, ire, ivi or ii, itum, 4, *v. n., to obey, yield obedience to, to be subject to,* used with the *dat.* and *absol.*—**obediens,** entis, *P. a., obedient, pliant,* used with the *dat.*—**obedienter,** *adv., obediently.*

obeo, ire, ii, itum, 4, *v. n.* and *a., to die.*

oberro, are, avi, atum, 1, *v. n., to go astray, to miss intellectual truth,* used fig.

obex, icis, *m.* and *f., a hindrance, impediment, obstacle.*

obfirmatus, a, um, *P. a., firm, resolute, fixed.*

obicio, ere, ieci, iectum, 3, *v. a.,* (1) in gen., *to object,* (a) *to bring forward* or *state in opposition;* to adduce as a reason against something, to urge as an objection, used with *in contrarium,* (b) to bring forward as a reason, ground, instance, *to adduce, say, remark, point out,* used with *de,* with *quod,* (2) in partic., (a) to bring as a charge against anyone; to attribute to anyone as a fault or crime, *cast in one's teeth, accuse one of, reproach*

with, used with *acc.* of the thing and *dat.* of the person, with the *acc.* alone, (b) *to impart* aliquid alicui.

obitus, us, *m., death.*

obiectio, onis, *f., an objection,* that which is or may be presented in opposition; *an adverse reason* or *argument.*

obiectum, i, *n., subject matter, subject, object* of an action or of a faculty or of a *habitus,* synonym of *materia circa quam, oppositum,* and *subiectum.* On **cognoscere in obiecto cognito,** see *cognoscere* under 2; on **frui sicut obiecto,** see *frui;* on **libertas quantum ad obiectum,** see *libertas* under 2.—**ratio seu ratio formalis obiecti,** *the formal relationship of a thing to a faculty* or *the precise aspect under which it is object.*—Kinds of *obiectum* are: (a), **obiectum formale seu formaliter acceptum** and **obiectum materiale seu materialiter acceptum,** *the formal object* or *the object formally considered,* i.e., precisely as object, and *the material object* or *the object materially considered as underlying many formalities,* i.e., that manner of being or relationship of being on the part of a thing whereby it is made the object of this or that action, which serves as regards the thing itself as form to matter, and this thing in relation to or for itself taking no account of that manner of being or relationship of being.—(b), **obiectum ma-**

teriale seu materialiter acceptum, see *obiectum formale.*—(c), **obiectum per accidens,** and **obiectum per se,** *an object indirectly through something else* and *an object directly* and *through itself,* i.e., that which is accidentally and that which is itself the object of an action or a faculty.—(d), **obiectum per se,** see *obiectum per accidens.*—(e), **obiectum primo seu principale** and **obiectum secundarium,** *the primary* or *principal object* (*formal*) and *the secondary object* (*formal*) *which is consequent upon the first.*—(f), **obiectum principale,** see *obiectum primo.*—(g), **obiectum proprium,** *the proper* or *characteristic object,* which is identical according to the subject with *obiectum primo seu principale* and is the opposite of *obiectum commune,* i.e., the object common to several actions and faculties.— (h), **obiectum secundarium,** see *obiectum primo.*—(i), **obiectum virtutis,** see *virtus* under 5.

obiurgatio, onis, *f., a chiding, reproof.*

obiurgo, are, avi, atum, 1, *v. a., to chide, upbraid, rebuke.*

oblatio, onis, *f., an offering, presenting, a giving* or *bestowing gratuitously, gift.*—On the difference between *oblatio* and *sacrificium,* see *sacrificium.*

oblectamentum, i, *n., a delight, pleasure,* used in the S.T. only in quot.

oblectatio, onis, *f., a delighting, delight;* **oblectatio carnis,** *the lust of the flesh;* used in the S.T. only in quot.

oblecto, are, avi, atum, 1, *v. a., to delight, to please.*

obligatio, onis, *f.,* (1) in gen., *a binding,* used fig., *a bond* by which one is held captive, (2) in partic., *an obligation,* (a) *an agreement,* a concurrence in an engagement that something shall be done or omitted, (b) *an obligation,* a formal and binding agreement or acknowledgement of a liability to pay a certain sum, (c) that which obligates or constrains; the binding power of a vow, oath, promise, etc., (d) that which a person is bound to do or forbear; any duty imposed by law, promise or contract, (e) the state of being obligated or placed under obligation because of a favor received.

obligativus, a, um, *adj., impeding, restraining.*

obligatorius, a, um, *adj., binding, obligatory.*

obligo, are, avi, atum, 1, *v. a.,* (1) in gen., *to bind, to restrain,* or *hold* by authority, law, duty, promise, vow or other moral tie, (2) in partic., (a) *to bind* or *devote* something to a particular use, (b) *to plight, to put* something in danger of forfeiture, (3) *pass.,* (a) *to be obliged* to do something by a legal or moral tie, (b) *to be bound* or *attached* to someone by allegiance or duty, (c) *to be bound* by the ties of gratitude; to be indebted to a person for something, (4) reflex., *to pledge, lay one's self* under constraint or obligation with respect to performance, (5) Jurid. t.t., *to pledge* something as security.—The following phrases are of frequent occurrence: **obligare aliquem ad peccatum mortale**, *to bind someone under pain of mortal sin.*—**obligare ad peccatum**, *to bind under pain of sin.*—**obligare se ad poenam**, *to bind oneself to punishment.*—**obligare ad mortale**, *to bind under pain of mortal sin.*—**obligatus**, a, um, *P. a.*, (1) *bondaged, enslaved, reduced to slavery*, (2) *bound, fettered*, (3) *bound, under obligation.*

oblique, *adv.*, see *obliquus*.

obliquitas, atis, *f.*, *obliqueness.*

obliquo, are, avi, atum, 1, *v. a.*, *to turn aside in an oblique direction*, used fig.—**obliquatus**, a, um, *P. a.*, *deflected.*

obliquus, a, um, *adj.*, (1) *sidelong, slanting, awry, oblique, collateral, parabolic*, when applied to motion as opposed to rectilineal, (2) *oblique case* in declension, the grammatical sense.—On **circulus obliquus**, see *circulus* under 1; on **motus obliquus**, see *motus* under 1; on **nomen obliquum**, see *nomen* under 1.—On **casus obliquus**, see *casus* under 5.—**in obliquo**, *in the grammatical case of an inflection or declension*, the opposite of *in recto*.

On **importare in obliquo**, see *importare* under 2; on **ponere in obliquo**, see *ponere* under 1; on **praedicare in obliquo**, see *praedicare* under 2; on **significare in obliquo**, see *significare.*—**oblique**, *adv., in an indirect manner, in a round-about way, obliquely*, synonym of *indirecte*, the opposite of *directe.*

oblitus, a, um, *P. a.*, see *obliviscor.*

oblivio, onis, *f.*, (1) *lit., a being forgotten, oblivion, forgetfulness*, (2) transf., *a forgetting, forgetfulness.*

obliviosus, a, um, *adj., forgetful.*

obliviscor, i, litus, 3, *v. dep., to forget*, used with (1) *acc.* of the thing, (2) *gen.* of the thing, (3) the *inf.*—**oblitus**, a, um, *adj., forgotten.*

oblongus, a, um, *adj., longish, protruding.*

obloquor, i, locutus, 3, *v. dep., to speak evil about someone.*

obmutesco, ere, tui, 3, *v. inch., n., to be speechless, mute, silent.*

obnoxio, are, 1, *v. a., to render subject* or *obnoxious* to any thing, used in the S.T. only in quot.

obnoxius, a, um, *adj.*, (1) *lit.*, (a) *subject, liable to punishment, obnoxious to punishment, punishable*, (b) *obnoxious, reprehensible, blameworthy*, (c) *subject to, liable, exposed* to sin, death etc., (2) transf., (a) *answerable, responsible, the occasion of*, (b) *subject* to the authority of, *answerable* to some authority, (c) *subject to* or *influenced by.*

obnubilo, are, avi, atum, 1, *v. a., to darken, cloud, obscure.*

oboedientia, ae, *f.*, (1) *obedience* in general, opposite to *inoboedientia*, (2) voluntary *obedience* to an ecclesiastical superior.—On **debitum oboedientiae**, see *debitus* under 1; on **potentia oboedientiae**, see *potentia* under 4.—On **consilium oboedientiae**, see *consilium* under 2; on **necessitas oboedientiae seu oboedientia consequens**, see *necessitas* under 1; on **servitus oboedientiae**, see *servitus* under 2; on **votum oboedientiae**, see *votum* under 1.—Kinds of *oboedientia* in this (2) sense are: (a), **oboedientia discreta** and **oboedientia indiscreta**, *the discrete obedience* and *the indiscrete obedience*, or *the obedience connected with discretion* and *that with indiscretion.*—(b), **oboedientia imperfecta** and **oboedientia perfecta**, *the imperfect* and *the perfect obedience.*—(c), **oboedientia indiscreta**, see *oboedientia discreta.*—(d), **oboedientia perfecta**, see *oboedientia imperfecta.*

oboedientialis, e, *adj., obeying, obedient,* not found in the S.T. of St. Thomas. On **potentia oboedientialis**, see *potentia* under 4; on **ratio oboedientialis**, see *ratio* under 11 and 12.

obolus, i, *m., an obol, a small Greek coin, the sixth part of a drachma,* equivalent to three and a half cents.

obrepo, ere, psi, ptum, 3, *v. n., to steal upon,* used with the *dat.*

obruo, ere, rui, utum, 3, *v. a., to overcome, overpower, eclipse.*

obscoenitas, atis, *f., moral impurity, obscenity, unchastity.*

obscoenus, a, um, *adj., obscene.*

obscuratio, onis, *f.*, (1) lit., *a being dark, darkness,* (2) fig., *obscurity, indistinctness, uncertainty.*

obscure, *adv.*, of speech, *obscurely, indistinctly.*

obscuritas, atis, *f.*, (1) lit., *a being dark, darkness, obscurity,* (2) fig., *obscurity, indistinctness, uncertainty.*

obscuro, are, avi, atum, 1, *v. a.*, (1) lit., (a) *to render dark, to darken, obscure,* (b) transf., *to bedim, diminish, lessen,* (2) fig., (a) *to obscure, darken, becloud,* (b) *to obscure, render unknown.*

obscurus, a, um, *adj.*, (1) lit., (a) of places, *dark,* (b) of a body or surface not reflecting or emitting light, *opaque,* (c) of violence, *harmful, derogatory,* (d) of lowly things, *hidden, obscure,* (2) fig., (a) of knowledge, words, speech, *obscure, unintelligible,* (b) of God's image in the sinner's soul, *dim.*

obsecratio, onis, *f., obsecration, supplication, earnest entreaty.*

obsecro, are, avi, atum, 1, *v. a., to pray, supplicate, implore,* used with the *acc.* of the *person* or *thing.*

obsequium, ii, *n.*, (I) in gen., (1) *obsequiousness, compliance to excess,* (2) *obedience, compli-*

ance, deference, (II) in partic., *service, duty, occupation, employment,* the performance of labor for the benefit of another or at another's command or in fulfillment of duty, (1) *service* to God and to the Church, spiritual serving as shown by obedience, good works and love, (2) *service* to creatures, (a) of a servant or slave, (b) of a child to its parents, *help* of a material nature, *assistance, service* of any kind, (c) of a mother to its child, *care, attention,* (d) to a neighbor, (e) to authority, (3) *service, occupation, employment,* that set of duties upon which one is regularly employed.—**corporale obsequium,** *bodily homage* or *courtesy rendered.*

obsequor, i, cutus, 3, *v. dep., to accommodate one's self* to the will of a person; *to comply with, yield to, submit to,* (1) *to submit* to something, *discharge* the duty of, (2) *to obey* someone, (3) *to wait on* someone, serve, (4) *to help, aid* someone, used with the *dat.* of the *person* or *thing.*—**obsequens,** entis, *P. a., obedient, yielding, compliant.*

observantia, ae, *f.,* (1) *observance, attentive consideration,* synonym of *observatio,* (2) as a potential part of the virtue of justice, *the esteem* and *respect due to authority,* (3) *observance, following, performance,* (4) *observance, exercise, performance, practice,* esp. the magical arts of discovering secrets and foretelling the future.—On the difference between *observantia* and *pietas,* see *pietas* under 1. On **pars observantiae,** see *pars* under 1.—Kinds of *observantia* in this (3) sense are: (a), **observantia caeremonialis,** *observance of a ceremonial prescription of the Old Testament,*—(b), **observantia legalis seu legis,** *the observance of the Mosaic law,* by which is understood first law in general, then the law of the Old Testament.—(c), **observantia legis,** see *observantia legalis.*—On **superstitio observantiarum,** see *superstitio.*—Kinds of *observantia* in this (4) sense are: (a), **observantia carnalis,** and **observantia spiritualis,** *the bodily* or *physical* and *the immaterial* or *spiritual performance.*—(b), **observantia illicita,** *fortune-telling.*—(c), **observantia regularis,** *regular observance,* i.e., living according to rule.—(d), **observantia spiritualis,** see *observantia carnalis.*—(e), **observantia vana,** *fortune-telling.*

observatio, onis, *f.,* (1) *observance, attentive consideration,* synonym of *observantia,* (2) *observance, following, performance,* (3) *observance, exercise, performance, use.*—On **superstitio observationum,** see *superstitio.*—Kinds of *observatio* in this (3) sense are: (a), **observatio illicita,** *fortune-telling.*—(b), **observatio legalis,** *the observance of the prescriptions of the Old Testament.*—(c),

observatio superstitiosa, *the superstitious exercise.*—(d), **observatio vana,** *fortune-telling.*

observator, oris, *m., an observer;* **observator legis,** *an observer of the law,* i.e., *one who obeys it.*

observo, are, avi, atum, 1, *v. a.,* (I) *to observe, to attend to* in practice; *to keep, follow,* (1) *to observe* a law, command, custom, practice, covenant or anything prescribed or fixed, (2) *to follow* a principle or rule of action, (3) *to observe, celebrate duly, to solemnize* in the prescribed way a religious rite, ceremony, etc., (4) *to follow the practice, be in the habit of doing something,* (II) *to observe, to attend to* with the mind, *to mark, perceive, observe,* (1) *to give close attention to* with the purpose of hearing, (2) *to inspect* or *regard with attention* for the purpose of divination, (3) *to watch for* in order to take advantage of a proper time or opportunity, (4) *to consider, take into consideration,* (5) *to take notice of* any astronomical feature, (III) *to observe, utter* by way of remark, (IV) by catachresis, *to keep, hold, retain* something.

obsessus, a, um, *P. a.,* (1) lit., of a city, *beseiged,* (2) of an evil spirit, *obsessed, assailed* or *harassed* by an evil spirit.

obsidio, onis, *f., a siege, blockade* of a place, used in the S.T. only in quot.

obsisto, ere, stiti, stitum, 3, *v. n., to set one's will against; to oppose, resist, withstand.*

obsolesco, ere, levi, letum, 3, *v. inch. n., to grow dim, fall into disuse, lose value.*—**obsoletus,** a, um, *P. a., obsolete.*

obsoletus, a, um, *P. a.,* see *obsolesco.*

obstaculum, i, *n., an obstacle, hindrance,* used lit and fig.

obstetrix, icis, *f., a midwife.*

obstinate, *adv.,* see *obstinatus.*

obstinatio, onis, *f., determination, stubbornness, obstinacy.*—One kind of *obstinatio* is: **obstinatio imperfecta,** *the imperfect obstinacy.*

obstinatus, a, um, *P. a., firmly set, fixed,* in a bad sense, *stubborn, obstinate.*—**obstinate,** *adv., wilfully.*

obsto, are, stiti, atum, 1, *v. n.,* (1) lit., *to stand before* or *against* anything, (2) in partic., *to withstand, thwart, hinder, oppose,* used with the *dat.,* absol.—*impers.,* **nec obstat,** *it doesn't matter.*

obstrictus, a, um, *P. a.,* see *obstringo.*

obstringo, ere, strinxi, strictum, 3, *v. a., to bind, fetter, hamper; to oblige, lay under obligation.*—**obstrictus,** a, um, *P. a., bound, obliged.*

obstupescibilis, e, *adj., possible of being confounded, amazed, benumbed,* used in the S.T. only in quot.

obstupesco, ere, ui, 3, *v. inch. n.* and *a.,* (1) lit., *to become senseless, lose feeling,* (2) fig., *to be astonished, amazed.*

obsum, obesse, obfui or offui, *v. n., to injure, hurt, be prejudicial to,* used with the *dative.*

obtego, ere, xi, ctum, 3, *v. a.,* (1) lit., *to cover over,* for concealment, (2) fig., *to veil, conceal, keep secret.*

obtempero, are, avi, atum, 1, *v. a., to comply with, attend to, submit to, obey,* used with the *dat.*

obtenebratio, onis, *f., darkness,* used fig.

obtenebresco, ere, *v. inch. n., to become* or *grow dark.*

obtenebro, are, avi, atum, *v. a., to make dark, to darken,* used lit. and fig.

obtentus, us, *m., a pretext, pretence.*

obtestans, antis, *P. a., imploring, supplicating.*

obtineo, ere, tinui, tentum, 2, *v. a.* and *n.,* (1) *act.,* (a) *to hold, have, possess; to preserve, keep, maintain,* (b) *to get possession of; to gain, acquire, obtain* something, (2) *neutr., to obtain, prevail, stand.*

obtundo, ere, tudi, tusum, 3, *v. a., to weaken, dull.*—obtusus, a, um, *P. a., dull, blunt.*

obtusio, onis, *f., bluntness, dullness.*

obtusus, a, um, *P. a.,* see *obtundo.*

obtutus, us, *m.,* (1) *the eye,* (2) fig., *act of viewing attentively, contemplation.*

obumbrate, see *obumbro.*

obumbratio, onis, *f., a shadow, darkness,* used fig., used in the S.T. only in quot.

obumbratus, a, um, see *obumbro.*

obumbro, are, avi, atum, 1, *v. a., to overshadow, shade, obscure, darken.*—obumbratus, a, um, *P. a., obscured, darkened.* On **cognitio obumbrata,** see *cognitio* under 2; on **ratio obumbrata,** see *ratio* under 3.—obumbrate, *adv., obscurely, under a veil.*

obvenio, ire, veni, ventum, 4, *v. n., to fall to one's lot.*

obviam, *adv., in the way,* hence, with verbs of motion (in a good or bad sense) *towards, against, to meet.*

obviatio, onis, *f., a saluting, a salutation.*

obvio, are, avi, 1, *v. n.,* (1) in gen., *to meet,* (2) in partic., (a) in a hostile sense, *to withstand, resist, oppose,* (b) *to obviate.*—(1), quia superiores caeteris apparebunt in iudicio obviantes Christo in aera, PTS. Q. 89. Art. 1 c.

obvius, a, um, *adj., in the way so as to meet, meeting.*

obvolvo, ere, vi, utum, 3, *v. a., to entangle,* used fig.

occasio, onis, *f., occasion, occasional cause, accidental cause, inducement.*—Kinds of *occasio* are: (a), **occasio accepta** and **occasio data,** *the accepted* and *the given occasion.*—(b), **occasio coniuncta** and **occasio praecedens,** *the occasion connected with an action* and *that preceding it.*—(c), **occasio data,** see *occasio accepta.*—

(d), **occasio praecedens,** see *occasio coniuncta.*

occasionaliter, *adv., as occasions arise, occasionally, after the manner* or *in the sense of an occasional* or *accidental cause* or *inducement.* On **causa occasionaliter dicta,** see *causa* under 2.

occasionatus, a, um, see *occasiono.*

occasiono, are, avi, atum, 1, *v. a., to occasion, cause accidentally, induce.*—**occasionatus,** a, um, *P., a., occasioned, induced.*

occasus, us, *m.,* (1) *a falling down, going down, a setting of the heavenly bodies,* esp., the sun, (2) *that quarter of the heavens in which the sun sets, the west.*

occidens, entis, *P. a.,* see *occido,* (2).

occidentalis, e, *adj., western, westerly.*

occido, (1), ere, cidi, cisum, 3, *v. a.,* (1) lit., *to kill, slay, deprive of life, put to death,* (2) fig., *to kill the soul, to kill spiritually.*

occido, (2), ere, cidi, casum, 3, *v. n.,* of the heavenly bodies, *to go down, set.*—**occidens,** entis, *m., the quarter of the setting sun, the occident, the west.*

occiduus, a, um, *adj., fleeting, perishable.*

occisio, onis, *f., a killing, slaying, murder.*

occisor, oris, *m., a slayer, murderer.*

occultatio, onis, *f., concealment,* (1) *cover* or *protection* from observation, (2) *hidden knowledge.*

occulte, *adv.,* see *occultus.*

occulto, are, avi, atum, 1, *v. freq. a., to hide, to conceal, secrete,* (1) with a *pers. pron.,* (2) the place of concealment expressed by (a) *adv. of place,* (b) *sub* with the *abl.,* (c) *in* with the *abl.,* (d) the *abl. alone.*

occultus, a, um, *P. a., hidden, concealed, secret.*—**occulta,** orum, *n., plur., secret things, secrets.*—**occultum,** i, *n., secrecy.*—*in adverb. phrase,* **in occulto,** *in secret, secretly.*—**occulte,** *adv., in secret, secretly, privately.*

occupatio, onis, *f.,* (1) *a care,* an object of watchful attention, (2) *consideration,* continuous and careful thought, (3) *business, employment, occupation,* the being occupied or employed with, or engaged in something; that in which one is engaged.

occupo, are, avi, atum, 1, *v. a.,* (I) lit., (1) *to possess, take possession of, seize anything,* (2) transf., (a) *to fill, occupy, use up space,* (b) of disease, *to possess, occupy; cover the body, overwhelm, oppress,* (II) fig., *to engross, employ, busy, engage* the mind, attention, person, often in *pass.;* also *refl.*

occurro, ere, curri, cursum, 3, *v. n.,* (1) lit., of persons, (a) *to go* or *come to, to meet* someone, (b) *to come upon, attack,* (2) transf., (a) *to alight on, fall in with,* (b) *to occur, to appear* in any place, (c) *to come to* any place, (3) fig., (a) *to lie in way of, meet* as an obstacle, (b) *to obviate* or *seek*

days of Jeroboam II the son of Joas, king of Israel.

Osee, *n.,* indecl., see *Oseas.*

ostendo, ere, di, sum, 3, *v. a.,* (I) lit., *to expose to view, to show, exhibit, display,* (II) fig., (1) in gen., *to show, disclose, exhibit, manifest,* (2) *to show, express, indicate* by speech or signs; *to give, to understand, to declare, say, tell, make known,* used with (a) *acc.,* (b) with *obj.* or *rel. clause,* (c) *absol.*—**ostendere se,** *to show one's self, to appear.*

ostensio, onis, *f.,* (1) *proof,* (2) *argument,* a kind of *demonstratio.* —A kind of *ostensio* in this (1) sense is: **ostensio exemplaris,** *the exemplary proof* or *the proof with an example.*—A kind of *ostensio* in this (2) sense is: **ostensio ad hominem,** *the argument for this* or *that man.*

ostensive, *adv.,* see *ostensivus.*

ostensivus, a, um, *adj., proving, ostensive.* On **demonstratio ostensiva,** see *demonstratio* under 3; on **ratio ostensiva,** see *ratio* under 3.—**ostensive,** *adv., after the manner* or *in the sense of a proof, ostensively,* does not occur in the S.T. of St. Thomas. On **demonstrare ostensive,** see *demonstrare* under 3.

ostentatio, onis, *f., an idle show, vain display, pomp, parade, ostentation;* any kind of display intended to attract notice or attention.

ostento, are, avi, atum, 1, *v. freq. a.,* (1) *to show off with vanity* or

boastfulness, to display, make a display of, (2) *to show* by speech or signs; *to reveal, disclose.*

ostiarius, ii, *m.,* (1) in gen., *a doorkeeper, porter,* (2) in partic., the *ostiary,* in the early Church the doorkeeper or janitor of a church. The office of ostiary is the lowest of minor orders. It is the duty of the ostiary to strike the cymbal and ring the bell, to open the Church and the sanctuary, and the book for him who preaches.

Ostiensis, e, *adj., of* or *belonging to Ostia, Ostian,* one of the suburban sees of Rome.

ostium, ii, *n., door.*

ostrea, ae, *f., an oyster.*

otior, ari, atus, 1, *v. dep., to have* or *enjoy leisure, to be at leisure, to keep holiday.*

otiose, *adv.,* see *otiosus.*

otiositas, atis, *f., leisure, idleness.*

otiosus, a, um, *adj.,* (1) in gen., of persons, (a) *idle, indolent, lazy,* (b) with respect to participation, *unconcerned, at leisure,* (2) transf., (a) of inanimate things, *idle, useless, unprofitable,* (b) *otiose, at leisure.*—**otiose,** *adv.,* (1) *otiosely, without any practical end,* (2) *idly, indolently.*

otium, ii, *n.,* (1) in gen., *leisure, time for anything,* (2) in partic., *idleness, ease, inactivity.*

ousia, (Grk. *ousia*), in St. Thomas the same as Latin *essentia, essence, nature.*

ousiosis, (Grk. *ousiosis*) *subsistence.*

Ovidius, ii, *m., P. Ovidius Naso* or *Ovid,* a celebrated Latin poet of the first century B.C.

ovile, is, *n.,* (1) lit., *a sheepfold,* (2) fig., *the Church* or *fold of Christ.*

ovis, is, *f., a sheep,* (1) lit., (2) fig.

ovum, i, *n., an egg.*

Oza, ae, *m., Oza,* a Levite in the time of David, and one of the sons of Abinadab, David ordered the Ark of God to be taken from the house of Abinadab; Oza guided the cart on which the ark was placed. At a certain point in the procession the oxen slipped; Oza stretched out his hand to hold the ark but was struck dead on the spot, Kings II. 6. 7.

Ozias, ae, *m., Ozias,* son and successor of Amasius, on the throne of Juda, same as Azarias.

P

pabulum, i, *n.,* (1) of men, *food, nourishment,* (2) of animals, *fodder.*

pacificatio, onis, *f., a peace-making, pacification.*

pacifice, *adv.,* see *pacificus.*

pacifico, are, avi, atum, 1, *v. a., to bring* or *reduce to a state of peace, pacify.*

pacificus, a, um, *adj., peaceful, peacemaking, pacific, peaceable.* —**hostia pacifica,** *a peace-offering.* Peace offerings were either *thank-offerings* or *votive offerings* or *impetratory-offerings.* In a sacrifice of thanksgiving the sacrificial meat had to be eaten the same day; in the votive and impetratory sacrifice, the meal must be continued on the second day, but no longer.—**pacificus usus agri,** *the unmolested use of land.*—**pacifici,** orum, *m., peacemakers.*—**pacifica,** orum, *n., peace-offerings.*—**pacifice,** *adv., peacefully, peaceably.*

paco, are, avi, atum, 1, *v. a., to make peaceful, pacify.*—**pacatus,** a, um, *P. a., peaceful, pacified.*

pactio, onis, *f., a compact, agreement.*

pactum, i, *n., an agreement, covenant, contract, pact.*—Kinds of *pactum* are: (a), **pactum cum daemone,** *the pact with the devil.*—(b), **pactum expressum** and **pactum tacitum,** *the pact expressed in words* or *the explicit pact* and *the pact entered upon silently* or *the silent pact.*—(c), **pactum tacitum,** see *pactum expressum.*

paedagogus, i, *m.,* (1) lit., *a pedagogue, tutor,* a man whose occupation is the instruction of children or youths, (2) transf., *a guide.*

paene, (pene), *adv., nearly, almost.*

paganus, i, *m., a pagan.*

pagina, ae, *f., a written page.*

Palaestinus, a, um, *adj., of* or *belonging to Palestine.*

palam, *adv., openly, publicly, plainly.*

palatium, ii, *n., a palace.*

palatum, i, *n., the palate,* as the organ of taste.

palea, ae, *f., chaff, straw, fibre,* used lit. and fig.

palla, ae, *f., an altar-cloth.*

Palladius, ii, *m., Palladius,* presbyter of Mount Sina in Arabia Petraea.

pallesco, ere, pallui, 3, v. inch., *n., to grow* or *turn pale.*

pallidus, a, um, *adj.,* of color, *pale, yellowish.*

pallium, i, *n.,* (1) in gen., *a cloak, mantle,* (2) in partic., *a pallium,* the name given by the Catholic Church to one of the ecclesiastical ornaments worn by the Pope, patriarchs, and archbishops, (3) fig., *a cover.*

pallor, oris, *m., pallor.*

palma, ae, *f., a palm-tree, a palm,* used lit. and fig.—**dominica die palmarum,** *Palm Sunday,* the last Sunday of Lent; it is so called from the custom of blessing branches of the palm tree, or of other trees substituted in those countries in which palms cannot be procured, and of carrying the blessed branches in procession, in commemoration of the triumphant entry of our Lord into Jerusalem.

palmus, i, *m., a span* or *twelve digits.*

palpabilis, e, *adj., tangible, palpable.* On **corpus palpabile,** see *corpus.*

palpebra, ae, *f., eye-lid.*

palpito, are, avi, atum, 1, v. freq. *n., to palpitate.*

palpo, are, avi, atum, 1, *v. a.,* (1) lit., *to touch softly, pat,* (2) fig., *to cajole, flatter.*

palpo, onis, *m., a flatterer.*

Pancratius, ii, *m., Pancratius.* Pope Pelagius I addressed a letter between 555 and 560, urging upon him and Viator the duty of abstaining from the sacrifices of schismatics, even more than from sacrilege.

pando, ere, pandi, pansum, 3, *v. a.,* (1) lit., *to open anything,* (2) fig., *to make known, relate.*

pango, ere, pepigi, pactum, 3, *v. a., to pledge, agree upon.*

panis, is, *m.,* (I) lit., (1) in gen., *bread,* (2) plural, *breads,* (3) liturgical, *bread,* the matter, as it is called, of the sacrifice of the Mass, composed of wheaten bread and wine of the grape, (4) in partic., *a loaf,* (II) transf., *food* in general.—The following phrases refer to the Holy Eucharist:—**panis angelorum,** *the bread of angels.*—**panis vivus,** *the living bread.*—**panis vitae aeternae,** *the bread of eternal life.*—**panis mysticus,** *the mystical bread.*—**panis caelestis,** *the heavenly bread.*—**panis sanctus vitae aeternae,** *the holy bread of eternal life.*—Other phrases are: **panis propositionis,** *the bread of proposition,* the twelve loaves of unleavened bread, which were placed on the table before the Lord to the right of the Altar of Incense, so called because they were always before the face of the Lord.— **panis hordeaceus,** *barley bread.*— **panis triticeus,** *wheaten bread.*— **panis azymus,** *unleavened bread.* —**panis fermentatus,** *fermented bread.*

pannus, i, *m.,* (1) in gen., as a material, *cloth,* a name given in the most general sense to every pliant fabric, woven, felted, or otherwise formed, of any animal or vegetable or even mineral filament, (2) in partic., (a) *a cloth,* a piece of pliable woven material suitable for spreading or folding over, covering, wrapping, etc., (b) plur.; *an infant's swaddling clothes.*

Panormitanus, a, um, *adj., Panormitan,* of Panormus, a city in Sicily, the modern Palermo.

papa, ae, *m., pope.*

Paphnutius, ii, *m., Paphnutius,* an anchorite of the *Thebaid* in the fourth century, commemorated by Palladius and Rufinus in the *Historia Lausiaca,* 62-5; and in the *Historia Monachorum,* 16.

par, paris, *adj.,* (1) in gen., *equal,* (2) in partic., (a) *equal* in rank, station, (b) *even, not odd;* capable of division by two without a remainder.—The following phrases occur frequently: **pari ratione,** *in like manner.*—**pari consensu,** *by mutual consent.*—**pari fastu,** *through parity of pride.*— **pari modo,** *equally, in an equal manner.*—**pari passu,** *with equal*

pace, on a par.—**pari celeritate,** *equally soon, with equal speed.*— **par,** paris, *n., a pair.*—**pariter,** *adv.,* (1) in gen., *in an equal degree, alike,* used freq. with *cum,* (2) in partic., like *simul,* of equality in time or in association, *at the same time, together.*

parabola, ae, *f., a parable.*

parabolicus, a, um, *adj., parabolical, figurative, expressed by a parable.* On **modus parabolicus,** see *modus* under 2; on **sensus parabolicus,** see *sensus* under 8.

paracletus or **paraclitus,** i, *m., the Paraclete,* an appellation of the Holy Ghost. Christ promised to the Apostles "another Paraclete", so that they might not be desolate orphans when He should depart. Christ was the first advocate or comforter and He continues His advocacy for us in Heaven.

paradisus, i, *m., paradise,* (1) *the dwelling place of the first human beings, the Garden of Eden,* (2) *the abode of the blessed.*

Paradoxa, orum, *n., the Paradoxa,* a philosophical treatise of Cicero setting forth the six striking theorems of the Stoic system. It was composed in 46 B.C.

Paralipomena, orum, *n., the Paralipomenon,* the name of two books of the Bible which from the Hebrew title are also known as Chronicles.

paralogismus, i, *m., false conclusion, false inference, paralogism,* synonym of *fallacia* and *sophis-*

ma, does not occur in S.T. of St. Thomas.—Kinds of *paralogismus* are: (a), **paralogismus disciplinae,** *the false argument of a positive science.*—(b), **paralogismus extra dictionem** and **paralogismus in dictione,** the *paralogismos exo tes lexeos* and the *paralogismos para ten lexin* of Aristotle, *the objective* or *dialectic* and *the linguistic* or *grammatical wrong conclusion.*—(c), **paralogismus in dictione,** see *paralogismus extra dictionem.*

paralysis, is, *f., palsy, paralysis.*

paralyticus, i, *m., a paralytic, a palsied person.*

paranymphus, i, *m., a groomsman.*

parasceve, es, *f., the parasceve,* day before the Sabbath, Friday; also the day before certain feasts of sabbatical rank; the day before the Pasch was observed more religiously than any other Friday.

paratus, a, um, *P. a.,* see *paro.*

parcimonia, ae, *f., sparingness, frugality, parsimony.*

parcitas, atis, *f., sparingness, lowliness,* quality or state of being lowly.

parco, ere, peperci, parsum, 3, *v. n.* and *a.,* (1) lit., of things, (a) *to spare, use frugally* or *stingily; forbear the use of,* (b) of persons, *to spare, forbear, injure, punish* or *accuse, preserve from punishment* or *other evil; have mercy upon,* used *absol.,* with *dat.,* (2) fig., (a) *to refrain from* doing a thing, used with the *dat.,* (b)

pass. impers. **sibi parci ab,** *to withhold oneself from, to be spared from,* (c) *to spare,* i.e., *to preserve by sparing, use carefully, not to injure.*

parcus, a, um, *adj., sparing, economical, niggardly.*

parens, entis, *m.,* (1) in gen., *a parent,* a person who has begotten or borne a child; *a father* or *mother,* (2) in partic., (a) *a progenitor, a forefather,* esp. *our first parents* (*primi parentes),* Adam and Eve, (b) plur., *ancestors.*

parentela, ae, *f., relationship, kinship.*

pareo, ere, ui, paritum, 3, *v. n.,* (1) lit., *to appear, be visible,* (2) transf., *to obey, be obedient to.*

paries, etis, *m., a wall,* used lit. and fig.

parifico, are, 1, *v. a., to make* or *represent as equal; to compare, liken.*

pario, ere, peperi, paritum and partum, 3, *v. a.,* (1) lit., *to bring forth, to bear,* (2) fig., *to produce, create, bring about.*

pariter, *adv.,* see *par.*

Parmenianus, i, *m., Parmenian,* successor to Donatus the Great, who followed Majorinus as Donatist bishop of Carthage. Optatus called him *peregrinus,* i.e., probably not a native of Africa. Having adopted Donatist opinions, he succeeded Donatus about 350, and having been banished A.D. 358, he returned under the decree of Julian A.D. 362. He published a work in defence of Donatism. About 372 Tichonius, a Donatist, wrote a book condemning the narrow views of the sect. Parmenian replied, condemning the doctrine of Tichonius. This reply fell into the hands of Augustine who discussed it in a treatise divided into three books.

paro, are, avi, atum, 1, *v. a.,* (1) in gen., (a) *to prepare, make* or *get something ready,* used with the *acc.,* (b) pass., *be prepared,* to be mentally or spiritually ready or disposed to do anything, used with the *inf.,* with *ad,* (2) in partic., (a) *to prepare, provide, furnish,* get something in readiness beforehand, (b) *to prepare, to fit* by preliminary instruction.—**paratus,** a, um, *P. a.,* (1) in gen., *prepared, ready,* (2) of mental preparation, *ready, prepared.*

parochia, ae, *f., an ecclesiastical district, a parish.*

parochialis, e, *adj., parochial, of* or *belonging to a parish.*

parochianus, i, *m., an inhabitant of a parish, a parishioner.*

parricidialis, e, *adj., pertaining to* or *producing the crime of parricide, parricidal.*

parricidium, ii, *n., parricide, the murder of one's father* or *parent.*

pars, partis, *f.,* (1) *a part, piece, portion, share,* the opposite of *totus,* (2) *side.* On **agere secundum partem,** see *agere* under 1; on **esse in parte,** see *esse;* on **generatio secundum partem,** see

generatio under 1; on **incommunicabilitas partis,** see *incommunicabilitas;* on **esse in loco ut pars,** see *locus* under 2; on **motus secundum partem,** see *motus* under 1; on **movere secundum partem,** see *movere;* on **multum partibus seu secundum partes,** see *multus* under 1; on **passio partis sensitivae,** see *passio* under 2; on **quaestio in parte,** see *quaestio.—* Kinds of *pars* in this (1) sense are: (a), **pars accidentalis** and **pars essentialis,** *the accidental* or *unessential* and *the essential part.—*(b), **pars affectiva seu appetitiva** and **pars apprehensiva seu cognitiva seu cognoscitiva** (**sc.** animae), *the part of the soul accessible to* or *desiring good* and *the part of the soul that comprehends* or *understands.—*(c), **pars animae,** *part of the soul,* i.e., *a power of the soul* or *a species of the powers of the soul which is considered as separate from the other powers of the soul* or *can exist apart from them,* the *morion psyches* of Aristotle.— (d), **pars appetitiva,** see *pars affectiva.—*(e), **pars apprehensiva,** see *pars affectiva.—*(f), **pars cognitiva seu cognoscitiva,** see *pars affectiva.—*(g), **pars completiva,** *the part that completes* or *brings something to a conclusion.* Cf. Verit. 5. 1 c; 1 Perih. 8 b.—(h), **pars consimilis seu similis seu similaris seu totius homogenei** and **pars dissimilis seu difformis seu totius heterogenei,** *the part* *which is like another* or *of a similar kind* and *that which is unlike another* or *dissimilar.*—(i), **pars continua seu continui** and **pars non continua seu decisa seu discerpta seu disiuncta**, *the part which is connected with others* and *that which is not so connected* or *is separated from others.*—(j), **pars decisa**, see *pars continua.* —(k), **pars definitionis**, *the part of a definition.*—(l), **pars difformis**, see *pars consimilis.*—(m), **pars discerpta**, see *pars continua.* —(n), **pars disiuncta**, see *pars continua.*—(o), **pars dissimilis**, see *pars consimilis.*—(p), **pars essentiae** and **pars quantitatis seu secundum quantitatem**, *part of the essence of a physical thing, part of a physical quantity.* Cf. *pars accidentalis* and *pars integralis.*— (q), **pars essentialis**, see *pars accidentalis.*—(r), **pars formalis seu secundum formam** and **pars materialis seu secundum materiam**, *the formal* and *the material part* or *the part acting after the manner of form* and *that after the manner of matter.*—(s), **pars generis, pars speciei,** and **pars habentis speciem seu individui**, *the part of a genus, the part of a species,* and *the part of an individual.*—(t), **pars habentis speciem**, see *pars generis.*—(u), **pars incidentalis, seu secundaria** and **pars praedominans seu principalis**, *the incidental* or *subordinate part* and *the predominant* or *principle part.*—(v), **pars indivi-**

dui, see *pars generis.*—(w), **pars integralis seu totius integralis, pars subiectiva,** and **pars potentialis seu secundum potentiam seu totius universalis,** *the part that integrates* or *that conditions the completeness of a thing, the subjective part* or *that which belongs to something as a species of the same,* and *the potential part* or *that which though not formally present is contained in the powers* or *faculties.*—(x), **pars intellectiva, pars sensitiva,** and **pars vegetativa seu vegetabilis seu nutritiva** sc. animae, *the intellectual, the sensitive,* and *the vegetative part of the soul.* Cf. *pars animae* above.—(y), **pars interior** sc. animae, *the inner part of the soul* which includes the *pars intellectiva* and in part also the *pars sensitiva.* Cf. *pars animae* above; also *pars intellectiva.* —(z), **pars irrationabilis seu irrationalis** and **pars rationabilis seu rationalis** sc. animae, *the irrational* and *rational part of the soul.*—(a^2), **pars logica,** *the logical part.*—(b^2), **pars materiae,** *the part of matter.*—(c^2), **pars materialis**, see *pars formalis.*—(d^2), **pars non-continua,** see *pars continua.*—(e^2), **pars nutritiva,** see *pars intellectiva.*—(f^2), **pars obaudibilis,** *the part that gives ear* or *that obeys.*—(g^2), **pars opinativa** and **pars ratiocinativa** sc. animae, *the thinking part of the soul* or *the part that forms opinions* and *certain conclusions.* Cf.

pars animae above.—(h²), **pars organica,** *the organic* or *instrumental part.*—(i²), **pars phantastica** sc. **animae,** *the phantasy* or *the power of imagination.* Cf. *pars animae* above.—(j²), **pars potentialis,** see *pars integralis.*—(k²), **pars praedominans,** see *pars incidentalis.*—(l²), **pars principalis,** see *pars incidentalis.*—(m²), **pars propinqua,** *the proximate* or *closer part.*—(n²), **pars quantitatis,** see *pars essentiae.*—(o²), **pars quantitativa,** see *pars essentiae.*—(p²), **pars ratiocinativa,** see *pars opinativa.*—(q²), **pars rationabilis seu rationalis,** see *pars irrationabilis.*—(r²), **pars rationis seu secundum rationem** and **pars rei seu secundum rem,** *the part existing in the mind* and *the part of a thing* or *the notional* or *factual part.*—(s²), **pars rei,** see *pars rationis.*—(t²), **pars secundaria,** see *pars incidentalis.*—(u²), **pars secundum formam,** see *pars formalis.*—(v²), **pars secundum materiam,** see *pars formalis.*—(w²), **pars secundum potentiam,** see *pars integralis.*—(x²), **pars secundum rationem,** see *pars rationis.*—(y²), **pars secundum rem,** see *pars rationis.*—(z²), **pars sensitiva,** see *pars intellectiva.*—(a³), **pars signata,** *the designated* or *definite part.*—(b³), **pars similaris seu similis,** see *pars consimilis.*—(c³), **pars situalis,** *the part of a thing according to its local situation.*—(d³), **pars speciei,** see *pars gene-*

ris.—(e³), **pars subiectiva,** see *pars integralis.*—(f³), **pars substantiae,** *the part of a substance.*—(g³), **pars superior** sc. **animae,** *the superior* or *higher part of the soul,* i.e., human reason in so far as it applies to divine things.—(h³), **pars totius heterogenei,** see *pars consimilis.*—(i³), **pars totius homogenei,** see *pars consimilis.*—(j³), **pars totius integralis,** see *pars integralis.*—(k³), **pars totius universalis,** see *pars integralis.*—(l³), **pars vegetabilis seu vegetativa,** see *pars intellectiva.*—(m³), **pars virtutis,** *the part of a virtue.* Cf. *virtus* under 5. Cf. *virtus* under 4.—**bonum est totius finis cuiuslibet partium,** see *totus* under 1.—**omne totum est maius sua parte,** see *totus* under 1.—**posito toto necesse est poni partem,** see *totus* under 1.—**resoluto toto in partes incipiunt partes esse in actu,** see *totus* under 1.—**totum dicitur esse in partibus,** see *totus* under 1.—**totum est prius in consideratione quam partes,** see *totus* under 1. On **infinitum ex parte formae materiae et post,** see *infinitus;* on **se tenere ex parte,** see *tenere* under 1.—**partim,** *adv., partly, in part.*

partialis, e, *adj., partial.*—**partialiter,** *adv., partially.*

partialitas, atis, *f.,* fact or *quality of being limited* or *local, partiality.*

partialiter, *adv.,* see *partialis.*

partibilis, e, *adj., divisible, partible, capable of being parted* or *separated.*

particeps, cipis, *adj.*, *sharing, partaking, participant*, with the *gen.*

participabilis, e, *adj.*, *participable, capable of being participated in or shared.*

participatio, onis, *f.*, *sharing, participation, taking part in.* On **bonitas per participationem**, see *bonitas* under 1; on **bonum per participationem**, see *bonus* under 2; on **commune secundum participationem**, see *communis* under 1; on **dicere participationem et per participationem**, see *dicere* under 3; on **ens per participationem**, see *ens;* on **esse per participationem**, see *esse;* on **humanus per participationem**, see *humanus;* on **infinitum participationis et per participationem**, see *infinitus;* on **malum per participationem**, see *malus* under 2; on **praedicare per participationem**, see *praedicare* under 2; on **ratio per participationem**, see *ratio* under 3; on **rationale per participationem**, see *rationalis* under 2; on **similitudo per participationem eiusdem formae seu qualitatis**, see *similitudo* under 1; on **tale per participationem**, see *talis;* on **verum per participationem**, see *verus* under 1; on **voluntas per participationem**, see *voluntas* under 2.—One kind of *participatio* is: **participatio deficiens**, *the deficient* or *imperfect participation.*

participative, see *participativus.*

participativus, a, um, *adj.*, *participating, capable of participating, participative.*—participative, *adv.*, *after the manner of participation, in the sense of participation, participatively,* synonym of *per participationem,* the opposite of *essentialiter seu per essentiam.* On **aeternum participative**, see *aeternus* under 1; on **beatus participative**, see *beatus* under 1; on **bonum participative**, see *bonus* under 2; on **dicere participative**, see *dicere* under 3; on **esse participative**, see *esse;* on **infinitum participative**, see *infinitus;* on **praedicare participative**, see *praedicare* under 2; on **rationale participative**, see *rationalis* under 2; on **voluntas participative dicta**, see *voluntas* under 2.

participatus, us, *m.*, *a sharing, participation, a taking part* in some action.

participium, ii, *n.*, *a verbal form which partakes of the function of a verb, a participle.*

participo, are, avi, atum, 1, *v. a.* and *n.*, (1) *to cause to partake of, impart,* (2) *participate, take part in,* (3) *have communion with, associate with.* On **actus participatus**, see *actus* under 2; on **aeternitas participata**, see *aeternitas;* on **beatitudo participata**, see *beatitudo* under 1; on **bonitas participata**, see *bonitas* under 1; on **bonum participatum et non-participatum**, see *bonus* under 3; on **esse participatum**, see *esse;* on **forma participata**, see *forma* under 2. On **actus participatus**, see *actus* under 1; on **aeternitas participata**, see *aeternitas;* on **beati-**

tudo participata, see *beatitudo* under 1; on **bonitas participata,** see *bonitas* under 1; on **bonum participatum et non-participatum,** see *bonus* under 3; on **contradictio participata in contrariis,** see *contradictio;* on **esse participatum,** see *esse;* on **forma participata,** see *forma* under 2; on **infinitum participatum,** see *infinitus;* on **veritas participata,** see *veritas* under 1; on **virtus participata,** see *virtus* under 1.—Kinds of *participare* in this (2) sense are: (a), **participare indivisibiliter seu secundum rationem indivisibilitatis** and **participare secundum magis et minus,** *to take part in something entirely* or *after the manner of being undivided* or *to take part in something after the manner of more* or *less.*—(b), **participare secundum magis et minus,** see *participare indivisibiliter.*—(c), **participare secundum rationem indivisibilitatis,** see *participare indivisibiliter.*—(d), **participare substantialiter,** *to take part in something according to its substance.*—**omne participans componitur ex participante et participato,** *everything which takes part in something is composed of that which takes part in* and *that which is taken part in.*—**omne participatum comparatur ad participans ut actus eius,** *everything shared in is related to that which shares in it as its reality.*—**omne participatum est in participante,** *everything*

participated in is in the thing that participates in it.—**participans est in potentia ad participatum,** *the participating thing is in the position of potentiality with reference to that which is participated in.*

particula, ae, *f.,* (1) *a small bit, a particle* in the general sense of the word, (2) in grammar, a *particle.* On **passio particulae sensitivae,** see *passio* under 2.

particularis, e, *adj., of* or *concerning a part, partial, particular,* synonym of *singularis* and *specialis,* the opposite of *universalis* and *generalis.* On **actus particularis,** see *actus* under 1; on **aestimatio particularis,** see *aestimatio;* on **agens particularis,** see *agens;* on **agibile particulare,** see *agibilis;* on **apprehensio particularis,** see *apprehensio* under 2; on **bonum particulare,** see *bonus* under 3; on **causa particularis,** see *causa* under 2; on **cognitio particularis,** see *cognitio* under 2; on **cognoscere in particulari,** see *cognoscere* under 2; on **communitas particularis,** see *communitas* under 1; on **conceptio particularis,** see *conceptio* under 4; on **conclusio particularis,** see *conclusio* under 2; on **confessio particularis,** see *confessio* under 2; on **consideratio particularis,** see *consideratio;* on **consilium particulare,** see *consilium* under 2; on **corpus particulare,** see *corpus;* on **demonstratio particularis,** see

demonstratio under 3; on differentia particularis, see differentia; on dominium particulare,
see dominium; on effectus particularis, see effectus; on ens
particulare, see ens; on enuntiatio particularis, see enuntiatio
under 2; on factio particularis,
see factio; on finis particularis,
see finis under 2; on forma particularis, see forma under 2; on
ignorantia particularis, see ignorantia under 1; on imaginatio
particularis, see imaginatio under 1; on iniustificatio particularis, see iniustificatio; on iniustitia particularis, see iniustitia;
on iniustum particulare, see iniustus; on intentio particularis,
see intentio under 3; on iustitia
particularis, see iustitia under
1; on iustum particulare seu
particulare dictum, see iustus;
on lex particularis, see lex under 1; on malitia particularis,
see malitia under 3; on malum
particulare, see malus under 3;
on materia particularis, see materia under 3; on natura particularis, see natura; on operabile
particulare, see operabilis; on
opinio particularis, see opinio;
on ordo particularis, see ordo
under 1; on organum particulare, see organum; on perfectio
particularis, see perfectio under
2; on persona particularis, see
persona under 3; on potentia
particularis, see potentia under
2; on potestas particularis, see
see potestas under 3; on propositio particularis, see propositio
under 2; on prudentia particularis, see prudentia under 2; on
ratio particularis, see ratio under
2 and 3; on regimen particulare,
see regimen; on sapientia particularis, see sapientia under 1; on
scientia particularis, see scientia under 1; on scire in particulari, see scire under 1; on sensus particularis, see sensus under 3; on signum particulare,
see signum under 1; on species
particularis, see species under
6; on subiectum particulare, see
subiectum under 3; on substantia particularis, see substantia
under 1; on syllogismus particularis, see syllogismus; on transmutatio particularis, see transmutatio under 1; on unitas particularis, see unitas; on veritas
particularis, see veritas under 1;
on verum particulare, see verus
under 1; on virtus particularis,
see virtus under 1 and 5; on voluntarium in particulari, see voluntarius under 3.—Kinds of particulare are: particulare in genere substantiae and particulare
in quolibet genere, the particular in the category of substance
and the particular in general
which can be spoken of also in
each of the other categories.—
actiones in particularibus sunt,
see actus under 1.—in particularibus est actus, see actus under
1.—in universali sunt in potentia
particularia, see universalis under 1.—operatio est in particula

ribus, see *operatio* under 2.—
operationes circa singularia sunt,
see *operatio* under 2.—**particularium non est scientia nec definitio,** *for particular things as such
there is neither a knowledge nor
a definition.*—universalia **non
movent, sed particularia,** see
universalis under 1.—**particulariter,** *adv., partly, in a special
manner, particularly.* On **iniustum particulariter,** see *iniustus;*
on **prudens particulariter,** see
prudens.

particularitas, atis, *f., particularity, individuality,* the quality of
being particular as opposed to
general or universal.

particulariter, *adv.,* see *particularis.*

particulatim, *adv., part after part,
bit by bit, one by one, sing-
ly, in detail.*

particulatio, onis, *f., a dividing
into particles, a restricting to a
particular thing.*

particulo, are, avi, atum, 1, *v. a.,
to make in a special way, to
make something in particular,
particularly.* On **bonum particulatum,** see *bonus* under 3; on
esse particulatum, see *esse; on*
similitudo particulata, see *similitudo* under 1; on **virtus particulata,** see *virtus* under 1.

partim, *adj.,* see *pars.*

partior, iri, partitus, 4, *v. dep., to
share, divide.*—**partitus,** a, um,
P. a., divided, parted.

partitio, onis, *f., a sharing, division.*

partitive, *adv.,* see *partitivus.*

partitivus, a, um, *adj., dividing,
expressing a separation, partitive.* On **nomen partitivum,** see
nomen under 1; on **terminus
partitivus,** see *terminus* under 5.
—**partitive,** *adv., in the sense* or
*manner of a partition, partitive-
ly.* On **dicere partitive,** see *dicere* under 3.

partitus, a, um, *P. a.,* see *partior.*

parturio, ire, ivi or ii, 4, *v. desid.,
a., to be in travail* or *labor,* said
of women and animals.—**partu-
riens,** entis, *P. a., travailing,
about to bring forth* or *give
birth.*

partus, us, *m.,* (1) in abstr. *a bringing forth, birth,* (2) in concr.,
the young or *offspring* of any
creature.

parum, *subst. indecl.* and *adv., too
little, not enough, not sufficiently, little.*

parumper, *adv., for a little while,
a moment.*

parvificentia, ae, *f., niggardliness,
stinginess,* the opposite of *magnificentia, apirocalia, banausia,
consumptio,* and *prodigalitas.*

parvificus, a, um, *adj., niggardly,
stingy,* the opposite of *banausus*
and *magnificus.*

parvipendo, ere, 3, *v. a.* and *n.,*
see *pendo.*

parvipensio, onis, *f., disdain, disregard, contempt, disparagement.*

parvissimus, a, um, *adj.,* see *parvus.*

parvitas, atis, *f., littleness, smallness, slightness, insignificance.*

parvulus, a, um, *adj.,* (1) *very small, little,* (2) of age, *little, young.*—**parvulus,** i, *m., a child, a little one.*

parvus, a, um, *small,* the opposite of *magnus.* On **mundus parvus,** see *mundus* under 1; on **passio parva,** see *passio* under 3; on **solutio parva,** see *solutio* under 2.—Kinds of *parvus* are: **parvus absolute** and **parvus secundum relationem,** *the small absolutely* and *the small relatively.*—**ex multis parvis non possunt fieri magna continua,** see *continuus* under 2.—Comp.: **minor,** us, *comp.* from *parvus,* (1) *smaller,* according to extent, (2) *smaller,* according to duration of time, i.e., *younger,* (3) *smaller* or *lower* in the sphere of thought, i.e., the lower or less extensive premise of a syllogism, the *minor,* (4) *less* according to perfection, *lower* according to rank, *less important, less.*—On **mundus minor,** see *mundus* under 1; on **terminus minor,** see *terminus* under 1.—**esse in minus,** *to extend over less, reach out less, have less value.* On **extremitas minor,** see *extremitas* under 2; on **propositio minor,** see *propositio* under 2; on **terminus minor,** see *terminus* under 4.—Kinds of *minor* in this (3) sense are: (a), **minor de contingenti,** *the minor premise concerned with what may or may not be.* Cf. C. G. 3. 86.— (b), **minor de inesse,** *the minor proposition which states that*

something subsists in a thing. On **abstractio minor,** see *abstractio* under 3; on **locus a minori,** see *locus* under 4; on **ordo minor,** see *ordo* under 4; on **religio minor,** see *religio* under 2; on **status minor,** see *status* under 4.—**probare a minori,** *to prove by concluding from the lower to the higher.*—*Sup.,* **minimus,** a, um, also **parvissimus,** *very small, very little, least, smallest.*—*Adv.,* —*comp.,* **minus,** *less.*—*sup.,* **minime,** *least of all, in the smallest degree, least, very little.*

pascha, ae, *f.,* and atis, *n.,* (1) *the Paschal lamb,* (2) *paschal food,* i.e., *unleavened bread,* (3) *Christ,* (4) *Easter, the feast of the Passover.*

paschalis, e, *adj., paschal, of* or *belonging to the Passover, Easter.*

Paschalis, is, *m., Paschal II,* Pope, succeeded Urban II and reigned from 1099 till his death in 1118. He was born in central Italy and was received at an early age as a monk in Cluny. St. Thomas refers to a decision of his relating to the payment of tithes by the clergy, and on the question of simony.

Paschasius, ii, *m., Paschasius,* deacon of Rome, saint and confessor, flourished at the end of the fifth century, and the beginning of the sixth. Gregory the Great in his Dialogues, bk. IV, chap. 40, speaks of him as a man of great sanctity. Gregory likewise gives an account of his deliverance from Purgatory, where he was expiating his sin of resisting the judgment of the Church in the anti-pope Laurentius.

pasco, ere, pavi, pastus, 3, *v. a.* and *n.,* and *pascor,* pastus sum, 3, *v. dep.,* (I) lit., (1) of animals, (a) *to graze, browse, feed,* (b) *in pass. reflex.* with *dep.* force, (c) *to feed, supply food with* their own flesh, (2) of persons, *to feed, nourish, maintain, support,* (II) fig., (1) *to guide, rule, govern,* (2) in *pass. reflex.* with *dep.* force, *to feast, gratify.*

pascor, pastus sum, 3, *v. dep.,* see *pasco.*

pascuum, i, *n., a pasture.*

passer, eris, *m., a sparrow.*

passibilis, e, *adj., capable of feeling* or *suffering, passible,* the opposite of *impassibilis.* On **caro passibilis,** see *caro* under 1; on **corpus passibile,** see *corpus;* on **intellectus passibilis,** see *intellectus* under 1; on **qualitas passibilis,** see *qualitas;* on **transmutatio passibilis,** see *transmutatio* under 1.

passibilitas, atis, *f.,* (1) *capability of suffering, passibility,* the opposite of *impassibilitas,* (2) *emotion, affection,* synonym of *passio,* (3) *painful suffering,* likewise a synonym of *passio.*

passim, *adv.,* (1) lit., *at different places,* (2) *transf.,* (a) *everywhere, far* and *wide,* (b) *at random, indiscriminately, in many cases.*

passio, onis, *f.,* generally speaking, but not always, the correlative of *activity, receptivity, passivity, a result.* Thus (1) as the third species of *qualitas* (q.v.), *those accidents which change by alteration,* e.g., color. Hence (2) any quality, impression or effect characteristic of the nature of a thing, *a property,* (3) the category of *passivity,* of *receiving action,* the opposite of *actio,* (4) in the psychological order, the sensitive appetites and their operations, *emotion, an act of the sensitive appetite with some bodily change,* synonym of *affectio, concitatio animi, motus animi,* (5) spec., *detrimental change, injurious affection, suffering.*—A kind of *passio* in this (1) sense is: **passio perpetua** and **passio transiens,** *the perpetual* or *permanent impression* and *the transient* or *temporary impression.* On **transmutatio circa seu secundum passiones,** see *transmutatio* under 1.—Kinds of *passio* in this (2) sense are: (a), **passio composita seu divisibilis** and **passio simplex,** *the composite* or *divisible* and *the simple* or *indivisible property.*—(b), **passio divisibilis,** see *passio composita.*—(c), **passio generis** and **passio speciei,** *the peculiarity of a genus* and *that of a species.*—(d), **passio harmoniae,** *the peculiarity of harmony.*—(e), **passio muliebris,** *the peculiarity of woman.*—(f), **passio numeri,** *the property of number.*—(g), **passio per se seu propria,** *the property that be-*

longs to a thing through itself and *its own nature* or *that belongs to it as such,* thus its own peculiarity.—(h), **passio propria,** see *passio per se.*—(i), **passio quantitatis,** *the property of quantity* or *size.*—(j), **passio sensibilis seu sensibilium corporum,** *the sensibly perceptible peculiarity* or *the peculiarity of the sensibly perceptible body.*—(k), **passio sensibilium corporum,** see *passio sensibilis.*—(l), **passio simplex,** see *passio composita.*—(m), **passio speciei,** see *passio generis.* On **affectus passionis seu secundum passionem,** see *affectus* under 2; on **magnitudo passionis,** see *magnitudo* under 3; on **peccare ex passione,** see *peccare* under 2; on **peccatum ex passione,** see *peccatum* under 2; on **potentia passionis,** see *potentia* under 1; on **voluntarium secundum passionem,** see *voluntarius* under 3; on **voluntas passionem praecedens,** see *voluntas* under 3.—Kinds of *passio* in this (4) sense are: (a), **passio affectiva seu affectus seu secundum affectionem,** *the affection connected with physical emotion,* the opposite of *simplex affectus.* See *affectus* under 2.—(b), **passio affectus,** see *passio affectiva.*—(c), **passio animae seu in anima seu animi seu animalis seu interior passio carnis seu corporis seu corporalis seu corporea** and **passio naturae,** *the affection of the soul* or *spiritual affection,* by

which is understood generally and in the strictest sense of the word an agitation of the sensible faculty, at times also, however, the reception of the sensible or the intellectual representation of a thing upon the corresponding intellectual faculty, yet again every other activity of the soul, *the carnal* or *physical affection,* by which is usually meant a pain or sickness of the body, at times also, however, *an agitation of the sensible faculty,* and *the affection of nature* and *essence* or *the material affection.*—(d), **passio animae nutritivae** and **passio partis sensitivae seu particulae sensitivae seu passio sensibilis,** *the affection of the vegetative* or *plant part of the soul* and *that of the animal* or *the sensitive part of the soul.*—(e), **passio animae tantum** and **passio compositi seu coniuncti,** *the affection of the soul alone* and *that of the combined body* and *soul.*—(f), **passio animalis,** see *passio animae.*—(g), **passio animi seu appetitus sensitivi seu passio irrationalis,** *the affection of the spirit* or *of the sensitive faculty* or *the irrational affection,* because it belongs to the irrational part of the soul.—(h), **passio appetitus sensitivi,** see *passio animi.*—(i), **passio bona** and **passio mala seu defectiva seu vitiosa,** *the morally good* and *the morally bad* or *faulty affection.*—(j), **passio carnis,** see *passio animae.*—(k), **pas-**

sio communis and passio propria, *the affection common to one thing with another* and *the affection proper to it,* (cf. *passio propria* under 1.)—(l), passio communiter dicta seu sumpta seu large seu improprie accepta seu transumptive sumpta and passio proprie dicta seu sumpta, *passivity in general* or *in the proper sense of the word.*—(m), passio completa seu perfecta and passio inchoata, *the complete* or *perfect passion* and *the passion begun.*—(n), passio completiva in genere seu finalis in genere and passio completiva seu finalis simpliciter, *the completing* or *concluding passion in a definite genus* and *the simply* or *absolutely completing* or *concluding passion.*—(o), passio completiva simpliciter, see *passio completiva in genere.*—(p), passio composita, *the composed passion,* namely *anger.*—(q), passio compositi, see *passio animae tantum.*—(r), passio concupiscibilis and passio irascibilis, *the passion which belongs to the vis concupiscibilis,* i.e., *amor et odium, desiderium vel concupiscentia et fuga vel abominatio, gaudium vel delectatio et dolor vel tristitia,* and *the passion which belongs to the vis irascibilis,* i.e., *spes et desperatio, timor et audacia, ira.*—(s), passio coniuncti, see *passio animae tantum.*—(t), passio conservativa and passio laesiva, *the suffering that preserves* and *that that hinders* or *harms.*—(u),

passio consequens and passio praecedens seu praeveniens, *the passion which follows a judgment of the intellect* or *an act of the will* and *that which precedes such.*—(v), passio corporalis seu corporea, see *passio animae.*—(w), passio corporis, see *passio animae.*—(x), passio corruptiva and passio perfectiva seu perfectionis, *the suffering that corrupts* or *destroys* and *that which perfects.*—(y), passio debilis seu parva and passio dura seu fortis seu intensa, *the weak* or *small* and *the severe* or *strong passion.*—(z), passio defectiva, see *passio bona.*—(a^2), passio determinata, *the determined affection.*—(b^2), passio divinorum, *affection for God* and *divine things.*—(c^2), passio dura, see *passio debilis.*—(d^2), passio finalis in genere, see *passio completiva in genere.*—(e^2), passio finalis simpliciter, see *passio completiva in genere.*—(f^2), passio fortis, see *passio debilis.*—(g^2), passio generalis and passio specialis, *the general* and *the particular passion.*—(h^2), passio immunditiae, *the passion of impurity.* Cf. Nom. 12. 1.—(i^2), passio inchoata, see *passio completa.*—(j^2), passio inordinata and passio moderata, *the inordinate passion* and *that regulated* or *moderated by reason.*—(k^2), passio intellectus seu intellectus possibilis and passio sensus, *the passivity of reason* and *that of sense.* Cf. *passio sensitivi.*—(l^2), passio intellectus pos-

sibilis, see *passio intellectus.—*
(m²), passio interior, see *passio
animae.—*(n²), passio irascibilis,
see *passio concupiscibilis.—*(o²),
passio laudabilis and passio vituperabilis, *the praiseworthy* and
the blameworthy passion.—(p²),
passio mala, see *passio bona.—*
(q²), passio manifesta, *the manifest passion.—*(r²), passio moderata, see *passio inordinata.—*(s²),
passio parva, see *passio debilis.—*
(t²), passio perfecta, see *passio
completa.—*(u²), passio phantastici and passio sensitivi, *the affection of the power of imagination*
and *that of the sensible perceptive faculty.* Cf. *passio sensus.—*
(v²), passio praecedens, see *passio
consequens.—*(w²), passio praeveniens, see *passio consequens.—*
(x²), passio praevisa and passio
subita, *the foreseen* and *the sudden passion.—*(y²), passio primi
sensitivi, *the affection of the first
sensible perceptive faculty* or
common sense.—(z²), passio principalis, passio principalissima
and passio secundaria, *the chief*
or *fundamental passion,* i.e., *gaudium et tristitia, timor et spes,
the principal passion,* i.e., *gaudium et tristitia,* and *the subordinate* or *derived passion.—*(a³),
passio propria, see *passio communis.—*(b³), passio proprie dicta
seu sumpta, see *passio communiter dicta.—*(c³), passio secundaria,
see *passio principalis.—*(d³), passio secundum affectionem, see
passio affectiva.—(e³), passio sen-

sibilis, see *passio animae nutritivae.—*(f³), passio sensitivi, see
passio phantastici.—(g³), passio
sensus, see *passio intellectus.—*
(h³), passio specialis, see *passio
generalis.—*(i³), passio subita, see
passio praevisa.—(j³), passio transumptive sumpta, see *passio
communiter dicta.—*(k³), passio
virilitatis, *the virile* or *masculine
passion.—*(l³), passio vitiosa, see
passio bona.—(m³) passio vituperabilis, see *passio laudabilis.—*
Kinds of *passio* in this (5) sense
are: (a), passio ab extrinseco illata seu exterius illata seu exterior
and passio ab intrinseco causata
seu intrinseca, *the outer* and *the
inner suffering.—*(b), passio ab
intrinseco causata, see *passio ab
extrinseco illata.—*(c), passio
Christi, *the suffering of Christ.—*
(d), passio exterior, see *passio ab
extrinseco illata.—*(e), passio exterius illata, see *passio ab extrinseco illata.—*(f), passio humana,
human suffering.—(g), passio indetractibilis, *the suffering that
does not lack merit* or *grace.—*(h),
passio intrinseca, see *passio ab
intrinseco illata.—*(i), passio involuntaria seu violenta and passio
naturalis, *the involuntary suffering contrary to nature* and *the
natural suffering* or *the suffering
according to nature.* Cf. *passio
pura.—*(j), passio naturalis, see
passio involuntaria.—(k), passio
pura, *the pure* or *complete suffering.—*(l), passio violenta, see
passio involuntaria.

passive, *adv.*, see *passivus.*

passivus, a, um, *adj., suffering, capable of suffering, passible, passive,* synonym of *receptivus,* the opposite of *activus.* On alteratio passiva, see *alteratio;* on appetitus passivus, see *appetitus* under 2; on determinatio passiva, see *determinatio* under 1; on dispositio passiva, see *dispositio* under 4; on generatio passiva, see *generatio* under 1; on impotentia passiva, see *impotentia;* on intellectus passivus, see *intellectus* under 2; on omnipotentia passiva, see *omnipotentia* under 1; on origo passiva, see *origo;* on potentia passiva, see *potentia* under 1 and 2; on potestas passiva, see *potestas* under 1; on principium passivum et primum passivum, see *principium;* on privatio passiva, see *privatio* under 1; on processio passiva, see *processio;* on quale passivum, see *qualis;* on qualitas passiva, see *qualitas;* on relatio passiva, see *relatio;* on scandalum passivum, see *scandalum* under 2; on sphaera passiva, see *sphaera* under 3; on verbum passivum, see *verbum* under 2; on virtus passiva, see *virtus* under 1. —passiva recipiunt actionem activorum secundum proprium modum, *passive things receive upon themselves the action of active things according to a manner proper to them.* Cf. *recipere.—* passive, *adv., after the manner or in the sense of the suffering, passively,* synonym of *receptive,* the opposite of *active.* On creatio passive accepta, see *creatio* under 1; on dicere passive, see *dicere* under 3; on generatio passive accepta seu sumpta, see *generatio* under 1; on iustificatio passive accepta, see *iustificatio* under 1; on origo passive significata, see *origo;* on recipere passive, see *recipere;* on significare passive, see *significare.*

passus, a, um, *patior.*

passus, us, *m., a step, pace, track, trace.*

pastio, onis, *f., a feeding,* the action of nourishing as if by food, used fig.; cura pastionis, *pastoral care.*

pastor, oris, *m.,* (1) *a herdsman, a shepherd,* (2) eccl. Lat., (a) *a shepherd, pastor,* especially a bishop who is to feed, lead, and gently rule, like a shepherd, the flock committed to him, (b) esp. of Christ.

pastoralis, e, *adj., pastoral, of* or *pertaining to a shepherd* or *pastor of souls.—Liber Regulae Pastoralis,* of Gregory the Great, a treatise on the duties and responsibilities of the pastoral office, addressed to a bishop John, with the purpose of explaining and justifying the writer's former reluctance to undertake the burden of the papacy. St. Thomas quotes freely from this treatise.

patefacio, ere, feci, factum, 3, *v. a.* and in *pass.,* patefiet, *to disclose, bring to light.*

patefio, see *patefacio.*

patena, ae, f., *a paten,* the circular plate of silver, gilt, or gold, used from the earliest times to receive the Host consecrated at Mass.

pateo, ere, ui, 2, v. n., (1) lit., *to lie open, be open,* (2) fig., (a) *to be exposed* or *subject to anything* (b) *to be clear, plain, well-known, evident, manifest,* used *absol.,* with subject-clause.

pater, tris, m., *father,* the opposite of *filius.* On **limbus patrum,** see *limbus.*—Kinds of *pater* are: (a), **pater adoptans,** *the father who adopts someone as his child.*—(b), **pater caelestis,** and **pater terrenus,** *the heavenly* and *the earthly father.*—(c), **pater carnalis** and **pater spiritualis,** *the carnal* and *the spiritual father.*—(d), **pater spiritualis,** see *pater carnalis.*—(e), **pater terrenus,** see *pater caelestis.*

paterfamilias, ae, m., see *familia.*

paternalis, e, adj., *paternal.*

paternitas, atis, f., *paternity, the relation* or *quality of being a father, the relation of a father, fatherhood.* In discussions of the doctrine of the Holy Trinity, the Father is spoken of as the One Who created us, the Holy Ghost the One Who sanctifies us. This cannot be so, since all actions which terminate outside of God must be attributed to God's nature which is one and which is common equally to the three divine Persons. Hence, it is not true that the Father created us any more than the Son or the Holy Ghost. This way of speaking is permitted by the Church and is called appropriation. It means that the function of creating is attributed to the Father to commemorate His paternity which is in an especial way connected with the idea of creating.

paternus, a, um, adj., *of* or *belonging to a father, fatherly, paternal.* On **disciplina paterna,** see *disciplina* under 4; on **potestas paterna,** see *potestas* under 3; on **principatus paternus,** see *principatus* under 1; on **regimen paternum,** see *regimen.*

pathos, ous, n., *emotions, motus animi.*

pathicus, a, um, adj., *pathic, who submits to unnatural lust.*

patibilis, e, adj., *patible, liable to undergo something.*

patibulum, i, n., *a fork-shaped gibbet.*

patienter, adv., see *patior.*

patientia, ae, f., *the quality of bearing, suffering,* or *enduring, patience, endurance.* The virtue of *patientia* is also called *patientia sufferens,* i.e., *suffering patience,* in order to distinguish it from the act of *patientia* which is a *fructus Spiritus sancti.*

patior, pati, passus, 3, v. dep., (1) *to bear, undergo, suffer, endure,* synonym of *recipere,* the opposite of *agere,* (2) *suffer, bear, allow, permit.*—On **praeparatio patientis,** see *praeparatio* under 1; on **principium patientis,** see *principium;* on **sensus patientis,** see *sensus under* 3.—Kinds of *patior* in this (1) sense are: (a), **pati communiter, pati proprie,** and **pati propriissime,** *to suffer in the general* or *wider sense of the word, suffer in the proper* or *narrower sense of the word,* and *suffer in the most proper* or *narrowest sense of the word.*—(b), **pati improprie,** *to suffer in the improper* or *figurative sense of the word,* i.e., to accept something without losing anything.—(c), **pati per accidens** and **pati per se,** *to suffer by accident* and *for itself* or *as such.*—(d), **pati per se,** see *pati per accidens.*—(e), **pati proprie,** see *pati communiter.*—(f), **pati propriissime,** see *pati communiter.*—(g), **pati secundum quid** and **pati simpliciter,** *to suffer with respect to something* or *in a certain respect* and *suffer simply* or *absolutely.* —(h), **pati simpliciter,** see *pati secundum quid.*—**agens et patiens oportet esse simul,** see *agens.* —**mitis non patitur,** the translation of the Aristotelian passage, *paros ho apethes legetai, the gentle man has no (inordinate) affection.*—**omne agens assimilat sibi patiens,** see *agens.*—**omne agens est nobilius seu honorabilius seu praestantius patiente,** see *agens.*—**patiens,** ntis, *P. a., bearing, supporting, suffering, permitting, patient.*—**patienter,** *adv., patiently.*—**passus,** a, um, *P. a.,* (1) *having suffered,* (2) *suffering.* —**factum et passum consequitur**

dispositionem facientis et agentis, *the effect directs itself according to the disposition of the cause.*—**violentum est, cuius principium est extra, nihil conferente vim passo,** see *violentus.*

patria, ae, *f.,* (1) *fatherland, native land* or *country,* (2) *heavenly fatherland, heaven,* the opposite of *via.* On **bonum patriae,** see *bonus* under 3. On **beatitudo patriae,** see *beatitudo* under 1; on **caritas patriae,** see *caritas;* on **claritas patriae,** see *claritas;* on **cognitio patriae,** see *cognitio* under 2; on **contemplatio patriae,** see *contemplatio;* on **ecclesia secundum statum patriae,** see *ecclesia* under 1; on **gloria patriae,** see *gloria* under 1; on **gratia patriae,** see *gratia* under 2; on **perfectio patriae,** see *perfectio* under 3; on **status patriae,** see *status* under 3; on **visio patriae,** see *visio* under 1.

patriarcha, ae, *m., a patriarch, father* or *chief of a tribe,* (1) in the Septuagint the word means "chief" of the tribes; in the New Testament (Heb. VII, 4) it is applied to Abraham as a version of his title "father of many nations"; also to David (Acts II, 29) and to the twelve sons of Jacob (Acts VII, 8-9). This last became the special meaning of the word when used of Scriptural characters. The heads of the tribes were the "Twelve patriarchs", though the word is used in a broader sense of the Old Law in general, e.g., the invocation in the Litany, "all ye holy Patriarchs and prophets," (2) in early times bishops of special dignity were called patriarchs. The oldest canon law admitted only three bishops as having what later ages called patriarchal rights—the Bishops of Rome, Alexandria, and Antioch.—**De Patriarchis,** *on the Patriarchs,* a work by St. Ambrose.

patrimonialis, e, *adj., of* or *belonging to a patrimony, patrimonial.* On **bonum patrimoniale,** see *bonus* under 3.

patrimonium, ii, *n., an inheritance, patrimony, estate.*

patrinus, i, *m., a sponsor, God-parent,* one who at the baptism of an infant or child professes the Christian faith in its name and guarantees its religious education.

patrius, a, um, *adj., of* or *belonging to a father, fatherly, paternal.*

patro, are, avi, atum, 1, *v. a., do, perform, accomplish.*

patrocinium, ii, *n.,* (1) in gen., *patronage, protection, defence,* (a) *the guardianship, patronage,* tutelary care of a saint, (b) *spiritual assistance, suffrages* for the dead, (2) in partic., *a defence* in a court of justice, *a pleading.*

patrocinor, ari, atus, 1, *v. dep. n., to protect, defend, support, furnish a defence* or *protection to,* used *absol.,* with the *dat.*

patronatus, us, *m., patronage.* The *ius patronatus,* the right of pa-

tronage is the sum of the rights and obligations of a patron (one who erects or maintains a benefice) in connection with the assignment or administration of this benefice. Patronage may be acquired by inheritance, presentation by the patron to another, by exchange, purchase, prescription.

patronus, i, *m., an advocate, defender.*

patruus, i, *m., a father's brother, paternal uncle.*

paucitas, atis, *f., a small number, fewness, scarcity, paucity.*

paucus, a, um, *adj., few, little.*—**pauci,** orum, *m., few, a few.*—**pauca,** orum, *n., a few words.*

Paula, ae, *f., Paula,* a noble and wealthy Roman lady, who accompanied Jerome to Palestine in 385 and lived the rest of her life at Bethlehem where she died in 404. She was born in 347, and while quite young was married to the senator Taxatius, of the Julian family. Becoming a widow at the age of 31, she abandoned her riches and country to devote herself to a penitential life. In Bethlehem she founded several monasteries and also an asylum for pilgrims.

paulatim, *adv., little by little, by degrees, gradually.*

Paulianisti and **Pauliani,** orum, *m., the Paulianists,* heretics and followers of Paul of Samosata, the proud Bishop of Antioch about the year 360. He maintained that

Christ though begotten of the Holy Ghost and born of a virgin was no more than a mere man in which the divine Logos, the wisdom of God, dwelt not as a person but as a quality or power. The Samosatians or Paulianists, as his followers were called, continued as a distinct sect down to the fourth century.

Paulina, ae, *f., Paulina,* a Christian lady, wife of Armamentarius. She and her husband made a vow to renounce the world, on which St. Augustine wrote a letter approving heartily of their resolution. Paulina requested Augustine to explain to her the doctrine about "seeing God" on which he appears to have written to her a short letter, Ep. 147, 17. He again replies to her question at greater length and calls his letter a book, *de Videndo Deo.*

Paulinus, i, *m., Paulinus,* bishop of Nola. He was born at Bordeaux, France in 354 and died at Nola, Italy in 431. Educated under Ausonius, he became governor of the Province of Campania; he married a Spanish Christian lady named Therasia and was converted to Christianity. With his wife he retired to Spain in 390 and embraced the religious life. His poems and letters are valuable contributions to the literature of his day.

paulisper, *adv., for a little while, for a short time.*

paulo, *adv., by a little, a little, somewhat.*

Paulus, i, *m., Paul,* saint, apostle of the Gentiles. He was born in the year 2 A.D. of Jewish parents of the tribe of Benjamin, at Tarsus in Cilicia and martyred at Rome in 67. At the time of his circumcision he received the name Saul, but being a Roman citizen, he also had the name Paul by which he was known when he began his apostolate among the Gentiles. A Pharisee (Acts. 23, 6), he persecuted the Christians. The story of his miraculous conversion is related in Acts 9, 1-9; 22, 3-21; 26, 9-23. We have fourteen canonical letters from St. Paul, which are addressed partly to one or several congregations, partly to certain persons.

pauper, peris, *adj.,* (1) *poor,* i.e., *not wealthy, of small means,* (2) fig., **pauperes spiritu,** *poor in spirit,* i.e., *humble.*—**pauper,** eris, *comm., a poor person.*

pauperculus, a, um, *adj., dim, poor.*

paupertas, atis, *f.,* (1) *poverty, small means, moderate circumstances,* (2) *voluntary poverty.*—Kinds of *paupertas* in this (1) sense are: (a), **paupertas coacta seu involuntaria** and **paupertas voluntaria,** *the forced* or *involuntary poverty* and *the voluntary poverty.*—(b), **paupertas evangelica,** *the evangelical poverty.*—(c), **paupertas involuntaria,** see *paupertas coacta.*—(d), **paupertas spi-**

ritus, *the poverty of the spirit* or *according to the spirit.*—(e), **paupertas voluntaria,** see *paupertas coacta.*—On **consilium paupertatis perpetuae,** see *consilium* under 2; on **votum paupertatis,** see *votum* under 1.—Kinds of *paupertas* in this (2) sense are: **paupertas actualis** and **paupertas habitualis,** *the poverty according to the act* and *poverty that has become a habit.*

paveo, ere, pavi, 2, *v. n.* and *a.,* (1) *neutr., to be afraid, to tremble,* (2) *act., to fear, dread.*

pavesco, ere, *v. inch. n.* and *a., to become alarmed.*

pavidus, a, um, *adj., trembling, timorous, terrified, alarmed.*

pavimentum, i, *n., a floor* composed of small stones.

pavor, oris, *m., fear, dread.*

pax, pacis, *f.,* (1) *peace, tranquillity,* (2) *the greeting of peace, the kiss of peace. Pax* is one of the *beatitudines* (see *beatitudo* 2) and accordingly also one of the *fructus Spiritus sancti* (see *fructus* 2), both indeed according to different relationships. On **sacramentum pacis,** see *sacramentum* under 3.—Kinds of *pax* in this (1) sense are: (a), **pax apparens** and **pax vera,** *the apparent* and *the true peace.*—(b), **pax imperfecta** and **pax perfecta,** *the imperfect* and *the perfect (true) peace.*—(c), **pax perfecta,** see *pax imperfecta.*—(d), **pax vera,** see *pax apparens.*

peccamen, inis, *n., a fault, sin.*

peccator, oris, *m., a transgressor, sinner.*

peccatrix, icis, *f., a female sinner.* —*adj., sinful, sinning.*

peccatum, i, *n.,* (cf. *pecco,* are), (1) *fault, error, mistake,* in the general sense of the word, (2) *fault,* in the moral sense, *transgression, sin.*—Kinds of *peccatum* in this (1) sense are: (a), **peccatum artis seu in artificialibus, peccatum naturae seu in naturalibus,** and **peccatum morale seu in moralibus seu in moribus,** *the fault of art, of nature,* and *the moral fault* or *the fault which is committed in the field of art, of natural things* and *in moral actions* or *morals.*—(b), **peccatum in artificialibus,** see *peccatum artis.*—(c), **peccatum in moralibus,** see *peccatum artis.*—(d), **peccatum in moribus,** see *peccatum ꞏ artis.*—(e), **peccatum in naturalibus,** see *peccatum artis.*—(f), **peccatum in ratione seu rationis,** *the fault of reason* or *in reason.* Cf. *peccatum rationis* under 2.—(g), **peccatum morale,** see *peccatum artis.* —(h), **peccatum naturae,** see *peccatum artis.*—(i), **peccatum rationis,** see *peccatum in ratione.* On **amor peccati,** see *amor* under 1; on **confessio peccati,** see *confessio* under 1; on **corruptio peccati originalis,** see *corruptio* under 3; on **deformitas peccati,** see *deformitas* under 2; on **immunditia peccati,** see *immunditia;* on **impuritas peccati,** see *impuritas* under 1; on **libertas peccati seu li-**

bertas a peccato, see *libertas* under 1; on macula peccati, see *macula;* on magnitudo peccati, see *magnitudo* under 3; on opus peccati, see *opus* under 4; on poena concomitans peccatum et consequens ex peccato, see *poena;* on quantitas peccati, see *quantitas* under 2; on radix peccati, see *radix;* on reatus peccati, see *reatus;* on reliquiae peccati, see *reliquiae;* on sanctificatio a seu ex peccato, see *sanctificatio* under 1; on servitus peccati, see *servitus* under 2; on status peccati et post peccatum, see *status* under 3; on substantia peccati, see *substantia* under 8; on virtus peccati, see *virtus* under 7. – Kinds of *peccatum* in this (2) sense are: (a), peccatum actuale and peccatum originale seu originis, *the fault* or *sin consisting in an action,* or *actual sin* and *original sin.*–(b), peccatum aeternum, *the eternal sin, that lasting forever.*–(c), peccatum alienum and peccatum proprium, *the foreign* and *the proper sin.*–(d), peccatum capitale, *capital sin,* by which is understood either that sin which brings capital punishment with it or that which gives rise to and directs other sins.–(e), peccatum carnale seu corporale and peccatum spirituale, *the carnal sin* and *that of the spirit.*–(f), peccatum comissionis seu transgressionis seu commissum and peccatum omissionis, *the sin of commission* or *transgression* and *the sin of omission.*–(g), peccatum commissum, see *peccatum commissionis.*–(h), peccatum contra Deum, peccatum contra proximum, and peccatum contra seipsum, *the sin against God, that against neighbor,* and *that against self.*–(i), peccatum contra naturam, *the sin against nature.*–(j), peccatum contra proximum, see *peccatum contra Deum.*–(k), peccatum contra seipsum, see *peccatum contra Deum.*–(l), peccatum cordis, peccatum oris, and peccatum operis, *sin in thought, sin in word,* and *sin in action.*–(m), peccatum corporale, see *peccatum carnale.*–(n), peccatum curabile seu veniale and peccatum incurabile seu mortale, *the curable* or *venial sin* and *the incurable* or *mortal sin.*–(o), peccatum ex certa malitia seu malitiae seu industriae, peccatum ex ignorantia seu nescientiae and peccatum ex infirmitate seu passione seu imbecillitatis, *the sin of pure malice, that of ignorance,* and *that of weakness* or *excitement of the mind.* Cf. *peccare ex certa malitia* under *peccare* 2.–(p), peccatum ex deliberatione and peccatum ex subreptione, *the sin committed with deliberation* and *that committed in haste.*–(q), peccatum ex ignorantia, see *peccatum ex certa malitia.*–(r), peccatum ex infirmitate, see *peccatum ex certa malitia.*–(s), peccatum ex passione, see *peccatum ex certa malitia.*—(t), **peccatum ex subreptione,** see *peccatum ex deliberatione.*—(u), **peccatum generale** and **peccatum speciale,** *the general* and *the special sin.*—(v), **peccatum grave** and **peccatum leve seu minutum,** *the grave* and *the light* or *small sin.*—(w), **peccatum humanae seu totius naturae seu naturae seu naturale** and **peccatum humanum seu personae seu personale,** *the sin attached to human nature,* and *the sin committed by an individual* or *the personal sin.* Cf. *peccatum actuale.*—(x), **peccatum humanum,** see *peccatum humanae naturae.*—(y), **peccatum incurabile,** see *peccatum curabile.*—(z), **peccatum industriae,** see *peccatum ex certa malitia.*—(a²), **peccatum in Filium, peccatum in Patrem,** and **peccatum in Spiritum sanctum,** *the sin against God the Son, that against God the Father,* and *that against God the Holy Spirit.* —(b²), **peccatum in Patrem,** see *peccatum in Filium.*—(c²), **peccatum in Spiritum sanctum,** see *peccatum in Filium.*—(d²), **peccatum leve,** see *peccatum grave.*— (e²), **peccatum malitiae,** see *peccatum ex certa malitia.*—(f²), **peccatum minutum,** see *peccatum grave.*—(g²), **peccatum mortale,** see *peccatum curabile.*—(h²), **peccatum naturae,** see *peccatum humanae naturae.* Cf. *peccatum naturae* under 1.—(i²), **peccatum naturale,** see *peccatum humanae naturae.*—(j²), **peccatum nescien-**

tiae, see *peccatum ex certa malitia.*—(k²), **peccatum occultum** and **peccatum publicum,** *the secret* and *the public sin.*—(l²), **peccatum omissionis,** see *peccatum commissionis.*—(m²), **peccatum operis** see *peccatum cordis.*—(n²), **peccatum originale,** see *peccatum actuale.*—(o²), **peccatum originis,** see *peccatum actuale.*—(p²), **peccatum oris,** see *peccatum cordis.*—(q²), **peccatum personae,** see *peccatum humanae naturae.*—(r²), **peccatum personale,** see *peccatum humanae naturae.*—(s²), **peccatum proprium,** see *peccatum alienum.*—(t²), **peccatum publicum,** see *peccatum occultum.*— (u²), **peccatum rationis, peccatum sensualitatis,** and **peccatum voluntatis,** *the sin of reason* (cf. *peccatum in ratione* under 1), *that of the sensuous appetitive faculty* and *that of the will,* i.e., the sin that has its subject in the reason, or in the sensuous appetitive faculty, or in the will.—(v²), **peccatum sensualitatis,** see *peccatum rationis.*—(w²), **peccatum speciale,** see *peccatum generale.* —(x²), **peccatum spirituale,** see *peccatum carnale.*—(y²), **peccatum totius naturae,** see *peccatum humanae naturae.*—(z²), **peccatum transgressionis,** see *peccatum commissionis.*—(a³), **peccatum veniale,** see *peccatum curabile.*—(b³), **peccatum veniale ab eventu, peccatum veniale ex causa,** and **peccatum veniale in genere,** *the sin venial because of* *some event, that venial because of its cause,* and *the venial sin in general.*—(c³), **peccatum voluntarium,** *the voluntary sin* or *the sin committed with knowledge* and *will.*—(d³), **peccatum voluntatis,** see *peccatum rationis.*

pecco, are, avi, atum, 1, *v. a.* and *n.,* (cf. *peccatum*), (1) *to miss, fail, make a mistake,* in the general sense of the word, (2) *to err* or *fail* in the moral sense of the word, *sin.*—Kinds of *peccare* in this (2) sense are: (a), **peccare ex certa malitia seu scientia seu ex industria seu ex electione, peccare ex passione seu ex infirmitate,** and **peccare ex ignorantia,** *to sin out of pure malice* or *with full knowledge* or *with intention* or *from free choice,* and *to sin because of agitation of mind* or *from weakness* or *from ignorance.*—(b), **peccare ex certa scientia,** see *peccare ex certa malitia.*—(c), **peccare ex electione,** see *peccare ex certa malitia.* —(d), **peccare ex ignorantia,** see *peccare ex certa malitia.*—(e), **peccare ex industria,** see *peccare ex certa malitia.*—(f), **peccare ex infirmitate,** see *peccare ex certa malitia.*—(g), **peccare ex passione,** see *peccare ex certa malitia.*— (h), **peccare mortaliter** and **peccare venialiter,** *to sin with complete aversion from God, thereby destroying grace* and *charity,* and *to sin without complete aversion, grace* and *charity remaining.* Cf. *peccatum mortale*

under peccatum 2.—(i), **peccare venialiter,** see *peccare mortaliter.*

pectus, oris, *n.,* (1) *breast, the breastbone,* (2) transf., as the seat of *affection, courage,* etc., *the heart, feelings, disposition.*

pectusculum, i, *n., a little breastbone.*

peculatus, us, *m., peculation, embezzlement of public money.*

peculium, ii, *m., private property.*

pecunia, ae, *f.,* (sometimes **pecuniae,** arum, *f.,*), (1) in gen., *property, riches, wealth,* (2) in partic., *money.*

pecuniarius, a, um, *adj., pecuniary, of* or *belonging to money.*

pecus, oris, *n.,* (1) lit., (a) *cattle,* used in the sing. and pl., (b) of sheep, *a flock, sheep,* (2) transf., of a single animal, *a beast,* (3) fig., in the sing., *a flock, sheep.*— **pastor pecorum,** *a shepherd.*

pecus, udis, *f., a single head of cattle, a beast.*

pedalis, e, *adj., a foot in diameter.*

pedester, tris, tre, *adj., plain, common.*

pedetentim, *adv., gradually, by degrees, cautiously.*

peiero, are, avi, atum, 1, *v. n., to swear falsely, to forswear* or *perjure oneself.*

peior, us, see *malus.*

peioro, are, 1, *v. a.* and *n., to render worse.*

Pelagianus, a, um, *adj., Pelagian, of* or *pertaining to Pelagius* or *his doctrine.*—**Pelagiani,** orum, *m., the Pelagians,* followers of the doctrine of Pelagius.

Pelagius, ii, *m.*, *Pelagius*, (1) a famous heretic of the fifth century, A.D. He was probably born in England and came to Rome about the year 400 for the purpose of continuing his studies. Here he embraced the errors of Rufinus, concerning the exemption of human nature from inborn and inherited corruption. The fundamental error of Pelagius was the denial of original sin, and of the necessity of divine grace for man. (2) *Pelagius II,* Pope from 578-590. He was born at Rome, but the date of his birth is unknown. He succeeded Benedict I when the Lombards were besieging Rome. The most important acts of Pelagius have relation to the Lombards, or to the Istrian schism of the Three Chapters.

pelagus, i, *n.*, (1) lit., *the sea,* (2) fig., *for an immense mass* or *extent.*

pelliceus, a, um, *adj., made of skins.*

pellicula, ae, *f., a small skin, foreskin.*

pellis, is, *f., a skin, hide.*

pello, ere, pepuli, pulsum, 3, *v. a.,* (1) lit., *to excel, turn out,* used with *ab* and *abl.* of the place from which one is expelled, (2) fig., *to drive out* or *away, to banish, expel.*

pendeo, ere, pependi, 2, *v. n.,* (1) lit., (a) *to hang* on something, *to suffer death on a cross,* used with *in* and the *abl.,* (b) *to cling to*

something used with *ad* and *acc.,* (c) *to hang something, to fasten to* some object so as to allow free motion, (2) fig., *to hang, rest, depend* upon a person or a thing, used with *de, ex, ab* and *abl.*-- **pendens,** entis, *P. a.,* (1) *hanging, suspended* from the cross, (2) in econom. lang., of fruit not yet plucked or gathered.

pendo, ere, pependi, pensum, 3, *v. a.* and *n., to value, esteem, regard,* used in the S.T. only with *parvi,* a genitive of value in the sense of *to esteem lightly* or *of little value:* in some editions written as one word, *parvipendo.*

pene, adv., see *paene.*

penes, prep. with *acc., in, within, according to.*

penetratio, onis, *f., a piercing, penetrating.*

penetrativus, a, um, *adj., penetrating, penetrative.*

penetro, are, avi, atum, 1, *v. a.* and *n., to enter, penetrate;* (1) *act.,* (2) *neutr.*

penitus, *adv., entirely, wholly, utterly.*—**audire nihil penitus,** *to hear nothing at all.*

penna, ae, *f.,* (1) *a quill, a pen* for writing made by sharpening the point of the stalk of a feather, (2) plur., *wings, a wing,* synonym of *ala.*

pennula, ae, *f., a little wing.*

pensio, onis, *f., a paying, payment.*

penso, are, avi, atum, 1, *v. freq. a., to weigh, measure, ponder, consider, examine.*

pentagonus, a, um, *adj., pentago-
nal.—***pentagonum,** i, *n., a pen-
tagon.*

Pentateuchus, i, *m., the Pentateuch,*
the name for the first five books
of the Old Testament: Genesis,
Exodus, Leviticus, Numbers, and
Deuteronomy.

Pentecoste, es, *f., Pentecost, Whit-
Sunday,* the fiftieth day after
Easter.

penultimus, a, um, *adj., the last
but one, penultimate.*

penuria, ae, *f., want, need,* scarcity
of anything.

Pepuziani, orum, *m., the Pepuziani,* the name of a sect of Montanists in the second century, so
called from Pepuza in Phrygia.

per, *prep.* with *acc.,* (1) *through,
by means of, for the sake of,
on account of, as the result of,
from, in accordance with, with
respect to, by virtue of,* (2) *by,
in,* and *for,* (3) *after the way*
and *manner,* having the same
meaning as *per modum* with
which it is sometimes interchanged. On **per ordinem,** see
ordo under 1.—**per se,** *through
oneself* or *on account of oneself,
in consequence of* or *according
to one's own nature* and *essence.*
—**per seu propter seu secundum
aliud seu ab alio,** *through another* or *on account of another*
or *in consequence of another* or
by another, the opposite of *per
se.* On **bonitas per se,** see *bonitas* under 2; on **causa per se et
per aliud,** see *causa* under 2; on

cognoscere per se, see *cognoscere* under 2; on **debitum per se
seu secundum se et propter aliud,** see *debitus* under 1; on **divisio per se,** see *divisio;* on **esse
per se et per aliud seu ab alio,**
see *esse;* on **impossibilitas per se,**
see *impossibilitas;* on **intelligibile per se,** see *intelligibilis* under
2; on **meritorium per se,** see *meritorius;* on **necessarium per se
et per aliud,** see *necessarius*
under 1; on **notum per se et per
aliud,** see *notus;* on **oppositum
per se,** see *opponere;* on **perfectus per se,** see *perfectus* under
1; on **spirituale per se,** see *spiritualis* under 3; on **vanum per se,**
see *vanus* under 3; on **verbum
per se dictum,** see *verbum* under 2; on **verum per se et per
aliud notum,** see *verus* under 1.
—**per seu secundum accidens,**
through or *in accordance with
something accidental,* by which
is to be understood the accidental or the unessential of a thing
and one of its parts, *indirectly,*
the usual opposite of *per se, directly.* On **accidens per se,** see
accidens under 2; on **actus per
se, et actus per accidens bonus,**
see *actus* under 1; on **agens per
se et per accidens,** see *agens;*
on **agere per se et per accidens,**
see *agere* under 1; on **alius secundum accidens,** see *alius;* on
alter secundum accidens, see *alter;* on **amicitia per se et per
accidens,** see *amicitia* under 1;
on **bonum per se et per acci-**

dens, see *bonus* under 2; on causa per se et per accidens, see *causa* under 1; on causare per se et per accidens, see *causare;* on cognoscere per se et per accidens, see *cognoscere* under 2; on corrumpere per se et per accidens, see *corrumpere* under 1; on dicere per se et per accidens, see *dicere* under 3; on differentia per se et per accidens, see *differentia;* on distinguere per se, see *distinguere; on* dividere per se et per accidens, see *dividere* under 1; on dominus per accidens, see *dominus;* on effectus per se et per accidens, see *effectus;* on ens per se et per accidens, see *ens;* on esse per se et per accidens, see *esse;* on esse in loco per se et per accidens, see *locus* under 2; on facere per accidens, see *facere* under 1; on fieri per se et per accidens seu secundum accidens, see *fieri;* on generare per se et per accidens, see *generare;* on generatio per se seu per se intenta et per accidens, see *generatio* under 1; on impossibile per se et per accidens, see *impossibilis;* on incontinens per se et per accidens, see *incontinens;* on indivisus per se et per accidens, see *indivisus;* on inesse per se et per accidens, see *inesse;* on infinitum per se et per accidens, see *infinitus;* on intellegibile per se, see *intellegibilis* under 1; on locus per se et per accidens, see *locus* under 2; on malum per se et per

accidens, see *malus* under 2; on mobile per se et per accidens, see *mobilis;* on motus per se et per accidens, see *motus* under 1; on movens per se et per accidens, see *movens;* on movere per se et per accidens seu secundum accidens, see *movere;* on nonens per se et secundum accidens, see *non-ens;* on notum per se et per accidens, see *notus;* on obiectum per se et per accidens, see *obiectum;* on ordo per se et per accidens seu secundum accidens, see *ordo* under 1; on passio per se, see *passio* under 1; on pati per se et per accidens, see *pati* under 1; on praedicare per se et per accidens seu secundum accidens, see *praedicare* under 2; on praedicatio per se, see *praedicatio* under 2; on praedicatum per se et per accidens, see *praedicatum* under 1; on principium per se et per accidens, see *principium;* on prius per se et per accidens, see *prior* under 1; on probatio per se, see *probatio* under 2; on quantitas per se et per accidens, see *quantitas* under 1; on quantum per se et per accidens, see *quantus* under 2; on sanctus per se, see *sanctus;* on scire per se et per accidens, see *scire* under 2; on sensibile per se et per accidens, see *sensibilis* under 3; on sentire per se et per accidens, see *sentire* under 1; on terminus per se et per accidens, see *terminus* under 2; on totalitas per se et per accidens, see *totalitas;* on **transmutatio per se et per accidens,** see *transmutatio* under 1; on **unio per se et per accidens,** see *unio;* on **unitas per se et per accidens,** see *unitas;* on **verum per se et per accidens,** see *verus* under 1; on **volitum per se et per accidens,** see *volitus;* on **voluntarium per se et per accidens,** see *voluntarius* under 3.—There are four *modi dicendi per se,* i.e., four ways of mentioning something *per se,* of which three are as follows (For the fourth or rather the third according to St. Thomas, see below under 2): primus ergo modus dicendi "per se" est quando id quod attribuitur alicui, pertinet ad formam eius, et quia definitio significat formam et essentiam rei, primus modus eius quod est per se, quando praedicatur de aliquo definitio vel aliquid in definitione positum, . . ., sive ponatur in recto sive in obliquo; sicut in definitione trianguli ponitur linea; unde linea per se inest triangulo, . . ., secundus modus dicendi "per se" est quando haec praepositio *per* designat habitudinem causae materialis, prout scilicet id cui aliquid attribuitur est propria materia et proprium subiectum ipsius, . . ., quando subiectum ponitur in definitione praedicati, quod est proprium accidens eius, . . ., sicut rectum et circulare insunt lineae per se; nam linea ponitur in definitione

eorum, . . ., ponit quartum modum, secundum quod haec praepositio *per* designat habitudinem causae efficientis vel cuiuscumque alterius, et ideo dicit, quod quidquid inest unicuique propter seipsum "per se" dicitur de eo, quod vero non propter seipsum inest alicui per accidens dicitur; sicut cum dic "hoc ambulante coruscat," non enim propter id quod ambulat coruscavit, sed hoc dicitur secundum accidens, si vero quod praedicatur insit subiecto propter seipsum, per se inest, ut si dicamus, quod interfectum interiit; manifestum est enim quod propter id quod illud interfectum est, interiit, et non est accidens quod interfectum interierit. 1 Anal. 10 a and c.—**quod est per se, semper est prius eo quod est per aliud,** *that which is through itself is prior to that which is through something else.* —**per se,** *for itself* or *for itself alone* or *taken in itself,* synonym of *secundum se,* the opposite of *cum se seu in alio seu per respectum ad aliud seu secundum aliud.* Ponit alium (sc. *tertium,* see above under 1) modum eius, quod est "per se", prout "per se" significat aliquid solitarium, sicut dicitur quod per se est aliquod particulare quod est in genere substantiae, quod non praedicatur de aliquo subiecto, . . ., quae vero dicuntur de subiecto, scilicet in subiecto exsistentia, accidentia sunt; nam quae dicuntur de subiecto, sicut universalia de inferioribus, non semper accidentia sunt, 1 Anal. 10 b. On **agere per se,** see *agere* under 1; on **bonum per se,** see *bonus* under 2; on **ens per se,** see *ens;* on **exsistere per se,** see *exsistere;* on **forma per se,** see *forma* under 2; on **iniustum per se,** see *iniustus;* on **perfectum per se,** see *perfectus* under 1; on **vita per se,** see *vita* under 1.—Kinds of *per se* are: (a), **per se frustra,** *useless in itself,* see *frustra.*—(b), **per se homo,** *man-in-itself, subsisting manhood,* see *homo.*—(c), **per se pulchritudo,** see *pulchritudo.* —(d), **per se sapientia,** *subsistent wisdom,* see *sapientia* under 1. Cf. PP. Q. 44. Art. 3, in quot.— (e), **per se sufficiens,** *self-sufficient,* see *sufficiens.*—(f), **per se sufficientia,** *self-sufficiency,* see *sufficientia.*—(g), **per se vanum,** see *vanus* under 3.

pera, ae, *f., a bag, wallet.*

perago, ere, egi, actum, 3, *v. a., to carry through, to go through with, execute, finish, accomplish.* —*peragere vitam, to carry on life, live.*

perambulo, are, avi, atum, 1, *v. a., to go about.*

perceptibilis, e, *adj., perceptible.*

perceptibilitas, atis, *f., susceptibility, capacity for being acted upon, of receiving.*

perceptio, onis, *f.,* (1) *taking, receiving,* (2) *perception, observa-*

tion.—One kind of perception is: **perceptio visibilis,** *visual perception.*

perceptivus, a, um, *adj., perceptive, capable of perceiving.*

percipio, ere, cepi, ceptum, 3, *v. a.,* (1) lit., *to get, obtain, receive,* (2) fig., (a) *to perceive, observe, to obtain knowledge through the senses;* (b) *to apprehend,* with the mind; *to recognize* the nature of; *to comprehend, understand; note.*—**perceptus,** a, um, *adj.,* (1) *perceived* by the senses, (2) *received, obtained.*

percuncto, (**percunctor**), are, atum, 1, *v. a.* and *n., to question, to inquire earnestly.*

percurro, ere, percucurri or percurri, cursum, 3, *v. a.* and *n., to run over in speaking, to mention cursorily.*

percussio, onis, *f.,* (1) *a beating, striking, percussion,* the sharp striking of one body against another; violent collision especially such as causes a shock or sound, (2) *a striking,* the action of assailing or attacking some one with blows.

percussor, oris, *m., a striker, killer.*

percussura, ae, *f., blow, stroke, thrust.*

percutio, ere, cussi, cussum, 3, *v. a.,* (I) lit., with the notion of the *per* predominating, (II) with the idea of the verb predominating, (1) lit., (a) in gen., *to strike, beat, hit, smite,* (b) in partic., *to strike, stamp an image,* (2) fig., (a) *to smite, strike,* visit with calamity of any kind, (b) *to affect deeply, move, astound*, (c) *to condemn.*—PT. Q. 37. Art. 3 c. —(II) (1) (a).

perdisco, ere, didici, 3, *v. a.*, *to learn completely.*

perditio, onis, *f.*, *ruin, perdition.*

perdix, icis, *m.*, *a partridge.*

perdo, ere, didi, ditum, 3, *v. a.*, *to make away with, destroy, ruin, squander, dissipate, lose.*

perdoceo, ere, ui, ctum, 2, *v. a.*, *to teach thoroughly.*

perduco, ere, xi, ctum, 3, *v. a.*, *to lead, bring, conduct, guide* a person or thing to any place.

perduro, are, avi, atum, 1, *v. a.* and *n.*, *to last* or *hold out, to endure.*

peregre, *adv.*, *away from home.*

peregrinatio, onis, *f.*, *pilgrimage*, (1) life on earth as distinguished from life hereafter, (2) a journey taken by or with a group to a shrine or other sacred place, (3) the act of journeying as a traveller.

peregrinor, ari, atus, 1, *v. dep. n.*, (1) lit., *to travel about*, (2) fig., with *a*, *to be absent from*, *a stranger to.*

peregrinus, a, um, *adj.*, *strange, foreign, from without.*—**peregrinus,** i, *m.*, *a stranger, traveller, pilgrim.*

peremptio, onis, *f.*, *a destroying, a killing.*

perennis, e, *adj.*, *uninterrupted, continual.*

pereo, ire, ii, ivi, itum, 4, *v. n.*, (1) in gen., *to pass away, to be destroyed, to perish*, (2) in partic.,

(a) *to lose one's life, to perish*, (b) *to be lost, ruined, undone*, (3) fig., (a) of abstract things, *to die, perish, pass away*, (b) *to perish, to suffer spiritual* or *moral death; to be lost, to perish* in one's sins.

perfecte, see *perfectus.*

perfectibilis, e, *adj.*, *perfectible, capable of being made perfect; capable of arriving at the highest attainable perfection.*

perfectio, onis, *f.*, (1) *finish, accomplishment, completion, perfection*, on the level of essence and entity, synonym of *completio, consummatio*, and *terminatio*, the opposite of *corruptio*, (2) *completion, accomplishment, perfection*, on the level of action and operation, the opposite of *imperfectio*, (3) *moral accomplishment, spiritual perfection* of man, which consists in moral virtue, and for the Christian, charity, (4) *the moment of perfection, the perfection of the individual*, the opposite of *defectus, privatio*, and *vitium.* On **passio perfectionis**, see *passio* under 2.—(2), ad perfectionem alicuius rei dupliciter aliquid pertinet. On **finis perfectionis**, see *finis* under 1; on **magnitudo perfectionis**, see *magnitudo* under 3; on **ordo perfectionis**, see *ordo* under 1; on **prius perfectione seu secundum perfectionem seu ordine perfectionis**, see *prior* under 1; on **totalitas perfectionis**, see *totalitas;* on **unitas perfectionis**, see *unitas.*—There is a difference beween

perfectio propria seu **proprie** seu **simpliciter dicta** and **perfectio large** seu **transumptive dicta,** *the perfection so called properly or simply,* and *the perfection in the wider* or *transferred sense of the word* which is also called *perfectio in malitia.*—The following are kinds of *perfectio propria:* (a), **perfecto absoluta,** *the absolute* or *unconditioned perfection.* See *perfectio absoluta* under 3.—(b), **perfectio accidentalis** and **perfectio essentialis** seu **substantialis,** *the unessential and the essential perfection.*—(c), **perfectio actus,** *the perfection of an action.*—(d), **perfectio caritatis,** *the perfection of charity* or *love.*—(e), **perfectio causalis,** *the causal perfection* which consists in the exercise of causality.—(f), **perfectio complementi,** *the perfection of completion* or *conclusion.*—(g), **perfectio consummata** seu **summa,** *the highest perfection.*—(h), **perfectio debita,** *the due* or *befitting perfection.*—(i), **perfectio dispositionis, perfectio formae** and **perfectio finis** seu **ratione finis** seu **ex parte finis,** *the perfection of preparation, that of form, and that of the end* or *goal* or *with respect to the end* or *goal.*—(j), **perfectio divina** and **perfectio hominis,** *the perfection of God and that of man.*—(k), **perfectio essentialis,** see *perfectio accidentalis.*—(l), **perfectio ex ratione finis,** see *perfectio dispositionis.*—(m), **perfectio extrinseca** and **perfectio in-** trinseca seu **interior,** *the outer and the inner perfection.* Cf. *perfectio exterior et interior* under 3.—(n), **perfectio finis,** see *perfectio dispositionis.*—(o), **perfectio formae,** see *perfectio dispositionis.*—(p), **perfectio formalis** and **perfectio materialis,** *the perfection of a thing according to its form and that according to its material.*—(q), **perfectio gloriae, perfectio gratiae,** and **perfectio naturae** seu **naturalis,** *the perfection of heavenly glory, that of divine grace, and that of nature.* Cf. also *perfectio naturalis* under 4.—(r), **perfectio gratiae,** see *perfectio gloriae.*—(s), **perfectio hominis,** see *perfectio divina.*—(t), **perfectio imperfecta** and **perfectio omnimoda** seu **plena** seu **totalitatis,** *the imperfect* or *defective* and *the universal* or *complete* or *total perfection.* Cf. **perfectio particularis et universalis.**—(u), **perfectio intellectus** seu **secundum intellectum** and **perfectio secundum affectum,** *the perfection of reason* and *that of the will.*—(v), **perfectio interior,** see *perfectio extrinseca.*—(w), **perfectio intrinseca,** see *perfectio extrinseca.*—(x), **perfectio materialis,** see *perfectio formalis.*—(y), **perfectio multitudinis** and **perfectio unius personae** seu **personalis,** *the perfection of a multitude* or *of a crowd* and *that of a single person* or *personal perfection.*—(z), **perfectio naturae,** see *perfectio gloriae.*—(a²), **perfectio**

naturalis, see *perfectio gloriae.*
—(b²), **perfectio omnimoda,** see
perfectio imperfecta.—(c²), **perfectio operationis,** see *operatio*
under 2, *perfection of operation.*
—(d²), **perfectio particularis** and
perfectio universalis, *the partial*
and *the universal perfection.* Cf.
also *perfectio imperfecta* and
perfectio omnimoda.—(e²), **perfectio personalis,** see *perfectio
multitudinis.*—(f²), **perfectio plena,** see *perfectio omnimoda.*—
(g²), **perfectio prima,** and **perfectio secunda seu ultima,** *the first
and the second* or *last perfection
of a thing.* Cf. *perfectio ultima*
under 4. Cf. also *actus primus et
secundus* under *actus* 2.—(h²),
**perfectio prima hominis seu hu-
manae naturae** and **perfectio ultima hominis,** *the first perfection
of man,* and *the last* or *ultimate
perfection of man.*—(i²), **perfectio
prima humanae naturae,** see *perfectio prima hominis.*—(j²), **perfectio propria,** *the perfection
proper to a thing.*—(k²), **perfectio
scientiae** and **perfectio virtutis,**
the perfection of knowledge and
that of virtue.—(l²), **perfectio secunda,** see *perfectio prima.*—(m²),
perfectio secundum affectum, see
perfectio intellectus.—(n²), **perfectio secundum intellectum,** see
perfectio intellectus.—(o²), **perfectio speciei,** *the perfection of
the species.*—(p²), **perfectio spiritualis,** *the spiritual perfection.*
Cf. *perfectio spiritualis,* under 4.
—(q²), **perfectio substantialis,** see

perfectio accidentalis.—(r²), **perfectio summa,** see *perfectio consummata.*—(s²), **perfectio totalitatis,** see *perfectio omnimoda.*—(t²),
perfectio ultima, see *perfectio
prima.*—(u²), **perfectio ultima hominis,** see *perfectio prima hominis.*—(v²), **perfectio unius personae,** see *perfectio multitudinis.*
—(w²), **perfectio universalis,** see
perfectio particularis.—(x²), **perfectio universi,** *the perfection of
the universe.*—(y²), **perfectio virtutis,** see *perfectio scientiae.*—**in
via generationis semper incompletum est prius completo, licet
in via perfectionis sit totum e
contrario,** see *generatio* under 1.
On **opus perfectionis,** see *opus*
under 4; on **sacramentum superabundantis perfectionis,** see *sacramentum* under 2; on **status
perfectionis,** see *status* under 4.
—Kinds of *perfectio* in this (3)
sense are: (a), **perfectio absoluta,**
absolute perfection.—(b), **perfectio abundantiae** and **perfectio
sufficientiae,** *the perfection of
abundance,* and *the perfection
of sufficiency.*—(c), **perfectio
communis** and **perfectio superabundans,** *the common* and *the
superabundant* or *unusual perfection.*—(d), **perfectio comprehensoris seu patriae seu vitae
aeternae** and **perfectio viae seu
huius vitae,** *the perfection of the
possessor of heavenly happiness
or that of the heavenly fatherland or that of eternal life and
that on the way to heaven or that*

of this life.—(e), **perfectio consilii** and **perfectio iustitiae,** *the perfection of counsel* and *that of justice,* i.e., *the perfection that is suggested over and above the necessary perfection that is demanded.*—(f), **perfectio exterior** and **perfectio interior,** *the exterior perfection* and *the interior perfection.*—(g), **perfectio huius vitae,** see *perfectio comprehensoris.*—(h), **perfectio interior,** see *perfectio exterior.*—(i), **perfectio iustitiae,** see *perfectio consilii.*—(j), **perfectio patriae,** see *perfectio comprehensoris.*—(k), **perfectio secundum quid** and **perfectio simpliciter,** *relative perfection* and *simple perfection,* or *perfection in a certain respect* and *absolute perfection.*—(l), **perfectio simpliciter,** see *perfectio secundum quid.*—(m), **perfectio sufficientiae,** see *perfectio abundantiae.*—(n), **perfectio viae,** see *perfectio comprehensoris.*—(o), **perfectio vitae aeternae,** see *perfectio comprehensoris.*—Kinds of *perfectio* in this (4) sense are: (a), **perfectio adquisita** and **perfectio infusa,** *the acquired* and *the infused perfection.*—(b), **perfectio habitualis,** *perfection become a habit* or *state.*—(c), **perfectio infusa,** see *perfectio adquisita.*—(d), **perfectio intellectualis,** *the perfection belonging to reason.*—(e), **perfectio naturalis** and **perfectio supernaturalis seu superaddita,** *the natural* and *the supernatural* or *added* (to the nature of a thing)

perfection. Cf. *perfectio naturalis* under 2.—(f), **perfectio spiritualis,** *the spiritual perfection.* Cf. also *perfectio spiritualis* under 2.—(g), **perfectio superaddita,** see *perfectio naturalis.*—(h), **perfectio supernaturalis,** see *perfectio naturalis.*—(i), **perfectio ultima,** *the last perfection.* Cf. *perfectio ultima* under 2.—(j), **perfectio ut ad speciem habendam** and **perfectio ut habentis iam speciem,** *the perfection of a thing for the attainment* or *preservation of its species* and *the perfection of such as already possesses its species* and *essence.*—(k), **perfectio ut habentis iam speciem,** see *perfectio ut ad speciem habendam.*

perfectissime, *adv.,* see *perfectus.*

perfectissimus, see *perfectus.*

perfective, *adv.,* see *perfectivus.*

perfectivus, a, um, *adj., accomplishing, perfecting, perfective,* synonym of *completivus,* the opposite of *corruptivus.* On **alteratio perfectiva,** see *alteratio;* on **amor perfectivus,** see *amor* under 1; on **bonum perfectivum,** see *bonus* under 3; on **causa perfectiva,** see *causa* under 2; on **ordo perfectivus,** see *ordo* under 3; on **passio perfectiva,** see *passio* under 2; on **vis perfectiva,** see *vis* under 1.—**perfective,** *adv., in a manner conducive to perfection, perfectively.*

perfector, oris, *m., a finisher, perfecter.*

perfectus, a, um, *adj.,* (1) *finished, completed, perfect,* synonym of *completus, omnis,* and *totus,* the opposite of *imperfectus* and *incompletus,* (2) *morally* or *spiritually perfect.* On **actus perfecti et perfectus,** see *actus* under 1 and 2; on **adoptio perfecta,** see *adoptio;* on **agens perfectus,** see *agens;* on **amicitia perfecta,** see *amicitia* under 1; on **amor perfectus,** see *amor* under 1; on **animal perfectum,** see *animal* under 2; on **beatitudo perfecta,** see *beatitudo* under 1; on **blasphemia perfecta,** see *blasphemia;* on **bonitas perfecta,** see *bonitas* under 2; on **bonum perfectum,** see *bonus* under 2 and 3; on **caritas perfecta,** see *caritas;* on **castitas perfecta,** see *castitas* under 2; on **certitudo perfecta,** see *certitudo* under 2; on **coactio perfecta,** see *coactio;* on **cognitio perfecta,** see *cognitio* under 2; on **communitas perfecta,** see *communitas* under 3; on **comprehensio perfecta,** see *comprehensio* under 2; on **consilium perfectum,** see *consilium* under 2; on **contemplatio perfecta,** see *contemplatio;* on **continentia perfecta,** see *continentia* under 4; on **contrarietas perfecta,** see *contrarietas* under 2; on **conversio perfecta,** see *conversio* under 2; on **definitio perfecta,** see *definitio* under 2; on **delectatio perfecta,** see *delectatio;* on **differentia perfecta,** see *differentia;* on **dilectio perfecta,** see *dilectio* under 1; on **dispositio perfecta,** see *dispositio* under 4; on **dominium perfectum,** see *dominium;*

on **esse perfectum,** see *esse;* on **felicitas perfecta,** see *felicitas;* on **figura perfecta,** see *figura* under 1; on **forma perfecta,** see *forma* under 2; on **fruitio perfecta,** see *fruitio;* on **gloria perfecta,** see *gloria* under 2; on **gratia perfecta,** see *gratia* under 2; on **imago perfecta,** see *imago* under 1; on **immortalitas perfecta,** see *immortalitas;* on **intelligibile perfectum,** see *intelligibilis* under 2; on **iudicium perfectum,** see *iudicium* under 3; on **linea perfecta,** see *linea* under 1; on **magnitudo perfecta,** see *magnitudo* under 1; on **malum perfectum,** see *malus* under 2; on **matrimonum perfectum,** see *matrimonium;* on **motus perfectus,** see *motus* under 1; on **munditia perfecta,** see *munditia;* on **numerus perfectus,** see *numerus;* on **operatio perfecta,** see *operatio* under 2; on **oratio perfecta,** see *oratio* under 2 and 3; on **ordo perfectus,** see *ordo* under 3; on **passio perfecta,** see *passio* under 3; on **pax perfecta,** see *pax* under 1; on **persona perfecta,** see *persona* under 3; on **potentia perfecta,** see *potentia* under 4; on **potestas perfecta,** see *potestas* under 3; on **privatio perfecta,** see *privatio* under 2; on **prudentia perfecta,** see *prudentia* under 1; on **qualitas perfecta,** see *qualitas;* on **quantitas perfecta,** see *quantitas* under 1; on **ratio perfecta,** see *ratio* under 8; on **regimen perfectum,** see *regimen;* on **religio perfecta,** see *religio* under 2; on **resurrectio perfecta,** see *resurrectio;* on **sacerdotium perfectum,** see *sacerdotium;* on **sacramentum perfectum,** see *sacramentum* under 2; on **scientia perfecta,** see *scientia* under 2; on **sensus perfectus,** see *sensus* under 3; on **similitudo perfecta,** see *similitudo* under 1; on **species perfecta,** see *species* under 6; on **status perfectus,** see *status* under 3; on **subiectio perfecta,** see *subiectio* under 2; on **substantia perfecta,** see *substantia* under 2; on **veritas perfecta,** see *veritas* under 1; on **virtus perfecta, perfecta simpliciter et in comparatione ad alterum,** see *virtus* under 1 and 4; on **visio perfecta,** see *visio* under 1; on **vita perfecta,** see *vita* under 3; on **voluntas perfecta,** see *voluntas* under 3.—There are two kinds of *perfectum*: **perfectum vere** and **perfectum metaphorice seu translative seu secundum quandam similitudinem,** *the truly* or *properly perfect* and *the perfect in the transferred sense* or *after the manner of similarity.* —Kinds of *vere perfectum* are: (a), **perfectum a seipso,** *the perfect of itself.*—(b), **perfectum intellectu seu secundum intellectum,** and **perfectum secundum voluntatem,** *the perfect according to reason* and *that according to will.*—(c), **perfectum partialiter seu secundum aliquid sui seu secundum conditionem alicuius seu secundum quid** and

perfectum universaliter seu secundum se totum seu simpliciter, *the partially perfect* or *the perfect with reference to something* or *relatively* or *in a certain respect* and *the generally* or *wholly* or *simply* or *absolutely perfect.* —(d), **perfectum per aliquid exterius adveniens seu secundum aliquid exterius adiacens** and **perfectum per se seu secundum seipsum,** *the perfect through something coming upon one from the outside* or *in accordance with such* and *the perfect through itself* or *in accordance with itself.* Cf. *perfectum per respectum ad aliud.*—(e), **perfectum per respectum ad aliud seu secundum aliud,** and **perfectum per se seu secundum se,** *the perfect with respect to* or *according to something else* and *the perfect in itself* or *according to itself.* Cf. *perfectum per aliquid exterius adiacens.*—(f), **perfectum per se,** see *perfectum per aliquid exterius adveniens et per respectum ad aliud.*—(g), **perfectum secundum aliquid exterius adiacens,** see *perfectum per aliquid exterius adveniens.*—(h), **perfectum secundum aliquid sui,** see *perfectum partialiter.*—(i), **perfectum secundum aliud,** see *perfectum per respectum ad aliud.*—(j), **perfectum secundum conditionem alicuius,** see *perfectum partialiter.*—(k), **perfectum secundum intellectum,** see *perfectum intellectu.*—(l), **perfectum secundum na-**

turam seu secundum speciem, perfectum secundum statum and perfectum secundum tempus seu temporis conditionem, *the perfect according to its nature* or *essence, the perfect according to its condition* or *state,* and *the perfect according to the time of life.*—(m), perfectum secundum quid, see *perfectum partialiter.*—(n), perfectum secundum se, see *perfectum per respectum ad aliud.*—(o), perfectum secundum seipsum, see *perfectum per aliquid exterius adveniens.*—(p), perfectum secundum se totum, see *perfectum partialiter.*—(q), perfectum secundum speciem, see *perfectum secundum naturam.*—(r), perfectum secundum statum, see *perfectum secundum naturam.*—(s), perfectum secundum temporis conditionem seu secundum tempus, see *perfectum secundum naturam.*—(t), perfectum secundum voluntatem, see *perfectum intellectu.*—(u), perfectum simpliciter, see *perfectum partialiter.*—(v), perfectum universaliter, see *perfectum partialiter.*—imperfectum est prius quam perfectum in fieri, see *imperfectus.*—in omnibus generibus contingit aliquid esse dupliciter, vel sicut perfectum vel sicut imperfectum, *in all the categories of being something can occur in two ways, either as perfect or as imperfect.*—naturali ordine perfectum praecedit imperfectum, or, perfecta naturaliter sunt prio-

ra imperfectis, or, perfectum est prius imperfecto in rerum naturalium ordine, or, perfectum natura prius est imperfecto, or, perfectum naturaliter est prius imperfecto, or, perfectum secundum substantiam prius est imperfecto, *the perfect according to its nature* or *the natural order* or *its essence is prior to the imperfect.* —omne, quod est imperfectum, sub eodem genere cadit cum perfecto, non quidem sicut species, sed per reductionem, see *imperfectus.*—perfecta naturaliter sunt priora imperfectis, see above: *naturali ordine* etc.—perfectum est prius imperfecto et natura et tempore, *the perfect is according to nature* and *to time prior to the imperfect.*—perfectum est prius imperfecto in rerum naturalium ordine, see above: *naturali ordine* etc.—perfectum naturaliter est prius imperfecto, see above: *naturali ordine* etc.—perfectum natura prius est imperfecto, see above: *naturali ordine* etc.—perfectum secundum substantiam prius est imperfecto, see above: *naturali ordine* etc.—tanto est unumquodque perfectius quanto est ultimo fini propinquius, *a thing is the more perfect as it comes nearer to its last goal.*—unumquodque tanto perfectius est, quanto magis attingit ad propriam virtutem, *everything is the more perfect, the more it attains its own peculiar capacity.*—unusquisque maxime est illud, quod est in eo perfectissimum, *every-one is for the most part that which is the most perfect in him.* —veniente perfecto evacuatur imperfectum, quod ei opponitur, *when the perfect comes, the imperfect which is opposed to it is displaced.*—perfectior, ius, *more complete, more perfect.*—perfectissimus, a, um, *most complete, most perfect.*—perfecte, adv., *in a perfect manner* or *sense, perfectly,* synonym of *indeficienter,* the opposite of *defective* and *deficienter.* On cognoscere perfecte, see *cognoscere* under 2; on scire perfecte, see *scire* under 1; on velle perfecte, see *velle* under 1; on voluntarium perfecte, see *voluntarius* under 3.—perfectissime, adv., *most fully, most completely, most perfectly.*

perfero, ferre, tuli, latum, v. a., (I) lit., (A) *to bear, carry* something to a certain place or end, (B) transf., *to carry, bring, convey,* (II) fig., in gen., *to bear, suffer, put up with, endure.*

perficio, ere, feci, fectum, 3, v. a., *to achieve, execute, carry out, accomplish, perform, bring to an end* or *conclusion, finish, complete.*—perfectus, a, um, P. a., see under *perfectus.*

perfidia, ae, f., *perfidy, falsehood, dishonesty, faithlessness.*

perfidus, a, um, adj., *faithless.*

perflo, are, avi, atum, 1, v. a. and n., *to blow through* or *over,* used fig.

perforatio, onis, f., *a stab, a wound made by stabbing.*

perforo, are, avi, atum, 1, v. a., (1) lit.,, *to pierce* as with nails, (2) transf., *to tear* a garment or *dishonor* it in some way.

perfruor, i, ctus, 3, v. dep., *to enjoy fully* or *thoroughly.*

perfunctus, a, um, P. a., *enjoyed, experienced.*

perfundo, ere, fudi, fusum, 3, v. a., (I) lit., (A) *to pour over, wet, sprinkle, bedew, moisten,* (B) transf., (1) *to pass, spread, diffuse itself through,* (2) *to bathe* or *wash the face,* (3) *to cleanse* something with a liquid, (4) *to drench* someone, (5) of the sun's rays, *to flood,* (II) fig., *to imbue, inspire, fill* with anything.

perfusio, onis, f., *a perfusion, that which has been poured over.*—vinum perfusionis, *ablution-wine,* wine for the ablution of the chalice of the Mass.

pergo, ere, perrexi, perrectum, 3, v. a. and n., *to proceed, set forth, hasten, to go,* used with *ad* and acc., with *inf.*

perhibeo, ere, ui, itum, 2, v. a., *to say, assert anything.*—perhibere testimonium, *to bear witness.*

Periarchon, (peri archon) the Periarchon, De Principiis, one of the most important of the works of Origen. It treated in four books of the fundamental doctrines or principles of Christian faith. Only fragments of the original have been preserved, mostly in the *Philocalia Origenis.*

periclitor, ari, atus, 1, *v. dep., a.
and n., to be in danger* or *peril,
incur* or *be exposed to danger,
be endangered* or *imperilled.*

periculose, *adv.*, see *periculosus.*

periculosissime, *adv.*, see *periculosus.*

periculosus, a, um, *adj., dangerous,
hazardous, perilous.—periculose,
adv., dangerously, hazardously.*

periculum, i, *n., danger, risk, hazard,* the state of being exposed
to chance of evil of any kind;
exposure to injury or loss; *peril.*

Perihermenias, ae, *f.,* (*peri hermeneias*), the *Peri Hermenias* or *De
Interpretatione* of Aristotle, a
work on the doctrine of the judgment and on the proposition, important as an authority on logic
and philosophical terminology.

perimo, ere, emi, emptum, 3, *v. a.,*
(1) in gen., *to take away entirely,
to destroy, to cut off, hinder,* (2)
in partic., *to kill, slay.—peremptus,* a, um, *P. a.,* used in the S.T.
only once in the legal expression
*accusatio perempta, an accusation made by someone who is
absent,* described in one manuscript as, *accusatio ab absente
qui eam sustinere non potest.*

perinde, *adv.;* with *ac, just as.*

periodus, i, *f., a period, a lapse of
time, a series of years.*

Peripateticus, a, um, *adj., peripatetic,* of or belonging to the *Peripatetic* (*Aristotelian*) *philosophy.—*
Peripatetici, orum, *m., Peripatetics, philosophers of the Peripatetic* (*Aristotelian*) *school.*

perite, *adv.*, see *peritus.*

peritia, ae, *f., experience, knowledge gained by experience, practical knowledge, skill.*

peritus, a, um, *adj., experienced,
skilled, expert.—perite, adv., in
an experienced manner, skillfully, expertly.*

periurium, ii, *n., a false oath, perjury.*

periuro, are, avi, atum, 1, *v. n., to
swear falsely, forswear* or *perjure
one's self.*

periurus, a, um, *adj.*, in gen., *who
lies under oath, perjured.*

permanens, entis, *P. a.,* see *permaneo.*

permanentia, ae, *f., permanence,
permanentness.*

permaneo, ere, mansi, mansum, 2,
v. n., (1) *to hold out, last, continue, endure, remain, persist,
perceive,* (2) *to abide in* a way,
rule, or mode of life, *live by,
devote one's life to.—permanens,*
entis, *P. a., enduring, persisting,
abiding, permanent,* synonym of
manens, the opposite of *pertransiens, transiens* and *transitivus.*
On **actus permanens,** see *actus*
under 1 and 2; on **esse permanens,** see *esse;* on **forma permanens,** see *forma* under 2; on **materiale permanens,** see *materialis*
under 1; on **res permanens,** see
res.

permansio, onis, *f., a remaining,
persisting.*

permisceo, ere, scui, stum, and
xtum, 2, *v. a.,* (1) lit., *to mix* or
mingle together; to commingle,

intermingle, (2) fig., *to mix* or *mingle together*.—**permixtus,** a, um, *P. a.*, *mingled, mixed.*

permissio, onis, *f.*, *permission.*

permissive, *adv.*, *with permission, in the sense of a permission, permissively,* the opposite of *imperative,* not found in the S.T.

permitto, ere, misi, missum, 3, *v. a.*, *to give, have, let, allow, suffer, grant, permit.*

permixtio, onis, *f.*, *ingredients mixed together, mingling, a mixture,* used lit. and fig.

permoveo, ere, movi, motum, 2, *v. a.*, of the mind, *to move deeply, excite, trouble, astonish.*

permutatio, onis, *f.*, (1) *a changing, change,* (2) *an interchanging, barter, exchange.*

permuto, are, avi, atum, 1, *v. a.*, *to change throughout, to change completely.*

pernicies, ei, *f.*, *ruin, disaster, destruction, bane, pest.*

perniciosus, a, um, *adj.*, *destructive, ruinous, baleful, pernicious.*

pernocto, are, avi, 1, *v. n.*, *to pass the night.*

perpendo, ere, pendi, pensum, 3, *v. a.*, *to weigh mentally, ponder, consider.*

perperam, *adv.*, *perversely, wrongly.*

perpessio, onis, *f.*, *a bearing, suffering, enduring.*

perpetior, i, pessus, 3, *v. dep. n.* and *a.*, (1) of persons, *to bear steadfastly, suffer with firmness or patience; to abide, endure,* (2)

transf., of abstract things, *to endure, put up with.*

perpetratio, onis, *f.*, *performance, perpetration.*

perpetro, are, avi, atum, 1, *v. a.*, *to bring about, achieve, execute, perform, accomplish; to commit, perpetrate.*

perpetuitas, atis, *f.*, *uninterrupted* or *continual duration, uninterrupted progress* or *succession, continuity, perpetuity.*—**ad perpetuitatem,** *to perpetuity, forever.*

perpetuo, *adv.*, see *perpetuus.*

perpetuo, are, avi, atum, 1, *v. a.*, *to cause a thing to continue uninterruptedly, to proceed with continually, to make perpetual.*

perpetuum, *adv.*, see *perpetuus.*

perpetuus, a, um, *adj.*, *perpetual, lasting* or *destined to last forever; eternal; unceasing; permanent* (during life).—**perpetuum,** i, *n.*, *the abiding, permanent,* hence: **in perpetuum** (sc. **tempus**), *for all time, forever, in perpetuity, constantly.*—**perpetuo,** *adv.*, *perpetually, always, forever.*—**perpetuum,** *adv.*, *perpetually.*

perplexus, a, um, *adj.*, *doubtful, confused, ambiguous, perplexed.* On **dogma perplexum,** see *dogma.*—Kinds of *perplexus* are: **perplexus simpliciter** and **perplexus supposito quodam,** *the simply* or *absolutely perplexed* and *the relatively perplexed* or *the perplexed in a certain respect.*

perquiro, ere, sivi, situm, 3, *v. a.,*
to ask or *inquire after diligently,*
make a diligent search for any-
thing.

Persae, arum, *m., the Persians.—*
Persis, idis, *Persia.*

perscrutator, oris, *m., a thorough*
searcher, an examiner, investiga-
tor.

perscrutor, ari, atus, 1, *v. dep., to*
examine into, investigate.

persecutio, onis, *f., a persecution,*
esp., of Christians.

persecutor, oris, *m., a persecutor.*

persequor, i, cutus, 3, *v. dep. a.*
and *n.,* (1) lit., *to follow, pursue,*
(2) fig., (a) *to pursue, follow,* (b)
to persecute.

perseveranter, *adv.,* see *persevero.*

perseverantia, ae, *f., steadfast-*
ness, persistence, perseverance,
the opposite of *mollities* and *per-*
tinacia.

perseverativus, a, um, *adj., perse-*
vering, steadfast.

persevero, are, avi, atum, 1, *v. n.*
and *a.,* (1) neutr., *to abide by* or
adhere to strictly; to continue
steadfastly, to persist, persevere
in anything, a synonym of *per-*
sisto, permaneo, used with *in*
and *abl., abl.* alone, (2) act., *to*
go on or *proceed with steadily,*
to persevere in anything, used
with the *acc.—***perseverans,** antis, *P. a., persevering.—***perseve-**
ranter, *adv., perseveringly.*

Persis, idis, *f.,* see *Persae.*

persisto, ere, stiti, 3, *v. n., to con-*
tinue steadfastly, persist.

persolvo, ere, solvi, solutum, 3,
v. a., to pay what is due to another.

persona, ae, *f.,* (1) *face, disguise,*
mask, (2) *character, part,* a representation or likeness of, (3)
person, a supposition of an intellectual nature. That to which all
that is individual and particular,
as distinct from what is common
to the species, is referred as to
its sustaining principle. In general, it is that which is distinct in
a nature; cf. PP. Q. 29 Art. 4.
On **assumptio in persona,** see *as-*
sumptio under 1; on **communitas**
personae, see *communitas* under
1; on **corruptio personae,** see *cor-*
ruptio under 3; on **distinctio per-**
sonae, see *distinctio* under 2; on
iudicium de personis, see *iudici-*
um under 2; on **magnitudo per-**
sonae, see *magnitudo* under 3;
on **necessarium personae,** see *ne-*
cessarius under 1; on **nomen per-**
sonae, see *nomen* under 1; on
perfectio unius personae, see *per-*
fectio under 2; on **pluralitas per-**
sonarum, see *pluralitas;* on **ratio**
personae et notificans personam,
see *ratio* under 14; on **singulari-**
tas personae, see *singularitas* under 1; on **unio personae seu in**
persona seu secundum personam,
see *unio;* on **unire in persona seu**
secundum personam, see *unire;*
on **unitas personae,** see *unitas;*
on **vitium personae,** see *vitium*
under 1.—Kinds of *persona* in
this sense are: (a), **persona com-**
posita and **persona simplex,** *the*

composite and *the simple person of Christ.*—(b), **persona coniuncta** and **persona propria,** *the person connected* (with someone) and *the proper person.*—(c), **persona domestica,** *the person belonging to a house* or *belonging to a family.*—(d), **persona extranea** and **persona propinqua,** *the strange and the related person.*—(e), **persona illegitima,** *the illegal* or *illegitimate person.*—(f), **persona infamis,** *the notorious person.*—(g), **persona maior,** *the older person.*—(h), **persona particularis seu singularis,** *the single person who represents the opposite of a community of people.*—(i), **persona perfecta,** *the perfect person,* so-called because there is nothing lacking in him that belongs to the essence of a person.—(j), **persona privata** and **persona publica,** *the private* or *individual person* and *the public* or *official person.*—(k), **persona propinqua,** see *persona extranea.*—(l), **persona propria,** see *persona coniuncta.*—(m), **persona publica,** see *persona privata.*—(n), **persona simplex,** see *persona composita.*—(o), **persona singularis,** see *persona particularis.*—(p), **persona subsistens,** *the person existing for himself.*

personalis, e, *adj.,* (1) *personal,* i.e., *belonging to a person, concerning a person, proceeding from a person,* (2) *personal,* i.e., *constituting a person.* On **actio personalis,** see *actio* under 1; on **actus personalis,** see *actus* under 1; on **adiectivum personale,** see *adiectivus;* on **bonum personale,** see *bonus* under 3; on **communicatio personalis,** see *communicatio* under 3; on **communitas personalis,** see *communitas* under 2; on **demonstratio personalis,** see *demonstratio* under 1; on **distinctio personalis,** see *distinctio* under 2; on **donum personale,** see *donum* under 1; on **esse personale,** see *esse;* on **gratia personalis,** see *gratia* under 2; on **habitus personalis,** see *habitus* under 4; on **integritas personalis,** see *integritas;* on **nomen personale,** see *nomen* under 1; on **notio personalis,** see *notio* under 1; on **operatio personalis,** see *operatio* under 2; on **peccatum personale,** see *peccatum* under 2; on **perfectio personalis,** see *perfectio* under 2; on **praedicatum personale,** see *praedicatum* under 1; on **proprietas personalis,** see *proprietas* under 1; on **relatio personalis,** see *relatio;* on **res personalis,** see *res;* on **sanctificatio personalis,** see *sanctificatio* under 1; on **suppositio personalis,** see *suppositio* under 4; on **terminus personalis,** see *terminus* under 5; on **unio personalis,** see *unio;* on **unitas personalis,** see *unitas;* on **verbum personale,** see *verbum* under 1 and 2. On **amor personalis,** see *amor* under 1.—**personaliter,** *adv., personally, according to a person, after the manner of a person, in the sense of a person.*

personalitas, atis, *f.,* *personality,* i.e., that form or relation of being through which it is a person.

personaliter, *adv.,* see *personalis.*

persono, are, ui, itum, 1, *v. n.* and *a.,* (1) neutr., *to sound through,* (2) act., (a) *to represent, present in a different manner,* (b) *to utter, speak.*

perspectio, onis, *f., a seeing into, perception.*

perspectivus, a, um, *adj., looking through, examining, perspective, perplexive.* On **potentia perspectiva,** see *potentia* under 2; on **scientia perspectiva,** see *scientia* under 1.—**perspectiva sc. ars** or **scientia,** *optics,* a part of physics or natural science.—**perspectivus sc. philosophus,** *a specialist in the science of optics, an opticist.*

perspicacitas, atis, *f., perspicacity, discernment, discrimination.*

perspicaciter, *adv.,* see *perspicax.*

perspicax, acis, *adj., perspicacious, acute, sharp-sighted.*—**perspicaciter,** *adv., acutely, sharp-sightedly,* used here in the *comp.*

perspicio, ere, spexi, spectum, 3, *v. a.,* (1) lit., *to look at,* (2) fig., *to perceive, note, observe, ascertain.*

perspicue, *adv.,* see *perspicuus.*

perspicuitas, atis, *f., clearness.*

perspicuus, a, um, *adj., clear, evident.*—**perspicue,** *adv., evidently, clearly, manifestly, perspicuously.*

persto, are, stiti, statum, 1, *v. n.,* (1) *to stand fast* or *firm, persevere, persist in any thing,* used with *in*

and *abl.,* (2) with *absque* in the sense of *to refrain from.*

perstringo, ere, nxi, ctum, 3, *v. a.,* (1) *to bind tightly together,* (2) *to graze against, to confront.*—**perstrictus,** a, um, *P. a.,* in speaking, *narrated briefly.*

persuadeo, ere, si, sum, 2, *v. a.,* (1) in gen., *to convince* of the truth of any thing, *to persuade,* used absol., with an object clause, (2) in partic., *to prompt, induce prevail upon, persuade* to do anything.

persuadibilis, e, *adj., persuadable, amenable.*

persuasibilis, e, *adj., persuadable, capable of being persuaded* or *controlled.*

persuasio, onis, *f., persuasion,* an influencing to action by statement, argument, entreaty or anything that moves the intellect or the feelings.

persuasive, *adv., persuasively.*

persuasor, oris, *m., a convincer, one who persuades* or *prevails upon.*

persuasorius, a, um, *adj., persuasive.*

perterreo, ere, ui, itum, 2, *v. a., to terrify thoroughly.*

pertimesco, ere, mui, 3, *v. inch. a.* and *n., to fear greatly.*

pertinacia, ae, *f., obstinacy, pertinacity.*

pertinaciter, *adv.,* see *pertinax.*

pertinax, acis, *adj., obstinate, pertinacious, stubborn.*—**pertinaciter,** *adv., persistently.*

pertineo, ere, ui, 2, *v. n., to belong, relate, concern, pertain* or *have* *reference to,* constr. always with *ad* and *acc.*—**pertinens**, entis, *P. a., belonging to, relating to, concerning, pertaining to.*

pertingo, ere, *v. a., to stretch out, extend to, attain.*

pertracto, are, avi, atum, 1, *v. a.,* (1) lit., *to touch,* (2) fig., *to busy* or *occupy one's self* with anything: *to exercise* one's duty.

pertraho, ere, xi, ctum, 3, *v. a.,* (1) in a bad sense, *to draw, lead away, lead astray, induce,* (2) in a good sense, *to lead, help* someone to a good end.

pertranseo, ire, ivi, itum, *v. n., to go* or *pass through* or *over, go* or *pass by.*—**pertransiens**, entis, *P. a., passing, transient,* synonym of *transiens* and *transitivus,* the opposite of *manens* and *permanens.* On **accidens pertransiens**, see *accidens* under 2.—**pertranseunter,** *adv., in the manner of passing, transiently.*

pertransibilis, e, *adj., traversable.*

perturbatio, onis, *f., a disturbance, disquiet, perturbation,* of body, mind, or soul; *emotion, passion.*

perturbo, are, avi, atum, 1, *v. a., to disturb, discompose, embarrass, confound, confuse.*

perungo, ere, unxi, unctum, 3, *v. a., to anoint.*

pervenio, ire, veni, ventum, 4, *v. n., to come to, arrive at, reach, attain to,* followed usually by *ad,* sometimes *in* and the *acc.*

perventio, onis, *f., an arrival.*

perventor, oris, *m., a comer, arriver.*

perverse, *adv.,* see *perverto.*

perversitas, atis, *f.,* (1) *overturning, overthrow,* (2) *perversity, baseness.*

perversus, *P. a.,* see *perverto.*

perverto, ere, ti, sum, 3, *v. a., to overthrow, subvert, destroy, ruin, undo, corrupt.*—**perversus,** a, um, *P. a., perverse, not right, wrong, evil, bad.*—**perversus,** i, *m., the evil one, the perverse.*—**perverse,** *adv., perversely, wrongly, badly.*

pervicax, acis, *adj., firm, determined;* esp. in a bad sense, *stubborn, obstinate, headstrong.*

pervietas, atis, *f., penetrability, transparence.*

pervigil, is, *adj., ever watchful.*

pervius, a, um, *adj.,* (1) *accessible, passable, pervious,* (2) *penetrable, transparent.*

pes, pedis, *m., foot.*

pessumdo, dare, dedi, datum, 1, *v. a., to ruin, destroy.*

pestifer, era, erum, *adj.,* in gen., *that brings destruction, destructive, noxious, pernicious.*

pestilens, entis, *adj., pestilential, infected, unhealthy, unwholesome.*

pestis, is, *f., a plague, pest, pestilence, destruction, ruin.*

Petilianus, i, *m., Petilianus,* an eminent Donatist bishop, probably a native of Constantina or Cirta, chief town of Numidia. He was born of parents who were Catholics; but while he was still a catechumen he was carried off almost by force by the Donatists, and subsequently made, between 395 and 400, their bishop in Cirta.

petitio, onis, *f.,* (1) *an entreaty, request,* (2) *supposition, postulate,* the *aitema* of Aristotle (Anal. post. I. 10, 76. b. 23), i.e., the provisional acceptance of a demonstrable but not yet proven statement, which does not possess an opinion *pro* or *con* that which is to be proven from this statement.—Kind of *petitio* in this (1) sense are: (a), **petitio debiti,** *the entreaty* or *the request to perform the marital duty.*—(b), **petitio interpretata seu interpretativa,** *that considered as equivalent to an entreaty or request.*— One kind of *petitio* in this (2) sense is: **petitio principii,** *to assume as a valid starting point of reasoning precisely that proposition which is to be proved,* i.e., *to beg the question.*

petitivus, a, um, *adj., petitory,* characterized by asking or begging.

peto, ere, ivi, itum, 3, *v. a., to beg, beseech, ask, request, desire, entreat,* constr. with *ab* and *abl., of pers.*—**petitum,** i, *n., a prayer, desire, request, entreaty.*

petra, ae, *f., a rock, a crag, stone.*

petrinus, a, um, *adj., of stone, stone.*

Petrus, i, *m.,* (1) *Peter Lombard,* known as *Magister Sententiarum,* c. 1100 to c. 1160, appointed Bishop of Paris a few years before his death. He collected the opinions of the Fathers (*sententiae*) and arranged them under theological topics. This *Libri IV Sententiarum* was the standard text in the schools for 500 years, and many commentaries or explanations of it were written. It is from St. Thomas' commentary that the Supplement of the *Summa Theologica* was completed. The *Summa* contains many references to the *Master,* with whom St. Thomas does not always agree.—(2), *Peter, the Apostle.*

petulans, antis, *adj., insolent,*

petulantia, ae, *f., wantonness;* **petulantia carnis,** *lustfulness.*

phanos, (Grk. *phanos*), -ou, *m., apparition.*

phantasia, ae, *f.,* (1) *appearance, phenomenon,* synonym of *phantasma,* (2) *imagination, image,* i.e., the representation of a thing that has been experienced by the senses in its absence, synonym of *imago, phantasma,* and *theorema,* (3) *the power of imagination, the faculty of imagining,* i.e., the sense faculty of representing the image of a sensible thing in its absence, also a synonym of *imaginatio.*—Kinds of *phantasia* in this (2) sense are: **phantasia determinata** and **phantasia indeterminata,** *the definite* and *the indefinite* or *confused imaginative image.* On the difference between *phantasia* and *memoria,* see *memoria* under 2.—Kinds of *phantasia* in this (3) sense are: (a), **phantasia proterva,** *the shameless power of imagination.* —(b), **phantasia rationalis** and **phantasia sensibilis,** the translation of Aristotle's *phantasia lo-*

gistike kai aisthetike, the rational or intellectual and *the sensible power of imagination.*—(c), **phantasia sensibilis,** see *phantasia rationalis.*

phantasma, atis, *n.,* (1) *appearance, illusion, apparition,* synonym of *phantasia* and *visio,* (2) *image, fancy,* i.e., the representation of a thing in its absence, synonym of *imaginatio, phantasia,* and *theorema.*—Kinds of *phantasma* in this (1) sense are: **phantasma distortum seu inordinatum** and **phantasma ordinatum,** *distorted* or *disorderly* and *orderly* or *regulated phantasms.*—**anima intellectiva non potest intellegere sine phantasmatibus,** see *intellegere* under 1.—**anima non potest intellegere sine phantasmate,** see *intellegere* under 1.—**intellegere nostrum non est sine phantasmate,** see *intellegere* under 1.—**nequaquam sine phantasmate intellegit anima,** see *intellegere* under 1.—**nihil sine phantasmate intellegit anima,** see *intellegere* under 1.—**non contingit intellegere sine phantasmate,** see *intellegere* under 1.—**quamdiu est anima in corpore, non potest intellegere sine phantasmate,** see *intellegere* under 1.—**ratione naturali sine phantasmate nihil intellegit anima,** see *intellegere* under 1.

phantastice, *adv.,* see *phantasticus.*

phantasticus, a, um, *adj., imagining, imaginary, phantastic, apparent.* On **apprehensio phantastica,** see *apprehensio* under 2;

on **caro phantastica,** see *caro* under 1; on **corpus phantasticum,** see *corpus;* on **motus phantasticus,** see *motus* under 2; on **pars phantastica,** see *pars* under 1; on **passio phantastica,** see *passio* under 2; on **potentia phantastica,** see *potentia* under 2; on **similitudo phantastica,** see *similitudo* under 1; on **vis phantastica,** see *vis* under 1; on **visio phantastica,** see *visio* under 1 and 3.—**phantasticum** sc. **principium,** *the principle of the sensible representation* or *the power of imagination,* synonym of *phantasia* and *potentia seu vis phantastica.*—**phantastice,** *adv., by the imagination* or *fancy, phantastically.*

Pharao, onis, *m., Pharaoh, the title of the Egyptian Kings.*

Phares, *m., Phares* mentioned in Luke 3. 23.

Pharisaeus, i, *m., a Pharisee,* a member of the Jewish sect of that name, usually in plur.—**Pharisaei,** orum, *m., the Pharisees,* a Jewish sect.

Phase, *n., indecl., the Passover,* a Jewish feast commemorative of the rescue of the first-born among the Jews from the destruction which visited the Egyptians.

philanthropia, ae, *f., philanthropy.*

philargyria, ae, *f., philargyry, love of money, avarice.*

Philemo or - **on,** onis, *m., Philemon;* one of the epistles of St. Paul is addressed to a Greek of this name, as master of a fugitive slave.

Philippius, i, (**Philippensis,** is), *m., Philippian.* **Epistola Beati Pauli Apostoli ad Philippenses,** *Epistle of St. Paul to the Philippians.* The Philippians were the first among the Macedonians converted to the faith. When St. Paul was a prisoner in Rome, he was supplied with necessities by the Philippians through Epaphroditus. By this same Epaphroditus, he sent his Epistle to the Philippians.

Philippus, i, *m., Philip.* (1) Philip the Evangelist, one of the first seven deacons, mentioned in Acts 21, 8; 6, 5.

Philistaeus, i, *m., a Philistine.*

Philistini, orum, *m., the Philistines, the original inhabitants of Palestine.*

philokindynos, ou, *m.,* (*philokindunos*), *a lover of danger.*

philosophema, atis, *n., a philosophical tenet, philosophical problem, philosophical consideration,* does not occur in the Summa Theologica.—**Philosophema encyclium,** *the philosophical tenet which belongs to the sphere of general knowledge.*

philosophia, ae, *f., philosophy,* i.e., love of wisdom; the study of reality in the light of its ultimate causes. On **doctrina philosophiae,** see *doctrina* under 3; on **documentum philosophiae,** see *documentum* under 2.—Kinds of divisions of *philosophia* are: (a), **phi**losophia divina, *the philosophy concerning God* or *natural theology.*—(b), **philosophia mathematica,** *mathematics.*—(c), **philosophia moralis,** *ethics, moral philosophy.*—(d), **philosophia naturalis seu physica,** *natural philosophy* or *physics.*—(e), **philosophia physica,** see *philosophia naturalis.*—(f), **philosophia practica** and **philosophia theorica,** *the practical* and *theoretical* or *speculative philosophy.*—(g), **philosophia prima** and **philosophia secunda,** *the first philosophy* and *the second philosophy* or *Metaphysics* and *Physics.*—(h), **philosophia rationalis,** *the philosophy of reason* or *logic.*—(i), **philosophia secunda,** see *philosophia prima.*—(j), **philosophia theorica,** see *philosophia practica.*

philosophicus, a, um, *adj., of* or *belonging to philosophy, philosophical.* Cf. *philosophus* under 1. On **cognitio philosophica,** see *cognitio* under 2; on **compositio philosophica,** see *compositio* under 1; on **contemplatio philosophica,** see *contemplatio;* on **disciplina philosophica,** see *disciplina* under 3; on **documentum philosophicum,** see *documentum* under 2; on **ratio philosophica,** see *ratio* under 13; on **theologica philosophica,** see *theologia* under 1.

philosophor, ari, atus, 1, *v. dep., to apply one's self to philosophy, to play the philosopher, to philosophize.*

philosophus, i, *m.*, (1) *philosopher, a student of philosophy,* (2) *the philosopher,* i.e., Aristotle. —Kinds of *philosophus* in this (1) sense are: (a), **philosophus mathematicus,** *the mathematician.* —(b), **philosophus moralis,** *the moral philosopher* or *student of ethics.*—(c), **philosophus naturalis,** *the natural philosopher* or *physicist.*—(d), **philosophus primus,** *the first philosopher* or *the metaphysician.* Cf. *philosophia prima.*—(e), **philosophus probabilior,** *the philosopher who makes something more probable,* i.e., an adherent of the school of philosophy known as the New Academy.

philotimia, ae, *f., philotomy, excessive love of honor.*

philotimus, a, um, *adj.,* (1) *honorloving,* (2) *ambitious;* not used in the Summa Theologica.

Phinees, *indecl., m., Phineas,* son of Eleazar, mentioned in Num. 25, 7-14.

phlegma, atis, *n., phlegm, a clammy humor of the body.*

phlegmaticus, a, um, *adj., phlegmatic, full of phlegm.* On **homo phlegmaticus,** see *homo.*

Phlegon, ontis, *m., Phlegon,* a native of Tralles in Lydia. He was a freedman of the emperor Hadrian and not of Augustus as has been erroneously asserted by some writers.

Photiniani, orum, *m., the Photiniani,* followers of Photinus, bishop of Sirmium, who held that Jesus

Christ was not essentially divine but became so by a divine emanation which descended upon him.

Photinus, i, *m., Photinus,* bishop of Sirmium, founder of the *Photiniani.*

phrenesis, is, *f., madness, delirium, frenzy.*

phreneticus, a, um, *adj., mad, delirious, frantic.*

phronesis, is, *f.,* = Grk. *phronesis, understanding, good sense, prudence.*

phthisis, is, *f., phthisis, consumption.*

physice, *adv.,* see *physicus.*

physicus, a, um, *adj.,* (1) *physical, belonging to a being of nature* or to all the beings of nature, referring to one or the other, as distinct from mathematical or logical, synonym of *naturalis,* (2) *physical, philosophical,* i.e., pertaining to natural philosophy, synonym of *naturalis,* (3) pertaining to Aristotle's work, *physike akroasis.*—On **actio physica,** see *actio* under 1; on **agens physicus,** see *agens;* on **corpus physicum,** see *corpus;* on **documentum physicum,** see *documentum* under 2; on **movens physicus,** see *movens;* on **qualitas physica,** see *qualitas;* on **speculatio physica,** see *speculatio;* on **theologia physica,** see *theologia* under 1. On **definitio physica,** see *definitio* under 2; on **genus physicum,** see *genus* under 2; on **philosophia physica,** see *philosophia;* on **ratio**

physica, see *ratio* under 13; on **speculatio physica,** see *speculatio.*—**physica** sc. **philosophia seu scientia,** *the philosophy of nature* or *natural science.*—**physicus** sc. **philosophus,** *the philosopher of nature* or *also the philosopher absolutely.*—**physice,** *adv.,* *in the manner of natural philosophy or physics, physically,* synonym of *naturaliter,* the opposite of *logice.* On **considerare physice,** see *considerare;* on **unitas physica,** see *unitas;* on **unum physicum,** see *unus.*

pictor, oris, *m., a painter.*

pictura, ae, *f., a painting, picture.*

pie, *adv.,* see *pius.*

pietas, atis, *f.,* (1) *dutiful conduct,* as the result of which one shows proper respect and love to elders and fatherland, (2) *piety, devoutness,* i.e., the virtue of childlike reverence and love for God, synonym of *religio,* (3) *tenderness, pity, compassion.* On **donum pietatis,** see *donum* under 2.—The act of *pietas* in so far as it perfects the soul is a *beatitudo.* Cf. *fructus* under 2. On **voluntas pietatis,** see *voluntas* under 3.

pigeo, ere, gui and pigitum est, 2, *v. a., used impers, third pers. sing., it displeases, troubles one.*

piger, gra, grum, *adj., slow, lazy, slothful.*

pigmentarius, a, um, *adj., of or belonging to unguents.*

pigmentum, i, *n., paint.*

pignus, oris, *n., a pledge, security.*

pigresco, ere, *v.* inch. *n., to become slow, sluggish.*

pigritia, ae, *f., sloth, sluggishness, laziness,* a synonym of *segnities.*

Pilatus, i, *m.,* **Pontius Pilatus,** *Pontius Pilate,* a Roman governor of Judaea in the time of Jesus.

pilus, i, *m., a hair.*

Pimander, a work of Trismegistus or Hermes Trismegistus, an Egyptian philosopher of great antiquity, quoted by St. Thomas in PP. Q. 32. Art. 1 ob. 1.

pincerna, ae, *m., a cup-bearer, butler.*

pingo, ere, pinxi, pictum, 3, *v. a., to represent pictorially* with the pencil or needle, *paint, embroider.*—**pictus,** a, um, *P. a., painted, colored.*

pinguedo, inis, *f.,* (1) *fatness, fat.* (2) fig., *abundance, exuberance.*

pinguis, e, *adj., fat, rich.*

pinna, ae, *f., a pinnacle.*

pinnaculum, i, *n., a peak, pinnacle of a building.*

pinnula, ae, *f., dim., a little fin, a fin.*

piscator, oris, *m., a fisherman.*

piscis, is, *m., a fish.*

piscor, ari, atus, 1, *v. dep. n., to fish.*

pistor, oris, *m., a baker.*

Pittacus, i, *m., Pittacus,* one of the seven wise men of Greece from Mitylene, in Lesbos.

pituita, ae, *f., phlegm, rheum.*

pius, a, um, *adj., pious, devout, conscientious.*—**pie,** *adv., piously, religiously, devoutly.*

pixis, idis, *f., a pyx, a vessel* or *casket,* usually of precious metal, in which the host is reserved.

placentia, ae, *f., complacency, a cause of pleasure* or *satisfaction.*

placeo, ere, cui, citum, 2, *v. n., to please, to be pleasing* or *agreeable, to be welcome, acceptable, satisfy,* opposite of *displiceo.—* **placitus,** a, um, *P. a., pleasing, agreeable, acceptable.—***placitum,** i, *n., that which is pleasing* or *agreeable, an opinion, sentiment.*

placiditas, atis, *f., mildness, gentleness of nature* or *disposition, placidity.*

placidus, a, um, *adj.,* of persons, *peaceful, mild, placid.*

placo, are, avi, atum, 1, *v. a.,* in gen., *to reconcile, appease, pacify.*

plaga, ae, *f.,* (1) lit., (a) *a wound,* (b) *a blow* which wounds or injures, (c) *a stripe,* (2) fig., (a) *a plague,* (b) *an affliction, torture.*

plagium, ii, *n., kidnapping.*

planctivus, a, um, *adj., complaining.*

planctus, us, *m., a wailing.*

plane, *adv.,* see *planus.*

planeta, ae, *m., a wandering star, a planet.*

plango, ere, nxi, nctum, 3, *v. a.,* with *aliquid, to bewail, deplore* a thing.

planta, ae, *f., plant.* On **anima plantae,** see *anima* under 1; on **vita plantae,** see *vita* under 1.

plantatio, onis, *f., a setting, planting, transplanting.*

plantator, oris, *m., a planter.*

planto, are, avi, atum, *v. a., to plant, sow,* used lit. and fig.

planus, a, um, *adj., plain, clear, distinct, intelligible.—***plane,** *adv., plainly.*

planus, i, *m., astrologer.*

plasma, atis, *n., an image, figure, a creature.*

platea, ae, *f., a broad way in a city, a street.*

Plato, onis, *m., Plato,* a celebrated Grecian philosopher, the disciple of Aristotle and founder of the academic philosophy; also used to designate some individual man, as we would say "John Doe".

Platonicus, a, um, *adj., of* or *belonging to Plato, Platonic,* not used in the S.T. as adjective.— **Platonicus,** i, *m., follower of the Platonic philosophy, Platonist.*

plebanatus, us, *m., the district* and *territory of a plebanus* or *priest.*

plebanus, i, *m.,* in ecclesiastical law, *a rural dean, a priest.*

plebeius, a, um, *adj.,* (1) *of* or *belonging to the common people* or *commonality, plebeian,* (2) transf., *low, mean, common.*

plebiscitum, i, *n., a plebiscitum, a decree* or *ordinance of the people.*

plebs, is, *f.,* (1) *the plebeians, the commonality* as distinguished from the titled, the rich, or the learned; *the populace,* (2) *the people,* as opposed to those in authority, (3) *the people,* persons bound together by a common tie

as belonging to a congregation,
(4) *the whole people, nation.*

plecto, ere, xi, and xui, xum, 3, *v.
a.,* in pass., *to be punished, be
beaten.*

plenarie, *adv.,* see *plenarius.*

plenarius, a, um, *adj., plenary,* (1)
full, in all respects or requisites;
entire, absolute, (2) *having full
power.*—**plenarie,** *adv., plenarily,
fully.*

plene, *adv.,* see *plenus.*

plenitudo, inis, *f., a being full, fullness, plenitude.*

plenus, a, um, *adj., full, filled.*—
plenum, i, *n., space occupied by
matter, a plenum.*—**ad plenum,**
to the full, fully.—**plene,** *adv.,
fully, wholly, completely, thoroughly, largely;* also **plenius** and
plenissime.

plerumque, *adv.,* see *plerusque.*

plerusque, raque, rumque, *adj.,
very many, a very great part, the
most, most* used in plur. only.—
plerumque, *adv., for the most
part, mostly, commonly, very
often.*

ploratus, us, *m., a wailing, weeping, lamenting.*

ploro, are, avi, atum, *v. n.* and *a.,
to wail, lament, weep aloud.*

Plotinus, i, *m., Plotinus,* Egyptian
philosopher, the founder of Neo-
platonism; he flourished in the
third century, A.D.

pluma, ae, *f., a feather.*

plumbeus, a, um, *adj., made of
lead, leaden.*

plumbum, i, *n., lead.*

pluralis, e, *adj.,* (1) in gen., *belonging* or *relating to more than one,
relating to one,* (2) in partic.,
a gram. t.t., *plural.*—**pluraliter,**
adv., in the plural, gram. t.t.

pluralitas, atis, *f., plurality,* the opposite of *unitas.*—Kinds of *pluralitas* are: (a), **pluralitas enuntiationis,** *plurality of expression* or
statement.—(b), **pluralitas materialis,** *plurality according to matter.*—(c), **pluralitas personarum,**
the plurality of persons.—(d), **pluralitas rationis** and **pluralitas realis,** *plurality in the thought of
reason* and *plurality outside the
same.*

pluraliter, *adv.,* see *pluralis.*

pluries, *adv., often, oftentimes, frequently.*

pluvia, ae, *f., rain.*

pluvialis, e, *adj., of* or *belonging to
rain, rainy, rain-.*

pluviosus, a, um, *adj., full of rain,
rain-.*

podagra, ae, *f., the gout of the feet,
gout.*

podagricus, i, *m., a gouty person.*

poderes, is, *m., a long garment descending to the ankle, worn by
priests,* a synonym of *talaris vestis, a talaric vestment.*

poema, atis, *n., a poem.*

poena, ae, *f., compensation, satisfaction, expiation, punishment,
penalty,* synonym of *poenalitas.*
On **corruptio poenae,** see *corruptio* under 3; on **debitum poenae,**
see *debitus* under 1; on **defectus
poenae,** see *defectus* under 2; on
malitia poenae, see *malitia* under

3; on **malum poenae,** see *malum* under 3; on **reatus poenae,** see *reatus;* on **retributio poenae,** see *retributio.*—Kinds of *poenae* are: (a), **poena aeterna seu perpetua** and **poena temporalis,** *the eternal* or *everlasting punishment* and *temporal punishment,* i.e., that lasts for a time or that which deprives of a temporal good.—(b), **poena afflictiva seu sensus** and **poena damni,** *the punishment that hurts the body* or *punishment for the senses,* and *the punishment of bereavement.*—(c), **poena aliena** and **poena propria,** *the strange* or *foreign* and *the proper punishment.* —(d), **poena capitalis seu capitis seu mortis,** *capital punishment* or *punishment of death.*—(e), **poena capitis,** see *poena capitalis.*— (j), **poena concomitans peccatum** and **poena consequens ex peccato seu taxata pro peccato,** *the punishment that accompanies sin,* and *that which follows* or *is imposed upon it.*—(g), **poena condemnans seu ex toto exterminans** and **poena purgatoria,** *the condemning* or *entirely exterminating punishment* and *the purifying punishment,* i.e., the punishment which is inflicted simply *ad ultimam seu finalem damnationem,* and that which is inflicted *ad purgationem vel emendationem vitiorum.*—(h), **poena consequens ex peccato,** see *poena concomitans peccatum.*—(i), **poena corporalis** and **poena spiritualis,** *the corporal* and *the spiritual punishment.*—(j), **poena damni,** see *poena afflictiva.*—(k), **poena essentialis** and **poena secundaria,** *the essential* and *the secondary punishment.*—(l), **poena ex necessitate inflicta** and **poena voluntarie assumpta,** *the punishment inflicted of necessity* and *the punishment imposed on oneself voluntarily*—(m), **poena ex toto exterminans,** see *poena condemnans.*—(n), **poena finita** and **poena infinita,** *the limited* or *finite punishment* and *the unlimited* or *infinite punishment.*—(o), **poena infernalis, seu inferni, poena limbi** and **poena purgatorii,** *the punishment of hell, that of limbo, and that of purgatory.*—(p), **poena inferni,** see *poena infernalis.* —(q), **poena infinita,** see *poena finita.*—(r), **poena limbi,** see *poena infernalis.*—(s), **poena medicinalis** and **poena retributiva seu satisfactoria,** *the salutary* or *healing punishment, and the retaliating punishment* or *that satisfying justice.*—(t), **poena mortis,** see *poena capitalis.*—(u), **poena ordinata,** *the ordered punishment.*—(v), **poena pecunaria,** *the punishment of fines.*—(w), **poena perpetua,** see *poena aeterna.*—(x), **poena purgatoria,** see *poena condemnans.*—(y), **poena purgatorii,** see *poena infernalis.*—(z), **poena retributiva,** see *poena medicinalis.*—(a²), **poena satisfactoria,** see *poena medicinalis.*—(b²), **poena secundaria,** see *poena essentialis.*

—(c²), **poena sensibilis,** *the sensible punishment* or *the punishment consisting in the loss of sensible goods.*—(d²), **poena sensus,** see *poena damni.*—(e²), **poena spiritualis,** see *poena corporalis.*—(f²), **poena talionis,** *the punishment of like retaliation.*—(g²), **poena taxata pro peccato,** see *poena concomitans peccatum.*—(h²), **poena temporalis,** see *poena aeterna.*—(i²), **poena voluntarie assumpta,** see *poena ex necessitate inflicta.*

poenalis, e, *adj., of* or *belonging to punishment, penal.* On **defectus poenalis,** see *defectus* under 2; on **locus poenalis,** see *locus* under 1; on **malum poenale,** see *malus* under 3; on **opus poenale,** see *opus* under 4.—**poenaliter,** *adv., by punishment* or *penalty.*

poenalitas, atis, *f.,* (1) *culpability, punishableness,* (2) *punishment, penalty,* synonym of *poena.*

poenaliter, *adv.,* see *poenalis.*

poenitentia, ae, *f.,* (1) *the virtue of repentance, contrition,* (2) *the sacrament of penance,* synonym of *sacramentum poenitentiae,* see *sacramentum* under 2. On **sacramentum poenitentiae,** see *sacramentum* under 3.—Kinds of *poenitentia* in this (1) sense are: (a), **poenitentia ante baptismum, poenitentia mortalium,** and **poenitentia venialium,** *repentance before receiving baptism, repentance for mortal sins* post baptismum, and *repentance for venial sins.*—(b), **poenitentia exterior** and **poenitentia interior,** *the outer repentance* and *the inner repentance.*—(c), **poenitentia interior,** see *poenitentia exterior.*—(d), **poenitentia mortalium,** see *poenitentia ante baptismum.*—(e), **poenitentia publica,** *public repentance.*—(f), **poenitentia solemnis,** *solemn penance* by which is sometimes understood *public penance.*—The integrating parts of *poenitentia* in this sense are: *contritio, confessio,* and *satisfactio.*

poenitentialis, e, *adj., penitential, of* or *pertaining to* or *expressing penance.*—**psalmi poenitentiales,** *the penitential psalms,* a name given to seven psalms which give especial expression to the feelings of penitence.—**poenitentiale forum,** *the tribunal of the sacrament of penance.*—**Poenitentiale,** is, *n., a Penitential,* a book containing in codified form the canons of the Chuch relating to penance, its impositions, etc.; *a penitentiary manual.*

poenitentarius, ii, *m., a penitentiary,* a person appointed to deal with great penitents or penances; an officer vested with power to deal with cases over which the ordinary parish priest may not have sufficient jurisdiction to determine.

poeniteo, (**paeniteo**) ere, ui, 2, *v. a.,* and *impers., to repent, be sorry. Impers.,* found only in quot.; otherwise not used in S.T., *it repents one,* etc., i.e., *I, you, etc.*

repent.—**poenitens**, entis, *P. a.,*
repenting, repentant, penitent,
usually used as a substantive, *a*
penitent.—**poenitendum**, i, *n.,* re-
penting, sorrowing.

poenitivus, a, um, *adj., penitent.*

poenitudo, inis, *f., repentance.*

poenitus, *adv., entirely, completely.*

poenosus, a, um, *adj., painful.*

poeta, ae, *m., a poet.*

poetica, ae, *f.,* see *poeticus.*

poeticus, a, um, *adj., poetic, poeti-*
cal.—**poetica**, ae, *f., the poetic*
art, poetry.—**De Poetica**, *the Po-*
etics of Aristotle, a work devoted
to literary criticism.

polio, ire, ivi and ii, itum, 4, *v. a.,*
to smooth, polish.

politia, ae, *f.,* (1) *form of state,*
administration of the common-
wealth, state, synonym of *regi-*
men and *respublica,* (2) *poly-*
archy, government by several.—
On **corruptio politiae**, see *corrup-*
tio under 3.—Kinds of *politia* in
this (1) sense are: (a), **politia**
aristocratica, politia oligarchica,
and **politia democratica**, *the aris-*
tocratic, the oligarchic and *the*
democratic state.—(b), **politia**
corrupta seu perversa seu vitiata
seu iniusta seu iniqua and **politia**
iusta seu recta, *the corrupt* or
perverse or *unjust* and *the just* or
right state.—(c), **politia democra-**
tica, see *politia aristocratica.*—(d),
politia iniqua, see *politia corrup-*
ta.—(e), **politia iniusta**, see *politia*
corrupta.—(f), **politia iusta**, see
politia corrupta.—(g), **politia oli-**
garchica, see *politia aristocratica.*

—(h), **politia perversa**, see *politia*
corrupta.—(i), **politia recta**, see
politia corrupta.—(j), **politia vitia-**
ta, see *politia recta.*

politice, *adv.,* see *politicus.*

politicus, a, um, *adj.,* (1) *of* or *be-*
longing to a citizen, civic, synonym of *civilis* (see *civilis* under
1), (2) *of* or *belonging to civil*
polity or *to the state, political,*
social, synonym of *civilis,* (see
civilis under 2) and *socialis* (see
socialis), (3) relating to Aristotle's
work on the theory of the state
(circa doctrinam politicam, quam
Aristoteles in hoc libro tradit, 1
Pol. 1 a). On **amicitia politica,**
see *amicitia* under 1; on **domini-**
um politicum, see *dominium;* on
principatus politicus, see *princi-*
patus under 1; on **regimen politi-**
cum, see *regimen.* On **animal**
politicum, see *animal* under 1; on
ars politica, see *ars* under 2; on
bonum politicum, see *bonus* under 3; on **communicatio politica,**
see *communicatio* under 3; on
communio politica, see *commun-*
io under 1; on **communitas po**
litica, see *communitas* under 3;
on **congregatio politica**, see *con-*
gregatio under 2; on **conversatio**
politica, see *conversatio* under 1;
on **dilectio politica seu publicae**
virtutis, see *dilectio* under 1; on
doctrina politica, see *doctrina*
under 4; on **felicitas politica**, see
felicitas; on **fortitudo politica**, see
fortitudo under 3; on **habitus po-**
liticus, see *habitus* under 4; on
iustitia politica, see *iustitia* under

1; on **iustum politicum seu politicum proprie dictum seu politicum simpliciter**, see *iustus;* on
ordo politicus, see *ordo* under 1;
on **providentia politica**, see *providentia;* on **prudentia politica**,
see *prudentia* under 1; on **scientia politica**, see *scientia* under 1;
on **virtus politica**, see *virtus* under 5.—**politica**, when *ars* or *doctrina* or *scientia* is to be supplied,
signifies *political science* or *the
theory of politics*, i.e., that part
of philosophia moralis, quae considerat operationes multitudinis
civilis; when *virtus* is to be supplied, *the public* or *civic virtue*
which consists in recta ratio rerum agibilium circa bona vel mala totius multitudinis civilis.—**politicus** sc. **homo**, *the politician* or
statesman.—**homo est naturaliter
seu secundum suam naturam animal politicum**, see *homo.*—**politice** *adv., with respect to politics,
with reference to the state, politi-
cally.*

Pollentius, ii, *m., Pollentius,* a
friend of St. Augustine, known
through the treatise of St. Augustine, *De Coniugiis adulterinis.*

polleo, ere, 2, *v. n., to possess in
abundance, be rich in,* used with
the *abl.*

pollex, icis, *m.,* (1) *the thumb,* (2)
the great toe.

polliceor, eri, itus, 2, *v. dep. a.* and
n., to promise anything.

pollicitatio, onis, *f., a promising, a
promise.*

polluo, ere, ui, utum, 3, *v. a., to
soil, defile, pollute.*

pollutio, onis, *f., defilement, contamination, pollution.*

pompa, ae, *f.,* (1) in gen., *pomp,
display,* (2) in partic., (a) of
funeral rites, *solemnity,* (b) pl.,
pomps, in the baptismal formula,
pompae diaboli, originally the
processions, public shows, spectacles of the circus associated
with or sanctioned by pagan
worship; then more vaguely, any
"shows" held to be under the
patronage of the devil; finally,
tacitly transferred to those of the
"world", and associated with its
"vanities."

Pomponius, ii, *m., Pomponius,* bishop of Dionysiana in the Province
Bysacena. Epistle LXII of St.
Cyprian, De Virginitate, is addressed to him. Epistle IV of
St. Cyprian, De Virginibus Sub-
introductis, seems to be introduced to the same Bishop Pomponius. He lived during the middle of the third century.

pomum, i, *n., fruit of any kind, an
apple.*

ponderatio, onis, *f., a weighing, a
valuing, price.*

ponderator, oris, *m., a weigher,
evaluer.*

ponderositas, atis, *f., weight, pon-
derosity; state of being ponderous; weightiness.*

pondero, are, avi, atum, 1, *v. a., to
weigh in the mind, ponder, consider, reflect upon.*

ponderosus, a, um, *adj.,* (1) *of great weight, heavy, ponderous,* (2) *ruptured,* a synonym of *herniosus.*

pondus, eris, *n.,* (1) lit., (a) in abstr., *heaviness, weight of a body,* (b) in concr., *a weight, mass,* (2) fig., (a) *weight, consequence, importance, influence, authority,* (b) *oppressive weight, burden.*—**pondus gravitatis,** *the tread of authority.*

pono, ere, posui, positum, *v. a.,* (1) *to set, place, put, lay,* (2) *set down, put down,* (3) *place, construct, maintain,* the opposite of *removere,* (4) *stipulate, set up, determine,* (5) *accept as true, impute,* synonym of *sumere* and *supponere.*—Kinds of *ponere* in this (1) sense are: (a), **ponere in numerum,** Aristotle's *eis arithmon tithenai, to place, to combine in number* or *plurality.*—(b), **ponere in obliquo** and **ponere in recto,** *to place something in declension* and *to do so in the nominative case.*—(c), **ponere in recto,** see *ponere in obliquo.*—On **unitas posita,** see *unitas.*—Kinds of *ponere* in this (2) sense are: (a), **ponere adversative** and **ponere exceptive,** *to set something down in the sense of opposition and in the sense of exception.*—(b), **ponere causaliter** and **ponere consecutive,** *to set something down in the sense of cause* and *the sense of a result.*—(c), **ponere consecutive,** see *ponere causaliter.*—(d), **ponere distincte,** *to set*

something down with definiteness.—(e), **ponere exceptive,** see *ponere adversative.*—(f), **ponere explicite** and **ponere implicite,** *to set something down openly* or *explicitly and to do so in a restrained manner* or *implicitly.*—(g), **ponere implicite,** see *ponere explicite.*—(h), **ponere in actu** and **ponere in potentia,** *to set something down in the state of reality* and *in the state of potentiality.*—(i), **ponere in potentia,** see *ponere in actu.*—**posita actione sequitur effectus,** see *actio* under 1.—**posita causa sufficienti ponitur effectus,** see *causa* under 2.—**posita causa sufficienti necesse est effectum poni,** see *causa* under 2.—**posita causa sufficienti nihil aliud requiritur ad effectum inducendum seu nihil aliud videtur esse necessarium ad effectum,** see *causa* under 2.—**posito toto necesse est poni partem,** see *totus* under 1.—**ponere sub disiunctione,** *to maintain in the manner of a separation.* On **impossibile aliquo posito,** see *impossibilis.*—**ponens,** entis, *P. a., placing, setting down, maintaining, determining.*—**positus,** a, um, *P. a., placed, set down, maintained, determined.*

pons, ntis, *m., a bridge across a river, ditch* or *marsh.*

pontifex, ficis, *m.,* (1) *a pontiff, pope,* called distinctively the *summus pontifex, the supreme* or *sovereign pontiff,* and *Romanus pontifex, the Roman pon-*

tiff, (2) *a bishop*, (3) *a high priest*, the ecclesiastical head of the people of Israel, (4) *a high priest* of any religion, (5) *the high priest*, i.e., *Christ*.

pontificalis, e, *adj.*, *pontifical, episcopal*.

pontificatus, us, *m.*, *the episcopate*.

popularis, e, *adj.*, *of* or *belonging to the people, proceeding from* or *designed for the people, popular;* sc. *homo, citizen, common man.* On **status popularis**, see *status* under 5.

populor, ari, atus, 1, *v. dep.*, *to lay waste*, used fig.

populus, i, *m.*, *a people, the people*.

porcus, i, *m.*, *a hog, pig*.

porositas, atis, *f. porousness*.

porosus, a, um, *adj,. porous*.

Porphyrius, ii, *m.*, *Porphry, a Greek philosopher* of Syrian origin, of the Neo-platonic school (A.D. 233-306); disciple of Longinus and Plotinus.

porrectio, onis, *f.*, *a stretching out, extending, extension*.

Porretani, orum, *m.*, see *Porretanus*.

Porretanus, i, *m.*, *Gilbertus Porretanus* or *Gilbert de la Porrée*, bishop of Poiters, 1076-1154. He is author of *Liber Sex Principiorum*, quoted by St. Thomas (I. IX. 2), a commentary on the last six *Categories* of Aristotle; also of a Commentary on *De Trinitate of Boethius*. The *Liber de Causis*, frequently quoted in the *Summa*, is ascribed to him, though it is only an abridged

translation of the *Institutio Theologica* of Proclus.—**Porretani**, orum, *m.*, *The Porretani, followers of Porretanus*.

porrigo, ere, rexi, rectum, 3, *v. a.*, (1) lit., *to offer, present*, (2) fig., *to offer*, as a prayer.

porro, *adv.*, (1) lit., *afar off, far*, (2) transf., *but on the other hand*.

porta, ae, *f.*, (1) lit., (a) *a city-gate, a gate*, (b) transf., in gen., like our *gate of an avenue, entrance, door* of any kind, (2) fig., (a) in gen., *a gate*, (b) as the symbol of strength; *portae inferni, the powers of hell*.

portabilis, e, *adj.*, *that may be borne* or *endured*, a synonym of *moderatus*.

portatilis, e, *adj.*, *portatile, portable, movable*, especially in the phrase *portatile altar*.

portatio, onis, *f.*, *a carrying of anything*.

portentum, i, *n.*, *portent, wonder*, a synonym of *prodigium*.

portio, onis, *f.*, *a share, part, portion*.

porto, are, avi, atum, *v. freq. a.*, *to bear, carry, bring, endure, suffer*.

portus, us, *m.*, *a harbor, haven, port*.

porus, i, *m.*, *a pore, passage, channel* in the body.

posco, ere, poposci, 3, *v. inch. a.*, *to beg, demand, request, desire.* used with the *acc.*

positio, onis, *f.*, (1) *setting, position, place*, synonym of *disposi-*

tio and *situs*, (2) *setting down, putting down, affirmation*, synonym of *affirmatio*, the opposite of *negatio* and *remotio*, (3) *placement, construction, maintenance, position*, the opposite of *negatio* and *remotio*, (4) *establishment, settlement, decision*, (5) *imputation, assumption*, synonym of *suppositio*.—On **demonstratio positione differens**, see *demonstratio* under 3; on **quantitas positionem habens**, see *quantitas* under 1.—As a kind of *positio* in this (2) sense we have **positio absoluta**, *the unconditioned* or *absolute affirmation*. On **ratio disputantis contra positionem**, see *ratio* under 13.—Kinds of *positio* in this (3) sense are: (a), **positio absurda**, *the incongruous* or *absurd assertion*.—(b), **positio consequentis**, *the assertion of the result clause in a conditional sentence*.—(c), **positio extranea**, *the irrelevant assertion*. On **bonum secundum legis positionem**, see *bonus* under 2; on **iustum secundum legis positionem**, see *malus* under 2.

positive, *adv.*, see *positivus*.

positivus, a, um, *adj.*, (1) *stated without qualification*, the first degree of comparison, (2) *set, set down*, (within the sphere of reality), *positive*, the opposite of *negativus, privativus*, and *remotivus*. On **effectus positivus**, see *effectus;* on **ens positivum**, see *ens;* on **ius positivum**, see *ius* under 1; on **iustum positivum**,

see *iustus.*—**positive**, *adv.*, *after the manner of a setting down* or *affirmation*, *in the sense of setting* (into the sphere of reality), *positively*, the opposite of *negative, privative*, and *remotive*. On **accipere positive**, see *accipere* under 3; on **dicere positive**, see *dicere* under 3; on **ens positive dictum**, see *ens;* on **nominare positive**, see *nominare;* on **praedicare positive**, see *praedicare* under 2; on **significare positive**, see *significare*.

positor, oris, *m.*, *a founder*, **positor legis**, *a legislator*.

possessio, onis, *f.*, *a possessing, holding, possession*.

possessor, oris, *m.*, *a possessor, one who possesses, owns, enjoys* or *controls* anything.

possibilis, e, *adj.*, (1) *possible*, i.e., that which can be, the existence of which does not involve intrinsic contradiction, as would for instance a square circle. The context will determine which of these meanings is exact: (a), strictly, logical intrinsic possibility, that which could be, because there is no intrinsic contradiction implied in its existence, but which, as a matter of fact, never will exist; to be distinguished in this sense from *simple future* which not only can but will be, and from *potential* being; (b), thence, by extension, ontological intrinsic possibility, that which can be, because it is already contained potentially in actually existent causes; in this sense, synonymous with *potential,* and opposed to *actual;* (c), thence, that which is but can be other than it is; in this sense, synonymous with *contingent,* and opposed to *necessary,* (2) *possible* in the figurative sense, according to the mathematical power. On **enuntiabile possibile,** see *enuntiabilis;* on **intellectus possibilis,** see *intellectus* under 3; on **materia possibilis,** see *materia* under 3; on **propositio de possibili,** see *propositio* under 2; on **sensus possibilis,** see *sensus* under 3; on **solutio possibilis,** see *solutio* under 2; on **syllogismus de possibili,** see *syllogismus.—* Kinds of *possibile* in the proper sense of the word are: (a), **possibile absolute seu absolutum** and **possibile ex suppositione,** *the unconditioned and the conditioned possible.—*(b), **possibile absolutum,** see *possibile absolute.—*(c), **possibile active seu secundum potentiam activam seu per potentiam agentis** and **possibile secundum potentiam passivam seu per potentiam quae est in rebus,** *the actively and the passively possible,* or the possible with reference to a capacity to accomplish something, and that with reference to a capacity to be acted upon, which capacity is in things. Cf. *possibile per respectum ad aliquam potentiam.—*(d), **possibile alicui** and **possibile simpliciter,** *the possible for some-*

one and the simply or *absolutely possible.—*(e), **possibile ex suppositione,** see *possibile absolute.* —(f), **possibile per potentiam agentis,** see *possibile active.—* (g), **possibile per potentiam quae est in rebus,** see *possibile active.—*(h), **possibile per respectum ad aliquam potentiam seu secundum aliquam potentiam seu secundum potentiam** and **possibile secundum nullam potentiam, seu secundum se seu secundum seipsum,** *the possible considered in reference to the power of an effective cause and that apart from such a cause considered in itself,* i.e., *the extrinsically possible and the intrinsically possible.* Cf. *possibile active.—*(i), **possibile secundum aliquam potentiam,** see *possibile per respectum ad aliquam potentiam.—*(j), **possibile secundum causam inferiorem** and **possibile secundum causam superiorem,** *the possible with reference to an inferior* or *subordinate cause and the possible with reference to a higher* or *a superior cause.—*(k), **possibile secundum causam superiorem,** see *possibile secundum causam inferiorem.—*(l), **possibile secundum nullam potentiam,** see *possible per respectum ad aliquam potentiam.—*(m), **possibile secundum potentiam,** see *possibile per respectum ad aliquam potentiam.—*(n), **possibile secundum potentiam activam,** see *possibile active.—*(o), **possibile secundum** potentiam passivam, see *possibile active.*—(p), **possibile secundum se,** see *possibile per respectum ad aliquam potentiam.*—(q), **possibile secundum seipsam,** see *possibile per respectum ad aliquam potentiam.*—(r), **possibile simpliciter,** see *possibile alicui.*

possibilitas, atis, *f., ability to exist,* or *to act,* or *to be acted upon, possibility,* synonym of *facultas* and *potentia,* the opposite of *impossibilitas* and *impotentia.*— Kinds of *possibilitas* are: (a), **possibilitas ad esse seu essendi** and **possibilitas ad non esse seu non essendi,** *the possibility of being and the possibility of not being.*—(b), **possibilitas ad non esse,** see *possibilitas ad esse.*— (c), **possibilitas essendi,** see *possibilitas ad esse.*—(d), **possibilitas non essendi,** see *possibilitas ad esse.*—(e), **possibilitas secundum potentiam activam** and **possibilitas secundum potentiam passivam,** *possibility of doing something and of having something done.*—(f), **possibilitas secundum potentiam .passivam,** see *possibilitas secundum potentiam activam.*

possideo, ere, sedi, sessum, 2, *v. a.,* (1) lit., (a) *to have and hold, to be master of, to own, possess,* (b) transf., *to take possession of, to occupy,* (2) fig., (a) *to possess, to have a thing,* (b) *to possess, to hold in control* or *restrain.*

Possidius, ii, *m., Possidius,* bishop of Calama, a town of Numidia, to the southwest of Hippo. He appears to have been a convert from paganism, and on his conversion to have become an inmate of the monastery at Hippo, probably about 390 A.D. From that time he lived in intimate friendship with St. Augustine until his death in 430.

possum, posse, potui, *v. n.* irreg., *to be able, have power, can.* Cf. *contingens* under 2.—**ex posse seu pro posse seu secundum posse,** *according to possibility, according to powers.*—Kinds of *posse* are: (a), **posse ad aliquid,** *to be able with reference to something, to have some power.*—(b), **posse in aliquid,** *to attain something with one's own ability* or *power.* —(c), **posse super aliquid,** *to extend over something with one's own power.*—(d), **posse supra aliquid,** *to exceed something with one's own power.*—**potens,** entis, *P. a., able, mighty, powerful, potent.*—**potenter,** *adv., strongly, mightily, powerfully.*

post, *adv.,* and *prep.,* (1) *adv.,* (a) of place, *behind, back, backwards;* (b) of time, *afterwards, after;* (2) *prep* with *acc.,* (a) of place, *behind, after;* (b) of time, *after, since.*

postea, *adv., after this* or *that, hereafter, thereafter, afterwards.*

posterior, *posterius,* see *posterus.*

posterioritas, atis, *f., posteriority,* the state of being posterior or later in point of time; opposed to priority.

posteritas, atis, *f., posterity, succeeding generations.*
posterus, a, um, *adj., coming after,
following, next, ensuing, future,*
used in the Summa Theologica
in the positive only as substantive, thus: **in posterum** (sc. **tempus**), *in the future, for the future.*
—**posteri,** orum, *m., coming generations, descendants, posterity.*
—*Comp.,* **posterior, posterius,** (1)
latter, that behind, posterior, the
opposite of *anterior,* (2) *latter,
later,* the opposite of *prior,* (3)
Posteriora Analytica, *the Later*
or *Second Analytics of Aristotle,*
the opposite of *Priora Analytica.*
On **causa posterior,** see *causa* under 1 and 2; on **contraria posteriora,** see *contrarius* under 2; on
definire per posteriora, see *definire* under 2; on **dicere per
posteriora,** see *dicere* under 3;
on **differentia posterior,** see *differentia;* on **finis posterior,** see
finis under 2; on **necessitas a po-
steriore,** see *necessitas* under 1;
on **praedicare per seu secundum
posteriora,** see *praedicare* under
2; on **praedicatio posterior,** see
praedicatio under 2; on **processus
de priori ad posterius,** see *processus* under 1; on **quantitas per
posterius,** see *quantitas* under
1.—Kinds of *posterius* in this (2)
sense are: (a), **posterius in magnitudine seu secundum quantitatem** and **posterius motus seu in
motu,** *the later according to size
and quantity and that according
to movement.*—(b), **posterius in**

motu, see *posterius in magnitudine.*—(c), **posterius in tempore seu
tempore seu temporis seu via generationis,** *the later according to
time* or *according to origin.*—(d),
posterius motus, see *posterius in
magnitudine.*—(e), **posterius natura seu secundum naturam,** *the
later according to nature.*—(f),
posterius secundum actum, *the
later according to reality,* the
opposite of *posterius secundum
potentiam,* i.e., *the later according to potentiality.*—(g), **posterius
secundum naturam,** see *posterius
natura.*—(h), **posterius secundum
quantitatem,** see *posterius in
magnitudine.*—(i), **posterius tempore seu temporis,** see *posterius
in tempore.*—(j), **posterius via
generationis,** see *posterius in tempore.*—naturaliter prius est quod
est perfectius, licet in unoquoque
sit tempore posterius, see *prior*
under 1.—posito posteriori ponitur prius, *if the later is established* or *fixed, so also is the
earlier.*—posteriora non sunt de
intellectu priorum, sed e converso, *the later does not belong to
the conception of the earlier, but
this is true of the reverse.*—remoto posteriori non removetur
prius, *with the removal of the
later, the earlier upon which it
depends is not removed.*—remoto priori removetur posterius,
see *prior* under 1.—semper prius
salvatur in posteriori, see *pri-
or* under 1.—transmutato posteri-

ori non transmutatur prius, *the change of the later does not affect the earlier upon which it depends.*—**virtus prioris est in posteriori,** see *prior* under 1.— *Comp. adv.,* **posterius,** *later, afterwards.*—*Sup.,* **postremus,** a, um, *the hindmost, the last,* opposite of *primus.*—*Sup., adv.,* **postremo,** *at last, finally.*

postis, is, *m., a post, door post.*

postmodum, *adv., afterwards, presently, shortly.*

postpono, ere, posui, positum, 3, *v. a., to put after, set aside, postpone; to esteem less, to neglect, disregard.*

postpraedicamentum, i, *n., post-category,* general modes of being arising from the comparison of categories among themselves. There are five post-categories, namely: *oppositio, prioritas et posterioritas, simultas, motus,* and *habitus.* See article on *praedicamentum* under 2.

postquam, *conj., after that, after, as soon as, when,* constr. usually with *historical pres.,* or *perf.* or *imperf. indic.,* or *subj.*

postremus, a, um, *adj.,* see *posterus.*

postulatio, onis, *f., supplication, intercession.*

postulo, are, avi, atum, 1, *v. a.,* (1) in gen., *to ask, pray, desire something,* used with *acc.,* and *absol.,* (2) in partic., in jurid. lang., *to summon, arraign before a court.*

potatio, onis, *f., a drinking, potation.*

potator, oris, *m., a drinker, topor, bibber.*

potens, entis, *P. a.,* see *possum.*

potentatus, us, *m., power, rule, dominion.*

potenter, *adv.,* see *possum.*

potentia, ae, *f.,* (1) *power, the ability to be* or *become* or *to do something, possibility, potentiality, faculty for something,* synonym of *potestas,* (2) *faculty, power for an activity,* equivalent of *potentia agere* (see under 1), synonym of *potestas, virtus,* and *vis,* the opposite of *actus* and *impotentia,* (3) *power, strength, might, force, influence,* synonym of *dominium, potestas, principatus, regimen, virtus,* and *vis,* (4) *possibility* or *potentiality for being,* the equivalent of *potentia ad esse seu ad essendum* (see above, under 1), synonym of *possibilitas, potentialitas,* and *potestas,* the opposite of *impossibilitas, impotentia,* and *impotentialitas* on the one hand and of *actus* on the other.—Kinds of *potentia* in this (1) sense are: (a), **potentia actionis seu activa seu operativa seu agentis seu ad agere** and **potentia passionis seu passiva seu receptiva seu pure materialis seu ad esse seu ad essendum,** *the active* (cf. *potentia operativa* under 2) and *the passive potentiality* (cf. *potentia activa et passiva* under 2), i.e., *the faculty for an action and that for* a being or for the reception of a being or the mere potentiality belonging to the material of a thing (cf. *potentia materialis* under 2).—(b), **potentia activa,** see *potentia actionis.*—(c), **potentia ad agere,** see *potentia actionis.*—(d), **potentia ad esse seu ad essendum,** see *potentia actionis.*—(e), **potentia agentis,** see *potentia actionis.*—(f), **potentia mathematica seu secundum metaphoram,** *the mathematical* or *quasi-figurative potentiality.*—(g), **potentia operativa,** see *potentia actionis.*—(h), **potentia passionis,** see *potentia actionis.*—(i), **potentia passiva,** see *potentia actionis.*—(j), **potentia pure materialis,** see *potentia actionis.*—(k), **potentia receptiva,** see *potentia actionis.*—(l), **potentia secundum metaphoram,** see *potentia mathematica.* On **possibile secundum potentiam activam et passivam et secundum potentiam mathematicam,** see *possibilis* under 1 and 2; on **possibilitas secundum potentiam activam et passivam,** see *possibilitas.*—**proprius actus respondet propriae potentiae,** see *actus* under 2. On **impossibile per respectum ad potentiam, secundum potentiam et secundum nullam potentiam,** see *impossibilis;* on **possibile secundum potentiam seu secundum aliquam potentiam et secundum nullam potentiam,** see *possibilis* under 1; on **quantitas potentiae,** see *quantitas* under 2; on **subiectum**

potentiae, see *subiectum* under 1; on **substantia potentiae,** see *substantia* under 8; on **terminus potentiae,** see *terminus* under 1; on **ultimum potentiae,** see *ultimus.*—Kinds of *potentia* in this (2) sense are: (a), **potentia absoluta** and **potentia habitualis,** *unlimited power and that modified by a habit.* Cf. *potentia adaptata* and *potentia habitualis* under 3.—(b), **potentia acta, potentia tantum acta seu mota, potentia agens,** and **potentia tantum agens,** *the purely passive power, which acts only when acted upon and the spontaneously active power,* or *the power which once moved in a certain respect, moves itself.*—(c), **potentia activa** and **potentia passiva,** *the active and the passive power,* (cf. *potentia activa et passiva* under 1), i.e., the power of producing an effect on something else and the power of receiving the effect of another in the form of an action.—(d), **potentia adaptata seu assimilata** (*ad actum*) and **potentia nuda seu pura,** *the power accommodated to an act* or *made suitable* and *the bare* or *pure power,* i.e., the power provided with a *habitus* corresponding to the act and the power deprived of such. Cf. *potentia absoluta et habitualis.*—(e), **potentia aestimativa seu cogitativa, potentia imaginativa seu phantastica** and **potentia memorativa,** *the sense faculty of* *perceiving the goodness* or *harmfulness of an object,* (on the part of man or beast), *the faculty of imagination, the faculty of memory.*—(f), **potentia affectiva** and **potentia cognitiva seu cognoscitiva,** *the appetitive faculty* and *faculty of knowledge.* Cf. *potentia appetitiva et apprehensiva.*—(g), **potentia affixa organo corporali seu materiali seu utens corporali organo seu coniuncti** and **potentia non utens organo corporali seu incorporea seu solius animae,** *the organic and the inorganic power of the soul,* or the power which has its subject in the whole consisting of body and soul, and that which has its subject in the soul alone. —(h), **potentia agens,** see *potentia acta.*—(i), **potentia animae** and **potentia corporis seu corporalis,** *the power of the soul and that of the body.*—(j), **potentia appetitiva** and **potentia apprehensiva,** *the striving and the comprehending power* or *the power of the appetite and that of comprehension.* Cf. *potentia affectiva et cognitiva.*—(k), **potentia apprehensiva,** see *potentia appetitiva.*—(l), **potentia assimilata,** see *potentia adaptata.*—(m), **potentia augmentativa, potentia nutritiva,** and **potentia generativa,** *the power of growth, that of sustenance, and that of reproduction.*—(n), **potentia cogitativa,** see *potentia aestimativa.*—(o), **potentia cognitiva seu cognosci-**

tiva, see *potentia affectiva.*—(p), **potentia coniuncti,** see *potentia affixa organo corporali.*—(q), **potentia corporalis,** see *potentia animae.*—(r), **potentia corporis,** see *potentia animae.*—(s), **potentia cum ratione seu rationalis** and **potentia irrationalis,** the translation of the Aristotelian expression, *dynamis meta logou kai dynamis alogos* (Metaph. IX. 2, 1046. b. 2), *the rational and the irrational power,* i.e., the power which belongs to the rational part of the soul or is active under the influence of reason, and that with which neither of these is the case.—(t), **potentia defectiva seu diminutia** *the defective* or *diminished power.*—(u), **potentia diminuta,** see *potentia defectiva.*—(v), **potentia dirigens** and **potentia exsequens seu exsecutiva,** *the directing and the executing power.* Cf. *potentia imperans et imperata.*—(w), **potentia discurrens** and **potentia veritatem accipiens,** *the power that discusses and concludes a truth and that which grasps the truth directly.*—(x), **potentia exsecutiva seu exsequens,** see *potentia dirigens.*—(y), **potentia finita seu limitata** and **potentia infinita,** *the finite* or *limited power* and *the infinite* or *unlimited power.* —(z), **potentia generandi,** *the power of generating.*—(a²), **potentia generativa,** see *potentia augmentativa.*—(b²), **potentia habitualis,** see *potentia absoluta.*—(c²), potentia imaginativa, see *potentia aestimativa.*—(d²), potentia immaterialis and potentia materialis, *the immaterial* or *spiritual* and *the material* or *physical power.* Cf. *potentia pure materialis* under 1.—(e²), potentia imperans and potentia imperata, *the commanding power* and *the power that has received a command.* Cf. *potentia dirigens et exsequens.*—(f²), potentia incorporea, see *potentia affixa organo corporali.*—(g²), potentia infinita, see *potentia finita.*—(h²), potentia insensibilis, *the insensible power* or *that not consisting of any of the senses.*—(i²), potentia intellectiva seu intellegibilis, potentia sensitiva, and potentia vegetativa, *the intellectual, the sensitive,* and *the vegetative power.*—(j²), potentia interpretativa, *the interpretative power* or *the power of language.* —(k²), potentia irascibilis, *the power of irascibility.*—(l²), potentia irrationalis, see *potentia cum ratione.*—(m²), potentia libera and potentia ligata, *the free* and *the bound power* of which the latter is directed by nature to a definite activity; the former is not.— (n²), potentia ligata, see *potentia libera.*—(o²), potentia limitata, see *potentia finita.*—(p²), potentia materialis, see *potentia immaterialis.*—(q²), potentia memorativa, see *potentia aestimativa.*—(r²), potentia motiva, *the power moving locally.*—(s²), potentia naturalis, *the natural power* or *the*

power of nature.—(t²), potentia naturalis and potentia superaddita, *the natural power* or *that belonging to the nature of a being,* (cf. *potentia naturalis* under 4) and *the power added thereto.*—(u²), potentia non utens organo corporali, see *potentia affixa organo corporali.*—(v²), potentia nuda, see *potentia adaptata.*—(w²), potentia nutritiva, see *potentia augmentativa.*—(x²), potentia operativa seu practica and potentia perspectiva seu speculativa, *the power that aims at an action* or *deed* (cf. *potentia operativa* under 1) and *that which aims at comprehension.*—(y²), potentia originalis, *the original power* or *that given at the time of origin.*—(z²), potentia particularis and potentia universalis, *the particular* or *limited power* and *the general* or *unlimited power.*— (a³), potentia passiva, see *potentia activa.*—(b³), potentia perspectiva, see *potentia operativa.* —(c³), potentia phantastica, see *potentia aestimativa.*—(d³), potentia practica, see *potentia operativa.*—(e³), potentia pura, see *potentia adaptata.*—(f³), potentia rationalis, see *potentia cum ratione.*—(g³), potentia sensitiva, see *potentia intellectiva.*—(h³), potentia solius animae, see *potentia affixa organo corporali.*—(i³), potentia speculativa, see *potentia operativa.*—(j³), potentia spirativa, *the breathing power* or *the power of breath.*—(k³), potentia superactiva, *the superactive power* or *the power excessively active.*—(l³), potentia superaddita, see *potentia naturalis.*—(m³), potentia activa, *the power of touch* or *feeling.*—(n³), potentia tantum acta, potentia tantum agens, and potentia tantum mota, see *potentia acta.*—(o³), potentia universalis, see *potentia particularis.*—(p³), potentia utens corporali organo, see *potentia affixa organo corporali.*—(q³), potentia vegetativa, see *potentia intellectiva.*—(r³), potentia veritatem accipiens, see *potentia discurrens.*—(s³), potentia visiva, *the power of sight.*— actus cuiuslibet potentiae accipitur secundum ordinem potentiae ad suum obiectum, see *actus* under 1.—actus sunt praevii potentiis, see *actus* under 1.—cuius est actus, eius est potentia, see *actus* under 1.—cuius est potentia, eius est actio, or, cuius est potentia, eius est actus e contrario, or, eiusdem est potentia, cuius est actus procedens a potentia, or, eiusdem est potentia et actio, or, oportet quod eius sit potentia sicut subiecti, cuius est operatio, the translation of the Aristotelian passage: *hou gar he dynamis, toutou kai he energeia, that which is the subject of a power is evidently also the subject of the action arising from the latter and vice versa.*—diversitas actus quandoque indicat diversitatem potentiarum, quandoque non, see *actus* under 1.—eiusdem est

potentia, cuius est actus procedens a potentia, see above: *cuius est potentia* etc.—eiusdem est potentia et actio, see above: *cuius est potentia* etc.—non possunt esse unius potentiae simul plures actus, *one and the same power cannot perform several actions simultaneously.*—omnis potentia reducitur ad operationem sicut ad perfectionem propriam, *every power is directed toward a certain action as its proper perfection.*—oportet quod eius sit potentia sicut subiecti, cuius est operatio, see above: *cuius est potentia* etc.—quanto aliqua potentia est superior, tanto ad plura se extendit, *the higher a power is according to rank, the more things does it touch with its influence.*—Kinds of *potentia* in this (3) sense are: (a), potentia absoluta and potentia in ordine ad aliquid seu ordinata seu regulata sc. Dei, *the simple power* which extends to whatever is not intrinsically impossible, (cf. *potentia absoluta* under 2 and 4) *and the power of God with reference to His foreknowledge and predestination and the ordered or regulated power of God.*—(b), potentia creata seu creaturae and potentia creatoris seu divina, *the created power* or *the power of the creature* and *the power of the creator* or *the divine power.*— (c), potentia creatoris, see *potentia creata.*—(d), potentia creaturae, see *potentia creata.*—(e), po-

tentia divina, see *potentia creata.*
—(f), **potentia habitualis,** *the habitual power* or *the power in the form of a habit.* Cf. *potentia habitualis* under 2.—(g), **potentia in ordine ad aliquid,** see *potentia absoluta.*—(h), **potentia militaris,** *military power.*—(i), **potentia mundana seu secularis,** *worldly* or *temporal power.*—(j), **potentia mundana,** see *potentia absoluta.* —(k), **potentia regulata,** see *potentia absoluta.*—(l), **potentia saecularis,** see *potentia mundana.*— On **causa in potentia,** see *causa* under 2; on **cognoscere in potentia,** see *cognoscere* under 2; on **effectus in potentia,** see *effectus;* on **ens potentiae, ens in potentia, ens in potentia secundum quid et simpliciter,** see *ens;* on **esse in potentia,** see *esse;* on **infinitum potentiae seu in potentia,** see *infinitus;* on **contrarietas secundum potentiam,** see *contrarietas* under 1; on **convenientia potentiae ad actum,** see *convenientia* under 2; on **intellectus potentiae,** see *intellectus* under 3; on **possibile secundum potentiam mathematicam,** see *possibilis;* on **prius secundum potentiam,** see *prior* under 1; on **scientia in potentia,** see *scientia* under 1; on **scire in potentia,** see *scire* under 1; on **sensus in potentia,** see *sensus* under 3; on **verum secundum potentiam,** see *verus* under 1; on **vita secundum potentiam,** see *vita* under 2.—**in potentia,** *in the state of potentiality* with reference to

something. This state is a reality between non-existence and actual existence.—Kinds of *potentia* in this (4) sense are: (a), **potentia absoluta,** *the unconditioned* or *simple potentiality.* Cf. *potentia absoluta* under 2 and 3.—(b), **potentia accidentalis** and **potentia essentialis,** *the unessential and the essential potentiality,* or *the potentiality based on the essence of a thing.*—(c), **potentia completa seu perfecta** and **potentia non completa seu imperfecta,** *the complete* or *perfect and the incomplete* or *imperfect potentiality.*—(d), **potentia essentialis,** see *potentia accidentalis.*—(e), **potentia imperfecta,** see *potentia completa.*—(f), **potentia indisposita,** *the unprepared* or *disordered potentiality.*—(g), **potentia intellectiva seu intellectualis substantiae** and **potentia materiae,** *the intellectual potentiality* or *that consisting of an intellectual substance and the potentiality of the material of physical things.*—(h), **potentia materiae,** see *potentia intellectiva.*—(i), **potentia naturalis** and **potentia oboedientialis seu oboedientiae,** *the natural potentiality,* (cf. *potentia naturalis* under 2) and *the obediential potentiality* or *that which is reduced to act by nature* and *that which is actualized solely through obedience to the creator.* —(j), **potentia non completa,** see *potentia completa.*—(k), **potentia oboedientiae,** see *potentia natu-*

ralis.—(l), **potentia oboedientialis,** see *potentia naturalis.*—(m), **potentia perfecta,** see *potentia completa.*—(n), **potentia permixta** and **potentia pura seu tantum,** *the mixed (with actuality) potentiality* and *the pure* or *mere potentiality.*—(o), **potentia prima seu remota** and **potentia propinqua,** *the first* or *the remote and the proximate potentiality.*—(p), **potentia propinqua,** see *potentia prima.*—(q), **potentia pura,** see *potentia permixta.*—(r), **potentia remota,** see *potentia prima.*—(s), **potentia subiecti,** *the potentiality of a subject* or *that attached to a substance.*—(t), **potentia tantum,** see *potentia permixta.*—actus est prior potentia ratione, substantia seu secundum substantiam, id est, perfectione, et tempore, see *actus* under 2.—actus est prior quam potentia, secundum substantiam et formam, see *actus* under 2.—actus et potentia dividunt quodlibet genus entium, see *actus* under 2.—actus generatione et tempore est posterior potentia, see *actus* under 2.—actus secundum naturam est prior potentia, see *actus* under 2.—ens dividitur per potentiam et actum, see *ens.* —in bonis actus est melior potentia, . . . , in malis est actus peior potentia, see *actus* under 2.—nihil secundum idem est potentia et actu, *nothing exists in the state of potentiality and in that of reality according to one and the same relation.*—non reducitur quod est in potentia, in actum, nisi per id quod est in actu, or, omne quod est in potentia, reducitur ad actum per id quod est actu ens, or, quod est in potentia, naturaliter movetur ab alio, quod est actu, *all that exists in the state of potentiality is naturally transposed into the state of reality only by such as already exists in the state of reality.*—potentia et actus sunt de primis differentiis entis, *potentiality and reality belong to the first differences of being.*—proprius actus in propria materia fit, see *actus* under 2.— quod est in potentia, naturaliter movetur ab alio quod est actu, see above: *non reducitur* etc.— unumquodque genus dividitur per potentiam et actum, *every supreme genus of being is divided into the potentiality and into the reality of the genus in question.*

potentialis, e, *adj.,* (1) *pertaining to a power, to a force,* synonym of *virtualis,* (2) *potential,* synonym of *possibilis* and *virtualis,* the opposite of *actualis* on the one hand and of *impossibilis* on the other. On **pars potentialis,** see *pars* under 1; on **principium potentiale,** see *principium;* on **totum potentiale,** see *totus* under 1. On **cognitio potentialis,** see *cognitio* under 2; on **intellectus potentialis,** see *intellectus* under 3.—**potentialiter,** *adv., in potentiality, according to potentiality,* *potentially,* synonym of *virtualiter,* the opposite of *actualiter.*

potentialitas, atis, *f., potentiality,* synonym of *possibilitas, potentia,* and *potestas,* the opposite of *actus* on the one hand and of *impossibilitas, impotentia,* and *impotentialitas* on the other.

potentialiter, *adv.,* see *potentialis.*

potestas, atis, *f.,* (1) *possibility, potentiality for something,* synonym of *potentia,* (2) *potentiality, power for an action,* synonym of *potentia, virtus;* and *vis,* the opposite of *impotentia,* (3) *might, power, dominion,* synonym of *dominium, potentia, principatus,* and *regimen,* (4) *ruler, person in authority, the power,* (5) *potentiality* for a being, the equivalent of *potestas essendi* under 1, synonym of *possibilitas, potentialitas,* and *potentia,* the opposite of *impossibilitas* and *impotentialitas* on the one hand and of *actus* on the other.—Kinds of *potestas* in this (1) sense are: potestas activa and potestas passiva seu essendi, *the active and the passive potentiality,* i.e., the capacity for an action and that for an undergoing or for the reception of a being.—Kinds of *potestas* in this (2) sense are: (a), potestas adquisita, potestas infusa, and potestas naturalis, *the power* or *capacity acquired* (through practice), *that infused* or *bestowed* (by God), *and that lying within the nature of a thing and accompanying it.*—(b), potes-

tas gloriae and potestas naturae, *the power in the glory of heaven and that in the state of nature.*— (c), potestas infusa, see *potestas adquisita.*—(d), postestas naturae, see *potestas gloriae.*—(e), potestas naturalis, see *potestas adquisita.* —(f), potestas rationalis, *the rational power,* i.e., the power guided by or belonging to the rational part of the soul. Cf. *potentia rationalis,* under *potentia* 2. On nomen potestatis, see *nomen* under 1; on prius secundum potestatem, see *prior* under 1.—Kinds of *potestas* in this sense are: (a), potestas auctoritatis, potestas ministerii and ministerii principalis seu excellentiae, *the power of the author* (of the sacraments), *that of the minister, and that of the highest minister* (Christ), or *of him distinguished in service.*—(b), potestas clavium, *the ecclesiastical power of the keys.*—(c), potestas coactiva, *the compelling power* or *the power of exterior force.*—(d), potestas coarctata, *the restricted* or *limited power.*—(e), potestas commissa seu delegata seu per commissionem and potestas ordinaria, *the delegated* or *extraordinary power* and *the regular* or *ordinary power.*—(f), potestas corporalis and potestas spiritualis, *the physical* and *the spiritual power.* —(g), potestas delegata, see *potestas commissa.*—(h), potestas derivata, *the derived power.*—(i), potestas divina and potestas humana, *the divine and the human power.*–(j), **potestas dominativa** and **potestas paterna**, *the lordly and the paternal power* or *the power of the lord over his slaves and that of the father over his children.*–(k), **potestas episcopalis seu pontificalis** and **potestas sacerdotalis**, *the episcopal and the priestly power.*–(l), **potestas excellentiae**, see *potestas auctoritatis.*–(m), **potestas expedita seu libera**, *the unhindered* or *free power.*–(n), **potestas hierarchica**, *the hierarchical power* or *the power belonging to a member of the hierarchy.*–(o), **potestas humana**, see *potestas divina.*–(p), **potestas inferior** and **potestas superior**, *the lower* or *inferior and the higher* or *superior power.*–(q), **potestas infusa**, see *potestas adquisita.*–(r), **potestas iudiciaria**, *the judicial power.*–(s), **potestas iurisdictionis** and **potestas ordinis seu sacramentalis**, *the power of jurisdiction and that of the sacramental order.*–(t), **potestas libera**, see *potestas expedita.*–(u), **potestas ministerii**, see *potestas auctoritatis.*–(v), **potestas ministerii principalis**, see *potestas auctoritatis.* –(w), **potestas optimorum** and **potestas populi**, *the power of the best* or *of the aristocracy* and *that of the people.*–(x), **potestas ordinis**, see *potestas iurisdictionis.*–(y), **potestas particularis** and **potestas universalis**, *the particular* and *the universal power.*–(z),

potestas paterna, see *potestas dominativa.*–(a²), **potestas per commissionem**, see *potestas commissa.*–(b²), **potestas perfecta seu plenitudinis**, *the perfect* or *full power.*–(c²), **potestas plenitudinis**, see *potestas perfecta.*–(d²), **potestas pontificalis**, see *potestas episcopalis.*–(e²), **potestas populi**, see *potestas optimorum.*–(f²), **potestas propriae electionis**, *the power of proper choice* or *one's own chosen power.*–(g²), **potestas publica**, *the public power.*–(h²), **potestas regia seu regnativa** and **potestas tyrannica**, *the royal and the tyrannical power.*–(i²), **potestas regiminis**, *the power of the government.*–(j²), **potestas regnativa**, see *potestas regia.*–(k²), **potestas sacerdotalis**, see *potestas episcopalis.*–(l²), **potestas sacramentalis**, see *potestas iurisdictionis.*–(m²), **potestas saecularis seu temporalis**, *the secular* or *temporal power.*–(n²), **potestas spiritualis**, see *potestas corporalis.*– (o²), **potestas superior**, see *potestas inferior.*–(p²), **potestas temporalis**, see *potestas saecularis.* –(q²), **potestas tyrannica**, see *potestas regia.*–(r²), **potestas universalis**, see *potestas particularis.*– (s²), **potestas usurpata**, *the presumed power.*–**nulla res habet potestatem supra suum esse**, *nothing has a power which goes beyond its being.*–Kinds of *potestas* in this (4) sense are: (a), **potestas aerea**, *the aerial authority* or *the ruler of the air.*–(b),

potestas mundana seu saecularis, *the worldly authority.*

potestative, *adv.,* see *potestativus.*

potestativus, a, um, *adj., denoting* or *containing power.* On **totum potestativum,** see *totus* under 1. —**potestative,** *adv., with might, with power, powerfully,* synonym of *ex potestate seu per potestatem.*

potio, onis, *f.,* (1) in gen., *a drink, draught, potion,* (2) in partic., *a draught* or *potion given by physicians.*

potior, iri, itus, 4, *v. dep. n., to take possession of, to get, obtain, acquire, receive,* used with the *abl.*

potior, ius, see *potis.*

potis, e, *adj., able, capable, possible,* usually used in the positive with *est,* and rarely, if ever, declined, *able, capable, possible.*— **potior,** ius, comp. *adj., that may be preferred, preferred, better, preferable, stronger, more important.*—**potius,** *comp. adv., rather, preferably, more.*—**potissimus,** a, um, *sup. adj., the chief, principal, most prominent, most important.*—**potissime,** *sup. adv., chiefly, principally, especially, above all.*

potissime, *adv.,* see *potis.*

poto, are, avi, atum, or potum, 1, *v. a.,* and *n.,* causative, *to give to drink.*—**potatus,** a, um, *P. a.,* (1) *that has been drunk,* (2) *caused to drink, furnished with drink.*

potus, us, *m.,* (1) *drink,* any liquid that is taken into the stomach by swallowing, especially for the purpose of quenching the thirst, (2) as much as may be taken at one time; *a drink, a draft,* (3) specifically, *strong liquor, drink.*

practicus, a, um, *adj., active, acting, effecting,* pertaining to doing, acting, effecting; the opposite of *contemplativus, speculativus,* and *theoricus,* sometimes also of *operativus.* On **ars practica,** see *ars* under 1; on **cognitio practica,** see *cognitio* under 2; on **existimatio practica,** see *existimatio;* on **habitus practicus,** see *habitus* under 4; on **intellectus practicus,** see *intellectus* under 3; on **philosophia practica,** see *philosophia;* on **potentia practica,** see *potentia* under 2; on **ratio practica,** see *ratio* under 3; on **rectitudo practica,** see *rectitudo* under 3; on **scientia practica, practica secundum quid et practica simpliciter seu tantum,** see *scientia* under 1; on **vita practica,** see *vita* under 3.

prae, *prep.* with *abl., before, in front of, in advance of, in comparison with, compared with, in preference to.*

praeacceptio, onis, *f., preference.*

praeaccipio, ere, 3, *v. a.,* (1) *to possess, receive,* or *be the recipient of antecedently,* (2) *prefer.*

praeambulus, a, um, *adj., walking before, preceding, preparatory.*

praeassignatus, a, um, *P. a., aforesaid.*

praeassumptio, onis, *f., a receiving beforehand.*

praeassumptus, a, um, *P. a.,* *taken* or *received beforehand.*

praebeo, ere, bui, tum, 2, *v. a.,* *to give, grant, furnish, supply.*

praecantatio, onis, *f.,* *an enchantment, incantations.*

praecaveo, ere, cavi, cautum, 2, *v. a.,* (1) act., *to guard against, seek to avert,* (2) neutr., (a) *to beware, to use precaution,* (b) with *dat., to provide for, take precautions for one's safety.*

praecedo, ere, cessi, cessum, 3, *v. a.* and *n., to go before, precede.—* **praecedens,** entis, *P. a., going before, preceding.* On **finis praecedens,** see *finis* under 2; on **ignorantia praecedens,** see *ignorantia* under 1; on **intentio praecedens,** see *intentio* under 2; on **meritum praecedens,** see *meritum* under 1; on **occasio praecedens,** see *occasio;* on **passio praecedens,** see *passio* under 3; on **privatio praecedens,** see *privatio* under 2; on **qualitas praecedens,** see *qualitas.*

praecello, ere, *v. a.* and *n.,* (1) act., *to excel, surpass,* (2) neutr., *to excel.—***praecellens,** entis, *P. a., surpassing, excellent, distinguished.*

praecentor, oris, *m., a precentor, a leader in music.*

praeceps, cipitis, *adj., rash, hasty, precipitate,* used fig.—**praeceps lingua,** *a hasty tongue,* i.e., *hasty words.—***praeceps,** cipitis, *n., great danger.*

praeceptio, onis, *f., precept, injunction.*

praeceptivus, a, um, *adj., preceptive, mandatory, conveying a command.*

praeceptor, oris, *m., a preceptor, teacher, instructor.*

praeceptum, n., see *praecipio.*

praecido, ere, cidi, cisum, 3, *v. a.,* (1) lit., *to cut off,* used with the acc., (2) fig., *to cut off* from association.—**praecise,** *adv., positively, absolutely.*

praecipio, ere, cepi, ceptum, 3, *v. a., to give rules* or *precepts* (to any one), *to advise, admonish, warn, inform, instruct, teach; to enjoin, direct, bid, order,* synonym of *mando, impero, doceo.—* As subst.: **praecipiens,** entis, *m., teacher, adviser.—***praeceptum,** i, *n., rule, precept; an order, direction, command, bidding; an injunction.* On **opus praecepti,** see *opus* under 4; on **substantia praecepti,** see *substantia* under 8.— Kinds of *praeceptum* are: (a), **praeceptum affirmativum** and **praeceptum negativum seu prohibitivum,** *the command and the prohibition.—*(b), **praeceptum caeremoniale, praeceptum iudiciale,** and **praeceptum morale,** *the religious* or *ceremonial precepts, the judicial* or *civic precepts,* and *the moral* or *ethical precepts* of the old law.—(c), **praeceptum caritatis seu dilectionis** and **praeceptum iustitiae,** *the precepts* (governing the acts) *of love* and *those* (governing the acts) *of justice.—*(d), **praeceptum commune seu generale** and **prae-**

ceptum speciale, *the universal and the particular precept.*—(e), praeceptum Dei and praeceptum ecclesiae, *the commandment of God and that of the Church.*—(f), praeceptum democraticum, praeceptum regium, and praeceptum tyrannicum, *the democratic, the regal, and the tyrannical precepts,* i.e., the order issued by a democratic government, that by a king, and that by a tyrant. Cf. *politia democratia* and *ius tyrannicum.*—(g), praeceptum dilectionis, see *praeceptum caritatis.*—(h), praeceptum domesticum seu familiare, *the domestic or family precept.*—(i), praeceptum ecclesiae, see *praeceptum Dei.*—(j), praeceptum expressum and praeceptum interpretativum, *the expressed command and that interpreted as such.*—(k), praeceptum familiare, see *praeceptum domesticum.*—(l), praeceptum figurale, *the symbolical or typical precept.*—(m), praeceptum generale, see *praeceptum commune.*—(n), praeceptum interpretativum, see *praeceptum expressum.*—(o), praeceptum iudiciale, see *praeceptum caeremoniale.*—(p), praeceptum iuris naturalis seu legis naturalis seu naturae and praeceptum iuris positivi, *the precept of natural law or the law of nature and that of the positive or given law.*—(q), praeceptum iuris positivi, see *praeceptum iuris naturalis.*—(r), praeceptum iustitiae, see *praeceptum caritatis.*—(s),

praeceptum legis, *the prescription of a law in general or that of the Old Testament Law or of the Decalogue.*—(t), praeceptum legis naturae seu naturalis, see *praeceptum iuris naturalis.*—(u), praeceptum morale, see *praeceptum caeremoniale.*—(v), praeceptum negativum, see *praeceptum affirmativum.*—(w), praeceptum primae necessitatis, secundae, tertiae et quartae necessitatis, *the precept* (respecting the love of God) *of the first necessity, that of the second necessity, that of the third necessity, and that of the fourth necessity.*—(x), praeceptum primae tabulae and praeceptum secundae tabulae, *the precept of the first tablet,* i.e., the first three commandments, and that of *the second tablet of Moses,* i.e., the last seven commandments which are concerned with man's relation to other men. —(y), praeceptum prohibitivum, see *praeceptum affirmativum.*—(z), praeceptum pure caeremoniale and praeceptum pure morale, *the purely religious or devotional precept and the purely moral or ethical precept.*—(a²), praeceptum pure morale, see *praeceptum pure caeremoniale.*—(b²), praeceptum quartae necessitatis, see *praeceptum primae necessitatis.*—(c²), praeceptum regium, see *praeceptum democraticum.*—(d²), praeceptum secundae necessitatis, see *praeceptum primae necessitatis.*—(e²), praeceptum secundae tabulae, see *praeceptum primae tabulae.—(f²)*, **praeceptum speciale,** see *praeceptum commune.—(g²)*, **praeceptum tertiae necessitatis,** see *praeceptum primae necessitatis. —(h²)*, **praeceptum tyrannicum,** see *praeceptum democraticum.—* **praeceptum affirmatum obligat semper, sed non ad semper,** *an affirmative precept always holds its power of obligating, but not in such a way that one must fulfil it on every occasion, in every place, and under all circumstances; moreover, it grants exceptions.—***praecepta negative obligant semper et ad semper,** *a negative precept always binds under all circumstances, and never allows exceptions.*

praecipitanter, *adv.,* see *praecipito.*

praecipitatio, onis, *f., a following headlong, headlong hurry, inconsiderate haste, precipitation.*

praecipitium, ii, *n.,* (1) lit., *a falling headlong, a falling down,* (2) fig., *a downfall.*

praecipito, are, avi, atum, 1, *v. a.* and *n.,* (I) act., (A) lit., (1) *to throw* or *cast down headlong, to precipitate,* (2) with *reflex, pron., to throw* one's self from somewhere, (3) *to expose* someone to danger (B) fig., (1) *to precipitate, throw headlong,* (2) **praecipitare sententiam,** *to put forward an opinion, to pronounce judgment,* (II) neutr., (A) fig., (1) *to urge onward,* (2) *to be too hasty,* (3) *to precipitate, sway violently.—*

praecipitanter, *adv., hastily, precipitately.*

praecipue, *adv.,* see *praecipuus.*

praecipuus, a, um, *adj., that is taken before other things, particular, peculiar, especial.—***praecipue,** *adv., chiefly, principally, eminently, especially, particularly,* synonym of *praesertim.*

praecise, *adv.,* see *praecido.*

praecisio, onis, *f., a cutting off, excision.*

praeclarus, a, um, *adj., very beautiful physically* or *morally, magnificent, distinguished, excellent, famous, celebrated.*

praecludo, ere, si, sum, 3, *v. a., to close, forbid access to, shut up* or *off, hinder, stop, impede.*

praeco, onis, *m.,* (1) *a public crier* at an auction, (2) *a bearer* of important tidings.

praecogito, are, avi, atum, 1, *v. a., to think upon, ponder,* or *consider beforehand, to premeditate, precogitate.*

praecognitio, onis, *f., foreknowledge, precognition,* synonym of *praescientia.*

praecognosco, ere, gnovi, gnitum, 3, *v. a., to foreknow, foresee.—***praecognitus,** a, um, *P. a., foreknown, foreseen.*

praeconceptio, onis, *f., previous thought, preconception.*

praeconcipio, ere, cepi, ceptum, 3, *v. a., to preconceive, conceive* or *imagine beforehand; to anticipate in thought.—***praeconceptus,** a, um, *P. a., preconceived.*

praeconium, ii, *n.*, *a proclaiming, spreading abroad, publishing.*

praeconsideratus, a, um, *adj., foreknown, preconsidered, considered beforehand.*

praeconsiliatus, a, um, *adj., preconsidered.* On appetitus praeconsiliati, see *appetitus* under 1; on voluntarium praeconsiliatum, see *voluntarius* under 2.

praecordia, orum, *n., the heart,* used fig., *the thoughts.*

praecursio, onis, *f., the office* or *work of a forerunner, the mission of John the Baptist.*

praecursor, oris, *m., a forerunner, precursor.*

praeda, ae, *f.,* (1) lit., *property taken in war, booty, spoil,* (2) transf., (a) *prey, game,* (b) in gen., *booty, gain, profit.*

praedans, antis, *P. a., despoiling.*

praedecessor, oris, *m., a predecessor.*

praedefinitio, onis, *f., predetermination,* synonym of *praedestinatio* and *praedeterminatio.*

praedefinitus, a, um, *P. a., preordained, determined beforehand.*

praedestinatio, onis, *f.,* (1) *predestination, predetermination* in general, synonym of *praedefinitio* and *praedeterminatio,* (2) *direction of an intellectual being to a future supernatural end,* especially to eternal happiness, the opposite of *reprobatio.* On certitudo praedestinationis, see *certitudo* under 3; on notitia praedestinationis, see *notitia* under

2; on prophetia praedestinationis, see *prophetia.*

praedestinatus, a, um, *P. a.,* see *praedestino.*

praedestino, are, avi, atum, 1, *v. a.,* (1) *to determine beforehand, predestine* in general, (2) *predetermine* to supernatural happiness.—praedestinatus, a, um, *P. a., determined beforehand, predestined* (to eternal life).—praedestinatus, i, *m., the predestined* (for everlasting life).

praedeterminatio, onis, *f., predetermination, predestination,* synonym of *praedefinitio* and *praedestinatio.*

praedetermino, are, 1, *v. a., to fix beforehand, predetermine.*

praediales, e, *adj., predial, attached* or *pertaining to the globe* or *soil;* belonging to real estate or resulting from tenancy of farms; as predial tithes; tithes arising from the produce of the soil.

praedicabilis, e, *adj.,* (1) *predicable, affirmable,* (2) *predicable* or affirmable per eminentiam, the *kategoroumenon* of Aristotle (Top. 1. 8, 103 b. 8), one of the five ways in which universals are predicated. On genus praedicabile, see *genus* under 2.—One kind of *praedicabile* in this sense is: praedicabile per se, *that which is predicable of a thing in* or *for itself.* On the difference between *praedicabile* and *universale,* see *universalis* under 2.

praedicamentalis, e, *adj., belonging to* or *concerning one of the ten categories,* does not occur in the Summa Theologica. Cf. *praedicamentum* under 2. On **denominatio praedicamentalis,** see *denominatio;* on **genus praedicamentale,** see *genus* under 2; on **ordinatio praedicamentalis,** see *ordinatio* under 4.

praedicamentum, i, *n.,* (1) *predicate* in the sense of logic, synonym of *praedicatum,* (2) *one of the ten general classes of predicates and of being,* the translation of Aristotle's term *kategoria,* (3) Aristotle's work on the Categories, a part of the Organon.—The ten predicates mentioned are as follows: *substantia, quantitas, qualitas, relatio, passio, actio, quando seu tempus, ubi seu locus, situs, habitus.* On **figura praedicamenti,** see *figura* under 2.—**unum praedicamentum non continetur sub alio,** *the highest kinds of being exclude one another.*

praedicatio, onis, *f.,* (1) *public declaration, proclamation, sermon,* (2) *affirming* or *denying something of a subject,* (3) *the highest kind of predicate and of being,* synonym of *praedicamentum.*—On **commune per praedicationem,** see *communis* under 1; on **veritas praedicationis,** see *veritas* under 1.—Kinds of *praedicatio* in this (2) sense are: (a), **praedicatio absoluta,** *the unconditioned* or *absolute predicate.*—(b), **praedicatio abusiva,** *predication in a very wide sense.*

—(c), **praedicatio accidentalis seu per accidens** and **praedicatio essentialis seu per essentiam seu per se,** *the unessential and the essential predicate* or the predicate which applies only by reason of something over and above the essence and the predicate that belongs to a thing as such, i.e., through itself and its own essence, therefore of necessity. Cf. *praedicare per accidens et per se* under *praedicare* under 2.—(d), **praedicatio aequivoca, praedicatio analogica,** and **praedicatio univoca,** *applying the same in entirely different senses, relatively the same, and exactly the same sense,* secundum quod genera praedicantur de speciebus, in quarum definitionibus ponuntur.—(e), **praedicatio analogica,** see *praedicatio aequivoca.* —(f), **praedicatio concretiva seu denominativa,** *the uniting* or *denominative predicate,* per quem modum accidentia de substantia praedicantur.—(g), **praedicatio denominativa,** see *praedicatio concretiva.*—(h), **praedicatio de superiori,** *the predicate of the superior.*—(i), **praedicatio divina,** *the application of terms to God.*—(j), **praedicatio essentialis,** see *praedicatio accidentalis.*—(k), **praedicatio falsa** and **praedicatio vera,** *the false and the true predication.*—(l), **praedicatio immediata,** *the immediate predicate* or *the predicate apparent through itself.*—(m), **praedicatio imper-**

fecta, *the imperfect predicate.*— (n), **praedicatio impropria**, *the improper predication.*—(o), **praedicatio per accidens**, see *praedicatio accidentalis.*—(p), **praedicatio per causam** and **praedicatio per eminentiam**, *describing a thing by its cause rather than by its nature* and *describing a thing in the sense of preeminence.*—(q), **praedicatio per concomitantiam**, *the predicate of a thing as the coworker of another.*—(r), **praedicatio per denominationem seu informationem** and **praedicatio per identitatem**, *the predicate of a thing in the sense of the naming* or *forming of another and the predicate of a thing in the sense of identity.*—(s), **praedicatio per eminentiam**, see *praedicatio per causam.*—(t), **praedicatio per essentiam**, see *praedicatio accidentalis.*—(u), **praedicatio per identitatem**, see *praedicatio per denominationem.*—(v), **praedicatio per informationem**, see *praedicatio per denominationem.*— (w), **praedicatio per inhaerentiam**, *describing a thing by what belongs to its nature.*—(x), **praedicatio per posterius** and **praedicatio per prius**, *describing a thing through what is individual to it and through what is general.* —(y), **praedicatio per prius**, see *praedicatio per posterius.*—(z), **praedicatio per se**, see *praedicatio accidentalis.*—(a²), **praedicatio pluralis**, *the predicate in the plural.*—(b²), **praedicatio simplex**,

the simple predicate.—(c²), **praedicatio univoca**, see *praedicatio aequivoca.*—(d²), **praedicatio vera**, see *praedicatio falsa.*

praedicativus, a, um, *adj.*, (1) *predicating, predicating unconditionally,* synonym of *categoricus,* the opposite of *condicionalis,* does not occur in Summa Theologica. On **propositio praedicativa**, see *propositio* under 2.—(2), *predicating affirmatively, affirming,* the opposite of *negativus,* does not occur in the Summa Theologica. On **demonstratio praedicativa**, see *demonstratio* under 3.

praedicator, oris, *m.*, (1) in gen., *one who makes a thing publicly known, a proclaimer, publisher,* (2) *a preacher.*—**Fratres Praedicatores**, *Friars Preachers,* a name for the order of Dominican friars.

praedicatum, i, *n.*, see *praedico.*

praedico, are, avi, atum, 1, *v. a.*, (1) *to make known publicly, proclaim, preach,* (2) *predicate* in the sense of logic. On **modus praedicandi**, see *modus* under 2. —Kinds of *praedicare* in this (1) sense are: (a), **praedicare ab aeterno** and **praedicare ex tempore**, *to predicate something with respect to a thing from eternity and to do so in time.*—(b), **praedicare accidentaliter seu praedicatione accidentali** and **praedicare substantialiter seu per modum substantialis praedicati seu secundum modum substantiae**, *to predicate something in the sense of an accident and something in* *the sense of a substance.*—(c), **praedicare ad aliud seu relative,** *to predicate something with reference to something else.*—(d), **praedicare ad invicem seu aequaliter ad invicem seu aeque ad invicem seu de se invicem seu convertibiliter,** *to predicate something reciprocally* and *conversely.*—(e), **praedicare aequaliter,** *to predicate equally.*—(f), **praedicare aequaliter ad invicem seu de se invicem,** see *praedicare ad invicem.*—(g), **praedicare aeque ad invicem,** see *praedicare ad invicem.*—(h), **praedicare aequivoce seu omnino aequivoce seu pure aequivoce, praedicare analogice,** and **praedicare univoce,** *to predicate the same term in an entirely different sense, in relatively the same sense,* and *in exactly the same sense.*—(i), **praedicare analogice,** see *praedicare aequivoce.*—(j), **praedicare causaliter seu per causam** and **praedicare eminenter seu per eminentiam,** *to predicate of a thing its cause rather than its nature and something in the preeminent sense.*—(k), **praedicare concretive seu in concreto** and **praedicare in abstracto,** *to predicate something that pertains to the individual as individual,* i.e., *particularized, and something that pertains to its nature,* or *that it shares with other things.*—(l), **praedicare convertibiliter,** see *praedicare ad invicem.*—(m), **praedicare cum praecisione seu praecise,** *to pred-*

icate down to the ultimate difference.—(n), **praedicare de accidente** and **praedicare de subiecto,** *to predicate something of an accident and to do so of a real subject,* i.e., of a substance. Cf. *praedicare per accidens.*—(o), **praedicare denominative sive per modum denominationis seu per informationem,** *to predicate something denominatively* or *in the sense of a naming* or *of an informing.*—(p), **praedicare de omni, praedicare per se, praedicare primo,** and **praedicare universaliter,** *to predicate something of every member of a species as belonging to it, to do so of a thing as belonging to it of its very nature, to do so of a thing as belonging to it in the first place because constitutive of its nature,* and *to do so of a thing universally,* i.e., as belonging to everyone of its parts and to everyone in the first place.—(q), **praedicare de singulari** and **praedicare de universali,** *to predicate something of the singular* or *of the particular* and *something of the general.*—(r), **praedicare de subiecto,** see *praedicare de accidente.*—(s), **praedicare de superiori,** *to predicate what is less extensive of what is really more extensive.*—(t), **praedicare de universali,** see *praedicare de singulari.*—(u), **praedicare eminenter,** see *praedicare causaliter.*—(v), **praedicare essentialiter seu per essentiam seu substantialiter** and praedicare participative seu per participationem, *to predicate something of a thing as belonging wholly to it essentially and something as belonging to it through participation.* Cf. *praedicare accidentaliter.*—(w), praedicare ex tempore, see *praedicare ab aeterno.*—(x), praedicare falso, *to predicate something of a thing falsely.*—(y), praedicare improprie seu metaphorice and praedicare proprie, *to predicate something of a thing improperly or figuratively, and to do so properly.*—(z), praedicare in abstracto, see *praedicare concretive.*—(a^2), praedicare in communi, *to predicate something in the general sense.*—(b^2), praedicare in concreto, see *praedicare concretive.* —(c^2), praedicare in eo quod quale seu in quale quid and praedicare in eo quod quid est seu in quod quid est seu in quid, *to predicate a quality or in the sense of something qualitative,* and *the essence of a thing* (cf. *quod quid* under *quid* 2) or *as belonging to it,* (the equivalent of *en to ti esti kategorein* Aristotle's Anal. Post. 1. 22, 82 b. 37.—(d^2), praedicare in eo quod quid est, see *praedicare in eo quod quale.*—(e^2), praedicare in obliquo and praedicare in recto seu in principali, *to predicate something in an oblique case and something in the nominative case.*—(f^2), praedicare in plurali seu pluraliter and praedicare in singulari seu singulariter, *to predicate something in the plural and something in the singular.*—(g^2), praedicare in principali, see *praedicare in obliquo.*—(h^2), praedicare in quale quid, see *praedicare in eo quod quale.*—(i^2), praedicare in quid, see *praedicare in eo quod quale.*—(j^2), praedicare in quod quid est, see *praedicare in eo quod quale.*—(k^2), praedicare in recto, see *praedicare in obliquo.*—(l^2), praedicare in singulari, see *praedicare in plurali.*—(m^2), praedicare metaphorice, see *praedicare improprie.*—(n^2), praedicare negative seu privative seu remotive and praedicare positive, *to predicate something in the sense of a simple negation and in that of privation and in that of an affirmation.*—(o^2), praedicare omnino aequivoce, see *praedicare aequivoce.*—(p^2), praedicare participative, see *praedicare essentialiter.*—(q^2), praedicare per accidens seu secundum accidens and praedicare per se, *to predicate something of a thing as belonging to it by accident,* and *to predicate something as belonging to the same through itself and as such.*—(r^2), praedicare per causam, see *praedicare causaliter.*—(s^2), praedicare per eminentiam, see *praedicare causaliter.*—(t^2), praedicare per essentiam, see *praedicare essentialiter.*—(u^2), praedicare per informationem, see *praedicare denominative.*—(v^2), praedicare per modum ad aliud se habentis and **praedicare per modum inhaerentis,** *to predicate something in the sense of binding it to another, and something in the sense of adhering or clinging.*—(w²), **praedicare per modum denominationis,** see *praedicare denominative.*—(x²), **praedicare per modum inhaerentis,** see *praedicare per modum ad aliud se habentis.*—(y²), **praedicare per modum substantialis praedicati,** see *praedicare accidentaliter.*—(z²), **praedicare per participationem,** see *praedicare essentialiter.*—(a³), **praedicare per posterius seu secundum posterius seu secundario** and **praedicare per prius seu secundum prius,** *to predicate something in the sense of the less fundamental and something in the sense of the more fundamental.*—(b³), **praedicare per prius,** see *praedicare per posterius.*—(c³), **praedicare per se,** see *praedicare de omni et per accidens.*—(d³), **praedicare pluraliter,** see *praedicare in plurali.*—(e³), **praedicare positive,** see *praedicare negative.*—(f³), **praedicare praecise,** see *praedicare cum praecisione.*—(g³), **praedicare praedicatione accidentali,** see *praedicare accidentaliter.*—(h³), **praedicare primo,** see *praedicare de omni.*—(i³), **praedicare privative,** see *praedicare negative.*—(j³), **praedicare proprie,** see *praedicare improprie.*—(k³), **praedicare pure aequivoce,** see *praedicare aequivoce.* This is to distinguish it from *analogous predication,* which is sometimes called simply *aequivoce.*—(l³), **praedicare relative,** see *praedicare ad aliud.*—(m³), **praedicare remotive,** see *praedicare negative.*—(n³), **praedicare secundario,** see *praedicare per posterius.*—(o³), **praedicare secundum accidens,** see *praedicare per accidens.*—(p³), **praedicare secundum modum substantiae,** see *praedicare accidentaliter.*—(q³), **praedicare secundum posterius,** see *praedicare per prius.*—(r³), **praedicare secundum prius,** see *praedicare per prius.*—(s³), **praedicare secundum quid** and **praedicare simpliciter,** *to predicate something in a certain relation* or *in a certain respect and something simply or absolutely.*—(t³), **praedicare simpliciter,** see *praedicare secundum quid.*—(u³), **praedicare singulariter,** see *praedicare in plurali.*—(v³), **praedicare substantialiter,** see *praedicare accidentaliter et essentialiter.*—(w³), **praedicare universaliter,** see *praedicare de omni.*—(x³), **praedicare univoce,** see *praedicare aequivoce.*—**praedicatum, i,** *n.,* (1) *predicate, that which is affirmed* or *denied of a subject in a proposition,* the opposite of *subiectum,* (2) (rarely), *accident,* synonym of *accidens.*—On **affirmatio et affirmativa de praedicato finito et infinito,** see *affirmatio* and *affirmativus;* on **enuntiatio de praedicato finito, infinito et privativo,** see *enuntia-*

tio under 2; on **negativa de prae-dicato finito et infinito,** see *nega-tivus;* on **propositio de praedicato accidentali, substantiali, finito, infinito, et privativo,** see *propo-sitio* under 2.—Kinds of *praedi-catum* in this (1) sense are: (a), **praedicatum accidentale** and **praedicatum essentiale seu sub-stantiale,** *the accidental and the essential predicate,* or the predi-cate which expresses something not essential to the subject, *or not in the category of substance,* and that which expresses some-thing essentially belonging to it, or *substantial.*—(b), **praedica-tum affirmativum** and **praedica-tum privativum,** *the affirming and the depriving predicate* or the predicate that expresses something positive (e.g. *iustus*) and that expresses a lack (e.g. *iniustus*).—(c), **praedicatum co-pulatum,** *the connected* (with another) *predicate.*—(d), **praedi-catum essentiale,** see *praedica-tum accidentale.*—(e), **praedica-tum finitum** and **praedicatum in-finitum,** *the finite* or *limited predicate* (e.g. *iustus*) and *the infinite* or *unlimited predicate* (e.g. *non-iustus*).—(f), **praedica-tum infinitum,** see *praedicatum finitum.*—(g), **praedicatum notio-nale** and **praedicatum personale,** *the predicate that designates a notio* (q.v.) *and that designates a person* (in God).—(h), **praedi-catum per accidens** and **praedi-catum per se,** *that which is pred-*

icated by reason of something over and above the essence, or *something extrinsic, and that which is affirmed of it as such,* i.e., according to itself and its essence.—(i), **praedicatum per se,** see *praedicatum per accidens.* —(j), **praedicatum personale,** see *praedicatum notionale.*—(k), **praedicatum principale,** *the chief predicate.*—(l), **praedicatum pri-vativum,** see *praedicatum affir-mativum.*—(m), **praedicatum sub-stantiale,** see *praedicatum acci-dentale.*—(n), **praedicatum uni-versale,** *the universal predicate.* —(o), **praedicatum univocum,** *the univocal predicate,* or *the predi-cate always taken in the same sense.*

praedico, ere, xi, ctum, 3, *v. a., to say* or *mention beforehand, fore-tell, predict, forebode.*—**praedic-tus,** a, um, *P. a., previously named, before mentioned, pre-ceding.*—**praedictum,** i, *n., a fore-telling, prediction.*

praeditus, a, um, *P. a., endowed, gifted* or *provided with, pos-sessed of something.*

praedium, ii, *n., a farm, land, es-tate, manor.*

praedominor, ari, atus, 1, *v. dep. n., to rule, predominate,* of in-animate and abstract subjects, used *absol.,* with *in* and *abl.,* the *dat.*

praeeligo, ere, legi, 3, *v. a., to choose rather, to prefer.*

praeeminentia, ae, *f., pre-eminence.*

praeemineo, ere, *v. n.* and *a., to project forward, be prominent, excell, surpass*, constr. with *dat.*

praeeo, ire, ivi and ii, itum, *v. n.* and *a., to go before, precede*, used fig., (1) act., (2) neutr.

praeexcellens, entis, *adj., pre-eminent.*

praeexigo, ere, 3, *presuppose, pre-require.*

praeexistentia, ae, *f., pre-existence, earlier existence.*

praeexisto, ere, stiti, stitum, 3, *v. n., preexist, exist.*

praefatio, onis, *f.,* (1) *a preface, introduction* to a literary work usually containing some explanation of its subject, purpose, and scope, and of the method of its treatment, (2) *the preface of the Mass*, the prayer of thanksgiving ending with the *sanctus* which precedes and introduces the canon of the Mass, and is found in all liturgies.

praefator, oris, *m., a praefator, a foreteller.*

praefatus, a, um, *P. a., aforesaid.*

praefero, ferre, tuli, latum, *v. a.,* (1) *to place* a person or thing before another in esteem, *prefer*, regular meaning in S. T., (2) *display, manifest, reveal.*—**praelatus**, i, *subst.*, see *praelatus.*

praeficio, ere, feci, fectum, 3, *v. a., to place in authority over, place at the head, set over.*—**praefectus**, i, *m., an overseer, director, president, commander, prefect.*

praefigo, ere, xi, xum, 3, *v. a., prefix, fix, establish, mark.*—**praefix-**

us, a, um, *P. a., fixed, established.*

praefiguratio, onis, *f., prefiguration.*

praefigurativus, a, um, *adj., prefigurative, prefiguring, foreshadowing*, by a figure or type.

praefigurator, oris, *m., one who prefigures.*

praefiguro, are, avi, atum, 1, *v. a., to show, suggest, announce by antecedent types* or *similitudes; to prefigure.*

praefinio, ire, ivi and ii, itum, 4, *v. a., to determine, fix,* or *appoint beforehand, to prescribe.*

praefinitio, onis, *f., a determining* or *fixing beforehand.*

praeformatio, onis, *f., preformation, the act* or *process of forming* or *shaping beforehand, preshadowing.*

praefulgeo, ere, si, 2, *v. n., to shine, glitter*, used fig.

praegnans, antis, *adj., with child, pregnant.*

praehabeo, ere, ui, itum, 3, *v. a., to have* or *possess beforehand.*—**praehabitus**, a, um, *held* or *maintained before.*

praeintellego, ere, exi, ectum, 3, *v. a., to perceive, understand, comprehend beforehand; to presuppose.*

praeintentus, a, um, *P. a., preintended, intended previously.*

praeiaceo, ere, ui, 2, *v. n., to lie before, be situated in front of.* On **praeiacens materia**, see *materia* under 3.

praeiudicium, ii, *n.,* (1) *a preceding judgment, sentence* or *decision,*

(2) *a damage, disadvantage, prejudice.*

praeiudico, are, avi, atum, 1, *v. a., to prejudge, to be injurious, prejudicial,* with *dat.*

praelatio, onis, *f., superiorship, directorate, principalship,* synonym of *dominium, magisterium.* On **ius praelationis,** see *ius;* on **status praelationis,** see *status* under 4.—Kinds of *praelatio* are: **praelatio ecclesiastica seu spiritualis** and **praelatio saecularis,** *the ecclesiastical* or *spiritual* and *the secular* or *earthly superiorship.*

praelatus, i, *m., superior, prelate,* synonym of *praepositus.* On **status praelatorum,** see *status* under 4.—**praelatus ecclesiae seu ecclesiasticus,** *the true prelate of the Church,* i.e., the bishop.

praelibatio, onis, *f., a foretaste.*

praelior, ari, atus, 1, *v. dep. n., to fight, to join in battle.*

praelium (proelium), ii, *n., battle, combat, contest, strife.*

praeloquor, i, cutus, 3, *v. dep a.* and *n., to foretell, predict.*

praeludium, ii, *n., a prelude, an introduction, preface.*

praemeditatio, onis, *f., a considering beforehand, premeditation.*

praemeditor, ari, atus, 1, *v. dep. a., to think over, to muse* or *deliberate upon beforehand, to premeditate.*

praemiatio, onis, *f., a reward.*

praemio, are, avi, atum, 1, *v. a., to reward.*

praemissa sc. **propositio,** see *praemitto.*

praemitto, ere, misi, missum, 3, *v. a., to send forward* or *before, send out in advance, present before* or *in advance.*—**praemissa,** (*propositio*), ae, *f., each of the two statements made before the conclusio,* from which the conclusion is drawn, *premise.*—**praemissum,** i, *n., that which was said before, premise.*

praemium, ii, *n., reward, profit, recompense.* On **retributio praemii,** see *retributio.*—**praemium beatitudinis,** *the reward which consists of eternal happiness.*—**praemium beatitudinis** consists of two kinds: **praemium accidentale** and **praemium essentiale,** *an indeterminate* and *an essential reward.*

praemonitus, a, um, *P. a., forewarned.*

praemonstratio, onis, *f., a showing* or *indicating beforehand, a premonstration, example,* the translation of Aristotle's expression, *teretisma* (Anal. post. I. 22. 88 a 33); does not occur in the Summa Theologica.

praemonstro, are, avi, atum, 1, *v. a., to denote beforehand, foreshadow, predict.*

praenosco, ere, *v. a., to learn* or *become acquainted with beforehand, to foreknow.*

praenoto, are, avi, atum, 1, *v. a.,* (1) *to note, designate,* (2) *to entitle, name.*

praenuntiatio, onis, *f., a prediction.*

praenuntiativus, a, um, *adj.*, *that foretells* or *forebodes*, *announcing*. On **signum praenuntiativum**, see *signum* under 1.

praenuntio, are, avi, atum, 1, *v. a.*, *to announce* or *publish beforehand*, *to foretell*, *predict.*—**praenuntiatus**, a, um, *v. a.*, *foretold*, *predicted.*—**praenuntiatum**, i, *n.*, *something foretold* or *predicted*.

praenuntium, ii, *n.*, *a harbinger*, *token*.

praeoccupo, are, avi, atum, 1, *v. a.*, *to take possession of* or *occupy beforehand*, *preoccupy*, *forestall*, *anticipate*.

praeopto, are, avi, atum, 1, *v. a.*, *to wish rather*, *to desire more*, *to prefer*.

praeordinatio, onis, *f.*, *preordering*, *preordination*, *predirecting*.

praeordino, are, avi, atum, 1, *v. a.*, *to preordain*, *order beforehand*, *order.*—**praeordinatus**, a, um, *P. a.*, *ordered beforehand*, *preordained*.

praeparatio, onis, *f.*, (1) *a getting* or *making ready*, *a preparing*, *preparation*, *arrangement*, synonym of *dispositio*, (2) *readiness*, *willingness.*—Kinds of *praeparatio* in this (1) sense are: (a), **praeparatio agentis** and **praeparatio patientis seu materiae**, *the preparation of the agent* or *of the active principle, that of the patient* or *receptive thing* or *that of the material.*—(b), **praeparatio debita**, *the suitable preparation* or *that which is due.*— (c), **praeparatio materiae**, see *praeparatio*

agentis.—(d), **praeparatio patientis**, see *praeparatio agentis*.

praeparativus, a, um, *adj.*, *preparing*, *preparative*, *preparatory*, synonym of *praeparatorius*. On **actus praeparativus**, see *actus* under 1.

praeparatorius, a, um, *adj.*, *preparing*, *preparatory*, synonym of *praeparativus*. On **lex praeparatoria**, see *lex* under 1; on **purgatio praeparatoria**, see *purgatio*.

praeparo, are, avi, atum, 1, *v. a.*, *to get* or *make ready beforehand*, *make preparations for*, *prepare*. On **pausa praeparans**, see *causa* under 2.

praepedio, ire, ivi, ii, itum, 4, *v. a.*, (1) *to hinder*, *obstruct*, *impede*, (2) *to debar*, *preclude*, *render impossible by antecedent action*.

praepollens, entis, *P. a.*, see *praepolleo*.

praepolleo, ere, *v. n.*, 2, *to exceed* or *surpass in power*, *to be very remarkable* or *distinguished*.

praepollens, entis, *P. a.*, *very powerful*, *very distinguished*.

praepondero, are, 1, *v. n.*, and *n.*, *to be of greater weight*, *preponderate*, *outweigh*.

praepono, ere, posui, positum, 3, *v. a.*, *to place before*, *set first*, *prefer*, *to place* or *set over as chief* or *commander*, synonym of *praefero* and *praeficio*, opposite of *postpono.*—**praepositus**, a, um, *P. a.*, *placed before*, *preferred*, *placed over as chief* or *commander.*—**praepositus**, i, *m.*, *a* *prefect, president, director, commander.*

praepositio, onis, *f.,* *a putting* or *setting before;* in gram., *a preposition.*

Praepositivus, i, *m.,* *Prepositivus* (Gilbert Prevostin), a famous theologian from Cremona, who was Chancellor of the University of Paris from 1206 to 1209. He died in 1210.

praepostere, *adv.,* *in a reversed order, irregularly.*

praepropere, *adv.,* see *praeproperus.*

praeproperus, a, um, *adj.,* *too-quick* or *hasty.—***praepropere,** *adv.,* *very quickly, very hastily, with over-haste.*

praeputium, ii, *n.,* *transf., the retaining of the prepuce, uncircumcision.*

praeripio, ere, ripui, reptum, 3, *v. a., to snatch away before time.—***praeripere tempus loquendi,** *to be in a hurry to speak.*

praerogativa, ae, *f., preference, privilege, prerogative.*

praesagium, ii, *m., a presage, an indication of the future; prophetic token.*

praesanctificatus, a, um, *adj., presanctified, sanctified* or *consecrated beforehand.*

praescientia, ae, *f., foreknowledge, prescience.* On **certitudo praescientiae,** see *certitudo* under 2; on **prophetia praescientiae,** see *prophetia.*

praescindo, ere, scidi, 3, *v. a., to cut off in front.*

praescio, ire, ivi, itum, 4, *v. a., to know beforehand, to foreknow,* used to designate one who is not predestined, (2) esp. (in eccl. Lat.) of God's foreknowledge.

praescius, a, um, *adj., foreknowing, prescient.*

praescribo, ere, psi, ptum, 3, *v. a., to prescribe, ordain.—***praescriptus,** a, um, *P. a., prescribed, appointed.*

praescriptio, onis, *f., prescription, a claim based on long usage.*

praescriptus, a, um, *P. a.,* see *praescribo.*

praesens, entis, *adj.,* see *praesum.*

praesentia, ae, *f., being at hand, presence,* opposite of *absentia.—* Kinds of *praesentia* are: (a), **praesentia corporalis,** *bodily presence.—*(b), **praesentia temporalis,** *temporal presence.* Cf. 1 Cant. 8.

praesentialitas, atis, *f., presentiality, the condition* or *character of being presential.*

praesentialiter, *adv.,* see *praesens et praesum.*

praesentio, ire, sensi, sensum, 4, *v. a., to feel* or *perceive beforehand, to have a presentiment of, to presage, divine.*

praesento, are, no perf., atum, 1, *v. a., to place before, exhibit to view, show, present.*

praesepe, is, *n.,* and **praesepium,** ii, *n., a manger.*

praesertim, *adv., especially, chiefly, principally, particularly.*

praeservatio, onis, *f., preservation, the action of preserving and* keeping from injury and destruction.

praeservativus, a, um, *adj.*, *preservative.*

praeservo, are, avi, atum, 1, *v. a.*, *preserve, save, keep.*

praeses, idis, *m.*, *a ruler, governor.*

praesidentia, ae, *f.*, *presidence, the action* or *fact of presiding; superintendence, direction.*

praesideo, ere, sedi, −, 2, *v. n.* and *a.*, *to sit before* or *in front of, preside over, have the care* or *management of, superintend, direct, command*, with *dat.*—**praesidens**, entis, *P. a.*, as *subst.*, *a president, director, ruler.*

praesidium, ii, *n.*, in gen., *aid, help, assistance of any kind.*

praesignatio, onis, *f.*, *a presignifying.*

praesigno, are, avi, atum, 1, *v. a.*, *to mark* or *note before, foreshadow.*

praespicio, ere, −, −, 3, *v. a.*, *to look at beforehand, regard beforehand, foresee*, only in quot., in S.T.

praestans, antis, *P. a.*, *preeminent, superior, excellent, distinguished, extraordinary.*

praestigiosus, a, um, *adj.*, *full of deceitful tricks, delusive.*

praestigium, i, *n.*, *prophesying from illusions of the devil, prestigiation.*

praestituo, ere, ui, utum, 3, *v. a.*, *to determine* or *appoint beforehand, prescribe.*

praesto, *adv.*, *at hand, ready, present.*

praesto, are, iti, itum, 1, *v. n.* and *a.*, *to give, offer, furnish, present, expose.*

praesul, sulis, *m.*, *a presider, prelate, bishop*, used in the S.T. only in quotation.

praesulatus, us, *m.*, *the presulate, the tenure of the office of a bishop.*

praesum, esse, fui, *v. n.*, (1) *to be before a thing;* hence, *to be set over, to preside* or *rule over, to have charge* or *command of*, used with the *dat.*, (2) *transf.*, *to take the lead in anything.*—**praesens**, entis, *adj.*, (1) *senses relating to place*, (a) *being before, beside with* or *in the same place* as the person to whom the word has relation; being in the place considered or mentioned, (b) *present, actually in mind* or *under consideration*, (2) senses relating to time, (a) *present*, taking place of existing at the time of thought; falling or occurring in the passing moment or period of time; coincident in time with something begun and not ended; now going on, (b) *present instant, without delay, occurring at the very time.*—The following phrases occur frequently:—**de praesenti**, *of the present time.*—**ad praesens**, *at present, now.*—**praesentialiter**, *adv.*, *presentially, in a presential manner; in the way of actual presence; as being present.*

praesumo, ere, mpsi, mptum, 3, *v.*

a., *to presume, take for granted, suppose, believe, assume.*

praesumptio, onis, *f.*, *boldness, confidence, assurance, audacity, presumption.*—**praesumptio novitatum,** *the presumption of novelties,* i.e., the seeking to do or produce something new which arouses wonder or admiration but which is beyond the powers of the one concerned.

praesumptuose, see *praesumptuosus.*

praesumptuosus, a, um, *adj.*, *full of boldness, presumptuous.*—**praesumptuose,** *adv.*, *boldly, presumptuously.*

praesuppono, ere, posui, positum, 3, *v. a.*, *to presuppose.*—**praesuppositus,** a, um, *P. a.*, *presupposed.*—**praesuppositum,** i, *n.*, *something presupposed.*

praesuppositio, onis, *f.*, *presupposition.*

praetendo, ere, di, tum, 3, *v. a.*, *to hold out* or *bring forward as an excuse, allege, pretend, simulate.*

praeter, *prep.*, with *acc.*, *besides, together with, in addition to, except.*

praeterea, *adv.*, *besides, moreover, furthermore.*

praetereo, ire, ivi, or ii, itum, *v. n.* and *a.*, *to pass over, omit, leave out, go by, pass by, perish.*—**praeteritus,** a, um, *P. a.*, *gone by, past, past and gone, departed.*—**praeterita,** orum, *n.*, *things gone by, the past.*—**praeteritum,** (tempus), i, *n.*, *the past.*

praeteritio, onis, *f.*, *the condition of past, the past.*

praeteritus, a, um, *P. a.*, see *praetereo.*

praetermissio, onis, *f.*, *a leaving out, omission, passing over.*

praetermitto, ere, misi, missum, 3, *v. a.*, *to omit, neglect, pass over, omit, overlook.*

praeternaturalis, e, *adj.*, *beyond nature, against nature, unnatural,* synonym of *innaturalis,* the opposite of *naturalis,* does not occur in the Summa Theologica. On **causa praeternaturalis,** see *causa* under 2.

praeterquam, *adv.*, *beyond, besides, except, save, otherwise than.*

praetextus, us, *m.*, *a pretense, pretext.*

praetorium, ii, *n.*, *a magnificent building, hall of audience, hall.*

praetorius, a, um, *adj.*, *of* or *belonging to the praetor* or *praetor's, praetorian.*

praevaleo, ere, ui, —, 2, *v. n.*, *to have greater power* or *worth, be superior* or *distinguished, have the superiority, prevail.*

praevalidus, a, um, *adj.*, *very strong, very powerful, prevailing, prevalent,* used in the S.T. only in quotation.

praevaricatio, onis, *f.*, *collusion, prevarication, transgression, deviation* from duty or law.

praevaricator, oris, *m.*, *one who violates his duty, a sham accuser* or *defender, a prevaricator, a sinner, transgressor.*

praevaricor, ari, atus, 1, *v. dep.*, *to walk crookedly in the discharge of one's duties, to prevaricate, transgress, sin against, violate, collude.*

praevenio, ire, veni, ventum, 4, *v. n.* and *a.*, opposite of *subsequor*, *to come before, precede, outstrip, anticipate, prevent.*

praeverto, ere, ti, −, 3, *v. a.*, *to surpass, outweigh, exceed,* used only once in S.T. and in quot.

praevideo, ere, vidi, visum, 2, *v. a.*, *to foresee, anticipate, discern beforehand.*

praevisio, onis, *f.*, *foresight, anticipation.*

praevius, a, um, *adj.*, *going before, leading the way, previous.*

praevolatio, onis, *f.*, *a hurrying or hastening before, unbridled incontinence, impetuosity.*

praevolo, are, avi, −, 1, *v. n.*, *to fly before* or *in advance,* always in quot. in S.T.

prandeo, ere, di, sum, 2, *v. n.* and *a.*, *to take breakfast, breakfast.*

pratum, i, *n.*, *a broad field, a meadow.*

prave, *adv.*, see *pravus.*

pravitas, atis, *f.*, *viciousness, perversity, depravity.*

pravus, a, um, *adv.*, *perverse, irregular, improper, wrong, vicious,* synonym of *improbus, malus, nequam,* opposite of *rectus.−*prave, *adv.*, *improperly, wrongly, badly, perversely,* opposite of *recte.*

precatio, onis, *f.*, *praying, prayer,* occurs only in quotation.

precor, ari, atus, 1, *v. dep. n.* and *a.*, *to ask, beg, entreat, pray, supplicate, beseech,* always used in quotation in S.T.

premo, ere, essi, essum, 3, *v. a.*, *to press, press down, force,* only used in quotation in S.T.

presbyter, eri, *m.*, *an elder, presbyter, priest.*

pressura, ae, *f.*, *pressure, burden.*

pretiositas, atis, *f.*, *preciousness, costliness.*

pretiosus, a, um, *adj.*, *of great value, valuable, precious, expensive.*

pretium, ii, *n.*, *worth, value, price.*

prex, precis, *f.*, *prayer, request, entreaty.*

Priapus, i, *m.*, *Priapus,* the god of procreation.

pridem, *adv.*, *long ago, long since, a long time ago,* used only in quotation in S.T.

pridie, *adv.*, *on the day before,* used only in quotation in S.T.

primaevus, a, um, *adj.*, *first original,* synonym of *primitivus* and *primordialis.* On **auctoritas primaeva**, see *auctoritas* under 4; on **natura primaeva**, see *natura.*

primarius, a, um, *adj.*, *one of the first, of the first rank, chief, principal, primary,* synonym of *principalis.*

primas, atis, *comm.*, *one of the first, principal, chief, noble, primate,* used only in quotation in S.T.

primatus, us, *m.*, *the first place* or *rank, preference, pre-eminence, primary.*

primitia, ae, *f.*, (1) *firstness, being first, state of being first,* (2) in plural, *first things of their kind, first fruits.*

primitivus, a, um, *adj., the first, or earliest of its kind, primitive,* synonym of *primaevus* and *primordialis.*

primitus, *adv., at first, originally, for the first time.*

primo, *adv.,* see *primus.*

primogenitura, ae, *f., first-birth.* ius primo-geniturae, *the right of the first born.*

primogenitus, a, um, *adj., firstborn.*

primordialis, e, *adj., that is first of all, original, primordial,* synonym of *primaevus* and *primitivus.* On **causa primordialis,** see *causa* under 2; on **esse primordiale,** see *esse;* on **forma primordialis,** see *forma* under 2; on **origo primordialis,** see *origo;* on **principium primordiale,** see *principium.—* **primordialiter,** *adv., from the beginning, originally,* synonym of *principaliter.*

primordialiter, *adv.,* see *primordialis.*

primordius, a, um, *adj., original.—* **primordium,** ii, *n., the first beginning.*

primus, a, um, *adj., sup., first.* On **actus primus,** see *actus* under 2; on **agens primus,** see *agens;* on **alterans primus,** see *alterare* and *corpus;* on **animatum primum,** see *animatus* under 1; on **bonitas prima et bonitas prima actus moralis et rei naturalis,** see *bonitas* under 1; on **bonum primum,** see *bonus* under 2; on **caelum primum,** see *caelum;* on **causa pri-**

ma **et universaliter prima,** see *causa* under 2; on **cognitio prima,** see *cognitio* under 2; on **complementum primum,** see *complementum;* on **conceptio prima,** see *conceptio* under 4; on **consideratio prima,** see *consideratio;* on **contrarietas prima,** see *contrarietas* under 2; on **contrarium primum,** see *contrarius* under 1; on **corporeum primum,** see *corporeus;* on **corpus primum et primum alterans,** see *corpus;* on **creans primum,** see *creare* under 1; on **creatio prima,** see *creatio* under 2; on **differentia prima et prima contraria,** see *differentia;* on **donum primum,** see *donum* under 2; on **elementum primum,** see *elementum* under 2; on **ens primum,** see *ens;* on **esse primum,** see *esse;* on **forma prima et forma prima exemplaris,** see *forma* under 2; on **generatio prima,** see *generatio* under 1; on **genus primum,** see *genus* under 2; on **hierarchia prima,** see *hierarchia;* on **infinitum primum,** see *infinitus;* on **intellectum primum,** see *intellegere* under 1; on **intellectus primus,** see *intellectus* under 1; on **intellegentia prima,** see *intellegentia* under 1; on **intellegibile primum,** see *intellegibilis* under 2; on **intentio prima et prima naturae,** see *intentio* under 2 and 3; on **latio prima,** see *latio* under 1; on **locus primus,** see *locus* under 2; on **malum primum,** see *malus* under 2; on **materia prima,** see *materia* under 3; on mensura prima, see *mensura;* on mobile primum, see *mobilis* under 1; on motivum primum, see *motivus;* on motus primus, see *motus* under 1; on movens primum, see *movens;* on natura prima, see *natura;* on necessarium primum, see *necessarius* under 1; on numerus primus, see *numerus;* on oppositio prima, prima in genere et prima simpliciter, see *oppositio* under 2; on orbis primus, see *orbis;* on perfectio prima, prima hominis et prima humanae naturae, see *perfectio* under 2; on philosophia prima, see *philosophia;* on philosophus primus, see *philosophus;* on potentia prima, see *potentia* under 4; on principium primum, primum activum, primum cognoscendi, primum effectivum, primum essendi, primum exemplare, primum finale, primum formale, primum indemonstrabile, primum in genere, primum materiale, primum movens, primum passivum, primum productivum, primum rerum, primum simpliciter et primum universale, see *principium;* on propositio prima, prima in aliquo genere et prima simpliciter, see *propositio* under 2; on qualitas prima et prima tangibilis, see *qualitas;* on quantitas prima, see *quantitas* under 1; on regula prima, see *regula* under 1; on sanctificatio prima, see *sanctificatio* under 1; on sensitivum primum, see *sensitivus* under 2; on species prima, see *species* un-

der 8; on sphaera prima, see *sphaera* under 2; on subiectum primum, see *subiectum* under 2 and 3; on substantia prima, see *substantia* under 1; on tempus primum, see *tempus;* on umidum primum, see *umidus;* on veritas prima, see *veritas* under 1 and 3; on volitum primum, see *volitus;* on voluntas prima, see *voluntas* under 2.—prima, sc. praemissa seu propositio, *the major premise of a conclusion.*—prima, sc. hora, *prime* of the breviary.—Kinds of *primum* are: (a), primum cognitione seu secundum cognitionem, primum ratione seu secundum definitionem and primum tempore seu secundum tempus, *the first according to knowledge, the first according to conception or according to definition,* and *the first according to time.*—(b), primum exemplatum, *the first adduced as an example, the first representation, the world.*—(c), primum formale and primum materiale, *the first after the manner of form* and *the first after the manner of material.*—(d), primum in genere aliquo seu in ordine aliquo and primum simpliciter, *the first in a certain genus* or *order* and *the first simply* or *absolutely.*—(e), primum in ordine aliquo, see *primum in genere aliquo.*—(f), primum materiale, see *primum formale.*—(g), primum per ordinem ad aliquid extrinsecum and primum simpliciter secundum naturam, *the first ac-*

cording to its disposition to something oustide or exterior, and the simply or absolutely first according to its nature.—(h), **primum ratione,** see *primum cognitione.*—(i), **primum secundum cognitionem,** see *primum cognitione.*—(j), **primum secundum definitionem,** see *primum cognitione.*—(k), **primum secundum tempus,** see *primum cognitione.*—(l), **primum simpliciter,** see *primum in genere.*—(m), **primum simpliciter secundum naturam,** see *primum per ordinem ad aliquid extrinsecum.*—(n), **primum tempore,** see *primum cognitione.*—**demonstratio est ex primis,** see *demonstratio* under 3.—**quod est primum in constructione, est ultimum in resolutione,** *what is first in composition, is last in dissolution.*—**primum in generatione est postremum in corruptione,** see *generatio* under 1.—**quod est primum in intentione est ultimum in exsecutione,** see *intentio* under 2.—**ultimum in generatione est primum in resolutione et intentione,** see *generatione* under 1. —**uni primo non immediate adiungitur absoluta multitudo,** *an absolute plurality cannot be attached directly to a single first.* —**primo,** *adv.,* (1) *first, in the first place;* according to time, succession, rank; the opposite of *secundo, secundario, posterius seu per posterius,* (2) *first, in the first place,* i.e., *ratione sui ipsius seu secundum se totum,* some-

times joined with *per se,* the opposite of *ratione partis seu secundum partem.*—On **agere primo,** see *agere* under 1; on **contrarium primo,** see *contrarius* under 1; on **ens primo,** see *ens;* on **intellegere primo,** see *intellegere* under 1; on **mereri primo,** see *mereri;* on **meritorium primo,** see *meritorius;* on **motus primo primus,** see *motus* under 2; on **obiectum primo,** see *obiectum.* On **cognoscere primo,** see *cognoscere* under 2; on **dicere primo,** see *dicere* under 3; on **inesse primo,** see *inesse;* on **movere primo,** see *movere;* on **praedicare primo,** see *praedicare* under 2; on **significare primo,** see *significare.*—**in primo,** *in the first part* (i.e. of the Summa Theologica).

princeps, cipis, *m., a chief, superior, ruler, head.*

principalis, e, *adj., first, chief, principal,* the opposite of *accessorius, instrumentalis,* and *secundarius.* On **actus principalis ad vitam,** see *actus* under 1; on **agens principalis,** see *agens;* on **amicitia principalis,** see *amicitia* under 1; on **bonum principale,** see *bonus* under 3; on **causa principalis,** see *causa* under 2; on **circumstantia principalis,** see *circumstantia* under 2; on **clavis principalis,** see *clavis* under 2; on **continentia principalis,** see *continentia* under 4; on **dominium principale,** see *dominium;* on **esse principale,** see *esse;* on **exemplar principale,** see *exemplar* under 2; on **finis**

principalis, see *finis* under 2; on
forma principalis, see *forma* under 2; on fundamentum principale, see *fundamentum;* on intellectum principale, see *intellegere*
under 1; on intellectus principalis, see *intellectus* under 8; on
materia principalis, see *materia*
under 2; on movens principale,
see *movere;* on obiectum principale, see *obiectum;* on ordo principalis, see *ordo* under 4; on
organum principale, see *organum;* on pars principalis, see *pars*
under 1; on passio principalis,
see *passio* under 3; on praedicare
in principali, see *praedicare* under 2; on praedicatum principale,
see *praedicatum* under 1; on ratio principalis, see *ratio* under
13; on sacerdos principalis, see
sacerdos; on scientia principalis,
see *scientia* under 1; on sensus
principalis, see *sensus* under 3
and 8; on significatio principalis,
see *significatio* under 1; on substantia principalis, see *substantia*
under 1; on unitas principalis,
see *unitas;* on virtus principalis,
see *virtus* under 1 and 5; on volitum principale, see *volitus.*—principaliter, *adv.,* (1) *principally,
chiefly, in the first rank,* the opposite of *secundario* (2) *according to source* or *origin,* synonym
of *originaliter* and *primordialiter.* On agens principaliter, see
agens; on consistere principaliter,
see *consistere* under 3; on contrarium principaliter, see *contrarius* under 1; on movere princi-

paliter, see *movere;* on operari
principaliter, see *operari;* on significare principaliter, see *significare;* on tentare principaliter,
see *tentare.*

principalitas, atis, *f.,* (1) *essential
thing, chief matter,* (2) *the first
place, superiority, pre-eminence,
excellence.*

principaliter, *adv.,* see *principalis.*

principativus, a, um, *adj., having
superiority, ruling,* synonym of
architectonicus and *dominativus,*
not found in the Summa Theologica. On notitia principativa, see
notitia under 2; on ratio principativa, see *ratio* under 6.

principatus, us, *m.,* (1) *first place,
authority, principate, sovereign-
ty, dominion,* synonym of *dominium, potestas,* and *regimen,* (2)
ruler, chief, principalities.—Kinds
of *principatus* in this sense are:
(a), principatus despoticus and
principatus politicus, *the imperious* or *absolute authority* and *the
limited authority* or *that belonging to free citizens.*—(b), principatus dominativus and principatus oeconomicus, *the imperious*
or *absolute authority* and *the
domestic* or *family authority.*—
(c), principatus exterior, *the exterior authority* or *the authority
that exists outside.*—(d), principatus oeconomicus, see *principatus
dominativus.*—(e), principatus optimatum seu optimorum, principatus paucorum divitum et potentum, and principatus regalis
seu regius, *the authority of the*

highest class, that of a few rich and powerful, and *the royal authority,* i.e., *the aristocracy, the oligarchy,* and *the monarchy.*— (f), **principatus paternus,** *the paternal authority* or *the authority of elders over their children.*—(g), **principatus paucorm divitum et potentum,** see *principatus optimatum.*—(h), **principatus politicus,** see *principatus despoticus.*— (i), **principatus regalis, seu regius,** see *principatus optimatum.*— (j), **principatus sacer** and **principatus saecularis seu terrenus,** *the holy* or *spiritual authority* and *the worldly* or *secular authority.* —(k), **principatus saecularis,** see *principatus sacer.*—(l), **principatus terrenus,** see *principatus sacer.*

principio, are, avi, atum, *v. a., to furnish the beginning as origin to something, cause, produce, originate,* synonym of *originare.*

principium, ii, *n., beginning, commencement, origin, foundation, principle,* the *arche* of Aristotle, synonym of *inchoatio* and *primum,* i.e., that from which something takes its first (existence), *primum capit.* On **certitudo principiorum,** see *certitudo* under 2; on **cognoscere in cognitionis principio et secundum habitudinem principii,** see *cognoscere* under 2; on **habitus principiorum,** see *habitus* under 4; on **intellectus principiorum,** see *intellectus* under 6; on **necessitas principiorum, et principiorum essentiali-**

um, see *necessitas* under 1; on **petitio principii,** see *petitio* under 2; on **relatio principii et procedentis a principio,** see *relatio;* on **veritas primorum principiorum,** see *veritas* under 1; on **virtus principii,** see *virtus* under 6. —Kinds of *principium* are: (a), **principium actionis, principium factionis,** and **principium facti,** *the principle of an action in general, that of an action which produces something, and that of an accomplished work.*—(b), **principium activum seu agendi** and **principium passivum seu patiendi,** *the active* or *bestowing and the passive* or *receiving principle,* or *the principle for doing something and the principle for receiving something.*—(c), **principium agendi,** see *principium activum.*—(d), **principium agens seu effectivum, principium finale, principium exemplare, principium formale,** and **principium materiale sive susceptivum,** *the effective* or *productive cause, the motive* or *final, the exemplary, formal cause, and the cause acting after the manner of material* or *the receptive cause.*—(e), **principium agens propter finem,** *the cause active because of an end.* —(f), **principium a quo,** *the principle by which* or *the productive principle.*—(g), **principium circa quod** and **principium ex quo,** the translation of Aristotle's expression *arche peri hote kai ex hou* "*the principle about which*" and *"the principle from which"*.—(h), principium cognitionis seu cognoscendi seu cognoscitivum, principium essendi, and principium fiendi, *the principle of knowledge and that of being and that of becoming.*—(i), principium cognoscendi, see *principium cognitionis.*—(j), principium cognoscitivum, see *principium cognitionis.*—(k), principium commune and principium proprium, *the common and the particular or proper principle.*—(l), principium consubstantiale, *the principle of like nature and essence.*—(m), principium contingens and principium necessarium, *the not necessarily true and the necessarily true principle.*—(n), principium contractum and principium universale, *the restricted and the universal principle.*—(o), principium corporeum and principium incorporeum, *the corporeal and the incorporeal principle.*—(p), principium definiens, *the defining principle,* i.e., the principle which states or determines the essence of a thing.—(q), principium demonstrationis seu demonstrativum, *the principle of a proof,* which shows something as being necessarily true or the *apodeictic principle of a proof.*—(r), principium demonstrativum, see *principium demonstrationis.*—(s), principium de non principio, principium de principio, and principium de utroque principio, *the principle stemming*

from no principle, that from one and that from two.—(t), principium de principio, see *principium de non principio.*—(u), principium de utroque principio, see *principium de non principio.*—(v), principium dirigens, principium imperans, and principium exequens, *the guiding principle, the commanding or ruling principle,* and *the executing principle.*—(w), principium disponens seu dispositivum, *the preparing principle.*—(x), principium dispositivum, see *principium disponens.*—(y), principium effectivum, see *principium agens.*—(z), principium elementare, *the principle consisting of an essential element.*—(a^2), principium essendi, see *principium cognitionis.*—(b^2), principium essentiae seu essentiale seu substantiale, *the essential principle* or *that belonging to the essence of a thing.*—(c^2), principium essentiale, see *principium essentiae.*—(d^2), principium exemplare, see *principium dirigens.*—(e^2), principium ex quo, see *principium circa quod.*—(f^2), principium exequens, see *principium dirigens.*—(g^2), principium exterius seu extrinsecum and principium interius seu intrinsecum, *the outer and the inner principle.*—(h^2), principium extraneum, *the extraneous principle.*—(i^2), principium extrinsecum, see *principium exterius.*—(j^2), principium facti, see *principium actionis.*—

(k^2), **principium factionis,** see *principium actionis.*—(l^2), **principium falsum** and **principium verum,** *the false and the true principle.*—(m^2), **principium fiendi,** see *principium cognitionis.* —(n^2), **principium finale,** see *principium agens.*—(o^2), **principium finitum** and **principium infinitum,** *the finite* or *the limited* (in amount or size) and *the infinite* or *unlimited principle.* — (p^2), **principium fontale,** *the fontal* or *fundamental principle.* —(q^2), **principium formale,** see *principium agens.*—(r^2), **principium generationis, principium temporis, principium rei,** and **principium magnitudinis seu quantitatis,** *the beginning of a generation, that of time, that of a thing, and that of a quantity.*—(s^2), **principium immateriale** and **principium materiale,** *the principle which is free of matter and that which is attached to matter.*—(t^2), **principium immediatum** sc. **actionis seu actus seu motus,** *the immediate principle of an action* or *movement.*—(u^2), **principium immediatum,** and **principium mediatum** sc. **cognitionis,** *the direct and the indirect principle of knowledge* or *the principle of knowledge that is manifestly true directly* or *through itself and that indirectly* or *through something else.*—(v^2), **principium imperans,** see *principium dirigens.* —(w^2), **principium incorporeum,** see *principium corporeum.*—(x^2),

principium indeficiens, *the unfailing principle* or *that not failing of its perfection.*—(y^2), **principium indemonstrabile,** *the nonprovable principle* or *that not capable of an apodictic proof.*—(z^2), **principium individuale seu individuans seu individuationis** and **principium specificum seu speciei,** *the individual and the specific principle,* or *the principle which makes a thing an individual, and that which gives it its nature and essence and thereby places it in a definite species.* —(a^3), **principium individuans,** see *principium individuale.*—(b^3), **principium individuationis,** see *principium individuale.*—(c^3), **principium infinitum,** see *principium finitum.*—(d^3), **principium innatum,** *the inborn* or *inherent principle.*—(e^3), **principium in operativis seu operabilium** and **principium in speculativis seu speculabilium,** *the practical and the speculative* or *theoretical principle,* or *the principle in the sphere of action and deed, and that in the sphere of knowledge* or *investigation.*—(f^3), **principium in speculativis,** see *principium in operativis.*—(g^3), **principium insufficiens** and **principium sufficiens,** *the insufficient and the sufficient principle.*—(h^3), **principium integrans,** *the principle restoring something in its integrity.* —(i^3), **principium intellectivum seu intellectuale, principium sensitivum,** and **principium vegeta-**

tivum, *the transcendental* or *intellectual, the sensible, and the vegetative principle.*—(j³), **principium intellectus practici** and **principium intellectus speculativi,** *the principle of the practical and that of the speculative* or *theoretical intellect.*—(k³), **principium interius,** see *principium exterius.*—(l³), **principium intrinsecum,** see *principium exterius.*—(m³), **principium iuris naturalis,** *the principle of the natural law.*—(n³), **principium magnitudinis,** see *principium generationis.*—(o³), **principium materiale,** see *principium agens et principium immateriale.*—(p³), **principium mathematicum,** *the principle of mathematics.*—(q³), **principium mediatum,** see *principium immediatum.*—(r³), **principium motivum seu movens,** *the moving principle.*—(s³), **principium movens,** see *principum motivum.*—(t³), **principium naturae,** *the principle of nature* or *the principle of a thing of nature.*—(u³), **principium naturale** and **principium superadditum seu supernaturale,** *the natural principle* or *that existing from nature and the principle added to the nature of a thing* or *the supernatural principle.*—(v³), **principium naturaliter notum seu per se notum.**—(w³), **principium necessarium,** see *principium contingens.*—(x³), **principium numeri,** *the principle of number,* i.e., the unity of quantity.—(y³), **principium operabilium,** see *princi-*

pium operativis.—(z³), **principium operationis seu operativum seu operatorium seu potentiale,** *the principle of an operation* or *the principle representing a faculty.*—(a⁴), **principium operativum seu operatorium,** see *principium operationis.*—(b⁴), **principium originale seu originans seu originis seu secundum originem,** *the principle of origin* or *the principle giving origin.*—(c⁴), **principium originans,** see *principium originale.*—(d⁴), **principium originis,** see *principium originale.*—(e⁴), **principium passivum,** see *principium activum.*—(f⁴), **principium patiendi,** see *principium activum.*—(g⁴), **principium per accidens** and **principium per se,** *the principle existing accidentally* or *because of something else and that existing as such* or *because of itself.*—(h⁴), **principium per aliquam scientiam cognitum** and **principium per sensum acceptum,** *the intellectual and the sensible principle of knowledge.*—(i⁴), **principium per se,** see *principium per accidens.*—(j⁴), **principium per se notum,** see *principium naturaliter notum.*—(k⁴), **principium per sensum acceptum,** see *principium per aliquam scientiam cognitum.*—(l⁴), **principium potentiale,** see *principium operationis.*—(m⁴), **principium primordiale,** *the primitive principle.*—(n⁴), **principium primum,** *the first principle,* whether in the realm of thought or of being.—(o⁴), **principium**

primum seu remotum, and **principium propinquum seu proximum,** *the first* or *remote principle* (reckoned on the one hand from the performer, on the other hand from the action or effect), and *the proximate* or *next* (to the action or the effect) *principle.*—(p⁴), **principium primum activum** and **principium primum passivum,** *the first active and the first passive principle,* i.e., God and primary matter.—(q⁴), **principium primum cognoscendi** and **principium primum essendi seu rerum,** *the first principle of knowing and the first principle of the existence of things* or *the first principle of thought and that of being.*—(r⁴), **principium primum effectivum, principium primum exemplare, principium primum formale,** and **principium primum finale,** *the first effective, the first exemplary, the first formal, and the first final principle.*—(s⁴), **principium primum essendi,** see *principium primum cognoscendi.*—(t⁴), **principium primum exemplare,** see *principium primum effectivum.*—(u⁴), **principium primum finale,** see *principium primum effectivum.*—(v⁴), **principium primum formale,** see *principium primum effectivum.*—(w⁴), **principium primum indemonstrabile,** *the first indemonstrable principle.*—(x⁴), **principium primum in genere** and **principium primum simpliciter,** *the first principle in a certain area* and *the simple* or

the absolute first principle.—(y⁴), **principium primum materiale,** *the first material principle* or *the first material acting after the manner of material.*—(z⁴), **principium primum movens,** *the first moving principle* or *the first mover of the world.*—(a⁵), **principium primum passivum,** see *principium primum activum.*—(b⁵), **principium primum productivum,** *the first producing principle.*—(c⁵), **principium primum rerum,** see *principium primum cognoscendi.*—(d⁵), **principium primum simpliciter,** see *principium primum in genere.*—(e⁵), **principium primum universale,** *the first universal principle,* quod est Deus.—(f⁵), **principium propinquum,** see *principium primum.*—(g⁵), **principium proprium,** see *principium commune.*—(h⁵), **principium proximum,** see *principium primum.*—(i⁵.), **principium quantitatis,** see *principium generationis.*—(j⁵), **principium rei,** see *principium generationis.*—(k⁵), **principium remotum,** see *principium primum.*—(l⁵), **principium scientiae,** see *scientia* under l.—(m⁵), **principium secundum causas singulas, principium secundum intellectum** and **principium secundum situm,** *the principle of individual realities, that with reference to the process of reason, and the principle with reference to the place of a thing.*—(n⁵), **principium secundum intellectum,** see *principium secundum causas singu-*

las.—(o^5), **principium secundum originem**, see *principium originale.*—(p^5), **principium secundum situm**, see *principium secundum causas singulas.*—(q^5), **principium seminale**, *the seminal principle* or *that of germination.*—(r^5), **principium sensitivum**, see *principium intellectivum.*—(s^5), **principium separatum seu subsistens**, *the separated* (from material) *principle* or *the principle existing by itself.*—(t^5), **principium simpliciter**, *the simple* or *absolute principle*, i.e., that principle which is merely a principle for another but it itself has no principle.— (u^5), **principium speciei**, see *principium individuale.*—(v^5), **principium specificum**, see *principium individuale.*—(w^5), **principium speculabilium**, see *principium in operativis.*—(x^5), **principium subsistendi** and **principium substandi**, *the principle to exist for itself and not in another*, and *the principle to administer to another*, or *to serve as supporter.*—(y^5), **principium subsistens**, see *principium separatum.*—(z^5), **principium substandi**, see *principium subsistendi.*—(a^6), **principium substantiale**, see *principium essentiae.*—(b^6), **principium sufficiens**, see *principium insufficiens.*—(c^6), **principium superadditum**, see *principium naturale.*—(d^6), **principium supernaturale**, see *principium naturale.*—(e^6), **principium susceptivum**, see *principium agens.*—(f^6), **principium syllogis-**

mi, *the principle of a conclusion.* —(g^6), **principium temporis**, see *principium generationis.*—(h^6), **principium universale**, see *principium contractum.*—(i^6), **principium vegetativum**, see *principium intellectivum.*—(j^6), **principium verum**, see *principium falsum.*— (k^6), **principium virtuale**, *the principle according to power.*— (l^6), **principium vitae seu vitale**, *the life principle.*—(m^6), **principium vitale**, see *principium vitae.*— **Nihil est sui ipsius principium**, *nothing is the principle of its own self.*—**nullus sapiens disputat contra negantem principia suae artis**, see *sapiens* under 1.—**principium est potius eo quod ex principio derivatur**, *the principle is more excellent than that which is derived from the principle.*— **principium est virtute totum**, *the principle is virtually all that proceeds from it.*—**principium naturaliter prius est eo cuius est principium**, *the principle according to nature is antecedent to that of which it is the principle*, but *considered secundum relationem principii, the principle is simul naturaliter cum principiato.*— **quod est modicum in principio, in fine multiplicatur**, the translation of Aristotle's expression: *to en arche mikron en te teleute ginetai pammegethes, what is small in the beginning is very great in the end.*—See under *error.*—**unumquodque maxime videtur esse illud quod invenitur in eo** esse principium, *everything appears to be that especially which is found in it as the principle.*

principor, are, *v. dep. a., to hold superiority, rule.*—**principari dominative,** *to rule like a lord over his slaves.*

prior, prius, oris, adj. comp., (1) *former, previous, prior,* the opposite of *posterior,* (2) **Priora** sc. **Analytica,** *the Earlier* or *First Analytics of Aristotle,* the opposite of Posteriora. On **causa prior,** see *causa* under 1 and 2; on **contraria priora,** see *contrarius* under 1; on **dicere per prius,** see *dicere* under 3; on **differentia prior,** see *differentia;* on **necessarium a priori,** see *necessarius* under 1; on **necessitas a priori,** see *necessitas* under 1; on **praedicare per prius, seu secundum prius,** see *praedicare* under 2; on **praedicatio per prius,** see *praedicatio* under 2; on **processus de priori ad posterius,** see *processus* under 1.—Kinds of *prius* in this (1) sense are: (a), **prius a quo non convertitur essendi seu subsistendi consequentia,** the translation of Aristotle's expression, *proteron de dokei to toiouton einai, aph' hou me antistrephei he tou einai akoulethesis, the antecedent for which consequent being cannot* (logically) *be substituted.*—(b), **prius cognitione seu in cognitione seu ordine cognitionis seu secundum cognitionem seu secundum rationem nostrae apprehensionis,** *prior with*

respect to knowledge.—(c), **prius cognitione intellectiva seu ratione seu secundum rationem** and **prius secundum sensum,** *prior according to the intellectual* or *rational knowledge and according to the sensible knowledge.*—(d), **prius definitione seu secundum definitionem** and **prius ratione seu secundum rationem seu secundum intellectum,** *prior according to the definition and the conception.*—(e), **prius generatione seu in generatione seu ordine generationis seu secundum ordinem generationis seu in via generationis seu secundum viam generationis** and **prius tempore seu secundum tempus seu in via temporis seu secundum viam temporis,** *prior according to production and according to time.*—(f), **prius in causando,** *earlier according to activity.*—(g), **prius in esse seu in essendo seu secundum ordinem in essendo seu secundum naturalem ordinem in essendo** and **prius secundum rem seu ordine rei,** *earlier according to being* or *existing, and earlier according to the thing.*—(h), **prius in generatione,** see *prius generatione.*—(i), **prius in motu seu secundum motum seu secundum ordinem in motu** and **prius secundum quantitatem seu per ordinem quantitatis,** *prior according to movement and quantity.*—(j), **prius in ordine naturae seu ordine naturae seu secundum ordinem naturae seu secundum su-**

am naturam seu secundum naturam seu natura seu naturaliter
and **prius quoad nos,** *prior according to its nature* or *in itself,*
(cf. *prius secundum speciem*)
and *with reference to us* or *our
nature.*—(k), **prius in via generationis,** see *prius generatione.*—(l),
prius in via temporis, see *prius
generatione.*—(m), **prius natura,**
see *prius in ordine naturae.*—(n),
prius natura ex parte agentis and
prius natura ex parte materiae,
*prior according to nature on the
part of the active and on the part
of the material cause.*—(o), **prius
naturaliter,** see *prius in ordine
naturae.*—(p), **prius ordine cognitionis,** see *prius cognitione.*—
(q), **prius ordine dignitatis seu
secundum potestatem,** *prior according to dignity* or *power.*—(r),
prius ordine dispositionis, *prior
according to disposition* or *preparation.*—(s), **prius ordine naturae,** see *prius in ordine naturae.*
—(t), **prius ordine perfectionis
seu secundum perfectionem seu
perfectione seu secundum rationem complementi,** *prior according to perfection.*—(u), **prius ordine rei,** see *prius in esse.*—
(v), **prius per accidens** and **prius per se,** *prior according to
something else* and *prior according to itself* or *as such.*—(w), **prius perfectione,** see *prius ordine
perfectionis.*—(x), prius per ordinem quantitatis, see *prius in
motu.*—(y), **prius per se,** see
prius per accidens.—(z), **prius**

quoad nos, see *prius in ordine
naturae.*—(a²), **prius ratione,** see
*prius cognitione intellectiva and
prius definitione.*—(b²), **prius secundum actum** and **prius secundum potentiam,** *prior according to reality and according
to potentiality.*—(c²), **prius secundum cognitionem,** see *prius
cognitione.*—(d²), **prius secundum
definitionem,** see *prius definitione.*—(e²), **prius secundum intellectum,** see *prius definitione.*—
(f²), **prius secundum locum,** *prior
according to place.*—(g²), **prius
secundum motum,** see *prius in
motu.*—(h²), **prius secundum naturalem ordinem in essendo,** see
prius in esse.—(i²), **prius secundum naturam,** see *prius in ordine
naturae.*—(j²), **prius secundum nominis rationem,** and **prius secundum rei naturam,** *prior according to the meaning of the name
and prior according to the nature
of the thing.*—(k²), **prius secundum ordinem,** *prior according to
order.*—(l²), **prius secundum ordinem generationis,** see *prius generatione.*—(m²), **prius secundum
ordinem in essendo,** see *prius in
esse.*—(n²), **prius secundum ordinem in motu,** see *prius in motu.*
—(o²), **prius secundum ordinem
naturae,** see *prius in ordine naturae.*—(p²), **prius secundum perfectionem,** see *prius ordine perfectionis.*—(q²), **prius secundum
potentiam,** see *prius secundum
actum.*—(r²), **prius secundum potestatem,** see *prius ordine digni-*

tatis.—(s²), **prius secundum quantitatem,** see *prius in motu.*—(t²), **prius secundum quid** and **prius simpliciter,** *prior in a certain respect* or *with respect to something* and *prior simply* or *absolutely.*—(u²), **prius secundum rationem,** see *prius cognitione intellectiva* and *prius definitione.* —(v²), **prius secundum rationem complementi,** see *prius ordine perfectionis.*—(w²), **prius secundum rationem nostrae apprehensionis,** see *prius cognitione.*—(x²), **prius secundum rei naturam,** see *prius secundum nominis rationem.*—(y²), **prius secundum rem,** see *prius in esse.*—(z²), **prius secundum sensum,** see *prius cognitione intellectiva.*—(a³), **prius secundum speciem seu secundum substantiam seu substantia,** *prior according to essence* or *substance.* Cf., *prius in ordine naturae.*—(b³), **prius secundum suam naturam,** see *prius in ordine naturae.*—(c³), **prius secundum substantiam,** see *prius secundum speciem.*—(d³), **prius secundum tempus,** see *prius generatione.*—(e³), **prius secundum viam generationis,** see *prius generatione.*—(f³), **prius secundum viam temporis,** see *prius generatione.*—(g³) **prius simpliciter,** see *prius secundum quid.*—(h³), **prius substantia,** see *prius secundum speciem.*—(i³), **prius tempore,** see *prius generatione.*—**in quolibet genere quanto aliquid est prius, tanto est simplicius et in paucioribus**

consistens, *the earlier something is according to its nature in any genus of things, the simpler it is and in fewer examples does it consist.*—**naturaliter prius est quod est perfectius, licet in unoquoque sit tempore posterius,** *that which is perfect is earlier according to nature, although in any (created) thing according to time it is later.*—**posteriora non sunt de intellectu priorum, sed e converso,** see *posterior* under 2.—**posito posteriori ponitur prius,** see *posterior* under 2.—**quod est per se, semper est prius eo quod est per aliud,** see *per* under 1.—**remoto posteriori non removetur prius,** see *posterior* under 2.—**remoto priori removetur posterius,** or **remoto priori removentur ea quae consequenter sunt,** *with the removal of the earlier the later is also removed,* i.e., that which directly follows the former and results from it.—**semper prius salvatur in posteriori,** *the prior is always kept* or *preserved in the posterior.*—**transmutato posteriori non transmutatur prius,** see *posterior* under 2.—**virtus prioris est in posteriori, sed non convertitur,** *the power of the earlier is also in the later, but not vice versa.*

prioratus, us, *m.,* *priorship, office of prior.*

prioritas, atis, *f.,* *preference, priority,* synonym of *prioratus.*

Priscilla, ae, *f.,* *Priscilla,* sometimes called *Prisca,* a prophetess who together with Maximilla, another prophetess, and the prophet Montanus founded the Montanists or Montanism, a schism of the second century.

priscus, a, um, *adj.*, *of* or *belonging to former times, of many years ago, olden, ancient,* used only in quotation in the S.T.

pristinus, a, um, *adj.*, *former, early, original, primitive, pristine.*

prius, *adv.*, comp., *before, sooner, first, previously.*—With *quam,* and often joined in one word, **priusquam**, *before that, before, sooner, rather.*

priusquam, see *prius.*

privatim, *adv.*, *apart from state affairs, for one's self, as an individual, in private, privately, in a private capacity,* opposite of *publice.*

privatio, onis, *f.*, (1) *a taking away of that which is due, privation, removal,* synonym of *remotio,* (2) *privation, lack of what should be present,* synonym of *defectus,* the opposite of *habitus* and *perfectio.* On **effectus privationis,** see *effectus.*—Kinds of *privatio* in this (1) sense are: **privatio activa** and **privatio passiva,** *the active and the passive privation* or *depriving and the being deprived.* On **motus ad privationem,** see *motus* under 4; on **negatio per modum privationis seu secundum privationem,** see *negatio* under 2; on **oppositum secundum privationem seu ut privatio,** see *opponere.*—Kinds of *privatio* in this sense are: (a), **privatio ab-**

soluta and **privatio consequens aliquam potentiam,** *the absolute lack* which signifies the lack of all perfection, and *the lack adhering to a faculty.*—(b), **privatio communissime dicta, privatio communiter dicta,** and **privatio proprie dicta seu stricte accepta,** *lack in the most general, that in the general, and that in the proper* or *in the strict sense of the word.*—(c), **privatio communiter dicta,** see *privatio communissime dicta.*—(d), **privatio consequens aliquam potentiam,** see *privatio absoluta.*—(e), **privatio non simplex** and **privatio simplex seu pura seu perfecta seu totaliter aliquid privans,** *the not simple* or *partial lack connected with something of the corresponding perfection and the simple* or *the pure* or *the perfect* or *the complete lack of the same.*—(f), **privatio perfecta,** see *privatio non simplex.*—(g), **privatio praecedens** and **privatio sequens,** *the preceding and the following lack.*—(h), **privatio pura,** see *privatio non simplex.*—(i), **privatio sequens,** see *privatio praecedens.*—(j), **privatio simplex,** see *privatio non simplex.*—(k), **privatio stricte accepta,** see *privatio communissime dicta.*—(l), **privatio totaliter aliquid privans,** see *privatio non simplex.*—(m), **privatio vera,** *the true* or *real lack.*—**contrarietatis principium est oppositio privationis et habitus,** see *habitus* under 2.—**habitus naturaliter est prior**

privatione, see *habitus* under 2.—
omnis privatio praesupponit habitum, *every lack presupposes the possession of the same.*—**prima contrarietas est habitus et privatio,** see *habitus* under 2.—
principium contrarietatis est oppositio privationis et habitus, see *habitus* under 2.—**privatio et habitus est prima contrarietas,** see *habitus* under 2.—**privationes non suscipiunt magis et minus,** *lacks* or *privations do not permit a more or a less except secundum se.*—**privationis subiectum est potentia seu potentia materiae,** *the subject of the lack is the potentiality of the matter* or *that existing in the state of potentiality.*—
Privatio non habet causam per se agentem, *privation has no cause operating according to itself* or *as such,* and *privatio neither possesses a form nor is such.*—**privatio non ponit aliquid sed determinat sibi subiectum,** *lack is nothing positive,* i.e., nothing determined in the reality of things, but it demands a subject for itself to which it cleaves.

privative, *adv.,* see *privativus.*

privativus, a, um, *adj., depriving, removing, possessing a lack, denoting privation, privative, negative,* synonym of *remotivus,* the opposite of *affirmativus* and *positivus.* Cf. *privatio* under 2. Cf. *affirmatio privativa,* see *affirmatio* under 1; on **affirmativa privativa,** see *affirmativus;* on **demonstratio privativa,** see *de-*
monstratio under 3; on **effectus privativus,** see *effectus;* on **enuntiatio privativa,** see *enuntiatio* under 2; on **negatio privativa,** see *negatio* under 1 and 2; on **negativa privativa,** see *negativus;* on **nomen privativum,** see *nomen* under 1; on **praedicatum privativum,** see *praedicatum* under 1; on **res privativa,** see *res;* on **syllogismus privativus,** see *syllogismus.*—**privative,** *adv., in the manner* or *sense of privation, negatively, privatively,* synonym of *remotive,* the opposite of *affirmative* and *positive.* On **accipere privative,** see *accipere* under 3; on **dicere privative,** see *dicere* under 3; on **ignorantia privative accepta,** see *ignorantia* under 1; on **infinitum privative dictum seu sumptum,** see *infinitus,* on **intellegere privative,** see *intellegere* under 3; on **oppositum privative,** see *opponere;* on **praedicare privative,** see *praedicare* under 2; on **significare privative,** see *significare;* on **sumere privative,** see *sumere* under 3.

privatus, a, um, *P. a.,* see *privo.*

privilegiatus, a, um, *P. a., privileged, exceptional.*

privilegium, ii, *n., privilege, prerogative.*

privo, are, avi, atum, 1, *v. a., to bereave, deprive, rob, strip.*—**privatus,** a, um, *P. a.,* (1) *deprived, bereaved,* (2) *not in public* or *official life, private, deprived of office,* the opposite of *communis* and *publicus.* On **ens privatum,**

see *ens;* on **subiectum privatum,** see *subiectum* under 2.—On **actus privatus,** see *actus* under 1; on **bonum privatum,** see *bonus* under 3; on **homo privatus,** see *homo;* on **ius privatum,** see *ius* under 1; on **lex privata,** see *lex* under 1; on **libido privata,** see *libido* under 1; on **oratio privata,** see *oratio* under 3; on **persona privata,** see *persona* under 3; on **societas privata,** see *societas;* on **vita privata,** see *vita* under 3; on **votum privatum,** see *votum* under 1.

pro, *prep.* with *abl.,* (1) *for, in behalf of, in favor of, for the benefit of, on the side of,* opposite of *contra,* (2) *in the place of, instead of, for,* (3) *just the same as, even as, as though,* (4) *in exchange, in return for,* (5) *on account of, for the sake of,* (6) *in proportion, in comparison with, according to, as.*—**pro tanto,** *to such an extent, thus far.*

proairesis, eos, (Grk. *proairesis*), *f., choice,* used in quot. in S.T.

Proba, ae, *f., Proba,* Anicia Faltonia Proba, the widow of Sextus Petronius Probus, was of a very wealthy and noble Roman family. Three of her sons held the consulship, two of them together in 395 A.D. and the third in 406 A.D. Because of the Gothic invasions, Proba realized her ample fortune and sailed to Africa, accompanied by a retinue of widows and younger women, seeking protection under her es-

cort. After paying a large sum to secure the protection of Heraclianus, Count of Africa, she was permitted to establish herself with her community of pious women in Carthage. Her piety led her to seek the friendship and counsel of St. Augustine. How readily he gave it, we see from letters 130, 131, 150, and 188.

probabilis, e, *adj.,* (1) *likely, credible, probable,* synonym of *opinabilis,* (2) *making probable, probable.* On **certitudo probabilis,** see *certitudo* under 2; on **propositio probabilis,** see *propositio* under 2; on **suspicio probabilis,** see *suspicio* under 3.—On **medium probabile,** see *medium* under 2; on **philosophus probabilis,** see *philosophus* under 1; on **probatio probabilis,** see *probatio* under 2; on **ratio probabilis,** see *ratio* under 13.—**probabiliter,** *adv., with probability, probably, credibly.* On **cognoscere probabiliter,** see *cognoscere* under 2; on **dicere probabiliter,** see *dicere* under 3; on **scire probabiliter,** see *scire* under 2.

probabilitas, atis, *f., probability, credibility,* the opposite of *improbabilitas.* On **cognoscere per modum probabilitatis,** see *cognoscere* under 2; on **procedere secundum probalitatem,** see *procedere* under 2.—**probabilitas coniecturalis,** *the conjectural probability.*

probabiliter, *adv.,* see *probabilis.*

probatio, onis, *f.*, (1) *trying, proving, verification, testing,* (2) *proof, evidence, demonstration,* synonym of *ratio.*—Kinds of *probatio* in this (2) sense are: (a), **probatio argumentativa seu demonstrativa seu infallibilis** and **probatio probabilis,** *the proof which establishes something apodictically* or *unerringly and which establishes something as probable.*—(b), **probatio circularis,** *the circular proof* or *that moving in a circle.* Cf. **demonstratio circularis** under *demonstratio* 3.—(c), **probatio demonstrativa,** see *probatio argumentativa.*—(d), **probatio infallibilis,** see *probatio argumentativa.*—(e), **probatio logica,** *the logical proof* or *the proof developed in a logical way.* Cf. **logice.**—(f), **probatio per se, probatio per signum,** and **probatio propter quid,** *the proof from something which belongs to a thing through itself and its own nature, the proof from an outward sign* or *mark, and that from the cause.*—(g), **probatio per signum,** see *probatio per se.*—(h), **probatio probabilis,** see *probatio argumentativa.*—(i), **probatio propter quid,** see *probatio per se.*—(j), **probatio semiplena,** *the half finished* or *incompleted proof.*

problema, atis, *n.,* *a question proposed for solution, a problem, riddle, dispute,* synonym of *quaestio.* Kinds of *problema* are: (a), **problema de accidente** and **problem de genere,** *the problem concerning an accident and that concerning the genus* or *the essence of a thing.*—(b), **problema de genere,** see *problema de accidente.*—(c), **problema dialecticum,** *the dialectic problem,* or that which cannot be settled with certainty.

probo, are, avi, atum, *v. a., to show, prove, demonstrate.*—Kinds of *probare* are: (a), **probare demonstrative,** *to show proof,* in the sense of a necessarily true proof. —(b), **probare per signum,** *to prove by means of a sign.*

probus, a, um, *adj., upright, honest, virtuous,* used only in quot. in S.T.

procedo, ere, cessi, cessum, 3, *v. n.,* (1) *to go forward, advance,* (2) *proceed, act,* (3) *go out, commence,* (4) *to go out, emerge,* (5) *come off, progress, pass,* (6) *be possible, hold good, avails.*—Kinds of *procedere* in this (2) sense are: (a), **procedere demonstrative seu disciplinabiliter seu per certitudinem,** *to proceed after the manner of apodictic proof* or *with certainty.*—(b), **procedere disciplinabiliter,** see *procedere demonstrative.*—(c), **procedere intellectualiter seu intelligibiliter,** *to proceed after the manner of understanding the principles.*—(d), **procedere per certitudinem,** see *procedere demonstrative.*—(e), **procedere rationabiliter seu secundum probabilitatem,** *to proceed with probability* or *in the* *manner of the same.*—(f), **procedere secundum probabilitatem,** see *procedere rationabiliter.*— Kinds of *procedere* in this (3) sense are: (a), **procedere aequaliter seu communiter** and **procedere principaliter seu proprie,** *to proceed in an equal or common manner and in a superior or proper manner.*—(b), **procedere communiter,** see *procedere aequaliter.*—(c), **procedere immediate** and **procedere mediate,** *to proceed directly and indirectly.* —(d), **procedere mediate,** see *procedere immediate.*—(e), **procedere naturaliter seu per naturam seu per modum naturae,** *to proceed in a natural manner or after the manner of a natural being.*— (f), **procedere per modum amoris seu voluntatis seu per voluntatem** and **procedere per modum intelligibilis actionis seu intellectus,** *to proceed after the manner of love or of the will and after the manner of thought.*—(g), **procedere per modum intellectus,** see *procedere per modum amoris.*— (h), **procedere per modum intelligibilis actionis,** see *procedere per modum amoris.*—(i), **procedere per modum naturae,** see *procedere naturaliter.*—(j), **procedere per modum voluntatis,** see *procedere per modum amoris.*— (k), **procedere per naturam,** see *procedere naturaliter.*—(l), **procedere per voluntatem,** see *procedere per modum amoris.*—(m), **procedere principaliter,** see *pro-*

cedere aequaliter.—(n), **procedere proprie,** see *procedere aequaliter.* —(o), **procedere secundum rationem similitudinis,** *to proceed after the manner of similarity.*

processio, onis, *f., a going forward, an origin from some principle, procession, conclusion,* synonym of *processus.*—Kinds of *processio* are: (a), **processio ad extra** and **processio ad intra seu interior,** *the procession directed toward creatures and that directed inward* or *the exterior procession and that taking place within the divine nature.*—(b), **processio ad intra,** see *processio ad extra.*—(c), **processio aeterna** and **processio temporalis,** *the eternal and the temporal procession.*—(d), **processio amoris** and **processio verbi,** *the procession of love and the procession of the (divine) Word.* —(e), **processio immaterialis** and **processio materialis,** *the spiritual and the physical procession.*—(f), **processio intellectus seu per modum intellectus seu secundum intellectum seu intelligibilis** and **processio voluntatis seu per modum voluntatis,** *the procession after the manner of thought and that after the manner of desire.*— (g), **processio intelligibilis,** see *processio intellectus.*—(h), **processio interior,** see *processio ad extra.*—(i), **processio localis,** *the local procession.*—(j), **processio materialis,** see *processio immaterialis.*—(k), **processio mediata,** *the direct procession.*—(l), **processio**

naturae seu secundum naturam seu per modum naturae, *the procession after the manner of nature* or *of a being of nature.*—(m), processio originis, *a procession in the sense of origin.*—(n), processio passiva, *the passive procession* or *the procession in the sense of an enduring*, i.e., the procession being made.—(o), processio per modum naturae, see *processio naturae.*—(p), processio per modum voluntatis, see *processio intellectus.*—(q), processio secundum intellectum, see *processio intellectus.*—(r), processio secundum naturam, see *processio naturae.*—(s), processio substantialis, *the procession after the manner* or *in the sense of the essence.*—(t), processio temporalis, see *processio aeterna.*—(u), processio verbi, see *processio amoris.*—(v), processio voluntatis, see *processio intellectus.*

processionalis, e, *adj., processional*, used only in quot. in S.T.

processivus, a, um, *adj., progressive.*

processus, us, *m.*, (1) *a going forward, advance, progression*, (2) *procedure, process, method*, synonym of *modus and ratio*, (3) *going forth, issue*, synonym of *processio.*—Kinds of *processus* in this (1) sense are: (a), processus attinentiae, *the progression of relationship.*—(b), processus circularis, *the circular progression.*—(c), processus de priori ad posterius, *the progression from prior*

to posterior.—Kinds of *processus* in this (2) sense are: (a), processus ad impossibile, *the method leading to the impossible* or *the method of the indirect proof.*—(b), processus compositionis seu compositivus and processus resolutionis seu resolutorius, *the method of composition and that of resolution* or *the synthetic and the analytic method.*—(c), processus compositivus, see *processus compositionis.*—(d), processus demonstrativus, *the process of the apodictic proof.*—(e), processus mathematicus, *the mathematical method.*—(f), processus rationalis, *the process of inference.*—(g), processus resolutionis, see *processus compositionis.*—(h), processus resolutorius, see *processus compositionis.*—To be distinguished here are: processus rationis seu intellegibilis and processus rei seu realis, *the issue after the manner of thinking* or *in the sphere of reason, that of a thing* or *that taking place outside thinking.*

proclamatio, onis, *f., a calling out, proclamation.*

proclamo, are, avi, atum, 1, *v. a., call* or *cry out, proclaim.*

proclivis, e, *adj., inclined* or *disposed to a thing, liable, prone, subject*, synonym of *pronus.*

proconsul, is, *m., one who at the close of the consulship in Rome became governor of a province, a proconsul.*

procreatio, onis, *f.*, *a begetting, generation, procreation.*

procreo, are, avi, atum, 1, *v. a.*, *to bring forth, beget, generate, procreate, produce.*

procul, *adv.*, *at a distance, a great way off, far, afar off, from afar*, constr. with *ab* and *abl.*, with *abl.* alone, and absolutely.—**procul dubio**, *without doubt, undoubtedly.*

procuratio, onis, *f.*, *a caring for, taking care of, care.*

procurator, oris, *m.*, *a manager, procurator, keeper.*

procuro, are, avi, atum, 1, *v. a.* and *n.*, *to bring about, occasion, procure.*

prodeo, ire, ii, itum, *v. n.*, *to come forth, go forth, proceed, appear.*

prodigalitas, atis, *f.*, *wastefulness, prodigality, extravagance*, synonym of *apirocalia, banausia*, and *consumptio*, the opposite of *avaritia* and *illiberalitas.*

prodigium, ii, *n.*, *a prophetic sign, token, omen, portent, prodigy*, synonym of *portentum, signum.*

prodigus, a, um, *adj.*, *wasteful, lavish, prodigal, profuse*, opposite of *avarus.*—**prodigus**, i, *m.*, *a wasteful person, a spendthrift, a prodigal.*—**prodige**, *adv.*, *lavishly, extravagantly, prodigally.*

proditio, onis, *f.*, *a betrayal, treason, treachery.*

proditor, oris, *m.*, *a betrayer, traitor.*

proditorie, *adv.*, *treacherously.*

prodo, ere, didi, ditum, 3, *v. a.*, *to make known, disclose, betray.*

produco, ere, xi, ctum, 3, *v. a.*, *to bring forth, produce, make, prolong.*—**productus**, a, um, *P. a.*, *brought forth, produced, made, prolonged.*

productio, onis, *f.*, *a bringing forth, making production.*

productivus, a, um, *adj.*, *able to produce, productive.*

proemium, ii, *n.*, *proemium, foreword.*

proemium, see *praemium.*

profanus, a, um, *adj.*, *wicked, impious, profane.*

profecto, *adv.*, *actually, indeed, really, truly, surely, certainly, by all means.*

profectus, us, *m.*, *advance, progress, effect, increase, growth, profit, success*, the opposite of *defectus.*

profero, ferre, tuli, latum, *v. a.*, *to bring forth, produce, invent, discover, make known, reveal.*

professio, onis, *f.*, (1) *declaration, profession, expression*, (2) *profession* or *making of vows* on entering a religious community. —Kinds of *professio* in this (1) sense are: (a), **professio fidei**, *the profession of faith.*—(b), **professio monastica**, *the monastic profession* or *that made on entering a religious community.*—(c), **professio regulae**, *profession of a monastic rule.*—(d), **professio religionis**, *the profession of a religious community*, which is made on entering this religious community. On **votum professionis**, see *votum* under 1.

professor, oris, *m.,* (1) *professor, confessor,* (2) *professor, teacher.*

profestus, a, um, *adj., non-festival, common;* of days, *working* days.

proficio, ere, feci, fectum, 3, *v. n.* and *a., to go on, advance, make progress, profit, derive advantages, perform, effect, accomplish,* opposite of *deficio.*

proficiscor, i, fectuš, 3, *v. dep. n., to go, come, proceed.*

proficuus, a, um, *adj., beneficial, advantageous, conducive,* opposite of *nocivus.*

profiteor, eri, fessus, 2, *v. dep. a., to declare publicly, acknowledge, avow, confess openly, profess.*

profluo, ere, xi, xum, 3, *v. n.* and *a.,* (1) *to flow forth, issue, proceed,* (2) *pour forth, send out.*

profundatus, a, um, *adj., thoroughly grounded, steeped.*

profunditas, atis, *f., depth, profundity.*

profundo, ere, fudi, fusum, 3, *v. a., to pour out* or *forth, lavish.*—**profusus,** a, um, *P. a., lavish, profuse, excessive.*

profundus, a, um, *adj., deep, profound, vast.*—**profundum,** i, *n.,* (1) *depth, an abyss,* (2) figuratively, *depth,* e.g., of wisdom.—**profunde,** *adv., deeply, profoundly.*

progenies, ei, *f., descent, lineage, race, family, progeny.*

progenitor, oris, *m., the founder of a family, an ancestor, progenitor.*

progigno, ere, genui, genitum, 3, *v. a., to beget, bear, bring forth, produce.*

prognostico, are, avi, atum, 1, *v. a., foretell, prognosticate.*

prognosticon, or-**um,** i, *n., a sign,* or *token of the future, a prognostic,* a work of St. Julian, Bishop of Toledo (end of seventh century) to which St. Thomas refers (PTS. Q. 70. Art. 3 c) without naming the work, but as quoted by Peter Lombard.

prognosticus, a, um, *adj., forecasting the future, prophesying, prognostic,* does not occur in Summa Theologica. On **signum prognosticum,** see *signum* under 1.

progredior, i, gressus, 3, *v. dep. a., to come* or *go forth, go on, advance, proceed.*

progressio, onis, *f., a going forth* or *forward, progression.*

progressivus, a, um, *adj., progressing, progressive.* On **animal progressivum,** see *ánimal* under 2.

progressus, us, *m., a going forward, advance, progress, growth, increase.*

prohibeo, ere, ui, itum, 2, *v. a., to hold back, keep in check, restrain, prevent, forbid, prohibit,* used with *abl.* and *prep.* or with *abl.* alone; also with *inf.,* and with *ut, ne, quominus* and *subjunctive.*

prohibitio, onis, *f., a forbidding, prohibition.*

prohibitivus, a, um, *adj., that serves to prohibit* or *preclude prohibitive.*

prohibitor, oris, *m., a withholder, restrainer, preventor.*

prohibitorius, a, um, *adj.*, *restraining, prohibiting, prohibitory*, does not occur in the Summa Theologica. On **mandatum prohibitorium**, see *mandatum*.

proinde, *adv.*, *hence, therefore, accordingly, then.*

proiectio, onis, *f.*, *a throwing forward* or *forth, a stretching out, projection.*

proicio, ere, ieci iectum, 3, *v. a.*, *to fling away, throw down, throw, put out, stretch out.*—**proiectus**, a, um, *P. a.*, *stretched out, projected, projecting.*

prolabor, i, lapsus, 3, *v. n.*, *to slip, fall down.*

prolatio, onis, *f.*, *a bringing forward, putting forth, adducing, pronouncing.*

proles, is, *f.*, *offspring, progeny, child, descendant.*

prolixe, *adv.*, see *prolixus.*

prolixitas, atis, *f.*, *great length, breadth*, or *width;* temporis, *length of time;* of speech, *prolixity.*

prolixus, a, um, *adj.*, *long, extended, far-reaching, distant.*—**prolixe**, *adv.*, *abundantly, copiously, prolixly.*

prologus, i, *m.*, *a preface, introduction, prologue.*

prolongo, are, avi, atum, 1, *v. a.*, *to lengthen, prolong, extend.*

promano, are, avi, atum, 1, *v. n.*, *extend, spread.*

promereo, ere, ui, itum, 2, *v. a.*, and **promereor**, eri, itum, 2, *v. dep. a.*, *to deserve, be deserving of, merit.*

Prometheus, ei, *m.*, *Prometheus*, a son of Iapetus and Clymene, brother of Epimetheus and father of Deucalion. He formed men of clay, and animated them by means of fire brought from heaven, for which he was fastened to Caucusus, where a bird fed on his entrails until finally it was slain by Hercules.

promissio, onis, *f.*, *a promising, promise.*—Kinds of *promissio* are: (a), **promissio nuda**, *the bare* or *pure promise.*—(b), **promissio temporalis**, *the temporal promise* or *the promise of a temporal good.*

promissorius, a, um, *adj.*, *containing a promise* or *assurance that something will be done, promissory.*—**iuramentum promissorium**, *a promissory oath*, the opposite of *iuramentum assertorium.*

promitto, ere, misi, missum, 3, *v. a.*, *to promise, hold out, cause to expect, give hope* or *promise of, assure.*—**promissus**, a, um, *P. a.*, *assured, promised.*—**promissum**, i, *n.*, *promise.*

promo, ere, mpsi, mptum, 3, *v. a.*, *to bring to light, disclose, utter, tell, express, relate.*—**promptus**, a, um, *P. a.*, *at hand, prepared, ready, quick, prompt, inclined* or *disposed to.*—**prompte**, *adv.*, *readily, quickly, without delay, willingly, promptly.*

promotio, onis, *f.*, *advancement, preferment, promotion.*

promotivus, a, um, *adj.*, *furthering, promotive.*

promoveo, ere, movi, motum, 2, *v. a., to move forward, cause to advance, promote.*

prompte, *adv.*, see *promo.*

promptissime, *sup. adv.*, see *promo.*

promptitudo, inis, *f., promptitude, promptness.*

promptus, us, *m., readiness,* in S.T. used only in the phrase *in promptu* usually with *esse, habere,* or *apparere, to be at hand, have ready.*

promulgatio, onis, *f., a making publicly known, a proclaiming, publishing, promulgation.*

promulgator, oris, *m., one who publishes* or *proclaims, a promulgator.*

promulgo, are, avi, atum, 1, *v. a., to expose to public view, make known, publish, promulgate.*

pronepos, otis, *m., a great grandson.*

pronitas, atis, *f., inclination, propensity, proneness.*

pronomen, inis, *n., pronoun.*—Kinds of *pronomen* are: (a), **pronomen demonstrativum,** *the demonstrative pronoun.*—(b), **pronomen relativum,** *the relative pronoun.*

pronosticus, a, um, *adj., prognostic, foretelling,* synonym of *praenuntiativus.*

pronuntiatio, onis, *f., a public declaration, publication, expression, pronunciation.*

pronuntio, are, avi, atum, 1, *v. a., to make publicly known, publish, proclaim, declaim, pronounce.*

pronus, a, um, *adj.,* (1) *leaning* or *hanging forward, stooping, bending down,* opposite of *erectus, rectus,* (2) trop., *inclined, disposed, prone* to anything.

propagatio, onis, *f., propagating, propagation.*

propago, inis, *f., offspring, descendant, progeny.*

propago, are, avi, atum, 1, *v. a.,* (1) *to propagate, generate, continue by procreation,* (2) *extend, enlarge, increase.*

propalo, are, avi, atum, 1, *v. a., to make public* or *manifest, divulge.*

propassio, onis, *f., preëmotion, propassion.*

propatruus, i, *m., a grandfather's brother, a great uncle.*

prope, *adv.* and *prep.,* (1) *adv., near, nigh,* the opposite of *longe,* (2) *prep.* with *acc., near, near by, almost to.*

propero, are, avi, atum, 1, *v. n., to make haste, hasten, be quick.*

propheta, ae, *m., a foreteller, herald, prophet.*

prophetabilis, e, *adj., possible of being prophesied, prophesiable.*

prophetalis, e, *adj., prophetic, prophetical,* synonym of *propheticus.* On **donum prophetale,** see *donum* under 2; on **gratia prophetalis,** see *gratia* under 2; on **revelatio prophetalis,** see *revelatio;* on **visio prophetalis,** see *visio* under 1.

prophetia, ae, *f., foretelling, prediction, prophecy.* On **donum prophetiae,** see *donum* under 2; on **gratia prophetiae,** see *gratia* under 2; on **speculum prophetiae,** see *speculum* under 1; on

spiritus prophetiae, see *spiritus;*
on usus prophetiae, see *usus*
under 1; on visio prophetiae, see
visio under 1.—Kinds of *prophetia* are: (a), prophetia comminationis, seu comminatoria and prophetia promissionis, *the prophecy of threat and that of promise*
or *that threatening punishment
and that promising something
good.*—(b), prophetia comminatoria, see *prophetia comminationis.*
—(c), prophetia daemonis and
prophetia Dei seu divina, *the
prophecy inspired by the devil
and that inspired by God.*—(d),
prophetia Dei, see *prophetia daemonis.*—(e), prophetia divina, see
prophetia daemonis.—(f), prophetia naturalis, and prophetia supernaturalis, *natural* and *supernatural prophecy.*—(g), prophetia
praedestinationis and prophetia
praescientiae, *prophecy of salvation* and *prophecy of any foreknowledge,* but particularly of
damnation.—(h), prophetia praescientiae, see *prophetia praedestinationis.*—(i), prophetia promissionis, see *prophetia comminationis.*—(j), prophetia proprie dicta
seu simpliciter dicta seu vere dicta seu vera and prophetia secundum quid dicta, *the proper and
the simple* or *absolute* or *true
prophecy* and *prophecy in a certain respect* or *with respect to
something.*—(k), prophetia secundum quid dicta, see *prophetia
proprie dicta.*—(l), prophetia simpliciter dicta, see *prophetia pro-*

prie dicta.—(m), prophetia supernaturalis, see *prophetia naturalis.*
—(n), prophetia vera, see *prophetia proprie dicta.*—(o), prophetia
vere dicta, see *prophetia proprie
dicta.*

prophetice, *adv.,* see *propheticus.*

propheticus, a, um, *adj., predicting,
prophetic, prophetical,* synonym
of *prophetalis.* On lumen propheticum, see *lumen;* on res prophetica, see *res;* on revelatio prophetica, see *revelatio;* on spiritus
propheticus, see *spiritus.*—prophetice, *adv., prophetically.*

prophetissa, ae, *f., prophetess.*

prophetizo, are, avi, atum, 1, *v. a.,
to prophesy.*

propheto, are, avi, atum, 1, *v. a., to
foretell, predict, prophesy.*

propino, are, avi, atum, 1, *v. a., to
give one to drink, give, administer.*

propinque, *adv.,* see *propinquus.*

propinquitas, atis, *f.,* (1) *nearness,
vicinity, proximity, propinquity,*
(2) *relationship, affinity.*—Kinds
of *propinquitas* in this sense are:
(a), propinquitas attinentiae, *the
affinity of relationship.*—(b), propinquitas carnalis, and propinquitas spiritualis, *the physical*
or *carnal relationship,* and *the
spiritual relationship.*—(c), propinquitas consanguinitatis, *blood
relationship.*—(d), propinquitas
generis, and propinquitas similitudinis, *the relationship or genus*
or *essence and that of similarity.*
—(e), propinquitas naturalis, *the
natural relationship.*—(f), propin-

quitas similitudinis, see *propin-quitas generis.*—(g), **propinquitas spiritualis**, see *propinquitas carnalis.*

propinquo, are, avi, atum, 1, *v. n.*, to draw near, come nigh, approach, of persons with *dat.*

propinquus, a, um, *adj.*, (1) *near, neighboring*, (2) *kindred, related.* On **aequivocatio propinqua**, see *aequivocatio* under 1; on **agens propinquum**, see *agens;* on **beatitudo propinqua**, see *beatitudo* under 1; on **corruptio propinqua**, see *corruptio* under 3; on **dispositio propinqua**, see *dispositio* under 4; on **finis propinquus**, see *finis* under 2; on **genus propinquum**, see *genus* under 2; on **materia propinqua**, see *materia* under 2 and 3; on **pars propinqua**, see *pars* under 1; on **potentia propinqua**, see *potentia* under 4; on **principium propinquum**, see *principium;* on **regula propinqua**, see *regula* under 1. On **persona propinqua**, see *persona* under 3.—**propinque**, *adv.*, *near, at hand, hard by.*

propitiatio, onis, *f.*, *an appearing, atonement, propitiation.*

propitiator, oris, *m.*, *propitiator*, used only in quotation in S.T.

propitiatorius, a, um, *adj.*, *atoning, reconciling, propitiating*, not found in S.T. used as *adj.*—**propitiatorium**, ii, *n.*, *the propitiatory.*

propitiatus, a, um, *P. a.*, see *propitio.*

propitio, are, avi, atum, 1, *v. a.*, *to render favorable, appease, propitiate.*

propitius, a, um, *adj.*, *favorable, well-disposed, gracious, kind, propitious*, used only in quot. in S.T.

propono, ere, posui, positum, 3, *v. a.*, *to point out, relate, set forth, propose.*

proportio, onis, *f.*, (1) *comparative relation, proportion, symmetry*, synonym of *analogia*, (2) *relation, capacity, power.*—On **aequale secundum proportionem**, see *aequalis* under 1; on **aequalitas proportionis**, see *aequalitas* under 1; on **analogia secundum convenientiam proportionis**, see *analogia;* on **communitas secundum rationem proportionis**, see *communitas* under 1; on **convenientia proportionis et secundum proportionem**, see *convenientia;* on **medium proportionis**, see *medium* under 1; on **quantitas proportionis**, see *quantitas* under 1; on **similitudo proportionis**, see *similitudo* under 1; on **unum proportione seu in proportione seu secundum proportionem**, see *unus.*—Kinds of *proportio* in this (1) sense are: (a), **proportio aequalitatis** and **proportio inaequalitatis seu inaequalis**, *the proportion of equality and that of inequality.*—(b), **proportio arithmetica** and **proportio geometrica**, *the arithmetical* and *the geometrical proportion.* Cf. *proportionalitas arithmetica et geometrica.*—

(c), **proportio commutata seu permutata**, *the transformed* or *changed proportion.*–(d), **proportio conveniens** and **proportio non conveniens**, *the fitting and the unfitting proportion.*–(e), **proportio debita**, *the due proportion.*–(f), **proportio decupla** and **proportio subdecupla**, *the tenfold proportion and that subordinate to it,* i.e., the proportion of 10:1 and that of a part of 10:1.–(g), **proportio determinata**, *the determined proportion.*–(h), **proportio dupla seu duplex** and **proportio tripla**, *the twofold and threefold proportion* or *the proportion of* 2:1 *and that of* 3:1.–(i), **proportio finita**, *the finite* or *limited proportion.*–(j), **proportio geometrica**, see *proportio arithmetica.*–(k), **proportio inaequalis**, see *proportio aequalitatis.*–(l), **proportio inaequalitatis**, see *proportio aequalitatis.*–(m), **proportio non conveniens**, see *proportio conveniens.*–(n), **proportio numeralis**, *the numerical proportion* or *the proportion expressible in numbers.*–(o), **proportio permutata**, see *proportio commutata.*–(p), **proportio sesquialtera** and **proportio sesquitertia**, *the proportion of* 1½:1–(q), **proportio sesquitertia**, see *proportio sesquialtera.*–(r), **proportio subdecupla**, see *proportio decupla.*–(s), **proportio tripla**, see *proportio dupla.*

proportionabilis, e, *adj., possible of being proportionate* to some-

thing, *proportionable.* – **proportionabiliter**, *adv., proportionately, in proportion.*

proportionabiliter, *adv.*, see *proportionabilis.*

proportionalis, e, *adj., of* or *belonging to proportion, proportional.* On **quantitas proportionalis**, see *quantitas* under 1; on **retributio proportionalis**, see *retributio.*–**proportionaliter**, *adv., proportionally.*

proportionalitas, atis, *f., relationship of proportions,* i.e., the similar interrelationship of two things, one to the other, *proportional proportion.*–Kinds of *proportionalitas* are: (a), **proportionalitas arithmetica** and **proportionalitas geometrica**, *the arithmetic and the geometric proportionateness.*–(b), **proportionalitas coniuncta seu continua** and **proportionalitas disiuncta**, *proportionateness with a common term.* –(c), **proportionalitas continua**, see *proportionalitas coniuncta.*–(d), **proportionalitas diametralis**, *the diametrically opposed proportionateness.*–(e), **proportionalitas disiuncta**, see *proportionalitas coniuncta.*–(f), **proportionalitas geometrica**, see *proportionalitas arithmetica.*

proportionaliter, *adv.*, see *proportionalis.*

proportionatus, a, um, *P. a.*, see *proportiono.*

proportiono, are, avi, atum, 1, *v. a., to proportion*, *to make proportionate.*–**proportionatus**, a, um, *P. a.*, *proportioned, proportionate.*

propositio, onis, *f.*, (1) *proposition, representation*, (2) *statement, assertion, thesis* in the broader and in the narrower sense of the word; in the broader sense *propositio* is a synonym of *enuntiatio;* in the narrower sense on the other hand it is the expression of a judgment, consisting of a subject and predicate belonging to the matter of a conclusion, (3) *preposition*, synonym of the more common *praepositio*. On **compositio propositionis**, see *compositio* under 1; on **veritas propositionis**, see *veritas* under 1.—Kinds of *propositio* in this (2) sense are: (a), **propositio aequipollens**, *the equivalent assertion.*—(b), **propositio affirmativa** and **propostio negativa**, *the affirmative and the negative statement.*—(c), **propositio categorica seu praedicativa** and **propositio conditionalis**, *the unconditioned* and *the conditioned statement.*—(d), **propositio communis**, *the common assertion.*—(e), **propositio composita** and **propositio divisa**, *the assertion understood in sensu composito* and *that understood in sensu diviso.* Cf. *sensus* under 7. —(f), **propositio conditionalis**, see *propositio categorica.*—(g), **propositio contingens seu de contingenti, propositio necessaria seu de necessario, propositio de possibili** and **propositio de impossibili**, *the statement which expresses something that may or may not be, that which expresses something necessary, that which expresses something possible,* and *that which expresses something impossible.*—(h), **propositio copulativa** and **propositio disiunctiva**, *the copulative* and *the disjunctive statement,* or *the statement that contains a copulative and that which contains a disjunctive particle.*—(i), **propositio de contingenti**, see *propositio contingens.*—(j), **propositio de impossibili**, see *propositio contingens.*—(k), **propositio de inesse seu de inesse simpliciter seu simplicis inhaerentiae** and **propositio de modo seu modalis**, *the statement expressing a simple existence of the predicate* and *that containing a so-called modality* (see *modus* under 5), i.e., a statement which simply says that the predicate belongs to the subject, and that which also indicates the mood or manner of this relationship.—(l), **propositio demonstrabilis** and **propositio indemonstrabilis**, *the statement that can be proven apodictically* and *that which cannot be proven apodictically.*—(m), **propositio demonstrativa** and **propositio dialectica seu probabilis**, *the statement necessarily true* and *the debatable* or *probable statement.*—(n), **propositio de necessario**, see *propositio contingens.*—(o), **propositio de possibili**, see *propositio contingens.*—(p), **propositio de**

praedicato accidentali and propositio de praedicata substantiali, *the statement with an unessential* and *that with an essential predicate.*—(q), propositio de praedicato finito, propositio de praedicato infinito, and propositio de praedicato privativo, *the statement with a finite predicate, that with an infinite or undetermined predicate, and that with a predicate expressing a lack.*—(r), propositio de praedicato infinito, see *propositio de praedicato finito.*—(s), propositio de praedicato privativo, see *propositio de praedicato finito.*—(t), propositio praedicato substantiali, see *propositio de praedicato accidentali.*—(u), propositio dialectica, see *propositio demonstrativa.*—(v), propositio disiunctiva, see *propositio copulativa.*—(w), propositio divisiva, see *propositio composita.*—(x), propositio expositiva, *the expository statement.*—(y), propositio falsa and propositio vera, *the false and the true statement.*—(z), propositio immediata seu non individua and propositio mediata, *the immediate statement or that not concerning the particular* and *the mediate or derived statement.*—(a²), propositio immediata prima seu prima simpliciter and propositio immediata secunda seu prima in aliquo genere, *the first and the second immediate statement or the first simple statement and the first statement in some kind or discipline of sci-*

ence.—(b²), propositio immediata secunda, see *propositio immediata prima.*—(c²), propositio impropria, *the improper statement or the statement to be understood in the improper sense.*—(d²), propositio immediata secunda, see *propositio immediata prima.*—(e²), propositio incompacta, *the statement not entirely agreed upon.*—(f²), propositio indefinita, *the indefinite statement.*—(g²), propositio indemonstrabilis, see *propositio demonstrabilis.*—(h²), propositio inductiva seu particularis seu singularis and propositio universalis seu tota, *the statement belonging to induction or that concerning the part of a whole or an individual case and the general statement or that concerning a whole.*—(i²), propositio maior and propositio minor, *the statement containing the general and the particular term of a conclusion or the major and the minor propositions of a conclusion.*—(j²), propositio maxima, *the statement with the greatest range or the principal proposition.* Cf. *dignitas* under 2.—(k²), propositio mediata, see *propositio immediata.*—(l²), propositio minor, see *propositio maior.*—(m²), propositio modalis, see *propositio de inesse.*—(n²), propositio necessaria, see *propositio contingens.*—(o²), propositio negativa, see *propositio affirmativa.*—(p²), propositio non individua, see *propositio immediata.*—(q²), propositio particularis, see *propositio inductiva.* —(r²), **propositio per se nota,** *the proposition known through itself* or *the true proposition.*—(s²), **propositio per se nota in se seu quantum in se** and **propositio per se nota omnibus seu quoad omnes, seu quoad nos,** *the true statement in* or *for itself and that with reference to us all and our knowledge through itself.*—(t²), **propositio praedicativa,** see *propositio categorica.*—(u²), **propositio prima,** *the fundamental statement.*—(v²), **propositio prima in aliquo genere** and **prima simpliciter,** see *propositio immediata prima.*—(w²), **propositio probabilis,** see *propositio demonstrativa.* —(x²), **propositio simplicis inhaerentiae,** see *propositio contingens.*—(y²), **propositio singularis,** see *propositio inductiva.*—(z²), **propositio subcontraria,** *the statement subordinated to a contrary one.* Cf. 1 Gener. 19 c.—(a³). **propositio tota,** see *propositio inductiva.*—(b³), **propositio universalis,** see *propositio inductiva.*— (c³), **propositio vera,** see *propositio falsa.*

propositum, i, *n.,* (1) *proposition, the case in question,* (2) *undertaking, purpose, intention.*

proprie, *adv.,* see *proprius.*

proprietas, atis, *f.,* (1) *peculiarity, peculiar nature* or *quality, characteristic feature,* (2) *reality, true meaning,* the opposite of *metaphora* and *similitudo,* (3) *property, ownership,* the opposite of

usus. On **convenientia secundum proprietates naturae,** see *convenientia* under 2.—Kinds of *proprietas* in this sense are: (a), **proprietas absoluta** and **proprietas habitudinalis,** *the peculiarity proper to a thing without reference to anything else and that proper to it with reference to something else.*—(b), **proprietas accidentalis** and **proprietas essentialis,** *the unessential and the essential peculiarity.*—(c), **proprietas animalis** and **proprietas humana,** *the sensitive and the human peculiarity* or *the peculiarity of being endowed with senses and that of man.*—(d), **proprietas communis** and **proprietas individualis seu individuans,** *the common* or *general peculiarity* and *the single* or *particular peculiarity.*—(e), **proprietas coniuncti** and **proprietas solius animae,** *the property flowing from the combination of body and soul and that of the soul alone.*—(f), **proprietas habitudinalis,** see *proprietas absoluta.*—(g), **proprietas essentialis,** see *proprietas accidentalis.*—(h), **proprietas humana,** see *proprietas animalis.*—(i), **proprietas hypostatica sc. Christi,** *the peculiarity which belongs to Christ as the result of the union of his divinity and his humanity in one person.*—(j), **proprietas individualis seu individuans,** see *proprietas communis.*—(k), **proprietas intranea,** *the internal peculiarity.*—(l), **proprietas natura-**

lis and **proprietas personalis,** *the natural and the personal peculiarity,* i.e., the peculiarity which belongs to a rational being in accordance with his nature and that which belongs to him in accordance with his personality.— (m), **proprietas personalis,** see *proprietas naturalis.*—(n), **proprietas relativa,** see *proprietas absoluta.*—(o), **proprietas solius animae,** see *proprietas coniuncti.* On **dicere per seu secundum proprietatem,** see *dicere* under 3.

proprius, a, um, *adj.,* (1) *not common with others, one's own, special, particular, proper,* (2) *true, real, genuine,* the opposite of *similitudinarius.* On **accidens proprium,** see *accidens* under 2; on **actio propria,** see *actio* under 1; on **actus proprius,** see *actus* under 2; on **agens proprium,** see *agens;* on **apprehensio propria,** see *apprehensio* under 2; on **auctoritas propria,** see *auctoritas* under 4; on **bonum proprium et proprium individui,** see *bonus* under 3; on **causa propria,** see *causa* under 1 and 2; on **cognitio propria,** see *cognitio* under 2; on **concupiscentia propria,** see *concupiscentia* under 1; on **corpus proprium,** see *corpus;* on **corruptio propria,** see *corruptio* under 2; on **defectus proprius,** see *defectus* under 2; on **delectatio propria,** see *delectatio;* on **differentia propria,** see *differentia;* on **discretio propria,** see *discretio* under 2; on **dispositio propria,**

see *dispositio* under 4; on **disputatio propria,** see *disputatio;* on **effectus proprius,** see *effectus;* on **esse proprium,** see *esse;* on **essentia propria,** see *essentia* under 1; on **finis proprius,** see *finis* under 2; on **instantia propria,** see *instantia* under 1; on **instrumentum proprium,** see *instrumentum;* on **locus proprius,** see *locus* under 2; on **materia propria,** see *materia* under 2 and 3; on **medium proprium,** see *medium* under 2; on **motus proprius,** see *motus* under 1; on **natura propria,** see *natura;* on **nomen proprium,** see *nomen* under 1; on **obiectum proprium,** see *obiectum;* on **officium proprium,** see *officium* under 2; on **operatio propria,** see *operatio* under 2; on **organum proprium,** see *organum;* on **passio propria,** see *passio* under 1 and 2; on **peccatum proprium,** see *peccatum* under 2; on **perfectio propria,** see *perfectio* under 2; on **persona propria,** see *persona* under 3; on **principium proprium,** see *principium;* on **ratio propria,** see *ratio* under 11, 12, and 13; on **regula propria,** see *regula* under 1; on **sacerdos proprius,** see *sacerdos;* on **sensibile proprium,** see *sensibilis* under 3; on **sensus proprius,** see *sensus* under 3; on **similitudo propria,** see *similitudo* under 2; on **species propria,** see *species* under 5, 6, and 8; on **subiectum proprium,** see *subiectum* under 2 and 4; on **suppositum pro-**

prium, see *suppositum* under 2;
on **terminus proprius**, see *terminus* under 1; on **usus proprius**, see *usus* under 1; on **verbum
proprium**, see *verbum* under 1;
on **virtus propria**, see *virtus* under 1 and 4; on **vitium proprium**,
see *vitium* under 1.—**proprium**, i,
n., *characteristic mark, a sign,
peculiar quality, peculiarity,* synonym of *accidens proprium, accidens per se seu per se accidens, accidens naturale seu gratuitum totius naturae,* and *proprietas.* On **locutio propria**, see
locutio under 4; on **significatio
propria**, see *significatio* under 1.
—**proprie**, *adv., in the proper
manner, in the proper sense, pe-
culiarly, properly,* the opposite of
*communiter, figurate, improprie,
metaphorice,* and *similitudinarie.*
On **accipere proprie**, see *accipere* under 3; on **agere proprie**,
see *agere* under 1: on **communicabile proprie**, see *communicabilis;* on **communicare proprie**,
see *communicare* under 1; on
corrumpere proprie, see *corrumpere* under 1; on **dicere proprie**,
see *dicere* under 3; on **dividere
proprie**, see *dividere* under 1;
on **fides proprie accepta**, see
fides under 2; on **intellegere
proprie**, see *intellegere* under 2;
on **iustitia proprie dicta**, see *iustitia* under 1; on **locus proprie
dictus**, see *locus* under 1; on
mereri proprie, see *mereri;* on
nominare proprie, see *nominare;*
on **pati proprie**, see *pati* under

1; on **perfectio proprie dicta**, see
perfectio under 2; on **prophetia
proprie dicta**, see *prophetia;* on
praedicare proprie, see *praedicare* under 2; on **sumere proprie**,
see *sumere* under 3; on **tenere
proprie**, see *tenere* under 5; on
veritas proprie accepta seu dicta,
see *veritas* under 1: on **voluntas
proprie dicta**, see *voluntas* under 3.

propter, *prep.,* with the *acc., on
account of, by reason of, from,
for, because of, for the sake of,*
not used as adverb in the Summa
Theologica. On **appetere propter aliud et propter se**, see *appetere* under 1; on **debitum propter aliud**, see *debitus* under 1;
on **demonstratio propter quid**,
see *demonstratio* under 3; on
**instrumentum propter bene es-
se**, see *instrumentum;* on **notum
per se**, see *notus;* on **probatio
propter quid**, see *probatio* under 2; on **quaestio propter quid**,
see *quaestio;* on **scientia propter quid**, see *scientia* under 1;
on **scire propter quid**, see *scire*
under 1; on **velle propter aliud
et propter se**, see *velle* under 1.—
Kinds of *propter* are: (a), **propter
aliud seu alterum** and **propter se
seu seipsum**, *for the sake of
someone else* and *for the sake of
oneself.*—(b), **propter quid**, *precisely because of something.*—(c),
propter se seu seipsum, see *propter aliud.*—**propter quod unumquodque, et illud magis est, vel**

saltem non minus, the translation of the Aristotelian passage, *aei gar, di'ho hyparchei hekaston, ekeinon mallon hyparchei, that because of which* or *for the sake of which this* or *that exists is itself greater* or *at least not less than this* or *that,* it being implied of course that both belong to the same order of genus of causes.

propterea, *adv., therefore, for that cause, on that account.*

propugnatrix, icis, *f., she that defends, a protectress.*

propulso, are, avi, atum, 1, *v. freq. a., to ward off, avert, repel.*

proreta, ae, *m., the look-out man at the prow, under-pilot.*

prorsus, *adv., straightway, by all means, certainly, truly, precisely, utterly, absolutely.*

prorumpo, ere, rupi, ruptum, 3, *v. n., to rush* or *break forth, burst out.*

proruo, ere, rui, rutum, 3, *v. n., to rush forth, rush* or *fall upon.*

prosa, ae, *f., prose, sequence.*

prosapia, ae, *f., a stock, race, family.*

prosecutio, onis, *f., a following, pursuit,* opposite of *fuga.*

prosequor, i, cutus, 3, *v. dep. a., to follow after, tend, pursue,* opposite of *vito* and *fugio.*

prosilio, ire, ui, –, 4, *v. n., to spring* or *burst forth, break forth.*

Proslogium, ii, *n., the Proslogium of St. Anselm,* Abbot of Bec and Archbishop of Canterbury (1033-1109), where he sets forth his

well-known ontological proof of the existence of God.

prosopon, ou, *n., person,* Greek for Latin *persona,* used only in quot. in S.T.

prospectus, us, *m., sight, view.*

Prosper, i, *m., Prosper* of Aquitaine; saint, layman, and controversialist; correspondent of St. Augustine, born c. 403 and died 440. St. Thomas in the S.T. quotes from the *Liber Sententiarum Prosperi* or *Sententiae ex Augustino delibatae,* from the *Responsiones ad Capitula Gallorum,* as though they were the works of St. Augustine, and from the *De Vita Contemplativa,* which is of doubtful authenticity.

prospere, *adv.,* see *prosperus.*

prosperitas, atis, *f., desirable condition, good fortune, success, prosperity.*

prospero, are, avi, atum, 1, *v. a., to cause a thing to succeed, render fortunate* or *happy, prosper.*

prosperus, a, um, *adj., agreeable to one's wishes, favorable, fortunate, prosperous,* used in S.T. only in *subst.,* in plur.: prospera, orum, *n., favorable circumstances, good fortune, prosperity,* opposite of *adversa.*—**prospere,** *adv., agreeably to one's wishes, favorably, luckily, fortunately, prosperously.*

prospicio, ere, exi, ectum, 3, *v. n.* and *a., to see beforehand, look or see to beforehand, exercise, exercise foresight, look out for, take care of, provide for.*

prosterno, ere, stravi, stratum, 3, *v. a., to throw to the ground, throw down, overthrow, prostrate.*

prostibulum, i, *n., a prostitute.*

prostituo, ere, ui, utum, 3, *v. a., to expose publicly to prostitution, prostitute.*

prostitutio, onis, *f., prostitution,* used in the S.T. only in quot.

prostratio, onis, *f., an overthrowing, prostration.*

prosum, prodesse, fui, *v. n., to be useful* or *of use, do good, benefit, profit,* constr. with *dat.* or *absol.,* opposite of *obsum.*

prosyllogismus, i, *m., proconclusion,* i.e., that conclusion of a composite syllogism whose *conclusio* is a premise of the following conclusion. Does not occur in the Summa Theologica.

protectio, onis, *f., a protecting, protection.*

protego, ere, xi, ctum, 3, *v. a., to cover* or *shield from danger, defend, protect.*

protelo, are, avi, atum, 1, *v. a., to prolong, put off, protract.*

protendo, ere, di, sum, and tum, 3, *v. a., to stretch forth* or *out, extend.*

protensio, onis, *f., a stretching forth* or *out.*

Proterius, ii, *m., Proterius,* saint and patriarch of Alexandria, presbyter and church-steward under Dioscorus, and left in charge of the church when Dioscorus went to the council of Chalcedon.

protervia, ae, *f., wantonness, impudence.*

protervitas, atis, *f., perversity.*

protervus, a, um, *adj., shameless, perverted.*

protestatio, onis, *f., declaration, manifestation, protestation, profession.* One should distinguish **protestatio operis** and **protestatio oris,** *profession by work* and *profession by mouth.*

protestativus, a, um, *adj., declarative, manifestive, protestive.* On **signum protestativum,** see *signum* under 1.

protestor, ari, atus, 1, *v. dep. a., to declare in public, bear witness, testify.*

protinus, *adv., forthwith, immediately, directly,* used in the S.T. only in quot.

prototypus, a, um, *adj., original, primitive,* used in S.T. substantively only in quot.—**prototypum,** i, *n., the original, prototype.*

protractio, onis, *f., a drawing out, lengthening, protraction.*

protraho, ere, xi, ctum, 3, *v. a., to lengthen out, prolong, protract.*

prout, *adv., according as; in proportion, accordingly, proportionably as; just as; as.*

provectus, a, um, *Part.* and *P. a.,* see *proveho.*

provectus, us, *m., progress, increase, furtherance,* used in S.T. only in quot.

proveho, ere, xi, ctum, 3, *v. a., to carry* or *conduct forwards, convey, advance.*

provenio, ire, veni, ventum, 4, *v. n., to spring, originate, arise, come to pass, take place, occur.*

proventus, us, *m., a coming forth, produce, yield, crop.*

proverbium, ii, *n.,* (1) *an old saying, a saw, maxim, adage, proverb,* (2) Book of Proverbs.

provide, *adv.,* see *providus.*

providentia, ae, *f., foresight, directive care, providence.* On **certitudo providentiae,** see *certitudo* under 2.—Kinds of *providentia* are: (a), **providentia angeli, providentia daemonis,** and **providentia humana,** *the providence of the angel, that of the devil and that of man.*—(b), **providentia approbationis,** and **providentia concessionis,** *the providence of good which is approved and that of permission of evil.*—(c), **providentia concessionis,** see *providentia approbationis.*—(d), **providentia creaturae** and **providentia Dei seu divina,** *the providence of the creature and divine providence.*—(e), **providentia daemonis,** see *providentia angeli.*—(f), **providentia Dei seu divina,** see *providentia creaturae.*—(g), **providentia humana,** see *providentia angeli.*—(h), **providentia inferior** and **providentia superior,** *the inferior and the superior providence or the providence of an inferior and that of a superior being.*—(i), **providentia naturalis** and **providentia voluntaria,** *the natural and the wilful or voluntary providence.*—(j), **providentia oeconomica** and **providentia politica,** *the domestic providence,* and *the public providence.*—(k), **provi-**

dentia politica, see *providentia oeconomica.*—(l), **providentia superior,** see *providentia inferior.*—(m), **providentia voluntaria,** see *providentia naturalis.*

provideo, ere, vidi, visum, 2, *v. n.* and *a.,* (1) *to see to, look after, care for, provide, make preparation* or *provision for,* constr. *absol.,* with *dat., de,* (2) active, *to see* or *perceive beforehand, foresee,* (3) active, *to care for, give attention to, prepare* or *provide for.*—**provisus,** a, um, *P. a., provided, cared for, foreseen.*

providus, a, um, *adj., cautious, circumspect, provident.*—**provide,** *adv., carefully, prudently.*

provincia, ae, *f., a province, division.*

provisio, onis, *f., foresight, providence, supervision, care for.*

provisor, oris, *m., foreseer, provider.*

provocatio, onis, *f., a stimulus, provocation, encouragement.*

provocativus, a, um, *adj., calling forth, eliciting, provocative.*

provoco, are, avi, atum, 1, *v. a.* and *n., to challenge, incite, provoke, rouse.*

proxime, *adv.,* see *proximus.*

proximitas, atis, *f., relationship, connection, union,* used only in quot. in the S.T.

proximus, a, um, *sup.* of *comp. adj.,* **propior,** ius, which does not appear in the Summa Theologica, *nearest, next,* opposite of *remotus.* On **aequivocatio proxima,** see *aequivocatio* under 1; on agens proximus, see *agens;* on **bonum proximum,** see *bonus* under 3; on **causa proxima,** see *causa* under 2; on **effectus proximus,** see *effectus;* on **finis proximus,** see *finis* under 2; on **fundamentum proximum,** see *fundamentum;* on **genus proximum,** see *genus* under 2; on **materia proxima,** see *materia* under 2 and 3; on **mensura proxima,** see *mensura;* on **odium proximum,** see *odium;* on **peccatum contra proximum,** see *peccatum* under 2; on **principium proximum,** see *principium;* on **species proxima,** see *species* under 8; on **terminus proximus,** see *terminus* under 2.— Note anomalous form *proximior* (PP. Q. 104. 21.)—**proximus, i,** *m., a neighbor, fellow man,* opposite of *alienus.*—**proxime,** *adv., nearest, very near, next,* opposite of *remote.*

prudens, entis, *adj., foreseeing, foreknowing in the practical order, prudent,* (1) in the proper and (2) in the broader sense of the word.—Kinds of *prudens* are: **prudens in aliquo genere seu particulariter seu secundum quid** and **prudens simpliciter,** *prudent in some species of occupation* or *partially* or *relatively prudent* and *simply* or *absolutely prudent.* —**prudenter,** *adv., sagaciously, intelligently, discreetly, wisely, skilfully, prudently.*

prudenter, *adv.,* see *prudens.*

prudentia, ae, *f.,* (1) *prudence* in the narrower sense of the word, i.e., a virtue of the practical reason of man or of the reason turned to acting and doing and that which consists of the right relation of the reason to the immanent actions and deeds of man, (2) *prudence* in the broader sense of the word, under which is to be understood on the one hand human prudence with reference to evil, and on the other prudence and skill befitting alike beast and man. On the difference between *prudentia, ars, intellectus, sapientia,* and *scientia,* see *scientia* under 1. On **ratio prudentiae,** see *ratio* under 6; on **sensus prudentiae,** see *sensus* under 2.—Kinds of *prudentia* in this (1) sense are: (a), **prudentia adquisita** and **prudentia gratuita seu infusa,** *the self acquired prudence* and *prudence bestowed* or *infused by the grace of God.*—(b), **prudentia architectonica seu legis positivae** and **prudentia politica communi nomine dicta,** *the architectonic* or *commanding* or *the legislative prudence, and the prudence designated by the general terms of political* or *civic.*— (c), **prudentia carnis, prudentia diaboli,** and **prudentia mundi,** *the prudence of the flesh, that of the devil,* and *that of the world* or *the exterior goods of this world.*—(d), **prudentia diaboli,** see *prudentia carnis.*—(e), **prudentia falsa seu per similitudinem dicta** and **prudentia vera,** *the false prudence* or *that so* *called after the manner of similarity and the true prudence.*—(f), **prudentia gratuita,** see *prudentia adquisita.*—(g), **prudentia imperfecta,** and **prudentia perfecta,** *the imperfect and the perfect prudence.* Cf. *prudentia imperfecta* and *perfecta* under 2.—(h), **prudentia infusa,** see *prudentia adquisita.*—(i), **prudentia legis positiva,** see *prudentia architectonica.*—(j), **prudentia militaris, prudentia oeconomica, prudentia regnativa,** and **prudentia politica,** *the military, the domestic, the regal or executive,* and *the civic prudence,* or *the prudence of subjects.*—(k), **prudentia monastica seu regitiva unius** and **prudentia regitiva multitudinis,** *the prudence with which one rules himself and that with which he rules a multitude of men,* e.g., *familia exercitus et civitas vel regnum;* cf. *prudentia militaris.*—(l), **prudentia mundi,** see *prudentia carnis.*—(m), **prudentia oeconomica,** see *prudentia militaris.*—(n), **prudentia perfecta,** see *prudentia imperfecta.*—(o), **prudentia per similitudinem dicta,** see *prudentia falsa.*—(p), **prudentia politica,** see *prudentia militaris.*—(q), **prudentia politica communi nomine dicta,** see *prudentia architectonica.*—(r), **prudentia regitiva multitudinis,** see *prudentia monastica.*—(s), **prudentia regitiva unius,** see *prudentia monastica.*—(t), **prudentia regnativa,** see *prudentia militaris.*—(u), **pruden-**

tia simpliciter dicta, *the so-called simple* or *absolute prudence,* under which come *prudentia vera, prudentia monastica,* and *prudentia perfecta.*—(v), **prudentia vera,** see *prudentia falsa.*—Kinds of *prudentia* in this (2) sense are: (a), **prudentia imperfecta** and **prudentia perfecta,** *the imperfect and the perfect prudence.* Cf. *prudentia imperfecta et perfecta* above under 1.—(b), **prudentia naturalis,** *the natural prudence* or *the naturally inherent prudence,* i.e., the prudence of animals based on natural instinct.—(c), **prudentia particularis** and **prudentia universalis,** *the partial and the universal prudence.*—(d), **prudentia perfecta,** see *prudentia imperfecta.*—(e), **prudentia universalis,** see *prudentia particularis.*

pruna, ae, *f., a burning coal, live coal.*

prurio, ire, *v. n., to itch,* used only in quot. in S.T.

psallo, ere, i, 3, *v. n., to play upon a stringed instrument, play upon the cithara, sing to the cithara.*

psalmista, ae, *m., a composer* or *singer of psalms, a psalm-writer, psalm-singer, psalmist.*

psalmistatus, us, *m., the office of psalmist.*

psalmodia, ae, *f., psalmody,* used only in quot. in S.T.

psalmus, i, *m.,* (1) *a psalm,* (2) *the Book of Psalms.*

psalterium, ii, *n.,* (1) *a stringed instrument of the lute kind, a* *psaltery*, (2) *the songs of David, the Psalms, the Psalter.*

psaltes, ae, *m., a player on the cithara, a musician, minstrel,* used only in quot. in S.T.

pseudoapostolus, i, *m., a false apostle.*

pseudopropheta, ae, *m., a false prophet.*

Ptolemaeus, i, *m., Ptolemy,* an Egyptian astronomer of the second century A.D. Although not the founder, he was the chief exponent of the Ptolemaic system of astronomy, to which St. Thomas alludes frequently in the Summa Theologica and which remained in vogue until the sixteenth century.

pubertas, atis, *f., the age of manhood* or *womanhood, maturity, puberty.*

pubes, eris, *adj., that is grown up, of ripe age, adult, pubescent.*

publicanus, i, *m., a tax-gatherer, publican.*

publicatio, onis, *f., manifestation, publication.*

publice, *adv.,* see *publicus.*

publico, are, avi, atum, 1, *v. a., to make known, publish, reveal, disclose.*

Publicola, ae, *m., Publicola,* son of Melania, who from his station and fortune might have attained to senatorial rank but whom his mother wished to renounce the world and live a monastic life. However, he married Albania, daughter of Rufius Caionius Albinus, and by her had a daugh-

ter, Melania. He died before A.D. 406, for in that year his widow was residing for a time at Nola in the house of Paulinus, together with her mother-in-law, the elder Melania and others. He probably possessed considerable property in Africa, near Arzuges, a place of unknown site in the province of Byzacene in Africa, and wrote to St. Augustine to consult him as to his own conduct towards them and also on some other cases of conscience which troubled him. In answer to this St. Augustine wrote Letter XLVII about the year 398. St. Thomas refers to this letter several times in the S.T.

publicus, a, um, *adj., of* or *belonging to the people, state,* or *community, public, common,* the opposite of *privatus.* On **auctoritas publica,** see *auctoritas* under 4; on **bonum publicum,** see *bonus* under 3; on **disputatio publica,** see *disputatio;* on **iudicium publicum,** see *iudicium* under 1; on **ius publicum,** see *ius* under 1; on **iustitia publica et publicae honestatis,** see *iustitia* under 2 and 4; on **oratio publica,** see *oratio* under 3; on **persona publica,** see *persona* under 3; on **poenitentia publica,** see *poenitentia* under 1; on **potestas publica,** see *potestas* under 3; on **scandalum publicum,** see *scandalum* under 2; on **signum publicum iustitiae,** see *signum* under 1; on **societas publi-**

ca, see *societas;* on **via publica,**
see *via* under 1; on **votum publicum,** see *votum* under 1.—**publicum,** i, *n., a public place, publicity,* especially in the expressions
in publicum and *in publico* (opposite of in *occulto*), *publicly.—*
publice, *adv., before the people,
openly, publicly,* opposite of *occulte.*

pudenda, orum, *n.,* see *pudendus.*

pudendus, a, um, *P. a., of which
one ought to be ashamed, scandalous, disgraceful.* — **pudenda,**
orum, *n.,* (sc. *membra*), *the private parts.*

pudicitia, ae, *f., modesty, reserve,
propriety,* synonym of *verecundia.*

pudicus, a, um, *adj., chaste, pure,
undefiled.*

pudor, oris, *m., shame, a sense of
shame, shamefacedness, shyness;
modesty, decency, good manners, propriety.*

puella, ae, *f., a female child, a girl,
maiden, lass.*

puellaris, e, *adj., of or belonging to
a girl,* or *young woman, girlish,
maidenly.*

puer, eri, *m., a male child, a boy,
lad, young man.*

puerilis, e, *adj., boyish, childish,
youthful.*

pueritia, ae, *f., boyhood, childhood,
youth.*

puerperium, ii, *n., a new-born
child, an infant.*

pugil, ilis, *m., one who fights with
the cestus, a boxer, pugilist.*

pugna, ae, *f., a fight fist to fist, man
to man; a battle, combat, action,
engagement.*

pugnator, oris, *m., a fighter, com-
batant.*

pugno, are, avi, atum, 1, *v. n., to
fight,* either singly or in armies,
to *combat, give battle, engage,
contend.*

pugnus, i, *m., a fist,* used only once
and in quotation in S.T.

pulcher, chra, chrum, *adj., beautiful, fair, handsome.—***pulchrum,** i,
*n., beauty.—***pulchre,** *beautifully,
excellently,* used only in quot.
in S.T.

pulchritudo, inis, *f., beauty.—***per se
pulchritudo,** *beauty existing for
itself.—*Kinds of *pulchritudo* are:
**pulchritudo corporalis seu corpo-
ris seu exterior** and **pulchritudo
spiritualis seu interior,** *the physical* or *exterior beauty* and *the
spiritual* or *internal beauty.*

pullulatio, onis, *f., a bringing forth
young, a putting forth, sprouting
out, producing.*

pullulo, are, avi, atum, 1, *v. n.* and
*a., put forth, sprout out, come
forth.*

pullus, i, *m., a young animal,* especially of birds and fowl, *a chick,
chicken, young.*

pullus, a, um, *adj., black, dark-
colored.*

pulmentarius, a, um, *adj., of or belonging to relishes,* or *sauces,* or
condiments, or *food* in general.

pulmo, onis, *m., a lung.*

pulpa, ae, *f., the fleshy part, solid
flesh;* with *digiti, finger-tips.*

pulsatilis, e, *adj., pulsating, throbbing, pulsatile,* synonym of *pulsativus.*

pulsativus, a, um, *adj., pulsating, throbbing, pulsative,* synonym of *pulsatilis.*

pulso, are, avi, atum, 1, *v. freq. a., to strike, beat, attack, din.*

pulsus, us, *m., beating of the pulse, pulse.*

pulverizo, are, avi, atum, 1, *v. a., to reduce to dust, pulverize.*

pulvillus, i, *m., dim., a little cushion, a small pillow,* used in the S.T. only in quot.

pulvis, eris, *m., dust, powder.*

punctalis, e, *adj., of the nature of point,* or *small as a point, punctual.*

punctio, onis, *f., a pricking, puncture,* used in the S.T. only in quot.

punctualiter, *adv., exactly, precisely, punctually.*

punctum or **punctus,** i, *m., a point, small spot.* On the difference between *punctum* and *unitas,* see *unitas.*—Kinds of *punctum seu punctus* are: (a), **punctus motus** and **punctus non motus,** *the point moved* in the sensible motion, and the *point not moved* or *resting.*—(b), **punctus non motus,** see *punctus motus.*—(c), **punctum signatum,** *the designated* or *specified point.*—**duo puncta non sunt consequenter se habentia ad invicem,** *two points cannot immediately follow each other.*—**duo puncta simul coniuncta non sunt**

nisi unum, *two points immediately joined with each other are only one.*—**inter duo puncta semper est aliquod medium accipere,** or **inter duo puncta semper est linea media,** *between two points there is always a middle* or *intermediate line.*—**punctum additum puncto nihil maius efficit,** or **punctum nihil magnitudinis adicit lineae,** *if a point is added to a point* or *a line, there is no increase.*—**punctum stans est, et ideo potest bis accipi, semel ut principium et semel ut finis,** *the point is something static* or *resting and so can be viewed in two ways, as the beginning and as the end.*

pungo, ere, pupugi, punctum, 3, *v. a., to prick, puncture.*

Punicus, a, um, *adj., Punic, Carthaginian;* with *malum (apple),* pomegranate, synonym of *malum granatum (apple of many seeds),* used in S.T. only in quot.

punio, ire, ivi or ii, itum, 4, *v. a., to inflict punishment upon, punish.*

punitio, onis, *f., a punishment.*

punitivus, a, um, *adj., that inflicts* or *awards punishment, punitive.*

punitor, oris, *m., punisher.*

pupilla, ae, *f., the pupil of the eye, the eye.*

pupillus, i, *m., an orphan boy, an orphan.*

purbatio, onis, *f., cleansing, freeing, clearing.*

pure, *adv.,* see *purus.*

purgabilis, e, *adj., that can be eas-*

ily *cleansed* or *purified, cleansable, purifiable.*

purgamentum, i, *n.,* *a means of purgation, purification, dregs, offscouring.*

purgatio, onis, *f.,* *a cleansing, purging, purgation.* On **iudicium purgationis,** see *iudicium* under 1.— Kinds of *purgatio* are: (a), **purgatio a culpa** and **purgatio a nescientia seu a tenebris ignorantiae,** *the purgation from sin,* quae est per gratiam, 2 Sent. 9. 1. 2 ad 1; and *the purgation from the darkness of ignorance,* quae est per lumen doctrinae, 2 Sent. 9. 1. 2 ad 1. Cf. 4 Sent. 5. 1. 2 ad 5.—(b), **purgatio a nescientia,** see *purgatio a culpa.*—(c), **purgatio a tenebris ignorantiae,** see *purgatio a culpa.*—(d), **purgatio praeparatoria,** *the preparatory purgation.*

purgativus, a, um, *adj., purgative, cleansing, cathartic,* synonym of *purgatorius.* On **ordo purgativus,** see *ordo* under 3; on **vis purgativa,** see *vis* under 1.

purgatorius, a, um, *adj., cleansing, purgative, purgatory,* synonym of *purgativus.* On **poena purgatoria,** see *poena;* on **virtus purgatoria,** see *virtus* under 5.—**purgatorium,** ii, *n., place of cleansing, purgatory.* On **poena purgatorii,** see *poena.*

purgatus, a, um, see *purgo.*

purgo, are, avi, atum, 1, *v. a.,* (1) *to make clean, cleanse, purify,* (2) medic. lang., *to cleanse by stool, vomiting,* etc., *to purge,* (3)

to cleanse or *purge from a crime* or *sin with religious rites, to make expiation, purify.*—**purgatus,** a, um, *P. a., cleansed, purified, pure.*

purificatio, onis, *f., a purifying, purification.*

purifico, are, avi, atum, 1, *v. a., to purify with religious rites, expiate, atone for.*

puritas, atis, *f.,* (1) *purity, cleanness* in the proper sense of the word, i.e., freedom from stain, synonym of *munditia,* the opposite of *immunditia* and *impuritas,* (2) *purity* in the improper sense of the word, i.e., freedom from a mixture, synonym of *munditia,* the opposite of *immunditia* and *impuritas.*—Kinds of *puritas* in this (1) sense are: (a), **puritas contemplationis,** *the purity of observation* or *contemplation.*—(b), **puritas intellectualis cognitionis seu intellectus seu intellegentiae,** *the purity of intellectual knowledge.* —(c), **puritas intellectus,** see *puritas intellectualis cognitionis.*—(d), **puritas intellegentiae,** see *puritas intellectualis cognitionis.*—(e), **puritas naturae** and **puritas per gratiam,** *the purity supplied by nature and that bestowed by grace,* or *the natural and the supernatural purity.*—(f), **puritas per gratiam,** see *puritas naturae.* —(g), **puritas virginalis,** *the virginal purity.*—One kind of *puritas* in this (2) sense is **puritas actus,** *purity of reality* because not mixed with potentiality.

purpura, ae, *f., the purple,* i.e., *purple cloth, a purple garment.*

purpureus, a, um, *adj., purple-colored, purple.*

purus, a, um, *adj., clean, pure, unmixed,* synonym of *simplex,* opposite of *impurus.* On **actus purus,** see *actus* under 1 and 2; on **aequivocatio pura,** see *aequivocatio* under 1; on **bonitas pura,** see *bonitas* under 1; on **conscientia pura,** see *conscientia* under 3; on **esse purum,** see *esse;* on **forma pura,** see *forma* under 2; on **homo purus,** see *homo;* on **infinitum purum,** see *infinitus;* on **materia pura,** see *materia* under 3; on **naturalia pura,** see *naturalis;* on **negatio pura,** see *negatio* under 2; on **non-ens purum,** see *non-ens;* on **passio pura,** see *passio* under 2; on **potentia pura,** see *potentia* under 2; on **privatio pura,** see *privatio* under 2; on **quidditas pura,** see *quidditas;* on **veritas pura,** see *veritas* under 1. —**pure,** *adv., purely, clearly, without spot or mixture.*

pusillanimis, e, *adj., faint-hearted, timid, pusillanimous,* synonym of *pusillanimus.*

pusillanimitas, atis, *f., faintheartedness, timidity, pusillanimity,* the opposite of *magnanimitas. Pusillanimitas* is a daughter of *acidia.*

pusillanimus, a, um, *adj., faint-hearted, timid, pusillanimous,* synonym of *pusillanimis.*

pusillitas, atis, *f., littleness, smallness.*

pusillus, a, um, *adj., dim., little, small.*—**pusillus,** i, *m., little one.* —**pusillum,** *adv., a little while,* used in quot.

puta, see *puto.*

putative, *adv.,* see *putativus.*

putativus, a, um, *adj., imaginary, presumptive, putative.*—**putative,** *adv., by supposition, putatively,* used only in quot. in S.T.

puteus, i, *m., a well.*

puto, are, avi, atum, 1, *v. a., think, suppose, consider.*—**puta,** imperative of *puto,* (1) *suppose, namely,* (2) *for instance, for example.*

putredo, inis, *f.,* (1) *rottenness, putridity,* (2) also in fig. sense.

putrefacio, ere, feci, factum, 3, *v. a.,* and in *pass.* **putrefio,** factus, fieri, *to rot, moulder, putrefy, decay.*

putrefactibilis, e, *adj., capable of putrefaction, putrescible, putrefactible.*

putrefactio, onis, *f., a rotting, putrefaction.*

putresco, ere, *v. inch. n., to grow rotten* or *putrid, rot, putrify, moulder,* used lit. and fig.

putridus, a, um, *adj., rotten, decayed.*

pyromantia, ae, *f., pyromancy, divination by fire* or *by signs derived from fire.*

Pythagoras, ae, *m., Pythagoras,* a celebrated philosopher of Samos, about 550 B.C.; he taught in Lower Italy, and was the founder of the Pythagorean philosophy, which received its name

from him.—**Pythagorici,** orum,
m., the Pythagoreans.

Pythagorici, orum, *m.,* see *Pythagoras.*

Pythius, a, um, *adj., Pythian, Del-
phic, Apollonian.*

python, onis, *m., a python, a soothsayer,* or *soothsaying spirit,* from
the tradition that the Python delivered oracles at Delphi.

pythonissa, ae, *f., a possessed woman, a witch, sorceress.*

Q

quadragenarius, a, um, *adj., of* or
*belonging to the number forty,
consisting of forty, of forty.*

quadragesima, ae, *f.,* see *quadragesimus.*

quadragesimalis, e, *adj., quadrages-
imal, of* or *pertaining to the number forty,* especially *to the forty
days of Lent; Lenten.*

quadragesimus, a, um, *adj., the fortieth.*—**quadragesima,** ae, *f., the
Christian fast of forty days, Lent.*

quadraginta, num. *adj., forty.*

quadrangulus, a, um, *adj., four-
cornered, quadrangular.*

quadrans, antis, *m., the fourth part
of an as,* (as a coin) *three unciae,
a farthing.*

quadratum, i, *n.,* see *quadratus.*

quadratus, a, um, *P. a., squared,
square, quadrate.*—**quadratum,** i,
n., (1) *a square, a four-sided
figure,* (2) *the square, the product of a number* or *quantity by
itself.*

quadricolor, oris, *adj., quadricolor,
of four colors.*

quadrifariam, *adv., in a fourfold
manner.*

quadrilaterum, i, *n., a quadrilateral,
a figure bounded by four straight
lines.*

quadringenti, ae, *a, adj., four
hundred.*

quadripartitus, a, um, *P. a., divided
into four parts, fourfold, consisting of four parts, quadripartite.*

quadrupes, pedis, *adj., having four
feet.*—**quadrupes,** edis, *m.,* or *f.*
or *n., a quadruped, a four-footed
creature.*

quadruplex, icis, *adj., fourfold,
quadruple.*—**quadrupliciter,** *adv.,
four times, in a fourfold degree*
or *manner.*

quadrupliciter, *adv.,* see *quadruplex.*

quadruplum, i, *n., a fourfold
amount, four times as much.*

quadrus, a, um, *adj., square.*

quaero, ere, sivi or sii, situm, 3, *v.
a., to seek,* (1) lit., (2) in gen.:
aliquem, (b), *to seek, get, procure; to seek* or *search* for a
thing, (c), transf., of animals,
procure, seek, (2) fig., (a) in
partic., *to look for, seek to gain
anything; to get, acquire, obtain,
procure,* (b) = requirere, *to require,* (c) *to seek to learn from
anyone, to ask, interrogate,* used
with de, a rel. cl., (d) *to desire,*
used with inf., (e) *to examine,*

investigate.—**quaesitus,** a, um, *P. a., sought.*

quaeso, ere, ivi or ii; 3, *v. a.,* (1) *to seek to obtain anything, to seek,* (2) *to beg, pray, beseech, entreat,* mostly in the first pers. sing., (a) *absol.,* thrown parenthetically into the sentence, (b) with *acc.* of object sought.

quaestio, onis, *f., an inquiry, investigation, a questioning, question, subject of inquiry.* On **virtus quaestionis,** see *virtus* under 6.—Kinds of *quaestio* are: (a), **quaestio ad conclusionem,** *the question put for the sake of an inference* or *the inquiry.*—(b), **quaestio an est seu si est, quaestio propter quid, quaestio quia,** and **quaestio quid est,** *the question as to "whether something exists"* (cf. *quaestio de esse simpliciter*), *that as to "why or wherefore it is", the question to ascertain "that it is"* (cf. *quaestio de esse simpliciter*), *that is to ascertain "what it is."*—(c), **quaestio composita seu in numerum ponens** and **quaestio simplex seu non-ponens in numerum,** *the composite question* or *that put in numbers* and *the simple question* or *that not put in numbers.*—(d), **quaestio de esse simpliciter** and **quaestio in parte,** *the question as to the being of a thing simply* or *absolutely and that as to its being partially.*—(e), **quaestio incidens,** *the secondary* or *incidental question.*—(f), **quaestio in numerum ponens,** see *quaestio compo-*

sita.—(g), **quaestio in parte,** see *quaestio de esse simpliciter.*—(h), **quaestio moralis** and **quaestio naturalis,** *the ethical and the natural philosophical question.* Cf. Usur. pr.—(i), **quaestio naturalis,** see *quaestio moralis.*—(j), **quaestio non-ponens in numerum,** see *quaestio composita.*—(k), **quaestio propter quid,** see *quaestio an est.*—(1), **quaestio quia,** see *quaestio an est.*—(m), **quaestio quid est,** see *quaestio an est.*—(n), **quaestio si est,** see *quaestio an est.*—(o), **quaestio simplex,** see *quaestio composita.*—(p), **quaestio theologica,** *the theological question.*

quaestus, us, *m., gain, profit, advantage.*

qualifico, are, 1, *v. a., to qualify, invest with a quality* or *qualities.*

qualis, e, *pron. adj.,* (1) *interrog.: how constituted, of what sort, kind,* or *nature, what kind of,* (2) *rel.,* with or without the correlative *talis: so constituted of such a sort, kind* or *nature, such as, as,* (3) *indef.: having some quality* or *other, being in some condition* or *other, of some sort,* the Aristotelian *poios* by which can be understood something substantial or essential as well as something accidental or unessential.— **quale est unumquodque, talia operatur seu tale alterum facit,** *of whatever nature anything is, such things does it make* or *such another thing does it do.*—**qualis unusquisque est, talis et finis vi-**

detur ei, see *finis* under 2. On
numerus qualis, see *numerus;* on
**praedicare in eo quod quale seu
in quale quid**, see *praedicare* under 2.—**quale passivum**, *something of such a sort as to suffer*
or *to be capable of suffering.*—
qualiter, *adv., in what way* or
manner, how, just as, as.

qualiscumque, **qualecumque**, *adj.*,
(1) *rel., of what quality soever,
of whatever kind*, (2) transf., indef., *any without exception, any
whatever.*—**qualitercumque**, *adv.,
in what way soever, howsoever,
be it as it may.*

qualislibet, **qualelibet**, *pron., indef., of what quality it pleases,
of what sort you will.*

qualitas, atis, *f., a quality, property, modification, state, condition,*
in the narrower and in the wider
sense of the word. On **motus secundum qualitatem**, see *motus*
under 1; on **mutatio secundum
qualitatem**, see *mutatio;* on **significare cum qualitate**, see *significare;* on **similitudo per participationem eiusdem qualitatis**, see
similitudo under 1.—Kinds of
qualitas in the general sense of
the word are: (a), **qualitas accidentalis** and **qualitas essentialis
seu substantialis seu quae est differentia substantiae**, *the unessential and the essential quality.* The
unessential quality, one of the
ten categories of Aristotle, contains within itself four different
species: (1) habitus et dispositio-
nes, (2) potentiae et impotentiae

naturales with the charactere
sacramentales, (3) qualitates pas-
sibiles et passiones, and (4) figurae et formae.—(b), **qualitas activa** and **qualitas passiva**, *the
active qualities (calidum et frigidum)* and *the passive qualities
(umidum et siccum)* of the earthly body.—(c), **qualitas actus**, *the
quality* or *the kind and manner
of an action.* Cf. 1 Anim. 1 a.—
(d), **qualitas adquisita, qualitas
adventitia seu superveniens seu
non-naturalis** and **qualitas naturalis**, *the acquired, the added
quality* or *that not springing from
the nature of a thing* and *the natural quality* or *that supplied by
the nature of a thing.* Cf. *qualitas connaturalis.*—(e), **qualitas adventitia**, see *qualitas adquisita.*—
(f), **qualitas alterans seu alterativa seu passibilis seu sensibilis**,
*a quality which impresses a sense
by reason of alternating change.*
—(g), **qualitas alterativa**, see
qualitas alterans.—(h), **qualitas
complexionata seu composita** and
qualitas simplex, *the composite
and the simple quality.*—(i),
qualitas composita, see *qualitas
complexionata.* — (j), **qualitas
connaturalis** and **qualitas extranea**, *the quality corresponding
with the nature of a thing* and
that foreign to it. Cf. *qualitas adquisita.*—(k) **qualitas consequens**
and **qualitas praecedens** sc. **actum appetitus sensitivi**, *the quality of an animal body following
after a sensible desire* and *that*

preceding it.—(l), qualitas corporalis seu corporea and qualitas spiritualis, *the physical and the spiritual quality.* Cf. *qualitas immaterialis et materialis;* also *qualitas consequens.*—(m), qualitas deficiens, *the failing* or *deficient quality.*—(n), qualitas elementaris seu elementorum, *the quality of an element.*—(o), qualitas elementorum, see *qualitas elementaris.*—(p), qualitas enuntiationis, see *enuntiatio* under 2.—(q), qualitas essentialis, see *qualitas accidentalis.*—(r), qualitas extranea, see *qualitas connaturalis.*—(s), qualitas immaterialis and qualitas materialis, *the immaterial* or *incorporeal and the material* or *corporeal quality.* Cf. *qualitas corporalis et spiritualis.*—(t), qualitas imperfecta and qualitas perfecta, *the imperfect and the perfect quality.*—(u), qualitas materialis, see *qualitas immaterialis.*—(v), qualitas naturalis, see *qualitas adquisita.*—(w), qualitas nominis, *the quality* or *the origin of a name.*—(x), qualitas numeri, *the quality* or *property of a number.*—(y), qualitas passibilis, see *qualitas alterans.*—(z), qualitas passiva, see *qualitas activa.*—(a^2), qualitas perfecta, see *qualitas imperfecta.*—(b^2), qualitas physica seu tangibilis and qualitas tangentis, *the physical* or *tangible quality and the quality of the one who touches.*—(c^2), qualitas praecedens, see *qualitas*

consequens.—(d^2), qualitas prima and qualitas secunda, *the first* or *simple and the second* or *composite quality.*—(e^2), qualitas prima tangibilis, *the first tangible quality.*—(f^2), qualitas quae est differentia substantiae, see *qualitas accidentalis.*—(g^2), qualitas secunda, see *qualitas prima.*—(h^2), qualitas sensibilis, see *qualitas alterans.*—(i^2), qualitas simplex, see *qualitas complexionata.*—(j^2), qualitas spiritualis, see *qualitas corporalis.*—(k^2), qualitas substantialis, see *qualitas accidentalis.*—(l^2), qualitas superveniens, see *qualitas adquisita.*—(m^2), qualitas tangentis, see *qualitas physica.*—(n^2), qualitas tangibilis, see *qualitas physica.*—qualitas suscipit, magis et minus, or, qualitates possunt intendi et remitti, *the qualities of a thing can increase* or *decrease in intensity.*

qualiter, *adv.,* see *qualis.*

qualitercumque, *adv.,* see *qualiscumque.*

quam, *adv., in what manner, how, how much, as much as;* some special uses are: (1) with *magis the more . . . the more;* (2) *tam . . . quam, so . . . as;* (3) *after* comparatives or words of comparison, *than;* (4) after *alius, other than;* (5) after *aliter, otherwise than;* (6) after *potius, rather than;* (7) after *plus* or *minus, more* or *less than;* (8) after *quantum, as much . . . as.*

quamdiu, *adv.,* (1) of time, *as long as, until, during,* (2) of inference, *inasmuch as, in that.*

quamlibet, *adv.,* see *quilibet.*

quamobrem, *rel. adv.,* at the beginning of a sentence as a particle of transition, *on which account, wherefore.*

quamquam, (quam) *conj., though, although,* (1) with *indic.,* (2) with *subj.*

quamvis, *adv.* and *conj.,* (1) *adv., as you will, as much as you will* or *like, ever so much, ever so;* hence, to designate a very high degree, *as much as possible, very much, exceedingly,* (2) *conj., as much as ever you will,* i.e., *how much soever, however much, although;* (a) with *subj.,* (b) with *indic.*

quando, *adv.,* and *conj.,* (1) *adv ,* (a) *interrog., at what time, when,* (b) *rel., at what time, when,* (2) *conj.,* (a) *temp., when,* (b) in gen., *since, because, seeing that.*

quandocumque, *adv., at what time soever, at whatever time, whenever,* (1) with *indic.,* (2) with *subj.*

quandoque, *adv., indef.,* (1) *at times, now and then, sometimes,* (2) *at one time* or *other, at some time.*

quandoquidem, *adv., since, seeing that.*

quantitas, atis, *f.,* (1) *quantity, greatness, extent,* in the proper and narrower sense of the word, i.e., the sensibly realized or physical size resulting from extension of parts. Cf. *quantitas corporalis* under 2, (2) *quantity, greatness, extent* in the general and wider sense of the word, i.e., *strength, circumference, distance,* synonym of *magnitudo.—quantitas* in this the narrow sense of the word is one of the ten categories of Aristotle. See *praedicamentum* under 2. On **aequale secundum quantitatem et quantitatem absolutam,** see *aequalis* under 1; on **aequalitas quantitatis,** see *aequalitas* under 1; on **contactus quantitatis,** see *contactus;* on **divisio quantitatis, per quantitatem et secundum quantitatem,** see *divisio;* on **finis quantitatis,** see *finis* under 1; on **indivisibile quantitatis seu secundum quantitatem,** see *indivisibilis;* on **infinitum quantitatis, in quantitate et secundum quantitatem,** see *infinitus;* on **magnum quantitatis proportionis et secundum quantitatem absolutam,** see *magnus;* on **materia quantitatis subiecta,** see *materia* under 3; on **motus in quantitate seu secundum quantitatem,** see *motus* under 1; on **mutatio secundum quantitatem,** see *mutatio;* on **pars quantitatis,** see *pars* under 1; on **passio quantitatis,** see *passio* under 1; on **posterius secundum quantitatem,** see *posterior* under 1; on **principium quantitatis,** see *principium;* on **prius per ordinem quantitatis seu secundum quantitatem,** see *prior* under 1; on **tactus quantitatis,** see *tactus* under

1; on **terminus quantitatis**, see *terminus* under 1; on **totalitas quantitatis seu secundum quantitatem**, see *totalitas;* on **totum quantitatis**, see *totus* under 1; on **unitas quantitatis**, see *unitas.*— Kinds of *quantitas* in this sense are: (a), **quantitas absoluta** and **quantitas comparata seu proportionalis seu proportionis**, *the absolute* or *simple quantity and the compared* or *proportional quantity.*—(b), **quantitas comparata**, see *quantitas absoluta.*—(c), **quantitas completa seu perfecta** and **quantitas imperfecta**, *the complete* or *perfect* and *the incomplete* or *imperfect quantity.*—(d), **quantitas continua** and **quantitas discreta**, *the continuous quantity,* quae est magnitudo, 3 Phys. 7 d, and *the detached* or *separated quantity,* quae est multitudo, 3 Phys. 7 d. Cf. *quantitas dimensiva et numeralis.*—(e), **quantitas continua extrinseca** and **quantitas continua intrinseca**, *the extrinsic* (sc. *magnitudo*) and *the intrinsic continuous quantity* (sc. *locus et tempus*).*—*(f), **quantitas debita**, *the proper quantity.*—(g), **quantitas determinata** and **quantitas indeterminata**, *the determined quantity,* e.g., *bicubitum, tricubitum,* and *the undetermined quantity,* e.g., *magnum, parvum.*—(h), **quantitas dimensiva** and **quantitas numerabilis seu numeralis**, *the quantity of dimension and that of number.* Cf. *quantitas continua et discreta.*—(i), **quantitas discreta**, see *quantitas continua.*—(j), **quantitas finita seu terminata** and **quantitas infinita**, *the infinite* or *limited and the unlimited quantity.*—(k), **quantitas finita maxima**, *the greatest finite quantity.*—(l), **quantitas imperfecta**, see *quantitas completa.*—(m), **quantitas incommensurabilis**, *quantities which have no common measure with each other.*—(n), **quantitas indeterminata**, see *quantitas determinata.*—(o), **quantitas infinita**, see *quantitas finita.*—(p), **quantitas mathematica** and **quantitas naturalis**, *the mathematical quantity,* and *the natural* or *physical quantity.*—(q), **quantitas naturalis**, see *quantitas mathematica.*—(r), **quantitas numerabilis seu numeralis**, see *quantitas dimensiva.*—(s), **quantitas numeri**, *the quantity of a number.*—(t), **quantitas per accidens**, and **quantitas per se**, *indirectly* or *accidentally quantity* and *directly* or *essentially quantity,* i.e., that which is so because of something else and that which is so because of itself or as such.—(u), **quantitas perfecta**, see *quantitas completa.*—(v), **quantitas per posterius**, *quantity after the manner of the later.*—(w), **quantitas per se**, see *quantitas per accidens.*—(x), **quantitas positionem habens** and **quantitas positionem non habens**, *quantity which has a position,* e.g., the part of a line or of a surface or of a space or of a body of which it can be said that it is before, behind, about etc. another, and *quantity which does not have a position*, e.g., the part of a number, of a speech or of a time of which it cannot be said that it is before, behind, about etc. another.—(y), **quantitas prima**, *the first quantity*, i.e., number.—(z), **quantitas proportionalis**, see *quantitas absoluta.*—(a²), **quantitas proportionis**, see *quantitas absoluta.*—(b²), **quantitas terminata**, see *quantitas finita.* On **aequalitas secundum quantitatem virtualem**, see *aequalitas* under 2.—Kinds of *quantitas* in this (2) sense are: (a), **quantitas accidentalis**, *the unessential quantity.*—(b), **quantitas actus** and **quantitas potentiae**, *the quantity or energy of action or the extent in the objects of potentiality.*—(c), **quantitas cognitionis**, *the amount of knowledge.*—(d), **quantitas corporea seu corporis seu molis** and **quantitas virtualis seu virtutis**, *physical quantity or the quantity of the mass and the amount of power.*—(e), **quantitas corporis**, see *quantitas corporea.*—(f), **quantitas durationis**, *the greatness of duration.*—(g), **quantitas enuntiationis**, see *enuntiatio* under 2.—(h), **quantitas extensiva** and **quantitas intensiva**, *the quantity of extent and that according to energy or strength.*—(i), **quantitas fidei**, *the amount or strength of faith.*—(j), **quantitas formae**, see *forma* under 2.—(k),

quantitas habitus, see *habitus* under 4.—(l), **quantitas intensiva**, see *quantitas extensiva.*—(m), **quantitas intentionis**, *the strength of intention.*—(n), **quantitas molis**, see *quantitas corporea.*—(o), **quantitas peccati**, *the greatness or gravity of sin.*—(p), **quantitas potentiae**, see *quantitas actus.*—(q), **quantitas scientiae** and **quantitas virtutis**, *the amount or extent of knowledge, and the amount or extent of virtue.*—(r), **quantitas virtualis**, see **quantitas corporea**.—(s), **quantitas virtutis**, see *quantitas corporea et quantitas scientiae.*

quantitative, *adv.*, see *quantitativus.*

quantitativus, a, um, *adj.*, *pertaining or belonging to extension, chiefly physical, quantitative.* On **distinctio quantitativa**, see *distinctio* under 2; on **divisio quantitativa**, see *divisio;* on **mensura quantitativa**, see *mensura;* on **pars quantitativa**, see *pars* under 1; on **totalitas quantitativa**, see *totalitas;* on **totum quantitativum**, see *totus* under 1.—**quantitative**, *adv.*, *after the manner or in the sense of the proper size, quantitatively.*

quanto, *adv.*, see *quantus.*

quantum, *adv.*, see *quantus.*

quantumcumque, see *quantuscumque.*

quantus, a, um, (1) *how large, how great* Aristotelian *posos*, with *tantus, so great . . . as*, (2) *of a certain quantity or magnitude or* *number,* Aristotelian *posos.*—**in quantum,** *as far as, according as, to whatever extent, in so far as,* synonym of *secundum quod;* see *secundum.*—**quantum,** i, *n., how much, as much as.*—**quantum,** *adv., as much as, so much as, as far as.*—**quantum in** or **ad** with *acc., as far as* or *so far as concerns.*—**quanto,** *adv., by how much, by as much as, according as, usually,* used with correlative *tanto, by so much.* On **corpus quantum,** see *corpus;* on **totum quantum,** see *totus* under 1.— Kinds of *quantum* in this (2) sense are: **quantum per accidens** and **quantum per se,** *concrete extension indirectly by reason of some extended subject and extension directly.* Cf. *quantitas* under 1.

quantuscumque, tacumque, tumcumque, *adj., how great soever, of whatever size.*—**quantumcumque,** *neutr., adv., as much soever.*

quantuslibet, talibet, tumlibet, *adj., how great soever.*

quapropter, *adv., wherefore, on which account.*

quare, *adv., from what cause, on what account, wherefore, why,* (1) interrog., (2) indirect., (3) as a result of or an inference from which, *wherefore, hence, therefore.*

quarta, ae, *f.,* see *quartus.*

quarto, *adv.,* see *quartus.*

quartum, *adv.,* see *quartus.*

quartus, a, um, *num. adj., the fourth.*—**quarta,** ae, *f.,* (sc. *pars*),

a fourth part, a quarter.—**quarto,** *adv., fourthly.*—**quartum,** *adv., fourthly.*

quartus decimus, a, um, *num. adj., the fourteenth.*

quasi, *adv.,* (1) lit., (a) *as if, just as, as it were,* (b) after the comparative particles, *sic, inde,* (2) transf., *about, nearly.*

quatenus, *adv.,* (1) following *nisi, except, in so far as, to the extent,* (2) *so that, in order that, that.*

quater, *adv., num., four times.*

quaterdecies, num., *adv., forty times,* used in the S.T. only in quot.

quaternarius, a, um, *adj., consisting of four each, containing four, quaternary.*

quaterni, ae, a, *adj.,* plur., *fourfold.*

quatio, ere, no *perf.,* quassum, 3, *v. a., to agitate, shake, excite.*

quatuor, num. *adj., four.*

quatuordecim, *num. adj., fourteen.*

—que, *conj.* enclitic, a copulative particle affixed to the word that it connects; *and,* used rarely in the S.T.

quemadmodum, *adv., in what manner, how,* (1) interrog., (2) rel., (a) in gen., (b) in partic., corresponding with *sic, ita,* etc., *just as, as.*

qui, quae, quod, *pron. rel., who, which, what, that,* referring to a substantive or pronoun as antecedent. On **bonum cui fit,** see *bonus* under 2; on **finis cuius seu ut cuius et finis quo seu ut quo,** see *finis* under 2; on **intelligere id quo seu ut quo** and **intelligere**

id quod seu ut quod, see *intelle-gere* under 1; on **materia circa quam, ex qua et in qua,** see *ma-teria;* on **medium quo, in quo et sub quo,** see *medium* under 2; on **principium a quo, circa quod et ex quo,** see *principium;* on **quod quid seu quod quid est seu quod quid est esse** and **quod quid erat esse,** see *quis* under 1; on **secun-dum quod,** see *secundum;* on **sig-nificare ut quo et ut quod est,** see *significare.*—In every being one distinguishes *quo est* and *quod est,* i.e., that by which it is and that which possesses being or existence or the existence and the essence or the nature and the supposite.

quia, *conj.,* (1) *because* (2) *that,* introducing an indirect state-ment, Aristotelian *hoti,* synonym of *quod.* On **demonstratio quia,** see *demonstratio* under 3; on **quaestio quia,** see *quaestio;* on **scientia quia,** see *scientia* under 1; on **scire quia,** see *scire* un-der 1.

quicumque, quaecumque, quod-cumque, pron. rel., *whoever, whatever, whosoever, whatso-ever, every one who, every thing that, all that.*

quid, see *quis.*

quidam, quaedam, quoddam, (and *subst.* quiddam), pron. indef., (1) *a certain, a certain one, some-body, something,* (a) with an adj. to soften the assertion, (b) with-out an *adj.,* (2) *plur., some.*—

quiddam, *subst., something,* used with the *gen.,* without the *gen.*

quidditas, atis, *f., quiddity, what a thing is,* i.e., the essence of a thing, so called because in an-swer to the question, "quid est res", a statement of the essence of a thing is expected, synonym of *essentia, forma, natura, quod quid est, quod quid erat esse, species,* and *substantia.* On **com-positio quidditatis,** see *composi-tio* under 1; on **intellectus cogno-scitivus quidditatis rei seu quid-ditatem rei apprehendens,** see *in-tellectus* under 4.—Kinds of *quid-ditas* are: (a), **quidditas absoluta seu separata seu abstracta seu pura** and **quidditas recepta seu materialis,** *essence separated from matter* or *abstracted from it* or *pure* and *that united with matter* or *charged with it.*—(b); **quidditas abstracta,** see *quiddi-tas absoluta.*—(c), **quidditas com-posita seu compositi** and **quiddi-tas simplex,** *the composite and the simple essence* or *the essence of a composite and that of a sim-ple being.*—(d), **quidditas gene-ris, quidditas speciei,** and **quid-ditas individui,** *the quiddity* or *essence of a genus, that of a species, and that of an individual* or *single thing.*—(e), **quidditas individui,** see *quidditas generis.* —(f), **quidditas materialis,** see *quidditas absoluta.*—(g), **quiddi-tas pura,** see *quidditas absoluta.* —(h), **quidditas recepta,** see *quid-ditas absoluta.*—(i), **quidditas**

separata, see *quidditas absoluta.*
—(j), **quidditas simplex,** see *quidditas composita.*—(k), **quidditas
speciei,** see *quidditas generis.*—
(l), **quidditas subsistens,** *quiddity existing for itself.*

quidditativus, a, um, *adj., pertaining* or *belonging to quiddity* or
essence, does not occur in the
Summa Theologica. On **ratio
quiddativa,** see *ratio* under 8.

quidem, *adv.,* (1) *indeed, at least,
certainly, too, also,* (2) *ne . . .
quidem, not even.*

quies, etis, *f., rest, quiet, repose,
cessation,* in the proper and improper senses of the word, the
opposite of *motus.*—Kinds of
quies in the general sense of the
word are: (a), **quies animae et
quies corporalis seu corporis,** *repose of soul and repose of body.*
—(b), **quies corporalis seu corporis,** see *quies animae.*—(c), **quies
desiderii** and **quies motus,** *cessation of desire* and *that of motion*
in the proper sense of the word.—
(d), **quies extra naturam seu innaturalis seu violenta** and **quies
secundum naturam seu naturalis,**
quiet not according to nature or
the unnatural or *forced quiet and
that according to nature* or *the
natural quiet.*—(e), **quies innaturalis,** see *quies extra naturam.*—
(f), **quies mentis,** *peace of mind.*
—(g), **quies motus,** see *quies desiderii.*—(h), **quies naturalis,** see
quies extra naturam.—(i), **quies
secundum naturam,** see *quies extra naturam.*—(j), **quies spiritua-**
lis, *the spiritual peace.*—(k), **quies
violenta,** see *quies extra naturam.*

quiesco, ere, evi, and etum, 3, *v. n.*
and *a.,* (1) *to rest, stop, cease
from labor, desist from any effort,* used lit. and fig., (2) *rest, remain in a place, position* or *state,
lie still, be still.*

quietas, atis, *f., quiet, rest.*

quietatio, onis, *f., the action of
quieting; the state of being
quieted* or *quiet.*

quieto, are, 1, *v. a., to calm, to
quiet.*

quietus, a, um, *P. a., at rest, calm,
peaceful, quiet.* On **actus quietus,** see *actus* under 2; on **affectio quieta,** see *affectio.*

quilibet, quaelibet, quodlibet, *indef., pron., anyone who will,
anyone without distinction,
whom you will, no matter who,
any, all, every.*—**quamlibet,** *adv.,
how much soever, ever so much,
howsoever, as you will.*

quin, *conj.,* (1) as a *rel. particle,*
prop. qui or qui ne, and mostly,
where the relative stands for a
nom. masc. or for the *abl.* of
time, *who . . . not, that . . .not,
but . . . that, but, often* = Eng.
without followed by a *subj.
clause,* (a) in *gen.,* (b) after verbs
of *hindering, resisting, refusing,
delaying,* etc., (c) after expressions of *doubt, hesitation,* etc.,
(d) *introducing a pure result
clause* with the sense of *ut non,*
(e) with a *result clause* after
general negatives, (2) in corrections, *nay, rather.*

quindecim, *num. adj., fifteen.*

quingenti, ae, a, *num. adj., five-hundred.*

quinimo, *adv.,* (*quin* + *imo*), *nay rather.*

quinquagesimus, a, um, *num. adj., the fiftieth.*—**quinquagesima,** ae, *f., quinquagesima,* the period beginning with the Sunday immediately preceding Lent and ending with Easter.

quinquaginta, *num. adj., fifty.*

quinque, *num. adj., five.*

quinquennium, ii, *n., a period of five years, five years, a quinquennium.*

quinquies, *adv., five times.*

quintuplex, icis, *adj., fivefold, quintuple.*

quintuplus, a, um, *adj., five-fold.*

quintus, a, um, *adj., the fifth.* On **corpus quintum,** see *corpus;* on **essentia quinta,** see *essentia* under 2.

quinus, a, um, *adj., quinary.*

quippe, *adv.* and *conj.,* introducing an explanation, *for, for in fact, indeed, certainly, to be sure, by all means.*

Quirinus, i, *m.,* (a variant of Quiricus), *Quirinus,* bishop of Iberia. He wrote to Gregory the Great to inquire whether rebaptism was necessary in the case of priests and laymen who had renounced Nestorianism. Gregory replied in 601 A.D. by a letter addressed to Quirinus and the other bishops of Iberia.

quis, quid, *pron. interrog., who? which? what? why?* On **praedi-** care in quid, see *praedicare* under 2; on **quaestio quid,** see *quaestio.*—**quod quid seu quod quid est seu quod quid est esse,** the translation of the Aristotelian expression *to ti esti* = the essence of a thing, because in answer to the question, What is a thing? the statement of its essence is expected. Cf. *quidditas.* On **esse in eo quod quid est,** see *esse;* on **intellectus cognoscens quod quid est,** see *intellectus* under 4; on **intellegere in quod quid est,** see *intellegere* under 1; on **praedicare in quod quid est seu in eo quod quid est,** see *praedicare* under 2.—**indivisibile est quod est ipsius boni,** see *indivisibilis* under 1.—**quod quid erat esse,** *what kind of a being was it?* is the translation of the Aristotelian expression *to ti en einai* and has usually the same meaning as the expression *quod quid est seu quod quid est esse* with which it is often interchanged. Sometimes, however, it is used in a somewhat different sense, as when it is used as a kind of contrast to the aforementioned sense (e.g., 2 Anal. 3 f and 4 b), and then it indicates that to which the words *quid erat* refer, the essence of a thing before its state of actuality, i.e., the essence of an actually existing thing as it already was before the existence of this thing, not as something existing for itself, as Plato taught; but as a model idea in the intellect of the creator or an artist, while the expression *quod quid est seu quod quid est esse* indicates the essence of a thing *in statu exsistentiae*, i.e., as it actually is *in rerum natura*.

quis, quid, *pron. indef.*, anyone, anybody, anything; someone, somebody, something. On **infinitum quo,** see *infinitus;* on **propter quid,** see *propter;* on **secundum quid,** see *secundum.*

quisnam, quaenam, quidnam, *pron.*, *interrog.*, who, which, what pray, used in the S.T. only in quot.

quispiam, quaepiam, quodpiam, *indef. pron.*, any one, anybody, any thing, any; some one, something, some.—**ad alium quempiam,** to any one else.

quisquam, quaequam, quidquam or quodquam, *indef. pron.*, any, any one, any body, any thing, something, (1) in gen., (a) *adj.*, (b) *subst.*, (2) in partic., with *nec* (neque) *and non,* and *no one, and none, and nothing.*

quisque, quaeque, quodque, *indef. pron.*, whoever or whatever it be, each, every, every body, every one, everything.

quisquis, quaeque, quodque, and *subst.*, quicquid, quidquid, *pron. rel.*, whoever, whosoever, whatever, whatsoever, everyone who, each, every, all.—**quidquid** with the *gen.*

quivis, quaevis, quodvis, *pron. indef.*, who or whatever you please, any whatever, any one, any thing.

quo, *adv.*, to or in which place, whither, where (rel. and interrog.).

quoad, *adv.*, (1) with respect to, as to = quod attinet ad (with the *acc.* only, in the S.T.), (2) till, until.

quoadusque, *adv.*, until that, used in the S.T. only in quot.

quocirca, *conj.*, for which reason, wherefore.

quocumque, *adv.*, to whatever place, whithersoever.

quod, *conj.*, (1) that, in that, because, (2) the fact that, that, (3) that, after oporteret, videtur, manifestum est, etc., (4) that, with verbs of perceiving and declaring.

quodammodo, *adv.*, in a certain measure, in a measure.

quominus, *conj.*, that not, from, after verbs of hindering, preventing etc.

quomodo, *adv.*, in what manner, in what way, how, (1) interrog., (2) rel., (a) in gen., (b) esp. corresp. to *sic, in what manner, in the same manner, even as.*

quomodocumque, *adv.*, in what manner soever, howsoever.

quomodolibet, *adv.*, howsoever.

quonam, *adv.*, how, how far pray.

quondam, *adv.*, formerly, heretofore.

quoniam, *adv.*, since, seeing that, because, (1) with *indic.*, stating a fact (2) with *subj.*, introducing a reason conceived by the mind or given by another person,

(3) introducing an object-clause, *that.*

quoque, *conj., also, too.*

quoquomodo, *adv., in what way soever, howsoever.*

quot, *adj., indecl., how many, as many as.*

quotcumque, *adv., how many soever, as many as.*

quotidianus, a, um, *adj., of every day, daily.*—**quotidie,** *adv., daily.*

quotidie, *adv.,* see *quotidianus.*

quoties, *adv., as often as.*

quotiescumque, *adv., as often soever as.*

quotquot, *adj.,* indecl., *as many soever as.*

quotus, a, um, *adj., which* or *what in order.*

quousque, *adv., until what time, till when, how long.*

quum, *conj.,* see *cum.*

R

Raab, *indecl., f., Rahab,* a harlot of Jericho, who sheltered the Israelite spies.

Rabanus, i, *m., Rabanus Maurus,* Blessed Abbot of Fulda, Archbishop of Mainz (770-856). The Summa contains references to his De Sacramentis, De Clericorum Institutione and Enarrationes in Epist. Pauli.

rabbi, *indecl., noun,* (1) *rabbi, master, a teacher* who is not a priest, applied especially to learned doctors of the law ordained in Palestine, (2) *Rabbi Moyses,* see Moyses under 2.

rabies, em, e (gen. rabies, the other cases do not occur), *f., rage, fury, madness.*

raca, (*hraka*), *adj., worthless, contemptible,* an opprobrious Hebrew epithet.

racemus, i, *m., a cluster of grapes.*

racha, see *raca.*

Rachel, is, *f., Rachel, wife of Jacob,* mother of Joseph and Benjamin.

radicalis, e, *adj., having roots, rad-* ical, i.e., forming the root or primary beginning of something. On **umidum radicale,** see *umidus.* —**radicaliter,** *adv., in the manner* or *sense of the root, according to the root, radically,* the opposite of *consummative.* On **consistere radicaliter,** see *consistere* under 2; on **exsistere radicaliter,** see *exsistere.*

radicaliter, *adv.,* see *radicalis.*

radicatio, onis, *f., root-formation, taking root, radication.*

radicitus, *adv., by the roots, radically, utterly, completely.*

radico, are, avi, 1, *v. n.,* and **radicor,** atus, 1, *v. dep. n.,* used fig., *to strike root, take root.*—**radicatus,** a um, *rooted, having roots.*

radio, are, avi, atum, 1, *v. a., to furnish with beams, make beaming, irradiate,* used lit. and fig.

radius, ii, *m., a beam* or *ray of any shining object,* used lit. and fig.

radix, icis, *f., root* in the proper and improper sense of the word, in the latter sense the synonym of origin, first beginning, basis, fundamental doctrine, imputation, supposition. On **falsus quantum ad radicem,** see *falsus.*— Kinds of *radix* in the general sense of the word are: (a), **radix caritatis,** *the root of charity.*— (b), **radix gratiae,** *the root of grace.*—(c), **radix habitus,** *the root of a habit.* See *habitus* under 4.—(d), **radix meriti,** *the root of (supernatural) merit,* i.e., *the* grace of God.—(e), **radix peccati,** *the root of sin.*—(f), **radix quadrati,** *the square root.*—(g), **radix rationis,** *the foundation of a proof.*—(h), **radix relationis,** *the basis of the relation* (of one thing to another).—(i), **radix virtutis,** *the root of virtue.*

rado, ere, si, sum, 3, *v. a.,* (1) *to shave off with a razor,* (2) *to scrape.*—**rasus,** a, um, *P. a.,* torn down.

ramus, i, *m., a branch, bough, twig,* used lit. and fig.

rana, ae, *f., a frog.*

rancor, oris, *m., rancor, spite, an old grudge.*

rapacitas, atis, *f., greediness, rapacity.*

rapax, acis, *adj., grasping, greedy of plunder, rapacious.*

Raphael, is, *m., Raphael,* an angel mentioned in the Book of Tobias who accompanied Tobias into Media and overcame the demon Asmodeus.

rapina, ae, *f.,* in the sing. esp. *the act of robbery, to steal with vio-* lence, *the business* or *habit of plunder.*

rapio, ere, pui, ptum, 3, *v. a.,* (1) lit., (a) *to seize, carry off, draw or hurry away,* (b), with the idea of swiftness predominating, *carry off, hurry away, snatch up,* (c), *to ravish, carry off by force,* (2) *fig.,* (a), *to carry to* a state in which the mind is, as it were, freed from or raised above the body; carry to a state of mental exaltation, (b) used of abstract things, *to steal, rob.*

Rapsaces (Rabsaces), is, *m., Rapsaces.* This is not a proper name of a person, but is an Assyrian title of a superior or chief officer, and refers here to one sent by Sennacherib, King of Assyria to King Ezechias.

raptim, *adv., hastily, speedily.*

raptor, oris, *m., one who seizes by force, a robber, plunderer, abductor, ravisher.*

raptus, us, *m.,* (1) *a carrying off, robbing, plundering,* (2) *abduction* and *rape of a virgin,* (3) *rapture, ecstasy.*

rarefacio, ere, feci, factum, 3, *v. a., to make thin or rare, to rarefy* (*rarefieri* also in the S. T.).

rarefactio, onis, *f., rarefaction,* the process or act of making less rare or dense, increase of volume, the mass remaining the same, now usually of gases.

rarefactivus, a, um, *adj., rarefactive, rarefactional.*

raresco, ere, 3, v. inch. *n., to become rare, be rarefied.*

raritas, atis, *f., rarity, the state of being rare, thin or tenuous,* opposed to density.

rarus, a, um, *adj.,* (1) *rare, not dense, thin, rarefied,* (2) *rare, scarce, seldom,* occuring at remote intervals, (3) *choice, excellent, precious,* a synonym of *pretiosus.—raro, adv., rarely.*

rasio, onis, *f., a shaving, scraping.*

rasura, ae, *f., a scraping, a shaving.*

ratifico, are, avi, atum, 1, *v. a., to ratify, fix authoritatively, establish, declare or confirm the truth of.*

ratio, onis, *f., reason,* the human faculty of arriving at a truth, called a conclusion, from other previously known truths, called premises. From this proper meaning, the term is extended to many other things all more or less connected with man in his specific nature as *rational.* (1) *intelligence,* opposed to *sensus,* the faculties proper to intellectual substances, what is above the animal level, hence inclusive of volition, synonym of *intellectus* and *intelligentia,* (2) *mind, reason,* opposed to *appetitus,* any faculty of knowledge inclusive of *sensus,* (3) properly, *reason, human intelligence,* an inorganic faculty of knowledge designed for the perception of purely intelligible being, not sensible being, hence opposed to *sensus, appetitus,* and, in a sense, to *intellectus.* This faculty acts in two ways, *intuitionally,* when it apprehends truth directly, called by Aristotle *nous,* and *discursively,* when it arrives at truth indirectly through the medium of other truths, the *logistikon* of Aristotle, (4) the *act of reasoning,* the act of the faculty of reason, *discursive knowing,* as opposed to *intellectus* and *intelligentia,* synonym of *ratiocinatio,* (5) the result of the act of knowledge, *discursive knowledge, concept, notion, idea,* synonym of *conceptio, intentio, definitio, logos,* (6) *the essential elements of a thing* expressed in the rational concept, (7) *plan, pattern, mode of action* that has been reasoned out, *exemplar idea,* (8) *motive, reason,* synonym of *causa,* (9) *argumentation, proof, reasoning,* synonym of *ratiocinatio,* (10) *aspect, point of view, concept,* synonym of *intentio* and *formalitas,* (11) with *nominis,* meaning, *sense,* (12) *phrase* expressive of the essence, synonym of *oratio,* (13) *reckoning, account.—***virtus in ratione est,** *virtue is in the intellectual part of the human composite.—* Kinds of *ratio* in this (2) sense are: **ratio intellectiva seu universalis seu superior seu proprie accepta seu dicta** and **ratio particularis,** *the intellectual or universal or higher or properly so-called reason and the particular or individual reason or reason in the proper or improper senses of the term.* On **affectus secundum rationem,** see *affectus* under·2, on apprehensio rationis, see *apprehensio* under 2; on **bonum rationis seu secundum rationem**, see *bonus* under 3; on **compositio rationis**, see *compositio* under 1; on **concupiscentia cum ratione et sine ratione**, see *concupiscentia* under 1; on **dicere rationem**, see *dicere* under 1; on **ens rationis seu in rationem**, see *ens;* on **fructus rationis**, see *fructus* under 1; on **lumen rationis**, see *lumen;* on **iudicium rationis**, see *iudicium* under 4; on **medium rationis seu secundum rationem**, see *medium* under 1; on **motus rationis**, see *motus* under 2; on **negatio rationis tantum**, see *negatio* under 2; on **notum rationis seu secundum rationem**, see *notus;* on **peccatum rationis**, see *peccatum* under 1; on **pluralitas rationis**, see *pluralitas;* on **potentia cum ratione**, see *potentia* under 2; on **prius rationis seu secundum rationem**, see *prior* under 1; on **processus rationis**, see *processus* under 3; on **rectitudo rationis**, see *rectitudo* under 3; on **relatus rationis per rationem**, see *relatus;* on **res rationis seu rationis tantum**, see *res;* on **scintilla rationis**, see *scintilla;* on **usus rationis**, see *usus* under 1; on **veritas rationis** see *veritas* under 3; on **via rationis**, see *via* under 1; on **voluntas secundum rationem**, see *voluntas* under 2 and 3.—**cum ratione,** *with reason, rational.*—**praeter rationem,** *beyond reason, unattainable by reason.*—**secundum**

rationem, *according to reason, corresponding to the comprehensive power of reason.*—**supra rationem,** *above reason, beyond the comprehension of human reason.* —Kinds of *ratio* in this (3) sense are: (a), **ratio deliberans seu deliberativa seu ratio inquisitiva,** *reason moved by the will or investigating reason.*—(b), **ratio denuntians** and **ratio praecipiens,** the *logos delosas kai keleusas* of Aristotle (Problem. 38. 3, 949. b. 18), *the declaring* or *publishing reason and the prescribing* or *commanding reason.*—(c), **ratio factiva,** *the creative* or *productive idea according to which things are made;* a kind of the *ratio operativa.*—(d), **ratio fide informata** and **ratio naturalis,** *the reason formed or illuminated by faith and the natural reason or that without revelation or grace.* Cf. also *ratio naturalis* under 13. —(e), **ratio humana,** *human intelligence as opposed to divine and angelic intelligence.*—(f), **ratio inferior** and **ratio superior,** *the lower and the higher reason,* i.e., reason as concerned with earthly affairs, and as concerned with heavenly things.*—(g), **ratio inquisitiva,** see *ratio deliberans.*—(h), **ratio naturalis,** see *ratio fide informata.*—(i), **ratio obumbrata,** *the clouded* or *confused reason.*— (j), **ratio operativa seu practica** and **ratio speculativa seu scientifica,** *the nous praktikos pai the-*

oretikos of Aristotle, *reason concerned with action and deed and reason concerned solely with knowledge.*—(k), **ratio particularis** and **ratio universalis,** *the general and particular reason* or *that comprehending something general and that comprehending something special.*—(l), **ratio per essentiam** and **ratio per participationem,** *reason according to essence and reason according to participation* i.e., the faculty which according to its essence and that which through participation in such is rational.—(m), **ratio per participationem,** see *ratio per essentiam.*—(n), **ratio practica,** see *ratio operativa.*—(o), **ratio praecipiens,** see *ratio denuntians.*—(p), **ratio scientifica,** see *ratio operativa.*—(q), **ratio speculativa,** see *ratio operativa.*—(r), **ratio superior,** see *ratio inferior.*—(s), **ratio universalis,** see *ratio particularis.*—(t), **ratio ut natura** and **ratio ut ratio,** *reason as a nature* or *as a thing of nature and reason as reason or as a discursive intellectual power.*—(u), **ratio ut ratio,** see *ratio ut natura.*—**ratio contra naturam dividitur,** *reason is differentiated as opposed to nature.*—**ratio est universalium, sensus vero particularium,** *reason has the universal as its object, sense the special* or *particular.* Cf. *intellectus* under 3, and *scientia* under 3.—**voluntas in ratione est,** the translation of the Aristotelian passage: *en to logistiko he*

boulesis ginetai, the will as appetite follows the objects presented by the reason, and is therefore rooted in the intellect as its principle and subject. Cf. *voluntas* under 3; *intellectus* under 1.—One kind of *ratio* in this (4) sense is: **ratio prudentiae,** *the comprehension* which is *pars integralis* of *prudentia.*—Kinds of *ratio* in this (5) sense are: (a), **ratio absoluta** and **ratio dependens,** *concept without relation* (to anything else), and *dependent concept,* or essence understood without relation to anything else, and that which is understood in relationship to something.—(b), **ratio adaequata seu per modum adaequationem,** *concept wholly expressive of the essence,* or *serving as such.*—(c), **ratio appropriata,** *the appropriated concept.*—(d), **ratio definitiva seu quidditativa seu significans quid est seu significativa illius quod quid est,** the translation of Aristotle's expression: *logos horistikos; to ti en einai;* and *logos ho ti en einai, the rational representation that designates* or *expresses the essence of a thing,* i.e. the definition.—(e), **ratio exponens nominis significationem seu expositiva nominis seu significationis nominis seu interpretativa nominis** and **ratio expositiva seu manifestativa ipsius rei nominatae,** *the rational representation that explains* or *expresses a name or* *its meaning and that which explains or makes known the thing mentioned itself.*—(f), **ratio expositiva ipsius rei nominatae,** see *ratio exponens nominis significationem.*—(g), **ratio expositiva nominis,** see *ratio exponens nominis significationem.*—(h), **ratio expositiva significationis nominis,** see *ratio exponens nominis significationem.*—(i), **ratio generis** and **ratio speciei seu specifica,** *the concept of genus and that of species.*—(j), **ratio idealis,** *essence existing in a mind.*—(k), **ratio imperfecta,** and **ratio perfecta,** *the imperfect and the perfect concept.*—(l), **ratio in materia,** the *logos enylos* of Aristotle, *the concept in matter* or *the essential concept joined with matter* (habens esse in materia). Cf. *ratio concreta* above.—(m), **ratio intellecta seu intellegibilis,** *the essence perceived by the intellect* or *perceivable by it.*—(n), **ratio perfecta,** see *ratio imperfecta.*—(o), **ratio per modum adaequationis,** see *ratio adaequata.*—(p), **ratio quidditativa,** see *ratio definitiva.*—(q), **ratio scibilis,** *the knowable* or *rationally perceptible notion.*—(r), **ratio significans quid est,** see *ratio definitiva.*—(s), **ratio significativa illius quod quid est,** see *ratio definitiva.*—(t), **ratio speciei,** see *ratio generis.*—(u), **ratio specifica,** see *ratio generis.*—**ratio cuiuslibet speciei substantiae consistit in indivisibili,** *the concept of*

every species of substance is something indivisible. On **ad aliquid secundum rationem tantum,** see *ad* under 2; on **alius secundum rationem,** see *alius;* on **alter secundum rationem,** see *alter* under 2; on **communicare rationem,** see *communicare under* 1; on **communis ratio,** see *communis* under 1; on **communitas rationis et rationis fundatae in re,** see *communitas* under 1; on **compositio secundum rationem,** see *compositio* under 1; on **differre ratione seu secundum rationem,** see *differre* under 2; on **discretio secundum rationem,** see *discretio* under 2; on **distinctio secundum rationem tantum,** see *distinctio* under 2; on **distingui ratione,** see *distinguere;* on **diversitas rationis,** see *diversitas;* on **diversus ratione,** see *diversus;* on **divisio secundum rationem,** see *divisio;* on **eiusdem rationis est,** see *idem;* on **filiatio rationis tantum,** see *filiatio;* on **idem ratione seu secundum rationem,** see *idem;* on **incommunicabile ratione seu secundum rationem,** see *incommunicabilis;* on **pars rationis,** see *pars* under 1; on **primum ratione,** see *primus;* on **prius rationem seu secundum rationem,** see *prior* under 1; on **relatio rationis seu rationis tantum seu secundum rationem seu solum secundum rationem,** see *relatio;* on **res rationis,** see *res;* on **simul secundum rationem,** see *simul;* on **terminus rationis,** see *terminus* under 1; on **unum ratione seu secundum rationem,** see *unus;* on **veritas rationis,** see *veritas* under 1.—Kinds of *ratio* in this (6) sense are: (a), **ratio absoluta** and **ratio concreta,** *essence abstracted from matter,* and *essence united with matter.* Cf. also *ratio in materia.*—(b), **ratio aeternitatis** and **ratio temporis,** *the essential notion of eternity and that of time.* —Kinds of *ratio* in this (7) sense are: (a), **ratio aeterna seu divina** and **ratio temporalis seu humana,** *the eternal* or *divine and the temporal* or *human plans.*—(b), **ratio agibilium, ratio factibilium** and **ratio scibilium seu speculabilium,** *the reasonable plan* or *mode which should guide man in his actions (agibilia), his works (factibilia)* and *his knowledge (scibilia).*—(c), **ratio architectonica seu principativa seu dominativa,** *the architectural* or *ruling* or *commanding plan by which is meant the virtus politica.*—(d), **ratio corrupta seu perversa seu errans seu falsa seu non recta** and **ratio recta,** *the corrupt* or *perverse* or *false* or *not right and the right (because reasonable) norm* or *mode of activity.*—(e), **ratio dominativa,** see *ratio architectonica.*—(f), **ratio errans,** see *ratio corrupta.*—(g), **ratio factibilium,** see *ratio agibilium.*—(h), **ratio falsa,** see *ratio corrupta.*—(i), **ratio non recta,** see *ratio corrupta.*—(j), **ratio perversa,** see *ratio corrupta.*—(k), **ratio principativa,**

see *ratio architectonica.*—(l), **ratio recta,** see *ratio corrupta.*—(m), **ratio scibilium,** see *ratio agibilium.*—(n), **ratio speculabilium,** see *ratio agibilium.*—**ars est recta ratio factibilium,** see *ars* under 2.—**prudentia est recta ratio agibilium,** see *prudentia* under 1.—**scientia est recta ratio scibilium seu speculabilium,** see *scientia* under 1.—Kinds of *ratio* in this (8) sense are: (a), **ratio cognoscendi** and **ratio volendi,** *the cause* or *reason for knowing something* and *the cause* or *reason* or *motive for wishing for something.*—(b), **ratio creata** and **ratio divina,** *the created and the divine motive.*—(c), **ratio disponens,** *the preparing cause.*—(d), **ratio divina,** see *ratio creata.*—(e), **ratio oboedientialis seu seminalis,** *the obedient* or *the seminal cause.*—(f), **ratio seminalis,** see *ratio oboedientialis.*—(g), **ratio volendi,** see *ratio cognoscendi.* On **radix rationis,** see *radix;* on **virtus rationis,** see *virtus* under 6; on **vis rationis,** see *vis* under 2.—Kinds of *ratio* in this (9) sense are: (a), **ratio analytica** and **ratio logica,** *demonstrative and the merely dialectical proof,* (cf. *ratio logica* under 10).—(b), **ratio argumentativa seu ostensiva** and **ratio deducens seu ducens ad impossibile seu ad inconveniens,** *the proof that shows something is true directly* and *the proof that leads to the impossible* or *the absurd* or *the proof that shows the contra-*

dictory proposition to be an absurdity or *unfitting,* i.e., *the direct* and *indirect proof.*—(c), ratio astrologica and ratio mathematica, *the astronomical* and *the mathematical argumentation.*—(d) ratio circularis, *the circular proof.*—(e), ratio coadiuvans, *the cooperative* or *supporting proof.* —(f), ratio communis seu universalis and ratio propria, *the general and the special proof,* i.e., the proof based on the general principles and that based on the proper principle of a science. Cf. *ratio communis et propria* under 10.—(g), ratio demonstrativa seu necessaria and ratio probabilis seu non necessaria seu topica seu verisimilis, *the proof demonstrating something as necessarily true* and *the persuasive proof that shows something probable* or *the proof of probability.*—(h), ratio deducens ad impossibile seu ad inconveniens, see *ratio argumentativa.*—(i), ratio disputantis contra positionem seu disputativa, *the dialectical proof employed in the disputation* or *serving as the refutation of an assertion.*—(j), ratio disputativa, see *ratio disputantis contra positionem.*—(k), ratio ducens ad impossibile seu ad inconveniens, see *ratio argumentativa.*—(l), ratio efficax, *the efficacious* or *convincing proof.*—(m), ratio exterior and ratio interior, *the exterior* or *spoken proof* and *the interior* or *contemplated proof.*—(n), ratio extranea, *the ex-*

terior or *extraneous proof.*—(o), ratio frivola, *the insignificant* or *absurd proof.*—(p), ratio humana, *the human proof* or *the proof brought forth by human means.* Cf. *ratio humana* under 3.—(q), ratio improbabilis, *the improbable proof.*—(r), ratio inductiva, *the inductive proof.*—(s), ratio intelligibilis, *the rational proof.*— (t), ratio interior, see *ratio exterior.*—(u), ratio irrefragabilis, *the irrefutable proof.*—(v), ratio litigiosa, *the disputable proof.*—(w), ratio logica, see *ratio analytica.*— (x), ratio mathematica, see *ratio astrologica.*—(y), ratio metaphysica and ratio physica, *the metaphysical* and *the physical proof.* —(z), ratio naturalis, *the proof from the physical sciences* or *the natural proof,* i.e., the proof that does not go beyond nature and its course. Cf. also *ratio physica.* —(a²), ratio necessaria, see *ratio demonstrativa.*—(b²), ratio non necessaria, see *ratio demonstrativa.*—(c²), ratio ostensiva, see *ratio argumentativa.*—(d²), ratio persuasoria, *the persuasive proof.* See *ratio demonstrativa.*—(e²), ratio philosophica, *the philosophical reason.*—(f²), ratio physica, see *ratio metaphysica.*—(g²), ratio principalis, *the principal reason.* —(h²), ratio probabilis, see *ratio demonstrativa.*—(i²), ratio profunda, *the profound reason.*—(j²), ratio propria, see *ratio communis.* —(k²), ratio sacramentalis, *the sacramental reason* or *that taken from a sacrament.*—(l²), **ratio so-phistica,** *the sophistic proof.*—(m²), **ratio topica,** see *ratio demonstrativa.*—(n²), **ratio universalis,** see *ratio communis.*—(o²), **ratio verisimilis,** see *ratio demonstrativa.*—Kinds of *ratio* in this (10) sense are: (a), **ratio appetibilitatis,** *the aspect of desirability* or *appetibility.*—(b), **ratio boni** and **ratio mali,** *the aspect of good* and *that of evil.*—(c), **ratio causae efficientis, ratio causae finalis seu finis,** and **ratio causae formalis,** *the aspect* or *the concept of agent cause, that of final cause, and that of formal cause* or *that acting after the manner of form.*—(d), **ratio causae finalis,** see *ratio causae efficientis.*—(e), **ratio causae formalis,** see *ratio causae efficientis.*—(f), **ratio cognoscibilis seu scibilis,** *the aspect under which a thing is knowable* or *considered.* (cf. *diversa ratio cognoscibilis diversitatem scientiarum inducit* under *scientia* under 1).—(g), **ratio communis seu indeterminata** and **ratio propria seu determinata,** *the general* or *undetermined aspect* and *the proper* or *determined aspect.*—(h), **ratio convenientis** and **ratio non convenientis,** *the aspect of the advantageous* or *advantageousness* and *the aspect of the disadvantageous* or *disadvantageousness.*—(i), **ratio determinata,** see *ratio communis.*—(j), **ratio finis,** see *ratio causa efficientis.*—(k), **ratio formalis,** *the formal* or

proper aspect or *consideration.*—(l), **ratio formalis obiecti,** see *obiectum.*—(m), **ratio indeterminata,** see *ratio communis.*—(n), **ratio logica,** *the logical aspect* or *that arising from the consideration by the mind.*—(o), **ratio mali,** see *ratio boni.*—(p), **ratio non convenientis,** see *ratio convenientis.* —(q), **ratio notificans personam,** *the concept that identifies a divine person.*—(r), **ratio obiecti,** see *obiectum.*—(s), **ratio personae,** *the aspect of person* or *personality.*—(t), **ratio propria,** see *ratio communis.*—(u), **ratio scibilis,** see *ratio cognoscibilis.*—(v), **ratio singularitatis,** *the aspect of singleness* or *individuality.*—Kinds of *ratio* in this (11) sense are: **ratio figuralis, ratio litteralis,** and **ratio mystica,** *the figurative, the literal, and the mystical sense.*

ratiocinatio, onis, *f.,* (1) *rational act of discursive knowledge, activity of concluding* or *deducting,* synonym of *discursus* and *ratio,* the opposite of *intellectus,* (2) *the habit of concluding* or *deducting,* synonym of *ratio,* the opposite of *intellectus,* (3) *deducting, computation,* synonym of *ratio* and *ratiocinium.*—Kinds of *ratiocinatio* in this (1) sense are: **ratiocinatio falsa** and **ratiocinatio recta,** *the wrong and the right drawing of conclusion.*

ratiocinativus, a, um, *adj., of* or *belonging to reason* and *concluding, knowing discursively,* synonym of *discursivus*, the opposite of *intellectivus*. On **cognitio ratiocinativa**, see *cognitio* under 2; on **consideratio ratiocinativa**, see *consideratio;* on **intellectus ratiocinativus**, see *intellectus* under 3; on **pars ratiocinativa**, see *pars* under 1; on **scientia ratiocinativa**, see *scientia* under 2.—**ratiocinativum** sc. **principium animae**, the translation of the Aristotelian expression *logistikon*, synonym of *opinativum*, the opposite of *scientificum*, *the principle of calculative* or *deliberative knowledge*, i.e., the faculty or the aptitude for pondering variable and contingent things.

ratiocinium, i, *n.*, *a reckoning, computation, calculation, account*, synonym of *ratio* and *ratiocinatio.*

ratiocinor, ari, atus, 1, *v. dep. n.* and *a.*, *to think discursively, perceive discursively, conclude, infer*, synonym of *discurrere*, the opposite of *intellegere*. On the difference between *ratiocinari* and *intellegere* we read: ratiocinari comparatur ad intellegere, sicut moveri ad quiescere vel adquirere ad habere, quorum unum est perfecti, aliud autem imperfecti. On **agere ut ratiocinans**, see *agere* under 1; on **intellectus ratiocinans seu ratio discurrens**, see *intellectus* under 4; on **intellegere ratiocinando**, see *intellegere* under 1.

rationabilis, e, *adj.*, *reasonable, rational*, the opposite of *irrationa-*bilis and *irrationalis*. On **causa rationabilis**, see *causa* under 3; on **instantia rationabilis**, see *instantia* under 1; on **natura rationabilis**, see *natura;* on **pars rationabilis**, see *pars* under 1; on **voluntas rationabilis**, see *voluntas* under 1.—**in rationabili est voluntas**, *the will is in the rational part of the human soul*. Cf. *ratio* under 3.—**rationabiliter**, *adv.*, (1) *rationally, reasonably*, synonym of *rationaliter*, (2) *with probability, probably*. On **procedere rationabiliter**, see *procedere* under 2; on **sumere rationabiliter**, see *sumere* under 3.

rationabilitas, atis, *f.*, *reasonableness, rationalization*, synonym of *rationalitas*, the opposite of *irrationabilitas*.

rationabiliter, *adv.*, see *rationabilis*.

rationalis, e, *adj.*, (1) *rational*, i.e., belonging to the rational part of the human nature, *being of a rational nature*, synonym of *intellectualis* and *intellegibilis*, the opposite of *animalis, irrationalis*, and *sensibilis*, (2) *rational*, i.e., having reason, *concerning reason*, (3) *knowing rationally* in the general and broader sense of the word, i.e., knowing intuitively as well as discursively with the mind, synonym of *intellectivus* and *intellectualis*, the opposite of *sensibilis* and *sensitivus*, (4) *knowing rationally* in the proper and narrower sense of the word, i.e., knowing discursively with the mind, the opposite of *intel-*

lectualis, (5) *conceivable, intel-*
lectually imaginable, the opposite of *irrationalis*, (6) *ornament*
worn in giving a judicial deci-
sion, i.e., the breastplate of the
high priest in the Old Testament,
Rational. On **amor rationalis**,
see *amor* under 1; on **animal ra-**
tionale, see *animal* under 1; on
appetitus rationalis, see *appetitus*
under 1 and 2; on **pars rationalis**,
see *pars* under 1; on **phantasia**
rationalis, see *phantasia* under 3;
on **potentia rationalis**, see *poten-*
tia under 2; on **potestas rationa-**
lis, see *potestas* under 2; on **vir-**
tus rationalis, see *virtus* under 1;
on **vita rationalis**, see *vita* under 1; on **voluntas rationalis**,
see *voluntas* under 1 and 3.—
Kinds of *rationalis* in this (2)
sense are: **rationalis essentialiter**
seu per essentiam and **ratio par-**
ticipative seu per participatio-
nem, *rational essentially* or *ac-*
cording to its essence and ration-
al through participation. On **an-**
ima rationalis, see *anima* under
1; on **natura rationalis**, see *natu-*
ra; on **spiritus rationalis**, see *spi-*
ritus; on **substantia rationalis**, see
substantia under 2. On **conside-**
ratio rationalis, see *consideratio;*
on **natura rationalis**, see *natura;*
on **processus rationalis**, see *pro-*
cessus under 2. On **linea ratio-**
nalis, see *linea* under 1.—**rationa-**
liter, *adv., in a reasonable man-*
ner, reasonably, rationally, synonym of *rationabiliter.*

rationalitas, atis, *f., reasonableness,*
faculty of rational reason, ration-
ality.
rationaliter, *adv.*, see *rationalis.*
ratus, a, um, *P. a.*, (1) *valid*, (2)
ratified, (3) *conferred.*
Razias, used only in the *nom.*,
Razias, an elder of Jerusalem,
called "Father of the Jews" for
his goodness towards them.
rea, ae, *f.*, with a statement of the
punishment or crime, *one guilty*
of any crime.
reaedificatio, onis, *f., a rebuilding.*
reaedifico, are, 1, *v. a., to build*
again, rebuild.
realis, e, *adj., real, extramental,* existing or present, even though
only potentially as a state of
quality of things; having a foundation in fact; not merely in the
mind. Real is not synonymous
with actual.—**realiter**, *adv., real-*
ly, in a real manner.
realiter, *adv.*, see *realis.*
reamo, are, avi, atum, 1, *v. a., to*
love reciprocally.
reappareo, ere, ui, itum, 2, *v. n., to*
reappear.
reassumo, ere, mpsi, mptum, 3, *v.*
a., to take back.
reatus, us, *m., the condition of the*
accused person, a state of im-
peachment, state of guilt, punish-
able state.—Kinds of *reatus* are:
(a), **reatus ingratitudinis**, *the*
guilty state of ungratefulness.—
(b), **reatus peccati** and **reatus**
poenae, *the guilty state of sin*
and that of punishment.—(c),
reatus poenae, see *reatus peccati.*

rebaptizator, oris, *m.,* *a rebaptist,* one who baptizes or is baptized again.

rebaptizo, are, 1, *v. a., to baptize again, rebaptize.*

rebellio, onis, *m., a revolt, rebellion,* used lit. and fig.

rebellis, e, *adj., that makes war afresh, insurgent, rebellious.*

rebello, are, avi, atum, 1, *v. n., to rebel.*

recapitulatio, onis, *f., recapitulation.*

recedo, ere, cessi, cessum, 3, *v. n., to go back, fall back, give ground, retire, withdraw, recede.*

recens, entis, *adj., that has not long existed, fresh, recent, new.—recenter,* adv., *newly, recently.*

recenter, adv., see *recens.*

receptaculum, i, *n.,* (1) *a refuge,* any place into which persons are received or retire esp. for shelter or security, a synonym of *domus,* (2) *an abode,* a place of abiding for the soul after death, (3) *a receptacle,* that which receives and holds something, here, the womb of the Blessed Virgin.

receptator, oris, *m., in a bad sense, a hider, harborer, concealer.*

receptibilis, e, *adj., that may be received, suitable for reception* or *belief, receivable.*

receptio, onis, *f., a receiving, reception.*

receptive, adv., see *receptivus.*

receptivus, a, um, *adj., receiving, receptive,* synonym of *passivus, recipiens,* and *susceptivus,* the opposite of *activus.* On **operatio**

receptiva, see *operatio* under 2; on **potentia receptiva,** see *potentia* under 1.—**receptive,** *adv., in the manner* or *in the sense of receiving, receptively,* synonym of *passive,* the opposite of *active.*

recepto, are, avi, 1, *v.* freq. *a., to receive back.*

recessio, onis, *f., a going back, withdrawal.*

recessus, us, *m.,* (1) *the act of retiring, withdrawing* or *departing, withdrawal, departure,* (2) *a withdrawal from some state* or *standard.*

recidivo, are, avi, atum, 1, *v. n., to fall back, relapse.*

recidivum, i, *n., relapse into sin* or *error.*

recido, ere, reccidi, casum, 3, *v. n., to fall back, return.*

recipio, ere, cepi, ceptum, 3, *v. a., to take to oneself, accept, receive,* synonym of *pati,* the opposite of *agere.* On **quidditas recepta,** see *quidditas;* on **unitas recepta in aliquo,** see *unitas;* on **unum in aliquo receptum,** see *unus.*—Kinds of *recipere* are: (a), **recipere active** and **recipere passive,** *to receive in the active and in the passive sense of the word.* —(b), **recipere divise seu multipliciter,** *to receive in a divided and in a manifold manner.*—(c), **recipere immaterialiter seu spiritualiter** and **recipere materialiter,** *to receive in an immaterial* or *spiritual way* and *to receive in a material* or *physical way.*—(d), **recipere materialiter,** see *reci-*

pere immaterialiter.—(e), **recipere multipliciter,** see *recipere divise.* —(f), **recipere passive,** see *recipere active.*—(g), **recipere spiritualiter,** see *recipere immaterialiter.*—(h), **recipere univoce,** *to receive univocally.*—**recipiens** sc. **principium,** the translation of the Aristotelian expressions *dechomenon* and *dektikon,* designates the subject or the matter of something.—**nihil recipitur in aliquo nisi secundum proportionem recipientis,** or, **omne quod recipitur in aliquo, recipitur seu est in eo per modum recipientis,** or, **quod est in altero, est in eo per modum recipientis,** or, **quod recipitur in aliquo, est in eo per modum recipientis,** or, **quod recipitur in aliquo, recipitur in eo per modum eius in quo est,** or, **receptum est in recipiente secundum seu per modum recipientis,** or, **unumquodque recipitur in altero per modum recipientis,** *that which is received in a thing, is received into the same and has in it the same manner of existence as the thing that receives.*

reciprocus, a, um, *adj., reciprocal.*

recitatio, onis, *f., recitation,* the act of rehearsing, detailing, or enumerating; *recital.*

recitative, *adv., of the nature of, in the style of a recital; recitatively.*

recito, are, avi, atum, 1, *v. a.,* (1) *to relate, go through* or *over in detail,* (2) *to relate, mention, narrate, tell,* (3) *to repeat* or *ut-*

ter aloud something previously composed or heard.

reclamo, are, avi, atum, 1, *v. n.* and *a., to demur, offer objections* or *difficulties; cry out against.*

reclino, are, avi, atum, 1, *v. a., to recline, lie.*

recludo, ere, si, sum, 3, *v. a., to shut up.*

recogitatio, onis, *f., a recollection, reflection.*

recogito, are, avi, atum, 1, *v. a., to think over, consider, reflect upon.*

recognitio, onis, *f., recognition,* formal acknowledgement that one knows or accepts something.

recognosco, ere, gnovi, gnitum, 3, *v. a.,* (1) *to recognize, know again, call to mind, recollect,* (2) *to recognize, admit to oneself.*

recolligo, ere, legi, lectum, 3, *v. a., to shelter, harbor, to give refuge* or *shelter to.*

recolo, ere, colui, cultum, 3, *v. a., to recollect, remember.*

recompensatio, onis, *f.,* (1) *acknowledgement, compensation, a return* in gratitude, justice or friendship, for something received, (2) *reparation* made to someone for some wrong done to him; *atonement* or *satisfaction* for some offense.

recompenso, are, aturus, 1, *v. a., to recompense, to repay, give compensation to, to reward* for something done or given; *make compensation* for a misdeed or wrong; *to make up for* some loss or injury suffered, used with the *dat., acc., absol.*

reconciliatio, onis, *f., a reconciling, reconciliation.*

reconcilio, are, avi, atum, 1, *v. a., to reconcile, bring together again, reunite,* (1) in religious use, of God and man, *to reconcile,* (2) Eccl., *to reconcile,* purify a church by a special ritual after profanation; a church is said *reconciliari, to be reconciled,* when it is consecrated afresh after being polluted or profaned, (3) *to bring back, restore* or *readmit to the Church* (4) *to win over again to friendship with one's self* or *another.*

reconditus, a, um, *P. a.,* see *recondo.*

recondo, ere, didi, ditum, 3, *v. a.,* (1) *to hide away* in a purse, (2) *to bury,* (3) *to put away* in a hiding place.—**reconditus,** a, um, *P. a., put away.*

recordatio, onis, *f., recollection, a recalling to mind;* the act, process or power of recalling to mind the mental images or ideas of past experience.

recordativus, a, um, *adj., of* or *belonging to recollection, recordative.*

recordor, ari, atus, 1, *v. dep.* and *n., to remember, call to mind, recollect,* used with *gen., acc., absol., obj. clause.*

recreatio, onis, *f.,* (1) *re-creation,* in religious use, the process or fact of being born again in a

spiritual sense; the state resulting from this in which only the just are found, (2) *recreation, comfort, refreshment* or *consolation,* (3) *re-creation,* a second creation of human nature.

recreo, are, avi, atum, 1, *v. a., to create anew, recreate.*

rectificatio, onis, *f., rectification, a setting straight* or *right; improvement, correction.*

rectifico, are, avi, atum, 1, *v. a., to rectify, regulate, control, govern* or *direct by rule* or *regulations.*

rectilineus, a, um, *adj., rectilinear.*

rectitudo, inis, *f.,* (1) *straightness, rectilinearity, directness,* (2) *right position, vertical position,* (3) *rectitude, rightness, truth.*—Kinds of *rectitudo* in this (3) sense are: (a), **rectitudo bonitatis, rectitudo iustitiae,** and **rectitudo veritatis,** *measure of goodness, that of justice, and that of truth.*—(b), **rectitudo in intentione seu intentionis** and **rectitudo in opere,** *rectitude of intention and that of deed.*—(c), **rectitudo in opere,** see *rectitudo in intentione.*—(d), **rectitudo iustitiae,** see *rectitudo bonitatis.*—(e), **rectitudo naturalis,** *rectitude according to nature* or *natural rectitude.*—(f), **rectitudo practica,** *practical rectitude* or *truth.*—(g), **rectitudo rationis** and **rectitudo voluntatis,** *the rectitude of reason* (in the act of thinking) and *the rectitude of the will* (in act of its desiring). —(h), **rectitudo veritatis,** see *rec-*

titudo bonitatis.—(i), **rectitudo voluntatis,** see *rectitudo rationis.*

recto, *adv.,* see *rectus.*

rector, oris, *m., a guide, leader, ruler, master.*

rectus, a, um, *adj.,* (1) *straight, rectilinear, going straight forward,* the opposite of *curvus,* (2) *going straight upward, upright, vertical,* the opposite of *obliquus,* (3) *the case which stands upright* in the grammatical sense, the *nominative,* the opposite of *obliquus,* (4) *upright, conformed to some measure, just, true.* On **corpus rectum,** see *corpus;* on **fieri in rectum,** see *fieri;* on **generatio recta seu secundum rectum,** see *generatio* under 1; on **linea recta,** see *linea* under 1; on **magnitudo recta,** see *magnitudo* under 1; on **motus rectus,** see *motus* under 1. —In **recto,** *in the nominative,* the opposite of *obliquo.* On **importare in recto,** see *importare* under 2; on **ponere in recto,** see *ponere* under 1; on **praedicare in recto,** see *praedicare* under 2; on **significare in recto,** see *significare.* On **conscientia recta,** see *conscientia* under 3; on **dilectio recta et non recta,** see *dilectio* under 1; on **divisio recta,** see *divisio;* on **electio recta,** see *electio* under 1; on **existimatio recta,** see *existimatio;* on **fides recta,** see *fides* under 2; on **intellectus rectus,** see *intellectus* under 8; on **iudicium rectum,** see *iudicium*

under 2; on **motus rectus,** see *motus* under 2; on **operatio recta et non recta,** see *operatio* under 2; on **opinio recta,** see *opinio;* on **opus rectum,** see *opus* under 4; on **ordo rectus,** see *ordo* under 1; on **politia recta,** see *politia* under 1; on **ratio recta et non recta,** see *ratio* under 6; on **ratiocinatio recta,** see *ratiocinatio* under 1; on **regimen rectum,** see *regimen;* on **regula recta,** see *regula* under 1; on **scientia recta,** see *scientia* under 1; on **sensus rectus,** see *sensus* under 3; on **vita recta,** see *vita* under 3.—**recte,** *adv.,* (1) lit., *in a straight line, straightly,* (2) trop., *rightly, correctly, properly, duly, suitably, well, advantageously, accurately.*

recumbo, ere, cubui, 3, *v. n., to recline at table.*

recuperatio, onis, *f., a getting back, regaining, recovery, recuperation.*

recupero, are, avi, atum, 1, *v. a., to recover, regain, get* or *obtain,* (1) a material thing, (2) an immaterial thing, (3) health.

recurro, ere, curri, 3, *v. n.,* (1) lit., *to go back, hasten back,* (2) fig., in partic., *to have recourse to, resort to.*

recursus, us, *m., resort,* or *application to some person* or *thing for assistance, help* or *safety,* freq. in the phrase, **habere recursum,** *to have recourse to.*

recusatio, onis, *f., a declining, refusal.*

recuso, are, avi, atum, 1, *v. a.*, *to refuse, reject, decline, be reluctant* or *unwilling to do a thing.*

redamatio, onis, *f.*, *the action of returning love.*

redamo, are, 1, *v. a.*, *to love in return, return love for love.*

redarguo, ere, ui, 3, *v. a.*, *to disprove, refute, contradict, find fault with, condemn, reprove.*

redarguitio, onis, *f.*, *a refutation, reproof, defence,* used in the S.T. only in quot.

redargutive, *adv.*, *in the manner* and *sense of a refutation.* On **demonstrare redargutive,** see *demonstrare* under 3.

redditio, onis, *f.*, *a giving back, returning.*—**debiti redditio,** *payment of a debt.*

redditor, oris, *m.*, *one who pays, a payer.*

reddo, ere, didi, ditum, 3, *v. a.*, (1) *to give up, hand over, yield, render, give, grant, pay,* (2) *to make* or *cause a thing to be* or *appear* something or somehow, *render.*—**reddere debitum,** *pay a debt.*

redemptio, onis, *f.*, (1) *redemption, deliverance from* sin and its consequences by the atonement of Jesus Christ, (2) *ransom,* the act of freeing a prisoner, captive or slave by payment, (3) *freedom* from vows, possession of particular privileges.

redemptor, oris, *m.*, *a redeemer,* one who rescues from sin and its consequences.

redeo, ire, ivi or itum, 3, *v. n.*, *to go back, return* in the proper and improper sense of the word.

redigo, ere, egi, actum, 3, *v. a.*, (1) *in gen.*, *to bring* or *reduce* a thing to any condition or circumstance, used with *in* and *acc.*, *in* and *abl.*, *ad* and *acc.*, (2) *to make* or *fashion* something from something else, (3) **redigere in scriptum,** *to reduce to writing, express in writing.*

redimo, ere, emi, emptum, 3, *v. a.*, (1) in gen., *to buy back, redeem, ransom,* (2) in partic., (a) *to buy back, ransom, release, redeem* a prisoner, slave, etc., (b) as Christ, *to ransom, deliver from sin and its consequences,* (3) fig., (a) *to buy off* something abstract, (b) *to make amends for sins, atone, compensate* a wrong.

redintegratio, onis, *f.*, *a restoration, renewal.*

redintegro, are, avi, atum, 1, *v. a.*, *to make whole again, to restore, renew.*

reditus, us, *m.*, *a returning, return,* (1) *lit.*, (a) *a return* of the soul to immortality, to the body, (b) of the revolution of the heavenly bodies, (2) *fig.*, (3) *a revenue, income, proceeds, returns.*

redoleo, ere, ui, 3, *v. a.* and *n.*, *to emit a scent, diffuse an odor, be redolent* of anything, used *lit.* and *fig.*

reduco, ere, xi, ctum, 3, *v. a.*, (1) *to lead back, reduce,* (2) *conduct, lead.* On **reducere de po-**

tentia materiae in actum, see *educere*.

reductio, onis, *f.,* (1) *a leading* or *bringing back, a restoring, restoration,* (2) *a leading, conducting.*

redundanter, adv., *redundantly, excessively.*

redundantia, ae, *f., an overflowing, superfluity, excess,* used fig.

redundo, are, avi, atum, 1, *v. a., of water,* from being over full, *to run back* or *over, to pour over, overflow,* (1) transf., **redundare aliqua re,** *to be over full of, to overflow with* anything, (2) fig., *to flow over in excess, superabound, redound, to be superfluous, redundant.*

reduplicatio, onis, *f., repetition, understanding a term precisely as such.*

reeligo, ere, legi, lectum, 3, *v. a., to choose again.*

refamulor, ari, atus, 1, *v. dep. n., to repay.*

refectio, onis, *f., a refreshment, refection, repair, recreation, recovery,* used (1) *lit.,* and (2) *fig.*

refello, ere, felli, 3, *v. a., to prove to be false; to disprove, rebut, confute, refute.*

referibilis, e, *adj., referable.*

referiens, entis, *P. a., striking back,* used in the S.T. only in quot.

referio, ire, 4, *v. a., to strike back, or in return,* used in the S.T. only in quot.

refero, ere, retuli, relatum, 3, *v. a.,* irr., *to bear, carry, bring, draw,* or *give back, report, refer to,* used *lit* and *fig.*

refert (or separately **re fert**), referre, retulit, *v. n.,* and *impers.,* it is for *one's interest* or *advantage, it profits, it befits, matters, imports, concerns, it is of importance* or *consequence.*

reficio, ere, feci, fectum, 3, *v. a., to make again, make anew, put in condition again; to remake, restore, renew, rebuild, repair, refit,* (1) *lit.,* (2) *fig.,* (a) *in gen.,* (b) *in partic.,* of the body and mind.

reflecto, ere, xi, xum, 3, *v. a.,* and *n.,* (1) *to bend back, bend over,* in the proper sense of the word; (2) *bend back, bend over,* in the improper sense of the word, *reflect.*—On **deductio reflexa,** see *deductio* under 3; on **linea reflexa,** see *linea* under 1; on **motus reflexus,** see *motus* under 1. On **cognitio reflexa,** see *cognitio* under 2.

reflexio, onis, *f.,* (1) *a bending* or *turning back* in the proper sense of the word, (2) *a bending* or *turning back* in the improper sense of the word. On **apprehendere per reflexionem,** see *apprehendere* under 2.

refluentia, ae, *f., overflow.*

refluo, ere, 3, *v. n., to flow* or *run back; to flow off; overflow.*

refluxus, us, *m., a flowing back, return refluence,* used especially of the *sea,* the opposite of *fluxus.*

refocillatio, onis, *f., refreshment, reinvigoration.*

reformatio, onis, *f., a reformation, refashioning,* used *lit.* and *fig.*

reformativus, a, um, *adj., reformative.*

reformido, *no perf.,* atum, 1, *v. a., to fear greatly, to dread, to stand in awe of, to shun* or *avoid through fear,* used with the *inf.,* the *acc.*

reformo, are, avi, atum, 1, *v. a., reform, remake.*

refoveo, ere, fovi, fotum, 2, *v. a.,* (1) *lit., to renew,* (2) *fig., to refresh.*

refractus, a, um, *P. a., weakened, fig.*

refrenatio, onis, *f., a bridling, curbing, restraining.*

refreno, are, avi, atum, 1, *v. a., to check, bridle, curb, restrain,* used *fig.*

refrigerium, ii, *n., refreshment, consolation.*

refrigero, are, avi, atum, 1, *v. a.,*

refrigesco, ere, frixi, 3, *v. inch. n., to grow cold, to flag in zeal,* used *fig.*

refugio, ere, fugi, 3, *v. n.,* and *a.,* (1) *lit., to run away, flee, escape,* (2) *fig., to shun, avoid, shrink from,* (a) *neutr.,* (b) *act.*

refugium, ii, *n., a refuge, place of refuge,* used (1) lit., (2) fig.

refulgentia, ae, *f., a reflected lustre, refulgence.*

refulgeo, ere, si, 2, *v. n., to flash back, reflect a shining light; shine bright, glitter, glisten.*

refundo, ere, fudi, fusum, 3, *v. a., to cause to overflow.*

refusio, onis, *f., a restitution.*

refutatio, onis, *f., a refutation.*

refuto, are, avi, atum, 1, *v. a.,* (1) lit., *to refuse, renounce,* (2) fig., (a) *to repress, reject, oppose, resist, repel,* (b) in partic., *to refute, confute, disprove.*

regalis, e, *adj., of* or *belonging to a king, kingly, regal, royal.* On **dominium regale,** see *dominium;* on **principatus regalis,** see *principatus* under 1; on **regimen regale,** see *regimen;* on **sacerdotium regale,** see *sacerdotium.* —**regaliter,** *adv., in a regal* or *royal manner, royally.*

regaliter, *adv.,* see *regalis.*

regeneratio, onis, *f., a being born again, regeneration, rebirth.*

regenerativus, a, um, *adj., regenerating, renewing, regenerative.* On **vis regenerativa,** see *vis* under 1.

regenero, are, avi, atum, 1, *v. a., to regenerate, renew spiritually by the power of the Holy Ghost.*

regimen, inis, *n., a guiding, governing, directing, rule, guidance, government, command,* synonym of *dominium, potestas,* and *principatus.* On **iustitia regiminis,** see *iustitia* under 1; on **potestas regiminis,** see *potestas* under 3. —Kinds of *regimen* are: (a), **regimen animarum,** *the guidance of souls.*—(b), **regimen corruptum seu perversum** and **regimen rectum,** *the deteriorated* or *corrupt and the right* or *good government.*—(c), **regimen despoticum** and **regimen oeconomicum seu paternum,** *the despotic* or *impe-*

rious government and *the domestic* or *paternal government of a family.*—(d), **regimen divinum** and **regimen humanum seu hominum,** *the divine and the human government.*—(e), **regimen domus,** *the government of a house* or *of a family.*—(f), **regimen hominum,** see *regimen divinum.* —(g), **regimen humanum,** see *regimen divinum.*—(h), **regimen imperfectum** and **regimen perfectum,** *the imperfect and the perfect government.*—(i), **regimen iniquum seu iniustum** and **regimen iustum,** *the unjust and just government.*—(j), **regimen iniustum,** see *regimen iniquum.*— (k), **regimen iustum,** see *regimen iniquum.*—(l), **regimen multitudinis seu multorum seu plurium** and **regimen unius,** *the government of many* or *of several and that of an individual.*—(m), **regimen multorum,** see *regimen multitudinis.*—(n), **regimen naturale,** *the natural government* or *that existing in the nature of things* (*in rerum natura*).—(o), **regimen oeconomicum,** see *regimen despoticum.*—(p), **regimen particulare** and **regimen universale,** *the particular and the general government.*—(q), **regimen paternum,** see *regimen despoticum.*—(r), **regimen perfectum,** see *regimen imperfectum.*—(s), **regimen perversum,** see *regimen corruptum.*—(t), **regimen plurium,** see *regimen multitudinis.*—(u), **regimen politicum, regimen re-**

gale seu regis, and **regimen tyrannicum seu tyranni,** *the civic government* or *that worthy of a citizen, the royal, and the tyrannical government.*—(v), **regimen populi,** *the government by the people.*—(w), **regimen rectum,** see *regimen corruptum.*—(x), **regimen regale,** see *regimen politicum.*—(y), **regimen regis,** see *regimen politicum.*—(z), **regimen tyranni,** see *regimen politicum.*— (a²), **regimen tyrannicum,** see *regimen politicum.*—(b²), **regimen unius,** see *regimen multitudinis.* —(c²), **regimen universale,** see *regimen particulare.*

regina, ae, *f., a queen, mistress,* used lit. and fig.

regio, onis, *f., a region, a portion of the earth* or *heavens* of indefinite length, (1) *region,* one of the strata into which the air is divided by imaginary boundaries as upper and lower regions; the ancients held the opinion that heaven lay within these boundaries, (2) *a region, country, district.*—**de regione propinqua,** *from a neighboring country.*—**in regione Orientis,** *in the east.*—**in extraneas regiones,** *into a foreign country.*

registrum, i, *n.,* (1) *a record, list,* (2) as a title: the Epistles of Gregory the Great and Gregory VII, which St. Thomas quotes.

regitivus, a, um, *adj., guiding, leading, governing, ruling.* On **causa regitiva,** see *causa* under 2; on **prudentia regitiva multitudinis et**

unius, see *prudentia* under 1; on
scientia regitiva, see *scientia* under 1; on **virtus regitiva**, see *virtus* under 1; on **vis regitiva**, see
vis under 1.

regius, a, um, *adj., of* or *belonging
to a king, kingly, royal.—***regia**,
ae, *f.*, (sc. domus), *a royal palace.*

regnativus, a, um, *adj., regnant,
ruling, governing.*

regnator, oris, *m., a prince, sovereign.*

regno, are, avi, atum, 1, *v. n.* and
a., (1) in partic., (a) *to have royal
power, be king*, (b) as God, *to
rule, reign, govern, be supreme*,
(3) in gen., *to reign, hold sway*,
(4) fig., *to rule, have the mastery, prevail.*

regnum, i, *n., royal power, kingdom, kingship, realm.* On **clavis
regni seu regni caelestis**, see
clavis under 2; on **ius regni**, see
ius under 1.—Kinds of *regnum*
are: (a), **regnum caeleste seu
caelorum**, *the kingdom of heav-
en.*—(b), **regnum caelorum**, see
regnum caeleste.—(c), **regnum
Dei**, *the kingdom of God.*—(d),
regnum spirituale and **regnum
temporale**, *the spiritual and the
worldly kingdom.*—(e), **regnum
temporale**, see *regnum spirituale.*

rego, ere, xi, ctum, 3, *v. a., to
guide, manage, rule, govern,
have the supremacy over* any
thing.

regredior, i, gressus, 3, *v. dep. n.,
to go* or *come back; to turn back,
return.*

regressus, us, *m., a going back, return.*

regula, ae, *f.*, (1) *rule, precept,
measure, norm*, (2) *the rule of a
religious order, regula monastica.*
—Kinds of *regula* in this (1) sense
are: (a), **regula creata** and **regula
increata seu divina**, *the created
or made norm*, and *the uncreated
or divine norm.*—(b), **regula divina**, see *regula creata.*—(c), **regula homogenea**, *the homogeneous norm* (of a thing).—(d), **regula increata**, see *regula creata.*—
(e), **regula monastica**, *rule of the
cloister* or *of a religious order.*—
(f), **regula perversa** and **regula
recta**, *the perverse* and *the right
rule.*—(g), **regula prima** and **regula propinqua**, *the first* or *highest
norm* and *the proximate* or *the
norm closest to a thing.*—(h),
regula propinqua, see *regula prima.*—(i), **regula propria**, *the proper* or *particular norm of a thing.*
—(j), **regula recta**, see *regula perversa.*—(k), **regula regulata**, *the
norm of a thing regulated* or *determined by something else.* On
professio regulae, see *professio*
under 1.

regularis, e, *adj.*, (1) *according to
rule, regular*, the opposite of *irregularis*, (2) *existing under the
rule of an order, cloistered; pertaining to, connected with a monastic rule.* On **magnitudo regularis**, see *magnitudo* under 1; on
motus regularis, see *motus* under
1. On **canonicus regularis**, see
canonicus under 3; on **observan-**

tia **regularis**, see *observantia* under 4.—**habitus regularis**, *a religious habit* or the distinctive garment worn by members of a religious order.—**regularis**, is, *m.*, *one living under a religious rule, a regular, a religious.*—**regulariter**, *adv.*, *according to rule, regularly.*

regulariter, *adv.*, see *regularis.*

regulatio, onis, *f.*, *regulation*, the act of regulating, or the state of being regulated, used in the S.T. only in quotation.

regulatus, a, um, *P. a.*, *regulated, governed by rule*, properly controlled or directed, adjusted to some standard.

regulo, are, avi, atum, 1, *v. a.*, *to direct, regulate.*

reintegro, are, avi, atum, 1, *v. a.*, (1) *to restore, re-establish, renew.*

reinvito, are, avi, atum, 1, *v. a.*, *to invite again* or *in return.*

reiteratio, onis, *f.*, *repetition*, (1) of statements, (2) of actions.—(1), nec reiteratio facit iniuriam sacramento.

reitero, are, avi, atum, 1, *v. a.*, *to repeat, reiterate.*

rejicio, ere, ieci, iectum, 3, *v. a.*, *to reject* used lit. and fig.

relabor, i, lapsus, 3, *v. dep. n.*, *to sink* or *fall back; to relapse; to return.*

relatio, onis, *f.*, *relation, proportion*, synonym of *habitudo, intentio, ratio, relativum*, and *respectus*, one of the ten categories of Aristotle, see *praedicamentum* under 2. On **communitas relationis**, see *communitas* under 1; on **distinctio relationis**, see *distinctio* under 2; on **extremum relationis**, see *extremus* under 2; on **finis relationis**, see *finis* under 1; on **fundamentum relationis**, see *fundamentum;* on **magnus secundum relationem**, see *magnus;* on **nomen relationis**, see *nomen* under 1; on **parvus secundum relationem**, see *parvus;* on **radix relationis**, see *radix;* on **significare cum relatione**, see *significare;* on **subiectum relationis**, see *subiectum* under 2; on **terminus relationis**, see *terminus* under 1; on **unitas relationis**, see *unitas;* on **unum per relationem ad alterum**, see *unus.*—Kinds of *relatio* are: (a), **relatio absoluta**, *the simple relation*, i.e., that which is simply or purely a relation.—(b), **relatio activa** and **relatio passiva**, *relation in the active and in the passive sense of the word*, i.e., relating and being related.—(c), **relatio actualis**, *the actual relation* or *that existing in reality.*—(d), **relatio aequalitatis seu aequiparantiae** and **relatio identitatis**, *the relation of equality* or *equalization and that of identity.*—(e), **relatio aequiparantiae**, see *relatio aequalitatis.*—(f), **relatio assistens seu exterius affixa seu extrinsecus affixa**, **relatio inhaerens seu intrinsecus affixa** and **relatio subsistens**, *the incidental* or *exteriorly attached relation, the inherent* or *interiorly attached* or *indwelling relation and that which exists* not in a subject, but in itself alone.—(g), **relatio disparata**, *the unpaired relation*, i.e., that relation which cannot be paired with another.—(h), **relatio distinguens personam**, *the relation that distinguishes a (divine) person*. Cf. **relatio personalis**.—(i), **relatio divina**, *the divine relation or the relation in God*.—(j), **relatio dominii**, *the relation of proprietorship or the relation according to which someone is called a lord.* —(k), **relatio exterius seu extrinsecus affixa**, see *relatio assistens.* —(l), **relatio filiationis** and **relatio paternitatis**, *the relation of sonship and that of fatherhood.*— (m), **relatio generationis** and **relatio nativitatis**, *the relation of (active) generation and that of birth or being born.*—(n), **relatio generis** and **relatio speciei seu specifica**, *the relation of genus and that of species*, i.e., that relation according to which something belongs to a genus and that according to which something belongs to a species.*—(o), **relatio idealis**, *the ideal relation.*—(p), **relatio identitatis**, see *relatio aequalitatis.*—(q), **relatio inhaerens**, see *relatio assistens.*—(r), **relatio intellecta seu intellegibilis seu rationis** and **relatio realis seu realiter exsistens seu realiter substantiae adveniens seu rei seu secundum rem**, *the subjective or intellectual relation or that produced by the mind and existent only in the mind and the objec-* *tive relation or that independent of the mind or thinking*. (See below, *relatio rationis*).—(s), **relatio mutua**, *correlativeness, mutual relation.*—(t), **relatio nativitatis**, *the relatio generationis.*—(u), **relatio originis**, *the relation of the origin of a thing.*—(v), **relatio passiva**, see *relatio activa.*—(w), **relatio paternitatis**, see *relatio filiationis.*—(x), **relatio personalis**, *the relation as person*, cf. *relatio distinguens personam*, i.e., concerning or forming a divine person.—(y), **relatio principii** and **relatio procedentis a principio**, *the relation of principle and that of procession*, i.e., the relation according to which something is a principle and that according to which it flows from a principle. — (z), **relatio prioritatis**, *the relation of priority.*—(a²), **relatio procedentis a principio**, see *relatio principii.*—(b²), **relatio rationis**, see *relatio intellecta.*—(c²), **relatio rationis tantum seu secundum rationem tantum seu solum secundum rationem seu secundum rationem intellegentiae tantum**, *the relation placed in the thought of the intellect only or the purely subjective relation.*— (d²), **relatio realis**, *real, objective relation*, see *relatio intellecta.*— (e²), **relatio realiter exsistens**, see *relatio intellecta.*—(f²), **relatio realiter substantiae adveniens**, see *relatio intellecta.*—(g²), **relatio rei**, see *relatio intellecta.*—(h²), **relatio secundum dici ad aliquid** and **relatio secundum esse ad aliquid,** *the relation according to supposition* and *that according to reality.*—(i²), **relatio secundum esse ad aliquid,** see *relatio secundum dici ad aliquid.*—(j²), **relatio secundum rationem tantum,** see *relatio rationis tantum.*—(k²), **relatio secundum rationem intellegentiae tantum,** see *relatio rationis tantum.*—(l²), **relatio secundum rem,** see *relatio intellecta.*—(m²), **relatio secundum rem,** see *relatio intellecta.*—(n²), **relatio solum secundum rationem,** see *relatio rationis tantum.*—(o²), **relatio speciei,** see *relatio generis.*—(p²), **relatio specifica,** see *relatio generis.*—(q²), **relatio subsistens,** see *relatio assistens.*—(r²), **relatio temporalis,** *the temporal relation.* **—idem ad seipsum non refertur aliqua relatione reali,** *nothing is brought into relationship with itself except in thought.*—**relationes non recipiunt magis et minus,** *the relations do not become more or less.*—**relatio non potest esse absque aliquo absoluto,** *a relation or an existence of the relation is not possible without something that is absolute,* i.e., without a perspective.—**relatio non refertur per aliam relationem,** *a relation or a being of the relation is not taken with reference to something through another relation or through another being of the relation but through itself.*—**relatio sicut non incipit esse de novo absque mutatione alterius rela-**torum, ita nec absque alterius mutatione de novo desisti, *just as a new relation does not begin without a change of both things standing in relation one to the other or at least of one of the two, so does an already existing relation not cease without such a change.*

relative, *adv.,* see *relativus.*

relativus, a, um, *adj., having reference* or *relation, referring, relative,* synonym of *relatus* and *respectivus,* the opposite of *absolutus.* On **forma relativa,** see *forma* under 2; on **habitudo relativa,** see *habitudo;* on **nomen relativum et relativum secundum dici et esse,** see *nomen* under 1; on **oppositio relativa,** see *oppositio* under 2; on **pronomen relativum,** see *pronomen;* on **proprietas relativa,** see *proprietas* under 1; on **res relativa,** see *res;* on **verbum relativum,** see *verbum* under 1.—**relativum,** i, *n.,* synonym of *ad aliquid,* the Aristotelian *on pros ti, that which has reference to something, the being of the relation, that which has a relation to something* or *presents it,* which forms one of the ten categories of Aristotle.—Kinds of *relativum* are: (a), **relativum diversitatis** and **relativum identitatis,** *that which presents the relativeness of difference and that which presents the relativeness of identity.*—(b), **relativum identitatis,** see *relativum diversitatis.*—(c), **relativum reciprocum,** *that* *which presents the relation of reciprocity, the reciprocal relative.*—(d), **relativum secundum dici** and **relativum secundum esse,** *that which is relative only in thought or word, and that which is really so.*—(e), **relativum secundum esse,** see *relativum secundum dici.*—**interempto uno relativorum interimitur aliud,** *if one related term goes out of existence, so does that which corresponds to it.*—**omne relativum dependet a suo correlativo,** *everything that presents a relation to something, depends as such upon that to which it stands in relation;* cf. below: *relativum non potest etc.*—**relativum non potest esse sine correlativo,** *that which presents a relation to something, cannot exist without it;* cf. above: *omne relativum dependet etc.*—**relative,** *adv., after the manner* or *in the sense of a relation, relatively,* the opposite of *absolute.* On **dicere relative,** see *dicere* under 3; on **oppositum relative,** see *opponere;* on **praedicare relative,** see *praedicare* under 2; on **significare relative,** see *significare.*

relatus, a, um, *adj., related to something, relating to something, related,* synonym of *relativus* and *respectivus,* the opposite of *absolutus.*—Kinds of *relatus* are: **relatus per essentiam suam** and **relatus per rationem,** *related to something through its own essence* and *related to something through the intellect.*—**quod est**

per essentiam suam relatum posterius est absoluto, *that which presents a relationship to something according to its own essence is subsequent to that which has no relation to anything.*

relaxatio, onis, *f., a relaxation, an easing.*

relaxo, are, avi, atum, 1, *v. a.,* (1) lit., *to stretch out* or *widen again; to unloose, loosen, open,* (2) fig., *to slacken, ease, lighten, alleviate.*

relectio, onis, *f., reperusal, frequent reading.*

relego, ere, legi, lectum, 3, *v. a.,* (1) *to go through* or *over again* in reading, in speech, or in thought, (2) *to travel over* or *through again, to return.*

relevo, are, avi, atum, 1, *v. a., to relieve, set free from* any evil; or, *to alleviate, mitigate, lessen* the evil itself; *to relieve.*

religatio, onis, *f., a binding up, bond.*

religio, onis, *f.,* (1) *religion, the virtue of rendering the worship to God that is due Him,* (2) *state of Christian perfection, state of the religious (community) life, a religious order,* (3) *religion* in sense of a doctrine revealed by God. On **apostasia religionis,** see *apostasia;* on **professio religionis,** see *professio* under 1; on **status religionis,** see *status* under 4; on **votum religionis,** see *votum* under 1.—Kinds of *religio* in this (2) sense are: (a), **religio activa** and religio contemplativa, *the order active* in the works of mercy, and *the contemplative order.*—(b), religio contemplativa, see *religio activa.*—(c), religio eremitica and monastica, *the state of the hermit* and *that of the monk.*—(d), religio maior seu perfectior and religio minor, *the more perfect* and *the less perfect order,* (according to the severity of the Rule).—(e), religione minor, see *religio maior.*—(f), religio monastica, see *religio eremitica.*—(g), religio perfectior, see *religio maior.*

religiosus, a, um, *adj.,* (1) *religious, Godfearing, devout, pious,* (2) *religious,* i.e., belonging to the state of religious perfection, members of a religious order, synonym of *regularis,* the opposite of *saecularis.* On status religiosorum, see *status* under 4.

religo, are, avi, atum, 1, *v. a., to bind, fasten.*

relinquo, ere, liqui, lictum, 3, *v. a., to leave behind by removing one's self, to leave, move away from, abandon.*

reliquiae, arum, *f., the leavings, remains, relics, remnant, rest, remainder of anything.*

reliquus, a, um, *adj., that is left or remains, that is left behind, remaining.*

reluceo, ere, xi, 2, *v. n., to shine back, shine out; to reflect, shine, glow, give light.*

reluctor, ari, atus, 1, *v. dep. n., to struggle against* anything, *to resist.*

remaneo, ere, mansi, mansurus, 2, *v. n., to stay, remain, be left, continue, abide, endure.*—remanens, entis, *P. a., remaining, continuing, enduring.*

remediabilis, e, *adj., reparable.*

remedium, ii, *n.,* (1) lit., (a) *a remedy, medicine,* a cure for a disease or other disorder of body or mind; any medicine or treatment which alleviates pain and promotes restoration to health, (b) *a nostrum, a medicine,* the formula of which is a secret, (2) transf., or fig., *a means of aid, assistance* or *relief.*

rememoratio, onis, *f., remembrance, recollection.*

rememorativus, a, um, *adj., rememorative, serving to remind.* On signum rememorativum, see *signum* under 1; on virtus rememorativa, see *virtus* under 1.

rememoror, ari, atus, 1, *v. dep. n.* and *a., to call to mind,* used with *acc.,* with *rel. clause.*

Remigius, ii, *n., Remigius* of Auxerre, Benedictine monk and exegete in the latter half of the ninth century. There is a reference to him from the *Catena Aurea* of St. Thomas.

reminiscentia, ae, *f., arbitrary remembrance,* i.e., the action of remembering something, *reminiscence,* the deliberate use of *memoria.*

reminiscitivus, a, um, *adj., recalling something, reminiscent.* On vis reminiscitiva, see *vis* under 1.

reminiscor, sci, *v*. dep. *n*. and *a*., *to recall to mind, recollect, remember*.

remisse, *adv*., see *remitto*.

remissibilis, e, *adj*., *pardonable, remissible*.

remissio, onis, *f*., (1) *a slackening, relaxing, abatement,* the opposite of *intensio*, (2) *remission, cancellation, forgiveness.* On **remissio formae**, see *forma* under 2; on **remissio habitus**, see *habitus* under 4.

remissivus, a, um, *adj*., *remissive, inclined to, of the nature of remission* or *pardon*.

remissus, a, um, *P. a.*, see *remitto*.

remitto, ere, misi, missum, 3, *v. a.*, (1) lit., *to send back, cause to return,* (2) fig., (a) *to remit, to cancel a debt,* (b) *to remit, pay back,* (c) *to modify,* change more or less in character, properties or form, (d) *to forgive* or *pardon a sin, offence, fault, punishment,* etc., (e) *to refer* or *have recourse* to some one, (f) *to relax, relieve, release, abate, remit, lessen.*—**remittere veniam,** *to grant pardon.* —**remissus,** a, um, *P. a.*, (1) *slack, negligent, remiss,* (2) *rush,* (3) of sin, *forgiven.*—**remisse,** *adv.*, (1) *gently, mildly,* (2) *slightly*.

remordeo, ere, no perf., rsum, 2, *v. a.*, *to vex, torment, rebuke, disturb*.

remorsio, onis, *f.*, *remorse*.

remorsus, us, *m.*, *with conscientiae, remorse of conscience*.

remote, *adv.*, see *removeo*.

remotio, onis, *f.*, *a putting back, withdrawing, removal,* in the ontological sense of the word, synonym of *negatio* and *privatio,* the opposite of *affirmatio* and *positio.* On **cognoscere per modum remotionis seu per remotionem,** see *cognoscere* under 2; on **via remotionis seu quae est per viam,** see *via* under 2; on **ad remotionem causae sequitur remotio effectus,** see *causa* under 2.

remotive, *adv.*, see *remotivus*.

remotivus, a, um, *adj.*, *withdrawing, removing,* the opposite of *positivus.* On **effectus remotivus,** see *effectus.*—**remotive,** *adv.*, *in the manner and sense of withdrawal* or *removal, remotively,* the opposite of *positive,* does not occur in the Summa Theologica. On **accipere remotive,** see *accipere* under 3; on **dicere remotive,** see *dicere* under 3; on **praedicare** see *dicere* under 3; on **praedicare remotive,** see *praedicare* under 2.

remotus, a, um, *Part.* and *P. a.*, see *removeo*.

removeo, ere, movi, motum, 2, *v. a.*, *to move back, withdraw, remove* in the ontological and logical senses of the word, the opposite of *attribuere* and *ponere.*— **removens prohibens,** *the principle that removes an impediment.* —**remotus,** a, um, *Part.* and *P. a., moved back, withdrawn, removed.* On **causa remota et removens prohibens,** see *causa* under 2; on **cognitio remota,** see *cognitio* under 2; on **corruptio remota**, see *corruptio* under 3; on **definitio remota**, see *definitio* under 2; on **disponere remotum prohibens**, see *disponere* under 2; on **dispositio remota**, see *dispositio* under 4; on **finis remota**, see *finis* under 2; on **fundamentum remotum**, see *fundamentum;* on **genus remotum**, see *genus* under 2; on **materia remota**, see *materia* under 2 and 3; on **mensura remota**, see *mensura;* on **motor remotus**, see *motor;* on **movens remotum**, see *movens;* on **potentia remota**, see *potentia* under 4; on **principium remotum**, see *principium;* on **similitudo remota**, see *similitudo* under 1.— **remota causa removetur effectus**, see *causa* under 2.—**remoto posteriori non removetur prius** and **remoto priori removetur posterius**, see *posterius* under 1.—**remoto priori removentur ea, quae consequenter sunt**, see *prior* under 1.—**remote**, *adv.*, *at a distance, afar off, remotely.*

remuneratio, onis, *f.*, *a repaying, recompense, reward, remuneration.*

remunero, are, 1, *v. a.*, *to reward, repay,* (1) act., (2) pass.

renascor, i, atus, 3, *v. dep. n.*, (1) *lit., to be born again,* (2) *fig.*, (in eccl. Latin) *to be renewed in heart, to be born again.*

Renatus, i, *m., Renatus*, a monk and layman of Caesarea in Mauritania, the bearer of a letter to

Augustine from Optatus, bishop of Mileum, which he delivered to him at Caesarea, 418, A.D.

renes, renum, *m.*, (1) *lit., the loins,* (2) *fig., the seat of affections.*

renisus, us, *m., resistance.*

renitentia, ae, *f., resistance, reluctance.*

renitor, niti, *v. dep. n., to strive* or *struggle against, resist.*

renovatio, onis, *f., a renewing, renewal.*

renovo, are, avi, atum, 1, *v. a., to renew, restore,* used *lit.* and *fig.*

renuntiatio, onis, *f., a renunciation,* the act of giving up or surrendering, a possession, right etc.

renuntio, are, avi, atum, 1, *v. a., to give up, break off, protest against, disclaim, renounce.*

renuo, ere, ui, 3, *v. n.* and *a., to refuse, decline.*

reordino, are, avi, atum, 1, *v. a., to reordain, ordain anew.*

reparabilis, e, *adj., reparable,* capable of being set right again.— **reparabiliter**, *adv., reparably.*

reparabiliter, *adv.*, see *reparabilis.*

reparatio, onis, *f., a restoration, renewal.*

reparo, are, avi, atum, 1, *v. a., to restore, repair, renew, make good, refresh, revive,* used *lit.* and *fig.*

repello, ere, reppuli, repulsum, 3, *v. a., to drive, crowd,* or *thrust back; to reject, repulse, repel.*

rependo, ere, di, sum, 3, *v. a., to pay back, repay, requite, recompense, return, reward.*

repente, *adv.*, *suddenly*, *unexpectedly*.

repentinus, a, um, *adj.*, *sudden*, *hasty*, *unlooked for*, *unexpected*. —ex **repentino**, *suddenly*.

repercutio, ere, cussi, cussum, 3, *v. a.*, *to strike back*.

reperio, ire, repperi, repertum, 4, *v. a.*, (1) *lit.*, *find*, *meet with*, *find out*, either by searching or by accident, (2) *fig.*, *to find out*, *perceive*, *learn*, *discern*, *discover*.

repetitio, onis, *f.*, *repetition*.

repetitus, a, um, *P. a.*, see *repeto*.

repeto, ere, ivi or ii, itum, 3, *v. a.*, *to take hold of* or *undertake again*; *to enter upon again*; *to recommence*, *resume*, *repeat* an action, a speech, etc.—**repetitus**, a, um, *P. a.*, *repeated*.

repleo, ere, evi, etum, 2, *v. a.*, *to fill up*, *make full*, *to fill*, *to satisfy*, *satiate*.—**repletus**, a, um, *P. a.*, *filled*, *full*.

repletio, onis, *f.*, (1) *repletion*, the action of eating or drinking to excess, (2) *fulness*, the state or quality of being full in any sense.

repletivus, a, um, *adj.*, *causing repletion*, *replenishing*.

repletus, a, um, *P. a.*, see *repleo*.

replicatio, onis, *f.*, (1) *unrolling*, *repetition*, (2) *limitation*, *restriction*, does not occur in the Summa Theologica.

replico, are, avi, atum, 1, *v. a.*, in *jurid.* and *late Lat.*, *to make a reply* or *replication*, (2) *to turn back*, *return*, used *fig.*

repo, ere, psi, ptum, 3, *v. n.*, *to crawl*.

repono, ere, posui, positum, 3, *v. a.*, *to lay*, *place*, *put*, *to lay aside* or *away*, *preserve*, *reserve*.

reporto, are, avi, atum, 1, *v. a.*, *to bear*, *carry* or *bring back*; *to carry off*, *bear away*; *to get again*, *obtain*.

reposco, ere, poposci, —, 3, *v. a.*, and *absol.*, *to demand back*, *ask for again*, *to ask for*, *claim*, *demand*, *exact*, *require*.

repraesentatio, onis, *f.*, *a bringing before one*; *a showing*, *exhibiting*, *manifesting*, *representation*. On **similitudo repraesentationis seu quantum ad repraesentationis seu quantum ad repraesentationem**, see *similitudo* under 1.— Kinds of *repraesentatio* are: (a), **repraesentatio actualis**, *the real representation*.—(b), **repraesentatio expressa**, *the expressed* or *impressed representation*.—(c), **repraesentatio imaginis seu per modum imaginis** and **repraesentatio vestigii seu per modum vestigii**, *representation after the manner of a picture* or *image and that after the manner of a trace*. —(d), **repraesentatio libri** and **repraesentatio speculi**, *the representation of a book and that of a mirror*, i.e., the representation of a thing as a book describes it and that as a picture shows it.—(e), **repraesentatio per modum imaginis**, see *repraesentatio imaginis*.— (f), **repraesentatio per modum vestigii**, see *repraesentatio imaginis*.—(g), **repraesentatio speculi**, see *repraesentatio libri*.—(h), **re-**

praesentatio vestigii, see *repraesentatio imaginis*.

repraesentativus, a, um, *adj.*, *presenting, representing, representative*.

repraesento, are, avi, atum, 1, *v. a.*, *to bring before one, to bring back; to show, exhibit, display, manifest, represent.—*repraesentans, ntis, *P. a.*, *showing, representing.—*repraesentatus, a, um, *P. a.*, *shown, represented, presented*.

reprehendo, ere, di, sum, 3, *v. a.*, *to blame, censure, find fault with, reprove, rebuke, reprehend*.

reprehensibilis, e, *adj.*, *blamable, reprehensible, discreditable*.

reprehensio, onis, *f.*, *blame, censure, reprimand, reproof, reprehension*.

repressio, onis, *f.*, *restraining, curbing, repression*.

reprimo, ere, pressi, pressum, 3, *v. a.*, *to press back, keep back; to check, curb, restrain*.

reprobabilis, e, *adj.*, *worthy of rejection*.

reprobatio, onis, *f.*, (1) *rejection, declaration of guilt*, (2) *rejection of a rational being, determination of eternal damnation*, the opposite of *praedestinatio*.

reprobo, are, no perf., atum, 1, *v. a.*, *to disapprove, reject, condemn.—*reprobatus, a, um, *P. a.*, *disapproved, rejected, condemned*.

reprobus, a, um, *adj.*, *false, spurious.—*reprobus, i, *n.*, *the condemned, the damned*.

repromissio, onis, *f.*, *a counter-promise*.

repromitto, ere, misi, missum, 3, *v. a.*, *to promise in return, engage* or *bind one's self*.

reptile, is, *n.*, *a reptile, creeping creature*.

repto, are, avi, atum, 1, *v. freq. n.* and *a.*, *to crawl, creep*.

repudio, are, avi, atum, 1, *v. a.*, (1) *to reject, refuse, to scorn, disdain, repudiate*, (2) of persons married or betrothed, *to cast off, put away, divorce, repudiate*.

repudium, ii, *n.*, (*pudet*), t. t., of marriage or betrothed persons, *a casting off, putting away* of the opposite party; *a dissolution of the marriage contract, a separation, divorce, repudiation.—*repudium maledictionis, *the removal of the curse.—*libellus repudii, *a bill of divorce*.

repugnantia, ae, *f.*, (1) *a resistance, opposition, clashing*, (2) *repugnance, a contraction, contrariety, incompatibility*.

repugnatio, onis, *f.*, *a resistance, opposition*.

repugno, are, avi, atum, 1, *v. n.*, (1) *to repugn, be contrary to* or *contradictory to, be inconsistent with, oppose, resist, militate against*, used with the dative, with *ut* and *subj.*, (2) *to refute, overcome* by argument, (3) *to rage*.

repulsio, onis, *f.*, *repulsion*.

repulsivus, a, um, *adj.*, *repulsive*.

repurgo, are, avi, atum, 1, *v. a.*, *to clear again*.

reputatio, onis, *f.,* (1) *opinion, sup-
postion,* (2) *imputation,* whatever is charged or ascribed.

reputo, are, avi, atum, 1, *v. a., to
reckon, calculate, compute; to
think over, ponder, meditate, reflect upon.*

requies, etis, *f.,* (1) *rest, repose
from labor, suffering, care,* etc.;
*relaxation, respite, intermission,
recreation,* (2) *rest* as applied to
enjoyment of heaven, **requies
beatorum,** *the rest of the blessed;*
requies ventura, *the coming rest;*
sempiterna requies animarum,
the everlasting rest of souls; **requies sanctorum,** *the rest of the
saints;* **requies beatorum paupe-
rum,** *the rest of the blessed poor,*
all synonyms of **sinus Abrahae,**
i.e., the Limbo of the Fathers,
and after the death of Christ, (3)
rest, the Sabbath, (4) *the repose*
of the dead.

requiesco, ere, evi, etum, *v. n.* and
*a., neutr., to rest one's self, to
rest, repose.*

requiro, ere, sivi, or sii, situm, 3, *v.
a., to look after, seek* or *search
for, to ask* or *inquire after, to
need, lack, miss, require.*

res, rei, *f., a thing, object, concrete
being, matter, affair, event, fact,
circumstance, occurrence, deed,
condition.* On **ad aliquid secundum rem,** see *ad* under 2; on
**bonitas rei naturalis et bonitas
prima rei naturalis,** see *bonitas*
under 2; on **bonum in re et in rebus naturalibus,** see *bonus* under
2; on **cognitio ad rem et a re ac-**
cepta, see *cognitio* under 2; on
**communicabile secundum rei ve-
ritatem,** see *communicabilis;* on
communicare rem, see *communicare* under 1; on **communis res
seu secundum rem,** see *communis* under 1; on **communitas rei,**
see *communitas* under 1; on **compositio rei,** see *compositio* under
1; on **contraria in rerum natura,**
see *contrarius* under 1; on **contrarietas rerum,** see *contrarietas*
under 1; on **differre re seu secundum rem,** see *differre* under 2;
on **distinctio secundum rem,** see
distinctio under 2; on **ens in re
extra animam,** see *ens;* on **esse
rei,** see *esse;* on **falsum in re,** see
falsus; on **fundamentum in re,**
see *fundamentum;* on **gaudium
rei,** see *gaudium;* on **idem re
seu secundum rem,** see *idem;* on
identitas re seu secundum rem,
see *identitas;* on **incommunicabile re seu secundum rem,** see *incommunicabilis;* on **iudicium de
re,** see *iudicium* under 2; on **malum in rebus naturalibus et voluntariis,** see *malus* under 2; on
medium rei, see *medium* under
1; on **nomen rei seu res significans,** see *nomen* under 1; on **numerus rerum,** see *numerus;* on
ordo secundum rem, see *ordo*
under 1; on **pars rei seu secundum rem,** see *pars* under 1; on
**principium rei et principium pri-
mum rei,** see *principium;* on **prius secundum rem,** see *prior* under 1; on **processus rei,** see *processus* under 3; on **relatio rei seu**

secundum rem, see *relatio;* on simul secundum rem, see *simul;* on substantia rei, see *substantia* under 8; on ultimum rei, see *ultimus;* on unio secundum rem, see *unio;* on unitas rei, see *unitas;* on unum rei seu secundum rem, see *unus;* on verbum rei, see *verbum* under 1; on veritas rei, see *veritas* under 1; on verum in re, see *verus* under 1.—Kinds of *res* are: (a), res absoluta and res relativa, *the thing which is related to nothing and that which is related to something.*—(b), res animata and res inanimata, *the animated or living thing and the inanimate or lifeless thing.*—(c), res artificialis, and res naturalis, *the artificial and the natural thing or that produced by art and that produced by nature.*—(d), res casualis, *the accidental event or that produced contrary to expectation and intention.*—(e), res composita and res simplex, *the composite and the simple thing.*—(f), res coniuncta and res exterior seu extrinseca, *the thing connected with something and the thing exterior or foreign to something.*—(g), res corporalis seu corporea seu materialis and res incorporalis seu spiritualis seu immaterialis, *the corporal and the incorporal or spiritual thing.*—(h), res divina, *divine affair.*—(i), res essentialis, *the essential thing.*—(j), res exterior seu extrinseca, see *res coniuncta.*—(k), res extra animam seu in esse naturali exsis-

tens and res rationis seu rationis tantum, *the thing existing outside the mind and its thoughts* or *in reality and the thing of thought* or *of pure thought.*—(l), res falsa and res vera, *the false* or *non-genuine and the true* or *genuine thing.*—(m), res falsa secundum quid and res falsa simpliciter, *the thing false in a certain respect* and *the simply* or *absolutely false thing.*—(n), res falsa simpliciter, see *res falsa secundum quid.*—(o), res familiaris, *the family* or *domestic affair.*—(p), res figurata, *the thing with a definite form.*—(q), res humana, *the human affair.*—(r), res immaterialis, see *res corporalis.*—(s), res inanimata, see *res animata.*—(t), res incorporalis seu incorporea, see *res corporalis.*—(u), res indivisibilis, *the indivisible thing.*—(v), res in esse naturali exsistens, see *res extra animam.*—(w), res inhaerens and res subsistens, *the thing attached* or *connected with another* and *a thing existing for itself.* —(x), res intellegibilis and res sensibilis, *the intellectually perceptible thing* and *the thing recognizable through the senses.*— (y), res irrationabilis seu irrationalis, *the irrational thing* or *that without a mind.*—(z), res materialis, see *res corporalis.*—(a²), res mota and res permanens, *the moved thing and permanently resting thing.*—(b²), res mundana, *the worldly* or *earthly thing.*— (c²), res naturae, *the thing of na-*

ture or *the thing with a definite nature.*—(d²), res naturalis, see *res supernaturalis.*—(e²), res permanens, see *res mota.*—(f²), res personalis, *the personal thing.*—(g²), res privativa, *the thing consisting of a privation.*—(h²), res prophetica, *the prophetic thing* or *the thing of prophecy.*—(i²), res rationis seu rationis tantum, see *res extra animam.*—(j²), res relativa, see *res absoluta.*—(k²), res sacramenti, see *sacramentum* under 3. —(l²), res sensibilis, see *res intellegibilis.*—(m²), res simplex, see *res composita.*—(n²), res simpliciter, *the so-called simple* or *absolute thing,* i.e., the substance, the opposite of *secundum quid,* i.e., to the thing respectively so called under which is to be understood any predicamental accident.— (o²), res situalis, *the thing that has a location.*—(p²), res spiritualis, see *res corporalis.*—(q²), res subsistens, see *res inhaerens.*— (r²), res supernaturalis and res naturalis, *the supernatural* and *the natural thing* or *the thing according to nature.*—(s²), res universalis, *the universal thing.*—(t²), res vera, see *res falsa.*—(u²), res voluntaria, *the voluntary thing.* —ens et res convertuntur, see *convertere* under 2.—res non cognoscitur ab anima nisi per aliquam sui similitudinem exsistentem vel in sensu vel in intellectu, *a thing is not recognized* or *understood, sensibly* or *intellectually, unless by means of a likeness which exists either in the senses* or *in the mind.*—unaquaque res illud videtur esse, quod in ea est potissimum, *everything seems to be that which is most active in it.*—revera, the *abl. sing.* strengthened by *vera, in fact, in truth, indeed, in reality.*

resarcio, ire, *no perf.,* sartum, 4, *v. a.,* (1) *lit., to fill up again, regain, recover,* (2) *fig., to fill, enrich.*

rescindo, ere, scidi, scissum, 3, *v. a., to break down, cut loose, cut off,* used *fig.*

rescribo, ere, psi, ptum, 3, *v. a., to impress deeply,* used *fig.*

reseco, are, cui, ctum, 1, *v. a.,* (1) *lit., cut off,* (2) *fig., to check, stop.*

reseratio, onis, *f., reseration, the action of opening up.*

resero, are, avi, atum, 1, *v. a., to unlock, open.*

reservo, are, avi, atum, 1, v. a., *to keep back,* as if for future use; *to reserve,* used with *in* and *acc.,* in with *abl.,* the *dat., ad* and *acc.,* with *acc.*

resideo, ere, sedi, 2, *v. a.,* (1) *lit., to sit back, to remain sitting* anywhere; *to reside,* (2) fig., *to rest, reside, dwell.*

residuus, a, um, *adj., that is left behind, that remains over and above, remaining, residuary.*

resigno, are, avi, atum, 1, *v. a., to resign.*

resilio, ire, ui, 4, *v. n., to shrink from, recoil,* used fig.

resipisco, ere, ivi, or ii, 3, *v. inch. n.*, *to recover one's senses*, used fig.

resistentia, ae, *f.*, *resistance, opposition.*

resisto, ere, stiti, 3, *v. n.*, *to withstand, to oppose, resist; to make opposition* or *resistance*, u s e d with the *dat.*, or *absol.*, (1) of p e r s o n s, (2) of immaterial things.

resolutio, onis, *f.*, (1) *disintegration, resolution, analysis*, the opposite *of compositio*, (2) *release, escape, separation, abstraction*, synonym of *abstractio*. On **modus resolutionis**, see *modus* under 3; on **processus resolutionis**, see *processus* under 2; on **via resolutionis**, see *via* under 3.—**quod est primum in constructione, est ultimum in resolutione,** see *primus*.—**ultimum in generatione est primum in resolutione,** see *generatio* under 1.

resolutivus, a, um, *adj.*, *resolutive, dissolvent*, used fig.

resolutorius, a, um, *adj.*, (1) *disintegrating, resolving, analysing*, synonym of *analyticus*, the opposite of *compositivus*, (2) *Resolutoria*, the Analytics of Aristotle. On **modus resolutorius,** see *modus* under 3; on **ordo resolutorius,** see *ordo* under 1; on **processus resolutorius,** see *processus* under 2.—**Resolutoria** sc. **pars logice,** *analytics*, a part of logic; cf. *analyticus* under 1.

resolvo, ere, solvi, solutum, 3, *v. a.*, (1) lit., (a) *to dissolve, decom-*

pose, to separate into its constituent parts or elements as by means of *natural decay, to reduce to ashes;* (b) *to resolve*, to alter or change a thing from one form into another, (c) *to loose, release, resolve.* (2) fig., (a) *to destroy*, (b) *to resolve, to reduce* by mental analysis into more elementary forms and principles or relations, (c) *to examine* critically, (d) *to scatter, frustrate.*—

resolutus, a, um, *P. a.*, (1) *resolved, distilled,* changed from one thing into another, (2) *disintegrated, loosened*, (3) *decomposed.*

resonantia, ae, *f.*, *an echo.*

respectivus, a, um, *adj.*, *referring to, taking consideration of, relative to*, synonym of *relativus* and *relatus*. On **comparatio respectiva,** see *comparatio* under 2.

respectus, us, *m.*, *relation, proportion*, synonym of *relatio*, *abl.*, **respectu,** *by a regard, with regard*, with *gen.* On **perfectus per respectum ad aliquid,** see *perfectus* under 1; on **possibile per respectum ad aliquam potentiam,** see *possibilis*.—Kinds of *respectus* are: (a), **respectus actualis** and **respectus habitualis,** *the relation depending on an action* and *that at hand after the manner of a lasting condition.*—(b), **respectus habitualis,** see *respectus actualis.* —(c), **respectus idealis,** *ideal relation.*—(d), **respectus realis,** *the real relation.*

respicio, ere, spexi, spectum, 3, *v. n.* and *a.*, (1) *to look back* or *behind*, (2) *to look at with solicitude*, i.e., *to have a care for, regard, consider.*

respirans, ntis, *P. a., breathing out.*

respiratus, us, *m., a drawing breath, inhaling, inspiration.*

resplendeo, ere, ui, 2, *v. n., to shine brightly; to glitter, be resplendent*, used lit. and fig.

respondeo, ere, di, sum, 2, *v. a.*, (1) *to answer, reply, respond*, (2) *to meet, agree, accord* or *correspond with;* constr. usually with *dat.* or *absol.*

responsio, onis, *f., a reply, an answer.*

responsorium, ii, *n., responsory.*

responsum, i, *n.*, see *respondeo.*

res publica, ae, *f.*, (1) *the common weal, commonwealth, state;* synonym of *politia*, (2) *republic, free state.*

respuo, ere, ui, 3, *v. a., to reject, to refuse.*

restauratio, onis, *f., a restoration, renewal.*

restauro, are, avi, atum, 1, *v. a., to restore, repair, rebuild.*

restinguo, ere, nxi, nctum, 3, *v. a., to destroy*, used *fig.;* used in the S.T. only in quot.

restituibilis, e, *adj., restorable, capable of being restored.*

restituo, ere, ui, utum, 3, *v. a.*, (1) lit., (a) of things, *to deliver up again, to give back, make restitution, restore*, (b) *to grant to* or *obtain* for a person *reinstatement* to former rank, office, etc., (c) *to*

restore or *return* something to its original position, (d) *to restore, to bring back* a person or part of the body to a healthy state, (e) *to restore*, make good loss or damage, (2) fig., (a) *to restore, reestablish*, (b) *to restore* to grace, virtue, etc., to free from the effects of sin.

restitutio, onis, *f.*, (1) in gen., *restoration*, the action of restoring or giving back something to its proper owner, or of making reparation to one for loss or injury previously inflicted, (2) in *partic.*, (a) *restoration* of one's good name, (b) *recovery* of virtue, (c) *restoration* of former vigor, (d) *renewal* of friendship.—**facere restitutionem,** *to make restitution.*

resto, are, stiti, —, 1, *v. n.*, (1) *to withstand, resist, oppose*, constr. with *dat.*, (2) *to be left, remain*, constr. with *inf., ut* and *subjunctive, gerund, quod clause*, and used *absol.*

restricte, *adv.*, see *restringo.*

restringo, ere, inxi, ictum, 3, *v. a., to restrict, restrain, confine, check*, etc.—**restricte,** *adv., closely, sparingly.*

resultatio, onis, *f., a resultance, a result, effect, outcome.*

resulto, are, atum, 1, *v. freq. n.* and *a.*, (1) *result*, to arise as a consequence, effect, or conclusion from some action, process etc., (2) *to reflect, to return an image of*, as in a mirror, used lit. and fig.

resumo, ere, mpsi, mptum, 3, *v. a.,* (1) *to resume, assume, put on* or *take* to oneself anew something previously given up, as some appearance, form, condition, or act, (2) *to resume,* to say or write further or in addition, (3) *to go on again* with a discourse or remark.

resumptio, onis, *f., resumption,* the action of assuming, putting on, or taking to oneself anew something previously lost, given up, or discarded.

resurgo, ere, surrexi, surrectum, 3, *v. n.,* (1) *lit.,* (a) *to rise again, rise from the grave,* (b) of plants and seed, *to rise again,* (2) *fig.,* (a) *to rise again* from sin, (b) illness, (c) a lowly condition, etc.

resurrectio, onis, *f., a rising again from the dead, rising, resurrection.* On **status resurrectionis, ante et post resurrectionem,** see *status* under 3.—Kinds of *resurrectio* are: (a), **resurrectio animae seu spiritualis** and **resurrectio carnis seu corporis seu corporalis,** *the resurrection of the soul* (a morte peccati, C. G. 4. 79) and *that of the flesh,* or *the spiritual* and *the corporal resurrection.*— (b), **resurrectio carnis,** see *resurrectio animae.*—(c), **resurrectio communis seu generalis seu universalis,** *the common* or *the general resurrection.*—(d), **resurrectio corporalis,** see *resurrectio animae.*—(e), **resurrectio corporis,** see *resurrectio animae.*—(f), **resurrectio generalis,** see *resurrec-*

tio communis.—(g), **resurrectio gloriosa,** *the glorious resurrection.*—(h), **resurrectio imperfecta** and **resurrectio perfecta seu vera,** *the imperfect* and *the perfect* or *true resurrection.*—(i), **resurrectio integra,** *the undamaged resurrection* or *the resurrection after the manner of the integral whole.*— —(j), **resurrectio miraculosa** and **resurrectio naturalis,** *the miraculous* and *the natural resurrection* or *the resurrection taking place in the supernatural* and *in the natural manner.*—(k), **resurrectio naturalis,** see *resurrectio miraculosa.*—(l), **resurrectio perfecta,** see *resurrectio imperfecta.*—(m), **resurrectio spiritualis,** see *resurrectio animae.*—(n), **resurrectio ultima,** *the last resurrection,* or *the resurrection at the end of the world.*—(o), **resurrectio universalis,** see *resurrectio communis.*— (p), **resurrectio vera,** see *resurrectio imperfecta.*—(q), **resurrectio virtuosa,** *the powerful resurrection.*

resuscitatio, onis, *f., a raising again from the dead, resuscitation.*

resuscito, are, *v. a.,* to resuscitate, to restore a person to life physical or spiritual.

retardatio, onis, *f., a hindering, delaying, retarding.*

retardo, are, avi, atum, 1, *v. a.* and *n.,* used fig., (1) *to retard, delay, keep back, impede,* (2) *put off, delay to do something.*

rete, is, *n., a net.*

retentio, onis, *f.*, *retention*, (1) the fact of retaining things in the mind, (2) the action of keeping to oneself or in one's own hands.

retentivus, a, um, *adj.*, (1) *retentive*, tending or inclined to the keeping of something, (2) *retentive*, the retentive virtue or faculty, the ability to retain the physical secretions, or to keep food within the stomach.

reticeo, ere, cui, 2, *v. n.* and *a.*, (1) neutr., *to be silent*, (2) act, *to keep a thing silent, to conceal*.

retineo, ere, ui, tentum, 2, *v. n.*, *to hold* or *keep back, not let go; to detain; to restrain*.

retorqueo, ere, si, tum, 2, *v. a.*, (1) lit., *to twist* or *cast back*, (2) fig., (a) of persons in respect to the mind and feelings, *to recoil*, (b) of words, *to twist, give a wrong meaning to*, (c) **retorquere ad quaestum,** *to turn into gain*.

retractatio, onis, *f.*, *a taking in hand again; a retouching, revision, correction;* so only Retractationes, the title of a work of St. Augustine, (2) **absque retractatione,** *without withdrawal*.

retractio, onis, *f.*, (1) *a withdrawal of the sun's rays*, (2) of mental influences, *retraction*, the action of drawing or pulling in.

retracto, are, avi, atum, 1, *v. a.*, (1) *to retract, to withdraw, recall, revoke*, rescind a statement, promise, etc., (2) *to reconsider, to ponder over*.

retraho, ere, xi, ctum, 3, *v. a.*, *to draw back, withdraw, remove*.

retribuo, ere, ui, utum, 3, *v. a.*, *to give back, return, restore, repair, repay, requite*, used lit. and fig.

retributio, onis, *f.*, *recompense, restitution, retribution*. On **iudicium retributionis,** see *iudicium* under 2.—Kinds of *retributio* are: (a), **retributio gloriae,** *the recompense of eternal glory*.—(b), **retributio poenae** and **retributio praemii,** *the recompense of punishment* and *that of reward* or *the punishing* and *the rewarding recompense*.—(c), **retributio praemii,** see *retributio poenae*.—(d), **retributio proportionalis,** *the proportional recompense*.

retributivus, a, um, *adj.*, *recompensing, retributive*. On **poena retributiva,** see *poena*.

retro, *adv.*, of place, *backwards, back; behind*.

retroactus, a, um, *P. a.*, *retroacted, having a retrospective effect, past*.

retrocedo, ere, *v. n.*, *to go back, retire, recede*.

retrocessio, onis, *f.*, *a retrocession*.

retroeo, ire, *v. n.*, *to go back* or *backwards, to recede, retire*.

retrorsum, *adv.*, *back, backwards, behind*.

retrudo, ere, no *perf.*, sum, 3, *v. a.*, *to thrust back*.

retundo, ere, tudi, tusum, 3, *v. a.*, *to blunt, dull, deaden*.

reunio, iri, ii, itum, 4, *v. a.*, *to reunite*.

reus, i, *m.*, and **rea,** ae, *f.*, (1) originally, *a party to an action* either plaintiff or defendant; afterwards restricted to *the party accused, defendant,* (2) transf., *one who is bound* by anything.—**rea voti, reus voti,** *bound by vow;* **reus voti fracti,** *a vow breaker,* (3) *one guilty of any crime, one condemned to any punishment,* used with the *gen.* and *abl.,* (a) in *fem.,* (b) *masc.*

revelabilis, e, *adj., revealable, capable of being revealed.*

revelatio, onis, *f., an uncovering, manifestation of truth, revelation.* On **lumen divinae revelationis,** see *lumen;* on **via revelationis,** see *via* under 1.—Kinds of *revelatio* are: (a), **revelatio angelica** and **revelatio daemonum,** *revelation through an angel* and *that through the devil.*—(b), **revelatio daemonum,** see *revelatio angelica.*—(c), **revelatio divina,** *divine revelation.*—(d), **revelatio gratiae,** *the revelation from grace.*—(e), **revelatio imaginaria, revelatio intellectualis,** and **revelatio sensibilis,** *revelation solely through images in the imagination, solely through ideas in the mind,* and *that perceived through the senses.*—(f), **revelatio intellectualis,** see *revelatio imaginaria.*—(g), **revelatio prophetalis seu prophetica,** *revelation by means of a prophet.*—(h), **revelatio sensibilis,** see *revelatio imaginaria.*—(i), **revelatio spiritualium substantiarum,** *revelation by means of disembodied spirits.*

revelator, oris, *m., a revealer.*

revelo, are, avi, atum, 1, *v. a., to disclose, reveal.*

revera, see *res.*

reverberatio, onis, *f., reverberation,* the reflecting of light, heat, etc.

reverberatus, a, um, *adj., struck* or *beaten back,* used fig.

reverenter, *adv.,* see *revereor.*

reverentia, ae, *f., timidity,* arising from high respect or (more rarely) from fear, *respect, regard, fear, awe, reverence.*

revereor, eri, itus, 2, *v. dep. a., to stand in awe* or *fear of; to regard, respect, honor; to fear, be afraid of; to reverence, revere.*—**reverenter,** *adv., respectfully.*—**reverendus,** a, um, *P. a., inspiring awe.*

reverto, ere, 3, *v. n., to turn back* or *about, return, revert.*

revinco, ere, vici, victum, 3, *v. a., to convict; disprove, refute.*

revivisco, ere, vixi, —, 3, *v. inch. n., to come to life again, to be restored to life, to revive.*

revocatio, onis, *f., a withdrawal* of something.

revoco, are, avi, atum, 1, *v. a., to call back, recall, resume, to withdraw, retire; to regain, recover; to draw back, draw off* or *away; to withhold, restrain.*

revolutio, onis, *f., a revolving, revolution.*

revolvo, ere, volvi, volutum, 3, *v. a.,* (1) *to roll back; to unroll, unwind,* (2) *to brood, reflect upon.*

rex, regis, *m.,* (1) *a ruler of a country, a king,* (2) **Libri Regum,** *the*

Books of Kings in the Old Testament, (3) **Rex regum,** *the King of Kings, Dominus dominantium.*

Rhegium, ii, *n., Reggio,* a seaport and cathedral town; capital of Reggio di Calabria province.

Rhemensis, e, *adj., Rhemish,* of or pertaining to the city of *Rheims,* now *Reims,* France.

rhetor, oris, *m., one who argues on grounds that most appeal to men, even though untrue; a rhetorician.*

Rhetorica, ae, *f., the art of oratory, rhetoric,* the art of persuasion as distinct from conviction. Books on rhetoric, such as the *De Rhetorica of Aristotle* and the *De Rhetorica ad Herrenium of Cicero,* both quoted by St. Thomas.

rhetoricus, a, um, *adj., rhetoric,* i.e., belonging to the rhetor or the rhetorical art. On **disciplina rhetorica,** see *disciplina* under 3; on **disputatio rhetorica,** see *disputatio;* on **oratio rhetorica,** see *oratio* under 1; on **scientia rhetorica,** see *scientia* under 1.—**rhetorica,** sc. **ars seu pars logicae,** *Rhetoric,* persuasive argumentation.

Richardus, i, *m., Richard,* a monk of Scotch birth and Prior of the abbey of St. Victor, theologian, disciple of Hugh of St. Victor, died in 1173. St. Thomas quotes from his treatise *De Trinitate, De Mystica Contemplatione, De Potestate Solvendi et Ligandi, De Judiciaria Potestate.*

rictus, us, *m.,* of animals, *distended jaws,* here *snarling.*

rideo, ere, si, sum, 2, *v. n.* and *a., to smile, laugh,* used lit. and fig.

ridiculosus, a, um, *adj., laughable, droll, facetious.*

ridiculus, a, um, *adj., laughable, silly, absurd, ridiculous.*

rigidus, a, um, *adj., rigid, austere.*

rigor, oris, *m., severity, rigor, rigidity.*

rimor, ari, atus, 1, *v. dep. a., to examine thoroughly, investigate.*

Riparius, ii, *m., Riparius,* a learned presbyter of Aquitaine, in the beginning of the fifth century. He solicited the aid of Jerome in combating the views of Pelagius. Jerome replied in a short letter of encouragement.

risibilis, e, *adj., that can laugh, risible.*

risus, us, *m., a laughing, laughter, laugh.*

rite, *adv., in a proper* or *just manner, fitly, duly, rightly.*

ritus, us, *m., the form* and *manner of religious observances; a religious usage* or *ceremony, a rite.*

rivus, i, *m., a small stream of water, a brook.*

rixa, ae, *f., quarrel, brawl, dispute.* —*rixa* is *filia irae,* cf. *ira.*—Kinds of *rixa* are: **rixa factorum** and **rixa verborum,** *a quarrel of deeds* and *one of words.*

rixor, ari, 1, *v. dep. n., to quarrel, brawl, wrangle, dispute.*

rixose, *adv.,* see *rixosus.*

rixosus, a, um, *adj., quarrelsome, pugnacious.*—**rixose,** *adv., quarrelingly, in a quarrelsome manner.*

Roboam, *indecl. n. m.,* *Roboam* (Rehoboam), a son of Solomon against whom Jeroboam with ten tribes revolted successfully leaving Roboam only the kingdom of Judah.

roboro, are, avi, atum, 1, *v. a.,* *to make strong; to strengthen, invigorate, confirm.—roboratus,* a, um, *P. a., strengthened, vigorous, strong.*

robur, oris, *n., power, strength, force, vigor,* (1) *physical strength, spiritual strength,* (3) of fortitude, *law, courage, hope, the passions, authority, grace;* of contracts, **habere robur,** *to have force, to take effect, have validity;* of vows, **addere robur,** *to add force.*

robustus, a, um, *adj., robust, strong.* —**robuste,** *adv., stoutly, strongly.*

rodo, ere, si, sum, 3, *v. a., to gnaw.*

rogo, are, avi, atum, 1, *v. a., to ask, question, interrogate* one about a thing, *to ask for, pray,* synonym of *oro.*

Roma, ae, *f., the city of Rome.*

Romanus, a, um, *adj., of* or *belonging to Rome, Roman.*—**Romanus,** i, *m.; plur. the Romans.*

ros, roris, *m.,* (1) *dew,* (2) *of blood,* **ros,** the humidity found in the cavities of the smaller veins.

rosa, ae, *f., a rose.*

rosaceus, a, um, *adj., rose.* **Aqua rosacea,** *rose-water.*

rostrum, i, *n., the bill* or *beak of a bird.*

rota, ae, *f., a wheel, orb.*

rotunditas, atis, *f., roundness.*

rotundus, a, um, *adj., round, rounded.*

ruber, bra, brum, *adj., red, ruddy,* as *adj. prop.,* **Rubrum mare,** *the Red Sea.*

rubesco, ere, bui, 3, *v.* inch, *to turn red, blush.*

rubeus, a, um, *adj., red, reddish.*

rubicundus, a, um, *adj., red, ruddy.*

rubigo, inis, *f., rust* of metals.

rubor, oris, *m., redness* of all shades, (1) **rubor faciei,** *a blush,* (2) *rouge.*

rubricatus, a, um, *part.* of *rubrico, colored red,* used in the S.T. only in quot.

rubus, i, *m., a bramble bush.*

rudimentum, i, *n.,* used usually in the plural, *the elements, first principles, rudiments.*

rudis, e, *adj.,* (1) *rude, unpolished, unskilled, awkward, ignorant, inexperienced,* (2) *those ignorant of Christian doctrine, the uninitiated, catechumen,* e.g., the De Catechizandis Rudibus of St. Augustine.

ruditas, atis, *f., ignorance, crudity.*

rufus, a, um, *adj., red, reddish, red-haired, red-headed.*

ruga, ae, *f., a wrinkle,* used fig.

rugatus, a, um, *P. a., wrinkled.*

rugio, ire, *v. n., to roar,* as a lion.

rugitus, us, *m., a roaring of lions.*

ruina, ae, *f., a fall, downfall, ruin, spiritual ruin.*

ruinosus, a, um, *adj., tumbling down, going to ruin, ruinous,* also *spiritually ruinous.*

ruminatio, onis, *f., chewing the cud, rumination.*

rumino, are, 1, *v. n.* and *a., to chew over again, chew the cud.*

rumor, oris, *m., rumor, report.*

rumpo, ere, rupi, ruptum, 3, *v. a.,* (1) lit., *to burst, break,* (2) fig., *to break, violate, annul, interrupt.*

ruo, ere, ui, utum, 3, *v. n., to fall down, fail,* used only in spiritual sense in S.T.

ruptio, onis, *f., breaking, an opening.*

rursus, *adv., on the contrary, on the other hand, in return, again.*

rusticanus, a, um, *adj., of* or *pertaining to the country, rustic.*

rusticitas, atis, *f., rusticity.*

rusticus, a, um, *adj., rustic, plain, coarse.*—**rusticus,** i, *m.,* (1) *a countryman, a rustic, peasant,* (2) *a vassal,* one who held land of a superior lord by a feudal tenure.

Rusticus, i, *m., Rusticus,* bishop of Narbonne in the first half of the fifth century. In early youth he was attracted to the monastic life, but appears to have looked on it mainly as a preparation for the active ministry. St. Jerome in epistle 125 to Rusticus praises the coenobitic life.

Ruth, indecl. *n., f., Ruth,* a Moabitess who afterwards became the wife of Booz of Bethlehem, and was the great grandmother of David.

rutilo, are, avi, atum, 1, *v. a., to glisten with a reddish glow, to be reddish.*

S

Saba, ae, *f., Saba,* the largest town in Arabia Felix, especially celebrated for its myrrh, frankincense, etc.

sabbatum, i, *n., the Sabbath,* the Jewish Sabbath was the weekly day of rest with which the week ended. In commemoration of Christ's resurrection the Church observes the sabbath on Sunday, the first day of the week.

Sabellianus, a, um, *adj., of Sabellius, Sabellian,* the name of an heretical sect founded by Sabellius. The Catholic Church teaches that there are three divine Persons really distinct from each other, and yet one God. The Sabellians denied that the persons were really distinct, believing that they were merely different manifestations or different roles of one and the same person.

Sabellius, i, *m., Sabellius,* an elder of the Christian Church at Rome, and afterwards at Ptolemais, in the third century, the founder of the heretical sect of Sabellians.

saccus, i, *m., a garment of haircloth* or *sackcloth.*

sacer, sacra, sacrum, *adj., sacred, holy,* (1) *consecrated,* as the sacred elements, (2) *sacred,* religious in nature, association or use, of or pertaining to religion, its doctrines, history, etc., not secular or profane, as sacred vestments, sacred history, sacred seasons, (3) *holy, sacred, hallowed* by association with the divine, the consecrated or the like.—sacra, orum, *n., sacred things.*

sacerdos, otis, *m., priest.* On **ordo sacerdotis,** see *ordo* under 3 and 4.—Kinds of *sacerdos* are: (a), **sacerdos curatus,** *priest entrusted with care of souls,* as in a parish.—(b), **sacerdos degradatus** and **sacerdos excommunicatus,** *the priest stripped of the exercise of his priestly powers* and *the priest upon whom excommunication has been pronounced.* —(c), **sacerdos discretus seu proprius,** *the distinguished* or *special* or *proper priest.*—(d), **sacerdos excommunicatus,** see *sacerdos degradatus.*—(e), **sacerdos evangelicus seu novae legis** and **sacerdos legalis seu veteris legis,** *the priest of the Gospel* and *the priest of the law* or *the priest of the old* and *of the new law.*—(f), **sacerdos figuralis,** *the figurative priest.*—(g), **sacerdos legalis,** see *sacerdos evangelicus.*—(h), **sacerdos novae legis,** see *sacerdos evangelicus.*—(i), **sacerdos parochialis,** *the parish priest.*—(j), **sacerdos principalis,** *the High Priest,* i.e., Christ.—(k), **sacerdos proprius,** see *sacerdos discretus.* —(l), **sacerdos simplex, sacerdos superior,** and **sacerdos summus,** *the simple, the higher* (bishop), and *the highest* (pope) *priest.*— (m), **sacerdos summus,** see *sacerdos simplex.*—(n), **sacerdos superior,** see *sacerdos simplex.*—(o), **sacerdos veteris legis,** see *sacerdos evangelicus.*

sacerdotalis, e, *adj., of* or *belonging to priests, priestly, sacerdotal.*—**sacerdotalis dignitas,** *sacerdotal dignity.*—**sacerdotale officium,** *priestly office.*—**sacerdotalis stirps,** *priestly race.*—**sacerdotale genus,** *priestly tribe.*—**ordo sacerdotalis,** *priestly office.*—**sacerdotalis absolutio,** *the priestly absolution.*—**sacerdotalis potestas,** *priestly power.*—**sacerdotalis vestis,** *priestly vestment.*—**sacerdotalis character,** *priestly character.*

sacerdotium, ii, *n., priesthood.* On **character sacerdotii,** see *character* under 2; on **ordo sacerdotii,** see *ordo* under 4.—Kinds of *sacerdotium* are: (a), **sacerdotium aeternum seu perpetuum** and **sacerdotium temporale,** *the eternal* and *the temporal priesthood.* —(b), **sacerdotium Christi seu novem** and **sacerdotium leviticum seu legale seu veteris legis seu veteris testamenti seu vetus,** *the priesthood of Christ* and *the Levitic priesthood* or *the priesthood of the New Testament* and *that of the Old Testament.*—(c), **sacerdotium figurale,** *the figurative priesthood.*—(d), **sacerdotium gentilium** and **sacerdotium Iudaeorum,** *the priesthood of the Gentiles* and *that of the Jews.*—

(e), **sacerdotium Iudaeorum,** see *sacerdotium gentilium.*—(f), **sacerdotium legale,** see *sacerdotium Christi.*—(g), **sacerdotium Leviticum,** see *sacerdotium Christi.* —(h), **sacerdotium Melchisedech seu secundum ordinem Melchisedech,** *the priesthood of Melchisedech* or *according to the order of Melchisedech.*—(i), **sacerdotium novum,** see *sacerdotium Christi.* —(j), **sacerdotium perfectum,** *the perfect priesthood.*—(k), **sacerdotium perpetuum,** see *sacerdotium aeternum.*—(l), **sacerdotium regale,** *the royal priesthood.*—(m), **sacerdotium secundum ordinem Melchisedech,** see *sacerdotium Melchisedech.*—(n), **sacerdotium temporale,** see *sacerdotium aeternum.*—(o), **sacerdotium veteris legis,** see *sacerdotium Christi.*—(p), **sacerdotium veteris testamenti,** see *sacerdotium Christi.*

sacramentalis, e, *adj., belonging to* or *concerning a sacrament, sacramental;* cf. *sacramentum* under 3. On **actio sacramentalis,** see *actio* under 1; on **actus sacramentalis,** see *actus* under 1; on **causa sacramentalis,** see *causa* under 2; on **character sacramentalis,** see *character,* under 2; on **confessio sacramentalis,** see *confessio* under 1; on **gratia sacramentalis,** see *gratia* under 2; on **potestas sacramentalis,** see *potestas* under 3; on **ratio sacramentalis,** see *ratio* under 13; on **satisfactio sacramentalis,** see *satisfactio* under 1; on **signum**

sacramentale, see *signum* under 1; on **species sacramentalis,** see *species* under 2; on **verbum sacramentale,** see *verbum* under 1; on **virtus sacramentalis,** see *virtus* under 1; on **vis sacramentalis,** see *vis* under 1.—**sacramentale, is,** *n., a sacramental,* i.e., an action or a thing, the devout use of which is productive of spiritual benefit. On the difference between *sacramentale* and *sacramentum,* see *sacramentum* under 3.—**sacramentaliter,** *adv., in the manner* or *sense of a sacrament, by means of a sacrament, sacramentally, by way of sign.*

sacramentaliter, *adv.,* see *sacramentalis.*

sacramentum, i, *n.,* (1) *sacrament* in the wider sense of the word, i.e., that which is sanctified or consecrated, (2) *sacrament* in the proper sense of the word, i.e., sign of a holy thing which sanctifies man or concerns him, (3) *sacrament* in the narrowest sense of the word, excluding the sacraments of the Old Law, a visible sign or rite, instituted by Christ to confer grace.—A kind of *sacramentum* in this (1) sense is: **sacramentum militare,** *the oath of a soldier.*—Kinds of *sacramentum* in this (2) sense are: (a), **sacramentum ecclesiae seu ecclesiasticum,** *the sacrament of the* (*Catholic*) *church* or *the ecclesiastical sacrament.*—(b), **sacramentum ecclesiasticum,** see *sacramentum ecclesiae.*—(c), **sacra-**

mentum evangelicum seu novae legis, sacramentum legale seu legis Mosaicae seu veteris legis and sacramentum legis naturae, *the sacrament of the Gospel or of the new law, that of the Mosaic or of the old law* and *that of nature or the unwritten law.*—(d), sacramentum gratiae, *the sacrament producing or bestowing grace.*— (e), sacramentum legale, see *sacramentum evangelicum.*—(f), sacramentum legis Mosaicae, see *sacramentum evangelicum.*—(g), sacramentum legis naturae, see *sacramentum evangelicum.*—(h), sacramentum Melchisedech, *the sacrament of Melchisedech.*—(i), sacramentum novae legis, see *sacramentum evangelicum.*—(j), sacramentum perfectum, *the perfect sacrament.*—(k), sacramentum veteris legis, see *sacramentum evangelicum.* On agere sacramentum, see *agere* under 1; on forma sacramenti, see *forma* under 2; on gratia sacramenti, see *gratia* under 2; on materia sacramenti, see *materia* under 3.— Kinds of *sacramentum* in this (3) sense are: (a), sacramentum altaris seu eucharistae, *the sacrament of the altar or the sacrament of the Eucharist.*—(b), sacramentum caritatis and sacramentum fidei, *the sacrament of love or the Eucharist and the sacrament of faith or baptism,* with which is connected a *professio fidei.*—(c), sacramentum exeuntium and sacramentum in-

trantium, *the sacrament of those who depart this world* and *of those who enter it.*—(d), sacramentum fidei, see *sacramentum caritatis.*—(e), sacramentum intrantium, see *sacramentum exeuntium.*—(f), sacramentum necessitatis and sacramentum superabundantis perfectionis, *the sacrament of necessity* and *that of overflowing perfection,* i.e., a sacrament which is necessary for the acquisition of eternal salvation, i.e., baptism, and for an adult in mortal sin, penance, and that upon which an outstanding perfection depends, e.g., confirmation, Eucharist.—(g), sacramentum ordinis, *the sacrament of the priesthood or holy orders.*— (h), sacramentum pacis et unitatis, *the sacrament of peace* and *of union,* namely, *the Eucharist.* —(i), sacramentum plenitudinis gratiae, *the sacrament of the fullness of grace,* i.e., confirmation. —(j), sacramentum poenitentiae, *the sacrament of penance.*—(k), sacramentum superabundantis perfectionis, see *sacramentum necessitatis.*—(l), sacramentum unitatis, see *sacramentum pacis.*

sacrarium, ii, n., (1) *a sacrarium,* a place for the decent disposal of remnants of sacred things, (2) *a shrine sanctuary,* used fig.

sacrificium, ii, n., *sacrifice.* On agere per modum sacrificii, see *agere* under 1.—Kinds of *sacrificium* are: (a), sacrificium carnale, *the carnal sacrifice or the sacrifice consisting of the flesh of the animal.*—(b), **sacrificium corporale seu exterius seu sensibile seu visibile** and **sacrificium spirituale seu interius seu invisibile**, *the corporal,* or *exterior* or *sensible* or *visible sacrifice* and *the spiritual* or *interior* or *invisible sacrifice.*—(c), **sacrificium exterius**, see *sacrificium corporale.*—(d), **sacrificium figurale** and **sacrificium verum**, *the figurative* and *the true* or *real sacrifice.*—(e), **sacrificium interius**, see *sacrificium corporale.*—(f), **sacrificium invisibile**, see *sacrificium corporale.*—(g), **sacrificium pacificorum**, *the peace offering.* Cf. Hebr. 10. 1.—(h), **sacrificium sensibile**, see *sacrificium corporale.*—(i), **sacrificium spirituale**, see *sacrificium corporale.*—(j), **sacrificium visibile**, see *sacrificium invisibile.*—(k), **sacrificium zelotypiae**, *the sacrifice of jealousy* (described in Numbers, 5, 12 ff).

sacrifico, are, avi, atum, 1, *v. n.* and *a., to make* or *offer a sacrifice, to sacrifice,* (1) *neutr.,* (a) *absol.,* (b) with *dat.,* (2) *act.,* (3) *pass.*

sacrilegium, ii, *n.,* (1) *in gen., sacrilege,* (2) *in partic.,* (a) *sacrilege,* the crime of stealing, misusing, violating, or desecrating that which is sacred, or holy or dedicated to sacred uses, (b) the sin of violating the conditions for the worthy reception of a sacrament, (c) *sacrilege,* robbery from a Church or sacred place.

sacrilegus, a, um, *adj., sacrilegious.* —**sacrilegus**, i, *m., one who commits a sacrilege, a sacrileger.*

sacro, are, avi, atum, 1, *v. a., to declare* or *set apart as sacred; to consecrate, dedicate.*—**sacratus**, a, um, *P. a., hallowed, consecrated, holy, sacred.*

sacrosanctus, a, um, *adj., sacred, sacrosanct.*

Sadducaei, orum, *m., the Sadducees,* a politico-religious sect among the Jews during the late post-Exilic and New Testament period. They became the dominant priestly party during the Greek and Roman period of Jewish history, and the name originated in their pretensions to be the descendants of Sadoc, the high priest prominent in the time of David and Solomon.

saecularis, e, *adj., temporal, earthly, worldly, secular,* synonym of *mundanus,* the opposite of *regularis, religiosus,* and *spiritualis.* On **desiderium saeculare,** see *desiderium* under 1; on **industria saecularis,** see *industria* under 3; on **officium saeculare,** see *officium* under 2; on **potentia saecularis,** see *potentia* under 3; on **potestas saecularis,** see *potestas* under 3 and 4; on **principatus saecularis,** see *principatus* under 1; on **sapientia saecularis,** see *sapientia* under 1; on **societas saecularis,** see *societas;* on **status saecularis,** see *status* under 4; on **unitas saecularis,** see *unitas;* on **vita saecularis,** see *vita* under 3.—

saeculariter, *adv., in a worldly manner, in a worldly sense.*

saeculariter, *adv.,* see *saecularis.*

saeculum, i, *n.,* (1) *limit of existence, duration of life, age of man,* synonym of *aeternum* and *aevum,* (2) *an age, a century, a millenium,* (3) *time, earthly time,* (4) *the earth, the world,* (5) *the world, worldliness, worldly life, worldly sense,* the opposite of *religio* and *spiritualitas.*—Kinds of *saeculum* in this (3) sense are: **saeculum futurum** and **saeculum hoc,** *the future* and *the present time.* Cf. *saeculum hoc* under 4. —Kinds of *saeculum* in this (4) sense are: **saeculum altius seu superius seu intellegibile** and **saeculum hoc seu praesens,** *the higher* or *transcendental world* and *the present* or *sensible world.* Cf. *saeculum hoc* under 3. On **homo saeculi,** see *homo;* on **sapientia saeculi,** see *sapientia* under 1; on **tristitia saeculi,** see *tristitia* under 1.

saepe, *adv., often, oft, oftentimes, many times, frequently,* at definite intervals, while *crebro* denotes in close succession.

saevio, ire, ii, itum, 4, *v. n., to rage, to be fierce* or *furious.*

saevitia, ae, *f.,* of persons, (1) for any violent, passionate excitement, *fierceness, violence, harshness, cruelty, barbarity, severity,* (2) *wildness,* (3) *uncouthness.*

saevus, a, um, *adj., fierce, cruel, wild, violent, harsh, severe, fell, dire, barbarous.*

sagacitas, atis, *f.,* of animals, *keenness, acuteness.*

sagaciter, *adv.,* see *sagax.*

sagax, acis, *adj., sagacious.*—**sagaciter,** *adv., acutely, shrewdly, sagaciously.*

sagitta, ae, *f., an arrow, shaft, bolt.*

sagittans, antis, *Part.* used as *noun,* *m., an archer, bowman,* synonym of *sagittarius* and *sagittator.*

sagittator, oris, *m., an archer, bowman,* synonym of *sagittarius* and *sagittans.*

sagum, i, *n., a curtain, tent-cover.*—**cilicina saga,** *curtains of goats' hair.*

sal, salis, *m.,* (1) lit., *salt,* (2) poet., *the salt water, sea.*

salamandra, ae, *f., a salamander.*

salio, ire, ui, saltum, 4, *v. n.* and *a., to leap, bound, twitch, jump, spring forth.*

saliva, ae, *f., spittle, saliva.*

salix, icis, *f., a willow-tree, willow, sallow.*

Sallustius, ii, *m., Sallust, C. Sallustius Crispus,* the celebrated Roman historian, author of a Conspiracy of Cataline, the Jugurthine War, and the Histories.

Salomon, onis, *m., Solomon,* son of David and King of Israel and Judah in the tenth century B.C., noted for his superior wisdom and magnificent reign.

salsedo, inis, *f., a salt taste, saltiness.*

salsus, a, um, *P. a., salted, salt, salty.*

saltem, *adv., at least, at the least, at all events, anyhow.*

salto, are, avi, atum, 1, *v.* freq. *n.* and *a., to dance,* (in the widest sense of the word, including pantomine and gesticulation; mostly with a contemptuous accessory significance.)

saltus, us, *m.,* (1) *a leaping, leap, spring, bound,* (2) **per saltum,** lit., by a bound or jump, regularly used in a figurative sense, with *ordinari,* to receive a higher order without having taken a lower order, e.g., to receive the diaconate without having taken the sub-diaconate.

salubris, e, *adj., healthful, salutary, wholesome, beneficial, saving.—* **salubriter,** *adv., healthfully, wholesomely, profitably, advantageously.*

salubriter, *adv.,* see *salubris.*

Salumi (Salu) *indecl. n., Salu,* mentioned in Num. XXV, a prince of the kindred and tribe of Simeon. He is called Salomi in I Mach. II, 26.

salus, utis, *f., a being safe* and *sound; a sound* or *whole condition, health, welfare, prosperity, preservation, safety, deliverance,* etc., (1) of the body, (2) eccl. Lat., *salvation, deliverance from sin* and *its penalities, spiritual welfare.—***consilium salutis,** *salutary advice.*

salutaris, e, *adj., salutary, serviceable, beneficial, wholesome, advantageous, of* or *belonging to well-being,* in the most general sense, while the predominant meaning of *salubris* in classical

language is *healthy* in a medical sense.—**salutare,** is, *n., safety.*

salutatio, onis, *f., a greeting, saluting, salutation.*

salutifer, fera, ferum, *adj., health-bringing, healing, salubrious, beneficial, helpful.*

saluto, are, avi, atum, 1, *v. a., to salute any one, to greet, wish health to, pay one's respect to.*

salvatio, onis, *f., deliverance, salvation.*

salvator, oris, *m., in partic.,* in the Vulg. and Christian fathers, as a transl. of *soter* and Jesus, *the Saviour, Redeemer.*

salveo, ere, *v. n., to be well* or *in good health;* in partic., *salve, God save you, hail;* sometimes on one's sneezing, *God bless you!* Also with *vale* in taking leave, *farewell, goodby, adieu.*

salvo, are, avi, atum, 1, *v. a. to save.*

salvus, a, um, *adj., saved, preserved, unharmed, safe, unhurt, well, sound,* (1) freq. with a noun in the *abl. absol., without violation of, saving,* (2) in eccl Lat., *saved from sin, saved by Christ.*

Samaria, ae, *f., Samaria,* the middle district of Palestine.—**Samaritanus,** a, um, *adj., Samaritan.*

Samaritanus, a, um, *adj.,* see *Samaria.*

Sampson, or **Samson,** *indecl. noun, Samson,* an Israelite judge of Bible record, (see Judges XIII), distinguished for his great strength.

Samuel, is, *m., literally,* his name is El (God), *Samuel,* a famous He-brew judge and prophet.

sanabilis, e, *adj., that can be healed, curable, remediable,* used lit. and fig.

sanabilitas, atis, *f., sanability, sanableness,* susceptible of being cured or remedied.

sanatio, onis, *f., a healing, curing,* in a physical and spiritual sense.

sanativus, a, um, *adj., sanative, having the power to cure* or *heal, curative; tending to heal.*

sancio, ire, xi, sanctum or sancitum, 4, *v. a., to sanction, enact, confirm, ratify.*—**sancitum,** *Part. perf.,* (1) *sanctioned,* (2) *sacred, inviolable.*

sancte, *adv.,* see *sanctus.*

sanctificatio, onis, *f.,* (1) *sanctification, sanctifying,* (2) *religious observation.*—Kinds of *sanctificatio* in this (1) sense are: (a), **sanctificatio actualis,** *the real sanctification* or *that taking place in reality.*—(b), **sanctificatio adul-terorum** and **sanctificatio puer-orum,** *the sanctification of adults* and *that of children.*—(c), **sancti-ficatio a seu ex peccato,** *the sanc-tification of sinners,* the opposite of *sanctificatio a sancto,* i.e., to the sanctification of the sancti-fied or to the increase of their sanctification.—(d), **sanctificatio naturae** and **sanctificatio perso-nalis,** *the sanctification of nature* and *species and that of person* or *of the individual man.*—(e), **sanc-tificatio personalis,** see *sanctifi-*

catio naturae.—(f), **sanctificatio prima** and **sanctificatio secunda** sc. **sacramenti,** *the first* and *the second sanctification of a sacra-ment,* of which one is through the blessing of its matter and the other through its distribution as in the use of the sacrament.—(g), **sanctificatio puerorum,** see *sanc-tificatio adulterorum.*—(h), **sanc-tificatio secunda,** see *sanctificatio prima.*

sanctificator, oris, *m., a sanctifier.*

sanctifico, are, avi, atum, 1, *v. a., to make holy* or *treat as holy, to sanctify, consecrate, dedicate.*

sanctimonia, ae, *f., holiness, sanc-tity.*

sanctimonialis, is, *f., a nun.*

sanctio, onis, *f., a decree, ordi-nance, sanction.*

sanctitas, atis, *f., sacredness, sanc-tity.*—One kind of *sanctitas* is: **sanctitas absoluta,** *the absolute sanctity.*

sanctuarium, ii, *n., a sanctuary, shrine.*

sanctus, a, um, *holy.* On **sapientia sanctorum,** see *sapientia* under 1. —**sanctus,** i, *m., a saint, a holy man.*—**sancte,** *adv., religiously, with holy awe.*—**sancta sancto-rum,** *in pl., holy of holies.*

sandalium, ii, *n., a slipper, sandal.*

sane, *adv.,* see *sanus.*

sanguineus, a, um, *adj.,* (1) *of blood, consisting of blood, bloody.* (2) *sanguine.*

sanguinifluus, a, um, *adj., blood-flowing.*

sanguis, inis, *m., blood,* (1) *lit.,* (2) *plur.,* (a) late Lat.: *vir sanguinum,* i.e., *bloody, violent, cruel,* (b) used for sing., (3) transf., *blood,* i.e., *consanguinity, descent, race, family.*—**sanguine coniuncti,** *blood-relations, relatives by blood.*—**effundere humanum sanguinem,** *to shed human blood.*—**effundere sanguinem,** *to shed another's blood.*—**effusio sanguinis,** *the shedding of* (*one's*) *blood.*—**iudicium sanguinis,** *a sentence of blood,* i.e., *capital punishment.*—**in causa sanguinis,** *on trial for life.*—**baptismus sanguinis,** *baptism of blood,* i.e., *martyrdom.*—**poena sanguinis,** *the punishment of blood,* i.e., *death.*

sanies, em, e, *f., sanies, bloody matter.*

sanitas, atis, *f.,* (1) lit., *soundness of body, health,* (2) fig., *health* in a spiritual sense.

sano, are, avi, atum, 1, *v. a.,* (1) lit., *to make sound, to heal, cure, restore to health,* (2) fig., *to heal, correct, restore, repair, allay, quiet,* etc.

sanus, a, um, *adj., sound, whole, healthy, physically* or *mentally,* (1) lit., *sound in body, whole, healthy, well,* (2) fig., *sound in mind, in judgment, in belief,* etc. —**sane,** *adv., reasonably, rightly.*

Saphira, ae, *f., Saphira,* the wife of Ananias, in the days of the Apostles.

sapidus, a, um, *adj.,* (1) lit., *well-tasted, savory,* (2) fig., *sweet.*

sapiens, entis, *Part.* and *P. a.,* see *sapio.*

sapienter, *adv.,* see *sapiens.*

sapientia, ae, *f.,* (1) *wisdom* in the sense of a *habitus,* the opposite of *stultitia,* (2) *wisdom* in the sense of an act, *a judgment in the light of the ultimate causes,* (3) *wisdom* in the sense of the highest kind of science, (4) *wisdom* in the sense of a person, i.e., the second person of God. On the difference between *sapientia* and *scientia,* see *scientia* under 1. —**per se sapientia,** *wisdom existing for itself.* On **concupiscentia sapientiae,** see *concupiscentia* under 1; on **contemplatio sapientiae,** see *contemplatio;* on **discretio sapientiae,** see *discretio* under 3; on **donum sapientiae,** see *donum* under 2; on **gratia sapientiae,** see *gratia* under 2; on **veritas sapientiae,** see *veritas* under 1.—**initium sapientiae,** *the beginning of wisdom,* understood in the sense of the theologians.— **sermo sapientiae,** *the charismatic gift of wisdom.* Cf. also **donum sapientiae** under *donum* b.— Kinds of *sapientia* in this (1) sense are: (a), **sapientia adquisita** and **sapientia infusa,** *the studied wisdom* and *that infused* (by God).—(b), **sapientia animalis, sapientia diabolica,** and **sapientia terrena,** *the carnal, the diabolic,* and *the earthly wisdom.*—(c), **sapientia apparens seu visa** and **sapientia exsistens,** *the apparent wisdom* or *that according to* *appearance* and *the existing in reality.*—(d), **sapientia appropriata,** *the appropriated wisdom.*—(e), **sapientia creata** and **sapientia increata,** *the created wisdom* or *that with which God has endowed creatures* and *the divine wisdom.*—(f), **sapientia diabolica,** see *sapientia animalis.*—(g), **sapientia divina seu sanctorum** and **sapientia hominum seu humana,** *the wisdom of God* (see *sapientia increata*), *that of the saints,* and *that of men.*—(h), **sapientia essentialis,** and **sapientia exemplata,** *wisdom by nature* and *by participation.*—(i), **sapientia exemplata,** see *sapientia essentialis.*—(j), **sapientia exsistens,** see *sapientia apparens.*—(k), **sapientia genita** and **sapientia ingenita,** *the generated* and *the ungenerated wisdom* (in God).—(l), **sapientia hominum,** see *sapientia divina.*—(m), **sapientia humana,** see *sapientia divina.*—(n), **sapientia in aliquo genere seu quaedam seu particularis** and **sapientia simpliciter seu universalis,** *wisdom in any genus of things* or *the highest knowledge of any particular class* or *kind of things* and *the simple* or *absolute* or *universal wisdom.*—(o), **sapientia increata,** see *sapientia creata.*—(p), **sapientia infusa,** see *sapientia adquisita.*—(q), **sapientia ingenita,** see *sapientia genita.*—(r), **sapientia mala** and **sapientia stulta,** *the morally bad wisdom* (because directed toward something created as the

highest goal) and *the foolish wisdom.*—(s), **sapientia mundana seu mundi seu saeculi seu saecularis seu temporalis** and **sapientia spiritualis seu secundum Deum,** *the worldly* or *the temporal wisdom* or *the wisdom of this world* or *of the children of the world* and *spiritual wisdom* or *the wisdom that is according to God* or *that of the children of God.*—(t), **sapientia mundi,** see *sapientia mundana.*—(u), **sapientia particularis,** see *sapientia in aliquo genere.*—(v), **sapientia quaedam,** see *sapientia in aliquo genere.*—(w), **sapientia saecularis,** see *sapientia mundana.*—(x), **sapientia saeculi,** see *sapientia mundana.*—(y), **sapientia sanctorum,** see *sapientia divina.*—(z), **sapientia secundum Deum,** see *sapientia mundana.* —(a^2), **sapientia simpliciter,** see *sapientia in aliquo genere.*—(b^2), **sapientia stulta,** see *sapientia mala.*—(c^2), **sapientia temporalis,** see *sapientia mundana.*—(d^2), **sapientia terrena,** see *sapientia animalis.*—(e^2), **sapientia universalis,** see *sapientia in aliquo genere.*— (f^2), **sapientia visa,** see *sapientia apparens.*—Kinds of *sapientia* in this (3) sense are: **sapientia divina** and **sapientia mundana,** *the divine* and *worldly wisdom* or *the wisdom of the world,* i.e., the science of theology, quae considerat causas superiores, id est, divinas secundum quas iudicat, dicuntur autem superiores causae divina attributa, ut sapientia, bonitas et voluntas divina et huiusmodi, and the science of philosophy quae considerat causas inferiores scilicet causas causatas, et secundum eas iudicat.

sapio, ere, ivi or ii, 3, *v. n.* and *a.,* (1) lit., *to taste, savor; to smack,* or *savor of,* (2) fig., (a) *to taste* or *relish* something eternal, spiritual, earthly or some abstract thing; (b) *to know, understand,* (c) *be wise, show good sense;* (d) *to agree with;* (e) *to be highminded,* or *proud.*—**sapiens,** entis, *P. a., wise, knowing, sensible.*— Kinds of *sapiens* are: (a), **sapiens huius vel illius rei seu in aliquo genere** and **sapiens simpliciter seu maxime,** *wise in this* or *that thing* or *in some respect,* and *simply* or *absolutely wise* or *especially wise.*—(b), **sapiens in aliquo genere,** see *sapiens huius vel illius rei.*—(c), **sapiens maxime,** see *sapiens huius vel illius rei.* —(d), **sapiens simpliciter,** see *sapiens huius vel illius rei.*—(e), **sapiens vere,** *truly wise,* the opposite of *sapiens secundum quandam similitudinem,* i.e., *wise according to a certain similarity with the truly wise.*—**sapiens,** entis, *m., a shrewd, wise person.* —**nullus sapiens disputat contra negnatem principia suae artis,** *no wise man disputes with him who denies the principles of his science.*—**sapiens dominatur astris,** *the wise man rules above the stars,* id est, inclinationi,

quae ex astrorum dispositione relinquitur.—**Sapiens,** entis, *m., the Wiseman of the Old Testament,* the author of the Book of Wisdom.—**sapienter,** *adv., discreetly, prudently, wisely.*

sapor, oris, *m.,* (1) lit., *flavor, relish, savor, taste,* (2) fig., (a) *savor, distinctive property,* (b) *the sweetness of wisdom,* (c) *feeling, something that indicates the presence of.*

saporosus, a, um, *adj., of good flavor, palatable.*

Sara, ae, *f., Sara,* the wife of Abraham and the mother of Isaac.

Sarabaita, ae, *m., a Sarabaite* one of certain vagrant and unruly Oriental monks in the early church.

Saraceni, orum, *m., the Saracens* a people of Arabia Felix.

sarcina, ae, *f., a burden* used lit. and fig.

sartago, inis, *f., a pan for baking; a frying-pan,* used lit. and fig.

satago, ere, see *satis.*

Satanas, ae, and **Satan,** *indecl. m., an adversary, Satan, the Devil.*

satelles, itis, comm., *an attendant.*

satietas, atis, *f., a sufficiency, abundance,* used lit. and fig.

satio, are, avi, atum, 1, *v. a.,* (1) lit., *to fill, satisfy; to sate, satiate* with food, (2) fig., *to satisfy, glut, satiate a desire,* in a good or bad sense.

satis, sat, *adj.,* and *adverb,* (1) *adj., enough, sufficient,* (2) *adv., sufficiently, enough,* (a) with verbs, (b) adjectives, (c) with adverbs. —**satis facio** or in one word, **satis-**

facio, (1) *to give satisfaction, to satisfy, content, to gratify;* (2) *to give satisfaction* (by word or deed); *to make amends* or *reparation* for sin, *to ask pardon,* used with *de, pro,* the *dat.;* (3) *to give satisfaction* by suffering a penalty as Christ did for the sins of men.—**sat ago,** also in one word, **satago,** ere, 3, *n., to bustle about, to strive, busy about, be anxious to do something.*

satisfacio, see *satis* under (3).

satisfactio, onis, *f., satisfaction.* On **opus satisfactionis,** see *opus* under 4.—Kinds of *satisfactio* are: (a), **satisfactio imperfecte sufficiens** and **satisfactio perfecte sufficiens,** *the imperfectly sufficing* and *the perfectly sufficing satisfaction.*—(b), **satisfactio perfecte sufficiens,** see *sapientia imperfecte sufficiens.*—(c), **satisfactio sacramentalis,** *the sacramental satisfaction* or *that belonging to the sacrament of penance.*

satisfactivus, a, um, *adj., satisfying, satisfactive,* synonym of *satisfactorius.* On **vis satisfactiva,** see *vis* under 1.

satisfactor, oris, *m., a satisfier, a person* or *thing that satisfies.*

satisfactorie, see *satisfactorius.*

satisfactorius, a, um, *adj., satisfying, satisfactory,* synonym of *satisfactivus.* On **opus satisfactorium,** see *opus* under 4; on **oratio satisfactoria,** see *oratio* under 3; on **poena satisfactoria,** see *poena.* —satisfactorie, *adv., satisfactorily.*

saturitas, atis, *f., fulness, plenty, abundance, satiety.*

Saturnus, i, *m., Saturn,* the planet Saturn.

saucio, are, avi, atum, 1, *v. a., to wound, hurt,* used lit. and fig.

Saul, ulis, or *indecl. m.,* (*gen.* Saulis, *dat.* Sauli, *acc.* Saulem), *Saul,* the first King of the Jews.

saxeus, a, um, *adj., of rock, stone, rocky, stony.*

saxum, i, *n., a rock.*

scabellum, i, *n., dim., footstool, a low stool.*

scabies, em, e, *f.,* (1) in partic., as a disease *the scab, itch,* (2) *pruriency, lustfulness* of the flesh.

scabiosus, a, um, *adj., scabby, mangy.*

scaenicus, a, um, *adj.,* see *scenicus.*

scala, ae, *f., a ladder, scaling-ladder.*

scalpo, ere, psi, ptum, 3, *v. a., to scratch.*

scamnum, i, *n., a bench.*

scandalizo, are, avi, atum, 1, *to cause to stumble, tempt to evil, scandalize.*

scandalum, i, *n.,* (1) *stumbling block* in the broader sense of the word, (2) *stumbling block* in the narrower sense of the word, a word or act which occasions the downfall of someone, *scandal* (= *scandalum spirituale*).—Kinds of *scandalum* in this sense are: **scandalum corporale** and **scandalum spirituale,** *the corporal* and *the spiritual stumbling block* or *scandal.*—Kinds of *scandalum* in this (2) sense are: (a), **scanda-**

lum activum and scandalum passivum, *the scandal that is given*
and *that which is received.*—(b),
scandalum activum per accidens
and scandalum activum per se,
unintentional scandal or *that
given accidentally,* and *deliberate, intentional scandal.*—(c),
scandalum activum per se, see
scandalum activum per accidens.
—(d), scandalum passivum, see
scandalum activum.—(e), scandalum Pharisaeorum and scandalum pusillorum, *the Pharisaic
scandal* and *that taken by the
weak* and *ignorant.*—(f), scandalum publicum, *public scandal.*—
(g), scandalum pusillorum, see
scandalum Pharisaeorum.

scapulae, arum, *f., the shoulder-
blades.*

sceleratissime, *adv., sup.,* see *sceleratus.*

sceleratus, a, um, *P. a., wicked, vicious.*—sceleratissime, *adv., sup.,
very impiously, very wickedly.*

scelus, eris, *n., an evil deed; a wicked, heinous,* or *impious action; a
crime, sin, enormity, wickedness*
(the strongest general term for a
morally bad act or quality).

scena, ae, *f., a scene in a play,* a
division of an act during which
there is no change of place or
lapse in continuity of time.

scenicus, i, *m., a player, actor.*

scenopegia, ae, *f.,* = *skenopegia,*
the Jewish Feast of Tabernacles,
which was kept for seven days,
to commemorate the blessing of
being protected and led by God

through the desert, where they
lived in tents.

sceptrum, i, *n.,* = *skeptrum, a
sceptre.*

schedula, ae, *f., dim., a small leaf
of paper.*

schisma, atıs, *n., a split, separation,
disunion, schism,* in particular,
*separation from the Catholic
Church.* On the difference between *schisma* and *haeresis,* we
read: haeresis et schisma distinguuntur secundum ea quibus
utrumque per se et directe opponitur, nam haeresis per se opponitur fidei; schisma autem per se
opponitur unitati ecclesiasticae
charitatis. et ideo sicut fides et
charitas sunt diversae virtutes,
quamvis quicumque caret fide,
careat charitate; ita etiam schisma et haeresis sunt diversa vitia,
quamvis quicumque est haereticus, sit etiam schismaticus; sed
non convertitur, SS. Q. 39. Art.
1 ad 3.

schismaticus, i, *m.,* = *schismatikos,
a separatist, seceder, schismatic.*
On the difference between
schismaticus and *haereticus,* see
schisma.

schola, ae, *f., a place of learning, a
school.*

scholares, ium, *m., scholars.*

scibilis, e, *adj., that can be known
with certainty, knowable, discernible,* the opposite of *opinabilis.* On ratio scibilis seu scibilium, see *ratio* under 6, 8, and 14;
on substantia (sc. *scibilis*), see
substantia under 2.—scientia est

recta ratio scibilium, see *scientia* under 1.—**scientiae distinguuntur secundum diversas rationes scibilium,** see *scientia* under 1.

scienter, *adv.,* see *scio.*

scientia, ae, *f.,* (1) scientific knowledge in the narrow and proper sense of the word, as distinct from *ars, intellectus, prudentia,* and *sapientia,* i.e., *the absolutely certain knowledge of a derived truth in the speculative order, or certain* and *evident knowledge acquired by reasoning strictly from indisputable principles,* (2) *science* in a broad sense, i.e., intellectual knowledge that is certain, and evident, the opposite of *fides* and *opinio* on one hand, and of *ignorantia* and *nescientia* on the other, (3) *the gift of knowledge,* see *donum,* 2 (n), (4) *the charismatic gift of knowledge,* see *gratia,* 2 (h²). On the difference between the five intellectual habits, *scientia, ars, intellectus, prudentia,* and *sapientia,* we read: scientia est conclusionum et intellectus principiorum, 1 Anal. 7 d; tria eorum, scilicet sapientia, scientia et intellectus important rectitudinem cognitionis circa necessaria, scientia quidem circa conclusiones, intellectus autem circa principia, sapientia autem circa altissimas causas, quae sunt causae divinae, alia vero duo scilicet ars et prudentia important rectitudinem rationis circa contingentia, prudentia quidem circa agibilia, id est,

circa actus qui sunt in operante, puta amare, odire, eligere et huiusmodi, quae pertinet ad actus morales, quorum est directiva prudentia, ars autem importat rectitudinem rationis circa factibilia, id est, circa ea quae aguntur in exteriorem materiam, sicut est secare et alia huiusmodi opera, in quibus dirigit ars, hic autem addit rationem, quae pertinet ad deductionem principiorum in conclusiones, 1 Anal. 44 i.—**actus scientiae seu usus scientiae,** *the activity* or *use of the habitus of knowledge* or *science,* i.e., considering or pondering; cf. *considerare* and *consideratio.*—**principium scientiae,** *the principle of science.*—**semen scientiae,** *the seed* or *grain of science.*—**sermo scientiae,** *the charismatic gift of knowledge of divine things.* Cf. **gratia sermonis scientiae** under 2.—**spectamina scientiae,** *the mode* or *example of science,* i.e., *divine ideas.*—**subiectum scientiae,** *the object as well as the subject of science;* cf. *actus scientiae* above. On **certitudo scientiae,** see *certitudo* under 2; on **clavis scientiae,** see *clavis* under 2; on **donum scientiae,** see *donum* under 2; on **gratia sermonis scientiae,** see *gratia* under 2; on **habitus scientiae,** see *habitus* under 4; on **modus scientiae,** see *modus* under 3; on **peccare ex certa scientia,** see *peccare* under 2; on **perfectio scientiae,** see *perfectio* under 2; on **quantitas**

scientiae, see *quantitas* under 2; on **speculatio scientiae adquisitae,** see *speculatio;* on **terminus scientiae,** see *terminus* under 2; on **unitas scientiae,** see *unitas;* on **veritas scientiae,** see *veritas* under 1.—Kinds of *scientia* in this (1) sense are: (a), **scientia activa** and **scientia factiva,** *moral science which is concerned with doing (agere) and actions,* i.e., the practical sense, and *technical knowledge of making (facere) or producing things.*—(b), **scientia actualis, seu in actu, scientia habitualis seu in habitu,** and **scientia in potentia,** *knowledge actually in use, knowledge possessed but not being used,* and *knowledge not possessed but possible of acquisition.*—(c), **scientia afficiens,** *knowledge that foments love.*—(d), **scientia analytica,** *demonstrative logic.* Cf. *analyticus* under 1.—(e), **scientia architectonica seu regitiva seu principalis** and **scientia famulans seu servilis,** *the commanding* or *guiding* or *principal science* and *the serving* or *servile science.*—(f), **scientia astrologica seu astronomica, scientia harmonica** and **scientia perspectiva seu speculativa,** *astronomy, theory of harmony,* and *descriptive geometry.* Cf. *scientia doctrinalis.*—(g), **scientia astronomica,** see *scientia astrologica.*—(h), **scientia civilis, •seu politica, scientia oeconomica** and **scientia ethica seu monastica,** *teaching regarding civic life* or *political*

science, science of domestic life or *the family,* social science, and *moral philosophy* or *the science on the individual life of a man.* —(i), **scientia communis seu universalis** and **scientia particularis,** *the general* or *universal* and *the particular science* or *the general* or *universal* and *the particular knowledge.*—(j), **scientia disciplinalis seu mathematica, scientia metaphysica seu metaphysicae** and **scientia naturalis,** *the discipline per eminentiam* (see *disciplina* under 4) or *mathematics, metaphysics* and *natural science.* —(k), **scientia disparata,** *the unlike* or *entirely different science.* —(l), **scientia divina,** *the divine science* or *the science about God* and *divine things,* (cf. *scientia divina* under 2) or *theology, supernatural as well as natural,* which latter is usually identified with all metaphysics.—(m), **scientia divinativa seu sperativa,** *the science which foretells* (the future) or *that permits one to hope.*—(n), **scientia doctrinalis seu speculativa seu theorica** and **scientia operativa seu practica,** *the science that instructs* or *that aims merely at knowing* and *the practical science which has as its purpose action* or *regulation of action.*—(o), **scientia ethica,** see *scientia civilis.*—(p), **scientia factiva,** see *scientia activa.*—(q), **scientia falsa** and **scientia vera seu recta,** *the false and the true* or *right science.*—(r), **scientia famu-**

lans, see *scientia architectonica.* —(s), scientia harmonica, see *scientia astrologica.*—(t), scientia humanitus tradita, *the science learned in a human manner* or *the generally human science.*— (u), scientia in actu, see *scientia actualis.*—(v), scientia inferior seu subalterna seu subalternata and scientia superior seu subalternans, *a science is superior if its conclusions are used as principles by an inferior.*—(w), scientia in habitu, see *scientia actualis.* —(x), scientia in potentia, see *scientia actualis.*—(y), scientia inquisitiva and scientia iudicativa, *the experimental* and *the investigating science* and *the exact, true science.*—(z), scientia intellectualis, *intellectual science* or *the science of purely intelligible things.*—(a^2), scientia iudicativa, see *scientia inquisitiva.*—(b^2), scientia iuris, *jurisprudence* or *the science of law.*—(c^2), scientia legispositiva and scientia militaris, *the science of legislation* and *the military science.*—(d^2), scientia libera seu liberalis and scientia serva seu servilis, *the free* and *the servile knowledge.*—(e^2), scientia logicalis, *logic.*—(f^2), scientia mathematica, see *scientia disciplinalis.*—(g^2), scientia media, scientia pure mathematica, and scientia pure naturalis, *the middle* or *mathematical-physical science, the pure mathematical* and *the pure physical science.*—(h^2), scientia metaphysica seu meta-

physicae, see *scientia disciplinalis.*—(i^2), scientia militaris, see *scientia legispositiva.*—(j^2), scientia monastica, see *scientia civilis.*— (k^2), scientia moralis, *science of morality of human acts.*—(l^2), scientia naturalis, see *scientia disciplinalis.*—(m^2), scientia oeconomica, see *scientia civilis.*—(n^2), scientia particularis, see *scientia communis.*—(o^2), scientia perspectiva, see *scientia astrologica.*— (p^2), scientia politica, see *scientia civilis.*—(q^2), scientia practica, see *scientia doctrinalis.*—(r^2), scientia practica secundum quid and scientia practica simpliciter seu tantum, *the science practical in a certain respect* and *the simple* or *purely practical science,* cf. *scientia doctrinalis.* Cf. *scientia doctrinalis.*—(s^2), scientia practica simpliciter seu tantum, see *scientia practica secundum quid.*—(t^2), scientia principalis, see *scientia architectonica.*—(u^2), scientia propter quid and scientia quia, *knowledge of why a thing is so and cannot be otherwise,* and *knowledge merely that it is so.*— (v^2), scientia pure mathematica, see *scientia media.*—(w^2), scientia pure naturalis, see *scientia media.*—(x^2), scientia quae est ex additione seu appositione seu quae se habet ex additione and scientia quae est ex paucioribus, *the science whose matter includes the matter of another science after the manner of an addition* and *that which treats* simpler things.—(y^2), scientia quae est ex paucioribus, see scientia quae est ex additione.—(z^2), scientia quae se habet ex additione, see scientia quae est ex additione.—(a^3), scientia quia, see scientia propter quid.—(b^3), scientia rationalis, and scientia realis, the science of reason or logic.—(c^3), scientia realis, see scientia rationalis.—(d^3), scientia recta, see scientia falsa.—(e^3), scientia regitiva, see scientia architectonica.—(f^3), scientia rhetorica, rhetoric or the science of eloquence.—(g^3), scientia serva, see scientia libera.—(h^3), scientia servilis, see scientia architectonica and scientia libera.—(i^3), scientia sophistica, sophistic science or sophism, training in outwitting through the art of disputation.—(j^3), scientia speculative, see scientia doctrinalis.—(k^3), scientia speculativa secundum quid and scientia speculativa simpliciter, speculative science with respect to something or practical speculative science and the simple or purely speculative science.—(l^3), scientia speculativa simpliciter seu tantum, see scientia speculativa secundum quid.—(m^3), scientia sperativa, see scientia divinativa.—(n^3), scientia subalterna, see scientia inferior.—(o^3), scientia subalternans, see scientia inferior.—(p^3), scientia subalternata, see scientia inferior.—(q^3), scientia superior, see scientia inferior.—(r^3), scientia theorica, see scientia doctrinalis.—(s^3), scientia universalis, see scientia communis.—(t^3), scientia vera, see scientia falsa.—ad scientiam pertinet, considerare non solum subiectum, sed etiam partes et passiones subiecti, or, cuiuslibet scientiae est considerare subiectum et passiones et causas, it is proper to a science to consider not only its object but also its sub-divisions and its characteristics and its causes.—aliae scientiae sunt de rebus, et aliae de intentionibus intellectus, or, sunt scientiae de rebus, non autem de speciebus vel intentionibus intelligibilibus nisi sola scientia rationalis, some sciences treat of things outside the mind, others, e.g., logic with its special discipline treat of ideas and concepts or the intellectual representation of things.—contrarorum eadem est scientiae, see contrarius under 1.—cuiuslibet scientiae est, considerare subiectum et passiones et causas, see above: ad scientiam pertinet etc.—diversae ratio cognoscibilis diversitatem scientiarum inducit or scientiae distinguuntur secundum diversas rationes scibilium, the different aspects of a knowable thing causes a differentiation of the sciences, or the sciences are differentiated according to the formally different aspects of knowable things.—diversae scientia ex diversis principiis procedunt, different sciences come from different principles, and

*these are different when neither
the principles of one science proceed from those of another nor
the principles of both sciences
proceed from any principles
which are common to both.*—**habitus scientiarum, quibus intellectus perficitur, distinguuntur
secundum differentiam separationis a materia,** *the habitus of sciences by which the intellect is
perfected are distinguished according to the degree of abstraction from matter.*—**nulla scientia
probat sua principia,** *no science
proves its principles,* i.e., *those
truths on which it bases its conclusions.*—**particularium non est
scientia,** *science deals with universals,* see *particularis.*—**scientia
dicitur una ex hoc quod est unius
generis subiecti,** the translation
of the Aristotelian passage: *mia
d'episteme estin he henos genous,*
(Anal. post. 1. 28, 87. a. 28),
*the unity of a science comes from
the common class of thing which
it studies as its subject.*—**scientiae
distinguuntur secundum diversas
rationes scibilium** see above: *diversa ratio cognoscibilis* etc.—**scientia est quodammodo scibilia,**
the translation of the Aristotelian
passage: *estin d'he episteme men
ta episteta pos, science is in a
certain degree the knowable;* cf.
intellectus and *sensus* under 3.
—**scientia est universalium,** or,
scientia non est de singularibus,
the translation of the Aristotelian
passage: *he d'episteme ton ka-*

*tholou, a science treats only of
the general* and *not of the individual.* Cf. *intellectus* and *sensus* under 3.—**scientia non est
corruptibilium,** *there is no science of changeable things as
such.*—**scientia non est de singu-
laribùs,** see above: *scientia est
universalium.*—**scientia non est
eorum quae cognoscuntur per
sensum,** *there is no science of
sensible things as such.*—**scientia
non est eorum quae sunt a fortuna,** *there is no science of such
as occurs from chance* or *accidentally* but only *of that which
always* or *usually takes place.*—
**sunt scientiae de rebus non au-
tem de speciebus vel intentionibus intellegibilibus, nisi sola scientia rationalis,** see above: *aliae
scientia sunt* etc.—**una scientia est
alia certior,** *one science gives
greater certainty than another.*—
Kinds of *scientia* in this (2) sense
are: (a), **scientia absoluta seu
simplex** and **scientia collativa seu
discursiva seu ratiocinativa,** *independent* (of a principle of knowledge) *knowledge* or *simple
knowledge* (i.e., not composed
through a *discursus rationis*), and
*knowledge achieved through a
comparison* or *a derivation of
reason.*—(b), **scientia adquisita
seu experimentalis seu experientiae, scientia innata seu connaturalis seu naturalis** and **scientia
indita seu infusa,** *knowledege
acquired by use of faculties,
knowledge inborn* or *bestowed*

by nature, and *knowledge additionally infused* or *bestowed* by God or one of His angels.—(c), **scientia angelica seu angelorum, scientia beata seu beatitudinis seu beatorum** and **scientia Dei seu divina,** *the knowledge of the angels, that of the blessed in heaven,* and *the knowledge of God* or *about God.* Cf. **scientia divina** under 1.—(d), **scientia angelorum,** see *scientia angelica.*—(e), **scientia approbationis, scientia simplicis intellegentiae seu notitiae,** and **scientia visionis,** *the divine knowledge of things ordained to existence, which are good, knowledge of both possible* and *real things according to a kind of simple representation* or *understanding* (cf. *scientia absoluta*), and *knowledge of things ordained to real existence, even though morally evil, in the manner of objective consideration* and *contemplation.*—(f), **scientia beata,** see *scientia angelica.*—(g), **scientia beatitudinis,** see *scientia angelica.*—(h), **scientia beatorum,** see *scientia angelica.*—(i), **scientia certa** and **scientia incerta,** *certain* and *uncertain knowledge.*—(j), **scientia collativa,** see *scientia absoluta.*—(k), **scientia completa seu perfecta** and **scientia incompleta seu imperfecta seu inchoata,** *the complete* or *completed* or *perfect knowledge,* and *the incomplete* or *imperfect knowledge* or *knowledge begun.*—(l), **scientia comprehensiva seu supersubstan-**

tialis, *the comprehensive* or *supersubstantial knowledge,* i.e., that which surpasses a created substance.—(m), **scientia conclusionum,** *the science* or *knowledge of conclusions.*—(n), **scientia coniecturalis,** *conjectural knowledge.* —(o), **scientia connaturalis,** see *scientia adquisita.*—(p), **scientia creata** and **scientia increata,** *the created* or *creatural knowledge* and *the uncreated* or *divine knowledge.*—(q), **scientia credendorum, scientia desiderandorum,** and **scientia operandorum,** *the knowledge of believable things, that of desirable things,* and *that of things to be done.*—(r), **scientia demonstrativa, scientia dialectica,** and **scientia indemonstrabilis,** *the science that proves with complete certainty* or *the science about proof,* which forms a part of logic, *the science that gives only probability* and *the unprovable knowledge,* i.e., *intuitive.*— (s), **scientia desiderandorum,** see *scientia credendorum.*—(t), **scientia despotica seu dominativa** and **scientia servilis,** *the imperial* or *domineering and servile* or *slavish knowledge,* i.e., *the knowledge to rule over other men* and *that to do servile* or *slavish work for others.*—(u), **scientia dialectica,** see *scientia demonstrativa.*— (v), **scientia discursiva,** see *scientia absoluta.*—(w), **scientia divina,** see *scientia angelica.*—(x), **scientia dominativa,** see *scientia despotica.*—(y), **scientia experien-**

tiae, see *scientia adquisita.*—(z).
scientia experimentalis, see *scientia adquisita.*—(a²), **scientia imperfecta,** see *scientia completa.*—(b²), **scientia incerta,** see *scientia certa.*—(c²), **scientia inchoata,** see *scientia completa.*—(d²), **scientia incompleta,** see *scientia completa.*—(e²), **scientia increata,** see *scientia creata.*—(f²), **scientia indemonstrabilis,** see *scientia demonstrativa.*—(g²), **scientia indita,** see *scientia adquisita.*—(h²), **scientia infusa,** see *scientia adquisita.*—(i²), **scientia innata,** see *scientia adquisita.*—(j²), **scientia magica,** *the art of magic.*—(k²), **scientia naturalis,** see *scientia adquisita.*—(l²), **scientia operandorum,** see *scientia credendorum.*—(m²), **scientia perfecta,** see *scientia completa.*—(n²), **scientia ratiocinativa,** see *scientia absoluta.*—(o²), **scientia servilis,** see *scientia despotica.*—(p²), **scientia simplex,** see *scientia absoluta.*—(q²), **scientia simplicis intellegentiae,** see *scientia approbationis.*—(r²), **scientia simplicis notitiae,** see *scientia approbationis.*—(s²), **scientia supersubstantialis,** see *scientia comprehensiva.*—(t²), **scientia visionis,** see *scientia approbationis.*—**naturaliter unusquisque desiderat scientiam,** the translation of the Aristotelian passage: *pantes anthropoi tou eidenai eregontai physei, every man by nature desires knowledge.* Cf. *scire* under 2.—**quanto scientia est perfectior, tanto est magis unita,** *the more perfect a knowledge is, the more unified it is in itself,* i.e., *tanto minus est distincta per plures habitus.*

scientialis, e, *adj., belonging to* or *concerned with science, producing knowledge, scientific,* synonym of *scientificus,* does not occur in the Summa Theologica. On **demonstratio scientialis,** see *demonstratio* under 2; on **syllogismus scientialis,** see *syllogismus.*

scientificus, a, um, *adj.,* (1) *belonging to* or *concerned with science, producing knowledge, scientific,* synonym of *scientialis,* (2) *scientifically educated, learned.* On **demonstratio scientifica,** see *demonstratio* under 2; on **ratio scientifica,** see *ratio* under 3.— **scientificum** sc. **genus** seu **principium,** the translation of Aristotelian *epistomonikon, the habitus* or *the faculty for receiving the habitus to know necessary things.*

scilicet, *adv.,* (1) lit., *it is evident, plain, clear,* or *manifest; of course, naturally, evidently, certainly, undoubtedly,* (2) transf., *namely, to wit, that is to say,* (3) *evidently, because.*

scindo, ere, scidi, scissum, 3, *v. a.,* (1) *to cut, tear, rend,* or *break asunder; to split, cleave, divide,* (2) *to divide,* used fig.

scintilla, ae, *f., a spark;* trop., *a spark, glimmer, faint trace.*— Kinds of *scintilla* are: (a), **scintilla conscientiae,** *a spark of con-*

science.—(b), **scintilla rationis,** *the spark of reason.*

scio, ire, ivi, itum, 4, (1) *to know* in the narrower and proper sense of the word, i.e., to know something from its principles, to know something with certainty as necessarily true, as distinct from *cognoscere,* (2) *know* in the broad sense of the word, i.e., to know intellectually, synonym of *cognoscere,* the opposite of *nescire.*—Kinds of *scire* in this (1) sense are: (a), **scire addiscendo** and **scire inveniendo,** *to know by learning* and *to know by experimenting.*—(b), **scire in actu, scire in habitu,** and **scire in potentia,** *to know actually, to have science in the form of a habitus,* and *according to potentiality.*—(c), **scire in habitu,** see *scire in actu.*—(d), **scire in particulari** and **scire in universali,** *to know something in particular* and *to know something in general.*—(e), **scire in potentia,** see *scire in actu.*—(f), **scire in universali,** see *scire in particulari.*—(g), **scire inveniendo,** see *scire addiscendo.*—(h), **scire per effectum seu quia** and **scire propter quid,** *to know the existence of a cause by the effect and the nature of an effect by its causes,* or *to know the existence and the reasons why,* or *to know in an a posteriori manner* and *in an a priori manner.*—(i), **scire perfecte,** *to know in a perfect manner.*—(j), **scire propter quid,** see *scire per effectum.*—(k), **scire quia,** see

scire per effectum. On **modus sciendi,** see *modus* under 2.—Kinds of *scire* in this (2) sense are the following: (a), **scire demonstrative seu ex necessitate** and **scire probabiliter,** *to know something as being true of necessity* and *something as being probably true.*—(b), **scire ex necessitate,** see *scire demonstrative.*—(c), **scire expliciter,** *to know something in an explicit manner.*—(d), **scire immaterialiter** and **scire materialiter,** *to know something in an immaterial* or *incorporeal way* and *to know something in a material way,* or *to know something according to its matter.*—(e), **scire indistincte,** *to know something in an indistinct manner.*—(f), **scire materialiter,** see *scire immaterialiter.*—(g), **scire per accidens seu secundum accidens** and **scire per se,** *to know something because of something else* or *to know by accident* and *to know something according to its essence* or *as such.*—(h), **scire per se,** see *scire per accidens.*—(i), **scire probabiliter,** see *scire demonstrative.*—(j), **scire secundum accidens,** see *scire per accidens.*—(k), **scire secundum quid** and **scire simpliciter,** *to know something with respect to something* or *in a certain respect* and *to know something simply* or *absolutely.*—(l), **scire simpliciter,** see *scire secundum quid.*—**omnibus hominibus naturaliter desiderium inest ad sciendum,** the translation of the

Aristotelian passage: *pantes anthropoi tou eidenai oregontai physei, all men have by nature a desire for knowing or knowledge.* Cf. *scientia* under 2. —**sciens**, entis, *P. a., knowing.*— **scitus**, a, um, *P. a., known.*—**scienter**, *adv., knowingly, understandingly; wisely, skillfully, expertly.*

Scipio, onis, *m., Scipio,* Publius Cornelius Scipio Africanus the Younger, conqueror of the Carthaginians in the third Punic War (46 B.C.). The **Somnium Scipionis,** *the Dream of Scipio.* Cicero closes the *De Republica* with the *Dream of Scipio* which extends the theme beyond the world and the brief span of human life into the universe and eternity.

sciscitor, ari, atus, 1, *v. dep. a., to ask, inquire, question, examine, interrogate.*

scissio, onis, *f., a cleaving, dividing, scission* of a number.

scissura, ae, *f., a tearing, rending; a rent, cleft, scissure.*

scissus, a, um, *P. a., split, rent, broken asunder.*

scopus, (*skopos*), i, *m., a watching.*

scortum, i, *n., a prostitute, harlot.*

scriba, ae, *m.,* (1) *a notary,* (2) *a Scribe,* a doctor of the Jewish law, one whose duty it was to guard and expound the sacred text.

scribo, ere, psi, ptum, 3, *v. a., to write,* (1) in gen., (1) in Eccl. Lat. as a formula of quotation

from the Scripture: *scriptum est,* i.e., it is written in Holy Scripture.—**scribens,** entis, *P. a., writing.*—**scriptus,** a, um, *P. a., written.*—**scriptus libellus repudii,** *a written bill of divorce.*—**scriptum,** i, *n., written statement.*

scriptor, oris, *m.,* (1) *one who writes, a writer, composer, reporter, narrator,* (2) *a person writing anything.*

scriptura, ae, *f.,* (1) *writing, handwriting, written presentation,* (2) *a writing, a written book, a written work,* (3) *Sacred Scripture* both in the collective sense of the word and in that of a single writing, (4) *a scriptural passage.* On **lex scripturae,** see *lex* under 1; on **veritas sacrae scripturae,** see *veritas* under 1.—Kinds of *scriptura* in this (2) sense are: (a), **scriptura apocrypha,** and **scriptura authentica,** *the apocryphal* or *unauthentic writing* and *the authentic writing.*—(b), **scriptura authentica,** see *scriptura apocrypha.*—(c), **scriptura canonica,** *the writing accepted in the official canon of the Bible,* drawn up at Council of Carthage.—(d), **scriptura divina, seu sacra,** *divine* or *sacred scripture,* i.e., inspired by God.—(e), **scriptura evangelica,** *the writings of the gospels* or *of the new law.*—(f), **scriptura sacra,** see *scriptura divina.* On **canon Scripturae,** see *canon* under 2.

scriptus, a, um, *P. a.,* see *scribo.*

scrutator, oris, *m., a searcher, scrutinizer, examiner, investigator.*

scrutor, ari, atus, *v. dep. a., fig.*, (1) *to search, examine thoroughly, explore*, (2) *to read carefully, scrutinize.*

sculptile, is, *n., a carved image, statue.*

sculptura, ae, *f., a cutting out, carving in relief, sculpture.*

sculptus, a, um, *P. a., carved, cut, graven, chiseled* in stone, brass, wood, etc.

scurrilis, e, *adj., scurrilous.*

scurrilitas, atis, *f., buffoonery, scurrility.*

scutum, i, *n., a shield,* i.e., *a defense, protection, shelter,* used fig., used in the S.T. only in quot.

scyphus, i, *m., a cup, goblet* (cf.: *calix, poculum*).

Scytha, ae, *m., a Scythian.*

se, *pron. reflex.*, see *sui.*

Sebastianus, i, *m., Sebastian,* military martyr at Rome under Diocletian.

secerno, ere, crevi, cretum, 3, *v. a.*, (1) lit., *to separate, put apart,* (2) fig., (a) *to separate, set apart,* (b) *to discern, distinguish.*—**secretus**, a, um, *P. a., private, secret.*—**secreta oratio**, see under (c).—**secretum**, i, *n.*, (a) *a solitude, solitary place,* (b) *secret conversation, a secret mystery,* (c) either **secreta**, n., pl., *secret things,* or **secreta oratio**, *a prayer* or *prayers,* said by the celebrant in a low voice, which cannot be heard except by himself, after the Offertory and before the Preface.—**in secreto**, *in a secret*

place, secretly.—**sacrum secretum**, *sacred secret,* or *sacrament.* —**secrete**, *adv., in secret, secretly.* —**secreto**, *adv., in secret, secretly.*

secessus, us, *m., a privy, drain.*

secludo, ere, si, sum, 3, *v. a., to shut off, seclude,* used lit. and fig.

seco, are, cui, ctum, 1, *v. a.*, (1) lit., *to cut, cut off,* (2) fig., *to divide.* —**secans**, ntis, Part. used as *subst., one who saws.*

secrete, *adv.*, see *secerno.*

secreto, *adv.*, see *secerno.*

secretum, i, *n.*, see *secerno.*

secretus, a, um, *P. a.*, see *secerno.*

secta, ae, *f.*, (1) *scholastic opinion, heresy,* synonym of *haeresis,* (2) *a party faction, sect, school.*

sectator, oris, *m., a follower, adherent.*

sectio, onis, *f., a cutting, cutting off.*

sector, ari, atus, 1, *v. dep. freq. a.*, (1) lit., *to follow continually* or *eagerly,* in a good or bad sense, *to run after, follow after,* (2) fig., (a) *to follow* or *strive after, to pursue eagerly,* (b) *to busy one's self about,* used with the *acc.*

secularis, e, *adj., worldly, secular.*

secundarie, *adv.*, see *secundarius.*

secundario, *adv.*, see *secundarius.*

secundarius, a, um, *adj., coming in second place, subordinate, secondary,* the opposite of *principalis.* On **auctoritas secundaria**, see *auctoritas* under 4; on **bonum secundarium**, see *bonum* under 3; on **continentia secundaria**, see *continentia* under 4; on **finis se-**

cundarius, see *finis* under 2; on
forma secundaria, see *forma* under 2; on fundamentum secundarium, see *fundamentum;* on
intellectum secundarium, see *intellegere* under 1; on pars secundaria, see *pars* under 1; on
passio secundaria, see *passio* under 3; on poena secundaria, see
poena; on tempus secundarium,
see *tempus;* on virtus secundaria,
see *virtus* under 5; on volitum
secundarium, see *volitus;* on subiectum secundarium, see *subiectum* under 2.—secundarie, *adv.,
in second place, in a subordinate
manner, secondarily,* synonym of
secundario, the opposite of *principaliter.*—secundario, *adv., in
second place, in a subordinate
manner, secondarily,* synonym of
secundarie, the opposite of *principaliter.* On contraria secundario, see *contraria* under 1; on
mereri secundario, see *mereri;* on
praedicare secundario, see *praedicare* under 2; on sanctus secundario, see *sanctus.*

Secundinus, i, *m., Secundinus,* a
recluse to whom a long letter of
Gregory the Great is addressed
in 559 (lib. IX. and II. 52, in
Migne, Patr. Lat. LXXVII, 982).

secundum, prep. with *acc., agreeably to, in accordance with, according to.* On secundum accidens, see *accidens* under 1.—secundum quid (= aliqui), *according to something, in a certain respect,* the opposite of *absolute*
and *simpliciter.* On aequalitas

secundum quid, see *aequalitas*
under 1; on aeternum secundum
quid, see *aeternus* under 1; on
agere secundum quid, see *agere*
under 1; on alius secundum quid,
see *alius;* on beatus secundum
quid, see *beatus* under 1; on
bonum secundum quid, see *bonus* under 2 and 3; on cognoscere secundum quid, see *cognoscere* under 2; on conformitas secundum quid, see *conformitas*; on
consilium secundum quid, see
consilium under 2; on continens
secundum quid, see *continens*
under 3; on continentia secundum quid, see *continentia* under
2; on corrumpere secundum
quid, see *corrumpere* under 2;
on corruptio secundum quid, see
corruptio under 2; on dicere secundum quid, see *dicere* under
3; on divisio secundum quid, see
divisio; on ens secundum quid,
see *ens;* on esse secundum quid,
see *esse;* on essentia secundum
quid, see *essentia* under 1; on
falsus secundum quid, see *falsus;* on fieri secundum quid, see
fieri; on generare secundum
quid, see *generare;* on generatio
secundum quid, see *generatio*
under 1; on idem secundum
quid, see *idem;* on incontinens
secundum quid, see *incontinens;*
on incontinentia secundum quid,
see *incontinentia;* on infinitas secundum quid, see *infinitas;* on
infinitum secundum quid, see *infinitus;* on involuntarium secundum quid, see *involuntarius;* on

iudicare secundum quid, see *iudicare* under 2; on iudicium secundum quid, see *iudicium* under 3; on iustum secundum quid, see *iustus;* on libertas secundum quid, see *libertas* under 1; on esse in loco secundum quid, see *locus* under 2; on malum secundum quid, see *malus* under 1 and 2; on multum secundum quid, see *multus* under 1; on necessarium secundum quid, see *necessarius* under 1; on negativa secundum quid, see *negativus;* on nominare secundum quid, see *nominare;* on notum secundum quid, see *notus;* on pati secundum quid, see *pati* under 1; on perfectio secundum quid, see *perfectio* under 3; on perfectum secundum quid, see *perfectus* under 1; on praedicare secundum quid, see *praedicare* under 2; on prius secundum quid, see *prior* under 1; on prophetia secundum quid dicta, see *prophetia;* on prudens secundum quid, see *prudens;* on sanctus secundum quid, see *sanctus;* on scire secundum quid, see *scire* under 2; on tale secundum quid, see *talis;* on totum secundum quid, see *totus* under 1; on ultimum secundum quid, see *ultimus;* on unum secundum quid, see *ultimus;* on unum secundum quid, see *unus;* on velle secundum quid, see *velle* under 1; on violentum secundum quid, see *violentus;* on virtus secundum quid, see *virtus* under 5; on vita se-

cundum quid, see *vita* under 3; on voluntabile secundum quid, see *voluntabilis.*—secundum quod, synonym of *inquantum, in as far as, as.*—secundum se, *according to itself, in itself,* synonym of *per se.* On ad aliquid secundum se, see *ad* under 2; on falsum secundum se, see *falsus;* on notum secundum se, see *notus;* on perfectum secundum se seu seipsum, see *perfectus* under 1; on possibile secundum se, see *possibilis* under 1; on unum secundum se, see *unus;* on velle secundum se, see *velle* under 1; on volitum secundum se, see *volitus;* on voluntarium secundum se, see *voluntarius* under 3.

securis, is, *f., axe* or *hatchet.*

securitas, atis, *f.,* (1) *freedom from care, unconcern, composure,* (2) *freedom from danger, safety, security,* (3) mercant. t.t., *a guarantee, pledge for a debt* or *obligation.*

securus, a, um, *adj., free from care, careless, unconcerned, untroubled, fearless, easy, quiet.*—secure, *adv., safely, securely.*

secus, (1) *adv.* (*prop., following, later in rank* or *order,* i.e., *less* than something mentioned before; hence; in gen.), *otherwise, differently, not so,* (2) *prep.* with *acc. by, beside, along, on.*

sed, *conj., but, yet.*—(1), With *non.* —(2), after negative clauses, to limit the negative statement, i.e., either to indicate that the assertion does not hold good at all, but something else does, or else that it is not exclusively true, but something else holds good in addition, *but, on the contrary;* and in ascending significance *but also, but even, but in fact.*—(3), **non modo ... sed etiam,** *not only ... but also.*

sedatio, onis, f., *an allaying, assuaging, calming* of the passions.

sedecim, *num., adj.,* see *sexdecim.*

sedeo, ere, sedi, sessum, 2, *v. n., to sit,* used (1) *absol.,* (2) with *ad,* with *supra.*

sedes, is, f., (1) lit., (a) *that on which one sits, a bench, chair, throne,* (b) eccl., *a see,* the official chair or throne of a bishop; the seat or center of the power or authority of a bishop; the rank, office, power, authority etc. of a bishop, in case of Rome, the Pope or papal court, (2) transf., in gen., in relation to inanimate subjects, that upon which anything sits fast or rests, *ground, land.*—**sedes honoris,** *position of honor.*—**in perpetua sede,** *in their everlasting seats,* i.e., *heaven.*—**sedes iudicis,** (1) *judicial bench.*—(2), *a see,* the seat or center of the power or authority of a bishop whether of ordinary or of higher rank (archbishop, pope); hence the rank, office, power, authority etc. of a bishop (in case of Rome the Pope or Papal court).—**in sede Alexandrina,** *in the Alexandrian See.*

seditio, onis, f., *dissension, civil discord, sedition* (political or military).

seditiosus, a, um, *adj., seditious, factious, turbulent.*

sedo, are, avi, atum, 1, *v. a.,* and *n., to appease, quiet.*

seduco, ere, xi, ctum, 3, *v. a., to lead astray, mislead, seduce.*

seductio, onis, f., *a misleading, seduction* (eccl. Lat.).

seductor, oris, m., *a misleader, seducer.*

sedulitas, atis, f., *officiousness.*

sedulo, *adv., diligently, assiduously.*

seges, etis, f., (1) lit., (a) plur., *harvest, crops,* (2) transf., *standing corn,* (3) fig., *sheaves.*

segnis, e, *adj., weak, slack.*

segnities, em, e, *laziness, inactivity, slowness.*

segregatio, onis, f., *a parting, separation, segregation.*

segrego, are, avi, atum, 1, *v. a.,* (1) lit., *to set apart, lay aside, put away, to separate, remove, segregate,* (2) fig., *to separate, remove away from; to divide.*

seiuntus, a, um, *P. a., separated.*

Seleuciana, ae, f., *Seleuciana,* a servant of God, addressed by Augustine (Ep. 265) concerning baptism and the repentance of St. Peter.

seligens, ntis, *P. a., choosing.*

Sellum, m., *indecl., Sellum,* son of Thecuath and husband of Holda (4 Reg. XXII. 14).

semel, *adv. num., once, a single time.*—**simul et semel,** *at one and* *the same time.*—**semel aut bis,** *once or twice.*

semen, inis, *f.,* (1) lit., *seed,* (a) of men, animals, (b) of plants, (2) trans., *a stock, race,* (3) fig., (a) *a spiritual seed,* i.e., the word of God, (b) *doctrine, teaching.*

sementinus, a, um, *adj., of seed, seeded.*

sementis, is, *f.,* (1) *a sowing,* (2) transf., *seed-time.*

seminalis, e, *adj., of* or *belonging to seed, good for seed, seminal.* On **causa seminalis,** see *causa* under 2; on **forma seminalis,** see *forma* under 2; on **principium seminale,** see *principium;* on **ratio seminalis,** see *ratio* under 12; on **umidum seminale,** see *umidus.*—**seminale,** is, *n., seed, germ, origin,* synonym of *seminarium.*—**seminaliter,** *adv., in the manner of the seed* or *germ, by means of the seed or germ, seminally.*

seminaliter, *adv.,* see *seminalis.*

seminarium, ii, *n., seed, germ, origin,* synonym of *seminale.*

seminatio, onis, *f., a sowing, a bringing forth from seed,* used lit. and fig.

seminativus, a, um, *adj.,* (1) *bringing forth seeds,* (2) *belonging to the seed, being in the seed, seminative.* Does not occur in the Summa Theologica.—(1), on **vis seminativa,** see *vis* under 1.—(2), on **virtus seminativa,** see *virtus* under 1.

seminifluus, a, um, *adj., seminifluous, a flowing off.*

semino, are, avi, atum, 1, *v. a.,* (1) lit., *to sow,* (2) fig., *to plant, propagate, disseminate.*

semiplenus, a, um, *adj., incomplete.*

semotus, a, um, *P. a., removed, set aside.*

semper, *adv., ever, always, at all times, forever.*

sempiternus, a, um, *adj., everlasting, ever-during, perpetual, continual, imperishable, eternal, sempiternal.* — **in sempiternum,** *forever.*

senarius, a, um, *adj., with numerus, the number six.*

senator, oris, *m., a senator.*

senatus, us, *m., the senate.*—**senatus consultum,** *a decree of the Senate.*

Seneca, ae, *m., Seneca, Lucius Annaeus,* a Roman statesman and philosopher (3 B.C.-65 A.D.), St. Thomas quotes from De Beneficiis, De Ira, De Clementia, De Quatuor Virtutibus, De Vita Beata.

senecta, ae, *f., old age,* synonym of *senectus.*

senectus, utis, *f., old age, extreme old age,* synonym of *senecta.*

senesco, ere, nui, 3, *v. inch. n., to grow old, become aged.*

senex, senis, *comp., senior, old, age, advanced in years;* and *subst., an aged person, an old man, an ancient,* (1) adj., (2) subst.—**senes,** *the ancients.*—*Comp.,* **seniores,** (a), *elders,* referring to the Greek *episkopos* and *presbyteros* from which the English bishop and priest are derived.—(b), *supe-*

riors.—(3), in eccl. Lat., *elders* in the synagogue.

senilis, e, *adj., senile, aged.*

senior, oris, see *senex.*

senium, ii, *n., the feebleness of age, decline, decay, debility.*

sensatio, onis, *f. knowledge through the senses, perception, observation;* does not occur in the Summa Theologica.

sensatus, a, um, *adj.,* (1) *known through the senses, perceived,* (2) *gifted with sense, intelligent,* the opposite of *insensatus.* On forma sensata, see *forma* under 2; on **signum sensatum,** see *signum* under 2; on **species sensata,** see *species* under 5.

sensibilis, e, *adj.,* (1) *sensitive,* i.e., belonging to the sensible part of the soul, synonym of *sensitivus,* the opposite of *intellectivus; intellectualis,* and *intelligibilis* on the one hand and to *vegetabilis* on the other, (2) *sensitive,* i.e., perceiving by the senses, endowed with senses, capable of perceiving, synonym of *sensitivus,* the opposite of *intellectivus* and *intellectualis* on the one hand and of *sensualis* on the other, (3) *sensible,* i.e., obvious, perceptible by the senses, *perceptible,* the opposite of *intellegibilis.* On **appetitus sensibilis,** see *appetitus* under 2; on **cognitio sensibilis,** see *cognitio* under 2; on **concupiscentia sensibilis,** see, *concupiscentia* under 1; on **delectatio sensibilis,** see *delectatio;* on **dolor sensibilis,** see *dolor;*

on **esse sensibile,** see *esse;* on **immutatio sensibilis,** see *immutatio* under 2; on **motus sensibilis,** see *motus* under 2; on **operatio sensibilis,** see *operatio* under 2; on **phantasia sensibilis,** see *phantasia* under 3; on **visio sensibilis,** see *visio* under 1; on **visus sensibilis,** see *visus;* on **vita sensibilis,** see *vita* under 1. On **anima sensibilis,** see *anima* under 1; on **natura sensibilis,** see *natura;* on **spiritus sensibilis,** see *spiritus;* on **substantia sensibilis,** see *substantia* under 2. On **accidens sensibile,** see *accidens* under 2; on **bonum sensibile,** see *bonus* under 3; on **causa sensibilis,** see *causa* under 2; on **certitudo sensibilis,** see *certitudo* under 2; on **claritas sensibilis,** see *claritas* under 3; on **corpus sensibile,** see *corpus;* on **elementum sensibile,** see *elementum* under 2; on **esse sensibile,** see *esse;* on **experimentum sensibile,** see *experimentum* under 1; on **figura sensibilis,** see *figura* under 3; on **finis sensibilis,** see *finis* under 2; on **forma sensibilis** see *forma* under 2; on **fructus sensibilis,** see *fructus* under 1; on **homo sensibilis,** see *homo;* on **individuum sensibile,** see *individuum;* on **lux sensibilis,** see *lux* under 1; on **magnitudo sensibilis,** see *magnitudo* under 2; on **materia sensibilis communis seu in communi et materia sensibilis individualis seu signata,** see *materia* under 3; on **medium sensibile,** see *medium* under 2; on mundus sensibilis, see *mundus* under 1; on numerus in sensibili exsistens, see *numerus;* on passio sensibilis, see *passio* under 1; on poena sensibilis, see *poena;* on qualitas sensibilis, see *qualitas;* on res sensibilis, see *res;* on revelatio sensibilis, see *revelatio;* on sacrificium sensibile, see *sacrificium;* on signum sensibile, see *signum* under 1; on similitudo sensibilis, see *similitudo* under 2; on species sensibilis, see *species* under 3, 5, and 6; on subiectum sensibile, see *subiectum* under 2; on substantia sensibilis et sensibilis quanta, see *substantia* under 2; on totum sensibile, see *totum* under 1.—Kinds of *sensibile* in this (3) sense are: (a), sensibile commune and sensibile proprium, the Aristotelian *koinon kai idion aistheton, the sensible object perceptible by more than one sense, called common,* and *that peculiar to only one sense, called proper.*—(b), sensibile excellens and sensibile minus, *the very strongly* and *the less strongly perceptible by the senses.*—(c), sensibile exterius, *the exterior perceptible or the object of an exterior sense.* Cf. *sensus exterior* under *sensus* under 3.—(d), sensibile minus, see *sensibile excellens.*—(e), sensibile per accidens, and sensibile per se, the Aristotelian *aistheton kata symbebekos kai, kath' auto, the perceptible according to something else and that accord-*

ing to itself, or *the accidentally perceptible and the perceptible as such.*—(f), sensibile per se, see *sensibile per accidens.*—(g), sensibile proprium, see *sensibile commune.* On sensibile in actu est seu fit sensus in actu, see *sensus* under 3; on sensus est quodammodo ipsa sensibilia, see *sensus* under 3; on sensus in actu est seu fit sensibile in actu, see *sensus* under 3.—sensibiliter, *adv., by the senses, sensibly, obviously, visibly,* the opposite of *intellectualiter* and *intellegibiliter.*

sensibilitas, atis, *f., sensibility,* the opposite of *intellegibilitas* and *sensualitas;* does not occur in the Summa Theologica.

sensibiliter, *adv.,* see *sensibilis.*

sensifico, are, 1, *v. a., to make sensible, endow with sensation, sensitize.*

sensitivus, a, um, *adj.,* (1) *sensitive,* i.e., belonging to the sensitive part of the soul, synonym of *sensibilis,* the opposite of *intellectivus, intellectualis,* and *intelligibilis* on the one hand and *vegetabilis* on the other, (2) *sensitive,* i.e., knowing through the senses, perceiving, synonym of *sensibilis,* the opposite of *appetitivus* and *sensualis.* On affectio sensitiva, see *affectio;* on amor sensitivus, see *appetitus* under 1 and 2; on apprehensio sensitiva, see *apprehensio* under 2; on cognitio sensitiva, see *cognitio* under 2; on delectatio sensitiva, see *delectatio;* on forma sensitiva, see *forma*

under 2; on **notitia sensitiva,** see
notitia under 2; on **operatio sen-**
sitiva, see *operatio* under 2; on
passio sensitivi et primi sensitivi,
see *passio* under 2.—**sensitivum**
sc. genus potentiarum animae,
the Aristotelian *aisthetikon,*
the totality of the sensitive cogni-
tive power.—**primum sensitivum,**
the translation sometimes of the
Aristotelian expression (1) *pro-*
ton aisthetikon and sometimes of
the expression (2) *proton aisthe-*
terion, and signifies in the
first case the primary or highest
sensitive faculty, namely the
sensus communis, but in the latter instance the first or highest
sense organ. On **anima sensiti-**
va, see *anima* under 1; on **natura**
sensitiva, see *natura;* on **pars**
sensitiva, see *pars* under 1; on
potentia sensitiva, see *potentia*
under 2; on **principium sensiti-**
vum, see *principium;* on **virtus**
sensitiva, see *virtus* under 1; on
vis sensitiva, see *vis* under 1.

sensualis, e, *adj., sensual,* i.e., *de-*
siring sensually, belonging to
sensual desire. Cf. *sensualitas.*

sensualitas, atis, *f., sensuality, the*
sensitive appetitive part of the
soul, the totality of the sensitive
faculty of desire, synonym of
appetitus sensitivus, the opposite
of *voluntas* on the one hand and
of *sensibilitas* on the other. On
the difference between *sensuali-*
tas and *sensibilitas,* see *sensibili-*
tas. On **appetitus sensualitatis,**
see *appetitus* under 2; on **con-**

cupiscentia sensualitatis, see *con-*
cupiscentia under 1; on **corrup-**
tio sensualitatis, see *corruptio*
under 3; on **impetus sensualita-**
tis, see *impetus;* on **motus sensu-**
alitatis, see *motus* under 2; on
peccatum sensualitatis, see *pec-*
catum under 2; on **voluntas sen-**
sualitatis, see *voluntas* under 1.
—Kinds of *sensualitatis* are: **sen-**
sualitatis brutalis and **sensuali-**
tatis humana, *the sensuality of*
the beast and *that of man.*

sensus, us, *m.,* (1) *sensitive soul,*
sensitive part of the soul,
sensitive nature, the opposite of
intellectus and *ratio,* (2) *mind,*
i. e., the faculty of knowledge
in the broader conception of the
word, synoynm of *intellectus,*
and *ratio,* (3) *sense,* i.e., the
physical or organic faculty of
knowledge, the word understood alike in the collective
sense and in that of an individual faculty, the opposite of *intel-*
lectus and *ratio,* (4) *sense,* i.e.,
feeling, opinion, comprehension,
(5) *sense, sensation,* i.e., sensitive knowledge, perception, (6)
sense, i.e., the act of desire, (7)
opinion, view, synonym of *sen-*
tentia, (8) *sense, meaning, con-*
ception, comprehension, synonym of *intellectus, ratio, signifi-*
catio, virtus, and *vis.* On **delec-**
tabile sensus et secundum şe, see
delectabilis; on **delectatio sensus**
et secundum sensum, see *delec-*
tatio; on **desiderium sensus,** see
desiderium under 1; on **passio**

sensus, see *passio* under 2.— Kinds of *sensus* in this meaning are: (a), **sensus acutus** and **sensus hebetatus,** *the sharpened* and *the dulled sense.*—(b), **sensus carnis seu corporalis** and **sensus spiritualis,** *the carnal* and *the spiritual sense.*—(c), **sensus corporalis,** see *sensus carnis.*—(d), **sensus exterior** and **sensus interior,** *the outer* or *physical sense* and *the inner* or *spiritual sense.* Cf. *sensus exterior et interior* under 3.—(e), **sensus hebetatus,** see *sensus acutus.*—(f), **sensus interior,** see *sensus exterior.*—(g), **sensus iudicandi,** *the sense* or *power of judgment.*—(h), **sensus perspicax,** *the discerning sense.*—(i), **sensus prudentiae,** *the prudential sense* or *the practical sense.*—(j), **sensus spiritualis,** see *sensus corporalis.* Cf. *sensus spiritualis* under 8j.—(k), **sensus subtilis,** *the subtle sense* or *the finely distinguishing sense.* On **appetibile secundum sensum,** see *appetibilis;* on **apprehendere per se,** see *apprehendere* under 2; on **apprehensio sensus,** see *apprehensio* under 2; on **bonum sensus et secundum sensum,** see *bonus* under 3; on **cognitio sensus,** see *cognitio* under 2; on **iudicare secundum sensum,** see *iudicare* under 3; on **iudicium sensus,** see *iudicium* under 4; on **malum secundum sensum,** see *malus* under 3; on **motus sensus,** see *motus* under 2; on **notum sensus seu secundum sensum,** see *notus;*

on **opus sensus,** see *opus* under 4; on **passio sensus,** see *passio* under 2; on **poena sensus,** see *poena.*—Kinds of *sensus* in this sense are: (a), **sensus agens** and **sensus patiens,** *an effective* or *active sense* (*which does not exist since it is a contradiction*) and *the susceptive* or *passive sense.* —(b), **sensus auditus** and **sensus visus,** *the sense of hearing* and *the sense of sight.*—(c), **sensus communis** and **sensus particularis seu proprius,** the *koine kai idia aisthesis* of Aristotle, *the common sense* or *the sense of sensation,* and *the particular sense* for each individual sense object or *special sense.*—(d), **sensus depuratus** and **sensus elevatus,** *the purified sense* and *the elevated sense.*—(e), **sensus disciplinabilis,** *the sense that informs* or *furnishes knowledge.*—(f), **sensus elevatus,** see *sensus depuratus.* —(g), **sensus exterior** and **sensus interior,** *the exterior sense* or *the sense that observes something external* (sight, hearing, smell, taste, feeling), and *the inner sense* or *the sense that acts upon the sensations of the external senses,* (*sensus communis, imaginatio seu phantasia, vis aestimativa seu cogitativa, vis memorativa*). Cf. *sensus exterior et interior* above under 2.—(h), **sensus in actu** and **sensus possibilis seu in potentia,** *sense in the act of sensing* and *that in the state of potentiality* or *that could* *be active.*—(i), **sensus in potentia,** see *sensus in actu.*—(j), **sensus interior,** see *sensus exterior.*—(k), **sensus magis seu maxime cognoscitivus,** *the sense that perceives most,* i.e., the cause of sight and that of hearing.—(l), **sensus particularis,** see *sensus communis.*—(m), **sensus patiens,** see *sensus agens.*—(n), **sensus perfectior,** *the more perfect sense,* (because more perceptive). Cf. also *magis cognoscitivus.*—(o), **sensus possibilis,** see *sensus in actu.*—(p), **sensus principalis,** *the principal* or *chief sense,* i.e., *sensus communis.*—(q), **sensus proprius,** see *sensus communis.*—(r), **sensus rectus** and **sensus vanus,** *the correct sense* or *the sense that judges correctly,* and *the vain sense* or *the sense that judges falsely.*—(s), **sensus solutus,** *the released* or *alert sense.*—(t), **sensus vanus,** see *sensus rectus.*—(u), **sensus visus,** see *sensus auditus.*—**ratio est universalium, sensus vero particularium,** see *ratio* under 3.—**sensus cognitio est singularium,** or, **sensus non est cognoscitivus nisi singularium,** *a sense knows only singular, individual things.*—**sensus est quodammodo etiam ipsius universalis,** the translation of the Aristotelian expression: *he de aisthesis tou katholou estin, sense in a certain measure also recognizes the general.*—**sensus est quodammodo ipsa sensibilia,** or, **sensus in actu est seu fit sen-**

sibile in actu, the translation of the Aristotelian passage: *he de aisthesis esti ta aistheta, sense in the act of sensation is in a certain measure identical with that perceived by sense;* cf. **intellectus** under 3, and *scientia* under 1.—**sensus non componit vel dividit,** *sense does not compound* or *divide,* i.e., make judgements.—**sensus non est cognoscitivus nisi singularium,** see above: **sensus cognitio** etc.—One kind of *sensus* in this (4) meaning is **sensus bonus,** *the good* or *sound sense.* On **via sensus,** see *via* under 1.—**ad seu secundum sensum,** *with reference to sensible knowledge* or *according to perception.* On **demonstrare quantum ad sensum,** see *demonstrare* under 1; on **demonstratio ad sensum,** see *demonstratio* under 1; on **mixtio ad sensum,** see *mixtio;* on **prius secundum se,** see *prior* under 1.—Kinds of *sensus* in this (7) meaning are: (a), **sensus perversus,** *the perverse* or *bad opinion.*—(b), **sensus reprobus,** *the unacceptable opinion.*—Kinds of *sensus* in this (8) meaning are: (a), **sensus allegoricus seu typicus, sensus anagogicus,** and **sensus moralis seu tropologicus,** *the allegorical* or *symbolic sense, the anagogic* and *the moral* or *tropologic sense.*—(b), **sensus anagogicus,** see *sensus allegoricus.*—(c), **sensus compositus** and **sensus divisus,** *the composite* and *the divided sense* or *the sense of* composition and *that of separation.*—(d), **sensus divisus,** see *sensus compositus.*—(e), **sensus historicus seu litteralis** and **sensus spiritualis,** *the historical* or *literary sense* and *the spiritual sense.* —(f), **sensus litteralis,** see *sensus historicus.*—(g), **sensus moralis,** see *sensus allegoricus.*—(h), **sensus parabolicus,** *figurative litteral sense.*—(i), **sensus principalis,** *the principal sense.*—(j), **sensus spiritualis,** see *sensus historicus.*—(k), **sensus tropologicus,** see *sensus allegoricus.*—(l), **sensus typicus,** see *sensus allegoricus.*

sententia, ae, *f.,* (1) *view, opinion,* synonym of *sensus* (2) *a judge's sentence, judicial opinion,* synonym of *iudicium,* (3) *utterance, opinion, pronouncement,* synonym of *iudicium,* (4) *aphorism, sentence, teaching,* (5) the *Sententiae* of Peter Lombard.—One kind of *sententia* in this (1) sense is: **sententia communis,** *general opinion.*—Kinds of *sententia* in this (2) sense are: (a), **sententia capitalis,** *the sentence of death.*— (b), **sententia condemnans** and **sententia praemians,** *the sentence that pronounces a punishment* and *that which pronounces a reward.*—(c), **sententia definitiva,** *the concluding* or *final judgment.* —(d), **sententia praemians,** see *sententia condemnans.*—(e), **sententia vocalis,** *the judgment expressed in words.* On **magister sententiarum,** see *magister* under 2.—One kind of *sententia* in this

(4) sense is: **sententia fidei,** *the teaching of the Christian faith.*

sententialis, e, *adj., pertaining to a judicial sentence, based on a pronounced judgment, not on statute nor canon.* On **iustum sententiale,** see *iustus.*—**sententialiter,** *adv., after the manner of a judicial sentence, by the authority of a judicial sentence, sententiously.*

sententialiter, see *sententialis.*

sententio, are, 1, *n., to utter sentences* or *opinions.*

sentio, ire, si, sum, (4), (1) *to discern by the senses, perceive, be sensible of,* (2) *be of the opinion, think, deem,* (3) *take up favorably, agree.*—Kinds of *sentire* in this (1) sense are: (a), **sentire actu,** *to perceive actually,* the opposite of *sentire in potentia,* i.e., *to be able to perceive.*—(b), **sentire aliquid delectabile aut triste** and **sentire solum,** *to feel something pleasant* or *unpleasant* and *simply to feel.*—(c), **sentire per accidens** and **sentire per se,** *to perceive something accidentally, indirectly, as attached to what is perceived directly as the object of sense faculty.* Cf. also *sensibile per accidens.*—(d), **sentire per se,** see *sentire per accidens.*—(e), **sentire solum,** see *sentire delectabile aut triste.*

seorsum, *adv., asunder, separately, apart.*

separabilis, e, *adj., that may be separated, separable.* On **accidens**

separabile, see *accidens* under 2; on ens separabile, see *ens;* on substantia separabilis, see *substantia* under 6.

separatim, *adv., asunder, apart, separately.*

separatio, onis, *f., a sundering, severing, separation.*

separo, are, avi, atum, 1, *v. a., to disjoin, sever, part, divide, separate,* synonym of *absolvo* and *abstraho* and the opposite of *coniungo* and *unio.*—separatus, a, um, *P. a., separated, separate, disembodied, immaterial,* synonym of *absolutus* and *abstractus,* the opposite of *coniunctus* and *unitus.* On animal separatum, see *animal* under 1; on dimensio separata, see *dimensio;* on essentia separata, see *essentia* under 1; on exemplar separatum, see *exemplar* under 2; on forma separata, see *forma* under 2; on homo separatus, see *homo;* on infinitum separatum, see *infinitus;* on instrumentum separatum, see *instrumentum;* on intellectus separatus, see *intellectus* under 1; on motor separatus, see *motor;* on organum separatum, see *organum;* on principium separatum, see *principium;* on quidditas separata, see *quidditas;* on species separata, see *species* under 6; on spiritus separatus, see *spiritus;* on substantia separata, see *substantia* under 2; on unitas separata, see *unitas;* on vacuum separatum, see *vacuus* under 1; on vita separata, see *vita* under 1; on

voluntas separata, see *voluntas* under 3.

sepelio, ire, pelivi or ii, pultum, 4, (*perf.* sepeli, *part. perf.* sepelitus), *v. a., to bury, inter.*

septem, *num. adj. indecl., seven.*

septempliciter, *adv., in a sevenfold manner.*

septenarius, a, um, *adj., containing seven, consisting of seven, septenary;* septenarius numerus, *the number seven.*

septennis, e, *adj., of seven years, seven years old.*

septennium, ii, *n., a period of seven years.*

septentrio, onis, *m., the north* (as a quarter of the heavens).

septentrionalis, e, *adj., of or belonging to the north, northern.*

septies, *num. adv., seven times.*

septiformis, e, *adj., sevenfold* (eccl. Lat.).

septimana, ae, *f.,* late Lat. for *hebdomas, a week.*

septimo, *adv.,* see *septimus.*

septimus, a, um, *num. ord. adj., the seventh.*—septimo, *adv., a seventh time.*

septuagesimus, a, um, *num. ord. adj., a period of seventy days.* Septuagesima, *Eccl.,* the third Sunday before Lent, also called *Septuagesima Sunday.*

septuagies, *adv., seventy times.*

septuaginta, *num. adj., seventy.*

septuplum, i, *n., a septuple, sevenfold.*

sepulcrum, i, *n., a burial-place, grave, tomb.*

sepultura, ae, *f.*, *a burial, interment, funeral, obsequies, sepulture.*

sequax, acis, *m.*, *a follower.*

sequela, ae, *f.*, (1) *a following, that which follows,* (2) fig., *a result, consequence.*

sequentia, ae, *f.*, *sequence,* a rhythm sometimes sung between the Epistle and the Gospel; also called a "prose" because not in any regular metre.

sequester, tris, (orig. form *sequester,* tri, ante-and post-class., and in the poets), *m.*, *a mediator.*

sequestro, are, avi, atum, 1, *v. a.*, *to remove, separate from anything.*

sequor, i, secutus, 3, *v. dep.*, (1) lit., (a) *to follow, to come* or *go after, follow after, attend, come after,* (b) *to follow, result, ensue,* (2) *to follow* or *come naturally* or *easily, to be obtained without effort.*

sera, ae, *f.*, *lock, a bar* for fastening doors.

Seraphim, *plur, indecl.*, *the Seraphim,* one of an order of celestial beings ranking next above the cherubim in celestial hierarchy.

Serapion, onis, *m.*, *Serapion, abbot,* solitary, of Scete, and leader of the Anthropomorphites against the festal epistle of Theophilus, patriarch of Alexandria. The monks of Scete rejected the orthodox view as to God's nature, with the one exception of Paphnutius, an abbot. Serapion, however, was converted by the ef-

forts of Photinus, an oriental deacon.

serenitas, atis, *f.*, (1) lit., *clear, fair* or *serene weather,* (2) fig., *serenity* of disposition.

serenus, a, um, *adj.*, *clear, fair, bright, serene.*

Sergius, i, *m.*, (1) *Sergius,* patriarch of Constantinople, consecrated on Easter Eve, A.D. 610. The event that marked the patriarchate of Sergius was the origin of the Monothelite heresy, (2) *Sergius,* bishop of Rome after Conon from December, 687 A.D., to September, 701 A.D.

sericum, i, *n.*, *Seric stuff, silk.*

series, (no *gen.* or *dat.*), em, e, (1) lit., *a band, a succession, series,* (2) fig., *a chain, series, connection, train, sequence,* (3) in partic., *an unbroken line of descent, lineage, genealogy,* (4) *context,* those parts of a discourse, book, written or printed article, which are closely connected with any special sentence or word, and which should be taken into consideration in determining its meaning.

serio, *adv.*, see *serius.*

seriose, *adv.*, see *seriosus.*

seriosus, a, um, *adj.*, *serious.*—**seriose,** *adv.*, *seriously.*

serium, i, *n.*, see *serius.*

serius, a, um, *adj.*, *grave, earnest, serious.*—**serium,** and more freq. **seria,** orum, *n.*, *earnestness, seriousness, serious matters* or *discourse.*—**serio,** *adv.*, *in earnest, seriously.*

sermo, onis, *m.*, (1) *a sermon,* a dis-course delivered in public, or written out and circulated, for the purpose of religious instruc-tion and grounded generally on some passage of Scripture, (2) *a word, expression, speech, saying, conversation, talk,* (3) *an idiom.* —Common phrases are: **solus sermo,** *a mere word.*—**communis sermo,** *ordinary speech.*—**sermo comis et iucundus,** *affable* and *pleasant conversation.*—**ser-mo laudis,** *a word of praise.*— **sermo sapientiae, sermo scienti-ae, interpretatio sermonum,** *the word of knowledge, the word of wisdom, the interpretation of speeches.*

sermocinor, ari, atus, 1, *v. dep. n.,* *to talk with anyone, to discourse about anything, to preach.*—**ser-mocinans,** antis, *Part.* used as a *subst., one speaking.*

sero, *adv.,* see *serus.*

sero, ere, evi, satum, 3, *v. a., to sow, plant.*

serotinus, a, um, *adj., in the eve-ning.*

serpens, entis, *m.,* see *serpo.*

serpentinus, a, um, *adj., of* or *be-longing to a serpent, serpent-like.*

serpo, psi, ptum, 3, *v. n., to creep, crawl,* used fig.—**serpens,** entis, *f., a creeping thing, a creeper, snake, serpent.*

serra, ae, *f., a saw.*

serum, i, *n.,* see *serus.*

serus, a, um, *adj., late,* not used as an adjective in the S.T.—**sero,** *adv., late.*—**serum,** i, *n., late hour* (of the day or night).—**de sero,** *too late.*—**in sero,** *at evening.*

serva, ae, *f., a slave, servant.*

servatio, onis, *f., an observance.*

servilis, e, *adj.,* (1) *serving, ancil-lary,* the opposite of *architecton-cus, dominativus,* and *principa-tivus,* (2) *servile, slavish,* the opposite of *dominativus* and *li-beralis.*—(1), on **ars servilis,** see *ars* under 2; on **disciplina servilis,** see *disciplina* under 3; on **forma servilis,** see *forma* under 2; on **scientia servilis,** see *scientia* un-der 1 and 2. On **amicitia servi-lis,** see *amicitia* under 1; on **de-lectatio servilis,** see *delectatio;* on **opus servile,** see *opus* under 4; on **subiectio servilis,** see *sub-iectio* under 2; on **timor servilis,** see *timor.*—**serviliter,** *adv., like a slave, slavishly, servilely,* the op-posite of *liberaliter* and *libere.*

servilitas, atis, *f., servile opinion, servile being, servility,* the oppo-site of *libertas.*

serviliter, see *servilis.*

servio, ire, ivi and ii, itum, 4, *v. n.,* (1) lit., *to be a servant* or *slave, to serve, be in service,* (2) in gen. with the *dat.* of an object, (a person or thing), *to be devoted* or *subject to; to be of use* or *service to; to serve for, be fit* or *useful for, to do a service to, to comply with, gratify, humor* or *care for; to consult, aim at, to accommodate one's self to.*

servitium, ii, *n.,* (1) lit., (a) *the condition of a slave* or *servant, slavery, servitude, bondage,* (b) transf., *subjection, obedience,* (c) *servitude, service, worshipping,* a state of subjection to any work, claim, aim or demand, (2) *service* of God, spiritual devotion of obedience, reverence, public exercises of worship, (3) *a service,* the rendering of any duty to another.

servitus, utis, *f.,* (1) *slavery, servitude,* the opposite of *dominatio* and *dominium,* and also of *libertas,* (2) *submission, bondage, service,* the opposite of *dominatio* and *dominium,* (3) *being subject, being exposed, affability.* On **debitum servitutis,** see *debitus* under 1; on **lex servitus,** see *lex* under 1; on **status servitutis,** see *status* under 4; on **subiectio servitutis,** see *subiectio* under 2.-- Kinds of *servitus* in this (1) sense are: (a), **servitus amoris** and **servitus timoris,** *the servitude of love* and *that of fear.*—(b), **servitus carnalis seu corporalis** and **servitus spiritualis seu quantum ad animam,** *the carnal* or *corporal* and *the spiritual servitude* or *the servitude that pertains to the soul.*—(c), **servitus corporalis,** see *servitus carnalis.*—(d), **servitus legalis** and **servitus naturalis,** *legal servitude* or *that established through a positive law* and *natural servitude* or *that based on the different dispositions* and *capabilities of man.*—(e), **servitus naturalis,** see *servitus legalis.*—(f), **servitus quantum ad animam,** see *servitus carnalis.*—(g), **servi-tus spiritualis,** see *servitus carnalis.*—(h), **servitus timoris,** see *servitus amoris.*—Kinds of *servitus* in this (2) sense are: (a), **servitus civilis,** *civic service,* or *service in which citizens of a state are under their rules.*—(b), **servitus Dei** and **servitus hominis,** *the service of God* or *in relation to God* and *the service of man* or *of one man in relation to another man.*—(c), **servitus hominis,** see *servitus Dei.*—(d), **servitus immunditiae,** *the service of impurity.*—(e), **servitus iustitiae** and **servitus peccati,** *the service of justice* and *that of sin.*—(f), **servitus latriae,** *the service of adoration* or *the service of man by which he shows the virtue of his worship of God,* the opposite of *servitus duliae,* i.e., the service of reverence or that of service which man as the result of the virtue of *dulia* exhibits to the man who is over him.—(g), **servitus oboedientiae,** *the service of obedience,* i.e., *voluntary obedience.*—(h), **servitus peccati,** see *servitus iustitiae.*

servo, are, avi, atum, 1, *v. a.,* (1) *to observe,* to take notice of by appropriate conduct; to conform one's actions or practice to; *to keep, hold, comply, to keep* or *observe* anything prescribed or obligatory, (2) *to keep, preserve, maintain* any course of action, (3) *to sustain,* (4) *to fulfill* a duty etc.

servulus, i, *m., dim., a young slave, a servant lad.*

servus, i, *m.,* and **serva,** ae, *f., slave, menial, servant,* the opposite of both *liber* and *dominus.* On **scientia serva,** see *scientia* under 1; for **serva,** see under *serva.*—Kinds of *servus* are: **servus amoris** and **servus timoris,** *the slave of love* and *the slave of fear.*

servus, a, um, *adj., slavish, servile, subject.*

sessio, onis, *f., a sitting.*

sessor, oris, *m., a sitter upon a horse, a horseman, rider.*

seta, ae, *f., bristle, stiff hair.*

Seth, *indecl. noun, m., Seth,* the third son of Adam and Eve.

Sethim, (Setim), *indecl. noun. n., Sethim,* a place in the plains of Moab, opposite Jericho.—**Sethim lignum,** *Sethim wood* or *Setim wood.*

seu, *adv.,* see *sive.*

Severianus, i, *m., Severianus,* bishop of Gabala on the northern seabord of Syria, 400 A.D., and an intriguing opponent of St. John Chrysostom.

severitas, atis, *f., severity, seriousness, gravity, sternness, strictness.*

severus, a, um, *adj., serious, grave, strict, austere, stern, severe* in aspect, demeanor, conduct etc. (of persons and things).

Severus, i, *m., Severus,* patriarch of Antioch, 512-519 A.D.: a monophysite intruded into the see by Anastatius on the deposition of Flavian.

sex, num. *adj., six.*

sexagenarius, a, um, *adj., of* or *containing sixty, sixty, sixty-fold.*

sexagesima, ae, *f.,* see *sexagesimus.*

sexagesimus, a, um, *num. ord. adj., the sixtieth.*—**sexagesima,** ae, *f.,* (sc. *pars*), *the sixtieth part.*

sexaginta, num. *adj., sixty.*

sexdecim, num. *adj., sixteen.*

sexies, num. *adj., six times.*

Sextus, i, *m., Sextus* Julius Frontinus, superintendent of the Roman aqueducts under Nerva, in the latter half of the first century of the Christian era; author of Stratagemata.

sextus, a, um, *num. ord. adj., the sixth.*

sexus, us, *m., a sex, male* or *female* (of men and beasts).

si, a conditional particle, *if.* Common phrases involving *si* are: (a), **ac si,** *as if.*—(b), **si autem,** *if however,* or *if on the other hand.*—(c), **si enim,** *for if.*—(d), **si ergo,** or **si igitur,** *if therefore* or *if then.*—(e), **etiam si,** *even if.*—(f), **puta si,** *if for example,* or *for instance.*—(g), **si quidem,** *if indeed* or *truly.*—(h), **sicut si,** *just as if.*—(i), **similiter si,** *similarly* or *likewise if.*—(j), **si tamen,** *if however* or *yet if* or *nevertheless if.*—(k), **unde si,** *wherefore if.*—(l), **si vero,** *if indeed* or *truly.*

Siagrius, ii, *m., Siagrius,* bishop of Autun, who held a position of some eminence in France in the latter half of the sixth century.

Sibylla, ae, *f., a female soothsayer, a prophetess, a Sibyl.*

sic, *adv.*, *so, thus, in this* or *that manner, in such a manner.*

sicarius, ii, *m., a murderer, an assassin.*

siccatio, onis, *f., a drying.*

siccitas, atis, *f.*, (1) in gen., *dryness,* (2) of the weather, *dryness, drought.*

sicco, are, avi, atum, 1, *v. a.* and *n.*, (1) in gen., *to make dry, dry up,* (2) of trees, *to wither.*

siccus, a, um, *adj., dry.*—sicci oculi, *dry eyes.*

sicera, *n.*, = *sikera,* a kind of *spirituous, intoxicating drink.*

Sichem, *indecl., Sichem,* son of Hemor, a Hevite prince in the time of Jacob.

siclus, i, *m., a sicle, a shekel,* a Hebrew coin.

sicubi, *adv., if in any place, if anywhere, wheresoever.*

sicut, sicuti, *adv., so as, just as, as.*

sicuti, see *sicut.*

sidereus, a, um, *adj., sidereal, starry, of* or *belonging to the constellations* or *to the stars.*

Sidonii, orum, *m., the Sidonians.*

sidus, eris, *n., stars united in a figure, a group of stars, a constellation,* and hence mostly plural.—Sing., *a heavenly body, a star;* and collect., *a group of stars, a constellation.*

sigillatim, see *singillatim.*

sigillatio, onis, *f., sigillation, the action of sealing, a seal,* used *fig.*

sigillum, i, *n., dim., a seal,* used *lit.* and *fig.*—sigillum confessionis, *the seal of confession, an obliga-*tion *that prevents disclosure of confession as if by sealing the lips.*

signaculum, i, *n., a seal, mark, sign,* used *lit.* and *fig.*

signanter, *adv.,* see *signo.*

signatio, onis, *f., a marking, signing, sealing.*

signatus, a, um, *P. a.,* see *signo.*

signifer, feri, *m., a standard bearer.*

significatio, onis, *f.,* (1) *mark, meaning, sense,* synonym of *intellectus, ratio, sensus, virtus,* and *vis,* (2) *signification, pointing out, indication,* (3) *omen, foreboding.* On diversitas significationis, see *diversitas;* on veritas significationis, see *veritas* under 1.—Kinds of *significatio* in this (1) sense are: (a), significatio allegorica, significatio anagogica, and significatio moralis seu mystica, *the allegorical, the anagogic,* and *the moral* or *mystical meaning.*—(b), significatio anagogica, see *significatio allegorica.*—(c), significatio figurativa and significatio propria, *the figurative* or *symbolic* and *the proper meaning.*—(d), significatio formalis and significatio materialis, *the meaning of a thing according to its form* and *that according to its matter.*—(e), significatio materialis, see *significatio formalis.*—(f), significatio moralis, see *significatio allegorica.*—(g), significatio mystica, see *significatio allegorica.*—(h), significatio principalis, *the principal meaning.*—(i), significatio propria, see *significatio figurativa.*—

(j), significatio sacramentalis, *the sacramental meaning.*

significative, see *significativus.*

significativus, a, um, *adj.*, (1) *distinctive, significant,* (2) *denoting, signifying, significative.* On **ratio significativa illius quod quid est,** see *ratio* under 8; on **vox significativa,** see *vox* under 1. On **vis significativa,** see *vis* under 1.—significative, *adv.,* (1) *according to the mark* or *the sign,* (2) *after the manner of denoting* or *signifying, significatively.* On **sumere significative,** see *sumere* under 3.

significo, are, avi, atum, *v. a., to show by signs, signify, indicate, make known.* On **dictio per se significans et significans per aliquam rem conceptam,** see *dictio* under 2; on **forma significans,** see *forma* under 2; on **id ad quod significandum nomen imponitur et id a quo imponitur nomen ad significandum,** see *nomen* under 1; on **modus significandi,** see *modus* under 2; on **oratio significandi quod quid,** see *oratio* under 2; on **ratio significandi quid est,** see *ratio* under 8; on **vox significandi et non significandi,** see *vox* under 1.—Kinds of *significare* are: (a), **significare absolute** and **significare relative seu cum relatione,** *to signify something absolutely* or *without relation to anything else* and *to signify something relatively implying a connection with something else.*—(b), **significare abstracte**

seu in abstracto seu ut in abstracto and **significare concretive seu in concreto seu in concretione,** *to signify something in a state of absence of its individual determinants* and *to signify something in a state of combination with the same.*—(c), **significare active** and **significare passive,** *to signify something in the active sense* and *something in the passive sense.*—(d), **significare adiective** and **significare substantive,** *to signify something in the sense of an adjective* or *accident* and *something in the sense of a substantive* or *a substance.*—(e), **significare affirmative seu positive** and **significare negative seu privative,** *to signify something in the sense of an affirmation* or *an addition* and *something in the sense of a negation* or *deprivation.*—(f), **significare circumscriptive** and **significare definitive,** *to signify something in the sense of a description* or *in the sense of an explanation.* —(g), **significare concretive,** see *significare abstracte.*—(h), **significare cum demonstratione, significare cum qualitate,** and **significare cum tempore,** *to signify something with reference to something else, to signify something with a statement of a characteristic, to signify something with a statement fixing a time.*—(i), **significare cum qualitate,** see *significare cum demonstratione.*—(j), **significare cum relatione,** see *significare absolute.*—(k), **signifi-**

care cum tempore, see *significare cum demonstratione*.—(l), significare definitive, see *significare circumscriptive*.—(m), significare determinate and significare indeterminate, *to signify something in a definite manner* and *something in an indefinite manner*.—(n), significare ex aequo and significare per modum aequivocationis, *to signify something in an equal manner* and *something in the sense of a homonymy*.—(o), significare ex consequenti and significare primo seu principaliter, *to signify something in a subsequent* or *second place* and *something in the first* or *chief place*.—(p), significare ex institutione seu ex institutione hominum and significare naturaliter, *to signify something on the basis of convention* and *to signify something naturally*.—(q), significare formaliter and significare materialiter, *to signify something according to its form* and *something according to its matter*.—(r), significare in abstracto, see *significare abstracte*.—(s), significare in concretione, see *significare abstracte*.—(t), significare indeterminate, see *significare determinate*.—(u), significare in obliquo and significare in recto, *to signify something in an inflectional* or *declensional case* and *something in a case standing erect* or *the nominative case*.—(v), significare in recto, see *significare in obliquo*.—(w), significare materiali-

ter, see *significare formaliter*.—(x), significare naturaliter, see *significare ex institutione hominum*.—(y), significare negative, see *significare affirmative*.—(z), significare passive, see *significare active*.—(a^2), significare per modum actus, *to signify something after the manner of an action*.—(b^2), significare per modum, aequivocationis, see *significare ex aequo*.—(c^2), significare per modum formae seu ut forma suppositi and significare per modum suppositi seu ut suppositum, *to signify something in the sense of form* or *as form* and *something in the sense of suppositum* or *as a single substance*.—(d^2), significare per modum suppositi, see *significare per modum formae*.—(e^2), significare positive, see *significare affirmative*.—(f^2), significare primo, see *significare ex consequenti*.—(g^2), significare principaliter, see *significare ex consequenti*.—(h^2), significare privative, see *significare affirmative*.—(i^2), significare relative, see *significare absolute*.—(j^2), significare substantive, see *significare adiective*.—(k^2), significare ut ad aliquid and significare ut in aliquo, *to signify something as related to another* or *standing in relation to another* and *something as being in another*.—(l^2), significare ut in abstracto, see *significare abstracte*.—(m^2), significare ut in aliquo, see *significare ut ad aliquid*.—(n^2), significare ut forma suppositi, see *significare per modum formae.*—(o²), **significare ut in fieri**, *to signify something as in process of becoming.* —(p²), **significare ut quo est** and **significare ut quod est**, *to signify something as that by which a thing is that which it is,* and *something as that which is* or *exists,* i.e., to signify something in the sense of *form* or *nature* and *something in the sense of substance.*—(q²), **significare ut quod est**, see *significare ut quo est.*— (r²), **significare ut simplex**, *to signify something as simple.*—(s²), **significare ut subsistens**, *to signify something as existing for itself* and *not in another.*—(t²), **significare ut suppositum**, see *significare per modum formae.*— **significans**, ntis, *P. a., signifying, indicating, making known.*—**significatus**, a, um, *P. a., signified, indicated, made known.*

signo, are, avi, atum, 1, *v. a., to mark, designate, signify, determine.*—**signatus**, a, um, *P. a., marked, designated, signified, determined.* On **ens signatum**, see *ens;* on **forma signata**, see *forma* under 2; on **materia signata et non signata**, see *materia* under 3; on **hoc signatum**, see *hic;* on **materiale signatum fluens et refluens et permanens**, see *materialis* under 1; on **nunc signatum**, see *nunc;* on **pars signata**, see *pars* under 1; on **punctum signatum**, see *punctum.*—**signan-**

ter, *adv., expressly, clearly, distinctly.*

signum, i, *n.,* (1) *sign, characteristic, feature,* (2) *supernatural sign, miraculous sign,* (3) *fixed sign, designated place,* (4) *sign of the zodiac, constellation.* On **cognoscere per signum**, see *cognoscere* under 2; on **demonstratio signi**, see *demonstratio* under 3; on **probare per signum**, see *probare;* on **probatio per signum**, see *probatio* under 2; on **syllogismus per signum**, see *syllogismus;* on **veritas signi**, see *veritas* under 1; on **verum in signo**, see *verus* under 1; on **voluntas signi**, see *voluntas* under 3.— Kinds of *signum* in this sense are: (a), **signum ambiguum** and **signum certum**, *the doubtful* or *uncertain sign* and *the certain* or *indubitable sign.*—(b), **signum certum**, see *signum ambiguum.*— (c), **signum configurativum** and **signum distinctivum**, *the characteristic which makes a thing like another* and *that distinguishes it.* —(d), **signum Christi**, *the sign of Christ* or *the belonging to Christ.*—(e), **signum corporale seu visibile seu sensibile** and **signum spirituale seu signum intellectuale**, *the corporal* or *visible* or *perceptible sign* and *the spiritual* or *intellectual sign.*—(f), **signum demonstrativum, signum praenuntiativum seu prognosticum**, and **signum rememorativum**, *the demonstrative* or *indicative sign of something present,* and *an-*

nouncing or *prophesying sign of something future,* and *the commemorative sign of something past.*—(g), **signum distinctivum,** see *signum configurativum.*—(h), **signum distributivum,** *the dividing sign* or *sign of decision.*—(i), **signum expressum** and **signum interpretativum,** *the expressed* or *explicit sign* and *that interpreted as a sign of something.*—(j), **signum fructuosum** and **signum inane seu supervacuum,** *the fruitful* or *effective sign* and *the empty* or *purely vain sign.*—(k), **signum inane,** see *signum fructuosum.*—(l), **signum intellectuale,** see *signum corporale.*—(m), **signum interpretativum,** see *signum expressum.*—(n), **signum particulare** and **signum universale,** *the special* or *particular sign* and *the general sign.*—(o), **signum praenuntiativum,** see *signum demonstrativum.*—(p), **signum prognosticum,** see *signum demonstrativum.*—(q), **signum protestativum,** *the sign of confession* or *avowal.*—(r), **signum publicae iustitiae,** *the sign of public justice.*—(s), **signum rememorativum,** see *signum demonstrativum.*—(t), **signum sacramentale,** *the outward sign signifying interior effect.*—(u), **signum sensibile,** see *signum corporale.*—(v), **signum spirituale,** see *signum corporale.*—(w), **signum speciei,** *the sign of the species.*—(x), **signum supervacuum,** see *signum fructuosum.*—

(y), **signum visibile,** see *signum corporale.*—(z), **signum voluntatis,** *the sign of the will* or *of purpose.* One kind of *signum* in this sense (2) is **signum mendacii seu mendax,** *the false miracle* or *the miracle of deception.*—One kind of *signum* in this sense is: **signum sensatum,** *the perceptive sign.*

silens, entis, *P. a.,* see *sileo.*

silentium, ii, *n., silence,* the fact of abstaining or forbearing from speech or utterance.

sileo, ere, ui, 2, *v. n.* and *a.,* to be *noiseless, still* or *silent, to keep silence; act, not to speak of, to keep silent* respecting a thing.—**silens,** entis, *P. a., still, calm, quiet, silent.*

siligo, inis, *f., a kind of very white wheat, winter wheat.*

Silonites, is, *m., a native of Silo, a Silonite.*

silva, ae, *f., a wood, forest, woodland.*

Silverius, ii, *m., Silverius,* bishop of Rome after Agapetus, during the reign of Justinian I.

Silvester, tri, *m., Silvester,* bishop of Rome after Miltiades from 314 to 335 A.D.

silvestris, e, *adj., wild, savage.*

Simeon, onis, *m., Simeon,* a devout Jew of Jerusalem in the time of the birth of Christ.

similago, inis, *f., the finest wheat flour.*

similis, e, *adj., like, resembling, similar.* Cf. *similitudo* under 1. On **locus a simili,** see *locus* under

4; on **pars similis,** see *pars* under
1; on **totum similium partium,**
see *totus* under 1.—**omne agens
agit sibi simile,** see *agens.*—**simile,** is, *n., a comparison, likeness,
parallel case,* or *example.*—**similiter,** *adv., in like manner, similarly.*

similiter, *adv.,* see *similis.*

similitudinarie, *adv.,* see *similitudinarius.*

similitudinarius, a, um, *adj., similar,
of like kind, resembling,* the opposite of *proprius,* and *verus.* On
esse similitudinarium, see *esse;*
on **homo similitudinarius,** see
homo under 2; on **unitas similitudinaria,** see *unitas.*—**similitudinarie,** *adv., in the manner* or
sense of singularity, similarly, the
opposite of *proprie* and *per proprietatem.* On **veritas similitudinarie accepta seu dicta,** see *veritas* under 1.

similitudo, inis, *f.,* (1) *similarity,
similitude,* a likeness in some aspect, the opposite of *differentia,*
(2) *a likeness, picture,* synonym
of *species,* (3) *a carved* or *sculp-
tured figure.* On **approximatio
per similitudinem,** see *appoxima-
tio;* on **bonum secundum quandam similitudinem,** see *bonus*
under 2; on **communicabile secundum similitudinem et similitudinis participationem,** see *communicabilis;* on **comparatio similitudinis,** see *comparatio* under 2;
on **dicere per similitudinem,** see
dicere under 3; on **imago similitudinis,** see *imago* under 1; on

incontinens per similitudinem,
see *incontinens;* on **incontinentia
per similitudinem,** see *incontinentia;* on **perfectum secundum
quandam similitudinem,** see *perfectus* under 2; on **propinquitas
similitudinis,** see *propinquitas*
under 2; on **unio similitudinis,**
see *unio.*—Kinds of *similitudo* in
this (1) sense are: (a), **similitudo
aequiperantiae seu secundum aequiperantiam** and **similitudo imitationis,** *similarity of equalization*
and *that of imitation.*—(b), **similitudo analogiae seu proportionis,**
the similarity of analogy or *according to relation* or *proportionally.*—(c), **similitudo apparentiae
seu phantastica** and **similitudo
vera,** *the apparent* and *the real
similarity.*—(d), **similitudo conformitatis in natura seu secundum convenientiam in natura**
and **similitudo repraesentationis
seu quantum ad repraesentationem,** *similarity after the manner
of conformity* or *agreement in
nature* and *that after the manner
of representation* or *presentation.*
—(e), **similitudo confusa** and **similitudo expressissima,** *the confused* and *the fully expressed
similiarity.*—(f), **similitudo deficiens seu imperfecta** and **similitudo plena seu perfecta seu omnimoda,** *the deficient* or *imperfect* and *the full* or *perfect* or
complete similarity.—(g), **similitudo divina,** *divine similiarity* or
similarity with God.—(h), **similitudo exemplaris seu idealis** and

similitudo exemplata, *the exemplary* or *ideal* and *the portrayed similarity.*—(i), similitudo exemplata, see *similitudo exemplaris.*—(j), similitudo expressissima, see *similitudo confusa.*—(k), similitudo formalis, *similarity according to form.*—(l), similitudo generis and similitudo speciei, *similarity according to genus* and *according to species.*—(m), similitudo gloriae and similitudo gratiae, *similarity of heavenly glory* and *that of divine grace.*—(n), similitudo gratiae, see *similitudo gloriae.*—(o), similitudo idealis, see *similitudo exemplaris.*—(p), similitudo imaginis and similitudo vestigii, *similarity of an image* and *that of a foot-print.*—(q), similitudo imitationis, see *similitudo aequiparantiae.*—(r), similitudo imperfecta, see *similitudo deficiens.*—(s), similitudo mutua, *mutual similarity.*—(t), similitudo omnimoda, see *similitudo deficiens.*—(u), similitudo particulata and similitudo universalis, *the particular* and *the general similarity.*—(v), similitudo perfecta, see *similitudo deficiens.*—(w), similitudo per participationem eiusdem formae seu qualitatis and similitudo proportionabilitatis seu proportionalitatis seu per quandam proportionalitatem seu secundum proportionalitatem, *similarity of things through participation in the same form* or *characteristic,* and *similiarity of relations according to proportion-*al *likeness.*—(x), similitudo per quandam proportionalitatem, see *similitudo per participationem eiusdem formae.*—(y), similitudo phantastica, see *similitudo apparentiae.*—(z), similitudo plena, see *similitudo deficiens.*—(a^2), similitudo proportionabilitatis seu proportionabilitatis, see *similitudo per participationem eiusdem formae.*—(b^2), similitudo proportionis, see *similitudo analogiae.* —(c^2), similitudo quantum ad repraesentationem, see *similitudo conformitatis in natura.*—(d^2), similitudo remota, *the remote similarity.*—(e^2), similitudo repraesentationis, see *similitudo conformitatis in natura.*—(f^2), similitudo secundum aequiperantiam, see *similitudo aequiperantiae.*—(g^2), similitudo secundum convenientiam in natura, see *similitudo conformitatis in natura.*—(h^2), similitudo secundum proportionalitatem, see *similitudo per participationem eiusdem formae.*—(i^2), similitudo speciei, see *similitudo generis.*—(j^2), similitudo transumptiva, *the transferred similarity.*—(k^2), similitudo universalis, see *similitudo particulata.*—(l^2), similitudo univocorum, *the similarity of homogeneous things.*—(m^2), similitudo vera, see *similitudo apparentiae.*—(n^x), similitudo vestigii, see *similitudo imaginis.*—Kinds of *similitudo* ın this (2) sense are: (a), similitudo abstracta seu impressa and similitudo affluxa, *the likeness drawn* *from something* or *impressed on another* and *that which has come from something.*—(b), **similitudo adquisita** and **similitudo innata**, *the acquired* and *the innate likeness.*—(c), **similitudo corporalis seu sensibilis** and **similitudo intellegibilis**, *the corporal* or *sensible likeness* and *the intellectual likeness.*—(d), **similitudo creata**, *the created likeness.*—(e), **similitudo effluxa**, see *similitudo abstracta.*—(f), **similitudo impressa**, see *similitudo abstracta.*—(g), **similitudo innata**, see *similitudo adquisita.*—(h), **similitudo intellegibilis**, see *similitudo corporalis.*—(i), **similitudo naturalis**, *the natural likeness* or *that according to nature.*—(j), **similitudo propria**, *the proper likeness.*—(k), **similitudo sensibilis**, see *similitudo corporalis.*—(l), **similitudo vera**, *the true* or *correct likeness.*

similo, are, see *simulo.*

simitas, atis, *f.*, *a curvature of the nose.*

Simon, onis, *m.*, *Simon Magus* or *the sorcerer.*

simonia, ae, *f.*, *spiritual usury, simony.*

simoniace, *adv.*, see *simoniacus.*

simoniacus, a, um, *adj.*, *pertaining to* or *guilty of* or *tainted with simony, simoniacal.* On **collatio simoniaca**, see *collatio* under 3; on **intentio simoniaca**, see *intentio* under 2.—**simoniace**, *adv.*, *after the manner of* or *according to simony, simoniacally.*

simplex, icis, *adj.*, (1) *simple, uncomposed*, without parts, synonym of *indivisibilis*, the opposite of *compositus*, (2) *simple, absolute, not connected with anything*, synonym of *incomplexus*, the opposite of *complexus*, (3) *simple* in a moral sense, *without dissimulation, frank, artless.* On **accidens simplex**, see *accidens* under 2; on **affectus simplex**, see *affectus* under 2; on **causa simplex**, see *causa* under 2; on **consideratio simplex**, see *consideratio;* on **corpus simplex**, see *corpus;* on **delectatio simplex**, see *delectatio;* on **dictio simplex**, see *dictio* under 2; on **elementum simplex**, see *elementum* under 2; on **enuntiatio simplex et enuntiatio una simplex**, see *enuntiatio* under 2; on **essentia simplex**, see *essentia* under 1; on **fieri ut simplex**, see *fieri;* on **forma simplex**, see *forma* under 2; on **idea simplex**, see *idea;* on **linea simplex**, see *linea* under 1; on **magnitudo simplex**, see *magnitudo* under 1; on **materia simplex**, see *materia* under 3; on **motus simplex**, see *motus* under 1; on **natura simplex**, see *natura;* on **nomen simplex**, see *nomen* under 1; on **oratio simplex**, see *oratio* under 2; on **passio simplex**, see *passio* under 1; on **praedicatio simplex**, see *praedicatio* under 2; on **quaestio simplex**, see *quaestio;* on **qualitas simplex**, see *qualitas;* on **quidditas simplex**, see *quidditas;* on **res simplex**, see *res;* on **sacer-**

dos simplex, see *sacerdos;* on **significare ut simplex**, see *significare;* on **substantia simplex**, see *substantia* under 2; on **terminus simplex**, see *terminus* under 5; on **unitas simplex**, see *unitas;* on **unum simplex**, see *unus;* on **veritas simplex**, see *veritas* under 1; on **vita simplex**, see *vita* under 3. —Kinds of *simplex* in this (1) sense are: (a), **simplex apprehensum**, *the comprehended* or *recognized simple substance,* i.e., the comprehensively represented essence of a thing, which in reality is indivisible; cf. *indivisibilis.*— (b), **simplex omnino**, *the completely* or *wholly simple.*—**compositum se habet ad simplicia, ut perfectum ad imperfecta,** see *componere* under 1.—**ei quod est omnino simplex, non convenit aliquid in concretione dictum,** *to that which is completely simple no predicate can be added in reality.*—in **unoquoque genere simplex est prius compositis,** or, **simplex est prius composito,** *in every genus the simple precedes the compounded.*—**nihil est formalius aut simplicius quam esse,** see *esse.*—**quanto aliquid est magis simplex, tanto est maioris virtutis et principium plurium,** or, **quanto aliquid est simplicius, tanto virtus est minus limitata,** or, **quanto aliquid est simplicius, tanto virtute ad plura se extendit,** *the simpler something is according to substance* and *essence, the greater its effective power.*—

Quanto aliquid est simplicius et abstractius tanto secundum se est nobilius et altius, see *abstractus.* —**quanto aliquid est simplicius, tanto virtus est minus limitata,** see above: *quanto aliquid est magis* etc.—**quanto aliquid est simplicius, tanto virtute ad plura se extendit,** see *above:* *quanto aliquid est magis* etc.—**simplex simplici additum non facit maius,** *when something simple is added to something else that is simple, it does not make it greater.*— **simplex si attingitur, totum attingitur,** *when something simple is touched, it is touched in its entirety.* On **acceptio simplex**, see *acceptio* under 2; on **actus simplex**, see *actus* under 1; on **adoptio simplex**, see *adoptio;* on **appetitus simplex**, see *appetitus* under 1; on **apprehendere per modum simplex**, see *apprehendere* under 2; on **canonicus simplex**, see *canonicus* under 3; on **cognitio simplex**, see *cognitio* under 2; on **corruptio simplex**, see *corruptio* under 2; on **demonstratio simplex**, see *demonstratio* under 1; on **fornicatio simplex**, see *fornicatio* under 1; on **generatio simplex**, see *generatio* under 1; on **intellectus simplex**, see *intellectus* under 3 and 9; on **intellegentia simplex**, see *intellegentia* under 2; on **intuitus simplex**, see *intuitus* under 1; on **negatio simplex**, see *negatio* under 2; on **negativa simplex**, see *negativus;* on **numerus sim-**

plex, see *numerus;* on **operatio simplex,** see *operatio* under 2; on **persona simplex,** see *persona* under 3; on **privatio simplex et non simplex,** see *privatio* under 3; on **propositio simplex inhaerentiae,** see *propositio* under 2; on **sacerdos simplex,** see *sacerdos;* on **scientia simplex, simplicis intellegentiae et simplicis notitiae,** see *scientia* under 2; on **suppositio simplex,** see *suppositio* under 3 and 4; on **univocatio simplex,** see *univocatio* under 1; on **vita simplex,** see *vita* under 3; on **voluntas simplex,** see *voluntas* under 3; on **votum simplex,** see *votum* under 1.—**simpliciter,** *adv.,* (1) *in a simple, not complex manner,* synonym of *unite,* the opposite of *composite* and *multipliciter,* (2) *simply, purely,* sometimes *absolutely,* the opposite of *secundum quid.* On **accidens simpliciter,** see *accidens* under 2; on **aequale simpliciter,** see *aequalis* under 1; on **aequalitas simpliciter,** see *aequalitas* under 1; on **aeternum simpliciter,** see *aeternus* under 1; on **agere simpliciter,** see *agere* under 1; on **alius simpliciter,** see *alius;* on **beatus simpliciter,** see *beatus* under 1; on **bonum simpliciter et simpliciter acceptum,** see *bonus* under 2 and 3; on **cognoscere simpliciter,** see *cognoscere* under 2; on **concludere simpliciter,** see *concludere* under 4; on **conformitas simpliciter,** see *conformitas;* on **consilium simpliciter,** see *consi-*

lium under 2; on **continens simpliciter,** see *continens* under 2; on **continentia simpliciter,** see *continentia* under 2; on **contradictio simpliciter,** see *contradictio* under 1; on **corrumpere simpliciter,** see *corrumpere* under 2; on **corruptio simpliciter,** see *corruptio* under 2; on **demonstrare simpliciter,** see *demonstrare* under 3; on **demonstratio simpliciter,** see *demonstratio* under 3; on **dicere simpliciter,** see *dicere* under 3; on **diversus simpliciter,** see *diversus;* on **divisio simpliciter,** see *divisio;* on **ens simpliciter,** see *ens;* on **enuntiatio una simpliciter,** see *enuntiatio* under 2; on **esse simpliciter, esse simpliciter acceptum et esse in loco simpliciter,** see *esse;* on **falsus simpliciter** see *falsus;* on **fieri simpliciter,** see *fieri;* on **generare simpliciter,** see *generare;* on **generatio simpliciter,** see *generatio* under 2; on **idem simpliciter,** see *idem;* on **impossibile simpliciter,** see *impossibilis;* on **incontinens simpliciter,** see *incontinens;* on **incontinentia simpliciter,** see *incontinentia;* on **indivisum simpliciter,** see *indivisus;* on **infinitas simpliciter,** see *infinitas;* on **infinitum simpliciter,** see *infinitus;* on **involuntarium simpliciter,** see *involuntarius;* on **iudicare simpliciter,** see *iudicare* under 2; on **iudicium simpliciter,** see *iudicium* under 3; on **iustificatio simpliciter,** see *iustificatio* under 1; on **iustum simpliciter,** see *iustus;*

on **libertas simpliciter,** see *libertas* under 1; on **malitia simpliciter,** see *malitia* under 3; on **malum simpliciter et simpliciter acceptum,** see *malus* under 2 and 3; on **miraculum simpliciter et simpliciter loquendo,** see *miraculum* under 1; on **multum simpliciter,** see *multus* under 1; on **necessarium simpliciter,** see *necessarius* under 1; on **necesse simpliciter,** see *necesse* under 1; on **negatio simpliciter,** see *negatio* under 2; on **nominare simpliciter,** see *nominare;* on **non-ens simpliciter,** see *non-ens;* on **notum simpliciter,** see *notus;* on **numerus, simpliciter et simpliciter probatus,** see *numerus;* on **pati simpliciter,** see *pati* under 1; on **perfectio simpliciter, et simpliciter dicta,** see *perfectio* under 2 and 3; on **perfectum simpliciter,** see *perfectus* under 1; on **perplexus simpliciter,** see *perplexus;* on **possibile simpliciter,** see *possibilis* under 1; on **praedestinari simpliciter,** see *praedestinare* under 2; on **praedicare simpliciter,** see *praedicare* under 2 ; on **primum simpliciter et simpliciter secundum naturam,** see *primus;* on **principium simpliciter et primum simpliciter,** see *principium;* on **prius simpliciter,** see *prior* under 1; on **prophetia simpliciter dicta,** see *prophetia;* on **propositio prima simpliciter,** see *propositio* under 2; on **prudens simpliciter,** see *prudens;* on **prudentia simpliciter dicta,** see *prudentia*

under 1; on **res simpliciter,** see *res;* on **sanctus simpliciter,** see *sanctus;* on **sapiens simpliciter,** see *sapiens* under 1; on **sapientia simpliciter,** see *sapientia* under 1; on **scire simpliciter,** see *scire* under 2; on **syllogismus simpliciter,** see *syllogismus;* on **ultimum simpliciter,** see *ultimus;* on **velle simpliciter,** see *velle* under 1; on **verum simpliciter,** see *verus* under 1; on **violentum simpliciter,** see *violentus;* on **virtus simpliciter et simpliciter dicta,** see *virtus* under 5; on **vita simpliciter,** see *vita* under 4; on **voluntabile simpliciter,** see *voluntabilis;* on **voluntarium simpliciter,** see *voluntarius* under 3; on **voluntas simpliciter,** see *voluntas* under 3.

Simplicianus, i, *m., Simplicianus, Simplician,* St., bishop of Milan after St. Ambrose.

simplicitas, atis, *f.,* (1) *simpleness, simplicity, lack of composition,* synonym of *indivisibilitas,* the opposite of *compositio,* (2) *simplicity, foolishness,* (3) *sincerity, candor,* the opposite of *duplicitas.* On **abstrahere per modum simplicitatis,** see *abstrahere* under 1 c; on **unitas simplicitatis,** see *unitas.*—One kind of **simplicitas** in this (1) sense is: **simplicitas substantialis,** *simplicity according to substance.*

simpliciter, *adv.,* see *simplex.*

Simplicius, ii, *m., Simplicius,* a peripatetic philosopher of the sixth century A.D. St. Thomas quotes from his *Commentaries on the Categories of Aristotle.*

simplum, i, *n.*, see *simplus.*

simplus, a, um, *adj.*, *simple, single.* —**simplum**, i, *n.*, *the simple sum, the exact sum.*

simul, *adv.*, *at the same time, simultaneously.*—Kinds of *simul* are: (a), **simul naturaliter**, *simultaneously by nature* or *according to nature.*—(b), **simul secundum locum** and **simul tempore**, *simultaneously according to place* and *simultaneously in time.*—(c), **simul secundum rationem** and **simul secundum rem**, *simultaneously according to reason* and *simultaneously according to fact.* —(d), **simul secundum rem**, see *simul secundum rationem.*— (e), **simul tempore**, see *simul secundum rem.*—**movens et motum oportet esse simul**, see *movens.*

simulacrum, i, *n.*, of images formed by art, esp. of statues of the gods, an *image, effigy, statue.*

simulate, *adv.*, see *simulo.*

simulatio, onis, *f.*, *a falsely assumed appearance, a false show, feigning, shamming, pretence, feint, insincerity, deceit, hypocrisy, simulation.*

simulator, oris, *m.*, (1) *a feigner, pretender, simulator,* a synonym of *hypocrita; a hypocrite,* (2) *a copier, imitator.*

simulatorie, *adv.*, *simulatively, in a pretended manner.*

simulo, are, avi, atum, 1, *v. a.*, (1) *in gen., make like, liken,* (2) *in*

partic., to assume the appearance of a thing, to feign, pretend, counterfeit, simulate, used with (a) *acc.,* (b) with *obj. cl.,* and (c) *absol.*—**simulatus**, a, um, *P. a., simulated, pretended, feigned.* —Common phrases are: **simulata confessio**, *deceitful confession.*— **simulata religio**, *a hypocritical religion.*—**simulata sanctitas**, *pretended holiness.*—**simulate**, *adv., feignedly, deceitfully.*

simus, a, um, *adj.,* = *simos, flatnosed, snub-nosed.*

sin, *conj., but if not, unless.*

Sinai, *indecl. noun, Sinai,* Mount, a mountain where the commandments and law were given to Moses.

sinapi, sinape, is, *n., mustard.*

sincere, *adv.*, see *sincerus.*

sinceritas, atis, *f.*, (1) lit., of body, *soundness,* (2) fig., *sincerity, honesty, integrity.*

sincerus, a, um, *adj., pure, sincere, single-minded, genuine.*—**sincere**, *adv., sincerely.*

sindon, onis, *f., a kind of fine cotton stuff, muslin.*

sine, *prep.* with *abl., without.*

singillatim or **sigillatim**, *adv., one by one, singly.*

singularis, e, *adj.*, (1) *single, particular,* synonym of *particularis* and *unus,* the opposite of *communis, multus,* and *universalis,* (2) *belonging to singular number, singular* in the sense of grammar, opposite of *pluralis.*— On **actus singularis**, see *actus* under 1; on **bonum singulare**, see *bonus* under 3; on **causa singularis,** see *causa* under 2; on **conclusio singularis,** see *conclusio* under 2; on **enuntiatio singularis,** see *enuntiatio* under 2; on **gratia singularis,** see *gratia* under 2; on **homo singularis,** see *homo;* on **iudicium singulare,** see *iudicium* under 1; on **nomen singularis designati,** see *nomen* under 1; on **oratio singularis,** see *oratio* under 3; on **persona singularis,** see *persona* under 3; on **praedicare de singulari,** see *praedicare* under 2; on **propositio singularis,** see *propositio* under 2; on **species singularis,** see *species* under 5; · on **substantia singularis,** see *substantia* under 1; on **suppositum singulare,** see *suppositum* under 2; on **terminus singularis,** see *terminus* under 5; on **unum singulare,** see *unus.*—Kinds of *singulare* in this (1) sense are: (a), **singulare contingens,** *the contingent particular.*—(b), **singulare demonstratum seu designatum,** *the demonstrated* or *indicated particular.*—(c), **singulare designatum,** see *singulare demonstratum.*—actiones in singularibus sunt, see *actio* under 2.—actus circa singularia sunt, see *actus* under 2.—humani actus in singularibus contingentibus consistunt, see *contingens* under 2.—sensus non est cognoscitivus nisi singularium, see *sensus* under 3.—singulare est prius et notius quoad nos, quam universale, *the particular as far as we are concerned is*

prior to and better known than the universal.—singularia sunt priora quoad nos et posteriora simpliciter, *singulars are in themselves consequent upon a universal but with respect to us are previous in knowledge.* On **numerus singularis,** see *numerus;* on **praedicare in singulari,** see *praedicare* under 2;—**singulariter,** *adv.,* (1) *one by one, individually, singly, separately,* (2) *in the sense of the singular, in the singular number,* opposite of *pluraliter.* On **accipere singulariter,** see *accipere* under 3; on **praedicare singulariter,** see *praedicare* under 2.

singularitas, atis, *f.,* (1) *singularity, particularity,* synonym of *unitas,* the opposite of *communitas, multitudo,* and *universalitas,* (2) the *singular,* the opposite of *multiplicitas* and *pluralitas.* On **ratio singularitatis,** see *ratio* under 14. —Kinds of *singularitas* in this (1) sense are: (a), **singularitas naturae,** and **singularitas subsistentis in natura,** *the singularity of nature,* and *that of a being with a definite nature.*—(b), **singularitas personae,** *the singularity of a person.*—(c), **singularitas subsistentis in natura,** see *singularitas naturae.*

singulariter, *adv.,* see *singularis.*

singuli, ae, a, *num., distr. adj., separate, one to each, single, individual.*

sinister, tra, trum, *adj.,* (1) *left, on the left, on the left hand* or *side,*

(2) fig., *bad, evil.*—sinistra, ae, *f.,* (sc. *manus*), *the left hand, the left.*

sinistrorsum, *adv., towards the left, to the left.*

sino, ere, sivi, situm, 3, *v. a., to allow, let, suffer, permit, give leave,* used with (1) *obj. cl.,* (2) *ut* and *subj.,* (3) *acc.*—situs, a, um, *P. a., placed.*

sinus, us, *m., the bosom, lap,* used *fig.*—sinus terrae, *the bosom of the earth, an inner recess.*—sinus tranquillitatis, *the bosom of tranquillity, peaceful seclusion.*—sinus caelestis patriae, *the bosom of the heavenly country.*—sinus matris Ecclesiae, *the bosom of the church, a loving enclosure.*—sinus Abrahae, *Abraham's bosom,* a reposing in heaven as a child in its father's lap.

Sion, *indecl. noun, n., Sion, a hill of Jerusalem,* and by meton., *Jerusalem.*

siquidem (or separate, si quidem), *adv.,* like *quandoquidem, since indeed, since that.*

sisto, ere, stiti, 3, *v. n.,* (1) lit., *stand still, to stand immovable,* (2) fig., *to rest, stop, remain, stand.*

sitio, ire, ivi or ii, 4, *v. n.* and *a.,* (1) lit., *to thirst, be thirsty,* (2) fig., *to long for, thirst for, desire eagerly, covet.*—sitiens, entis, *P. a.,* (1) lit., *thirsting.*—(2) fig., *thirsty.*

sitis, is, *f.,* (1) lit., *thirst,* (2) fig., *trong* or *ardent desire, greediness.*

situalis, e, *adj., having a position, concerning* or *belonging to a local position, situal, positional.* On forma situalis, see *forma* under 2; on pars situalis, see *pars* under 1; on res situalis, see *res.*

situatus, a, um, *adj., situated, placed.*

situs, us, *m., the manner of lying, the situation, local position, site of a thing,* synonym of *dispositio* and *positio.* On the difference between *situs* and *ubi,* see *ubi* under 2. On motus secundum situm, see *motus* under 1; on principium secundum situm, see *principium.*

sive, seu, *conj., a disjunctive cond-particle, or if* = *vel si.*—(1), without a preceding *si.*—(2), repeated, with a disjunctive sense predominant. Connecting words or phrases in the same construction, or conditional clauses which have the same predicate, sive . . .sive, seu . . . seu, *whether . . . or,* i.e., *in either case, be it that . . . or that.*

Sixtus, i, *m., Sixtus,* bishop of Rome after Stephanus for about one year, martyred under Valerian on Aug. 6, 258 A.D.

soboles, is, *f., offspring,* used lit. and fig.

sobrie, *adv.,* see *sobrius.*

sobrietas, atis, *f., temperance in drinking, moderation, temperance, continence,* in anything.

sobrius, a, um, *adj.,* (1) lit., *sober, not drunk,* (2) in gen., *sober,*

moderate, temperate, continent.
—**sobrie,** *adv., soberly.*

socerinus, a, *m., father-in-law.*

socia, ae, *f., a companion.*

sociabilis, e, *adj., that may be easily united* or *joined together, sociable, social.*

socialis, e, *adj., companionable, sociable, social,* the opposite of *solitarius.* On **amor socialis,** see *amor* under 1; on **animal sociale,** see *animal* under 1; on **vita socialis,** see *vita* under 3.—**homo est naturaliter seu secundum suam naturam animal sociale,** see *homo.*—**socialiter,** *adv., for the sake of company, socially.*

socialiter, *adv.,* see *socialis.*

societas, atis, *f., fellowship, association, union, community, society.* —Kinds of *societas* are: (a), **societas oeconomica** and **societas politica,** *domestic* and *political society.*—(b), **societas perpetua** and **societas temporalis,** *perpetual* and *temporal society.*—(c), **societas politica,** see *societas oeconomica.* —(d), **societas privata** and **societas publica,** *the private* or *closed* and *the public society.*—(e), **societas publica,** see *societas privata.* —(f), **societas saecularis,** *secular* or *worldly society.*—(g), **societas temporalis,** see *societas perpetua.*

socio, are, avi, atum, 1, *v. a., to join* or *unite together; to associate; to do* or *hold in common, to share a thing with another.*

socius, i, *m.,* in gen., *a fellow sharer, partner, comrade, companion, associate.*

Socrates, is, *m., Socrates,* the celebrated Greek philosopher, (469-399 B.C.). The name however signifies any individual man, John Doe.—**Socraticus,** a, um, *adj., of* or *belonging to Socrates, Socratic.*

Socraticus, a, um, *adj.,* see *Socrates.*

socrus, us, *m.,* either *a father-in-law* or *mother-in-law.*

sodalis, is, *comm., companion.*

Sodoma, orum, *n.,* = Grk. *Sodoma, the city of Sodom* in Palestine; also **Sodoma,** ae, *f.,* and **Sodomi,** orum, *m.*—**Sodomitae,** arum, *m.,* = *Sodimitai, the inhabitants of Sodom, the Sodomites.*—**Sodomiticus,** a, um, *adj., of* or *belonging to Sodom, Sodomitic.*

Sodomitae, arum, *m.,* see *Sodoma.*

Sodomiticus, a, um, *adj.,* see *Sodoma.*

sol, solis, *m., the sun* as a heavenly body—**sol iustitiae,** *the Sun of Justice,* i.e., *Christ.*—**solis ortus,** *sunrise* and **solis occasus,** *sunset.*

solaris, e, *adj., solar, of* or *belonging to the sun.*

solatium, ii, *n., a soothing, assuaging; a comfort, relief, consolation, solace, assistance.*

solea, ae, *f., the uncloven hoof* of an animal.

solemnitas, atis, *f., solemnization, solemnity, festival, celebration* of a day.

solemnis, e, *adj.,* (1) *stated, established, appointed,* (2) transf., according as the idea of the religious or that of the established, stated nature of the thing quali-fied predominates, (a) with the idea of its religious character predominating, *religious, festive, solemn,* (b) of days or seasons; marked by the celebration of special observance or rites (esp. of a rel. character); distinguished by, or set apart for, special cere-monies, *solemn,* (c) of vows, *solemn;* a solemn vow implies an absolute and irrevocable sur-render, and the acceptance of it as such by lawful authority, (d) *solemn* penance. When a pen-ance was accompanied by certain rites as prescribed in the canons, it was a solemn penance.—**solem-ne,** i, *n., ceremony, solemn rite.* —**solemniter,** *adv.*

solemniter, *adv.,* see *solemnis.*

solemnizatio, onis, *f., solemnization.*

solemnizo, are, avi, atum, *v. a., to solemnize, to dignify* or *honor by ceremonies; to celebrate* or *com-memorate* by special observance or with special formality.

soleo, ere, itum, 2, *v. n., be wont, be accustomed,* used with *inf.,* with *pass. inf.*—**solitus,** a, um, *P. a., wonted, accustomed, usual, habitual.*

solers, tis, *adj., shrewd, clever, expert.*

soliditas, atis, *f.,* (1) lit., *solidness, solidity,* (2) transf., *solidity, firm-ness.*

solido, are, avi, atum, 1, *v. a., to make firm* or *solid; to season.*

solidus, a, um, *adj.,* (1) lit., *firm, compact, solid,* (2) fig., *sol-*

id, well-established, reliable.—**so-lidus,** i, *m.,* (sc. *nummus*), *a sol-do, coin.*

soliloquium, i, *n.,* (*solus-loquor*), *a talking to one's self, a soliloquy.*

soliltarius, a, um, *adj., alone, soli-tary, eremitical,* the opposite of *socialis.* On **homo solitarius,** see *homo;* on **vita solitaria,** see *vita* under 3.

solitudo, inis, *f., solitude, a being alone.*

solium, ii, *n., a throne, royal seat.*

sollertia, (**solert-**), ae, *f., skill, shrewdness, quickness of mind,* i.e., skill in discovering some-thing, especially the principle of a thing, the *agchinoia* of Aris-totle.

sollicitator, oris, *m., a tempter, se-ducer.*

sollicite, *adv.,* see **sollicitus.**

sollicito, are, avi, atum, 1, *v. a.,* (1) *to cause distress, anxiety; to dis-tress, disturb,* used lit. and fig., (2) *to incite one to do something; to urge to wrong-doing, seduce, tempt.*

sollicitudo, inis, *f., uneasiness of mind, care, disquiet, anxiety, solicitude, forethought, duty, re-sponsibility.*

sollicitus, a, um, *adj., of restless-ness* from fear, suspense etc., *so-licitous, full of anxiety, agitated, disturbed.*—**sollicite,** *adv., care-fully, punctiliously.*

soloecismus, i, *m., soloikismos,* a grammatical fault in the con-struction of a sentence, *a sole-cism.*

solor, ari, atus, 1, *v. dep. a., to comfort, console.*

solstitium, ii, *n.,* the time when the sun seems to stand still, either in Cancer or in Capricorn, the summer or winter, *solstice.*

solubilis, e, *adj., that can be solved,* as a problem; *soluble.*

solummodo, see *solus* under *adv. solum.*

solus, a, um, *adj., alone, only, single, sole.*—**solum,** *adv., alone, only, merely, barely.*—Strengthened by *modo,* and joined with it in one word, **solummodo.**—Negatively: **non solum . . . sed etiam,** *not only . . . but also.*

solutio, onis, *f.,* (1) *loosing* as of a debt, *demolition, payment,* (2) *solution, analysis, explanation.*— Kinds of *solutio* in this (2) sense are: (a), **solutio ad hominem** and **solutio ad veritatem,** *the solution* (of a question) *for this* or *that person* and *that according to truth which is meant for all.* Cf. also **solutio vera.**—(b), **solutio ad veritatem,** see *solutio ad hominem.*—(c), **solutio defectiva, solutio topica,** and **solutio vera,** *the defective, the probable, and the true* or *proper solution.*—(d), **solutio parva,** *the small* or *weak solution,* because not exhaustive. —(e), **solutio possibilis,** *the possible solution,* ex qua non sequatur aliquod inconveniens.—(f), **solutio topica,** see *solutio defectiva.* —(g), **solutio vera,** see *solutio defectiva.*

solvo, ere, solvi, solutum, 3, *v. a.,* (1) *to loosen* an object from anything, *to release,* or *loose, remove* anything which binds or restrains another, *set free,* (a) from bands, ties, etc., (b) an organ of the body, (c) of liquids, *to destroy, change* the nature of, (d) from any fastening, **funem solvere,** *to loosen the rope* that holds the ship, (2) fig., *to free, release, loose, emancipate, set free,* (a) from guilt, sin, *to acquit, absolve, cleanse,* (b) from excommunication, *to loose, free from,* (c) from punishment, *to release,* (d) of difficulties, questions, *to solve, explain,* (e) of the mind, *to relax,* (f) of marriage, *to dissolve, void, cancel,* (g) of feelings, *to dispel,* (h) of duties and obligations, *to set free from,* (i) *to cancel* anything that binds, (j) of time, *to blot out,* (k) of the fetters of sin, *to destroy,* (3) in partic., of obligations, *to fulfill, pay,* (4) *to break, violate.*— **solvere pecuniam,** *to pay money.* —**solvere primitias,** *to pay the first-fruits.*—**solvere decimas,** *to pay tithes.*—**solvere tributum,** *to pay tax.*—**solvere sanguinem,** *to pay one's blood as a price.*— **solvere pretium,** *to pay the price.* —**solvere debitum,** *to pay the debt.*—**solvere ieiunium,** *to break the fast.*—**solvere sabbatum,** *to break the sabbath.*—**solutus,** a, um, *P. a.,* (1) *paid,* (2), *loosed, freed from,* excommunication, (3) *freed from* duties, obligations, etc., (4) *free* in the sense of un-married.

somniator, oris, *m., a dreamer.*

somnio, are, avi, atum, 1, *v. a., to dream, to dream of,* or *see in a dream.*

somnium, ii, *n., a dream.*

somnolentia, ae, *f., sleepiness, drowsiness, somnolence.*

somnolentus, a, um, *adj., full of sleep, drowsy, dozy, somnolent.*

somnus, i, *m.,* (1) *sleep,* (2) *a dream.*

sonabilis, e, *adj., sounding, noisy.*

sonabilitas, atis, *f., capability of sound.*

sonitus, us, *m., a noise, sound, din.*

sono, are, ui, itum, 1, *v. n.* and *a.,* (1) *to make a noise, to sound, resound,* (2) *to utter, speak, say, pour forth, sound,* (3) *to de-note, signify, imply.*—**sonare,** *to stand for.*—**sonantia verba,** *audible words.*

sonus, i, *m., a noise, sound.*

sophisma, atis, *n., a false conclu-sion, fallacy, sophism,* synonym of *fallacia* and *paralogismus.*—Kinds of *sophisma* are: (a), **so-phisma accidentis,** *the sophism of an accident,* as if it were some-thing that belongs to a thing of necessity.—(b), **sophisma conse-quentis,** *the sophism of a conclu-sion of a conditional sentence.*

sophista, ae, *m., an apparent phi-losopher* or *wise man, a sophist.*

sophisticatio, onis, *f., sophistry, ap-pearance,* the opposite of *veritas,* not used by St. Thomas in the S.T.

sophisticatus, a, um, *adj., sophisti-cated, adulterated, mixed with some foreign substance.*

sophisticus, a, um, *adj., sophistic, sophistical.* On **disputatio sophis-tica,** see *disputatio;* on **instantia sophistica,** see *instantia* under 1; on **locus sophisticus,** see *locus* under 4; on **modus sophisticus,** see *modus* under 2; on **ratio so-phistica,** see *ratio* under 13; on **scientia sophistica,** see *scientia* under 1; on **syllogismus sophisti-cus,** see *syllogismus.*—**sophistica,** ae, *f., sophistic,* a part of the logical works of Aristotle, or *sophistical refutation,* in which he treats of argumentation which appears to arrive at truth, by the use of fallacies, paradox and the like; also *apparent science* or *wisdom,* i.e., *scientia sophistica.*—Kinds of *sophistica* in this last sense are: **sophistica docens** and **sophistica utens,** *the teaching so-phistic* and *the useful sophistic* or *sophism,* or sophism in theory and sophism in practice.

Sophonia, ae, *m., Sophonia,* one of the minor prophets.

Sophroniscus, i, *m., Sophroniscus,* the father of Socrates.

sopitus, a, um, *P. a., lulled to sleep, settled, quiet.*

sopor, oris, *m., a deep sleep.*

sorbeo, ere, ui, 2, *v. a., to suck in, sup up.*

sordes, is, *f.,* (1) lit., (a) *filth, dirt, squalor, uncleanness,* (b) transf., *mourning garment,* *coarse clothes,* (2) fig., *unclean-ness, filth.*

sordesco, ere, dui, 3, *v. inch. n., to depreciate.*

sordidus, a, um, *adj., sombre, poor.*

sorex, icis, *m., a shrew-mouse.*

soror, oris, *f., a sister.*

sors, tis, *f.,* (1) *lot,. fate, destiny, chance,* (2) *capital, invested money, principal.* On **divinatio sortium,** see *divinatio* under 2.—Kinds of *sors* in this (1) sense are: **sors consultoria, sors divinativa, seu divinatoria,** and **sors divisoria,** *the advisory lot, the prophesying lot,* and *the distributive lot.* On **usura sortis,** see *usura.*

sortialis, e, *adj., pertaining to divination by lots, sortilegious.*

sortiaria, ae, *f., a diviner by lots, sortileger, sorcerer.*

sortilegus, a, um, *adj., divining by lots, prophetic, foretelling.*

sortior, iri, 4, *v. dep. n.* and *a., to draw* or *cast lots for, to fix, assign, allot,* also *to obtain* or *receive a thing.*

sospitas, atis, *f., a sospitation, a preserving.*

Soter, eris, *m., Soter,* saint (167-175). He is quoted on the precept of Holy Communion, and as forbidding a priest to say Mass without the presence of two other persons.

spado, onis, *m., a castrated person, a eunuch.*

spargo, ere, si, sum, 3, *v. a.,* (1) lit., (a), *to scatter, sow* (b) *to sprinkle,* (2) fig., *to distribute.*

sparsim, *adv., scatteredly, dispersedly, here and there.*

spatiosus, a, um, *adj., comely.*

spatium, ii, *n.,* (1) *space, distance, interval,* (2) *declaration, statement.*—Kinds of *spatium* in this (1) sense are: (a), **spatium infinitum,** *infinite space.* Cf. 3 Phys. 7 a.—(b), **spatium plenum** and **spatium vacuum,** *the full* or *filled space* and *the empty space.* —(c), **spatium separatum,** *the space separated from a body* or *abstract space.*—(d), **spatium vacuum,** see *spatium plenum.*

spatula, ae, *f., dim., a little palm-branch, branch.*

spatulamantia, ae, *f., spatulamancy,* divination by means of the shoulder blade of an animal.

specialis, e, *adj.,* (1) *belonging to* or *concerning species, special,* the synonym of *specificus,* the opposite of *generalis,* (2) *individual, particular, special,* synonym of *particularis,* the opposite of *communis, generalis.* On **forma specialis,** see *forma* under 2; on . **ratio specialis,** see *ratio* under 11. —**specialiter,** *adv., particularly, specially, specifically,* opposite of *generaliter.*—**specialissime,** *supl. adv., in a most special manner, most especially.*—**in speciali,** *in particular,* the opposite of *in generali.* On **cognitio specialis,** see *cognitio* under 2; on **cognoscere in speciali,** see *cognoscere* under 2; on **condicio specialis,** see *condicio* under 3; on **confessio specialis,** see *confessio* under

2; on **dispensatio specialis**, see *dispensatio* under 2; on **distinctio specialis**, see *distinctio* under 2; on **donum speciale**, see *donum* under 2; on **eleemosyna specialis**, see *eleemosyna*, on **genus speciale**, see *genus* under 2; on **iniustitia specialis**, see *iniustitia* under 1; on **iustitia specialis**, see *iustitia* under 1; on **malatia specialis**, see *malatia* under 3; on **modus specialis**, see *modus* under 2; on **necessitas specialis**, see *necessitas* under 3; on **nomen speciale**, see *nomen* under 1; on **oppositum in speciali**, see *opponere;* on **origo in speciali**, see *origo;* on **passio specialis**, see *passio* under 3; on **peccatum speciale**, see *peccatum* under 2; on **praeceptum speciale**, see *praeceptum;* on **ratio specialis**, see *ratio* under 11; on **species specialis**, see *species* under 8; on **suffragia specialia**, see *suffragium;* on **virtus specialis**, see *virtus.*

specialitas, atis, *f., particularity, peculiarity.*

specialiter, *adv.*, see *specialis.*

species, ei, *f.,* (1) *spectacle, sight, vision,* (2) *outward appearance, shape, form,* (3) *beautiful appearance, splendor, beauty,* (4) *seeming, semblance, appearance,* (5) *a form of knowledge, a representation* of an object in a faculty of knowledge, synonym of *intentio,* (6) *species,* in ontological sense, synonym of *essentia,* not exact synonym of *species,* as distinct from *genus,* (7)

essence in the general and broader sense of the word, (8) a *particular sort, kind,* or *quality, a species* in the logical or proper and in the improper sense of the word, the opposite of *individuum* and *genus.* Species in this sense exists only in the mind.— One kind of *species* in this (2) sense is: **species sacramentalis**, *sacramental appearance,* i.e., *of bread and wine.* On the relation of *species* to *intentio,* see *intentio* under 4. On **abstracti speciei a materia**, see *abstractio* under 3; on **abstrahere speciem a materia**, see *abstrahere;* on **cognoscere per speciem**, see *cognoscere* under 2; on **locus speciei**, see *locus* under 1; on **verbum speciei vocis**, see *verbum* under 1; on **visio speciei seu per speciem**, see *visio* under 1.—Kinds of *species* in this (5) sense are: (a), **species adquisita seu a re abstracta seu accepta, species indita seu influxa seu infusa** and **species connaturalis seu innata**, *the intelligible form acquired* or *abstracted from a thing, that bestowed* or *infused directly by God,* and *that given along with the nature at the time of its production.*—(b), **species a re abstracta seu accepta**, see *species adquisita.*—(c), **species concreata inhaerens** and **species creata inhaerens**, *the form created simultaneously with the being* and *adhering to it,* and *the form created afterwards* and *adhering to it.*—(d), **species connaturalis,** see *species adquisita.*—(e), **species continentis** and **species propria**, *the form of that in which a thing is contained* and *the proper form of a thing.*—(f), **species creata inhaerens**, see *species concreata.*—(g), **species depurata**, *the purified* or *separated* (from matter) *form.*—(h), **species imaginata**, *the form sensibly represented.* —(i), **species indita**, see *species adquisita.*—(j), **species individualis seu singularis**, and **species universalis**, *the form representing the individual*, and *representing the universal nature.*—(k), **species infusa**, see *species adquisita.*—(l), **species influxa**, see *species adquisita.*—(m), **species innata**, see *species adquisita.*—(n), **species intellecta seu intellectualis seu intellegibilis seu spiritualis** and **species sensata seu sensibilis**, *the form received upon the intellect* or *the intellectual* or *spiritual form* and *the form received upon one of the senses* or *the sensible form.*—(o), **species propria**, see *species continentis.*—(p), **species sensata seu sensibilis**, see *species intellecta.*—(q), **species singularis**, see *species individualis.*—(r), **species specierum**, *the form of forms*, i.e., the soul so called, inquantum per intellectum agentem facit species intellegibiles actu et recipit eas secundum intellectum possibilem.—(s), **species spiritualis**, see *species intellectualis.*—(t), **species superexcedens**, *form containing more than*

is proper to an individual.—(u), **species universalis**, see *species individualis.*—(v), **species visibilis**, *the form of the sense of sight, the visible form.* On **indivisibile secundum speciem**, see *indivisibilis;* on **integritas speciei**, see *integritas;* on **pars speciei et habentis speciem**, see *pars* under 1; on **passio speciei**, see *passio* under 1; on **perfectio ut ad speciem habendam et ut habentis iam speciem**, see *perfectio* under 4; on **perfectus secundum speciem**, see *perfectus* under 1; on **principium speciei**, see *principium;* on **prius secundum speciem**, see *prior* under 1.—Kinds of *species* in this sense are: (a), **species completa seu perfecta** and **species incompleta seu imperfecta**, *the complete* or *perfect* and *the incomplete* or *imperfect essence.*— (b), **species corporalis seu sensibilis**, *the corporal essence* or *the essence of the sensibly perceptible thing.*—(c), **species deficiens** and **species superexcedens**, *the essence deficient* as compared to another and *the essence exceeding another.*—(d), **species exemplaris seu idealis**, *the model* or *ideal essence.*—(e), **species factiva**, *the factitive* or *producing essence*, i.e., the model of a thing in the mind of an artist.—(f), **species generativa**, *the generative essence.*—(g), **species idealis**, see *species exemplaris.*—(h), **species imperfecta**, see *species completa.* —(i), **species incompleta**, see *spe-*

cies completa.—(j), **species indifferens,** *the notion that is applicable to diverse things.*—(k), **species integra,** *the integral essence.*—(l), **species particularis,** *the particular essence.*—(m), **species perfecta,** see *species completa.*—(n), **species per se exsistens seu separata,** *essence existing by itself* or *separated* (from material, as Plato assumed it).—(o), **species propria,** *the proper sense.* Cf. *species propria* under 7.—(p), **species sensibilis,** see *species corporalis.*—(q), **species separata,** see *species per se exsistens.*—(r), **species superexcedens,** see *species deficiens.* On **bonum speciei seu secundum speciem suam,** see *bonus* under 2 and 3; on **circumstantia constituens et mutans speciem,** see *circumstantia* under 2; on **communitas speciei,** see *communitas* under 1; on **contrarium secundum speciem,** see *contrarius* under 1; on **differentia speciei seu secundum speciem,** see *differentia;* on **differre speciem seu secundum speciem,** see *differre* under 2; on **distinctio speciei,** see *distinctio* under 2; on **distinguere secundum speciem,** see *distinguere;* on **diversitas speciei seu secundum speciem,** see *diversitas;* on **diversus specie seu secundum speciem,** see *diversus;* on **forma speciei seu secundum speciem,** see *forma* under 2; on **idem specie seu in natura speciei seu per speciem suppositi,** see *idem;* on **indifferens secundum speciem,** see *indifferens* under 1; on **indifferentia speciei,** see *indifferentia;* on **infinitum secundum speciem,** see *infinitus;* on **intentio speciei,** see *intentio* under 3; on **malum secundum speciem suam,** see *malus* under 2; on **multum specie,** see *multus* under 1; on **oppositio secundum speciem,** see *oppositio* under 2; on **natura speciei,** see *natura* under 9; on **nomen speciei,** see *nomen* under 1; on **perfectio speciei,** see *perfectio* under 2; on **quidditas speciei,** see *quidditas;* on **ratio speciei,** see *ratio* under 11; on **relatio speciei,** see *relatio;* on **signum speciei,** see *signum* under 1; on **similitudo speciei,** see *similitudo* under 1; on **totalitas speciei,** see *totalitas;* on **unitas speciei,** see *unitas;* on **unum speciei seu in specie seu secundum speciem,** see *unus;* on **virtus speciei,** see *virtus* under 1. —Kinds of *species* in this (7) sense are: (a), **species attinentiae,** *the species of belonging* or *relationship.*—(b), **species communis** and **species propria,** *the general* and *the particular species.* Cf. *species propria* under 6.—(c), **species contraria, species media,** and **species disparata,** *the species contrarily opposed to another, but in same genus, that in the middle* (between two), and *the dissimilar* or *different species,* because in different genera.—(d), **species disparata,** see *species contraria.*—(e), **species individua** seu **specialissima**, *the individual* or *ultimate species* (quae non dividitur in alias species). Cf. *species individualis* under 5.—(f), **species loci**, see *locus* under 1.— (g), **species mathematica**, *the mathematical species*, i.e., *forms.* —(h), **species media**, see *species contraria.*—(i), **species propria**, see *species communis*, also *species propria*, under 5.—(j), **species specialissima**, see *species individua.*—(k), **species subalterna**, *the subordinate species.*—(l), **species vera**, *the true* or *proper species.* — **actus speciem recipiunt ex obiectis**, see *actus* under 1.—**nihil agit ultra seu nisi secundum suam speciem**, see *agere* under 1.— **ratio cuiuslibet speciei substantiae consistit in indivisibili**, see *ratio* under 11.

specificatio, onis, *f.*, *classification* in a species, *presentation* of a species.

specifico, are, avi, atum, 1, *v. a.*, *to make according to a species, include in a species.* On **differentia specificans**, see *differentia;* on **dispositio specificans**, see *dispositio* under 4.

specificus, a, um, *adj.*, *of* or *pertaining to* or *characterizing* or *constituting a species, specific*, synonym of *specialis.* On **cognitio specifica**, see *cognitio* under 2; on **differentia, specifica et specifica ultima**, see *differentia;* on **esse specifica**, see *esse;* on **forma specifica**, see *forma*, under 2; on **principium specificum**, see *principium;* on **ratio specifica**, see *ratio* under 11; on **relatio specifica**, see *relatio.*

specimen, inis, *n.*, *that by which a thing is seen, known* or *recognized, a proof, evidence, sign.*

speciosus, a, um, *adj.*, (1) *goodlooking, showy, beautiful, splendid*, (2) *having a form, formed.*

spectaculum, i, *n.*, (1) lit., *stageplay*, (2) in gen., pl., *sights* of any kind.

specto, are, avi, atum, 1, *v. freq. a.*, (1) lit., *to look at, behold; to gaze at, watch, observe*, (2) in partic., *to look to a thing*, as to an end or guide of action; hence, *to have in view, bear in mind; to aim, strive*, or *endeavor after; to tend, incline, refer, pertain* or *have regard to* a thing.—**ex alio spectare**, *to keep one's eye on another.*

speculabilis, e, *adj.*, *that may be seen, visible, explorable, speculative, cognoscible.* On **principium speculabilium**, see *principium;* on **ratio speculabilis**, see *ratio* under 6.—**scientia est ratio recta speculabilium**, see *scientia* under 1.

specularis, e, *adj.*, *of* or *belonging to a mirror, like a mirror, indirect, occuring by means of a mirror, being in a mirror.* On **cognitio specularis**, see *cognitio* under 2; on **corpus speculare**, see *corpus;* on **visio specularis**, see *visio* under 1.

speculatio, onis, *f.*, *spying out, investigation, contemplation, ob-*

servation. On **cognoscere per modum speculationis,** see *cognoscere* under 2.—Kinds of *speculatio* are: (a), **speculatio physica,**
the physical contemplation.—(b),
speculatio prophetiae and **speculatio scientiae adquisitae,** *the infused contemplation of prophesy*
and *that of acquired knowledge*
or *the prophetic* and *the scientific contemplation.*—(c), **speculatio scientiae adquisitae,** see *speculatio prophetiae.*

speculative, *adv.,* see *speculativus.*

speculativus, a, um, *adj., contemplative, concerned with truth for
its own sake, speculative,* synonym of *theoricus,* the opposite of
operativus and *practicus.* On **ars
speculativa,** see *ars* under 1; on
cognitio speculativa, see *cognitio*
under 2; on **consideratio speculativa,** see *consideratio;* on **existimatio speculativa,** see *existimatio;* on **felicitas speculativa,** see
felicitas; on **habitus speculativus,**
see *habitus* under 4; on **intellectus speculativus,** see *intellectus*
under 3; on **opinio speculativa,**
see *opinio;* on **potentia speculativa,** see *potentia* under 2; on **principium in speculativis,** see *principium;* on **ratio speculativa,** see
ratio under 3; on **scientia speculativa, speculativa secundum
quid et simpliciter seu tantum,**
see *scientia* under 1; on **veritas
speculativa,** see *veritas* under 1;
on **via speculativa,** see *via* under
3; on **virtus speculativa,** see *virtus* under 5; on **vita speculativa,**

see *vita* under 3.—**speculative,**
adv., in the manner or *sense
of contemplation, speculatively,
contemplatively,* the opposite of
practice. On **cognoscere speculative,** see *cognoscere* under 2.

speculator, oris, *m., a watchman, a
looker-out.*

speculor, ari, atus, 1, *v. dep. a., to
observe, watch, examine, explore.*

speculum, i, (1) *a looking-glass, a
mirror,* in the proper and in the
improper senses of the word, (2)
reflection, image. On **cognoscere in speculo,** see *cognoscere*
under 2; on **visio per speculum,**
see *visio* under 1.—Kinds of *speculum* in this (1) sense are: (a),
**speculum aeternitatis seu aeter-
num** and **speculum temporale,**
the mirror of eternity and *the
temporal mirror.*—(b), **speculum
aeterum,** see *speculum aeternitatis.*—(c), **speculum coniunctum**
and **speculum distans,** *the mirror
connected with sense of sight* or
the eyes and that distant from it.
—(d), **speculum distans,** see *speculum coniunctum.*—(e), **speculum igneum,** *the fiery mirror.*—
(f), **speculum increatum,** *the uncreated mirror.*—(g), **speculum
intellegibile seu intellegibilium
substantiarum seu intellegentiarum,** *the intellectual mirror* or
*the mirror of the intellectual
substances* or *of the intelligences.*
—(h), **speculum intellegentiarum,**
see *speculum intellegibile.*—(1),
speculum intellegibilium, see
speculum intellegibile.—(j), **spe-**

culum materiale, and speculum spirituale seu mentis, *the physical* or *material mirror* and *the spiritual mirror.*—(k), speculum prophetiae, *the mirror of prophecy.*—(l), speculum spirituale, see *speculum materiale.*—(m), speculum temporale, see *speculum aeternitatis.*—(n), speculum trinitatis, *the mirror of the Trinity.*—(o), speculum voluntarium, *the voluntarily* or *freely reflecting mirror.*

specus, us, *m., a cave.*

spelta, ae, *f., spelt.*

spelunca, ae, *f., a cave, cavern.*

sperativus, a, um, *adj., hoping, causing hope,* does not occur in S.T. On scientia sperativa, see *scientia* under 1.

sperma, atis, *n.,* = Grk. *sperma, seed, semen, sperm.*

sperno, ere, sprevi, spretum, 3, *v. a., to despise, condemn, reject, scorn, spurn.*

spero, are, avi, atum, 1, *v. a., to hope, look for, expect,* used (a) *absol.,* (b) with *acc.,* (c) with *obj.-clause,* (d) with *in* and *acc.,* (e) with *de,* (f) with *inf.-fut.,* (g) with *inf.-pres.*

spes, ei, *f., hope.* On beatitudo spei, see *beatitudo* under 1; on delectatio spei et per spem, see *delectatio;* on fortitudo quae est per spem, see *fortitudo* under 2; on gaudium spei, see *gaudium.*— Kinds of *spes* in the sense of a virtue are: spes formata and spes informis, *hope formed* (by love) and *the formless* or *unformed*

hope, i.e., hope supported by charity and that not supported by charity.

sphaera, ae, *f.,* (1) *globe, ball* in the sense of a solid body (*corpus sphaericum*), synonym of *globus,* (2) *hollow globe, the celestial hollow globe* (*sphaera caelestis,* 2 Cael. 10 b; 2 Meteor. 10 b), synonym of *globus* and *orbis,* (3) *the form of a globe* (*figura sphaerica*), (4) *sphere, region,* synonym of *globus.*—Kinds of *sphaera* in this (2) sense are: (a), sphaera concentrica and sphaera excentrica, *a sphere concentric with another* and *that not concentric with it.*—(b), sphaera deferens seu ferens seu volvens and sphaera revolvens, *the sphere moving a heavenly body forward* or *carrying it along* and *that turning it over* or *revolving it.*—(c), sphaera excentrica, see *sphaera concentrica.*—(d), sphaera ferens, see *sphaera deferens.*— (e), sphaera inferior and sphaera superior, *the inferior* and *the superior* or *the lower* and *the higher sphere.*—(f), sphaera lunaris and sphaera solis, *the sphere of the moon* and *that of the sun.* —(g), sphaera nona, *the ninth sphere* which is to be found beyond the sphere of the fixed stars.—(h) sphaera prima seu suprema seu ultima, *the first* (counting from above) or *the highest* or *the last* (counting from below), i.e., the sphere of the fixed stars.—(i), sphaera revol-

vens, see *sphaera deferens.*—(j),
sphaera solis, see *sphaera luna-*
ris.—(k), **sphaera superior,** see
sphaera inferior.—(l), **sphaera**
suprema, see *sphaera prima.*—
(m), **sphaera ultima,** see *sphaera*
prima.—(n), **sphaera volvens,**
see *sphaera deferens.*—Kinds of
sphaera in this sense are: **sphaera**
activorum and **sphaera passivo-**
rum, *the region of the active* and
that of the passive things of na-
ture, i.e., the sublunary region.

sphaericus, a, um, *adj., of* or *be-*
longing to a ball, globe-shaped,
spherical. On **corpus sphaericum,**
see *corpus;* on **figura sphaerica,**
see *figura* under 1; on **motus**
sphaericus, see *motus* under 1.

spica, ae, *f., of grain, an ear.*

spina, ae, *f., a thorn.*

spiraculum, i, *n., breath of life.*

spiratio, onis, *f., breathing, breath,*
respiration, and in the Holy Trinity, the procession of the Holy
Spirit, from the Father and Son.
—One kind of *spiratio* in this
sense is: **spiratio communis,** *spi-*
ration shared by two as one
principle.

spirativus, a, um, *adj., breathing,*
respiring, respirative. On **poten-**
tia spirativa, see *potentia* under
2; on **virtus spirativa,** see *virtus*
under 1; on **vis spirativa,** see *vis*
under 1.

spirator, oris, *m., a spirator,* applied
to the Holy Trinity to denote
who spirates, or gives origin to
the procession of the Holy Spirit.

spiritualis, e, *adj.,* (1) *spiritual, in-*
corporeal, synonym of *immateria-*
lis, incorporalis, and *incorporeus,*
the opposite of *carnalis, materia-*
lis, corporalis, corporeus, and *na-*
turalis, (2) *spiritual, spiritualized,*
spirit-like, the opposite of *natura-*
lis, (3) *spiritual,* corresponding
to the spirit in its superiority over
sensible nature, the opposite of
animalis and *carnalis,* (4) *spirit-*
ual, i.e., belonging to the spiritual state, concerning it, synonym
of *eccelsiasticus,* the opposite of
civilis, saecularis, and *mundanus.*
On **actio spiritualis,** see *actio*
under 1; on **actus spiritualis,** see
actus under 1; on **adoratio spiri-**
tualis, see *adoratio* under 1; on
adulterium spirituale, see *adulte-*
rium; on **approximatio spiritualis,**
see *approximatio;* on **beatitudo**
spiritualis, see *beatitudo* under
1; on **bonum spirituale,** see *bonus*
under 3; on **castitas spiritualis,**
see *castitas* under 1; on **causa**
spiritualis, see *causa* under 2; on
character spiritualis, see *charac-*
ter under 2; on **claritas spiritua-**
lis, see *claritas* under 3; on **com-**
municatio spiritualis, see *com-*
municatio under 3; on **congrega-**
tio spiritualis, see *congregatio*
under 2; on **contactus spiritualis,**
see *contactus;* on **contemplatio**
spiritualis, see *contemplatio;* on
cultus spiritualis, see *cultus* under 2; on **defectus spiritualis,** see
defectus under 2; on **delectatio**
spiritualis, see *delectatio;* on **di-**
vitiae spirituales, see *divitiae;* on

dolor spiritualis, see *dolor;* on
donum spirituale, see *donum* under 1; on eleemosyna spiritualis,
see *eleemosyna;* on esse spirituale, see *esse;* on filius spiritualis,
see *filius* under 1; on finis spiritualis, see *finis* under 2; on forma spiritualis, see *forma* under 2;
on fornicatio spiritualis, see *fornicatio* under 2; on fortitudo spiritualis, see *fortitudo* under 1; on
fructus spiritualis, see *fructus*
under 2; on fundamentum in
spiritualibus spiritualis aedificii
et spiritualis doctrinae, see *fundamentum;* on gaudium spirituale, see *gaudium;* on generatio
spiritualis, see *generatio* under
1; on gloria spiritualis, see *gloria*
under 1 and 2; on gratia spiritualis, see *gratia* under 2; on ieiunium spirituale, see *ieiunium;*
on individuum spirituale, see *individuum;* on intentio spiritualis,
see *intentio* under 4; on locus
spiritualis, see *locus* under 1; on
locutio spiritualis, see *locutio* under 2; on lumen spirituale, see
lumen; on lux spiritualis, see *lux;*
on magnitudo spiritualis, see
magnitudo under 2; on malum
spirituale, see *malus* under 3; on
materia spiritualis, see *materia*
under 3; on matrimonium spirituale, see *matrimonium;* on miraculum spirituale, see *miraculum*
under 1; on modus spiritualis,
see *modus* under 2; on mors spiritualis, see *mors;* on motus spiritualis, see *motus* under 2; on
multiplicatio spiritualis, see *mul-*

tiplicatio; on natura spiritualis,
see *natura;* on observantia spiritualis, see *observantia* under 4;
on oculus spiritualis, see *oculus;*
on opus spirituale, see *opus* under 4; on pater spiritualis, see
pater; on peccatum spirituale,
see *peccatum* under 2; on perfectio spiritualis, see *perfectio*
under 2; on poena spiritualis, see
poena; on propinquitas spiritualis, see *propinquitas* under 2; on
pulchritudo spiritualis, see *pulchritudo;* on qualitas spiritualis,
see *qualitas;* on quies spiritualis,
see *quies;* on regnum spirituale,
see *regnum;* on res spiritualis,
see *res;* on resurrectio spiritualis,
see *resurrectio;* on sacrificium
spirituale, see *sacrificium;* on
scandalum spirituale, see *scandalum;* on sensus spiritualis, see
sensus under 2; on servitus spiritualis, see *servitus* under 1; on
signum spirituale, see *signum*
under 1; on species spiritualis,
see *species* under 5; on speculum
spirituale, see *speculum* under
1; on substantia spiritualis, see
substantia under 2; on tactus
spiritualis, see *tactus* under 1; on
via spiritualis, see *via* under 1;
on virtus spiritualis, see *virtus*
under 1 and 5; on vis spiritualis,
see *vis* under 1; on visio spiritualis, see *visio* under 1; on visus
spiritualis, see *visus;* on vita spiritualis, see *vita* under 1 and 3;
on vitium spirituale, see *vitium*
under 2. On amor spiritualis,
see *amor* under 1; on corpus

spirituale, see *corpus;* on **esse spirituale,** see *esse;* on **forma spiritualis,** see *forma* under 2; on **immortalitas spiritualis,** see *immortalitas;* on **immutatio spiritualis,** see *immutatio* under 2; on **sensus spiritualis,** see *sensus* under 8; on **transmutatio spiritualis,** see *transmutatio* under 1. On **homo spiritualis,** see *homo;* on **vita spiritualis,** see *vita* under 3.—Kinds of *spiritualis* in this (3) sense are: **spirituale per causam** and **spirituale per essentiam seu per se,** *the spiritual by reason of causality,* and *the spiritual according to its essence or according to itself.* On **dominium spirituale,** see *dominium;* on **iudicium spirituale,** see *iudicium* under 1; on **officium spirituale,** see *officium* under 2; on **potestas spiritualis,** see *potestas* under 3; on **praelatio spiritualis,** see *praelatio.*—**spiritualiter,** *adv., in a spiritual manner or respect, spiritually,* synonym of *invisibiliter.* On **recipere spiritualiter,** see *recipere.*

spiritualitas, atis, *f.,* (1) *spirituality, incorporeality,* synonym of *immaterialitas* and *incorporeitas,* the opposite of *materialitas, carnalitas,* and *corporeitas,* (2) *spirituality, the state of being spiritualized, spiritualization,* (3) *spiritual state, spiritual being, spiritual life,* (4) *spiritual relation* or *relationship.*—Kinds of *spiritualitas* in this (2) sense are: (a), **spiritualitas coniugatorum,** **spiritualitas viduarum,** and **spiritualitas virginum,** *the spiritual life of the married, that of widows,* and *that of virgins.*—(b), **spiritualitas necessaria** and **spiritualitas superabundans,** *the necessary* and *the superbundant* or *more than necessary spiritual life.*—(c), **spiritualitas superabundans,** see *spiritualitas necessaria.*—(d), **spiritualitas viduarum,** see *spiritualitas coniugatorum.*—(e), **spiritualitas virginum,** see *spiritualitas coniugatorum.*

spiritualiter, *adv.,* see *spiritualis.*

spiritus, us, *n., air, exhalation, breath, power, spirit, mind.* On **incorruptio spiritus,** see *incorruptio* under 2; on **paupertas spiritus,** see *paupertas* under 1.— Kinds of *spiritus* are: (a), **spiritus animalis seu sensibilis,** *the animal* or *sensible spirit of life.*—(b), **spiritus bonus** and **spiritus malus seu malignus,** *the good* and *the evil spirit.*—(c), **spiritus caelestis,** and **spiritus terrenus,** *the heavenly* and *the earthly spirit.*—(d), **spiritus complantatus,** the Aristotelian *symphyton pneuma, the implanted breath.*—(e), **spiritus concupiscentiae,** *the spirit* or *force of concupiscence.*—(f), **spiritus coniunctus** and **spiritus separatus,** *the spirit joined with a body* or *the pure spirit.*—(g), **spiritus corporalis seu corporeus,** *the corporal spirit.*—(h), **spiritus Dei seu divinus seu Domini seu sanctus,** *the spirit of God* or *of the Lord* or *the Holy Spirit.*—(i), **spiritus divinus,** see *spiritus Dei.*

—(j), **spiritus Domini,** see *spiritus Dei.*—(k), **spiritus falsitatis seu mendacii seu mendax** and **spiritus veritatis,** *the spirit of falsehood* or *of lies* and *that of truth.* —(l), **spiritus gratiae,** *the spirit of grace* or *grace.*—(m), **spiritus inferior** and **spiritus superior,** *the inferior* or *subordinate spirit* and *the higher* or *superior spirit.*—(n), **spiritus intellegibilis,** *the spirit* or *power of intellectual knowledge.* —(o), **spiritus interior,** *inner spirit* (of life).—(p), **spiritus invisibilis,** *the invisible spirit.*—(q), **spiritus malignus,** see *spiritus bonus.*—(r), **spiritus malus,** see *spiritus bonus.*—(s), **spiritus mendacii,** see *spiritus falsitatis.*—(t), **spiritus mendax,** see *spiritus falsitatis.*— (u), **spiritus miraculorum,** and **spiritus prophetiae seu propheticus,** *the power* or *gift of working miracles* and *that of prophecy.*— (v), **spiritus prophetiae,** see *spiritus miraculorum.*—(w), **spiritus propheticus,** see *spiritus miraculorum.*—(x), **spiritus rationalis,** *the rational spirit.*—(y), **spiritus sanctus,** see *spiritus Dei.*—(z), **spiritus sensibilis,** see *spiritus animalis.*—(a²), **spiritus separatus,** see *spiritus coniunctus.*—(b²), **spiritus spumosus,** *the effervescent spirit* (of life).—(c²), **spiritus superior,** see *spiritus inferior.*—(d²), **spiritus terrenus,** see *spiritus caelestis.*— (e²), **spiritus veritatis,** see *spiritus falsitatis.*—(f²), **spiritus vitae seu vitalis,** *the spirit of life.*—(g²), **spiritus vitalis,** see *spiritus vitae.*

spiro, are, avi, atum, 1, *v. n.* and *a.,* (1) *to breathe out, exhale, emit* used *lit.* and *fig.,* (2) *to spirate,* to give origin to the Holy Spirit through the motion of the will in loving.

spissitudo, inis, *f., thickness, density, consistency.*

spissus, a, um, *adj., thick, compact, dense.*

splendeo, ere, 2, *v. n., to shine, gleam, glitter, glisten,* used *lit.* and *fig.*

splendide, *adv.,* see *splendidus.*

splendidus, a, um, *adj., splendid, magnificent, fine.*—**splendide,** *adv., sumptuously.*

splendor, oris, *m., brightness, brilliance, lustre, splendour,* used *lit.* and *fig.*

spoliatio, onis, *f., a passing away.*

spoliator, oris, *m., a robber, pillager, plunderer, despoiler.*

spolio, are, avi, atum, 1, *v. a.,* (1) in gen., *to strip, to deprive of clothing,* used with the *abl.,* (2) *to despoil, deprive, rob* aliquem or aliquid.

spolium, ii, *n.,* in gen., *anything taken from the enemy, booty, prey, spoil.*

spondeo, ere, spopondi, sponsum, 2, *v. a., to promise* or *engage in marriage, betroth, to plight one's troth.*—**sponsus,** i, *m., a betrothed man, a bridegroom.*—**sponsa,** ae, *f., a betrothed woman, a bride.*

sponsa, ae, *f.,* see *spondeo.*

sponsalia, ium, *n., a betrothal, espousal.*

sponsalitius, a, um, *adj., of* or *belonging to betrothal, sponsal.*

sponsio, onis, *f., a solemn promise* or *engagement* to some performance, *an obligation.*

sponsor, oris, *m., a bondsman, surety.*

sponsus, i, *m.,* see *spondeo.*

spontaneus, a, um, *adj., from* an *intrinsic principle, voluntary, spontaneous,* not strictly a synonym of *voluntarius* because reflex actions are spontaneous but involuntary, the opposite of *invitus, coactus,* and *violentus.* On **donum spontaneum,** see *donum* under 1; on **generatio spontanea,** see *generatio* under 1; on **voluntas spontanea,** see *voluntas* under 3.—**spontanee,** *adv., of one's own mind, willingly,* synonym of *sponte,* the opposite of *coacte* and *violenter.*

sponte, *adv., of one's own accord, freely, spontaneously,* synonym of *spontanee,* the opposite of *coacte* and *violenter.*

spumosus, a, um, *adj., full of foam, frothy.*

spuo, ere, spi, utum, 3, *v. n.* and *a., to spit, spit out, spew.*—**sputum,** i, *n., spit, spittle.*

spurcitia, ae, *f., filth, dirt.*

spurius, i, *m., an illegitimate* or *spurious child, a bastard.*

sputum, i, *n.,* see *spuo.*

squalor, oris, *m., squalor, filthiness.*

squama, ae, *f., a scale* (of a fish).

stabilio, ire, ivi, itum, 4, *v. a., to make firm, steadfast,* or *stable;*

to fix, stay, establish, used *lit.* and *fig.*

stabilis, e, *adj., firm, enduring, durable, stable,* used *lit.* and *fig.*— **stabiliter,** *adv., firmly, durably, permanently.*

stabilitas, atis, *f., a standing fast* or *firm, steadfastness, firmness, durability, immovability, stability,* used *lit.* and *fig.*

stabiliter, *adv.,* see *stabilis.*

stadium, ii, *n., a stadium,* used *fig.*

stamen, inis, *n., the warp in* the upright loom of the ancients.

stanneus, a, um, *adj.,* (stannum) *made of stannum.*

stannum, i, *n., tin.*

stater, eris, *m.*=Grk. *stater,* a small silver coin of the Jews, of the value of four drachmae, *a stater.*

statim, *adv.,* like our *on the spot, forthwith, straightway, at once, immediately, instantly.*

statio, onis, *f.,* (1) *a station,* a church in Rome in which the procession of the clergy halted on stated days to say prayers, (2) *a standing still.*

statua, ae, *f., an image, statue.*

statuo, ere, statui, statutum, 3, *v. n.* and *a.,* (1) *corporeally, cause to stand, set forth* persons or things, (2) *fig.,* (a) *to determine,* give a definite direction or bias to, (b) *to establish,* place one on a firm basis, (c) *to institute, cause to be,* (d) *to fix, establish,* (e) *decide* on something, (f) *to establish, constitute, enact, ordain,* (g) *to hold, maintain,* (h) *to order, command, decree, prescribe,*

(i) *to appoint* a time.—statutus, a, um, *P. a.*, (1) *fixed, appointed.* —statutum, i, *n.*, *a statute, law, decision, determination.*

staturae, ae, *f.*, (*status*, from *sto;* prop. a standing upright, an upright posture; hence), *height* or *size* of the body, *stature.*

status, us, *m.*, (1) *stand, standing, standing upright,* (2) *stand-still, standing still,* (3) *condition, state,* (4) *stand, position,* (5) *state,* synonym of *politia* and *republica.* On perfectum secundum statum, see *perfectus* under 1.—Kinds of *status* in this (3) sense are: (a), status altior and status inferior, *the higher* and *the lower state.*— (b), status ante resurrectionem and status post resurrectionem, *the state* (of the human soul) *before* and *that after the resurrection of the body.*—(c), status communis and status eminens, *the common* and *the eminent state.*—(d), status corruptionis and status generationis, *the state of corruption* and *that of coming into being* or *originating.*—(e), status creationis, *the state of creation* or *of being created.*—(f), status culpae and status peccati, *the state of guilt* and *that of sin.* (g), status demerendi and status merendi seu meriti, *the state of demerit* or *of acquiring demerit* and *the state of merit* or *of acquiring merit.*—(h), status eminens, see *status communis.*—(i), status finalis seu futurae beatitudinis, *the state of final* or *future*

happiness.—(j), status futurus and status praesens seu praesentis seu istius vitae, *the future* and *the present state* or *the state of men in the future* and *in the present* or *this life.*—(k), status generationis, see *status corruptionis.*—(l), status gloriae seu gloriae consummatae and status miseriae, *the state of consummate glory in heaven* and *that of misery.*—(m), status gratiae seu iustitiae seu rectitudinis and status malitiae, *the state of sanctifying grace* or *of justice* or *of moral righteousness* and *that of moral depravity* or *corruption.*—(n), status imperfectus and status perfectus, *the imperfect* and *the perfect state.* —(o), status incorruptionis, *the state of incorruption.*—(p), status inferior, see *status altior.*—(q), status innocentiae and status post peccatum, *the state of innocence* or *before original sin* and *that after sin.*—(r), status integritatis naturae seu naturae integrae and status naturae corruptae, *the state in which sense appetites were subject to reason* or *of unimpaired human nature, i.e., before the Fall,* and *that of corrupted nature as now.*—(s), status istius vitae, see *status futurus.*— (t), status iustitiae, see *status gratiae.*—(u), status legis naturae, status legis veteris,* and status legis novae, *the state of nature, that of the old and that of the new law* or *the state of the human world under the natural law* *alone, that under the Mosaic Law* and *that under the law of Christ.*—(v), status malitiae, see *status gratiae.*—(w), status merendi seu meriti, see *status demerendi.*—(x), status meriti, see *status demerendi.*—(y), status militiae seu pugnae and status recipiendi praemium vel poenam, *the state of military service* or *of battle* and *the state of receiving reward* or *punishment.*—(z), status miseriae, see *status gratiae.*—(a²), status mundi, *the state of the world,* by which is to be understood the entire visible world and the human world.—(b²), status mutabilis, *the changeable* or *transient state.*—(c²), status naturae, *the state of nature,* by which is to be understood the state of the nature and of the essence of a thing and the natural state of all things.—(d²), status naturae conditae seu status primae conditionis, *the state of created nature* or *that of the first creation of being,* i.e., the state of the nature of a being as it was given him at his first creation.—(e²), status naturae corruptae and status naturae integrae, see *status integritatis naturae.*—(f²), status patriae and status viae seu viatoris, *the state in the heavenly fatherland* and *that on earth* or *of pilgrimage there.*—(g²), status peccati, see *status culpae.*—(h²), status perfectus, see *status imperfectus.*—(i²), status poenae and status praemii, *the state of punishment* and *that of reward.*—(j²), status post peccatum, see *status innocentiae.*—(k²), status post resurrectionem, see *status ante resurrectionem.*—(l²), status praemii, see *status poenae.*—(m²), status praesens seu praesentis vitae, see *status futurus.*—(n²), status primae condicionis, see *status naturae conditae.*—(o²), status pugnae, see *status militiae.*—(p²), status recipiendi praemium vel poenam, see *status militiae.*—(q²), status rectitudinis, see *status gratiae.*—(r²), status resurgentium seu resurrectionis, *the state of resurrection* or *that of man at his resurrection from the dead.*—(s²), status viae, see *status patriae.*—(t²), status virtutis, *the state of virtue.* On perfectum secundum statum, see *perfectus* under 1.—Kinds of *status* in this (4) sense are: (a), status clericalis seu clericorum, status curatorum, and status monasticus seu monachorum, *the clerical, the parochial,* and *the monastic state.*—(b), status coniugalis seu matrimonii, status vidualis, and status virginalis, *the married state, the widow's state, the virgin's state.*—(c), status curatorum, see *status clericalis.*—(d), status episcopalis seu episcoporum seu pontificalis seu praelationis seu praelatorum, *the episcopal state and that of ecclesiastical prelates.*—(e), status libertatis and status servitutis, *the state of freedom* and *that of slavery.*—(f), status maior and status minor, *the higher* and *the lower state of perfection.*—(g), status matrimonii, see *status coniugalis.*—(h), status minor, see *status maior.*—(i), status monachorum, see *status clericalis.*—(j), status monasticus, see *status clericalis.*—(k), status perfectionis, *the state of perfection.*—(l), status plebanorum seu saecularum and status religionis seu religiosorum, *the laic* or *secular state* and *the religious state.*—(m), status pontificalis, see *status episcopalis.*—(n), status praelationis, see *status episcopalis.*—(o), status praelatorum, see *status episcopalis.*—(p), status religionis, see *status plebanorum.*—(q), status religiosorum, see *status plebanorum.*—(r), status saecularium, see *status plebanorum.*—(s), status servitutis, see *status libertatis.*—(t), status supererogationis, *the state of supererogation* or *that state in which more is accomplished than is demanded,* i.e., the state of perfection.—(u), status vidualis, see *status coniugalis.*—(v), status virginalis, see *status coniugalis.*—Kinds of *status* in this (5) sense are: (a), status optimatum, *the aristocracy,* in quo pauci virtuosi principantur.—(b), status paucorum, *oligarchy.*—(c), status popularis, *democracy,* in quo multitudo agricolarum, vel opificum vel ministrorum principantur.

statutum, i, *n.,* see *statuo.*

stella, ae, *f., a star.*

Stephanus, i, *m.,* (1) *Stephen,* one of the seven deacons, (2) Stephen V, Pope. He is quoted on the question of superstitious observances, and against extorting confession.

stercus, oris, *m., dung, excrement.*

sterilis, e, *adj.,* (1) *sterile, barren,* (2) *sterile,* incapable of, or unfitted for reproduction.

sterilitas, atis, *f., barrenness, sterility.*

sterno, ere, stravi, stratum, 3, *v. a., overthrow, prostrate.*

sternutatio, onis, *f., a sneezing, sternutation.*

sternuto, are, avi, 1, *v. freq. n., to sneeze.*

sterquilinium, ii, *n., a cess-pool.*

stilla, ae, *f., a drop.*

stillatio, onis, *f., a dropping down, falling in drops.*

stillo, are, avi, atum, 1, *v. n., to drop, fall, drip, trickle.*

stimulo, are, avi, atum, 1, *v. a., to stimulate to any action.*

stimulus, i, *m.,* (1) *lit., a goad, spur,* (2) *fig.,* (a) *a sting, torment,* (b) *an incentive.*

stipendium, ii, *n., pay, stipend, salary,* use *lit.* and *fig.*

stipes, itis, *m.,* (1) *lit., a log, stock, post, trunk* of a tree, (2) *stock, ancestor.*

stips, stipis, *f., an alms.*

stipula, ae, *f., dim.,* of the stalks of grain left behind in reaping, *straw, stubble.*

stirps, pis, *f.,* also *m.,* of persons, *a stem, stock, race, family, lineage.*

sto, are, steti, statum, 1, *v. n.*, (1) *lit.*, (a) *to stand*, in opposition to sitting, walking, or lying prostrate, *to stand still, stand upright, remain standing,* (b) of things, *to stand, to stand firm* or *immovable; to remain, continue,* (2) *fig.*, (a) *to stand still, cease activity,* (b) *to persist, stand steadfast,* (c) *to stand, hold, to conform* to fact or truth, (d), *to fall under, be subordinate to* in the way of classification, (e) *to stand, coexist, exist* at the same time, (f) of time, *to stand still,* (g) *to stand for, represent.*

Stoicus, i, *m., a* Stoic *philosopher, a* Stoic.

stola, ae, *f.*, (1) *a robe,* (2) *a stole, a vestment* consisting of a long narrow band, esp. of silk, worn around the neck and falling over the shoulders.

stoliditas, atis, *f., dullness, obtuseness, stupidity, stolidity.*

Strabus, i, *m., Strabo* Walafred, (809-849). He was a pupil of Hraban, and a child of humble parents who devoted himself from his earliest years to the church. Having received his first training in the Monastery of Reichenau under Jatto and Wettin he became the common authority on the sense of Holy Scripture, by his *Glossa.*

strangulatus, a, um, *P. a., suffocated, choked, strangled.*

stratagema, atis, *n., a stratagem, a piece of generalship.*

strenue, *adv.,* see *strenuus.*

strenuitas, atis, *f., nimbleness, briskness, vivacity, activity.*

strenuus, a, um, *adj., strenuous, vigorous, active.—***strenue,** *adv., briskly, promptly, quickly, strenuously.*

strepitus, us, *m.*, (1) *lit., a rattling, clattering,* (2) *fig., noise.*

stricte, *adv.,* see *strictus.*

strictus, a, um, *P. a.*, (1) *narrow, tight,* (2) *strict, exact, precise, rigid* in interpretation.—**stricte,** *adv., strictly, accurately.*

stridor, oris, *m., a gnashing* of the teeth.

structura, ae, *f., structure, arrangement, order,* used *fig.*

struthio, onis, *m., an ostrich.*

studeo, ere, ui, 2, *v. a.* and *n.*, (1) in gen., *to be eager* or *zealous, to take pains about, be diligent in, anxious about, busy one's self with, strive after, to apply one's self to* or *pursue* some course of action, etc.; *to desire, wish,* etc., (2) *to apply one's self to learning, to study, be diligent in study.*

studiositas, atis, *f., desire for knowledge, studiousness, diligence.*

studiosus, a, um, *adj.*, (1) *deliberate, ardent, eager,* (2) *desirous of knowledge, studious,* (3) *worth desiring, desirable, good,* Aristotelian *spoudaios.* On **inquisitio studiosa,** see *inquisitio;* on **operatio studiosa,** see *operatio* under 2.—**studiose,** *adv., eagerly, zealously, anxiously, carefully, studiously.*

studium, ii, *n.*, (1) in gen., *a busying one's self about* or *application to* a thing, *assiduity, zeal, eagerness, fondness, inclination, desire, exertion, endeavor, study,* (a) *effort, zeal, striving, exertion, endeavor, study, fondness, earnestness,* (b) pl., *aims, pursuits, occupations, purposes* of a person, (c) *study, considerable effort* towards some thing, (2) in partic., *application to learning* or *studying, study,* in the pl., *studies.—*summo studio, *with greater zeal.—*parvum studium, *little trouble.—*proprium studium, *personal study.*

stulte, *adv.*, see *stultus.*

stultiloquium, ii, *n.*, *silly talk, babbling, stultiloquence.*

stultitia, ae, *f.*, *folly, foolishness, simplicity, silliness, fatuity,* the opposite of *sapientia.—*Kinds of *stultitia* are: (a), **stultitia apud Deum** and **stultitiae humana seu mundana**, *foolishness before God* and *foolishness before the children of the world.—*(b), **stultitia bona**, *the morally good foolishness.—*(c), **stultitia humana**, see *stultitia apud Deum.—*(d), **stultitia mundana**, see *stultitia apud Deum.—*(e), **stultitia quae est peccatum**, *sinful foolishness, filia luxuriae.*

stultus, a, um, *adj., foolish, silly, simple, fatuous.—*stultus, i, *m., a fool.—*stulte, *adv., foolishly, sillily.*

stupefacio, ere, feci, factum, 3, *v.*

a., to make stupid or *senseless, to benumb, deaden, stun, stupefy.*

stupeo, ere, ui, 2, *v. n.* and *a., to be stupified, astonished, amazed, confounded, stunned.*

stupidus, a, um, *adj., stupid.*

stupor, oris, *m., stupor, numbness, dullness, insensibility, stupefaction, astonishment, wonder, amazement.*

stuprator, oris, *m., a defiler, debaucher, ravisher.*

stuprum, i, *n.*, (1) *seduction, act of seducing, enticement to wrong doing; enticing* a woman to unlawful sexual intercourse by promise of marriage or other means of persuasion without the use of force; if force is used, it becomes *raptus, rape,* (2) *disgrace* by unchastity of any sort, often translated by *incest, rape.*

suadeo, si, sum, 2, *v. n.* and *a., to advise, urge, persuade, exhort,* used (a) *absol.,* (b) *acc.,* (c) with *inf.,* (d) the *dat.*

suadibilis, e, *adj.,* late Lat., *that may be persuaded.*

suasio, onis, *f., counselling, advice, exhortation, suasion, persuasion.*

suavesonans, antis, *P. a., sweet-attuned.*

suavis, e, *adj., sweet, pleasant, agreeable, grateful, delightful,* (1) as affecting the senses, (2) as affecting the mind or feelings.—**suaviter**, *adv., sweetly, agreeably, pleasantly,* to the mind.

suavitas, atis, *f., sweetness, pleasantness, agreeableness,* (1) to the senses, (2) to the mind or feelings.

suaviter, *adv.*, see *suavis*.

sub, *prep.*, *under, beneath, below, at, by, near, before*, (1) in gen., (2) of space, *under, beneath*, (3) of time, *within, during, at, by, in*, (4) *under*, to point out the object under which a thing goes, (5) *under* indicating subjection, guidance, control, subject to the authority of, (6) *under* the form, appearance etc. of, indicating the form or manner of appearance assumed or presented.—Common phrases are: **sub dio**, *under the open sky, in the air*.—**sub poena**, *under penalty of*.—**sub sigillo confessionis**, *under the seal of confession*.

subactivus, a, um, *adj.*, *indirectly active*, not used in the S.T.

subalternatim, *adv.*, *after the manner* or *in the sense of subordination*.

subalterno, are, avi, atum, *v. a.*, *to subordinate*. On **ars subalternata**, see *ars* under 2; on **scientia subalternans et subalternata**, see *scientia* under 1.

subalternus, a, um, *adj.*, *subaltern, subordinate*. On **genus subalternum**, see *scientia* under 1; on **species subalterna**, see *species* under 8.

subarrhatio, onis, *f.*, *subarrhation*, an ancient form of betrothal in which pledges in the form of money, rings, etc. were bestowed by the man upon the woman.

subauctoritas, atis, *f.*, *subordination*.

subcontrarius, a, um, *adj.*, *subcontrary, contrary in an inferior degree*, because both may be true. On **enuntiatio subcontraria**, see *enuntiatio* under 2; on **propositio subcontraria**, see *propositio*.

subdiaconatus, us, *m.*, *subdiaconate, the rank of subdeacon, the first of major orders*.

subdiaconus, i, *m.*, *a sub-deacon*.

subdo, ere, didi, ditum, 3, *v. n.*, (1) *to subject, make subservient* or *submissive*, (2) *to append, add, say*.—**subditus**, a, um, *P. a.*, *subject*.—**subditi**, orum, *m.*, *subjects*, those subject to a monarch, ruler or superior.

subdolus, a, um, *adj.*, *somewhat crafty, cunning, sly, subtle, deceptive* or *deceitful*.

subduco, ere, xi, ctum, 3, *v. a.*, (1) *to withdraw, lead away*, (2) esp. with *se*, *to take one's self away by stealth, withdraw*, (3) in partic., naut. t.t., *to draw* or *haul up on land*.

subductio, onis, *f.*, *withdrawal, removal*, here *suspended animation*.

subeo, ire, ii, itum, 4, *v. n.* and *a.*, *to subject one's self to, take upon one's self* an evil; *to undergo, submit to, sustain, endure, suffer, bear*.—**subire iudicium**, *to go to law*.—**subito**, *adv.*, *suddenly, unexpectedly*.

subficio, ere, see *sufficio*.

subflavus, a, um, *adj.*, *light, yellow, yellowish*.

subicio, ere, ieci, iectum, 3, *v. a.,* (1) *bow down,* (2) *to make subject, to subject, submit.*—**subiectus,** a, um, *P. a., subjected, subject.*

subinfero, ferre, tuli, irreg. *v. a.,* to *subjoin, add.*

subintellectus, a, um, *P. a.,* see *subintelligo.*

subintelligo, ere, exi, ectum, 3, *v. a.,* to *supply* in thought, *understand* in addition.

subintratio, onis, *f., unobtrusive entrance, permeation.*

subintro, are, avi, atum, 1, *v. n.,* to *go into secretly, to enter by stealth, steal into.*

subintroduco, ere, xi, ctum, 3, *v. a.,* late Lat., *to introduce in secret.*

subinvicem, *adv., each other, mutually.*

subitaneus, a, um, *adj., sudden.*

subito, *adv.,* see *subitus,* a, um.

subitus, a, um, *adj., sudden, unexpected,* synonym of *instantaneus* and *momentaneus,* the opposite of *successivus.* On **motus subitus,** see *motus* under 2.—**ad subitum,** *suddenly, unexpectedly.*—**subito,** *adv., suddenly, unexpectedly.*

subiaceo, ere, cui, 2, *v. n.,* (1) *to lie under* or *near* anything, (2) *to be under, subject* to anything.

subiectio, onis, *f.,* (1) *a laying, putting* or *placing under,* (2) *subordination, subjection, submissiveness,* (3) *subordination* in the logical sense.—Kinds of *subiectio* in this (2) sense are: (a), **subiectio civilis seu oeconomica** and **subiectio dominativa seu servilis seu**

servitutis, *the civic* or *economic* and *the servile* or *slavish subjection,* i.e., *the subjection that the citizens of a free state show to the ruler, the members of a family to the head of the house,* and *slaves to the master.*—(b), **subiectio corporalis,** *physical subjection* or *subjection according to body.*—(c), **subiectio dominativa,** see *subiectio civilis.*—(d), **subiectio involuntaria** and **subiectio voluntaria,** *involuntary* and *voluntary subjection.*—(e), **subiectio oeconomica,** see *subiectio civilis.* —(f), **subiectio perfecta seu plena,** *perfect* or *complete subjection.*—(g), **subiectio plena,** see *subiectio perfecta.*—(h), **subiectio servilis seu servitutis,** see *subiectio civilis.*—(i), **subiectio temporalis,** *temporal subjection* or *subjection in a temporal way.*

subiective, *adv.,* see *subiectivus.*

subiectivus, a, um, *adj.,* of or belonging to the subject, in logic of a proposition, in morals of an act, *subjective,* the opposite of *obiectivus, subordinate,* as a species to a genus, as in subjective parts of cardinal virtues.—**subiective,** *adv., according to* or *in the sense of* or *in the manner of the subpect, subjectively,* the opposite of *obiective.*

subiectum, i, *n.,* (1) *subject* in the general sense of the word, i.e., the subjected, the subordinated, that laid underneath, the bearer, the holder, (2) *subject* in the ontological sense of the word, i.e., that upon which accidental determinations depend for existence, or that in which forms are received, synonym of *hypostasis, substantia,* and *suppositum* on the one hand and in corporeal things of *materia* on the other, (3) *subject* in the logical sense of the word, i.e., that of which something is expressed, (4) *object* of an action, *a faculty,* that concerning which, or about which action takes place, as distinct from the object-motive of an action, synonym of *materia.* On **genus subiectum,** see *genus* under 2.—Kinds of *subiectum* in this (1) sense are: **subiectum enuntiationis** and **subiectum receptivum seu substans,** *the subject of a statement* and *the receiving* or *the supporting subject,* i.e., the subject in the logical and that in the ontological sense. On **alius secundum subiectum,** see *alius;* on **alter secundum subiectum,** see *alter* under 2; on **dicere de subiecto,** see *dicere* under 2; on **esse in subiecto,** see *esse;* on **fieri ex subiecto,** see *fieri;* on **idem subiectum,** see *idem;* on **mutatio de subiecto ex non-subiecto in subiectum, mutatio de subiecto ex subiecto in non-subiectum et mutatio de subiecto ex subiecto in subiectum,** see *mutatio;* on **negatio in subiectum,** see *negatio* under 2; on **potentia subiecti,** see *potentia* under 4; on **praedicare de subiecto,** see *praedicare* under 2; on **verus in**

subiecto, see *verus* under 1.— Kinds of *subiectum* in this (2) sense are: (a), **subiectum affirmatum** and **subiectum privatum,** *the affirmative* or *positive subject* and *the deprived subject* or *the subject lacking something due it.*—(b), **subiectum formatum** and **subiectum informe,** *the formed subject* or *that supplied with a form* and *the unformed* or *formless subject.*—(c), **subiectum informe,** see *subiectum formatum.*—(d), **subiectum primum** and **subiectum secundarium,** *the primary subject* which, reckoned from that which it serves as subject, is also called the *proximate subject* and *the secondary subject,* likewise reckoned from that which it serves as subject called *remote.*—(e), **subiectum privatum,** see *subiectum affirmatum.* —(f), **subiectum proprium,** *the special* or *proper subject.* Cf. also *subiectum proprium* under 4.— (g), **subiectum proximum** and **subiectum ultimum,** *the proximate* or *closest* and *the last subject of thing,* reckoned from the thing.—(h), **subiectum relationis,** *the subject of a relationship.*—(i), **subiectum scientiae,** *the subject of knowledge.* See *scientia* under 1.—(j), **subiectum secundarium,** see *subiectum primum.*—(k), **subiectum sensibile,** *the sensible* or *perceptible subject.*—(l), **subiectum ultimum,** see *subiectum proximum.*—**accidens non excedit suum subiectum seu non extendit** se ultra suum subiectum, see *accidens* under 2.—subiectum comparatur ad accidens, ut potentia ad actum, *the subject is related to the accident connected with or attached to it, as a potentiality to its corresponding actuality.*—subiectum est causa propria passionis, quae ei per se inest, *the subject is the determining cause of the particular characteristic which belongs to it as such.*—subiectum naturaliter est prius accidente, or, subiectum naturaliter prius est eo quod est in subiecto, *the subject according to nature is earlier than the accident belonging to it.* On enuntiatio de subiecto infinito, see *enuntiatio* under 2.—Kinds of *subiectum* in this (3) sense are: (a), subiectum infimum seu ultimum and subiectum primum, *the lowest* or *the last,* and *the first,* i.e., the most particular and the most general subject. Cf. also *subiectum primum* under 2.—(b), subiectum infinitum, *the undefined subject.*—(c), subiectum particularissimum and subiectum universalissimum, *the most particular* or *individual* and *the most general subject.*—(d), subiectum primum, see *subiectum infimum.*—(e), subiectum ultimum, see *subiectum infimum.*—(f), subiectum universalissimum, see *subiectum particularissimum.* On subiectum scientiae, see *scientia* under 1.—One kind of *subiectum* in this (4) sense is: subiectum proprium, *the particular* or *proper subject.* Cf. also *proprium* under 2.

subiugo, are, avi, atum, 1, *v. a., to subject, subjugate.*

subiungo, ere, xi, ctum, 3, *v. a.,* of speech, *to add, subjoin, make a statement.*

sublatus, a, um, *P. a., cancelled, removed.*

sublevamentum, i, *n., an uplifter.*

sublevatio, onis, *f., a lightening, alleviation.*

sublevo, are, avi, atum, 1, *v. a.,* (1) lit., *to lift up* from beneath, *to raise up, hold up, support,* (2) fig., (a) *to lift up,* (b) *to relieve, lessen* an evil.

sublimatio, onis, *f.,* (1) *lifting up, raising,* (2) *refinement, fineness.*

sublimis, e, *adj.,* (1) lit., *high, lofty, exalted, elevated,* (2) fig., *lofty, exalted, eminent, distinguished.*—sublime, is, *n., height.*—adv., comp., sublimius.

sublimitas, atis, *f., sublimity, loftiness.*

sublimo, are, avi, atum, 1, *v. a., to lift up on high, to raise, elevate, exalt,* used fig.

submergo, ere, si, sum, 3, *v. a., to dip* or *plunge under, to sink, submerge, submerse.*

submersio, onis, *f., a sinking, drowning, submersion.*

subministratio, onis, *f., subministration, the act of subministering.*

subministro, are, avi, atum, 1, *v. a., to aid by giving; to give, furnish, afford, supply.*

submitto, ere, misi, missum, 3, *v. a.* (1) in gen., *to submit, yield,* (2) *to offer* previously as something to explain or aid in understanding what follows, (3) *to lower, moderate,* **submittere vocem,** *to speak low,* (4) *to put in the place of, substitute.—***submissus,** a, um, *P. a., let down, lowered.*

submotus, a, um, *P. a., withdrawn, withheld.*

submultiplex, icis, *n., submultiple, a number* or *quantity that divides another exactly, an aliquot part of a number,* i.e., 8 is a sub-multiple of 72; does not occur in the S.T.

suboles, is, *f., offspring.*

subrepo, ere, psi, ptum, 3, *v. n.* and *a., to creep under, to creep* or *steal along, creep softly on, steal upon, to come on unawares, insensibly* or *by degrees.*

subreptio, onis, *f., subreption, a sudden* or *enforced attack,* as of a temptation.

subreptitius, a, um, *adj., sudden* and *unforeseen, stolen, creeping unawares.*

subripio, ere, see *surripio.*

subrogo, are, avi, atum, 1, *v. a., to put in another's place, substitute.*

subruo, ere, ui, utum, 3, *v. a., to undermine, subvert, corrupt.*

subsannatio, onis, *f., mockery, laughing to scorn, derision in pantomine.*

subsanno, are, 1, *v. a., to insult by derisive gestures, to deride, mock.*

subscribo, ere, psi, ptum, 3, *v. a., to sign, subscribe.*

subscriptio, onis, *f., anything written underneath, a subscription.*

subsequor, i, cutus, 3, *v. n.* and *a., to follow close after* or *immediately, to follow, succeed, ensue,* used of *abstr. subjects.*

subservio, ire, 4, *v. n., to be subject to, to serve.*

subsidium, ii, *n.,* (1) in gen., *aid, support, assistance, help, protection,* (2) abstr., *support* in battle, *aid, help, relief, succour, assistance.*

subsido, ere, sedi, sessum, 3, *v. n.* and *a., to set one's self down, to be susceptible* to something.

subsistentia, ae, *f., subsistence,* that mode of existence which is self-contained and independent of any subject, and also a being that exists in this manner, synonym of *hypostasis, res subsistens, persona,* i.e., both that which exists for itself and not in another and also the manner of existence and the relation of being belonging to it. On **unio secundum subsistentiam,** see *unio.*—One kind of *subsistentia* in this sense is: **subsistentia naturalis,** *the natural subsistence* or *the subsistence existing for itself in the nature of things.*

subsisto, ere, stiti, 3, *v. n.,* (1) *to stand under,* (2) *exist* as a substance, synonym of *exsistere,* (3) *subsist,* i.e., to exist for itself not in another. On **esse per se subsistens seu esse separatum subsistens,** see *esse;* on **forma per se subsistens,** see *forma* under 2; on

individuum per se subsistens, see *individuum;* on **prius est a quo non convertitur subsistens consequentia,** see *convertere* under 1; on **unitas per se subsistens,** see *unitas.* On **bonum subsistens,** see *bonus* under 2; on **ens subsistens,** see *ens;* on **esse subsistens et non subsistens,** see *esse;* on **filiatio subsistens,** see *filiatio;* on **forma subsistens et non subsistens,** see *forma* under 2; on **persona subsistens,** see *persona* under 3; on **principium subsistens,** see *principium;* on **quidditas subsistens,** see *quidditas;* on **relatio subsistens,** see *relatio;* on **res subsistens,** see *res;* on **significare ut subsistens,** see *significare;* on **suppositum subsistens,** see *suppositum* under 2; on **virtus subsistens,** see *virtus* under 1.— Kinds of *subsistens* in this sense of self-existent are: (a), **subsistens completum seu completum in natura alicuius speciei** and **subsistens quodcumque,** *that subsistent which is specifically complete, and not merely a part of some other subsistent, e.g., man, and any subsistent,* e.g., the human soul.—(b), **subsistens completum in natura alicuius speciei,** see *subsistens completum.*—(c), **subsistens distinctum,** *the distinct* or *differentiated existing for itself.*—(d), **subsistens quodcumque,** see *subsistens completum.*

substantia, ae, *f.,* (1) *substance in the general sense of the word,* i.e., that which stands under, basis, foundation, principle, *support,* of the manifold appearances (accidents), synonym of *hypostasis, subiectum,* and *suppositum,* (2) *first substance, individual substance, an entity existing of itself and not in another as subject,* (3) *the substance principle,* i.e., the inner or constituting principle of a substance, (4) *the substance part, the substance element,* (5) *the substance germ, the substance beginning* or *start,* (6) *substance in the sense of the universal,* (7) *second substance, the predicament of substances,* i.e., genus or species of substance, in other words the general or most common manner of existence by and of themselves of things according to which they are called substance, (Cf. *substantia secunda et universalis* under 1), the opposite of *accidens,* (8) *essence, being, nature,* synonym of *essentia, forma, natura, quidditas, quod quid est, quod quid erat esse,* and *species,* (9) *property, possession.*—Kinds of *substantia* in this (1) sense are: (a), **substantia distincta seu incommunicabilis seu individua,** *the defined substance* or *that cannot be communicated to another* or *the individual substance.* Cf. *substantia prima et singularis.*—(b), **substantia incommunicabilis,** see *substantia distincta.*—(c), **substantia individua,** see *substantia distinc-*

ta.—(d), **substantia media seu particularis seu singularis** and **substantia universalis**, *the middle, the particular* or *individual,* and *the universal substance.*—(e), **substantia particularis**, see *substantia media.*—(f), **substantia prima** and **substantia secunda,** *the ousia prote kai deutera* of Aristotle, *the first* and *the second substance* or *that which is called substance in the first place, concrete* and *individual,* and *that which is so called in the second place, abstract* and *general,* i.e., *the single substance* (cf. *substantia individua et singularis*) or the single being of reality existing for itself and the category of substance or that general manner of existence of a thing according to which it is called a substance.—(g), **substantia principalis,** *the principal substance* or *that which chiefly* and *especially deserves the name of substance,* i.e., *substantia prima.*—(h), **substantia secunda,** see *substantia prima.*—(i), **substantia singularis,** see *substantia media.*—(j), **substantia supersubstantialis,** *the supersubstantial substance,* i.e., that substance which is elevated above the category of substance, namely God.—(k), **substantia universalis,** see *substantia media.*—**tribus modis substantia est primum inter omnia entia, scilicet secundum cognitionem, secundum definitionem et secundum tempus,** *substance is of all*

beings the first in a threefold manner, according to knowledge, definition, and time.—Kinds of *substantia* in this (2) sense are: (a), **substantia animata seu vivens,** *the animated* or *living substance.*—(b), **substantia caelestis seu mundana,** *the heavenly* or *cosmic substance.*—(c), **substantia cognoscens seu cognoscitiva,** *the cognitive substance.*—(d), **substantia completa seu perfecta** and **substantia incompleta,** *the complete* or *perfect,* i.e., that which by nature is not part of a composite, and *the incomplete substance,* which, like human soul, is part of a composite, or which, like substantial form, is unable to exercise existence outside of composite.—(e), **substantia composita** and **substantia simplex,** *the composite* and *the simple substance.* —(f), **substantia coniuncta** and **substantia separata,** *substance designed for union with matter* and *that substance independent of matter* or *existing separated from it,* i.e., an angel.—(g), **substantia corporalis seu corporea** and **substantia incorporalis seu incorporea seu spiritualis,** *the corporeal* and *the incorporeal* or *spiritual substance.*—(h), **substantia corruptibilis seu generabilis** and **substantia incorruptibilis,** *the substance which can come to be* and *pass away by generation* and *corruption because composed* and *the changeless* and *incorruptible substance because* *not a composite.*—(i), **substantia creata** and **substantia divina,** *the created* and *the divine substance;* under the latter may be understood in an Aristotelian context any spiritual being.—(j), **substantia divina,** see *substantia creata.* —(k), **substantia finita** and **substantia infinita,** *the limited* or *finite* and *the unlimited* or *infinite substance.*—(l), **substantia generabilis,** see *substantia corruptibilis.*—(m), **substantia immaterialis,** and **substantia materialis,** *immaterial substance* or *that which is free of matter* and *the material substance* or *that consisting of material;* cf. *substantia coniuncta.*—(n), **substantia immobilis** and **substantia mobilis,** *the unchangeable* and *the changeable substance.*—(o), **substantia incompleta,** see *substantia completa.*—(p), **substantia incorporalis seu incorporea,** see *substantia corporea.*—(q), **substantia incorruptibilis,** see *substantia corruptibilis.*—(r), **substantia inferior** and **substantia superior,** *the lower* or *subordinate* and *the higher* or *superior substance.*—(s), **substantia infinita,** see *substantia finita.*—(t), **substantia intellectiva seu intellectualis seu intelligens,** *the intellectually discerning substance* which is considered both as purely intuitively and as intuitively and discursively discerning. Cf. *substantia rationalis.*—(u), **substantia materialis,** see *substantia immaterialis.*

—(v), **substantia mobilis,** see *substantia immobilis.*—(w), **substantia modificata,** *the modified substance* or *the substance provided with a definite manner of existence.* Cf. *pelagus substantiae infinitum* under 1.—(x), **substantia movens,** *the moving substance.*—(y), **substantia mundana,** see *substantia caelestis.*—(z), **substantia naturalis,** *the substance belonging to visible nature.*—(a²), **substantia orbis,** *the substance of a celestial sphere.*—(b²), **substantia perfecta,** see *substantia completa.*—(c²), **substantia perpetua seu sempiterna,** *the lasting* or *perpetual substance,* by which is to be understood both a spiritual being and a heavenly body. Cf. *substantia incorruptibilis.*—(d²), **substantia rationalis,** *the rational substance* or *the substance endowed with reason.* Cf. *substantia intellectiva.*—(e²), **substantia scibilis,** *the knowable substance,* i.e., that which can be made the object of knowledge.—(f²), **substantia sempiterna,** see *substantia perpetua.*—(g²), **substantia sensibilis,** *the substance perceptible by the senses* and *the substance perceiving by the sense.*—(h²), **substantia sensibilis quanta,** *a substance of any magnitude perceptible by the senses.*—(i²), **substantia separata,** see *substantia coniuncta.*—(j²), **substantia simplex,** see *substantia composita.*—(k²), **substantia spiritualis,** see *substantia corporalis.*—(l²), **sub-**

stantia superior, see *substantia inferior.*—(m²), **substantia vivens,** see *substantia animata.*—Kinds of *substantia* in this (3) sense are: (a), **substantia corpulenta,** *the corporal substance* or *matter.*—(b), **substantia prima,** *the first form,* because form gives existence to the substantial composite.—A kind of *substantia* in this (6) sense is: **substantia separabilis,** *the separable universal.*—**pelagus substantiae infinitum,** *the infinite sea of substance,* an expression originating with John Damascene, by which God is meant. On **bonum in substantia seu per suam substantiam seu quantum ad substantiam,** see *bonus* under 2; on **definitio substantiae,** see *definitio* under 2; on **dicere secundum substantiam,** see *dicere* under 3; on **differre secundum substantiam,** see *differre* under 2; on **distinctio substantiae et in substantiam,** see *distinctio* under 2; on **diversitas substantiae seu secundum substantiam,** see *diversitas;* on **diversus secundum substantiam,** see *diversus;* on **esse substantiae,** see *esse;* on **indifferens secundum substantiam,** see *indifferens;* on **individuum substantiae,** see *individuum;* on **malum in substantia,** see *malus* under 2; on **multum secundum substantiam,** see *multus* under 1; on **mutatio secundum substantiam,** see *mutatio;* on **pars substantiae,** see *pars* under 1; on **prior substantia seu**

prius secundum substantiam, see *prior* under 1; on **transmutatio circa seu secundum substantiam et ex substantia ente in potentia in substantiam entem in actu,** see *transmutatio* under 1; on **unitas substantiae,** see *unitas;* on **unum secundum substantiam,** see *unus.* —Kinds of *substantia* in this (8) sense are: (a), **substantia absoluta,** *the independent essence of a thing.*—(b), **substantia actus,** *the essence of an activity* or *deed.*—(c), **substantia formae sacramentalis,** *the essence of the sacramental form.*—(d), **substantia habitus,** *the essence of a habit.*—(e), **substantia imaginis,** *the essence of the image.*—(f), **substantia legis,** *the essence of the law.*—(g), **substantia loci,** *the essence of the place* or *space.*—(h), **substantia nominis,** *the essence of name.*—(i), **substantia numeri,** *the essence of number.*—(j), **substantia operis,** *the essence of a work.*—(k), **substantia peccati,** *the essence of sin.*—(l), **substantia potentiae,** *the essence of power* or *potentiality.*—(m), **substantia praecepti,** *the essence of a precept.*—(n), **substantia rei,** *the essence of a thing.*—**operatio rei demonstrat substantiam et esse ipsius,** see *operatio* under 1.— **substantia non recipit seu suscipit magis et minus,** *the essence of a thing is capable neither of increase nor of decrease.*

substantialis, e, *adj.,* (1) *belong to* or *concerning the substance, sub-*

stantial, the opposite of *acciden-talis* and *supersubstantialis,* (2) *belonging to* or *concerning the essence, substantial,* synonym of *essentialis,* the opposite of *acci-dentalis.* On **compositio substan-tialis,** see *compositio* under 1; on **conceptio substantialis,** see *con-ceptio* under 2; on **conversio sub-stantialis,** see *conversio* under 2; on **corruptio substantialis,** see *corruptio* under 3; on **distingui secundum esse substantiale,** see *distinguere;* on **forma substantia-lis,** see *forma* under 2; on **gene-ratio substantialis,** see *generatio* under 1; on **mutatio substantialis seu secundum esse substantiale,** see *mutatio;* on **simplicitas sub-stantialis,** see *simplicitas* under 1; on **terminus substantialis,** see *terminus* under 5; on **transmuta-tio substantialis,** see *transmutatio* under 1; on **unio substantialis,** see *unio.* On **bonitas substantia-lis,** see *bonitas* under 1; on **bo-num substantiale,** see *bonus* un-der 2; on **conceptio substantialis,** see *conceptio* under 3; on **deme-ritum substantiale,** see *demeri-tum;* on **designatio substantialis,** see *designatio;* on **differentia substantialis,** see *differentia;* on **modus substantialis,** see *modus* under 1; on **perfectio substantia-lis,** see *perfectio* under 2; on **praedicatum substantiale,** see *praedicatum* under 1; on **princi-pium substantiale,** see *principi-um;* on **processio substantialis,** see *processio;* on **qualitas sub-**

stantialis, see *qualitas.*—**substan-tialiter,** *adv.,* (1) *in the manner* or *in the sense of a substance, substantially,* the opposite of *es-sentialiter* as well as *accidentali-ter* and *supersubstantialiter,* (2) *in the manner* or *in the sense of an essence, substantially,* syno-nym of *essentialiter,* the opposite of *accidentaliter.* On **consistere substantialiter,** see *consistere* un-der 3; on **dicere substantialiter,** see *dicere* under 3; on **distingui substantialiter,** see *distinguere;* on **fieri substantialiter,** see *fieri;* on **participare substantialiter,** see *participare* under 2; on **praedi-care substantialiter,** see *praedi-care* under 2; on **unire substan-tialiter,** see *unire.* On **dicere sub-stantialiter,** see *dicere* under 3; on **participare substantialiter,** see *participare* under 2; on **praedi-care substantialiter,** see *praedi-care* under 2.

substantialitas, atis, *f., substantiali-ty,* i.e., that respect of being ac-cording to which something is called a substance, the opposite of *supersubstantialitas.*

substantialiter, *adv.,* see *substan-tialis.*

substantificator, oris, *m., a maker of substance, creator of sub-stances, substantiator,* not used in the S.T.

substantifico, are, avi, atum, 1, *v. a., to make a substance, substan-tiate, concretize, substantify.* On **corpus substantificatum,** see *cor-pus.*

substantive, *adv.*, see *substantivus.*

substantivo, are, avi, atum, 1, *v. a.*, to make or use substantively, substantize, substantivize. On **genus substantivatum**, see *genus* under 1.

substantivus, a, um, *adj.*, *substantive*, noun directly designating individual possessing some attribute, the opposite of *adiectivus*. On **genus substantivum**, see *genus* under 1.—**substantive**, *adv.*, *after the manner* or *in the sense of a substantive, substantively*, the opposite of *adiective*. On **dicere substantive**, see *dicere* under 3; on **significare substantive**, see *significare;* on **sumere substantive**, see *sumere* under 3; on **tenere substantive**, see *tenere* under 7.

substerno, ere, stravi, stratum, 3, *v. a.*, (1) *to underlie, lay under*, (2) *to submit to.*

substituo, ere, ui, utum, 3, *v. a.*, to put instead or in the place of another, to substitute.

substo, are, 1, *v. n.*, *to substand, to stand, be under* or *among, to be present.*

subsum, esse, no perf., *v. n.*, (1) *to be subject to, submit to*, (2) *to be, exist under*, (3) *to underlie, be at the basis of, come under.*

subtegmen, inis, *n.*, *that which is wrought* or *woven in, the woof, weft,* of a web.

subter, *prep.* with *acc.*, *below, beneath, under.*

subterfugio, ere, fugi, 3, *v. n.* and *a.*, *to escape, evade, shun, avoid.*

subtilio, are, 1, *v. a.*, *to subtiliate, to make thin* as iron, *to sharpen; to rarefy.*

subtilis, e, *adj.*, (1) lit., *fine, subtle, not thick* or *coarse, thin, slender*, (2) transf., of the senses, *fine, acute, delicate, subtle*, (3) fig., *fine, nice, precise, exact, accurate, minute, subtle.*—**subtilis aqua**, *plain water.*—**subtiliter**, *adv.*, *minutely, accurately.*

subtilitas, atis, *f.*, (1) lit., *subtlety, thinness, tenuity, exility, penetrativeness* arising from lack of density, (2) fig., (a) *subtlety, obstruseness, intricacy*, (c) *craftiness, duplicity, cunning*, esp. of a treacherous kind, (c) *subtlety, acuteness, penetration* chiefly with implication of delicate or keen perception of fine distinction or nice points.

subtiliter, *adv.*, see *subtilis.*

subtractio, onis, *f.*, *a drawing back, subtraction.*

subtractus, a, um, *Part. a.*, see *subtraho.*

subtraho, ere, xi, ctum, 3, *v. a.*, *to draw away from underneath* or *by stealth*, also in gen., *to draw off, carry off, withdraw, take away, steal*, used (1) lit., (2) fig.

subtriplus, a, um, *adj.*, *contained three times in a larger number, a third part of a whole*, not used in the S.T.

subtus, *adv.*, *below, beneath, underneath.*

subvectio, onis, *f.*, *a carrying, transporting.*

subveho, ere, vexi, vectum, 3, *v. a.,* *to bring* or *carry up.*

subvenio, ire, veni, ventum, 4, *v. n.,* *to come to one's assistance, to aid, assist, relieve, succor; to obviate, remedy, heal, cure* a disease, evil, etc., used with the *dat., absol.*

subventio, onis, *f., a rendering aid, assistance.*

subversio, onis, *f.,* (1) lit., *overthrow, destruction,* (2) fig., *perversion, destruction.*

subversus, a, um, *Part.* of *subverto.*

subverto, ere, ti, sum, 3, *v. a.,* (1) lit., *to overturn, overthrow,* (2) fig., *to subvert, pervert, overthrow, destroy.*

succedo, ere, cessi, cessum, 3, *v. n.* and *a.,* (1) lit., (a) *to follow, succeed, follow* (one next after), as by being the heir or the elected or appointed successor, (b) *to succeed,* take the place of something by natural necessity, (2) fig., (a) of abstract things, *to succeed, come after,* (b) of festivals, *to succeed each other, follow after,* (c) of time, *follow after, succeed.*

succendo, ere, di, sum, 3, *v. a.,* (1) lit., *to kindle* or *set on fire,* (2) *to kindle, inflame with passion.*— **succensus,** a, um, *P. a.,* boiling.

succenseo, ere, sui, sum, 2, *v. n.,* *to be angry, irritated.*

succensio, onis, *f., a setting on fire, kindling.*

successio, onis, *f., a coming into the place of another, a following after, succeeding, succession.*

successive, *adv.,* see *successivus.*

successivus, a, um, *adj., following one another, gradual,* the opposite of *instantaneus, momentaneus,* and *subitus.* On **conversio successiva,** see *conversio* under 2; on **factio successiva,** see *factio;* on **motus successivus,** see *motus* under 2; on **mutatio successiva,** see *mutatio.*—**successive,** *adv., in the manner* or *sense of a succession, successively,* opposite of *instanti* and *simul.*

successor, oris, *m., a successor, follower.*

succido, ere, cidi, cisum, 3, *v. a., to cut off* or *away below, cut down,* used lit. and fig.

succinctorium, ii, *n., a succintory, a cincture* for confining the alb.

succresco, ere, 3, *v.* inch. *n., to grow up,* used lit. and fig.

succubus i, *m., a succubus,* a demon in female form supposed to have carnal intercourse with men in their sleep.

succumbo, ere, cubui, cubitum, 3, *v. n.,* (1) lit., *to yield* in a fight, *to submit,* (2) fig., *to succumb.*

succurro, ere, curri, cursum, 3, *v. n., to help, aid, assist, succor.*

sudarium, ii, *n., a cloth for wiping off perspiration, a handkerchief.*

sudor, oris, *m.,* (1) lit., *sweat, perspiration,* (2) fig., *sweat,* i.e., *toil, severe labor.*

suffero, sufferre, sustuli, sublatum, 3, *v. a., to undergo, bear, endure, suffer* an evil or grievance.

sufficiens, entis, part. of *sufficio.*

sufficienter, *adv.,* see *sufficio.*

sufficientia, ae, *f.,* *sufficiency, enough.* On **perfectio sufficientiae,** see *perfectio* under 3.—**per se sufficientia,** *sufficiency unto itself.*

sufficio, ere, feci, fectum, 3, *v. a.,* *to be sufficient, suffice, avail for, meet the need of, satisfy.*—**sufficiens,** entis, *P. a., sufficient, adequate.* On **causa sufficiens,** see *causa* under 2 and 4; on **coactio sufficiens,** see *coactio;* on **definitio sufficiens,** see *definitio* under 2; on **principium sufficiens,** see *principium;* on **satisfactio imperfecte et perfecte sufficiens,** see *satisfactio;* on **vita per se sufficiens,** see *vita* under 1.—**sufficienter,** *adv., sufficiently, enough.* On **demonstrare sufficienter,** see *demonstrare* under 3; on **dicere sufficienter,** see *dicere* under 3.—**quod potest sufficienter fieri per unum, superfluum est, quod fiat per multa,** see *fieri.*—**quod sufficienter fit uno posito, melius est per unum fieri, quam per multa,** see *fieri.*—**quod sufficienter potest fieri per unum, non oportet, quod per aliquid aliud inducatur,** see *fieri.*

sufflavus, a, um, *adj.,* see *subflavus.*

sufflo, are, avi, atum, 1, *v. a.* and *n., to blow up.*

suffoco, are, avi, atum, 1, *v. a.,* (1) lit., *to choke, stifle, strangle, suffocate* by compressing the throat, (2) fig., *to choke, stifle.*

suffodio, ere, fodi, fossum, 3, *v. a.,* *to dig* or *pierce underneath, to dig under.*

suffragium, i, *n., intercession, prayer* or *good work* done for the benefit of someone else. On **virtus suffragiorum,** see *virtus* under 6.—Kinds of *suffragia* are: (a), **suffragia communia** sc. **ecclesiae,** *the universal intercessions of the Church.*—(b), **suffragia specialia** sc. **ecclesiae,** *special intercessions* of the Church.

suffragor, ari, atus, 1, *v. dep. n.,* (1) lit., *to support,* (2) transf., *to support, assist.*

suggero, ere, gessi, gestum, 3, *v. a.,* *to suggest, advise, prompt, bring to mind.*

suggestio, onis, *f., a hint, intimation, suggestion.*

sugillatio, onis, *f., an insulting.*

sugo, ere, xi, ctum, 3, *v. a., to suck.*

sui (gen). *dat.,* **sibi,** *acc.* and *abl.* **se** or *sese,* sing. and plur. **Sui,** *of himself, herself, itself, themselves.*—**sibi,** (*dat.*), *to himself, herself, itself, themselves.*—**se,** (*acc.*), *himself, herself, itself, themselves.*—**se** (*abl.,*) *by himself, herself, itself, themselves.*

sulfureus, a, um, *adj., of* or *like sulphur, sulphurous, sulphureous.*

sulphur, uris, *n., sulphur.*

summarie, *adv.,* see *summarius.*

summarius, a, um, *adj., comprising* or *containing the main thing, summary.* On **cognitio summaria,** see *cognitio* under 2.—**summarie,** *adv., according to the main facts, in the manner of a summary, summarily.* Aristotelian en *kephalaio,* synonym of *capitulatim* and *summatim.*

summatim, *adv.*, *according to the main facts, in the manner of a summary, summarily,* synonym of *capitulatim* and *summarie,* not used in the S.T.

summe, *adv.,* see *superus.*

summergo, ere, see *submergo.*

summitas, atis, *f., the highest part, height, top, summit.*

summitto, ere, see *submitto.*

summopere, see *summus,* under *superus.*

summus, a, um, see *superus.*

sumo, ere, sumpsi, sumptus, 3, (1) *to take, take to oneself, seize,* (2) *take, take from, draw from,* (3) *take, grasp, understand,* synonym of *accipere* and *tenere,* (4) *take to, add,* (5) *take to, adopt, place under,* synonym of *ponere* and *supponere.*—Kinds of *sumere* in this (3) sense are: (a), **sumere abstracte seu abstractive** and **sumere concrete seu concretive,** *to take something in an abstract sense* or *in the sense of a generalization* and *to take something in a concrete sense* or *in the sense of the particular.*—(b), **sumere adiective** and **sumere substantive,** *to take something adjectively* and *something substantively.*—(c), **sumere aequivoce** and **sumere analogice,** *to take something in the sense of a pure equivocation* and *something in the sense of relative likeness.*—(d), **sumere analogice,** see *sumere aequivoce.*—(e), **sumere categorematice** and **sumere syncategorematice,** *to take something in a*

categorematic or *restricted sense* and *something in a syncategorematic* or *unrestricted sense.* Cf. *categorematice* and *syncategorematice.*—(f), **sumere concrete seu concretive,** see *sumere abstracte.*—(g), **sumere distributive seu divise,** *to take something in the sense of distribution* or *division.*—(h), **sumere divise,** see *sumere distributive.*—(i), **sumere essentialiter, seu notionaliter,** and **sumere personaliter,** *to take something in the sense of essence,* and *something in the sense of the mark of a Divine Person,* and *something in the sense of a Divine Person.*—(j), **sumere materialiter,** *to understand something according to its matter.*—(k), **sumere mathematice** and **sumere naturaliter,** *to take something in the sense of mathematics* and *something in the sense of natural science.*—(l), **sumere metaphorice seu transumptive** and **sumere proprie,** *to take something in a metaphorical* and *something in the proper meaning.*—(m), **sumere naturaliter,** see *sumere mathematice.*—(n), **sumere negative** and **sumere privative,** *to take something in the sense of a mere negation* and *something in the sense of a deprivation.*—(o), **sumere notionaliter,** see *sumere essentialiter.*—(p), **sumere participialiter,** *to take in the sense of a participle.*—(q), **sumere personaliter,** see *sumere essentialiter.*—(r), **sumere privative,** see *sumere negative.*—(s), **sumere** probabiliter seu rationabiliter, *to take something in the sense of a probability.*—(t), **sumere proprie,** see *sumere metaphorice.*—(u), **sumere rationabiliter,** see *sumere probabiliter.*—(v), **sumere significative,** *to take in the sense of illusion.*—(w), **sumere substantive,** see *sumere adiective.*—(x), **sumere syncategorematice,** see *sumere categorematice.*—(y), **sumere transumptive,** see *sumere metaphorice.*

sumptio, onis, *f., a taking.*

sumptuosus, a, um, *adj., very expensive* or *costly, lavish,* (1) of persons, *lavish, extravagant;* (2) of things, *dear, expensive.*

sumptus, us, *m., expense, cost, charge.*

Sunamitis, idis, *adj., a native* or *inhabitant of Sunam, Sunamitess.*

sunetoi = Grk. *synetoi,* i.e., *persons of good sense* or *eusynetoi,* i.e., *men of good sense.*

supellex, lectilis, *f., chattel, household, utensils, stuff, furniture* or *goods.*

super, *prep.* with (1) *acc.,* (2) *abl., over, above, on the top of, on, upon.*

superabundanter, *adv.,* see *superabundo.*

superabundantia, ae, *f., superabundance, excess, surplus.*

superabundo, are, avi, 1, *v. n., to be very abundant, to superabound, surpass.*—**superabundanter,** *adv., very abundantly.*

superaccensus, a, um, *P. a.,* lit., *kindled, lighted.*

superaccresco, ere, evi, etum, 3, *v. n., to be added to* by way of increase or augmentation.

superadditio, onis, *f., an adding to, addition, superadding.*

superaddo, no *perf.,* ditum, 3, *v. a., to add over* and *above, to superadd.*

superaedifico, are, 1, *v. a., to build upon* or *over.*

superbe, *adv.,* see *superbus.*

superbia, ae, *f.,* (1) in a bad sense, *pride, arrogance, haughtiness,* the opposite of *humilitas,* (2) in a good sense, *lofty pride, honorable pride.* On the difference between *superbia* and *inanis gloria* (see *gloria* under 1), we read: superbia non est idem inani gloriae, sed causa est; nam superbia inordinate excellentiam appetit, sed inanis gloria appetit excellentiae manifestationem. On **defectus superbiae,** see *defectus* under 2.—Kinds of *superbia* in this (1) sense are: (a), **superbia completa,** *the completed* or *complete pride.*—(b), **superbia praesumptuosa,** *the pride bound with presumption.*—(c), **superbia summa,** the *highest* or *greatest pride.*— (d), **superbia vitae,** *the pride of life.*—One kind of *superbia* in this (2) sense is: **superbia bona,** *the morally good pride.*

superbio, ire, 4, *v. n., to be haughty* or *proud, to take pride in a thing.*

superbitricia, ae, *f.,* = *superbitertia,* i.e., a number which contains a given number plus two thirds of that number, or what stands in such a relation to another number.

superbus, a, um, *adj.*, *haughty, proud, arrogant, insolent, discourteous, uncivil, rude, supercilious, domineering.—***superbe**, *adv.*, *haughtily, proudly, superciliously.*

supercado, ere, cecidi, 3, *v. n.*, *to fall upon* or *over.*

supercaelestis, e, *adj.*, *that is above the heavens, supercelestial.*

supercilium, ii, *n.*, *sternness, severity.*

superduco, ere, xi, ctum, 3, *v. a.*, *to add, subjoin.*

supereminenter, *adv.*, *supereminently, in a supereminent manner* or *degree.*

supereminentia, ae, *f.*, *supereminence.*

superemineo, ere, 2, *v. a.* and *n.*, *to overtop, to appear* or *be above, to rise above.*—***supereminens**, entis, *P. a.*, *superior, brilliant, prominent.*

supererogatio, onis, *f.*, *a payment in addition, performing more than necessary, supererogation,* the opposite of *necessitas.* On **gloria supererogationis**, see *gloria* under 1; on **operatio supererogationis**, see *operatio* under 2; on **opus supererogationis**, see *opus* under 4; on **status supererogationis**, see *status* under 4.

supererogo, are, avi, 1, *v. a.*, *to spend* or *pay out over* and *above.*

superexcedenter, *adv.*, see *superexcedo.*

superexcedo, ere, 3, *v. a.*, *to surpass.*—***superexcedenter**, *adv.*, *surpassingly.*

superexcellentia, ae, *f.*, *excellence in a high degree, great excellence.*

superexcello, ere, cellui, celsum, 3, *v. a.* and *n.*, *to be eminent, to excel, surpass,* in a good or in a bad sense.—***superexcellens**, entis, *P. a.*, *excelling* in a high degree.

superexcessus, us, *m.*, *excess* of any kind in a high degree.

superexcrescentia, ae, *f.*, *immoderate increase, great increase.*

superexcresco, ere, crevi, cretum, 3, *v. inch. n.*, *grow beyond, exceed.*

superextensio, onis, *f.*, *a stretching out.*

superextolo, ere, 3, *v. a.*, *to raise, exalt.*

superfero, ferre, *v. a.*, *pass.*, *to move over.*

superfervens, entis, *P. a.*, *glowing, most fervent.*

superficialis, e, *adj.*, *superficial.*

superficiatus, a, um, *adj.*, *having a surface, supplied with a surface.*

superficies, ei, *f.*, (1) *the outside of a thing, top, surface, the exterior part* or *face*, (2) *species*, the appearance of bread or of wine which the respective transubstantiated Eucharistic elements have; hence the consecrated elements so appearing, (3) of a test, *on the surface, surface meaning.*

superflue, *adv.*, see *superfluus.*

superfluitas, atis, *f.*, *surplus, what remains over* and *above what has been taken* or *used; an amount remaining in excess; superfluity, excess.*

superfluo, ere, 3, *v. n.* and *a.*, (1) *to be superfluous,* (2) *to superabound.*

superfluus, a, um, *adj.*, (1) lit., *superfluous,* an excess of what is sufficient, necessary, normal or desirous; *superabundant; surplus, not needed,* (2) *superfluous, unnecessary.*—superfluum, i, *n.*, *a superfluity.*—superflue, *adv.*, *superfluously.*

superfugio, ere, 3, *v. a.*, *to flee away over a thing, evade.*

supergredior, i, gressus, 3, *v. dep. a.* and *n.*, *to transcend, to pass over; surpass, excel, exceed.*

superhumanus, a, um, *adj.*, *superhuman,* the opposite of *humanus.* On virtus superhumana, see *virtus* under 5.

superhumerale, is, *n.*, i.e., *over the shoulders, the ephod.*

superinductio, onis, *f.*, *an introduction.*

superintendo, ere, 3, *v. n.*, *to have the oversight of, to superintend.*

superioritas, atis, *f.*, *superiority, elation, authority.*

superliminare, is, *n.*, *a lintel.*

superluceo, ere, 2, *v. n.*, *to shine.*

supermundanus, a, um, *adv.*, *unworldly,* the opposite of *mundanus.* On amor supermundanus, see *amor* under 1.

supernaturalis, e, *adj.*, *supernatural,* that which is absolutely beyond the unaided powers of any creature, the opposite of *naturalis.* On acceptio supernaturalis, see *acceptio* under 1; on agens supernaturale, see *agens;* on beatitudo supernaturalis, see *beatitudo* under 1; on cognitio supernaturalis, see *cognitio* under 2; on communicatio supernaturalis, see *communicatio* under 1; on conversio supernaturalis, see *conversio* under 2; on donum supernaturale, see *donum* under 1; on effectus supernaturalis, see *effectus;* on finis supernaturalis, see *finis* under 2; on forma supernaturalis, see *forma* under 2; on inspiratio supernaturalis, see *inspiratio;* on intellectus supernaturalis, see *intellectus* under 3; on iudicium supernaturale, see *iudicium* under 3; on lumen supernaturale, see *lumen;* on operatio supernaturalis, see *operatio* under 2; on perfectio supernaturalis, see *perfectio* under 4; on principium supernaturale, see *principium;* on prophetia supernaturalis, see *prophetia;* on res supernaturalis, see *res;* on veritas supernaturalis, see *veritas* under 3; on virtus supernaturalis, see *virtus* under 1.—supernaturaliter, *adv.*, *in a supernatural manner, supernaturally,* the opposite of *naturaliter.* On operari supernaturaliter, see *operari.*

supernaturaliter, *adv.*, see *supernaturalis.*

supernus, a, um, *adj.*, *heavenly, celestial.*

supero, are, avi, atum, 1, *v. n.,* (1) *to surpass, overcome, excel, rise above,* used lit. and fig.

superplenus, a, um, *adj., over-full.*

superpono, ere, posui, positum, 3, *v. a.,* lit., *to put* or *place over* or *place upon, to set up, to superimpose, add.*

superpositio, onis, *f., imposition, the act of laying on the hands* as in a religious ceremony, in ordination, used in the S.T. only in quot.

superradio, are, avi, atum, 1, *v. a ,* *to emit beams, to beam, shine, radiate.*

superstes, itis, *adj., that remains alive after another's death, surviving.*

superstitio, onis, *f., superstition.*—Kinds of *superstitio* are: (a), **superstitio divinationis seu divinativa,** *the superstition of fortune-telling* or *that occasioned by fortune-telling.*—(b), **superstitio idololatriae,** *the superstition of idolatry* or *that committed through idolatry.*—(c), **superstitio indebiti cultus veri Dei,** *the superstition of the unlawful veneration of the true God* or *the superstition which is committed through the unlawful veneration of the true God.*—(d), **superstitio noxia** and **superstitio nugatoria,** *the harmful* and *the foolish superstition.*—(e), **superstitio nugatoria,** see *superstitio noxia.*—(f), **superstitio observantiarum seu observationum,** *the superstition that is committed through certain practices* and *performances.*

superstitiosus, a, um, *adj., full of superstition, superstitious.*

supersubstantialis, e, *adj., supersubstantial,* i.e., raised above the category of substance, the opposite of *substantialis.* On **cognitio supersubstantialis,** see *cognitio* under 2; on **scientia supersubstantialis,** see *scientia* under 2; on **substantia supersubstantialis,** see *substantia* under 1; on **theologia supersubstantialis,** see *theologia* under 2.—**radius supersubstantialis,** *the supersubstantial ray of divine light.*—**supersubstantialiter,** *adv., in a supersubstantial way,* i.e., in the manner of a being which is raised above the category of the substance, the opposite of *substantialiter.*

supersubstantialitas, atis, *f., supersubstantiality,* i.e., elevation above the category of substance, the opposite of *substantialitas.*

supersubstantialiter, *adv.,* see *supersubstantialis.*

supersum, fui, esse, *v. n.,* (1) *to be left, to remain, to exist still,* (2) *to be in excess.*

superus, a, um, *adj., that is above, upper, higher,* not used in the S.T.—I comp.: *superior,* ius, *adj.,* (1) of place, *higher, upper,* the opposite of *inferior,* (2) of time, or order of succession, *former, past, previous, earlier,* (3) of quality or condition, *higher, more distinguished, greater, superior,* the opposite of *inferior.*—

On **corpus superius,** see *corpus;* on **elementum superius,** see *elementum* under 1; on **sphaera superior,** see *sphaera* under 2. On **agens superius,** see *agens;* on **appetitus superior,** see *appetitus* under 2; on **ars superior,** see *ars* under 2; on **causa superior,** see *causa* under 2; on **genus superius,** see *genus* under 2; on **intellectus superior,** see *intellectus* under 1; on **iurisdictio superior,** see *iurisdictio;* on **ordo superior,** see *ordo* under 3 and 4; on **pars superior,** see *pars* under 1; on **potestas superior,** see *potestas* under 3; on **praedicare de superiore,** see *praedicare* under 2; on **praedicatio de superiore,** see *praedicatio* under 2; on **providentia superior,** see *providentia;* on **ratio superior,** see *ratio* under 2 and 3; on **sacerdos superior,** see *sacerdos;* on **scientia superior,** see *scientia* under 1; on **spiritus superior,** see *spiritus;* on **substantia superior,** see *substantia* under 2; on **virtus superior,** see *virtus* under 1; on **visio superior,** see *visio* under 1.—**in superiori semper includitur virtus inferioris,** *in the superior the power of the inferior corresponding to it is always included.*— **perfectiones, quae attribuuntur inferiori per multa, superiori attribuuntur per unum,** see *inferior* under 3. —**quanto aliqua causa est superior, tanto ad plura se extendit in causando,** see *causa* under 2.— **quanto est causa superior, tanto**

eius virtus ad plura se extendit, see *causa* under 2.—**semper inferior participat aliquid de perfectione superioris,** see *inferior* under 3.—**superius,** *comp., adv., before, formerly.*—II. Sup. in two forms, (1), **supremus,** a, um, *adj.,—highest, loftiest, topmost.—* (2) **summus,** a, um, *uppermost, highest, topmost; the top of, highest part of.*—**Summus Pontifex,** *the sovereign Pontiff.*—**summus Deus,** *the most high God.* —**summe,** *adv., in the highest degree, most highly or greatly, extremely.*—**summopere,** *adv., with the greatest care, diligently.*

supervacuus, a, um, *adj., useless, needless, unnecessary, superfluous.*

supervendo, ere, didi, ditum, 3, *v. a., to sell, to vend at a high price.*

supervenio, ire, veni, ventum, 4, *v. n.* and *a.,* (1) lit., *to add, superadd, supervene, come over or upon, come upon, fall upon,* (2) fig., *to add, superadd, come upon.*—**superveniens,** entis, *P. a., adventitious, supervenient.*

supervestio, ire, ivi, itum, 4, *v. a., to clothe upon, clothe.*

supervinco, ere, 3, *v. a., to overcome, conquer.*

supervivo, ere, xi, 3, *v. a., to outlive, survive.*

suppeto, ere, ivi or ii, itum, 3, *v. n., to be at hand or in store, to be present.*

supplanto, are, avi, atum, 1, *v. a., to deceive.*

supplementum, i, *n., that with which any thing is made full* or *whole; a filling up, supply, supplement.*

suppleo, ere, evi, etum, 2, *v. a., to fill up, make full* or *whole, to make good, to complete, supply.*

suppletio, onis, *f., supplementation, restitution, supplement.*

supplex, icis, *adj., humbly begging* or *entreating.*—**suppliciter,** *adv., humbly, submissively, suppliantly.*

supplicans, antis, *P. a., begging humbly, beseeching, imploring.*

supplicatio, onis, *f., a public prayer* or *supplication.*

suppliciter, *adv.,* see *supplex.*

supplicium, ii, *n., punishment, torture, torment, pain, distress, suffering.*

suppono, ere, posui, positum, 3, *v. a.,* (1) *to put, place, set under,* (2) *to subject, subordinate,* (3) *place, accept, take,* synonym of *ponere* and *sumere,* (4) *stand in place of something, place* or *state a definite subject of activity.*—On **impossibile suppositis quibusdam,** see *impossibilis;* on **perplexus suppositus,** see *perplexus.*—**confuse et indistincte supponere,** *to stand for something confusedly* and *indefinitely.*—**suppositum,** i, *n.,* (1) *something placed under, subjected, subordinated, accepted, assumed,* (2) *that which underlies all the accidents of a thing,* i.e., *the individual substance of a certain kind* which is the subject of existence and all

accidental modifications which constitute the individual, synonym of *hypostasis, subiectum,* and *substantia.* On **differre supposito,** see *differre* under 2; on **distinctio suppositi,** see *distinctio* under 2; on **distingui supposito,** see *distinguere;* on **diversitas suppositi seu secundum suppositum,** see *diversitas;* on **idem per naturam suppositi, in ratione suppositi, per rationem suppositi, per speciem suppositi et secundum suppositum,** see *idem;* on **significare per modum suppositi seu ut suppositum,** see *significare.*—Kinds of *suppositum* in this (2) sense are: (a), **suppositum aeternum seu increatum** and **suppositum temporale seu creatum,** *the eternal* or *uncreated* and *the temporal* or *created individual substance.*—(b), **suppositum completum ultima completione,** *the individual substance of highest completion.*—(c), **suppositum creatum,** see *suppositum aeternum.* (d), **suppositum determinatum seu distinctum** and **suppositum indistinctum,** *the definite* or *distinguished,* i.e., *individual,* and *the indefinite* or *undistinguished,* i.e., *specific substance.*—(e), **suppositum distinctum,** see *suppositum determinatum.*—(f), **suppositum divinae naturae** and **suppositum humanae naturae,** *the individual substance of divine nature* and *that of human nature.*—(g), **suppositum humanae naturae,** see *suppositum divinae na-*

turae.—(h), **suppositum increatum**, see *suppositum aeternum.* —(i), **suppositum indistinctum,** see *suppositum determinatum.*—(j), **suppositum locutionis** and **suppositum realiter distinctum,** *the substance distinguished in words* and *that distinguished in reality.*—(k), **suppositum proprium,** *the proper* or *particular individual substance.*—(l), **suppositum realiter distinctum,** see *suppositum locutionis.*—(m), **suppositum singulare,** *the single* or *individual substance.*—(n), **suppositum subsistens,** *the individual substance as something existing by* and *for itself.*—(o), **suppositum temporale,** see *suppositum aeternum.*—**actiones seu actus sunt suppositorum,** see *actio* under 1 and *actus* under 1.—**actus referuntur ad supposita,** see *actus* under 1.—**quanto suppositum est prius in agendo, tanto virtus eius est immediatior effectui,** *the more an individual substance is prior in action, the more immediate is its power as regards the effect, since the power of the first cause joins the second cause to its effect.*

supportatio, onis, *f., endurance, bearing, tolerance.*

supporto, are, avi, atum, 1, *v. a., to bear, carry, support, bear with.*

suppositio, onis, *f.,* (1) *putting under, supposition,* (2) *subordination, assumption,* synonym of *positio,* (3) *basic assumption, presupposed principle,* synonym

of *positio,* (4) *standing for something, signifying something, meaning of an expression.* On **bonum ex suppositione alterius,** see *bonus* under 3; on **falsum ex suppositione,** see *falsus;* on **impossibile ex suppositione,** see *impossibilis;* on **malum ex suppositione alterius,** see *malus* under 3; on **necessarium ex suppositione et ex suppositione finis,** see *necessarius* under 1 and 2; on **necessitas suppositionis et ex suppositione,** see *necessitas* under 1; on **possibile ex suppositione,** see *possibilis* under 1; on **velle ex suppositione,** see *velle* under 1; on **verum ex suppositione,** see *verus* under 1; on **voluntarium ex suppositione,** see *voluntarius* under 3.—Kinds of *suppositio* in this (3) sense are: **suppositio ad aliquem** and **suppositio simpliciter,** *the principal supposition* and *the simple* or *absolute supposition.* On **diversitas suppositionis,** see *diversitas.*—Kinds of *suppositio* in this (4) sense are: (a), **suppositio accidentalis** and **suppositio naturalis,** *the accidental* and *the natural meaning of an expression.*—(b), **suppositio confusa** and **suppositio determinata,** *the indefinite* and *the definite meaning of an expression.*—(c), **suppositio determinata,** see *suppositio confusa.*—(d), **suppositio naturalis,** see *suppositio accidentalis.*—(e), **suppositio personalis** and **suppositio simplex,** *the meaning of an expression directed towards a* *person* and *the simple* or *absolute meaning of an expression.*—(f), **suppositio simplex**, see *suppositio personalis*.

suppositivus, a, um, *adj.*, *supposing*. On **oratio suppositiva**, see *oratio* under 2.

suppositum, i, *n.*, see *suppono*.

supra, *adv.*, and *prep.*, (1) *adv.*, of time, *before, formerly, previously*, especially of anything previously said or written.—(2) *prep.* with *acc.*, *above, over*.

supradictus, a, um, *P. a.*, *said before*.

suprapositus, a, um, *P. a.*, *aforesaid*.

supremus, see *superus*, a, um.

surditas, atis, *f.*, *deafness*.

surdus, a, um, *adj.*, *deaf*.

surgo, ere, surrexi, surrectum, 3, *v. a.* and *n.*, (1) lit., (a) *to rise*, move from a lower to a higher position, (b) *to rise, ascend* from the grave, come to life, (c) *to rise*, get up from a bed after rest or sleep, (d) of water *to rise*, to reach a higher level, (e), *to rise, emerge*, above the horizon, (2) fig., (a) *to rise*, (b) *to rise* in figures, *amount to*, (c) *to exalt* to pride.

surrectio, onis, *f.*, *a rising again, resurrection*.

surrepo, ere, see *subrepo*.

surreptio, onis, *f.*, (1) *theft, a getting in a surreptitious manner*, (2) *a coming unperceived, surreption*.

surrigo, ere, see *surgo*.

surripio, ere, ripui, reptum, 3, *v. n.* and *a.*, *to snatch* or *take away* *secretly, to withdraw privily, to steal, pilfer*, used lit. and fig.

surrogo, are, see *subrogo*.

sursum, *adv.*, (1) *from below*, i.e., *up, upwards*, (2) pleon., *joined with versus*.—**sursum corda**, *lift up your hearts*.

Susanna, ae, *f.*, *Susanna*, wife of Joachim whose story is found in the Vulgate in Daniel, c. XIII. Accused of adultery by two Jewish elders who had vainly attempted her chastity, she was proved innocent by Daniel and her accusers were put to death.

susceptibilis, e, *adj.*, *receptive, susceptive, susceptible*, synonym of *receptivus, recipiens*, and *susceptivus*.—**susceptibile** sc. **principium**, the Aristotelian *dechomenon seu dektikon*, synonym of *recipiens* (see *recipere*) and *susceptivum, the subject for something* or *the material for something*.

susceptibilitas, atis, *f.*, *susceptibility*.

susceptio, onis, *f.*, (1) *an assuming, assumption; a taking in hand, undertaking*, (2) *an acceptance, reception*.

susceptivus, a, um, *adj.*, *receiving, accepting, admitting, susceptive*, synonym of *receptivus, recipiens*, and *susceptibilis*.—**susceptivum** sc. **principium**, Aristotelian *dektikon* or *dechomenon*, synonym of *recipiens* (see *recipere*) and *susceptibile, the subject for something* or *the matter for something*.

susceptor, oris, *m.,* (1) *a recipient,* (2) *a sponsor, guardian, protector.*

suscipio, ere, cepi, ceptum, 3, *v. a.,* (1) in *gen.,* (a) *to get, beget,* or *bear a child,* (b) *to assist* from the waters of baptism, said of sponsors, (c) *to receive* a stranger into one's house, (d) *to receive* money, (e) *to receive* a sacrament, (f) *to receive* a blow, wound, (2) of actions, *obligations,* etc., *to take upon, undertake a war,* (3) in *gen., to receive, get, acquire,* etc.,

suscitatio, onis, *f., an awakening, resurrection, resuscitation* from death.

suscito, are, avi, atum, 1, *v. a.,* (1) in gen., *to raise* the dead to life, *to awaken, resuscitate,* (2) (a) *to raise up* a saviour for the people, (b) *to raise* affliction, (c) *to raise* strife, (3) *to stir up,* (a) *to stir up* a friend, (4) *to raise* seed, (5) *to arise from, result from.*

suspendo, ere, di, sum, 3, *v. a.,* (1) lit., (a) *to hang, choke* to death, (b) *to hang,* esp. to hang so as to be free on all sides except at the point of support, (2) fig., (a) *to debar* usually for a time, from the exercise of a function or enjoyment of a privilege, (b) *to make uncertain* or *doubtful, to keep in suspense,* (c) *pass., to be lifted up* in contemplation, (d) *to suspend, put a stop to* for a time.—**suspensus,** a, um, *P. a.,* (1) *deferred* to a later time, (2) *in*

suspense, (3) *lifted up* to spiritual things.

suspensio, onis, *f.,* (1) *suspension, crucifixion,* (2) *suspension,* the action of debarring or state of being debarred, esp. for a time, from a function or privilege.

suspensus, a, um, *P. a.,* see *suspendo.*

suspicatio, onis, *f., a suspicion.*

suspicio, onis, *f.,* (1) *supposition, guess, conjecture* in particular cases, the *hypoleipsis* of Aristotle, (2) *mistrust, distrust, suspicion.*—Kinds of *suspicio* in this (2) sense are: **suspicio praesumptuosa, suspicio probabilis,** and **suspicio violenta,** *the almost groundless, the well-informed suspicion,* and *the incontrovertible suspicion.*

suspiciosus, a, um, *adj., based on suspicion, suspicious.*

suspicor, ari, atus, 1, *v. dep. a.,* in gen., *to suspect, apprehend, surmise, suppose, conjecture.*

suspiro, are, avi, atum, 1, *v. n.* and *a., to sigh for, long for.*

sustentamentum, i, *n., sustenance.*

sustentatio, onis, *f., sustenance, maintenance, upkeep.*

sustento, are, avi, atum, 1, *v. freq. a.,* (1) lit., *to hold up* or *upright, to uphold, support, prop, sustain,* (2) fig., (a) *to keep up, uphold, sustain, maintain, support, bear, uplift,* (b) in partic., *to support, sustain, maintain, preserve* by food, money, etc.

sustinentia, ae, *f., an endurance.*

sustineo, ere, tinui, tentum, 2, *v. a.*, (1) *to bear, undergo, endure, suffer,* (2) *to maintain, uphold, sustain.*

susurratio, onis, *f., tale-bearing, a whispering.*

susurro, are, 1, *v. n.* and *a., to whisper.*

susurro, onis, *m., a tale-bearer, mutterer, whisperer.*

suus, a, um, *pron. poss., 3rd pers.* (referring back to subject), *his, hers, its, theirs,* etc.—omnia sua, *all one has.*

sycomorus, i, *f., a wild fig tree.*

syllaba, ae, *f., a syllable.*

syllogismus, i, *m., syllogism,* the external expression of the internal act of reasoning in which a conclusion is reached from two or more premises. On figura syllogismi, see *figura* under 2; on forma syllogismi, see *forma* under 1 and 2; on materia syllogismi, see *materia* under 3; on medium syllogismi, see *medium* under 2; on modus syllogismi, see *modus* under 2; on principium syllogismi, see *principium.*— Kinds of *syllogismus* are: (a), syllogismus ad contradicendum seu contradicens seu contradictionis, *the argument made for contradiction* or *disproof.*—(b), syllogismus ad impossibile seu ducens ad impossibile and syllogismus ostensivus, *the argumentation leading to the assertion of something impossible* and *that directly manifesting truth.*—(c), syllogismus affirmativus and syllogismus negativus seu privativus, *the argumentation that affirms* and *that which denies* or *that with an affirming* and *that with a denying final sentence.*—(d), syllogismus apparens, *the apparent conclusion* or *false conclusion.* Cf. *parasyllogismus.*—(e), syllogismus categoricus seu condicionalis seu hypotheticus and syllogismus disiunctivus seu divisivus, *the categorical, the hypothetical,* and *the disjunctive* or *divisive argument* or *the syllogism with a categorical, that with a hypothetical,* and *that with a disjunctive* or *divisive major proposition.* Cf. propositio categorica, condicionalis, and disiunctiva under *propositio.*—(f), syllogismus circularis, *the argument turning in a circle.*—(g), syllogismus condicionalis, see *syllogismus categoricus.*—(h), syllogismus contingens seu de contingenti, syllogismus necessarius seu de necessario, syllogismus de impossibili and syllogismus de possibili, *the syllogism with contingent, that with necessary, that with impossible,* and *that with a possible matter in its premises and consequently in its conclusion.* Cf. propositio de contingenti, de necessario, de impossibili et de possibili under *propositio.*—(i), syllogismus contradicens seu contradictionis, see *syllogismus ad contradicendum.*—(j), syllogismus deceptionis seu deceptivus, *the deceptive* or *il-*

lusive argumentation.—(k), **syllogismus de contingenti,** see *syllogismus contingens.*—(l), **syllogismus de impossibili,** see *syllogismus contingens.*—(m), **syllogismus de inesse, de modo seu de modalibus** and **syllogismus mixtus,** *the argument in which something is derived from propositiones simplicis inhaerentiae* (see *propositio*), *that in which something is derived from propositiones modales,* and *that in which one premise represents a propositio simplicis inhaerentiae and the other a propositio modalis.*—(n), **syllogismus de modo seu de modalibus,** see *syllogismus de inesse.*—(o), **syllogismus demonstrativus** and **syllogismus dialecticus,** *the demonstrative argument proving something necessarily and with certainty or the proper proof, which constitutes the syllogismus disciplinalis seu scientialis,* and *the argument which proceeding from contingent and probable premises arrives only at probability.*—(p), **syllogismus de necessario,** see *syllogismus contingens.*—(q), **syllogismus de possibili,** see *syllogismus contingens.* —(r), **syllogismus detruncatus,** *the abbreviated argument,* i.e., one in which one of the two premises is not expressed in words.—(s), **syllogismus dialecticus,** see *syllogismus demonstrativus.*—(t), **syllogismus directe concludens** and **syllogismus indirecte concludens,** *the direct* and *the*

indirect argumentation, the conclusion of the latter can be logically converted into the same conclusion as the former.—(u), **syllogismus disciplinalis, seu scientialis,** and **syllogismus simpliciter,** *the argument that instructs or produces absolutely certain knowledge because of the nature of the premises,* and *the argumentation considered simply as such, the formal arrangement of propositions without reference to what they express.*—(v), **syllogismus disiunctivus,** see *syllogismus categoricus.*—(w), **syllogismus divisivus,** see *syllogismus categoricus.*—(x), **syllogismus ducens ad impossibile,** see *syllogismus ad impossibile.*—(y), **syllogismus expositivus,** *the explanatory syllogism.*—(z), **syllogismus falsitatis seu falsus** and **syllogismus verus,** *the objectively false* and *the objectively true argumentation.*—(a^2), **syllogismus hypotheticus,** see *syllogismus categoricus.*—(b^2), **syllogismus ignorantiae seu secundum ignorantiam,** *the argument arranged from ignorance as to the form or material of the subject.*—(c^2), **syllogismus indirecte concludens,** see *syllogismus directe concludens.*— (d^2), **syllogismus inutilis** and **syllogismus utilis,** *the useless* and *the useful argument,* or a syllogism that derives a true conclusion from premises of any matter and that which does so only from premises of a definite matter.—

(e²), **syllogismus litigiosus**, the *syllogismos eristikos* of Aristotle, also called *syllogismus contentiosus, the controversial* or *disputative argument,* i.e., that syllogism, which deduces from premises which are probable or may be considered such, a conclusion which is valid only on the grounds admitted by the adversary but not in reality.—(f²), **syllogismus mixtus**, see *syllogismus de inesse.*—(g²), **syllogismus necessarius**, see *syllogismus contingens.*—(h²), **syllogismus negativus**, see *syllogismus affirmativus.* —(i²), **syllogismus operativus**, *the practical argumentation* or *the argument in a practical field.*— (j²), **syllogismus ostensivus**, see *syllogismus ad impossibile.*—(k²), **syllogismus particularis** and **syllogismus universalis**, *the particular* and *the general syllogism,* or the syllogism with a particular and that with a general conclusion.—(l²), **syllogismus per signum**, the *syllogismos dia semeiou* of Aristotle, *the syllogism through a sign* or *by analogy.*—(m²), **syllogismus privativus**, see *syllogismus affirmativus.*—(n²), **syllogismus scientialis**, see *syllogismus disciplinalis.*— (o²), **syllogismus secundum ignorantiam**, see *syllogismus ignorantiae.*—(p²), **syllogismus simpliciter**, see *syllogismus disciplinalis.* —(q²), **syllogismus sophisticus**, *the sophistic* or *the deceptive argument,* cf. *paralogismus* and

sophisma.—(r²), **syllogismus universalis**, see *syllogismus particularis.*—(s²), **syllogismus utilis**, see *syllogismus inutilis.*—(t²), **syllogismus verus**, see *syllogismus falsitatis.*

syllogistice, *adv.,* see *syllogisticus.*

syllogisticus, a, um, *adj., syllogistic, of* or *belonging to a syllogism.* On **actus syllogisticus**, see *actus* under 1; on **forma syllogistica**, see *forma* under 2; on **medium syllogisticum**, see *medium* under 2.—**syllogistice**, *adv., syllogistically, in syllogisms.*

syllogizo, are, avi, atum, 1, *v. a., to conclude* from universal principles to conclusions, *syllogize,* the opposite of *induco.*—**syllogizare demonstrative** and **syllogizare dialectice**, *to conclude something with certainty* and *to do so with mere probability.*

Sylvanus, i, *m., Silvanus, a satyr; a deity presiding over woods* and *all places planted with trees, the god of the woods, the rural Mars.* Christians considered such creatures demons.

symbolice, *adv.,* see *symbolicus.*

symbolicus, a, um, *adv., figurative, symbolic.* On **locutio symbolica**, see *locutio* under 4; on **nomen symbolicum**, see *nomen* under 1; on **theologia symbolica**, see *theologia* under 2.—**symbolice**, *adv., figuratively, symbolically,* not in the S.T. On **dicere symbolice**, see *dicere* under 3; on **nominare symbolice**, see *nominare.*

symbolum, i, *n.,* (1) *mark, signal, sign,* (2) *arrangement, settlement, agreement,* (3) *token of agreement,* (4) *creed, articles of faith, confession of faith,* (5) *the Nicaean confession of faith.*—Kinds of *symbolum* in this (4) sense are: (a), **symbolum apostolorum seu primum,** *the apostolic* or *first confession of faith,* the Apostolic Creed.—(b), **symbolum Athanasii,** *the Athanasian confession of faith,* drawn up at time of Arian controversies, reputedly by St. Athanasius.—(c), **symbolum Chalcedonensis synodi,** *the Chalcedonian confession of faith,* the same as (d) and (e).—(d), **symbolum Constantinpolitanum seu Constantinopolitanae synodi,** *the Constantinopolitan confesson of faith,* which is a slight amplification of the Nicene creed.—(e), **symbolum Nestorianorum,** *the Nestorian confession of faith.*—(f), **symbolum Nicaenum,** *the Nicene creed.*—(g), **symbolum patrum,** *the confession of faith of the fathers* or *bishops.* —(h), **symbolum primum,** see *symbolum apostolorum.*

Symmachus, i, *m., Symmachus,* saint (498-514). A letter of his to Caesarius, Archbishop of Arles is quoted.

synagoga, ae, *f., a congregation, synagogue* of Jews.

synaxis, is, *f., a gathering, collecting, communion.*

syncategorema, atis, *n., syncatego-* *rema, kategorema,* extrapredicamental, uncategoric.

syncategorematice, a, um, *adj.,* see *syncategorematicus.*

syncategorematicus, a, um, *adj., syncategorematic, syncategorematical, uncategorical, not capable of standing alone as a name in a proposition, having significance only in conjunction with another word, extra-predicamental,* the opposite of *categorematicus.* On **dictio syncategorematica,** see *dictio* under 2.—**syncategorematice,** *adv., in a syncategorematic manner, syncategorematically,* the opposite of *categorematice.*

synderesis, is, (*synteresis*), *f., the guarding* or *keeping of the natural principles of the moral law, the habit of understanding these primary principles* or *precepts, synderesis* or *synteresis.* On **iudicium synderesis,** see *iudicium* under 3.

synecdoche, es, *f., a figure of speech by which a part is put for the whole, the cause for the effect,* or *the contrary, a proper for a common noun, etc., synecdoche.*

synecdochicus, a, um, *adj., synedochic* or *synedochiacal, in the sense of a synecdoche,* i.e., a figure of speech by which a part is put for the whole, the cause for the effect, or the contrary, a proper for a common noun. On **locutio synecdochica,** see *locutio* under 4.

synesis, is, *f.*, *the virtue of common sense in practical affairs*, i.e., the habit of judging rightly about practical individual cases according to the customary rules of life, of like meaning with *eusynesia*. It is a potential part of the virtue of prudence.—On the difference between *synesis* and *eubulia*, we read: synesis (est eminentior), quam eubulia, inquisitio enim ordinatur ad iudicium sicut ad finem et iudicium ad praeceptum.

synodalis, e, *adj.*, *of* or *belonging to a synod, synodal.*

synodicus, a, um, *adj.*, *synodical.*

synodus, i, *f.*, *an ecclesiastical assembly of local bishops with limited scope, a synod.*

synonymus, a, um, *adj.*, *of like meaning, synonymous,* the *sy-*nonymos* of Aristotle, of like meaning with *univocus*. On **nomen synonymum**, see *nomen* under 1.— **synonymum**, i, *n.*, *a word having the same meaning with another, a synonym.*

syntagema, atis, *f.*, *a syntagma, a regular* or *orderly collection of statements, propositions, doctrines, etc.*

syntagmaticus, a, um, *adj.*, *well ordered, orderly, put together, standing in relation to something, syntagmatic,* not in S.T. On **dogma syntagmaticum**, see *dogma.*

synteresis, see *synderesis.*

Syri, orum, *m.*, *the Syrians.*

Sryia, ae, *f.*, *Syria, a country in Asia, on the Mediterranean Sea.*

systole, es, *f.*, = Grk. *systole, systole,* i.e., *contraction.*

T

tabernaculum, i, *n.*, *a tabernacle,* (1) lit., (a) *the Jewish tabernacle,* the portable tent-like structure that served the Jews as a sanctuary during their wanderings in the wilderness and the early period of their life in Palestine, also later the *Jewish temple,* (b) **aeterna tabernacula,** *the everlasting dwellings,* i.e., heaven, (c) *a tent,* fixed or portable, (d) *the dwelling place* of the Christ, such as the stable, the cave, etc., (2) fig., (a) the Blessed Virgin as *the tabernacle* of God, (b) *a tent* of splendor or glory which will cover the saints in heaven, (c) **De Tabernaculo et Vasis eius,** *the Tabernacle and its utensils,* a work of Bede's quoted by St. Thomas.

tabesco, ere, bui, 3, *v. inch. n.*, *to pine, repine, melt away,* used fig.

Tabita, ae, *f.*, *Tabita* or *Tabitha,* (Greek, *Dorcas*), the pious widow whom St. Peter raised from the dead at Joppa. Cf. Acts. 9. 36 ff.

tabula, ae, *f.*, (1) in gen., *a board, a plank,* (a) lit., (b) fig., (2) in partic., (a) lit., *plur., tables* of the law on which the ten commandments were written, (b) fig., *tables* of your heart, (3) *a writ-*

ing-tablet, (4) *the table* of a consecrated altar, (5) *any table* in the tabernacle or temple of the Old Law, either to support the Shekinah, or the loaves of proposition, (6) *a picture.*

taceo, ere, cui, citum, 2, *v. n.* and *a.*, (1) neutr., *to be silent*, i.e., *not to speak, to say nothing, hold one's peace*, (2) act., *to pass over in silence*, be silent respecting a thing.—**pactum tacitum**, *a tacit agreement.*—**tacitum praeceptum**, *a tacit command.*

taciturnitas, atis, *f.*, *taciturnity, disinclination to talk.*

taciturnus, a, um, *adj., speechless.*

tactivus, a, um, *adj., touching, feeling, coming in contact with,* not in S.T. On **corpus tactivum**, see *corpus*; on **potentia tactiva**, see *potentia* under 2.

tactus, us, *m.*, (1) *touching, touch* as an action in the proper and figurative sense of the word, synonym of *contactus*, (2) *sense of feeling,* the faculty of touch, the most fundamental of the five external senses.—Kinds of *tactus* in this (1) sense are: (a), **tactus corporalis seu corporeus** and **tactus spiritualis,** *the physical touch* (sicut duo corpora se tangunt, PP. Q. 105. Art. 2 ad 1), and *the spiritual touch* (for example, that which prevails between soul and body, cf. 4 Sent. 44. 3. 3. 3 ad 7).—(b), **tactus mathematicus** and **tactus physicus,** *the mathematical* and *the physical touch.*—

(c), **tactus physicus**, see *tactus mathematicus.*—(d), **tactus quantitatis,** and **tactus virtutis seu virtualis,** *touch* or *contact which is physical* and *material,* and *touch* or *contact only by power* or *influence.*—(e), **tactus spiritualis,** see *tactus corporalis.*—(f), **tactus virtualis seu virtutis,** see *tactus quantitatis.* On **delectabile secundum tactum,** see *delectabilis;* on **delectatio tactus et secundum tactum,** see *delectatio.*

taediosus, a, um, *adj., wearisome, irksome, tedious.*

taedium, ii, *n., weariness, tediousness.*

talaris, e, *adj., of* or *belonging to the ankles, with tunica,* or *vestis,* i.e., *long, talaric.*

talentum, i, *n., a talent, a sum of money,* varying in amount according to state or country.

talio, onis, *f.,* in jurid. lang., *a punishment similar* and *equal to injury sustained, like for like, retaliation in kind.*

talis, e, *adj., such, of such a kind, nature,* or *quality, such like.* On **ens tale,** see *ens;* on **esse tale,** see *ens.*—Kinds of *tale* are: (a), **tale per essentiam** and **tale per participationem,** *being such essentially* or *according to essence* and *according to participation.*—(b), **tale per participationem,** see *tale per essentiam.*—(c), **tale secundum quid** and **tale secundum se seu simpliciter,** *being such in a certain respect* or *according to something* and *being such sim-*

ply.—(d), **tale secundum se,** see *tale secundum quid.*—(e), **tale simpliciter,** see *tale secundum quid.*—**omne quod est totaliter aliquale, est essentialiter tale,** see *aliqualis.*—**propter quod unumquodque tale, est illud magis,** see *propter.*—**quale est unumquodque, talia operatur seu tale alterum facit,** see *qualis* under 1.—**quale ipsum est, talia facit,** see *qualis* under 1.—**qualis unusquisque est, talis et finis videtur ei,** see *finis* under 2.—**taliter,** *adv., in such a wise, in such sort, so.*

taliter, *adv.,* see *talis.*

talpa, ae, *f., a mole.*

talus, i, *m., the ankle.*

tam, *adv., so, so much, as,* (1) as comparative adverb, demonstrative with correlative *quam,* introducing comparative clauses of like intensity; in comparison between two adjectives, or two adverbs, etc., *as . . . as, as much . . . as,* (2) with *adj., so,* (3) with *adv., so,* (4) as demonstr. *adv.* of intensity, correlative with *ut, that,* and its equivalents *qui, quin.*

tamdiu, *adv.,* (1) *so long, for so long a time, as long,* (2) as antecedent of temporal clause introduced by *quam diu: tam diu . . . quam diu, as long as.*

tamen, *adv., notwithstanding, nevertheless, for all that, however, yet, still,* (1) in gen., with a corresponding concessive or conditional particle (*quamvis, etsi, licet, si, ut, cum* etc.), (a) with *quamvis,* (b) with *etsi,* (c) with *licet,* (d) with *ut,* (e) with *si,* (f) with *cum,* (g) without correlative particle, (2) esp., (a) with *sed,* in transitions, in resuming the thought after a parenthesis, or in limiting or correcting something already said, or some inference from it, *but yet, but nevertheless, but still,* (b) *si tamen, if at least, if only,* (c) *ne tamen, that by no means,* (d) with *rel. pron. qui tamen,* etc., *who however, although he* (she, it, they), (3) strengthened by *nihilominus.*

tamquam, and **tanquam,** *adv., as if, as much as, so as, just as, like as, as it were, so to speak,* (1) in gen. (2) esp., (a) with a corres. *sic* or *ita,* (b) with *si,* in a hypothetical comparison, *as if, just as if* etc., (always with *subj.*), (c) sometimes *tamquam* alone, without *si,* is joined immediately to a conditional clause of comparison, *as if, just as if.*

tandem, *adv.,* implying the end of long delay or expectation, *at length, at last, in the end, finally.*

tangibilis, e, *adj., that may be touched, tangible.* On **contrarietas tangibilis,** see *contrarietas* under 2; on **corpus tangibile,** see *corpus;* on **qualitas tangibilis,** see *qualitas.*

tango, ere, tetigi, tactum, 3, (1) *to touch,* (2) *feel, handle,* (3) *touch upon, mention.* On **unitas tangentium,** see *unitas.*—**corpora tangendo agunt,** see *corpus.* On **qualitas tangentis,** see *qualitas.*

tantus, a, um, *adj., of such size* or *measure, so great.* On *esse* **tantum,** see *esse.*—**tanto,** (*abl.,* with comparatives), *by so much, so much the.*—**tantum,** *adv., so much, so greatly, to such a degree, so.*—**tantum,** *adv., only, alone, merely.*—**tantummodo, tantum,** (adv.), strengthened by *modo, only now, now only, only.*—**tantumdem,** *adv., just so much, just as much.*—**in tantum,** *so far, so much, to such a degree, so greatly.*—**pro tanto,** *in so far as.*

tarde, *adv.,* see *tardus.*

tarditas, atis, *slowness, tardiness.*

tardo, are, avi, atum, 1, *v. a.* and *n., to delay, postpone.*

tardus, a, um, *adj.,* (1) of motion or action, *slow, not swift, sluggish, tardy,* (2) of the intellect, will, desires, passions etc. *slow, sluggish.*—**tarde,** *adv., slowly, tardily.*

taurus, i, *m., a bullock, ox, steer.*

taxatio, onis, *f.,* (1) *a fixing, arrangement of anything,* (2) *an appointment* to office.

taxillus, i, *m., a small die.*

taxo, are, avi, atum, 1, *v. freq. a., to decide definitely, make sure, settle, determine, fix, reckon.*

tecmerion, ou, *n.* (*tekmerion*), *an evident sign affording positive proof, a demonstrative proof.*

tectum, i, *n., a roof.*

tegmen, inis, *n., a cover, covering.*

tego, ere, xi, ctum, 3, *v. a., to cover, hide, conceal.*

tegumentum, i, *n.,* (1) lit., *a covering, cover, clothing,* (2) fig.

telum, i, *n., a dart, weapon, missile.*

temerarie, *adv.,* see *temerarius.*

temerarius, a, um, *adj., rash, thoughtless.*—**temerarie,** *adv., rashly.*

temeratus, a, um, *P. a., dishonored.*

temere, *adv., rashly, at random.*

temeritas, atis, *f., temerity, rashness, excessive boldness.*

temperantia, ae, *f.,* (1) *physical* and *psychological complexion,* the opposite of *distemperantia,* (2) *moderate temperature, moderate climate,* synonym of *temperies,* (3) the general virtue of *moderation, temperance,* (4) the cardinal virtue of *temperance* in sense pleasure, of which the opposed vices are *intemperantia, gula,* and *luxuria.*—Kinds of *temperantia* in this (4) sense are: **temperantia adquisita** and **temperantia infusa,** *the acquired moderation* and *that bestowed by God* with the infusion of grace.

temperamentum, i, *n.,* (1) *a mixture in due proportion, a proper measure, disposition,* or *constitution; temperament,* synonym of *temperantia,* the opposite of *distemperantia,* (2) *moderation, temperance.*—Kinds of *temperamentum* in this (1) sense are: (a), **temperamentum commixtionis,** *the right measure* or *proportion in mixture.*—(b), **temperamentum complexionis,** *the right relationship in the mixture of the juices of an animal body* (or the temperament) of which there are four.

temperans, antis, *P. a.,* see *tempero.*

temperate, *adv.*, see *temperatus.*

temperatio, onis, *f., a means of moderating, qualifying* or *tempering.*

temperatus, a, um, *P. a.*, (1) *having the right proportion, properly arranged,* the opposite of *intemperatus,* (2) *tempered, moderated,* the opposite of *intemperatus,* (3) *moderate, having moderation,* the opposite of *intemperatus,* (4) *temperate, moderate,* the opposite of *intemperatus,* (5) *a temperate man.* On **complexio temperata,** see *complexio* under 2. – **temperate,** *adv., in due proportion, with moderation, moderately, temperately.*

temperies, ei, *f.,* of climatic conditions, *temperature,* (2) *temperateness,* the quality of being temperate.

tempero, are, avi, atum, 1, *v. a.* and *n.,* (1) lit., *to temper, modify,* (2) fig., *temper, regulate, rule.*—**temperans,** antis, *P. a., sober, moderate, temperate.*

tempestas, atis, *f.,* esp., of bad or stormy weather, *a storm, tempest.*

tempestuosus, a, um, *adj., stormy, tempestuous.*

templum, i, *n., a consecrated* or *sacred place, a temple, a shrine.*

temporalis, e, *adj., of* or *belonging to time, lasting but for a time, temporary, temporal,* synonym of *saecularis,* the opposite of *aeternus* and *spiritualis.* On **bonum temporale,** see *bonum* under 3; on **causa temporalis,** see *causa*

under 2; on **dominium temporale,** see *dominium;* on **electio temporalis,** see *electio* under 2; on **filiatio temporalis,** see *filiatio;* on **generatio temporalis,** see *generatio* under 1; on **iudicium temporale,** see *iudicium* under 1; on **malum temporale,** see *malus* under 3; on **missio temporalis,** see *missio;* on **mors temporalis,** see *mors;* on **poena temporalis,** see *poena;* on **potestas temporalis,** see *potestas* under 3; on **praesentia temporalis,** see *praesentia;* on **processio temporalis,** see *processio;* on **promissio temporalis,** see *promissio;* on **ratio temporalis,** see *ratio* under 8; on **regnum temporale,** see *regnum;* on **relatio temporalis,** see *relatio;* on **sacerdotium temporale,** see *sacerdotium;* on **sapientia temporalis,** see *sapientia* under 1; on **societas temporalis,** see *societas;* on **speculum temporale,** see *speculum* under 1; on **subiectio temporalis,** see *subiectio* under 2; on **verbum temporale,** see *verbum* under 1; on **vita temporalis,** see *vita* under 1; on **votum temporale,** see *votum* under 1.—**temporaliter,** *adv., for a time, temporarily.* On **dicere temporaliter,** see *dicere* under 3.

temporarius, a, um, *adj., of* or *belonging to time, lasting but for a time, temporary.*

tempus, oris, *n., time, the measure of the succession in motion.* The only actual time is the present, now; the past and the future exist only in the mind at present. On the difference between *tempus* and *aevum,* see *aevum.* *Quando* is one of the ten categories of Aristotle (see *praedicamentum* under 2). On **dicere de seu ex tempore,** see *dicere* under 3; on **nunc temporis,** see *nunc;* on **ordo temporis seu secundum viam temporis,** see *ordo* under 1; on **perfectum secundum tempus seu secundum conditionem temporis,** see *perfectus* under 1; on **posterius tempore seu temporis seu in tempore,** see *posterior* under 2; on **praedicare ex tempore,** see *praedicare* under 2; on **primum temporis seu secundum tempus,** see *primus;* on **principium temporis,** see *principium;* on **prius tempore seu in via temporis seu secundum tempus,** see *prior* under 1; on **ratio tęmporis,** see *ratio* under 14; on **significare cum tempore,** see *significare;* on **simul tempore,** see *simul;* on **unitas temporis,** see *unitas.*—Kinds of *tempus* are: (a), **tempus aeternum seu infinitum** and **tempus determinatum seu finitum,** *the eternal* or *endless time* and *the limited* or *finite time.*—(b), **tempus continuum** and **tempus non-continuum seu discretum,** *the continuous* and *the discontinuous* or *broken time.*—(c), **tempus determinatum,** see *tempus aeternum.*—(d), **tempus discretum,** see *tempus continuum.*—(e), **tempus enuntiationis,** see *enuntiatio* under 2.—(f), **tempus finitum,** see

tempus aeternum.—(g), **tempus imaginarium** and **tempus reale seu verum,** *the imagined time* and *the actually existing* or *real time.*—(h), **tempus infinitum,** see *tempus aeternum.*—(i), **tempus non-continuum,** see *tempus continuum.*—(j), **tempus primum, tempus secundarium,** and **tempus ultimum,** *the first time* or *the beginning time, the second* or *the following time,* and *the last time* or *the ending time.*—(k), **tempus reale,** see *tempus imaginarium.*—(l), **tempus secundarium,** see *tempus primum.*—(m), **tempus ultimum,** see *tempus primum.*—(n), **tempus verum,** see *tempus imaginarium.*

tenax, acis, *adj., holding fast, gripping, tenacious.*

tendo, ere, tetendi, tentum and tensum, 3, *v. n., to direct one's self* or *one's course; to aim, strive, go, travel, march, tend, bend one's course in any direction.*—**tendens,** entis, *P. a., aiming, striving, tending.*

tenebra, ae, *f.,* usually in plur., **tenebrae,** arum, synonym of *nox, darkness, the darkness of death, shades, death-shades.*

tenebrarius, a, um, *adj., of* or *belonging to darkness.*

tenebresco, ere, *v. inch. n., to grow* or *become dark.*

tenebro, are, 1, *v. a., to make dark, to darken.*

tenebrositas, atis, *f., darkness, obscurity.*

tenebrosus, a, um, *adj., dark, gloomy.*

tenellus, a, um, *adj.,* dim., *somewhat tender* or *delicate.*

teneo, ere, tenui, tentum, 2, *v. a.,* and *n.,* (1) *to hold, have,* (2) *keep in, confine, possess,* (3) *hold fast, preserve,* (4) *hold one's own, defend,* (5) *urge one to do something, bind, oblige,* (6) *hold to something, understand,* synonym of *accipere* and *sumere,* (7) *stand firmly, remonstrate, prevail.*—Kinds of *tenere* in this (5) sense are: (a), **tenere directe** and **tenere indirecte,** *to oblige directly* and *indirectly to something.*—(b), **tenere indirecte,** see *tenere directe.*—(c), **tenere proprie,** *to hold to something in the proper sense of the word.*—Kinds of *tenere* in this (7) sense are: (a), **tenere adiective** and **tenere substantive,** *to understand something in the sense of an adjective,* and *to do so in the sense of a noun.*—(b), **tenere causaliter** and **tenere consecutive,** *to understand something in the sense of a cause* and *to do so in the sense of a result.*—(c), **tenere collective** and **tenere divise,** *to understand something in the sense of a collection* or *combination* and *to do so in the sense of a separation* or *division.*—(d), **tenere consecutive,** see *tenere causaliter.*—(e), **tenere divise,** see *tenere collective.*—(f), **tenere formaliter** and **tenere materialiter,** *to understand something in the sense of form* and *to do so in the sense of matter.*—(g), **tenere materialiter,** see *tenere formaliter.*—(h), **tenere substantive,** see *tenere adiective.*

tener, era, erum, *adj.,* (1) lit., (a) in gen., *soft, delicate, tender,* (b) in partic., *tender of age, young,* (2) fig., *tender, delicate.*

teneritudo, inis, *f., softness, tenderness.*

tenor, oris, *m.,* (1) *sense, meaning,* (2) *view, intention.*

tentamentum, i, *n., temptation.*

tentatio, onis, *f.,* (1) *experiment, trial, attempt,* (2) *temptation, enticement to evil.*—Kinds of *tentatio* in this (1) sense are: (a), **tentatio Dei,** *the trial of God by a creature who puts God to a test.*—(b), **tentatio interpretativa,** *that which amounts to a trial of God although it may not be direct.*—Kinds of *tentatio* in this (2) sense are: (a), **tentatio a carne seu carnis, tentatio mundi seu a mundo,** and **tentatio diabolica seu diaboli seu hostis seu a diabolo seu ab hoste,** *the temptation to sin arising from the flesh, that from the world,* and *that from the devil* or *the evil enemy.*—(b), **tentatio ab hoste,** see *tentatio a carne.*—(c), **tentatio a diabolo,** see *tentatio a carne.*—(d), **tentatio a mundo,** see *tentatio a carne.*—(e), **tentatio carnis,** see *tentatio a carne.*—(f), **tentatio diaboli,** see *tentatio a carne.*—(g), **tentatio diabolica,** see *tentatio a carne.*—(h), **tentatio exterior** and

tentatio interior, *the exterior* and *the interior temptation.*—(i), **tentatio hostis,** see *tentatio a carne.* —(j), **tentatio interior,** see *tentatio exterior.*—(k), **tentatio mundi,** see *tentatio a carne.*

tentativus, a, um, *adj., making trial, tentative.* On **disputatio tentativa,** see *disputatio.*

tentator, oris, *m.,* (1) *a tempter,* (2) esp., *the tempter,* i.e., *the devil.*

tentio, onis, *f., a holding, taking hold of.*

tento, are, avi, atum, 1, *v. freq. a., to attempt, submit to experiment, prove, put on trial,* and in part. *to lead into sin.*—Kinds of *tentare* are: (a), **tentare expresse** and **tentare interpretative,** *to try expressly* and *to try in an interpretative manner.*—(b), **tentare factis** and **tentare verbis,** *to try by actions* and *to try by words.*—(c), **tentare instrumentaliter** and **tentare principaliter,** *to try in the manner of an instrument,* and *to do so as a main cause.*—(d), **tentare interpretative,** see *tentare expresse.*—(e), **tentare materialiter,** *to try in the sense* or *manner of material* (used as a means). —(f), **tentare principaliter,** see *tentare instrumentaliter.*—(g), **tentare verbis,** see *tentare factis.*

tentorium, i, *n., a tent.*

tenuis, e, *adj.,* (1) lit., (a) of substance, *thin, rare, fine, clear,* (b) means of living, *poor, small,* (2) fig., *slight.*

tenus, *prep., according to, by,* with the *acc., abl.*—**tenus verbo,** *as far as the meaning of the word extends, in name, nominally.*—**tenus ore,** *by word of mouth, orally.*

tepesco, ere, pui, 3, *v. inch. n., to cool off, decrease in ardor,* used fig.

tepide, *adv.,* see *tepidus.*

tepiditas, atis, *f., tepidity.*

tepidus, a, um, *tepid, moderately warm.*—**tepide,** *adv., half-heartedly.*

tepor, oris, *m., tepidity.*

ter, *adv., adv. num., three times, thrice.*

Terentius, i, *m., Terence,* the celebrated comic poet, born at Carthage A.U.C. 569.

tergiversatio, onis, *f.,* (1) *a declining, refusing, a shift, subterfuge, tergiversation,* (2) *an unlawful withdrawal of an accusation.*

tergivesor, ari, atus, 1, *v. dep. n., to decline, refuse; to boggle, shuffle, seek a shift* or *evasion; to shift, tergiversate.*

tergum, i, *n., the back of men.*—**a tergo,** *behind.*—**terga vertere,** *to turn the back.*

terminatio, onis, *f.,* (1) *limitation, boundary,* (2) *finishing, completion, termination,* synonym of *perfectio,* (3) *direction, aim.*—Kinds of *terminatio* in this (1) sense are: (a), **terminatio ex parte recipientis,** *the limitation of a thing on the part of the one receiving it.*—(b), **terminatio formalis,** *the limitation of a thing according to its form.*—(c), **termina-**

tio partium durationis and terminatio totius durationis, *the limitation of the part of duration* and
that of the whole duration.—(d),
terminatio potentiae, *the limitation of a power.*—(e), **terminatio
propria,** *the proper* or *particular
termination.*—(f), **terminatio totius durationis,** see *terminatio
partium durationis.*

terminativus, a, um, *adj., termina-
tive, bringing* or *coming to an
end, finishing, concluding.*

termino, are, avi, atum, 1, *v. a.,* (1)
to bound, limit, (2) *define, determine,* (3) *terminate, complete,*
(4) *permit to end in something,
permit to aim at, direct at something.* On **corpus terminatum,**
see *corpus;* on **dimensio terminata,** see *dimensio;* on **quantitas
terminata,** see *quantitas* under 1.
On **esse terminatum,** see *esse.*

terminus, i, *m.,* (1) *a boundary, extreme, outer-most member, ter-
minus,* synonym of *extremitas,
extremum, finis,* and *ultimum,*
(2) *end, goal,* synonym of *finis,*
(3) *purpose,* synonym of *finis,*
(4) *conception, conceivable essence,* synonym of *definitio* and
ratio, (5) *the vocal* expression of
a *conception,* synonym of *dictio,
locutio* and *nomen.* On **contrarietas secundum accessum et recessum ab eodem termino et contrarietas terminorum,** see *contrarietas* under 1; on **esse in loco
ut terminus,** see *locus* under 2. -
Kinds of *terminus* in this (1)
sense are: (a), **terminus affirma-**

tus and **terminus negatus,** *the affirmative* and *the negative terminus.*—(b), **terminus alienus** and
terminus proprius, *the foreign*
and *the proper boundary.*—(c),
terminus ad quem seu in quem
and **terminus a quo seu ex quo,**
the boundary to which and *that
from which,* i.e., the end or ending point and *the beginning* or
starting point.—(d), **terminus a
quo,** see *terminus ad quem.*—
(e), **terminus essentialis seu quantum ad essentiam,** *the essential
boundary.*—(f), **terminus ex quo,**
see *terminus ad quem.*—(g), **terminus indivisibilis,** *the indivisible boundary,* e.g., the point.—
(h), **terminus in maius** and **terminus in minus,** *the boundary according to the greater* and *that
according to the smaller,* or *the
maximum* and *the minimum
boundary.*—(i), **terminus in minus,** see *terminus in maius.*—(j),
terminus in quem, see *terminus
ad quem.*—(k), **terminus localis,**
the local boundary or *the limit of
place.*—(l), **terminus motus** and
terminus mutationis, *the boundary of motion* and *that of change.*
—(m), **terminus mutationis,** see
terminus motus.—(n), **terminus
negatus,** see *terminus affirmatus.*
—(o), **terminus proprius,** see *terminus alienus.*—(p), **terminus
quantitatis,** *limitation of size,* sicut punctus lineae.—(q), **terminus
quantum ad essentiam,** see *terminus essentialis.*—(r), **terminus
rationis,** *the limitation of concep-*

tion.—(s), **terminus relationis,** *an extreme member of a relation.*—Kinds of *terminus* in this (2) sense are: (a), **terminus extremus seu ultimus** and **terminus proximus,** *the ultimate* or *the last* and *the proximate aim.*—(b), **terminus per accidens** and **terminus per se,** *the accidental aim* and *the aim as such,* or *that which is an aim according to something else* and *that which is an aim in itself.*—(c), **terminus per se,** see *terminus per accidens.*—(d), **terminus proximus,** see *terminus extremus.*—(e), **terminus scientiae,** *the aim* or *object of a science.*—(f), **terminus ultimus,** see *terminus extremus.*—Kinds of *terminus* in this (3) sense are: (a), **terminus aequalis seu convertibilis,** *a term like* another in extent or *a term exchangeable* with another. —(b), **terminus coniunctus** and **terminus disiunctus,** *the term connected with another* or *including it* (e.g., man and animal.) and *the term separated from another* or *excluding it* (e.g., man and ass).—(c), **terminus convertibilis,** see *terminus aequalis.*—(d), **terminus disiunctus,** see *terminus coniunctus.*—(e), **terminus maior, terminus medius,** and **terminus minor,** *the major, middle,* and *minor terms of a syllogism, in the conclusion of which the minor is subject,* and *the major predicate.*—(f), **terminus medius,** see *terminus maior.*—(g), **terminus minor,** see *terminus maior.*—

Kinds of *terminus* in this (4) sense are: **terminus communis** and **terminus discretivus,** *the common expression* and *the selecting* or *separating* or *discriminating expression.*—(b), **terminus complexus seu compositus** and **terminus simplex,** *the complex expression,* or *that consisting of at least two words* and *the simple expression* or *that consisting of only one word.*—(c), **terminus compositus,** see *terminus complexus.*—(d), **terminus discretivus,** see *terminus communis.*—(e), **terminus essentialis** and **terminus personalis,** *the expression designating the essence of a thing* and *that designating a person.*—(f), **terminus infinitus,** *the infinite term.*—(g), **terminus numeralis,** *the expression signifying a number* or *plurality.*—(h), **terminus partitivus,** *the expression signifying a separating* or *separation.*—(i), **terminus personalis,** see *terminus essentialis.*—(j), **terminus simplex,** see *terminus complexus.*—(k), **terminus singularis** and **terminus universalis,** *the expression signifying a single thing* and *that signifying something general.*—(l), **terminus substantialis,** *the term that signifies a substance.*—(m), **terminus substantivus,** *the substantival expression.*—(n), **terminus universalis,** see *terminus singularis.*

ternarius, a, um, *adj., containing* or *consisting of three, ternary.*

terni, ae, *a., num. distr. adj.; triple.*

tero, ere, trivi, tritum, 3, *v. a., to crush.*

terra, ae, *f.,* (1) *the earth, land, ground, soil,* (2) *a country, land.* —ubique terrarum, *in the whole world, anywhere in the world.*

terrenus, a, um, *adj.,* (1) *consisting of earth, earthy, earthen,* synonym of *terrestris,* (2) *being on earth, belonging to earth, earthly,* synonym of *terrestris,* the opposite of *caelestis.* On **corpus terrenum,** see *corpus.* On **affectio terrena,** see *affectio;* on **affectus terrenus,** see *affectus* under 2; on **altitudo terrena,** see *altitudo;* on **animal terrenum,** see *animal* under 2; on **beatitudo terrena,** see *beatitudo* under 1; on **bonus terrenus,** see *bonus* under 2; on **corpus terrenum,** see *corpus;* on **felicitas terrena,** see *felicitas;* on **filius terrenus,** see *filius* under 1; on **homo terrenus,** see *homo;* on **pater terrenus,** see *pater;* on **principatus terrenus,** see *principatus* under 1; on **sapientia terrena,** see *sapientia* under 1; on **spiritus terrenus,** see *spiritus.*

terreo, ere, ui, itum, 2, *v. a.,* (1) lit., *to terrify, frighten, put in fear* or *dread, alarm,* (2) transf., *to frighten, deter by terror, scare,* from any action.

terrestreitas, atis, *f., terreity, earthiness.*

terrestris, e, *adj.,* (1) *consisting of earth, earthy, earthen,* synonym of *terrenus,* (2) *being on earth, belonging to earth, earthly,* synonym of *terrenus,* the op-

posite of *caelestis.* On **complexio terrestris,** see *complexio* under 2; on **corpus terrestre,** see *corpus;* on **elementum terrestre,** see *elementum;* on **natura terrestris,** see *natura.* On **animal terrestre,** see *animal* under 2; on **corpus terrestre,** see *corpus;* on **ecclesia terrestris,** see *ecclesia* under 1; on **materia terrestris,** see *materia* under 3.

terreus, a, um, *adj., of earth, earthen.*

terribilis, e, *adj., frightful, dreadful, terrible.*—**terribiliter,** *adv., fearfully, dreadfully, terribly*

territorium, ii, *n., the land round a town, a domain, district, territory.*

terror, oris, *m.,* (1) lit., *affright, dread, alarm, terror,* (2) transf., *an object of fear* or *dread, a terror.*

tertianus, a, um, *adj., tertianae febres,* i.e., *the tertian fever.*—**tertiana,** ae, *f.,* (sc. *febris) the tertian fever.*

tertius, a, um, *num. ord. adj., the third.*—**tertio,** *adv.,* (1) *in the third place, thirdly.*

testamentum, i, *n.,* (1) *agreement, will, alliance, legacy,* (2) *agreement, alliance, legacy of God.*— Kinds of *testamentum* in this (2) sense are: **testamentum novum** and **testamentum vetus,** *the New* and *the Old Testament.* On **hierarchia veteris testamenti,** see *hierarchia;* on **sacerdotium veteris testamenti,** see *sacerdotium.*

testiculus, i, *m., dim., a testicle.*

testificatio, onis, *f.*, *a giving evidence, attestation, proof, evidence.*

testificor, ari, atus, 1, *v. dep. a.*, *to bear witness, give evidence, attest, testify,* used *absol., subst. clause* with *indic.*, with *acc.*, with *de.*

testimonium, ii, *n.*, (1) *witness, evidence, attestation, testimony,* oral or written, (2) transf., *that which serves as a proof of any thing, proof, evidence.*

testis, is, *comm.*, *one who attests any thing* (orally or in writing), *a witness.*

testor, ari, atus, 1, *v. a.*, in gen., *to make known, show, prove; to give to understand, to declare, assert, bear witness to.*

tetragonismus, i, *m.*, *quadrature,* means of measurement or comparison of areas by constructing squares and diagonals, *act* or *process of making a square* or *of determining areas in time quadrature* and *in space quadrature,* not in S.T.

tetragonus, a, um, *adj.*, *tetragonal, four-sided.—***tetragonum,** i, *n.*, *a quadrangle, a tetragon.*

tetragrammaton, i, *n.*, = Grk. *tetragrammaton,* the tetragrammaton, the group of four letters representing the holy name (Jahveh) of God in Hebrew texts, consisting of four consonants, JHVH, JHWH, Y H V H or Y H W H. From reverence and other reasons the word JHVH was almost never uttered in later Jewish traditions antedating the Christian era, Adonai or Elohim being used instead, and therefore in Masoretic texts the vowels of these words are found accompanying the tetragrammaton in the text.

texo, ere, ui, xtum, 3, *v. a.*, *to weave;* transf., in gen., *to join or fit together anything, to construct, make, fabricate, build.*

textus, us, *m.*, *text, context.*

thalamus, i, *n.*, *a resting place,* used in the S.T. only in quot.

Thamar, indecl. *n.*, *f.*, *Thamar* I, wife of Er, the eldest son of Judas, and mother of Phares and Zaras.

theandrikos, (Grk. *theandrikos*), *adj. theandric,* relating to the God-man or Christ, combining the natures of both God and man.

thearchia, ae, *f.*, = Grk. *thearchia, the supreme deity.*

thearchicum, (Grk. *thearchichos, e, on*), *adj.*, *belonging to the thearchia.*

theastai, = *theasthai, to consider all things.*

theatralis, e, *adj.*, *of* or *belonging to the theatre, theatrical.*

theatricus, a, um, *adj.*, = *theatrikos, of* or *belonging to the theatre, theatrical.*

theatrum, i, *n.*, *a theatre.*

Thebae, arum, *f.*, *Thebes,* the name of several ancient cities of antiquity.—**Thebanus,** a, um, *adj.*, *of* or *belonging to Thebes, Theban.*

Thebanus, a, um, *adj.*, see *Thebae.*

thelesis (*thelesis, eos, he*), *a willing, will.*

theletum, (*theleton*), *a thing desired, invention,* a synonym of *operatio,* used in the S.T. only in quot.

Themistius, ii, *m., Themistius,* neoplatonic philosopher (A.D. 317-387), author of commentaries on Aristotle. St. Thomas quotes his paraphrase of *De Anima.*

Theodoretus, i, *m., Theodoretus,* bishop of Cyrrhus or Cyrus, one of the most conspicuous of the heretics of the fifth century.

Theodoricus, i, *m., Theodoric,* Theodoric the Great, King of the Ostrogoths, born probably in 454 and died August, 26, 526; the son of Theodomir, of the royal Ostrogothic family of Amali, by his concubine Erelieva.

Theodorus, i, *m.,* (1) *Theodorus,* fourth bishop of Frejus. On the death of St. Leontius about 432, the people elected St. Maximus as his successor, but he fled to the woods to escape the honor, and thereupon Theodorus, an abbot in the neighboring group of the Stoechades was chosen in his place.—(2), *Theodore,* bishop of Mopsuestia in Cilicia. Of his numerous writings which were condemned by the Fifth General Council 553 only fragments have been preserved.

Theodosius, i, *m., Theodosius* (Flavius Theodosius) Roman emperor, born in Spain about 346, died in Milan, Jan. 17, 395.

Theodotus, i, *m., Theodotus* of Ancyra, saint, martyr. Theodotus was a married man who kept an inn at Ancyra, the Capital of Galatia. He is a patron of innkeepers.

theologia, ae, *f.,* (1) *theology,* i.e., the science of God and divine things, (2) *Christian theology,* the science which by the light of reason deduces conclusions from the data of revelation.—Kinds of *theologia* in this (1) sense are: (a), **theologia civilis, theologia fabularis,** and **theologia naturalis seu physica,** *the theology of the state, that of fables,* and *the natural theology* or *that depending on nature.*—(b), **theologia fabularis,** see *theologia civilis.*—(c), **theologia gentilium,** *the theology of the pagans.*—(d), **theologia naturalis,** see *theologia civilis.*—(e), **theologia philosophica seu quae pars philosophiae ponitur** and **theologia sacrae Scripturae seu quae ad sacram doctrinam pertinet,** *the philosophical* and *the sacred theology* or *the theology which forms a part of philosophy* and *the theology of sacred scripture.*—(f), **theologia physica,** see *theologia civilis.*—(g), **theologia quae ad sacram doctrinam pertinet,** see *theologia philosophica.*—(h), **theologia quae pars philosophiae ponitur,** see *theologia philosophiae.*—(i), **theologia sacrae scripturae,** see *theologia philosophica.*—Kinds of *theologia* in this (2) sense are: (a), **theolo-**

gia discreta and theologia unita, *the distinguished* or *particular theology* and *the combined* or *general theology.*—(b), theologia mystica seu occulta, *the mystical* or *hidden theology* or *the teaching of the mysterious* or *hidden in God.*—(c), theologia occulta, see *theologia mystica.*—(d), theologia supersubstantialis, *the supersubstantial theology* or *the theology about God.*—(e), theologia symbolica, *the symbolic theology* or *that which is found in figures of speech.*—(f), theologia unita, see *theologia discreta.*

theologicus, a, um, *adj., of or belonging to theology, theological.* On cognitio theologica, see *cognitio* under 2; on consideratio theologica, see *consideratio;* on determinatio theologica, see *determinatio* under 2; on disciplina theologica, see *disciplina* under 3; on disputatio theologica, see *disputatio;* on quaestio theologica, see *quaestio;* on virtus theologica, see *virtus* under 5.

theologus, i, *m.,* (1) *one who treats of the deity* and *of divine things, a theologian,* (2) *Christian theologian.* On contemplatio theologorum, see *contemplatio.*

Theophilus, i, *m., Theophilus,* Patriarch of Alexandria, uncle of St. Cyril. His writings were quoted in the Council of Ephesus; St. Thomas refers to them.

Theophrastus, i, *m., Theophrastus,* Greek philosopher, (372-288 B.C.) disciple of Aristotle and Plato, succeeded the former as head of the Peripatetic school. St. Thomas refers to him as quoted by St. Jerome.

Theophylactus, i, *m., Theophylact,* Greek archbishop and exegete. St. Thomas quoted from his *Enarrationes in Lucam* referring to St. John Chrysostom.

theorema, atis, *n.,* (1) *something perceived, appearance, imagination,* synonym of *phantasia, phantasma,* and *imaginatio,* (2) *tenet, dogma, teaching, proposition to be proved, theorem.*

theoria, ae, *f.,* = Grk. *theoria, a philosophic speculation, theory.*

theoricus, a, um, *adj., observing, considering, relating to observation* or *consideration, serving it, belonging to it, theoric, theorical,* synonym of *speculativus,* the opposite of *operativus* and *practicus,* not in S.T. On intellectus theoricus, see *intellectus* under 3; on philosophia theorica, see *philosophia;* on scientia theorica, see *scientia* under 1.

theosebia, ae, *f.,* = *theosebeia, theosebia, divine worship, the service* or *fear of God, religiousness.*

therapeutae, arum, *m.,* = Grk. *therapeutae, servants, attendants, ministers.*

Therasia, ae, *f., Therasia,* wife of Paulinus of Nola. Letter 31 of St. Augustine is addressed to Paulinus and Therasia.

thesaurizo, are, 1, *v. n.* and *a., to gather* or *lay up treasure.*

thesaurus, i, *m.,* (1) lit., (a) *any-thing laid* or *stored up, a hoard, treasure, provision, store,* (b) *a treasury, treasure-vault,* (2) fig., (a) *repository, storehouse,* (b) *a treasure in a spiritual sense,* (c) **thesaurus Ecclesiae,** *treasury of the Church* or treasury of merit consisting of the superabundant merits of Jesus Christ and His saints. It is out of this treasury that indulgences are granted. ⁻

Thesbes, itis, *m., an inhabitant of Thesba,* a city in the tribe of Gad, and the country of Elias, *a Thesbite,* used in the S.T. only in quot.

Thessalonicenses, ium, *m., the in-habitants of Thessalonica,* a city of Macedonia, *Thessalonians.* Two of the epistles addressed by St. Paul to the Christians of that city are extant.

theurgicus, a, um, *adj., spirit-sum-moning, magic, theurgic,* used in the S.T. only in quot.

Thomas, ae, *m.,* (1) *Thomas,* one of the twelve apostles, (2) Thomas Cantuariensis, saint, martyr, Archbishop of Canterbury, born at London, 21 Dec. 1118, died at Canterbury, 29 Dec. 1170.

Threnus, i, *m.,* = Grk. *threnos, a song of mourning, a lamentation, dirge, elegy.* One of the lyrical poetic books of the Old Testa-ment, (The Lamentations of Jere-mias) bewailing the destruction of Jerusalem by the Chaldeans.

thronus, i, *m.,* (1) *an elevated seat,* *a throne,* (2) *an angelic order, an order of angels.*

thurificatio, onis, *f., incense.*

thurifico, are, avi, atum, 1, *v. a., to burn incense to, to offer incense to, to incense.*

thus, thuris, *n., incense, frankin-cense.*

thymiama, atis, *n.,* = Grk. *thymia-ma, a composition for fumigat-ing, incense.*

thymos, ou, *m.,* = Grk. *thymos, irascibility,* a kind of anger that arises and subsides intermittent-ly, a synonym of *furor, quickness to anger* and *firmness of purpose in being avenged.*

tiara, ae, *f., the head-dress of the Orientals, a turban, tiara.*

Tiberias, adis, *n.,* Tiberias, other-wise known in the Bible as "the sea of Galilee," or as "the lake of Genesareth," or as "the sea of Cenereth," or as "the water of Genesar," a sea in Galilee, in the course of the Jordan, frequented by Christ and his disciples.

Tiberius, ii, *m., Tiberius,* the sec-ond Roman Emperor (A.D. 14-37). He was the son of Tiberius Claudius Nero and Livia. The ministry and death of John the Baptist and of Jesus Christ oc-curred during the reign of Ti-berius.

tibia, ae, *f., large shin-bone, tibia, leg.*

Tiburtius, ii, *m., Tiburtius,* son of Agrestius Chromatius, vicar to the prefect of Rome. He was thrown into the flames, but after making the sign of the Cross, he walked on the burning coal. He was beheaded on the Lavicanian Way in 286.

Ticonius, ii, *m., Tichonius,* a Donatist writer of the fourth century, author of the *Liber de Sex Regulis,* to which work a reference is made by St. Thomas quoting St. Augustine.

tignum, i, *n., a beam.*

Timaeus, i, *m.,* = *Timaios, Timaeus,* a Pythagorean philosopher, a contemporary of Plato; the Platonic dialogue of Timaeus, was named after him.

timeo, ere, ui, 2, *v. a.* and *n., to fear, be afraid of, to dread, apprehend; to be afraid* or *in fear, to be fearful, apprehensive,* or *anxious;* constr. in S.T. with (1) *acc.,* (2) *de,* and *abl.,* (3) *inf.,* (4) *ne* or *ut,* and (5) *absol.*—**ti-mens,** ntis, *P. a., fearing, timid.*

timiditas, atis, *f., fearfulness, timidity, cowardice.*

timidus, a, um, *adj., fearful, afraid, faint-hearted, cowardly, timid.*

timocratia, (*timokratia*), ae, *f., timocracy,* in the Aristotelian sense, a polity with a property qualification for the ruling class.

timor, oris, *m., fear, dread, apprehension, alarm, anxiety.* On **donum timoris,** see *donum* under 2; on **lex timoris,** see *lex* under 1; on **servitus timoris,** see *servitus* under 1; on **servus timoris,** see *servus.*—*Species timoris, quae accipiuntur secundum divisionem propriam obiecti ipsius timoris*

are the following: *admiratio,* admiration or wonder (admiratio et stupor refugiunt difficultatem considerationis rei magnae et insolitae, sive sit bona sive mala; *agonia,* anxiety over future evil; *erubescentia,* blushing at the moment when committing a shameful action; *segnities,* laziness (refugit laborem exterioris operationis; *stupor,* bewilderment, stupefaction; *verecundia,* shame (si autem sit de turpi iam facto, est verecundia.—Kinds of *timor* are: (a), **timor amicabilis seu actus seu filialis** and **timor servilis,** *the amicable* or *chaste* or *filial fear,* called "chaste" with reference to 1 Corinth. 11. 2 and "filial" with reference to Rom. 8. 15, and *the servile* or *slavish fear.*—(b), **timor castus,** see *timor amicabilis.*—(c), **timor filialis,** see *timor amicabilis.*—(d), **timor humanus seu mundanus,** *fear of man* or *fear of the world.*—(e), **timor initialis,** *the initial fear* (of God), so called quia solet esse in hominibus in initio suae conversionis ad Deum, Rom. 8. 3; si ergo aliquis convertatur ad Deum et ei inhaereat propter timorem poenae, erit "timor servilis"; si autem propter timorem culpae, erit "timor filialis;" nam filiorum est timere offensam patris, si autem propter utrumque, est timor initialis qui est medius inter utrumque timorem.—(f), **timor mundanus,** see *timor humanus.*—(g), **timor natu-**

ralis and **timor non-naturalis,** *the spontaneous* and *the cognitive fear.*—(h), **timor non naturalis,** see *timor naturalis.*—(i), **timor non-sanctus** and **timor sanctus,** *the unholy fear* which falls into *timor mundanus* and *timor servilis,* and *the holy fear* which ıs *identical* with *timor castus seu filialis.*—(j), **timor sanctus,** see *timor non-sanctus.*—(k), **timor servilis,** see *timor amicabilis.*

Timotheus, ei, *m.,* (*Timotheos* = honoring God), *Timothy,* a disciple and companion of St. Paul. He· was born at Lystra in Asia Minor of a Gentile and a Jewess who embraced the faith. On the arrival of St. Paul at Lystra the youthful Timothy became his companion. He was made the first Bishop of Ephesus, and here he received from St. Paul the two epistles which bear his name, the first from Macedonia and the second from Rome, in which St. Paul from his prison gives vent to his longing desire to see his "dearly beloved son," once before his death.

tinctio, onis, *f., a dipping.*

tinctura, ae, *f., a dyeing.*

tingo, ere, nxi, nctum, 3, *v. a.,* (1) lit., *to dip, wet, moisten, bathe* or *sprinkle* with or in any liquid, (2) in partic., *to soak in color, to dye, color, tinge,* (3) fig., *to soak.*

tintinnabulum, i, *n., a bell.*

titubans, ntis, *P. a., hesitating, wavering.*

titulus, i, *m., title,* the descriptive heading of each section or subdivision of a book.

Titus, i, *m., Titus,* (1) ordained bishop of Crete by St. Paul. Afterward the Apostle on a journey to Nicopolis, a city of Macedonia, wrote an epistle to Titus. (2) *Titus Livius,* a Roman historian (59 B.C.-17 A.D.), (3) *Titus* Flavius Sabinus Vespasianus. A Roman emperor A.D. 79-81, commonly called by his praenomen *Titus.* Titus laid siege to Jerusalem in 70 A.D.; its temple was destroyed.

Tobias, ae, *m., Tobias,* (1) *Tobias* the Elder, chief character in the Book of Tobias. He was a Jew of the tribe of Nephtali, and was carried to Ninive by Salmanasar in 722 B.C., (2) *Tobias* the Younger, son of the above. The story of his journey to Media under the guidance of an angel is well known; he married his cousin Sara during the journey and upon his return cured his father of blindness, (3) *Tobias* Book of. A canonical book of the O.T., containing a most interesting story about the Elder Tobias.

tolerabilis, e, *adj., endurable, tolerable, bearable.*—**tolerabiliter,** *adv., tolerably.*

tolerabiliter, *adv.,* see *tolerabilis.*

tolerantia, ae, *f., a bearing, supporting, endurance.*

toleratio, onis, *f., a bearing, supporting enduring.*

tolero, are, avi, atum, 1, *v. a., to bear, endure, tolerate, sustain, support.*

Toletanus, a, um, *adj., pertaining to Toledo, in Spain.*

Toletum, i, *n., a town in Spain, Toledo.*

tollo, ere, sustuli, sublatum, 3, *v. a., to take off, carry off, make away with, kill, destroy, to abolish, annul, abrogate, cancel.*

tondeo, ere, totondi, tonsum, 2, *v. a., to clip, crop, shave the head.* See *tonsura.*

tonitruum, ii, (*gen.* tontitrui), *n., thunder*, used in *plur.*

tonsura, ae, *f., a clipping* of the hair; an ecclesiastical ceremony, by which a baptized and confirmed preson is made a cleric, admitted to the clerical state and prepared for the reception of orders.

Tophet, *indecl. n., Tophet, the valley of hell.*

topica, orum, *n.,* = *topika*, (1) the title of a work of Aristotle on the sources of probable arguments, (2) *De Differentiis Topicis*, a work of Boethius.

topicus, a, um, *adj.,* (1) *concerning the place of merely probable as distinct from demonstrative arguments, referring to such, belonging to such, topical*, synonym of *dialecticus*, (2) the *Topica* or *Liber Topicorum* of Aristotle. On **ratio topica**, see *ratio* under 13; on **solutio topica**, see *solutio* under 2.—**topica** sc. **ars seu scientia**, synonym of *dialectica*, the

art or science which devotes itself to scientific common places, in so far as it directs the use of such common places for scientific discussion. Cf. 1 Anal. 1 a.

tormentum, i, *n.*, in gen., *torture, anguish, pain, torment.*

torneamentum, i, *n., a tournament.*

torpesco, ere, pui, 3, *v. inch. n., to slacken*, used fig.

torpor, oris, *m., laziness, sluggishness.*

torqueo, ere, torsi, tortum, 2, *v. a.,* (1) *to rack, torment, torture*, (2) *to wrestle*, to attempt to conquer some question.—**tortus**, a, um, *P. a., crooked.*—**torta**, ae, *f., a twisted loaf, a twist.*

torquis or **torques**, *m.* and *f., a chain, collar.*

torrens, entis, *m., a torrent, brook.*

tortor, oris, *m., an executioner, torturer.*

tortuca, ae, *f., a tortoise.*

torus, i, *m.*, transferred like *thalamus* as a designation for *marriage; a bed, couch.*—**ex illegitimo toro nati**, *born of an illegitimate marriage.*—**alienum torum**, *another's marriage bed.*

tot, *num. adj. indecl., so many, so great a number*, in the S.T. usually with a corresponding *quot*, also *ut* clause.

totalis, e, *adj., total, whole, entire.*

totalitas, atis, *f., wholeness, totality.* On **perfectio totalitatis**, see *perfectio* under 2.—Kinds of *totalitas* are: (a), **totalitas absoluta**, *the totality without respect to anything* or *absolute totality*, which

is opposed to the *totalitas relativa seu secundum quid,* i.e., the
totality in a certain respect.—(b),
**totalitas essentiae seu perfectio-
nis,** *the totality of essence* or *according to perfection,* as opposed
to **totalitas virtutis.**—(c), **totalitas
loci,** *totality according to place.*—
(d), **totalitas per accidens** and
totalitas per se, *the totality which
is incidental to a thing* and *that
which is according to itself* or
belonging to it as such.—(e),
totalitas perfectionis, see *totalitas essentiae.*—(f), **totalitas per
se,** see *totalitas per accidens.*—
(g), **totalitas quantitatis seu
quantitativa seu secundum quantitatem,** *totality according to
quantatative parts.*—(h), **totalitas quantitativa,** see *totalitas
quantitatis.*—(i), **totalitas secundum quantitatem,** see *totalitas
quantitatis.*—(j), **totalitas secundum virtutem seu virtutis,** *the
totality of power* or *according to
power.*—(k), **totalitas speciei,** *the
totality of species.*—(l), **totalitas
virtutis,** see *totalitas secundum
virtutem.*

totaliter, *adv., altogether, totally,
wholly, completely, entirely.*

totalus, a, um, *adj., whole-winged,*
i.e., with undivided wings, not
used in the S.T.

totidem, *num. adj., indecl., just as
many.*

toties, *adv., num., so often, so
many times, as often, as many
times,* (1) *absol.,* (2) with a cor-

responding *quotiens,* (3) with
quot.

totus, a, um, *adj.,* (1) *all, whole,
entire,* synonym of *omnis* and
perfectus, the opposite of *pars,*
(2) *the whole world,* the uni-
verse, synonym of *omne* and *universum.* On **abstrahere totum a
parte,** see *abstrahere;* on **actus
totus,** see *actus* under 2; on **agere
secundum se totum,** see *agere*
under 1; on **bonum totum,** see
bonus under 3; on **infinitum secundum totum,** see *infinitus;* on
malitia tota, see *malitia* under 3;
on **perfectum secundum se totum,** see *perfectus* under 1; on
poena ex toto excerminans, see
poena; on **propositio tota,** see
propositio under 2.—Kinds of *totum* in this (1) sense are: (a),
**totum anhomoeomerum seu he-
terogenum seu dissimilium partium** and **totum homoeomerum seu
homogeneum seu similium partium,** *the unlike* and *the like
whole.*—(b), **totum contiguum**
and **totum continuum,** *the whole
accomplished through contact
with its parts,* and *the whole co-
herent in itself.*—(c), **totum continuum,** see *totum contiguum.*—
(d), **totum dissimilium partium,**
see *totum anhomoeomerum.*—(e),
**totum essentiale seu secundum
essentiae perfectionem, totum
potentiale seu potestativum** and
**totum quantum seu quantitati-
vum seu secundum quantitatem,**
the whole found in the essence or
according to the perfection of

essence, the whole found perfectly in one part and imperfectly in others which are ordered to it, and *that whole found in quantity.*—(f), **totum heterogeneum,** see *totum anhomoeomerum.*—(g), **totum homoeomerum,** see *totum anhomoeomerum.*—(h), **totum homogeneum,** see *totum anhomoeomerum.*—(i), **totum integrale** and **totum universale,** *the whole which consists of integral parts* and *that which is an abstracted universal.*—(j), **totum intelligibile** and **totum sensibile,** *the intelligible whole* and *the sensible whole* or *the sensibly perceived whole.* —(k), **totum potentiale,** see *totum essentiale.*—(l), **totum potestativum,** see *totum essentiale.*—(m), **totum quantitativum,** see *totum essentiale.*—(n), **totum quantum,** see *totum essentiale.*—(o), **totum secundum essentiae perfectionem,** see *totum essentiale.*—(p), **totum secundum quantitatem,** see *totum essentiale.*—(q), **totum secundum quid,** *the whole with respect to something* and *that in a certain respect.*—(r), **totum sensibile,** see *totum intelligibile.*— (s), **totum similium partium,** see *totum anhomoeomerum.*—(t), **totum universale,** see *totum integrale.*—**bonum totius finis est cuiuslibet partium,** *the good of a whole is the purpose of everyone of its parts.*—**omne totum est maius sua parte,** *every whole is greater than one of its parts.*— **posito toto necesse est poni par-**

tem, *if the whole is established, so must its parts be established.*— **resoluto toto in partes incipiunt partes esse in actu,** *when the whole is resolved into its parts, the parts,* (hitherto existing only theoretically), *begin to exist actually.*—**totum dictur esse in partibus,** *the whole is said to be in its parts,* i.e., non est praeter partes.—**totum est prius in consideratione quam partes,** *in the consideration of something the whole is prior to its parts.*—**unumquodque totum videtur esse id quod est principalius in eo,** *every whole seems to be that which is the more important in it.*

trabs, trabis, *f., a beam, plank.*

tractabilis, e, *adj., tractable.*

tractatus, us, *m., a treatise, tractate, tract,* in eccl. Lat., *a sermon, homily.*

tracto, are, avi, atum, 1, *v.* freq. *a.,* (I) lit., *to touch, handle,* (2) fig., (a) *to handle, treat, investigate, discuss anything,* used with *de,* with *acc.,* (b) *to treat, use,* or *conduct one's self* toward a person in any manner, (c) *to plot* or *plan,* used with an interrog. clause, (d) *to handle, manage* or *conduct* business, secular affairs etc.

tractus, us, *m.,* used fig., (1) of time, *lapse, space,* (2) in gen., *course, progress.*

Tractus, us, *m., the Tract,* a verse or verses from Scripture recited in the Mass following the Graduale and taking the place of the

Alleluia on days of sorrow or penance, e.g., in the ferial Masses of Lent; so named because it is usually long or drawn out.

traditio, onis, *f.*, (1) *a giving over, delivery, surrender,* (2) *a handing down, tradition.*

traditor, oris, *m.*, *a traitor.*

trado, ere, didi, ditum, 3, *v. a.*, *to give up, hand over, deliver, transmit, surrender, consign.* – **traditus**, a, um, *P. a.*, *transmitted, surrendered, consigned.*

traducibilis, e, *adj.*, *transmissible, capable of being transmitted.*

traduco, ere, xi, ctum, 3, *v. a.*, *to lead, bring* or *conduct across; to lead, bring,* or *carry over anything.*—**traductus**, a, um, *P. a.*, *conducted across, carried over.*

traductio, onis, *f.*, (1) *exposure to disgrace,* (2) *bringing over, leading over, transferring,* (3) *production* or *generation through the transferring of seed.*

tradux, ucis, *m.*, originally, *a vine-branch* or *vine-layer* trained for propagation; hence *a parent* and so used in S.T.

tragoedia, ae, *f.*, = *tragodia*, *a tragedy.*

tragoedus, i, *m.*, = *tragodus*, *a tragic actor, tragedian.*

traho, ere, xi, ctum, 3, *v. a.*, *to draw, drag,* or *haul, to drag along; to draw off, forth,* or *away.*

traicio, ere, ieci, iectum, 3, *v. a.* and *n.*, (1) *to transmit,* as evil, (2) *to traject, swallow.*

Traianus, i, *m.*, *Trajan,* a Roman emperor, who reigned A.D. 98-118.

traiectio, onis, *f.*, *a passing over.*

trames, itis, *m.*, *a way, path, road,* used in the S.T. only in quotation.

tranquille, *adv.*, see *tranquillus.*

tranquillitas, atis, *f.*, *calmness, quiet, serenity, tranquillity.*— **tranquillitas ordinis**, *tranquillity of order,* consisting in all the appetitive movements in one man being set at rest together.

tranquillo, are, 1, *v. a.*, *to calm, compose, tranquillize.*

tranquillus, a, um, *adj.*, *calm, quiet, placid.*—**tranquille**, *calmly, quietly.*

trans, *prep.* with *acc., across, over, beyond.*

transactio, onis, *f.*, in jurid. Lat., *a transaction, a kind of legal compromise.*

transactus, a, um, *P. a.*, see *transigo.*

transcendo, ere, di, sum, 3, *v. a.* and *n.*, (1) *to pass over, overstep, exceed, transcend,* (2) *excel, exceed, surpass, transcend.*—**transcendens**, ntis, *P. a., passing over, overstepping, exceeding, transcending, excelling.* On **multitudo transcendens**, see *multitudo* under 1.—**transcendens**, ntis, *n., the transcendental,* i.e., that which because of the analogical nature of being cannot be determined to any category or predicament or the *modus generaliter consequens omne ens.* There are five transcendentals—*res, aliquid, unum, verum, bonum,* or when *ens* is added six.

transcorporatio, onis, *f., transmigration,* the translocation of the soul from one body to another.

transcribo, ere, psi, ptum, 3, *v. a., to transcribe.*

transcurro, ere, curri, or cucurri, cursum, 3, *v. n.* and *a., touch briefly upon.*

transeo, ire, ivi or ii, itum, *v. n.* and *a., to go over* or *cross, cross over, pass over, pass by, pass,* the opposite of *maneo* and *permaneo.* —**transiens,** ntis, *P. a., going over, passing, transient,* synonym of *pertransiens* and *transitivus,* the opposite of *manens* and *permanens.* On **actus transiens,** see *actus* under 1; on **materia transiens,** see *materia* under 3; on **operatio transiens,** see *operatio* under 2; on **passio transiens,** see *passio* under 1.

transfero, ferre, tuli, latum, *v. a.,* (1) lit., *to transfer, convey* from one place, person, or thing to another; *to transport, remove,* or cause to pass to another place, person or thing, (2) fig., (a) *to transfer, direct, transport, convey,* (b) *to translate* to another language.

transfigo, ere xi, xum, 3, *v. a., to pierce, transfix* a thing, used fig. and lit.

transfiguratio, onis, *f.,* (1) *a change of shape, transformation,* (2) *glorification, transfiguration.* On **fieri transfiguratione,** see *fieri.*

transfiguro, are, avi, atum, 1, *v. a.,* (1) lit., *to change in shape, to transform, transfigure,* (2) fig., *to change, transform.*

transformo, are, avi, atum, 1, *v. a., to change in shape, transform,* used lit. and fig.

transfreto, are, avi, atum, 1, *v. n.* and *a., to cross over the sea.*

transfundo, ere, fudi, 3, *v. a., to transmit, transfuse.*

transfusio, onis, *f., a transmission.*

transglutio, ire, 4, *v. a., to swallow down, gulp down.*

transgredior, i, gressus, 3, *v. dep. a.* and *n.,* (1) lit., *to step over, pass over,* (2) eccl. Lat., *to transgress.*

transgressio, onis, *f., transgression,* the action of transgressing or passing beyond the bounds of legality or right; a violation of law, duty, or command; *disobedience, trespass, sin.*

transgressor, oris, *m., an infringer,* transgressor of the law.

transigo, ere, egi, actum, 3, *v. a.,* with *vita, to lead, pass, spend.*—**transactus,** a, um, *P. a., completed.*

transilio, ire, ivi, or ui, 4, *v. n.* and *a., to pass over.*

transitio, onis, *f., transition.*

transitivus, a, um, *adj., going over, passing, transitive, transient,* synonym of *transiens* and *pertransiens,* the opposite of *manens* and *permanens.* On **motus transitivus,** see *motus* under 1.

transitorius, a, um, *adj., passing, transitory.*

transitus, us, *m.*, (1) lit., (a) of a river, *a passing over, passing, crossing,* (b) of time, from this life, through purgatory, *a passage,* (2) fig., *a passing over unobserved.*

translatio, onis, *f.*, (1) lit., (a) *transference,* the giving over of anything from one person to another, (b) *a removal* of anything, (2) fig., of speech or writing, *a version, translation* into another language.

translative, *adv.*, see *translativus.*

translativus, a, um, *adj., of* or *belonging to transference, that is to be transferred, translative, metaphorical,* synonym of *metaphoricus* and *transumptivus.* On **ars translativa,** see *ars* under 2; on **nomen translativum,** see *nomen* under 1.—**translative,** *adv., in the manner* or *sense of transference, metaphorically* synonym of *metaphorice* and *transumptive.* On **dicere translative,** see *dicere* under 3.

translator, oris, *m., one who carries* or *hands over, transferrer, translator,* not in S.T.

transluceo, ere, *v. n., to shine through, show through; to be transparent* or *translucent.*

transmigratio, onis, *f., a removing from one country to another, a transmigration.*

transmigro, are, avi, 1, *v. n., to remove from one place to another, transmigrate.*

transmissio, onis, *f., transmission,* *the action of passing over,* used fig.

transmitto, ere, misi, missum, 3, *v. a.*, (1) *to send, carry; to send off, dispatch, transmit* from one place or person to another, (2) *to transmit* by writing, (3) *to transmit* something to one's successor, used lit. and fig.

transmutabilis, e, *adj., changeable.*

transmutabilitas, atis, *f., changeableness, transmutability.*

transmutatio, onis, *f.*, (1) *transmutation,* change in the proper sense of the word, i.e., the change from one being to another being, synonym of *conversio, immutatio,* and *mutatio,* (2) *transmutation, change,* in the improper sense of the word, i.e., change from being to non-being, synonym of *annihilatio.* On the relationship of *transmutatio* to *transubstantiatio,* see *transubstantiatio.*—Kinds of *transmutatio* in this (1) sense are: (a), **transmutatio circa magnitudinem, transmutatio circa passiones seu secundum passiones seu passibilium qualitatum** and **transmutatio localis seu secundum locum,** *the quantitative, the qualitative,* and *the local change.* Cf. *transmutatio secundum accidentia.*—(b) **transmutatio circa passiones,** see *transmutatio circa magnitudinem.*—(c), **transmutatiio circa substantiam seu secundum substantiam seu ex substantia ente in potentia in substantiam entem in actu seu substantialis seu ex**

hoc, in hoc and **transmutatio se-cundum accidentia,** *the substantial* and *the accidental change* or *the change of a thing according to its substance* and *that according to one of its accidents.*—(d), **transmutatio corporalis,** *the physical change.*—(e), **transmutatio ex hoc in hoc,** see *transmutatio circa substantiam.*—(f), **transmutatio ex substantia ente in potentia in substantiam entem in actu,** see *transmutatio circa substantiam.*—(g), **transmutatio formalis seu secundum formam** and **transmutatio secundum materiam,** *the change of a thing according to its form* and *that according to its matter.*—(h), **transmutatio innaturalis, transmutatio miraculosa,** and **transmutatio naturalis,** *the unnatural, the miraculous* or *supernatural,* and *the natural change.* Cf. *transmutatio materialis et quae fit a natura.*—(i), **transmutatio localis,** see *transmutatio circa magnitudinem.*—(j), **transmutatio materialis seu naturalis** and **transmutatio spiritualis** sc. organi animae, *the material* or *physical change of an organ of the soul.*—(k), **transmutatio miraculosa,** see *transmutatio innaturalis,*—(l), **transmutatio mutua,** *the mutual change of two things into each other.*—(m), **transmutatio naturalis,** see *transmutatio innaturalis et materialis.*—(n), **transmutatio particularis,** *the special change* or *a special kind of* change.—(o), **transmutatio passibilium qualitatum,** see *transmutatio circa magnitudinem.*—(p), **transmutatio per accidens** and **transmutatio per se,** *the accidental change in a thing* and *that which takes place in it as such* or *according to itself.*—(q), **transmutatio per se,** see *transmutatio per accidens.*—(r), **transmutatio quae est per artem** and **transmutatio quae fit a natura,** *the artistic* and *the natural change,* or the change which is accomplished through the art of man and that through the power of nature.—(s), **transmutatio quae fit a natura,** see *transmutatio quae est per artem.*—(t), **transmutatio secundum accidentia,** see *transmutatio circa substantiam.*—(u), **transmutatio secundum formam,** see *transmutatio formalis.*—(v), **transmutatio secundum locum,** see *transmutatio circa magnitudinem.*—(w), **transmutatio secundum materiam,** see *transmutatio formalis.*—(x), **transmutatio secundum passiones,** see *transmutatio circa magnitudinem.*—(y), **transmutatio secundum substantiam,** see *transmutatio circa substantiam.*—(z), **transmutatio spiritualis,** see *transmutatio materialis.*—(a²), **transmutatio substantialis,** see *transmutatio circa substantiam.*

transmuto, are, avi, atum, 1, *v. a.,* *to change, transform, transmute.*

transparens, entis, *adj., transparent.*

transpositio, onis, *f., transposition, alteration or order,* or *interchange* of position, especially words in a sentence; the result of such action.

transubstantiatio, onis, *f., total change of substance, transubstantiation,* i.e., that change by which a thing is changed into another not merely according to its form but also according to its matter, thus according to its whole substance.

transubstantio, are, 1, *to transubstantiate, to change from one substance to another.*

transumo, ere, 3, *v. a., to take from one to another; to adopt, assume.*

transumptio, onis, *f., a taking* or *assuming of one thing for another, a representation, comparison.*

transumptive, *adv.,* see *transumptivus.*

transumptivus, a, um, *adj., transferring the sense, understood in the transferred sense, transumptive, metaleptic,* synonym of *metaphoricus* and *translativus,* not in S.T. On **locutio transumptiva,** see *similitudo* under 1.—**transumptive,** *adv., after the manner* or *in the sense of change, transumptively, metaphorically,* synonym of *metaphorice* and *translative.* On **passio transumptive sumpta,** see *passio* under 1; on **perfectio transumptive dicta,** see *perfectio* under 2; on **sumere transumptive,** see *sumere* under 3; on **uti transumptive,** see *uti* under 1.

transversalis, e, *adj., genealogy, collateral.*

transversus, a, um, *P. a., crosswise, transverse.*

transvolo, are, avi, atum, 1, *v. a.,* and *n., to fly away,* used fig.

Trebatius, ii, *m., Trebatius* C. Testa, a lawyer, a friend of Cicero, to whom the latter dedicated the Topica.

trecenti, ae, *a., num. adj., three-hundred.*

tredecim, *num., adj., thirteen.*

tremo, ere, ui, 3, *v. n.,* and a., (1) neutr., *to shake, quake, quiver, tremble,* etc., (2) act., *to quake* or *tremble* at a thing.—**tremendus,** a, um, *P. a., awe-inspiring, terrible.*

tremor, oris, *m., a trembling, shaking.*

trepidatio, onis, *f., a state of confused hurry* or *alarm, agitation, confusion, trepidation.*

trepido, are, avi, atum, 1, *v. n.,* and *a., to hurry with alarm, to bustle about anxiously, be in a state of confusion, agitation* or *trepidation.*

tres, tria, num. *adj., three.*

Trevirensis, e, *adj., of* or *pertaining to Treves,* a district in the Rhine Province.

triangularis, e, *adj., of* or *belonging to a triangle, triangular.*

triangulum, i, *n.,* and **triangulus,** i, *m., a triangle.*

tribulatio, onis, *f., distress, trouble, tribulation.*

tribulus, i, *m., a thistle.*

tribunal, alis, *n.*, *tribunal, judgment seat.*

tribunus, i, *m.*, *a tribune, captain, commander.*

tribuo, ere, ui, utum, 3, *v. a.*, *to assign, impart, allot, bestow, give,* used lit. and fig.—**tributum,** i, *n.*, *a stated payment, a contribution, tribute.*

tribus, us, *f.*, *a tribe, a division of the people.*

tributarius, a, um, *adj.*, *subject to tribute, tributary.*

tributivus, a, um, *adj.*, *contributive, contributory.*

tributum, i, *n.*, see *tribuo.*

tricenarius, a, um, *adj.*, *of or containing thirty.*

tricesimus, a, um, *num. ord. adj.*, see *trigesimus.*

tricubitus, a, um, *adj.*, *tricubital, of three cubits.*

triduum, i, *n.*, *the space of three days.*

triennium, ii, *n.*, (sc. spatium), *the space of three years, three years.*

trifariam, *adv.*, *triply, in a threefold manner.*

triformis, e, *adj.*, *having three forms, shapes* or *natures; threefold.*

trigenarius, a, um, *adj.*, *of or containing thirty.*

trigesimus, a, um, *num. ord. adj.*, *the thirtieth.*

triginta, *num. adj. indecl.*, *thirty.*

trigonum, i, *n.*, = *trigonon, a triangle, trigon.*

trilaterus, a, um, *adj.*, *three sided, trilateral.*

trinarius, a, um, *adj.*, *threefold, triple.*

trinitas, atis, *f.*, (1) *the number three, a triad, a trinity,* (2) *the Blessed Trinity, Holy Trinity.*— One kind of *trinitas* is: **trinitas divina seu increata seu sancta,** *the divine* or *uncreated* or *Holy Trinity.* On **caelum sanctae trinitatis,** see *caelum.* On **caelum Trinitatis,** see *caelum;* on **speculum Trinitatis,** see *speculum* under 1; on **vestigium Trinitatis,** see *vestigium.*

trinus, a, um, *adj.*, *three, triune, triple, three each.*

tripartitus, a, um, *adj.*, *three-fold.*

triplex, icis, *adj.*, *three-fold, triple.* —**tripliciter,** *adv.*, *in a threefold manner, in three ways.*

triplicitas, atis, *f.*, *triplicity.*

tripliciter, *adv.*, see *triplex.*

triplus, a, um, *adj.*, *num.*, *threefold, triple.*

Trismegistus, i, *m.*, *Thrice Greatest,* thus *Hermes Trismegistus,* an Egyptian philosopher of great antiquity. St. Thomas refers to him.

tristabilis, e, *adj.*, *disagreeable, painful.*

tristis, e, *adj.*, *dejected, sorrowful, mournful, melancholy, disconsolate.*

tristitia, ae, *f.*, (1) *sorrow, sadness, grief* in the sense of an affection, the opposite of *delectatio, gaudium,* and *laetitia,* (2) *pain* in the general use of the word, synonym of *dolor.*—Kinds of *tristitia* in the improper sense of the species of the word are four: *acidia, anxietas, invidia,* and *misericordia.* Other kinds of *tristitia* are: **tristitia saeculi** and **tristitia secundum Deum,** *sadness because of the world* and *sadness because of God.*

tristor, ari, atus, *v. dep. n., to be sad, grieved,* or *downcast.*

triticeus, a, um, *adj., of wheat, wheaten, wheat.*

triticum, i, *n., wheat.*

trituro, are, 1, *v. a., to thresh.*

triumphator, oris, *m., a triumpher.*

triumpho, are, avi, atum, 1, *v. n.* and *a., to conquer, overcome, to triumph over.*—**triumphans,** antis, *P. a., triumphant, graced with triumph, victorious.*—**Ecclesia triumphans,** *the Church triumphant,* the portion of the Church which has overcome the world and entered into glory.

triumphus, i, *m., a triumph, victory.*

trivium, i, *n., cross-road.*

tropice, *adv.,* see *tropicus.*

tropicus, a, um, *adj., figurative, metaphorical, tropical, tropological,* synonym of *tropologicus,* not in S.T. On **locutio tropica,** see *locutio* under 4.—**tropice,** *adv., figuratively.*

tropologicus, a, um, *adj., figurative, metaphorical, tropical, tropological,* synonym of *tropicus.* On **sensus tropologicus,** see *sensus* under 8.

trucido, are, avi, atum, 1, *v. a., to slay, kill.*

trunco, are, avi, atum, 1, *v. a., to cut off.*

tu, *tui; plu., vos, vestrum* or *vestrorum, c., thou, you,* usually used for emphasis; the gentive plural is sometimes used for the possessive pronoun.—**tibi.** – **te.** – **vobis** (*dat.*).—(*abl.*).

tuba, ae, *f., a trumpet.*—**festum Tubarum,** see *festum.*

tueor, eri, tutus, 2, *v. dep. a., to look to, care for, keep up, maintain, support, guard, preserve, defend, protect.*—**tutus,** a, um, *P. a., safe, secure, out of danger.*—**tute,** and **tuto,** *adv., safely, securely, in safety, without danger.*

tuitio, onis, *f., a taking care of, keeping, guarding, preserving, defense, protection, perservation.*

Tullius, ii, *m., M. Tullius Cicero,* the renowned statesman and orator.

tum, *adv., then,* with *etiam, then also; then too, besides.*—**tum quia** . . . **tum quia,** *both because . . . and because.*—**tum propter,** . . . **tum propter,** *both on account of . . . and on account of.*

tumeo, ere, 2, *v. n.,* (1) *to swell, burst out* in passionate excitement, (2) *to be puffed up* with pride.

tumidus, a, um, *adj., puffed up* with pride.

tumor, oris, *m., a swelling from pride, pride.*

tumulo, are, avi, atum, 1, *v. a., to cover with a mound, to bury.*

tumultus, us, *m., tumult, disturb-*

ance, violent commotion, used lit. and fig.

tumulus, i, *m., a tomb, a sepulchral mound.*

tunc, *adv., then, at that time,* the opposite of *nunc.*

tundo, ere, tutudi, tunsum, tussum- and tusum, 3, *v. a., to beat, strike.*

tunica, ae, *f., a tunic, garment,* (1) *a garment* resembling a shirt or gown, worn by both sexes among the Greeks and Romans; in medieval times, a body-garment or coat over which a loose mantle or cloak was worn, (2) the long outer vestment of the subdeacons, worn when they assist the priest at solemn functions, (3) in the Old Law, one of the eight vestments worn by the highpriests while presiding at the altar of the temple.

tunicatus, a, um, *P. a., clothed with a tunic.*

tunsio, onis, *f., the action of beating* or *striking.*

turba, ae, *f., a crowd, throng, multitude, mob.*

turbatio, onis, *f., confusion, disorder, disturbance.*

turbidus, a, um, *adj.,* (1) lit , *cloudy,* (2) fig., (a) *haughty,* (b) *impure.*

turbo, are, avi, atum, 1, *v. a.,* (1) lit., *to disturb, agitate; to throw into disorder* or *confusion,* (2) physically, *to disturb,* (3) mentally, *to trouble, disturb.*

turbo, inis, *m., a whirlwind, a storm,* used lit. and fig.

turbulentia, ae, *f., trouble, disquiet, turbulence.*

turpiloquium, ii, *n., obscene* or *immodest speech.*

turpis, e, *adj., unseemly, shameful, disgraceful, base, infamous, scandalous, dishonorable.—***turpe,** is, *n., a base* or *shameful thing.—***turpiter,** *adv., basely, shamefully, dishonorably.*

turpiter, *adv.,* see *turpis.*

turpitudo, inis, *f., baseness, shamefulness, disgrace, dishonor, infamy, turpitude.*

turris, is, *f.,* = *tyrris, a tower.*

turtur, uris, *m., a turtle-dove.*

Tusculanus, a, um, *of* or *belonging to Tusculum; Tusculan,* hence, *Tusculanae Disputationes,* the title of a work written there by Cicero.

tutela, ae, *f., care, protection, charge, defence.*

tutor, oris, *m., a guardian, tutor.*

tutus, a, um, see *tueor.*

tuus, a, um, *pron. poss., thy, thine, your, yours.*

typicus, a, um, *adj., typical, exemplary.* On **sensus typicus,** see *sensus,* under 8.

typus, i, *m.,* = *typos, a type, figure, character* of something.

tyrannicus, a, um, *adj., tyrannous, tyrannical,* synonym of *despoticus.* On **dominium tyrannicum,** see *dominium;* on **lex tyrannica,** see *lex* under 1; on **potestas tyrannica,** see *potestas* under 3.

tyrannis, idis, *f.,* = Grk. *tyrannis, the sway of a tyrant, arbitrary* or *despotic rule, tyranny.*

tyrannus, i, *m., tyrant,* one who rules not for the common weal but for his own benefit.

Tyrii, orum, *m., the inhabitants of Tyre, the Tyrians.*

tyrocinium, ii, *n., tirocinium, first* *military service* or *campaign, warlike exercise.*

Tyrus, i, *f.,* = *Tyros, Tyre,* a famous maritime and commercial city of the Phoenicians.

U

uber, eris, *n., a breast that gives suck.*

uber, eris, *adj., abundant, plentiful, copious,* (1) lit., (2) fig.

ubertas, atis, *f., plenty, richness, fruitfulness,* used lit. and fig.

ubi, *adv.,* (1) *where, in what place, in which place,* (2) *anywhere,* synonym of *alicubi* one of the ten categories of Aristotle (see *praedicamentum* under 2).—ubi supra, *somewhere above, loco citato.*

ubicumque, *adv., wherever, wheresoever.*

ubique, *adv., wherever, wheresoever, in any place whatever, anywhere, everywhere.*—ubique terrarum, *everywhere, throughout the world.*

ulciscor, i, ultus, 3, *v. inch. dep. to avenge one's self on, take vengeance on,* or *punish for wrong doing,* (1) absol., (2) with a non-personal object.

ullus, a, um, *gen. ullius; dat. ulli* (*gen. sing. ulli*), *adj. dim.* (for *unulus,* dim. of *unus*), *any, anyone,* used in negative declarations and affirmative clauses.

ulna, ae, *f., an ell.*

ulter, tra, trum, *adj.,* the *posit.* is not found but the *comp.* and the *sup.* are very frequent, *farther, on the farther side,* that is, *beyond, ulterior.* For *adverbs* see under *ultra.* For *sup.* see *ultimus*

ultimus, a, um, *adj., the farthest, most distant, most remote, the uttermost, extreme, last,* synonym of *extremus.* On actus ultimus, see *actus* under 2; on beatitudo ultima, see *beatitudo* under 1; on bonitas ultima, see *bonitas* under 1; on bonum ultimum see *bonus* under 3; on cognitio ultima, see *cognitio* under 2; on complementum ultimum, see *complementum;* on differentia ultima, see *differentia;* on dispositio ultima, see *dispositio* under 4; on esse ultimum, see *esse;* on felicitas ultima, see *felicitas;* on finis ultimus, ultimus quoad aliquem seu hunc et ultimus simpliciter, ultimus secundum rationem ultimi finis et ultimus secundum id, in quo finis ultimi ratio invenitur, see *finis* under 4; on forma ultima, see *forma* under 2; on generatio ultima, see *generatio* under 1; on hierarchia ultima, see *hierarchia;* on infinitum in ultimum,

see *infinitus;* on **iudicium ultimum,** see *iudicium* under 1; on
materia ultima, see *materia* under 3; on **movens ultimum,** see
movens; on **necessitas ultima,** see
necessitas under 3; on **perfectio
ultima et ultima hominis,** see
perfectio under 2 and 4; on **resurrectio ultima,** see *resurrectio;*
on **sphaera ultima,** see *sphaera*
under 2; on **subiectum ultimum,**
see *subiectum* under 2 and 3; on
terminus ultimus, see *terminus*
under 2.—**ultimum,** i, *n.,* the last,
the end, synonym of *terminus.*—
Kinds of *ultimum* are: (a), **ultimum potentiae** and **ultimum rei,**
the utmost of a potentiality and
that of a thing or *the highest,* in
quod potentia elevari potest, and
the utmost in or of a thing which
has to be taken into account.—
(b), **ultimum rei,** see *ultimum potentiae.*—(c), **ultimum secundum
quid** and **ultimum simpliciter,**
the ultimate in a certain respect
and *the ultimate simply* or *absolutely.*—(d), **ultimum simpliciter,**
see *ultimum secundum quid.*

ultio, onis, *f.,* a taking vengeance,
avenging, revenge.

ultor, oris, *m.,* a punisher, avenger,
revenger.

ultra, *prep.* and *adv.,* (1) *prep.* beyond, past, over, more than.—(2),
adv., beyond, farther, over, more,
besides.—**ulterius,** *comp.* beyond,
farther on, farther.

ultro, *adv.,* spontaneously, of one's
own accord.

ululo, are, avi, atum, 1, *v. n.* and *a.,*
to shout, howl, yell.

umbilicus, i, *m.,* (1) lit., *the navel,*
(2) transf., *the navel, middle,
centre.*

umbra, ae., *f.,* a shade, a shadow,
(1) lit., (2) fig.

umbraliter, *adv.,* in outline as in a
shadow.

umbrositas, atis, *f.,* umbrosity, the
state or condition of being shady.

umerus, i, *m.,* see *humerus.*

umidus, a, um, *adj.,* see *humidus.*

umor, oris, *m.,* see *humor.*

unanimis, e, *adj.,* unanimous.—unanimiter, *adv.,* unanimously, in a
unanimous manner.

unanimiter, *adv.,* see *unanimis.*

unctio, onis, *f.,* (1) anointing, be-
smearing, unction, (2) anointing
or *unction* of man.—Kinds of *unctio* in this (2) sense are: (a),
unctio extrema seu ultima, the
last anointing, extreme unction.
—(b), **unctio invisibilis** and **unctio visibilis,** the invisible and
visible anointing.—(c), **unctio ultima,** see *unctio extrema.*—(d),
unctio visibilis, see *unctio invisibilis.*

unctus, a, um, *P. a.,* see *ungo.*

unda, ae, *f.,* (1) *a wave,* (2) *a spring,
a flow of water.*

unde, *adv.,* whence, wherefore,
therefore, so.

undecim, *num. adj.,* eleven.

undecimus, a, um, *num. adj.,* the
eleventh.

undecumque, *adv.,* from wherever,
whencesoever.

undenarius, a, um, *adj., containing eleven.*

undique, *adv., indef., from all parts, sides* or *places; on all sides, everywhere, on every part.*

ungo, or unguo, nxi, nctum, 3, *v. a., to anoint* by pouring or rubbing with oil as a sign of consecration. Anointing was extensively practised by the Jews even at the time of Christ Who is called the Messias or anointed. In the Catholic Church unctions with oil are prescribed in a number of sacraments as well as in many benedictions. This verb is used both *lit.* and *fig.* in the S.T.

unguentum, i, *n., an ointment, unguent, perfume.*

unguis, is, *m., nail* of a person's finger or toe.

ungula, ae, *f.,* (1) *the hoof, claw, talon* of an animal, (2) *a claw,* an instrument of torture.

unibilis, e, *adj., unible, capable of being united; unitable.*

unibilitas, atis, *f., compatibility.*

unicus, a, um, *adj., one* and *no more, only, sole, single.*

uniformis, e, *adj., having only one shape* or *form, uniform,* synonym of *conformis,* the opposite of *difformis.* On cognitio uniformis, see *cognitio* under 2; on motus uniformis, see *motus* under 1.— uniformiter, *adv., in one* and *the same manner, uniformly.* On movere uniformiter, see *movere.*

uniformitas, atis, *f., uniformity, monotony,* synonym of *conformitas,* the opposite of *difformitas.*

On motus uniformitatis, see *motus* under 1.

uniformiter, *adv.,* see *uniformis.*

unigenitus, a, um, *adj., eccl. Lat., only-begotten, only.*

unio, onis, *f., oneness, unity, union,* synonym of *unitio,* the opposite of *discretio.* On gratia unionis, see *gratia* under 2.—Kinds of *unio* are: (a), unio accidentalis seu per accidens seu secundum accidens and unio per se seu secundum essentiam seu naturae seu in natura seu secundum naturam, *the non-essential* and *the essential union.*—(b), unio affectiva seu affectualis seu affectus seu secundum affectum and unio realis seu secundum rem, *union according to emotion* or *longing* and *that taking place according to reality.*—(c), unio affectus, see *unio affectiva.*—(d), unio amoris, *the union effected through love.* —(e), unio condignativa seu dignativa and unio consentanea sc. in Christo, *the union worthy of Christ,* and *that corresponding to Him.*—(f), unio congregatorum se superficialiter tangentium and unio continuorum, *the union by touching* and *that by coherence.* —(g), unio consentanea, see *unio condignativa.*—(h), unio continuorum, see *unio congregatorum se superficialiter tangentium.*—(i), unio dignativa, see *unio condignativa.*—(j), unio exigitiva, *the necessary union.*—(k), unio in hypostasi seu secundum hypostasim seu in substantia seu substantialis seu secundum subsistentiam seu in supposito and unio in persona seu secundum personam seu personae seu personalis, *the union according to the individual substance or according to the substance* and *that according to the person.*—(l), unio in natura, see *unio accidentalis.* —(m), unio in persona, see *unio in hypostasi.*—(n), unio in substantia, see *unio in hypostasi.*— (o), unio in supposito, see *unio in hypostasi.*—(p), unio naturae, see *unio accidentalis.*—(q), unio naturalis and unio non-naturalis, *the natural union or that according to nature* and *the unnatural union or the union not according to nature.*—(r), unio non-naturalis, see *unio naturalis.*—(s), unio per accidens, see *unio accidentalis.*—(t), unio per modum commensurationis, and unio per modum confusionis and unio per modum commixtionis, *the union after the manner of a right proportion, that after the manner merely of a mixture,* and *that after the manner of a chemical combination.*—(u), unio per modum commixtionis, see *unio per modum commensurationis.*—(v), unio per modum confusionis, see *unio per modum commensuratio nis.*—(w), unio per se, see *unio accidentalis.*—(x), unio personae, see *unio in hypostasi.*—(y), unio personalis, see *unio in hypostasi.* —(z), unio realis, see *unio affectiva.*—(a²), unio secundum acci-

dens, see *unio accidentalis.*—(b²), unio secundum affectum, see *unio affectiva.*—(c²), unio secundum essentiam, see *unio accidentalis.*—(d²), unio secundum naturam, see *unio accidentalis.*—(e²). unio secundum personam, see *unio in hypostasi.*—(f²), unio secundum rem, see *unio affectiva.* —(g²), unio secundum subsistentiam, see *unio in hypostasi.*—(h²), unio similitudinis, *the union (with something) through similarity (with it).*—(i²), unio substantialis, see *unio in hypostasi.* unio, ire, ii, itum, 4, *v. a., to join together, unite, combine, make uniform, simplify.* On consideratio unita, see *consideratio;* on discretio unita, see *discretio* under 2; on instrumentum unitum, see *instrumentum;* on theologia unita, see *theologia* under 2; on virtus unita, see *virtus* under 1.— Kinds of *unire* are: (a), unire accidentaliter seu modo accidentali and unire essentialiter seu substantialiter, *to unite in an unessential manner* and *to do so in an essential manner.*—(b), unire essentialiter, see *unire accidentaliter.*—(c), unire immediate seu sine medico and unire mediante aliquo seu per medium, *to unite directly* and *to do so indirectly.*— (d), unire in individuo and unire integritate speciei, *to unite in an individual* and *to do so in the preservation of a species* or *to unite according to the indivdual* and *according to the species.*—

45

(e), **unire in integritate speciei,** see *unire in individuo.*—(f), **unire in natura seu secundum naturam** and **unire in persona seu secundum personam seu personaliter seu secundum hypostasim,** *to unite in a nature* and *in a person* or *according to nature* and *according to person.*—(g), **unire in persona,** see *unire in natura.*—(h), **unire mediante aliquo,** see *unire immediate.*—(i), **unire modo accidentali,** see *unire accidentaliter.*—(j), **unire per contactum virtutis, unire per modum contactus,** and **unire per modum mixtionis,** *to unite after the manner of contact by a power, after the manner of* (physical or actual) *touch,* and *after the manner of mixing.*—(k), **unire per medium,** see *unire immediate.*—(l), **unire per modum contactus,** see *unire per contactum virtutis.*—(m), **unire per modum mixtionis,** see *unire per contactum virtutis.*—(n), **unire personaliter,** see *unire in natura.*—(o), **unire secundum hypostasim,** see *unire in natura.*—(p), **unire secundum naturam,** see *unire in natura.*—(q), **unire secundum personam,** see *unire in natura.*—(r), **unire sine medio,** see *unire immediate.*—(s), **unire substantialiter,** see *unire accidentaliter.*—**abstractio non est nisi unitorum,** see *abstractio* under 3.—**omnis virtus, quanto est fortior, tanto est magis unita,** *the stronger a power is* or *the more it is capable, the more it is united* or *simplified* (in its activity).—**omnis virtus, quanto plus est omnis virtus, quanto plus est unita, tanto efficacior est ad agendum,** *the more a power is united* or *simplified* (in its activity), *the more efficacious it is in its activity.*—**omnis virtus unita plus est infinita, quam multiplicata,** *every power united* or *simplified* (in its activity) is more unrestricted (in its activity) than a manifold power; cf. also: *virtus unita est,* etc.—**quanto aliquo virtus est magis unita, tanto est magis infinita et ad plura se potest extendere,** *the more a power is united* or *simplified* (in its activity,) *the more unrestricted* and *simplified it is* and *the more things it extends itself over.*—**quanto aliquid est superius, tanto habet virtutem magis unitam et ad plura se extendentem,** *the higher and the more perfect something is, the more united* or *simplified is its power* (in activity), and *the more things does it extend itself over.*—**quanto aliquid magis unitum est, tanto eius virtus et bonitas perfectior est,** *the more something is united or simplified, the more perfect is its power and goodness.*—**quanto virtus est superior, tanto est magis unita,** or, **virtus quanto est superior, tanto magis colligitur et unitur,** *the higher and the more perfect a power is, the more collected and united it is in its activity.*—**quod est in supremo unitum, multiplex** in infimis invenitur, *that which is found united in the highest, is found manifold among the lowest things.*—virtus, **quanto est magis unita, tanto est fortior,** *the more a power is united and simplified in its activity, the more effective it is.*—virtus, **quanto est superior, tanto magis colligitur et unitur,** see above: *quanto virtus est,* etc. —virtus **unita magis est potens quam multiplicata,** *the power united or simplified in itself and in its activity is more effective than a power that is manifold in itself and in its activity or a power that presents manifold things.*

unitas, atis, *f., oneness, unity* in the general sense of the word, on the one hand *unitas numeralis seu secundum numerum* quae scilicet est principium numeri, i.e., the numerical or mathematical unity, in other words *oneness* or *singleness,* the opposite of *multiplicitas, multitudo,* and *pluralitas;* on the other hand *unitas transcendens,* i.e., the transcendental or metaphysical unity, in other words, the *oneness of indivisibility,* the opposite of *distinctio, diversitas,* and *multitudo.* On **numerus unitatum,** see *numerus;* on **sacramentum unitatis,** see *sacramentum* under 3.—Kinds of *unitas* are: (a), **unitas absoluta,** *the simple* or *unconditioned unity.*—(b), **unitas affectus,** *the unity of affection* or *inclination.*—(c), **unitas collectiva,** *the collective unity,* id est, quasi ex pluribus

congregata, sicut multi homines dicuntur unus populus et multi fideles dicuntur una ecclesia.— (d), **unitas utilitatis** and **unitas iuris,** *the unity of common use and that of law.*—(e), **unitas completa seu omnimodo,** *the complete* or *total unity.*—(f), **unitas connexionis,** *the unity of connection or of combination.*—(g), **unitas continuitatis seu continuorum** and **unitas tangentium,** *the unity of continuity or of the continuous and that of things that touch one another.*—(h), **unitas continuorum,** see *unitas continuitatis.*— (i), **unitas corporis,** and **unitas spiritus seu spiritualis,** *the unity of the body* and *that of the Spirit or corporal and spiritual unity.*—(j), **unitas creata** and **unitas increata,** *the created* and *the uncreated unity or the unity of the creature and that of the created.*—(k), **unitas definitionis** and **unitas enuntiationis,** *the unity of definition* and *that of opinion.* Cf. also *enuntiatio* under 2.— (l), **unitas ecclesiastica** and **unitas saecularis seu temporalis,** *the ecclesiastical* and *the secular or temporal unity.*—(m), **unitas enuntiationis,** see *unitas definitionis.*—(n), **unitas essentiae seu essentialis seu naturae** and **unitas personae seu personalis,** *the unity of essence or nature* and *that of person or the essential or natural and the personal unity.*— (o), **unitas essentialis,** see *unitas essentiae.*—(p), **unitas hypostasis** seu substantiae, *unity according to substance.*—(q), unitas increata, see *unitas creata.*—(r), unitas instantis and unitas temporis, *the unity of the moment and that of time.*—(s), unitas iuris, see *unitas communis utilitatis.*—(t), unitas moris, *the unity of morality or of moral character.*—(u), unitas motus, *the unity of motion.*—(v), unitas multitudinis, *the unity of the multitude,* e.g., of a people or of a state.—(w), unitas naturae, see *unitas essentiae.*—(x), unitas naturalis, *the natural unity or that according to nature.*—(y), unitas numeralis seu secundum numerum and unitas speciei, *the unity according to number* and *that according to the individual,* and *unity according to species.*—(z), unitas operationis and unitas virtutis, *unity of action* and *that of power.*—(a²), unitas ordinis, *unity according to order.*—(b²), unitas particularis, *the particular unity,* which is opposed to the general unity.—(c²), unitas per se subsistens seu separata and unitas recepta in aliquo, *the unity existing for itself* or *separated from things and the unity received in something.*—(d²), unitas personae, see *unitas essentiae.*—(e²), unitas personalis, see *unitas essentiae.*—(f²), unitas posita, *the set unity* or *the point.*—(g²), unitas principalis, *the principal* or *chief unity.*—(h²), unitas quantitatis, *the unity of quantity.*—(i²), unitas realis seu rei, *the objective unity* or *the unity according to the thing.*—(j²), unitas recepta in aliquo, see *unitas per se subsistens.*—(k²), unitas rei, see *unitas realis.*—(l²), unitas saecularis, see *unitas ecclesiastica.*—(m²), unitas scientiae, *the unity of science.*—(n²), unitas secundum numerum, see *unitas numeralis.*—(o²), unitas separata, see *unitas per se subsistens.*—(p²), unitas similitudinaria and unitas vera, *the apparent* and *the true unity.*—(q²), unitas simplex seu simplicitatis, *the unity of simplicity.*—(r²), unitas simplicitatis, see *unitas simplex.*—(s²), unitas speciei, see *unitas numeralis.*—(t²), unitas spiritualis, see *unitas corporis.*—(u²), unitas spiritus, see *unitas corporis.*—(v²), unitas substantiae, see *unitas hypostasis.*—(w²), unitas tangentium, see *unitas continuitatis.*—(x²), unitas temporis, see *unitas instantis.*—(y²), unitas vera, see *unitas similitudinaria.*—(z²), unitas virtutis, see *unitas operationis.*

unite, *adv., after the manner* or *in the sense of union* or *unity,* synonym of *unitive,* the opposite of *discrete, divise,* and *divisim.*

unitio, onis, *f., unification, combination, union,* synonym of *unio,* the opposite of *discretio* and *distinctio.* Kinds of *unitio* are: (a), unitio communis and unitio propria, *the general* and *the particular unification* or *the general* and *the particular species of unification,* communis et proprius mo-

dus unitionis.—(b), **unitio divina
seu in divinis,** *the divine unification* or *the unification taking
place in God.*—(c), **unitio in divinis,** see *unitio divina.*—(d), **unitio propria,** see *unitio communis.*
unitivus, a, um, *adj.,* *uniting, making united, characterized or tending to produce union, unitive.*
On **amor unitivus,** see *amor;* on
virtus unitiva, see *virtus* under 1;
on **vis unitiva,** see *vis* under 1.—
**amor est vis unitiva et concreti-
va seu congregativa,** see *amor.*—
unitive, *adv., after the manner*
or *in the sense of uniting, uni-
tively,* synonym of *unite,* the opposite of *discrete, discretive, divise,* and *divisim.*
universalis, e, *adj.,* (1) *of or belonging to all or the whole, universal,* synonym of *communis*
and *generalis,* the opposite of
*individualis, particularis, singula-
ris,* and *specialis,* (2) *universal
per eminentiam* synonym of *praedicabilis.* On **abstractio universalis,** see *abstractio* under 3; on
abstrahere universale, see *abstrahere;* on **agens universale,** see
agens; on **apprehensio universalis,** see *apprehensio* under 2; on
bonitas universalis, see *bonitas*
under 1; on **bonum universale,**
see *bonus* under 3; on **causa universalis,** see *causa* under 2; on
cognitio universalis, see *cognitio*
under 2; on **cognoscere in universali,** see *cognoscere* under 2;
on **communitas universalis,** see
communitas under 1; on **concep-**

tio universalis, see *conceptio* under 4; on **consideratio universalis,** see *consideratio;* on **definitio
universalis,** see *definitio* under 2;
on **demonstratio universalis,** see
demonstratio under 1; on **effectus universalis,** see *effectus;* on
elementum universale, see *elementum* under 3; on **ens universale et in universale,** see *ens;* on
enuntiatio universalis, see *enuntiatio* under 2; on **esse universale,**
see *esse;* on **finis universalis,** see
finis under 2; on **forma universalis,** see *forma* under 2; on **habitudo universalis,** see *habitudo;*
on **ignorantia universalis et universalis iuris,** see *ignorantia* under 1; on **incommunicabilitas
universalis,** see *incommunicabilitas;* on **instantia universalis,** see
instantia under 1; on **intellegibile
universale,** see *intellegibilis* under 2; on **intentio universalis,**
see *intentio* under 3; on **iudicium
universale,** see *iudicium* under 1
and 3; on **lex universalis,** see *lex*
under 1; on **locus universalis,** see
locus under 2; on **natura universalis,** see *natura;* on **opinio universalis,** see *opinio;* on **ordo universalis,** see *ordo* under 1; on
perfectio universalis, see *perfectio* under 2; on **potentia universalis,** see *potentia* under 2; on **potestas universalis,** see *potestas*
under 3; on **praedicare de universali,** see *praedicare* under 2;
on **praedicatum universale,** see
praedicatum under 1; on **principium universale et primum uni-**

versale, see *principium;* on **propositio universalis,** see *propositio* under 2; on **prudentia universalis,** see *prudentia* under 2; on **ratio universalis,** see *ratio* under 2 3, 11, 13; on **regimen universale,** see *regimen;* on **res universalis,** see *res;* on **resurrectio universalis,** see *resurrectio;* on **sapientia universalis,** see *sapientia* under 1; on **scientia universalis,** see *scientia* under 1; on **scire in universali,** see *scire* under 1; on **similitudo universalis,** see *similitudo* under 1; on **species universalis,** see *species* under 5; on **subiectum universale,** see *subiectum* under 3; on **substantia universalis,** see *substantia* under 1; on **syllogismus universalis,** see *syllogismus;* on **terminus universalis,** see *terminus* under 5; on **totum universale,** see *totus* under 1; on **virtus universalis,** see *virtus* under 1; on **vitium universale,** see *vitium* under 2; on **voluntarium in universali,** see *voluntarius* under 3. —**intellectus est universalium et non singulorum,** see *intellectus* under 3. **in universali sunt in potentia particularia,** *in the general is the particular contained as to potentiality.* **ratio est universalium,** see *ratio* under 3. **scientia est universalium,** see *scientia* under 1. **universalia non movent, sed particularia,** *universal things are not moved to action but only the particular or individual things.*—There are five universals, namely, *genus, species, differen-*

tia, proprium, accidens. On the difference between *universale* and *praedicabile,* we read: de quibus secundis intentionibus nunc dicamus, scilicet de quinque universalibus seu praedicabilibus, quae universalia dicuntur, prout intellectus attribuit eis esse in pluribus, praedicabilia vero dicuntur, prout intellectus attribuit eis dici de pluribus.—**universaliter,** *adv., in the manner or in the sense of the universal, all together, in general.* On **cognoscere universaliter,** see *cognoscere* under 2; on **dicere universaliter,** see *dicere* under 3; on **ens universaliter,** see *ens;* on **ferre universaliter,** see *ferre* under 4; on **intellegere universaliter,** see *intellegere* under 1; on **perfectum universaliter,** see *perfectus* under 1; on **praedicare universaliter,** see *praedicare* under 2; on **verum universaliter,** see *verus* under 1.

universalitas, atis, *f.,* (1) *universality,* synonym of *communitas,* (2) *totality.*

universaliter, *adv.,* see *universalis.*

universitas, atis, *f.,* (1) *the whole body, aggregate or number of creatures, persons, things* etc., (2) *the universe,* (3) *a company of persons specifically addressed.*

universum, i, *n.,* see *universus, a, um.*

universus, a, um, *adj., all together, all taken collectively, whole, entire, general, universal,* synonym of *omnis* and *totus.*—**universum,** i, *n., the whole world, the uni-*

verse, synonym of *omne* and *totum.* On **communitas universi,** see *communitas* under 3; on **complementum universum,** see *complementum;* on **ordo universi,** see *ordo* under 1; on **perfectio universi,** see *perfectio* under 2.—**universi,** orum, *m., *the whole body of citizens, all men together.*

univocatio, onis, *f.,* (1) *of like name, homonymity,* synonym of *aequivocatio,* (2) *of like name and likewise of the same nature, homogeneousness.* On **idem secundum univocationem,** see *idem.* — A kind of *univocatio* in this sense is *univocatio simplex, the simple or absolute homonymity,* i.e., that likeness of name which occurs with two or more things simply or absolutely and not with reference to anything else. On **communitas univocationis,** see *communitas* under 1.

univoce, *adv.,* see *univocus.*

univoco, are, avi, atum, 1, *v. a., to designate by the same name* and *to reckon under the same species.*

univocus, a, um, *adj.,* (1) *all agreeing, of one voice,* (2) *of the same name and of the same nature, homogeneous,* the Aristotelian, *synonymos,* the opposite of *aequivocus.* On **agens univocum,** see *agens;* on **causa univoca,** see *causa* under 2; on **commune univocum,** see *communis* under 1; on **communitas univoca,** see *communitas* under 1; on **divisio univoca,** see *divisio;* on **effectus univocus,** see *effectus;* on **generans**

univocum, see *generare;* on **generatio univoca et non univoca,** see *generatio* under 1; on **genus univocum,** see *genus* under 2; on **praedicatio univoca,** see *praedicatio* under 2; on **praedicatum univocum,** see *praedicatum* under 1; on **similitudo univoca,** see *similitudo* under 1.—**univoce,** *adv., after the manner or in the sense of the same name and of the same nature, after the manner or in the sense of homogeneity.* On **accipere univoce,** see *accipere* under 3; on **commune univoce,** see *communis* under 1; on **dicere univoce,** see *dicere* under 3; on **generare univoce,** see *generare;* on **praedicare univoce,** see *praedicare* under 2; on **recipere univoce,** see *recipere.*

unquam, *adv. temp., at any time, ever; most frequently* in negative clauses, rarely in conditional clauses.

unum, see *unus, a, um.*

unus, a, um, *num. adj., single, a* or *an,* one in the general sense of the word, synonym of *idem, indivisus, singularis,* and *unicus,* the opposite of *diversus, divisus, multiplex, multus,* and *plus.* On **affirmatio una,** see *affirmatio* under 1; on **bonum unum seu unum hominis seu unum individui,** see *bonus* under 3; on **debitum unum,** see *debitus* under 1; on **enuntiatio una, unum absolute seu simpliciter seu simplex et unum coniunctione,** see *enuntiatio* under 2; on **modus unus,** see *modus* under 2; on **motus unus,** **unus genere seu secundum genus,** **unus specie seu secundum speciem,** **unus numero seu secundum substantiam,** **unus secundum quid et unus simpliciter,** see *motus* under 1; on **negatio una,** see *negatio* under 1; on **perfectio unius personae,** see *perfectio* under 2; on **regimen unum,** see *regimen;* on **scientia una,** see *scientia* under 2.—**unum,** i, *n., one.*— Kinds of *unum* in general are: (a), **unum absolute seu simpliciter** and **unum aliqualiter seu secundum quid,** *absolute or simple one and in some manner or relative one.*—(b), **unum abstractum** and **unum in aliquo receptum,** *one abstracted from matter or existing for itself or one received in something.*—(c), **unum actu** and **unum potentia seu virtute,** *one according to reality and one according to potentiality or power.*—(d), **unum aggregatione,** **unum coniunctione,** and **unum indivisibilite seu simplex,** *one through aggregation,* sicuti acerbus lapidum est unus; *one through combination* and *one in the sense of the indivisible or the simple,* quod nec actu nec potentia est plura, ut punctus et unitas. —(e), **unum aliqualiter,** see *unum absolute.*—(f), **unum analogia seu secundum analogiam seu secundum proportionem seu in proportione seu proportione,** *one according to analogy or according to proportion.*—(g), **unum colli-** gatione seu per commissionem, **unum contactu seu continuatione seu continuitate seu ex continuitate** and **unum compositione,** *one through exterior composition,* and *through lasting continuity,* and *one through inner combination.*—(h), **unum commune** and **unum singulare,** *the common and particular one.*—(i), **unum compositione,** see *unum colligatione.*— (j), **unum coniunctione,** see *unum aggregatione.*—(k), **unum continuatione seu continuitate,** see *unum colligatione.*—(l), **unum formaliter** and **unum perfective seu perfectione seu toto,** *one according to form or essence,* and *one according to perfection or totality.*—(m), **unum genere seu in genere,** **unum specie seu in specie seu secundum speciem** and **unum numero seu secundum numerum,** *one according to genus, one according to species,* and *one according to number or individual.*—(n), **unum in aliquo receptum,** see *unum abstractum.* —(o), **unum indivisibilite,** see *unum aggregatione.*—(p), **unum in genere,** see *unum genere.*— (q), **unum in rerum natura seu secundum esse seu secundum rem seu re** and **unum secundum rationem seu ratione,** *one in the reality of things or according to existence or according to a thing* and *one according to conception or thought.*—(r), **unum in specie,** see *unum genere.*—(s) **unum logice** and **unum physice,** *the logical* *and the physical one.*—(t), unum numero, see *unum genere.*—(u), unum ordine seu unum secundum ordinem, *one according to order.*—(v), unum **per accidens** seu secundum accidens and unum per se seu secundum substantiam, *one according to something else* and *one according to itself or according to substance.*—(w), unum **perfectione**, see *unum formaliter.*—(x), unum **perfective**, see *unum formaliter.*—(y), unum per naturam and unum per violentiam, *one by nature and one by violence.*—(z), unum **per relationem ad alterum** and unum **secundum se**, *one through relationship with another and one by itself.*—(a²), unum **per se**, see *unum per accidens.*—(b²), unum per violentiam, see *unum per naturam.*—(c²), unum **physice**, see *unum logice.*—(d²), unum **principio** and unum **subiecto seu supposito**, *one according to beginning or origin* and *one according to subject or bearer or supporter.*—(e²), unum **proportione**, see *unum analogia.*—(f²), unum **ratione**, see *unum in rerum natura.*—(g²), unum **re**, see *unum in rerum natura.*—(h²), unum **secundum accidens**, see *unum per accidens.*—(i²), unum **secundum analogiam**, see *unum analogia.*—(j²), unum **secundum esse**, see *unum in rerum natura.*—(k²), unum **secundum numerum**, see *unum genere.*—(l²), unum **secundum proportionem**, see *unum*

analogia.—(m²), unum **secundum quid**, see *unum absolute.*—(n²), unum **secundum rationem**, see *unum in rerum natura.*—(o²), unum **secundum rem**, see *unum in rerum natura.*—(p²), unum **secundum speciem**, see *unum genere.*—(q²), unum **secundum substantiam**, see *unum per accidens.*—(r²), unum **simplex**, see *unum aggregatione.*—(s²), unum **simpliciter**, see *unum absolute.*—(t²), unum **singulare**, see *unum commune.*—(u²), unum **specie**, see *unum genere.*—(v²), unum **toto**, see *unum formaliter.*—(w²), unum **virtute**, see *unum actu.*—**ens et unum convertuntur**, see *convertere* under 1. unum **consequitur ad ens**, see *consequi* under 1. unum **et ens se consequuntur**, see *consequi* under 2. **unusquisque**, see under the word.

unusquisque, *distrib. pron., every single one.*

upupa, ae, *f., a hoopoe,* an Old World *upupoid bird.*

urbanitas, atis, *f., urbanity, refinement.*

urbanus, a, um, *adj., of or belonging to the city, civil.*

Urbanus, i, *m.,* (1) *Urban I,* bishop of Rome under the emperor Alexander Severus, from A.D. 223 to A.D. 230, (2) Urban II, pope 1088-89. Born at Chatillon-sur-Marne, France about 1042. He was a Benedictine, Archdeacon to Rheims, Cardinal Bishop to Ostia and legate to Germany 1082-85.

urbs, urbis, *f., a city.*

urceolus, i, *m., a little pitcher or water-pot.*

urgeo, ere, ursi, 2, *v. a., to urge, press, force, drive,* used lit. and fig.

Uria, ae, *m., Uria,* one of David's warriors, whose wife, Bethsabee, David took.

urina, ae, *f., urine.*

urna, ae, *f., a pot.*

uro, ere, ussi, ustum, 3, *v. a., to burn, blaze,* used lit., and fig.

ursus, i, *m., a bear.*

usitor, ari, atus, 1, *v. freq. dep., to use often, be in the habit of using.*—**usitatus,** a, um, *P. a., usual, wonted, customary, common, ordinary.*

uspiam, *adv., at or in any place, anywhere, somewhere.*

usque, *adv., up to, as far as, even, until,* used with (1) *ad,* in (2) with adverbs, such as *modo, adeo, tunc, hodie, adhuc, quo.*—(3), esp., with *quaque,* less correctly as one word, **usquequaque,** *always, on every occasion.*—with **adeo,**—with **tunc,**—with **hodie,**—with **adhuc,**—with **quo.**

usquequaque, *adv.,* see *usque.*

usquequo, *adv.,* see *usque.*

ustio, onis, *f., a burning, searing* or *cauterizing.*

ustivum, i, *n., heat.*

usualis, e, *adj., that is for use, fit for use, usual,* not in S.T. On ars **usualis,** see *ars* under 2; on arti**fex usualis,** see *artifex.*

usura, ae, *f., interest* paid for the use of money, *usury,* in the prop-

er and improper use of the word, synonym of *interesse.*—Kinds of *usura* are: (a), **usura corporalis,** *physical or material interest.*—(b), **usura sortis** and **usura usurarum,** *interest of capital and interest upon interest.*—(c), **usura usurarum,** see *usura sortis.*

usurarius, a, um, *adj., of* or *belonging to interest or usury, that pays usurious interest,* used especially with *pecunia.*—**usurarius,** i, *m., usurer.*

usurpatio, onis, *f., usurpation,* the action of seizing or holding in possession by force, or without right; applied to seizure of functions, powers, rights, possessions etc., used lit. and fig.

usurpo, are, avi, atum, 1, *v. a., to take, usurp,* to hold in possession by force or without right, applied to seizure of office, place, functions, powers, rights.

usus, us, *m.,* (1) *use, employment, exercise* of anything, the opposite of *fruitio* and *possessio,* (2) *use, enjoyment, fruition,* synonym of *fruitio,* (3) *use, custom, practice,* (4) *use, usefulness, value, utility, advantage,* synonym of *utilitas,* —Kinds of *usus* in this sense are: (a), **usus communis** and **usus proprius,** *the general and the particular use.*—(b), **usus miraculorum,** *the use of the gift to perform miracles.*—(c), **usus pecuniae,** *the use of money.*—(d), **usus prophetiae,** *the use of the gift of prophesy.*—(e), **usus proprius,** see *usus communis.*—(f), **usus ratio-**

nis, *the use of reason.*—(g), **usus scientiae**, *the use of knowledge.* —**ususfructus**, us, *m., usufruct.*

ususfructus, us, *m.*, see *usus.*

ut or **uti**, (1) *that, in order that, so that*, (2) *as, for example*, (3) *as, just as.* On **considerare ut**, see *considerare;* on **contingens ut**, see *contingens* under 2; on **significare ut**, see *significare.*

utcumque, *adv.*, simply limiting a verb or adj., *in any way whatever, in one way or another.*

uter, tris, *m.*, *a bag or bottle* made of an animal's hide, *a skin* for wine, oil, water etc.

uterinus, a, um, *adj.*, *born of the same mother, uterine.*

uterlibet, utralibet, utrumlibet, *pron.* indef., *either one* (of two), *either of two.*

uterque, utraque, utrumque (gen. utriusque) *pron. each* (of two), *either, each one, one and the other, one as well as the other, both* (applied to two subjects regarded severally, while *ambo* regards the two as a pair—(1), in gen., (a) with a subst., (b) absol. (2) in partic., (a) in reciprocal uses, *one . . . the other, each . . . the other, either . . . the other, one another* etc., (b) with a case of *alter.*—**in utramque partem**, *to either side, on either side.*

uterus, i, *m.*, *the womb, matrix,* used (1) lit., (2) fig.

utervis, utravis, utrumvis, *pron.* indef., *which of the two you will, either one of the two, either* (be it which it may) *of the two.*

utibilis, e, *adj., usuable, useful, advantageous,* synonym of *utilis,* the opposite of *fruibilis.*

utilis, e, *adj., usable, useful, advantageous,* synonym of *utibilis,* the opposite of *fruibilis.*—**utiliter**, *adv., usefully, profitably, beneficially, advantageously.*

utilitas, atis, *f.*, (1) *usefulness, utility,* (2) *use, advantage, profitableness, profit.* On **unitas communis utilitatis**, see *unitas.*—Kinds of *utilitas* in this (2) sense are: (a), **utilitas formalis** and **utilitas liberalis**, *formal utility and utility in the sense of liberality.*—(b), **utilitas legalis** and **utilitas moralis**, *the legal utility or that relating to laws or the moral utility or that according to good morals.*—(c), **utilitas liberalis**, see *utilitas formalis.*—(d), **utilitas moralis**, see *utilitas legalis.*

utiliter, *adv.*, see *utilis.*

utinam, *adv.*, a particle of wishing, *oh that!, I wish that!, if only!, would to heaven!, would that!.*

utique, *adv.*, a restrictive particle of confirmation, *in any case, at any rate, certainly, surely, assuredly, by all means, particularly, especially, at least, without fail, undoubtedly.*

utor, i, usus, sum, 3, *v. dep.* (1) *to use* in the proper and narrower senses of the word, i.e., to make use of a thing as a means to attaining an end, the opposite of *frui*, (2) *to use* in the broader and more general sense of the word, (3) *be accustomed to, be*

used to. On **dialectica utens,**
see *dialecticus* under 2; on **logica
utens,** see *logicus;* on **potentia
utens corporali organo,** see *potentia* under 2; on **sophistica
utens,** see *sophisticus.*—**uti** transumptive, *to use something in a
figurative sense.*

utpote, *adv., as namely, namely, as
being, as, seeing that, inasmuch
as, since.*—(1) with rel. pron., (2)
with *cum,* (3) with adj. phrases,
(4) with participles.

utrinque, *adv., from or on both
sides or parts, on the one side
and on the other,* used lit. and
fig.

utrobique, *adv., on both parts or
sides, on the one side and the
other.*

utrum, *adv.,* introducing an alternative question with *an* beginning
the second clause; in Engl. repre-

sented in direct questions simply
by the tone of voice, and in indirect questions by *whether.*—(1),
indirect question (a) with *an* introducing the second clause, (b)
alternative questions in themselves single, but of which some
detail is alternative and introduced by *aut, vel,* (2) *indirect
question* without an expressed alternative.

uva, ae, *f., the fruit of the vine, a
grape.*

uxor, oris, *f., a spouse, wife, consort.*

uxoratus, a, um, *adj., married.*

uxoricidium, i, *n., uxoricide, the
murder of one's wife.*

uxorius, a, um, *adj., of or belonging
to a wife or married woman, excessively fond of one's wife, uxo-
rious.* On **affectus uxorius,** see
affectus.

V

vacatio, onis, *f., rest, freedom from
business or activity,* (2) *rest, the
quiet of contemplation, stillness
of mind.*

vacca, ae, *f., a cow, heifer.*

vacillo, are, avi, atum, 1, *v. n., to
waver, vacillate.*

vaco, are, avi, atum, 1, *v. n.,* (1)
transf., *to rest, to be free from
labor,* (2) in partic., (a) *vacari
alicui rei, to be free to attend,
apply, or devote one's self to
something, to have leisure or
time for a thing,* (b), *vacare ad
aliquid, to be free for something,*

(3) *to be free from, without,* (4)
vacatur, it is permitted.

vacuo, are, avi, atum, 1, *v. a., to
make void.*

vacuus, a, um, *adj.,* (1) *empty, free
from,* synonym of *inanis,* the opposite of *plenus,* (2) *useless, futile,* synonym of *frustra, inanis,*
and *vanus,* the opposite of *efficax,* (3) *free from labor, at leisure, idle.*—On **spatium vacuum,**
see *spatium* under 1.—**vacuum,** i,
*n., an empty space, an open or
vacant place, a void, a vacuum.*
—Kinds of *vacuum* are: **vacuum**

corporibus inditum and **vacuum separatum,** *the empty space found in bodies and that found outside them.*

vado, ere, 3, *v. n., to go, walk,* used lit. and fig.

vae, *interj.,* (*ouai*), an exclamation of pain or dread, *woe! ah! alas!*

vagacitas, atis, *f., unsteadiness, vacillation.*

vagatio, onis, *f., a roaming, wandering,* used fig.

vagina, ae, *f., a sheath, scabbard.*

vagio, ire, ivi or ii, 4, *v. n.,* of young children, *to cry, squall.*

vago, are, 1, *v. n., to lead astray.*

vagor, ari, atus, 1, *v. dep. n.* and *a., to roam, wander.*

vagus, a, um, *adj.,* (1) lit., *wandering,* (2) fig., *wandering, wavering, vague, random.*

valde, *adv.,* see *validus.*

Valentinianus, i, *m., Valentinian II,* emperor A.D. 375-392, son of Valentinian I and of Justina his wife.

Valentinus, i, *m., Valentinus,* founder of one of the Gnostic sects which originated in the first half of the second century.

valeo, ere, ui, itum, 2, *v. n.,* (1) *to be strong, excel, have power or force, avail, be of use or service, profit,* with the *inf., have the power, be able, can,* (2) with *adv.* qualifications expressing the degree of power or influence exerted, with *nihil, tantum, plurimum, minus* etc.—(3), idiomatic

use, of money, *to be of the value of, be worth.*

Valerius, ii, *m.,* (1) *Valerius Maximus,* the writer of the *Memorabilia,* (2) Valerius Bishop of Hippo, predecessor of Augustine, whom he admitted to the priesthood at the earnest desire of the people; against Augustine's wish as expressed in a letter to Valerius, but in answer, as Valerius thought, to his own prayers, (3), Valerius, count of Africa, a firm upholder of Catholic truth against heretical attack, who wrote to Augustine three letters, in return for which Augustine sent him the first book of his work *De Concupiscentia et Gratia.* To this book Julian of Eclana replied in four books, in which he accused Augustine of denying the divine institution of marriage. The entire book by Julian was sent to Augustine by Claudius. On another occasion Augustine wrote to Valerius commending to him a bishop named Felix.

valetudinarius, ii, *m., an invalid, a valetudinarian.*

valetudo, inis, *f., habit, state, or condition of body, state of health,* whether good or bad.

validus, a, um, *adj.,* (1) *strong, stout, able, powerful, robust, vigorous,* (2) fig., *powerful, effective,* (3) of vows, *valid.*—**valde,** *an intens. adv., strongly, vehemently, vigorously, intensely, very, very much, exceedingly,* used (a) with *adjectives*, (b) with *adverbs*.

valles, or *vallis,* is, *f.,* (1) *a valley, vale,* (2) transf., *the valley of hell.*

vallo, are, avi, 1, *v. a., to fortify, protect.*

valor, oris, *m., value.*

vane, *adv.,* see *vanus.*

vanesco, ere, *v. inch. to disappear.*

vaniloquium, ii, *n., empty or idle talk, gabble, prate, vaunting.*

vanitas, atis, *f.,* (1) *vanity, vainglory,* (2) esp. in the pl., *senseless idea, foolish notions, trifles, worldly vanities.*—**vanitas sensus,** *vanity of understanding.*—**saeculares vanitates,** *worldly vanities.*

vanus, a, um, *adj.,* (1) *worthless, vain, void,* (2) *inconsistent, having no firm consistency,* (3) *fruitless, useless, futile,* synonym of *fustra, inanis,* and *vacuus,* (4) *sinful, iniquitous.* On **cogitatio vana,** see *cogitatio* under 2; on **gloria vana,** see *gloria* under 1; on **observantia vana,** see *observantia* under 4; on **observatio vana,** see *observatio* under 3; on **sensus vanus,** see *sensus* under 3. —in **vanum,** *vainly, in vain.*—**per se vanum,** Aristotle's *automaton,* synonym of **per se frustra,** *futile in itself* or *futile as such.*—**impossibile est,** naturae appetitum va-num esse, *it is impossible that the desire of nature or the natural desire of a thing be futile,* in so far, indeed, as it does not attain the goal of its desire. Cf. *deside-*

rium under 1.—**vane,** *adv., idly, vainly.*

vapor, oris, *m., vapor, steam, exhalation.*

vaporabiliter, *adv., vaporously, in the manner of vapor.*

vapulatio, onis, *f., vapulation, a beating or flogging,* used fig.

vapulo, are, avi, 1, *v. neutral pass., to be lashed, scourged, punished,* used fig.

variabilis, e, *adj., changeable, variable.*—**variabiliter,** *adv., variably, in a variable, inconstant* or *uncertain manner.*

variabilitas, atis, *f., variability, capacity for variation or change.*

variabiliter, *adv.,* see *variabilis.*

variatio, onis, *f., a difference, variation.*

varicator, oris, *m., one that walks with his legs spread apart, a straddler.*

varie, *adv.,* see *varius.*

varietas, atis, *f.,* (1) *difference, diversity, variety,* (2) *a variety or that which is various, a number or collection of things,* (3) *change or variation,* (4) *changeableness.*

vario, are, avi, atum, 1, *v. a.,* and *n.,* (1) lit., *to change, variegate,* (2) fig., *to cause to change, make different or various; to alter, change, vary, interchange.*—**variare sensum verborum,** *to change the sense of words.*

varius, a, um, *adj., various, different, manifold.*—**varie,** *adv., variously, in various ways, differently.*

Varro, onis, *m., Varro, a surname in the gens Terentia,* e.g., *M. Terentius Varro,* a contemporary of Cicero. He was born at Reate in the Sabine country in 116 B.C. St. Augustine quotes him in the City of God and St. Thomas in turn refers to those passages.

vas, vasis; *plur.* **vasa,** orum, *n., a vessel, dish.*

vasculum, i, *n., dim., a small vessel.*

vasto, are, avi, atum, 1, *v. a., to harass, to perplex,* used fig.

vates, (vatis), is, *comm., a soothsayer, prophet.*

vaticinor, ari, atus, 1, *v. dep. n.* and *a., to foretell, predict.*

ve (perih, from the same root as *vel, volo;* but cf. Sanscr. *va, or*), *or;* leaving the choice free between two things or among several (always enclitic).

vectis, is, *m., a bar, bolt.*

vegetabilis, e, *adj., animating, enlivening, vegetative,* synonym of *nutritivus* and *vegetativus.* On **anima vegetabilis,** see *anima* under 1; on **forma vegetabilis,** see *forma* under 2; on **pars vegetabilis,** see *pars* under 1.

vegetativus, a, um, *adj., animating, enlivening, vegetative,* synonym of *nutritivus* and *vegetabilis.* On **anima vegetativa,** see *anima* under 1; on **pars vegetativa,** see *pars* under 1; on **potentia vegetativa,** see *potentia* under 2; on **principium vegetativum,** see *principium.—vegetativum (sc. genus potentiarum animae),* synonym of *nutritivum,* Aristotelian

threptikon, the genus of the vegetative potentialities of the soul.

Vegetius, (Flavius Vegetius Renatus), ii, *m., Vegetius,* a Roman author of the fourth century A.D. He wrote *Epitoma Rei Militaris* which St. Thomas quotes.

vegeto, are, avi, atum, 1, *v. a., to invigorate, animate, enliven, quicken, arouse.*

vehemens, entis, *adj.,* (1) lit., *very eager, furious, impetuous, ardent, vehement,* (2) transf., *active, forcible, vigorous, powerful, mighty, strong.—vehementer, adv., vehemently.*

vehementer, *adv.,* see *vehemens.*

vehementia, ae, *f., eagerness, fervency, vehemence.*

vehiculum, i, *n., a means of transport, a carriage, conveyance, vehicle.*

veho, ere, xi, ctum, 3, *v. a.,* and *n., to bear, carry, convey.*

vel, (prob. imperative of *volo*), *conj., or* (less exclusive than *aut*), **vel ... either ... or;** as intensifying *adv., even.*—With *etiam,* or *even.*—With *potius,* to correct or make more precise what has been said, *or rather.*

velamen, inis, *n., a cover, covering, clothing, robe, garment, veil,* used lit. and fig.

velleitas, atis, *f., the conditioned, the imperfect, that does not lend to deeds, that does not attain the aim of the will, velleity,* the opposite of *voluntas, absoluta et completa seu perfecta.*

vellicans, antis, *P. a., plucking.*

vello, ere, vulsi, vulsum, 3, *v. a., to pluck, pull or tear out.*

velo, are, avi, atum, 1, *v. a.,* (1) lit., *to wrap up, veil,* (2) fig., *to hide, conceal.*

velocitas, atis, *f., swiftness, fleetness, speed, rapidity, velocity,* used lit. and fig.

velociter, *adv.,* see *velox.*

velox, ocis, *adj.,* (1) lit., *swift, quick, fleet, rapid, speedy,* (2) fig.—**velociter,** *adv., swiftly, quickly, speedily.*

velum, i, *n., a cloth, covering, curtain, veil,* (1) *a veil or curtain* used in the Old Law to divide the outer tabernacle from the court, (2) *a veil,* one of the veils in modern use in the Catholic Church, either the paten veil, the chalice veil, the superhumeral veil etc.

velut, (veluti), *adv., (even as), just as:* **veluti si,** *just as if.*

vena, ae, *f.,* (1) *a vein, blood-vessel,* (2) transf., of things that resemble veins, *a water-course* used (a) lit., and (b) fig.

venalis, e, *adj., for sale, to be sold.*

venatio, onis, *f., hunting the chase.*

venativus, a, um, *adj., chasing, hunting, searching for, investigating, venatic,* not in S.T. On **cognitio venativa,** see *cognitio* under 2.

vendico, are, avi, atum, 1, *v. a., to lay claim to as one's own, claim.*

venditio, onis, *f., a selling, sale, a vending.*

venditor, oris, *m., a seller, vendor.*

vendo, ere, didi, ditum, 3, *v. a.,* (1) *to sell, vend anything,* (2) *eccl., to sell, to traffic in sacred things.*

veneficium, ii, *n.,* (1) *poisoning,* (2) *witchcraft, sorcery.*

venenatus, a, um, *P. a., poisonous, venomous.*

venenosus, a, um, *adj., full of poison, very poisonous.*

venenum, i, *n., poison,* lit. and fig.

veneo, ire, ivi, ii, itum, 4, *v. n., to go to sale,* i.e, *to be sold.*

venerabilis, e, *adj., worthy of respect, reverence, veneration.*

veneratio, onis, *f., the highest respect, reverence, veneration.*

venereus, a, um, *adj., sexual, venereal.* On **concupiscentia venerea,** see *concupiscentia* under 2; on **delectabile venereum,** see *delectabilis;* on **delectatio venerea,** see *delectatio;* on **voluptas venerea,** see *voluptas.*

veneror, ari, atus, 1, *v. dep. a.,* (1) of God, *to reverence with religious awe; to worship, adore, revere, venerate,* (2) of men or things, as objects, *to revere, do homage to, reverence, honor.*

venia, ae, (1) *forbearance* in view of any wrong that has been done, *forgiveness, pardon, remission,* (2) *kindness, obliging disposition.*

venialis, e, *adj., pardonable, venial.* On **culpa venialis,** see *culpa;* on **delectatio venialis,** see *delectatio;* on **peccatum veniale, veniale ab eventu, veniale ex causa, et veniale in genere,** see *peccatum* under 2.—**venialiter,** *adv., in an easily pardoned or venial* *manner, venially.* On **peccare ve-nialiter**, see *peccare* under 2.

venialiter, *adv.,* see *venialis.*

venio, ire, veni, ventum, 4, *v. n.,* (1) lit., *to come,* (2) in fig., (3) in partic., **venire in aliquid,** *to come into, fall into* any state or condition.—**ad mentem venire,** *to occur to one.*

venor, ari, atus, 1, *v. dep. n.,* and *a., to chase, hunt, seek after, search for.*

venter, tris, *m.,* (1) *the belly,* used lit. and fig., (2) transf., *the womb.*

ventilo, are, avi, atum, 1, *v. a.,* used fig., (1) *to set in motion, agitate,* (2) *to bring forward.*

ventosus, a, um, *adj., windy, vain, conceited.*

ventus, i, *m., wind,* used lit. and fig.

venumdo, are, dedi, datum, 1, *v. a., to sell, put up for sale.*

Venus, eris, *f., the goddess of love, the goddess Venus.*

ver, veris, *n., spring,* used in the S.T. only in quot.

veracitas, atis, *f., truthfulness.*

veraciter, *adv.,* see *verax.*

verax, acis, *adj., speaking truly, true, veracious.*—**veraciter,** *adv., truly, veraciously.*

verbalis, e, *adj.,* (1) *concerning the word in general, consisting of words, wordy, verbal,* (2) *of or belonging to verbs, verbal;* not in S.T.—(1), on **compositio verbalis,** see *compositio* under 1.—(2), on **nomen verbale,** see *nomen* under 1.

verber, eris, *n., a stripe, blow, stroke, a lashing, flogging.*

verberatio, onis, *f., a striking, beating.*

verbero, are, avi, atum, 1, *v. a., to lash, scourge, whip, flog, beat.*

verbositas, atis, *f., multiplicity of words, wordiness, verbosity.*

verbum, i, *n.,* (1) *word* in general under which can be understood a verb as well as a noun or name (see *nomen* under 1), synonym of *vox,* (2) *verb,* the opposite of nomen, (3) *the word* in the sense of a divine person, i.e., the second person of the Deity (= verbum Dei seu divinum), (4), *word* in the proper sense, *command.*— On **processio verbi,** see *processio* under 1.—Kinds of *verbum* in this sense are: (a), **verbum aedificatorium,** *the edifying or instructive word.*—(b), **verbum aeternum,** *the eternal word of God.* —(c), **verbum alterius** and **verbum proprium,** *the word of another* and *the proper word,* or *the name of another and the proper name.*—(d), **verbum animae impressum seu rei, verbum animi sinu cogitatum seu in corde enuntiatum seu speciei vocis** and **verbum vocis seu quod est angelus,** *the word or the name of a thing impressed upon the soul* (of a thing), *the word thought in the inner part of the soul or spoken in the heart,* which consists of an image of the word spoken with the mouth, and *the word of the mouth* or *the word expressing* a message of the thought.—(e), verbum animi sinu cogitatum, see *verbum animae impressum.*—(f), **verbum cordis seu mentis seu intellectus seu mentale seu intellegibile, verbum interius** and **verbum vocis seu vocale seu vocabile seu exterius,** *the word of reason, the word spoken within,* by which is to be understood both the word of reason and the sensible representation of the word spoken outside, and *the word of mouth* or *the outer word.*—(g), **verbum essentiale, verbum notiale,** and **verbum personale,** *the word signifying the essence of God, that signifying a divine notio,* and *that signifying a person in God.*—(h), **verbum expressivum seu manifestativum seu repraestativum,** and **verbum factivum seu operativum,** *the word expressing or declaring a thought and that creating or effecting a thought.*—(i), **verbum exterius,** see *verbum cordis.*—(j), **verbum factivum,** see *verbum expressivum.*—(k), **verbum incarnatum,** *the Incarnate Word (of God).*—(l), **verbum in corde enuntiatum,** see *verbum animae impressum.*—(m), **verbum increatum,** *the uncreated word (of God).*—(n), **verbum intellectus,** see *verbum cordis.*—(o), **verbum intellegibile,** see *verbum cordis.* —(p), **verbum interius,** see *verbum cordis.*—(q), **verbum iocosum** and **verbum otiosum,** *the facetious word and the idle and*

useless word.—(r), **verbum manifestativum,** see *verbum expressivum.*—(s), **verbum mentale,** see *verbum cordis.*—(t), **verbum mentis,** see *verbum cordis.*—(u), **verbum notionale,** see *verbum essentiale.*—(v), **verbum operativum,** see *verbum expressivum.* —(w), **verbum otiosum,** see *verbum iocosum.*—(x), **verbum personale,** see *verbum essentiale.*— (y), **verbum proprium,** see *verbum alterius.*—(z), **verbum rei,** see *verbum animae impressum.*— (a²), **verbum relativum,** *the word expressing a relationship.*—(b²), **verbum repraesentativum,** see *verbum expressivum.*—(c²), **verbum sacramentale,** *the word which produces a sacrament.*— (d²), **verbum speciei vocis,** see *verbum animae impressum.*—(e²), **verbum temporale,** *the verb.*— (f²), **verbum tertium,** *the third word* in an expression, i.e., that word which in an expression is to be distinguished beside the subject and the predicate, namely the copula.—(g²), **verbum vocabile seu vocale,** see *verbum cordis.*—(h²), **verbum vocis,** see *verbum cordis* and *verbum animae impressum.* On **casus verbi,** see *casus* under 5.—Kinds of *verbum* in this (2) sense are: (a), **verbum activam** and **verbum passivum,** *the active and the passive verb.*— (b), **verbum exceptae actionis seu impersonale** and **verbum personale,** *the verb freed from action or the impersonal verb,* e.g., *tonat, pluit,* and *the personal verb;* see *verbum personale* under 1.—(c), **verbum finitum** and **verbum infinitum,** *the finite or definite verb* and *the infinite or indefinite verb,* the *hrema aoriston* of Aristotle's *De Interpr.* 3. 16. b. 14.—(d), **verbum imperativum** and **verbum infiniti modi,** *the imperative verb or the imperative and the verb of the indefinite form or the infinitive.*—(e), **verbum infiniti modi,** see *verbum imperativum.*—(f), **verbum infinitum,** see *verbum finitum.*—(g), **verbum negativum,** *the negative verb.*—(h), **verbum passivum,** see *verbum activum.*—(i), **verbum per se dictum,** *the verb spoken for itself alone.*—(j), **verbum personale,** see *verbum exceptae actionis.*—(k), **verbum substantivum,** *the substantive verb or the verb which is used as a substantive.* On **processio Verbi,** see *processio.*

vere, *adv.,* see *verus.*

verecundabilis, e, *adj., shameful.*

verecundia, ae, *f., the natural feeling of shame, shamefacedness, bashfulness, shyness.*

verecundor, ari, atus, 1, *v. dep. n., to feel bashful, or ashamed, to be shy or diffident.*

verecundus, a, um, *adj., shamefaced, bashful, shy.*

vereor, eri, itus, 2, *v. dep. a* and *n., to feel awe of, to reverence, revere, respect; to fear, be afraid of anything; to fear or be afraid*

to do a thing, used with (a) *inf.,* (b) with *ne* (c) with *acc.*

vergo, ere, (*perf.* and *sup.* wanting), *to turn, incline, verge, bind.*

veridicus, a, um, *adj., truth-telling, veracious, veridical, that speaks the truth.*

verifico, are, 1, *v. a., to confirm the truth or authenticity of; to show to be true by evidence, verify.*

verisimilis, more correctly written separately, **veri similis,** etc. see under *verus* and *similis.*

verisimilitudo, inis, *f., likelihood, probability,* not in S.T. On **cognitio per verisimilitudinem,** see *cognitio* under 2.

veritas, atis, *f.,* (1) *truth* in the general sense of the word, the opposite of *falsitas,* (2) *truth per eminentiam* in the sense of a *veritas rei,* (3) *truth, true opinion, true statement,* (4) *reality,* (5) *truthfulness.* On **confessio veritatis,** see *confessio* under 1; on **mutabilitas veritatis,** see *mutabilitas;* on **rectitudo veritatis,** see *rectitudo* under 3; on **solutio ad veritatem,** see *solutio* under 2; on **verum veritatis naturalis speciei et significationis,** see *verus* under 1; on **voluntabile secundum veritatem,** see *voluntabilis.*—Kinds of *veritas* in this (1) sense are: (a), **veritas absoluta** and **veritas confesse se habens,** *the truth comprehended in and for itself or the absolute truth* and *truth corresponding with the right will,* i.e., *the relative or corresponding truth.*—(b), **veritas**

accidentalis and veritas inseparabiliter communicata, *the truth imparted accidentally or separately and that imparted inseparably.*–(c), veritas actionis seu operis and veritas vocis, *the truth of action or of deed,* and *the truth of word.*–(d), veritas aeterna, *the eternal or divine truth.*–(e), veritas cognitionis adquisitae, veritas cognitionis infusae, and veritas cognitionis naturalis, *the truth of acquired knowledge, that of infused knowledge,* and *that of natural knowledge.*–(f), veritas cognitionis infusae, see *veritas cognitionis adquisitae.*–(g), veritas cognitionis naturalis, see *veritas cognitionis adquisitae.*–(h), veritas communis and veritas particularis, *the general and the particular truth.*–(i), veritas confesse se habens, see *veritas absoluta.*–(j), veritas contingens and veritas necessaria, *the unnecessary and the necessary truth.*–(k), veritas creata and veritas increata, *the created and the uncreated or divine truth.*–(l), veritas divina, *the divine truth,* i.e., God Himself or the truth in the mind of God.–(m), veritas divinorum, *the truth of divine things.*–(n) veritas doctrinae, veritas iustitiae, and veritas vitae, *the truth of teaching, the truth of justice,* and *the truth of life.*–(o), veritas enuntiabilium seu enuntiationis seu praedicationis, *the truth of opinion or of a statement or of a*

predicate. Cf. veritas opinionis and veritas propositionis.–(p), veritas enuntiationis, see *veritas enuntiabilium.*–(q), veritas essentialiter dicta seu per essentiam and veritas participata, *the essential truth and the truth participated in.*–(r), veritas extrinseca and veritas inhaerens, *the truth exteriorly attached to a thing,* and *the truth connected with or dwelling in itself.*–(s), veritas immortalis seu incorruptibilis seu perpetua, *the immortal or incorruptibile or perpetual truth.*–(t), veritas immutabilis seu incommutabilis and veritas mutabilis, *the unchangeable and the changeable truth.*–(u), veritas improprie seu metaphorice seu similitudinarie and veritas proprie accepta seu dicta, *the truth comprehended in the improper or figurative or allegorical sense and that comprehended in the proper sense or the so called truth.*–(v), veritas incorruptibilis, see *veritas immortalis.*–(w), veritas increata, see *veritas creata.*– (x), veritas inhaerens, see *veritas extrinseca.*–(y), veritas inseparabiliter communicata, see *veritas accidentalis.*–(z), veritas intellectus and veritas rei, *the truth of reason or of knowledge* and *the truth of the thing or fact.*– (a²), veritas intellectuum seu rationum and veritas rerum, *the truth of the conceptions or ideas of things* and *the truth of the things themselves.*–(b²), veritas intellegibilis seu intellegibilium, *the truth of the intelligibile or transcendental.*—(c²), veritas interminabilis, *the undetermined or infinite truth.*—(d²), veritas iustitiae, see *veritas doctrinae.*—(e²). veritas litteralis, *the literal truth.* —(f²), veritas metaphorice accepta seu dicta, see *veritas improprie accepta seu dicta.*—(g²), veritas mutabilis, see *veritas immutabilis.*—(h²), veritas naturae, *the truth of the nature and essence of a thing.*—(i²), veritas naturalis speciei and veritas significationis, *the truth of a natural species or the truth of something belonging to a species of a natural thing, and the truth of a signification.*—(j²), veritas necessaria, see *veritas contingens.*—(k²), veritas operis, see *veritas actionis.*—(l²), veritas opinionis and veritas propositionis, *the truth of an opinion and that of an assertion.*—(m²), veritas participata, see *veritas essentialiter dicta.*—(n²), veritas particularis, see *veritas communis.*—(o²), veritas per essentiam, see *veritas essentialiter dicta.*—(p²), veritas perfectissima seu prima seu summa, *the most perfect or first or highest truth.*—(q²), veritas perpetua, see *veritas immortalis.*—(r²), veritas praedicationis, see *veritas enuntiabilium.*—(s²). veritas prima, see *veritas perfectissima.*—(t²), veritas propositionis, see *veritas opinionis.*—(u²), veritas proprie accepta seu dicta, see *veritas improprie accepta.*—

(v²), veritas pura seu purissima, *the (absolutely) pure or the purest truth,* i.e., *God.*—(w²), veritas rationum, see *veritas intellectuum.*—(x²), veritas rei, see *veritas intellectus.*—(y²), veritas rerum, see *veritas intellectuum.*—(z²), veritas sacrae Scripturae, *the truth of Holy Scripture.*—(a³), veritas sapientiae, *the truth of (divine) wisdom.*—(b³), veritas scientiae, *the truth of science.*—(c³), veritas signi, *the truth of a sign.*—(d³), veritas significationis, see *veritas naturalis speciei.*—(e³). veritas similitudinarie accepta seu dicta, see *veritas improprie accepta.*—(f³), veritas simplex, *the simple truth,* i.e., *God.*—(g³), veritas speculativa, *the speculative truth or the truth of speculative knowledge.*—(h³), veritas summa, see *veritas perfectissima.* —(i³), veritas vitae, see *veritas doctrinae.*—(j³), veritas vocis, see *veritas actionis.*—On certitudo veritatis, see *certitudo* under 1; on potentia veritates accipiens, see *potentia* under 2.—Kinds of *veritas* in this (2) sense are: (a), veritas demonstrativa, *the demonstrable truth.*—(b), veritas fidei seu fidei Christianae seu supernaturalis and veritas rationis, *the truth of the Christian faith or the supernatural truth,* and *the rational truth.*—(c), veritas intellegibilis, *the intelligible truth.* Cf. *intellegibilis,* under 1.—(d) veritas prima, *the first truth,* i.e., *the truth first known by us.*—(e), veritas primorum principiorum, *the truth consisting of the first principles* of knowledge.—(f), veritas rationis, see *veritas fidei.*—(g), veritas supernaturalis, see *veritas fidei.* On communicabile secundum rei veritatem, see *communicabilis;* on felicitas secundum veritatem, see *felicitas;* on incommunicabile secundum rei veritatem, see *incommunicabilis.* —Kinds of *veritas* in the sense of reality are: veritas aeternitatis and veritas gratiae, *the reality of eternity* and *that of grace.*

vermiculus, i, *m. dim.,* in the Vulgate, *the scarlet worm,* for coccum (*scarlet color*).

vermis, is, *m., a worm,* used lit., and fig.

vernaculus, a, um, *adj., born in slavery.*

vernalis, e, *adj., of or belonging to spring, vernal.*

vero, *adv.,* see *verus.*

versatilis, e, *adj., that turns or moves around, revolving, movable.*

versiculus, i, *m.,* dim., *a little line, a mere line.*

versio, onis, *f., a turning;* bona versio, *a happy turn.*

versor, ari, atus, 1, *v. n.,* prop. *to move about in a place,* i.e., to *dwell, live, remain, stay,* be in a place or among certain persons, used with *inter,* (2) *in partic., to occupy or busy one's self* with any action, *to be engaged* in any thing, used with *circa, in,* (3), *to*

be, to be circumstanced or situated.

versus, us, *m.,* in partic., *a line of writing;* and *in poetry, a verse.*

versus, *adv.* and *prep.,* see *verto.*

vertex, icis, *m.,* (1) lit., *the top or crown of the head,* (2) fig., *the highest source, uttermost, greatest.*

vertibilis, e, *adj., vertible, capable of turning or being turned; changing, inconstant, mutable.*

vertibilitas, atis, *f., changeableness, inconstancy.*

verto, ere, ti, sum, 3, *v. a.* and *n.,* (1) lit., *to turn round or about,* (2) in partic., (a) *to change or turn* into something else, (b) of literary productions, *to turn into another language, to translate.* (3) fig., (a) *to turn,* (b) impers, vertitur in quaestionem, *a question is moved,* (c), *to refer, ascribe.*—versus, *adv., turned in the direction of, towards a thing,* (1) after *acc.,* (2) after *adv.*

verum, *adv.,* see *verus.*

verumtamen, *conj., but yet, notwithstanding, however, nevertheless.*

verus, a, um, *adj.,* (1) *true, real,* the opposite of *falsus, apparens,* and *similitudinarius,* often used as a substantive, verum, i, *n., the truth,* the opposite of *falsum,* (2) *genuine, truth-loving, frank, honest.* On aestimatio vera, see *aestimatio;* on animal verum, see *animal* under 2; on apprehensio vera, see *apprehensio* under 2; on bonitas vera, see *bonitas* under 1; on **bonum verum**, see *bonus* under 3; on **caro vera**, see *caro* under 1; on **claritas vera**, see *claritas* under 3; on **conclusio vera**, see *conclusio* under 2; on **corpus verum**, see *corpus;* on **definitio vera**, see *definitio* under 2; on **delectatio vera**, see *delectatio;* on **demonstratio vera**, see *demonstratio* under 3; on **differentia vera**, see *differentia;* on **divitiae verae**, see *divitiae;* on **ecclesia vera**, see *ecclesia* under 1; on **existimatio vera**, see *existimatio;* on **fortitudo vera**, see *fortitudo* under 3; on **gloria vera**, see *gloria* under 1; on **homo verus**, see *homo;* on **intellectus verus**, see *intellectus* under 8; on **iudicium verum**, see *iudicium* under 3; on **iustitia vera**, see *iustitia* under 1; on **iustum verum**, see *iustus;* on **libertas vera**, see *libertas* under 1; on **locutio vera**, see *locutio* under 2; on **malum verum**, see *malus* under 3; on **matrimonium verum**, see *matrimonium;* on **miraculum verum**, see *miraculum* under 1; on **mixtio vera**, see *mixtio;* on **opinio vera**, see *opinio;* on **opus verum**, see *opus* under 1; on **oratio vera**, see *oratio* under 2; on **pax vera**, see *pax;* on **praedicatio vera**, see *praedicatio* under 2; on **principium verum**, see *principium;* on **privatio vera**, see *privatio* under 2; on **prophetia vera**, see *prophetia;* on **propositio vera**, see *propositio* under 2; on **prudentia vera**, see *prudentia* under 1; on

res vera, see *res;* on **resurrectio vera**, see *resurrectio;* on **scientia vera**, see *scientia* under 1; on **similitudo vera**, see *similitudo* under 2; on **solutio vera**, see *solutio* under 2; on **species vera**, see *species* under 8; on **syllogismus verus**, see *syllogismus;* on **tempus verum**, see *tempus;* on **unitas vera**, see *unitas;* on **virtus vera**, see *virtus* under 5; on **vox vera**, see *vox* under 2.—Kinds of *verum* in this (1) sense are: (a), **verum absolute seu absolutum seu simpliciter** and **verum ex suppositione**, *the unconditioned or simple or absolute truth*, and *the conditioned truth.*—(b), **verum a contingenti seu contingens seu non necessarium** and **verum ex necessitate seu necessarium**, *the unnecessarily true* and *the necessarily true.*—(c), **verum actu** and **verum secundum potentiam**, *the true in reality* and *that according to potentiality.*—(d), **verum commune** and **verum particulare**, *the common truth* and *the particular truth* or *the truth in general* and *the truth in particular.*—(e), **verum contemplabile**, *the true which can be made the object of contemplation.*—(f), **verum contingens**, see *verum a contingenti.* —(g), **verum effective** and **verum essentialiter**, *the true according to its effect* and *that according to its essence.*—(h), **verum enuntiabile seu in enuntiatione**, **verum intellectus seu in intellectu seu in mente** and **verum in re seu in**

rebus, *the true in a sentence spoken with audible words, the true in the thought of the intellect, the true in a thing or in things.*—(i), **verum ex necessitate**, see *verum a contingenti.*—(j), **verum ex suppositione**, see *verum absolute.*—(k), **verum formaliter** and **verum materialiter**, *the formally* and *the materially true* or *the true according to essence* and *that according to matter.*—(l), **verum in causa, verum in signo**, and **verum in subiecto**, *the true in its cause, that in its signification*, and *that in its subject.*—(m), **verum in compositione** and **verum in divisione**, *the true in an affirmation of a statement* and *that in a negation.*—(n), **verum in compositis** and **verum in simplicibus**, *the true in that composed through the thought of reason* or *in opinion* and *the true in the simple or in representations* (not expressed by another) *of reason.* —(o), **verum in divisione**, see *verum in compositione.*—(p), **verum in enuntiatione**, see *verum enuntiabile.*—(q), **verum in intellectu**, see *verum enuntiabile.*—(r), **verum in mente**, see *verum enuntiabile.*—(s), **verum in re seu in rebus**, see *verum enuntiabile.*—(t), **verum in signo**, see *verum in causa.*—(u), **verum in simplicibus**, see *verum in compositis.*—(v), **verum in subiecto**, see *verum in causa.*—(w), **verum intellectus**, see *verum enuntiabile.*—(x), **verum intellectus practici** and **verum intellectus speculativi**, *the true of the practical* and *that of the speculative or theoretical reason.*—(y), **verum intellectus speculativi**, see *verum intellectus practici.*—(z), **verum maxime**, *that which is mostly true, the truest.* —(a^2), **verum necessarium**, see *verum a contingenti.*—(b^2), **verum non necessarium**, see *verum a contingenti.*—(c^2), **verum particulare**, see *verum commune.*— (d^2), **verum per accidens** and **verum per se seu secundum se**, *the accidentally true or true through an accident* and *true according to itself.*—(e^2), **verum per alia notum** and **verbum per se notum**, *the true known through something else*, and *that known through itself.*—(f^2), **verum per participationem**, *the true after the manner of participation or the true by participation*, which is the opposite of *verum per essentiam*, i.e., *the essentially true.*—(g^2), **verum per se**, see *verum per accidens.*—(h^2), **verum per se notum**, see *verum per alia notum.*—(i^2), **verum secundum potentiam**, see *verum actu.*—(j^2), **verum secundum se**, see *verum per accidens.*—(k^2). **verum simpliciter**, see *verum absolute.*—(l^2), **verum universaliter**, *the universally true.*—(m^2), **verum veritate naturalis speciei**, and **verum veritate significationis**, *the true through the truth of a natural species* and *the true through the truth of signification.* Cf. *veritas naturalis speciei* and *veritas significationis*, under *ve- ritas* under 1.—(n²), **verum veri- tate significationis**, see *verum veritate naturalis speciei*.—**ens et verum convertuntur**, see *conver- tere* under 1.—**esse et verum con- vertuntur**, see *convertere* under 1.—**nihil est adeo verum, quin voce possit negari, . . . , quaedam autem adeo vera sunt, quod eo- rum opposita intellectu capi non possunt**, *nothing is so very true that it cannot be denied in words, but somethings are true to the extent that their opposites cannot be conceived.*—**verum et bonum subiecto quidem conver- tuntur, . . . , sed secundum ratio- nem invicem se excedunt**, see *bo- nus* under 1.—**verum**, *adv., truly, just so, certainly*; in the con- struction **non modo** (**solum, tan- tum**)**, . . . , verum etiam** (**quo- que**), *not only . . . but also.*—**vero**, *adv., in truth, in fact, certainly, truly, to be sure, surely, assured- ly.*—**vere**, *adv., according to truth, truly, really, in fact, prop- erly, rightly.*

vesania, ae, *f., madness, insanity.*

vescor, vesci, *v. dep. n.* and *a., to take food, feed, eat*, used with the *abl.* and *absol.*

vesper, eris, eri, *m.*, (in class. prose mostly *acc. vesperum*, and *abl. vespere* or *adv. vesperi*; the plu- ral is found only in the phrase **in vesperis**, *the evening, even, eve, even-tide.*—**vespere et mane**, *evening* and *morning*, here *vespere* is *indecl.* like *mane.*—

vespere, *abl. adverb., in the eve- ning.*—**in vesperis**, *in the evening.*

vespera, ae, *f., the evening, even- tide.*

vespertilio, onis, *m., a bat.*

vespertinus, a, um, *adj., of* or *belonging to evening* or *even- tide, evening.*—**cognitio vesperti- na**, *evening knowledge*. The ex- pression *morning* and *evening knowledge* is derived from St. Augustine, who interprets the six days wherein God made all things, not as ordinary days measured by the solar circuit, since the sun was not made until on the fourth day, but as one day, namely, the day of angel- ic knowledge as directed to six classes of things. Just as in the ordinary day, morning is the be- ginning and evening the close of day, so their knowledge of the primordial being of things is called *morning knowledge*. But their knowledge of the very be- ing of the thing created, as it stands in its own nature, is termed *evening knowledge*, be- cause the being of things flows from the Word as from a kind of primordial principle, and this flow is terminated in the being which they have in themselves.

vestibulum, i, *n., a vestibule, en- trance-court.*

vestigium, i, *track, trace*, in the proper and the improper sense of the word. On **repraesentatio ves- tigii seu per modum vestigii**, see *repraesentatio;* on **similitudo vestigii,** see *similitudo* under 1.

vestimentum, i, *n., clothing, a garment, vestment.*

vestio, ire, ivi or ii, itum, 4, *v. a., to cover with a garment, to dress, clothe, vest.*—(1) lit., (2) of vegetation, (3) fig., *to clothe.*—**vestitus,** a, um, *P. a., clothed, clad.*

vestis, is, *f.,* (1) lit., *the covering for the body, clothes, clothing, attire, vesture;* in sing. = *vestes;* in plur., *clothing, garments,* (2) transf., *a vestment,* a liturgical garment; any article of the ceremonial attire and insignia worn by officiants and assistants during divine service as appropriate to the rite and indicative of their hierarchial rank.

vestitus, us, *m., clothing, clothes, dress, attire, vesture.*

veteranus, a, um, *adj., old, veteran.*

veterasco, ere, ravi, 3, *v. inch. n., to grow old.*

veteratio, onis, *f., veteration, waxing old.*

veto, are, ui, vetitum, 1, *v. a., to forbid, prohibit* a thing.—**vetitus,** a, um, *P. a., forbidden.*—**vetitum,** i, *n., a veto, a forbidden* or *prohibited thing.*

vetula, ae, *f., a little old woman, witch.*

vetus, eris, *adj.,* (1) *old, worn out,* (2) *old, of long standing,* (3) *old, belonging to times past;* of a remote period, or of an early date in history, (4) *old,* unregenerate human nature, (5) *old, former,* (6) *prior, preceding, former,*

known earlier, designating or distinguishing that one of two or more things of the same kind or periods or stages of the same thing which precedes the other or others in time or occurrence.

vetustas, atis, *f., oldness, old age, age long existence.*

vetustus, a, um, *adj., that has existed for a long time, aged, old.*

vexatio, onis, *f., a grievance, trouble, vexation.*

vexillum, i, *n., a standard, banner, flag,* used lit., and fig.

vexo, are, avi, atum, 1, *v. freq., to injure, damage, molest, annoy, distress, plague, trouble, maltreat, abuse, vex, harass, disquiet, disturb, torment.*—**vexatus,** a, um, *adj., sickly, injured.*

via, ae, *f.,* (1) *way, walk, course,* in the general sense of the word, (2) *way of life, journey to the heavenly fatherhood,* the opposite of *patria,* (3) *method, procedure,* synonym of *modus, processus,* and *ratio.* On **prius in via generationis et temporis,** see *prior* under 1.—Kinds of *via* in this (1) sense are: (a), **via apprehensionis,** *the way of comprehension.*—(b), **via communis seu publica,** *the common or the public way.*—(c), **via corporalis** and **via spiritualis,** *the physical and the spiritual way.*—(d), **via fidei,** and **via rationis,** *the way of* (Christian) *faith and that of reason.*—(e), **via infinitatis,** *the way of infinity.*—(f), **via intellegibilis** and **via sensus,** *the intellectual way and* *the sensible way.*—(g), via iudicii, *the way or course of judgment.*—(h), via meriti and via orationis, *the way of merit and that of prayer.*—(i), via morum and via pedum, *the way of morals and that of feet,* or *the way of the moral life* and *the way to be travelled by foot.*—(j), via naturae, *the way of nature.*—(k), via naturalis cognitionis and via revelationis, *the way of natural cognition and that of knowledge.* —(l), via pedum, see *via morum.* —(m), via persuasiva, *the way of persuasion* or *convincing.*—(n), via publica, see *via communis.*— (o), via regia, *the royal way.*—(p), via rationis, see *via fidei.*—(q), via sensus, see *via intellegibilis.*— (r), via spiritualis, see *via corporalis.*—(s), via revelationis, see *via naturalis cognitionis.* On beatitudo viae, see *beatitudo* under 1; on caritas viae, see *caritas;* on cognitio viae, see *cognitio* under 2; on contemplatio viae, see *contemplatio;* on ecclesia secundum statum, see *ecclesia* under 1; on perfectio viae, see *perfectio* under 3; on status viae, see *status* under 3; on visio viae, see *visio* under 1.—Kinds of *via* in this (3) sense are: (a), via abstractionis, *the method of abstraction.*—(b), via affirmationis, via negationis seu remotionis seu quae est per remotionem, via causalitatis seu quae est per causalitatem and via eminentiae seu quae est per eminentiam, *the method of affirma-*

tion, the method of negation, that of cause, and *that of excellence,* i.e., the method by which something is affirmed by a thing, that by which something is denied by it, that by which something is affirmed by it as its cause, and that by which something is affirmed by it in a form of an endless increase.—(c), via assimilationis, *the method of assimilation.*—(d), via causalitatis, see *via affirmationis.*—(e), via compositionis and via resolutionis, *the method of composition* and *that of solution* or *the synthetic and the analytical methods.* Cf. *via procedendi ad cognitionem veritatis.*—(f), via definitionis and via demonstrationis, *the method of definition and that of demonstration,* which presents something as being necessarily true.—(g), via demonstrationis, see *via definitionis.*—(h), via divisionis and via inductionis, *the method of division* in the formation of a conclusion and *that of induction,* in which the conclusion is drawn *per singularia ad universale.*—(i), via eminentiae, see *via affirmationis.*—(j), via inductionis, see *via divisionis.*—(k), via inquisitionis seu inventionis and via iudicii, *the method of discovery or invention* and *that of judgment or opinion.*—(l), via inventionis, see *via inquisitionis.* —(m), via iudicii, see *via inquisitionis.*—(n), via motus, *the method of motion.*—(o), via negationis,

see *via affirmationis.*—(p), via
procedendi ad cognitionem veri-
tatis, *the method of proceeding
to the knowledge of truth.*—(q),
via quae est per causalitatem, see
via affirmationis.—(r), **via quae
est per eminentiam,** see *via affirmationis.*—(s), **via quae est per
remotionem,** see *via affirmationis.*—(t), **via remotionis,** see *via
affirmationis.*—(u), **via resolutionis,** see *via compositionis.*—(v),
via speculativa, *the method aiming purely at knowledge.*

viaticum, i, *n.,* (1) *viaticum,* Holy
Communion given to those in
danger of death. The word "viaticum" came into Church use as
a translation of the Greek *epho·
dion,* meaning provision for the
journey, and, metaphorically,
provision for the journey of life.
Next the metaphor was extended
to the provision for the last journey, viz. from this world to the
next, and so it occurs as an epithet of Holy Communion given
to the dying, (2) *provision for
the journey.*

viator, oris, *m.,* (1) *a wayfarer,
traveler,* (2) *a traveler on earth,
a pilgrim to the heavenly fatherland,* the opposite of *comprehensor.* On **cognitio viatoris,** see
cognitio under 2; on **gaudium
viatoris,** see *gaudium;* on **gratia
viatoris,** see *gratia* under 2; on
status viatoris, see *status* under 3.

vicarius, ii, *m., a vicar, deputy,
substitute.*

vicesimus, a, um, *adj.,* see *vigesimus.*

vicia, ae, *f., triumph* or *ultimate
success* in any contest, struggle
or enterprise, a synonym of *victoria.*

vicinitas, atis, *f., nearness, proximity, vicinity.*

vicinus, a, um, *adj., nearness,
neighboring, in the neighborhood
or vicinity.*—**vicinum,** i, *n., a
neighboring place, the neighborhood, vicinity.*—**e vicino,** *from
close quarters.*

vicis, (as a *gen.;* the *nom.* does not
occur, *vicem, vice;* in *plur., vices*
(*nom.* and *acc.*) and *vicibus* (*dat.*
and *abl.*), *f.,* (1) in gen., (a) in
particular, *a time, a turn,* (b)
reciprocal behavior or conduct,
i.e., *return, remuneration, retaliation,* (2) transf., *the position,
place, room, stead, post, duty* of
one person or thing as assumed
by another.—**vices comestionum,**
number of meals.—**vice,** *adv.,* (1)
like, (2) *instead of.*

vicissim, *adv., in turn.*

vicissitudo, inis, *f., vicissitude,
change, interchange, alternation.*

victima, ae, *f., a beast for sacrifice,
a sacrifice, victim.*

Victor, oris, *m., Victor (St.), Abbey of St. Victor.* In the year
1108, the famous William of
Champeaux, archdeacon of Notre Dame in Paris who had been
lecturing to crowds of students,
retired to a small hermitage dedicated to Saint Victor, near the
city. Here he was followed by

many of his disciples, Abelard among them, and induced to take up his lectures. Hence the origin of the Royal Abbey and School of Saint Victor. To that celebrated school students from every country came, among them Hugh of St. Victor and Richard of St. Victor.

victor, oris, *m., a conqueror, vanquisher, victor.*

victoria, ae, *f., victory,* the overcoming of an enemy in battle or of an antagonist in any contest; a gaining of superiority in any struggle.

victoriosus, a, um, *adj., conquering, victorious.*

victrix, icis, *f., she that is victorious, a conqueress;* used in the S.T. as an *adj., conquering, victorious.*

victus, us, *m.,* (1) *that upon which one lives; food, sustenance, nourishment, provision, victuals,* (2) *a way of living, mode of living, support.*

vicus, i, *m., a town, a row of houses in town or country.*

videlicet, *adv.,* (1), *it is easy to see, it is clear or evident, in truth, clearly, evidently, manifestly,* (2) transf., as a mere complementary or explanatory particle, *to wit, namely.*

video, ere, vidi, visum, 2, *v. a.,* and *n.,* (1) *to see, perceive* by the eye, (2) *to see, meet and converse with,* (3) *to perceive by mental insight; to form an idea or conception of; to note with the*

mind; to discern, (4) impers. pass., *seem, appear.*

vidua, ae, *f., a widow.*

vidualis, e, *adj., of or belonging to a widow, vidual.* On **castitas vidualis,** see *castitas* under 2; on **continentia vidualis,** see *continentia* under 4; on **status vidualis,** see *status* under 4.

viduitas, atis, *f., widowhood.*

vigeo, ere, 2, *v. n., to thrive, flourish, bloom.*

vigesimus, a, um, ord. num. adj., *the twentieth.*

vigil, ilis, *m., a watchman.*

vigilanter, *adv., watchfully, carefully, vigilantly.*

vigilantia, ae, *f., vigilance, watchfulness.*

Vigilantius, ii, *m., Vigilantius,* a presbyter of Comminges and Barcelona in the end of the fourth and beginning of the fifth century, known by his protests against the superstitious practices then creeping into the Church. He wrote with a certain zeal for religion, but was led astray by the praise of men. He interpreted in a perverse manner the second vision of Daniel, and put forth other works of no value, which must be placed in the catalogue of heretical writings. Jerome wrote the *Contra Vigilantium.* This was a treatise in answer to statements made by Vigilantius.

vigilia, ae, *f.,* (1) in gen., *wakefulness, sleeplessness, a lying awake.* (2) *vigil, a watch* kept in the night before a feast, spent in prayer or other devotions, later *the eve* of any feast.

vigilo, are, avi, atum, 1, *v. n.* and *a.,* (1) lit., *to watch, be awake, to be or continue without sleep, to awake; keep vigil,* (2) in partic., *to keep watch over* a person, (3) *to keep watch, to keep awake* for the purpose of guarding, protecting, attending or the like; *to watch* as a sentinel, (4) *to watch out, to see or attend to* or *take measures* or *precautions.*—**vigilare de sero,** *to sit up late at night.*

viginti, *num. adj., twenty.*

vigor, oris, *m., force, strength, vigor.*

vilesco, ere, 3, *v. inch. n., to become worthless, bad, vile.*

vilis, e, *adj.,* (1) lit., *of small price or value, purchased at a low rate, cheap,* (2) transf., *of trifling value, cheap, poor, paltry, common, mean, base, vile.*—**viliter,** *adv., cheaply.*

vilitas, atis, *f.,* (1) *trifling value of a thing, meanness, baseness, worthlessness, vileness,* (2) *contempt, low esteem.*

villa, ae, *f., dim., a village.*

villicus, i, *m., a steward.*

Vincentius, ii, *m.,* (1) *Vincentius,* one of St. Augustine's friends, to whose letter the Saint replied at length. He was successor of Rogatus at Cartenna. In his reply Augustine defends repression by legal means of Donatists whose conduct is violent and vexatious. —(2), *Vincentius,* Deacon of

Saragossa, suffered death for the Faith under Diocletian in 300 A.D.

vincibilis, e, *adj., vincible, that can be conquered.*

vinco, vincere, vici, victum, 3, *v. a.* and *n.,* (1) lit., *to conquer, overcome, get the better of, defeat, subdue, vanquish,* (2) fig., in gen., *to prevail, be superior, overcome, surpass, outdo.*

vinctus, a, um, *P. a., bound, fettered.*

vinculum, i, *n.,* (1) esp. in the *plur.,* of the *fetters* of prisoners, and hence sometimes to be rendered *prison, chains,* (2) fig., *a bond, fetter, tie, band.*

vindemia, ae, *f., vintage, grape-gathering.*

vindicatio, onis, *f., revenger, an avenging, punishment* of an offence.

vindicativus, a, um, *adj., avenging, punishing, vindictive.* On **iustitia vindicativa,** see *iustitia* under 1; on **iustum vindicativum,** see *iustus.*

vindico, are, avi, atum, 1, *v. a.,* (1) *to lay claim to as one's own, to make a claim upon, to demand, claim, assume, appropriate* a thing, (2) with respect to some wrong perpetrated, *to avenge, revenge, punish; to take vengeance* on any one, (3) transf., (after the analogy of *ulcisci*): **vindicare se ab (de) aliquo,** *to revenge one's self upon one.*

vindicta, ae, *f., revenge, vengeance, punishment.* On **zelus vindictae,**

see *zelus* under 1.—Kinds of *vindicta* are: **vindicta iusta** and **vindicta iniusta,** *the just and the unjust vengeance.*

vinea, ae, *f., a plantation of vines, a vineyard.*

vinolentus, a, um, *adj., full of or drunk with wine, drunk, intoxicated.*

vinum, i, *n., wine.*—**vinum vitis,** *wine of the grape,* the wine used at the Consecration of the Mass.

violatio, onis, *f., an injury, violation.*

violator, oris, *f., a violator, profaner.*

violenter, *adv., in a violent manner, with force, impetuously, vehemently, violently,* the opposite of *naturaliter, per naturam,* and *voluntarie.*

violentia, ae, *f.,* (1) *power, force* in the wider sense of this word, synonym of *coactio* and *vis,* the opposite of *natura naturale,* and *voluntarium,* (2) *violence, outrage.* On **continuum per violentiam,** see *continuus* under 2; on **involuntarium per violentiam,** see *involuntarius;* on **movere per violentiam,** see *movere;* on **necessitas violentiae,** see *necessitas* under 1. Kinds of *violentia* in this sense are: **violentia absoluta** and **violentia voluntario mixta,** *the unconditioned or simple,* i.e., the physical force and *that mixed with something voluntary,* i.e., the moral force. *Violentia* in this (2) sense is a *filia* of *avaritia.* Cf. *avaritia.*

violentus, a, um, *adj., forceful, impetuous, forced* in the wider and narrower sense of the word, synonym of *coactus* and *involuntarius,* the opposite of *naturalis* and *voluntarius.*—**violentum est cuius principium est extra, nihil conferente vim passo,** the translation of the Aristotelian passage: *biaion de hou he arche exothen, toiaute ousa en he meden symballetai ho pratton e ho paschon.* On **causa violenta,** see *causa* under 2; on **corruptio violenta,** see *corruptio* under 2; on **generatio violenta,** see *generatio* under 1; on **habitudo violenta,** see *habitudo;* on **mors violenta,** see *mors;* on **motus violentus,** see *motus* under 1; on **mutatio violenta,** see *mutatio;* on **operatio violenta,** see *operatio* under 2; on **passio violenta,** see *passio* under 4; on **quies violenta,** see *quies;* on **suspicio violenta,** see *suspicio* under 2.—Kinds of *violentum* in the broader sense of the word are: **violentum absolute seu simpliciter** and **violentum secundum quid seu mixtum,** *the absolutely or simply,* i.e., *the physically forced* and *the forced in a certain respect* or, *the forced in a mixed manner,* i.e., the morally forced.

violo, àre, avi, atum, 1, *v. a., to treat with violence, to injure, dishonor, outrage, violate,* (1) lit., (a) with persons and (b) things as object, (2) with abstract objects, *to violate, outrage, break,* *injure.—*violare sabbatum, *to break the sabbath.*

vipereus, a, um, *adj., of a viper, poisonous.*

vir, viri, (gen., plur., *virum*), *m.,* (1) *a male person, a man,* (2) *a man* as related to a woman, *a husband.*

virens, entis, P. a., *fresh, green, verdant.*

viresco, ere, 3, *v. inch. n., to become green or verdant, to grow.*

virga, ae, *f.,* (1) *a rod, the rod* of Moses, of Aaron, (2) *a switch for flogging.—*virga pastoris, *a pastor's rod.*

Virgilius, ii, *m.,* P. *Virgilius Maro,* a celebrated Roman poet, born on October 15, 70 B.C. in the township of Andes, near Mantua, north of the Po. His outstanding works were the *Eclogues, Georgics,* and the famous epic, the *Aeneid.* In 19 B.C. having worked out a draft of the whole Aeneid the poet set out for Greece intending to spend three years in polishing the poem. On his return from Athens he fell ill of a fever and died a few days after reaching Brundisium, September 21, 19 B.C.

virginalis, e, *adj., of or belonging to a maiden or virgin, maidenly, virgin, virginal.* On castitas virginalis, see *castitas* under 2; on continentia virginalis, see *continentia* under 4; on integritas virginalis, see *integritas;* on puritas virginalis, see *puritas;* on status virginalis, see *status* under 4.

virgineus, a, um, *adj., of or belonging to a maiden or virgin, virginal.*

virginitas, atis, *f., maidenhood, virginity,* the opposite of *commixtio virilis,* (cf. Pot. 1. 3 ad 6 c). On consilium virginitatis seu de virginitate, see *consilium* under 2; on votum virginitatis, see *votum* under 1.

virgo, inis, *f., a maid, maiden, virgin.* On spiritualis virginum, see *spiritualis* under 3.—Virgo beata seu gloriosa seu virginum, *the Blessed or Glorified Virgin per eminentiam* or *the Virgin of all virgins,* i.e., the Virgin Mary.

virgultum, i, *n., a bush, thicket, plant, shrubbery.*

viridis, e, *adj., green.*

viriditas, atis, *f., green color, greenness, verdure.*

virilis, e, *adj.,* (1) *of or belonging to a man, manly, virile, having the nature, properties or qualities of an adult man,* (2) with respect to sex, *male, masculine,* (3) with respect to strength, vigor, age, etc., *manly,* (4) of attire, *male,* (5) of the virtues, mind, *manly, virile.—*(6), Deus virilis, *God-man like.*

virilitas, atis, *f., manliness, manly vigor.*

viror, oris, *m., green color, greenness, verdure.*

virtualis, e, *adj.,* (1) *pertaining to the power of a thing, coming from it,* synonym of *potentialis,* (2) *being according to the power or the might or the potentiali-*

ty, the opposite of *actualis* and *habitualis,* synonym of *potentialis,* (3) *virtuous,* synonym of *virtuosus,* the opposite of *vitiosus.* On cóntactus virtualis, see *contactus;* on quantitas virtualis, see *quantitas* under 2; on tactus virtualis, see *tactus* under 1. On operatio virtualis, see *operatio* under 2.—virtualiter, *adv., according to power or might or potentiality,* synonym of *potentialiter,* the opposite of *actualiter* and *habitualiter.* On infinitum virtualiter, see *infinitus.*

virtualiter, see *virtualis.*

virtuose, *adv.,* see *virtuosus.*

virtuosus, a, um, *adj.,* (1) *powerful, strong,* (2) *virtuous, good,* synonym of *virtualis,* the opposite of *vitiosus.* On resurrectio virtuosa, see *resurrectio.* On actus virtuosus, see *actus* under 1; on conversatio virtuosa, see *conversatio* under 2; on habitus virtuosus, see *habitus* under 4; on ira virtuosa, see *ira* under 1; on opus virtuosum, see *opus* under 4.—virtuose, *adv., virtuously.*

virtus, utis, *f.,* (1) *power, faculty, aptitude* or *capacity,* the proximate principle of an activity, synonym of *potentia, potestas,* and *vis,* (2) *personified power,* i.e., power in the sense of a personal being, (3) *power, might, potentiality* in a being, synonym of *potentia* and *potestas,* the opposite of *actus,* and *habitus,* (4) *ability, virtue,* synonym of *bonitas* and *perfectio,* (5) *the virtue*

of man in the sense of a *habitus,* the opposite of *malitia* and *vitium,* (6) *power, strength, might,* synonym of *fortitudo, potentia,* and *vis,* (7) *the highest feat of strength, the highest accomplishment,* synonym of *fortitudo* and *potentia,* (8) *a wonderful feat of strength, wonder,* synonym of *miraculum,* (9) *sense, meaning,* synonym of *intellectus, ratio, sensus, significatio,* and *vis.* On contactus virtutis, see *contactus;* on defectus virtutis, see *defectus* under 2; on magnitudo virtutis, see *magnitudo* under 3; on motus virtutis, imperantis et imperatae, see *motus* under 2; on quantitas virtutis, see *quantitas* under 2; on tactus virtutis, see *tactus* under 1; on totalitas virtutis seu secundum virtutem, see *totalitas;* on unitas virtutis, see *unitas;* on unum virtutis, see *unus;* on vitium virtutis, see *vitium* under 1.— Kinds of *virtus* in this (1) sense are: (a), virtus absolute, *absolute power or power taken by itself;* (b), virtus activa and virtus passiva, *the power to produce something and the power to suffer something.* Cf. *potentia activa et passiva under potentia* under 1.— (c), virtus adiuncta, *the added power.*—(d), virtus aestimativa and virtus cogitativa, *the faculty of judgment through the senses* of animal and of men.—(e), virtus affectiva seu appetitiva and virtus apprehensiva, *the appetitive power* and *the comprehensive*

power. Cf. *virtus cognitiva.*—(f),
virtus aliena and **virtus propria**,
strange and proper power. Cf.
vitus propria under 4.—(g), **virtus
animae** and **virtus corporis**, *the
power of the soul* and *that of the
body.*—(h), **virtus animalis** and
virtus naturalis, *the sensitive* and
the (rough) natural power. Cf.
virtus gratuita et naturalis.—(i),
virtus appetitiva, see *virtus affectiva.*—(j), **virtus apprehensiva**,
see *virtus affectiva.*—(k), **virtus
apprehensiva deforis** and **virtus
apprehensiva deintus**, *the power
perceiving from without* and *that
perceiving from within.*—(l), **virtus apprehensiva deintus**, see
virtus apprehensiva deforis.—(m),
virtus attractiva and **virtus repulsiva**, *the power of attraction* and
that of repulsion.—(n), **virtus augmentativa**, **virtus nutritiva**, and
virtus generativa, *the power of
increase, that of growth or nourishing*, and *that of production or
generating.*—(o), **virtus caelestis
seu corporis caelestis seu caeli**
and **virtus corporum inferiorum**,
*the heavenly power or the pow-
er of a heavenly body* and *that
of the lower or sublunary body.*—
(p), **virtus caeli**, see *virtus caelestis.*—(q), **virtus clavium**, *the
power of the keys of the Church.*
—(r), **virtus cogitativa**, see *virtus
aestimativa.*—(s), **virtus cognitiva
seu cognoscitiva** and **virtus operativa**, *the cognitive power* and
the effective or creative power.—
(t), **virtus collativa**, *the power of*

comparison by which is understood not only reason but also the
sensible faculty of evaluation.—
(u), **virtus communis seu universalis** and **virtus particularis seu
particulata seu propria seu contracta seu determinata**, *the general and the particular or the re-
tricted power.*—(v), **virtus completa** and **virtus incompleta seu
imperfecta**, *the complete* and *the
incomplete or imperfect power.*—
(w), **virtus concretiva seu unitiva**,
the coalescing or uniting power.
—(x), **virtus consecrativa**, *the consecrating power.*—(y), **virtus contracta**, see *virtus communis.*—(z),
virtus conversiva, *the converting
power.*—(a²), **virtus corporalis seu
corporea** and **virtus incorporea
seu spiritualis**, *the corporeal and
the incorporeal or spiritual power.*—(b²), **virtus corpore utens seu
organo utens seu organi corporei
seu organo affixa** and **virtus organo corporeo non utens**, *the power making use of a body or of a
bodily organ for its action* and
*the power not making use of
such.*—(c²), **virtus corporea**, see
virtus corporalis.—(d²), **virtus corporis**, see *virtus animae.*—(e²),
virtus corporis caelestis, see *virtus caelestis.*—(f²), **virtus corporum inferiorum**, see *virtus caelestis.*—(g²), **virtus corruptibilis** and
virtus incorruptibilis, *the corruptible and the incorruptible power.*
—(h²), **virtus creata seu creaturae**
and **virtus increata seu Dei seu
divina**, *the created and the un-*

created or divine power or the power of the creature and that of the Creator or God.—(i^2), **virtus creativa** and **virtus productiva,** *the creative power or the power that brings something forth out of nothing* and *the power that brings something forth from something else.*—(j^2), **virtus creaturae,** see *virtus creata.*—(k^2), **virtus defectiva seu deficiens** and **virtus effectiva,** *the defective power or that deficient in its effect* and *the power producing its full effects.*—(l^2), **virtus Dei,** see *virtus creata.*—(m^2), **virtus determinata,** see *virtus communis.*—(n^2), **virtus diffusiva,** *the diffusive or spreading power.*—(o^2), **virtus divina,** see *virtus creata.*—(p^2), **virtus effectiva,** see *virtus defectiva.*—(q^2), **virtus elementaris seu elementi,** *the elemental power or the power of an element of nature.*—(r^2), **virtus elementi,** see *virtus elementaris.*—(s^2), **virtus excellentiae,** *the power of excellence or the excellent power.*—(t^2), **virtus expulsiva,** *the expulsive power.*—(u^2), **virtus exsecutiva seu exsequens seu imperata** and **virtus imperativa seu imperans,** *the power executing something* and *that demanding something.*—(v^2), **virtus finita** and **virtus infinita,** *the finite and the infinite power.*—(w^2), **virtus formativa seu seminativa,** *the formative or generative power.*—(x^2), **virtus generativa,** see *virtus augmentativa.*—(y^2), **virtus germina-** tiva, *the power of germination or germinal power.*—(z^2), **virtus gratuita seu infusa** and **virtus naturalis,** *the power bestowed or infused by grace and the natural power or that existing from nature.* Cf. *virtus gratuita seu infusa* under 5; *virtus animalis et naturalis.*—(a^3), **virtus gressiva,** *the hierarchical power or that belonging to the hierarchy.*—(b^3), **virtus illuminativa,** *the illuminating power in the proper and in the figurative senses of the word.* (c^3), **virtus imaginaria seu imaginativa,** *the power of imagination.*—(d^3), **virtus immaterialis** and **virtus materialis,** *the immaterial or incorporeal and the material or corporeal power.* Cf. *virtus corporalis.*—(e^3), **virtus imperans seu imperativa,** see *virtus exsecutiva.*—(f^3), **virtus imperata,** see *virtus exsecutiva.*—(g^3), **virtus imperfecta,** see *virtus completa.*—(h^3), **virtus incompleta,** see *virtus completa.*—(i^3), **virtus incorporea,** see *virtus corporalis.*—(j^3), **virtus incorruptibilis,** see *virtus corruptibilis.*—(k^3), **virtus increata,** see *virtus creata.*—(l^3), **virtus inferior** and **virtus superior,** *the inferior and the superior power.*—(m^3), **virtus infinita,** see *virtus finita.*—(n^3), **virtus infusa,** see *virtus gratuita.*—(o^3), **virtus inquisitiva, virtus interpretativa,** and **virtus manifestativa,** *the investigating, the interpretative,* and *the manifesting power,* or *the power of investigation, that of interpreting* or *of the spoken expression of thought,* and *that of making known.*—(p³), **virtus instrumentalis** and **virtus principalis agentis,** *the power of the instrument and that of the main cause.*—(q³), **virtus intellectiva seu intellectualis seu intellegibilis,** and **virtus sensitiva seu sensualis,** *the intellectually cognitive* and *the sensibly perceptive power.*—(r³), **virtus intellectualis,** see *virtus intellectiva.*—(s³), **virtus intellegibilis,** see *virtus intellectiva.*—(t³), **virtus intentionalis** and **virtus quiescens in aliquo** (Unio 5 ad 12), *the imitative power or the power after the manner of a copy which has gone over to something else,* and *the power that remains in a thing.*—(u³), **virtus interpretativa,** see *virtus inquisitiva.*—(v³), **virtus intranea,** *the inner power.*—(w³), **virtus locativa,** *the power that makes local or spacious,* i.e., the faculty that brings about that something is in a place or in a space.—(x³), **virtus manifestativa,** see *virtus inquisitiva.*—(y³), **virtus materialis,** see *virtus immaterialis.*—(z³), **virtus memorativa seu rememorativa,** *the power of remembrance.*—(a⁴), **virtus motiva,** *the moving power* by which is understood not only the power moving locally but also any other kind of moving power, e.g., the will.—(b⁴), **virtus multiplicata** and **virtus unita,** *the multiplied and the united power or the power presenting something manifold*

in itself or that presenting something simple in itself.—(c⁴), **virtus naturalis,** see *virtus animalis* and *virtus gratuita.*—(d⁴), **virtus naturalis** and **virtus supernaturalis,** *the natural* (cf. *virtus animalis* and *virtus gratuita*) and the *supernatural power* or the power which is according to the nature of a thing and that which surpasses it.—(e⁴), **virtus nutritiva,** see *virtus augmentativa.*—(f⁴), **virtus operativa,** i.e., the active power or the power for an action by which is understood both a producing and an effecting in contrast to a knowing and an action in general.—(g⁴), **virtus organi corporei,** see *virtus corpore utens.*—(h⁴), **virtus organo affixa,** see *virtus corpore utens.*—(i⁴), **virtus organo utens et organo corporeo non utens,** see *virtus corpore utens.*—(j⁴), **virtus participata** and **virtus pura seu subsistens,** *the participated or shared power* and *pure power or the power existing for itself as such.*—(k⁴), **virtus particularis,** see *virtus communis.*—(l⁴), **virtus particulata,** see *virtus communis.*—(m⁴), **virtus passiva,** see *virtus activa.*—(n⁴), **virtus principalis,** see *virtus instrumentalis.*—(o⁴), **virtus productiva,** see *virtus creativa.*—(p⁴), **virtus propria,** see *virtus aliena et communis.*—(q⁴), **virtus pura,** see *virtus participata.*—(r⁴), **virtus quiescens in aliquo,** see *virtus intentionalis.*—(s⁴), **virtus rationalis,** *the power belonging to the ra-*

tional power of the soul.—(t⁴), virtus regitiva, *the governing or the ruling power.*—(u⁴), virtus rememorativa, see *virtus memorativa.*—(v⁴), virtus repulsiva, see *virtus attractiva.*—(w⁴), virtus resuscitandi seu resuscitativa, *the power of awakening or of resuscitation.*—(x⁴), virtus sacramentalis seu sacramentaria, *the sacramental power.*—(y⁴), virtus seminativa, see *virtus formativa.*—(z⁴), virtus sensitiva, see *virtus intellectiva.*—(a⁵), virtus sensualis, see *virtus · intellectiva.*—(b⁵), virtus solaris, *the power of the sun.*—(c⁵), virtus speciei, *the power of the species,* i.e., the power which belongs to a thing according to its species.—(d⁵), virtus spirandi seu spiritiva, *the power of breathing.*—(e⁵), virtus spiritualis, see · *virtus corporalis.*—(f⁵), virtus subsistens, see *virtus participata.*—(g⁵), virtus superior, see *virtus inferior.*—(h⁵), virtus supernaturalis, see *virtus naturalis.*—(i⁵), virtus unita, see *virtus multiplicata.*—(j⁵), virtus unitiva, see *virtus concretiva.*—(k⁵), virtus universalis, see *virtus communis.*—(l⁵), virtus visiva, *the power of sight,* spiritual as well as corporeal.—(m⁵), virtus vitalis, *the power of life.*—nulla virtus activa agit ultra suum genus, or nulla virtus activa se extendit ad ea, quae sunt supra speciem et naturam agentis, *no active or creative power is active above its genus or above the species and essence*

of its subject. nulla virtus datur alicui rei frustra, *no power is given to anything in vain.* nulla virtus finita extendi se in infinitum, *no power extends itself with its activity into the infinite.* nullius causae naturalis intentio se extendit ultra virtutem eius, *in no cause of nature does the striving go beyond its power,* esset enim frustra.—omnis virtus, quanto est fortior, tanto est magis unita, see *unire.*—omnis virtus, quanto est universalior, tanto est potentior, *the more universal a power is, the greater it is.*—omnis virtus, quanto magis est a corpore separata, tanto est fortior in operationibus suis, *the more a power is separated from or independent of the body, the stronger it is in its activity.* omnis virtus una operatione vel uno actu fertur in obiectum et in rationalem formalem obiecti, *every power aims with one and the same action at its object and at the formal relationship according to which it is its object.* omnis virtus unita plus est infinita quam multiplicata, see *unire.* quanto aliqua virtus activa est fortior, tanto in remotiora suam actionem extendit, *the stronger a producing or effecting power is, the farther it reaches with its actions.* quanto aliqua virtus est altior, tanto ad plura se extendit, *the higher a power stands according to its essence or its rank, the more objects does it extend itself over.* quanto aliqua virtus est magis unita, tanto est magis infinita et ad plura se potest ex tendere, see *unire.* quanto virtus est superior, tanto est magis unita, see *unire.* tanto maior virtus requiritur in agente, quanto potentia est magis remota ab actu, *the greater a power must be for the production of a thing, the farther must it be from the exercise of its activity in relation to the effect.* unaquaeque virtus tanto excellentior est, quanto ad altius bonum ordinatur, *a power is the more excellent, the higher its object.* virtus facientis non solum consideratur ex substantia facti, sed etiam ex modo faciendi, *the power of an activity is not known merely from the substance of what is produced but from the species and the manner of the producing.* virtus, quanto est magis unita, tanto est fortior, see *unire.* virtus quanto est superior, tanto magis colligitur et unitur, e contrario vero virtus inferior dividitur et multiplicatur, *the higher a power is according to its rank and essence, the more it is collected and unified in itself and in its action,* and *vice versa a lower power is divided and diversified in itself and in its action.* virtus rei demonstrat substantiam eius, *the power of a thing demonstrates its substance and essence.* virtus sequitur naturam rei, *the power of a thing is directed according to its nature and essence.*—Kinds of *virtus* in

this (4) sense are: (a), virtus divina and virtus humana seu hominis, *the divine and the human virtue.*—(b), virtus exemplaris and virtus exemplata, *the exemplary and the exemplified virtue, or the virtue as it is in God and as it is in man.*—(c), virtus exemplata, see *virtus exemplaris.*—(d), virtus hominis, see *virtus divina.*—(e), virtus humana, see *virtus divina.*—(f), virtus propria, *the proper or special virtue.* On the relationship between *virtus* and *fructus,* see *fructus* under 2. On altitudo virtutis, see *altitudo;* on bonum virtutis, see *bonus* under 2 and 3; on complementum virtutis, see *complementum;* on forma virtutis, see *forma* under 2; on gratia virtutis, see *gratia* under 2; on habitus virtutis, see *habitus* under 4; on imperfectio virtutis, see *imperfectio;* on inchoatio virtutis, see *inchoatio* under 1; on perfectio virtutis, see *perfectio* under 2; on status virtutis, see *status* under 3.—actus virtutis, *an act of virtue.*—modus virtutis, *the art and manner in which a virtue is active.*—obiectum virtutis, *the object of a virtue.*—pars virtutis, *part of virtue.*—Kinds of *virtus* in this (5) sense are: (a), virtus activa and virtus contemplativa seu speculativa, *the active and the contemplative or speculative virtue,* i.e., *virtue in acting and doing* and *virtue in knowing and comprehending.*—(b), virtus adiuncta seu secundaria and virtus principalis, *the virtue added* (to another virtue) *or subjected* (to it) and *the main or principal virtue.*—(c), virtus adquisita and virtus gratuita seu infusa, *the virtue acquired* (through practice) and *the virtue bestowed by grace or infused* (by God).—(d), virtus animosa, *the virtue of courage.*—(e), virtus architectonica seu imperans seu praecipiens seu praeceptiva and virtus ministrans seu eliciens seu exsecutiva, *the architectonic or ruling or prescribing virtue and the serving or eliciting* (a commanded action from itself) *or executing virtue.*—(f), virtus bene consiliativa seu consiliativa and virtus bene iudicativa, *the virtue of giving good advice and the virtue of forming good judgment.*—(g), virtus bene iudicativa, see *virtus bene consiliativa.*—(h), virtus cardinalis, *the cardinal virtue.*—(i), virtus civilis seu politica, virtus purgatoria and virtus purgati animi, *the civic or political virtue, that purifying the heart and the virtue of the purified heart.*—(j), virtus communis seu generalis and virtus determinata seu particularis seu specialis, *the general and the restricted or particular virtue.*—(k), virtus communis seu humana seu simpliciter and virtus heroica seu superhumana seu divina, *the common or usual or (purely) human or simply so-called and the heroic or superhuman or divine virtue.*—(l), virtus

completa seu perfecta and virtus inchoata seu imperfecta seu deficiens, *the complete or perfect virute* and *virtue at its beginning or imperfect or deficient virtue.*—(m), virtus consiliativa, see *virtus bene consiliativa.*—(n), virtus contemplativa, see *virtus activa.*—(o), virtus deficiens, see *virtus completa.*—(p), virtus determinata, see *virtus communis.*—(q), virtus divina, see *virtus communis* and *virtus intellectiva.*—(r), virtus eliciens, see *virtus architectonica.*—(s), virtus exsecutiva, see *virtus architectonica.*—(t), virtus generalis, see *virtus communis.*—(u), virtus gratuita, see *virtus adquisita.*—(v), virtus heroica, see *virtus communis.*—(w), virtus humana, see *virtus communis.*—(x), virtus imperans, see *virtus architectonica.*—(y), virtus imperfecta, see *virtus completa.*—(z), virtus inchoata, see *virtus completa.*—(a^2), virtus informis, *the unformed virtue or that not penetrated by love.*—(b^2), virtus infusa, see *virtus adquisita.*—(c^2), virtus intellectiva seu intellectualis, virtus moralis and virtus theologica seu divina, *the virtue of reason, the moral virtue,* and *the theological or divine virtue.*—(d^2), virtus ministrans, see *virtus architectonica.*—(e^2), virtus moralis, see *virtus intellectiva.*—(f^2), virtus motiva, *the virtue stimulating another to action,* cf. *virtus architectonica.*—(g^2), virtus particularis, see *virtus communis.*—(h^2), virtus perfecta, see *virtus completa.*—(i²), virtus perfecta in comparatione ad alterum and virtus perfecta simpliciter, *the virtue in comparison with something or the respective virtue and the simple or absolutely perfect virtue.*—(j²), virtus perfecta simpliciter, see *virtus perfecta in comparatione ad alterum.*—(k²), virtus politica, see *virtus civilis.*—(l²), virtus praecipiens seu praeceptiva, see *virtus architectonica.*—(m²), virtus principalis, see *virtus adiuncta.*—n²), virtus purgati animi, see *virtus civilis.*—(o²), virtus purgatoria, see *virtus civilis.*—(p²), virtus secundaria, see *virtus adiuncta.*—(q²), virtus secundum quid and virtus simpliciter seu simpliciter dicta, *the respective virtue or that in a certain respect and the simple or absolute virtue so called.*—(r²), virtus simpliciter, see *virtus communis et secundum quid.*—(s²), virtus simpliciter dicta, see *virtus secundum quid.*—(t²), virtus specialis, see *virtus communis.*—(u²), virtus spiritualis, *the spiritual virtue.*—(v²), virtus superhumana, see *virtus communis.*—(w²), virtus theologica, see *virtus intellectiva.*—(x²), virtus vera, *the true or genuine virtue.* —virtus in medio seu in mediocritate consistit, *virtue consists of a medium or in adhering to a middle course,* namely, the middle course between faults such as excess and want.—virtus in ratione est, see *ratio* under 1.—virtus

moralis est habitus electivus in medietate consistens seu exsistens, ut sapiens determinabit, the translation of the Aristotelian passage: *estin ara he arete hexis proairetike, en mesoteti ousa, . . ., hos an ho phronimos horiseien, moral virtue consists of a selecting habitus or the habitus of selection which rests in the middle as the wise man determines it,* i.e., a habitus of selecting which holds the middle course between two faults, according to the view of the wise man. virtus moralis est quaedam medietas et est medii coniectatrix, the translation of the Aristotelian passage: *mesotes tis ara he arete, stochastiche ge ousa tou mesou, moral virtue is a kind of middle,* i.e., the middle between two faults, and *also aims at the middle,* inquantum scilicet respicit medium et medium operatur. virtus moralis in medio consistit quoad nos determinato ratione, the translation of the Aristotelian passage: *estin ara he arete hexis proairetike, en mesoteti ousa te pros hemas, horismene logo, moral virtue consists in the middle with reference to us, as it is determined by the reason,* i.e., in a habitus of choice of that which according to the decision of our reason holds the middle course with reference to us between two opposite faults.—Kinds of *virtus* in this (6) senes are: (a), virtus affirmationis and virtus negationis, the power of affirmation and th*at* of negation.—(b), **virtus coactiva**, *the coercive power.*—(c), **virtus conclusionis seu inferendi**, *the power of conclusion or inference.* —(d), **virtus fomitis**, *the power of evil desire.*—(e), **virtus inferendi**, see *virtus conclusionis.*—(f), **virtus negationis**, see *virtus affirmationis.*—(g), **virtus principiorum**, *the power of principle.*—(h), **virtus quaestionis**, *the power or importance of the question.*—(i), **virtus rationis**, *the power of argument.* —(j), **virtus suffragiorum**, *the power of intercession.*—Kinds of *virtus* in this (7) sense are: (a), **virtus demonstrationis**, *the highest performance of proof.*—(b), **virtus motus**, *the highest performance of movement.*—(c), **virtus peccati**, *the highest performance of sin or the height of sin.*

virus, i, *n., venom.*

vis, vis, *f.,* (1) *energy, force, potency, faculty, virtue,* i.e., the proximate principle of an action, synonym of *potentia, potestas,* and *virtus,* (2) *mental strength, power, force, vigor,* synonym of *fortitudo, potentia,* and *virtus,* (3) *power, force, violence,* synonym of *coactio* and *violentia,* (4) of abstract things in transferred sense, *force, notion, meaning, sense, import,* synonym of *intellectus, ratio sensus, significatio,* and *virtus.*—Kinds of *vis* in this (1) sense are: (a), **vis aestimativa** and **vis cogitativa**, *the sensitory power of judgment on*

the part of animals, and that on the part of man.—(b), **vis affectiva seu appetitiva** and **vis cognitiva seu cognoscitiva seu apprehensiva**, *the appetitive faculty and the faculty of knowledge.*— (c), **vis animalis seu sensitiva** and **vis intellectiva**, *the sensitory faculty and the intellectual faculty.*—(d), **vis appetitiva**, see *vis affectiva.*—(e), **vis apprehensiva**, see *vis affectiva.*—(f), **vis augmentativa, vis nutritiva,** and **vis generativa**, *the power of growth, that of nutrition,* and *that of generation.*—(g), **vis clavium**, *the power of the keys of the Church.* —(h), **vis cogitativa**, see *vis aestimativa.*—(i), **vis cognitiva seu cognoscitiva**, see *vis affectiva.*— (j), **vis collativa**, *the collating power.*—(k), **vis concretiva seu unitiva** and **vis discretiva**, *the coalescing or uniting power* and *the severing or separating power.* —(l), **vis concupiscibilis** and **vis irascibilis**, *the power of concupiscible and of irascible striving.*— (m), **vis constrictiva**, *the constricting power.*—(n), **vis continuativa**, *the power causing connection.* Cf. *vis concretiva.*—(o), **vis corporalis seu materialis** and **vis spiritualis**, *the corporal or the material and the spiritual force.* —(p), **vis deliberativa**, *the deliberating power or the power of deliberation.*—(q), **vis deordinata**, *the disordered force.*—(r), **vis discretiva**, see *concretiva.*—(s), **vis electiva**, *the selecting power or* *the selective faculty.*—(t), vis **exterior** and vis **interior**, *the exterior* and *the interior force.*—(u), vis **factiva** and vis **significativa**, *the effective power and the designating power.*—(v), vis **formativa seu seminativa**, *the forming power or the power of production.*—(w), vis **generativa**, see *vis augmentativa.*—(x), vis **illativa**, *the concluding power or the power of conclusion.*—(y), vis **illuminativa**, vis **purgativa** and vis **perfectiva**, *the illuminating, the purifying, and the perfecting power.*—(z), vis **imaginaria seu imaginativa seu phantastica**, *the power of imagination or phantasy.*—(a²), vis **immutativa** and vis **productiva**, *the changing and the producing power or the power of change and the power of production.*—(b²), vis **imperativa**, *the commanding or ruling power.*—(c²), vis **inferior**, *the inferior power.*—(d²), vis **intellectiva**, see *vis animalis.*—(e²), vis **interior**, see *vis exterior.*—(f²), vis **irascibilis**, see *vis concupiscibilis.*—(g²), vis **irrationalis**, *the irrational power or the power withdrawn from the influence of reason.*—(h²), vis **materialis**, see *vis corporalis.*—(i²), vis **memorativa** and vis **reminiscitiva**, *the power of involuntary and that of voluntary remembrance.*—(j²), vis **motiva**, *the moving force* by which may be understood not only a locally moving force but any other kind of a moving force.*—(k²), vis **na-**

turae seu naturalis, *the natural power or the power which is according to the nature of a thing.*—(l²), vis **naturalis**, see *vis naturae.*—(m²), vis **perfectiva**, see *vis illuminativa.*—(n²), vis **phantastica**, see *vis imaginaria.*—(o²), vis **productiva**, see *vis immutativa.*—(p²), vis **purgativa**, see *vis illuminativa.*—(q²), vis **regenerativa**, *the regenerating power or the power of regeneration.*—(r²), vis **regitiva**, *the guiding or leading power.*—(s²), vis **reminiscitiva**, see *vis memorativa.*—(t²), vis **sacramentalis**, *the sacramental power.*—(u²), vis **satisfactiva**, *the satisfying power or the power of satisfaction.*—(v²), vis **seminativa**, see *vis formativa.*—(w²), vis **sensitiva**, see *vis animalis.*—(x²), vis **significativa**, see *vis factiva.*—(y²), vis **spirativa**, *the breathing power or the power of breath.*—(z²), vis **spiritualis**, see *vis corporalis.*—(a³), vis **unitiva**, see *vis concretiva.*—Kinds of *vis* in this (2) sense are: (a), vis **coactiva** and vis **directiva**, *the compelling power* and *the power that directs.*—(b), vis **demonstrationis**, *the power of proof* which presents something as being necessarily true.*—(c), vis **directiva**, see *vis coactiva.*—(d), vis **rationis**, *the power of an argument.*—vis **naturae**, *the power of nature.*—**violentum est, cuius principium est extra, nihil conferenti vim passo**, see *violentus.*

viscus, eris, and more frequently in the plur.; **viscera**, um, *n., the in-*

ner parts of the animal body, *the internal organs, the inwards, viscera* (the nobler parts, the heart, lungs, liver, as well as the ignobler, the stomach, entrails, etc. (a) of the uterus, *womb*, (b) of animals, the *bowels* of an animal, (c) of man, *the heart* regarded as the seat of emotions.— (2) *fig. the bowels of the earth, of charity, etc.*—viscera cordis, *the inmost recesses of the heart.* —viscera animae meae, *my inmost soul.*

visibilis, e, *adj., that may be seen, visible,* the opposite of *invisibilis.* On essentia visibilis, see *essentia* under 1; on sacramentum visibile, see *sacramentum* under 1; on sacrificium visibile, see *sacrificium;* on signum visibile, see *signum* under 1; on species visibilis, see *species* under 5; on spiritus visibilis, see *spiritus;* on unctio visibilis, see *unctio* under 2.—visibiliter, *adv., visibly.*

visibilitas, atis, *f., visibility.*

visibiliter, *adv.,* see *visibilis.*

visio, onis, *f.,* (1) *the act or sense of seeing, sight, vision, observation,* (2) *a thing seen, an appearance, apparition, vision,* synonym of *phantasia* and *phantasma.* On certitudo visionis, see *certitudo* under 2; on cognoscere per modum visionis, see *cognoscere* under 2; on notitia visionis, see *notitia* under 2; on scientia visionis, see *scientia* under 2.—Kinds of *visio* in this (1) sense are: (a), visio actualis, *observation after*

the manner of an action.—(b) visio aenigmatica seu specularis and visio aperta seu manifesta seu faciei, *the reflective or mirror-like* and *the open view* or *that taking place face to face.*— (c), visio aperta, see *visio aenigmatica.*—(d), visio beata seu beatificans seu beatitudinis, *the blessed or sanctifying view or* that of eternal blessedness.—(e), visio beatificans, see *visio beata.* —(f), visio beatitudinis, see *visio beata.*—(g), visio comprehendens seu comprehensiva seu comprehensionis, *the view embracing the goal of man* or *that including heaven or the view of the possession of heaven,* i.e., the view bound with the possession of heaven.—(h), visio comprehensionis, see *visio comprehendens.* —(i), visio comprehensiva, see *visio comprehendens.*—(j), visio continua and visio intercisa, *the continued* and *the interrupted view.*—(k), visio corporalis seu corporea seu exterior seu sensibilis, visio spiritualis seu imaginationis seu imaginaria seu imaginativa seu phantastica and visio intellectiva seu intellectualis seu intellegibilis seu mentalis, *the physical or exterior or sensory view, the spiritual view of the imaginative faculty and immaterial or intellectual view.*—(l), visio Dei seu divina, *the view of God.*—(m), visio Dei per creaturam and visio Dei per essentiam, *the seeing of God in His crea-*

tures and *the seeing of God according to His essence.*—(n), visio **Dei per essentiam**, see *visio Dei per creaturam.*—(o), visio **divina**, see *visio Dei.*—(p), visio **exterior**, see *visio corporalis.*—(q), visio **faciei**, see *visio aenigmatica.*—(r), visio **fidei**, *the sight of faith.*—(s), visio **gloriae seu gloriosa**, *the view in the glory of heaven.*—(t), visio **gloriosa**, see *visio gloriae.*—(u), visio **imaginaria**, see *visio corporalis.*—(v), visio **imaginationis**, see *visio corporalis.*—(w), visio **imaginativa**, see *visio corporalis.*—(x), visio **immediata** and visio **mediata**, *the direct and the indirect view.*—(y), visio **imperfecta** and visio **perfecta**, *the imperfect* and *the perfect view.*—(z), visio **inferior** and visio **superior**, *the lower* and *the higher views.*—(a²), visio **intellectiva**, see *visio corporalis.*—(b²), visio **intellectualis**, see *visio corporalis.*—(c²), visio **intellegibilis**, see *visio corporalis.*—(d²), visio **intercisa**, see *visio continua.*—(e²), visio **manifesta**, see *visio aenigmatica.*—(f²), visio **mediata**, see *visio immediata.*—(g²), visio **mentalis**, see *visio corporalis.*—(h²), visio **patriae** and visio **viae**, *the view in the heavenly fatherland* and *that on the way to it.*—(i²), visio **per essentiam**, visio **per speciem seu speciei** and visio **per speculum**, *the view of a thing according to its essence, that according to its species, the view taking place as in a mirror.*—(j²), visio **per spe-**

ciem, see *visio per essentiam.*—(k²), visio **perfecta**, see *visio imperfecta.*—(l²), visio **phantastica**, see *visio corporalis.*—(m²), visio **prophetalis seu prophetiae seu prophetica**, *the prophetic vision.*—(n²), visio **prophetiae**, see *visio prophetalis.*—(o²), visio **prophetica**, see *visio prophetalis.*—(p²), visio **raptus**, *the vision in the state of rapture.*—(q²), visio **sensibilis**, see *visio corporalis.*—(r²), visio **somnii**, *the vision in a dream.*—(s²), visio **speciei**, see *visio per essentiam.*—(t²), visio **specularis**, see *visio aenigmatica.*—(u²), visio **spiritualis**, see *visio corporalis.*—(v²), visio **superior**, see *visio inferior.*—(w²), visio **supermundana seu supernaturalis**, *the supermundane or supernatural view.*—(x²), visio **supernaturalis**, see *visio supermundana.*—(y²), visio **viae**, see *visio patriae.* On the difference between *visio* and *revelatio* see *revelatio.*—visio **phantastica**, *the appearance of the power of imagination.*

visitatio, onis, f., (1) *a visit, act of visiting someone,* (2) *a visitation, punishment.*

visito, are, avi, atum, 1, *v. freq. a.* (1) *to go to see, to visit* anyone. —(2) *eccl. Lat., to punish.*

visivus, a, um, *adj., seeing, visive.*

visualis, e, *adj., concerning seeing or sight, attained by sight;* does not occur in S.T. On *linea visualis*, see *linea* under 1.

visus, us, *m., the faculty or act of seeing, vision, sight.* On **delecta-**

tio visus, see *delectatio;* on sensus visus, see *sensus* under 3; on vitium visus, see *vitium* under 1. —Kinds of *visus* are: **visus corporalis seu sensibilis, visus intellectualis,** and **visus spiritualis,** *the physical or sensory, the intellectual, and the spiritual power of sight.*

vita, ae, *f.,* (1) *life* in the proper sense of the word, i.e., the proper existence of a being which possesses the ability to move itself in a certain manner, (2) *life* in the improper and broader sense of the word, i.e., action of life or action which consists in self-action, (3) *life* in the improper and narrower sense of the word, i.e., the particular action of life or manner of life of man, the chief occupation of man, the chief direction in his life in general. On **gloria vitae aeternae,** see *gloria* under 1; on **gradus vitae,** see *gradus* under 1; on **liber vita,** see *liber* under 2; on **necessitas vitae et vitae humanae seu temporalis,** see *necessitas* under 3; on **operatio vitae,** see *operatio* under 2; on **perfectio vitae aeternae et huius vitae,** see *perfectio* under 3; on **principium vitae,** see *principium;* on **spiritus vitae,** see *spiritus;* on **status istius seu praesentis vitae,** see *status* under 3; on **veritas vitae,** see *veritas* under 1. Kinds of *vitae* in this (1) sense are: (a), **vita aeterna seu sempiterna** and **vita temporalis,** *the eternal or everlasting and the*

temporal life.—(b), **vita angeli** and **vita Dei seu divina,** *the life of the angel and the life of God or the divine life.* Cf. *vita divina* under 3.—(c), **vita animae seu spiritualis** and **vita corporis seu corporalis,** *the life of the human soul or the spiritual life* and *the life of the body or the corporeal life.*—(d), **vita animalis seu animalium, vita plantae,** and **vita hominis seu humana,** *the sensitive life or the life of the beast, that of the plant,* and *that of man or human life.* Cf. *vita intellectiva.* —(e), **vita animalium,** see *vita animalis.*—(f), **vita beata** and **vita misera,** *the happy life,* and *the wretched or unhappy life.*—(g), **vita corporalis,** see *vita animae.*—(h), **vita corporis,** see *vita animae.*—(i), **vita corruptibilis seu mortalis** and **vita incorruptibilis seu immortalis,** *the corruptible or mortal* and *the incorruptible or immortal life.*—(j), **vita creata** and **vita increata,** *the created and the uncreated life.*— (k), **vita Dei,** see *vita angeli.*—(l), **vita divina,** see *vita angeli.*—(m), **vita futura** and **vita praesens,** *the future and the present life.*—(n), **vita gloriae seu gloriosa vita gratiae** and **vita naturae seu naturalis,** *the life of heavenly glory or the heavenly glorified life, the life of grace and that of nature or the natural life.*—(o), **vita gloriosa,** see *vita gloriae.*—(p), **vita gratiae,** see *vita gloriae.*—(q), **vita hominis,** see *vita animalis.*—(r), vita humana, see *vita animalis*.—(s), vita immortalis, see *vita corruptibilis*.—(t), vita imperfecta and vita perfecta, *the imperfect life,* e.g. that of plants and the *perfect life*.—(u), vita incorruptibilis, see *vita corruptibilis*.—(v), vita increata, see *vita creata*.—(w), vita indeficiens, *the everlasting life*.—(x), vita intellectiva seu rationalis vita sensibilis, and vita nutritiva, *the intellectual or immaterial, the sensitive or sensible,* and *the vegetative or plant life*.—(y), vita iustitiae, *the life of justice*.—(z), vita materia permixta and vita separata seu per se, *life mixed with matter or sharing it* and *life separated from it or life for itself*.—(a²), vita misera, see *vita beata*.—(b²), vita mortalis, see *vita corruptibilis*.—(c²), vita naturae, see *vita gloriae*.—(d²), vita naturalis, see *vita gloriae*.—(e²), vita nutritiva, see *vita intellectiva*.—(f²), vita perfecta, see *vita imperfecta*.—(g²), vita per se, see *vita materiae permixta*.—(h²), vita per se sufficientissima, *life most sufficient for itself alone*.—(i²), vita plantae, see *vita animalis*.—(j²), vita plena, *the full life* quando est virtuosa, Praec. 4.—(k²), vita praesens see *vita futura*.—(l²), vita rationalis, see *vita intellectiva*.—(m²), vita resurgentium, *the life of the resurrected or of those risen from the dead*.—(n²), vita sempiterna, see *vita aeterna*.—(o²), vita sensibilis, see *vita intellectiva*.—(p²), vita sepa-

rata, see *vita materiae permixta*.—(q²), vita spiritualis, see *vita animae*.—(u²), vita temporalis, see *vita aeterna*. On superbia vitae, see *superbia* under 1.—Kinds of *vita* in this (2) sense are: vita secundum actum, and vita secundum potentiam, *life according to action* and *life according to potentiality*.—Kinds of *vita* in this (3) sense are: (a), vita abiecta and vita honesta, *the despised or despicable life* and *the honorable life*.—(b), vita absoluta, *the separated or retired life*.—(c), vita activa seu practica seu moralis and vita contemplativa seu speculativa, *the active* and *the contemplative life or life after the manner of a moral virtue* and *that after the manner of a virtue of reason*.—(d), vita aeterna, *the eternal life*. Cf. *vita aeterna,* under 1.—(e), vita austera seu districta and vita laxa seu voluptuosa seu luxuriosa, *the austere or mortified life* and *the unrestrained or pleasurable or sensual life*.—(f), vita bestialis seu brutalis and vita spiritualis, *the animal or brute life* and *the spiritual life*. Cf. *vita spiritualis* under 1.—(g), vita brutalis, see *vita bestialis*.—(h), vita caelestis, *the heavenly life*.—(i), vita civilis and vita domestica, *the civic or public* and *the home or family life*.—(j), vita communis seu consueta and vita peregrina, *the common or customary life* and *the strange or unusual life.*—(k), **vita communis** seu **socialis,** and **vita privata** seu **solitaria** seu **eremetica,** *the common or social life* and *the private or eremetical life.*—(l), **vita coniugalis,** *the married life.*—(m), **vita consueta,** see *vita communis.* —(n), **vita contemplativa,** see *vita activa.*—(o), **vita districta,** see *vita austera.*—(p), **vita divina** seu **superhumana** and **vita proprie humana,** *the divine or superhuman life,* and *the properly human life.* —(q), **vita domestica,** see *vita vitalis.*—(r), **vita eremetica,** see *vita communis.*—(s), **vita exterior,** *the outer or exterior life.*—(t), **vita honesta,** see *vita abiecta.*—(u), **vita inops** seu **pauper** and **vita opulenta,** *the needy or the poor life* and *the rich or opulent life.*— (v), **vita laboriosa,** *the laborious life.*—(w), **vita laxa,** see *vita austera.*—(x), **vita luxuriosa,** see *vita austera.*—(y), **vita monastica** and **vita saecularis,** *the monastic life or life in a monastery* and *the worldly life or life in the world.*— (z), **vita moralis,** see *vita activa.*— (a²), **vita opulenta,** see *vita inops.* —(b²), **vita pauper,** see *vita inops.* —(c²), **vita peregrina,** see *vita communis.*—(d²), **vita practica,** see *vita activa.*—(e²), **vita privata,** see *vita communis.*—(f²), **vita proprie humana,** see *vita divina.*— (g²), **vita recta,** *the right life.*— (h²), **vita saecularis,** see *vita monastica.*—(i²), **vita secundum quid** and **vita simpliciter,** *life of man with respect to something* and

life of man simply lived.—(j²), **vita simplex,** *the simple life.*—(k²), **vita simpliciter,** see *vita secundum quid.*—(l²), **vita socialis,** see *vita communis.*—(m²), **vita solitaria,** see *vita communis.*—(n²), **vita speculativa,** see *vita activa.*—(o²), **vita spiritualis,** see *vita bestialis.* —(p²), **vita voluptuosa,** see *vita austera.*

vitabilis, e, *adj., that may or ought to be shunned.*

vitalis, e, *adj., of or belonging to life, vital.* On **esse vitale,** see *esse;* on **motio vitalis,** see *motio;* on **motio vitalis,** see *motus* under 2; on **operatio vitalis,** see *operatio* under 2; on **principium vitale,** see *principium;* on **spiritus vitalis,** see *spiritus;* on **virtus vitalis,** see *virtus* under 1.

vitatio, onis, *f., a shunning, avoiding, avoidance.*

vitio, are, avi, atum, 1, *v. a., to make faulty, to injure, spoil, mar, taint, corrupt, infect.*

vitiositas, atis, *f., viciousness, corruption.*

vitiosus, a, um, *adj., full of faults or defects, faulty, defective, bad, corrupt, vicious,* the opposite of *virtualis* and *virtuosus.* On **actus vitiosus,** see *actus* under 1; on **habitus vitiosus,** see *habitus* under 4; on **ignorantia vitiosa,** see *ignorantia* under 2; on **ira vitiosa,** see *ira* under 1; on **iudicium vitiosum,** see *iudicium* under 2; on **passio vitiosa,** see *passio* under 3.

vitis, is, *f., a vine, grape-vine.*

vitium, ii, *n.*, (1) *fault, defect,* in the general sense of the word, synonym of *defectus* and *privatio,* the opposite of *perfectio,* (2) *sinful habit, vice,* synonym of *malitia.*—Kinds of *vitium* in this (1) sense are: (a), **vitium alienum** and **vitium proprium,** *the strange and the proper defect.*—(b), **vitium intellectus,** *the defect of intellect.*—(c), **vitium morale seu moris** and **vitium naturae,** *the moral defect* and *the defect of nature.*—(d), **vitium moris,** see *vitium morale.*—(e), **vitium naturae,** see *vitium morale.*—(f), **vitium naturae** and **vitium personae,** *the defect connected with the nature of man* and *the personal defect.*—(g), **vitium originis,** *the defect connected with the origin of a thing.*—(h), **vitium personae,** see *vitium naturae.*—(i), **vitium proprium,** see *vitium alienum.*—(j), **vitium virtutis,** *the defect of a power or faculty.*—(k), **vitium visus,** *the defect of the sense of sight.* On **actus vitii,** see *actus* under 1; on **ira per vitium,** see *ira* under 1.—Kinds of *vitium* in this (2) sense are: (a), **vitium animi seu spirituale** and **vitium carnale,** *the vice rooted in the soul or the spiritual vice* and *that rooted in the flesh or the carnal vice.*—(b), **vitium capitale seu principale,** *the principal vice.*—(c), **vitium carnale,** see *vitium animi.*—(d), **vitium contra naturam,** *the unnatural vice.*—(e), **vitium principale,** see *vitium capitale.*—(f), **vitium spirituale,** see *vitium animi.*—(g), **vitium universale,** *the common vice,* namely, *superbia.*

vito, are, avi, atum, 1, *v. a.,* and *n.,* *to shun, to seek to escape, avoid, evade.*

vitreus, a, um, *adj.,* *of glass, glass-, vitreous.*

vitrum, i, *n.,* *glass, crystal.*

vitta, ae, *f.,* *a band,* esp., *a fillet* or *chaplet* worn round the head; and in relig. lang. *a head-band,* a sacrificial or sacerdotal fillet.

vitula, ae, see *vitulus.*

vitulus, i, *m.,* and *vitula,* ae, *f.,* (1) *lit., calf,* (a) *a bull-calf,* (b) *a cow-calf,* (2) *in partic.,* **vitulus marinus,** *a sea-calf, seal.*—**vitulus conflatilis,** *a molten calf.*

vituperabilis, e, *adj.,* *blameworthy, blamable, censurable.*

vituperatio, onis, *f.,* *vituperation, reproof.*

vituperium, ii, *n.,* *blame, censure.*

vitupero, are, avi, atum, 1, *v. a.,* *to inflict censure, to blame, censure, vituperate.*

vivacitas, atis, *f.,* *natural vigor, vivacity, quickness,* used in S.T. only in quot.

vivaciter, *adv.,* see *vivax.*

vivax, acis, *adj.,* *restless.*—**vivaciter,** *adv., with liveliness or spirit, vigorously.*

vivicabilis, e, *adj.,* *life-giving, quickening.*

vivificatio, onis, *f.,* *a making alive, quickening, vivification.*

vivificativus, a, um, *adj.,* *life-giving, vivifying.*

vivificator, oris, *m.*, *he who makes alive, a quickener, vivifier.*

vivificatrix, tricis, *adj.*, *life-giving.*

vivifico, are, avi, atum, 1, *v. a.*, *to make alive, restore to life, quicken, vivify,* used *lit.* and *fig.*

vivificus, a, um, *adj.*, *making alive, quickening, vivifying, vivific.*

vivo, ere, vixi, victus, 3, *to live, be alive, have life.* On **fides vivens,** see *fides* under 2; on **gradus vivens,** see *gradus* under 1; on **substantia vivens,** see *substantia* under 2.

vivus, a, um, *adj.*, *alive, living, that has life,* synonym of *animatus,* opposite of *mortuus.* On **corpus vivum,** see *corpus;* on **opus vivum,** see *opus* under 4.—**aqua viva,** *living water, water that flows continually.* **argentum vivum,** *living silver, quick silver, mercury.* **panis vivus,** *living bread,* i.e., Christ.

vix, *adv.*, *with difficulty, with much ado, hardly, scarcely, barely.*

vocabulum, i, *n.*, *an appellation, designation, name of anything.*

vocalis, e, *adj.*, *that utters a voice, vocal, resounding, sonorous, speaking, consisting of words.* On **instrumentum vocale,** see *instrumentum;* on **laus vocalis,** see *laus;* on **oratio vocalis,** see *oratio* under 2; on **sententia vocalis,** see *sententia* under 2.—**vocaliter,** *adv.*, *in words, aloud, vocally.*

vocaliter, *adv.*, see *vocalis.*

vocatio, onis, *f.*, *a calling, vocation* on the part of God.

voco, are, avi, atum, 1, *v. a.* and *n.*, *to call* (in a wide variety of senses), *lit.* and *fig.*, *summon, invite, welcome; call by name, name.*

volatilis, e, *adj.*, *flying, winged.* —**volatile,** is, *n.*, *a fowl.*

volatus, us, *m.*, *a flying, flight.*

volenter, *adv.*, *willingly.*

volibilis, e, *adj.*, *desirable,* i.e., that which can be made the object of *wishing,* synonym of *voluntabilis,* not in the S.T.

volito, are, avi, atum, 1, *v. freq. n.*, *to fly to and fro, to fly or flit about.*

volitus, a, um, *adj.*, see *volo.*

volo, are, avi, atum, 1, *v. n.*, *to fly* used *lit.* and *fig.*

volo, velle, volui, volitus, (1) *to wish* in the wider sense of the word, i.e., every act of the will, synonym in nominal use of *voluntas,* (2) *wish* in the narrow sense of the word, i.e. in so far as it is the goal of the will, likewise, a synonym in nominal use of *voluntas.*—Kinds of *velle* in this (1) sense are: (a), **velle absolute seu simpliciter** and **velle secundum quid seu ex suppositione seu sub condicione,** *to want without respect to anything or unconditionally or absolutely* and *to want with respect to something or according to some condition.*—(b), **velle actu,** *to want in reality or after the manner of an action.*— (c), **velle antecedenter** and **velle consequenter,** *to wish before and after,* before or after a certain circumstance has been taken into consideration.—(d), **velle appetitu naturali seu naturali instinto seu naturaliter seu necessario seu ex necessitate** and **velle per electionem,** *to want from a natural desire or a natural urge or of necessity and to want with free choice.*—(e), **velle consequenter,** see *velle antecedenter.*—(f), **velle directe** and **velle indirecte,** *to want directly or immediately and to want indirectly or mediately.*—(g), **velle ex necessitate,** see *velle appetitu naturali.*—(h), **velle ex ordine ad alterum seu propter aliud,** and **velle propter se seu secundum se,** *to want with reference to something else or for the sake of something else* and *to want on account of oneself or for the sake of oneself.*—(i), **velle ex suppositione,** see *velle absoluta.*—(j), **velle imperfecte** and **velle perfecte,** *to want imperfectly and to do so perfectly.*—(k), **velle in causa** and **velle secundum se,** *to want (something) in its cause and to want (something) in itself.* Cf. *velle ex ordine ad alterum.*—(l), **velle indirecte,** see *velle directe.*—(m), **velle naturali instinctu,** see *velle appetitu naturali.*—(n), **velle naturaliter,** see *velle appetitu naturali.*—(o), **velle necessario,** see *velle appetitu naturali.*—(p), **velle per electionem,** see *velle appetitu naturali.*—(q), **velle perfecte,** see *velle imperfecte.*—(r), **velle propter aliud,** see *velle ex ordine ad alterum.*—(s), **velle propter se,** see *velle ex ordine ad alterum.*—(t), **velle secundum quid,** see *velle absolute.*—(u), **velle secundum se,** see *velle ex ordine ad alterum* and *velle in causa.*—(v), **velle simpliciter,** see *velle absolute.*—(w), **velle sub condicione,** see *velle absolute.*—**volitus,** a, um, *P. a.,* longed for, wanted in the wider sense of the word.—On *ignorantia directe et indirecte volita,* see *ignorantia* under 1.—Kinds of *volitum* as substantive are: (a), **volitum actu,** *that wanted in reality.*—(b), **volitum ex ordine ad alterum** and **volitum secundum se,** *that wanted with respect to something else* and *that wanted according to itself or that wanted for the sake of itself.*—(c), **volitum formaliter** and **volitum materialiter,** *that wanted according to its form or essence* and *that wanted according to its matter.*—(d), **volitum materialiter,** see *volitum formaliter.*—(e), **volitum per accidens** and **volitum per se,** *that wanted accidentally and that wanted for itself or as such.*—(f), **volitum per se,** see *volitum per accidens.*—(g), **volitum primum seu principale** and **volitum secundarium,** *that wanted first or chiefly* and *that wanted secondarily.*—(h), **volitum principale,** see *volitum primum.*—(i), **volitum secundarium,** see *volitum primum.*—(j), **volitum secundum se,** see *volitum ex ordine ad alterum,* volubilis, e, *adj., movable, change-able*. On **cogitatio volubilis,** see *cogitatio* under 2; on **cognitio volubilis,** see *cognitio* under 2.

volucris, is, *f., a bird, a flying creature*.

volumen, inis, *n., book, volume,* used *lit.* and *fig.*

voluntabilis, e, *adj., desirable,* i.e., that which can be made the object of wishing, synonym of *volibilis,* not in S.T.—Kinds of *voluntabile* are: (a), **voluntabile secundum naturam,** *the desirable according to its nature.*—(b), **voluntabile secundum quid** and **voluntabile simpliciter,** *the desirable in a certain respect and the simply desirable.*—(c), **voluntabile secundum veritatem,** *the desirable in truth.*—(d), **voluntabile simpliciter,** see *voluntabile secundum quid.*

voluntarie, *adv.,* see *voluntarius.*

voluntarius, a, um, *adj.,* (1) *at one's pleasure, arbitrary,* i.e., arising from a will in the wider sense of the word, synonym of *spontaneus,* the opposite of *coactus* and *violentus,* (2) *intentional,* arising from or belonging to the will in the narrow and proper sense of the word whether freely or of necessity, the opposite of *involuntarius* and *non voluntarius,* (3) *voluntary, freely desired,* i.e., arising from a will in a narrow and proper sense of the word on the basis of deliberation and choice, (4) *ready, willing.* On **motus voluntarius,** see *motus* un-

der 1 and 2.—As kinds of *voluntarium* in this sense we have: **voluntarium secundum rationem imperfectam** and **voluntarium secundum rationem perfectam,** *the voluntary according to the imperfect* and *that according to the perfect conception.*—One kind of *voluntarium* in this (2) sense is **voluntarium praeconsiliatum,** the Aristotelian *hekousion probebouleumenon, the deliberately intentional* or *the voluntary.* On **actio voluntaria,** see *actio* under 1; on **actus voluntarius,** see *actus* under 1; on **agens voluntarius,** see *agens;* on **appetitus voluntarius,** see *appetitus* under 1; on **causa voluntaria,** see *causa* under 2; on **commutatio voluntaria,** see *commutatio* under 2; on **defectus voluntarius,** see *defectus* under 2; on **error voluntarius,** see *error;* on **habitudo voluntaria,** see *habitudo;* on **ignorantia directe et indirecte, per accidens et per se malum in rebus voluntaria,** see *malus* under 2; on **ignorantia voluntaria,** see *ignorantia* under 1; on **iustificatio voluntaria,** see *iustificatio* under 1; on **opus voluntarium,** see *opus* under 4; on **paupertas voluntaria,** see *paupertas* under 1; on **peccatum voluntarium,** see *peccatum* under 2; on **providentia voluntaria,** see *providentia;* on **res voluntaria,** see *res;* on **speculum voluntarium,** see *speculum* under 1; on **subiectio voluntaria,** see *subiectio* under 2; on **violentia voluntaria**

mixta, see *violentia* under 1.—
Kinds of *voluntarium* in this (3)
sense are: (a), voluntarium absque condicione seu voluntate
absolute and voluntarium sub
condicione seu ex suppositione
seu voluntate condicionata, *the
voluntary without respect to anything else or unconditional voluntary* and *the conditioned voluntary.*—(b), voluntarium absoluta
seu de se, and voluntarium relative seu per comparationem ad
aliud, *the voluntary taken by itself,* i.e., as it is, without respect
to anything else, and *the voluntary placed with reference to
something else or in comparison
with something else.*—(c), voluntarium de se, see *voluntarium absolute.*—(d), voluntarium directe
and voluntarium indirecte, *the
directly voluntary,* and *the indirectly voluntary.*—(e), voluntarium ex suppositione, see *voluntarium absque conditione.*—(f),
voluntarium indirecte, see *voluntarium directe.*—(g), voluntarium
in particulari and voluntarium in
universali, the *voluntary with
reference to a particular case* and
*the voluntary with reference io
the general contained in this
case.*—(h), voluntarium in universali, see *voluntarium in particulari.*—(i), voluntarium mixtum,
and voluntarium simpliciter, *the
mixed* and *the simply or absolutely voluntary.*—(j), voluntarium per accidens and voluntarium
per se, *the accidentally voluntary*

and *the voluntary in itself or as
such.*—(k), voluntarium per comparationem ad aliud, see *voluntarium absolute.*—(l), voluntarium
per se, see *voluntarium per accidens.*—(m), voluntarium perfecte
and voluntarium quocumque modo, *the perfectly voluntary* and
the voluntary in some way.—(n),
voluntarium quocumque modo,
see *voluntarium perfecte.*—(o),
voluntarium relative, see *voluntarium absolute.*—(p), voluntarium secundum actionem and voluntarium secundum passionem,
the freely desired in the sense of
an action, and *that in the sense
of a suffering.*—(q), voluntarium
secundum causam and voluntarium secundum se, *that desired in
its cause,* and *that freely desired
in itself.*—(r), voluntarium secundum passionem, see *voluntarium
secundum actionem.*—(s), voluntarium secundum se, see *voluntarium secundum causam.*—(t),
voluntarium simpliciter, see *voluntarium mixtum.*—(u), voluntarium sub condicione, see *voluntarium absque condicione.*—(v),
voluntarium voluntate absoluta,
see *voluntarium absque condicione.*—(w), voluntarium voluntate
condicionata, see *voluntarium
absque condicione.*—voluntarie,
adv., (1) *of free will, of itself,*
synonym of *spontanee* and *sponte,* the opposite of *coacte* and
violenter, (2) *voluntarily, with
free will,* the opposite of *involun-*

tarie. On **poena voluntarie as-sumpta,** see *poena.*

voluntas, atis, *f.,* (1) *will* in the broader sense of the word, i.e., every appetitive faculty, synonym of *appetitus,* (2) *will* in the narrower and proper sense of the word, i.e., transcendental or spiritual appetitive faculty, also *voluntas potentiae,* i.e., will in the sense of a faculty, the opposite of *appetitus sensitivus* and *sensualitas,* (3) *wishing* in the broader sense of the word, i.e., every activity of the will, also *voluntas actus,* i.e., will in the sense of an action, synonym of *velle,* (4) *wishing* in the narrower sense of the word, i.e., simple or absolute wishing, **voluntas simplex seu simpliciter,** synonym of *velle,* the opposite of *voluntas consiliativa seu deliberativa seu deliberans seu deliberata seu ut deliberata, electio,* and *eligere.*— (5), *that which is wanted, the desired.*—Kinds of *voluntas* in this (1) sense are: **voluntas rationabilis seu rationalis seu rationis** and **voluntas sensualitatis,** *the will of the rational and that of the sensatory part of the soul or the intellectual and the sensatory appetitive faculty.*—**actus voluntatis,** *the action of the will.* On **actio voluntatis,** see *actio* under 1; on **agens per voluntatem,** see *agens;* on **agere per voluntatem,** see *agere;* on **causa per voluntatem,** see *causa* under 2; on **consilium voluntatis,** see *consilium* un-

der 1; on **imperium voluntatis,** see *imperium* under 1; on **libido voluntatis,** see *libido* under 2; on **motus voluntatis,** see *motus* under 2; on **opus voluntatis,** see *opus* under 4; on **peccatum voluntatis,** see *peccatum* under 2; on **perfectus secundum voluntatem,** see *perfectus* under 1; on **processio voluntatis seu per modum voluntatis,** see *processio;* on **rectitudo voluntatis,** see *rectitudo* under 3.—Kinds of *voluntas* in this (2) sense are: (a), **voluntas absolute considerata** and **voluntas secundum rationem,** *the will considered absolutely or without respect to anything else* and *the will acting according to reason.*— (b), **voluntas creata** and **voluntas Dei seu divina,** *the created or creature-like will and the divine or creative will.*—(c), **voluntas Dei,** see *voluntas creata.*—(d), **voluntas divina,** see *voluntas creata.*—(e), **voluntas essentialiter dicta seu per essentiam** and **voluntas participative dicta seu per participationem,** *the will which is called will according to its essence* and *that which is so called through participation in or subordination to it.*—(f), **voluntas humana,** *the human will.* Cf. *voluntas humana* under 3.—(g), **voluntas participative dicta,** see *voluntas essentialiter dicta.*—(h), **voluntas per essentiam,** see *voluntas essentialiter dicta.*—(i), **voluntas per participationem,** see *voluntas essentialiter dicta.*—(j), voluntas prima, *the first or highest will.*–(k), voluntas secundum rationem, see *voluntas absolute considerata.*–in rationabili est voluntas, see *rationabilis.* summa diffusio voluntatis est per modum amoris, *the greatest emission or communication of will occurs by means of love.* Cf. *diffusivus.* voluntas in ratione est, see *ratio* under 1. voluntas proprie in intellectu est, see *intellectus* under 1. On complementum voluntatis, see *complementum;* on modus voluntatis, see *modus* under 2; on signum voluntatis, see *signum* under 1; on voluntarium voluntate absoluta et condicionata, see *voluntarius* under 3.–Kinds of *voluntas* in this (3) sense are: (a), voluntas absoluta and voluntas condicionata, *the unconditioned and the conditioned wishing.* Cf. *velleitas.* (b), voluntas accedens, voluntas antecedens, voluntas concomitans, and voluntas consequens, *the wishing attached to an action, that preceding it, that accompanying it,* and *that following it.*–(c), voluntas actualis seu secundum actum and voluntas habitualis seu secundum habitum, *the actual and the habitual wishing or the wishing in the manner of an action* and *that in the manner of a habit.*–(d), voluntas aeterna and voluntas mutabilis, *the eternal and the changeable wishing.*–(e), voluntas affectionis and voluntas ef-

fectionis, *the wishing of affection and that of effect,* or the wishing that has for its result an *actus interior* and that which has an *actus exterior.* voluntas amicitiae, *the wishing of friendship or benevolence.*–(f), voluntas antecedens, see *voluntas accedens.*– –(g), voluntas beneplaciti and voluntas signi, *the wishing of complacency and that of the sign,* i.e., wishing which consists of the complacency of the will in something or of the inclination to something and the sign that someone wishes something (= *signum voluntatis*).–(h), voluntas bona and voluntas mala, *the morally good and the morally bad wishing.*–(i), voluntas completa seu consummata seu perfecta and voluntas incompleta seu non completa, *the complete or perfect* and *the incomplete or imperfect wishing.*–(j), voluntas coniuncta and voluntas separata, *the wishing* connected (with an exterior action) and *that separated from it.*–(k), voluntas concomitans, see *voluntas accedens.*–(l), voluntas condicionata, see *voluntas absoluta.*–(m), voluntas consequens, see *voluntas accedens.*–(n), voluntas consiliativa seu deliberativa seu deliberans seu deliberata seu ut deliberata and voluntas non deliberata seu simplex seu simpliciter, *the deliberating or deliberated wishing* and *the undeliberated or simple or absolute wishing.*–(o), voluntas consummata, see *voluntas completa.*—(p), voluntas cordis, *the wishing of the heart and of the soul.*—(q), voluntas deliberans seu deliberata seu deliberativa, see *voluntas consiliativa.* —(r), voluntas deordinata seu inordinata and voluntas ordinata, *the disordered* and *the ordered wishing.*—(s), voluntas divina and voluntas humana, *divine and human wishing.* Cf. *voluntas divina et humana* under 2.—(t), voluntas effectionis, see *voluntas affectionis.*—(u), voluntas ex libero arbitrio rationis proveniens seu spontanea seu non necessaria and voluntas necessaria, *wishing from the free decision of reason or unnecessary wishing* and *necessary wishing.*—(v), voluntas gratuita, *the gratuitous or undeserved wishing or the wish from grace.*—(w), voluntas habitualis, see *voluntas actualis.*—(x), voluntas humana, see *voluntas divina.*—(y), voluntas incompleta, see *voluntas completa.*—(a²), voluntas inordinata, see *voluntas deordinata.*—(b²), voluntas mala, see *voluntas bona.*—(c²), voluntas mera, *pure or simple wishing.*—(d²), voluntas metaphorice dicta and voluntas proprie dicta, *wishing in the transferred sense of the word* and *wishing in the proper sense of the word.*—(e²), voluntas mutabilis, see *voluntas aeterna.*—(f²), voluntas naturalis seu ut natura seu per modum naturae and voluntas rationalis seu ut ratio

seu per modum rationis, *natural and rational wishing or the wishing of the will as of a natural thing, wishing of the will as of a spiritual faculty.*—(g²), voluntas necessaria, see *voluntas ex libero arbitrio proveniens.*—(h²), voluntas non completa, see *voluntas completa.*—(i²), voluntas non deliberata, see *voluntas consiliativa.* —(j²), voluntas non necessaria, see *voluntas ex libero arbitrio proveniens.*—(k²), voluntas ordinata, see *voluntas inordinata.*— (l²), voluntas perfecta, see *voluntas completa.*—(m²), voluntas per modum naturae, see *voluntas naturalis.*—(n²), voluntas per modum rationis, see *voluntas naturalis.*—(o²), voluntas pietatis, *wishing after the manner of merciful love or pity.*—(p²), voluntas praecedens actum and voluntas praecedens passionem, *wishing preceding an action and that preceding an emotion.*—(q²), voluntas praecedens passionem, see *voluntas praecedens actum.*—(r²), voluntas proprie dicta, see *voluntas metaphorice dicta.*—(s²), voluntas rationalis, see *voluntas naturalis.*—(t²), voluntas secundum actum, see *voluntas actualis.*—(u²), voluntas secundum habitum, see *voluntas actualis.*—(v²), voluntas separata, see *voluntas coniuncta.*—(w²), voluntas signi, see *voluntas beneplaciti.*—(x²), voluntas simplex seu simpliciter, see *voluntas consiliativa.*—(y²), voluntas spontanea, see *voluntas ex*

libero arbitrio proveniens.—(z^2),
voluntas ut deliberata, see *volun-*
tas consiliativa.—(a^3), **voluntas ut**
natura, see *voluntas naturalis.*—
(b^3), **voluntas ut ratio,** see *volun-*
tas naturalis.

voluptas, atis, *f., pleasure, satisfac-*
tion, enjoyment, delight, lust.
Kinds of *voluptas* are: (a), **volup-**
tas carnalis seu carnis seu cor-
poralis, *carnal or corporal lust.*—
(b), **voluptas carnis,** see *voluptas*
carnalis.—(c), **voluptas corpora-**
lis, see *voluptas carnalis.*—(d),
voluptas inordinata, *inordinate*
lust.—(e), **voluptas libidinis seu**
libidinosa seu venerea, *sensual or*
sexual enjoyment.—(f), **voluptas**
libidinosa, see *voluptas libidinis.*
—(g), **voluptas meretricia,** *un-*
chaste lust.—(h), **voluptas vene-**
rea, see *voluptas libidinis.*

voluptuosus, a, um, *adj., full of*
gratification, enjoyment, pleasure
or *delight, sensual, voluptuous.*
On **vita voluptuosa,** see *vita* under 3.

Volusianus, i, *m., Volusianus,* son
of Albinus and brother to Albina,
and thus maternal uncle to her
daughter Melania the younger.
His mother was a devout Christian. He may have been the same
as Caius Coeonius Rufus Valusi-
anus, *praefectus urbi* in the time
of Valentinian who died A.D.
375. At the time when Marcellinus went to Africa the mother of
Volusianus wrote to St. Augustine entreating him to use his in-

fluence with him to become a
Christian.

voluto, are, avi, atum, 1, *v. freq. a.*
and *n., to toss about, consider.*

volva, ae, *f.,* see *vulva.*

volvo, ere, volvi, volutum, 3, *v. a.,*
(1) *to roll out* as sound, (2) *fig.*
(a) *to roll off,* (b) *in partic., to*
turn over or revolve in the mind.

vomer, eris, *m., a ploughshare.*

vomitus, us, *m., a throwing up,*
used *lit.* and *fig.*

vomo, ere, ui, itum, 3, *v. n.* and *a.,*
(1) *lit., to vomit, throw up* or
discharge by vomiting, (2) *fig.,*
to discharge, pour out in abundance.

vorax, acis, *adj., voracious, swal-*
lowing greedily.

vos, *pron.* see *tu.*

votivus, a, um, *adj., votive, prom-*
ised by a vow.

votum, i, *n.,* (1) *a solemn promise,*
vow, (2) *wanting, wish, desire.*
On **commutatio voti,** see *commu-*
tatio under 1; on **necessitas voti,**
see *necessitas* under 1.—Kinds of
votum in this (1) sense are: (a),
votum abstinentiae and **votum**
ieiunii, *the vow to abstain* (from
meat) and *the vow to fast.*—(b),
votum commune and **votum sin-**
gulare, *the common* or *custom-*
ary vow, and *the individual or*
particular vow.—(c), **votum con-**
templationis and **votum oratio-**
nis, *the vow to observe medita-*
tion and that to say a prayer.—
(d), **votum continentiae, votum**
oboedientiae, and **votum pauper-**
tatis, *the vow of (sexual) renun-*

ciation or *chastity, that of obedi-*
ence (to an ecclesiastical or religious superior) and that of (voluntary) *poverty.*—(e), **votum ie-**
iunii, see *votum abstinentiae.*—
(f), **votum interpretativum seu**
intepretatum and **votum ore te-**
nus emissum, *the intepreted vow*
and that made with the mouth.—
(g), **votum large acceptum seu**
largo modo dictum and **votum**
proprie dictum, *the vow in the*
broader and in the narrower sen-
ses of the word.—(h), **votum lar-**
go modo dictum, see *votum large*
acceptum.—(i), **votum oboedien-**
tiae, see *votum continentiae.*—(j),
votum orationis, see *votum con-*
templationis.—(k), **votum ore te-**
nus emissum, see *votum interpre-*
tativum.—(l), **votum paupertatis,**
see *votum continentiae.*—(m), **vo-**
tum peregrinationis terrae sanc-
tae seu terrae sanctae, *the vow of*
a pilgrimage to the Holy Land.—
(n), **votum perpetuum** and **votum**
temporale, *the perpetual or final*
vow and *the temporal vow or*
that binding only for a time.—(o),
votum per posterius dictum, and
votum per prius dictum, *the vow*
which is so called after the man-
ner of earlier and *that which is*
so called after the manner of
later.—(p), **votum per prius dic-**
tum, see *votum per posterius dic-*
tum.—(q), **votum privatum** and
votum publicum, *the private vow*
or that made in private and the
public vow.—(r), **votum profes-**
sionis, *the vow of profession or*

that made on entering the reli-
gious life.—(s), **votum proprie**
dictum, see *votum large accep-*
tum.—(t), **votum publicum,** see
votum privatum.—(u), **votum re-**
ligionis and **votum vitae saecu-**
laris, *the vow to enter a religious*
order and the vow to continue
the secular life or life in the
world.—(v), **votum simplex** and
votum solemne seu solemniza-
tum, *the simple vow or that con-*
nected with no solemnity and the
solemn vow or that connected
with solemnity.—(w), **votum so-**
lemne seu solemnizatum, see *vo-*
tum simplex.—(x), **votum tem-**
porale, see *votum perpetuum.*—
(y), **votum terrae sanctae,** see *vo-*
tum peregrinationis terrae sanc-
tae.—(z), **votum virginitatis,** *the*
vow of virginity.—(a^2), **votum vi-**
tae saecularis, see *votum religio-*
nis.

voveo, ere, vovi, votum, 2, *v. a.* and
n., to vow, to bind oneself to do,
give or the like, by a solemn
promise to God.

vox, vocis, *f.,* (1) *sound, sound of*
the voice, (2) *articulated sound,*
word, linguistic expression, synonym of *verbum.* On **dicere voce,**
see *dicere* under 1; on **verbum**
vocis et speciei, see *verbum* under 1.—Kinds of *vox* in this (1)
sense are: (a), **vox articulata seu**
litterata and **vox non articulata**
seu non litterata, *the voice as*
heard in syllables, i.e., *separated*
by consonants, and *the voice not*
syllabificated or separated by

consonants, e.g. the hissing of a snake.—(b), vox **brutorum,** and vox **humana,** *the voice of animals and that of man.*—(c), vox **humana,** see *vox brutorum.*—(d), vox **litterata,** see *vox articulata.*—(e), vox **naturalis,** *the natural voice.*—(f), vox **non articulata,** see *vox articulata.*—(g), vox **non litterata,** see *vox articulata.*—(h), vox **non significans** and vox **significativa,** *the voice that does not signify anything* and *the voice that signifies something.*—(i), vox **significans seu significativa ad placitum seu secundum placitum seu ex proposito** and vox **significans seu significativa naturaliter,** *the sound according to the desire or intention of man* and *the sound* signifying something by nature.—(j), vox **significans cum imaginatione aliquid significandi,** *the sound bound with the imagination to express something.*—(k), vox **significans ex proposito,** see *vox significans ad placitum.*—(l), vox **significans seu significativa naturaliter,** see *vox significans ad placitum.*—(m), vox **significativa,** see *vox non significans.*—(n), vox **significativa secundum placitum,** see *vox significans ad placitum.*—(o), vox **turbae,** *the sound of the trumpet at the last judgment.* On **elementum vocis,** see *elementum* under 1; on **veritas vocis,** see *veritas* under 1.—Kinds of *vox* in this (2) sense are: (a), vox **complexa** and vox **incomplexa,** *the*

legomenon kata symbloken and *legomenon aneu symblokes* of Aristotle, *the verbal expression composed of two or more independent words and that consisting of a single word.*—(b), vox **exterior,** *the exterior word or that expressed by the mouth.*—(c), vox **falsa** and vox **vera,** *the false and the true word.*—(d), vox **incomplexa,** see *vox complexa.*—(e), vox **vera,** see *vox falsa.*

vulgaris, e, *adj., of or belonging to the great mass or multitude, general, usual, ordinary, common, vulgar.*—**vulgariter,** *adv., after the ordinary or common manner, commonly, vulgarly.*

vulgariter, *adv.,* see *vulgaris.*

vulgo, *adv.,* see *vulgus.*

vulgus, i, *n., the great mass, the multitude, the people, public.*—**vulgo,** *adv., generally, commonly.*

vulneratio, onis, *f., a wounding, wound.*

vulnero, are, avi, atum, 1, *v. a.,* (1) *lit., to wound, hurt or injure by a wound,* (2) *fig., to wound, hurt, injure, pain,* etc.

vulnus, eris, *n., a wound, blow, misfortune, calamity.*—One kind of *vulnus* is: vulnus **naturae seu naturae humanae seu naturae ex peccato consequens seu inflictum toti humanae naturae ex peccato primi parentis,** *the wound or* wounding of human nature through the sin of our forefathers which consists in this, that omnes vires animae remanent quodammodo destitutae proprio ordine quo naturaliter ordinantur ad virtutem. Of these there are four: inquantum ergo ratio destituitur suo ordine ad verum est vulnus ignorantiae; inquantum vero voluntas destituitur ordine ad bonum, est vulnus malitiae; inquantum vero irascibilis destituitur suo ordine ad arduum, est vulnus infirmitatis; inquantum vero concupiscentia destituitur ordine ad delectabile moderatum ratione est vulnus concupiscentiae.

vulpes, is, *f., a fox.*

vultur, uris, *m., a vulture.*

vultus, us, *m., an expression of countenance, the countenance, visage,* as to features and expression; hence often to be translated by *features, looks, air, mien, expression, aspect,* (1), *in gen., face, countenance, look,* (2) *the brow,* (3) *complexion.*—**respicere se mutuis vultibus,** *to look at one another, mutually.*—**cognoscere vultum,** *to know by sight.*

vulva, ae, *f., the womb, matrix of women.*

X

xenius, ii, *n., a gift, present.*

ɪ **xenodochium,** i, *n., guest-house.*

Z

Zacharias, ae, *m.,* (1) *Zachary,* the father of John the Baptist.

Zacheus, i, *m., Zacheus,* a publican and tax gatherer, who lived in Jericho in the time of our Lord.

Zambri, *indecl. noun, Zambri,* a chief of Simeon, slain by Phinees.

Zara, ae, *m., Zara,* son of Iuda and Thamar, and twin brother of Phares.

Zebedaeus, i, *m., Zebedee,* husband of Salome, and father of the apostles John and James the Greater.

zelo, are, 1, *v. a.,* (1) *to be jealous of, to be envious,* (2) *to be zealous for.*

zelotes, ae, *m., a zealot, one that loves with jealousy, one that is jealous* (eccl. Lat.).

zelotypia, ae, *f., jealousy.*

Zelpha, ae, *f., Zelpha,* a Syrian servant of Lea, given as a secondary wife to Jacob, to whom she bore Gad and Aser.

zelus, i, *m.,* (1) *zeal, emulation,* (2) *jealousy.* On **ira per zelum,** see *ira* under 1.—Kinds of *zelus* in this (1) sense are: (a), **zelus invidiae,** *the zeal of envy or jealousy.*—(b), **zelus iustitiae,** *the zeal for justice.*—(c), **zelus vindicta,** *the zeal for revenge.*

Zephirinus, i, *m.,* Zephyrinus, Saint, Pope, (198-217). He is quoted on the material of which chalices were to be made.

zizania, orum, *n., darnel, cockle,* (Eccl. Lat.).

Zodiacus, i, *m.,* = *Zodiakos,* the *zodiac* (pure Lat. orbis signifer).

DAUGHTERS OF ST. PAUL

Missionary Sisters of the Catholic Editions

50 St. Paul's Ave.
BOSTON 30, MASS.

315 Washington Street
BOSTON 8, MASS.

381 Dorchester Street
SO. BOSTON 27, MASS.

78 Fort Place
STATEN ISLAND 1, N. Y.

325 Main Street
FITCHBURG, MASS.

39 Erie Street
BUFFALO 2, N. Y.

141 West Rayen Ave.
YOUNGSTOWN 3, OHIO

114 East Main Plaza
SAN ANTONIO 5, TEXAS

827 Fifth Ave.
SAN DIEGO 1, CALIF.

86 Bolton Ave.
ALEXANDRIA, LA.

2700 Biscayne Blvd.
MIAMI 37, FLORIDA

33 West Notre Dame
MONTREAL, CAN.

134 Westmount Ave.
TORONTO, CAN.